The Business Consultancy Project

The Business Consultancy Project

Selected chapters from:

The Management Consultant
Richard Newton

The Business Student's Hand Book
Sixth Edition
Sheila Cameron

Project Management
Fourth Edition
Harvey Maylor

Project Management Achieving Competitive Advantage
Fourth Edition and Global Edition
Jeffrey K. Pinto

The Seven Cs of Consulting
Third Edition
Mick Cope

Strategic Management
Eighth Edition
Richard Lynch

Research Methods for Business Students
Seventh Edition
Mark Saunders, Philip Lewis, and Adrian Thornhill

The Study Skills Book
Third Edition
Kathleen Mcmillan, and Jonathan Weyers

Pearson

Harlow, England • London • New York • Boston • San Francisco • Toronto • Sydney • Dubai • Singapore • Hong Kong
Tokyo • Seoul • Taipei • New Dehli • Cape Town • São Paulo • Mexico City • Madrid • Amsterdam • Munich • Paris • Milan

Pearson
KAO Two
KAO Park
Harlow
Essex CM17 9SR

And associated companies throughout the world

Visit us on the World Wide Web at:
www.pearson.com/uk

Compiled from:

The Management Consultant
Richard Newton
ISBN 978-0-273-73087-3
© Richard Newton 2010

The Business Student's Hand Book
Sixth Edition
Sheila Cameron
ISBN 978-1-292-08864-8
© Sheila Cameron 2009, 2016

Project Management
Fourth Edition
Harvey Maylor
ISBN 978-1-292-23706-0
© Pearson Education Limited 1996, 2010

Project Management Achieving Competitive Advantage
Fourth Edition and Global Edition
Jeffrey K. Pinto
ISBN 978-1-292-09479-3
© Pearson Education Limited 2016

The Seven Cs of Consulting
Third Edition
Mick Cope
ISBN 978-0-273-73108-5
© Pearson Education Limited 2003, 2010

Strategic Management
Eighth Edition
Richard Lynch
ISBN 978-1-292-21140-4
© Richard Lynch 2018

Research Methods for Business Students
Seventh Edition
Mark Saunders, Philip Lewis, and Adrian Thornhill
ISBN 978-1-292-01662-7
© Mark Saunders, Philip Lewis, and Adrian Thornhill 2016

The Study Skills Book
Third Edition
Kathleen Mcmillan, and Jonathan Weyers
ISBN 978-0-273-77331-3
© Pearson Education Limited 2012

ISBN 978-1-78764-527-1

Printed and bound in Great Britain by CPI Group.

CONTENTS

chapter

1

What is a Consultant?

This chapter answers the questions: what is a management consultant and what is management consultancy?

You may be an experienced consultant who wants to pick up a few new tricks. On the other hand, maybe you are new to consulting and want to gain a better understanding of what it is all about. This chapter is aimed primarily at the novice consultant, whether you are considering joining a major consultancy, are starting out as an independent consultant, or have been recruited as an internal consultant. It provides an overview of some of the fundamental concepts in consulting. Most of the book is about *how* to be a consultant. As an opening to the subject this chapter answers *what* being a consultant means.

To gain the most from this book it is important to understand what a management consultant is, to be familiar with some common consulting terminology, and to appreciate the difference between being a consultant and other roles. If you want to be a management consultant, it is helpful to recognise why you want to be a consultant and to think through whether or not it is a profession that can meet your desires. To achieve this it is useful to have at least a basic grasp of the economics of a consulting business. This chapter sets out to do all of this. There is nothing complex here, but it is important as it provides the foundations for the rest of the book. This chapter covers a disparate range of topics that combined give a basic, but essential, picture of consulting.

One small, but noteworthy point: rather than write the phrases 'management consultant' and 'management consultancy' repeatedly, I shorten these to 'consultant' and 'consultancy'. There are other types of consultants and consultancy, and many of them could find something useful in this book, but the focus is on the management variety.

What is a management consultant?

There is a large and growing band of people who call themselves management consultants. Some people are management consultants but do not use this title, preferring labels such as *business advisor, strategy consultant, operational consultant* or even *leadership consultant*. These and related job titles encompass a divergent and eclectic group of individuals.

The work such people do varies enormously. The fee rates range from low to very high, and the length a consulting project may vary from hours to years. Clients who use consultants can be the owners of firms, managers of one level of seniority or another, or the main board directors of major corporations. Clients can also be staff in the public sector and not-for-profit organisations. Some consultants are employees of the firms the consulting takes place in, others are external but regular faces within an organisation, while many are individuals who appear in a client organisation for a short time and never reappear again. Their areas of specialist expertise go from obscure pieces of business to generalist management advice. Given this huge variety, what is it that is similar that enables them to be bundled together as *management consultants*? It is not easy to come up with a concise definition that covers this assortment of roles.

“it is not easy to come up with a concise definition”

The problem with describing the role of a management consultant is compounded by the fact that some existing definitions have been written by people who are not consultants, and who do not understand fully what consultants do. But listening to professional consultants can equally be misleading. Those who are consultants have a vested interest in making the role sound majestic and magical, and to bias any description towards the type of work they specifically do. I have read definitions of management consultancy in sales brochures, books, dictionaries and various online encyclopaedias. A few definitions are the hopeless summarisations of people without any real understanding, some are correct but focus on irrelevant aspects of the role, many are good, but do not quite manage to encapsulate the role and its variations.

Given the wide variety of consultants, rather than starting with a definition, I will list characteristics to provide an appreciation of the role of a consultant. As little in this world is absolutely black and white there are caveats with each one of these characteristics.

Consultants do the following seven things:

1. They provide advice and recommendations to managers, and may provide assistance with the implementation of the recommendations.
   Caveat: Consulting companies may provide a whole range of services, from pure consulting to training and outsourcing. Not all of this is consulting. Consulting is about providing useful advice, and helping managers to implement the advice.
2. They base their advice and recommendation on a set of skills and expertise, or intellectual property they have available to them.
   Caveat: This is what should happen. However, ask any experienced manager and they can probably tell you of the time they spoke to or even engaged someone who purported to be a consultant but who had very limited skills, experience or intellectual property.
3. They consult. This may sound obvious given the name, but it is often forgotten. What I mean by this is that consultants engage in dialogue with an organisation and its staff, and apply their expertise to develop recommendations, taking account of the specific needs and context of that organisation.
   Caveat: Some firms called consultancies do not consult. Such firms may be very successful in selling research, benchmarking data or other types of information. Consultants do not sell products or give the same advice to everyone. There is nothing wrong with selling a product, but irrespective of how it is branded, it is not management consulting.
4. They are involved with a given client on a temporary basis.
   Caveat: The length of a consulting project may be anything from hours to months. Occasionally, it may be years, although it is difficult to argue that someone who has worked continuously in one organisation for years is still working as a consultant. (Internal consultants work for one organisation, but they will be working on different projects across a range of departments or divisions.) It is not unusual for a consultant to work regularly for the same client, but each piece of work is of a limited duration.
5. They are independent. A consultant should be providing advice or recommendations irrespective of the internal politics and vested interests of an organisation or the managers who are their client.

Caveat: Consultants are human, have their own business interest to consider, and naturally have their own biases. But a consultant's biases should be independent of a client's biases.

6 They are not paid for from an organisation's normal staff budgets.
Caveat: A manager who wants to employ a consultant needs a budget for it. This is often true even for internal consultants who charge back their time, and if they do not, they remain an overhead to the rest of the business.

7 They add value to a manager and the client organisation by helping them to change. Value can take many forms, such as improved decision making, faster change implementation, reduced business risk and so on.
Caveat: At least they should do! Reality is not always so clear cut.

If we take these seven characteristics of a consultant and take the most pertinent points it is possible to develop a definition of a consultant that is true in most situations:

Definition

A consultant is an independent advisor who adds value by helping managers to identify and achieve beneficial change appropriate to their situation.

Essential consulting jargon

To get the most from this book it is important that we start with a common understanding of the basic terminology surrounding management consultancy. Some words, or pieces of consulting jargon, will be used repeatedly through the book, and if you are new to the industry then it's important you become familiar with these concepts. I am not generally a big advocate of jargon, but there are words and phrases that are continuously used by consultants. Most of these may be obvious and intuitively understandable, some are not specific to the consulting industry, but they are essential to know.

Consultants tend to talk about ***clients***, rather than customers. The concept of a client is explored in the next chapter. In general terms, the word is used both to refer to a specific manager who gives the consultant direction on a consulting project, and the organisation in which that manager works. Hence a consultant may think of the client as Mr Peter Smith of the XYZ Company, or may consider it to be the XYZ Company. To differentiate, when I refer to a client I am talking about a person (or group of people), when I am talking about the organisation the client works for I use the term ***client organisation.***

Once employed by a client, the specific consulting project being undertaken is usually referred to as an ***engagement*** or sometimes a ***live engagement.*** A client is one of a larger group of ***stakeholders*** a consultant must deal with. Stakeholders form a set of individuals who consultants must take into consideration when delivering an engagement.

To win some work consultants engage in ***business development.*** Business development relates to time that is not (usually) ***chargeable*** to a client, and includes activities that are associated with marketing a business and pursing specific sales. The aim of business development is to identify ***opportunities,*** and then convert these opportunities into live engagements and hence have some chargeable time. An opportunity is the situation in which a client has a need for some consulting support. To convert an opportunity into an engagement and hence be able to charge fees, consultants must normally write a description of the service they will provide to the client. This description is called a ***proposal. Chargeable time*** is the time when a consultant is billing fees to the client. Once an engagement is complete, consultants often seek to ***sell on***, that is to sell a subsequent consulting engagement to the client so the consultant can remain chargeable.

“consultants must normally write a description of the service they will provide”

In order to sell regularly, and for proposals to be successful, consultants may have ***service lines.*** A service line is a specific area of expertise that a consultant or a consultancy company invests in. For instance, one consultancy may have a service line in improving the management of IT departments, and another may have a service line to increase innovation in business. Service lines may be the informal labelling of expertise of individual consultants, but they can also be the formal documentation of processes and approaches to consulting by larger consulting companies. Service lines and any other knowledge or approaches are often called ***intellectual property*** or ***intellectual capital*** by consultants. Intellectual property has a specific legal meaning, but many consultants use this phrase in a looser fashion than the legal definition requires.

One of the most important measures of a consulting business is ***utilisation*** or ***chargeable utilisation.*** Utilisation is a measure of the proportion of time a consultant is working on fee-paying work on a client site. Hence, a consultant who is billing three days a week is 60 per cent utilised. It is normally not possible for a consultant to be 100 per cent utilised because some time must be spent on business development, the creation and maintenance of service lines, and holiday.

How does consulting differ from other roles?

Developing a full understanding of the role of the consultant is helped by understanding the difference between a consultant and an employee, a manager or a business leader. The boundaries between being a consultant and, for example a manager, are grey, but there are important and definite differences.

Let's start by considering the role of a consultant versus an employee in the organisation using consultants. The obvious point is that a consultant is not an employee of the organisation they are helping, but an employee of a consulting business. Why does this matter? Most consultants want to do a good job that satisfies a client, but their performance assessments, pay increases, promotions, ongoing praise and criticism are not done by the client organisation. All these are influenced by their performance with clients, but consultants have different motivations from client staff. Consultants are never fully part of a client organisation's team. For example, a client may regard a consultant as having done a brilliant job by providing fantastic advice. A consulting company may judge the same consultant to have only done an average job because he did not manage to make any additional consulting sales.

A consultant can be part of a client organisation's project team, and in doing this share some goals with other client staff, but consultants are always to some extent independent from the client organisation. Their incentives and performance drivers are different. This is true even for an internal consultant. Obviously, an internal consultant is employed by the same company as their clients, but is not employed by the same department or part of the same management hierarchy. This is not necessarily a bad thing – a consultant who is as much part of your team as any other employee will struggle to give truly independent advice.

What about the difference between being a consultant and a line manager? Like managers, consultants often are hard working and want to produce a quality result, but this is relative to the scope of a consulting engagement. They do not and arguably cannot deliver an end result in a client organisation, and do not live with the outcomes of their recommendations. If a consultant is providing advice, then, if the advice is accepted, a line manager has to implement this advice somehow. Even if consultants help with implementation planning or a change implementation project, they do not end up working with the results following the implementation. Consultants are temporary visitors to an organisation – it is line managers who must live with the results of any consulting engagement.

There is another point about consultants compared to managers. Many consultants are ex-senior managers with a good understanding of the challenge of managing a department. On the other hand, whilst all consultants advise, some have never managed anything of any significant complexity. Even relatively senior career consultants, who became consultants from university, may never have managed a team of more than 20 people. For someone in an operational role with several thousand staff and a budget of hundreds of millions, a consultant's understanding of the reality of dealing with this number of people and scale of budget will appear limited. The consultant's response to this should not even attempt to be an expert line manager, but to provide focused specialist expertise beyond that of a normal manager.

Finally, what about a consultant compared to a business leader? Many consultants fancy themselves to be great leaders, and some have the potential. There are well regarded business gurus who have come from a consulting background, but a guru is not a leader – a guru is an influencer and a shaper of opinions. Sometimes you see a successful chief executive with a background in consulting, and they are probably a great leader. But on the whole I am sceptical about professional consultants as leaders. The consultancy profession encourages the development of a range of skills which sometimes can be mistaken for leadership, such as strong communication and influencing skills. Normally though, consulting does not require significant leadership skills. You can be a very good consultant without having the ability to lead or inspire.

“you can be a very good consultant without having the ability to lead or inspire”

The fact that consultants are different from employees, managers and business leaders should not be taken as a criticism of consultants. Consultants are not employees, managers or leaders – because that is not what the role entails or requires. Consulting is a very different role from being an employee, manager or leader. Consultants must appreciate these roles, be able to work with them and be able to influence them. Some consultants may have a background in organisations which required them to manage or to lead, but this is not universally true. Consultants should not forget that the role of the consultant is to consult, not to manage or to lead.

Now, having said all this, comparing consulting to other roles does to some extent depend on the type of consultant being talked about. There are two dimensions of consulting we should be aware of and differentiate:

1. ***Internal or external consultants***: An internal consultant is a full-time employee of an organisation who has a role as a consultant to the business. Typical examples include human resources (HR) or internal change management specialists. An external consultant is someone who is engaged for a specific consulting project, but otherwise is independent of an organisation. Internal consultants tend to have a greater understanding of an organisation's culture and are familiar with many aspects of a business that an external consultant will take some time to learn or understand. External consultants will typically have a broader range of experience and have done work similar to their current engagement in other organisations.
2. ***Strategic, operational, implementation or specialist***: Many consultants work in a wide range of roles and float between providing strategic advice, helping with implementing it and supporting operational managers. But generally we can differentiate between consultants (and consulting companies) who advise organisations at a strategic level – what direction a business should be taking; at an operational level – how the business should be run on a daily basis efficiently and effectively; or at an implementation level – how to deliver projects and changes (which may be derived from the advice of a strategic or operational consultant). There are also specialist consultants who focus on a particular area of advice. Arguably all consultants should be specialists, but what I mean here are, for example, consultants who focuses on very specific areas such as regulatory compliance advice or on minimising technology costs.

Another thing to consider is whether the work being done is consulting or another related profession. There are several job titles in common use which are often employed in relation to consultants, or in relation to people doing work that can seem similar to that of a consultant. The main examples are:

- *Contractor*: A contractor is a temporary employee who is usually paid a day rate to complete some work which is of a transitory nature, where it is not appropriate or not possible to employ a permanent member of staff. This covers a wide range of areas – from office cleaners to very short-term senior staff. The overlap with management consultants is that many projects require temporary staff, and these are often contractors. Organisations are often left with a choice of whether to use contractors or consultants. A rough difference is that a consultant is employed to advise or provide skills the client does not have access to, and a contractor is employed as an extra pair of hands to increase the capacity of an organisation beyond that available with existing permanent staff.
- *Interim manager*: An interim manager is a specialised form of senior contractor. An expert manager is engaged to perform a management role for a limited period of time – for example because a senior manager is ill or on maternity leave. Interim managers should be expert managers, who fit quickly into even the most senior management roles. It is really impossible to define hard and fast boundaries with consultants, as many consultancies offer interim management services and some consultants regularly work as interim managers – but when they do they are not working as a consultant.
- *Coach/mentor*: It is common to pay for professional coaching and mentoring, to help individual managers. Such work is normally done on a one-to-one basis. Coaches and mentors are slightly different, but they are both concerned with helping individuals to reach their full potential. A consultant may work as a coach or mentor to individual managers, but there are also professional coaches and mentors, who rightly do not consider themselves consultants.
- *Facilitator*: A facilitator is someone who uses facilitation skills to help a group or team resolve some issue or problem. Facilitation is one of the most misused words in business and is explored. Facilitation is often closely associated with workshops, but it is possible to use facilitation in other situations. Facilitators do not advise directly, but help clients to solve their own problems. I regard facilitation skills both as an expert profession in its own right, but to a certain degree also a core skill of all consultants.

It is worth understanding the differences in these roles, which can be real, but the boundaries are often exaggerated for commercial or personal reasons. Professional interim managers, facilitators and coaches have valid reasons related to the nature of the roles to differentiate themselves from management consultants, but it also makes commercial sense to do so as well. Many consultants have the necessary skills and often work in one or more of these roles, but you should not assume that all consultants can or even need to be able to perform such roles effectively. Put another way, you can be a successful consultant without, for example, having the capability to coach or be an interim manager.

Varieties of consulting organisations

There are many different organisational structures you can work in as a consultant, and the choice is important as it will affect the type of projects you do, the nature of the day-to-day work, and the level of risk and uncertainty you expose yourself to. There are essentially four ways you can work as a consultant:

1. as a solo or independent consultant working for yourself or your own company
2. as an employee of a major consulting company
3. as part of an organisation offering a portfolio of services of which consulting is only one – the most common is the consulting, IT development and outsourcing company, but there are other variants
4. as part of a small consultancy company.

To some extent the choice depends on personal preferences, and what opportunities are open to you. I have worked in organisations in all these models.

The independent consultant is usually either someone who has worked in a larger consultancy but wants a more self-sufficient lifestyle, or an ex-senior manager who now wants to advise rather than manage. There are many reasons for choosing to become independent. I now prefer to work for my own company as it enables me to maximise my personal flexibility. The cost is that I am completely dependent on my own ability to find projects and generate an income. However, once you have an established reputation this is not that hard. Organisations always need help. Additionally, as my business costs are comparatively low, and I have other revenues, should I choose not to work for a few months I do not need to generate significant revenues to cover my

“organisations always need help”

business costs. I have access to a wide variety of work. I even undertake some very large engagements as I have a network of trusted colleagues, and we work together often to deliver larger engagements than a single consultant can manage.

At the other extreme are the major consulting companies. If you have little experience, are a recent graduate or like to combine consulting with a corporate culture these are the organisations for you. The big consultancies can be attractive places to work. For example, they tend to give great opportunities for professional development, international working and arguably reduce your personal risk as you have teams of people around you also helping to win and deliver engagements. Additionally, the larger firms often win massive projects which may require leading-edge thinking and techniques, although on the largest projects you can feel like a cog in the machine rather than a real consultant. If you become a senior manager (or partner) in such organisations the rewards can be high. But it does mean all the baggage that comes with corporate life such as annual appraisals, fitting in with company culture and worrying about things like brand risk. Big consultancies are also notoriously political environments. Some are focused on people who fit their specific organisational culture, which can give the consultancy a very defined feeling that will not suit everyone.

Companies offering a portfolio of services beyond consultancy provide a large variety of career options. However, if your firm is not purely a consultancy, there is always the tension over how independent the consulting advice is and whether it is really just a sales channel for other services. Some outsourcing firms have very successful consulting divisions, but there is always a doubt in some clients' minds as to whether the consulting is impartial advice or a funnel to win outsourcing contracts.

Whilst I am happy not to work for a large firm any more it is fair to say that I probably could not do what I do now had I not learnt what I did working for the major consultancies I was employed by. It is by no means a bad place to start.

There are many smaller consultancies, which offer a compromise between the complete self-sufficiency of the sole trader and the corporate hierarchies of the larger firms. Some of the smaller consultancies are industry leaders in specific consulting niches. For instance you can find consulting firms who specialise solely in financial regulation, telecommunications, customer services or cost control in manufacturing. If you have a particularly focused specialisation there may be a firm for whom you are a perfect fit.

Why do you want to be a consultant?

If you roughly understand what a consultant is, then it is time to reflect on whether and why you want to be one, and if your reasons have a realistic chance of being fulfilled.

The best reason for wanting to become a management consultant is simply because you enjoy the process of consulting with clients. Of course, if you have never worked as a consultant what 'consulting with a client' means will be unclear. If you do know, and this is the reason for becoming a consultant, then you are well set for a successful career. However, most people have more pragmatic grounds for becoming a consultant.

A common reason to join the profession is the potential variety of the work. Although as a consultant you may work in a specialist area, you will work in many organisations. The context and culture of the organisations and details of the problems will vary significantly. I find consulting work highly varied. I have worked all around the world, for companies in a wide variety of sectors, with clients of differing levels of seniority, to help resolve a divergent range of problems. However, if the service you will provide to organisations is very specialised – for example, helping them to be compliant with a specific piece of industrial regulation – what variety you gain from different clients you may also lose in essentially doing the same piece of work again and again.

Some people join consulting for skills development. This typically arises from one of two sources. Development may happen because of the wide variety of challenging work you are involved in. And there is no quicker way of improving your skills than doing a wide variety of challenging work. Alternatively, and this is most true for graduates coming into consulting, it is because you join a company who understands that its key asset is people and hence is willing to invest significantly in their development. Consulting does provide a great way to develop a powerful set of useful skills, such as problem analysis, communication skills and influencing skills. One important exception to this is that if you want to learn how to manage people then you will be better off seeking an operational line management role.

However, this brings me to another potential advantage of consulting. If you want to, you can avoid much of the burden of line management that goes with a corporate role. Some individuals love managing people, some hate it. If you work for a large consultancy you may still have staff whom you have to performance manage and motivate, but the teams tend to be small. As an independent consultant staff management is not something you have to worry about.

Graduates often want to join consultancies for the lifestyle and travel. There are a few professions which enable you to travel even more and to wilder places, such as mining and oil exploration, but generally there is a fantastic opportunity to travel as a consultant if you want to – especially if you are multi-lingual. Such travel can be exciting and rewarding. Working in foreign countries gives you a perspective that other travellers never gain, but it is a double-edged sword. Travelling all the time can be dull. You have to be a little shallow to be really interested in having gold frequent flyer cards with several airlines. Often the locations sound exotic, but an office is an office wherever it is in the world. Continuous travel will also play havoc with your social life.

> “working in foreign countries is a double-edged sword”

Some people want to enter consulting for the money. The money earned as a consultant can be good, but of course it depends what you are used to. Few consultants achieve the rewards of the chief executive of a major company, unless they happen to become a senior partner in a big firm. On the other hand, most reasonably successful consultants earn more than senior middle managers and junior executives in most other industries.

There are much more down-to-earth explanations for becoming a consultant. Some people just fall into it. I was recruited by Coopers & Lybrand out of industry, and frankly I had no idea what consulting was but it was better money, which for a young man with a family seemed an attractive proposition. I was lucky in that it is a career that has suited me immensely. Other people come into consulting because they feel they have no other choice. Perhaps they have been senior managers who find themselves late in their careers having been made redundant and, irrespective of age discrimination laws, cannot find a suitable alternative role. These are not necessarily bad reasons for entering the consulting profession. We are all, at times, hard-nosed about our careers, and just because you entered the profession as way of overcoming redundancy does not mean it will not be a huge success. On the other hand, simply because you have some business skills does not mean you will thrive as a consultant.

A phrase that has become common recently is the 'portfolio career'. This is a career in which you mix various different types of work together. This is definitely possible as a consultant, especially if you are self-employed. Some types of work can complement consulting very well. I know many people who manage to control this mix very successfully. I have several professions: as well as running my consulting business I write, deliver training courses and seminars and take regular time out to study.

Whatever your reasons for considering consulting, don't fool yourself that it is always an easy ride, or that it will give you a completely flexible lifestyle. For example, as a self-employed consultant you may well be able to take more holiday, you may well be able to work part time – but, and it is a big but, within the constraints of your clients' needs. You may decide to work only nine months a year, but that does not mean you can definitely choose the three months you don't work to be 1 November to 31 January every year whilst you are in the South Pacific, and expect at the same time to be 100 per cent fee earning until 31 October, and have an immediate start again on 1 February of the following year. Clients won't usually wait for a particular consultant: if they have a problem they want someone to fix it, and if you are not available they can usually find someone else to do the work just as well. Consulting opportunities cannot simply be turned on and off. They have to be searched out and won. Clients and engagements do not easily fit a predictable pattern. If you want flexibility you do need to have some flexibility yourself.

Whatever flexibility you want from consulting is effectively a constraint on your ability to service clients. If you are clever and pragmatic there is no reason why the constraints cannot be overcome and you can manage to balance your own and your client's desires very well. But you cannot both maximise your income and maximise your personal flexibility (unless, perhaps, you really are a world renowned industry guru).

I know many people who love working as a consultant. But consulting does not suit everyone's personalities. If you are constantly working in different organisations, it changes the relationship with the place you are working. To some extent you will always be an outsider, which does not suit everyone's personality. Consulting can leave many people with an ongoing feeling of uncertainty and risk. As one project ends, where is the next and when will it start? If you are an independent consultant there is no career path as such – you may want to vary your work, and may over time increase your rates, but there is no management hierarchy to be promoted through. If you work in one of the large consultancies, promotion is possible, but for most firms seniority beyond a certain level does not just depend on your consulting skills and expertise, but on your ability to sell.

Consulting offers great opportunity, but it is different from other types of employment. It offers potentially high rewards and significant flexibility. If unmanaged, it can intrude into your personal life, but arguably so does any senior role. If you are pragmatic and flexible, then you can get a good level of rewards and flexibility in return.

The economics of consulting

The past few decades have brought an increasing stress on the work–life balance and less on the financial factors of employment. However, a key aspect in deciding whether to be a consultant is whether you will make the income you desire. Whether a career in consulting can provide you with the money you want depends on your expectations (or income needs), your degree of success, but also the inherent economics of consulting. Before entering this profession you should understand your potential income. I am going to look at this only very, very simply. This is not a business plan for a consulting business, but it does explain the basics.

“this is not a business plan for a consulting business”

Let's start by considering the case of a single independent consultant as this is the simplest to understand. I will only look at revenues. Costs for independent consultants are generally low, and most of those that are incurred are attributable to clients and can be recharged as expenses. So, I am going to ignore them for now. This is of course a gross generalisation, but it is fine to begin with as it will not change the overall outcome. There are two factors that determine how much money you generate as a consultant:

1. the number of chargeable days a year you achieve
2. your daily charge-out rate.

(Not all consulting projects are charged on a daily basis, but this basis is accurate enough to understand the general economics of the business.)

It is really as simple as that. So how do you know how many days a year you will work for and what daily charge-out rate you will achieve? There are huge variations between different consultants. Taking account of fee rates and number of chargeable days it is quite easy to find two apparently similar consultants, one of whom has an income three or four times higher than the other. At the extremes, comparing the lowest to highest revenue-generating consultant then the multiples are much greater.

Some estimates

To estimate the daily rate you will achieve it is best to do a little research, but it is not straightforward finding accurate information. There is no easily available database of rates as there is no transparent market in consultancy, and it is generally not in consultants' interests to make it transparent. A good place to start is the internet. There are websites dedicated to sourcing consultants and other temporary staff that will give you a rough idea of potential daily rates, but they do tend to focus on the lower end of the market. There are studies of the industry, but they are not always freely available. Even if you get hold of one, their categorisations of consultants may give you some ideas, but generally are too broad to base your own fees on. A good source of information is your personal network. Ask a few friends who hire consultants regularly, and you may be able to get a feel for the sort of rates the big firms charge. These tend to be higher than independents achieve, although this is not always true. The best way to get a feel for rates is to find someone with some experience of the industry and ask them what they think you will be able to charge. Never forget, whatever fee rate you expect or want, it actually depends on a client being willing to pay it.

Next you need to estimate how many days a year you will work. If you are new to consulting, do not be overly optimistic. Can you really work 5 days a week for 52 weeks a year? That gives you 260 chargeable days a year, but you should never assume that what you make is 260 times your daily rate. You will rarely be 100 per cent utilised – and even if you can be, do you really want to be? As a rule of thumb, assume you will be busy 100 days a year. You may well be a lot busier, but if you cannot afford to be a consultant working only this many days you are taking a significant risk. Many consultants make a very comfortable living on this, and many more are busy for considerably more than 100 days a year. But it is best to be conservative at the start of your career.

Other factors

There are several other factors you must consider. There are possible tax efficiencies of being self-employed or running your own business. You need professional advice to understand these fully, and tax legislation can change at any time. Remember, if you are becoming a self-employed consultant after a career in industry there are none of the benefits that you may have received in your previous job. There are no extra pension contributions, no bonus, no paid holiday, no health care or sick pay, no car allowance, etc. Additionally, you should not confuse income with cash flow. Consulting tends to pay big bills in dribs and drabs, and some clients can be very slow in delivering cash into your bank account. I am usually paid reasonably promptly, but some invoices have languished for six months before finally being paid. You need to have a float of money to cover for these periods.

For a consulting firm with multiple employees the economics are much more complex. Costs cannot be ignored. Business costs for premium office space and facilities may be high. Staff you employ will naturally expect many benefits on top of salaries. There will be the costs of non-fee-earning staff and senior staff: although they may be able to charge some fees, these may not cover the full cost of their salary and expenses. Bad debt has to be considered – that is clients who will not or cannot pay. I have never (yet!) experienced this and it does seem to be rare. However, in the largest firms, simply because of the volume of work they undertake, occasionally a client may not pay. Whatever the size of firm, slow payment remains a far bigger issue.

Profitability of consultancy companies can be very high when chargeable utilisation is above a certain level, but drop below this level and all those large salaries and fancy offices can soon lead to big losses. Hence the tendency of some firms to recruit heavily in the boom times, but also to be quick to make staff redundant when the economy is struggling. In the end, although an accountant could find a million flaws in my simple views, the profit of a consulting company can be approximated by a very simple piece of arithmetic:

Profit = (days charged × average charge-out rate) – cost of business

The rate you charge and the number of days you work are dependent on clients, but your costs are largely under your own control. With modern technology and services you can run a consultancy on a shoestring, and still look completely professional. Therefore the most important considerations will always be making sure you charge enough days at a high enough fee rate to generate the income you require. If you are committing yourself to significant costs before you have started to generate revenue, think again. You can always make those commitments once you are sure of your income.

Finally, what about the situation in which you take a job within a consultancy, as an employed consultant, rather than someone who runs their own business? Here your salary is to some extent divorced from the economics of the consulting business, and is down to what you can negotiate. The big firms tend to have a standard package for graduates. For more senior staff the salary and package will depend on how valuable you are to the consultancy and what you can negotiate. At a more senior level your value to a consultancy is more related to your relationships and personal network than your pure consulting skills. Generally, the large consultancies pay well and provide a good set of other benefits. There are professions paying higher, but consulting has to be considered as towards the top end of the market in terms of salaries. As an internal consultant it is different, and your salary will depend on the market rates associated with your specialisation and the remuneration policies of the specific firm you are being employed by. Generally, salaries are lower than in the consultancy companies.

“big firms tend to have a standard package for graduates”

What is a good consultant?

By this point you know what a consultant is, why you might want to consider it as a profession and whether you will make any money. In this final section I want to consider what makes a good consultant. Much of this book is taken up with giving advice on how to be a good consultant; this short section is concerned with what would be assessed as a good consultant.

When I told a friend of mine, who is a successful and experienced consultant, about this book he responded with the comment that there is little to write. He said the book would only be about 10 pages long, but then went on to advise that I should not write a book, but a haiku! The truth behind this jibe is that it is quite simple to define what a good consultant is – but most of this book is about how to achieve this rather than defining it. My poetry skills are limited, so I will stick to prose rather than the haiku. A good consultant: *continuously adds value to clients commensurate with his or her fees.*

We will explore what adding value means in later chapters.

There is a significant difference between being good at something and being a good consultant. There is an old joke, aimed rather unfairly at teachers, saying: *those who can, do; those who can't, teach.* This joke can be extended to become: *those who can, do; those who can't, teach; and those who can't teach, consult.* The joke for teachers is unfair, but it hides an important truth – there is a difference between being good at something and being a good teacher. As many students will attest, being a good university lecturer is quite a different skill from being a brilliant academic. I am sure we have all experienced the giant brain who cannot explain anything, and the person with a nominally lesser grasp who explains it very well. While most teachers are perfectly capable of doing, that is not what they are employed for – they are employed to impart and embed knowledge and skills in their students. Whether or not they can actually 'do' is to some extent irrelevant. It is similar for consultants. There are many advantages in having management experience, but consulting is not about managing. Equally, having been a great manager is an advantage for consulting, but it does not guarantee that you will be a successful consultant.

From your perspective you are a good consultant if you achieve your personal objectives through consulting. I cannot tell you what your personal goals should be, and the rest of this book is about how you can continuously add value for your clients. However, you may wonder whether you have the right type of personality to succeed as a consultant. There is no single personality type who makes the best consultant, but I will pick on a few factors which I think are important.

Firstly, as a consultant you should be a people person. It is not necessary to be a natural extrovert, but you must be happy engaging with others. You will constantly be working and interacting with people, and if this does not excite you then consulting is not for you. Next, you should be flexible and adaptable. Client needs and expectations vary enormously, and you need to flex to the situation. It may surprise some people, but it also helps if you are not status conscious. Although you may end up as a hugely successful consultant earning much more than most of your clients, when you are on a client's site you are just a consultant doing a job for them. Consultants must be orientated to resolving problems. A client has engaged you to help; there are many forms this help can take, but all of them must result in resolving a client's problems. Next, whilst a consultant is there to help, they must not be over hasty in determining solutions. You must have the personality that wants to solve problems properly, rather than resolve the most apparent symptoms. You want to be like the doctor who finds out why a patient has spots rather than the one who just gives a cream to make them less itchy. Finally, you must be someone who listens. To be objective and to provide a diagnosis that is most helpful to the client requires listening and assessing the situation. Solutions must be tailored to the specific context.

There are many other factors which influence your ability to be a great consultant, but the above are critical.

Summary

If you are new to consulting there are some essential concepts you must understand. You should now be familiar with the main concepts covered in this chapter. They are:

- The role of a consultant and the difference between it and other roles, especially that of a line manager.
- The skills of a consultant in relation to those of other professions such as contractor or interim manager.
- The core consulting jargon.
- The variety of consulting organisations.
- Why you want to be a consultant and whether it is a profession that can fulfil those needs.
- The economics of consulting.
- What a good consultant is.

The rest of this book explains how to be a good and successful consultant.

chapter

2

The Ethical Dimensions of Operating as a Consultant

Until comparatively recently, few people regularly used the phrase *business ethics* and few worried about managing a business ethically. This is not to deny that individuals in business had ethics or that some commercial enterprises have a long history of shaping their work based on clear moral stances. But this was usually about individual views and not a universally shared acceptance of the need for ethical business practices. This has changed. Study for any MBA, and sooner or later you will find yourself considering business ethics. In any modern company today it is ethics as well as commercialism that influences decisions and actions. The management consulting industry is no exception.

Of course, there has always been a foundation of rules defined in the law. Further rules exist in commercial regulations, which have become generally more specific and onerous over time. Remaining compliant with the law can be considered as an ethical issue, but this is not the concern of this chapter. With the number of consultants there are in the world, no doubt some are charlatans who take a relaxed attitude to adhering to legislation, but I think these are a small minority. Legal and regulatory compliance are not trivial issues, but I am going to assume that if you know the law you want to remain compliant with it. But is that sufficient? The answer is easy and simple: no. Ethics goes beyond legal issues. It is not difficult to imagine many scenarios which are legal, but which most people agree are unethical.

Thinking about ethics opens many complex debates – for instance, absolute moral principles versus relative and culturally specific values.

There are deeply conflicting views on whether an action is ethically sound simply because it adheres to some fundamental principle; or if actions should be judged on their intentions or on their consequences, irrespective of underlying moral principles. No matter how clear you feel you are on ethical principles (e.g. 'stealing is always wrong'), you can very soon find yourself challenged in valid ways (e.g. 'Ah, but what about the pen you are writing with – didn't you take that from the office stationery cupboard? Isn't that stealing?'). These are deep waters and areas where there is definitely no universal consensus. Other than acknowledging the complexity of ethical considerations, it is significantly outside the scope of a book like this to even discuss issues of this complexity. My aims are much more modest. I want to raise the issue of ethics so that it is a conscious part of your consulting perspective.

Ethics can be trivialised or on the contrary made overly complex. In this chapter I will show that ethics should not be a trivial concern for the consultant, but neither should ethics be an intensely complex piece of analysis. Commonsense, pragmatism and reasoned judgement lie at the heart of most good ethical decisions. I have split this chapter into three sections reflecting these introductory thoughts:

- ***Ethical basics***: What are the basic guidelines we should try to adhere to as consultants?
- ***Application of ethics***: Having ethical concepts is one thing, applying them is another. This section considers two specific aspects of consulting – the privileged position of the consultant, and the relationship between the consultant and client.
- ***Ethics and dilemmas in consulting***: If all we needed to do was list some ethical rules and adhere to them, life might be comparatively simple. The real challenge is when different ethical guidelines or other objectives conflict, and deciding how to deal with this.

Irrespective of what you take from this chapter and how much consideration you choose to give to ethical issues, there is a simple practical stance to take. You always have a choice as to what work you do and how you interact with a client. Part of this is an ethical choice. Engagements can usually be shaped in different ways and ethics taken into account during this shaping. In the rare case that the engagement cannot be shaped appropriately, never forget that you can always say no to any engagement you feel ethically compromised on.

Ethical basics

A simple way to think of ethics is to look at the concepts which enable you to decide how to do good and, as important, how to avoid doing harm. Considering the consultancy context, what does this mean in practice? I have chosen seven examples which reflect a simple set of ethical guidelines or can be seen as areas of temptation for consultants:

1. Ensuring fair fees for the engagement.
2. Performing only appropriate engagements relative to skills and experience.
3. Only performing work that the client needs and is in the client's interest.
4. Avoiding building a dependency of the client upon the consultant.
5. Respecting client information.
6. Using fair contracts.
7. Avoiding conflicts of interest arising from simultaneous commercial involvement in a consulting and client business.

Let's explore each one of these in a little more detail.

Fair fees

The fees a consultant charges are part of a commercial relationship between the client and consultant. We should not confuse what is commercially reasonable with ethical fairness. If you have a particularly rare and valuable skill that you have developed over years of consulting, it is perfectly reasonable for you to charge a fee rate in line with what the market will bear. If you are lucky enough for this to be 10 times what your less skilful competitors can charge, this is purely a commercial issue. Fairness is concerned with how the fees are presented and handled. The client should have an understanding of what the fee rates will be at the start of the engagement, what any extras that will be charged for are, and what the total level of fees for the engagement are likely to be. If the engagement changes, then there is time for debate on the fees again. If the client wants to enter an uncapped time and materials engagement, then again there is nothing unethical in charging the client for every second you have worked, as long as the client appreciates what they are

“fairness is concerned with how the fees are presented and handled”

committing to. Similarly, you should not be charging clients for any time on an engagement where you are developing your company's intellectual property and not directly adding value to the client.

One particular issue associated with fees is the charging for time working in a client office or on work related to a client engagement, when the consultant is not actually progressing the engagement but is engaged in business development. Your sales activities should be at your cost, not charged as hours to the client. Of course, you will recoup this one way or another from the client, otherwise you would not stay in business, but that should be recouped from the margin you make on your legitimate chargeable hours.

An area that often causes tension between clients and consultants is the recharge of expenses. Part of this comes down to the apparently lavish lifestyle of some consultants. This is not an ethical issue. What your expenses policy is remains an issue for you and your company. A client has the option when signing up to your services to negotiate what are acceptable levels of expenses to them. You may damage your relationship with your client by having an overly lavish expenses policy, but that is your choice. However, where it becomes an ethical issue is when expenses recharged to a client were not actually accrued related to the engagement. Typical examples are:

- Charging all expenses for travel and accommodation to a certain geographic region to one client who is currently being billed for a live engagement, when one of the reasons for travel was to visit other clients for sales meetings, without the opportunity to recharge travel costs to the latter group.
- Inviting clients out for drinks or dinner, and then recharging them for the privilege.

Performing appropriate work

The second ethical issue involves performing only appropriate work. But what is appropriate work? All consulting engagements require competencies and knowledge. These include any combination of functional, sector, geographic, and service line skills and experience. Loosely defined, appropriate work is engagements that you have the correct skills and experience for. What skills are appropriate depends significantly on the role you are taking on in an engagement. If you are selling yourself as an expert then it is not unreasonable for the client to expect you to have in-depth expertise in a specific area or business. On the other hand, if you are putting yourself forward as a process consultant or facilitator, then whilst you must have process consulting and facilitation skills, specific functional or industry knowledge is less relevant.

It is relatively easy to convince some clients that you have skills which you do not, and unfortunately there are many consultants who seem to just about get away with this. I call this type of consultants *chancers*. They will win the work and take the chance that they will get away with it, irrespective of real competence. These chancers may not sell on very often, but survive on the basis that the pool of clients with problems is very big and they may never need to work with the same people twice. Such chancers are more common in certain parts of the world, where clients have less experience of working with consultants.

What actually is an appropriate level of skill or experience is clearly a judgement. No engagement is a copy of a previous one. Even if it could be, the client situation will vary in some ways, so there are elements of unpredictability, exploration and learning on each engagement. There will be clear-cut cases when you are confident your skills are sufficient and there will be situations which you walk away from because you are not the right person. But there are many ambiguous situations when it is not certain, and in my experience this constitutes a large proportion of engagements. There is a fine difference between a legitimate stretch in your skills and a leap into the unknown. If you are even the slightest bit unsure, the most ethical position is to explain to your client what you do and do not have experience of, and how confident you are of being able to stretch this to meet the situation. Then leave the choice to the client. Clients will usually respond positively to consultants who are open enough to admit their limitations as well as their expertise. Such openness can be the basis of a long-term trusting relationship.

A related but slightly different issue is using the client as an experimental testing ground for a new service line, or using the client engagement as service line development. Consultancies do need to develop service lines, and client experience forms the base of such service line development. This is reasonable. It is even reasonable to develop the service line as part of the work, if this is agreed with the client. It becomes unethical when:

- As part of the engagement's sale it was claimed that there was a service line when it does not exist, and it is developed 'on the hoof' while on the engagement: in this situation, the client is subject to risk and being charged for the service line development.

- You claim that a service line provides proven value, when in fact if it is a new service line and so effectively an experimental product whose value has no evidential base.
- You claim you have a service line, when in reality you have minimal understanding of a topic but have read an article or two and sound convincing to the client.

An appropriate service is also one in which the consultant has access to sufficient data and information to draw the right conclusions from. If you do not have or cannot find the skills to analyse the situation, then you are not offering an appropriate service. Without the right data, no matter what skills or experience you have, the results of your engagement are unlikely to be correct.

Consulting services are appropriate only if they are based on an understanding of the specific, unique situation of the client. Of course a consultant brings experience from other situations, but simply giving exactly the same advice or the same plan in every situation is not appropriate. Value-adding consulting is always bespoke. Providing a 'cookie cutter' approach is not adding value. There is nothing wrong with a company that sells a standard service to a client which is not tailored to the individual situation. But it is not management consulting – the very word *consulting* implies consultation and hence dialogue and interaction. If you are selling a plain vanilla service then good luck, but do not call it management consulting.

> “value-adding consulting is always bespoke”

Only doing necessary work

The third issue for ethical consideration relates to only doing work that a client needs and is in the client's interest. One situation in which this matters is with follow-on work, when you have been fortunate enough to complete an engagement successfully and part of the recommendations are for subsequent work using your skills. There is an obvious moral hazard when the person with an interest in future work is also the person advising a client as to what the future work should be. I do not see any problem with advising follow-on work that requires your skills, or winning it. The problem comes only if the advice you gave has been deliberately skewed to favour the sell-on. The easiest answer is to point out your inherent conflict to the client. Most clients see the conflict of interest, and pointing it out does not change anything other than making it clear that you are being open and honest.

There are some situations in which the bias is more covert. A classic example is that some consultants design engagements to overcome client issues by starting with the generation of hypotheses. The hypotheses are used as a starting point to explore what the client issues and solutions might be. The engagement then seeks data to prove or disapprove the hypotheses. This is common practice, especially amongst the more strategic consultancies. There is nothing intrinsically wrong with it, as long as the selection of hypotheses and the search for data is not biased to come out with a result that is in the consultant's commercial interest. Unfortunately, sometimes the selection of hypotheses is biased. This problem can run very deep. Some consultants so strongly believe their own skills, service lines and views on management that the bias is unconscious. Unproven assumptions are made about how a business should and should not be run, and these are reflected into the hypotheses and data collection approach selected. There is then an inherent bias which results in recommendations that unsurprisingly(!) match other services the consultancy can offer. This problem can be compounded by some consultants' lack of understanding of the difference between a hypothesis, a conviction, an evidence-based conjecture and a fact.

Another problem can arise when the strength of a consulting company's brand is used to pressurise a client to undertake work. When a partner or other senior member of a major consultancy looks a manager in the eye and says 'we are advising you to do this', this can be the quality advice of a good consultancy sticking to its guns, but it can easily veer into an implicit threat. The unspoken statement is really: 'Follow our advice and the risk is not yours, go against it and everyone will know it was your choice – if it goes wrong you will pay the penalty.' Great care is needed here, because in some situations this is a legitimate position to take. To me, the difference between an unethical threat and a reasonable statement comes down to intentions. If it is given as a valid warning to the client, then it is ethical. If the threat is given purely to bully the client into purchasing your services, it is not.

Often consultants remain working with a client well after an engagement has really finished. Sometimes they stay beyond the time they are required, without adding value that is commensurate with their fees, simply because the client has not got round to terminating the engagement. If you keep on working beyond the natural end point, you should question whether you are still really offering sufficient value to the client. If you aren't, then move on.

Avoiding client dependency

My fourth ethical concern is client dependency on the consultant. It is quite easy, with some clients, to develop a dependency on your skills. It may be accidental, but it can also be engineered. There is a point on any engagement, whether it is an engagement delivering recommendations, a plan or implemented change, when the question to answer is 'so what should the client do next?' Answering this question is the source of many ethical challenges. A dependency on the consultant can be developed by not providing all the information to enable a client to progress work, so they have to keep coming back to you for more. It can also be through inappropriate advice, for example selling proposals or ideas that are unnecessarily complex relative the client's level of skill and which you know they will need your help to implement.

As so often with ethical issues, there is balance required. A client may legitimately want to retain your skills for a period of time because they continue to add value in various ways. This is the basis of long-term consultant–client relationships. But, this is quite different from the deliberate manipulation of recommendations or plans relative to the client's skills so that they need to retain you – either to interpret the recommendations to plans, or simply because they are written in such a way that you are the only person who can fulfil them.

Handling confidential information

The fifth point on my ethical list relates to the correct use, and avoiding the misuse, of client confidential information. This must be based on a general respect for the confidentiality of data you collect as part of the engagement. This is another complex issue, as clients have to have sensible expectations with respect to information as well. Of course, you cannot take specific data and sell it to your client's competitors. Also consultants should not be secretly collecting data on client sites which then will form part of their consultancy's benchmarking database. But your client hired you because of some specific expertise – expertise you developed at other clients. It is inherent in hiring a consultant that they will learn whilst working for a client, and what they learn will be used on future clients. Consultants should not be embarrassed about this. It is effectively part of the definition of the profession of consultancy. If a client does not like this aspect of consultants, then

“clients have to have sensible expectations with respect to information” they have a simple commercial decision – there is no compulsion to engage consultants. But there is a significant difference between learning on a client's site and actually walking off with specific client ideas and business information which you use to support selling to or delivering engagements for other clients.

Using fair contracts

The sixth ethical issue boils down to the consulting contract. Clients should know better, but it is easy to fill contracts with all sorts of inappropriate small print. Of course, a client should really have the contract checked (see next page). But the fact that important clauses are hidden in the small print and not explicit in the proposal reflects the suspicion that some consultancies are trying to pull the wool over their client's eyes. I have noticed two areas where I think some consultancies push the boundaries of ethics:

1. ***Ownership of intellectual property (IP)***: Many consultancies, including some of the blue chip names, have contractual clauses stating that they own the IP from any consulting engagement. What grates with many clients is that the IP (if there is any) was developed when working with client staff. Ask anyone if they think it is ethical that person A owns the IP for a piece of work they developed in conjunction with person B, when person B paid for all the work. Most people will say no! Yet this is precisely what giving ownership of IP to the consultant means. Of course, consultants may bring IP on to the client site which they should retain ownership of, so it can be difficult to disentangle really original IP arising from an engagement with what the consultant owned before. However, whenever I am employed to choose and manage consultants, I insist that any clause giving the consultant full ownership of IP is taken out or at least renegotiated for shared IP.
2. ***Recharging for expenses and supporting activities***: The actual amount charged to a client may significantly exceed the pure consultant time costs. There are expenses on top, sometimes administration fees and all sorts of other fees. Often these fees are reasonable, but sometimes they are completely unreasonable. I have heard of partners in some firms recharging proportions of their club fees to clients. Also some simple administrative support can be very profitable for consultants – for example, photocopying at massively inflated rates, well above the usual commercial rate. I have seen six-figure charges for photocopying.

Conflicts of interest

The final ethical concern relates to conflicts of commercial interest. This is almost turning the ethical problem around, as its root lies with the client. I have come across situations where company directors are simultaneously directors of consultancy companies and lobbying for the use of the consultancy in the business they are a director of. I have come across a senior IT manager pushing the services of an IT consultancy that he had a direct shareholding in. These are clear ethical breaches, and probably fall foul of most organisations' corporate governance regulations. Requiring staff to register such commercial conflicts of interest and penalising rapidly and heavily for breaches is usually sufficient to remove most of these temptations. One possible solution that clients and consultants can adopt is to simply rule that any company the individual works for cannot be provided services by the consultancy they also have a commercial interest in.

I want to end this section on ethical guidelines by looking at it from the opposite perspective. Whilst you have an ethical responsibility as a consultant, the client also has a responsibility to behave in a sensible and competent manner. Clients have lawyers who should read the small print and accept the contract, modify it or suggest a completely different contract. Managers should only ask for appropriate services for their business, and in the end it's their job to buy what their business needs – not only yours to ensure it is right. Managers should review findings, recommendations and plans and ensure they are fit for purpose for their organisation. You are not selling door-to-door products to vulnerable groups. You are selling a professional service to a commercial enterprise, and the working principle of *caveat emptor* (buyer beware) must to some extent hold. However, ethics cannot be shrugged off with the view that the clients are 'big boys' who should know better than to accept unethical practice. As a consultant, you have a clear ethical responsibility to your client.

Application of ethics

Ethics is interesting as a theoretical subject and one for debate with friends over dinner. But what makes ethics real is its impact on the decisions we make and the actions we take. There are two factors which can make the applications of ethics in consulting quite complex:

1 the privileged position of the consultant
2 the lack of clarity over who the client is.

As a consultant you operate in a privileged position of trust. Imagine the scenario of a client you have worked with on and off for many years. A client who values your skills and the way you execute engagements. You are regularly advising the client. You are a *trusted advisor*. As a trusted advisor to the client you face one of the classic moral hazards in business. It is your advice that often leads to you gaining more work. You will know when you are selling on if it is right for your client, and if it is right for you. That is the opportunity to make the right ethical choice. If you do not know, you are not thinking clearly enough, as it is usually obvious. When you legitimately sell on, your interests and those of your client align, and this is a good outcome for both of you. When your interests are not aligned, don't try to sell on.

“when your interests are not aligned, don't try to sell on”

The privileged position can run deeper than this. We now enter distinctly muddy waters – and that is whether as a trusted consultant you have a *duty of care* to your client. Technically, duty of care is a legal term referring to the need for professionals to conform to a reasonable standard of care when executing their profession. I do not literally mean a legal duty of care, but the ethical duty of care a consultant has to their client. What is the difference between a commercial duty and a duty of care? To me, your commercial duty is to fulfil the terms of your contract and proposal. A duty of care goes beyond this and means upholding the standards expected of a profession. By duty of care I mean a responsibility actively to ensure your client gets the best advice, irrespective of the precise boundaries of your engagement, and to execute all your work to a high-quality standard. If you have a duty of care you cannot turn a blind eye to anything you think is substandard or inappropriate, irrespective of the scope of your consulting engagement.

There are several dangers once a consultant reasons they have a duty of care. The first is simply that you can get lost flagging a myriad of problems to a client. No business is perfect and there are always hundreds of substandard ways of working. If not, there would never be the possibility of any business improvement. Additionally, the label 'duty of care' is often used spuriously by consultants to barge into all sorts of areas of the business that really have nothing to do with their work. Therefore consider seriously whether you have a duty of care to your client or not. If you do, it is not a stick to beat the client into doing work they would not otherwise accept, but it is a responsibility to work professionally and advise on related matters that you are competent to advise them on.

What about the lack of clarity over who the client is? Throughout this chapter I have considered *the client* as the focus of our ethical considerations. But as I described in earlier chapters, the identification of the client is not a trivial matter. Consultants tend to think of the client as an organisation, but an organisation is an abstract entity. On the other hand, consultants may think of the client as an individual, but the interests of no one individual in an organisation may actually align perfectly with all the interests of the organisation. So, there is the odd situation that an organisation is made up of people, you can only interact with people and judge the organisation's interest from those people, but the organisation's interest may not completely align with any of those people's interest.

Of course, for many engagements we can, in practice, say that there is no ethical dilemma. The scope of the engagement is such that the interest we should consider as described by individuals in the organisation is to all practical purposes the interest of the organisation. But this will not always be true. Consider the following questions:

- If your work leads to someone being made redundant, have you harmed the client? Usually consultants answer no. Often this is right – but thinking about the grounds on which this judgement is made is often not as clear cut as it should be and can be suspiciously abstract.
- Should you go above the individual who engaged you to their boss without their knowledge, to comment on the individual's skills and ability? This sometimes is legitimate and sometimes unethical. Which it is must be determined by assessing the reasons you have for going to the boss and what alternatives are available to you. Generally, it is best to avoid such action except as a last resort.
- Does the engagement you are working on help a senior but incompetent manager to keep their job? At one level, if managers had all the skills required, consultants would not be needed. But if the primary reason for the engagement is to support a person who should not have a job, then this must be regarded as unethical.
- Are you providing advice for the benefit of an individual client manager over the organisation as a whole? This is veering not only into ethical issues, but potentially into straightforward corruption.

- If the engagement results in recommendations on redundancy or job changes, are you giving unbiased advice, ignoring your commercial interest? You can envisage consultant's advice being biased against staff who oppose or inhibit the consultant's work or ability to win further work. Sometimes, as part of a change activity, people do need to be moved into different roles or removed from an organisation, but this must only be because it is in the organisation's interest. Doing it for the commercial interest of the consultancy is never ethical. I am sure this practice is rare: it is completely unacceptable.

Some consultants avoid the issue of conflicting client interests by saying that they are working for a higher authority; no, not God, but the shareholders' interests. This is just dodging the issue, and is one of the great intellectual evasions of consulting. Generally, a consultant is not engaged by the shareholders. The consultant has probably never spoken to the shareholders and does not understand their interests other than some vague and generic need to increase value in some way or another. Thinking that you are working for the interests of a group of people you have never spoken to, never specifically analysed, and whom you have no relationship with, has to be considered as highly dubious.

So what classifies an engagement as in the interests of the organisation? The answer can only be for you to make a judgement of the situation based on the information that is available to you. Moreover, if you assume that you have a duty of care to the client, you should not only consider the information that is available to you, but also actively seek out the information you require to make the ethical choice.

Ethics can seem a burden, yet can also be an advantage or selling point for consultants. As always with consulting, for every problem there is also a commercial opportunity. Understand the ethical issues and how to make balanced ethical decisions well, and there is an opportunity for ethical consulting as a service in its own right. Many clients face a range of ethical issues which they are not equipped to handle and benefit from consultants to help them along.

“for every problem there is also a commercial opportunity”

Ethics and dilemmas in consulting

So far in this chapter I have described basic ethical guidelines for consultants and considered aspects of being a consultant that must be taken into account when making ethical judgements. This final section goes beyond and looks at situations in which different ethical guidelines are conflicting, or when the consultant faces a conflict between ethics and other considerations.

There are many ambiguous situations when it comes to ethical decisions, where clear thinking and sharp judgement is required. With some dilemmas there may never be a truly satisfactory answer, only the least wrong one. But the ability to make a balanced decision in such situations, whilst not unique to consulting, is a regular part of the challenge of being a successful consultant.

There are three common situations where dilemmas involving ethics arise:

1. balancing the interests of different stakeholders
2. constraints the client puts on the engagement
3. the conflict between commercial interest and ethical guidelines.

Let's look at each of these in turn.

Balancing the interests of different stakeholders

Balancing the interests of different stakeholders, both within the client and also within the consulting organisation, is a very common challenge. We have already discussed the concept of a client as being complex, and that there may be more than one client. When the role of the client is made up of different people, they will often have different interests and hence there is a risk of conflict. Examples where this can cause dilemmas for the consultant are:

- When two (or more) client representatives want different and incompatible things covered in an engagement. Often, different client needs can be catered for in a single engagement, but it is possible that they can conflict irreconcilably.
- If an individual member of a client organisation, who is paying for your work, wants you to do something that is not in their business's interest.

There is no single solution to these sorts of issues, but the answer is to be found by a combination of the following:

- Having a clear primary client who arbitrates and makes decisions when there is a conflict of interest.

- Not hiding or ignoring the issue of conflict. Be explicit with your client: it is the client's problem and although you can help they must in the end fix it. If you try and ignore or hide a conflict, this may often lead to greater problems, which you are then party to.
- Negotiating a solution that is acceptable to all parties, involving the different clients in the negotiation. A single meeting bringing the interested parties together is usually the best way to do this.

Finally, if nothing else works and you are left with either an impossible engagement, one in which you will not be perceived to deliver value, or one in which you feel unacceptably ethically compromised, walk away. This may not be easy to do, and I do not underestimate how difficult some clients can be if you say you do not want the work. But you should uphold your own standards.

Constraints the client puts on the engagement

The second type of dilemma which faces consultants is connected to the constraints clients put on engagements. As part of scoping an engagement, or during carrying it out, the client may specify a range of factors which constrain the consultant's freedom to decide how to pursue the engagement. Many of these requirements will be perfectly reasonable. For example, the client may need the work completed within a certain timeframe. Clients will usually have a limited budget and the engagement must be performed for whatever the client can afford. The client may be a busy manager and so may want to limit how much time the consultant can have to work with them. Similarly, clients have limits as to how many people they can allocate to work with consultants. These types of constraints are all part of a normal consulting engagement.

Most clients are reasonable and will negotiate on such constraints and listen to reasoned argument from the consultant. But in the haste to earn money or for an easy life, consultants can sometimes agree to all sorts of conditions which, in reality, are unworkable. Generally, this is a mistake. From a commercial perspective the consultant needs to think through any constraints and decide if it is still possible to complete an engagement and be paid for it profitably. The ethical perspective is different. Even if you can complete the engagement and are paid for it, you must decide at what point is the engagement so constrained that it will add no value to the client? A sensible consultant is only interested in commercially viable engagements. An ethical consultant is only interested in engagements that are of value to the client. It is possible, if sometimes difficult, to be both sensible and ethical.

Experienced consultants can think of many examples of client behaviours which reduce the value the consultant may give. Some clients regularly engage consultants, never listen to the consultant's advice, but still pay the bill. I have no problem with clients who engage, debate and disagree with the consultant's findings – but if the client simply ignores the advice all the time, you are taking money from an organisation for nothing. Another example is that it is not unusual for clients to want findings without giving you enough time to do proper research or analysis. Of course, it is always possible to give some advice on even minimal information. But its validity and value are questionable. Consultants can be tempted to take the risk and provide advice without sufficient information, when in reality the answer should be to decline the work unless sufficient time is allowed for data collection and analysis.

Conflict between commercial interest and ethical guidelines

Throughout this chapter I have looked at examples of the possible conflict between commercial and ethical interests. I would like to complete the chapter by looking at two further conflicts of this kind in a little more detail. The first concerns the sustainability of consulting advice, and the second the application of knowledge from one client to another.

To add value to a client, a consultant must not only create whatever the agreed deliverables are – reports, plans, recommendations and implemented change – but also needs to ensure that the result is helpful to the client. For something to be helpful, it must be usable and appropriate to the client. Additionally, recommendations must be practical and workable in the client's environment. There is no point giving advice which you know will not be possible for the client to achieve. Your aim should not merely be to fulfil the letter of the proposal and deliver whatever you agreed to deliver, but the contents of the deliverables must have a lasting impact on the client.

> “for something to be helpful, it must be usable and appropriate to the client”

Effective consultants base their knowledge on the experience they have gained working in many businesses and many different situations. That is often the reason for engaging a consultant. The client starts by thinking, 'I have a problem of type X, which I do not know how to handle.'

The client then goes on to think, 'I will get help from a consultant who has dealt with problems of type X in many situations.' The ethical problem arises from the issue of understanding when it is appropriate to take knowledge and experience from one client and apply it to another. If you are a public sector consultant, there is probably no ethical issue, but as a consultant advising clients in the commercial field, there is. Is it ethical to help multiple clients by taking the knowledge from one business and selling it to their competitors? Even if we exclude directly sharing current business data, the consultant still has an ethical dilemma. Management approaches, business processes and other intangibles are the source of most competitive edge in business, but these things are the very currency of consulting.

One possible ethical line to take is to avoid working with direct competitors, at least in areas of the business that provide competitive differentiation. If you work for company A, you will not work for their main competitor, company B. This may be fine if you are a sole trader who has a much larger list of possible clients than capacity to do work, but this is impractical for a major consulting firm with tens of thousands of staff. The big firms, simply because of their scale, must at times work for direct competitors. In some industries there are fewer and fewer major players. To survive as a specialist consultant, you are bound at times to provide services to competing organisations.

An answer may be to challenge the validity of massive consultancies providing services to competing businesses. If you are so big that you must provide services to competitors, perhaps you really are too big to maintain a clean bill of ethical health. I think this is a valid challenge, but I know it is impractical. The huge services firms are here to stay. A more realistic answer is the concept of a *Chinese wall*. A Chinese wall is the term used for an internal division within a business in which certain information may not pass. Individuals working on one side of the Chinese wall may not work on the other. Companies such as financial services and auditors, where information from competitors or information about possible market sensitive changes are handled, use Chinese walls all the time. I applaud the concept. In practice, I am cynical about how strong such walls really are.

I think the solution must lie in an open dialogue with the client. If the client challenges you, you should commit to keeping their real secrets secret, but you must also be open to the fact that sometime you are likely to work for a competitor. That is just the way the world is and the nature of consulting. If the client expects you to bring direct experience of competitors, then they have no ethical grounds for complaining if you share your ever-growing experience with their competitors as well. If a client wants you to guarantee your experience is never used elsewhere, you need some guarantee from them as to an ongoing income stream!

Summary

Ethics provides you with an understanding of what you should and should not do, and how you can achieve good and avoid harm.

- There are a range of situations in which consultants have the opportunity to do good, and conversely there are situations in which consultants can be strongly tempted to undertake activities which are in their interests but which do harm to their clients.
- Each situation is unique and a range of factors must be considered before deciding what the most ethical approach to take is. However, making ethical decisions is a central part of being a good and client-centric consultant.
- Ethics is a complex matter for consultants because of the privileged position they occupy with a client, but also because the needs of different stakeholders may be very varied and yet must be addressed.

3
SELLING YOURSELF AND PITCHING YOUR IDEAS

Learning outcomes

By the end of this chapter you should:

- be alert to the things that can go wrong with presentations
- have assessed your own strengths and weaknesses in this area
- be able to structure a presentation in a way that is appropriate to your audience
- be developing your delivery technique
- be using appropriate software and other visual aids to good effect
- be confident in handling questions from your audience
- be able to control nervousness.

Introduction

Most managers will need to give talks or make presentations as part of their job, and such presentations are often an opportunity to raise your profile in an organisation. Your presentation skills may be tested at a job interview. Becoming better at making presentations can therefore make you more employable, and accelerate your career, as well as being useful to you as a student. Many people are terrified of public speaking at first, yet, with practice, most come to enjoy it, though usually with an element of nervousness. This chapter looks at the necessary skills and suggests ways in which you can improve your skills as a presenter. You may not become brilliant at it – such people are rare – but you can become good enough to get high marks on your course and impress potential employers.

The final face-to-face communication skill you need is that of making a presentation to a group. Poor presentations can be an ordeal for speaker and audience; good ones can be a delight for both. Furthermore, both good and bad presentations are *remembered*. Whether you are presenting your research results to a group of potential collaborators, talking to a group of senior managers in your own organisation, making a pitch to a potential major client or giving an after-dinner speech for a professional association, it is important to make a good impression. You may pay an invisible price for years to come if you do not. On the other hand, if you do well, unexpected opportunities may come your way in the future. You will also have an immediate feeling of power and euphoria from having had your audience exactly where you want them.

This chapter addresses the problem of nervousness and the skills that you need to make a good presentation. Again, these overlap with skills already covered. Being clear about your objectives, understanding your listeners' (albeit now in the plural) needs, expressing yourself appropriately and clearly and checking understanding will be as important as in one-to-one talking or in making a contribution to a group discussion. But additionally, you need to know how to ensure that your audience can see and hear you, to gain and hold their attention and to use visual aids to good effect. The bulk of the chapter looks at presenting formally to a captive audience. However, there is a short section on presenting more informally via a poster display with a passing audience.

The Risks in Presentation

Presentations, like written papers or reports, showcase you to a wider audience so it is important to do all you can to avoid the risks of anything going wrong. Because you are operating in real time, the risks of this may be greater than for a written report. If something is difficult to express in writing, you can keep trying until you get it right. If your reader finds that concentration has lapsed, they can go and make a cup of tea, then try reading again from where they 'switched off'. In a live presentation, neither presenter nor audience has a second chance.

There is normally less interchange between speaker and listeners in a formal presentation than in one-to-one or group discussion. Keeping the audience awake, interested and involved is therefore a considerable challenge. You probably know all too well how easy it is to stop concentrating in a lecture and have found sitting still and being 'talked at' a fairly stressful experience. Unfortunately, the older you get, the harder it becomes to be a member of an audience.

As in other areas, the best way to become more aware of what is required is to look at what other people do less than well. You can then look at how those who are more competent do the same thing. Once you are more alert to the different dimensions required, you will be better able to reflect on, and develop, your own skills.

Activity 3.1

Think of an unsatisfactory presentation that you have attended recently (lectures are fair game here, as well as presentations by fellow students). List all the factors which contributed to your dissatisfaction. Now think of an experience of a good presentation. List any additional features which distinguished this. (You can go on to do this again at the next presentation you attend.)

Good features: ______________________________

____

Bad features: ______________________________

____

If your experience is anything like mine, your list of bad practice might include occasions when the speaker did some or even all of the following:

- read a prepared speech in 'written' rather than 'spoken' English
- mumbled, whispered, went too fast or was otherwise inaudible
- used illegible visual aids – perhaps with far too much text in the smallest font
- faced away from you, perhaps while writing on the board or flipchart
- used a hypnotic monotone making sleep irresistible, probably with no visual aids at all
- distributed handouts during the presentation, so that you read these rather than listened
- was muddled incomprehensible, or said nothing you did not already know
- 'lost the thread' by responding at length to barely relevant questions
- went on long beyond the scheduled end
- got into an argument with a single member of the audience.

The remainder of the chapter addresses these common faults as well as covering features which may well have appeared on your list of 'good' points.

Activity 3.2

Did you mention presentation skills as a strength in your SWOT? If not, use the following questionnaire to assess your skill level (score 5 if the statement is completely true, 4 if mostly true, 3 if it is neither true nor untrue, 2 if it is not very true, and 1 if it is totally untrue)

I have lots of experience in giving presentations	____
The presentations I give are usually very well received	____
I always think carefully about what I need to communicate, and how best to do it to any particular audience	____
I am good at thinking of how to use visual aids to reinforce my message	____
I am confident in using PowerPoint to produce effective overheads	____
I think it is really important to watch the audience, and modify a presentation if it does not seem to be working	____
Total	____

If your score is 25 or above you should not need this chapter – assuming your assessment of your skills is accurate. Below this, you might think about developing an action plan to improve aspects of your skills.

Structure

A clear structure is perhaps even more important in a presentation than a written report. It is very easy for your audience to lose the thread of what you are saying and very hard for them to find it again if they do. They cannot go back and read the difficult bit again. So the classic advice of 'Say what you are going to say, say it, then tell them what you have said' still holds good.

Good presentations:

- have a clear structure
- are clearly signposted
- are clearly delivered
- use varied visual aids
- interest the audience throughout
- do not overrun.

Introduction

At the beginning you need to settle your audience, so say who you are, what you are aiming to achieve, how long you will be talking and how you plan to operate. Do you want to save all questions except those for clarification to the end, for example, or are you happy to take questions at any point? Will you be handing out copies of your overhead transparencies (OHTs) at the end or do people need to take notes? Once the ground rules have been established, you then need to outline the main points that you will be covering during your presentation. If you can say something that catches your audience's attention at the outset and makes them *want* to hear what follows, then the presentation is likely to go well.

Main presentation

As with a written report, you need to make clear what situation or topic you are addressing and use evidence to support the arguments you are making. Because of the difficulty of following a spoken argument, you need to make your structure absolutely clear and give your audience as much help as possible on this: 'What I have established thus far is . . . (brief summary). The next point I want to make is . . .' If you give such pointers at regular intervals, perhaps with slides or other visual aids to reinforce them, your audience will find it easier to maintain concentration and to stay with your argument.

Conclusion

This is the 'tell them what you have said' section. You need to summarise the points you have made, again using visual aids to reinforce them if possible. If you are making a proposal, then it is worth emphasising the main points of this again. It is also good practice to thank the audience for their patience and to invite questions or discussion.

Delivery Technique

If you do come across good presenters, study them carefully to see if there are ways in which you could improve your own performance. Even if you are not exposed to skilled practitioners, the following guidelines will give you a good foundation.

Relate to your audience

How well do you relate to a speaker who seems to be talking to a point on the back wall, in a monotone? Try to sound human in your introduction. Look at people. Say things in the way that they are most likely to understand. Check with them that you are on the right lines: 'Was that point clear?' 'Can you all see this slide?' 'Am I going too fast?'

Make it easy for people to hear

Speak clearly, not too fast, and vary your tone. Use short sentences and straightforward language, avoiding unnecessary jargon. Use 'spoken language' not 'written language'. If you have ever heard someone (literally) read a paper they have written, you will probably be all too aware of the difference. If not, try reading part of a journal article out loud, and then rephrase it using words you would normally use in talking. Avoid turning your back on your audience (whiteboards are a real hazard here) or being hidden by equipment.

Try to be interesting

Vary your pace and use a variety of visual aids if there are appropriate ones; showing something as simple as showing a pile of books on a subject can reinforce the point that there has been a lot written on it. Occasional humour can be useful, but don't overdo it (unless you are making an after-dinner speech, when a high proportion of jokes seem to be the norm). Above all, make the relevance of what you are saying clear. It may be less obvious to your audience why something is significant than it is to you: you need to *work* at making sure that they see it too.

Beware of becoming bogged down in detail

It is far harder to absorb detail from a spoken presentation than from a written report. Indeed, detail is likely to obscure the main point. Try to give only as much detail as you need to make your point. If a fine detail is crucial, it is probably better to give this as a handout. (If you are doing this at the end, let people know so that they do not take unnecessary notes.)

Avoid giving handouts while you speak

If you give out handouts while you are talking it distracts people, and you will lose your audience; everyone will be reading rather than listening. It doesn't matter how often you say of a handout 'don't read this now' – the temptation to look at it immediately seems universally irresistible. If you distribute handouts before you start, early arrivals will have something to do while they wait. It will also be clear to them how many additional notes (if any) they need to take. Handouts distributed at the end can be a good way of concluding, but you need to tell people at the outset that you are going to do this; otherwise they can feel annoyed if they have taken careful notes which the handout makes superfluous.

Keep your notes brief

Particularly if you are new to giving presentations, it is tempting to write out – and then read – the whole thing. Such a script can be reassuring as you know that if you dry up you can simply read the rest. But resort to reading only as an emergency measure. And if you do write out a full-text version, write briefer notes from which, barring the onset of total panic, you will actually speak.

These notes should indicate the key points to be made, in order. Hard copy notes are ideally made on index cards, numbered and joined with a treasury tag or similar in case you drop them. (Trying to reorder a hopeless jumble of cards while facing an audience can be deeply embarrassing.) Alternatively use a phone or small tablet – this is better than staring at a laptop. Indicate in your notes each point at which you need to use a visual aid. And cross-refer to your transcript so that you can easily switch to that if necessary. (After a few presentations, when you have never used the full notes, you will probably feel confident enough to dispense with them.)

It may seem obvious to use your slides as notes. But what will help your audience grasp and remember key points from your presentation is likely to be very different from what will help you remember what to say next. Slides should serve the first purpose!

Watch your audience

You need feedback on your delivery as you go along, so that you can adjust accordingly. People may not tell you in words, but their body language will speak volumes. If a glaze of incomprehension is stealing over your audience you may need to slow down and explain more, or perhaps check understanding by asking a question. If eyelids are drooping, you may be going too slowly already or have underestimated the prior knowledge of people there. Or you may need to vary your delivery more. If people are tense, tapping feet or fingers with restrained force, you are seriously getting on their nerves. You need to find out why. Unless you are fairly sure what you are doing wrong, *ask* what the problem is – and adapt your presentation in the light of the answers.

Be honest

Trying to fool people seldom works. If there is a weakness in your case, admit it rather than hoping that no one will notice. If they do notice, they will not think well of you for seemingly failing to spot the weakness yourself. But if you admit to it and have formed a good relationship with your audience, they may help you to strengthen the point. Similarly, pretending to know something when in fact you don't may make you look foolish. But admitting your ignorance may allow someone in the audience who does know to contribute their knowledge – to everyone's advantage.

Manage your time

Inexperienced presenters are often surprised at how little it is possible to communicate in a specified time. This is because they do not allow for speech being slower than reading, for questions of clarification, for introductions, for interim summaries or for use of visual aids. Do a 'dry run' in front of a friend to judge how long a presentation will take and adjust it if your guess is wrong. Aim to undershoot slightly. It is generally better to risk allowing slightly too long for questions than to run out of time, and to stop before you have said everything necessary.

Effective Visual Aids

Communication will be far more effective in either writing or speaking if you use images to reinforce your words. Visual aids have already been mentioned several times: this should have indicated that they are essential in formal presentations of any length or complexity. Such aids have three main functions: they can help the audience *understand* a point; they can help the audience *remember* a point and they can keep your audience

Visual aids can:

- reinforce key points
- clarify meaning
- aid retention
- keep audience awake.

awake. To make good use of visual aids, you need to think about how each of your points could be reinforced by an action, an object or a picture, and then how best to achieve this reinforcement. The best visual aid to use will depend on both the point you are making and the audience to whom you are making it.

Some things can be conveyed far more effectively by means other than words alone. Relationships are more clearly shown in diagrams, whereas trends are clearly demonstrated in graphs. Video clips can provide powerful and memorable examples. Other chapters cover representing data visually and diagramming other aspects of a situation. You can incorporate such visuals into your presentation as you would in a written report. The same principles apply, though within the restrictions of what can be seen from a distance. Revise these principles if you are in doubt. But although you will probably use visual aids similar to those suitable for a report for most of your points, your scope in a spoken presentation is potentially far wider.

Video clips of products, processes, people or places can be hugely effective. Concrete objects can also make a lasting impression. To take an example, when running open events to attract potential Open University students, I needed to explain how distance learning works, especially for a subject like management. *Showing* the audience a course pack, with written units, and print-outs of course assignments covered in teaching comments from the tutor, together with extracts from teaching videos or a video of a seminar (or recording of an online event) conveyed far more about the course than would a mere spoken description.

I have seen speakers hold up broken items to make a point about quality, or a new product to make a different point. Cognitive psychologist Stephen Pinker held up a comb to make a point about the innate distastefulness of using a comb to stir coffee. Such images make a lasting impression – though the point they demonstrated is not always clearly remembered. If the image is too strong, then it may overshadow the point (what *was* the significance of the comb-related distaste?). Even for points which might be adequately made in words, an appropriate visual aid might help people remember the point.

It is also important to incorporate variety to keep people awake and interested. For any presentation longer than, say, half an hour, it is worth using a range of visual aids for this reason alone. You can mix PowerPoint or Prezi slides with diagrams you draw on a board or flipchart at an appropriate point (do this quickly and avoid talking while drawing), and add photos and video clips to enliven your presentation. Because visual aids can be so powerful it is important to make sure that any you use will reinforce rather than distract from your message.

If your talk is short, you do not need to work so hard at keeping people's attention, and too much variety in visual aids can be counterproductive. It is better to reserve them for points that are best made visually, plus those which you really wish to emphasise.

TECHSkills 3.1 Choosing and using presentation software

It is now normal to use presentation software: PowerPoint is perhaps the most widely used, as it comes as part of Microsoft Office, but there are several other popular options. PowerPoint is basically designed to deliver a series of slides, stored on your own device, downloaded onto a data stick for portability, or stored a cloud for access from anywhere with internet access. Similar tools include Apple's Keynote, and for those with a Gmail or Google account, the web driven Google Drive slides, which since they exist on the Google cloud can be shared with 'friends'.

A popular alternative for those who find PowerPoint or comparable systems too linear is Prezi. Instead of a series of discrete slides, Prezi allows you to assemble your presentation on something akin to a giant board, constructing frames at different places and then zooming in and out from the big picture to individual frames as you give your presentation. The 'track' of the focus is pre-programmed, so you decide on the order the frames will appear beforehand, just as you decide on the order of your slides in PowerPoint, but what the audience sees is much more dynamic and visually interesting that a series of discrete PowerPoint slides.

Prezi provides a much wider range of templates, too, and makes it easy to use frames for pictures, video clips or other non-textual material to add variety, and to resize, move or rotate frames. The ability to see the 'big picture' is the visual equivalent of the summary in a report, and zooming out at intervals enable the structure of the presentation to be clear. A basic version of Prezi is (at the time of writing) free and there are many free tutorials online (see online resources for suggestions). This basic version should be adequate for your use until presentations become a key part of your job, at which point their hope is that you will purchase the more advanced system, which offers far more features.

If you want something even more different from PowerPoint, PowToon is another popular system. This allows you to create animated presentations, and if you love graphics you may enjoy playing with it.

As well as software that helps you directly create the visual aspect of your presentation, there are programmes such as SlideDog, which help you create the equivalent of a playlist of videos, documents or other things you might want to use in a presentation, and then link them to Prezi or other presentation software.

In recent years the range of options has increased hugely, and your choice of presentation software becomes correspondingly harder. What is best for you will depend on answers to a number of questions:

- What packages do you already have? (For example, PowerPoint comes as part of Microsoft Office, and your university might provide other options.)
- Do you want to be able to access slides or the whole presentation remotely?

- How important is it to create a good impression with your visual aids?
- How much time (and money) do you want to spend on acquiring new software and the skills to use it? (Though as noted, there are often free basic versions available usually offering only a limited number of features, and therefore perhaps less learning time.)

You will find online reviews of the main presentation software packages, and may like to check some of these out (see online resources for a suggestion). Check who is writing the review. If it written by the company selling one of the packages being reviewed you might expect a degree of bias!

Whatever presentation software and other visual aids you are using, it is important to consider how to use these to engage your audience and convey your message in a way they will understand, be convinced by and remember. Your aim is to communicate, and your visual aids are a tool for this, not something to be considered in isolation.

Resist using the features of your system just because you can. While it is important to know what the system can do, you need to choose those features which will best serve your objectives for the presentation. Only use features that are impressive in their own right rather than there to make your message more powerful if your main aim is to show your technical competence rather than to communicate a more substantive message.

If using PowerPoint or a similar system you need to be careful it does not constrain your presentation to an endless series of bullet points. As Naughton (2003) pointed out, PowerPoint was conceived in a software sales environment, so it tends to turn everything into a sales pitch. There was a version of the Gettysburg address doing the email rounds a while ago that demonstrated this limitation (see **www.norvig.com/Gettysburg** for some light relief on this topic, or explore versions fitting the actual speech to the slides or critiquing PowerPoint, which you can easily find online).

Tufte, a Yale professor and expert on visual communication argues that PowerPoint's ready-made templates tend to weaken verbal and spatial reasoning and corrupt statistical analysis. He attributes the Columbia space shuttle disaster to a slide that led Nasa to overlook the destructive potential of the crucial loose tile (see 'PowerPoint does rocket science', on Tuft's website **www.edwardtufte.com**). His analysis may also add to your understanding of the idea of argument mapping.

General requirements for visual aids

There is often a temptation to cram too much onto a slide. The amount of effective information people can absorb from any one screen is surprisingly small. Before finalising your visual aids, check that they will be visible to the normal eye from the same distance as the back of the room in which you will make your presentation. A good rule of thumb is to aim at no more than four points per slide.

Colour can either enhance or hinder clarity. Think about how you use it. I have seen tasteful but totally useless slides in shades of blue on blue, the words invisible from more than three paces. Use both colour and light/dark contrast to enhance legibility and emphasise key points. And be careful about fancy backgrounds and too much animation of slides: they may look good in themselves but they can distract, and obscure your message.

For 'transient' presentations, for example on group work, where all you are seeking is to convey your thought processes to fellow students, it is fine to use flip charts. But it is still important that you manage the amount of information per chart, and ensure that charts will be legible from the farthest seat. (Avoid using red pen, or any light colour, as these are not easily visible at a distance.) You can prepare flipchart sheets in the same way as slides and ask a fellow student to be responsible for displaying the right one on cue. (Trying to talk and manage a flipchart is possible but not easy. It helps considerably to split the responsibility.)

Activity 3.3

You can easily assemble an exhibit for your portfolio that addresses both your ability to use images and your ability to read and respond to materials. Take as the basis for this a presentation you make in class, perhaps summarising something you have studied. The exhibit should include the notes for your talk and copies of the images used, together with a description of how you selected the content and images, any feedback on their effectiveness from tutor and other students, and your reflections on what you would do differently next time.

Handling Questions

Sometimes questions are helpful, but I have seen them wreck a presentation completely. Until you are fairly experienced, it is safer to take substantive questions at the end. Make it clear at the outset that during your presentation you will deal only with requests for clarification and that there will be time for questions at the end.

Otherwise, you risk being completely sidetracked from your main argument or disconcerted by challenges to what you are saying before you have completed your case. If you want to postpone a question, either take a note of it so that you do not forget or, better still, ask the questioner to ask it again at the end. This means that your brain is not distracted by trying to remember the question while giving the talk.

When you do accept a question, your listening skills will be important. It is hard to listen carefully when you are nervous, particularly if someone is asking a complex question with many, perhaps not closely related parts. If this happens, jot down the key parts of the question, otherwise it is easy to answer the first part and forget all the rest. If you are at all uncertain what the question means, clarify this with the questioner. You may feel that it makes you look stupid if you don't understand. But if the questioner is far from clear it is sensible to pick up on this. You may tie yourself in knots if you try to answer a question that you have only partially understood: this does not look all that impressive either.

If a question challenges what you have said, resist the temptation to become either defensive or aggressive. Take their view seriously, looking for ways to develop your position in the light of it, unless you are convinced that the questioner really has missed or misunderstood your point or is misinformed. If the point has been missed by the questioner, others may have missed it too, so it is worth trying to repeat it in a slightly different way. If you cannot quickly satisfy the questioner, suggest that you discuss it after the presentation is finished. This avoids getting into an argument that will be of little interest to most of the audience.

People ask questions for many reasons. In work presentations, there will be some who are trying to make an impression on the audience, perhaps with a view to establishing themselves as a rival expert or advertising their own business. Or they may simply like being the centre of attention. Where questions are clearly being asked in the questioner's personal interest, it is simplest to thank them for raising their point, agree with as much of the point as you can, perhaps suggest a discussion outside the meeting and move on to the next question.

If questions reveal a genuine weakness in your presentation, it is usually better to accept this and ask for suggestions from the questioner and the audience for ways around the difficulty. You may find that someone can suggest a way forward. If, however, the difficulty seems to you to be much less significant than the questioner is suggesting, you will need to make sure that the audience does not end up devaluing the bulk of what you have said.

Virtual Presentations and Podcasts

Virtual presentations are becoming increasingly common for reasons similar to those driving growth in virtual meetings. Again they may be take place in real time, with scope for some at least of the scattered audience to email or phone in questions. Such presentations are often recorded to allow access by people not available at the time of the podcast, or there may be no live version, only a recording. Such presentations may be 'broadcast' through a conferencing system or made available (via Dropbox or Google Drive) for people to access on demand.

If you are studying online using a 'virtual classroom' you may be asked to make presentations on group work within this system. If not, you may well need to make virtual presentations at some point in your career, so can usefully think about any modifications that may be needed. If you are presenting privately, the general principles above may be enough, although it is worth using any 'voting' or other option to check understanding as you go along.

If you are 'broadcasting' your presentation on a public platform you will need to think about copyright implications. Video clips, music, quotations and images copied from elsewhere are all likely to be subject to copyright legislation, so should not be used without permission. You can find some music which is not copyrighted, but need to hunt for it. Podcasting is an excellent form of advertising if you eventually choose to set up your own business. A wealth of podcasting tips are available online should you wish to develop your skills in this direction.

Poster Presentations

Thus far the chapter has addressed formal presentations to a (normally) seated audience. At conferences it is common to supplement the formal presentation programme with less formal poster presentations. A large space will be made available, and each presenter will be allocated wall space for a poster. The audience will wander round the room, looking at the various displays and stopping to discuss those of particular interest with the 'presenter', who will be standing by the poster ready to answer questions.

This allows participants to access a much greater number of presenters than would otherwise be the case, and is often used to allow students to present their research. If you are doing a dissertation you may have the opportunity to take part in a poster session within the university or at a larger conference. This sort of presentation is also sometimes used in organisational contexts, at meetings between members of different project groups, so it is worth extending your presentation skills to include this format. In either case the poster presentation tends to be aimed primarily at peers and/or colleagues.

Poster presentations present different communication challenges to the presenter. The 'talking' part tends to be less intimidating: you are talking to people individually or in very small groups. On the other hand, these conversations are equivalent to the 'questions' part of a formal presentation, which is in many respects the most challenging part as much of the control passes to the questioner.

The real challenge for most, however, is in poster design. Typically you will have a space 1 metre high, and 1.5–1.75 metres wide. This space has to work hard for you. As with any communication, your first task is to clarify your objectives. What do you want the poster to achieve? Clearly this will depend on what you are presenting upon and the context in which you are presenting. Are you simply aiming to inform as many participants as possible? If so, what are the key points you are trying to get across? Are you trying to sell yourself or your research, and if so, to whom? Are you aiming to engage colleagues in conversation? If so, what would you particularly like to talk with them about? Are you seeking like-minded people from other universities with whom to network? If so, what would be most likely to interest such people? This is not an exhaustive list. It merely indicates the sort of objectives you might have. You need to be absolutely clear of your objectives on each occasion.

Posters aim to:

- attract
- inform
- start conversations
- advertise your work
- summarise achievements.

Clarity is paramount because 1.5 square metres is not very big, and anything within this space has to be visible from around 1.5 metres away. So every word needs to count, and you need to use pictures (or graphs or whatever) as much as possible. Aim to 'show' rather than 'tell'. A good rule of thumb is 20 per cent text, 40 per cent graphics and 40 per cent space. Do not underestimate the importance of this white space, on slides, as well as in posters. It is what gives the other 60% its impact.

Given overall space limitations, and the need to include a lot of white space, you need to think very carefully about what to include. Useful questions to answer include.

- What are your (very few) key points?
- How can you convey these graphically?
- How can you lay these out on a poster so that they will communicate to someone walking past at a distance of up to 2 metres?

Remember, you may be in competition with dozens of other posters, and participants will not look in any detail at more than a small proportion of these. You will not have time to talk to everybody even if you attract them. So, how can you ensure that you engage those people with whom you are likely to have the most profitable conversations, prime them to ask the most useful questions, and leave a favourable impression both of you personally and of the work that you have done?

If you Google 'poster presentations' you will find a wealth of information on how to lay out posters for maximum impact. The essential messages are:

- You need to say who you are, where you come from and the topic covered by your poster – IN VERY LARGE WRITING.
- You need to have a clear 'path' through the poster so that people can follow the narrative easily.
- You cannot afford to waste a single word – 'Findings' or 'methodology' do not convey information by themselves. Something like '80% misunderstand age legislation' carries a message. Think newspaper headlines here. Write large, and with bar charts or other simple graphics to support them.
- You need a way of continuing the exchange when you have 'engaged' someone's interest. At the very least show your email address clearly on the poster. But it is even better to have a handout expanding on key points, with your email address on it. Safest of all, particularly if your key aim is to network, is to have people write *their* email address (or write it for them) and email a more substantial document – the text behind the headlines – a couple of days later, with a note saying how much you enjoyed talking to them.

Figure 3.1 shows two possible layouts for poster presentations for a standard research presentation. You may be able to be far more creative – but do remember the need for clarity from 2 metres distance. Messy and cluttered do not, on the whole, attract.

Controlling Your Nerves

It is natural to be nervous when standing up in front of a group of people, whether for a formal presentation or a poster display. The adrenaline it generates can give your performance an excitement that it would otherwise lack, so do not aim to become totally blasé about it. But excess nerves can be a liability, drying your throat and making you physically and verbally clumsy. If you think that you are worrying more than is reasonable, there are several things that can help considerably: get as much practice as you can; concentrate on exposing yourself to similar situations; practise deliberate relaxation and prepare for each specific presentation.

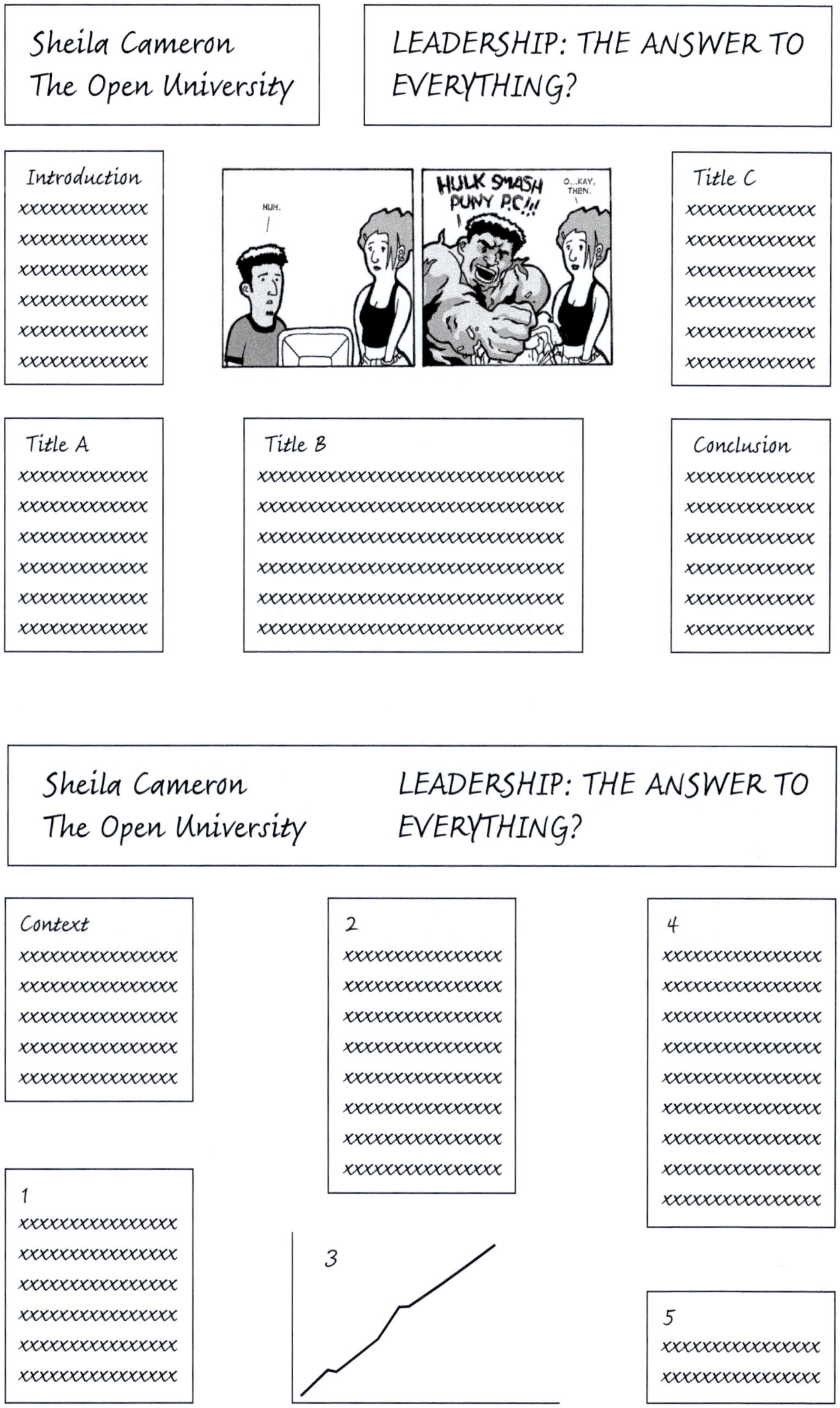

Figure 3.1 Possible layouts for poster presentations

Increase your confidence in presenting by:

- **frequent practice**
- **relaxation techniques**
- **thorough preparation.**

If you *are* over-nervous, you probably avoid situations where you need to talk in front of people. But the best way to reduce nervousness is to seek out such situations and force yourself to talk. Find the least threatening situations first – talking to a small group of students before addressing the whole class, getting used to the class before giving a paper at a conference would be good ways to start. But *do* it. Each time you will feel less nervous.

This is one form of practice which 'desensitises' you to the general trauma of the situation. Another form is to have one or more 'practice runs' of a specific presentation. This will mean that you are confident about the structure of the talk, have practised some of the phrases you will use, know where to use your OHTs or other visual aids and have checked how long it takes, so that you are not worried about having too much or too little material.

Relaxation techniques, discussed as part of stress management, can help reduce this sort of stress too, though you need to be familiar with the techniques for best effect. If you have not yet practised them, a short period of deep breathing will help. And a *small* alcoholic drink can sometimes be useful.

But your best weapon against nerves is the knowledge that you have done everything possible to prepare for the event. If you have carefully researched your subject and audience, your talk (or poster) is well structured and your notes are well organised, your visual aids are well chosen and you have at your fingertips supporting evidence and examples, you have little to fear. Dry runs, described above, can be part of your preparation. Remember, a presentation is a challenge, but it can be exciting and rewarding, and can provoke interesting discussion on a subject dear to your heart. Preparation is so important that more detail is given below.

Even if you have prepared, you may well experience an initial onrush of nerves when you stand up to make a formal presentation. To get you over this, make sure that you have your introductory remarks written out in full, preferably learned by heart. Take a sip of water and a deep breath, go over your introduction and by then you will have calmed down enough to enjoy yourself.

Preparation

Preparation is the key to successful presentation and you cannot afford to cut corners if you want to do well. You need to have thought carefully about what to communicate, how to structure it and how to add impact to your arguments by examples and visual aids. For important presentations, you will want to rehearse your arguments several times. Much of this can be done piecemeal, for example while exercising or in a waiting room, *sotto voce*. But you will need one full-scale, real-time rehearsal to check timing, use of aids and flow of arguments – or responses to a poster and likely questions. Ideally, find colleagues or friends to act as an audience and ask them to give you feedback afterwards. If this is impossible, then, for a formal presentation, tape yourself and replay the tape after a decent interval, listening critically and noting points where you need to change something. For a poster, come back to it a few days later and try to pretend that you know nothing about the topic.

If you are giving a presentation at work, to clients or potential customers, or a paper at a conference, your preparation needs to extend to ensuring that the location is set up as you want it, temperature is appropriate and equipment working properly. You do not want to be struggling to get your laptop to talk to the data projection system in front of your audience! So arrive early and make all the necessary checks.

Preparation for your *next* presentation should be informed by feedback from the last, so it is important to capture as much feedback as possible. Make a note of your immediate reactions in the light of audience response. Do this as soon as possible after the event, noting in your learning journal your feelings and points for future action. If possible, have a friend in the audience charged with giving you their reactions and suggestions. You may even be able to design and distribute a short questionnaire for the audience to complete on leaving. If the presentation is one of a series, this can be extremely useful in helping you to adjust future events to meet audience needs more effectively. If you are likely to have the chance to participate in more than one poster display, feedback may have the same benefits. If you are preparing an exhibit on your presentation skills, it will be important to include all such feedback.

SUMMARY

This chapter has argued the following:

- Presentation skills are an important part of communication in the work context and may indeed be tested during selection procedures.
- During your studies you will have many opportunities to develop these skills and they may even influence some of your marks.
- Successful presentation depends on adequate preparation. You need to be clear on your objectives and those of your audience, and structure is even more important here than with written communications.
- Good visual aids help audience concentration, comprehension and retention. A range of presentation software is available, but it is important to use it to reinforce your message rather than to flaunt your technical skills.
- Audibility, visibility and ability to pace your delivery to suit your audience and your content are essential.
- Questions can be an asset or a disruption. Substantive ones are probably best taken at the end.
- Poster displays present major challenges of distilling the core message into words and graphics visible from 1.5 to 2 metres away.
- Extreme nervousness can be disabling but lower levels can help. Practice, relaxation and preparation will help you to reduce excessive nerves.

Further information

Bradbury, A. (2010) *Successful Presentation Skills*, 4th edn, Kogan Page.

Conradi, M. and Hall, R. (2001) *That Presentation Sensation*, Financial Times Prentice Hall.

Kermode, R. (2013) Speak So Your Audience Will Listen, Pendle Publishing.

Leech, T. (2013) *Say It Like Shakespeare*, 2nd edn, Presentations Press. This gives an interestingly different slant on presenting.

http://guides.nyu.edu/posters – there are many useful websites but try this one.

Customshow (2015) for a review of alternatives to PowerPoint at http://www.customshow.com/best-powerpoint-alternatives-presentation-programs/ for another 2015 comparison of alternatives to PowerPoint and explanation of how SlideDog works – but better still, look for a range of up-to-date alternatives to this (assuming you are reading the book a year or two after publication).

https://www.youtube.com/playlist?list=PL09A34EF19596B7BB for a series of tutorials on using Prezi.

4 Project Management to Achieve Strategic Aims

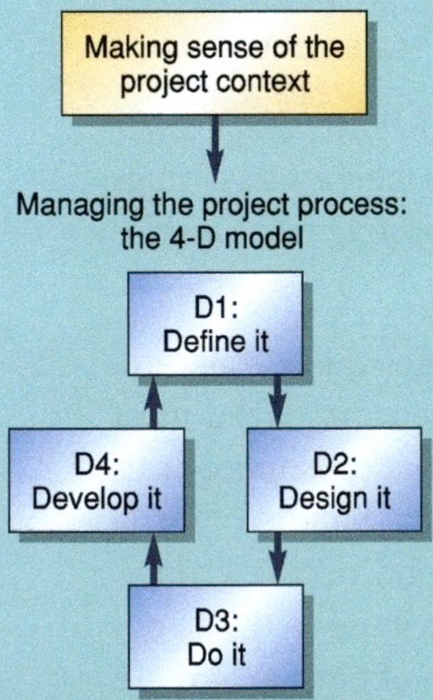

'After more than 30 years of evolution, from a planning methodology associated with PERT and CPM, project management has finally come of age. No longer simply a middle management tool for planning, organising and controlling human and other resources, project management can now be regarded as an essential means of turning strategic objectives into organisational ventures.'[1]

Principles

1. There should be coherence between the objectives of the organisation and the work being carried out in projects.
2. Resources are scarce: the time, money and effort committed to projects need to be managed.
3. Project management is best carried out in an environment that recognises and supports the needs of the people carrying out the activities.

Learning objectives

By the time you have completed this chapter, you should be able to:

➔ define the role of organisational strategy in projects
➔ recognise a process for the deployment of strategy
➔ demonstrate the role of portfolios and programmes of projects and the possible support roles that an organisation can offer to portfolio, programme and project managers.

Contents

Source: Steven May/Alamy

Following the rise of budget airlines (e.g. Southwest Airlines) in the US, Europe and Australia in particular have seen new carriers emerging as major players in the markets. In Europe, easyJet and Ryanair have been the main players in this burgeoning market.

A notable feature of easyJet has been its focus. Right from its humble beginnings, its limited resources (certainly compared with the established competition) have been focused on achieving results in its key corporate objectives, as expressed in its mission statement:

> *'To provide our customers with safe, good value, point-to-point air services. To effect and to offer a consistent and reliable product and fares appealing to leisure and business markets on a range of European routes. To achieve this we will develop our people and establish lasting relationships with our suppliers.'*

This provides a good steer for the business: safety is critical – if they get this wrong and aircraft crash, they will lose business. Good value, or how to move passengers in the most efficient (cheapest) manner possible, is what wins them business. Projects that support this efficiency, for instance by improving the speed with which transactions are handled on the website, or changes that will reduce the amount of time that planes spend on the ground between flights, are readily approved. Anything that does not directly contribute to this is not allowed to progress. The result is that everyone in the firm has a clear sense of purpose – there is no doubt what the firm is about.

Introduction

Walking around some organisations, you get the sense of everything being very purposeful, with people somehow connected, each in their own way, with the organisation in which they work. Such an event is rare, but when it occurs there is always a common element – a clear organisational direction that everyone in the organisation understands, and a demonstrable link between activities and this direction.

The opening quotation in this chapter illustrates the role of project management in creating such a connection. Such a conversion of strategic objectives into operational ventures, and then activities, requires the active participation of project managers in the process. To achieve such participation requires that the process, purpose and language of strategy and the organisational strategist be understood. That is the purpose of this chapter. The reason is that behind every organisational strategy are a huge number of individual decisions that have to be made. As will be shown, these need to carry forward that strategy into the day-to-day activities of a project and also inform the future direction of an organisation through the evolution of that organisation's capabilities.

4.1 Organisational strategy and projects

It has been recognised for a long time that *'the organisation that attempts a narrow mission, will outperform one that attempts a wider* **mission**'.[3] Put another way, don't try to be good at everything. In organisational terms this means that the things that the organisation decides to be good at should be the **focus** of what it does. There are a number of elements to achieving this focus that will be explored in this and section 4.2. These elements build into the **strategy process** shown in Figure 4.1. Each of the elements will be discussed here.

At the top of Figure 4.1, there is the Chief Executive Officer (CEO) or leader of the organisation who is responsible (amongst other things) for providing the **vision** of where the organisation is going. For the organisation, this has been well described as:

'We're standing on this hill here. The vision is that we want to be on that hill over there.'

The description implies that there is knowledge of the organisation's current position and a notion of where its leader(s) wants it to be at a point in the future. The vision is expressed as a **mission statement** for the organisation. Often clichéd, they are none the less a good guide to the effectiveness of the strategy process in an organisation, as the example from easyJet showed at the start of this chapter. Formulating the content of that mission requires input from the current capabilities of the organisation, and analysis of the threats and opportunities that it faces. In this book, we consider two major inputs to the process – the organisation itself feeding in opportunities and the organisation's leadership. Traditionally, **strategy** was considered to be a one-way process – organisational strategy would be implemented from the top down. Figure 4.2 shows the differences between this and the strategy processes of world-class organisations today that combine this with feedback from the organisation.[4]

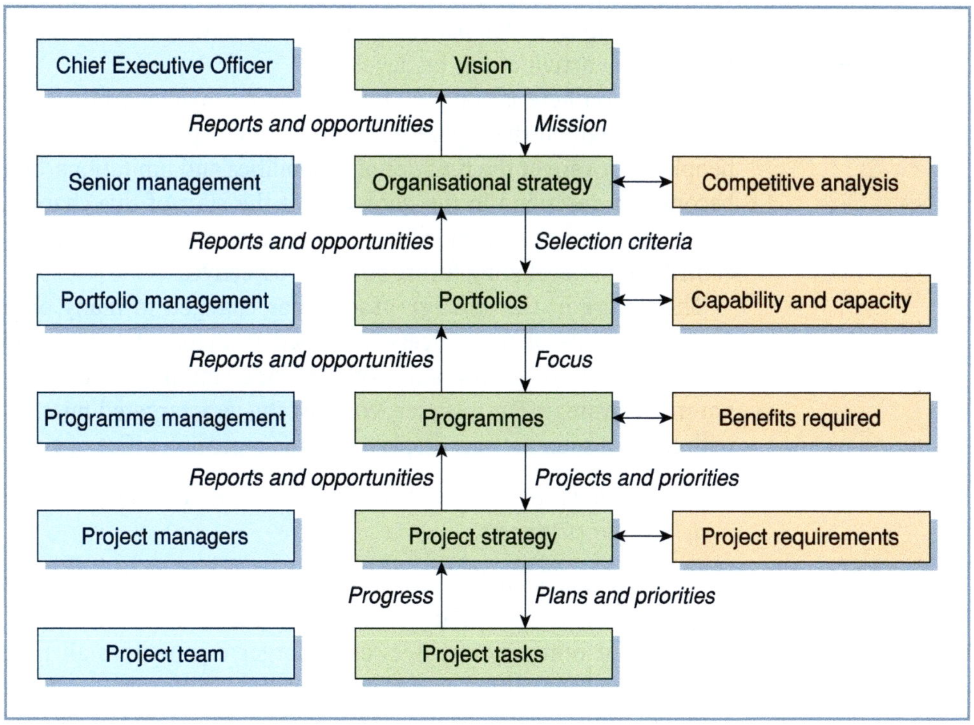

Figure 4.1 Organisational strategy process

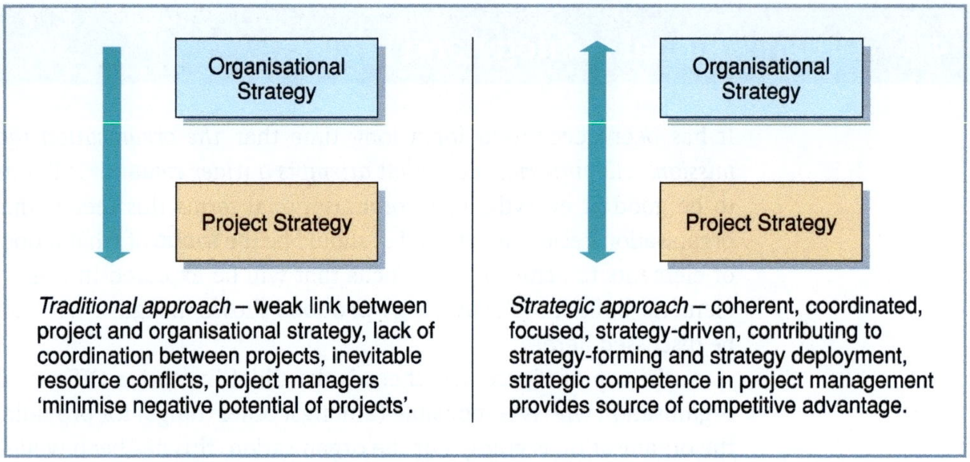

Figure 4.2 Traditional versus strategic approaches

Using a traditional approach, it is often found that rather than aiming to create competitive advantage through projects, project managers are forced into the mode of trying to 'minimise the negative potential' of projects.[5] In this mode the focus is on **conformance** regardless of the real needs of **performance** of the organisation (this is discussed further below) and an attitude of 'just don't mess up'. Strategy is the concern of senior management only and is implemented in a top-down manner, often regardless of the realities of what is possible at a project level.

The strategic approach has a number of important differentiating features. These include the strong link between strategy and activities at the project level. Strategy formulation is still carried out by senior management in the organisation, but importantly, there are inputs from all levels of the organisation. These include progress reports on existing work, current workloads and capacities, limitations of existing capabilities and potential new capabilities, and in particular ideas as to how new opportunities that have emerged from project activities can be developed.

The notion here is simple – by creating an involving process of two-way communication throughout the organisation, the strategy process becomes more consensual and people are aware of the realities of capabilities and limitations 'on the ground'.[6] Projects become, as described in the quotation at the start of this chapter, the '*essential means of turning strategic objectives into organisational ventures*'. More than this, they will also contribute to developing future strategic objectives.

The nature of the strategy process has changed in many organisations. Returning to the elements of the process identified in Figure 4.1, the mission statement of an organisation is often revealing of the understanding of that organisation about the nature of strategy. For instance, contrast the very targeted mission statement of easyJet with the one seen proudly displayed in the reception office of a small firm:

> *'Our mission is to be the best producer in the world of high-technology solutions which delight our customers.'*

The firm was a small player in a large market, which survived through its ability to supply quickly to local markets. It did not need to be the 'best in the world' – indeed this was not remotely credible, as its larger competitors all had superior technology and delivery capabilities. The employees and the customers all knew this. The firm was excellent at providing capacity for manufacturing complex printed circuit board (PCB) assemblies at short notice. A more appropriate mission might have been:

'To be the most responsive supplier of PCBs and associated design services to our customers.'

Being the best wasn't necessary – the firm didn't have to be the best quality or the cheapest. It did have to be responsive to gain advantage from its geographical position close to a number of original equipment manufacturers (OEMs – the people who make branded electronic equipment). Setting the vision identifies where the organisation is heading. Using the hill metaphor, the direction or course has been set. The next layer down in the strategy process is the *organisational strategy*. In one sense this is 'the route to get to the other hill'. The process here is now concerned with delivery – turning the ideas into reality. This part of the strategy process is known as **strategy deployment** – providing a focused set of activities that the organisation will work on.

In addition to the vision providing an input to the deployment, an analysis of the environment contributes – as described in Chapter 7. Further tools for providing this input include **SWOT** (strengths, weaknesses, opportunities and threats) and analysis of 5-Forces (bargaining power of customers and suppliers, threats of new entrants and substitutes and competitive rivalry between existing players).[7] Henry Mintzberg, one of the founders of modern thinking in strategic management and more recently one of its most ardent critics,[8] defined strategy in terms of 5-Ps[9] – a plan, a pattern of consistent behaviour over time, a position created by an organisation in a market, a perspective or approach that is identified with that organisation ('the HP Way', Ericsson's PROPPS system) and a ploy. The last is reminiscent of militaristic strategy and would be intended to outmanoeuvre a competitor. All of these are evident in the analogy of how to get to 'that hill over there'.

Deploying strategy results in two key things – the priorities for the way that products and services are delivered today (*direct revenue-earning* activities) and what the organisation will be doing tomorrow (resulting in **organisational change**). The first category includes completing a consultancy assignment, a construction project or any work carried out for a third party for which you or your organisation is paid. The second category would include changes to an organisation's structure, IT system, a merger or a new business start-up. These projects do not directly earn anything, though they should be yielding benefits to the organisation, for instance in obtaining cost savings or opening up a new market to the organisation. Their cases do have some overlap, but the strategic aspects of each are essentially different.

Figure 4.3 shows this split and the different approaches that are taken to deploying strategy in each case.

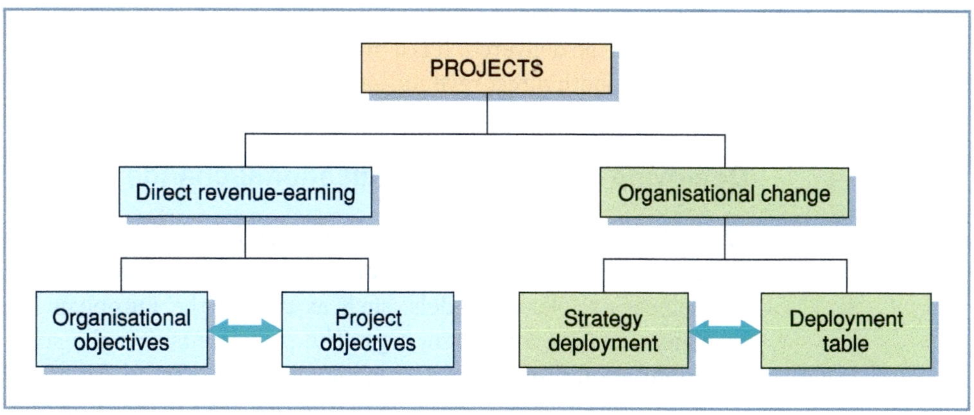

Figure 4.3 Projects and organisational strategy

Strategy and direct revenue-earning projects

The strategic input here is the organisational **objectives**, as Figure 4.3 shows. This would be of the form – we are in business to be the fastest OR the best OR the cheapest providers of these projects. This can then be reflected into the project objectives, usually starting with such time, cost and quality objectives. An organisation that sells itself on being the cheapest should have this as the objective of the project – to deliver the cheapest solution. As will be shown, such a decision has far-reaching consequences and will impact practically every aspect of how the project is managed. This should include the other players in the supply chain – both suppliers and customers. This is illustrated in the following example.

REAL WORLD Speed is key

Pearce Retail is a lead contractor for several organisations, including Asda/Walmart, Tesco and Marks and Spencer, in the provision of new retail spaces (also called 'sheds' by those less favourably disposed to the aesthetics of such buildings). The design and erection of these buildings is one of its key revenue-generating processes. For its main client, Asda, the time that such projects take, from acquisition of land to the opening of a new store, needs to be as short as possible. It is only once the store is opened that the investment in the facility starts to be repaid. As a result, Pearce has had to develop relationships with its suppliers (suppliers of designs, materials, labour, legal services, site support facilities and so on) consistent with this objective. In addition, all internal processes need to be consistent with this objective. For instance, there is no point having a highly responsive supplier able to deliver materials at 24 hours' notice if it takes 6 weeks to process a purchase order.

Project strategy

The topic of project strategy is covered in much more detail in Chapter 14. For the purpose of this book, the definition of project strategy that will be used is as follows:

> ***Project strategy is the definition of position, the means and the guidelines of what to do and how to do it, to achieve the highest competitive advantage and the best value from a project.***[10]

This approach focuses more on the benefits and value of a project than the mechanics of how it is to be delivered. It is a higher-order consideration and one that is fundamental to success in both direct revenue earning and organisational change projects.

Deploying strategy in organisational change projects

The task of strategy deployment is well established in a few world-class organisations.[11] It was a central feature of the Total Quality Management movement and more recently in business excellence models, such as that of the European Foundation for Quality Management (see www.efqm.org). The principle is that the strategies and projects of an organisation should show a high level of **coherence**. This is where, as a minimum, all projects are part of some overall plan for the organisation and form a recognisable contribution to that plan.

Masters of this particular art include the Toyota Motor Company where projects must demonstrate contribution to QCD – Quality, Cost or Delivery performance – as a prime, qualifying requirement. Features of its process of deployment are:

- objectives aligned throughout the organisation by making strategy highly visible and well understood. Conflicts between functional and project objectives are resolved at a high level;
- all members of the organisation are responsible for the process – strategy is no longer the domain of senior management alone and individuals can show the impact of their contribution to organisational objectives through their contribution to change projects;
- progress towards objectives monitored through highly visible measures;
- objectives based on customer needs – retaining the customer-focused nature of the organisation.

The strategy deployment table (Table 4.1) provides a means for project managers to agree objectives for their projects and illustrate how these relate to organisational objectives. This is ideal where an organisation has a large number of projects ongoing and a manager is responsible for more than one project. It can be used both between and within organisations to ensure consistency of objectives.

Table 4.1 shows the deployment of a strategy by a firm to reduce its new product lead-time (how long it takes to bring a new product through from the initial idea to when it is launched into a market) by 20 per cent. It is important that the objective set is quantifiable wherever possible – particularly a higher-level objective. This is then deployed into a series of second-level objectives. These include achieving balanced workloads, that is, a balance between the amount of time available and the amount of work that is required to be carried out. As is the case for 'increase level of concurrency in processes', objectives may have more than one activity associated with them.

Having determined the strategic objectives of the organisation and specifically the nature of both current and future activities that it carries out, the next level in the strategy process shown in Figure 4.1 is the design of *portfolios* and *programmes*.

Table 4.1 Strategy deployment table

Objectives Level 1	*Activities Level 1*	*Objectives Level 2*	*Activities Level 2*	*Objectives Level 3*	*Activities Level 3*
Reduce new product lead-time by 20 per cent	1 Establish managed portfolio of projects	Achieve balanced work allocations	Determine workload due to current projects		
		Close down 80 per cent of projects that are over 2 years old	Examine potential of all projects over 2 years old		
	2 Re-engineer project processes	Understand current processes	Map current processes	Identify strengths and weaknesses in processes	Conduct review of all major projects over the past 3 years
		Increase level of concurrency in processes	Co-locate staff for major projects		
			Train project facilitators		
	3 Implement new design technology	Reduce prototyping time by 80 per cent	Install rapid-prototyping equipment		
		Reduce product engineering time by 38 per cent	Install new version of design software		

4.2 Portfolios and programmes

> *'Managing projects is, it is said, like juggling three balls – cost, quality and time. Programme management (portfolio management, multi-project management) is like organising a troupe of jugglers all juggling their three balls and swapping balls from time to time.'*[12]

The previous section showed how organisations were developing current and future activities under the first principle 'it is not possible to be good at everything'. This reflects the reality for both organisations and individuals that they have to make choices about 'what is important'.

The second principle is that 'it is not possible to do everything'. In practice, organisations and individuals have to make choices about what they do, not just how well they are going to do it. This is part of the strategy process known as **portfolio management**. Ideally, an organisation will choose the activities it undertakes such that it will gain maximum benefit from its investment in those activities.

In the Real World box below, an organisation goes through the change from no recognition of the role of portfolio management to having this capability.

REAL WORLD **Abbey**

Source: Maurice Savage

Abbey (formerly Abbey National) is one of the UK's largest retail banks and now part of the Spanish banking conglomerate, Grupo Santander. During a review of the performance of its corporate operations during 2002, it was noted that the functionally based structure[13] prevailed – people were based in operating functions, but it was evident that any customer-beneficial change was delivered cross-functionally. In project terms, during 2001, 127 projects had been started but only 27 finished. Many projects were noted to be competing and overlapping. In addition, no one knew which projects were the most important or even the real benefits of any project. A director commented: 'When we added up the claimed benefits of the projects we had ongoing, had they all delivered, they would have resulted in us having 110 per cent of the retail mortgage market.' Clearly the claims being made to justify projects were not realistic. The other major finding of this review was that project management was treated as a 'home for difficult people' – it was the job you were sent to if you were perceived to be a problem.

A short transition period began, during which 75 per cent of the existing projects in the company's portfolio were cancelled in one day. A programme structure was introduced whereby key priorities for the business were identified, and projects were identified under each of these priorities or programmes. Programme managers were appointed from the senior project staff to head one of five programme areas, and resources from the cancelled projects were re-deployed onto the new prioritised projects.

During 2002, there was a distinct change in the performance of the operations. The average cycle time for projects dropped by 60 per cent, and as importantly for an organisation in a very dynamic market, of 47 projects started under the 5 programmes, 47 were finished. From the point of view of the business, it was now able to measure the delivery, with benefits realised of over £500 million. For the project staff, things had changed too. From the 'home for difficult people' they became the most head-hunted people in the organisation, because of their new-found ability to deliver projects.

This example demonstrates clearly the effect of having this portfolio management approach in place. It is worth noting as well the positive impact of having such a clear-out of projects, both as individuals and organisations; it seems to be a common characteristic of both that we take on more projects than we can reasonably handle.

This illustrates the first principle of this chapter and a major reason why 'we can't do everything' is that, as the economists would say, 'resources are scarce'. That is, they are finite, not necessarily flexible or easily transferred between activities, and particularly where these resources are 'people', are not 100 per cent available. To take account of this, programme management therefore requires the following step: aggregation of resource plans.

The sanity check: aggregate resource plan

> *'The first time we assessed our total project load, we found that we had scheduled three times as much work in one year as we could reasonably handle. The results weren't very pleasant or productive.'*
> (Programme manager – automotive supply firm)

The above scenario is very typical of many organisations that have no mechanism for determining their total workload. The **aggregate resource plan** is essential to keep control of the activities that the organisation is undertaking, both projects and repetitive operations – aka business-as-usual work. Firms often have a good picture of their repetitive operations – these have a relatively high level of visibility, particularly in a manufacturing setting. Projects, meanwhile, require some overall view to be maintained of what is going on in the organisation. Providing a concise statement of the resource requirements of the expected activities, both project and operational, is the objective of the aggregate resource plan.

An aggregate plan is another step in the process of determining what projects can be undertaken and in what order. It determines the *capacity* of the organisation to carry out projects and allocates this capacity to projects that fit with the organisational priorities. Imagine a production line that can produce 11 000 drinks cans per hour for 23 hours a day. The capacity of that line is 11 000 × 23 = 253 000 cans per day. In organisational terms, the role of management then becomes to make sure that this capacity is used to generate the best return for the organisation – and schedule jobs on the machine accordingly. If there is a changeover time between jobs on the machine, this needs to be considered too, as such a changeover will reduce the productive time of the machine and therefore the overall capacity. This becomes part of the expectation for the scheduling of the work around that machine – you would not schedule, for instance, 300 000 or 500 000 cans per day without adding new resources (another machine, for instance). Indeed, where, for instance, a new design of can was being trialled, you might significantly reduce the working capacity of the machine. Therefore in managing the capacity of the machine, the role of management is to limit the demands placed on it to be less than or equal to the capacity of the machine and to schedule the jobs accordingly, taking account of the needs of the specific job and changeover times.

Organisations that manage their work capacity follow the same approach. The capacity of people and machines is finite, they need to work on the most important jobs first, and there is a significant changeover time between tasks. The following example shows how one organisation treats this capacity issue.

What do you do the rest of the time?

A large engineering consultancy wanted to manage its capacity. Its main and certainly most expensive resources were its people – mostly graduate engineers, designers and planners. Capacity for them would be determined by the availability of those people for work tasks, both within the company (e.g. in operational improvement work) and as part of

→

delivering work to clients. People always seemed very busy in the company and a number of departmental heads had asked for more staff to be able to deal with the workloads. Did they need more people or should they be able to manage with the people they already had? The first stage in determining this was to assess the capacity for work of the people they had. The result was quite a surprise to them – it was considerably less than they had predicted.

In calculating their capacity they calculated that one person would be available for productive work for no more than 40 weeks per year (allowing for holidays, training, sick leave and other disturbances) and in each week would be productive for 30 hours, to allow for meetings, briefings, dealing with administration, emails, etc. This gave a capacity figure of 1200 hours per person per year. Project requirements were always estimated in person hours and the firm now had a basic assessment of the hours required to do the work and what it had available to do it. It was now able to make an assessment of the loadings of the different departments and determine that it did indeed need more people in certain key areas.

Having assessed the workload of project staff (which in many cases will include ongoing work in addition to project tasks), just as the firm in the example did, many firms are surprised to find just how overloaded their personnel are. Keeping track of the workload is an important contribution that programme management can make. The means for this is to keep a log of the available person-hours (number of people multiplied by the hours they are available in a time period) and to allocate these by project. There is frequently a tendency to underestimate the amount of time required for activities (particularly where there is some uncertainty regarding the outcome), resulting in an overcommitment of resources. Where resources are overcommitted, the scope for any flexibility becomes very limited and will stifle innovation – a key component of success for many projects.

The capabilities or competencies required for the project portfolio should also be considered at this level. There may be key resources or people that are critical to the processes. In addition, many firms do not consider their key competencies, trying instead to do everything themselves. This is rarely a successful strategy, particularly where technology is concerned. Where a requirement is outside the firm's set of core competencies, the requirements of external partners or contractors should be discussed.

There is an additional consideration for the aggregate project plan. People rarely know the relative importance of the projects on which they are working or their contribution to organisational strategy. Furthermore, taking on too many projects causes stress for the people carrying them out. This is compounded by confusion about what is urgent and what is important. There should be only a restricted set of activities that any individuals undertake that is both urgent and important. It is the responsibility of the senior management team to ensure this. Otherwise, the changeover time between projects will become significant.

So, just how many projects can a firm undertake at any one time? There is, of course, no universal answer. However, one firm, visited as part of a research project, had 72 development projects ongoing at the time, with one manager and eight staff. The result was an obvious confusion about the relative priorities of the projects and a highly stressful work environment. Furthermore, the task for the manager was enormous. For instance, which projects should each person be working on at any one time? Inevitably, the projects worked on were those where the customers were screaming the loudest. The knock-on effect was that staff would start work on one project and then be moved on to another as the priorities changed, to appease the latest angry customer. The effects of this are very stressful for the individual and highly unproductive for the organisation.[14]

For the development organisation, a move away from the old system of 'whoever shouts loudest' to a clear system of priorities reduced the workload from 72 projects to 12. This sounds draconian, as many projects had to be put on hold or abandoned. The positive effect was incredible – the firm successfully completed twice as many projects that year as it had ever done in the past with the same resources. In addition, the working conditions improved immeasurably and the workload and flow through the department became not only faster but more predictable.[15]

EPM

EPM (Enterprise programme/project management) has emerged and grown in importance over the past 10 years. It is defined as:

> ***the capability to lead and manage resources, knowledge and skills in the effective deployment of multiple projects designed collectively to deliver enhanced value.***[16]

EPM concerns the resourcing and managing of programmes across an entire organisation. While a small organisation or business unit can manage using spreadsheets for instance, for larger organisations it is usually associated with enterprise-wide software applications, such as Microsoft Project[17] or SAP.[18] These are necessary to integrate the vast amount of data, including the number of projects, the resource requirements and timings of those requirements, and to handle these in a dynamic manner. Schedules, availability of people and resources, priorities and project requirements can all change and frequently do in reality. Working through the implications of all the changes on the ability of an organisation to deliver a portfolio of projects and routine operations requires significant processing power. However, these are still not panacea for organisations. As with any software, it is the thinking behind it and the way that it is used that will determine whether it provides the solution being sought or just adds another headache for those in the organisation.

Programme management

The photo shown here illustrates beautifully the need for **programme management**. As can be seen, two projects have been completed – the road building and the erection of telegraph poles. However, in order for the community to get any *benefits* from these projects, someone needs to have integrated the work. Clearly this hasn't happened.

Source: Courtesy of Michael Trolove

Programme management provides this layer of coordination between projects, ensuring that the higher-level benefits are realised.[19]

As for project management, the professional institutes have generated considerable discussion around the nature of definitions of a programme. The main ones are shown in Table 4.2.

Table 4.2 Definitions of 'programme'

Institution	*Definition*
APM BoK (2004)	A group of related projects, which may include related business-as-usual activities that together achieve a beneficial change of a strategic nature for an organisation.
PMI BoK (2008)	A group of related projects managed in a coordinated way to obtain benefits and control not available from managing them individually. Programmes may include elements of related work outside the scope of the discrete projects in a programme.
Managing Successful Programmes (2007)[20]	A temporary flexible organisation created to coordinate, direct and oversee the implementation of a set of related projects and activities in order to deliver outcomes and benefits related to the organisation's strategic objectives. A programme is likely to have a life that spans several years.

A summary of the characteristics of these provides the definition for programme that will be used in this book:

> ***An [organisational] framework for grouping existing or defining new projects, and for focusing all the activities required to achieve a set of major benefits. These projects are managed in a coordinated way, either to achieve a common goal, or to extract benefits which would otherwise not be realised if they were managed independently.***[21]

However, there is considerable disparity between and even within organisations as to what constitutes 'a programme'.[22] Currently, there is no scientific or rigorous method that would allow us to identify a piece of work as a project or a programme. At one level, programmes can be considered simply as 'big projects'. This is not entirely without foundation – in one organisation, a unit of work that is labelled a 'programme' would be a 'large project' in another. In general though, the larger the organisation, the larger the unit of work that is termed 'a programme'.

Consistent with this variation in definition of the unit of work, programme management is viewed by some as 'the management of multiple projects', while by others as 'the management of organisational change through projects that bring about change'.[23] Part of this variation is explained by the differences in the nature of the programme. For instance, the projects in a programme may be represented as a chain of projects, one occurring after another, a portfolio of projects taking place at one point in time, or as a network of interlinked projects.[24] These are shown in Figure 4.4.

In reality, large organisations use a blend of these different types of programmes in deploying their strategies.

Organising multiple projects into programmes allows commonalities between projects to be exploited (e.g. knowledge obtained from one project being transferred to another similar project) and coordination of objectives and resources. *Programme management* can also be viewed as a means of management gaining greater control of the activities in the organisation. Indeed, the creation of programme management in many organisations has resulted in a new layer of management being added – an interesting phenomenon at

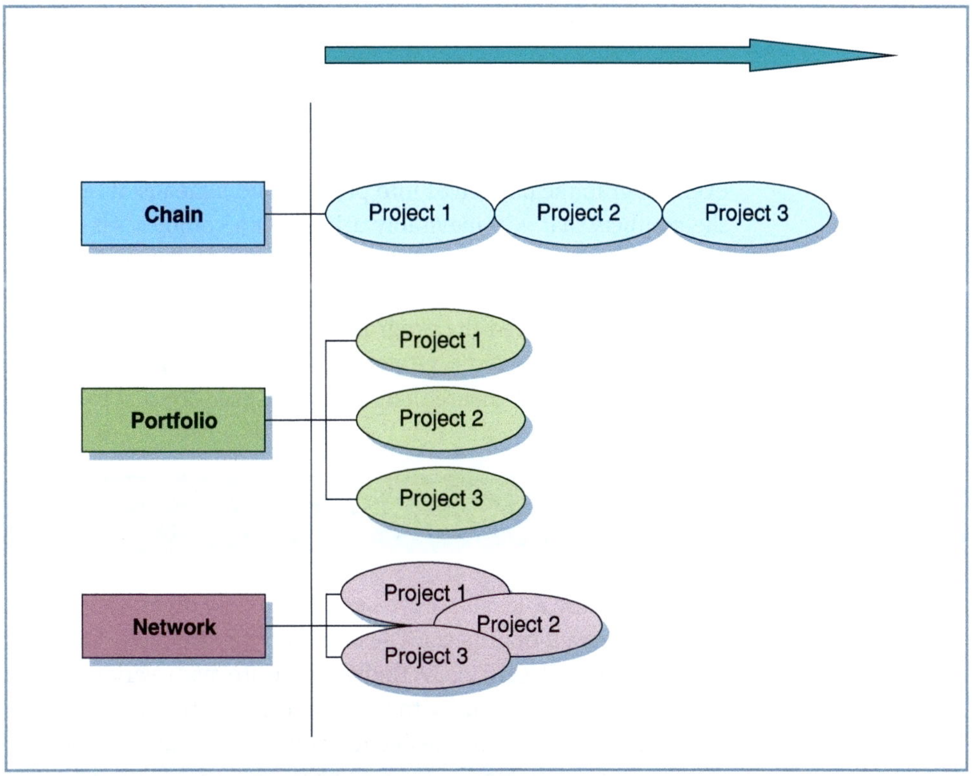

Figure 4.4 Arrangements of projects in programmes

a time when most organisations have been removing layers of management. However, there are instances, such as the Abbey case shown earlier, where this approach has yielded considerable benefits over and above the additional costs that this extra layer of management activity will incur. Another view of programme management is that it is a *sense-making* process – it is a method by which those running an organisation will seek to understand the complexities of that organisation and its activities, by adding structures that put some order to what otherwise will appear chaotic.

The issue of project selection is considered in more detail in Chapter 14. The prime issues concern the relation of the potential and existing projects to the organisational objectives and the use of a strategy matrix to balance the objectives.

An example of a **strategy matrix** is shown in Table 4.3. The matrix shows the relationship between three projects and three key strategic objectives. Each of the projects addresses one of the key strategic objectives. However, project 2 will have a negative effect on objective 1. For instance, if objective 1 is 'to improve the quality of customer service' and project 2 is 'cut costs by 20 per cent', it is likely that this objective and this project will

Table 4.3 Strategy matrix

	Objective 1	*Objective 2*	*Objective 3*
Project 1	++	+	
Project 2	−−	++	
Project 3	+	+	++

Key: ++ Strong positive relationship
\+ Positive relationship
− Negative relationship
−− Strong negative relationship

conflict. This indicates that the project should be reconsidered to see precisely the nature of this impact and whether the negative effect can be removed. Having determined the project objectives, these are then implemented through the measurement system that is put in place.

The matrix therefore provides a sense of the deployment of the organisation's or even programme objectives into projects and a means of resolving or at least identifying the conflicts that will inevitably arise with a complex set of projects and objectives. In addition, gaps can be identified where objectives have no projects contributing to their achievement.

Having established the programme or portfolio of projects that the organisation will undertake in any given time period, the issue is then how to support these projects in their execution and ensure their continued contribution to organisational objectives.

4.3 Project roles and governance

There are many roles that have been created by organisations in an attempt to facilitate the management of projects. The roles and the structure that they can operate in are well illustrated in PRINCE 2 2009, though there are many variants on this.[25] The roles and their relationships as defined by the project organisation are termed the *project governance*. This sets out who is responsible for doing what and to whom they are responsible. The structure shown in Figure 4.5 is an expansion of that shown in Figure 4.1.

The **project board** is run by the **executive** or **senior responsible owner**. This is the person, also referred to as the '**sponsor**', who ultimately wants the result and has the budget for the project to be carried out. The **senior user** provides high-level input to the project from those who will ultimately be using the output of the project (e.g. the users of an IT system being delivered through a project). The **senior supplier** is the representative of those who will be delivering the project. For instance, if the work to deliver the project is being carried out by an outside contractor, a senior manager from that firm would be represented on the project board.

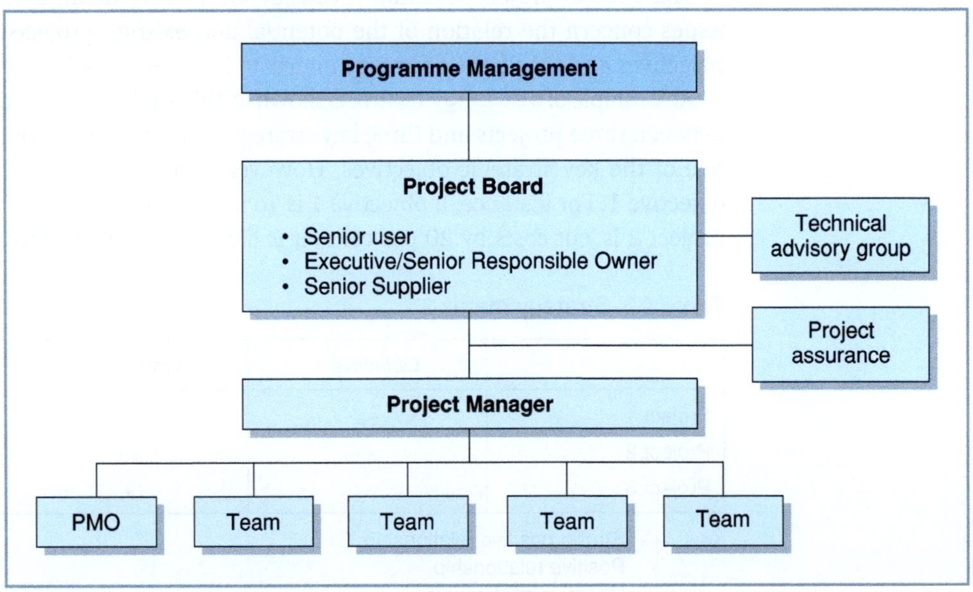

Figure 4.5 Basic project governance structure

A **technical advisory group** may be added where the project is of a highly technical nature. For instance, in scientific research projects, a group of scientists external to the project may be asked to provide advice to the project board on the status of the project and the viability of science being considered.

Also reporting into the project board and not under the direct control of the project manager may be a **project assurance** function. This may be as extensive as the project itself, particularly where security or safety is concerned. For instance, in running projects for London Underground (a highly safety-critical environment), all projects have to pass through extensive assurance processes. These will include engineering assurance – ensuring that any potential impact on the working of the underground system has been properly evaluated.

The project manager then has a number of direct reports, including the various teams carrying out the work of the project. In addition, we are increasingly seeing that they will have at their disposal a PMO – a **project management office**.

The project management office (PMO)

Many organisations, particularly from sectors that regularly run large-scale projects, use project offices to assist in all aspects of the management of project work. This is constituted as a function alongside other functions within the organisation. At one time, it was limited to large-scale engineering firms, but the project office is a regular feature in most major organisations globally today. This function has been added to run alongside other functions in the organisation and provides recognition of the importance of project activities, and in particular the need for project management professionals to run projects. The relationship between the project and the project office is shown in Figure 4.6.[26]

The office provides a central facility with the skills and knowledge of how to run project processes. This can be drawn on by the project manager to help ensure that the project is given the best chance of success. The office can provide key project staff, often including the project manager, but also including project planners, accountants, staff to carry out review activities and consultants. Resources that may be under the control of the project office include any project planning software system that is used. The support role includes one of personal support to individuals, including training and mentoring (personal counselling and assistance) and sharing of experience where problems are encountered that have occurred elsewhere. The project office can also provide checks

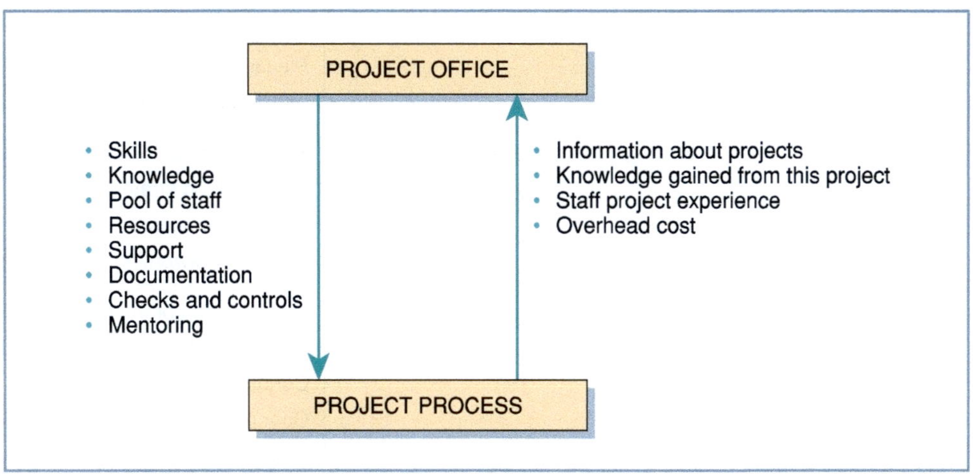

Figure 4.6 Relationship between the project and the project office

and controls on the project processes, assisting in the establishment of checkpoints and control measures.

The project management office can also be called:

- project support office;
- programme management office;
- enterprise project/programme management office.

The role that any PMO covers is incredibly varied – between and within organisations and also over time. Work carried out by Professor Brian Hobbs at the University of Quebec in Montreal has identified 24 roles which have been grouped into five categories, as shown in Table 4.4.[27]

Three further roles did not fit with the other categories shown here:

1 Manage customer interfaces.
2 Execute specialised tasks for project managers.
3 Recruit, select, evaluate and determine salaries for project managers.[28]

All this additional support to the project process does not come free. Organisations that do use this way of working usually maintain that any downside element, including the increased overhead cost, is more than compensated for by the increased project success.

Table 4.4 PMO roles

Category	*Role*
1 Monitoring and control of project performance	Report status to upper management Monitor and control project performance Implement and operate a project information system Develop and maintain a project scoreboard
2 Development of project management capabilities and methodologies	Develop and implement a standard methodology Develop competency of personnel, including training Promote project management within organisation Provide mentoring for project managers Provide a set of tools without an effort to standardise
3 Multi-project management	Coordinate between projects Manage one or more portfolios Identify, select and prioritise new projects Manage one or more programmes Allocate resources between projects
4 Strategic management	Provide advice to senior management Participate in strategic planning Manage benefits Conduct networking and environmental scanning
5 Organisational learning	Monitor and control performance of PMO Manage archives of project documentation Conduct project audits Conduct post-project reviews Implement and manage database of lessons learned Implement and manage risk database

Experience has also shown that there is considerable benefit from having a consistent approach to running projects and the advice provided prevents problems such as teams overpromising on project deliverables or failing to analyse the risks associated with their work properly. Other contributions from the project to the office include the stream of knowledge and experience that the projects generate. The role of the office in this respect is marshalling and managing this knowledge. People who have been working on projects and show an interest in a project management career can use the project office as a way of moving to take a greater role in future projects. For example, a marketing person may enjoy the project environment more than the day-to-day activities of the marketing function and wish to become more involved with projects. The professionalisation of the role through the project office provides a route for such an individual to progress within the organisation and research has shown that this should be a separate career path from that of either a project or programme manager, as it requires a distinct and different skillset.

However, finding the correct location for this function within an organisation is not always straightforward, as the case below shows.

REAL WORLD **Lloyds TSB – where's the project office?**

Lloyds TSB is one of the UK's largest banking and financial services groups and carries out hundreds of large projects every year. Programme management is fundamental to the delivery of business benefits from these projects and during the 1990s led to the development of a corporate programme management function. Its role was to resource and control the projects being carried out within and across each of the business units. During 2003, it became clear that this centralisation of control and resources was not ideal for the business – the overhead to costs that this represented to the business units was perceived to be too high and less than the benefits of the office. Also, there was a perceived loss of autonomy by the business units that the office served.

During 2004, the central PMO was broken up and the functions devolved to the individual business units. This resulted in the characteristics and roles of each PMO being more closely linked to the needs of each business unit, with greater cost transparency.

There are many publicly available examples of governance structures.[29] Further structural and governance issues.

Summary

- The strategy process identified in Figure 4.1 shows how the vision created for an organisation is reflected through to the project activities. The input from competitive analysis might include, for example, an analysis of the organisation's strengths, weaknesses, opportunities and threats (SWOT). It may also consider the impact of changes in technology, new entrants to the market (if a commercial organisation) and other market force changes (e.g. currency movements, legal changes) that will affect the organisation. The other input to this process comes from the organisation itself, demonstrating that strategy is a two-way process.

- The vision is to be realised through the organisational strategy in the first instance. This provides a focus for all the activities of the organisation, including all projects. Focus is an important concept here, which we define as those aspects of our product or service offering into which we are going to invest time, money and effort, with the objective of securing improved/superior performance.

- Having determined the intended focus, it has been observed that many senior management teams make the mistake of assuming that this will automatically be followed through by those who make decisions within the organisation. This does not always happen and results in problems for project managers trying to operate in the middle of interdepartmental conflicts, where different views of the mission and focus prevail. The alternative is to instigate programme or portfolio management. As part of this process of evaluating the strategic contribution of each project, overlaps and gaps in the programme need to be identified. An aggregate resource plan ensures that the capacity and capability exist to do the work required by the strategy and to keep an overview of the many projects going on in an organisation at any one time.

- Programmes consist of a number of projects. These may be externally generated – as direct revenue earners which will require their own set of strategies. This must be in line with corporate objectives regarding the basis on which the organisation will compete in order to meet customer needs. The project strategy in this case would include both conformance and performance objectives. In addition, organisational change projects should be part of the strategy deployment of the organisation and their objectives should be put through a strategy matrix to remove conflicts before the project starts.

- The objective of this process is to clear the way for project activities to be undertaken in a coherent manner with the organisational objectives, focused and with minimal conflict. This process is simple in concept, but very challenging in application. It is notable that in organisations where this does happen, there is an almost palpable feeling of everybody working in the one direction, with many of the stresses and failures that are caused by 'the system' avoided. This is surely a worthwhile objective for our organisations.

Key terms

aggregate resource plan
coherence
conformance
EPM (enterprise project/programme management)
executive
focus
mission
mission statement
objectives
organisational change
performance
programme/portfolio management
project assurance
project board
project management office
senior responsible owner
senior supplier
senior user
sponsor
strategy
strategy deployment
strategy matrix
strategy process
SWOT
technical advisory group
vision

Relevant areas of the Bodies of Knowledge

There is little in either of the Bodies of Knowledge concerning the strategic context or aspects of projects. Given the importance of this area and the impact that it has on projects in general, this is a significant omission. There are some points of relevance in the APM version for programme management and these are given in Table 4.5.

The PMI Body of Knowledge covers some descriptions and definitions of the terms used in this chapter, in section 1.

Table 4.5 Relevant areas of the APM Body of Knowledge

Relevant section	*Title*	*Summary*
11	Programme management	Defines programme management and some of the tasks that are done under this heading.
20	Project success criteria	Defines some of the terms used here, including requirements, critical success factors and key performance indicators.

PROJECT MANAGEMENT IN PRACTICE

The Airbus A380 development

The 27 April 2005 was a huge day for the Airbus A380 as the brand-new plane took to the skies for its maiden test flight. With six crew and 20 tonnes of test equipment, it successfully completed the first stage in its flight trials, that will take several more years to complete before the plane can enter commercial service. That it has ever flown at all is an enormous achievement on the part of the individuals and organisations taking part in the development. The technical and managerial challenges have been and continue to be significant.

The plane is considerably larger than Boeing's 747 (see Figure 4.7), in basic form being able to accommodate over 550 passengers in three classes on two decks, up to a version for the Japanese market which will carry 840 passengers. Technically, this additional size does create new constraints. The

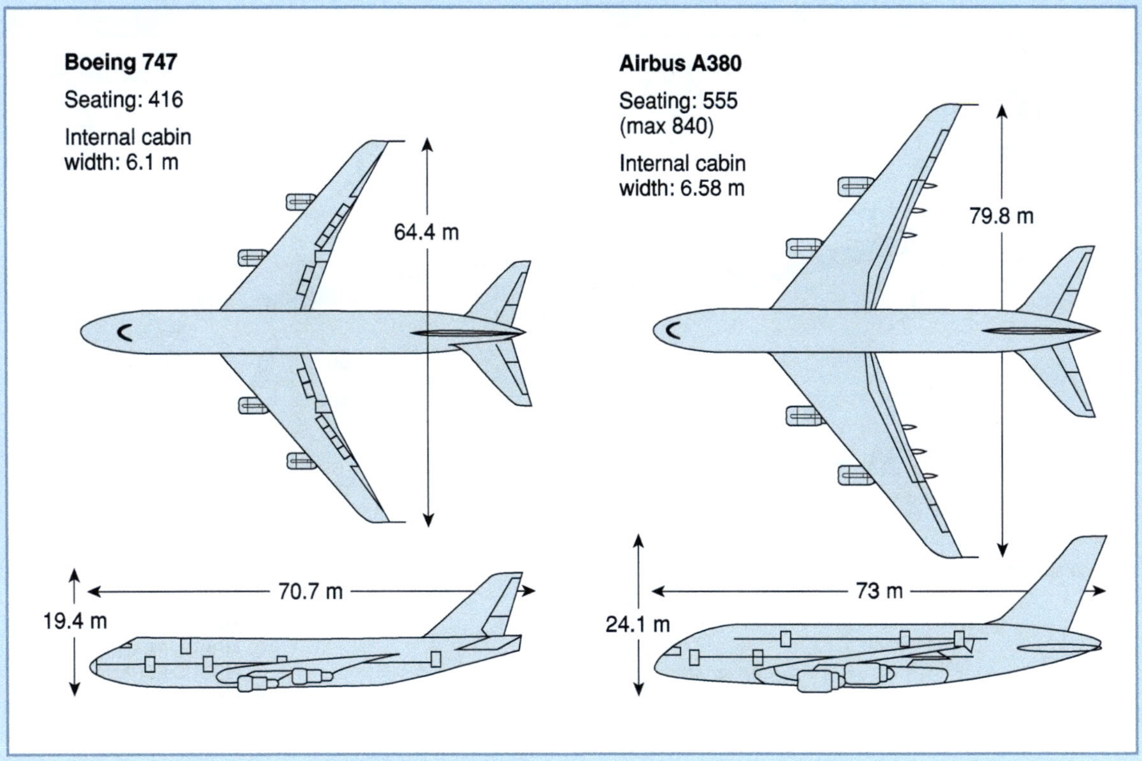

Figure 4.7 Comparative size of Boeing 747 and Airbus A380

Source: Boeing corp. (www.boeing.com); Airbus S.A.S. (www.airbus.com)

→

wings, for instance, at 36.6 m long, are considerably longer than the previously largest wing that Airbus has built. The fuel capacity of the aircraft is 310 000 litres. On landing, the undercarriage and brake systems will have to bring the 560 tonne aircraft to a standstill from over 320 km/h in just 32 seconds. While some of this increase in scale of the product is being achieved by incremental innovation, there are limits to some of the technology that is being applied, and new technological solutions, particularly in the avionics, materials and manufacturing processes, that are having to be developed.

It is a significant commercial risk for Airbus, as the business case for the A380's development is hotly contested in the industry – Airbus claiming a market of 1100 planes, Boeing, its main rival, claiming that it is nearer to 300. The latter figure would be commercially disastrous for Airbus, given the development budget of US$13 billion.

While the technological and business risks are significant for the A380, the organisation of the programme adds another dimension to the risks. Firstly, there are in place existing agreements for the percentage of value of the work that will be undertaken by the countries that have been part of the Airbus consortium – the UK, France, Germany and Spain. These have had to be incorporated into the new organisation set up to run the A380 programme. Within each organisation, there are a variety of procurement mechanisms for each of the major systems. For instance, Rolls-Royce (which developed the Trent 900 engines used on the maiden flight) provides most engines to airlines on a 'power by the hour' basis – the owner of the plane will not actually own the engines but will buy the capability that they provide on an hourly chargeable basis. Other major components are provided, as shown in Figure 4.8.

All the components have to be transported to the assembly plant in Toulouse, France and then the completed planes will be flown to Hamburg, Germany for fitting out. The logistics of moving the major aircraft components alone is huge – and significant projects in their own right. Whilst much of the manufacture takes place in Europe, significant sub-assemblies are brought in from all over the world.

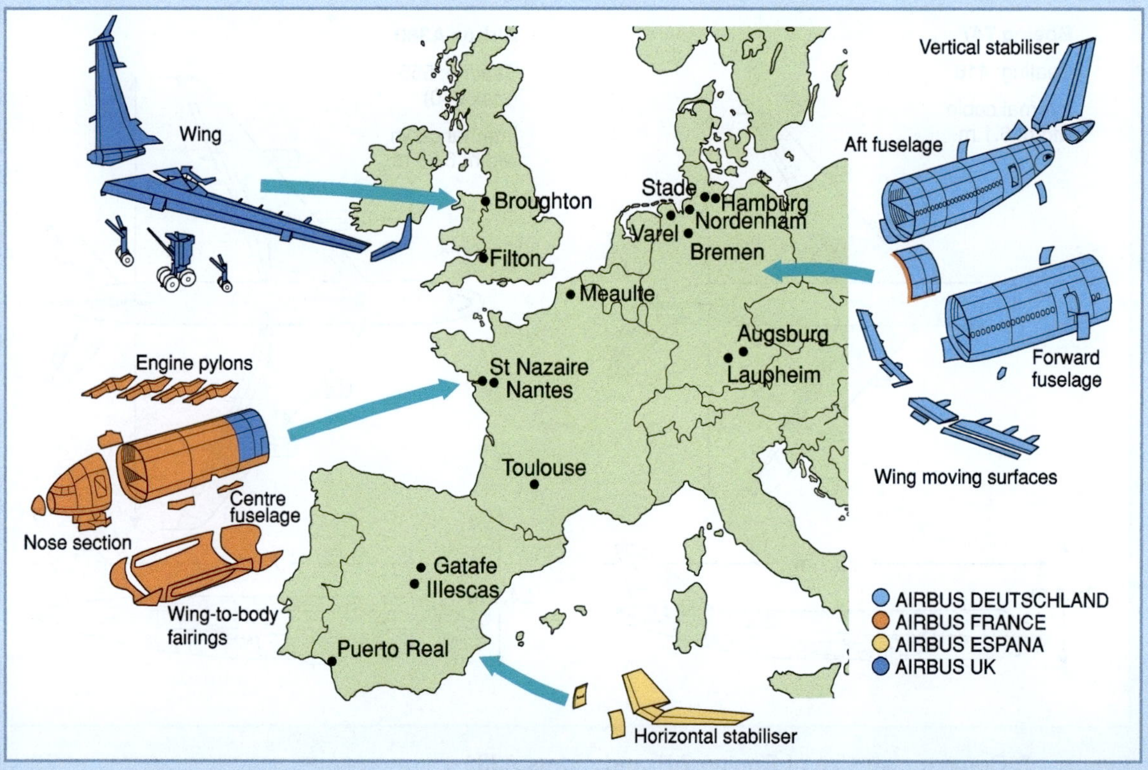

Figure 4.8 Sourcing the components of the A380

This is to make sure that local manufacturing content requirements are kept up to ensure saleability of the aircraft, particularly in China, and Boeing's own backyard, in the US. Wing tips, for instance, come into Broughton in the UK. These are assembled onto the wings and these loaded onto specially adapted barges. They meet with parts of the fuselage that have been pre-assembled in Germany at Mostyn docks for the journey to Bordeaux. En route the ship stops at St Nazaire in France to deliver one forward section of fuselage and collect a completed forward and nose assembly. From Bordeaux, the assemblies are transferred to barge and then road to Toulouse for final assembly.

For further information, see www.airliners.net/info/stats.main?id=29 and www.airbus.com/en/aircraftfamilies/a380.

Points for discussion

1 Was the A380 development a project or a programme?

2 Using the notation of Figure 4.5, how has the development been managed?

3 Suggest what the 'challenges to the management of this development' might be.

4 Review the performance of the development to date using relevant websites. Has this been a success to date?

5 Suggest the role that project/programme offices could take in such a development.

PROJECT MANAGEMENT IN PRACTICE
Selecting a personal project

A group of students, as part of their coursework, has to carry out a group project where they run an event or perform a particular task to demonstrate their ability to plan, execute and review a project. They are assessed on the basis of originality of their idea, the quality of the planning process and the content of a report following the project that reflects on their experiences of the project. They had a meeting and came up with a number of ideas. These were:

- produce a yearbook for their class group;
- develop a short video promoting the course that they are studying;
- run a formal ball for the entire department;
- organise a treasure hunt one Sunday;
- organise an 'accident awareness' day for schoolchildren.

The group then had to consider which one of these was the first choice. The next activity was to establish the decision criteria by which each of the proposals would be judged. The first three were given by the requirements of the assessment – that of originality of idea, whether the idea would allow demonstration of project management skills and whether it would enable them to produce a good report. The students added some further characteristics that they felt they wanted their project to have. These were:

- it should be sufficiently stretching of the group;
- it should not depend too heavily on other people for its success;
- it must not require them to undertake any large financial risk;
- it must be fun for the group to do.

They then put this together as shown in Table 4.6.

→

Table 4.6 Decision matrix

	Originality	*Demonstrate skills*	*Produce good report*	*Stretching*	*Independent of others*	*Avoids financial risk*	*FUN*
Yearbook	✗	✓	✓	–	–	✗	✗
Video	✓	✓	✓	✓	✓	–	✓
Ball	–	✓	✓	✓	✗	✗✗✗	✓
Treasure hunt	✗	–	–	✗	–	✓	–
Accident awareness day	✓	✓	–	–	✗	✓	–

You may disagree with the rating that the group gave some of the items, but this is how the students saw the options. They also saw very clearly as a group that there was one clear choice for them: the video. It also told them that the financial risk element (cost of hiring editing facilities and production of the finished product) needed to be minimised.

Points for discussion

1 Under what circumstances might this approach to selection be beneficial?

2 How might the measures of success change over time?

3 Suggest other applications for this approach to decision-making.

Topics for discussion

1 You have been asked to advise the 2012 London Olympics team on running the games. Firstly, is this a project or a programme and why?

2 What are the impacts at a project level of poor strategy processes?

3 What is coherence and why is it worth pursuing?

4 What is the role of strategy in project management?

5 Do a web search and identify the mission statements of some organisations that you know. Would you recognise that mission statement from the experience that you have of that organisation?

6 What is the difference between programme and portfolio management?

7 Why is an aggregate project plan beneficial for an organisation that pursues a number of projects at the same time?

8 Investigate the potential for EPM – what problems is it claimed to solve for an organisation?

9 Compile a list of project roles based on one of the project management standards (PMI, APM or PRINCE 2 2009). Which is the most important role in your view for the success of a project?

10 What are the costs and benefits to an organisation of having a PMO?

Further information

Bernstein, S. (2000) 'Project Office in Practice', *Project Management Journal*, Vol. 31, No. 4, pp. 4–6.

Block, T.R. and Frame, J.D. (1998) *The Project Office*, Crisp Learning, Menlo Park, CA.

Cooper, R.G. and Edgett, S.E. (2003) 'Overcoming the Crunch in Resources for New Product Development', *Research Technology Management*, May–June, pp. 48–58.

Elonen, S. and Artto, K.A. (2003) 'Problems in Managing Internal Development Projects in Multi-project Environments', *International Journal of Project Management*, Vol. 21, No. 6, pp. 395–402.

Grundy, A. and Brown, L. (2001) *Strategic Project Management: Creating Organisational Breakthroughs*, Thomson Learning, London.

Hill, G.M. (2007) *The Complete Project Management Office Handbook*, 2nd edition, Auerbach Publications, New York.

Lycett, M., Rassau, A. and Danson, J. (2004) 'Programme Management: A Critical Review', *International Journal of Project Management*, Vol. 22, pp. 289–299.

Partington, D. (2000) 'Implementing Strategy through Programmes of Projects', in Turner, J.R. and Simister, S.J. (eds), *Gower Handbook of Project Management*, Gower, Aldershot, pp. 33–46.

Partington, D., Pellegrinelli, S. and Young, M. (2005) 'Attributes and Levels of Programme Management Competence: An Interpretive Study', *International Journal of Project Management*, Vol. 23, No. 2, pp. 87–95.

Pelegrinelli, S. (2008) *Thinking and Acting as a Great Programme Manager*, Palgrave Macmillan, Basingstoke.

Thorn, M.E. (2003) 'Bridge Over Troubled Water: Implementation of a Program Management Office', *SAM Advanced Management Journal*, Autumn, pp. 48–59.

Website

www.efqm.org for more information on the European Foundation for Quality Management Business Excellence Model.

References

1 Lord, M.A. (1993) 'Implementing Strategy Through Project Management', *Long Range Planning*, Vol. 26, No. 1, pp. 76–85.

2 Throughout this book, the spelling of programme will be with the ending 'me'. North America and Australia in particular use the spelling 'program'.

3 Skinner, W. (1969) 'Manufacturing – Missing Link in Corporate Strategy', *Harvard Business Review*, May–June, pp. 136–145.

4 It is not intended to provide a detailed consideration of the many and varied views of strategy here. For this, you should refer to dedicated texts, such as Johnson, G., Scholes, K. and Whittington, R. (2007) *Exploring Corporate Strategy*, 8th edition, FT Prentice Hall, Harlow.

5 This follows the terminology of Hayes and Wheelwright (1984) in describing the relationship between operations strategy and organisational strategy – see Hayes, R.H. and Wheelwright, S.C. (1984) *Restoring Our Competitive Edge: Competing Through Manufacturing*, Wiley, New York.

6 The nature of this two-way process is further described in Shenhar, A.J., Milosevic, D., Dvir, D. and Thamhain, H. (2007) *Linking Project Management to Business Strategy*, Project Management Institute, Newtown, PA.

7 See Porter, M.E. (2004) *Competitive Strategy: Techniques for Analyzing Industries and Competitors*, Free Press, New York.

8 See Mintzberg, H. (2000) *The Rise and Fall of Strategic Planning*, FT Prentice Hall, Harlow.

9 Mintzberg, H. and Ghoshal, S. (2002) *The Strategy Process*, FT Prentice Hall, Harlow.

10 Shenhar, A.J., Milosevic, D., Dvir, D. and Thamhain, H. (2007) *Linking Project Management to Business Strategy*, Project Management Institute, Newtown, PA, p. 65.

11 Another term that is used to describe this process is *Hoshin Kanri* or policy deployment – see Akao Akao, Y. (ed) (1991) *Hoshin Kanri – Policy Deployment for Successful TQM*, Productivity Press, New York.

12 Reiss, G. (1996) *Programme Management Demystified*, E & FN Spon, London.

13 See Chapter 11 for a description of this kind of structure.

14 The effects of this are discussed further in Chapter 7.

15 For further examples of this type of change, see Newbold, R. (1999) *Project Management in the Fast Lane*, St Lucie Press, Boca Raton, FL.

16 Williams, D. and Parr, T. (2004) *Enterprise Programme Management*, Palgrave Macmillan, Basingstoke.
17 See www.microsoft.com.
18 See www.sap.com.
19 For a discussion of the emergence of the use of programmes in organisations, see Maylor, H., Brady, T., Cooke-Davies, T. and Hodgson, D. (2006) 'From Projectification to Programmification', *International Journal of Project Management*, Vol. 24, pp. 663–672.
20 MSP is a programme management standard – often referred to as 'the big brother of PRINCE 2'. See Office of Government Commerce (OGC) (2007), *Managing Successful Programmes*, The Stationery Office, London.
21 Pellegrinelli, S. (1997) 'Programme Management: Organising Project Based Change', *International Journal of Project Management*, Vol. 15, No. 3, pp. 141–149.
22 Murray-Webster, R. and Thiry, M. (2000) 'Managing Programmes of Projects' in Turner, J.R. and Simister, S.J. (eds), *Gower Handbook of Project Management*, Gower, Aldershot, pp. 33–46.
23 Vereecke, A., Pandelaere, E., Deschoolmeester, D. and Stevens, M. (2003) 'A Classification of Development Programmes and Its Consequences for Programme Development', *International Journal of Operations and Production Management*, Vol. 23, No. 10, pp. 1279–1290.
24 Gareis, R. (2000) 'Programme Management and Project Portfolio Management: New Competences of Project-oriented Organizations', presented at PMI Symposium, Houston, and available at http://debian.p-m-a.at/docs/programme_management_PMA.pdf.
25 Office of Government Commerce (2009) *Managing Successful Projects with PRINCE 2 2009* The Stationery Office, Norwich, pp. 395–407.
26 The OGC has published a 'best practice guide' on the use of PMOs – OGC (2008) *For Successful Portfolio, Programme and Project Offices: Think P3O*, The Stationery Office, Norwich.
27 Hobbs, J.B. (2007) *The Multi-Project PMO: Global Analysis of the Current State of Practice*, Project Management Institute, Newtown Square, PA.
28 See also Hobbs, B., Aubry, M. and Thuillier, D. (2008) 'The Project Management Office as an Organisational Innovation', *International Journal of Project Management*, Vol. 26, No. 5, pp. 547–555.
29 See for instance www.cornwall.gov.uk/media/word/o/e/Project_Governance_Structure_and_Roles_and_Responsibilities.doc.

The Organizational Context

Strategy, Structure, and Culture

Chapter Outline

Chapter Objectives

After completing this chapter, you should be able to:

1. Understand how effective project management contributes to achieving strategic objectives.
2. Recognize three components of the corporate strategy model: formulation, implementation, and evaluation.
3. See the importance of identifying critical project stakeholders and managing them within the context of project development.
4. Recognize the strengths and weaknesses of three basic forms of organizational structure and their implications for managing projects.
5. Understand how companies can change their structure into a "heavyweight project organization" structure to facilitate effective project management practices.
6. Identify the characteristics of three forms of project management office (PMO).

7. Understand key concepts of corporate culture and how cultures are formed.
8. Recognize the positive effects of a supportive organizational culture on project management practices versus those of a culture that works against project management.

PROJECT MANAGEMENT BODY OF KNOWLEDGE CORE CONCEPTS COVERED IN THIS CHAPTER

1. Project Procurement Management
2. Identify Stakeholders (PMBoK sec. 18.1)
3. Plan Stakeholder Management (PMBoK 18.2)
4. Manage Stakeholder Engagement (PMBoK 18.3)
5. Organizational Influences on Project Management (PMBoK sec. 4.1)
6. Organizational Structures (PMBoK sec. 4.1.3)
7. Organizational Cultures and Styles (PMBoK sec. 4.1.1)
8. Enterprise Environmental Factors (PMBoK sec. 4.1.5)

PROJECT PROFILE

Case—Tesla's $5 Billion Gamble

Tesla Motors, developer of the iconic Model S "electric sports car," recently unveiled plans to create a "gigafactory" in order to produce batteries to power its automobiles. The concept was introduced by Tesla's owner, Elon Musk, who called the proposed battery plant the world's largest, and would lead to hiring 6,500 new workers and creating thousands of ancillary jobs in the process. Musk's plan is to develop a factory that will cover 10 million square feet of space with a manufacturing capacity to produce 35 gigawatt hours of batteries per year. To put this in perspective, Tesla's closest competitor in producing car batteries would be Nissan's battery factory in Tennessee, which employs only 300 workers and can turn out 4.8 gigawatt hours of batteries. In setting their sights on building the world's largest battery factory, Tesla (and Elon Musk) are gambling that demand for electric cars is rapidly growing. Musk's plan is for the plant to start producing batteries by 2017, which puts pressure on the company to break ground by the end of 2014.

Tesla's first car, the Tesla Model S, is a fully-electric powered sports car that has generated huge publicity for its performance, styling, and quality. *Consumer Reports* gave the car a "99" rating; its highest score ever. Selling for over $80,000 per car, however, has limited the market for the Tesla Model S to the very affluent. As a result, Tesla has already announced plans for a mid-priced car, the Gen III, which is expected to have a starting price of around $35,000. Tesla's challenge lies in reducing the cost of its batteries. For example, the 85 kilowatt-hour battery pack for the Model S can cost over $25,000. Clearly, for a mid-priced car to be a possibility, Tesla has to find a way to lower battery costs, with an initial target of a 30% reduction.

With the promise of such a massive factory, including the thousands of jobs the project would bring, it is no surprise that a number of western states are actively competing to be the host site for the structure. Officials in Arizona, Nevada, New Mexico, and Texas have all promised tax breaks, the opportunity for Tesla to open their own retail stores statewide, and a list of other incentives for them to agree to build in their state.

Not everyone has greeted Tesla's plan with enthusiasm, however. For example, Volkswagen CEO Martin Winterkorn recently observed that the current supply of car batteries was more than enough, given the slow acceptance rate with which electric cars are entering the American marketplace. Sales of electric vehicles remain small—less than 1% of the total U.S. market. The U.S. government spent more than $1 billion on new electric-vehicle battery plants as part of the Obama administration's economic stimulus, but many of those plants now run at just 15% to 20% of capacity. Numerous CEOs of car companies, battery makers, and others with a stake in the automotive industry share concerns about the advisability of devoting such huge capital investment in one factory for a market that is, at best, slowly developing.

Tesla, with sales of just over 22,400 cars last year, is already the largest buyer of lithium-ion battery cells in the world. Its plans to sell 500,000 vehicles means that its own demand would be greater than the demand for every laptop, mobile phone, and tablet sold in the world. To help meet this demand, as well as offset some of the cost of the huge factory project, Elon Musk has been negotiating with some skeptical potential partners, including Panasonic's automotive and industrial systems subsidiary, to invest in the new Gigafactory and run battery-cell production. Tesla executives

(continued)

FIGURE 4.9 The Tesla Model S "Skateboard" design with the flat battery pack located in the base of the car

Source: Car Culture/Corbis

argue that they need a plant to guarantee future supplies of the millions of battery cells they need at the reduced costs that come from economies of scale and logistics savings.

The risks in taking on this huge project are not solely technical or demand-based. Given Tesla's tight timetable for completion of the factory, there is concern that it may not be possible to complete a structure within the window Mr. Musk envisions. While it may be doable, there is no doubt that the vision to imagine, design, and build a Gigafactory makes this a unique opportunity, coupled with significant risks.[30]

INTRODUCTION

For successful project management, the *organizational setting matters*—its culture, its structure, and its strategy each play an integral part, and together they create the environment in which a project will flourish or founder. For example, a project's connection to your organization's overall strategy, the care with which you staff the team, and the goals you set for the project can be critical. Similarly, your organization's policies, structure, culture, and operating systems can work to support and promote project management or work against the ability to effectively run projects. Contextual issues provide the backdrop around which project activities must operate, so understanding what is beneath these issues truly contributes to understanding how to manage projects. Issues that affect a project can vary widely from company to company.

Before beginning a project, the project manager and team must be certain about the structure of the organization as it pertains to their project and the tasks they seek to accomplish. As clearly as possible, all reporting relationships must be specified, the rules and procedures that will govern the project must be established, and any issues of staffing the project team must be identified. General Electric's efforts to acquire French conglomerate Alstom for $17 billion has been an enormously complicated undertaking, involving the combined efforts of multiple business units, financial analysis, and constant interaction with Alstom's principle stakeholders, especially the French government. As part of their strategy, GE must identify the business groups that can be blended in with their own organization, units that are redundant to GE operations, and a logical organizational structure to best link the combined organization together in as efficient a manner as possible. Integrating Alstom's nearly 85,000 employees and global business units with their own operations makes GE's efforts a showcase in the project management of a strategic acquisition.

For many organizations, projects and project management practices are not the operating norm. In fact, as Chapter 1 discussed, projects typically exist outside of the formal, process-oriented activities associated with many organizations. As a result, many companies are simply not structured to allow for the successful completion of projects in conjunction with other ongoing corporate activities. The key challenge is discovering how project management may best be employed, regardless of the structure the company has adopted. What are the strengths and weaknesses of various structural forms and what are their implications for our ability to manage projects? This chapter will examine the concept of organizational culture and its roots and implications for effective project management. By looking closely at three of the most important contextual issues for project management—strategy, organizational structure, and culture—you will see how the variety of structural options can affect, either positively or negatively, the firm's ability to manage projects.

4.4 PROJECTS AND ORGANIZATIONAL STRATEGY

Strategic management is the science of formulating, implementing, and evaluating cross-functional decisions that enable an organization to achieve its **objectives**.[31] In this section we will consider the relevant components of this definition as they apply to project management. Strategic management consists of the following elements:

1. ***Developing vision statements and mission statements.*** Vision and mission statements establish a sense of what the organization hopes to accomplish or what top managers hope it will become at some point in the future. Vision statements describe the organization in terms of where it would like to be in the future. Effective vision statements are both inspirational and aspirational. A corporate vision serves as a focal point for members of the organization who may find themselves pulled in different directions by competing demands. In the face of multiple expectations and even contradictory efforts, an ultimate vision can serve as a "tie breaker," which is highly beneficial in establishing priorities. A sense of vision is also an extremely important source of motivation and purpose. As the *Book of Proverbs* points out: "Where there is no vision, the people perish" (Prov. 29:18).[32] Mission statements explain the company's reason for existence and support the vision. Many firms apply their vision and mission statements to evaluating new project opportunities as a first screening device. For example, Bechtel Corporation, a large construction organization, employs as its vision the goal of being "the world's premier engineering, construction, and project management company."[33] For Bechtel, this means (1) Customers and partners will see Bechtel as integral to their success; (2) People will be proud to work at Bechtel; and (3) Communities will regard Bechtel as "responsible—and responsive." Projects they undertake must support this vision and those that do not are not pursued.
2. ***Formulating, implementing, and evaluating.*** Projects, as the key ingredients in strategy implementation, play a crucial role in the basic process model of strategic management. A firm devotes significant time and resources to evaluating its business opportunities through developing a corporate vision or mission, assessing internal strengths and weaknesses as well as external opportunities and threats, establishing long-range objectives, and generating and selecting among various strategic alternatives. All these components relate to the formulation stage of strategy. Within this context, projects serve as the vehicles that enable companies to seize opportunities, capitalize on their strengths, and implement overall corporate objectives. New product development, for example, fits neatly into this framework. New products are developed and commercially introduced as a company's response to business opportunities. Effective project management enables firms to efficiently and rapidly respond.
3. ***Making cross-functional decisions.*** Business strategy is a corporate-wide venture, requiring the commitment and shared resources of all functional areas to meet overall

TABLE 4.7 Projects Reflect Strategy

Strategy	Project
Technical or operating initiatives (such as new distribution strategies or decentralized plant operations)	Construction of new plants or modernization of facilities
Development of products for greater market penetration and acceptance	New product development projects
New business processes for greater streamlining and efficiency	Reengineering projects
Changes in strategic direction or product portfolio reconfiguration	New product lines
Creation of new strategic alliances	Negotiation with supply chain members (including suppliers and distributors)
Matching or improving on competitors' products and services	Reverse engineering projects
Improvement of cross-organizational communication and efficiency in supply chain relationships	Enterprise IT efforts
Promotion of cross-functional interaction, streamlining of new product or service introduction, and improvement of departmental coordination	Concurrent engineering projects

objectives. Cross-functional decision making is a critical feature of project management, as experts from various functional groups come together into a team of diverse personalities and backgrounds. Project management work is a natural environment in which to operationalize strategic plans.

4. ***Achieving objectives.*** Whether the organization is seeking market leadership through low-cost, innovative products, superior quality, or other means, projects are the most effective tools to allow objectives to be met. A key feature of project management is that it can potentially allow firms to be effective in the external market as well as internally efficient in operations; that is, it is a great vehicle for optimizing organizational objectives, whether they incline toward efficiency of production or product or process effectiveness.

Projects have been called the "stepping-stones" of corporate strategy.[34] This idea implies that an organization's overall strategic vision is the driving force behind its project development. For example, 3M's desire to be a leading innovator in business gives rise to the creation and management of literally hundreds of new product development projects within the multinational organization every year. Likewise, Rubbermaid Corporation is noted for its consistent pursuit of new product development and market introduction. The manner in which organizational strategies affect new project introductions will be addressed in greater detail in the chapter on project selection (Chapter 12). Projects are the building blocks of strategies; they put an action-oriented face on the strategic edifice. Some examples of how projects operate as strategic building blocks are shown in Table 4.7. Each of the examples illustrates the underlying theme that projects are the "operational reality" behind strategic vision. In other words, they serve as the building blocks to create the reality a strategy can only articulate.

The **TOWS matrix** (See Figure 4.10) is a useful way to see the links between projects and an organization's strategic choices. TOWS comes from the acronym for "Threats–Opportunities–Weaknesses–Strengths" and refers to the challenges companies face in both their internal environment (within the organization) and their external environment (outside the company). In first identifying and then formulating strategies for addressing internal strengths and weaknesses and external opportunities and threats, firms rely on projects as a device for pursuing these strategic choices. As Figure 4.10 suggests, once an organization determines the appropriate strategies to pursue (e.g., "maxi-maxi" strategy), it can then identify and undertake project choices that support this TOWS matrix. Projects offer companies the ability to create concrete means for realizing strategic goals.[35]

	External Opportunities (O) 1. 2. 3.	External Threats (T) 1. 2. 3.
Internal Strengths (S) 1. 2. 3.	SO *"Maxi-Maxi" Strategy* Develop projects that use strengths to maximize opportunities	ST *"Maxi-Mini" Strategy* Develop projects that use strengths to minimize threats
Internal Weaknesses (W) 1. 2. 3.	WO *"Mini-Maxi" Strategy* Develop projects that minimize weaknesses by taking advantage of opportunities	WT *"Mini-Mini" Strategy* Develop projects that minimize weaknesses and avoid threats

FIGURE 4.10 TOWS Matrix

An organization's strategic management is the first important contextual element in its project management approaches. Because projects form the building blocks that allow us to implement strategic plans, it is vital that there exist a clear sense of harmony, or complementarity, between strategy and projects that have been selected for development. In a later section, we will add to our understanding of the importance of creating the right context for projects by adding an additional variable into the mix: the organization's structure.

4.5 STAKEHOLDER MANAGEMENT

Organizational research and direct experience tell us that organizations and project teams cannot operate in ways that ignore the external effects of their decisions. One way to understand the relationship of project managers and their projects to the rest of the organization is through employing stakeholder analysis. **Stakeholder analysis** is a useful tool for demonstrating some of the seemingly irresolvable conflicts that occur through the planned creation and introduction of any new project. **Project stakeholders** are defined as all individuals or groups who have an active stake in the project and can potentially impact, either positively or negatively, its development.[36] Project stakeholder analysis, then, consists of formulating strategies to identify and, if necessary, manage for positive results the impact of stakeholders on the project.

Stakeholders can affect and are affected by organizational actions to varying degrees.[37] In some cases, a corporation must take serious heed of the potential influence some stakeholder groups are capable of wielding. In other situations, a stakeholder group may have relatively little power to influence a company's activities but its presence may still require attention. Contrast, for example, the impact that the government has on regulating the tobacco industry's activities with the relative weakness of a small subcontractor working for Oracle on new software development. In the first case, the federal government has, in recent years, strongly limited the activities and sales strategies of the tobacco companies through the threat of regulation and litigation. On the other hand, Oracle, a large organization, can easily replace one small subcontractor with another.

Stakeholder analysis is helpful to the degree that it compels firms to acknowledge the potentially wide-ranging effects, both intended and unintended, that their actions can have on various stakeholder groups.[38] For example, the strategic decision to close an unproductive manufacturing facility may make good business sense in terms of costs versus benefits that the company derives from the manufacturing site. However, the decision to close the plant has the potential to unleash a torrent of stakeholder complaints in the form of protests and challenges from local unions, workers, community leaders in the town affected by the closing, political and legal groups, environmental concerns, and so forth. Sharp managers will consider the impact of stakeholder reaction as they weigh the possible effects of their strategic decisions.

Just as stakeholder analysis is instructive for understanding the impact of major strategic decisions, project stakeholder analysis is extremely important when it comes to managing projects. The project development process itself can be directly affected by stakeholders. This relationship is essentially reciprocal in that the project team's activities can also affect external stakeholder groups.[39] Some common ways the client stakeholder group has an impact on project team operations include agitating for faster development, working closely with the team to ease project transfer problems, and influencing top management in the parent organization to continue supporting the project. The project team can reciprocate this support through actions that show willingness to closely cooperate with the client in development and transition to user groups.

The nature of these various demands can place them seemingly in direct conflict. That is, in responding to the concerns of one stakeholder, project managers often unwittingly find themselves having offended or angered another stakeholder who has an entirely different agenda and set of expectations. For example, a project team working to install a new software application across the organization may go to such levels to ensure customer satisfaction that they engage in countless revisions of the package until they have, seemingly, made their customers happy. However, in doing so, the overall project schedule may now have slipped to the point where top management is upset by the cost and schedule overruns. In managing projects, we are challenged to find ways to balance a host of demands and still maintain supportive and constructive relationships with each important stakeholder group.

Identifying Project Stakeholders

Internal stakeholders are a vital component in any stakeholder analysis, and their impact is usually felt in relatively positive ways; that is, while serving as limiting and controlling influences (in the case of the company accountant), for example, most internal stakeholders want to see the project developed successfully. On the other hand, some external stakeholder groups operate in manners that are quite challenging or even hostile to project development. Consider the case of spikes in the price of oil. With oil prices remaining unstable, ranging from \$60 to above \$100 per barrel through much of 2014, the impact on the global economy, attempting to emerge from the Great Recession, has been severe. Many groups in the United States have advocated taking steps to lessen the country's dependence on foreign oil, including offshore exploration and the development of a new generation of nuclear power plants. Hydraulic fracturing ("fracking") technology has been widely embraced as a means for developing shale deposits across the country, resulting in projections that the United States will go from a net importer of 1.5 trillion cubic feet of natural gas in 2012 to an exporter by 2016. Environmental groups, however, continue to oppose these steps, vowing to use litigation, political lobbying, and other measures to resist the development of these alternative energy sources. As a recent example of the danger, they cite the Deepwater Horizon disaster that leaked thousands of barrels of oil into the Gulf of Mexico. Political efforts by environmentalists and their supporters have effectively delayed for years the development of the 1,700-mile-long Keystone XL oil pipeline from Canada's oil sands region to refineries in Texas. Cleland refers to these types of external stakeholders as **intervenor groups**, defined as groups external to the project but possessing the power to effectively intervene and disrupt the project's development.[40]

Among the set of project stakeholders that project managers must consider are:

Internal

- Top management
- Accounting
- Other functional managers
- Project team members

External

- Clients
- Competitors
- Suppliers
- Environmental, political, consumer, and other intervenor groups

CLIENTS Our focus throughout this entire book will be on maintaining and enhancing client relationships. In most cases, for both external and internal clients, a project deals with an investment. Clients are concerned with receiving the project from the team as quickly as possible because the longer the project implementation, the longer the money invested sits without generating any returns. As long as costs are not passed on to them, clients seldom are overly interested in how much expense is involved in a project's development. The opposite is usually the case, however. Costs typically must be passed on, and customers are avidly interested in getting what they pay for. Also, many projects start before client needs are fully defined. Product concept screening and clarification are often made part of the project scope of work. These issues—costs and client needs—are two strong reasons why many customers seek the right to make suggestions and request alterations in the project's features and operating characteristics well into the schedule. Customers feel, with justification, that a project is only as good as it is acceptable and useful. This sets a certain flexibility requirement and requires willingness from the project team to be amenable to specification changes.

Another important fact to remember about dealing with client groups is that the term *client* does not in every case refer to the *entire* customer organization. The reality is often far more complex. A client firm consists of a number of internal interest groups, and in many cases they have different agendas. For example, a company can probably readily identify a number of distinct clients within the customer organization, including the top management team, engineering groups, sales teams, on-site teams, manufacturing or assembly groups, and so on. Under these normal circumstances, it becomes clear that the process of formulating a stakeholder analysis of a customer organization can be a complex undertaking.

The challenge is further complicated by the need to communicate, perhaps using different business language, with the various customer stakeholder groups (see Figure 4.11). Preparing a presentation to deal with the customer's engineering staff requires mastery of technical information and solid specification details. On the other hand, the finance and contractual people are looking for tightly presented numbers. Formulating stakeholder strategies requires you first to acknowledge the existence of these various client stakeholders, and then to formulate a coordinated plan for uncovering and addressing each group's specific concerns and learning how to reach them.

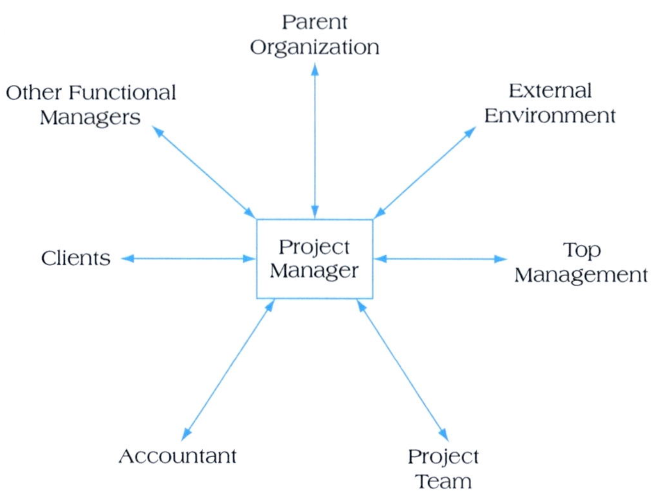

FIGURE 4.11 **Project Stakeholder Relationships**

COMPETITORS Competitors can be an important stakeholder element because they are affected by the successful implementation of a project. Likewise, should a rival company bring a new product to market, the project team's parent organization could be forced to alter, delay, or even abandon its project. In assessing competitors as a project stakeholder group, project managers should try to uncover any information available about the status of a competitor's projects. Further, where possible, any apparent lessons a competitor may have learned can be a source of useful information for a project manager who is initiating a similar project. If a number of severe implementation problems occurred within the competitor's project, that information could offer valuable lessons in terms of what to avoid.

SUPPLIERS *Suppliers* are any group that provides the raw materials or other resources the project team needs in order to complete the project. When a project requires a significant supply of externally purchased components, the project manager needs to take every step possible to ensure steady deliveries. In most cases this is a two-way street. First, the project manager has to ensure that each supplier receives the information necessary to implement its part of the project in a timely way. Second, the project manager must monitor the deliveries so they are met according to plan. In the ideal case, the supply chain becomes a well-greased machine that automatically both draws the input information from the project team and delivers the products without excessive involvement of the project manager. For example, in large-scale construction projects, project teams daily must face and satisfy an enormous number of supplier demands. The entire discipline of supply chain management is predicated on the ability to streamline logistics processes by effectively managing the project's supply chain.[41] When this process fails or is disrupted the consequences can be severe, as in the case of the catastrophic tsunami that struck the northeastern coast of Japan in March 2011, The supply chains and product development capabilities of Japanese corporations were badly damaged. Economists estimate that the natural disaster cost the country's economy over $300 billion. Further, numerous corporations (both Japanese companies and those that are their supply chain partners) were affected by the disaster. Japan manufactures 20% of the world's semiconductor products, leading to serious shortages and delivery delays for companies such as Intel, Toshiba, and Apple.

INTERVENOR GROUPS Environmental, political, social, community-activist, or consumer groups that can have a positive or negative effect on the project's development and successful launch are referred to as intervenor groups.[42] That is, they have the capacity to intervene in the project development and force their concerns to be included in the equation for project implementation. There are some classic examples of intervenor groups curtailing major construction projects, particularly in the nuclear power plant construction industry. As federal, state, and even local regulators decide to involve themselves in these construction projects, intervenors have at their disposal the legal system as a method for tying up or even curtailing projects. For example, while wind farms supply more than half of the electricity needs for the country of Denmark, an alternative energy "wind farm" project being proposed for sites off the coast of Cape Cod, Massachusetts, have encountered strong resistance from local groups opposed to the threat from these farms ruining the local seascape. Litigation has tied this wind farm project up for years and shows no sign of being approved in the near future. Prudent project managers need to make a realistic assessment of the nature of their projects and the likelihood that one intervenor group or another may make an effort to impose its will on the development process.

TOP MANAGEMENT In most organizations, top management holds a great deal of control over project managers and is in the position to regulate their freedom of action. Top management is, after all, the body that authorizes the development of the project through giving the initial "go" decision, sanctions additional resource transfers as they are needed by the project team, and supports and protects project managers and their teams from other organizational pressures. Top management requires that the project be timely (they want it out the door quickly), cost-efficient (they do not want to pay more for it than they have to), and minimally disruptive to the rest of the functional organization.

ACCOUNTING The accountant's *raison d'être* in the organization is maintaining cost efficiency of the project teams. Accountants support and actively monitor project budgets and, as such, are sometimes perceived as the enemy by project managers. This perception is wrong minded. To be able to manage the project, to make the necessary decisions, and to communicate with the customer, the project manager has to stay on top of the cost of the project at all times. An efficient cost control and reporting mechanism is vital. Accountants perform an important administrative service for the project manager.

FUNCTIONAL MANAGERS Functional managers who occupy line positions within the traditional chain of command are an important stakeholder group to acknowledge. Most projects are staffed by individuals who are essentially on loan from their functional departments. In fact, in many cases, project team members may only have part-time appointments to the team; their functional managers may still expect a significant amount of work out of them per week in performing their functional responsibilities. This situation can create a good deal of confusion, conflict, and the need for negotiation between project managers and functional supervisors and lead to seriously divided loyalties among team members, particularly when performance evaluations are conducted by functional managers rather than the project manager. In terms of simple self-survival, team members often maintain closer allegiance to their functional group than to the project team.

Project managers need to appreciate the power of the organization's functional managers as a stakeholder group. Functional managers are not usually out to discourage project development. Rather, they have loyalty to their functional roles, and they act and use their resources accordingly, within the limits of the company's structure. Nevertheless, as a formidable stakeholder group, functional managers need to be treated with due consideration by project managers.

PROJECT TEAM MEMBERS The project team obviously has a tremendous stake in the project's outcome. Although some may have a divided sense of loyalty between the project and their functional group, in many companies the team members volunteer to serve on projects and, hopefully, receive the kind of challenging work assignments and opportunities for growth that motivate them to perform effectively. Project managers must understand that their project's success depends on the commitment and productivity of each member of the project team. Thus, team members' impact on the project is, in many ways, more profound than that of any other stakeholder group.

Managing Stakeholders

Project managers and their companies need to recognize the importance of stakeholder groups and proactively manage with their concerns in mind. Block offers a useful framework of the political process that has application to stakeholder management.[43] In his framework, Block suggests six steps:

1. Assess the environment.
2. Identify the goals of the principal actors.
3. Assess your own capabilities.
4. Define the problem.
5. Develop solutions.
6. Test and refine the solutions.

ASSESS THE ENVIRONMENT Is the project relatively low-key or is it potentially so significant that it will likely excite a great deal of attention? For example, when EMC Corporation, a large computer manufacturer, began development of a new line of minicomputers and storage units with the potential for either great profits or serious losses, it took great care to first determine the need for such a product. Going directly to the consumer population with market research was the key to assessing the external environment. Likewise, one of the shapers of autonomous and near-autonomous care technology (driverless cars) has been companies such as Google working closely with consumers to determine their expectations and comfort level with the technology. In testing to date, autonomous vehicles have driven over 700,000 miles with only one accident (which was human-caused). Current projections are that a safe and workable driverless car could be ready for release as early as 2017. Ultimately, it is estimated that over 1 billion automobiles and trucks worldwide and over 450,000 civilian and military aircraft could be affected by this new technology.[44]

IDENTIFY THE GOALS OF THE PRINCIPAL ACTORS As a first step in fashioning a strategy to defuse negative reaction, a project manager should attempt to paint an accurate portrait of stakeholder concerns. Fisher and Ury[45] have noted that the positions various parties adopt are almost invariably based on need. What, then, are the needs of each significant stakeholder group regarding the project? A recent example will illustrate this point. A small IT firm specializing in network solutions and software development recently contracted with a larger publishing house to develop a simulation for college classroom use. The software firm was willing to negotiate a lower-than-normal price for the job because the publisher suggested that excellent performance on this project would lead to future business. The software organization, interested in follow-up business, accepted the lower fee because its more immediate needs were to gain entry into publishing and develop long-term customer contacts. The publisher needed a low price; the software developer needed new market opportunities.

Project teams must look for hidden agendas in goal assessment. It is common for departments and stakeholder groups to exert a set of overt goals that are relevant, but often illusionary.[46] In haste to satisfy these overt or espoused goals, a common mistake is to accept these goals on face value, without looking into the needs that may drive them or create more compelling goals. Consider, for example, a project in a large, project-based manufacturing company to develop a comprehensive project management scheduling system. The project manager in charge of the installation approached each department head and believed that he had secured their willingness to participate in creating a scheduling system centrally located within the project management division. Problems developed quickly, however, because IT department members, despite their public professions of support, began using every means possible to covertly sabotage the implementation of the system, delaying completion of assignments and refusing to respond to user requests. What was their concern? They believed that placing a computer-generated source of information anywhere but in the IT department threatened their position as the sole disseminator of information. In addition to probing the overt goals and concerns of various stakeholders, project managers must look for hidden agendas and other sources of constraint on implementation success.

ASSESS YOUR OWN CAPABILITIES As Robert Burns said, "Oh wad some Power the giftie gie us/To see oursels as ithers see us!"[47] Organizations must consider what they do well. Likewise, what are their weaknesses? Do the project manager and her team have the political savvy and a sufficiently strong bargaining position to gain support from each of the stakeholder groups? If not, do they have connections to someone who can? Each of these questions is an example of the importance of the project team understanding its own capacities and capabilities. For example, not everyone has the contacts to upper management that may be necessary for ensuring a steady flow of support and resources. If you realistically determine that political acumen is not your strong suit, then the solution may be to find someone who has these skills to help you.

DEFINE THE PROBLEM We must seek to define problems both in terms of our own perspective and in consideration of the valid concerns of the other party. The key to developing and maintaining strong stakeholder relationships lies in recognizing that different parties can have very different but equally legitimate perspectives on a problem. When we define problems not just from our viewpoint but also by trying to understand how the same issue may be perceived by stakeholders, we are operating in a "win-win" mode. Further, we must be as precise as possible, staying focused on the specifics of the problem, not generalities. The more accurately and honestly we can define the problem, the better able we will be to create meaningful solution options.

DEVELOP SOLUTIONS There are two important points to note about this step. First, developing solutions means precisely that: creating an action plan to address, as much as possible, the needs of the various stakeholder groups in relation to the other stakeholder groups. This step constitutes the stage in which the project manager, together with the team, seeks to manage the political process. What will work in dealing with top management? In implementing that strategy, what reaction is likely to be elicited from the accountant? The client? The project team? Asking these questions helps the project manager develop solutions that acknowledge the interrelationships of each of the relevant stakeholder groups. The topics of power, political behavior, influence, and negotiation will be discussed in greater detail in Chapter 17.

As a second point, it is necessary that we do our political homework prior to developing solutions.[48] Note the late stage at which this step is introduced. Project managers can fall into a trap if they attempt to manage a process with only fragmentary or inadequate information. The philosophy of "ready, fire, aim" is sometimes common in stakeholder management. The result is a stage of perpetual firefighting during which the project manager is a virtual pendulum, swinging from crisis to crisis. Pendulums and these project managers share one characteristic: They never reach a goal. The process of putting out one fire always seems to create a new blaze.

TEST AND REFINE THE SOLUTIONS Implementing the solutions implies acknowledging that the project manager and team are operating under imperfect information. You may assume that stakeholders will react to certain initiatives in predictable ways, but such assumptions can be erroneous. In testing and refining solutions, the project manager and team should realize that solution implementation is an iterative process. You make your best guesses, test for stakeholder reactions, and reshape your strategies accordingly. Along the way, many of your preconceived notions about the needs and biases of various stakeholder groups must be refined as well. In some cases, you will have made accurate assessments. At other times, your suppositions may have been dangerously naive or disingenuous. Nevertheless, this final step in the stakeholder management process forces the project manager to perform a critical self-assessment. It requires the flexibility to make accurate diagnoses and appropriate midcourse corrections.

When done well, these six steps form an important method for acknowledging the role that stakeholders play in successful project implementation. They allow project managers to approach "political stakeholder management" much as they would any other form of problem solving, recognizing it as a multivariate problem as various stakeholders interact with the project and with one another. Solutions to political stakeholder management can then be richer, more comprehensive, and more accurate.

An alternative, simplified stakeholder management process consists of planning, organizing, directing, motivating, and controlling the resources necessary to deal with the various internal and external stakeholder groups. The various stakeholder management functions are interlocked and repetitive; that is, this stakeholder management process is really best understood as a cycle. As you continually assess the environment, you refine the goals of the principal stakeholders. Likewise, as you assess your own capabilities, define the problems and possible solutions, you are constantly observing the environment to make sure that your proposed solutions are still valid. Finally, in testing and refining these solutions, it is critical to ensure that they will be the optimal alternatives, given likely changes in the environment. In the process of developing and implementing your plans, you are likely to uncover new stakeholders whose demands must also be considered. Further, as the environment changes or as the project enters a new stage of its life cycle, you may be required to cycle through the stakeholder management model again to verify that your old management strategies are still effective. If, on the other hand, you deem that new circumstances make it necessary to alter those strategies, you must work through this stakeholder management model anew to update the relevant information.

4.6 ORGANIZATIONAL STRUCTURE

The word *structure* implies organization. People who work in an organization are grouped so that their efforts can be channeled for maximum efficiency. **Organizational structure** consists of three key elements:[49]

1. ***Organizational structure designates formal reporting relationships, including the number of levels in the hierarchy and the span of control of managers and supervisors.*** Who reports to whom in the structural hierarchy? This is a key component of a firm's structure. A span of control determines the number of subordinates directly reporting to each supervisor. In some structures, a manager may have a wide span of control, suggesting a large number of subordinates, while other structures mandate narrow spans of control and few individuals reporting directly to any supervisor. For some companies, the reporting relationship may be rigid and bureaucratic; other firms require flexibility and informality across hierarchical levels.
2. ***Organizational structure identifies the grouping together of individuals into departments and departments into the total organization.*** How are individuals collected into larger groups? Starting with the smallest, units of a structure continually recombine with other units to create larger groups, or organizations of individuals. These groups, referred to as departments, may be grouped along a variety of different logical patterns. For example, among the most common reasons for

creating departments are (1) *function*—grouping people performing similar activities into similar departments, (2) *product*—grouping people working on similar product lines into departments, (3) *geography*—grouping people within similar geographical regions or physical locations into departments, and (4) *project*—grouping people involved in the same project into a department. We will discuss some of these more common departmental arrangements in detail later in this chapter.

3. ***Organizational structure includes the design of systems to ensure effective communication, coordination, and integration of effort across departments.*** This third feature of organizational structure refers to the supporting mechanisms the firm relies on to reinforce and promote its structure. These supporting mechanisms may be simple or complex. In some firms, a method for ensuring effective communication is simply to mandate, through rules and procedures, the manner in which project team members must communicate with one another and the types of information they must routinely share. Other companies use more sophisticated or complex methods for promoting coordination, such as the creation of special project offices apart from the rest of the company where project team members work for the duration of the project. The key thrust behind this third element in organizational structure implies that simply creating a logical ordering or hierarchy of personnel for an organization is not sufficient unless it is also supported by systems that ensure clear communication and coordination across the departments.

It is also important to note that within the project management context two distinct structures operate simultaneously, and both affect the manner in which the project is accomplished. The first is the overall structure of the organization that is developing the project. This structure consists of the arrangement of all units or interest groups participating in the development of the project; it includes the project team, the client, top management, functional departments, and other relevant stakeholders. The second structure at work is the internal structure of the project team; it specifies the relationship between members of the project team, their roles and responsibilities, and their interaction with the project manager. The majority of this chapter examines the larger structure of the overall organization and how it pertains to project management. The implications of internal project team structure will be discussed here but explored more thoroughly in Chapter 17.

4.7 FORMS OF ORGANIZATIONAL STRUCTURE

Organizations can be structured in an infinite variety of ways, ranging from highly complex to extremely simple. What is important to understand is that typically the structure of an organization does not happen by chance; it is the result of a reasoned response to forces acting on the firm. A number of factors routinely affect the reasons why a company is structured the way it is. Operating environment is among the most important determinants or factors influencing an organization's structure. An organization's **external environment** consists of all forces or groups outside the organization that have the potential to affect the organization. Some elements in a company's external environment that can play a significant role in a firm's activities are competitors, customers in the marketplace, the government and other legal or regulatory bodies, general economic conditions, pools of available human or financial resources, suppliers, technological trends, and so forth. In turn, these organizational structures, often created for very sound reasons in relation to the external environment, have a strong impact on the manner in which projects are best managed within the organization. As we will see, each organizational type offers its own benefits and drawbacks as a context for creating projects.

Some common structural types classify the majority of firms. These structure types include the following:

1. *Functional organizations*—Companies are structured by grouping people performing similar activities into departments.
2. *Project organizations*—Companies are structured by grouping people into project teams on temporary assignments.
3. *Matrix organizations*—Companies are structured by creating a dual hierarchy in which functions and projects have equal prominence.

Functional Organizations

The **functional structure** is probably the most common organizational type used in business today. The logic of the functional structure is to group people and departments performing similar activities into units. In the functional structure, it is common to create departments such as accounting,

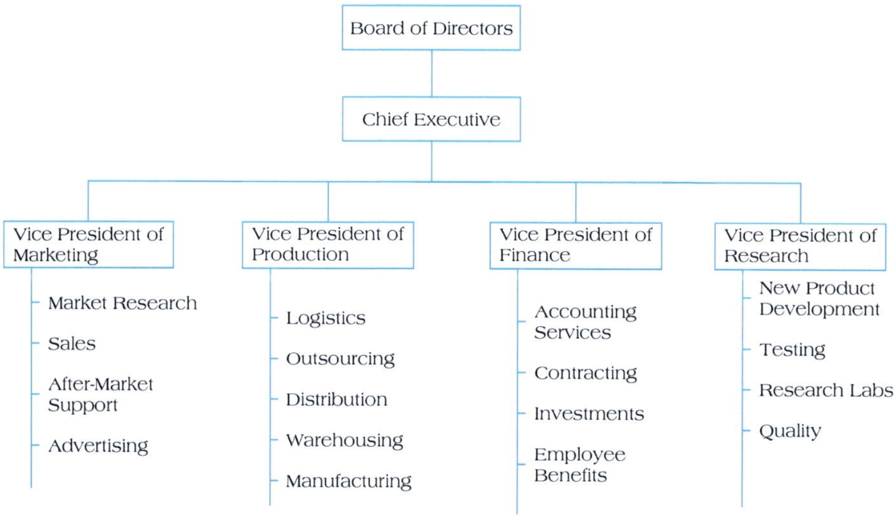

FIGURE 4.12 Example of a Functional Organizational Structure

marketing, or research and development. Division of labor in the functional structure is not based on the type of product or project supported, but rather according to the type of work performed. In an organization having a functional structure, members routinely work on multiple projects or support multiple product lines simultaneously.

Figure 4.12 shows an example of a functional structure. Among the clear strengths of the functional organization is efficiency; when every accountant is a member of the accounting department, it is possible to more efficiently allocate the group's services throughout the organization, account for each accountant's work assignments, and ensure that there is no duplication of effort or unused resources. Another advantage is that it is easier to maintain valuable intellectual capital when all expertise is consolidated under one functional department. When you need an expert on offshore tax implications for globally outsourced projects, you do not have to conduct a firmwide search but can go right to the accounting department to find a resident expert.

The most common weakness in a functional structure from a project management perspective relates to the tendency for employees organized this way to become fixated on their concerns and work assignments to the exclusion of the needs of other departments. This idea has been labeled *functional siloing*, named for the silos found on farms (see Figure 4.13). Siloing occurs when similar people in a work group are unwilling or unable to consider alternative viewpoints, collaborate with other groups, or work in cross-functional ways. For example, within Data General Corporation, prior to its acquisition by EMC, squabbles between engineering and sales were constant. The sales department complained that its input to new product development was minimized as the engineering department routinely took the lead on innovation without meaningful consultation with other departments. Likewise, Robert Lutz, former President of Chrysler, argued that an ongoing weakness at the automobile company was the inability of the various functional departments to cooperate with and recognize the contributions of each other. Another weakness of functional structures is a generally poor responsiveness to external opportunities and threats. Communication channels tend to run up and down the hierarchy, rather than across functional boundaries. This vertical hierarchy can overload, and decision making takes time. Functional structures also may not be very innovative due to the problems inherent in the design. With siloed functional groups typically having a restricted view of the overall organization and its goals, it is difficult to achieve the cross-functional coordination necessary to innovate or respond quickly to market opportunities.

For project management, an additional weakness of the functional structure is that it provides no logical location for a central project management function. Top management may assign a project and delegate various components of that project to specialists within the different functional groups. Overall coordination of the project, including combining the efforts of the different functions assigned to perform project tasks, must then occur at a higher, top management level. A serious drawback for running projects in this operating environment is

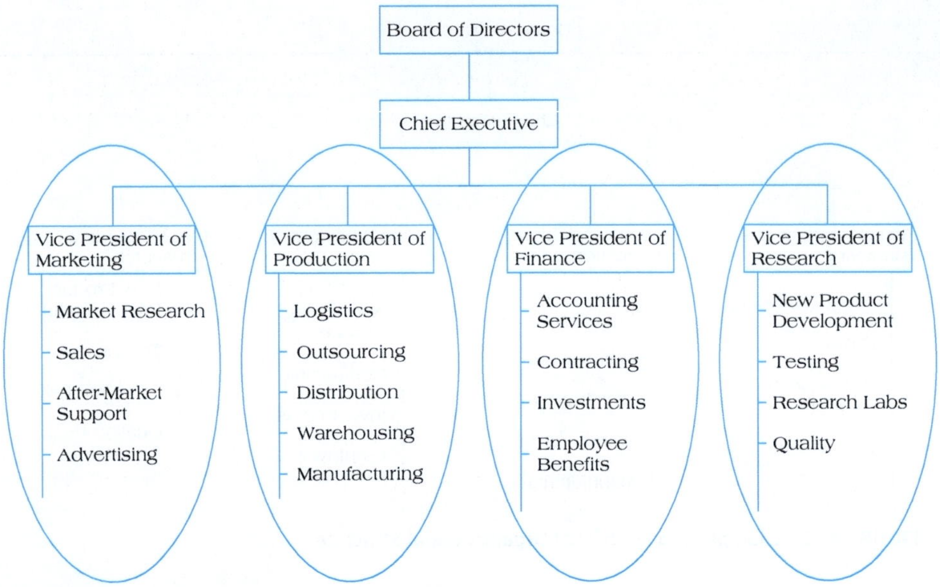

FIGURE 4.13 The Siloing Effect Found in Functional Structures

that they often must be *layered,* or applied on top of the ongoing duties of members of functional groups. The practical effect is that individuals whose main duties remain within their functional group are assigned to staff projects; when employees owe their primary allegiance to their own department, their frame of reference can remain functional. Projects can be temporary distractions in this sense, taking time away from "real work." This can explain some of the behavioral problems that occur in running projects, such as low team member motivation or the need for extended negotiations between project managers and department supervisors for personnel to staff project teams.

Another project-related problem of the functional organization is the fact that it is easy to suboptimize the project's development.[50] When the project is developed as the brainchild of one department, that group's efforts may be well considered and effective. In contrast, departments not as directly tied to or interested in the project may perform their duties to the minimum possible level. A successful project-based product or service requires the fully coordinated efforts of all functional groups participating in and contributing to the project's development.

Another problem is that customers are not the primary focus of everyone within the functionally structured organization. The customer in this environment might be seen as someone else's problem, particularly among personnel whose duties tend to be supportive. Customer requirements must be met, and projects must be created with a customer in mind. Any departmental representatives on the project team who have not adopted a "customer-focused" mind-set add to the possibility of the project coming up short.

Summing up the functional structure (see Table 4.8), as it relates to the external environment, the functional structure is well suited to firms with relatively low levels of external uncertainty because their stable environments do not require rapid adaptation or responsiveness. When the environment is relatively predictable, the functional structure works well because it emphasizes efficiency. Unfortunately, project management activities within the functionally organized firm can often be problematic when they are applied in settings for which this structure's strengths are not well suited. As the above discussion indicates, although there are some ways in which the functional structure can be advantageous to managing projects, in the main, it is perhaps the poorest form of structure when it comes to getting the maximum performance out of project management assignments.[51]

Project Organizations

Project organizations are those that are set up with their exclusive focus aimed at running projects. Construction companies, large manufacturers such as Boeing or Airbus, pharmaceutical firms, and many software consulting and research and development organizations are organized as pure

TABLE 4.8 Strengths and Weaknesses of Functional Structures

Strengths for Project Management	Weaknesses for Project Management
1. Projects are developed within the basic functional structure of the organization, requiring no disruption or change to the firm's design.	1. Functional siloing makes it difficult to achieve cross-functional cooperation.
2. Enables the development of in-depth knowledge and intellectual capital.	2. Lack of customer focus.
3. Allows for standard career paths. Project team members only perform their duties as needed while maintaining maximum connection with their functional group.	3. Projects generally take longer to complete due to structural problems, slower communication, lack of direct ownership of the project, and competing priorities among the functional departments.
	4. Projects may be suboptimized due to varying interest or commitment across functional boundaries.

project organizations. Within the project organization, each project is a self-contained business unit with a dedicated project team. The firm assigns resources from functional pools directly to the project for the time period they are needed. In the project organization, the project manager has sole control over the resources the unit uses. The functional departments' chief role is to coordinate with project managers and ensure that there are sufficient resources available as they need them.

Figure 4.14 illustrates a simple form of the pure **project structure**. Projects Alpha and Beta have been formed and are staffed by project team members from the company's functional groups. The project manager is the leader of the project and the staff all report to her. The staffing decisions and duration of employees' tenure with the project are left to the discretion of the project manager, who is the chief point of authority for the project. As the figure suggests, there are several advantages to the use of a pure project structure.

- First, the project manager does not occupy a subordinate role in this structure. All major decisions and authority remain under the control of the project manager.
- Second, the functional structure and its potential for siloing or communication problems are bypassed. As a result, communication improves across the organization and within the project team. Because authority remains with the project manager and the project team, decision making is speeded up. Project decisions can occur quickly, without lengthy delays, as functional groups are consulted or allowed to veto project team decisions.

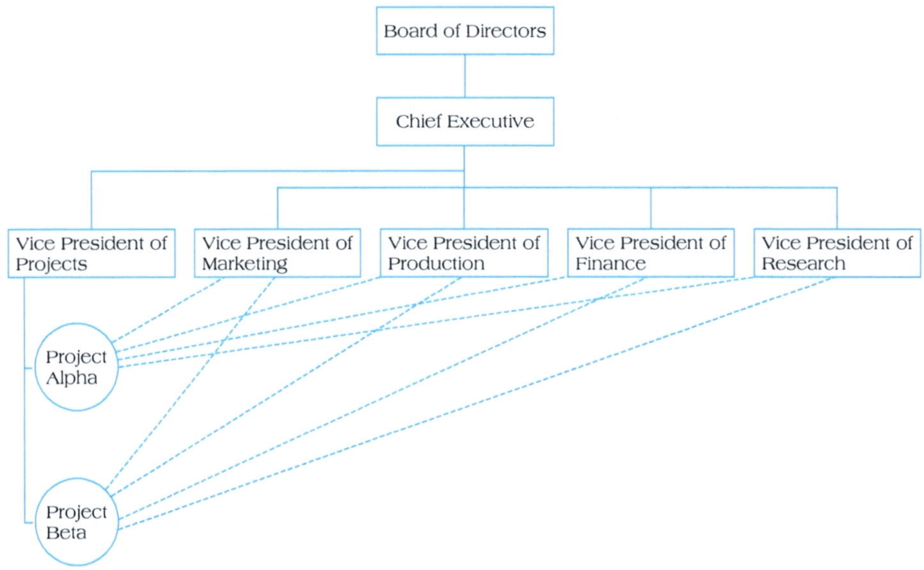

FIGURE 4.14 **Example of a Project Organizational Structure**

TABLE 4.9 Strengths and Weaknesses of Project Structures

Strengths for Project Management	Weaknesses for Project Management
1. Assigns authority solely to the project manager.	1. Setting up and maintaining teams can be expensive.
2. Leads to improved communication across the organization and among functional groups.	2. Potential for project team members to develop loyalty to the project rather than to the overall organization.
3. Promotes effective and speedy decision making.	3. Difficult to maintain a pooled supply of intellectual capital.
4. Promotes the creation of cadres of project management experts.	4. Concern among project team members about their future once the project ends.
5. Encourages rapid response to market opportunities.	

- Third, this organizational type promotes the expertise of a cadre of project management professionals. Because the focus for operations within the organization is project-based, everyone within the organization understands and operates with the same focus, ensuring that the organization maintains highly competent project management resources.
- Finally, the pure project structure encourages flexibility and rapid response to environmental opportunities. Projects are created, managed, and disbanded routinely; therefore, the ability to create new project teams as needed is common and team formation can be quickly undertaken.

Although there are a number of advantages in creating dedicated project teams using a project structure (see Table 4.9), this design does have some disadvantages that should be considered.

- First, the process of setting up and maintaining a number of self-contained project teams can be expensive. The different functional groups, rather than controlling their resources, must provide them on a full-time basis to the different projects being undertaken at any point. This can result in forcing the project organization to hire more project specialists (e.g., engineers) than they might need otherwise, with a resulting loss of economies of scale.
- Second, the potential for inefficient use of resources is a key disadvantage of the pure project organization. Organizational staffing may fluctuate up and down as the number of projects in the firm increases or decreases. Hence, it is possible to move from a state in which many projects are running and organizational resources are fully employed to one in which only a few projects are in the pipeline, with many resources underutilized. In short, manpower requirements across the organization can increase or decrease rapidly, making staffing problems severe.
- Third, it is difficult to maintain a supply of technical or intellectual capital, which is one of the advantages of the functional structure. Because resources do not typically reside within the functional structure for long, it is common for them to shift from project to project, preventing the development of a pooled knowledge base. For example, many project organizations hire technically proficient contract employees for various project tasks. These employees may perform their work and, once finished and their contract is terminated, leave the organization, taking their expertise with them. Expertise resides not within the organization, but differentially within the functional members who are assigned to the projects. Hence, some team members may be highly knowledgeable while others are not sufficiently trained and capable.
- A fourth problem with the pure project form has to do with the legitimate concerns of project team members as they anticipate the completion of the project. What, they wonder, will be in their future once their project is completed? As noted above, staffing can be inconsistent, and often project team members finish a project only to discover that they are not needed for new assignments. Functional specialists in project organizations do not have the kind of permanent "home" that they would have in a functional organization, so their concerns are

justified. In a similar manner, it is common in pure project organizations for project team members to identify with the project as their sole source of loyalty. Their emphasis is project-based and their interests reside not with the larger organization, but within their own project. When a project is completed, they may begin searching for new challenges, and may even leave the company for appealing new assignments.

Matrix Organizations

One of the more innovative organization designs to emerge in the past 30 years has been the **matrix structure**. The **matrix organization**, which is a combination of functional and project activities, seeks a balance between the functional organization and the pure project form. The way it achieves this balance is to emphasize both function and project focuses at the same time. In practical terms, the matrix structure creates a *dual hierarchy* in which there is a balance of authority between the project emphasis and the firm's functional departmentalization. Figure 4.15 illustrates how a matrix organization is set up; note that the vice president of projects occupies a unique reporting relationship in that the position is not formally part of the organization's functional department structure. The vice president is the head of the projects division and occupies one side of the dual hierarchy, a position shared with the CEO and heads of functional departments.

Figure 4.15 also provides a look at how the firm staffs project teams. The vice president of projects controls the activities of the project managers under his authority. They, however, must work closely with functional departments to staff their project teams through loans of personnel from each functional group. Whereas in functional organizations project team personnel are still almost exclusively under the control of the functional departments and to some degree serve at the pleasure of their functional boss, in the matrix organizational structure these personnel are shared by both their departments and the project to which they are assigned. They remain under the authority of both the project manager and their functional department supervisor. Notice, for example, that the project manager for Project Alpha has negotiated the use of two **resources** (personnel) from the vice president of marketing, 1.5 resources from production, and so forth. Each project and project manager is responsible for working with the functional heads to determine the optimal staffing needs, how many people are required to perform necessary project activities, and when they will be available. Questions such as "What tasks must be accomplished on this project?" are best answered by the project manager. However, other equally important questions, such as "Who will perform the tasks?" and "How long should the tasks take?", are matters that must be jointly negotiated between the project manager and the functional department head.

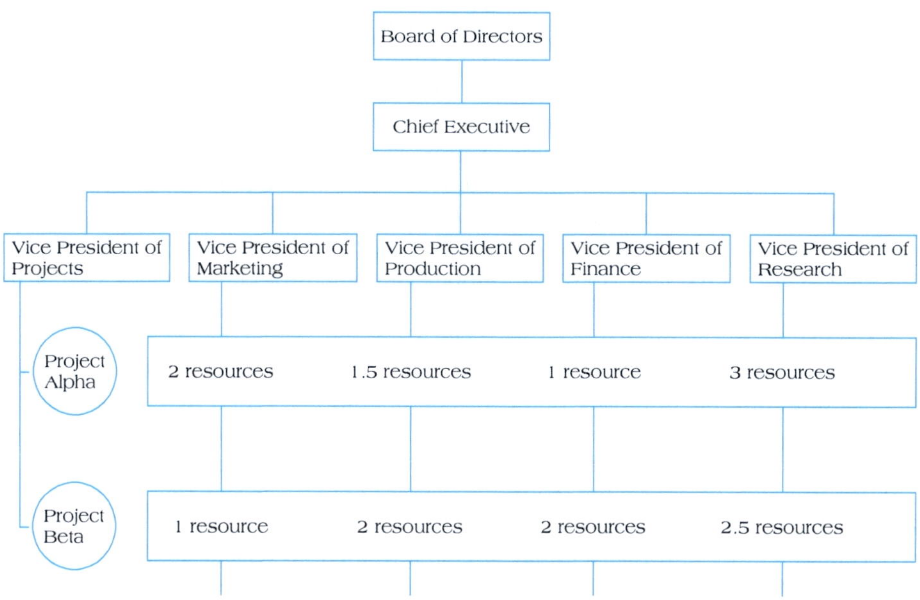

FIGURE 4.15 Example of a Matrix Organizational Structure

It is useful to distinguish between three common forms of the matrix structure: the **weak matrix** (sometimes called the *functional matrix*), the **balanced matrix**, and the **strong matrix** (sometimes referred to as a *project matrix*). In a weak matrix, functional departments maintain control over their resources and are responsible for managing their components of the project. The project manager's role is to coordinate the activities of the functional departments, typically as an administrator. She is expected to prepare schedules, update project status, and serve as the link between the departments with their different project deliverables, but she does not have direct authority to control resources or make significant decisions on her own. The goal of the balanced matrix is to equally distribute authority and resource assignment responsibility between the project manager and the functional department head. In a strong matrix, the balance of power has further shifted in favor of the project manager. She now controls most of the project activities and functions, including the assignment and control of project resources, and has key decision-making authority. Although functional managers have some input into the assignment of personnel from their departments, their role is mostly consultative. The strong matrix is probably the closest to a "project organization" mentality that we can get while working within a matrix environment.

Creating an organizational structure with two bosses may seem awkward, but there are some important advantages to this approach, provided certain conditions are met. Matrix structures are useful under circumstances in which:[52]

1. ***There is pressure to share scarce resources across product or project opportunities.*** When an organization has scarce human resources and a number of project opportunities, it faces the challenge of using its people and material resources as efficiently as possible to support the maximum number of projects. A matrix structure provides an environment in which the company can emphasize efficient use of resources for the maximum number of projects.
2. ***There is a need to emphasize two or more different types of output.*** For example, the firm may need to promote its technical competence (using a functional structure) while continually creating a series of new products (requiring a project structure). With this dual pressure for performance, there is a natural balance in a matrix organization between the functional emphasis on technical competence and efficiency and the project focus on rapid new product development.
3. ***The environment of the organization is complex and dynamic.*** When firms face the twin challenges of complexity and rapidly shifting environmental pressures, the matrix structure promotes the exchange of information and coordination across functional boundaries.

In the matrix structure, the goal is to create a simultaneous focus on the need to be quickly responsive to both external opportunities and internal operating efficiencies. In order to achieve this dual focus, equal authority must reside within both the project and the functional groups. One advantage of the matrix structure for managing projects is that it places project management parallel to functional departments in authority. This advantage highlights the enhanced status of the project manager in this structure, who is expected to hold a similar level of power and control over resources as department managers. Another advantage is that the matrix is specifically tailored to encourage the close coordination between departments, with an emphasis on producing projects quickly and efficiently while sharing resources among projects as they are needed. Unlike the functional structure, in which projects are, in effect, layered over a structure that is not necessarily supportive of their processes, the matrix structure balances the twin demands of external responsiveness and internal efficiency, creating an environment in which projects can be performed expeditiously. Finally, because resources are shared and "movable" among multiple projects, there is a greater likelihood that expertise will not be hoarded or centered on some limited set of personnel, as in the project organization, but will be diffused more widely across the firm.

Among the disadvantages of the matrix structure's dual hierarchy is the potentially negative effect that creating multiple authority points has on operations. When two parts of the organization share authority, the workers caught between them can experience great frustration when they receive mixed or conflicting messages from the head of the project group and the head of their functional departments. Suppose that the vice president of projects signaled the need for workers to concentrate their efforts on a critical project with a May 1 deadline. If, at the same time, the head of finance were to tell his staff that with tax season imminent, it was necessary for his employees to ignore projects for the time being to finish tax-related work, what might happen? From the team member's perspective, this dual hierarchy can be very frustrating. Workers daily experience

TABLE 4.10 Strengths and Weaknesses of Matrix Structures

Strengths for Project Management	Weaknesses for Project Management
1. Suited to dynamic environments.	1. Dual hierarchies mean two bosses.
2. Emphasizes the dual importance of project management and functional efficiency.	2. Requires significant time to be spent negotiating the sharing of critical resources between projects and departments.
3. Promotes coordination across functional units.	3. Can be frustrating for workers caught between competing project and functional demands.
4. Maximizes scarce resources between competing project and functional responsibilities.	

a sense of being pulled in multiple directions as they receive conflicting instructions from their bosses—both on projects and in their departments. Consequently, ordinary work often becomes a balancing act based on competing demands for their time.

Another disadvantage is the amount of time and energy required by project managers in meetings, negotiations, and other coordinative functions to get decisions made across multiple groups, often with different agendas. Table 4.10 summarizes the strengths and weaknesses of the matrix structure.

Although matrix structures seem to be a good solution for project management, they require a great deal of time to be spent coordinating the use of human resources. Many project managers comment that as part of the matrix, they devote a large proportion of their time to meetings, to resolving or negotiating resource commitments, and to finding ways to share power with department heads. The matrix structure offers some important benefits and drawbacks from the perspective of managing projects. It places project management on an equal footing with functional efficiency and promotes cross-functional coordination. At the same time, however, the dual hierarchy results in some significant behavioral challenges as authority and control within the organization are constantly in a state of flux.[53] A common complaint from project managers operating in matrix organizations is that an enormous amount of their time is taken up with "playing politics" and bargaining sessions with functional managers to get the resources and help they need. In a matrix, negotiation skills, political savvy, and networking become vital tools for project managers who want to be successful.

Moving to Heavyweight Project Organizations

The term **heavyweight project organization** refers to the belief that organizations can sometimes gain tremendous benefits from creating a fully dedicated project organization.[54] The heavyweight project organization concept is based on the notion that successful project organizations do not happen by chance or luck. Measured steps in design and operating philosophy are needed to get to the top and remain there. Taking their formulation from the "Skunkworks" model, named after the famous Lockheed Corporation programs, autonomous project teams represent the final acknowledgment by the firm of the priority of project-based work in the company. In these organizations, the project manager is given full authority, status, and responsibility to ensure project success. Functional departments are either fully subordinated to the projects or the project teams are accorded an independent resource base with which to accomplish their tasks.

In order to achieve the flexibility and responsiveness that the heavyweight organization can offer, it is important to remember some key points. First, no one goes directly to the autonomous team stage when it comes to running projects. This project organizational form represents the last transitional stage in a systematically planned shift in corporate thinking. Instead, managers gradually move to this step through making conscious decisions about how they are going to improve the way they run projects. Successful project firms work to expand the authority of the project manager, often in the face of stiff resistance from functional department heads who like the power balance the way it currently exists. Part of the process of redirecting the power balance involves giving project managers high status, authority to conduct performance evaluations of team members, authority over project resources, and direct links to the customers. Project managers who are constantly forced to rely on the good graces of functional managers for their team staffing, coordination, and financial and other resources are operating with one hand tied behind their backs.

Second, heavyweight project organizations have realigned their priorities away from functional maintenance to market opportunism, a realignment that can occur only when the resources needed to respond rapidly to market opportunities rest with the project team rather than being controlled by higher level bureaucracies within a company. Finally, as noted throughout this book, the shift in focus for many firms toward project-based work profoundly affects the manner in which the project organization, manager, and the team operate. The new focus on the external customer becomes the driving force for operations, not simply one of several competing demands that the project team must satisfy as best they can.

Ultimately, the decision of which organizational structure is appropriate to use may simply come down to one of expediency; although it may, in fact, be desirable to conduct projects within a structure that offers maximum flexibility and authority to the project manager (the pure project structure), the fact remains that for many project managers it will be impossible to significantly influence decisions to alter the overall organizational structure in support of their project. As a result, perhaps a more appropriate question to ask is: What issues should I be aware of, given the structure of the organization within which I will be managing projects? The previous discussion in this chapter has developed this focus as our primary concern. Given the nature of the structure within which we must operate and manage our projects, what are the strengths and weaknesses of that form as it pertains to our ability to do our job as best we can? In formulating a thoughtful answer to this question, we are perhaps best positioned to understand and adapt most effectively to finding the link between our organization's structure and project management success.

BOX 4.1

Project Management Research in Brief

The Impact of Organizational Structure on Project Performance

It is natural to suppose that projects may run more smoothly in some types of organizational structures than in others. Increasingly, research evidence suggests that depending on the type of project being initiated, some structural forms do, in fact, offer greater advantages in promoting successful completion of the project than others. The work of Gobeli and Larson, for example, is important in highlighting the fact that the type of structure a firm has when it runs projects will have either a beneficial or detrimental effect on the viability of the projects.

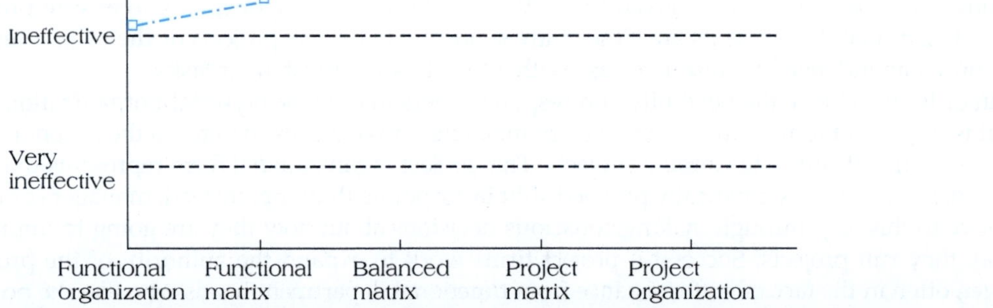

FIGURE 4.16 Managers' Perceptions of Effectiveness of Various Structures on Project Success

Source: D. H. Gobeli and E. W. Larson. (1987). "Relative Effectiveness of Different Project Management Structures," *Project Management Journal*, 18(2): 81–85, figure on page 83. Copyright and all rights reserved. Material from this publication has been reproduced with the permission of PMI.

Larson and Gobeli compared projects that had been managed in a variety of structural types, including functional, matrix, and pure project. They differentiated among three subsets of matrix structure, labeled functional matrix, balanced matrix, and project matrix, based on their perception of whether the matrix structure of a firm leaned more heavily toward a functional approach, an evenly balanced style, or one more favorable toward projects. After collecting data from a sample of more than 1,600 project managers, they identified those who were conducting projects in each of the five organizational types and asked them to assess the effectiveness of that particular structure in promoting or inhibiting effective project management practices. Their findings are shown in Figure 4.16, highlighting the fact that, in general, project organizations do promote an atmosphere more supportive of successful project management.

Interestingly, when Gobeli and Larson broke their sample up into new product development projects and those related to construction, their findings were largely similar, with the exception that construction projects were marginally more effective in matrix organizations. This suggests that structure plays a significant role in the creation of successful projects.[55]

4.8 PROJECT MANAGEMENT OFFICES

A **project management office** (PMO) is defined as a centralized unit within an organization or department that oversees or improves the management of projects.[56] It is seen as a center for excellence in project management in many organizations, existing as a separate organizational entity or subunit that assists the project manager in achieving project goals by providing direct expertise in vital project management duties such as scheduling, resource allocation, monitoring, and controlling the project. PMOs were originally developed in recognition of the poor track record that many organizations have demonstrated in running their projects. We cited some sobering statistics on the failure rates of IT projects, for example, in Chapter 6, indicating that the majority of such projects are likely to fail.

PMOs were created in acknowledgment of the fact that a resource center for project management within a company can offer tremendous advantages. First, as we have noted, project managers are called upon to engage in a wide range of duties, including everything from attending to the human side of project management to handling important technical details. In many cases, these individuals may not have the time or ability to handle all the myriad technical details—the activity scheduling, resource allocation, monitoring and control processes, and so forth. Using a PMO as a resource center shifts some of the burden for these activities from the project manager to a support staff that is dedicated to providing this assistance. Second, it is clear that although project management is emerging as a profession in its own right, there is still a wide gap in knowledge and expectations placed on project managers and their teams. Simply put, they may not have the skills or knowledge for handling a number of project support activities, such as resource leveling or variance reporting. Having trained project management professionals available through a PMO creates a "clearinghouse" effect that allows project teams to tap into expertise when they need it.

Another benefit of the PMO is that it can serve as a central repository of all lessons learned, project documentation, and other pertinent record keeping for ongoing projects, as well as for past projects. This function allows all project managers a central access to past project records and lessons learned materials, rather than having to engage in a haphazard search for these documents throughout the organization. A fourth benefit of the PMO is that it serves as the dedicated center for project management excellence in the company. As such, it becomes the focus for all project management process improvements that are then diffused to other organizational units. Thus, the PMO becomes the place in which new project management improvements are first identified, tested, refined, and finally, passed along to the rest of the organization. Each project manager can use the PMO as a resource, trusting that they will make themselves responsible for all project management innovations.

A PMO can be placed in any one of several locations within a firm.[57] As Figure 4.17 demonstrates, the PMO may be situated at a corporate level (Level 3) where it serves an overall corporate support function. It can be placed at a lower functional level (Level 2) where it serves the needs within a specific business unit. Finally, the PMO can be decentralized down to the actual project level (Level 1) where it offers direct support for each project. The key to understanding the function of the PMO is to recognize that it is designed to *support* the activities of the project manager and staff, not *replace* the manager or take responsibility for the project. Under these circumstances, we see that the PMO can take a lot of the pressure off the project manager by handling the

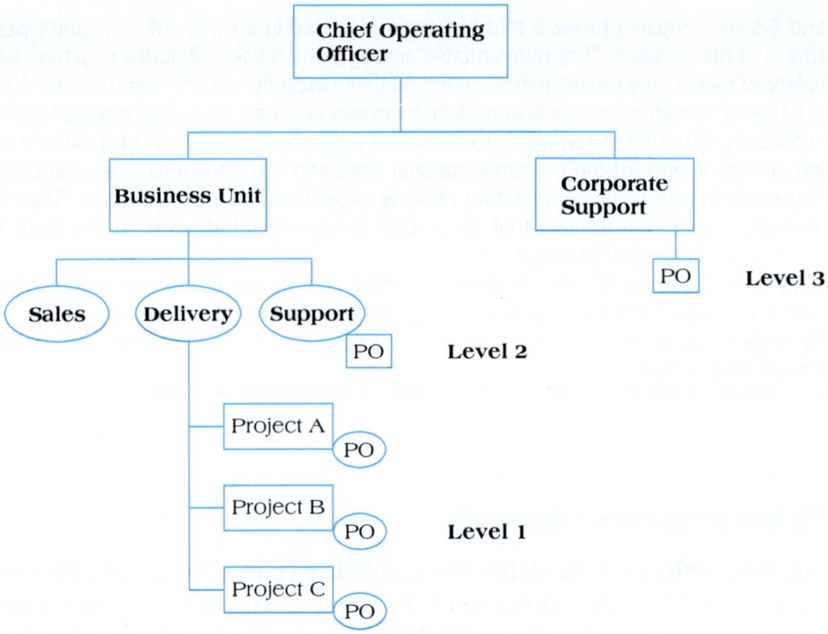

FIGURE 4.17 Alternative Levels of Project Offices

Source: W. Casey and W. Peck. (2001). "Choosing the Right PMO Setup," *PMNetwork*, 15(2): 40–47, figure on page 44. Copyright and all rights reserved. Material from this publication has been reproduced with the permission of PMI.

administration duties, leaving the project manager free to focus on the equally important people issues, including leading, negotiating, customer relationship building, and so forth.

Although Figure 4.17 gives us a sense of where PMOs may be positioned in the organization and, by extension, clues to their supporting role depending on how they are structured, it is also helpful to consider some of the PMO models. PMOs have been described as operating under one of three alternative forms and purposes in companies: (1) weather station, (2) control tower, and (3) resource pool.[58] Each of these models has an alternative role for the PMO.

1. ***Weather station***—Under the weather station model, the PMO is typically used only as a tracking and monitoring device. In this approach, the assumption is often one in which top management, feeling nervous about committing money to a wide range of projects, wants a weather station as a tracking device, to keep an eye on the status of the projects without directly attempting to influence or control them. The weather station PMO is intended to house independent observers who focus almost exclusively on some key questions, such as:
   - What's our progress? How is the project progressing against the original plan? What key milestones have we achieved?
   - How much have we paid for the project so far? How do our earned value projections look? Are there any budgetary warning signals?
   - What is the status of major project risks? Have we updated our contingency planning as needed?
2. ***Control tower***—The control tower model treats project management as a business skill to be protected and supported. It focuses on developing methods for continually improving project management skills by identifying what is working, where the shortcomings exist, and how to resolve ongoing problems. Most importantly, unlike the weather station model, which monitors project management activities only to report results to top management, the control tower is a model that is intended to directly work with and support the activities of the project manager and team. In doing so, it performs four functions:
   - ***Establishes standards for managing projects***—The control tower model of the PMO is designed to create a uniform methodology for all project management activities, including duration estimation, budgets, risk management, scope development, and so forth.

- *Consults on how to follow these standards*—In addition to determining the appropriate standards for running projects, the PMO is set up to help project managers meet those standards through providing internal consultants or project management experts throughout the development cycle as their expertise is needed.
- *Enforces the standards*—Unless there is some process that allows the organization to enforce the project management standards it has developed and disseminated, it will not be taken seriously. The control tower PMO has the authority to enforce the standards it has established, either through rewards for excellent performance or sanctions for refusal to abide by the standard project management principles. For example, the PMO for Accident Fund Insurance Co. of America has full authority to stop projects that it feels are violating accepted practices or failing to bring value to the company.
- *Improves the standards*—The PMO is always motivated to look for ways to improve the current state of project management procedures. Once a new level of project performance has been created, under a policy of continuous improvement, the PMO should already be exploring how to make good practices better.

3. *Resource pool*—The goal of the resource pool PMO is to maintain and provide a cadre of trained and skilled project professionals as they are needed. In essence, it becomes a clearinghouse for continually upgrading the skills of the firm's project managers. As the company initiates new projects, the affected departments apply to the resource pool PMO for assets to populate the project team. The resource pool PMO is responsible for supplying project managers and other skilled professionals to the company's projects. In order for this model to be implemented successfully, it is important for the resource pool to be afforded sufficiently high status within the organization that it can bargain on an equal footing with other top managers who need project managers for their projects. Referring back to Figure 4.7, the resource pool model seems to work best when the PMO is generally viewed as a Level 3 support structure, giving the head of the PMO the status to maintain control of the pool of trained project managers and the authority to assign them as deemed appropriate.

The PMO concept is rapidly being assimilated in a number of companies. However, it has some critics. For example, some critics contend that it is a mistake to "place all the eggs in one basket" with PMOs by concentrating all project professionals in one location. This argument suggests that PMOs actually inhibit the natural, unofficial dissemination of project skills across organizational units by maintaining them at one central location. Another potential pitfall is that the PMO, if its philosophy is not carefully explained, can simply become another layer of oversight and bureaucracy within the organization; in effect, rather than freeing up the project team by performing supporting functions, it actually handcuffs the project by requiring additional administrative control. Another potential danger associated with the use of PMOs is that they may serve as a bottleneck for communications flow across the organization,[59] particularly between the parent organization and the project's customer.

Although some of the criticisms of PMOs contain an element of truth, they should not be used to avoid the adoption of a project office under the right circumstances. The PMO is, at its core, recognition that project management skill development must be encouraged and reinforced, that many organizations have great need of standardized project practices, and that a central, supporting function can serve as a strong source for continuous project skill improvement. Viewed in this light, the PMO concept is likely to gain in popularity in the years to come.

4.9 ORGANIZATIONAL CULTURE

The third key contextual variable in how projects are managed effectively is that of organizational culture. So far, we have examined the manner in which a firm's strategy affects its project management, and how projects and portfolios are inextricably tied to a company's vision and serve to operationalize strategic choices. Structure constitutes the second piece of the contextual puzzle, and we have demonstrated how various organizational designs can help or hinder the project management process. Now we turn to the third contextual variable: an organization's culture and its impact on managing projects.

One of the unique characteristics of organizations is the manner in which each develops its own outlook, operating policies and procedures, patterns of thinking, attitudes, and norms of behavior. These characteristics are often as unique as an individual's fingerprints or DNA signature; in the same way, no two organizations, no matter how similar in size, products, operating environment, or profitability, are the same. Each has developed its own unique method for indoctrinating its employees, responding to environmental threats and opportunities, and supporting or discouraging operating behaviors. In other settings, such as anthropology, a culture is seen as the collective or shared learning of a group, and it influences how that group is likely to respond in different situations. These ideas are embedded in the concept of **organizational culture**. One of the original writers on culture defined it as "the solution to external and internal problems that has worked consistently for a group and that is therefore taught to new members as the correct way to perceive, think about, and feel in relation to these problems."[60]

Travel around Europe and you will quickly become immersed in a variety of cultures. You will discern the unique cultural characteristics that distinguish nationalities, such as the Finnish and Swedish. Differences in language, social behavior, family organization, and even religious beliefs clearly demonstrate these cultural differences. Even within a country, cultural attitudes and values vary dramatically. The norms, attitudes, and common behaviors of northern and southern Italians lead to differences in dress, speech patterns, and even evening dining times. One of the key elements in courses on international business identifies cultural differences as patterns of unique behavior, so that business travelers or those living in other countries will be able to recognize "appropriate" standards of behavior and cultural attitudes, even though these cultural patterns may be very different from those of the traveler's country or origin.

For project team members who are called upon to work on projects overseas, or who are linked via the Internet and e-mail to other project team members from different countries, developing an appreciation for cross-border cultural differences is critical. The values and attitudes expressed by these various cultures are strong regulators of individual behavior; they define our belief systems and work dedication, as well as our ability to function on cross-cultural project teams.

Research has begun to actively explore the impact that workplace cultures have on the performance of projects and the manner in which individual project team members decide whether or not they will commit to its goals. Consider two contrasting examples the author has witnessed: In one *Fortune* 500 company, functional department heads for years have responded to all resource requests from project managers by assigning their worst, newest, or lowest-performing personnel to these teams. In effect, they have treated projects as dumping grounds for malcontents or poor performers. In this organization, project teams are commonly referred to as "leper colonies." It is easy to imagine the response of a member of the firm to the news that he has just been assigned to a new project! On the other hand, I have worked with an IT organization where the unspoken rule is that all departmental personnel are to make themselves available as expert resources when their help is requested by a project manager. The highest priority in the company is project delivery, and all other activities are subordinated to achieving this expectation. It is common, during particularly hectic periods, for IT members to work 12-plus hours per day, assisting on 10 or more projects at any time. As one manager put it, "When we are in crunch time, titles and job descriptions don't mean anything. If it has to get done, we are all responsible—jointly—to make sure it gets done."

The differences in managing projects at the companies illustrated in these stories are striking, as is the culture that permeates their working environment and approach to project delivery. Our definition of **culture** can be directly applied in both of these cases to refer to the unwritten rules of behavior, or norms that are used to shape and guide behavior, that are shared by some subset of organizational members, and that are taught to all new members of the company. This definition has some important elements that must be examined in more detail:

- ***Unwritten***—Cultural norms guide the behavior of each member of the organization but are often not written down. In this way, there can be a great difference between the slogans or inspirational posters found on company walls and the *real*, clearly understood culture that establishes standards of behavior and enforces them for all new company members. For example, Erie Insurance, annually voted one of the best companies to work for, has a strong, supportive culture that emphasizes and rewards positive collaboration between functional groups. Although the policy is not written down, it is widely held, understood by all, and taught to new organization members. When projects require the assistance of personnel from multiple departments, the support is expected to be there.
- ***Rules of behavior***—Cultural norms guide behavior by allowing us a common language for understanding, defining, or explaining phenomena and then providing us with guidelines

as to how best to react to these events. These rules of behavior can be very powerful and commonly held: They apply equally to top management and workers on the shop floor. However, because they are unwritten, we may learn them the hard way. For example, if you were newly hired as a project engineer and were working considerably slower or faster than your coworkers, it is likely that one of them would quickly clue you in on an acceptable level of speed that does not make you or anyone else look bad by comparison.

- ***Held by some subset of the organization***—Cultural norms may or may not be companywide. In fact, it is very common to find cultural attitudes differing widely within an organization. For example, blue-collar workers may have a highly antagonistic attitude toward top management; members of the finance department may view the marketing function with hostility and vice versa; and so forth. These "subcultures" reflect the fact that an organization may contain a number of different cultures, operating in different locations or at different levels. Pitney-Bowes, for example, is a maker of postage meters and other office equipment. Its headquarters unit reflects an image of stability, orderliness, and prestige. However, one of its divisions, Pitney-Bowes Credit Corporation (PBCC), headquartered in Shelton, Connecticut, has made a name for itself by purposely adopting an attitude of informality, openness, and fun. Its décor, featuring fake gas lamps, a French café, and Internet surfing booths, has been described as resembling an "indoor theme park." PBCC has deliberately created a subculture that reflects its own approach to business, rather than adopting the general corporate vision.[61] Another example is the Macintosh project team's approach to creating a distinct culture at Apple while they were developing this revolutionary system, to the point of being housed in different facilities from the rest of the company and flying a pirate flag from the flagpole!
- ***Taught to all new members***—Cultural attitudes, because they are often unwritten, may not be taught to newcomers in formal ways. New members of an organization pick up the behaviors as they observe others engaging in them. In some organizations, however, all new hires are immersed in a formal indoctrination program to ensure that they understand and appreciate the organization's culture. The U.S. Marines, for example, take pride in the process of indoctrination and training for all recruits, which develops a collective, committed attitude toward the Marine Corps. Google takes its new indoctrination procedures ("onboarding") seriously. The company, which onboarded over 7,000 new hires in 2013, has experimented with its orientation procedures to help new employees, called "Nooglers," make more social connections and get up to speed more quickly. General Electric also sends new employees away for orientation, to be "tattooed with the meatball," as members of the company refer to the GE logo.

On the other hand, when allowed to get out of control, a culture can quickly become toxic and work against the goals of the organization. For example, the Australian Olympic swim team has historically been one of the strongest competitors at the summer competition and yet, in London in 2012, the team managed to win just one gold medal, a stunningly poor result. An independent review, commissioned in the aftermath of their performance, focused the blame on a failure of leadership and culture on the team. The report cited a "toxic" culture involving "bullying, the misuse of prescription drugs, and a lack of discipline." The worst performance in 20 years was directly attributable to a lack of moral authority and discipline among team members.[62]

How Do Cultures Form?

When it is possible to view two organizations producing similar products within the context of very individualistic and different cultures, the question of how cultures form gets particularly interesting. General Electric's Jet Engine Division and Rolls-Royce share many features, including product lines. Both produce jet engines for the commercial and defense aircraft industries. However, GE prides itself on its competitive, high-pressure culture that rewards aggressiveness and high commitment, but also has a high "burnout" rate among engineers and mid-level managers. Rolls-Royce, on the other hand, represents an example of a much more paternalistic culture that rewards loyalty and long job tenure.

Researchers have examined some of the powerful forces that can influence how a company's culture emerges. Among the key factors that affect the development of a culture are technology, environment, geographical location, reward systems, rules and procedures, key organizational members, and critical incidents.[63]

TECHNOLOGY The **technology** of an organization refers to its conversion process whereby it transforms inputs into outputs. For example, the technology of many project organizations is the project development process in which projects are developed to fill a current need or anticipate a future opportunity. The technical means for creating projects can be highly complex and automated or relatively simple and straightforward. Further, the projects may be in the form of products or services. Research suggests that the type of technology used within a project organization can influence the culture that it promotes. "High-technology" organizations represent an example of how a fast-paced, technologically based culture can permeate through an organization.

ENVIRONMENT Organizations operate under distinct environmental pressures. A firm's environment may be complex and rapidly changing, or it may remain relatively simple and stable. Some firms are global, because their competition is literally worldwide, while other companies focus on regional competition. Regardless of the specific circumstances, a company's environment affects the culture of the firm. For example, companies with simple and slow-changing environments may develop cultures that reinforce low risk taking, stability, and efficiency. Firms in highly complex environments often develop cultures aimed at promoting rapid response, external scanning for opportunities and threats, and risk taking. In this way, the firm's operating environment affects the formation of the culture and the behaviors that are considered acceptable within it. For example, a small, regional construction firm specializing in commercial real estate development is likely to have more stable environmental concerns than a Fluor-Daniel or Bechtel, competing for a variety of construction projects on a worldwide basis.

GEOGRAPHICAL LOCATION Different geographical regions develop their own cultural mores and attitudes. The farther south in Europe one travels, for example, the later the evening meal is typically eaten; in Spain, dinner may commence after 9 pm. Likewise, in the business world, culturally based attitudes often coordinate with the geographical locations of firms or subsidiaries. It can even happen within countries: Xerox Corporation, for example, had tremendous difficulty in trying to marry the cultures of its corporate headquarters in Connecticut with the more informal and down-to-earth mentalities of its Palo Alto Research Center (PARC) personnel. Projects at one site were done much differently than those undertaken at another location. It is important not to overstate the effect that geography can play, but it certainly can result in cultural disconnects, particularly in cases where organizations have developed a number of dispersed locations, both within and outside of their country of origin.

REWARD SYSTEMS The types of rewards that a firm offers to employees go a long way toward demonstrating the beliefs and actions its top management truly values, regardless of what official company policies might be. Reward systems support the view that, in effect, a company gets what it pays for. An organization that publicly espouses environmental awareness and customer service but routinely promotes project managers who violate these principles sends a loud message about its real interests. As a result, the culture quickly forms around acts that lead to pollution, dishonesty, or obfuscation. One has only to look at past business headlines regarding corporate malfeasance at Enron, WorldCom, Goldman Sachs, or Adelphia Cable Company to see how the culture of those organizations rewarded the type of behavior that ultimately led to accounting fraud, public exposure, and millions of dollars in fines.

RULES AND PROCEDURES One method for influencing a project management culture is to create a rulebook or system of procedures for employees to clarify acceptable behavior. The idea behind rules and procedures is to signal companywide standards of behavior to new employees. The obvious problem arises when public or formal rules conflict with informal rules of behavior. At Texas Instruments headquarters in Dallas, Texas, a formal rule is that all management staff works a standard 40-hour workweek. However, the informal rule is that each member of the company is really expected to work a 45-hour week, at a minimum, or as one senior manager explained to a newly hired employee, "Here, you work nine hours each day: eight for you and one for TI." In spite of the potential for disagreements between formal and informal rules, most programs in creating supportive project-based organizations argue that the first step toward improving patterns of behavior is to formally codify expectations in order to alter dysfunctional project cultures. Rules and procedures, thus, represent a good starting point for developing a strong project culture.

KEY ORGANIZATIONAL MEMBERS Key organizational members, including the founder of the organization, have a tremendous impact on the culture that emerges within the company. When the founder is a traditional entrepreneur who encourages free expression or flexibility, this attitude becomes ingrained in the organization's culture in a powerful way. The founders of Ben and Jerry's Ice Cream, two proud ex-hippies, created a corporate culture that was unique and expressed their desire to develop a "fun" alternative to basic capitalism. A corporate culture in which senior executives routinely flaunt the rules or act contrary to stated policies demonstrates a culture in which there is one rule for the people at the top and another for everyone else.

CRITICAL INCIDENTS Critical incidents express culture because they demonstrate for all workers exactly what it takes to succeed in an organization. In other words, critical incidents are a public expression of what rules *really* operate, regardless of what the company formally espouses. Critical incidents usually take the form of stories that are related to others, including new employees, illustrating the types of actions that are valued. They become part of the company's lore, either for good or ill. In a recent year, General Electric's Transportation Systems Division built up a large backlog of orders for locomotives. The company galvanized its production facilities to work overtime to complete this backlog of work. As one member of the union related, "When you see a unit vice president show up on Saturday, put on an environmental suit, and work on the line spray painting locomotives with the rest of the workers, you realize how committed the company was to getting this order completed on time."

Organizational Culture and Project Management

What are the implications of an organizational culture on the project management process? Culture can affect project management in at least four ways. First, it affects how departments are expected to interact and support each other in pursuit of project goals. Second, the culture influences the level of employee commitment to the goals of the project on balance with other, potentially competing goals. Third, the organizational culture influences project planning processes such as the way work is estimated or how resources are assigned to projects. Finally, the culture affects how managers evaluate the performance of project teams and how they view the outcomes of projects.

- ***Departmental interaction***—Several of the examples cited in this chapter have focused on the importance of developing and maintaining a solid, supportive relationship between functional departments and project teams. In functional and matrix organizations, power either resides directly with department heads or is shared with project managers. In either case, the manner in which these department heads approach their willingness to support projects plays a hugely important role in the success or failure of new project initiatives. Not surprisingly, cultures that favor active cooperation between functional groups and new projects are much more successful than those that adopt a disinterested or even adversarial relationship.
- ***Employee commitment to goals***—Projects depend on the commitment and motivation of the personnel assigned to their activities. A culture that promotes employee commitment and, when necessary, self-sacrifice through working extra hours or on multiple tasks is much more successful than a culture in which the unwritten rules seem to imply that, provided you don't get caught, there is nothing wrong with simply going through the motions. AMEC Corporation, for example, takes its training of employees seriously when it comes to instilling a commitment to safety. AMEC is a multinational construction company, headquartered in Canada. With annual revenues of nearly $7 billion and 29,000 employees, AMEC is one of the largest construction firms in the world. It takes its commitment to core values extremely seriously, impressing upon all employees their responsibilities to customers, business partners, each other, the company, and the wider social environment. From the moment new people enter the organization, they are made aware of the need to commit to the guiding principles of ethical behavior, fairness, commitment to quality, and safety.[64]
- ***Project planning***—We will explore the process of activity duration estimation in a later chapter; however, for now it is important just to note that the way in which employees decide to support the project planning processes is critical. Because activity estimation is often an imprecise process, it is common for some project team members to "pad" their estimates to give themselves as much time as possible. These people are often responding to a culture that reinforces the idea that it is better to engage in poor estimation and project planning than to be late with deliverables.

Conversely, when there is a culture of trust among project team members, they are more inclined to give honest assessments, without fearing that, should they be wrong, they will be punished for our mistakes.

- *Performance evaluation*—Supportive cultures encourage project team members taking the initiative, even if it means taking risks to boost performance. When a culture sends the signal that the goal of the firm is to create innovative products, it reinforces a project management culture that is aggressive and offers potentially high payoffs (and the occasional significant loss!). As noted earlier, organizations get what they pay for. If the reward systems are positive and reinforce a strong project mentality, they will reap a whirlwind of opportunities. On the other hand, if they tacitly support caution and playing it safe, the project management approaches will equally reflect this principle.

A culture can powerfully affect the manner in which departments within an organization view the process of project management. The culture also influences the manner in which employees commit themselves to the goals of their projects as opposed to other, potentially competing goals. Through symbols, stories, and other signs, companies signal their commitment to project management. This message is not lost on members of project teams, who take their cues regarding expected performance from supervisors and other cultural artifacts. Visible symbols of a culture that advocates cross-functional cooperation will create employees who are prepared and motivated to work in harmony with other groups on project goals. Likewise, when an IT department elevates some of its members to hero status because they routinely went the extra mile to handle system user complaints or problems, the company has sent the message that they are all working toward the same goals and all provide value to the organization's operations, regardless of their functional background.

To envision how culture can influence the planning and project monitoring processes, suppose that, in your organization, it was clear that those involved in late projects would be severely punished for the schedule slippage. You and your fellow project team members would quickly learn that it is critical to avoid going out on a limb to promise early task completion dates. It is much safer to grossly overestimate the amount of time necessary to complete a task in order to protect yourself. The organizational culture in this case breeds deceit. Likewise, it may be safer in some organizations to deliberately hide information in cases where a project is running off track, or mislead top management with optimistic and false estimates of project progress. Essentially, the issue is this: Does the corporate culture encourage authentic information and truthful interactions, or is it clear that the safer route is to first protect yourself, regardless of the effect this behavior may have on the success of a project?

PROJECT PROFILE

Electronic Arts and the Power of Strong Culture in Design Teams

Electronic Arts is one of the top computer gaming companies in the world, known for perennial console and PC bestsellers like Madden NFL, FIFA, Battlefield, Need for Speed, the Sims, and more. In the computer gaming industry, speed to market for new games is critical. Making award-winning games requires a combination of talented designers, graphic artists, programmers, and testers, all working to constantly update best-selling games and introduce new choices for the gaming community. It is a fast-paced environment that thrives on a sense of chaos and disruptive new technologies and ideas. In this setting, the former head of the EA Labels group, Frank Gibeau, has developed a winning formula for game design. He doesn't believe in large teams for developing games; instead his goal is to preserve each studio's culture by supporting its existing talent.

Gibeau's belief is that the best games come from small teams with strong cultures. One of his principles is to limit the size of project teams to promote their commitment to each other and to the quality of the games they design. Gibeau notes that when too many people get involved, there is a law of diminishing returns that sets in, because everything becomes too hard to manage – too many people, too many problems. In addition, it's easier to maintain a unique culture when teams are kept small and allowed to stay in place for an extended time. As a result, EA supports the use of smaller teams over a longer period of time to get the game right. As a result, he is careful to ensure that the different studios don't over-expand and get too big. Gibeau remains a firm believer in the "small is better" philosophy because it supports dynamic cultures and action-oriented attitudes.

Electronic Arts' approach to game design is centered on small teams, given the opportunity to work as freely as possible, maintain their distinctive group identities, and thereby promote a strong internal culture. EA executives have recognized that these unique team cultures are critical for encouraging the kind of creativity and commitment to the work that make for technologically advanced games, so necessary for maintaining a competitive edge in a rapidly evolving industry.[65]

What are some examples of an organization's culture influencing how project teams actually perform and how outcomes are perceived? One common situation is the phenomenon known as escalation of commitment. It is not uncommon to see this process at work in project organizations. **Escalation of commitment** occurs when, in spite of evidence identifying a project as failing, no longer necessary, or beset by huge technical or other difficulties, organizations continue to support it past the point an objective assessment would suggest that it should be terminated.[66] Although there are a number of reasons for escalation of commitment to a failed decision, one important reason is the unwillingness of the organization to acknowledge failure or its culture's working toward blinding key decision makers to the need to take corrective action.

The reverse is also true: In many organizations, projects are managed in an environment in which the culture strongly supports cross-functional cooperation, assigns sufficient resources to enable project managers to schedule aggressively, and creates an atmosphere that makes it possible to develop projects optimally. It is important to recognize that an organization's culture can be a strong supporter of (as well as an inhibitor to) the firm's ability to manage effective projects. Because of this impact, organizational culture must be managed, constantly assessed, and, when necessary, changed in ways that promote project management rather than discouraging its efficient practice.

The context within which we manage our projects is a key determinant in the likelihood of their success or failure. Three critical contextual factors are the organization's strategy, structure, and culture. Strategy drives projects; projects operationalize strategy. The two must work together in harmony. The key is maintaining a clear linkage between overall strategy and the firm's portfolio of projects, ensuring that some form of alignment exists among all key elements: vision, objectives, strategies, goals, and programs. Further, companies are recognizing that when they adopt a structure that supports projects, they get better results. Likewise, when the cultural ambience of the organization favors project management approaches, they are much more likely to be successful. Some of these project management approaches are the willingness to take risks, to think creatively, to work closely with other functional departments, and so forth. More and more we are seeing successful project-based organizations recognizing the simple truth that the context in which they are trying to create projects is a critical element in seeing their projects through to commercial and technical success.

Summary

1. **Understand how effective project management contributes to achieving strategic objectives.** This chapter linked projects with corporate strategy. Projects are the "building blocks" of strategy because they serve as the most basic tools by which firms can implement previously formulated objectives and strategies.
2. **Recognize three components of the corporate strategy model: formulation, implementation, and evaluation.** The chapter explored a generic model of corporate strategic management, distinguishing between the three components of strategy formulation, strategy implementation, and strategy evaluation. Each of these components incorporates a number of subdimensions. For example, strategy formulation includes the stages of:

   - Developing a vision and mission.
   - Performing an internal audit (assessing strengths and weaknesses).
   - Performing an external audit (assessing opportunities and threats).
   - Establishing long-term objectives.
   - Generating, evaluating, and selecting strategies.

   Strategy implementation requires the coordination of managerial, technological, financial, and functional assets to reinforce and support strategies. Projects often serve as the means by which strategy implementation is actually realized. Finally, strategy evaluation requires an ability to measure results and provide feedback to all concerned parties.
3. **See the importance of identifying critical project stakeholders and managing them within the context of project development.** The chapter addresses a final strategic question: the relationship between the firm and its stakeholder groups. Project stakeholders are either internal to the firm (top management, other functional departments, support personnel, internal customers) or external (suppliers, distributors, intervenors, governmental agencies and regulators, and customers). Each of these stakeholder groups must be managed in a systematic manner; the process

moves from identification to needs assessment, choice of strategy, and routine evaluation and adjustment. Stakeholder management, in conjunction with strategic management, forms the context by which projects are first evaluated and then managed.

4. **Recognize the strengths and weaknesses of three basic forms of organizational structure and their implications for managing projects.** We examined the strengths and weaknesses of three major organizational structure types, including functional, project, and matrix structures. The nature of each of the three structural types and their relationship to project management were addressed. The functional structure, while the most common type of organizational form, was shown to be perhaps the least effective type for managing projects due to a variety of limitations. The project structure, in which the organization uses its projects as the primary form of grouping, has several advantages for managing projects, although it has some general disadvantages as well. Finally, the matrix structure, which seeks to balance the authority and activities between projects and functions using a dual hierarchy system, demonstrates its own unique set of strengths and weaknesses for project management practice.
5. **Understand how companies can change their structure into a "heavyweight project organization" structure to facilitate effective project management practices.** The movements within many organizations to a stronger customer focus in their project management operations has led to the creation of a heavyweight project organization, in which the project manager is given high levels of authority in order to further the goals of the project. Because customer satisfaction is the goal of these organizations, they rely on their project managers to work toward project success within the framework of greater control of project resources and direct contact with clients.
6. **Identify the characteristics of three forms of project management office (PMO).** Project management offices (PMOs) are centralized units within an organization or department that oversee or improve the management of projects. There are three predominant types of PMO in organizations. The weather station is typically used only as a tracking and monitoring device. In this approach, the role of the PMO is to keep an eye on the status of the projects without directly attempting to influence or control them. The second form of PMO is the control tower, which treats project management as a business skill to be protected and supported. It focuses on developing methods for continually improving project management skills by identifying what is working, where the shortcomings exist, and methods for resolving ongoing problems. Most importantly, unlike the weather station model, which only monitors project management activities to report results to top management, the control tower is a model that is intended to directly work with and support the activities of the project manager and team. Finally, the resource pool is a PMO intended to maintain and provide a cadre of trained and skilled project professionals as they are needed. It serves as a clearinghouse for continually upgrading the skills of the firm's project managers. As the company initiates new projects, the affected departments apply to the resource pool PMO for assets to populate the project team.
7. **Understand key concepts of corporate culture and how cultures are formed.** Another contextual factor, organizational culture, plays an important role in influencing the attitudes and values shared by members of the organization, which, in turn, affects their commitment to project management and its practices. Culture is defined as the unwritten rules of behavior, or the norms that are used to shape and guide behavior, that are shared by some subset of organizational members and are taught to all new members of the company. When the firm has a strong culture that is supportive of project goals, members of the organization are more likely to work collaboratively, minimize departmental loyalties that could take precedence over project goals, and commit the necessary resources to achieve the objectives of the project.

   Organizational cultures are formed as the result of a variety of factors, including technology, environment, geographical location, reward systems, rules and procedures, key organizational members, and critical incidents. Each of these factors can play a role in determining whether the organization's culture is strong, collaborative, customer-focused, project-oriented, fast-paced, and so forth.
8. **Recognize the positive effects of a supportive organizational culture on project management practices versus those of a culture that works against project management.** Finally, this chapter examined the manner in which supportive cultures can work in favor of project management and ways in which the culture can inhibit project success. One common facet of a "sick" culture is the escalation of a commitment problem, in which key members of the organization continue to increase their support for clearly failing courses of action or problematic projects. The reasons for escalation are numerous, including our prestige is on the line, the conviction that we are close to succeeding, fear of ridicule if we admit to failure, and the culture of the organization in which we operate.

Key Terms

Balanced matrix
Culture
Escalation of commitment
External environment
Functional structure
Heavyweight project organization
Intervenor groups
Matrix organization
Matrix structure
Objectives
Organizational culture
Organizational structure
Project management office
Project organizations
Project stakeholders
Project structure
Resources
Stakeholder analysis
Strategic management
Strong matrix
Technology
TOWS matrix
Weak matrix

Discussion Questions

4.1 The chapter suggests that it is critical for projects to be aligned with the strategic focus of an organization. Table 4.1 gives some examples of projects that reflect strategy. Consider the following strategic objectives of a hotel chain:

a. Be a leader in customer service
b. Grow customer base by 20%
c. Improve employee satisfaction
d. Reduce energy costs

What project ideas can you identify to help achieve these objectives?

4.2 Your company is planning to upgrade a key piece of software that is used daily across the organization. Identify the potential stakeholders for this project and discuss some of the reasons why these stakeholders might influence the success of the project.

4.3 Your company is planning to construct a nuclear power plant in Oregon. Why is stakeholder analysis important as a precondition of the decision whether or not to follow through with such a plan? Conduct a stakeholder analysis for a planned upgrade to a successful software product. Who are the key stakeholders?

4.4 Consider a medium-sized company that has decided to begin using project management in a wide variety of its operations. As part of its operational shift, it is going to adopt a project management office somewhere within the organization. Make an argument for the type of PMO it should adopt (weather station, control tower, or resource pool). What are some key decision criteria that will help it determine which model makes the most sense?

4.5 The chapter presents three basic forms of organizational structure: functional, project, and matrix. Suppose you are responsible for advising an IT company on changes to an organizational structure, to embrace the growing need for effective project management in creating new software products. Conduct an assessment of the advantages and limitations of each of the three structure types. Which would you recommend?

4.6 You are a member of the senior management staff at XYZ Corporation. You have historically been using a functional structure setup with five departments: finance, human resources, marketing, production, and engineering.

a. Create a drawing of your simplified functional structure, identifying the five departments.
b. Assume you have decided to move to a project structure. What might be some of the environmental pressures that would contribute to your belief that it is necessary to alter the structure?
c. With the project structure, you have four ongoing projects: stereo equipment, instrumentation and testing equipment, optical scanners, and defense communications. Draw the new structure that creates these four projects as part of the organizational chart.

4.7 Suppose you now want to convert the structure from that in Question 6 to a matrix structure, emphasizing dual commitments to function and project.

a. Re-create the structural design to show how the matrix would look.
b. What behavioral problems could you begin to anticipate through this design? That is, do you see any potential points of friction in the dual hierarchy setup?

CASE STUDY 4.1

Rolls-Royce Corporation

Although the name Rolls-Royce is inextricably linked with its ultra-luxurious automobiles, the modern Rolls-Royce operates in an entirely different competitive environment. A leading manufacturer of power systems for aerospace, marine, and power companies, Rolls's market is focused on developing jet engines for a variety of uses, both commercial and defense-related. In this market, the company has two principal competitors, General Electric and Pratt & Whitney (owned by United Technologies). There are a limited number of smaller, niche players in the jet engine market, but their impact from a technical and commercial perspective is minor. Rolls, GE, and Pratt & Whitney routinely engage in fierce competition for sales to defense contractors

(continued)

and the commercial aviation industry. The two main airframe manufacturers, Boeing and Airbus, make continual multimillion-dollar purchase decisions that are vital for the ongoing success of the engine makers. Airbus, a private consortium of several European partner companies, has drawn level with Boeing in sales in recent years. Because the cost of a single jet engine, including spare parts, can run to several million dollars, winning large orders from either defense or commercial aircraft builders represents an ongoing challenge for each of the "big three" jet engine manufacturers.

Airlines in developing countries can often be a lucrative but risky market for these firms. Because the countries do not maintain high levels of foreign exchange, it is not unknown, for example, for Rolls (or its competitors) to take partial payment in cash with assorted commodities to pay the balance. Hence, a contract with Turkey's national airline may lead to some monetary payment for Rolls, along with several tons of pistachios or other trade goods! To maintain their sales and service targets, these jet engine makers routinely resort to creative financing, long-term contracts, or asset-based trading deals. Overall, however, the market for jet engines is projected to continue to expand at huge rates. Rolls-Royce projects a 20-year window with a potential market demand of 70,000 engines, valued at over $400 billion in civil aerospace alone. When defense contracts are factored in as well, the revenue projections for jet engine sales are likely to be enormous. As Rolls sees the future, the single biggest market growth opportunity is in the larger, greater thrust engines, designed to be paired with larger jet aircraft.

Rolls-Royce is currently engaged in a strategic decision that offers the potential for huge payoffs or significant losses as it couples its latest engine technology, the "Trent series," with Airbus's decision to develop an ultra-large commercial aircraft for long-distance travel. The new Airbus design, the 380 model, seats more than 550 people, flying long-distance routes (up to 8,000 miles). The Trent 900, with an engine rating of 70,000 pounds thrust per engine, has been created at great expense to see service in the large jet market. The project reflects a strategic vision shared by both Airbus and Rolls-Royce that the commercial passenger market will triple in the next 20 years. As a result, future opportunities will involve larger, more economically viable aircraft. Since 2007, Airbus has delivered a total of 40 A380s to its customers, with 17 in 2010. Their total order book currently sits at 234 aircraft ordered. Collectively, Airbus and Rolls-Royce have taken a large financial gamble that their strategic vision of the future is the correct one.

Questions

1. Who are Rolls's principal project management stakeholders? How would you design stakeholder management strategies to address their concerns?
2. Given the financial risks inherent in developing a jet engine, make an argument, either pro or con, for Rolls to develop strategic partnerships with other jet engine manufacturers in a manner similar to Airbus's consortium arrangement. What are the benefits and drawbacks in such an arrangement?

CASE STUDY 4.2

Classic Case: Paradise Lost—The Xerox Alto[67]

Imagine the value of cornering the technological market in personal computing. How much would a five-year window of competitive advantage be worth to a company today? It could easily mean billions in revenue, a stellar industry reputation, future earnings ensured—and the list goes on. For Xerox Corporation, however, something strange happened on the way to industry leadership. In 1970, Xerox was uniquely positioned to take advantage of the enormous leaps forward it had made in office automation technology. Yet the company stumbled badly through its own strategic myopia, lack of nerve, structural inadequacies, and poor choices. This is the story of the Xerox Alto, the world's first personal computer and one of the great "what if?" stories in business history.

The Alto was not so much a step forward as it was a quantum leap. Being in place and operating at the end of 1973, it was the first stand-alone personal computer to combine bit-mapped graphics, a mouse, menu screens, icons, an Ethernet connection, a laser printer, and word processing software. As a result of the combined efforts of an impressive collection of computer science geniuses headquartered at Xerox's Palo Alto Research Center (PARC), the Alto was breathtaking in its innovative appeal. It was PARC's answer to Xerox's top management command to "hit a home run." Xerox had profited earlier from just such a home run in the form of the Model 914 photocopier, a technological innovation that provided the impetus to turn Xerox into a billion-dollar company in the 1960s. The Alto represented a similar achievement.

What went wrong? What forces combined to ensure that no more than 2,000 Altos were produced and that none was ever brought to market? (They were used only inside the company and at some university sites.) The answer could lie in the muddled strategic thinking that took place at Xerox while the Alto was in development.

The history of Xerox during this period shows a company that stepped back from technological leadership into a form of incrementalism, making it content to follow IBM's lead in office automation. *Incrementalism* refers to adopting a gradualist approach that plays it safe, avoiding technological leaps, large risks, and consequently the possibility of large returns. In 1974, Xerox decided to launch the Model 800 magnetic tape word processor rather than the Alto because the Model 800 was perceived as the safer bet. During the next five years, a series of ill-timed acquisitions, lawsuits, and reorganizations rendered the Alto a casualty of inattention. What division would oversee its development and launch? Whose budget would support it, and PARC in general? By leaving such tough decisions unmade, Xerox wasted valuable time and squandered its technological window of opportunity. Even when clear indications showed that competitor Wang was in line to introduce its own line of office systems, Xerox could not take the step to bring the Alto to market. By 1979, Xerox's unique opportunity was lost. No longer was the Alto a one-of-a-kind technology, and the company quietly shelved any plans for its commercial introduction.

Perhaps the ultimate irony is this: Here was a company that had made its name through the phenomenal success of a highly innovative product, the Model 914 photocopier, but it did not know how to handle the opportunities presented by the next phenomenon. The Alto was so advanced that the company seemed unable to comprehend its possibilities. Executives did not have a strategic focus that emphasized a continual progression of innovation. Instead, they were directed toward remaining neck-and-neck with the competition in an incremental approach. When competitor IBM released a new electric typewriter, Xerox responded in the same incremental way. The organizational structure at Xerox did not allow any one division or key manager to become the champion for new technologies like the Alto.

In 1979 Steven Jobs, president of Apple Computer, was given a tour of the PARC complex and saw an Alto in use. He was so impressed with the machine's features and operating capabilities that he asked when it was due to be commercially launched. When told that much of this technology had been developed in 1973, Jobs became "physically sick," he later recounted, at the thought of the opportunity Xerox had forgone.

Questions

1. Do you see a logical contradiction in Xerox's willingness to devote millions of dollars to support pure research sites like PARC and its refusal to commercially introduce the products developed?
2. How did Xerox's strategic vision work in favor of or against the development of radical new technologies such as the Alto?
3. What other unforeseeable events contributed to making Xerox's executives unwilling to take any new risks precisely at the time the Alto was ready to be released?
4. "Radical innovation cannot be too radical if we want it to be commercially successful." Argue either in favor of or against this statement.

CASE STUDY 4.3

Project Task Estimation and the Culture of "Gotcha!"

I recently worked with an organization that adopted a mind-set in which it was assumed that the best way to keep project team members working hard was to unilaterally trim their task duration estimates by 20%. Suppose that you were asked to estimate the length of time necessary to write computer code for a particular software product and you determined that it should take about 80 hours. Knowing you were about to present this information to your supervisor and that she was going to immediately cut the estimate by 20%, what would be your course of action? You would probably first add a "fudge factor" to the estimate in order to protect yourself. The conversation with the boss might go something like this:

Boss "Have you had a chance to estimate that coding sequence yet?"

You Yes, it should take me 100 hours."

Boss "That's too long. I can only give you 80 hours, tops."

You (Theatrical sigh) "Well, if you say so, but I really don't know how I can pull this off."

Once you leave the office and shut the door, you turn with a smile and whisper, "Gotcha!"

Questions

1. How does the organization's culture support this sort of behavior? What pressures does the manager face? What pressures does the subordinate face?
2. Discuss the statement, "If you don't take my estimates seriously, I'm not going to give you serious estimates!" How does this statement apply to this example?

CASE STUDY 4.4

Widgets 'R Us

Widgets 'R Us (WRU) is a medium-sized firm specializing in the design and manufacturing of quality widgets. The market for widgets has been stable. Historically, WRU has had a functional organization design with four departments: accounting, sales, production, and engineering. This design has served the company well, and it has been able to compete by being the low-priced company in the industry.

In the past three years, the demand for widgets has exploded. New widgets are constantly being developed to feed the public's seemingly insatiable demand. The average life cycle of a newly released widget is 12–15 months. Unfortunately, WRU is finding itself unable to compete successfully in this new, dynamic market. The CEO has noted a number of problems. Products are slow to market. Many new innovations have passed right by WRU because the company was slow to pick up signs from the marketplace that they were coming. Internal communication is very poor. Lots of information gets kicked "upstairs," and no one seems to know what happens to it. Department heads constantly blame other department heads for the problems.

Questions

1. You have been called in as a consultant to analyze the operations at WRU. What would you advise?
2. What structural design changes might be undertaken to improve the operations at the company?
3. What are the strengths and weaknesses of the alternative solutions the company could employ?

Internet Exercises

4.1 Wegmans has been consistently voted one of the 100 best companies to work for in the United States by *Fortune* magazine. In fact, in 2005 it was ranked number 1, and in 2012 it was ranked number 4. Go to its Web site, www.wegmans.com, and click on "About Us." What messages, formal and informal, are being conveyed about Wegmans through its Web site? What does the Web site imply about the culture of the organization?

4.2 Go to the Web site www.projectstakeholder.com and analyze some of the case studies found on the Web site. What do these cases suggest about the importance of assessing stakeholder expectations for a project *before* it has begun its development process? In other words, what are the risks of waiting to address stakeholder concerns until after a project has begun?

4.3 Go to a corporate Web site of your choice and access the organizational chart. What form of organization does this chart represent: functional, project, matrix, or some other form? Based on our discussion in this chapter, what would be the likely strengths and weaknesses of this organization's project management activities?

4.4 Access the corporate Web site for Fluor-Daniel Corporation and examine its "Compliance and Ethics" section at www.fluor.com/sustainability/ethics_compliance/Pages/default.aspx. What does the "Fluor Code of Business Conduct and Ethics" suggest about the way the company does business? What are the strategic goals and directions that naturally flow from the ethical code? In your opinion, how would the ethics statement influence the manner in which the company manages its projects?

PMP CERTIFICATION SAMPLE QUESTIONS

1. What is the main role of the functional manager?
   a. To control resources
   b. To manage the project when the project manager isn't available
   c. To define business processes
   d. To manage the project manager
2. What is the typical role of senior management on a project?
   a. Support the project
   b. Pay for it
   c. Support the project and resolve resource and other conflicts
   d. Resolve resource and other conflicts
3. What is an organization that controls project managers, documentation, and policies called?
   a. Project management office
   b. Strong matrix
   c. Functional
   d. Pure project
4. A business analyst has a career path that has been very important to her throughout the 10 years of her career. She is put on a project with a strong matrix organizational structure. Which of the following is likely viewed as a negative of being on the project?
   a. Being away from the group and on a project that might make it more difficult to get promoted
   b. Working with people who have similar skills

c. Working long hours because the project is a high priority
d. Not being able to take her own certification tests because she is so busy

5. The functional manager is planning the billing system replacement project with the newest project manager at the company. In discussing this project, the functional manager focuses on the cost associated with running the system after it is created and the number of years the system will last before it must be replaced. What best describes what the functional manager is focusing on?
   a. Project life cycle
   b. Product life cycle
   c. Project management life cycle
   d. Program management life cycle

Answers: 1. a—The functional manager runs the day-to-day operations of his department and controls the resources; 2. c—Because senior managers usually outrank the project manager, they can help with resolving any resource or other conflicts as they arise; 3. a—The project management office (PMO) typically has all of these responsibilities; 4. a—Being away from her functional group may cause her to feel that her efforts on behalf of the project are not being recognized by her functional manager, since the project employs a strong matrix structure; 5. b—The functional manager is focusing on the product life cycle, which is developed based on an example of a successful project and encompasses the range of use for the product.

INTEGRATED PROJECT

Building Your Project Plan

EXERCISE 1—DEVELOPING THE PROJECT NARRATIVE AND GOALS

You have been assigned to a project team to develop a new product or service for your organization. Your challenge is to first decide on the type of product or service you wish to develop. The project choices can be flexible, consisting of options as diverse as construction, new product development, IT implementation, and so forth.

Develop a project scope write-up on the project you have selected. Your team is expected to create a project history, complete with an overview of the project, an identifiable goal or goals (including project targets), the general project management approach to be undertaken, and significant project constraints or potential limiting effects. Additionally, if appropriate, identify any basic resource requirements (i.e., personnel or specialized equipment) needed to complete the project. What is most important at this stage is creating a history or narrative of the project you have come up with, including a specific statement of purpose or intent (i.e., why the project is being developed, what it is, what niche or opportunity it is aimed to address).

The write-up should fully explain your project concept, constraints, and expectations. It is not necessary to go into minute detail regarding the various subactivities or subcomponents of the project; it is more important to concentrate on the bigger picture for now.

SAMPLE BACKGROUND ANALYSIS AND PROJECT NARRATIVE FOR ABCUPS, INC.

Founded in 1990, ABCups, Inc., owns and operates 10 injection-molding machines that produce plastic drinkware. ABCups's product line consists of travel mugs, thermal mugs, steins, and sports tumblers. The travel mugs, thermal mugs, and steins come in two sizes: 14 and 22 ounces. The sports tumblers are offered only in the 32-ounce size. All products except the steins have lids. The travel and thermal mugs consist of a liner, body, and lid. The steins and sports tumblers have no lining. There are 15 colors offered, and any combination of colors can be used. The travel and thermal mugs have a liner that needs to be welded to the outer body; subcontractors and screen printers weld the parts together. ABCups does no welding, but it attaches the lid to the mug. ABCups's customer base consists primarily of distributors and promotional organizations. Annual sales growth has remained steady, averaging 2%–3% each year. Last year's revenues from sales were $70 million.

CURRENT PROCESS

ABCups's current method for producing its product is as follows:

1. Quote job.
2. Receive/process order.
3. Schedule order into production.
4. Mold parts.
5. Issue purchase order to screen printer with product specifications.
6. Ship parts to screen printer for welding and artwork.
7. Receive returned product from screen printer for final assembly and quality control.
8. Ship product to customer.

At current processing levels, the entire process can take from two to four weeks, depending on order size, complexity, and the nature of current production activity.

OVERVIEW OF THE PROJECT

Because of numerous complaints and quality rejects from customers, ABCups has determined to proactively resolve outstanding quality issues. The firm has determined that by bringing welding and screen printing functions "in-house," it will be able to address the current quality problems, expand its market, maintain better control over delivery and order output, and be more responsive to customers. The project consists of adding three new processes (welding, screen printing, and improved quality control) to company operations.

ABCups has no experience in or equipment for welding and screen printing. The organization needs to educate itself, investigate leasing or purchasing space and equipment, hire trained workers, and create a transition from subcontractors to in-house operators. The project needs a specified date of completion so that the transition from outsourcing to company production will be smooth and products can be delivered to customers with as little disruption to shipping as possible.

Management's strategy is to vertically integrate the organization to reduce costs, increase market share, and improve product quality. ABCups is currently experiencing problems with its vendor base, ranging from poor quality to ineffectual scheduling, causing ABCups to miss almost 20% of its customers' desired ship dates. Maintaining complete control over the product's development cycle should improve the quality and on-time delivery of ABCups's product line.

Objectives

Goals	Targets
1. Meet all project deadlines without jeopardizing customer satisfaction within a one-year project time frame.	Excellent = 0 missed deadlines Good = 1–5 missed deadlines Acceptable = <8 missed deadlines
2. Deplete dependence on subcontracted screen printing by 100% within six months without increasing customer's price or decreasing product quality.	Excellent = 100% independence Good = 80–99% independence Acceptable = 60–79% independence
3. Perform all process changes without affecting current customer delivery schedules for the one-year project time frame.	Excellent = 0% delivery delays Good = <5% delivery delays Acceptable = 5–10% delivery delays
4. Decrease customer wait time over current wait time within one year without decreasing quality or increasing price.	Excellent = 2/3 decrease in wait time Good = 1/2 decrease in wait time Acceptable = 1/3 decrease in wait time
5. Stay within 10% of capital budget without exceeding 20% within the project baseline schedule.	Excellent = 1% variance Good = 5% variance Acceptable = 10% variance
6. Decrease customer rejections by 25% within one year.	Excellent = 45% reduction Good = 35% reduction Acceptable = 25% reduction

General Approach

1. **Managerial approach**—The equipment will be purchased from outside vendors; however, ABCups's internal employees will perform the assembly work. Given the type of equipment that is required, outside contractors will not be needed because the company's facility employs the necessary maintenance staff to set up the equipment and troubleshoot as required, once the initial training has been supplied by the vendor.
2. **Technical approach**—The equipment manufacturers will utilize CAD to design the equipment. Initially, the firm will require a bank of parts to be available once the equipment arrives in order to fine-tune the machinery. Fixtures will be designed as required, but will be supplied by the machine manufacturer.

Constraints

1. **Budget constraints**—This project must ultimately increase profitability for the company. In addition, the project will have a constraining budget. It must be shown that any additional expense for both the conversion and producing finished cups on-site will result in increased profitability.

2. **Limited plant space**—ABCups is assuming this conversion does not involve building a new plant or significantly increasing facility size. Space for new machinery, new employees, and storage for dyes and inventory must be created through conversion of existing floor space. If additional floor space is required, leasing or purchasing options will need to be investigated.
3. **Time**—Since this project will require the company to break existing contracts with vendors, any missed milestones or other delays will cause an unacceptable delay to customers. A back-up plan must be in place to avoid losing customers to competitors in case the time frame is not strictly met. The conversion must be undertaken with a comprehensive project scheduling system developed and adhered to.
4. **Safety regulations**—The installation and conversion activities must be in accordance with several agencies' specifications, including but not limited to guidelines from the Occupational Safety and Health Administration (OSHA), the insurance carrier, and the financing agency.
5. **Current orders must be filled on time**—All activities must be designed to avoid any delay in current orders. The transition should appear seamless to customers to avoid losing any part of the extant customer base.

Notes

30. Ramsey, M., 2014. Does Tesla Really Need a $5 Billion Battery? *Wall Street Journal*, April 2, pp. B1–B2.
31. David, F. R. (2001). *Strategic Management*, 8th ed. Upper Saddle River, NJ: Prentice Hall.
32. The Holy Bible, King James Version. Cambridge Edition: 1769; (Prov. 29:18).
33. Vision Statement of Bechtel Corporation
34. Cleland, D. I. (1998). "Strategic project management," in Pinto, J. K. (Ed.), *Project Management Handbook*. San Francisco, CA: Jossey-Bass, pp. 27–40.
35. Weihrich, H. (1982). "The TOWS matrix—A tool for situational analysis," *Long Range Planning*, 15: 54–66; Hillson, D. (2002), "Extending the risk process to manage opportunities," *International Journal of Project Management*, 20: 235–40.
36. Wheelen, T. L., and Hunger, J. D. (1992). *Strategic Management and Business Policy*, 4th ed. Reading, MA: Addison-Wesley.
37. Wiener, E., and Brown, A. (1986). "Stakeholder analysis for effective issues management," *Planning Review*, 36: 27–31.
38. Mendelow, A. (1986). "Stakeholder analysis for strategic planning and implementation," in King, W. R., and Cleland, D. I. (Eds.), *Strategic Planning and Management Handbook*. New York: Van Nostrand Reinhold, pp. 67–81; Winch, G. M. (2002). *Managing Construction Projects*. Oxford: Blackwell; Winch, G. M., and Bonke, S. (2001). "Project stakeholder mapping: Analyzing the interest of project stakeholders," in Slevin, D. P., Cleland, D. I., and Pinto, J. K. (Eds.), *The Frontiers of Project Management Research*. Newtown Square, PA: PMI, pp. 385–404.
39. Wideman, R. M. (1998). "How to motivate all stakeholders to work together," in Cleland, D. I. (Ed.), *Project Management Field Guide*. New York: Van Nostrand Reinhold, pp. 212–26; Hartman, F. T. (2000). *Don't Park Your Brain Outside*. Newtown Square, PA: PMI.
40. Cleland, D. I. (1988). "Project stakeholder management," in Cleland, D. I., and King, W. R. (Eds.), *Project Management Handbook*, 2nd ed. New York: Van Nostrand Reinhold, pp. 275–301.
41. Vrijhoef, R., and Koskela, L. (2000). "The four roles of supply chain management in construction," *European Journal of Purchasing and Supply Management*, 6: 169–78.
42. Cleland, D. I. (1988), as cited in note 12.
43. Block, R. (1983). *The Politics of Projects*. New York: Yourdon Press.
44. Manyika, J., Chui, M., Bughin, J., Dobbs, R., Bisson, P., and Marrs, A. (2013). *Disruptive technologies: Advances that will transform life, business, and the global economy*. McKinsey Global Institute. file:///C:/Users/jkp4/Downloads/MGI_Disruptive_technologies_Executive_summary_May2013.pdf.
45. Fisher, R., and Ury, W. (1981). *Getting to Yes: Negotiating Agreement Without Giving In*. New York: Houghton Mifflin.
46. Frame, J. D. (1987). *Managing Projects in Organizations*. San Francisco, CA: Jossey-Bass.
47. Robert Burns, a Scottish poet and lyricist. (1759–1796).
48. Grundy, T. (1998). "Strategy implementation and project management," *International Journal of Project Management*, 16(1): 43–50.
49. Daft, R. L. (2001). *Organization Theory and Design*, 7th ed. Mason, OH: Southwestern; Moore, D. (2002). *Project Management: Designing Effective Organizational Structures in Construction*. Oxford: Blackwell; Yourker, R. (1977). "Organizational alternatives for project management," *Project Management Quarterly*, 8(1): 24–33.
50. Meredith, J. R., and Mantel, Jr., S. J. (2003). *Project Management*, 5th ed. New York: Wiley.
51. Larson, E. W., and Gobeli, D. H. (1987). "Matrix management: Contradictions and insights," *California Management Review*, 29(4): 126–37; Larson, E. W., and Gobeli, D. H. (1988). "Organizing for product development projects," *Journal of Product Innovation Management*, 5: 180–90.
52. Daft, R. L. (2001). *Organization Theory and Design*, 7th ed. Mason, OH: Southwestern; Anderson, C. C., and Fleming,

M. M. K. (1990). "Management control in an engineering matrix organization: A project engineer's perspective," *Industrial Management,* 32(2): 8–13; Ford, R. C., and Randolph, W. A. (1992). "Cross-functional structures: A review and integration of matrix organization and project management," *Journal of Management,* 18: 267–94.

53. Larson, E. W., and Gobeli, D. H. (1987). "Matrix management: Contradictions and insights," *California Management Review,* 29(4): 126–37; Larson, E. W., and Gobeli, D. H. (1988). "Organizing for product development projects," *Journal of Product Innovation Management,* 5: 180–90; Engwall, M., and Kallqvist, A. S. (2000). "Dynamics of a multi-project matrix: Conflicts and coordination," Working paper, Chalmers University, www.fenix.chalmers.se/publications/2001/pdf/WP%202001-07.pdf.

54. Wheelwright, S. C., and Clark, K. (1992). "Creating project plans to focus product development," *Harvard Business Review,* 70(2): 70–82.

55. Gobeli, D. H., and Larson, E. W. (1987). "Relative effectiveness of different project management structures," *Project Management Journal,* 18(2): 81–85; Gray, C., Dworatschek, S., Gobeli, D. H., Knoepfel, H., and Larson, E. W. (1990). "International comparison of project organization structures," *International Journal of Project Management,* 8: 26–32.

56. Gray, C. F., and Larson, E. W. (2003). *Project Management,* 2nd ed. Burr Ridge, IL: McGraw-Hill; Dai, C. (2000). *The Role of the Project Management Office in Achieving Project Success.* PhD Dissertation, George Washington University.

57. Block, T. (1998). "The project office phenomenon," *PMNetwork,* 12(3): 25–32; Block, T. (1999). "The seven secrets of a successful project office," *PMNetwork,* 13(4): 43–48; Block, T., and Frame, J. D. (1998). *The Project Office.* Menlo Park, CA: Crisp Publications; Eidsmoe, N. (2000). "The strategic project management office," *PMNetwork,* 14(12): 39–46; Kerzner, H. (2003). "Strategic planning for the project office," *Project Management Journal,* 34(2): 13–25; Dai, C. X., and Wells, W. G. (2004). "An exploration of project management office features and their relationship to project performance," *International Journal of Project Management,* 22: 523–32; Aubry, M., Müller, R., Hobbs, B., and Blomquist, T. (2010). "Project management offices in transition," *International Journal of Project Management,* 28(8): 766–78.

58. Casey, W., and Peck, W. (2001). "Choosing the right PMO setup," *PMNetwork,* 15(2): 40–47; Gale, S. (2009). "Delivering the goods," PMNetwork, 23(7): 34–39.

59. Kerzner, H. (2003). *Project Management,* 8th ed. New York: Wiley; Englund, R. L., and Graham, R. J. (2001). "Implementing a project office for organizational change," *PMNetwork,* 15(2): 48–52; Fleming, Q., and Koppelman, J. (1998). "Project teams: The role of the project office," *Cost Engineering,* 40: 33–36.

60. Schein, E. (1985). *Organizational Culture and Leadership: A Dynamic View.* San Francisco, CA: Jossey-Bass, pp. 19–21; Schein, E. H. (1985). "How culture forms, develops and changes," in Kilmann, R. H., Saxton, M. J., and Serpa, R. (Eds.), *Gaining Control of the Corporate Culture.* San Francisco, CA: Jossey-Bass, pp. 17–43; Elmes, M., and Wilemon, D. (1989). "Organizational culture and project leader effectiveness," *Project Management Journal,* 19(4): 54–63.

61. Kirsner, S. (1998, November). "Designed for innovation," *Fast Company,* pp. 54, 56; Daft, R. L. (2001). *Organization Theory and Design,* 7th ed. Mason, OH: Southwestern.

62. "Australian London 2012 Olympic swim team 'toxic'" (2013, February 19). *BBC News Asia,*. www.bbc.com/news/world-asia-21501881.

63. Kilmann, R. H., Saxton, M. J., and Serpa, R. (1985). *Gaining Control of the Corporate Culture.* San Francisco, CA: Jossey-Bass.

64. "The US must do as GM has done." (1989). *Fortune,* 124(2): 70–79.

65. Hillier, B. (2013, July 24), "Gibeau: 'You get the best games from small teams with strong cultures,'" *VG 24/7.* www.vg247.com/2013/07/24/gibeau-you-get-the-best-games-from-small-teams-with-strong-cultures/; Takahashi, D. (2013, July 23). "EA exec Frank Gibeau: Betting on next-gen consoles, mobile, and doing right by consumers," *Venture Beat.* http://venturebeat.com/2013/07/23/eas-frank-gibeau-on-interview-part-1.

66. Staw, B. M., and Ross, J. (1987, March–April). "Knowing when to pull the plug," *Harvard Business Review,* 65: 68–74.

67. Smith, D. K., and Alexander, R. C. (1988). *Fumbling the Future: How Xerox Invented, Then Ignored, the First Personal Computer.* New York: Macmillan; Kharbanda, O. P., and Pinto, J. K. (1996). *What Made Gertie Galdop?* New York: Van Nostrand Reinhold.

5

Project Management as Change

Consider how hard it is to change yourself
and you'll understand what little chance you
have of trying to change others.

Jacob M. Braude

Change is the fun part of the whole process. This is where the action takes place, careers are made and reputations destroyed. At this stage, as a consultant you might put on your project management hat, pull out the 25-page work-structure breakdown and launch into a highly technical discussion about milestones, critical paths and percentage-completion factors. Clearly, these issues need to be included, but this aspect of the process has been sufficiently well documented elsewhere and so is not covered in this book.

The focus here is on the softer factors – the issues that have a subtle but significant impact on the change process. It is these intangible factors that are often pushed to one side. However, only by taking care of the soft issues will the hard deliverables be achieved. As Senge *et al.* (1999) suggest, most change initiatives fail. In many cases the supposed failure rate for total quality and re-engineering initiatives is around 70 per cent. Kotter's study of 100 top management-driven corporate transformations concluded that more than half did not survive the initial phase (Kotter, 1999).

The failure to recognize or resolve this problem is often shielded by a cloak of political intrigue, or the simple fact that organizations change so fast that the failures are lost in the mists of time. But effective change is not about increased technical or project management capability, it is more about the need to understand the meta-processes that drive and support change. These are the actions that need to be understood, irrespective of the nature of the change or the industry. However, these factors are often viewed as the soft processes, the intangible elements that are swept aside once the ball is in the air.

Yet within an engagement, the soft issues are often the hardest. Although the development and management of a project plan is difficult and often labour-intensive, it is important to ensure that the more intangible issues are not overlooked as the heat is turned up.

The Change stage of the Seven Cs model includes the following themes that seek to help to understand and address the human elements of change.

- **System dynamics** – what are the deep systemic issues that will cause the Change stage to hit problems?
- **Organization and disorganization** – what factors related to the organization of the system will impact on the success of the change?
- **Understand the resistance** – how can people be encouraged to be involved in the change?
- **Change spectrum** – what type of change interventions can be effected to help people through the change?
- **What makes 'Guide' work** – this includes the training, educating, facilitating and mentoring of the people involved in the change.
- **Consumer segmentation** – how can the consumers be segmented into groups based on their desire for change?
- **Methodology** – what methodology will be used to drive the engagement?
- **Energy mapping –** where are the forces that can impact on the change?

System dynamics

Look at the list of words in Table 5.1. Why is it that so many consultants sell their services using words from the left-hand column, while so many clients believe that the words on the right are more indicative of the outcome? Wherever you go, whatever industry, the role of the consultant is generally under attack. People are dissatisfied with their doctors, householders complain about builders and directors moan that yet another consultant has left them with a mundane solution. Clearly the consultancy industry might have a few rogues and the odd bad apple but the huge growth in consultancy spend over recent years seems to run counter to the view that consultants do not add value to the client and consumer.

Table 5.1 Intent and outcome

Consultant's intent	*Perceived outcome*
Action	Aberration
Better	Bluff
Cure	Chaos
Deliver	Delay
Easy	Embarrassment
Faster	Fails

One of the reasons is because so many consultants do not pay sufficient attention to the nature of the system in which they are working. They act on the evidence of a single event and give little consideration to the deeper issues that underpin the system. Consultancy projects are often designed on the premise that the issues revolve around a simple, predictable component. In reality, this is the tip of a problem that involves a complex, dynamic and integrated system. As Senge (1990) suggests:

Business and human endeavours are systems ... they are bound by invisible fabrics or interrelated actions, which often take years to fully play out their effects on each other. Since we are part of that lacework ourselves it is doubly hard to see the whole pattern of change. Instead we tend to focus on snapshots of isolated parts of the system and wonder why problems never seem to get solved.

For example, the incident the police most dread is a family dispute. In this situation they are being asked to dive into a situation that is volatile, emotional and unpredictable. There is often no 'solution' since the issue is probably about a perceived rather than an actual problem. No matter what action they might take they are likely to end up in the firing line, often being abused by both parties. They are effectively being asked to intervene in a system where they have little or no control over the process or outcome.

As a consultant asked to help resolve a problem within an organization, you are often in a similar position. You will be asked to unravel problems to which people are emotionally attached and will defend against outside interference. Moreover, you will rarely have to resolve an issue that involves just one person.

In all cases, the effective consultant will focus less on the issues (tasks, content or facts) than on trying to understand the relationship between them. For example, the only way a marriage guidance counsellor will be able to help in resolving a problem is by understanding the nature of the relationship between the husband and wife. Just understanding each partner in isolation will only produce a rubber-band solution, where the old problems bounce back after a few days. In the same way that 2 + 2 is vastly different from 2 × 2, the relationship is as much a part of the system as the component parts. In other words, the whole of the system is more than the sum of its parts. Unless you are able to see this then any project will be flawed from the outset.

“you must see (and help others see) the big picture”

You must see (and help others see) the big picture. The view that an individual, team or organization can be improved by focusing just on one part in isolation is seriously flawed. Senge (1990) makes this point when he suggests that:

From a very early age we are taught to break apart problems, to fragment the world. This apparently makes complex tasks and subjects more manageable, but we pay a hidden, enormous price. We can no longer see the consequences of our actions; we lose our intrinsic sense of connection to a larger whole. When we then try to 'see the big picture', we try to reassemble the fragments in our minds to list and organize the pieces.

Once this dissection has taken place it can be difficult to resolve the problem. Actions are taken on the separatist's principle with the result that a short-term fix might be delivered but a bigger long-term problem is planted. The consultant's failure to take account of the total system will often lead to one of the following scenarios.

- **Action/abort** – systems that are made up of people do not react passively to an outsider. They will fight back with all the energy they can muster. Change makes things worse – it is difficult for a stranger to fix a problem because they do not have sensitivity to the context and situation. Thus it is impossible to make a change in one area without some impact being felt elsewhere. The end result is that the consultant has to close down the project or call in other people to help untangle the mess. Interestingly, in many cases consultants will make a good living on the back of projects that previous people have failed to resolve.
- **Better/bluff** – things often get better before they get worse. Like the

car mechanic who changes the spark plugs when your car is running rough, you might get a short-term improvement in performance, but unless the mechanic realizes that the clogged-up spark plugs are caused by excessive oil being burnt, then the issue has not been resolved. The real problem is that the piston rings are worn and no amount of short-term fixes will produce a long-term improvement.

- **Cure/chaos** – in this case the cure is worse than the original problem. A doctor may happily prescribe valium for a depressed patient. But unless the doctor tries to understand the root cause of the depression, the individual is led down a rocky road to possible long-term addiction. An insidious cycle of shared dependency can be generated with this approach. As the system falls into chaos because of an inappropriate cure, so managers look to the consultant to help them resolve yet another problem. Dependency is created between the consultant, client and consumer, with each believing that the real cure is just around the corner – if only they can have just one more fix of the latest consultancy fad.
- **Deliver/delay** – when a change causes a problem for the system you can take immediate action to resolve the issue. However, the difficulty comes when a time delay creeps into the reaction and problems are caused downstream. You might make a change on the assumption that it has been effective, but you might not be around to see the impact of your actions. In 99 per cent of projects the consultant is not around after six months to understand the impact of the change.
- **Easy/embarrassment** – if you are asked to help in resolving a problem, the temptation can be to use tried and tested techniques on the basis that what worked before will work again. You are like someone with a hammer who believes that all problems can be fixed with a nail. The danger is that after trying for the fifth time to push 'a square peg into a round hole' you might have to accept (with some embarrassment) that the easy, quick-fix solution might not be the most appropriate. Just because one system looks like another, it does not mean that solutions can be easily replicated.
- **Faster/fails** – the pressure valve on a cooking pot or the governor on a steam engine are examples of how things are set to operate at their optimum level. In the same way, any system will have an optimum level at which it operates and any effort to push over the limit will be frustrating for you and damaging for the system. This can be seen in the way that people try to resolve difficult issues. Rather than stepping back from a situation to consider what deep structural issues

are causing the problem, the tendency is to work harder, do more research or involve more people. In many cases, it might be that the slower or lesser action would actually deliver the desired outcome. Rather than trying to overcome resistance and force a change through, it might be easier to understand what limiting factors are causing the resistance and try to eliminate them by more subtle means. You can spend an hour arguing with your daughter about the need to keep her bedroom tidy, but it might be simpler to suggest that the tidiness of her bedroom will be directly linked to her pocket money.

Although each template tells a different story, they have a common theme that has a serious implication for any consultant. They suggest that when embarking on an engagement, you need to ensure that the situation is understood from the whole perspective and not in isolation (see Figure 5.1).

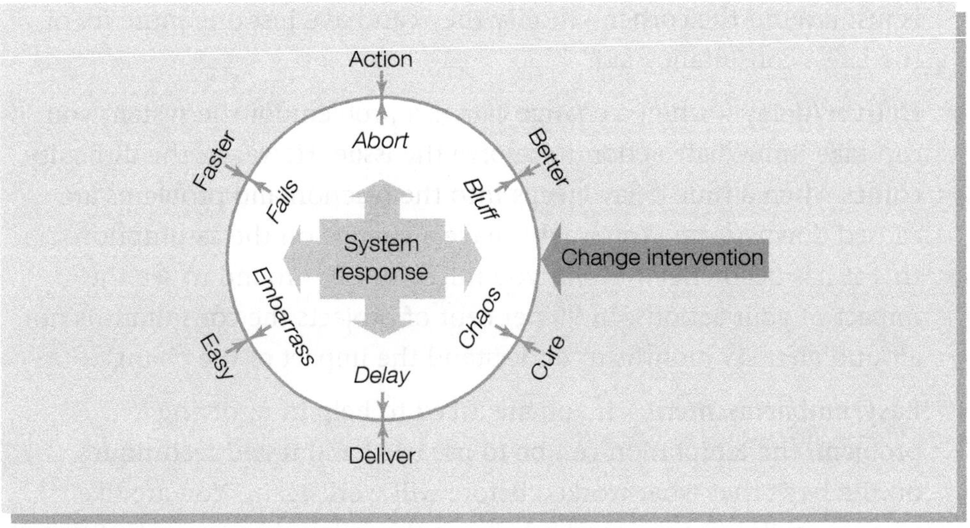

Figure 5.1 System responses

When undertaking any change engagement, you must pay careful attention to the systemic nature of the organization being changed. The systematic nature of the engagement can either fuel the drive towards a successful engagement or leave a problem legacy for the future – a problem that you, a colleague or client might be forced to resolve.

Organization and disorganization

Another issue that is beginning to have a significant impact on the way that change is deployed is the organization of the business unit. Historically, consultants may have been able to assume that the client group would have an organization build that was broadly based on a hierarchical business model. Today this assumption cannot be made. With a constant shift in organization shape, location and reporting structure there is often a move away from the formal hierarchical model to a more networked-based formation.

For those organizations based on mechanistic or machine-based operating principles they will have typical assumptions that drive the formation of an organization's management system (Cope, 1998):

- equilibrium, stability and control are the desired states;
- organizations can be separated into discrete components (function, department, product groups, etc.) and these elements can operate independently of any other unit within the business;
- organizations should always allocate resources in trying to determine what the market will look like in one, three and five years time;
- cause and effect relationships can be traced through the business;
- when something goes wrong in one part of the business, it can be isolated and repaired without affecting other areas.

These assumptions are driven by a set of deep underlying ideas.

- **We can know the future** – organizations are often awash with market forecasters, business planners, strategy builders and economists who advise the organization of what is likely to happen in the future. The whole premise on which these positions exist is that the future can be predicted and managed.
- **Divide and conquer** – there is often a desire to divide the organization into management chunks on the assumption that things can be taken apart, dissected and split asunder (as with business functions and academic disciplines). The conjecture is that by comprehending the workings of each piece, the whole can be managed (Wheatley, 1994). The chunking that might typically be seen in organizations is by function (marketing, engineering, finance, etc.), geography, hierarchy, product groups or project teams.
- **Let me tell you what is wrong** – most systems operate on negative feedback. Control systems such as objective setting, budgetary structures and resource allocations, are driven by a common approach. People are asked to forecast what is required, report any variance against the forecast, and then take action to rectify and limit the variance.

- **The boss knows best** – the common structural map is that the people at the top – the managers – know best and need only draw on the views of the lower teams to pick up a few tit-bits and give them a pat on the head.
- **Don't feel, think** – organizations are typically (overtly) driven by tasks, business goals, corporate objectives and the assumption that people come to work for the love of the business. Often there is a view that people's feelings are left at home. Many organizations work on a repressed model, where any mention of emotion or sentiment in a business meeting can be enough to cause an apoplexy for the traditional manager. The base (espoused) assumption is that business decisions are based on logical and sensible decision-making processes. The reality is that decisions are often driven by personal ambition, greed and fear as commonly as for the good of the business.

The network organization is founded on an entirely different set of operating principles. It is built around the idea of a community that can spontaneously self-organize itself and adapt to changing market conditions. It can be seen as the ability of group of people to manage itself without any intervention or control from an external agent. Self-organization demands that a system draws on its own resources, not that of the hierarchy, in order to meet the challenges that it faces (Goldstein, 1994). Like birds flocking in the sky, children in a playground, people leaving a football stadium or massed peace rallies, once the boundaries are set and simple rules are offered, then harmony can emerge from a situation that is apparently chaotic – this is essentially 'order for free' (Kauffman, 1995).

One of the significant factors with the mechanistic organization is the emphasis that is placed on the cogs in the system. This means that people have defined roles, objectives and their place in a robust hierarchy. With the self-organization model, the emphasis is placed more on the nature of connectivity within the system – on the interconnections, the configuration and the map of the relationship between the components, as well as the roles of the people. This can be seen as the network organization – one that is likely to increase with the proliferation of web-based connections, remote working and global expansion.

Organizations that operate according to network model have the following characteristics.

- **Self-stability** – there is a high degree of stability, not in the traditional sense of being fixed or unvarying, but in the capability to maintain the same overall structure in spite of any changes or replacement of component parts. The nature of the system means that it is able to remain steady, even when small disturbances occur. Since the inherent design of the system is based on adaptability and self-regulation, it is able to cope with any surprises that might have been disruptive. If the people in the network want to be in the network, then it will survive. It will change and adapt every day, week and month, but it will survive.

- **Self-reproduction** – the network can continually reproduce itself in order to meet its goals. While the overall structure of the community remains the same, the components or people in the network will continually change. Thus the network modifies its internal elements but retains its overall identity. An example of this can be seen in the way that people rebuild their pancreas every 24 hours, their stomach lining every three days and blood every month. The body is able to do this because it continually regenerates and changes the cell structure within the body (Capra, 1997).
- **Self-regulation** – underpinning this idea of the self-sustaining organization is the notion of intrinsic self-regulation. Intrinsic regulation is where the network has its own capacity to regulate its operation, and hence its output. Extrinsic regulation is where the control comes from outside the natural system. Networks will typically be intrinsically managed because no one person has the right to say what is and what is not right or wrong.
- **Self-organization** – natural organisms can have a tendency to be attracted to an instinctive style or pattern of working. This natural or stable state is often known as the attractor state – it is a way of operating where order naturally arises out of disorder. For example, look at a group of school children playing at lunchtime. There is apparent disorder and chaos, but if the picture is considered in terms of patterns and relationships, different shapes and behavioural patterns will emerge. It will be possible to see patterns in the guise of repeated games that instigate a set of behaviours. Football will set up one pattern, while the game of tag will drive another pattern. Networks will intuitively set up self-regulated patterns that form around a common point of interest. If you can understand the nature of the attractor then you will start to understand the nature of the network and how it self-organizes.

As people migrate from a mechanistic or organized system to operate in an open network they might need to lose some of the beliefs in the gods of direction, stability and consistency. If this is the case then consultants must develop the ability to effect change across organizations that do not have a network mentality. It is easy to 'install' a new vision, mission or strategy into a business where everyone meets in team meetings, logs in to the company website every morning and is paid through the same payroll system. The challenge will be for consultants to effect change across organizations where none of these things can be taken for granted – where people work with and not for the business, or where people log on at different times, depending on where they are based in the world.

In many cases the change style adopted as norms by many change agents (command and control) may need to shift towards a much more negotiated and softer style to ensure that sustainable change is realized. As the formal organization structures begin to change, so too will the resistance that people offer to change imposed by external agents.

Understand the resistance

People don't resist change – they resist being changed.

Resistance to change is one of the most significant but least considered issues. This is because many people view opposition as a negative issue – something to go into battle with and gain victory over. However, unless people are already moving in the direction of a proposed change then it is natural to expect some form of resistance. This might be minimal, such as the odd joke or sarcastic comment about the new corporate uniform; or major, such as company-wide industrial action triggered by proposed downsizing. Although these two examples are different in scale, they follow the same underlying process that is a natural response in reaction to something that people regard as unfair or inappropriate.

Although it is impossible to identify every type of behaviour where resistance is encountered, there are a number of common reactions that can be observed as people experience the adaption process (Kubr, 1976).

- **Lack of conviction that change is needed** – if people are not properly informed and the purpose of change is not explained, they are likely to view the present situation as satisfactory, and any effort to change as useless and upsetting.
- **Dislike of imposed change** – in general, people do not like to be treated as passive objects. They resent changes that are imposed on them and about which they cannot express any views.

- **Dislike of surprises** – people do not want to be kept in the dark about any change being prepared; changes tend to be resented if they come as a surprise.
- **Fear of the unknown** – people do not like to live in uncertainty and may prefer an imperfect present to an unknown and uncertain future.
- **Reluctance to deal with unpopular issues** – managers and other people often try to avoid unpleasant reality and unpopular actions even if they realize that they will not be able to avoid these for ever.
- **Fear of inadequacy and failure** – many people worry about their ability to adjust to change and to maintain and improve their performance in a new work situation. Some of them may feel insecure and doubt their ability to make a special effort to learn new skills and attain new performance levels.
- **Disturbed practices, habits and relations** – following change, well-established and mastered practices may become obsolete and familiar relationships may be altered or destroyed. This can lead to frustration and unhappiness.
- **Lack of respect in the person promoting change** – people are suspicious about change proposed by a manager they do not trust and respect, or by an external person whose competence and motives are not known and understood.

The common theme with all these issues is that resistance often occurs when people do not feel engaged in the change process. In general, people can live with what they know, but find it difficult to live with the unknown.

“resistance often occurs when people do not feel engaged in the change process”

The first reaction to such resistance is often to try to minimize any response to the proposed change. But all this means is that valuable time is spent on avoidance routines – trying to work out ways to hide the elements that people might not like. For example, think about the hours people spend trying to find a politically correct way to present an idea that is obviously not politically correct. Hence the rebadging of ‘downsizing’ to ‘rightsizing’, or ‘decruiting’ as a way of managing people out of a business in a controlled way. All these actions indicate a change process that is being squeezed through the back door rather than being presented honestly.

Natural resistance

It is normal for individuals, teams, organizations or even nations to react adversely when faced with something different or unexpected. This reaction can be mapped in the form of a Y-curve (see Figure 5.4 on p. 140), mapping time against the stages the individual(s) will pass through. The Y-curve is a powerful and effective change model that clearly illustrates many of the feelings associated with change and learning. People will especially feel these emotions where the change process affects their self-esteem or position in an organization.

Letting go

The Y-curve consists of two distinct stages (which may overlap). The first stage is the letting-go or disposal stage. This is where people learn that they will have to modify how they currently think, feel or behave and be expected to adopt a new set of behaviours (see Figure 5.2). Such a change in a person's lifestyle can push them over the edge of the cliff into a downward spiral. External events, or stressors such as the death of a significant other, personal injury, illness or change of residence, will tend to force a person out of secure patterns. While the loss of a loved one through death or divorce is unquestionably shattering, humans mourn other losses as well – the end of a secure relationship, loss of a homeland, loss of favourite job

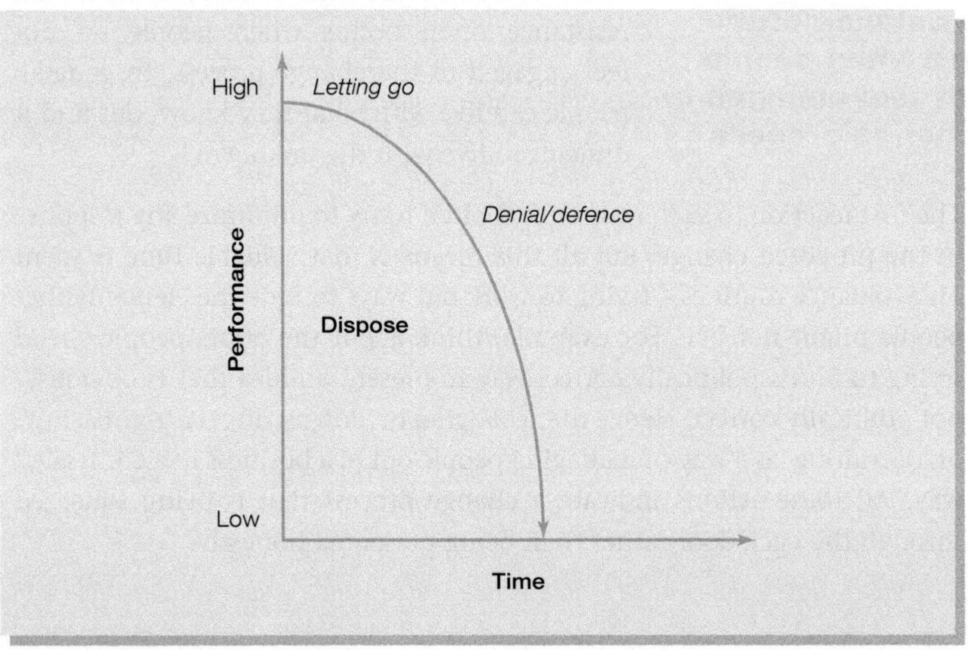

Figure 5.2 **Letting-go phase**

or even access to the local playing field to play soccer can be quite devastating for some people. Humans experience grief any time their life role is seriously changed and can be seen to move down the slope.

An important process in this stage is to allow the person to express their feelings. Don't try to 'sunshine' them out of their grief or distract them from what they need to express. Recognize outbursts of anger as a natural part of the grieving process and expect people to become selfish, childish and angry. They may well experience concern, denial, shock, worry, anger, grief, excitement, depression and frustration. This is normal and needs to be supported not shut down. Most importantly, watch out in case you or the client tend to avoid these grieving people just because they might be difficult to deal with.

Before people can adapt and adopt the new ways of thinking, feeling and behaving, they must unlearn – they have to let go of maps that are of no further use. This is not the same as throwing away ideas. The brain does not erase memories, it changes the connections – renewing some, letting others fade away – under a form of selection. When we remember, we recreate memories based on these strengthened or weakened connections. To rebuild our cognitive maps and emotional memories, we have to throw away the old pattern (Battram, 1999).

However, simply letting go of knowledge is not always as easy as it sounds. Because knowledge is associated with power, prestige and political clout, we are often loath to release it for others to use. In addition, unlearning is emotionally difficult because the old way of doing things has worked for a while and has become embedded in our beliefs and behaviours (Schein, 1993). We have to shift from the comfortable domain in the existing organizational environment and be prepared to migrate to the new form – we have to discard and forgo any existing mental models that might have held the status quo. This can be difficult because we often remain prisoners of our conceptual framework, where there is a general reluctance to leave the old way of thinking (Meznar, 1995).

The disposal process is critical to the change process, yet it is one that is rarely considered. Few change programmes really examine the process of unlearning and how to help people let go of redundant ideas and feelings. Unless we learn how to let go of past and redundant beliefs, then we will find it difficult to accept and embrace new forms of knowledge.

Looking forward

Once people have been able to let go and dispose of an old way of thinking and feeling, then they can start the journey to discover the new ways of being that is expected of them. The start of the discovery phase is the point when people will look forward in anticipation of what is to come (see Figure 5.3).

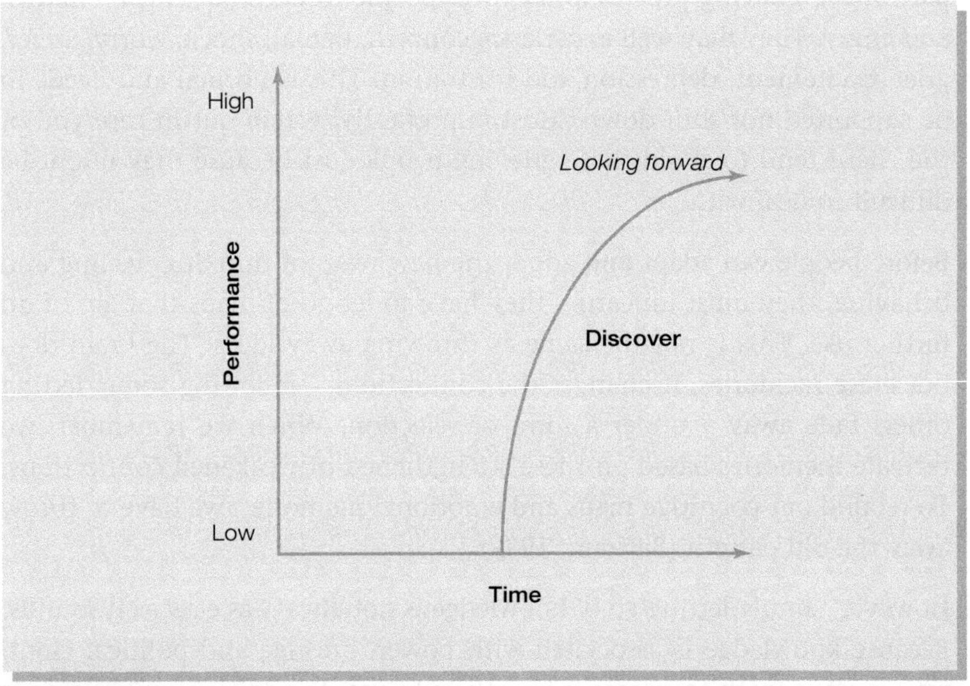

Figure 5.3 Looking-forward phase

Discovery is the process by which we enhance the quantity and quality of our ability to think, feel and behave. This might be through a range of processes, including reading, writing, conference presentations, working alongside someone, daydreaming or working in a management team. The one thing these processes all have in common is the acquisition of knowledge.

At this stage in the change cycle the new thoughts and feelings do not have to be newly created – they only need to be new to the individual or organization. BP gives a 'Thief of the Year Award' to the person who has 'stolen' the best ideas in application development. The company recognizes that, when it comes to organizational knowledge, originality is less important than usefulness. Texas Instruments has created a 'Not Invented Here, But I Did It Anyway' award for borrowing a practice from either inside or outside the company. A knowledge-focused firm needs to have appropriate knowledge available when and where it can be applied, not just generate new ideas for their own sake.

The important point about the discovery phase is that people have to make a decision to let go of the past and move forward. Critically, this is a choice that must be made by the individual and not imposed by an outside agent. This might be an explicit decision in the form of a conscious choice to accept that they have to think, feel or behave in a new way. This might be someone who looks in the mirror and realizes that they really do need to get fitter, or the company that finally accepts that the current processes are not up to scratch and they need to look for new operating models. Or it might be a tacit decision – an emerging acceptance that things must change. This might be the realization a couple come to when they accept that problems in their relationship need to be addressed or the organization that slowly begin to focus on the real issues as more and more people surface the shadows and talk about the problems they face. Critically it is the fact that the decision must be owned and internalized. Without this then the change will be short-lived. For example lots of people go on training courses – but few learn. So often they have been sent by the boss and they did not make the personal choice to change. Without this conscious choice to change then little knowledge acquisition or change will occur.

The looking-forward phase is important because it is a building block to the value to be created from the change. Unless people are helped to look forward and climb out of the dip that they may have hit in the letting-go phase then their personal performance will diminish over time. If the personal performance of people in an organization dips, then so will the business performance – no matter how robust the management systems and processes might be.

The Y-curve

As we bring the two stages of disposal and discovery together we see the emergence of the Y-curve – the pattern that people follow as they go through change (see Figure 5.4).

The Y-curve has a shaded area where the letting-go and looking-forward phases cross. This is the doldrums where nothing is moving. The person has disposed of the old way of thinking and feeling but has not yet climbed up the discover side to find a new way of being.

In *The Phantom Tollbooth* (Juster, 2008) the Doldrums is where the Lethargians live. These are minute creatures who live in perpetual boredom.

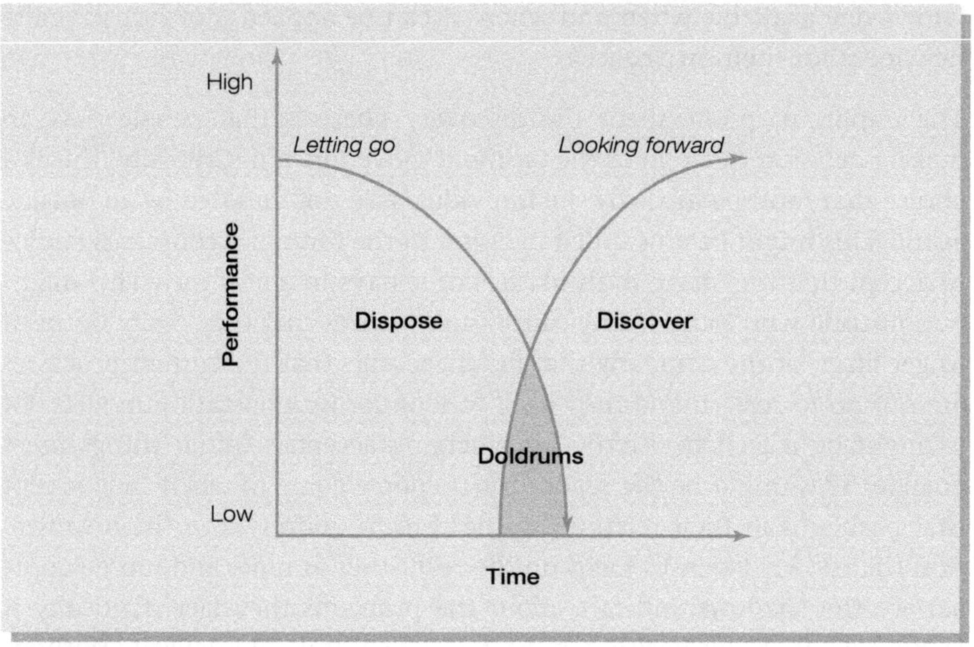

Figure 5.4 **Y-curve**

They change colours to match their surroundings and sometimes enforce laws against thinking and laughing. The Lethargians spend their life busily doing nothing:

'Well, if you can't laugh or think, what can you do?' asked Milo.

'Anything as long as it's nothing, and everything as long as it isn't anything,' explained another. 'There's lots to do; we have a very busy schedule.

At 8 o'clock we get up, and then we spend

From 8:0 to 9:0 daydreaming.

From 9:0 to 9:30 we take our early midmorning nap.

From 9:30 to 10:30 we dawdle and delay.

From 10:30 to 11:30 we take our late early morning nap.

From 11:00 to 12:00 we bide our time and then eat lunch.

From 1:00 to 2:00 we linger and loiter.

From 2:00 to 2:30 we take our early afternoon nap.

From 2:30 to 3:30 we put off for tomorrow what we could have done today.

From 3:30 to 4:00 we take our early late afternoon nap.

From 4:00 to 5:00 we loaf and lounge until dinner.

From 6:00 to 7:00 we dilly-dally.

From 7:00 to 8:00 we take our early evening nap, and then for an hour before we go to bed at 9:00 we waste time.

As you can see, that leaves almost no time for brooding, lagging, plodding or procrastinating, and if we stopped to think or laugh, we'd never get nothing done.'[1]

Walk through any organization that has embarked on a change process that is not working well, find business teams where people feel that they are not being supported, told what to do or where they are going and you will get a sense of the doldrums. These are people who are angry, moaning to each other, busily searching the web for the latest free software and doing anything they can to fill the day.

The theme of *The Phantom Tollbooth* story is that a mind is a terrible thing to waste. In the same way, it is a terrible waste to push people into the clutch of the Y-curve and not offer a ladder they can use to help themselves to climb out. This is the role of the consultant in the Seven Cs. It is to act as an expert – not to pull people out, but to offer strategies to the client by which people can be helped to find a way up the discovery curve and back to peak performance.

The D-spot

The one consistent activity that will help anyone who enters the Y-curve is to help them to understand *why*. Why has the change happened? Why does it affect them? Why should they give up what they are doing? Why do they have to do something new in the future? Without the why factor then people will often fail to step through the Y-curve and simply revert back to their old ways of thinking, feeling and behaving.

The critical point on the Y-curve is the point where the dispose phase meets the discover phase. This is the D-spot – the point where a conscious or subconscious choice needs to be made (see Figure 5.5). This is where to make the choice to move forward into the next stage or to reject the potential change and regress back to the previous way of thinking and feeling.

As people go down the disposal curve they will naturally get upset, angry and despondent. They will fall down the curve until they reach a point where they say enough is enough (either consciously or subconsciously)

1 From THE PHANTOM TOLLBOOTH by Norton Juster, Copyright © 1961, 1989, 2008 by Norton Juster. Used by permission of Brandt & Hochman Literary Agents, Inc., HarperCollins Publishers Ltd and Random House Children's Books, a division of Random House, Inc.

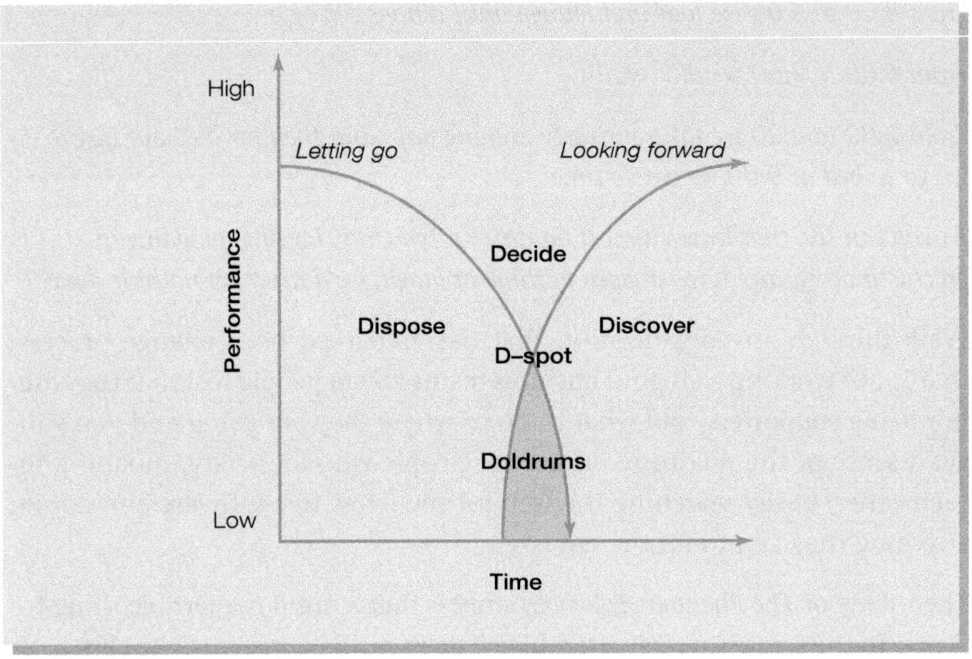

Figure 5.5 D-spot

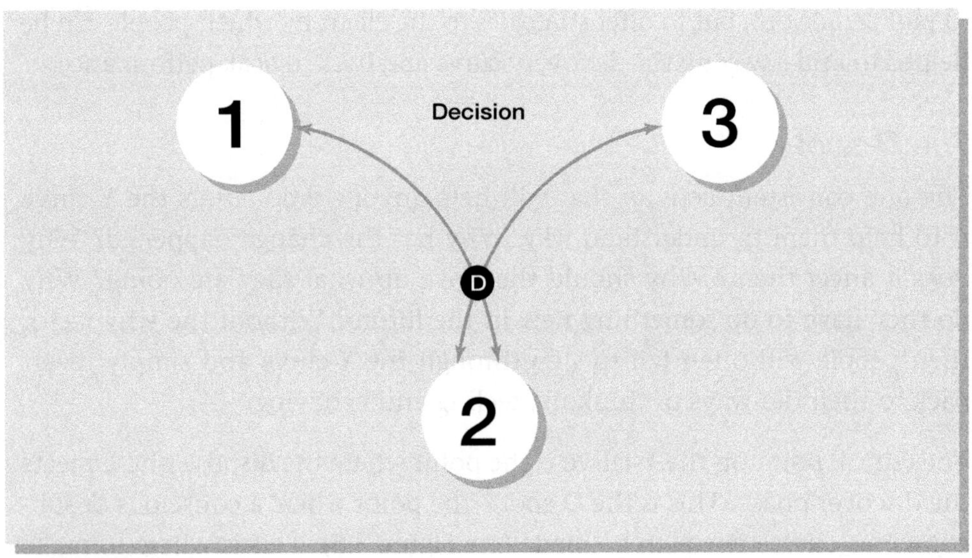

Figure 5.6 Choices at the D-spot

– this is the point where one of three decisions can be taken (see Figure 5.6). The first choice that people might make is to go back to point 1. In this case they will say this future position is not for me and refuse to go forward. This often happens in organizations that are embedded in rigid bureaucratic models – for example government organizations or family firms where change seems quite untenable for people who want to hold on to the current status quo. Point 2 is where people hit the low point and do not come out – they just sit feeling angry, upset and as a consequence can be quite disruptive. Point 3 is where people choose to internalize the future and move out of the dip and into a new way of thinking, feeling and behaving.

This is a choice, but not always a conscious one. The role of the consultant and client is to manage the D-spot and to help all the participants in the change process make the choice that will support the overall transformation the client wishes to achieve. It is a failure to consciously address what choices people are likely to make at the D-spot that often leads to successful short-term change but unsuccessful long-term change.

Change spectrum

Before setting out on any change, you have to consider the strategy that will be used to underpin the transition (Hersey and Blanchard, 1972) and help to make this decision to change. When push comes to shove, what rules will govern the decisions to be made? To decide this, you need to agree what ethos will underpin the assignment. Will it be one where the client and consumers are given the freedom to decide their personal rate of adaptation or will the consultant own the process and be responsible for controlling the change? Although there are degrees between the two extremes, any change will often have a bias in one direction (see Figure 5.7).

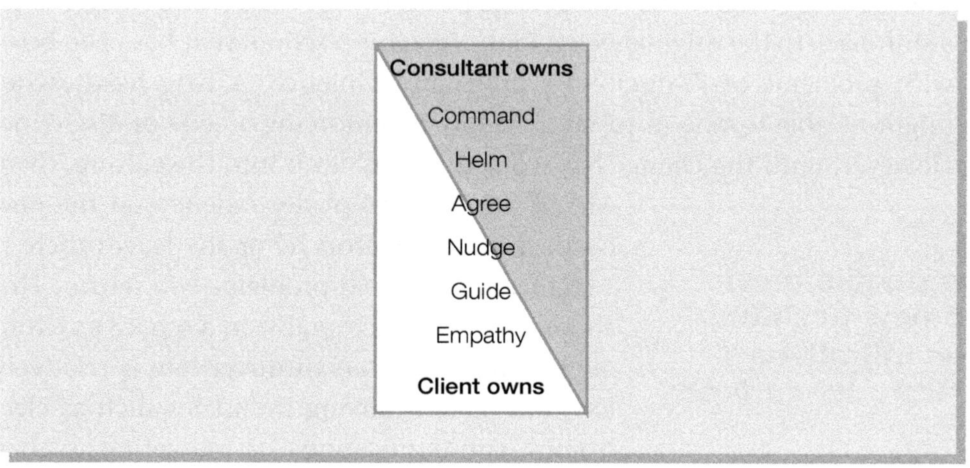

Figure 5.7 **Change spectrum**

At the 'client owns' end of the spectrum, the assumption is that giving people a new knowledge base modifies their behaviour. This is like the government campaign that tries to stop people smoking or avoid drinking and driving. The objective is to offer people information about the destructive impact of cigarettes or drink. In the same way, an organization might try to modify behaviour by offering people knowledge about a new quality system, ideas scheme or advanced competitor product. The problem with this approach is that it can take time and often requires a high level of back-up. The benefit is that the change will last over a period of time and is not dependent on a directive transformation process.

At the other end of the spectrum, the consultant decides that urgent change is necessary and stimulates rapid behavioural change across the organization in the expectation that everyone will quickly adopt a new range of behaviours. This is seen in the way that the UK government introduced car seatbelt and motorbike helmet laws to curb the high death rate on the roads. For an organization, this type of action is seen in the introduction of new process measures, quality audits or enhanced personal objectives. Each action will be reinforced by the idea that failure to reach the prescribed target will result in some form of disciplinary action. However, although behaviours will have been modified, people are doing it under duress. In many cases, deep-set attitudes and beliefs will not have been modified. Only over time might people start to embrace the new ways of working and accept that the new knowledge is valid as part of their normal working style.

Where the consultant owns the process, it is dependent on the people or system that originated the change. If the support mechanism is taken away, there is every chance that the change project will collapse and there will be a shift back to the original behaviours. Imagine a school that has been beset with problems of ill-discipline, drugs and violence. A new headteacher might be able to ride in to save the day by enforcing a code of discipline. However, until the change has worked its way deep into the culture, there will be a high level of dependency on the new head. If for any reason he or she leaves there is a chance that the old problems will return. This approach may be acceptable in a school environment, where the staff turnover rate is relatively low, but in fast-moving industries such as electronics, communications or marketing, such a strategy is risky. As people move on to new positions, so the initiatives they introduced fade away, with their replacement introducing a new set of changes.

“as people move on to new positions, so the initiatives they introduced fade away”

Therefore, when a client asks about the difficulty and length of time associated with a consultancy project, they might need to be educated about the trade-offs that must be made. You might be able to deliver speed and ease of implementation, but add the caveat that it might not include true and deep gain in the short term. For example, a company that wants to improve its level of quality has a decision to make. Does it look for a quick implementation, on the premise that it will be owned and driven by one of the senior managers? Or does it take a longer view and allow people to absorb and adapt to the new ideas at their own rate of change? Although you can help facilitate the decision, the ultimate responsibility for the judgement must be down to the client.

Change levels

One way to help the client to make sense of the change process is to offer a simple tool that can describe the levels of change that sit across the change spectrum. At one end of the spectrum the consultant takes charge, and at the other the consultant simply supports the client while they make all the choices. Working from one end of this spectrum to the other it is possible to identify six types of change.

- **Command** – the consultant owns the process and does not delegate any of the power to the client or consumers.
- **Helm** – the consultant gives away some level of control and does not have absolute power over the direction of the project, but still retains significant authority over the direction of the project.
- **Agree and negotiate** – the consultant gives away significant areas of the power, but does this through agreement (because of the desire to protect the change process).
- **Nudge** – the consultant has conceded over 50 per cent of the power to effect change to the client group. However, the consultant keeps a presence and encourages people to take small steps to try the change out – perhaps key people are encouraged to get involved so that others feel like joining in.
- **Guide** – the consultant's role is to help people to understand what is coming and how it might impact on them. This is primarily an education intervention where the role is to help the client and consumers to understand what is happening.
- **Empathy** – the consultant shows an understanding of potential problems – giving people time and space to acclimatize to the proposed change.

At any time in the change process, the consultant has to make a choice as to the most appropriate level of control they need to retain and how much is managed by the client. This raises an issue that must be clearly dealt with in the Client stage of the change process – just how much control will the consultant have to effect the change process and how much do they want or need? It is the failure to agree such a simple factor that can lead to confusion and chaos in the Change stage. When this happens consequences are guaranteed – the client will suffer in the short term as the change falls apart and the consultant will suffer in the long term as the value of their brand is eroded.

However, assuming that the consultant does have the necessary level of control, they will have to make choices about how to deploy the control and where to be on the change spectrum will be most effective. They do this by taking into account the change, the client's level of experience and the client's desire to accept control of the project. The implications of managing some of the levels are described below.

Command

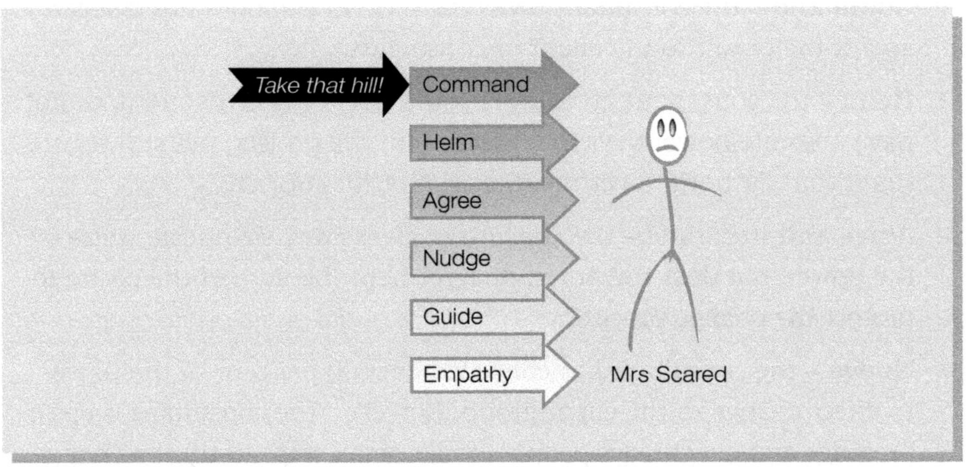

Clearly this is a powerful change process. It offers speed, simplicity and a power of autonomy that can ensure that things get done. However, the risk is that in getting things done people can get scared. They can be worried by the loss of jurisdiction and power and this can have a dramatic impact on the performance of the business. The moment people are scared then it might be beneficial to consider other options in the change spectrum – to help them to understand why you are taking absolute control over the change.

Helm

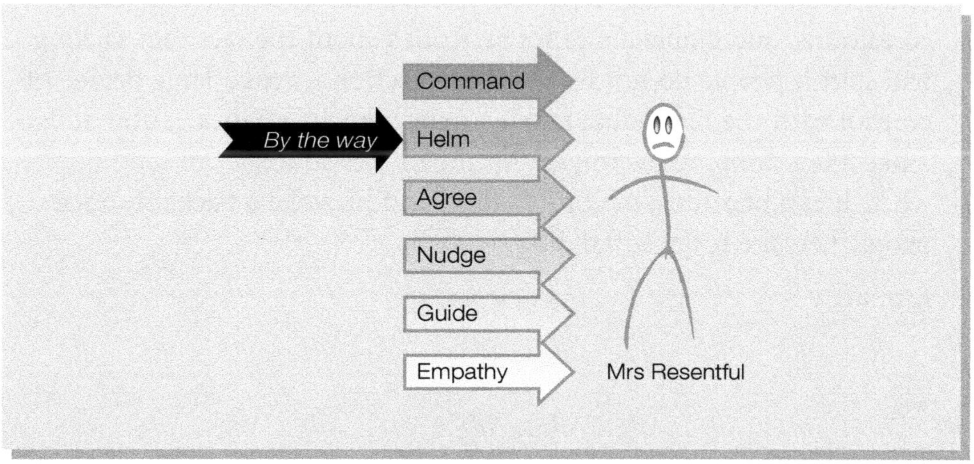

Where the helm style is being used, the consultant has handed over a degree of control to the client. This offers the benefit of signalling a desire to include others in the change process and so helps the movement towards independence. However, the risk with this approach is that by giving people a taste of the action they want more. Like the father who lets the young child play in the front garden, the child then wants to play in the street and feels resentment when the parent says no.

Nudge

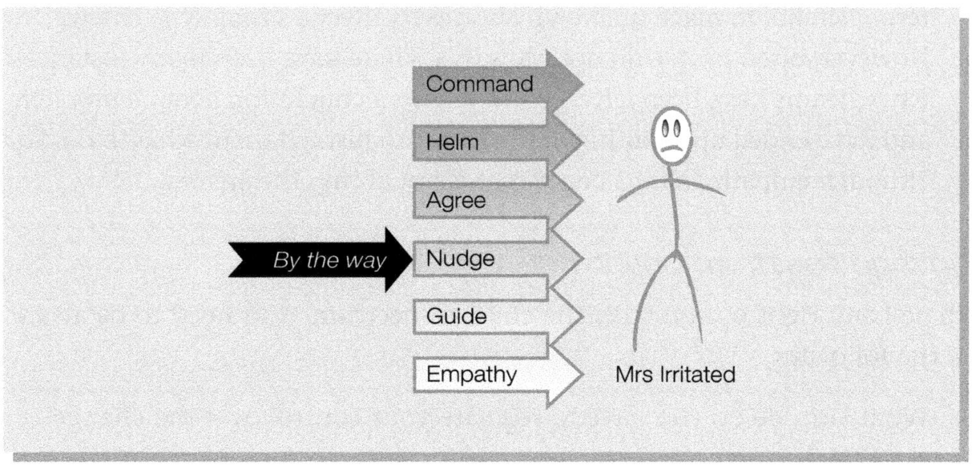

The nudge is often used where companies need to downsize. For example, there might be a combination of factors – including legislation, union power and political implications – that prevents a company from moving to a full-blown redundancy programme. However, it needs to lower the staff costs over time and so instigates a number of semi-soft actions to help nudge the people out of the door. These might include briefings in the company paper about poor market conditions, briefs to union representatives about poor trade conditions, and grapevine or lobby stories about the fact that sacking will start if people do not leave. All this action leaves a large degree of control with the individual but the management offers a gentle nudge – like a tap dripping overnight. Although this strategy can (and does) work, it can become a major irritation and provoke a backlash once people become really irritated.

- **Empathy**

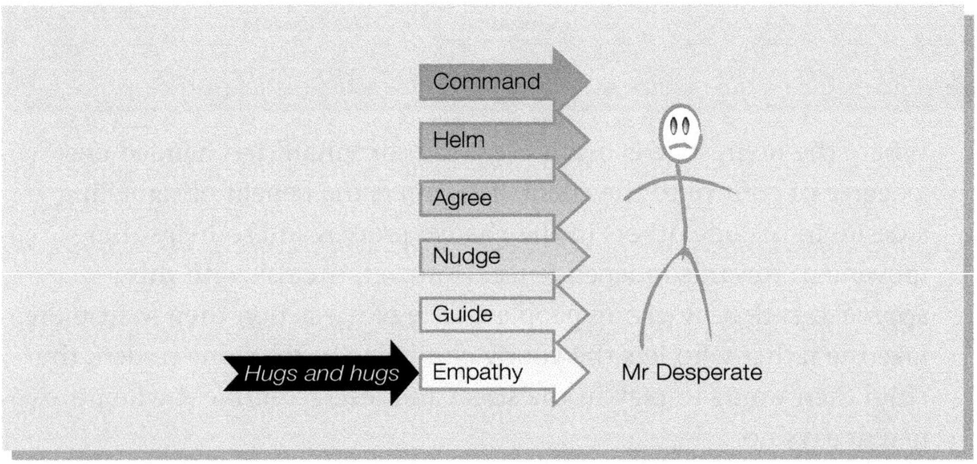

Many people would argue that it is important to give people time and responsibility to make their own choices to effect a sustainable change. However, often people do not want this. There have been many instances where teams have been left to find their own conclusion about a problem and have ended up shouting at the leader to just tell them what to do. So although empathy has its benefits, it is not always the answer.

Change spectrum options

There is no right option with the change spectrum. You need to be aware of the following:

- What latitude do you have to regulate your control over the change activities?
- What type of intervention does the client group prefer or expect?
- What preference do you have? Often consultants will favour one particular type of intervention based on their psychological preference and personal beliefs.
- What budget is available to support the intervention? The cost of

effecting each of the levels will vary quite considerably – both for short- and long-run costs.

- What internal support processes are available? This will vary, depending on the type of change effected.

In most cases there are no single miracle cures or single-shot solutions to deliver successful change. Single shots rarely hit a challenging target. The delivery of sustainable value through change involves introducing and sustaining multiple policies, practices and procedures across multiple units and levels. So one engagement might start with a command action by the consultant; be followed by a round of guidance or education sessions to help train the consumers and a series of nudge processes to stimulate action; finally there will be agreement with the staff associations to open the door for movement. The key is to be able to develop a cohesive and coherent change strategy that will help realize sustainable value and not introduce the knee-jerk change that delivers short-term fixes but long-term decay.

What makes 'Guide' work?

The CHANGE framework (p. 145) highlights the Guide aspect as one of the key factors that helps to create change programmes that are successful and sustainable. By 'guide' we mean the processes of training, educating, facilitating, mentoring and a whole host of activities that are designed to help people to change how they think, feel and behave.

This in itself seems a relatively easy process and one that is often noted as a task or milestone on a project plan. However, wrapped up in the task box that says 'People trained' hides a host of challenges. These challenges are in many, if not most, cases brushed over and hidden among the regular weekly updates that are fed to the senior managers. This is because at its very core the notion of 'training' someone is laced with very deep philosophical, psychological and humanistic issues that are rarely explored as part of the initial project proposal. Even worse, the whole notion of training is in many ways a major falsehood that is perpetuated because so many people do well out of the process! I make this (possibly contentious) argument based on three precepts.

- Over a one year period I challenged every single HR, OD and training manager I met with the deliberate statement, 'I don't think training is working and I believe there is limited return on investment'. During that period not one person fought back with any real argument.

I spoke with one senior HR manager who admitted they had spent two years putting all their managers through a company-wide programme with no discernable change in behaviour.

- Over a one year period I made the assertion to almost everyone on one of my programmes that I'd bet that they had recently been on a course where they made false promises – by completing an end of programme action plan that they never again touched. The result was cupboards full of dusty grey folders full of new quality-systems, customer-care techniques and personal-development plans. Hardly anyone disagreed!
- In one year alone official UK figures demonstrated that companies spent £38.5 billion on staff training. This was based on a skills survey that covered 79000 businesses. Along with this, a total of 218 million days were spent on training. (*National Employers Skills Survey*, Learning and Skills Council 2008)

I make this argument not because training doesn't add value – just that we have developed an accepted culture and regime where training is input based – so the notion prevails that getting bums on seats hits the target and everyone gets rewarded. Taking a view that training is not just about learning – and that learning implies not just knowing better – rather, it means doing better. So effective training should be about a clear shift in three areas:

- **Head** – cognition-based shift in what people know.
- **Heart** – an affective-based shift in that there is sufficient emotional connection with the learning for people to want to try it out for real.
- **Hands** – the behavioural or physiological component whereby people behave in a different way.

The argument is that if the consultant is embarking on a programme that will help the client change something in their organization – be it a new process, policy, system or reorganization – the chances are that people will be asked to know, feel or behave in a new way. If this is the case, then for some, training or education will probably be necessary and in most cases the potential success and sustainability of the project will be critically dependent on the ability and willingness of the people to behave in the new way.

To help in ensuring that this change process (that is key to the outcome and potentially very costly) adds real value there are three factors that do not necessarily guarantee a perfect outcome but can have a significant impact on the success and sustainability of the learning:

- Does the delegate's line manager support their attendance?
- Does the participant want to be there?
- Is the learning process focused on sustainable behavioural change – will there be a focus on doing better as well as knowing more?

The magic triangle

The first suggestion is that the effectiveness of any training intervention is driven heavily by the 'magic triangle' – namely the relationship that sits between delegation and the three points of a triangle. These are the tutor, the team leader and the training manager. When a training intervention works it is often because all three sides of the triangle interlace effectively. However, there are times (like the Bermuda triangle) when the value of the training simply disappears because the three groups do not interact well.

It is only by ensuring that the relationship is established and most importantly, that the line support is in place to help in reinforcing the new management behaviours that any real chance of sustainable behavioural change can be established. Making a significant investment in a person's development is often wasted simply because when they return to the office the line support does not reinforce or aid the development process. So there needs to be a tight and coherent framework of support established between the tutor, training manager and team leader from the very outset. For these three agents a number of key issues need to be considered.

- **Training manager**
  - Corporate needs being met by the overall programme.
  - Performance of the delivery agent is continually assessed.
  - Sustainability addressed with in-house support processes.
- **Tutor**
  - Clarity with the client on the required change and outcomes.
  - Clear about the derived business value from the training.
  - Ensure that dependency is avoided and hence change will stick.
- **Team leader**
  - Operational needs addressed.
  - Pre-and post-support established.
  - Clear added value for lost operational time.

It is the public airing of this magic triangle and its potential impact on the success of any training intervention that is paramount for the business. Without the interlaced support of the key agents then any chance of sustainable change is marginal at best. It is this gap that ultimately limits any chance of sustainable learning occurring.

This is not to point the finger or to lay the blame on any particular person or role – often, it is a more systemic issue where the failure to take development seriously at a senior and strategic level results in training becoming a weakened and undervalued cousin within the change processes.

10:20:30:40

One we have a participant on a training session who wants to be there and has clear and unambiguous support from their line manager, we can begin to explore the journey they will take. Ask what processes will help to deliver behavioural change and to ensure that they don't walk out the course with little intention of changing.

Let's consider the perfect learning journey and the path it takes. One example that happened recently for me was when, as part of middle age menopause, I decided to take my motorbike test and get a bike. This was one of the most powerful learning experiences I have ever encountered simply because so much was condensed into a single week. It is the condensed format and the freedom to deconstruct the journey afterwards that has offered the chance to reflect on the nature of learning within organizations.

The learning path to becoming a proficient rider involved four simple stages.

1 **Choose – owning the investment**

   This is the conscious and reasoned decision that I wanted to learn to ride a motorbike. Now, although this might appear to be a relatively simple process, in reality the choice is important because it is about owning and taking responsibility for the learning. I had to learn to ride, I had to study for the exam and I had to deal with the pain and embarrassment of the first fall. No one else could do that for me so the private and public choice to learn is a key factor in this journey.

   In the same way – for those of you who are trainers or run workshops – you know that the intent to listen and learn comes in the main from the mindset that people have when they walk through the door. Although we can sometimes transform 'anti' types into 'evangelists', ideally our role is to feed those who are hungry and not to force-feed those who don't have an appetite for what we can offer. This was so self-evident on the first stage of the motorbike course where some people were there to 'learn' to ride a bike, whereas others were there to simply get the certificate that allowed them to go out and pull wheelies. Two very different mindsets, and I suggest that the same training intervention delivered two very different outcomes!

2 **Train – gaining the knowledge**

The next stage of the bike journey was having to learn both the theoretical and practical aspects of riding. In itself this was a fascinating exercise because it combined a range of cognitive, affective and behavioural processes in such a condensed period of time.

One big lesson that I learned was that because I chose to learn and was not pressured I took time to study for the exam, I braved the cold, I went to learn, I didn't make excuses and fail to turn up. Also I made the sacrifice to pay for extra tuition when I became concerned that I might not pass the first time round.

3 **Coach – application with support**

It was interesting to watch how the bike tutors moved so easily from the role of instructor slowly migrating to a position where they were coaching us. So, in the first instance they gave us the basic safety first (school of) riding. This gave us confidence that we would not kill ourselves on the first outing – and also gave the instructor reassurance that they would not have to go through the hassle of taking us to hospital if we felled the bike.

A further example of this came when I went for a day's riding with the Bike Safe organization. This is a voluntary scheme set up by the Metropolitan Police offering riders coaching and feedback from professionals who have been riding for many years. With this scheme there are two riders allocated to each police motorcyclist – and they really push you to take the bike to its limits (safely) and then give feedback at the end of the day. The benefit is that they are not telling you what is right or wrong – they are just sharing their wisdom, ideas and thoughts that are not be found in the standard Highway Code book. So their goal is to help to foster a safe style of riding – one that fits with the rider's natural predisposition. Their role is to help translate the theoretical models offered in the training course into pragmatic behaviours that can be applied safely on the road.

4 **Do – embedding the learning**

It was interesting that, when in London recently, I was talking to a cabbie and he described his learning journey. First he spent four years

> studying his 'knowledge' of London routes (interestingly taking longer to learn than many degrees) and then rode round on a moped to familiarize himself with the physical characteristics of the land. This got him to the position where he proudly gained his cabbie badge and thought that all his worries were over.
>
> It was then that he had six months of hell – when he realized that the theory of driving a cab was very different to the daily experience. Although the theory might suggest an optimum route, just how do you deal with punters who know better? Who offer an endless stream of advice and who ridicule you because you don't know where a small cul-de-sac is in the far west of London.
>
> For him this embedded learning came from a number of experiences. First was going through the pain of doing it (like getting blisters on your fingers when learning to play the guitar). Second was the use of war stories within the cabbie community to share lessons learnt. This can be seen in the police force as a canteen culture, or for airline pilots where stories of flight problems feed the tacit learning systems.

It is this social learning theory considered by Bandura (1977) that emphasizes the importance of observing and modelling the behaviours, attitudes, and emotional reactions of others. He suggests that 'learning would be exceedingly laborious, not to mention hazardous, if people had to rely solely on the effects of their own actions to inform them what to do. Fortunately, most human behaviour is learned observationally through modeling: from observing others one forms an idea of how new behaviours are performed and on later occasions this coded information serves as a guide for action.' Social learning theory explains human behaviour in terms of a continuous reciprocal interaction between cognitive, behavioural, and environmental influences. It is this all-important aspect of the learning journey that is so often lost when significant training investments are made by organizations.

In summary I suggest that the perfect learning journey is an unfolding of four key processes.

- **Choose** – taking ownership of the need to learn and all the consequential activities to achieve that.
- **Train** – taking on board the cognitive, affective and behavioural traits necessary to deliver the outcomes.
- **Coach** – putting it all into practice and developing the necessary behaviours.

- **Do** – making it real and sustainable through experience, interaction and conversation.

The question that you need to consider as a consultant is to what extent do you help people move through all four stages? Do you responsibly help move people through all four stages and so create behavioural learning that is sustainable? Or do you just keep exposing them to yet another training solution – like waves lapping on the beach that will eventually erode the coastline and cause irreparable damage. I wonder to what extent failure to provide sustainable learning solutions is damaging both the organization and its people!

The investment journey

The training scale (see Figure 5.8) shows that the effective structure and form of a development programme is based on a simple premise. In any intervention, the total budget (100%) and investment capacity can be measured against a simple formula.

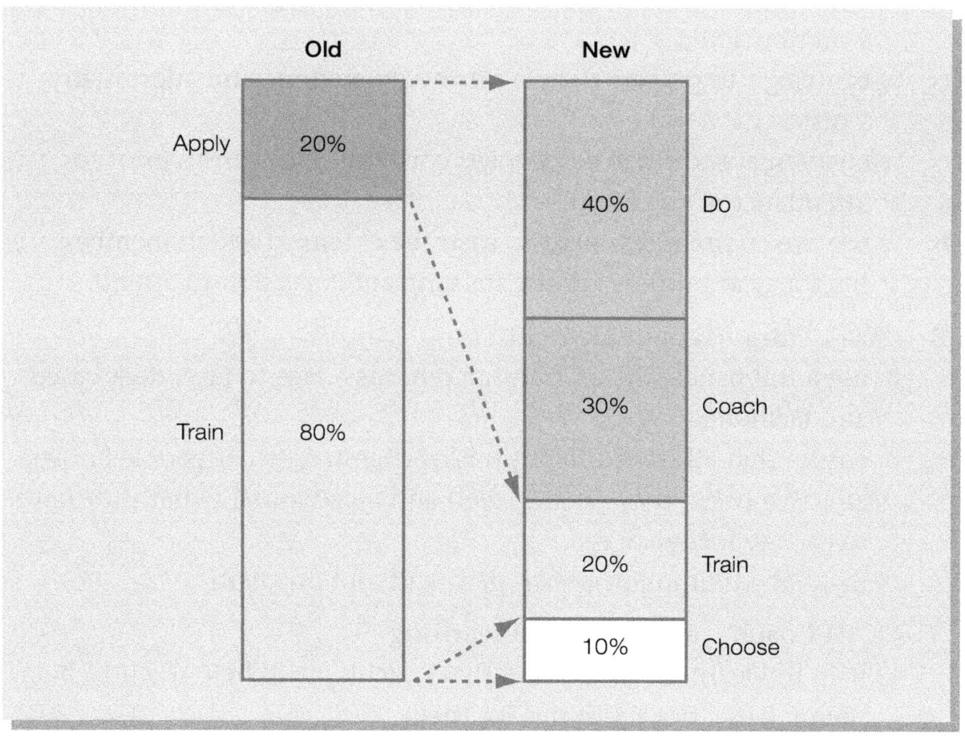

Figure 5.8 **Training model**

- **Choose** – 10% of investment in qualification and preparation of suitable candidates. This includes prebriefing on the programme and their role within it.

- **Train** – 20% on formalized tutor or class contact time designed to impact on the new way of thinking, feeling or behaving.
- **Coach** – 30% on collegiate coaching to reinforce the theories learnt in the formal environment and help in embedding behavioural change.
- **Do** – 40% for on-the-job reinforced learning based on practical experience, reflective processes and, quite simply, the school of hard knocks.

The suggestion with this model is that a failure to adequately deploy sufficient resources to all four areas will diminish the overall effectiveness and long-term sustainability of the intervention and investment. Only by ensuring that all four act together can the integrity of proportional balance be maintained and exploited.

Exmples of actions that the consultant can seek to drive within a development programme follow.

1 **(10%) Choose – candidates' choice**
   - differentiate those who can and want to change from those who won't or can't;
   - campaign to prepare people for the programme and address any worries;
   - create space to listen to peoples' concerns and worries prior to attendance at the event;
   - use pre-course assessment to map the extent to which members have a clear purpose for the training and a passion to attend.

2 **(20%) Train – taught element**
   - use a full bandwidth of training options – face to face, desk based and facilitated, etc.;
   - ensure that all three dimensions of cognitive (what people know), affective (what they need to feel) and behavioural (what they have to do) are included;
   - make the training personal, pertinent and pragmatic.

3 **(30%) Coach – application of learning**
   - help the learners understand that coaching will help them to help themselves – not fix things for them;
   - ensure that a core group of change agents are trained in basic coaching skills – only use real volunteers for this because it needs real passion and commitment;
   - ensure that post-event activities are embedded into the training programme;

- embed coaching review meetings to review learning about progress and outcomes.

4 (40%) **Do – embed the outcomes**
- integrate learning outcomes with any existing competency frameworks and performance reviews;
- develop experts and mentors who can refresh learning for the wider group;
- use after-action review groups to explore what the original goals were and how progress has been made against them.

Case example

Assume that a large retail company has identified that a major problem exists within its customer service department. A slow increase in customer complaints, linked with a perceived fall in morale within the division, has led the director to form the view that training is needed on a number of fronts. This is supported by the training manager who undertakes a training-needs analysis and identifies that there are three areas that need addressing with some urgency:

- call handling processes when dealing with more difficult clients;
- building rapid rapport;
- basic team management skills.

The decision is made to create a training intervention that takes place over a year. Using the training scale model, the training manager presents a proposal to the board, based on the following activities.

1 (10%) **Choose – candidates' choice**
- Use segmentation techniques to identify and separate out those who can and want to change from those who won't or can't.
- Put processes in place to harness the energy of the high impact and high involvers to lead communication and engagement sessions.
- Begin a campaign to prepare people for the programme and address any questions.
- Create space to listen to people's concerns and worries, and address these prior to attendance at the event.
- Use pre-course assessment to map the extent to which delegates have a clear purpose for the training and a passion to attend. Where gaps are identified then resolve them before the event.

2 (20%) **Train – taught element**

- Ensure that a full bandwidth of training options is used – face to face, desk based and facilitated etc.
- Ensure that all three dimensions of cognitive (what people know), affective (what they need to feel) and behavioral (what they have to do) are designed into the events.
- Ensure that the external tutor fully understands the culture of the organization and can match the needs of the delegates and the organization.
- If possible identify key line managers and include them in the development programme. Also try to use directors and senior managers as guest speakers.

3 (30%) **Coach – application of learning**

- Ensure that a core group of line managers are trained in basic coaching skills – only use 'real' volunteers for this because it takes time and energy.
- Use this group to act as agents of change and support for other line managers.
- Ensure that post-event activities are embedded into the training programme.
- Also ensure that members know who their coach or mentor will be when they leave the event.
- Embed coach review meetings to assess the value of their support and the programme across the division.
- Use simple tests across the members (independent of coaches' feedback) to map the application of learning.

4 (40%) **Do – embed the outcomes**

- Develop experts and mentors from the group who have adopted the new ways of working – train them to run top-up and refresh sessions for the wider group.
- Determine the learning preferences of the various members and try to match the embedding process to their preferred pattern.
- Develop after-action review groups to explore what the original goals were and how progress has been made against them.
- Use creative coffee sessions – where people are encouraged to socialize and share their thoughts on the learning.
- Allocate set time for problem identification and resolution using the new ways of working and the techniques introduced during the training – don't just assume it will happen.
- Foster the development of 'war' stories and examples of good practice.

- Use online help and support systems to enable instant access when problems are encountered.
- Ensure that line staff are involved in the building and running of the support system – and that it is not left only to the 'experts'.
- Ensure that the senior team are using and have shown adoption of the new behaviours.
- Highlight stories where people are putting new ways of working into place.
- Invite customers in to share the good news and new behaviours.
- Use blog technology to encourage people to write diaries about the change in their team.

The net result is that the focus has shifted from classroom-based training to applied learning. In many ways one might argue for the maxim 'train less – do more'.

Using the 10:20:30:40 model should give greater clarity of people's role in the development programme and how much time they need to allocate to enable a sustainable outcome. The message I hope it sends out is that organizational development is not just the responsibility of the external trainer or consultant. They are only there to help in facilitating change – real sustainable transformation is owned by the business and its managers and leaders.

After using the 10:20:30:40 model, people have indicated both its immense value in driving up the sustainable behavioural outcomes and also reducing the cost of failure. Of most interest and significance is the power and value of the 10% area – differentiating those participants who can and want to change from those who won't or can't. This continually proves to have a significant impact on the success and sustainability of the learning process. This highlights the importance of a relatively simple idea – the need to profile the participants who are attending a programme rather than following the more obvious sheep-dip process that has been so commonly used on change programmes.

Participant profile

In the 10% choose stage of the model, the key line was 'Differentiate those who can and want to change, from those who won't or can't'. This simple statement holds the key to so many change, training and development programmes. Ask any trainer or change agent and they will be able to instantly talk about programmes where members have been SENT by the manager to GET them to change and so FIX the problem. This is so often characterized under the guise of a sheep-dip programme where everyone is pulled through the same change pool with the expectation that everyone can get IT at the same time and so reduce the time taken to change and reduce the cost.

This is a terrible fallacy that has cost many organizations dearly and ruined the professional brand of so many change agents. We can't GET anyone to change – at best we can trigger an external manifestation of change that people rapidly learn to fake – and this faking begins from early school age when people are expected to conform to the socially expected norms. If you don't believe me then answer these questions for yourself. Thinking of the last three courses you attended:

- Did you want to go to them?
- For those that you wanted to attend – what was the outcome? Did you learn and then apply that learning?
- For those you where marginally interested in – what happened, both at the session and afterwards?
- For those you were not keen on – how did this lack of invitation impact on your learning and application of any knowledge?
- For those that you did not want to go to – what happened and did you (knowingly or unknowingly) disrupt the learning process in any way for others?

These are the shadow undisscusable questions that rarely get raised with clients and in most cases are never asked of the people that we wish to help change. If people do want to engage then it is important to provide a learning and change process that helps them to change in a way that works for them. For those who don't want to learn and change then we need to identify them as soon as possible in the change process and take immediate action.

A simple model that can help with this is to categorize all change participants along a simple 5P continuum:

- **Players** – those who wish to become actively involved in the change and are prepared to lead from the front.
- **Participants** – those who demonstrate involvement with a commitment to the change and want to make a difference.
- **Passengers** – those coming along for the ride who might engage if they find some value. The key thing is to have curiosity if not commitment.

- **Prisoners** – those not really interested who have been forced to attend. They may not knowingly disrupt, but will unintentionally affect the flow of the event and will probably erode value for others.
- **Protesters** – those forced to attend who will overtly use all their energy to disrupt the learning process for themselves and others.

The first step is to identify where members are on this spectrum. In a perfect world it is best to have this discussion with the client or line manager. But in reality this change is a challenge in the middle of frantic change processes – so often it is a case of dealing with people when they walk into the room and you meet them for the first time. A simple set of questions can help to identify where they are and what the impact is of that location on the model:

- Why are you here?
- What do you want to achieve?
- What have you heard about it?
- What do you plan to do at the end of it?
- Have you completed any pre-work?
- Do you see value in this investment?
- Do you feel free to leave if it is not seen to add value?
- What is your previous experience of this type of activity?

Clearly, in many cases participants in a change programme are not used to being asked if they want to be involved, but a failure to ask someone is like making the assumption that your partner will marry you, booking the wedding, paying for the cake and inviting people without checking it out with them. Pretty much a recipe for disaster – in the same way as not testing people's intent is for any change programme.

However, it may be easier to assume that your partner does want to marry you and to decide to propose on live prime-time TV – but what do you do if they say no or that they are not sure? Just how do you deal with the truth when someone says they are not engaged with the process (or in the proposal situation don't want to be engaged). I have had many different outcomes in using this approach – they range from:

- **Closure** – shut the programme down and restart when new motivations develop or new people are employed. Cleary this is a very high-risk high-impact choice but one that sends a clear signal about the seriousness of intent of both the consultant and the client.

- **Converse** – time is made to talk about people's level of intent, surface issues or concerns and deal with those before moving on.
- **Cooperate** – sometimes it is OK to agree to disagree. To accept that intent may not be there, but to work on the basis that they will give it a go. If things don't work out they may leave, or just stay to experience the programme out of interest.
- **Convert** – in one amazing case I had the most fervent protester who after three hours suddenly 'got it'. She understood that what was being proposed wasn't just a company initiative but that it would make her life so much easier. At that point she switched and became the greatest advocate for the change across the organization.
- **Challenge** – in some cases it becomes necessary to go back to the client and challenge their preconceptions and assumptions about the project, and feedback that ground-floor views indicate that the core ideas about the problem are wrong. This takes immense courage on the part of the members and the consultant – but can save immense amounts of pain, frustration and money in the long run.

As this short list of outcomes and actions shows, this can be a treacherous area that is potentially frustrating, scary, challenging and can significantly threaten the income and brand of the consultant. Choosing to use the 5P assessment model to check the validity and interests of the participants is a risk – but I would argue that the greater risk is to brush the chances of non-engagement under the carpet and to assume that all will be fine. When this happens the client, consultant and consumer all tend to suffer and so it pays to address the issue early on in the change process. If you don't want to look like an idiot in front of your friends, maybe check out if your boy-friend or girlfriend wants to get married before you pop the question!

In summary – the 'Guide' of the CHANGE model is underpinned by three simple questions.

- **Magic triangle** – is there congruence between the aims and ambitions of the participant, the training manager and the line manager.
- **10:20:30:40** – is the intervention designed to focus on sustainable long-term behavioural change rather than just knowing better now?
- **Participant profile** – have you got the right people at the right time in the right place (logically and emotionally)?

A 'yes' to these doesn't guarantee that the Guide process will work – but it does make a huge difference to the chances of success and sustainability.

Consumer segmentation

There will be occasions when resistance starts to stall the change. All consultants have war stories of the time they spent battling with a group or individual that refused to change. If this happens, it can help to segment the target audience to ensure that energy is applied in the right places. The worst thing that a client or consultant can do is to spend time and resources trying to change someone if that person does not really contribute to the end change process.

The change process can be considered along two specific lines of interest. First, the extent to which people are actively involved in the change. For a retail organization about to implement a new stock control system, it might be that certain groups of people are critical and need to be introduced to new ways of working at the outset. However, there will be other people who might need to know about the system but whose training can take place at a later date. Second, consider the level of resistance to change. This ranges from high (where there is a real blockage) down to low (where the people are quite happy to take on board the new ways of working). The different groups of people are shown in Figure 5.9.

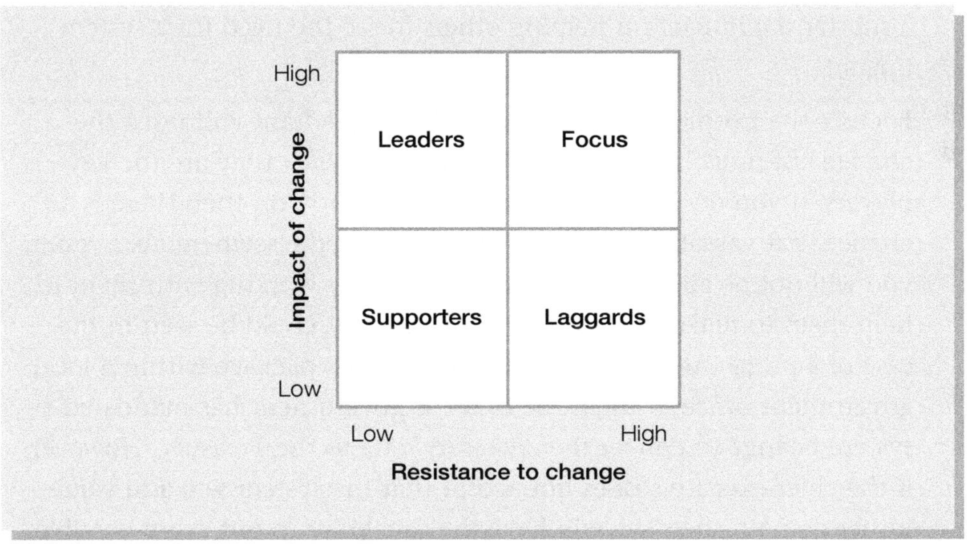

Figure 5.9 **Change segmentation matrix**

- **Leaders** – this quadrant includes those people who are viewed as the early adopters – people who will respond to the change initiative in a proactive and visible way. They have a critical role in the final change outcome and have a low resistance to change. Hooking in these people early gives a clear signal that the project is serious – people are buying into the new ways of working and the new model is socially acceptable. As an example, consider the cable TV company that has merged with another similar group and needs to relocate to a site over 100 miles away. Resistance to this shift is likely to be fierce and could lead to protracted negotiations and conflict. However, it will be useful to identify one or two people who are happy with the change and are willing to support the strategic need for relocation. Their visible support sends a positive signal so that other people will become more amenable to the change.

- **Supporters** – these are the people who have limited involvement in the change but are committed to its success. They are people who enthuse about the change but in reality it makes little difference if they decide to change or not. In the case of an IT upgrade, the small customer services team may be enthusiastic about the proposed shift to a new platform. However, the shift has actually been proposed to reduce the product delivery time. So their support is only a limited by-product of a shift elsewhere. However, if this team is committed then it makes sense to use their enthusiasm. You could use them as internal communicators, trainers or facilitators. Although their involvement might add little to the formal engagement, it might have a substantial impact on helping others to see the need for a system upgrade.
- **Focus** – the people who fall into the focus quadrant will resist the change but must be converted to ensure success – they are the key players. If you do not identify these people early on then there is a chance that valuable resources will be deployed elsewhere. As a result, you will not be able to spend time and energy working with them to help them to make the necessary change. This could be seen in the case of a project to implement a new financial package within a local government office. It might be that the government has mandated a system change to deliver the necessary data to the Treasury. However, if the chief executive does not accept that the system will add value in her domain then she will have the capability to put every possible obstacle in the way. You must put every available effort into working with the individual and her team to convince them of the benefits. Failure to shift their viewpoint will turn the project into a nightmare and might result in a loss of your future income.
- **Laggards** – these people will fiercely resist the change but have little involvement in the outcome. In many cases it is better to say, 'Fine, we will make the change in your absence and when the time is right

you can make the shift in your own way'. An example is a technical department that refuses to accept the need to attend customer skills training. While the chief executive has decreed that everyone should attend a two-day event, this group has little contact with other people. The consultant could force the situation, but the end result will be a great deal of game playing by the unit manager and a disruptive crowd of people at the change workshop. By giving them the option to adopt the new techniques at their own rate, these people are able to do so in a way that suits their needs. As a result, they might become leading exponents of the need to adopt a more customer-focused approach within their work and actively start to promote this ethos to their suppliers.

Methodology

In this context, methodology refers to the underlying ethos and approach that will be used to underpin all the decisions made and actions taken by the consulting team and client group.

In recent years, change has become a discipline in its own right. It is now recognized that it is important to pay attention to the underlying dynamics that drive successful business transformation. In particular, you must understand what choices you have when faced with change issues. Although these choices are many, two factors should be taken into consideration.

- Will the programme be planned in advance of the change? Should every detail be strapped down well in advance or can things be left to chance?
- Will receivers of the transition be aware of what is happening? Is the change to be conducted in the public domain or will it be hidden from view, so any shift is seen as happening naturally as opposed to an external change?

When considering these two drivers, it is possible to identify four schools of change management that are commonly seen in industry – accidental, backstage, controlled and debate. By looking in more detail at each of these four styles, it becomes possible to develop a simple change management matrix (see Figure 5.10). Each of the four quadrants has a particular management style that may be applied in different circumstances.

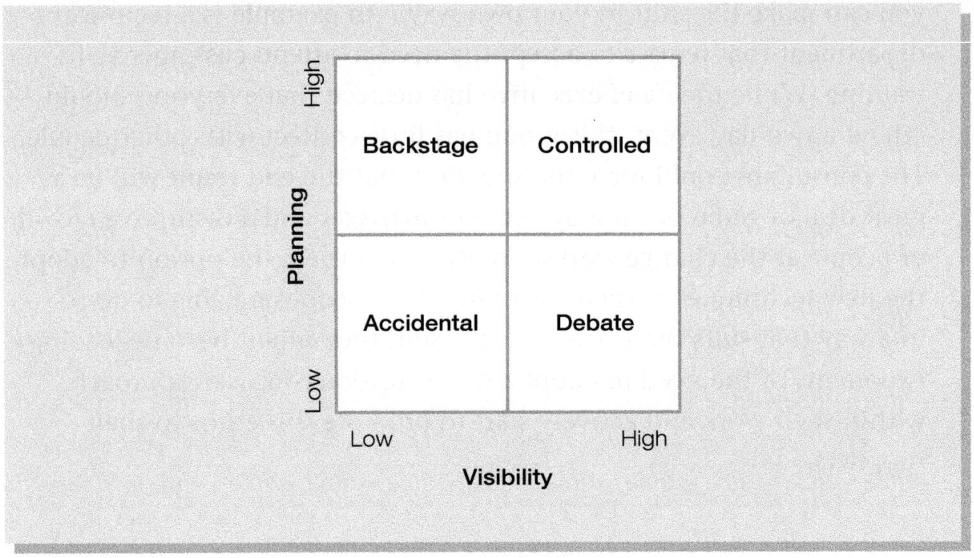

Figure 5.10 **Change management matrix**

Accidental style

When a group of young children play together, the overall behaviour of the group has a chaotic feel. An observer sees the chance of anything productive coming out of the antics as accidental in nature. It is often left to the capability of a single teacher to manage the demands, tantrums and excesses of over 200 apparently wild animals. However, within this zoo-like scenario, there are a number of powerful rules that control how the group operates.

The children are effectively operating as a self-organizing system. Although the teacher has set out ground rules, within these the children operate as free agents. Examples of these rules are keep on the hard surface, no swearing or fighting and everyone must line up for dinner at a certain time. Since the teachers are also aware of these rules, they can initiate a change and, within reason, guarantee that a desired outcome is achieved.

For example, if a football is left in the playground at the start of break then within minutes a football match will start and will keep the children amused for the duration of the break. Alternatively, just drawing some white lines will trigger specific games associated with the patterns. The children also understand that if the teacher suddenly walks out into the middle of the area and blows a whistle, they are expected to stop what they are doing and listen for instructions.

Let's assume that organizations can operate in a similar fashion by conforming to a shared set of common rules and norms. As a result, rather than trying to dominate and deliver an outcome, some consultants might choose to spend their time trying to understand the rules that drive an organization. Once understood, they can make engagements that might seem chaotic or random but which will deliver the desired outcome. The engagements are not highly planned and have little visibility – but they still have a clear purpose.

For example, a regional manager in a retail organization might have a level of stock wastage higher than the industry norm – it must be reduced to an acceptable level. Clearly one option is to issue dictates, discipline people or change the formal stock control procedures. Now this might 'apparently' work but the ingrained behaviours are likely to surface once the manager's attention is focused elsewhere. However, by using the accidental methodology, the manager might attempt to understand what rules or norms drive the wastage to happen and why it is seen to be acceptable by local managers. It might be that, at the store level, wastage costs are attributed to a hidden budget line, visible only to the regional manager and the finance department. This rule means that the operational managers are not actually affected by the wastage, so it is not part of their frame of reference. By simply changing the bonus indicators, for example, the regional manager might be able to deliver a radical reduction in wastage. The change will have been managed without any real control or planning and its visibility would have been limited, but the end result is a successful change.

This is clearly a high-risk strategy and is reliant on the trust of the organization to adopt any changes that are promoted by the management team. The consultant's role in this management style is more about helping to develop a suitable environment for the change to occur rather than formalizing any direct approach.

Backstage style

Millions of people watched the movie *Titanic*. The boat scenes are amazing, to the point where the audience believes they are actually part of the production. Although star actors play a critical frontstage role, it is often the backstage people that can make or break such a film. Compare the technical prowess of *Titanic* with the out-takes shown on television – doors won't open, walls fall over and props fail to perform. Taking these two scenarios together, the power of the backstage processes is apparent.

“the key to managing any backstage process is preparation, preparation and more preparation”

The key to managing any backstage process is preparation, preparation and more preparation. Just to generate a simple scene in a film will take hours of pre-production effort. This process is invisible to the audience – they just see a two-second jump off a cliff. In the same way, some change programmes are stage-managed by consultants. The installation of a new IT system, the shift to a new quality directive or the adoption of a new legal ruling will all be highly managed and planned but will in the main be invisible to the end user until the point of handover.

The change process is often concerned with the exercise of power, persuasion and political skills. It involves intervening in political and cultural systems, influencing, negotiating and selling ideas and meaning to the owners and recipients of the change and mobilizing the necessary power to effect the backstage activity (Buchanan and Body, 1992).

Imagine that you are to install a new quality system into a medium-sized manufacturing company. You might choose to operate across a number of backstage areas. The first step is to agree the content of the system with the directors of the company, since the structure of any quality system will potentially lock in a set of standards and processes. Next, you might need to undertake a degree of negotiation with all the key stakeholders to ensure that the content of the system fits with their map of the world. Firstly, much of the backstage work will be focused on managing people’s feelings. The quality system is right for the business, but if people ‘feel’ upset or concerned about its adoption then the whole change process will be fraught with problems. So although there will be effort applied in developing the new system, a large chunk of the work will be focused on the backstage issues – the unseen aspects that will never be apparent to the end user.

The backstage model is one that people use intuitively every day. Persuading a child to eat their cabbage, hiding a pill in the dog’s food or flirting with the boss’s PA so as to get some time in the diary. The question to consider is the extent to which such stage management is undertaken as a manipulative tool for personal gain. When it is overtly used, you must be careful that you are not seen as using the process in a duplicitous way just to further your personal goals. Working with a client group always involves a degree of suspicion about your actions. When this model is used it is therefore imperative that it is used openly and without any hidden agendas. This does not mean that you tell everyone what is happening, but that if people ask about the process being used then you take time to explain it.

Controlled style

This type of change is like the processes used to manage a large construction project such as the Channel Tunnel. The scale and risk of such projects mean that everything down to the last nut and bolt must be forecast and controlled to ensure that the change is managed to time, cost and quality.

The control model is based on a deterministic framework. The consultant makes the assumption that it is possible to predict and control the future according to a set of rules. Plans are made, resources booked and people hired, all on the premise that the change will follow a known path. The change is then managed using the exception method, where the goal is to minimize any variance or disturbance in the system. Accidents will be frowned on, deviation is not allowed and failure to hit a milestone will cause apoplexy.

Where the surrounding issues are managed by the consultant or client then this approach is clearly effective. However, where you or the client do not control all the levers then it is quite dangerous. Building a rigid plan and locking people into a controlled system puts all the eggs definitely in one basket and sudden changes in the environment can result in costly and time-consuming last-minute actions.

This methodology is perfect for the delivery of fixed outcomes, particularly where the plan is built using logical cause and effect reasoning. This is why it is used so frequently in the construction of missiles, houses and a host of other projects. However, its success is dependent on your ability to control all the environmental factors.

Debate style

Think about the case of a merger between two large organizations. Project managers, probably using the control methodology outlined above, will wrap up all the mechanistic issues. However, there will be elements of the merger that cannot be managed using a highly planned style. In particular, how will the two cultures come together?

When you try to merge cultures, the desired outcome is reasonably clear but it is very difficult to plan down to the last detail what will happen and when. People are people and have their biases, preferences and particular styles of thinking and behaving. Any action plan will have some critical milestones or tasks, but there is still likely to be much debate as people struggle to come to terms with new ways of working. Only through a process of sharing and working together will people start to understand what value their new partners will be able to contribute.

The debate style of change is seen in many areas. Think about the traditional way that a senior team will develop vision and values. It often falls to a consultant to organize a workshop. This will be preceded by a meeting with each of the directors to develop an understanding of their beliefs about company values. This initiates the debate process, in which each person is encouraged to talk about their views on what the company values should be and offers people the necessary time and space to share their schematic view of the world. As they talk to the consultant, people start to firm up their beliefs so that once they get to the workshop they will have a clearer view of their desired outcome. At the workshop, these personal schemas are displayed, shared and (if all goes well) will merge to become a shared schema – one that is communicated to a wider audience.

Another example is the way that strategy can slowly develop within an organization. One view is that the control approach should be used, where logical processes are used to build a corporate strategy. Another view is that strategy emerges from dialogue and debate that goes on between the key players in the business. This might happen in formal meetings, but in many cases it is the odd comment as people meet in corridors or coffee rooms.

The debate model happens all the time but is often not recognized. As a process it is difficult to recognize because it is so natural and embedded in the content of the change. Trying to understand how a decision was made, or a mission or strategy developed can be quite painful – people struggle to understand how the change took place. However, the benefit is that when this style of change is used, it is locked in at the desire level in the change ladder. Therefore, the change will have a greater degree of passion and permanence.

Four-quadrant model

Bringing these change styles together results in the four-quadrant model seen in Figure 5.10. In this simple matrix each quadrant represents one style – accidental, backstage, control or debate. This suggests that in many cases you might have to make a decision to use one particular style. Should the change be controlled or is it best to take the accidental route? Should the development of the outcome be through open debate or is it more appropriate to push the discussion into the backstage and develop answers that people are mandated to follow?

However, it is possible to offer a holistic framework – a hybrid model that builds on the strengths of each of the four quadrants and yet tries to avoid their weaknesses. By drawing on each of the four quadrants it becomes possible to develop another option, that of the emergent style – a fifth way that sits in the middle of the matrix (see Figure 5.11).

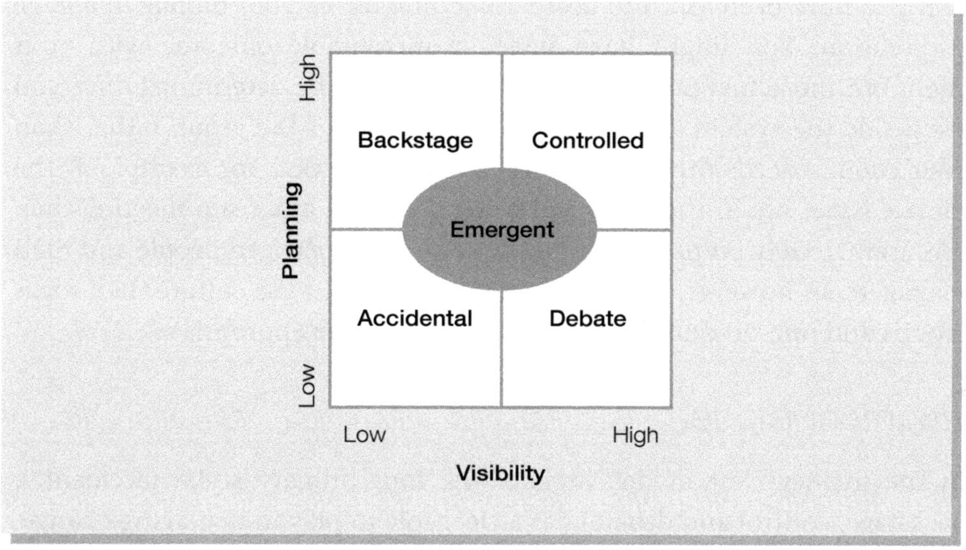

Figure 5.11 Emergent change

Emergent style

If a group of people decide to travel around the world on a backpacking holiday, which of the four styles would be appropriate? The accidental approach is exciting but could leave the group sitting as hostages in a war zone. The backstage model would be ineffective because only the travel agent would know the itinerary. The control model seems to be the most practical, but using a deterministic approach in a chaotic world will only lead to frustration and cost increases as the group struggles to get back in line with 'the plan'. Finally, the debate model is inappropriate because the group might have fun discussing where to go next but the trip will probably take three years longer than expected. The solution is to adopt a change process that allows for clearly defined outcomes but with the flexibility to be adaptive.

The emergent model allows an agreed outcome to be delivered through people interacting according to their own sets of behaviour. It creates a framework for action without specifying the action to be taken. As consultant, you will set the goals, boundaries and basic operating rules but leave the action and detail up to those directly involved in the engagement. The benefit is the development of a flexible plan that allows people to respond to changes.

This type of approach is often seen in culture development programmes where the end goal may be understood but the deployment process needs to be flexible enough to cope with the needs of different managers. Imagine that you have been asked to deal with a problem of poor morale in a large corporation. You might have agreed a measurable outcome with your client but the actual processes and tools can only be determined once you are inside the system. This is because the needs of the group rather than your client's needs drive the choice of a change tool. For example, if the morale issues are in the open and being discussed at a team meeting then it is useful to rely on peer review and open events between people and their managers. If, however, the issues are buried deep in the culture then focus groups and one-on-one coaching sessions are more appropriate.

Five-segment model

In the five-segment model, each of the four primary styles (accidental, backstage, control and debate) has a clear role to play in managing change. However, when change is being managed according to one of the four primary styles, any deviation from the preferred approach is viewed as a failure. Hence, the person running a project using the control model might view deviation and variability as a problem. Similarly, someone using the accidental style might forcibly resist any attempt by the organization to impose formal controls or milestones on the engagement.

The emergent school of change is something that people use all the time, but not always knowingly. For example, it is used in a manager's diary system. A manager's life is often in tension between planned and unplanned events. It is a battle between order and disorder, seen in the deletions and changes to most people's diaries. However, it is the practised ability to manage unplanned and emergent interactions that allows a manager to respond to changes in the marketplace. Once the boundaries are set and simple rules are understood then it is possible to create a balance between accidental and controlled change.

Although this model segments your approach into five different methodologies, clearly it is never so simplistic. Any change methodology must be focused entirely on the needs of the client and the context, so each change process is unique. However, what this model does highlight is that there are alternatives to the more typical command and control approach to managing change.

Usually the change process will employ all the options at different times. Imagine you have been asked to lead a project team to develop a new Christmas toy. You have only nine months left to design, develop and deliver the toy to the shops. With such a tight deadline, and with the fact that the environment is under your control, you may well opt to take a control approach – clearly setting out the goals, milestones and delivery dates for each of the project teams. However, you should also recognize that this is a creative process as well as a delivery process and as such it would be unwise to constrain people's freedom to innovate and make mistakes. Therefore, you may also try to ensure that the lower-level change processes have a degree of freedom and space so that people can experiment within the teams. A map of the change style used for different elements within the project might look like the list set out in Table 5.2.

> **“the decision to adopt a particular change style is not black and white”**

The decision to adopt a particular change style is not black and white and in many cases might not actually be a decision that has to be made. In some cases, it is best to let things happen naturally and simply be aware of the choice that is made if things start to go wrong.

Table 5.2 **Change styles within a project**

Project activity	*Change style*
Project plan	Control – this is necessary because of the fixed delivery date and the ability to manage the close environment
Review meetings	Debate – this allows the necessary flexibility to find out how the project is progressing, but with space for some shadow issues to surface
Design meetings	Accidental – the need to offer the designers space to innovate is paramount at this stage
Customer focus groups	Accidental – the primary goal is to understand the customers' expectations and to give them the space to talk and describe their feelings
Pilot trials	Control – since feedback from this stage will affect the launch decision, the marketing data must be very accurate and controlled
Measurement process	Backstage – since the primary focus should be on delivery of the product, the goal is to keep any project measurement procedures to a minimum: they will only operate in the background, using exception reports where issues surface

Energy mapping

By definition, change is about modifying the status quo – managing a shift from one state to another. This transfer requires energy. It might be the energy required to climb on the exercise bike; that burst of energy to read the latest management book; the physical and emotional energy required to run yet another quality workshop. Alternatively, it is the energy required to stop something or someone from taking action when they want to be a change inhibitor. Just think how often you work with an organization where people spend more time stopping action from happening rather than making a change work. In a change process you need to have a clear appreciation of where energy will come from and how it might affect the change. Carter (1999) makes this point when he suggests that:

The energy that people put into organizations is absorbed in a number of ways. Some of it is used for actually doing things for the customer, such as adding value to a product or service, but little of it is directly productive in this way. Much of it is spent communicating with other people within the organization, co-ordinating activities, planning, motivating, managing, being managed.

To understand how this energy can affect a change, you might map three aspects:

- the source;
- the mass;
- the direction.

You can then set out a strategy to harness the energy and use it to support the change. Or you might develop counteracting energies that will help to overcome any resisting forces.

Energy source

This is how and where energy is dissipated across an organization. Simplistically, power is bestowed as part of the formal governance system (in reality power germinates and accumulates in a range of areas within any system as a result of energy used). When you are dealing with an organization, you must determine where the power lies. Then you must use this knowledge to determine what strategy will be appropriate in influencing how the energy is directed and applied.

Consider a touring group performing Shakespeare. If you look closely it would be possible to deconstruct the energy within the group – to identify who owns and dispenses different types of energy, and so power. One of the group might manage the finances, another the interactions with the various theatre managers, yet another might act as the group's soul with the energy to ensure that effective relationships are maintained within the group. It is possible to map the various energy levels and, more importantly, how the energy is deployed within the group.

The same idea can be applied to organizational change. Looking around any organization, it is possible to see where the various streams of energy sit. Some of the possible groups are described below.

- **Financial** – in many organizations you only have to walk through the door to realize that the financial controllers have their hands on the tiller. Evidence is in the construction of the tender documents, the people that have to sign-off your contract or the extent to which financial prudence dictates the building decoration.
- **Operational** – in some types of business the operations managers are seen as the gods. In organizations where production lines are key to the business they will dictate what changes are acceptable and how programmes should be implemented.
- **Professional** – in some companies the professional groups hold control over the key decision-making processes. For example lawyers, IT specialists or marketing groups often feel that they are above change programmes and do not need to be involved.
- **Interest groups** – sometimes the power actually exists outside the organization. In the UK, for example, government regulatory bodies hold sway over the regulated industries. In other countries lobby groups have amassed power over the petroleum industry.
- **Customer-facing groups** – in professional service firms there is often an absolute focus on the customer experience. For example in large consulting or accounting firms the core driver for all resource allocation and decision making takes place on the yield figure, so the billable time booked to the customer is key. Since any change programme will take people away from this billing activity, you will have to justify the true business value of any change.

These groups may not be the absolute sources of energy within an organization, but they do highlight how energy can surface in different shapes and forms. Your role is to build an ability to sniff out where the sources of power originate when developing the change implementation programme. However, simply understanding where the power resides is not enough.

You also need to determine the extent of the power under each group's control.

Energy mass

The mass of a body in terms of the physical world is related to its weight, which is measured in terms of its inertia or resistance to acceleration. This mass is actually nothing more than a bundle of energy – even when an object is at rest it has energy stored in its mass. Within an organization, it is possible to consider the energy sources in terms of their ability to release energy.

In any organization, different functions will have differing energy levels. So for one company it might be that the finance department has a significant mass of energy and is able to exert a great deal of influence over the business. In another business it might be that the IT group has a significant energy level but its true ability to exert a force over the company is limited because the real energy is held by the customer-facing teams. To understand the energy mass within a system, it can help to calibrate it against a set of levels.

- **Dense** – absolute power and energy to drive or resist change within a business.
- **Medium** – some energy to effect a control over the change process but is subservient to the dense groups.
- **Light** – limited energy to effect change and will always lose out to the medium and dense groups.

Thus the IT department with a light mass level will not be able to force through an idea in opposition to a finance department that has a medium or dense mass. Although many groups with a light mass level do attempt to take on the stronger opponent, the reality is that unless they are adept political animals they will waste their time and energy in a fruitless battle.

Trying to find a way to map these energy levels accurately can be difficult. One way is to look at the profiles that the groups promote within the organization. Who is featured in the internal house magazines? Which people sit on the financial approval committees? Who has the ear of the managing director? Finally, and most important, whose budgets are cut first every time there is a reduction in expenditure? Across most industries, training is the first budget to be reduced when a downturn comes – this is indicative of the limited mass that the personnel function is seen to have.

This approach to mapping energy mass does not offer a definitive answer but it might help to point you in the right direction. The other approach is to follow the money – in the majority of cases the dominant group will have a significant amount of influence over the way that cash is received and distributed.

Energy direction

The final issue to consider when mapping the energy sources within an organization is their direction. Imagine a company facing a crisis. Sales are falling, costs are rising and the market does not look rosy. In the midst of this, the marketing director suggests that part of the problem is the fact that the espoused brand values are not being lived by the customer-facing teams. So while the company sells its products on the basis of 'a quality product with a quality service', the service end is not being delivered. There are reports from customers of rudeness and inefficiency, and the marketing director believes this is causing sales to fall. The marketing director therefore proposes that the company embarks on an organization-wide 'living what we value' programme, where everyone goes through an intensive series of workshop and coaching sessions. Clearly, in such a difficult time, this individual might find it difficult to introduce a change programme that will temporarily raise costs. The key point will be what energy other directors have in resisting his proposal, and in particular where the energy is directed. If the finance director has sufficient mass, and chooses to focus it in the marketing director's direction, then the change programme might well be blocked. However, it might be that the finance director has the mass to stop the proposition but chooses to focus energy on the engineering functions in the belief that their costs are the cause of the problems. If this is the case, then the marketing director can use this space to push the change programme through.

So when trying to understand how any one person or group is targeting their energy, it is possible to allocate it to one of three categories.

- **Driver** – a positive force that is supportive of the change.
- **Doubtful** – an in-between force – not quite a supporter but not quite willing to resist any change process.
- **Driven** – an energy source opposed to the ideas put forward by the consultant – so has to be pushed to take every action.

Allocating a person or group to one of these categories is bound to be at worst a guess and at best open to contradiction, but it does have some useful benefits. The first is that it offers a benchmark against which other stakeholders can be calibrated. Although as an absolute measure it is inaccurate, at a relational level it is possible to build an accurate picture of your supporters and opponents. Second, it offers a dialogue tool that helps to clarify the views of different individuals. Often when people come together to effect a change, each will have different experiences of the various power brokers and independent views of their orientation towards the project. Bringing these views together into a single picture helps to create consistency within the project team.

Energy map

By now you should have assessed where the energy is contained within the organization. This will indicate both the energy level and where this force is directed. Now you can construct a map, to bring this knowledge into a single view.

Imagine a company is being pressured into adopting an environmental quality programme. Figure 5.12 shows how an outside pressure group is threatening to take the company to court if it does not implement a new environmental directive. The legal department realizes that the company

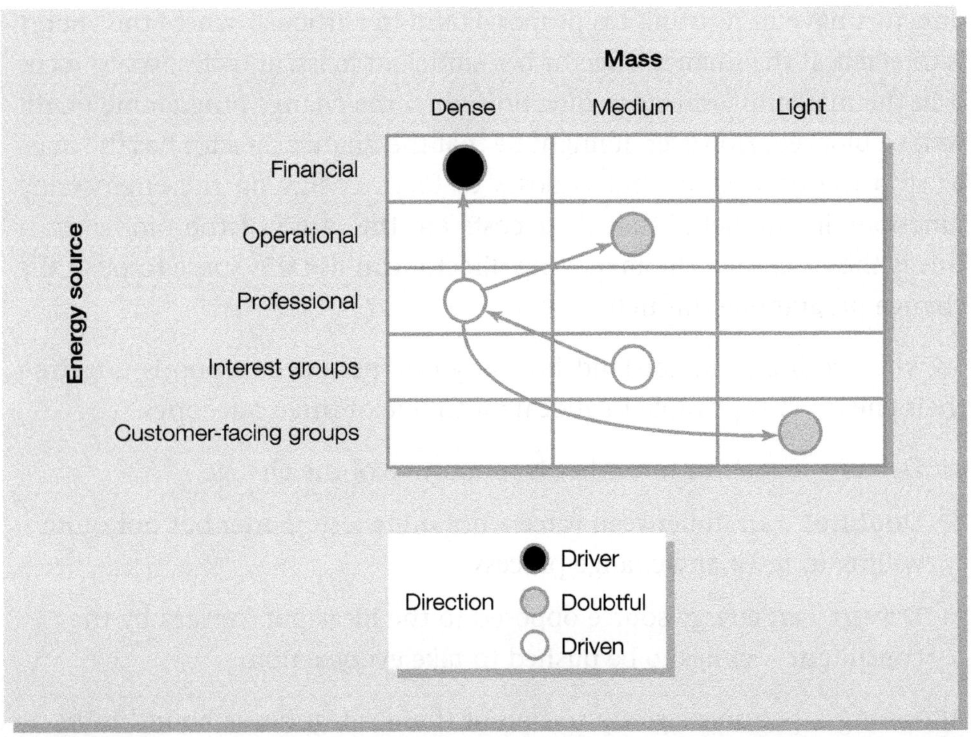

Figure 5.12 **Energy map**

must take urgent action, but also that the work will incur significant cost and disruption. The net result is that the legal department is applying pressure to three key organizational groups – the finance department, the operations managers and the customer-facing groups. The legal department has sufficient mass within the business to drive the latter two groups to change without much resistance. However, when dealing with the finance team it is tackling a group that has more mass and so will have a problem in trying to effect a change. The map indicates that in trying to take on the finance team, the professional unit is unlikely to succeed. However, if it uses the additional energy contained within the operations and customer-facing groups, the combined force might well offer sufficient power to effect a change.

This approach is not about accurately calculating the energy within any group in relation to another group. But it should be possible to assess such detail intuitively and use the knowledge to ensure that blockage does not occur.

6 Project Management Definitions

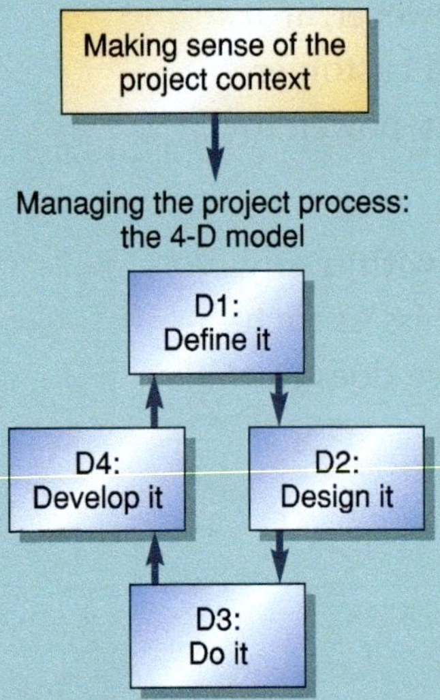

'Life is one big project.' The trick is in managing it.

Principles

1. What is and is not a project needs to be defined so that we know whether the practices known as 'project management' (PM) are relevant.
2. Project management has a fundamental role in modern organisations and the careers of the people working in them.
3. The past 50 years of PM development should be understood to help understand the current state and the opportunities for the future.

Learning objectives

By the time you have completed this chapter, you should be able to:

→ identify the definitions of a project and the task of management within a range of projects

→ demonstrate the importance of successful project management to individuals, organisations and economies

→ recognise the development of the modern subject along with some of the challenges and limitations.

Contents

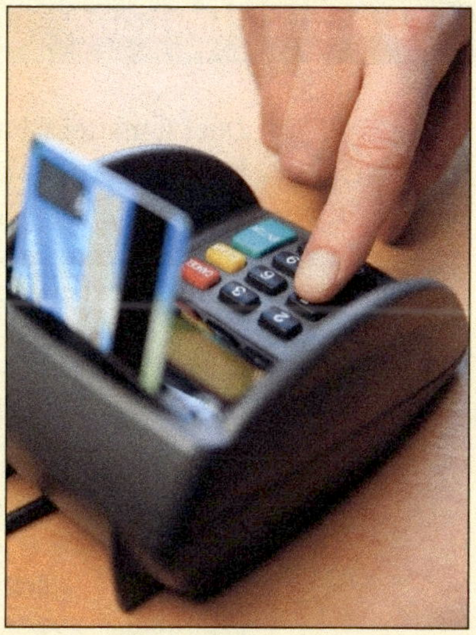
Source: Andrew Howe/iStockphoto

Chip and PIN day – 14 February 2006 – could have been a disaster of monumental proportions. To have up and running a new system, that would issue 138 million cards and security numbers, convert outlets that handle credit cards to use the new technology and have operational a system that will handle in excess of 150 transactions every second, was no small feat. Oh, and customers needed to be informed that this was happening and that they would need to remember their PINs. It was vital that the process of continuing to do business had minimal interruptions from the new system.

Twelve months on, the feared meltdown of the technology, and rejection by the customers and the staff who have to work with it, hasn't materialised. Instead, in the UK 99.8 per cent of all card transactions are now PIN verified, retailers report that it has speeded up transactions and it saved the banking industry £60 million in one year in fraud from lost or stolen cards. While there are still concerns about the security of the systems, the project has largely delivered the promised benefits. Interesting to see how much media coverage this success has achieved relative to some of the more notorious failures.

Introduction

The introduction of Chip and PIN technology is a good example of a highly successful project. With the press fascinated by a plentiful supply of project failure stories, it would be tempting to believe that all projects fail. This is certainly not the case – many projects (though certainly not all) do succeed in delivering what they promised. The Chip and PIN introduction project illustrates some of the features that we will see as being applicable to a wide range of other projects. It had a fixed duration – it had to deliver by 14 February 2006. It involved an array of interlinking activities – the technology development, the roll-out to stores, the IT systems to back it up, the issuing of cards, the training of staff and the gaining of support from card users. It had definable benefits – what the card issuers and retailers wanted to achieve from the change which provided a business case for the implementation. There were also considerable consequences of failure – it was important for all the organisations involved.

We will explore success and failure and some of the reasons for each in future chapters. For now, Chip and PIN is a good example of the art and science of managing a project and the importance of projects in general to the world in which we live.

In this chapter, we will begin with **definition**, stating what constitutes a project and its management. This is vital as it is possible, quite literally, to frame almost any activity as a project – indeed we can go as far as to say that the opening quotation of 'Life is one big project' does fit many of the accepted definitions. The challenge is more aptly stated as 'finding what is not a project' so that it is possible to discuss with some clarity the range of human activity that this covers. In the case of Chip and PIN, there were clearly many issues that required the coordination that the management role provides. We will explore the role of a project manager in outline here and the careers of project managers. Second, projects are important. They represent a significant part of all economic activity, being important to the individuals who carry them out, their organisations and, in many cases, society as a whole.

6.1 Basic definitions

Does it matter what activities do and do not constitute **projects**? Almost any activity can be claimed to be a project. One practitioner put it very simply: '***a project is whatever I call a project***'. One step on from this is the most basic of accepted definitions: ***a project is a task that has a beginning and an end.*** This is insufficient, as the two examples below will demonstrate.

> **Environmental health manager**
>
> The role of the environmental health department in a local authority (a county council in this case) includes visiting food premises (restaurants, cafés, school canteens and mobile catering outlets) to determine whether the practices that they are following in the preparation, storage and serving of food meet legal requirements. Inspectors have considerable powers (including closure of the premises) where deficiencies are identified. The manager of the department was convinced that he was a project manager. Each inspection lasted for several hours and was, therefore, an activity with a start and a finish. QED in his view it was a project.

> **Integrated Project Team (IPT) leader – UK Ministry of Defence – ship procurement**
>
> The prime role of the IPT leader is the management of the process from initial concept or identification of a requirement for a new capability, through the stages of approval, development, delivery into service, ongoing maintenance and finally disposal. The role is central to integrating the requirements (both current and future) of users, while making sure any equipment is compatible with other technology being used across the military. The provision of what is termed *through-life support* is vital, with upgrade paths being required for all equipment. The duration of the project was that of the ship. In the words of one IPT leader: '. . . end to end, this is a 60-year project.'

Both an inspection and the ship's life have a beginning and an end. However, it is not useful to define either of these as projects. Consider the requirements for managing each of these tasks. The first is relatively straightforward and would not require the input from the kind of approaches that will be discussed as 'project management' – they would simply be too cumbersome and costly for such a task. The process that was followed each time (arrange visit, visit, report and follow up) was the same and each inspector was visiting one or two premises a day. This was **operations** rather than project **management**.

It was, however, only one part of that manager's role. Other parts included planning and executing the response to public health issues, such as an outbreak of a particular disease (e-coli poisoning, for example). These were fortunately rare events and each one had its own characteristics. They also had to be preplanned, so that no time was wasted when they did occur. Other projects included regular initiatives to highlight particular aspects of public health – such as an autumn campaign of promoting influenza vaccination. The role of this manager was therefore split between the **general management** associated with the ongoing activities and the project management of both initiatives and reactions to 'crises'. He was advised to look to operations management as a subject to help with the management of the day-to-day tasks, but to build a relevant knowledge base and set of practices for the projects he ran.

The second case is a hugely complex task that will change significantly in nature over the 60-year period. Each part (e.g. designing the ship, building it, trials, hand-over, maintenance, refurbishing and disposal) is a project or series of projects in its own right, with each project needing appropriate management. This task is clearly very different from that of the inspections.

It clearly does matter what we call projects, as when they have to be managed, it is useful to know something about the approach that should be taken to the management task. To help clarify this task, the following definitions are useful:

> Association for Project Management (UK's largest professional body for project managers), 2004: ***Projects are unique, transient endeavours undertaken to achieve a desired outcome.***
>
> Project Management Institute (world's largest professional association), 2004: ***A project is a temporary endeavour undertaken to create a unique product, service or result.***
>
> British Standard 6079, 2000: ***A unique set of coordinated activities, with definite starting and finishing points, undertaken by an individual or organisation to meet specific performance objectives within defined schedule, cost and performance parameters.***
>
> PRINCE 2 2009 (PRojects IN Controlled Environments – UK government standard for project management), ***A management environment that is created for the purpose of delivering one or more business products according to a specified business case.*** And: ***A temporary organisation that is needed to produce a unique and predefined outcome or result at a given time using predetermined resources.***
>
> Project Management Association of Japan, 2005: ***A project refers to a value creation undertaking based on a specific mission, which is completed in a given or agreed timeframe and under constraints, including resources and external circumstances.***

Some common themes are evident here:

1 **Unique**: the exact project has not been performed before. The project has a degree of novelty, in terms of time, place, team carrying out the task, product or service being provided. However, something like it has almost certainly been done by someone somewhere before. For this reason, projects are said to have *aspects of uniqueness*.[1]
2 **Temporary**: the project does have a beginning and an end, as for our earlier definition, and requires a group of people to carry out the task (the establishment of a temporary organisation). When the project finishes, the team moves on. The financial resources available to the project are also temporary and almost always finite – when the project is completed the funding ceases.
3 **Focused**: the task of the project is to deliver a particular product, service or result (the specific mission). This is not to say that every project starts out with a complete and clear idea of exactly what will be achieved and how.

PRINCE 2 2009 projects require the production of a specific **business case**. While this is evident in many organisations (and required for UK government-funded information technology (IT) projects), there are still many areas where this is not appropriate. For instance, when a tsunami struck Asia at the end of 2004, the task of bringing aid to those regions devastated by the event fell to many non-governmental agencies which planned and executed life-saving projects in the weeks and months following the devastation. In each case, there was not the time to prepare a business case and indeed, given that there was no return envisaged, it is inappropriate to use this term, and the more generic notion of achieving a particular **mission** is more useful. It is useful to look further than this, with the mission being a means to an end. We say that projects are undertaken to **deliver benefits**. This characteristic is evident in both commercial and non-commercial projects.

In the relief projects undertaken after the tsunami, relief workers often said, 'We didn't know what we would encounter until we got there.' While this is an extreme example, it illustrates a further characteristic of projects – that of **emergence**. The high-level benefits that the projects were undertaking were known (save lives), but the exact objectives and means to achieve them could be determined only once a certain amount of work had been done. These included assessments of the needs of different groups of people (for instance, some needed life-saving medical treatment, some had no access to clean drinking water, others needed shelter). BS 6079 does not recognise this emergence (*A unique set of coordinated activities, with definite starting and finishing points, undertaken by an individual or organisation to meet specific performance objectives within defined schedule, cost and performance parameters)* and many projects would fail this definition test. It is not clear what they would then be called or what would be an appropriate toolset to manage them. It is a fact that many projects start with a limited or high-level view of what will constitute their performance measures and it is quite normal for such criteria to evolve as the project progresses.

Related to this characteristic, **uncertainty** is another fundamental of projects. The future cannot be predicted with certainty, and in many cases nor can the response to activities carried out in a project. Where emergence referred to the requirements of the project, uncertainty covers all of the environmental conditions in which a project has to operate. For instance, there may be uncertainty about costs of people or materials, or whether some part of the project is indeed achievable. We may not know how long tasks being undertaken for the first time will take. All of these provide the project manager with a major challenge: how they work with such uncertainty.

In addition to having uncertainty, projects have another characteristic – they usually involve **change**. It used to be the case that an IT project such as Chip and PIN would be viewed as a technical implementation of a new computer-based system. It is more usual now to consider it as an *IT-enabled change* project – the change brought about by any new system goes beyond the technology, to impact the way that people work.[2]

The change issue leads us to another facet of projects – they are not machines but are groups of people carrying out a (hopefully linked) set of tasks. We say that unlike a machine that is real and tangible, a project is a **social construction** – it was literally devised by people. It involves people and systems of people, both in the project team and associated with the project as customers, for instance. A project is intangible. This has implications for the way that we consider projects.[3] For instance, treating a project as a mechanical system that responds easily to changes may be inappropriate. Because there are people and groups of people involved, there are going to be complex, dynamic interactions between those people.

It is not just people though that interact through a project. A characteristic of Chip and PIN was that it required all of the parts of the project to be **integrated**. It would not have been sufficient to deliver a brilliant technological solution here, without the training of shop staff or the widespread media coverage to alert customers to the change. Similarly, in order for the project to work, the project manager needed to integrate the organisations and people with the necessary knowledge in a structure that would provide both resources and control of the overall task.

The characteristics and their implications are shown in Figure 6.1. They either describe the nature of the task (aspects of uniqueness, mission focused, involving change, having emergence and uncertainty) or the means by which it is delivered (through a temporary organisation, which is a social construction involving integration). Further exploration of the means for delivery shows that this is rarely entirely random (though there are exceptions) and that project managers use combinations or systems of activities, people and organisations to deliver the project. Such a system of delivery is termed a **process**. The process is the main unit of analysis here.

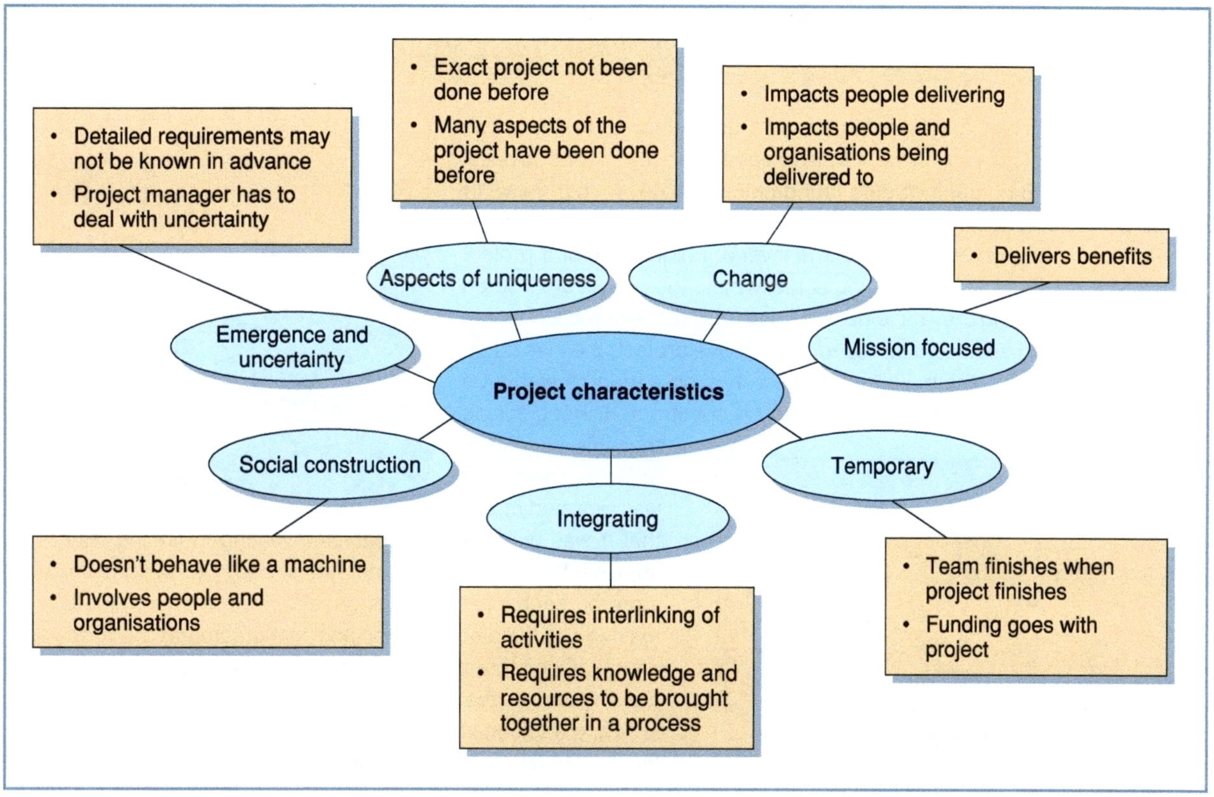

Figure 6.1 Project characteristics

Organising to deliver a project as a process

The characteristics described above are useful to determine what is and is not a project. Further description of a project comes from analysing the system of delivery, including consideration of how activities in the project were identified, planned and executed, and how issues such as change and uncertainty were handled by the project team.

There are significant advantages to considering projects in this way (see Real World box).

A basic classification of processes considers **volume** and **variety**.[4] The volume is the quantity of throughput for that process. For a petrochemical plant, this is very high, whereas for a chauffeur service, it is low. The variety is the number of different variations of process possible. For instance, a petrochemical process is likely to have relatively little flexibility, while for a small operation such as the chauffeur service, the process will have far more flexibility to respond to the needs of individual passengers.

The relationship between volume and variety is shown in Figure 6.2. As you can see, there is generally an inverse relationship between volume and variety. For example, a noodle bar is a good example of a high-volume, low-variety business – it provides a high volume of products with very little variety in the process. A management consultant, meanwhile, operates at the other end of the scale, providing a low volume of services, carried out according to the needs of each client, and is therefore a high-variety process.

The traditional project management area is low-volume, high-variety processes, where the notion of *uniqueness* prevails. These are indicated on the figure as **first-timers**. Examples of these are the first moon landing and the development of the first computer. It is noticeable with the wider adoption of project management that individuals and organisations are running projects, often over time periods as short as a few weeks or months, and that these are being carried out on a regular basis as part of ordinary

REAL WORLD Benefits of the application of process thinking

Source: Mark Richardson/Alamy

It is now possible to build a McDonald's drive-through restaurant in just 24 hours. One project went from 'clear site' to 'open for business' in less than 48 hours, including foundations. Whatever your views of the proliferation of these outlets, they do represent a good case of what can be achieved when the true level of uniqueness of a project is assessed. The contractors who actually build the outlets are Yorkon and Britspace, and they have done so over 300 times in the UK alone. If each one had been considered to be a unique project, then we could reasonably expect the build time to be very long – months would be completely normal for such a space to be constructed. Recognising that this was likely to be a project that was repeated meant that it was worth the companies investing in finding ways to improve the *process*. So, instead of trying to build a unique store on each site, the firms considered the opportunities for making the building *modular* and *manufacturing* the modules off site. One store typically consists of six modules and these are shipped to the site and 'assembled' on site, rather than involving traditional building techniques. Each time it was done, the processes for carrying this out could be improved.

Source: Alex Segre/Alamy

business activity. Here, the end product may be different, but the process by which it is delivered is often repeated over time. Two further scenarios are identified here. The first is where there is some similarity to previous work, in terms of either the process followed or the product being delivered. These are referred to in Figure 6.2 as '**as . . . but . . .**'s, that is, *as* the job we did last time, *but* with the following differences. The second of these is where there is a high degree of commonality in both process and outcome. These are termed **painting by numbers** projects[5] because the process and the outcome are well known. The project team has the task of following the path to the required outcome. Projects such as carrying out a financial audit of a company will be project-based, but the processes and the outcomes (a set of reports and accounts) are well known in advance. Marketing research projects are similarly painting by numbers projects in many instances and the construction of the drive-through also fits in this category.[6]

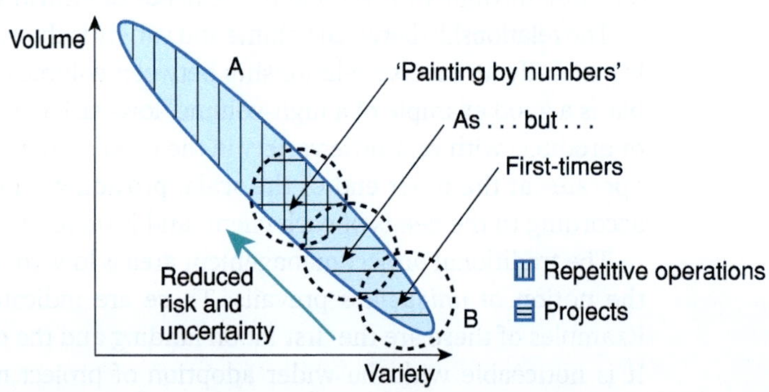

Figure 6.2 Volume versus variety and projects

Moving away from considering projects as first-timers can be beneficial. The more like repetitive operations a project is, the less the risk and uncertainty. It is a considerable challenge for many project managers to take this in, as projects that are definitely first-timers are allowed to have the allure of the more complex, difficult or risky, and therefore their skills as project managers need to be appreciated. From the point of view of most organisations, however, they are more likely to prefer the relative reliability that can come from projects that are 'painting by numbers'.

The two example projects used earlier in this section are classified as shown in Figure 6.2. The environmental health 'projects' are at the point marked 'A' on the diagram, in the region where the primary area of interest is in *repetitive operations* rather than projects. The 60-year product lifecycle 'project' is marked at point B, similarly outside the *projects* area.

For the purpose of this book, a project is from one of the three of the categories of projects from Figure 6.2.[7]

6.2 Importance of successful project management to an organisation and to you

For many organisations, projects are fundamental to the way they operate. Engineering group Siemens, for instance, estimated that 50 per cent of its revenue was from projects.[8] The major management consultancies earn over 90 per cent of their revenues from projects. The global data solutions firm HP Enterprise Services (EMEA) estimates that 60 per cent of its revenues are from projects. Whole sectors of industry are **project-based organisations** (PBOs), including much of the engineering and construction sectors, many public-sector bodies and much of the IT industry. Construction alone makes up in the region of 8 per cent of gross domestic product in the European Union. Government, from local up to European Union level, carries out a significant proportion of its business through projects. Projects are central to our economies. So, just how important are they to an organisation? The Real World box on page 188 demonstrates the extent of the impact of project performance to one organisation.

Projects and you – from accidental to professional PM

Who are these 'project managers'? There is one group which has the title – these are relatively easy to identify. Others examples are not so obvious. Organising a festival or a sporting event is a project (Glastonbury in the UK, Oktoberfest in Germany, Tour de France). Festival organisers may not give themselves the title of 'project manager', but many recognise the skills base is highly appropriate for what they have to do. Similarly for the medical consultant given the job of managing the opening of a new local hospital, or a politician the job of launching a new policy, PM is core to what they are doing.

For many years PM was regarded as the accidental **profession** – people got into it by accident. Typical in this respect is the scenario described in Table 6.1. This role change, from a technical role (in this case, engineering, but could equally well be for marketing, finance, IT, managerial or any technical specialism) to a project managerial role, used to be a transition that you were expected to manage, often with little by way of development and support. It used to be the case that in a group of 40 European project managers, 5 or fewer would have had any formal training or induction into what PM was. Today, it is more likely that most of the group will have that as a minimum. However, two recent experiences demonstrate that there is still a long way to go before the recognition of need is converted into recognised qualifications being mandated:

REAL WORLD Sometimes, it takes more than projects . . .

Source: David Wolff-Young/Alamy

The product that has led to the revival of Apple Inc's fortunes since 2000 is the iconic iPod. Launched in 2001, like most new products its development was managed through a *programme* of projects – that is, a coordinated set of projects with a common goal. These included:

1 The development of the hardware – from the electronics to the 'look and feel' of the product.
2 The development of the software – the user interface, the firmware.
3 Establishing *iTunes* – vital for the success of the product was the content that could be loaded onto it.
4 The production set-up – tooling up to produce prototypes to production of the final product and its subsequent upgrades.
5 The marketing – from identification of market needs to promotion of the product.

While all of these had to function together for the product to be a success at its launch, the collaboration and the projects did not stop there. In order to keep up with a highly innovative and competitive market, there needed to be continual refreshing of the product, new versions and cost-reduction projects on the existing versions. Ability to deliver this depends on Apple Inc's ability to manage its projects.

Table 6.1 Accidental profession or profession of choice?

Accidental profession	*Profession of choice*
Engineering Projects Manager: 'I did my degree in engineering and all my professional exams to get chartered. I still really want to be an engineer – it's the technology that I find really interesting. But I was in the office one day and the MD walks in – "You OK to manage this next project?" he says. Couldn't really say no.'	IT Programme Manager: 'I started as a technical specialist, but was frustrated at how fast we could move things along and so really wanted to be running the project. I did my first PM professional qualification and then joined the programme management office. After a short time as a planner, I moved into project management. I did further management qualifications while working and recently championed our change programme on excellence in project management.'

- Major defence contractor working on a major project, 1200 staff but not one professional PM qualification and only one general management qualification.
- Major government agency – running 800-plus projects, 20 recently qualified in PRINCE 2. With the number and size of the projects being run, this is not going to make a significant difference, but is a place to start.

So how does this fit with the traditional **career** path structure?

PM and line management

Figure 6.3 shows a conventional management hierarchy, with the lines representing lines of reporting or responsibility. At the head of each of the major functions within an organisation there will be functional or line managers. These managers have the responsibility for the people who work under them in their departments.

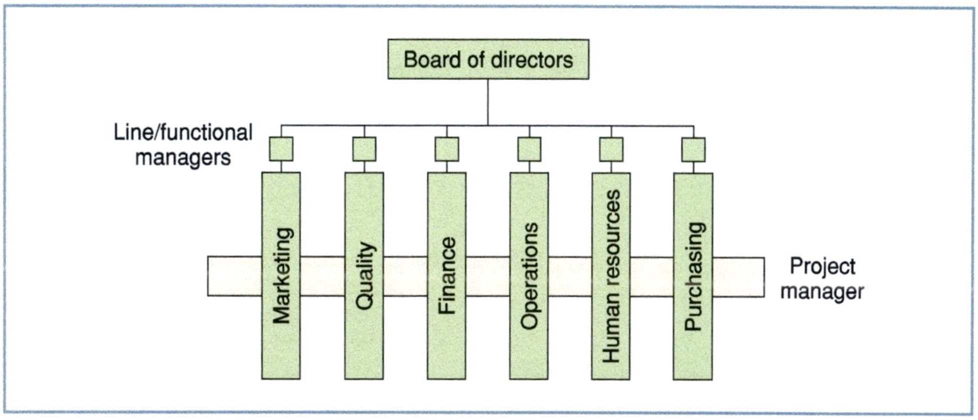

Figure 6.3 **Project organisational structure (for project of medium complexity)**

The project manager may have a line-management role as well, but is responsible for projects that may run across several functions. The figure shows the project manager being responsible for people drawn from every function in their activities in relation to that project.

The project manager's role differs from that of the line manager in the nature of the task being carried out. Table 6.2 establishes the major differences.

As Figure 6.4 shows, the split between tasks that can be considered as **maintenance** (maintaining the status quo) and **innovation** is changing. In the figure, the trend is for the line AB to move downwards – increasing the degree of innovation activities required from line managers. The result of this is a change in the role of line managers and a reduction in the difference in the roles of line and project managers. Indeed, as already stated, this blurring of project management into general management provides for considerable confusion. Reference back to the definitions of projects will show those activities that are and are not project-based. Table 6.2 illustrates this.

Many managers today have both project-management and line-management responsibility and it is frequently quoted that the project-related proportion is in excess of 50 per cent of their time. Their line responsibilities (finance, marketing, design) involve them in a variety of day-to-day activities plus longer-term projects. The skills and techniques used in the line-management function will differ from those required in projects, as we shall see. The more enlightened organisations will provide a basic skills

Table 6.2 **Project versus general management**

General management	*Project management*
• Responsible for managing the status quo	• Responsible for overseeing change
• Authority defined by management structure	• Lines of authority 'fuzzy'
• Consistent set of tasks	• Ever-changing set of tasks
• Responsibility limited to their own function	• Responsibility for cross-functional activities
• Works in 'permanent' organisational structures	• Operates within structures which exist for the life of the project
• Tasks described as 'maintenance'	• Predominantly concerned with innovation
• Main task is optimisation	• Main task is the resolution of conflict
• Success determined by achievement of interim targets	• Success determined by achievement of stated end-goals
• Limited set of variables	• Contains intrinsic uncertainties

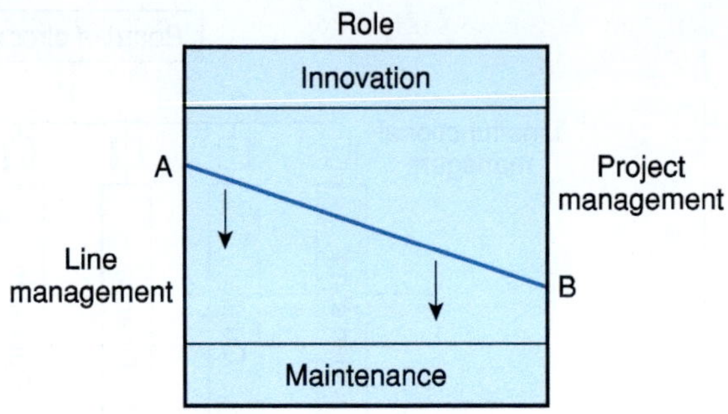

Figure 6.4 Innovation and maintenance activities in project and line management

grounding in the best ways to run projects, and help, coach and mentor individuals in recognising and developing their project roles.

Lastly, there are many other professional roles associated with the project manager. We see many organisations using project management offices (as in Table 6.1) or project support offices.[9] These are additional functions, often included in the organisation in the same manner as another internal function, alongside human resources, operations, finance and marketing. This gives recognition to the importance and prevalence of the roles required to support projects, described further in the next chapter. Indeed, we have seen three distinct career paths emerge in this area:

1 **Project manager**.
2 **Programme manager**.
3 **Project or Programme support office manager**.

For a project manager, the addition of a project-management function in this way provides a route for promotion as they develop their skills, knowledge and experience in managing projects. Without this, there is seen to be little continuity in the careers of project managers and crucial knowledge can leave with a manager when a project is completed. Career development could lead to positions of project director, programme manager, senior responsible owner, sponsor and others (we will be looking at these roles in more detail in future chapters). However, it is clear that the three main career paths do require fundamentally different skillsets and approaches to managing.[10]

6.3 Project management past and present

History

We should be able to learn from how humans have managed projects since the start of civilisation. This is an enlightening area for study, as projects are frequently treated as unique and in the process repeat the mistakes of the past.[11] However, looking at the knowledge base, there appears to be little that has been gleaned from millennia of this type of human activity – great construction projects, movements of people, engineering achievements and so forth. Perhaps the evidence is there, just without obvious signs and indicators to the provenance of the ideas that are so accepted today.

There are other explanations for the apparent lack of learning. For one, the constraints are hardly the same today as they were. One very successful civilisation – the Roman Empire – did not have the same resource constraints that project managers face today.

As one historian pointed out, if they wanted any more resources to complete their projects, they simply had to go and conquer the region that had those resources and take them. Maybe this is more reminiscent of industrial practice today than we credit . . . In later history, we see that project timescales were much longer and expectations were much less. For instance, construction of some of Europe's great churches was accomplished over many decades or longer. Lastly, we do have a 'survivor bias' for projects carried out by our ancestors – we do not find so much evidence of their failures as of their successes.

History should provide us with lessons that we can draw upon to improve our management of the present and the future. There are far more influences coming into modern project-management ideas and we should glean more from forensic analysis of past projects. For the present, major influences on modern project management can be identified as coming from work carried out in the 1950s. Obviously, small- and large-scale projects were undertaken before the 1950s. Individuals managed events and other situations. For example, the Pyramids were constructed, wars were fought and products were developed. Table 6.3 shows the progression of ideas in this area – from first-generation processes, developed for large engineering projects during the 1950s to the 1980s, through the development of a much wider range of approaches for many different projects in the 1990s, through to the third-generation processes of today. The features of each **generation of project practices** are described.

Table 6.3 Historical development of project management

Time	*Development*	*Generation*
Pre-1950s	No generally accepted methods or recognised processes. Much industry-specific custom and practice	
1950s	Development of planning processes and numerical methods for quantifying uncertainty in high-profile, military projects, predominantly in the US	First-generation PM
1960s	Further development of techniques and wider acceptance of their application. 1965 IPMA, 1969 PMI founded	
1970s	Recognition of role of project manager in large-scale projects, formation of UK's APM (as now known)	
1980s	Continued interest in project management as a formalised means to manage large-scale engineering and construction projects[12]	
1990s	Increasing recognition of role of **standards** in many industries and the profession as a whole, more work undertaken called projects[13] beyond engineering and construction. PMI and APM publish their **Bodies of Knowledge**[14]	Second-generation PM
2000s	Widespread acceptance of need for developing PM, burgeoning consultancy sector, further professionalisation including minimum standards required for taking the role of a project manager, development of ideas beyond traditional tools and techniques.[15] Rethinking project management takes place.[16] Development of lean and agile approaches to PM. Programme management becoming norm in organisations[17]	Third-generation PM

During the 1950s, formal tools and techniques were developed to help manage large, complex projects that were uncertain or risky. The chemical manufacturer Du Pont developed techniques (critical path analysis (CPA)) for scheduling maintenance shutdowns at the company's production facilities. In the same period, the defence contractor RAND Corp. created its tool (Programme Evaluation and Review Technique or PERT) for planning missile development. These tools focused almost exclusively on the project-planning phase and there were no close rivals for their use. The methods survived and became accepted practice.

The second-generation PM became evident in the 1990s, with an expanded array of tools and techniques beyond those of the first-generation processes. This was accompanied by the development of standards for PM processes in the US and Europe. Leading the development of such standards have been the major professional associations – specifically the Project Management Institute (PMI) in the US and the Association for Project Management (APM) in the UK. The International Project Management Association (IPMA) was founded in the 1960s as a networking group and since then has taken a greater coordinating role between 40 national professional bodies from around the world. The emergence of PM as a recognised profession with definable knowledge requirements to enter the profession began.

The third-generation processes recognised the requirement for a strategic approach to the design of the project process rather than the highly reactive approach that was prevalent. The variety of practices evident under the heading of 'project management' increased significantly, with the best organisations and managers continuing to develop new approaches and many more starting their 'project management journeys'.

Conventional methods developed to manage large-scale, direct-value-adding projects with timescales of years, such as heavy engineering, are too cumbersome when projects require short timescales to exploit market openings quickly, in particular in an information-based economy.

The third stage of project management emphasises the strategic role of projects, especially those processes that the project manager must put in place to deliver the end objective of the project and satisfy the needs of all the project's customers. In this new approach, project managers become project *integrators*, responsible for integrating the required resources, knowledge and processes from the project's beginning to end. This third stage has also been greatly influenced by the changes that have occurred in the context in which modern projects operate. In particular, the ready availability of technology (especially communications technology) has led to the emergence of *virtual teams* as a means of running projects. Similarly, there has been considerable development of powerful project planning tools software and the computer-processing power to support it. Both of these have the potential to change the way that we work in projects. In addition, as mentioned in the previous section, we have seen the emergence of the three career paths of project, programme and project support office managers.

This consideration of the evolution of the subject brings us to the issues that practitioners and academics are facing today.

Current issues

There are many areas where project management proves to be a huge challenge for individuals and organisations. Some of these are reflected in the list below:

'Ready, fire, aim.' A project is started with no clear objectives. The motto is *'shoot first – whatever you hit, call it the target'*. While we accept that emergence is a characteristic of projects, and some will be deliberately exploratory (but necessarily limited), this approach to managing projects is not associated with any great success for the organisation. However, if you do work in such an environment, setting your own targets at the end of the project is the easiest method for the project manager, without a doubt!

'It's all in my head.' The project manager will set out with all the information in their head. This may work well where the project is very small, but the lack of any system will soon start to tell on the individual and the results if there are any problems or if the scale of the project escalates. Here, the application of the structures and systems will greatly help, enabling better-grounded decisions to be made and avoiding many problems to which this approach will inevitably lead. It remains a challenge for many individuals and organisations to move away from this usually random approach to managing projects. This links to the next point.

'We work in a nanosecond environment, we don't have time to do this stuff.' This was a regular quotation from senior managers in fast-moving e-commerce firms in the late 1990s. Given the demise of so many of these, one can only speculate on the impact that the lack of good project management had on those businesses. Undoubtedly, changes to the basic practices of project managers are required under such circumstances, but this is more adaptation than radical re-invention. This scenario is in sharp contrast to the next one.

'Project management – we have a procedure for that.' Having procedures or a documented set of processes for projects provides a highly structured approach that is favoured in some industries. Indeed, there are many where the slavish dedication to highly restrictive methods is necessary as part of the requirements of customers (military procurement and areas where safety considerations are paramount are two such areas). The result is high levels of documentation (the procedures manual for projects at one international bank ran to several thousand pages) and considerable bureaucracy associated with it. Decision making can be very slow and the overhead costs associated with such systems significant. This represents the other end of the formalisation scale from the previous scenarios; it is a challenge for project managers to deal with this high degree of formalisation and yet try to engender creativity into the project and the people working on it. It is a constant theme among project management professionals just how much formalisation is required in systems. While some will have the levels specified by the requirements of the project, the vast majority, particularly for smaller projects, require an approach that is more appropriate to the particular situation.

'It's all just common sense, isn't it?' Well yes, but that depends on what you mean by common sense. If you mean 'the obvious after it has been explained',[18] then possibly. However, this statement usually just shows that things about which little or nothing is known appear obvious, as exemplified by the bar-room philosopher with easy answers to life, the universe and everything, if only they would listen . . . This is a great challenge for project management today. The past 50 years of the subject will be shown to have provided a substantial knowledge base for project managers to use. The art is in knowing the relevant parts of that base and tailoring that knowledge to the particular environment.

'I've got the badge, therefore I am a project manager.' The card-carrying project-management expert is a relatively recent phenomenon. Short courses, including PRINCE 2, provide some knowledge, at the end of which participants take an exam. If they pass it, they have the status of project management practitioner. This is regardless of whether they can actually apply any of the knowledge gained from their course or its relevance to their context. Such courses are valuable as first steps on the way to becoming a professional project manager and many people have benefited from them; however, they are only a starting point.

'We've done this lots of times before. It never worked then, why should it this time?' Here we see the experienced project worker showing the exasperation that comes with the application of many different approaches, only to be regularly confronted with the same results – projects running late, over budget or delivering less than was required of them. This is not at all uncommon, because organisations rarely address the real causes of failure. The failures deserve more careful study – they are a significant opportunity for learning and are generally very costly: to individuals, the organisation or both.

'It won't work here!' Lastly, a challenge for new methods that have been developed in other areas of business is to find how they might be applied with benefit to the project environment. These must overcome this often-heard rejection of anything new as it was 'not invented here, therefore it cannot be of any relevance to us'. The pressure for change in most organisations is such that ideas need to be brought in from wherever possible and adapted for projects and then the particular application. Examples of changes that are having an impact on the project environment include taking operations initiatives (including *lean* and *agile*) and applying the principles to the project environment. There is no longer just one best way to run a project; now there are many possible options and it is this choice of processes that will be discussed in subsequent chapters.

Academic subject

Alongside practice, what has been written and taught about project management has evolved considerably over the recent past. At one time, a project management course was a relatively novel addition to an engineering programme of study. Today, it is an emerging discipline and is taught extensively in management, engineering and science schools. Further, there is a growing band of academics researching, writing, teaching and consulting in the area, and more relevant papers appearing in a wide range of academic and practitioner journals.[19] The following Real World box describes a recent study that has been influential both in setting out the current state of the art in project management and in defining requirements for the future.

REAL WORLD Rethinking Project Management (2004–2006), a UK government-funded research initiative

Funded by the UK's Engineering and Physical Sciences Research Council (EPSRC), the main argument of the 'Rethinking Project Management' research centred on the growing criticisms of mainstream project management theory in relation to the developing practice across different sectors. Importantly, the main argument was not that mainstream project-management ideas should be abandoned, but rather a need exists to extend and enrich the discipline beyond its current intellectual foundations. Thus, the aim of the research was to identify directions for future research aimed at extending and enriching current project-management ideas in relation to the developing field of projects across all sectors. Led by the University of Manchester, the project was carried out between 2004 and 2006 involving a large group of academics and practitioners, with the main findings published in the *International Journal of Project Management* in November 2006. In summary, three key areas were identified in which new ideas and approaches are needed:

1 Value creation through projects and programmes.
2 Social complexity in project environments.
3 Practitioner development in the management of projects.

Starting with the first of these, the main focus of 20th-century project-management ideas has been on *product creation* – the engineering of physical assets, systems and facilities etc. to specification, cost and time – and hence the ideas that have taken root are lifecycle models and mainstream techniques for project management. In contrast, the focus in the 21st century is no longer just on product creation but increasingly that of value creation through projects and programmes. Here the concern is no longer just about doing projects right, but doing the right projects, which is a much more strategic view and a much broader concept than the traditional image of projects. Moreover, by value creation the focus is on not just wealth creation but other kinds of value and benefit too, such as improvements to public services and contributions towards protecting the environment.

The second theme to emerge from the research is how the reality of projects is much more socially complex and unpredictable than the traditional models in the literature. Practitioners are often left 'stranded' to deal with this complexity without much help from the literature. Hence, one of the main findings is for future research to focus on developing new ways of thinking which relate to the actual complexity of projects, covering aspects such as the complexity of social interaction and human action, and the framing and reframing of projects and programmes within an evolving flux of social agenda, practices, stakeholder relations, politics and power.

Finally, with regard to the knowledge and skills required of practitioners, the most important message of the research is the need for organisations to review their approaches to training and development. In contrast to mainstream training with its focus on methods and tools, organisations need to focus less on particular products and more on the development of practitioner capabilities linked to the realities of 21st-century projects. Examples of these capabilities are:

- dealing with complexity, ambiguity and uncertainty;
- understanding social and political aspects (stakeholder interests and power, etc.);
- handling multiple relationships in project environments;
- understanding value and its creation through projects and programmes;
- pragmatic use of theory in practice;
- working with multiple perspectives.

Many of these will be taken up in this book.

Source: *Mark Winter, Manchester Business School*. Reproduced with permission.

Summary

■ Projects are important issues to both individuals and organisations. There are some key questions to be answered if we are to understand the meaning and potential of the subject and profession of project management and the activity of managing projects today. The first is: what is it? For some people, the image that is conjured up is of large-scale construction projects – the many buildings for the millennium or major events such as the London Olympics. The second is: what is the role of management in this? For many, project management is often associated with its basic tools and techniques or a particular software package. These views are limiting and do not do justice to the range or scope of project management today. To counter the first point, project management is a live subject – going on around us all the time, and not just in organisations that undertake large-scale projects. On the second point, rather than just being a limited set of tools and techniques, it is also a true profession, with a growing recognition of its contribution to all walks of working life. The role of project management covers the entire spectrum of management knowledge, making it a broad-based study, not confined to tools and techniques or technical issues.

- On a business level, there are projects ongoing in every organisation. These are vital as they are the execution of all the visions, missions and strategies of that organisation. There are many books and distinguished articles written on strategy, but relatively little on how to deliver it. On a personal level, we all have a number of projects ongoing – pursuing a course of study, buying a house or organising a holiday. The level of complexity differs, the underlying principle of delivering the result at a given point in time is the same. At a commercial level, the effectiveness of the project management process will determine whether or not those projects play a role in providing a source of competitive advantage (or even continued existence) for an organisation. But this is not usually the case, as the opening of the chapter showed. There is a problem with projects and their management, as demonstrated by the large percentage of projects that run late, cost more than was expected, or fail to deliver what was required of them.

- The first step on the way to understanding projects was their definition. This showed that there was a considerable diversity in the characteristics of projects, and that these require different approaches to their management. After we identified the nature of projects, the next discussion was to see how we arrived at the current state of the subject. Having emerged from the 'one best way' era of project management, we are faced with a large number of challenges, not least in terms of where the subject is going now. This is both helped and constrained by the current knowledge base, with high-profile bodies of knowledge being at the core of the professional discipline.

Key terms

as . . . but . . .
benefits
Bodies of Knowledge and standards
business case
career
change
definition
emergence
first-timers
focused
general management
generation of project practices
innovation
integrated
maintenance
mission
operations management
painting by numbers
process
profession
programme/project/project support office manager
project-based organisations
projects
social construction
temporary
uncertainty
unique
volume and variety

PROJECT MANAGEMENT IN PRACTICE
Three project managers with distinctly different roles

1 The site manager of a housing development

'I am in charge of the construction of the buildings you see around you [he gestured with his hand to the mixture of partially and fully completed properties] and of making sure they go from this stage [he indicates a pile of drawings and building schedules] to the point where we can hand them over to the sales people to sell. Most of the work is supervisory, ensuring that orders are placed and materials arrive on time, people turn up, do the job properly and get paid for it at the end of the week. There are always arguments between the various tradespeople to resolve and problems just get dumped on the desk. Some of the toughest problems come with the people you have to work with. Some of them will do anything to try to get one over on you – they'll tell you a job is finished when you can see it is only half done. Unless you go and check it yourself you're in trouble. Also, they don't give a damn for my schedule. How do you get a roofer, at four o'clock in the afternoon when it is raining rather heavily [not the words actually used] when you know he has a long drive home, to get back on the roof and finish the job he is doing so that other jobs which rely on this being completed can start at eight o'clock the following morning? It wouldn't be the first time we had to block his car in with a pallet of bricks to stop him leaving.'

2 Implementing Total Quality Management – the quality director

'The quality director was appointed with the brief to introduce Total Quality Management (TQM) to the company. It was his responsibility to put the proposal as to how it could be done, and then to carry it out. As he described at the outset of the project "[this] is one of the most complex projects that we could undertake at this time". The complexity came because the project would hopefully change the way that everyone in the company thought and worked [i.e. both attitude and procedures]. This would have to be done through consultation, training and the demonstration through piloting small-scale improvement activities, that the move towards TQ was worthwhile. The initial phase as part of the proposal process was to carry out a company-wide quality audit to determine attitudes, knowledge and current practice. The results paved the way for the carrying out of targeted efforts where needed most. The first phase of execution was to take the board of directors of the company on awareness training – showing them how working under a TQ environment would benefit them, and what changes would be needed. The next level of management were then trained and so on down the hierarchy until the middle management level. These managers then trained their own people – a process known as "cascading". The project to introduce the new philosophy to the company took several years, and has now moved on to become an accepted way of working. The quality director was initially involved in the management of the introduction process, where the employees and suppliers needed to be convinced that this was a good route for the company to take. His role then became one of project sponsor of a variety of improvement projects, which may be considered as subprojects of the main one.'

3 Project manager in financial management system implementation

'The main roles of the job include:

- organisation – from the design of the system to determining support issues and providing training;
- anticipation of future requirements of the system;
- monitoring of progress of the implementation;
- communication and information – providing progress reports to local team members and national common-interest groups;
- audit – ensuring the housekeeping, procedures and system security are in order.

The initial system design work involved coordinating with external system designers, the providers of the software and the in-house IT group. Our local area network (LAN) needed upgrading to run the new system. Other organisational issues were the role that consultants would play in the system design and training of users and the allocation of the budget between activities.

Anticipation was required as the requirements of the system would change over its life. For example, higher-level monthly indicators of financial performance would need to be provided where they had not been needed before. In addition, a management accounting system would be required to provide budgetary controls.

→

The monitoring system we used for the project was PRINCE 2 2009. This provided a basic set of planning tools, and we filled in the blanks on the planning sheets. A team was set up to monitor progress against the plan.

Training was one area where I was personally involved with the users, showing them how to use the system. People are very frightened of technology and do not always grasp immediately ideas you think are very simple. This is where the greatest attribute of the project manager was needed in plenty – patience.'

Points for discussion

1 Identify the title which might be given to the project management role in each case.

2 Describe the role of the project manager in each of the cases.

3 Describe the desirable characteristics of each project manager using the set of skills and attributes as a starting point.

Topics for discussion

1 Carry out a search using a library or a good Internet search engine to find more examples of project success and failure. From your search, are there any common themes in each? What are the implications of success and failure in each case?

2 The Beijing 2008 Olympics were considered to be a great success by many people. Carry out a search of the news of the time and the relevant websites to identify the characteristics of the project management that led to the success. Compare with the example of failed projects you found in the answer to 1.

3 Explain the differences between project and general management.

4 In what you are doing at the moment which parts are project and which are ongoing or repetitive operations?

5 Identify five project managers that have the title 'project manager' and another five that are project managers but don't carry the title. Do you notice any differences in their roles?

6 Select a sector of interest. For this sector, identify the likely pressures on project managers and the implications for them as a result of these.

7 Find examples of projects that fit into each of the categories of project – first-timers, as . . . but . . . s, and painting by numbers. Briefly discuss how the category would influence how you would expect to manage the particular project.

8 Consider the definitions of 'project' provided by each of the professional bodies. What are the similarities and differences?

9 Does it matter what we call a project?

10 'A project manager should not have other managerial responsibilities.' Discuss.

Further information

Organisations of interest

Project Management Institute – see www.pmi.org for information about the Institute and referral to national organisations (known as *Chapters*).

The Association for Project Management (UK) – see www.apm.org.uk or contact the Association at 150 West Wycombe Road, High Wycombe, HP12 3AE, UK.

PRINCE 2 2009 – see www.prince2.com for description of the processes associated with PRINCE 2 2009.

International Project Management Association – see www.ipma.ch (see www.ipma.ch/membership/memberassociations/Pages/default.aspx for full list of national associations and relevant websites).

Indian Project Management Associates – see www.pma-india.org.

Swedish Project Management Association – see www.projektforum.se/.

Nordnet – association of the Swedish, Norwegian, Finnish, Danish and Icelandic national project management associations.

Project Management Research Committee China (PMRC) – see www.pm.org.cn.

General forum websites

www.pmforum.org

www.gantthead.com

Books of interest

Andersen, E. (2008) *Rethinking Project Management*, Financial Times Prentice Hall, Harlow.

Andersen, E., Grude, K.V. and Haug, T. (2004) *Goal Directed Project Management: Effective Techniques and Strategies*, Kogan Page, London.

Archibald, R.D. (2003) *Managing High Technology Programs and Projects*, 3rd edition, Wiley, New York.

Buttrick, R. (2005) *The Project Workout*, 3rd edition, Financial Times Management, London.

Collins, A. and Bicknell, D. (1998) *Crash: Ten Easy Ways to Avoid Computer Disaster*, Simon & Schuster, New York.

Frame, J.D. (2002) *The New Project Management: Tools for an Age of Rapid Change, Complexity, and Other Business Realities*, Jossey-Bass, San Francisco, CA.

Hodgson, D. and Cicmil, S. (eds) (2006) *Making Projects Critical*, Palgrave, Basingstoke.

Holmes, A. (2001) *Failsafe IS Project Delivery*, Gower, Aldershot.

Kerzner, H. (2006) *Project Management*, 9th edition, Van Nostrand Reinhold, New York.

Lock, D. (2000) *Project Management*, 7th edition, Gower, Aldershot.

Meredith, J.R. and Mantel, S.J. (2003) *Project Management: A Managerial Approach*, 5th edition, Wiley, New York.

Morris, P, and Pinto, J.K. (2007) *The Wiley Guide to Project, Program, and Portfolio Management*, Wiley, New York.

Murray-Webster, R. and Simon, P. (2009) *50 Lucid Thoughts: Shedding Light on Current Project Management Practice*, Lucidus, London.

Peters, T. (1999) *The Project 50*, Alfred Knopf, New York.

Pinto, J. (2006) *Project Management: Achieving Competitive Advantage*, Prentice Hall, New York.

PMI (2004) *A Guide to the Project Management Body of Knowledge*, PMI, Upper Darby, PA (parts are downloadable free from www.pmi.org).

Turner, J.R. (2007) *Gower Handbook of Project Management*, Gower, Aldershot.

Verzuh, E. (2003) *The Portable MBA in Project Management*, Wiley, Chichester.

Young, T.L. (2007) *The Handbook of Project Management: A Practical Guide to Effective Policies, Techniques and Processes*, Kogan Page, London.

Journals of interest

Project Management Journal – published four times a year by Wiley

International Journal of Project Management – published eight times a year by Elsevier

International Journal of Managing Projects in Business

PM Network – monthly publication of PMI

Project – monthly publication of APM

Project Management Today – professional journal

References

1 See Davies, A. and Brady, T. (2000) 'Organizational Capabilities and Learning in Complex Product Systems: Towards Repeatable Solutions', *Research Policy*, Vol. 29, pp. 931–953.

2 For a fuller description of IT-enabled change, see Benjamin, R.I. and Levinson, E. (1993) 'A Framework for Managing IT-Enabled Change', *Sloan Management Review*, Vol. 34, No. 4, pp. 23–33.

3 See for instance Cicmil, S., Williams, T., Thomas, J. and Hodgson, D. (2006) 'Rethinking Project Management: Researching the Actuality of Projects', *International Journal of Project Management*, Vol. 24, No. 8, pp. 675–686.

4 For a fuller description of process and various classifications, see Slack, N. et al. (2007) *Operations Management*, FT Prentice Hall, Harlow.

5 See Obeng, E. (1994) *All Change: The Project Leader's Secret Handbook*, FT Pitman Publishing, London.

6 Turner, J.R. and Cochrane, R.A. (1993) 'Goals-and-methods Matrix: Coping with Projects with Ill Defined Goals and/or Methods of Achieving Them', *International Journal of Project Management*, Vol. 11, No. 2, pp. 93–102.

7 For further categorisations of project systems, see Crawford, L., Hobbs, J.B. and Turner, J.R. (2005) *Project Categorization Systems: Aligning Capability With Strategy for Better Results*, PMI, Newtown Square, PA.

8 *The Economist*, 2005.

9 See for instance Hobbs, B. and Aubry, M. (2007) 'The Project Management Office as an Organizational Innovation', presented at IRNOP 2007, at http://centrim.mis.brighton.ac.uk/events/irnop-2007/papers-1/Hobbs%20et%20al.pdf/view.

10 Partington, D., Pellegrinelli, S. and Young, M. (2005) 'Attributes and Levels of Programme Management Competence: An Interpretive Study', *International Journal of Project Management*, Vol. 23, No. 2, pp. 87–95.

11 See www.lessons-from-history.com for some good examples of historical projects and lessons drawn from them.

12 See Morris, P. and Hough, M. (1987) *The Anatomy of Major Projects*, Gower, Aldershot.

13 This phenomenon is known as *Projectification* after Midler, C. (1995) 'Projectification of the Firm: The Renault Case', *Scandinavian Management Journal*, Vol. 11, No. 4, pp. 363–375.

14 PMI Body of Knowledge first published as a white paper in 1987. First edition formally published 1996. APM Body of Knowledge first published 1992.

15 See Hodgson, D. and Cicmil, S. (eds) (2006) *Making Projects Critical*, Palgrave, Basingstoke.

16 Winter, M., Smith, C., Cooke-Davies, T. and Cicmil, S. (2006) 'Directions for Future Research in Project Management: The Main Findings of a UK Government-funded Research Network', *International Journal of Project Management*, Vol. 24, No. 8, pp. 650–662.

17 See Maylor, H., Brady, T., Cooke-Davies, T. and Hodgson, D. (2006) 'From Projectification to Programmification', *International Journal of Project Management*, Vol. 24, No. 8, pp. 663–674.

18 I am indebted to Keith Sutton of Chelmsford Technical College for this definition.

19 See 'Further information' for the main project management journals.

Introduction

Why Project Management?

Chapter Outline

Chapter Objectives

After completing this chapter, you should be able to:

1. Understand why project management is becoming such a powerful and popular practice in business.
2. Recognize the basic properties of projects, including their definition.
3. Understand why effective project management is such a challenge.
4. Differentiate between project management practices and more traditional, process-oriented business functions.
5. Recognize the key motivators that are pushing companies to adopt project management practices.
6. Understand and explain the project life cycle, its stages, and the activities that typically occur at each stage in the project.
7. Understand the concept of project "success," including various definitions of success, as well as the alternative models of success.

8. Understand the purpose of project management maturity models and the process of benchmarking in organizations.
9. Identify the relevant maturity stages that organizations go through to become proficient in their use of project management techniques.

PROJECT MANAGEMENT BODY OF KNOWLEDGE CORE CONCEPTS COVERED IN THIS CHAPTER

1. Definition of a Project (PMBoK sec. 6.2)
2. Definition of Project Management (PMBoK sec. 6.3)
3. Relationship to Other Management Disciplines (PMBoK sec. 6.4)
4. Project Phases and the Project Life Cycle (PMBoK sec. 4.1)

The world acquires value only through its extremes and endures only through moderation; extremists make the world great, the moderates give it stability.[20]

PROJECT PROFILE

Development Projects in Lagos, Nigeria

Lagos is the capital of Nigeria and home to an estimated 15–20 million people, making its population larger than London or Beijing. As the largest and fastest-growing city in sub-Saharan Africa (estimates are that 600,000 people are added to Lagos' population each year), Lagos is in desperate need of developing and maintaining infrastructure to support its population, while supporting its claim as a high-technology hub on the African continent. Considering that about 85% of the world's population resides in the developing world and transitioning economies, and nearly two-thirds of that population is below the age of 35, the need for infrastructure to support critical human needs is immense. About 70% of the city's population is believed to live in slums, while a 2006 United Nations report estimated that only 10% of households in the Lagos Metropolitan area were directly connected to a municipal water supply. In spite of these problems, Nigeria is Africa's biggest economy, driven by economic growth in Lagos, home to film and fashion industries, financial markets, and consumer goods manufacturers.

The list of critical items on the list for urban improvement is large. For example, for a city of more than 15 million, electricity is scarcely to be found. Lagos power stations only generate a mere 2,000 megawatts of electricity—less than half of that available for a single city block in midtown Manhattan! "We have about two hours, maybe, of public power a day," says Kola Karim, CEO of Nigeria's Shoreline Energy International. "It's unbearable." Everywhere in the city people are using gasoline or diesel generators to supply power when the inevitable rolling blackouts resume.

Additionally, Lagos is critically short on housing. To overcome this shortage people of Lagos resort to living in shanty towns, one such shanty town is Makoko. Makoko is situated on the mainland's Lagos lagoon. Home to several hundred thousand inhabitants, Makoko lacks access to basic services, including clean drinking water, electricity, and waste disposal, and is prone to severe environmental and health hazards. Consisting of rickety dwellings on stilts perched over the foul-smelling lagoon, Makoko is one of the many chaotic human settlements that have sprouted in Lagos in recent years. As these cities spread out and move too close to major bridges or electrical towers, the government periodically sends in troops to demolish portions of the floating village.

How did the city get to this point? A big reason was a lack of forethought and development planning. In metropolitan Lagos there are 20,000 people per square kilometer with thousands more arriving each day. Given the physical constraints of the city, originally built on a narrow strip of land and bordering the ocean, there is just not enough space to absorb the new inhabitants. Urban planning, as we know it today, simply did not exist and the city swelled organically, without forethought or a sense of direction. Thus, Lagos has no urban transportation system, few functioning traffic lights, and a crumbling and outdated road system.

The problems do not stop there. Land prices in Lagos are extremely high, due to lack of space for commercial development. However, because of the unreliable electricity supply that makes elevator use questionable, there are few high-rise apartments or office buildings in the city. Banks have been reluctant to invest in real estate transactions because of past failures and general economic instability. Faced with the need to drastically change the direction of the city, Babatunde Fashola, Lagos' visionary governor who took power in 2010, has launched a series of urban development projects to address a variety of the city's needs. Fashola has announced $50 billion in new infrastructure projects for Lagos, to be developed over the next 10 years. These new project initiatives include the following:

Lagos Metro Blue Line

The blue line is a major cosmopolitan light-rail transport project to connect districts in Nigeria's largest city. Designed to ease congestion and speed up journey times for the city's inhabitants, the Blue Line will run between Marina and Okokomaiko, stopping at 13 stations, and is part of the Lagos Rail Mass Transit program implemented by the government. Originally proposed in 2008, funding issues have pushed the launch of the Blue Line back to at least 2015. The Line is set to cost $1.2 billion and will be funded by the Lagos State Government.

Eko Atlantic

Eko Atlantic is an ambitious land reclamation project, a pioneering residential and business development located on Victoria Island, along its upmarket Bar Beach coastline. The project is being built on three and a half square miles of land reclaimed from the Atlantic Ocean and is expected to provide accommodation for 250,000 people and employment opportunities for a further 150,000. The complex will function as a city-within-a-city, including recreational facilities, business and shopping districts, and modern conveniences.

Bus Rapid-Transit System

To ease the crush of public transportation, the Bus Rapid Transport (BRT) system was introduced 10 years ago to streamline and modernize the motley collection of buses that had transported residents around the city. Lagos has long suffered from an unregulated transportation system in which a variety of different "buses," ranging from battered minibuses to old, yellow-painted school buses, competed for customers. Fares were also unregulated, leaving

FIGURE 6.5 **Traffic Congestion in Lagos, Nigeria**

Source: Femi Ipaye/Xinhua Press/Corbis

(*continued*)

drivers free to charge whatever fares they chose. "They might charge $1 in the morning for one trip one way and by afternoon they can go to $3," says Dayo Mobereola, managing director of the Lagos Metropolitan Area Transport Authority, noting that commuters spend on average 40% of their income on transportation. Before the project was announced, the city had projected that it would transport 60,000 passengers daily, but now it transports over 200,000 passengers daily. The BRT system has reduced waiting times at bus stops, the travel time across the city, all at a reduced rate when compared to the old system.

Schools, Bridges, and Power Plants

Part of the aggressive infrastructure modernization includes improving traffic by building the first suspension bridge in West Africa, as well as adding a number of new schools around the city. Two new power plants are also slated to be constructed, bringing a more dependable source of power to the city, including powering street lights to ease crime and other problems. The city has even launched a fleet of brand new garbage trucks to deal with the 10,000 tons of waste generated every day.

Lagos' modernization efforts in recent years have come not a moment too soon in support of its citizens. As Professor Falade observed, these efforts to modernize the city's facilities are a breath of fresh air. "The difference is clear, the evidence is the improved landscape of Lagos in the urban regeneration project."[21]

INTRODUCTION

Projects are one of the principal means by which we change our world. Whether the goal is to split the atom, tunnel under the English Channel, introduce Windows 9, or plan the next Summer Olympic Games in Rio de Janeiro, the means through which to achieve these challenges remains the same: project management. Project management has become one of the most popular tools for organizations, both public and private, to improve internal operations, respond rapidly to external opportunities, achieve technological breakthroughs, streamline new product development, and more robustly manage the challenges arising from the business environment. Consider what Tom Peters, best-selling author and management consultant, has to say about project management and its place in business: "Projects, rather than repetitive tasks, are now the basis for most value-added in business."[22] Project management has become a critical component of successful business operations in worldwide organizations.

One of the key features of modern business is the nature of the opportunities and threats posed by external events. As never before, companies face international competition and the need to pursue commercial opportunities rapidly. They must modify and introduce products constantly, respond to customers as fast as possible, and maintain competitive cost and operating levels. Does performing all these tasks seem impossible? At one time, it was. Conventional wisdom held that a company could compete using a low-cost strategy *or* as a product innovator *or* with a focus on customer service. In short, we had to pick our competitive niches and concede others their claim to market share. In the past 20 years, however, everything turned upside down. Companies such as General Electric, Apple, Ericksson, Boeing, and Oracle became increasingly effective at realizing all of these goals rather than settling for just one. These companies seemed to be successful in every aspect of the competitive model: They were fast to market *and* efficient, cost-conscious *and* customer-focused. How were they performing the impossible?

Obviously, there is no one answer to this complex question. There is no doubt, however, that these companies shared at least one characteristic: They had developed and committed themselves to project management as a competitive tool. Old middle managers, reported *Fortune* magazine,

> are dinosaurs, [and] a new class of manager mammal is evolving to fill the niche they once ruled: project managers. Unlike his biological counterpart, the project manager is more agile and adaptable than the beast he's displacing, more likely to live by his wits than throwing his weight around.[23]

Effective project managers will remain an indispensable commodity for successful organizations in the coming years. More and more companies are coming to this conclusion and adopting project management as a way of life. Indeed, companies in such diverse industries as construction, heavy manufacturing, insurance, health care, finance, public utilities, and software are becoming project savvy and expecting their employees to do the same.

6.4 WHAT IS A PROJECT?

Although there are a number of general definitions of the term **project**, we must recognize at the outset that projects are distinct from other organizational processes. As a rule, a **process** refers to ongoing, day-to-day activities in which an organization engages while producing goods or services. Processes use existing systems, properties, and capabilities in a continuous, fairly repetitive manner.[24] Projects, on the other hand, take place outside the normal, process-oriented world of the firm. Certainly, in some organizations, such as construction, day-to-day processes center on the creation and development of projects. Nevertheless, for the majority of organizations, project management activities remain unique and separate from the manner in which more routine, process-driven work is performed. Project work is continuously evolving, establishes its own work rules, and is the antithesis of repetition in the workplace. As a result, it represents an exciting alternative to business as usual for many companies. The challenges are great, but so are the rewards of success.

First, we need a clear understanding of the properties that make projects and project management so unique. Consider the following definitions of projects:

> A project is a unique venture with a beginning and end, conducted by people to meet established goals within parameters of cost, schedule, and quality.[25]
>
> Projects [are] goal-oriented, involve the coordinated undertaking of interrelated activities, are of finite duration, and are all, to a degree, unique.[26]
>
> A project can be considered to be any series of activities and tasks that:
>
> - Have a specific objective to be completed within certain specifications
> - Have defined start and end dates
> - Have funding limits (if applicable)
> - Consume human and nonhuman resources (i.e., money, people, equipment)
> - Are multifunctional (i.e., cut across several functional lines)[27]
>
> [A project is] [o]rganized work toward a predefined goal or objective that requires resources and effort, a unique (and therefore risky) venture having a budget and schedule.[28]

Probably the simplest definition is found in the Project Management Body of Knowledge (PMBoK) guide of the Project Management Institute (PMI). PMI is the world's largest professional project management association, with more than 450,000 members worldwide as of 2014. In the PMBoK guide, a project is defined as "a temporary endeavor undertaken to create a unique product, service, or result".[29]

Let us examine the various elements of projects, as identified by these set of definitions.

- ***Projects are complex, one-time processes.*** A project arises for a specific purpose or to meet a stated goal. It is complex because it typically requires the coordinated inputs of numerous members of the organization. Project members may be from different departments or other organizational units or from one functional area. For example, a project to develop a new software application for a retail company may require only the output of members of the Information Systems group working with the marketing staff. On the other hand, some projects, such as new product introductions, work best with representation from many functions, including marketing, engineering, production, and design. Because a project is intended to fulfill a stated goal, it is temporary. It exists only until its goal has been met, and at that point, it is dissolved.
- ***Projects are limited by budget, schedule, and resources.*** Project work requires that members work with limited financial and human resources for a specified time period. They do not run indefinitely. Once the assignment is completed, the project team disbands. Until that point, all its activities are constrained by limitations on budget and personnel availability. Projects are "resource-constrained" activities.
- ***Projects are developed to resolve a clear goal or set of goals.*** There is no such thing as a project team with an ongoing, nonspecific purpose. The project's goals, or **deliverables**,

define the nature of the project and that of its team. Projects are designed to yield a tangible result, either as a new product or service. Whether the goal is to build a bridge, implement a new accounts receivable system, or win a presidential election, the goal must be specific and the project organized to achieve a stated aim.

- ***Projects are customer-focused.*** Whether the project is responding to the needs of an internal organizational unit (e.g., accounting) or intended to exploit a market opportunity external to the organization, the underlying purpose of any project is to satisfy customer needs. In the past, this goal was sometimes overlooked. Projects were considered successful if they attained technical, budgetary, and scheduling goals. More and more, however, companies have realized that the primary goal of a project is customer satisfaction. If that goal is neglected, a firm runs the risk of "doing the wrong things well"—pursuing projects that may be done efficiently but that ignore customer needs or fail commercially.

General Project Characteristics

Using these definitional elements, we can create a sense of the key attributes that all projects share. These characteristics are not only useful for better understanding projects, but also offer the basis for seeing how project-based work differs from other activities most organizations undertake. Projects represent a special type of undertaking by any organization. Not surprisingly, the challenges in performing them right are sometimes daunting. Nevertheless, given the manner in which business continues to evolve on a worldwide scale, becoming "project savvy" is no longer a luxury: It is rapidly becoming a necessity.

Projects are characterized by the following properties:[30]

1. ***Projects are ad hoc endeavors with a clear life cycle.*** Projects are nontraditional; they are activities that are initiated as needed, operate for a specified time period over a fairly well understood development cycle, and are then disbanded. They are temporary operations.
2. ***Projects are building blocks in the design and execution of organizational strategies.*** As we will see in later chapters, projects allow organizations to implement companywide strategies. They are the principal means by which companies operationalize corporate-level objectives. In effect, projects are the vehicles for realizing company goals. For example, Intel's strategy for market penetration with ever newer, smaller, and faster computer chips is realized through its commitment to a steady stream of research and development projects that allows the company to continually explore the technological boundaries of electrical and computer engineering.
3. ***Projects are responsible for the newest and most improved products, services, and organizational processes.*** Projects are tools for innovation. Because they complement (and often transform) traditional process-oriented activities, many companies rely on projects as vehicles for going beyond conventional activities. Projects are the stepping-stones by which we move forward.
4. ***Projects provide a philosophy and strategy for the management of change.*** "Change" is an abstract concept until we establish the means by which we can make real alterations in the things we do and produce. Projects allow organizations to go beyond simple statements of intent and to achieve actual innovation. For example, whether it is Chevrolet's Volt electric car or Apple's newest iPhone upgrade, successful organizations routinely ask for customer input and feedback to better understand their likes and dislikes. As the vehicle of change, the manner in which a company develops its projects has much to say about its ability to innovate and commitment to change.
5. ***Project management entails crossing functional and organizational boundaries.*** Projects epitomize internal organizational collaboration by bringing together people from various functions across the company. A project aimed at new product development may require the combined work of engineering, finance, marketing, design, and so forth. Likewise, in the global business environment, many companies have crossed organizational boundaries by forming long-term partnerships with other firms in order to maximize opportunities while emphasizing efficiency and keeping a lid on costs. Projects are among the most common means of promoting collaboration, both across functions and across organizations.
6. ***The traditional management functions of planning, organizing, motivation, directing, and control apply to project management.*** Project managers must be technically well versed,

proficient at administrative functions, willing and able to assume leadership roles, and, above all, goal-oriented: The project manager is the person most responsible for keeping track of the big picture. The nature of project management responsibilities should never be underestimated because these responsibilities are both diverse and critical to project success.

7. ***The principal outcomes of a project are the satisfaction of customer requirements within the constraints of technical, cost, and schedule objectives.*** Projects are defined by their limitations. They have finite budgets, definite schedules, and carefully stated specifications for completion. For example, a term paper assignment in a college class might include details regarding form, length, number of primary and secondary sources to cite, and so forth. Likewise, in the Disney's Expedition Everest case example at the end of the chapter, the executive leading the change process established clear guidelines regarding performance expectations. All these constraints both limit and narrowly define the focus of the project and the options available to the project team. It is the very task of managing successful project development within such specific constraints that makes the field so challenging.
8. ***Projects are terminated upon successful completion of performance objectives***—or earlier in their life cycle, if results no longer promise an operational or strategic advantage. As we have seen, projects differ from conventional processes in that they are defined by limited life cycles. They are initiated, completed, and dissolved. As important alternatives to conventional organizational activities, they are sometimes called "temporary organizations."[31]

Projects, then, differ from better-known organizational activities, which often involve repetitive processes. The traditional model of most firms views organizational activities as consistently performing a discrete set of activities. For example, a retail-clothing establishment buys, stocks, and sells clothes in a continuous cycle. A steel plant orders raw materials, makes steel, and ships finished products, again in a recurring cycle. The nature of these operations focuses our attention on a "process orientation," that is, the need to perform work as efficiently as possible in an ongoing manner. When its processes are well understood, the organization always seeks better, more efficient ways of doing the same essential tasks. Projects, because they are discrete activities, violate the idea of repetition. They are temporary activities that operate outside formal channels. They may bring together a disparate collection of team members with different kinds of functional expertise. Projects function under conditions of uncertainty, and usually have the effect of "shaking up" normal corporate activities. Because of their unique characteristics, they do not conform to common standards of operations; they do things differently and often reveal new and better ways of doing things. Table 6.4 offers some other distinctions between project-based work and the more traditional, process-based activities. Note a recurring theme: Projects operate in radical ways that consistently violate the standard, process-based view of organizations.

Consider Apple's development of the iPod, a portable MP3 player that can be integrated with Apple's popular iTunes site to record and play music downloads. Apple, headed by its former chairman, the late Steven Jobs, recognized the potential in the MP3 market, given the enormous popularity (and, some would say, notoriety) of file-sharing and downloading music through

TABLE 6.4 Differences Between Process and Project Management[32]

Process	Project
Repeat process or product	New process or product
Several objectives	One objective
Ongoing	One shot—limited life
People are homogenous	More heterogeneous
Well-established systems in place to integrate efforts	Systems must be created to integrate efforts
Greater certainty of performance, cost, schedule	Greater uncertainty of performance, cost, schedule
Part of line organization	Outside of line organization
Bastions of established practice	Violates established practice
Supports status quo	Upsets status quo

Source: R. J. Graham. (1992). "A Survival Guide for the Accidental Project Manager," *Proceedings of the Annual Project Management Institute Symposium.* Drexel Hill, PA: Project Management Institute, pp. 355–61.

the Internet. The company hoped to capitalize on the need for a customer-friendly MP3 player, while offering a legitimate alternative to illegal music downloading. Since its introduction in 2003, consumers have bought nearly 400 million iPods and purchased more than 25 billion songs through Apple's iTunes online store. In fact, Apple's iTunes division is now the largest U.S. market for music sales, accounting for 29% of all music sold in the United States and 64% of the digital music market.

In an interview, Jobs acknowledged that Apple's business needed some shaking up, given the steady but unspectacular growth in sales of its flagship Macintosh personal computer, still holding approximately 13% of the overall PC market. The iPod, as a unique venture within Apple, became a billion-dollar business for the company in only its second year of existence. So popular has the iPod become for Apple that the firm created a separate business unit, moving the product and its support staff away from the Mac group. "Needless to say, iPod has become incredibly popular, even among people who aren't diehard Apple fanatics," industry analyst Paolo Pescatore told *NewsFactor*, noting that Apple recently introduced a smaller version of the product with great success. "In short, they have been very successful thus far, and I would guess they are looking at this realignment as a way to ensure that success will continue."[33]

A similar set of events are currently unfolding, centered on Apple's introduction and successive upgrades of its iPad tablet. Among the numerous features offered by the iPad is the ability to download books (including college textbooks) directly from publishers, effectively eliminating the traditional middlemen—bookstores—from the process. So radical are the implications of the iPad that competitors have introduced their own models (such as Samsung's Galaxy tablet) to capture a share of this market. Meanwhile, large bookstores are hoping to adapt their business models to the new electronic reality of book purchase by offering their own readers (for example, Kindle for Amazon). Some experts are suggesting that within a decade, tablets and other electronic readers will make traditional books obsolete, capturing the majority of the publishing market. These are just some examples of the way that project-driven technological change, such as that at Apple, is reshaping the competitive landscape.

Given the enthusiasm with which **project management** is being embraced by so many organizations, we should note that the same factors that make project management a unique undertaking are also among the main reasons why successful project management is so difficult. The track record of project management is by no means one of uninterrupted success, in part because many companies encounter deep-rooted resistance to the kinds of changes needed to accommodate a "project philosophy." Indeed, recent research into the success rates for projects offers some grim conclusions:

- A study of more than 300 large companies conducted by the consulting firm Peat Marwick found that software and/or hardware development projects fail at the rate of 65%. Of companies studied, 65% reported projects that went grossly over budget, fell behind schedule, did not perform as expected, or all of the above. Half of the managers responding indicated that these findings were considered "normal."[34]
- A study by the META Group found that "more than half of all (information technology) IT projects become runaways—overshooting their budgets and timetables while failing to deliver fully on their goals."[35]
- Joe Harley, the Chief Information Officer at the Department for Work and Pensions for the UK government, stated that "only 30%" of technology-based projects and programs are a success—at a time when taxes are funding an annual budget of £14bn (over $22 billion) on public sector IT, equivalent to building 7,000 new primary schools or 75 hospitals a year.[36]
- The United States Nuclear Security Administration has racked up $16 billion in cost overruns on 10 major projects that are a combined 38 years behind schedule, the Government Accountability Office reports. For example, at Los Alamos National Laboratory, a seven-year, $213 million upgrade to the security system that protects the lab's most sensitive nuclear bomb-making facilities does not work. A party familiar with the organization cites a "pervasive culture of tolerating the intolerable and accepting the unacceptable."[37]
- According to the 2004 PriceWaterhouseCoopers Survey of 10,640 projects valued at $7.2 billion, across a broad range of industries, large and small, only 2.5% of global businesses achieved 100% project success, and more than 50% of global business projects failed. The Chaos Summary 2013 survey by The Standish Group reported similar findings: The majority of all projects were

either "challenged" (due to late delivery, being over budget, or delivering less than required features) or "failed" and were canceled prior to completion, or the product developed was never used. Researchers have concluded that the average success rate of business-critical application development projects is 39%. Their statistics have remained remarkably steady since 1994.[38]

- The Special Inspector General for Iraq Reconstruction (SIGIR) reported that more than $8 billion of the $53 billion the Pentagon spent on thousands of Iraqi reconstruction projects was lost due to "fraud, waste, and abuse." Hundreds were eventually canceled, with 42% of the terminated projects ended because of mismanagement or shoddy construction. As part of their final 2013 report, SIGIR noted: "We found that incomplete and unstandardized databases left us unable to identify the specific use of billions of dollars spent on projects."[39]

These findings underscore an important point: Although project management is becoming popular, it is not easy to assimilate into the conventional processes of most firms. For every firm discovering the benefits of projects, many more underestimate the problems involved in becoming "project savvy."

These studies also point to a core truth about project management: We should not overestimate the benefits to be gained from project management while underestimating the commitment required to make a project work. There are no magic bullets or quick fixes in the discipline. Like any other valuable activity, project management requires preparation, knowledge, training, and commitment to basic principles. Organizations wanting to make use of project-based work must recognize, as Table 6.4 demonstrates, that its very strength often causes it to operate in direct contradiction to standard, process-oriented business practices.

6.5 WHY ARE PROJECTS IMPORTANT?

There are a number of reasons why projects and project management can be crucial in helping an organization achieve its strategic goals. David Cleland, a noted project management researcher, suggests that many of these reasons arise from the very pressures that organizations find themselves facing.[40]

1. ***Shortened product life cycles.*** The days when a company could offer a new product and depend on having years of competitive domination are gone. Increasingly, the life cycle of new products is measured in terms of months or even weeks, rather than years. One has only to look at new products in electronics or computer hardware and software to observe this trend. Interestingly, we are seeing similar signs in traditional service-sector firms, which also have recognized the need for agility in offering and upgrading new services at an increasingly rapid pace.
2. ***Narrow product launch windows.*** Another time-related issue concerns the nature of opportunity. Organizations are aware of the dangers of missing the optimum point at which to launch a new product and must take a proactive view toward the timing of product introductions. For example, while reaping the profits from the successful sale of Product A, smart firms are already plotting the best point at which to launch Product B, either as a product upgrade or a new offering. Because of fierce competition, these optimal launch opportunities are measured in terms of months. Miss your launch window, even by a matter of weeks, and you run the risk of rolling out an also-ran.
3. ***Increasingly complex and technical products.*** It has been well-documented that the average automobile today has more computing power than the Apollo 11 space capsule that allowed astronauts to walk on the moon. This illustrates a clear point: the world today is complex. Products are complicated, technically sophisticated, and difficult to produce efficiently. The public's appetite for "the next big thing" continues unabated and substantially unsatisfied. We want the new models of our consumer goods to be better, bigger (or smaller), faster, and more complex than the old ones. Firms constantly upgrade product and service lines to feed this demand. That causes multiple problems in design and production as we continually seek to push the technical limits. Further, in anticipating future demand, many firms embark on expensive programs of research and development while attempting to discern consumer tastes. The effect can be to erroneously create expensive and technically sophisticated

projects that we assume the customer will want. For example, Rauma Corporation of Finland developed a state-of-the-art "loader" for the logging industry. Rauma's engineers loaded the product with the latest computerized gadgetry and technologies that gave the machine a space-age feel. Unfortunately, the chief customer for the product worked in remote regions of Indonesia, with logistics problems that made servicing and repairing the loaders impractical. Machines that broke down had to be airlifted more than 1,000 miles to service centers. Since the inception of this project, sales of the logging machinery have been disappointing. The project was an expensive failure for Rauma and serves to illustrate an important point: Unless companies find a way to maintain control of the process, an "engineering for engineering's sake" mentality can quickly run out of control.[41]

4. ***Global markets.*** The early twenty-first century has seen the emergence of enormous new markets for almost every type of product and service. Former closed or socialist societies, as well as rapidly developing economies such as Brazil, China, Vietnam, and India, have added huge numbers of consumers and competitors to the global business arena. The increased globalization of the economy, coupled with enhanced methods for quickly interacting with customers and suppliers, has created a new set of challenges for business. These challenges also encompass unique opportunities for those firms that can quickly adjust to this new reality. In the global setting, project management techniques provide companies with the ability to link multiple business partners, and respond quickly to market demand and supplier needs, while remaining agile enough to anticipate and respond to rapid shifts in consumer tastes. Using project management, successful organizations of the future will recognize and learn to rapidly exploit the prospects offered by a global business environment.
5. ***An economic period marked by low inflation.*** One of the key indicators of economic health is the fact that inflation has been kept under control. In most of the developed Western economies, low inflation has helped to trigger a long period of economic expansion, while also helping provide the impetus for emerging economies, such as those in India and China, to expand rapidly. Unfortunately, low inflation also limits the ability of businesses to maintain profitability by passing along cost increases. Companies cannot continue to increase profit margins through simply raising prices for their products or services. Successful firms in the future will be those that enhance profits by streamlining internal processes—those that save money by "doing it better" than the competition. As a tool designed to realize goals like internal efficiency, project management is a means by which to bolster profits.

These are just some of the more obvious challenges facing business today. The key point is that the forces giving rise to these challenges are not likely to abate in the near future. In order to meet these challenges, large, successful companies such as General Electric, 3M, Apple, Samsung, Bechtel, and Microsoft have made project management a key aspect of their operating philosophies.

PROJECT PROFILE

"Throwing Good Money after Bad": the BBC's Digital Media Initiative

The British Broadcasting Corporation (BBC) recently announced the cancelation of a major Information Technology (IT) project intended to update their vast broadcast operations. The project, called the Digital Media Initiative (DMI), was originally budgeted at £81.7 million ($140 million) and was developed to eliminate the outdated filing systems and use of old-fashioned, analog videotape with its expensive archival storage. The BBC is one of the world's largest and most widely recognized news and media organizations; it is publically funded and under British government oversight. The DMI project was intended to save the organization millions annually by eliminating the cost of expensive and outdated storage facilities, while moving all media content to a modern, digital format. As an example of a large-scale IT project, the plan for DMI involved media asset management, archive storage and retrieval systems, and media sharing capabilities.

The DMI project was begun in 2008 when the BBC contracted with technology service provider Siemens, with consulting expertise to be provided by Deloitte. Interestingly, the BBC never put the contract out for competitive bidding, reasoning that it already had a 10-year support contract with Siemens and trusted Siemens' judgment on project development. As part of this "hands-off" attitude, executives at the BBC gave Siemens full control of the project, and apparently little communication flowed back and forth between the organizations. The BBC finally grew concerned with the distant relationship that was developing between itself and the contractor when Siemens began missing important delivery milestones and encountering technical difficulties. After one year, the BBC terminated its $65 million contract with Siemens and sued the company for damages, collecting approximately $47 million in a court settlement. Still, losing nearly $20 million in taxpayer money after only one year, with nothing to show for it, did not bode well for the future.

Having been burned by this relationship with an outside contractor, the BBC next tried to move the project "in house," assigning its own staff and project manager to continue developing the DMI. The project was under the overall control of the BBC's Chief Technology Officer, John Linwood. It was hoped that the lessons learned from the first-round failure of the project would help improve the technology and delivery of the system throughout the organization. Unfortunately, the project did no better under BBC control. Reports started surfacing as early as 2011 that the project was way behind schedule, was not living up to its promises, and, in fact, had been failing most testing along the way. However, although there are claims that the BBC was well aware of the flaws in the project as early as 2011, the picture it presented to the outside world, including Parliamentary oversight committees, was relentlessly upbeat. The BBC's Director General, Mark Thompson, appeared before a committee in 2011 and told them DMI was definitely on schedule and was actually working already: "There are many programs that are already being made with DMI and some have gone to air and are going to air," he told Members of Parliament.

The trouble was, the project was not working well at all. Continual failures with the technology were widely known within the project team and company executives, but reports suggest that concerns were buried under a flood of rosy projections. In fact, a later report on the project by an outside consulting firm suggests that throughout 2012, the deteriorating fortunes of DMI were not accurately reported either within management or, critically, to the BBC Trust. For example, the BBC's own internal project management office issued a "code red" warning of imminent project failure in February that wasn't reported to the trust until six months later. The CTO, John Linwood, maintained that the project did work, would lead to a streamlined and more cost-effective method for producing media, and did not waver from that view throughout these years.

This rosy view hid a deeper problem: the technology just was not working well. Different views emerged as to why DMI was not progressing. To the "technologists," there was nothing wrong with the system; it did deliver working technology, but the project was undermined by would-be users who never bought into the original vision and who continually changed their requirements. They believed that DMI was failing not because it did not work, but as a result of internal politics. On the other side were those who questioned the development of the project because the technology, whether it had been "delivered" or not, never really worked, certainly not at the scale required to make it adopted across the whole organization. Further, it was becoming evident that off-the-shelf technology existed in the marketplace which did some of what DMI promised but which, critically, already worked well. Why, then, was the BBC spending so much time and money trying to create its own system out of thin air?

FIGURE 6.6 BBC Digital Initiative Project

Source: Roberto Herrett/Loop Images/Corbis

(*continued*)

According to a news report, it was not until April 2013 that events demonstrated the ongoing problems with DMI. During BBC coverage of the death and funeral of Margaret Thatcher, news staff worked feverishly to transfer old archived analog videotape to digital format in order to produce footage for background on the life and career of the former Prime Minister. So poorly did the new digital archive system work that it was reported that tapes had to be physically transported around London by taxi and subway system to get to their locations while video transfer work was being carried out by private production companies. All this after nearly four years working to develop DMI!

The failure of the system during Thatcher's funeral was the final straw. In May 2013 the new Director General of the BBC, Lord Hall, announced the cancellation of the project and that the BBC's chief technology officer, John Linwood, was to be suspended pending an external investigation into the management of the DMI project. It was later revealed that a senior BBC manager had expressed grave doubts about DMI to BBC Chairman Lord Patten one year before the project was cancelled. He had also claimed that there was a "very significant risk" that the National Audit Office had been misled about the actual progress of DMI in 2011. Other BBC executives had also voiced similar concerns for about two years before DMI was abandoned. The final cost of the project to the BBC and British taxpayers has been estimated at about $160 million. BBC Trust member Anthony Fry remarked that the DMI had been a "complete catastrophe" and said that the project was "probably the most serious, embarrassing thing I have ever seen."

Members of Parliament, looking into the failure of DMI, also had a number of very pointed criticisms of the project, executive oversight of DMI, and the operations of the BBC in general. Margaret Hodge MP, Chair of the Committee of Public Accounts, summed up the project in her Parliament report:

> "The BBC's Digital Media Initiative was a complete failure. License fee payers paid nearly £100 million ($160 million) for this supposedly essential system but got virtually nothing in return.
>
> The main output from the DMI is an archive catalogue and ordering system that is slower and more cumbersome than the 40-year-old system it was designed to replace. It has only 163 regular users and a running cost of £3 million ($5.1 million) a year, compared to £780,000 ($1.3 million) a year for the old system.
>
> When my Committee examined the DMI's progress in February 2011, the BBC told us that the DMI was "an absolutely essential have to have" and that a lot of the BBC's future was tied up in the successful delivery of the DMI.
>
> The BBC also told us that it was using the DMI to make many programs and was on track to complete the system in 2011 with no further delays. This turned out not to be the case.
>
> The BBC was far too complacent about the high risks involved in taking it in-house. No single individual had overall responsibility or accountability for delivering the DMI and achieving the benefits, or took ownership of problems when they arose.
>
> Lack of clearly defined responsibility and accountability meant the Corporation failed to respond to warning signals that the program was in trouble."

Bad planning, poor corporate governance, excessively optimistic projections, and a cloak of secrecy regarding the real status of the Digital Media Initiative project all resulted in a very public black eye for one of the most respected broadcasting organizations in the world. It is likely that the causes of the failure of the DMI project will be debated for years to come, but at a minimum this story should be a cautionary tale for organizations developing sophisticated IT projects.[42]

Project management also serves as an excellent training ground for future senior executives in most organizations. One unique aspect of projects is how they blend technical and behavioral challenges. The technical side of project management requires managers to become skilled in project selection, budgeting and resource management, planning and scheduling, and tracking projects. Each of these skills will be discussed in subsequent chapters. At the same time, however, project managers face the equally strong challenge of managing the behavioral, or "people," side of projects. Projects, being temporary endeavors, require project managers to bring together individuals from across the organization, quickly mold them into an effective team, manage conflict, provide leadership, and engage in negotiation and appropriate political behavior, all in the name of project success. Again, we will address these behavioral challenges in this text. One thing we know is: Project managers who emphasize one challenge and ignore the other, whether they choose to focus on the technical or behavioral side of project management, are not nearly as successful as those who seek to become experts in both. Why is project management such a useful training ground for senior executives? Because it provides the first true test of an individual's ability to master both the technical and human challenges that characterize effective leaders in business. Project managers, and their projects, create the kind of value that companies need to survive and prosper.

6.6 PROJECT LIFE CYCLES

Imagine receiving a term paper assignment in a college class. Our first step would be to develop a sense of the assignment itself—what the professor is looking for, how long the paper should be, the number of references required, stylistic expectations, and so forth. Once we have familiarized ourselves with the assignment, our next step would be to develop a plan for how we intend to proceed with the project in order to complete it by the due date. We make a rough guess about how much time will be needed for the research, writing the first draft, proofreading the paper, and completing the final draft; we use this information to create some tentative milestones for the various components of the assignment. Next, we begin to execute our plan, doing the library or online research, creating an outline, writing a draft, and so forth. Our goal is to complete the assignment on time, doing the work to our best possible ability. Finally, after turning in the paper, we file or discard our reference materials, return any books to the library, breathe a sigh of relief, and wait for the grade.

This example represents a simplified but useful illustration of a project's life cycle. In this case, the project consisted of completing the term paper to the standards expected of the instructor in the time allowed. A **project life cycle** refers to the stages in a project's development. Life cycles are important because they demonstrate the logic that governs a project. They also help us develop our plans for carrying out the project. They help us decide, for example, when we should devote resources to the project, how we should evaluate its progress, and so forth. Consider the simplified model of the project life cycle shown in Figure 6.7, which divides the life cycle into four distinct phases: conceptualization, planning, execution, and termination.

- *Conceptualization* refers to the development of the initial goal and technical specifications for a project. The scope of the work is determined, necessary resources (people, money, physical plant) identified, and important organizational contributors or **stakeholders** signed on.
- *Planning* is the stage in which all detailed specifications, schematics, schedules, and other plans are developed. The individual pieces of the project, often called *work packages*, are broken down, individual assignments made, and the process for completion clearly delineated. For example, in planning our approach to complete the term paper, we determine all the necessary steps (research, drafts, editing, etc.) in the process.
- During ***execution***, the actual "work" of the project is performed, the system developed, or the product created and fabricated. It is during the execution phase that the bulk of project team labor is performed. As Figure 6.7 shows, project costs (in man hours) ramp up rapidly during this stage.
- *Termination* occurs when the completed project is transferred to the customer, its resources reassigned, and the project formally closed out. As specific subactivities are completed, the project shrinks in scope and costs decline rapidly.

These stages are the waypoints at which the project team can evaluate both its performance and the project's overall status. Remember, however, that the life cycle is relevant only after the project has actually begun. The life cycle is signaled by the actual kickoff of project development,

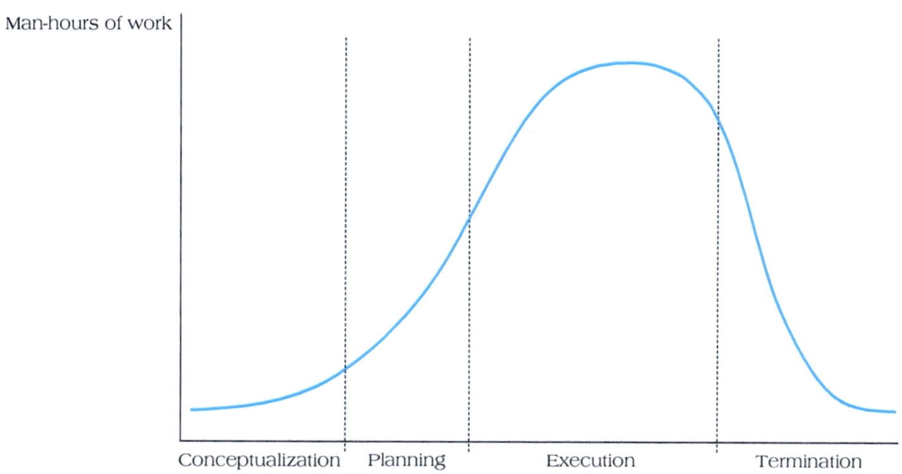

FIGURE 6.7 Project Life Cycle Stages

the development of plans and schedules, the performance of necessary work, and the completion of the project and reassignment of personnel. When we evaluate projects in terms of this life cycle model, we are given some clues regarding their subsequent resource requirements; that is, we begin to ask whether we have sufficient personnel, materials, and equipment to support the project. For example, when beginning to work on our term paper project, we may discover that it is necessary to purchase a PC or hire someone to help with researching the topic. Thus, as we plan the project's life cycle, we acquire important information regarding the resources that we will need. The life cycle model, then, serves the twofold function of project timing (schedule) and project requirements (resources), allowing team members to better focus on what and when resources are needed.

The project life cycle is also a useful means of visualizing the activities required and challenges to be faced during the life of a project. Figure 6.8 indicates some of these characteristics as they evolve during the course of completing a project.[43] As you can see, five components of a project may change over the course of its life cycle:

- ***Client interest:*** The level of enthusiasm or concern expressed by the project's intended customer. **Clients** can be either internal to the organization or external.
- ***Project stake:*** The amount of corporate investment in the project. The longer the life of the project, the greater the investment.
- ***Resources:*** The commitment of financial, human, and technical resources over the life of the project.
- ***Creativity:*** The degree of innovation required by the project, especially during certain development phases.
- ***Uncertainty:*** The degree of risk associated with the project. Riskiness here reflects the number of unknowns, including technical challenges that the project is likely to face. Uncertainty is highest at the beginning because many challenges have yet to be identified, let alone addressed.

Each of these factors has its own dynamic. Client interest, for example, follows a "U-shaped" curve, reflecting initial enthusiasm, lower levels of interest during development phases, and renewed interest as the project nears completion. Project stake increases dramatically as the project moves forward because an increasing commitment of resources is needed to support ongoing activities. Creativity, often viewed as innovative thought or applying a unique perspective, is high at the beginning of a project, as the team and the project's client begin developing a shared vision of the project. As the project moves forward and uncertainty remains high, creativity also continues to be an important feature. In fact, it is not until the project is well into its execution phase, with defined goals, that creativity becomes less important. To return to our example of the term

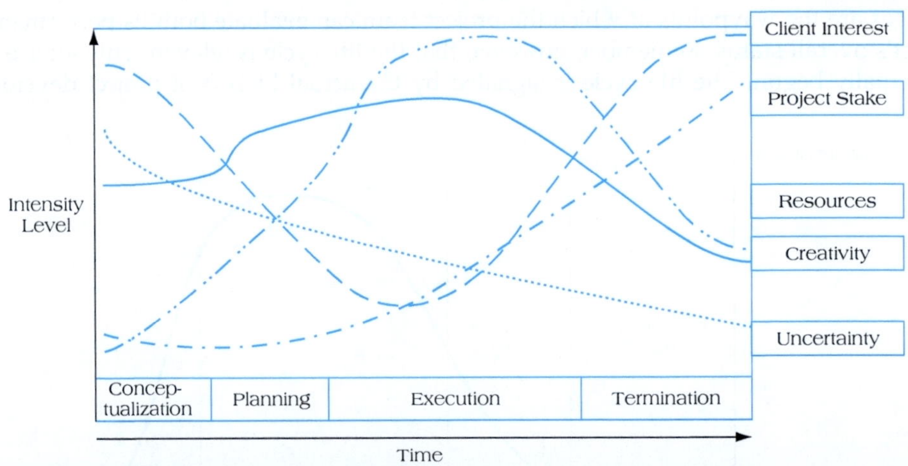

FIGURE 6.8 Project Life Cycles and Their Effects

Source: Victor Sohmen. (2002, July). "Project Termination: Why the Delay?" Paper presented at PMI Research Conference, Seattle, WA. Project Management Institute, Sohmen, Victor. "Project termination: Why the delay?" PMI Research Conference. Proceedings, p. 467–475. Paper presented at PMI Research Conference. Project Management Institute, Inc (2002). Copyright and all rights reserved. Material from this publication has been reproduced with the permission of PMI.

paper project, in many cases, the "creativity" needed to visualize a unique or valuable approach to developing the project is needed early, as we identify our goals and plan the process of achieving them. Once identified, the execution phase, or writing the term paper, places less emphasis on creativity per se and more on the concrete steps needed to complete the project assignment.

The information simplified in Figure 6.8 is useful for developing a sense of the competing issues and challenges that a project team is likely to face over the life cycle of a project. Over time, while certain characteristics (creativity, resources, and uncertainty) begin to decrease, other elements (client interest and project stake) gain in importance. Balancing the requirements of these elements across the project life cycle is just one of the many demands placed on a project team.

BOX 6.1

Project Managers in Practice

Stephanie Smith, Westinghouse Electric Company

Stephanie Smith is a project manager in the nuclear industry, working for Westinghouse Electric Company while living in Phoenix, Arizona. She earned her undergraduate degree in Biological Sciences from the University of Pittsburgh and subsequently a master's degree in Teaching. After teaching Biology and Environmental Sciences for four years, Stephanie decided on a career change and was hired as a Software Librarian at Westinghouse. Her job was to manage software created by multiple teams of engineers for use in nuclear power plants while also developing programmatic documentation such as program plans and program quality plans, document creation plans, and a program for technical editing of engineering documentation. After about a year of program-level support, she gained further experience working on large projects in nuclear protection and safety monitoring where, in addition to her other duties, she interacted with the members of the Nuclear Regulatory Commission.

As a project manager in the nuclear industry, the majority of the projects Stephanie has worked on are intended to perform first-of-a-kind engineering to develop products for use in nuclear power plants. This requires a strong technical skill set. However, Stephanie is quick to note that having the technical abilities alone does not prepare you for project management nor will it allow you to do your job to the best of your abilities. "Aside from the technical nature of this work, the majority of my effort is spent utilizing project management skills to develop and implement projects according to customer, internal quality, and regulatory requirements." Communication skills are critical, Stephanie argues, as "I regularly interact with my project team, upper management, and the customer to track project progress in terms of schedule, budget, and quality."

Stephanie is responsible for ensuring that technical problems are resolved as efficiently as possible, which is one of her greatest challenges, given the industry and the need to thoroughly think through problems,

FIGURE 6.9 Stephanie Smith—Westinghouse Electric

Source: Jeffrey Pinto/Pearson Education, Inc.

(continued)

effectively manage risks, and make prudent decisions regarding the safety of the product, all with an eye toward satisfying customers and regulatory agencies. "Risks must be effectively managed, particularly in the nuclear industry, for cost and safety reasons; therefore, I am always conscious that decisions we make have to be within carefully laid-out standards of safety." She is also responsible for contract management within her projects. This entails Stephanie working with customers and upper management to further define vague language in the contract so that work can be completed according to expectations. These meetings are also critical for project scope definition and control, skills project managers use on a daily basis.

"Without a strong foundation in project management fundamentals, I simply could not do my job," Stephanie argues. "My daily work is centered on the ability to effectively implement both the hard and soft skills of project management (i.e., the technical and people-oriented behaviors). Strong communication and leadership skills are very important in my daily work. Not a day goes by that I am not receiving and transmitting information among upper management, my team, and the customer. My work is dynamic, and regardless of how much planning is done, unanticipated events come up, which is where the need for flexibility comes in. The resolution of these problems requires significant communication skills and patience."

The greatest opportunity Stephanie sees in her work is supporting the development of clean energy worldwide. The nuclear industry has shed its old images and emerged in the current era as one of the cleanest and safest forms of energy. Nuclear power and project management are fast-growing and rapid-paced fields, and they require people interested in adapting to the unique challenges they offer. The work is demanding but, ultimately, highly rewarding. "In supporting a global effort for clean energy, I have the opportunity to work with very bright and energetic people, and I truly do learn something new every day. I encourage the novice or undergraduate to identify your greatest strengths, and try to develop a vision of how to apply those strengths to achieve the lifestyle you want. Do you see yourself in an office setting? Do you see yourself working in the field? One of the real advantages of project management careers is that they offer a level of flexibility and freedom that you rarely find in other office settings. Project management is challenging but the rewards can be impressive—both in terms of money and the satisfaction of seeing the results of your efforts."

6.7 DETERMINANTS OF PROJECT SUCCESS

Definitions of successful projects can be surprisingly elusive.[44] How do we know when a project is successful? When it is profitable? If it comes in on budget? On time? When the developed product works or sells? When we achieve our long-term payback goals? Generally speaking, any definition of **project success** *must* take into consideration the elements that define the very nature of a project: that is, time (schedule adherence), budget, functionality/quality, and customer satisfaction. At one time, managers normally applied three criteria of project success:

- ***Time.*** Projects are constrained by a specified time frame during which they must be completed. They are not supposed to continue indefinitely. Thus the first constraint that governs project management involves the basic requirement: the project should come in on or before its established schedule.
- ***Budget.*** A second key constraint for all projects is a limited budget. Projects must meet budgeted allowances in order to use resources as efficiently as possible. Companies do not write blank checks and hope for the best. Thus the second limit on a project raises the question: Was the project completed within budget guidelines?
- ***Performance.*** All projects are developed in order to adhere to some initially determined technical specifications. We know before we begin what the project is supposed to do or how the final product is supposed to operate. Measuring performance, then, means determining whether the finished product operates according to specifications. The project's clients naturally expect that the project being developed on their behalf will work as expected. Applying this third criterion is often referred to as conducting a "quality" check.

This so-called **triple constraint** was once the standard by which project performance was routinely assessed. Today, a fourth criterion has been added to these three (see Figure 6.10):

- ***Client acceptance.*** The principle of **client acceptance** argues that projects are developed with customers, or clients, in mind, and their purpose is to satisfy customers' needs. If client acceptance is a key variable, then we must also ask whether the completed project is

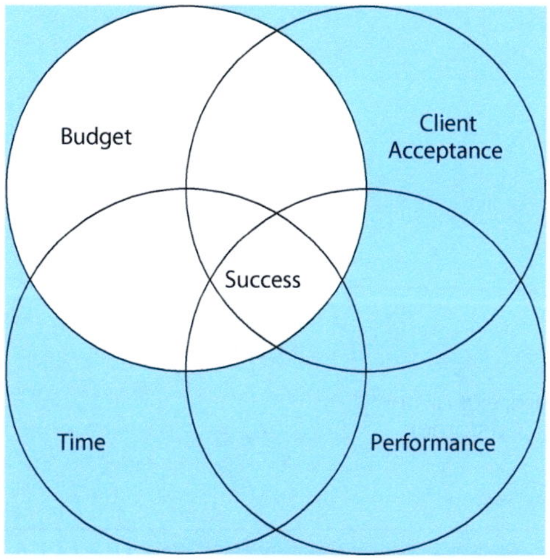

FIGURE 6.10 The New Quadruple Constraint

acceptable to the customer for whom it was intended. Companies that evaluate project success strictly according to the original "triple constraint" may fail to apply the most important test of all: the client's satisfaction with the completed project.

We can also think of the criteria for project success in terms of "internal" versus "external" conditions. When project management was practiced primarily by construction and other heavy industries, its chief value was in maintaining internal organizational control over expenditures of money and time. The traditional triple-constraint model made perfect sense. It focused internally on efficiency and productivity measures. It provided a quantifiable measure of personnel evaluation, and it allowed accountants to control expenses.

More recently, however, the traditional triple-constraint model has come under increasing criticism as a measure of project success. The final product, for example, could be a failure, but if it has been delivered in time and on budget and satisfies its original specifications (however flawed), the project itself could still be declared a success. Adding the external criterion of client acceptance corrects such obvious shortcomings in the assessment process. First, it refocuses corporate attention outside the organization, toward the customer, who will probably be dissatisfied with a failed or flawed final product. Likewise, it recognizes that the final arbiter of project success is not the firm's accountants, but rather the marketplace. A project is successful only to the extent that it benefits the client who commissioned it. Finally, the criterion of client acceptance requires project managers and teams to create an atmosphere of openness and communication throughout the development of the project.

Consider one example. In his book, *What Customers Really Want*, author Scott McKain relates how a coach bus company that transports music stars (i.e., clients either lease or purchase the company's buses) was originally planning to spend a great deal on a project to improve the interior of its vehicles because they believed that with these upgrades, customers would be willing to pay more to lease their buses. However, prior to starting a full-blown overhaul of their fleet, executives decided to ask past customers what they thought about this plan. Surprisingly, the company found that while its customers did want nice interiors, the single most important factor in selecting a coach company was the bus driver (i.e., a "nice guy," someone who could get the music stars to their destination safely, who would also serve as a good ambassador for the band with fans). Based on this information, the company dropped their original project and instead initiated a driver education program to teach their drivers how to communicate more effectively with customers and how to retain and grow customer goodwill. The company also started compensating drivers according to how well they served the customer and how well they cultivated long-term relationships with them. Once the company did that, it moved from fourth in the marketplace to first, and grew from 28 to 56 coaches.[45]

An additional approach to project assessment argues that another factor must always be taken into consideration: the promise that the delivered product can generate future opportunities, whether commercial or technical, for the organization.[46] In other words, it is not enough to assess

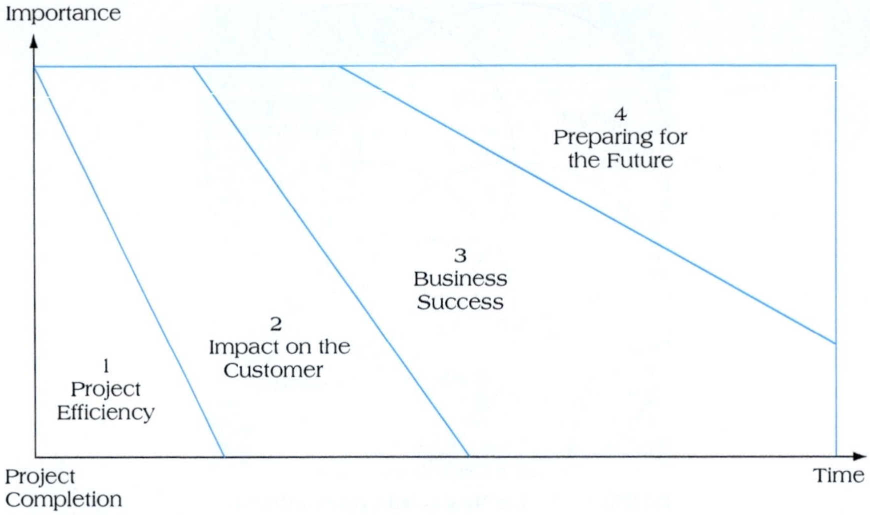

FIGURE 6.11 Four Dimensions of Project Success Importance

Source: A. J. Shenhar, O. Levy, and D. Dvir. (1997). "Mapping the Dimensions of Project Success," *Project Management Journal*, 28(2): 12. Copyright and all rights reserved. Material from this publication has been reproduced with the permission of PMI.

a project according to its immediate success. We must also evaluate it in terms of its commercial success as well as its potential for generating new business and new opportunities. Figure 6.11 illustrates this scheme, which proposes four relevant dimensions of success:

- *Project efficiency:* Meeting budget and schedule expectations.
- *Impact on customer:* Meeting technical specifications, addressing customer needs, and creating a project that satisfies the client's needs.
- *Business success:* Determining whether the project achieved significant commercial success.
- *Preparing for the future:* Determining whether the project opened new markets or new product lines or helped to develop new technology.

This approach challenges the conventional triple-constraint principle for assessing project success. Corporations expect projects not only to be run efficiently (at the least) but also to be developed to meet customer needs, achieve commercial success, and serve as conduits to new business opportunities. Even in the case of a purely internal project (e.g., updating the software for a firm's order-entry system), project teams need to focus both on customer needs and an assessment of potential commercial or technical opportunities arising from their efforts.

A final model, offered recently, also argues against the triple-constraint model as a measure of project success. According to Atkinson,[48] all groups that are affected by a project (stakeholders) should have a hand in assessing its success. The context and type of a project may also be relevant in specifying the criteria that will most clearly define its success or failure. Table 6.5 shows the Atkinson

TABLE 6.5 Understanding Success Criteria

Iron Triangle	Information System	Benefits (Organization)	Benefits (Stakeholders)
Cost	Maintainability	Improved efficiency	Satisfied users
Quality	Reliability	Improved effectiveness	Social and environmental impact
Time	Validity	Increased profits	Personal development
	Information quality	Strategic goals	Professional learning, contractors' profits
	Use	Organization learning	Capital suppliers, content
		Reduced waste	Project team, economic impact to surrounding community

BOX 6.2

Project Management Research in Brief

Assessing Information Technology (IT) Project Success

As noted earlier in this chapter, IT projects have a notoriously checkered history when it comes to successful implementation. Part of the problem has been an inability to define the characteristics of a successful IT project in concrete terms. The criteria for IT project success are often quite vague, and without clear guidelines for project success, it is hardly any wonder that so many of these projects do not live up to predevelopment expectations. In 1992 and again in 2003, two researchers, W. DeLone and E. McLean, analyzed several previous studies of IT projects to identify the key indicators of success. Their findings, synthesized from previous research, suggest that, at the very least, IT projects should be evaluated according to six criteria:

- ***System quality.*** The project team supplying the system must be able to assure the client that the implemented system will perform as intended. All systems should satisfy certain criteria: They should, for example, be easy to use, and they should supply quality information.
- ***Information quality.*** The information generated by the implemented IT must be the information required by users and be of sufficient quality that it is "actionable": In other words, generated information should not require additional efforts to sift or sort the data. System users can perceive quality in the information they generate.
- ***Use.*** Once installed, the IT system must be used. Obviously, the reason for any IT system is its usefulness as a problem-solving, decision-aiding, and networking mechanism. The criterion of "use" assesses the actual utility of a system by determining the degree to which, once implemented, it is used by the customer.
- ***User satisfaction.*** Once the IT system is complete, the project team must determine user satisfaction. One of the thorniest issues in assessing IT project success has to do with making an accurate determination of user satisfaction with the system. Yet, because the user is the client and is ultimately the arbiter of whether or not the project was effective, it is vital that we attain some measure of the client's satisfaction with the system and its output.
- ***Individual impact.*** All systems should be easy to use and should supply quality information. But beyond satisfying these needs, is there a specific criterion for determining the usefulness of a system to the client who commissioned it? Is decision making faster or more accurate? Is information more retrievable, more affordable, or more easily assimilated? In short, does the system benefit users in the ways that are most important to those users?
- ***Organizational impact.*** Finally, the supplier of the system must be able to determine whether it has a positive impact throughout the client organization. Is there, for example, a collective or synergistic effect on the client corporation? Is there a sense of good feeling, or are there financial or operational metrics that demonstrate the effectiveness or quality of the system?

DeLone and McLean's work provides an important framework for establishing a sense of IT project success. Companies that are designing and implementing IT systems must pay early attention to each of these criteria and take necessary steps to ensure that the systems that they deliver satisfy them.[47]

model, which views the traditional "iron triangle" of cost, quality, and time as merely one set of components in a comprehensive set of measures. Of course, the means by which a project is to be measured should be decided before the project is undertaken. A corporate axiom, "What gets measured, gets managed," suggests that when teams understand the standards to which a project is being held, they will place more appropriate emphases on the various aspects of project performance. Consider, for example, an information system setting. If the criteria of success are improved operating efficiency and satisfied users, and if quality is clearly identified as a key benefit of the finished product, the team will focus its efforts more strongly on these particular aspects of the project.

6.8 DEVELOPING PROJECT MANAGEMENT MATURITY

With the tremendous increase in project management practices among global organizations, a recent phenomenon has been the rise of project maturity models for project management organizations. **Project management maturity models** are used to allow organizations to benchmark the best practices of successful project management firms. Project management maturity models recognize that different organizations are currently at different levels of sophistication in their best

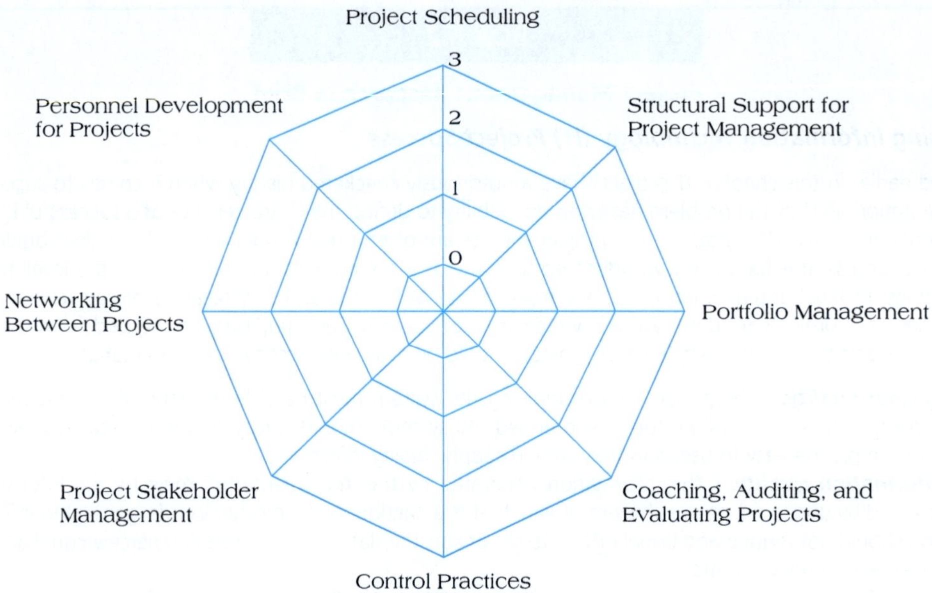

FIGURE 6.12 Spider Web Diagram for Measuring Project Maturity

Source: R. Gareis. (2001). "Competencies in the Project-Oriented Organization," in D. Slevin, D. Cleland, and J. Pinto, *The Frontiers of Project Management Research.* Newtown Square, PA: Project Management Institute, pp. 213–24, figure on p. 216. Copyright and all rights reserved. Material from this publication has been reproduced with the permission of PMI.

practices for managing projects. For example, it would be reasonable to expect an organization such as Boeing (aircraft and defense systems) or Fluor-Daniel (industrial construction) to be much more advanced in how they manage projects, given their lengthy histories of project initiatives, than a company that has only recently developed an emphasis on project-based work.

The purpose of **benchmarking** is to systematically manage the process improvements of project delivery by a single organization over a period of time.[49] Because there are many diverse dimensions of project management practice, it is common for a new organization just introducing project management to its operations to ask, "Where do we start?" That is, which of the multiple project management processes should we investigate, model, and apply to our organization? Maturity models provide the necessary framework to first, analyze and critically evaluate current practices as they pertain to managing projects; second, compare those practices against those of chief competitors or some general industry standard; and third, define a systematic route for improving these practices.

If we accept the fact that the development of better project management practices is an evolutionary process, involving not a sudden leap to top performance but rather a systematic commitment to continuous improvement, maturity models offer the template for defining and then achieving such progressive improvement.[50] As a result, most effective project maturity models chart both a set of standards that are currently accepted as state-of-the-art as well as a process for achieving significant movement toward these benchmarks. Figure 6.12 illustrates one approach to defining current project management practices a firm is using.[51] It employs a "spider web" methodology in which a set of significant project management practices have first been identified for organizations within a specific industry. In this example, a firm may identify eight components of project management practice that are key for success, based on an analysis of the firm's own needs as well as through benchmarking against competing firms in the industry. Note that each of the rings in the diagram represents a critical evaluation of the manner in which the organization matches up with industry standards. Suppose we assigned the following meanings to the different ratings:

Ring Level	Meaning
0	Not defined or poor
1	Defined but substandard
2	Standardized
3	Industry leader or cutting edge

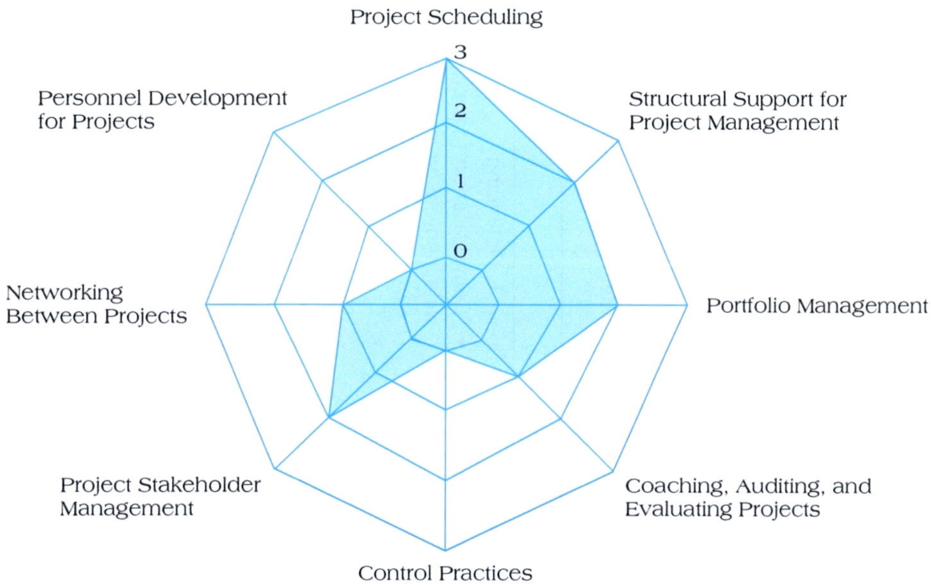

FIGURE 6.13 Spider Web Diagram with Embedded Organizational Evaluation

Source: R. Gareis. (2001). "Competencies in the Project-Oriented Organization," in D. Slevin, D. Cleland, and J. Pinto, *The Frontiers of Project Management Research*. Newtown Square, PA: Project Management Institute, pp. 213–24, figure on p. 216. Copyright and all rights reserved. Material from this publication has been reproduced with the permission of PMI.

Following this example, we may decide that in terms of project team personnel development or project control systems, our practices are poor relative to other competitors and rate those skills as 0. On the other hand, perhaps our scheduling processes are top-notch, enabling us to rate them as a 3. Figure 6.13 shows an example of the same spider web diagram with our relative skill levels assigned across the eight key elements of project management we have defined. This exercise helps us to form the basis for where we currently are in terms of project management sophistication, a key stage in any maturity model in which we seek to move to a higher level.

Once we have established a sense of our present project management abilities, as well as our shortcomings, the next step in the maturity model process is to begin charting a step-by-step, incremental path to our desired goal. Table 6.6 highlights some of the more common project maturity models and the interim levels they have identified en route to the highest degree of organization-wide project expertise. Several of these models were developed by private project management consultancies or professional project organizations.

It is interesting to compare and contrast the four maturity models highlighted in Table 6.6. These examples of maturity models are taken from the most well-known models in the field, including Carnegie Mellon University's Software Engineering Institute's (SEI) Capability Maturity Model, Harold Kerzner's Maturity Model, ESI International's Project Framework, and the maturity model developed by the Center for Business Practices.[52] Illustrating these dimensions in pyramid form, we can see the progression toward project management maturity (Figure 6.14). Despite some differences in terminology, a clear sense of pattern exists among these models. Typically they start with the assumption that project management practices within a firm are not planned and are not collectively employed; in fact, there is likely no common language or methods for undertaking project management. As the firm grows in project maturity, it begins to adopt common practices, starts programs to train cadres of project management professionals, establishes procedures and processes for initiating and controlling its projects, and so forth. Finally, by the last stage, not only is the organization "project-savvy," but it also has progressed beyond simply applying project management to its processes and is now actively exploring ways to continuously improve its project management techniques and procedures. It is during the final stage that the organization can be truly considered "project mature"; it has internalized all necessary project management principles and is actively seeking to move beyond them in innovative ways.

TABLE 6.6 A Comparison of Project Maturity Models and Incremental Stages

Center for Business Practices				
Level 1: Initial Process • Ad hoc process • Management awareness	Level 2: Structure, Process, and Standards • Basic processes, not standard on all projects • Management supports use • Estimates, schedules based on expert knowledge	Level 3: Institutionalized Project Management • All project processes are repeatable • Estimates, schedules based on industry standards	Level 4: Managed • Project management practices integrated with corporate processes • Solid analysis of project performance • Estimates, schedules based on corporate specifics	Level 5: Optimizing • Processes to measure project efficiency • Processes in place to improve project performance • Company focuses on continuous improvement
Kerzner's Project Management Maturity Model				
Level 1: Common Language • Sporadic use of project management • Small pockets of interest in the firm • No investment in PM training	Level 2: Common Processes • Tangible benefits made apparent • PM support throughout the firm • Development of a PM curriculum	Level 3: Singular Methodology • Integrated processes • Cultural and management support • Financial benefit from PM training	Level 4: Benchmarking • Analysis and evaluation of practices • Project office established	Level 5: Continuous Improvement • Lessons learned, files created • Knowledge transfer between teams • Mentorship program
ESI International's Project Framework				
Level 1: Ad Hoc • Processes ill-defined because they are applied individually • Little support by organization	Level 2: Consistent • Organization is well intentioned in its methods • No project control processes or lessons learned	Level 3: Integrated • Processes are tailored to enhance all PM aspects • Common use and understanding of methods across the firm	Level 4: Comprehensive • PM fully implemented across the firm • Information is used to evaluate processes and reduce variation • Advanced PM tools and techniques are developed	Level 5: Optimizing • Continual effort to improve and innovate project capability • Common failures are eliminated
SEI's Capability Maturity Model Integration				
Level 1: Initial • Ad hoc, chaotic processes	Level 2: Managed • Requirements management, project planning, and control occur • Process quality assurance occurs • Configuration management is used	Level 3: Defined • Requirements development and product integration occur • Verification and validation of processes • Risk management is emphasized	Level 4: Quantitative Management • Process performance is gauged • Quantitative PM highlighted	Level 5: Optimizing • Innovation and deployment accentuated • Causal analysis and resolution occur

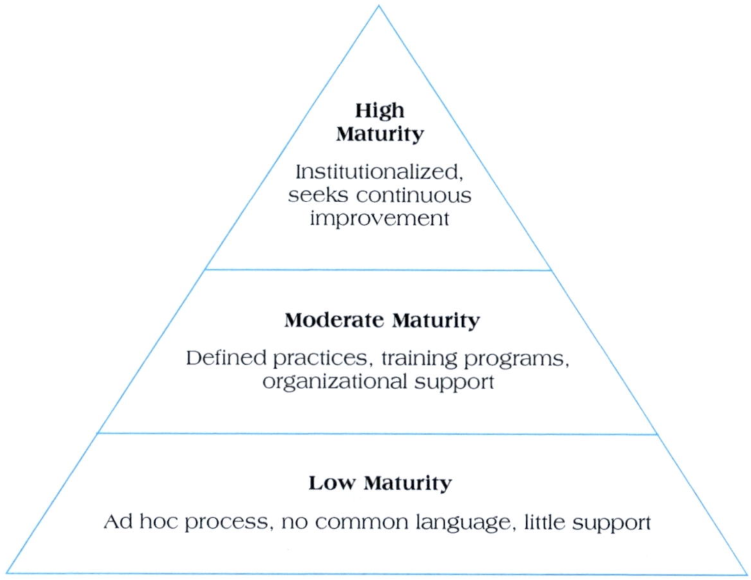

FIGURE 6.14 **Project Management Maturity—A Generic Model**

Project maturity models have become very useful in recent years precisely because they reflect the growing interest in project management while highlighting one of the recurring problems: the lack of clear direction for companies in adopting, adapting, and improving these processes for optimal use. The key feature of these models is the important recognition that change typically does not occur abruptly; that is, companies that desire to become skilled in their project management approaches simply cannot progress in immediate steps from a lack of project management understanding to optimal project practices. Instead, the maturity models illustrate that "maturity" is an ongoing process, based on continuous improvement through identifiable incremental steps. Once we have an accurate picture of where we fit into the maturity process, we can begin to determine a reasonable course of action to progress to our desired level. In this manner, any organization, no matter how initially unskilled in project management, can begin to chart a course toward the type of project organization it hopes to become.

6.9 PROJECT ELEMENTS AND TEXT ORGANIZATION

This text was written to provide a holistic, managerial-based approach to project management. The text is holistic in that it weaves together the wide variety of duties, responsibilities, and knowledge that successful project managers must acquire. Project management is a comprehensive and exciting undertaking. It requires us to understand aspects of management science in building schedules, assigning resources, monitoring and controlling our projects, and so forth. At the same time, successful project managers also must integrate fundamental issues of behavioral science, involving knowledge of human beings, leadership practices, motivation and team development, conflict resolution, and negotiation skills. Truly, a "science-heavy" approach to this subject will make us no more successful in our future project management responsibilities than will a focus that retains an exclusively "people-based" outlook. Project management is an exciting and challenging blend of the science and art of management.

Figure 6.15 offers a model for the organization of this text. The figure is a Gantt chart, a project scheduling and control device that we will become more familiar. For now, however, we can apply it to the structure of this book by focusing on some of its simpler features. First, note that all chapters in the book are listed down the left-hand column. Across the bottom and running from left to right is a simple time line that illustrates the point at which each of the chapters' topics will be introduced. For simplicity's sake, I have divided the X-axis time line into four distinct project phases that roughly follow the project life cycle discussed earlier in this chapter: (1) Foundation, (2) Planning, (3) Implementation, and (4) Termination. Notice how some of the topics we will cover are particularly relevant only during certain phases of the project while

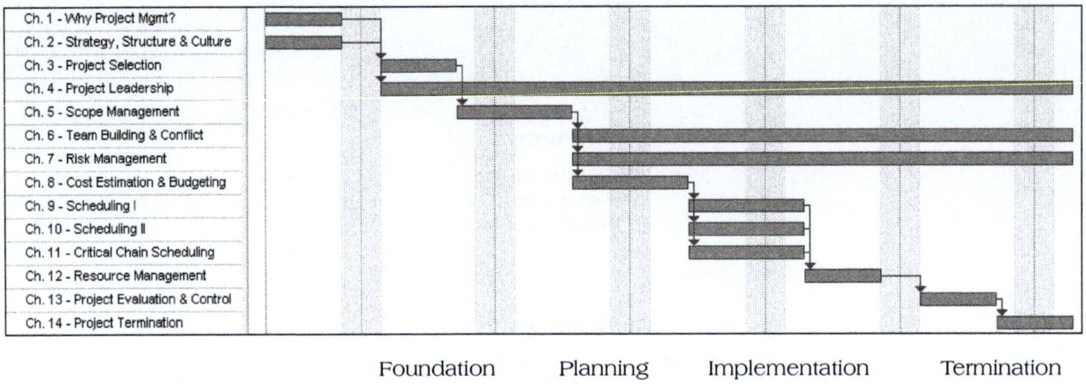

FIGURE 6.15 Organization of Text

others, such as project leadership, are significant across much of the project's life cycle. Among the benefits of setting up the text to follow this sequence are that, first, it shows the importance of blending the human-based topics (leadership and team building) directly with the more analytical or scientific elements of project management. We cannot compartmentalize our approach to project management as either exclusively technical or behavioral; the two are opposite sides of the same coin and must be appreciated jointly. Second, the structure provides a simple logic for ordering the chapters and the stage of the project at which we are most likely to concern ourselves with these topics. Some concepts, as illustrated by the figure, are more immediately concerned with project planning while others become critical at later phases in the project. Appreciating the elements of project management *and their proper sequencing* is an important learning guide. Finally, the figure offers an intuitively appealing method for visually highlighting the structure and flow we will follow across the topics in the text.

The foundation stage helps us with our fundamental understanding of what projects are and how they are typically managed in modern organizations. As part of that understanding, we must necessarily focus on the organizational setting within which projects are created, selected, and developed. Some of the critical issues that can affect the manner in which projects are successfully implemented are the contextual issues of a firm's strategy, structure, and culture. Either these elements are set up to support project-based work or they are not. In the former case, it is far easier to run projects and achieve positive results for the organization. As a result, it is extremely helpful for us to clearly understand the role that organizational setting, or context, plays in project management.

In Chapter 12 we explore the process of project screening and selection. The manner in which a firm selects the projects it chooses to undertake is often critical to its chances of successful development and commercial profitability. Project management is an extremely "leader-intensive" undertaking: The project manager is the focal point of the project, often functioning as a miniature CEO. The more project managers understand about project leadership and the skills required by effective project managers, the better companies can begin training project managers within their own ranks.

The second phase is related to the up-front issues of project planning. Once a decision to proceed has been made, the organization must first select a suitable project manager to oversee the development process. Immediately, this project manager is faced with a number of responsibilities, including:

1. ***Selecting a team***—Team building and conflict management are the first challenges that project managers face.
2. ***Developing project objectives and a plan for execution***—Identifying project requirements and a logical plan to develop the project are crucial.
3. ***Performing risk management activities***—Projects are not developed without a clear sense of the risks involved in their planning and implementation.
4. ***Cost estimating and budgeting***—Because projects are resource-constrained activities, careful budgeting and cost estimation are critical.

5. *Scheduling*—The heart of project planning revolves around the process of creating clear, aggressive, yet reasonable schedules that chart the most efficient course to project completion.
6. *Managing resources*—The final step in project planning is the careful management of project resources, including project team personnel, to most efficiently perform tasks.

"Project scope management" is something of an umbrella term under which we consider a number of elements in the overall project planning process. This chapter elaborates the variety of planning techniques and steps for getting a project off on the right foot.

Chapter 17 addresses some of the behavioral challenges project managers face in terms of effective team building and conflict management. This chapter looks at another key component of effective human resource management: the need to create and maintain high-performance teams. Effectively building and nurturing team members—often people from very different backgrounds—is a constant challenge and one that requires serious consideration. Conflict occurs on a number of levels, not just among team members, but between the team and project stakeholders, including top management and customers. This chapter will identify some of the principal causes of conflict and explain various methods for resolving it.

Chapter 13 deals with project risk management. In recent years, this area of project management has become increasingly important to companies that want to ensure, as far as possible, that project selection choices are appropriate, that all the risks and downside potential have been considered, and that, where appropriate, contingency plans have been developed. Chapter 18 covers budgeting and cost estimation. Because project managers and teams are held to both standards of performance and standards of cost control, it is important to understand the key features of cost estimation and budgeting.

These chapters offer an in-depth analysis of various project-scheduling tools, discuss critical software for project scheduling, and explain some recent breakthroughs in project scheduling. Once various project activities have been identified, we must make sure they work by allocating the resources needed to support them.

The third process in project management, *implementation,* is most easily understood as the stage in which the actual "work" of the project is being performed. For example, engineers and other technical experts determine the series of tasks necessary to complete the overall project, including their individual task responsibilities, and each of the tasks is actively managed by the manager and team to ensure that there are no significant delays that can cause the project to exceed its schedule. Chapter 18 addresses the project challenges of control and evaluation. During the implementation phase, a considerable amount of ambiguity regarding the status of the project is possible unless specific, practical steps are taken to establish a clear method for tracking and controlling the project.

Finally, the processes of project termination reflect the fact that a project is a unique organizational endeavor, marked by a specified beginning and ending. The process of closing down a project, whether due to the need to "kill" it because it is no longer viable or through the steps of a planned termination, offers its own set of challenges. A number of procedures have been developed to make this process as smooth and logical as possible. The phase in which the project is concluded and resources (both monetary and human) are reassigned.

This book was written to help create a new generation of effective project managers. By exploring the various roles of project managers and addressing the challenges and opportunities they constantly face, we will offer a comprehensive and integrative approach to better understand the task of project management—one that explores the full range of strategic, technical, and behavioral challenges and duties for project managers.

This text also includes, at the end of relevant chapters, a series of activities designed to help students develop comprehensive project plans. It is absolutely essential that persons completing a course in project management carry away with them practical knowledge about the steps involved in creating a project, planning its development, and overseeing its work. Future managers need to develop the skills to convert the theories of project management into the successful practice of the craft. With this goal in mind, the text contains a series of exercises designed to help professors and students construct overall project plans. Activities involve the development, from beginning to end, of a project plan, including narrative, risk analysis, work breakdown structure, activity estimation and network diagramming, resource leveling and project budgeting, and so forth. In order to add a sense of realism to the process, later chapters in the book also include a series of hypothetical problems. By the end of the course, students should have created a comprehensive project document that details the necessary steps in converting project plans into practical accomplishments.

As a template for providing examples, the text employs a hypothetical company called ABCups Inc., which is about to initiate an important project. Chapter-ending activities, including exercises in scheduling, budgeting, risk management, and so forth, will often include examples created from the ABCups project for students to use as a model for their own work. In this way, students will be presented both with a challenge and with an example for generating their own deliverables as they progressively build their project plans.

Several software packages are available for planning and tracking the current status of a project. Some of them (e.g., products by SAP and Oracle) are large, quite complex, and capable of linking project management functions to other critical through-put operations of a company. Other desktop software packages are more readily accessible and easier to interpret for the average novice interested in improving his or her project management skills. This text uses examples throughout from Microsoft's Project 2013, including screen captures, to illustrate how MSP 2013 can be used for a variety of planning and tracking purposes. Additionally, some simple tutorials are included in the appendices at the end of the text to give readers a feel for how the software works and some of the features it offers. As a method for learning the capabilities of the software, it's a start. For those committed to fully learning one of these project management scheduling packages, I encourage you to investigate alternative packages and, once you have made your choice, invest in a comprehensive training manual.

An additional feature of this text is the linkage between concepts that are discussed throughout and the Project Management Body of Knowledge (PMBoK), which was developed by the Project Management Institute (PMI). As the world's leading professional organization for project management and with nearly half a million members, PMI has been in the forefront of efforts to standardize project management practices and codify the necessary skills to be successful in our field. Now in its fifth edition, the PMBoK identifies ten critical "knowledge areas" of project management skills and activities that all practitioners need to master in order to become fully trained in their profession. These knowledge areas, which are shown in Figure 6.16, encompass a broad overview of the component processes for project management. Although it is not my intention to create a text to serve as a primer for taking a professional certification exam, it is important for us to recognize that the skills we develop through reading this work are directly applicable to the professional project management knowledge areas.

Students will find several direct links to the PMBoK in this text. First, the key terms and their definitions are intended to follow the updated, fifth edition PMBoK glossary (included as an appendix at the end of the text). Second, chapter introductions will also highlight references to the PMBoK as we address them in turn. We can see how each chapter not only adds to our knowledge of project management but also directly links to elements within the PMBoK. Finally, many end-of-chapter exercises and Internet references will require direct interaction with PMI through its Web site.

As an additional link to the Project Management Institute and the PMBoK, this text will include sample practice questions at the end of relevant chapters to allow students to test their in-depth knowledge of aspects of the PMBoK. Nearly 20 years ago, PMI instituted its Project Management Professional (PMP) certification as a means of awarding those with an expert knowledge of project management practice. The PMP certification is the highest professional designation for project management expertise in the world and requires in-depth knowledge in all nine areas of the PMBoK. To date, more than 600,000 project professionals worldwide have attained the PMP certification and the numbers are steadily growing each year. The inclusion of questions at the end of the relevant chapters offers students a way to assess how well they have learned the important course topics, the nature of PMP certification exam questions, and to point to areas that may require additional study in order to master this material.

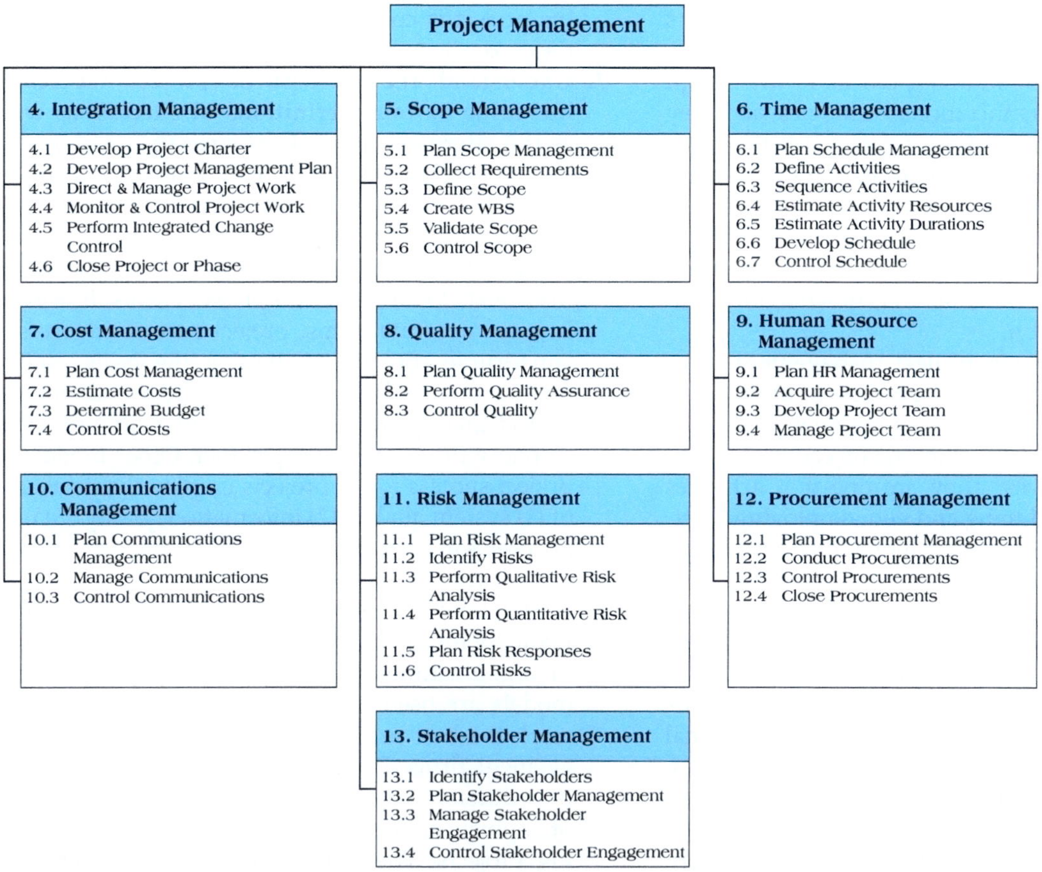

FIGURE 6.16 Overview of the Project Management Institute's PMBoK Knowledge Areas

Source: Project Management Institute. (2013). *A Guide to the Project Management Body of Knowledge (PMBoK Guide)*, 5th ed. Project Management Institute, Inc. Copyright and all rights reserved. Material from this publication has been reproduced with the permission of PMI.

This text offers an opportunity for students to begin mastering a new craft—a set of skills that is becoming increasingly valued in contemporary corporations around the world. Project managers represent the new corporate elite: a corps of skilled individuals who routinely make order out of chaos, improving a firm's bottom line and burnishing their own value in the process. With these goals in mind, let us begin.[53]

Summary

1. **Understand why project management is becoming such a powerful and popular practice in business.** Project management offers organizations a number of practical competitive advantages, including the ability to be both effective in the marketplace and efficient with the use of organizational resources, and the ability to achieve technological breakthroughs, to streamline new-product development, and to manage the challenges arising from the business environment.
2. **Recognize the basic properties of projects, including their definition.** Projects are defined as temporary endeavors undertaken to create a unique product or service. Among their key properties are that projects are complex, one-time processes; projects are limited by budget, schedule, and resources; they are developed to resolve a clear goal or set of goals; and they are customer-focused.
3. **Understand why effective project management is such a challenge.** Projects operate outside of normal organizational processes, typified by the work done by functional organizational units. Because they are unique, they require a different mindset: one that is temporary and aimed at achieving

a clear goal within a limited time frame. Projects are ad hoc endeavors with a clear life cycle. They are employed as the building blocks in the design and execution of organizational strategies, and they provide a philosophy and a strategy for the management of change. Other reasons why they are a challenge include the fact that project management requires the crossing of functional and organizational boundaries while trying to satisfy the multiple constraints of time, budget, functionality, and customer satisfaction.

4. **Differentiate between project management practices and more traditional, process-oriented business functions.** Projects involve new process or product ideas, typically with one objective or a limited set of objectives. They are one-shot activities with a defined beginning and end, employing a heterogeneous group of organizational members as the project team. They operate under circumstances of change and uncertainty, outside of normal organizational channels, and are intended to upset the status quo and violate established practice, if need be, in order to achieve project goals. Process-oriented functions adhere more closely to rigid organizational rules, channels of communication, and procedures. The people within the functional departments are homogenous, engaged in ongoing activities, with well-established systems and procedures. They represent bastions of established practice designed to reinforce the organization's status quo.
5. **Recognize the key motivators that are pushing companies to adopt project management practices.** Among the key motivators in pushing organizations to adopt project management are (1) shortened product life cycles, (2) narrow product launch windows, (3) increasingly complex and technical products, (4) the emergence of global markets, and (5) an economic period marked by low inflation.
6. **Understand and explain the project life cycle, its stages, and the activities that typically occur at each stage in the project.** The project life cycle is a mechanism that links time to project activities and refers to the stages in a project's development. The common stages used to describe the life cycle for a project are (1) conceptualization, (2) planning, (3) execution, and (4) termination. A wide and diverse set of activities occurs during different life cycle stages; for example, during the conceptualization phase, the basic project mission and scope is developed and the key project stakeholders are signed on to support the project's development. During planning, myriad project plans and schedules are created to guide the development process. Execution requires that the principal work of the project be performed, and finally, during the termination stage, the project is completed, the work is finished, and the project is transferred to the customer.
7. **Understand the concept of project "success," including various definitions of success, as well as the alternative models of success.** Originally, project success was predicated simply on a triple-constraint model that rewarded projects if they were completed with regard to schedule, budget, and functionality. This model ignored the emphasis that needs to be placed on project clients, however. In more accurate terms, project success involves a "quadruple constraint," linking the basic project metrics of schedule adherence, budget adherence, project quality (functionality), and customer satisfaction with the finished product. Other models of project success for IT projects employ the measures of (1) system quality, (2) information quality, (3) use, (4) user satisfaction, (5) individual impact, and (6) organizational impact.
8. **Understand the purpose of project management maturity models and the process of benchmarking in organizations.** Project management maturity models are used to allow organizations to benchmark the best practices of successful project management firms. Project maturity models recognize that different organizations are at different levels of sophistication in their best practices for managing projects. The purpose of benchmarking is to systematically manage the process improvements of project delivery by a single organization over a period of time. As a firm commits to implementing project management practices, maturity models offer a helpful, multistage process for moving forward through increasing levels of sophistication of project expertise.
9. **Identify the relevant maturity stages that organizations go through to become proficient in their use of project management techniques.** Although there are a number of project maturity models, several of the most common share some core features. For example, most take as their starting point the assumption that unsophisticated organizations initiate projects in an ad hoc fashion, with little overall shared knowledge or procedures. As the firm moves through intermediate steps, it will begin to initiate processes and project management procedures that diffuse a core set of project management techniques and cultural attitudes throughout the organization. Finally, the last stage in maturity models typically recognizes that by this point the firm has moved beyond simply learning the techniques of project management and is working at continuous improvement processes to further refine, improve, and solidify project management philosophies among employees and departments.

Key Terms

Benchmarking	Deliverables	Project life cycle	Project success
Client acceptance	Performance	Project management	Stakeholders
Clients	Process	Project management maturity models	Time
Budget	Project		Triple constraint

Discussion Questions

6.1 Describe the features of a project. How do they differ from day-to-day processes within an organization?

6.2 What do you see as being the primary challenges to introducing a project management philosophy in most organizations? That is, why is it difficult to shift to a project-based approach in many companies?

6.3 What are the advantages and disadvantages of using project management?

6.4 What key characteristics do all projects possess?

6.5 Consider and debate the usefulness of a project's life cycle as illustrated in Figure 6.4. What does this model suggest about the characteristics of projects and the impact they have on a project's life cycle?

6.6 Think of a successful project and an unsuccessful project with which you are familiar. What distinguishes the two, both in terms of the process used to develop them and their outcomes?

6.7 Consider the case on the BBC's Digital Initiative Media in this chapter. What do you see as some of the main problems associated with the BBC's approach to project management? What challenges did the project management team face in this project, and how can a firm responsible for large IT transformation projects overcome some of these challenges?

6.8 Consider the six criteria for successful IT projects. Why is IT project success often so difficult to assess? Make a case for some factors being more important than others.

6.9 As organizations seek to become better at managing projects, they often engage in benchmarking with other companies in similar industries. Discuss the concept of benchmarking. What are its goals? How does benchmarking work?

6.10 Explain the concept of a project management maturity model. What purpose does it serve?

6.11 Compare and contrast the four project management maturity models shown in Table 6.3. What strengths and weaknesses do you perceive in each of the models?

CASE STUDY 6.1

MegaTech, Inc.

MegaTech, Inc., designs and manufactures automotive components. For years, the company enjoyed a stable marketplace, a small but loyal group of customers, and a relatively predictable environment. Though slowly, annual sales continued to grow until recently hitting $300 million. MegaTech products were popular because they required little major updating or yearly redesign. The stability of its market, coupled with the consistency of its product, allowed MegaTech to forecast annual demand accurately, to rely on production runs with long lead times, and to concentrate on internal efficiency.

Then, with the advent of the North American Free Trade Agreement (NAFTA) and other international trade agreements, MegaTech found itself competing with auto parts suppliers headquartered in countries around the world. The company was thrust into an unfamiliar position: It had to become customer-focused and quicker to market with innovative products. Facing these tremendous commercial challenges, top management at MegaTech decided to recreate the company as a project-based organization.

The transition, though not smooth, has nonetheless paid big dividends. Top managers determined, for instance, that product updates had to be much more frequent. Achieving this goal meant yearly redesigns and new technologies, which, in turn, meant making innovative changes in the firm's operations. In order to make these adjustments, special project teams were formed around each of the company's product lines and given a mandate to maintain market competitiveness.

At the same time, however, MegaTech wanted to maintain its internal operating efficiencies. Thus

(continued)

all project teams were given strict cost and schedule guidelines for new product introductions. Finally, the company created a sophisticated research and development team, which is responsible for locating likely new avenues for technological change 5 to 10 years down the road. Today, MegaTech operates project teams not only for managing current product lines but also for seeking longer-term payoffs through applied research.

MegaTech has found the move to project management challenging. For one thing, employees are still rethinking the ways in which they allocate their time and resources. In addition, the firm's success rate with new projects is still less than management had hoped. Nevertheless, top managers feel that, on balance, the shift to project management has given the company the operating advantage that it needed to maintain its lead over rivals in its globally competitive industry. "Project management," admits one MegaTech executive, "is certainly not a magic pill for success, but it has started us thinking about how we operate. As a result, we are doing smarter things in a faster way around here."

Questions

1. What is it about project management that offers MegaTech a competitive advantage in its industry?
2. What elements of the marketplace in which MegaTech operates led the firm to believe that project management would improve its operations?

CASE STUDY 6.2

The IT Department at Hamelin Hospital

Hamelin Hospital is a large (700-bed) regional hospital in the northeastern United States. The information technology (IT) department employs 75 people and has an operating budget of over $35 million. The department is responsible for managing 30–40 projects, ranging from small (redesigning computer screens) to very large, such as multimillion-dollar system development projects that can run for over a year. Hamelin's IT department has been growing steadily, reflecting the hospital's commitment to expanding its information storage and processing capacities. The two principal functions of the IT department are developing new software applications and maintaining the current information system. Project management is a way of life for the department.

The IT department jobs fall into one of five categories: (1) help-desk technician, (2) programmer, (3) senior programmer, (4) systems analyst, and (5) project manager. Help-desk technicians field queries from computer system users and solve a wide range of problems. Most new hires start at the help desk, where they can become familiar with the system, learn about problem areas, become sensitive to users' frustrations and concerns, and understand how the IT department affects all hospital operations. As individuals move up the ladder, they join project teams, either as programmers or systems analysts. Finally, five project managers oversee a constantly updated slate of projects. In addition, the workload is always being supplemented by new projects. Team personnel finish one assignment and then move on to a new one. The typical IT department employee is involved in seven projects, each at a different stage of completion.

The project management system in place at Hamelin is well regarded. It has spearheaded a tremendous expansion of the hospital's IT capabilities and thus helped the hospital to gain a competitive advantage over other regional hospitals. Recently, in fact, Hamelin began "farming out" its IT services on a fee-for-service basis to competing hospitals needing help with their records, administration, order-entry systems, and so forth. Not surprisingly, the results have improved the hospital's bottom line: At a time when more and more health care organizations are feeling the effects of spiraling health care costs, Hamelin's IT department has helped the hospital sustain continuous budget increases, additional staffing, a larger slate of projects, and a track record of success.

Questions

1. What are the benefits and drawbacks of starting most new hires at the help-desk function?
2. What are the potential problems with requiring project team members to be involved in multiple projects at the same time? What are the potential advantages?
3. What signals does the department send by making "project manager" the highest position in the department?

CASE STUDY 6.3

Disney's Expedition Everest

One of the newest thrill rides to open in the Walt Disney World Resort may just be the most impressive. As Disney approached its 50th anniversary, the company wanted to celebrate in a truly special way. What was its idea? Create a park attraction that would, in many ways, serve as the link between Disney's amazing past and its promising future. Disney showed that it was ready to pull out all stops in order to get everything just right.

In 2006, The Walt Disney Company introduced Expedition Everest in Disney's Animal Kingdom Park at Lake Buena Vista, Florida. Expedition Everest is more than just a roller coaster. It is the embodiment of the Disney spirit: a ride that combines Disney's trademark thrills, unexpected twists and turns, incredible attention to detail, and impressive project management skills.

First, let's consider some of the technical details of Expedition Everest:

- With a peak of just under 200 feet, the ride is contained within the tallest of 18 mountains created by Disney's Imagineers at Disney parks worldwide.
- The ride contains nearly a mile of track, with twists, tight turns, and sudden drops.
- The Disney team created a Yeti: an enormous, fur-covered, Audio-Animatronics monster powered by a set of hydraulic cylinders whose combined thrust equals that of a Boeing 747 airliner. Through a series of sketches, computer-animated drawings, sculptures, and tests that took more than two years to perfect, Disney created and programmed its Abominable Snowman to stand over 10 feet tall and serve as the focal point of the ride.
- More than 900 bamboo plants, 10 species of trees, and 110 species of shrubs were planted to re-create the feeling of the Himalayan lowlands surrounding Mount Everest.
- More than 1,800 tons of steel were used to construct the mountain. The covering of the framework was done using more than 3,000 prefabricated "chips" created from 25,000 individual computer-molded pieces of steel.
- To create the proper color schemes, 2,000 gallons of stain and paint were used on rockwork and throughout the village Disney designed to serve as a backdrop for the ride.
- More than 2,000 handcrafted items from Asia are used as props, cabinetry, and architectural ornamentation.

Building an attraction does not come easily or quickly for Disney's Imagineers. Expedition Everest was several years in development as Disney sent teams, including Walt Disney Imagineering's Creative Executive Joe Rohde, on repeated trips to the Himalayas in Nepal to study the lands, architecture, colors, ecology, and culture in order to create the most authentic setting for the new attraction. Disney's efforts reflect a desire to do much more than provide a world-class ride experience; they demonstrate the Imagineers' eagerness to tell a story—a story that combines the mythology of the Yeti figure with the unique history of the Nepalese living in the shadow of the world's tallest mountain. Ultimately, the attraction, with all its background and thematic elements, took nearly five years to complete.

Riders on Expedition Everest gain a real feel for the atmosphere that Disney has worked so hard to create. The guests' adventure starts by entering the building of the "Himalayan Escape" tour company, complete with Norbu and Bob's booking office to obtain permits for their trip. Overhead flutter authentic prayer flags from monasteries in Nepal. Next, guests pass through Tashi's General Store and Bar to stock up on supplies for their journey to the peak of the mountain. Finally, guests pass through an old tea warehouse that contains a remarkable museum of artifacts reflecting Nepal's culture, a history of the Himalayas, and tales of the Yeti, which is said to inhabit the slopes of Mount Everest. It is only now that guests are permitted to board the Anandapur Rail Service for their trip to the peak. Each train is modeled after an aging, steam-engine train, seating 34 guests per train.

Over the next several minutes, guests are transported up the roller coaster track, through a series of winding turns, until their encounter with the Yeti. At this point another unique feature of the attraction emerges: The train begins rushing backward down the track, as though it were out of control. Through the balance of the ride, guests experience a landscape of sights and sounds culminating in a 50 mph final dash down the mountain and back to the safety of the Nepalese village.

Disney's approach to the management of projects such as Expedition Everest is to combine careful planning, including schedule and budget preparation, with the imagination and vision for which the company is so well known. Creativity is a critical element in the development of new projects at Disney. The company's Imagineers include some of the most skilled artists and computer-animation experts in the world. Although it is easy to be impressed by the technical knowledge of Disney's personnel, it is important to remember that each new project is approached with an understanding

(continued)

of the company's underlying business and attention to market projections, cost control, and careful project management discipline. New attraction proposals are carefully screened and researched. The result is the creation of some of the most innovative and enjoyable rides in the world. Disney does not add new attractions to its theme parks frequently, but when it does so, it does so with style!

Questions

1. Suppose you were a project manager for Disney. Based on the information in this case, what critical success metrics do you think the company uses when designing a new ride; that is, how would you prioritize the needs for addressing project cost, schedule, quality, and client acceptance? What evidence supports your answer?
2. Why is Disney's attention to detail in its rides unique? How does the company use the "atmosphere" discussed in the case to maximize the experience while minimizing complaints about length of wait for the ride?

CASE STUDY 6.4

Rescue of Chilean Miners

On October 13, 2010, Foreman Luiz Urzua stepped out of the rescue capsule to thunderous applause and cries of "Viva, Chile!"; he was the last of 33 miners rescued after spending 70 days trapped beneath 2,000 feet of earth and rock. Following a catastrophic collapse, the miners were trapped in the lower shafts of the mine, initially without contact with the surface, leaving the world in suspense as to their fate. Their discovery and ultimate rescue are a story of courage, resourcefulness, and ultimately, one of the most successful projects in recent times.

The work crew of the San Jose copper and gold mine near Copiapo, in northern Chile, were in the middle of their shift when suddenly, on August 5, 2010, the earth shook and large portions of the mine tunnels collapsed, trapping 33 miners in a "workshop" in a lower gallery of the mine. Though they were temporarily safe, they were nearly a half mile below the surface, with no power and food for two days. Worse, they had no means of communicating with the surface, so their fate remained a mystery to the company and their families. Under these conditions, their main goal was simple survival, conserving and stretching out meager food supplies for 17 days, until the first drilling probe arrived, punching a hole in the ceiling of the shaft where they were trapped. Once they had established contact with the surface and provided details of their condition, a massive rescue operation was conceived and undertaken.

The first challenge was simply keeping the miners alive. The earliest supply deliveries down the narrow communication shaft included quantities of food and water, oxygen, medicine, clothing, and necessities for survival as well as materials to help the miners pass their time. While groups worked to keep up the miners' spirits, communicating daily and passing along messages from families, other project teams were formed to begin developing a plan to rescue the men.

The challenges were severe. Among the significant questions that demanded practical and immediate answers were:

1. How do we locate the miners?
2. How quickly can we drill relief shafts to their location?
3. How do we bring them up safely?

The mine tunnels had experienced such damage in the collapse that simply digging the miners out would have taken several months. A full-scale rescue operation was conceived to extract the miners as quickly as possible. The U.S.-Chilean company Geotec Boyles Brothers, a subsidiary of Layne Christensen Company, assembled the critical resources from around the world. In western Pennsylvania, two companies that were experienced in mine collapses in the South American region were brought into the project. They had UPS ship a specialty drill, capable of creating wide-diameter shafts, large enough to fit men without collapsing. The drill arrived within 48 hours, free of charge. In all, UPS shipped more than 50,000 pounds of specialty equipment to the drilling and rescue site. The design of the rescue pod was the work of a NASA engineer, Clinton Cragg, who drew on his experience as a former submarine captain in the Navy and directed a team of 20 to conceive of and develop a means to carry the miners one at a time to the surface.

Doctors from NASA and U.S. submarine experts arrived at the mine site in mid-August, to assess the psychological state of the miners. Using their expertise in the physical and mental pressures of dealing with extended isolation, they worked with local officials to develop an exercise regimen and a set of chores for the workers in order to give them a sense of structure and responsibilities. The miners knew that help was being assembled, but they had no notion of the technical challenges of making each element in the rescue succeed. Nevertheless, with contact firmly established with the surface through the original contact drill shaft, the miners now began receiving news, updates from the surface, and a variety of gifts to ease the tedium of waiting.

The United States also provided an expert driller, Jeff Hart, who was called from Afghanistan, where he was helping American forces find water at forward operating bases, to man the specialty drilling machine. The 40-year-old drilled for 33 straight days, through tough conditions, to reach the men trapped at the mine floor. A total of three drilling rigs were erected and began drilling relief shafts from different directions. By September 17, Hart's drill (referred to as "Plan B") reached the miners, though the diameter of the shaft was only 5 inches. It would take a few weeks to ream the shaft with progressively wider drill bits to the final 25-inch diameter necessary to support the rescue capsules being constructed. Nevertheless, the rescue team was exuberant over the speed with which the shaft reached the trapped miners. Because of the special skills of the mining professionals, it is estimated that they cut more than two months off the time that experts expected this phase of the operation to take.

The first rescue capsule, named Phoenix, arrived at the site on September 23, with two more under construction and due to be shipped in two weeks. The Phoenix capsule resembled a specially designed cylindrical tube. It was 13 feet long and weighed 924 pounds with an interior width of 22 inches. It was equipped with oxygen and a harness to keep occupants upright, communication equipment, and retractable wheels. The idea was for the capsule to be narrow enough to be lowered into the rescue shaft but wide enough for one person at a time to be fitted inside and brought back to the surface. To ensure that all 33 miners would fit into the Phoenix, they were put on special liquid diets and given an exercise regimen to follow while waiting for the final preparations to be made.

Finally, after extensive tests, the surface team decided that the shaft was safe enough to support the rescue efforts and lowered the first Phoenix capsule into the hole. In two successive trips, the capsule carried down a paramedic and rescue expert who volunteered to descend into the mine to coordinate the removal of the miners. The first rescued miner broke the surface just after midnight on October 13 following a 15-minute ride in the capsule. A little more than 22 hours later, the shift manager, Urzua, was brought out of the mine, ending a tense and stressful rescue project.

The rescue operation of the Chilean miners was one of the most successful emergency projects in recent memory. It highlighted the ability of people to work together, marshal resources, gather support, and use innovative technologies in a humanitarian effort that truly captured the imagination of the world. The challenges that had to be overcome were significant: first, the technical problems associated with simply finding and making contact with survivors; second, devising a means to recover the men safely; third, undertaking special steps to ensure the miners' mental and physical health remained strong; and finally, requiring all parties to develop and rely on radical technologies that had never been used before. In all these challenges, the rescue team performed wonders, recovering and restoring to their families all 33 trapped miners. On November 7, just one month after the rescue, one of the miners, Edison Pena, realized his own personal dream: running in and completing the New York City marathon. Quite an achievement for a man who had just spent more than two months buried a half mile below the surface of the earth![54]

Questions

1. What does the story of the Chilean miners rescue suggest to you about the variety of ways that project management can be used in the modern world?
2. Successful project management requires clear organization, careful planning, and good execution. How were each of these traits shown in this rescue example?

Internet Exercises

6.1 The largest professional project management organization in the world is the Project Management Institute (PMI). Go to its Web site, www.pmi.org, and examine the links you find. Which links suggest that project management has become a sophisticated and vital element in corporate success? Select at least three of the related links and report briefly on the content of these links.

6.2 Go to the PMI Web site and examine the link "Membership." What do you discover when you begin navigating among the various chapters and cooperative organizations associated with PMI? How does this information cause you to rethink project management as a career option?

6.3 Go to www.pmi.org/Business-Solutions/OPM3-Case-Study-Library.aspx and examine some of the cases included on the Web page. What do they suggest about the challenges of managing projects successfully? The complexity of many of today's projects? The exciting breakthroughs or opportunities that projects allow us to exploit?

6.4 Using your favorite search engine (Google, Yahoo!, etc.), type in the keywords "project" and "project management."

Randomly select three of the links that come up on the screen. Summarize what you find.

6.5 Go to the Web site for the Software Engineering Institute of Carnegie Mellon University at https://resources.sei.cmu.edu/asset_files/SpecialReport/1994_003_001_16265.pdf and access the software process maturity questionnaire. What are some of the questions that IT companies need to consider when assessing their level of project management maturity?

PMP CERTIFICATION SAMPLE QUESTIONS

1. The majority of the project budget is expended upon:
   - a. Project plan development.
   - b. Project plan execution.
   - c. Project termination.
   - d. Project communication.
2. Which of the following is the most critical component of the triple constraint?
   - a. Time, then cost, then quality.
   - b. Quality, then budget, then time.
   - c. Scope.
   - d. They are all of equal importance unless otherwise stated.
3. Which of the following best describes a project stakeholder?
   - a. A team member.
   - b. The project manager.
   - c. Someone who works in an area affected by the project.
   - d. All of the above are stakeholders.
4. All of the following are elements in the definition of a project, except:
   - a. A project is time-limited.
   - b. A project is unique.
   - c. A project is composed of unrelated activities.
   - d. A project is undertaken for a purpose.
5. All of the following distinguish project management from other process activities, except:
   - a. There are no fundamental differences between project and process management.
   - b. Project management often involves greater certainty of performance, cost, and schedule.
   - c. Process management operates outside of line organizations.
   - d. None of the above correctly distinguish project from process management.

Answers: 1. b—The majority of a project budget is spent during the execution phase; 2. d—Unless otherwise stated, all elements in the triple-constraint model are equally critical; 3. d—All of the examples listed are types of project stakeholders; 4. c—A project is composed of "interrelated" activities; 5. d—None of the answers given correctly differentiates "process" from "project" management.

Notes

20. Valery, Paul, quoted in "Extreme chaos" (Boston: Standish Group International, 2001).
21. Duthiers, V., and Kermeliotis, T. (2012, August 22). "Lagos of the future: Megacity's ambitious plans." *CNN*. http://edition.cnn.com/2012/08/22/business/lagos-urbanization-regeneration-infrastructure/; Walt, V. (2014, June 30). "Africa's Big Apple," *Fortune*, pp. 92–94; Ogunbiyi, T. (2014, February 6). "On Lagos' investment in infrastructure development," *Business Day*. http://businessdayonline.com/2014/02/on-lagos-investment-in-infrastructure-development/#.U6hKwPldV8E; Joy, O. (2013, October 10). "Tech cities and mega dams: Africa's giant infrastructure projects," *CNN*. http://edition.cnn.com/2013/10/10/business/tech-cities-dams-africa-infrastructure/; Curnow, R. and Kermeliotis, T. (2012, April 5). "The daily grind of commuting in Africa's economic hubs," *CNN*. http://edition.cnn.com/2012/04/05/world/africa/commuting-africa/index.html?iref=allsearch
22. Peters, Thomas. (1994). *Liberation Management: Necessary Disorganization for the Nanosecond Nineties*. New York: Fawcett Books.
23. Stewart, Thomas H. (1995). "The corporate jungle spawns a new species," *Fortune*, July 10, pp. 179–80.
24. Gilbreath, Robert D. (1988). "Working with pulses not streams: Using projects to capture opportunity," in Cleland, D., and King, W. (Eds.), *Project Management Handbook*. New York: Van Nostrand Reinhold, pp. 3–15.
25. Buchanan, D. A., and Boddy, D. (1992). *The Expertise of the Change Agent: Public Performance and Backstage Activity*. London: Prentice Hall.
26. Frame, J. D. (1995). *Managing Projects in Organizations*, 2nd ed. San Francisco, CA: Jossey-Bass. See also Frame, J. D. (2002). *The New Project Management*, 2nd ed. San Francisco, CA: Jossey-Bass.
27. Kerzner, H. (2003). *Project Management*, 8th ed. New York: Wiley.
28. Field, M., and Keller, L. (1998). *Project Management*. London: The Open University.
29. Project Management Institute. (2013). *A Guide to the Project Management Body of Knowledge*, 5th ed. Newtown Square, PA: PMI.
30. Cleland, D. I. (2001). "The discipline of project management," in Knutson, J. (Ed.), *Project Management for Business Professionals*. New York: Wiley, pp. 3–22.
31. Lundin, R. A., and Soderholm, A. (1995). "A theory of the temporary organization," *Scandinavian Journal of Management*, 11(4): 437–55.
32. Graham, R. J. (1992). "A survival guide for the accidental project manager." *Proceedings of the Annual Project Management Institute Symposium*. Drexel Hill, PA: Project Management Institute, pp. 355–61.
33. Sources: http://macs.about.com/b/a/087641.htm; Mossberg, W. S. (2004). "The music man," *Wall Street Journal*, June 14, p. B1. Project Management Institute, Sohmen, Victor. "Project termination: Why the delay?" PMI Research Conference. Proceedings, p. 467–475. Paper presented at PMI Research Conference. Project Management Institute, Inc (2002). Copyright and all rights reserved. Material from this publication has been reproduced with the permission of PMI.

34. Pinto, J. K., and Millet, I. (1999). *Successful Information Systems Implementation: The Human Side,* 2nd ed. Newtown Square, PA: PMI.

35. Kapur, G. K. (1998). "Don't look back to create the future." Presentation at the Frontiers of Project Management Conference, Boston, MA.

36. Ted Ritter (2007, May 17). Public sector IT projects have only 30% success rate - CIO for Department for Work and Pensions. Retrieved from: http://www.computerweekly.com/blogs/public-sector/2007/05/public-sector-it-projects-have.html

37. Clausing, J., and Daly, M. (2013, September 14). "US nuclear agency faulted for laxity and overspending," *Boston Globe.* www.bostonglobe.com/news/nation/2013/09/13/nation-bloated-nuclear-spending-comes-under-fire/O2uP7gv06vTAEw0AIcCIlL/story.html

38. "How to establish an organizational culture that promotes projects," www.bia.ca/articles/HowToEstablishaProjectManagementCulture.htm; Standish Group. (2006). *The Trends in IT Value* report; Standish Group. (2013). *Chaos Manifesto 2013.* Boston, MA.

39. Kelley, M. (2008, November 18). "$600M spent on canceled contracts," *USA Today,* p. 1; Francis, D. (2014, June 12). "How squandered U.S. money fuels Iraqi insurgents," *Fiscal Times.* www.thefiscaltimes.com/Articles/2014/06/12/How-Squandered-US-Money-Fuels-Iraq-s-Insurgents; Mulrine, A. (2013, July 12). "Rebuilding Iraq: Final report card on US efforts highlights massive waste," *Christian Science Monitor.* www.csmonitor.com/USA/Military/2013/0712/Rebuilding-Iraq-Final-report-card-on-US-efforts-highlights-massive-waste

40. Cleland, D. I. (1994). *Project Management: Strategic Design and Implementation.* New York: McGraw-Hill; Pinto, J. K., and Rouhiainen, P. (2001). *Building Customer-Based Project Organizations.* New York: Wiley; Gray, C. F., and Larson, E. W. (2003). *Project Management,* 2nd ed. Burr Ridge, IL: McGraw-Hill.

41. Petroski, H. (1985). *To Engineer Is Human—The Role of Failure in Successful Design.* London: St. Martin's Press.

42. Hewlett, S. (2014, February 3). "BBC's Digital Media Initiative failed because of more than poor oversight," *The Guardian.* www.theguardian.com/media/media-blog/ 2014/feb/03/bbc-digital-media-initiative-failed-mark-thompson; Conlan, T. (2013, May 24). "BBC axes £98m technology project to avoid 'throwing good money after bad,'" *The Guardian.* www.theguardian.com/media/2013/may/24/bbc-technology-project-digital-media-initiative; Commons Select Committee. (2014, April 10). "BBC's Digital Media Initiative a complete failure." www.parliament.uk/business/committees/committees-a-z/commons-select/public-accounts-committee/news/bbc-dmi-report-substantive/; BBC. (2013, December 18). "BBC 'not effective' in running failed £100m IT scheme." www.bbc.com/news/entertainment-arts-25433174; Daniel, E., and Ward, J. (2013, June). "BBC's DMI project failure is a warning to all organisations," *Computer Weekly.* www.computerweekly.com/opinion/BBCs-DMI-project-failure-is-a-warning-to-all-organisations

43. Sohmen, Victor. (2002, July). "Project termination: Why the delay?" Paper presented at PMI Research Conference, Seattle, WA.

44. Freeman, M., and Beale, P. (1992). "Measuring project success," *Project Management Journal,* 23(1): 8–17.

45. Morris, P. W. G. (1997). *The Management of Projects.* Thomas Telford: London; McKain, S. (2005). *What Customers Really Want.* Thomas Nelson: Nashville, TN.

46. Shenhar, A. J., Levy, O., and Dvir, D. (1997). "Mapping the dimensions of project success," *Project Management Journal,* 28(2): 5–13.

47. DeLone, W. H., and McLean, E. R. (1992). "Information systems success: The quest for the dependent variable," *Information Systems Research,* 3(1): 60–95; Seddon, P. B. (1997). "A respecification and extension of the DeLone and McLean model of IS success," *Information Systems Research,* 8(3): 249–53; DeLone, W. H., and McLean, E. R. (2003). "The DeLone and McLean model of information system success: A ten-year update," *Journal of Management Information Systems,* 19(4): 9–30.

48. Atkinson, R. (1999). "Project management: Cost, time and quality, two best guesses and a phenomenon, it's time to accept other success criteria," *International Journal of Project Management,* 17(6): 337–42; Cooke-Davies, T. (2002). "The 'real' success factors on projects," *International Journal of Project Management,* 20(3): 185–90; Olson, D. L. (2001). *Introduction to Information Systems Project Management.* Burr Ridge, IL: Irwin/McGraw-Hill.

49. Pennypacker, J. S., and Grant, K. P. (2003). "Project management maturity: An industry benchmark," *Project Management Journal,* 34(1): 4–11; Ibbs, C. W., and Kwak, Y. H. (1998). "Benchmarking project management organizations," *PMNetwork,* 12(2): 49–53.

50. Reginato, P. E., and Ibbs, C. W. (2002). "Project management as a core competency," *Proceedings of PMI Research Conference 2002,* Slevin, D., Pinto, J., and Cleland, D. (Eds.), *The Frontiers of Project Management Research.* Newtown Square, PA: Project Management Institute, pp. 445–50.

51. Crawford, K. (2002). *Project Management Maturity Model: Providing a Proven Path to Project Management Excellence.* New York: Marcel Dekker; Foti, R. (2002). "Implementing maturity models," *PMNetwork,* 16(9): 39–43; Gareis, R. (2001). "Competencies in the project-oriented organization," in Slevin, D., Cleland, D., and Pinto, J. (Eds.), *The Frontiers of Project Management Research.* Newtown Square, PA: Project Management Institute, pp. 213–24; Gareis, R., and Huemann, M. (2000). "Project management competencies in the project-oriented organization," in Turner, J. R., and Simister, S. J. (Eds.), *The Gower Handbook of Project Management,* 3rd ed. Aldershot, UK: Gower, pp. 709–22; Ibbs, C. W., and Kwak, Y. H. (2000). "Assessing project management maturity," *Project Management Journal,* 31(1): 32–43.

52. Humphrey, W. S. (1988). "Characterizing the software process: A maturity framework," *IEEE Software,* 5(3): 73–79; Carnegie Mellon University. (1995). *The Capability Maturity Model: Guidelines for Improving the Software Process.* Boston, MA: Addison-Wesley; Kerzner, H. (2001). *Strategic Planning for Project Management Using a Project Management Maturity Model.* New York: Wiley; Crawford, J. K. (2002). *Project Management Maturity Model.* New York: Marcel Dekker; Pritchard, C. (1999). *How to Build a Work Breakdown Structure: The Cornerstone of Project Management.* Arlington, VA: ESI International.

53. Jenkins, Robert N. (2005). "A new peak for Disney," *St. Petersburg Times Online,* www.sptimes.com/2005/12/11/news_pf/travel/A_new_peak_for_Disney.

54. www.cnn.com/2010/WORLD/americas/10/15/chile.mine.rescue.recap/index.html; www.cnn.com/2010/OPINION/10/12/gergen.miners/index.html; www.thenewamerican.com/index.php/opinion/sam-blumenfeld/5140-how-americans-engineered-the-rescue-of-the-chilean-miners

7 Project Management Process

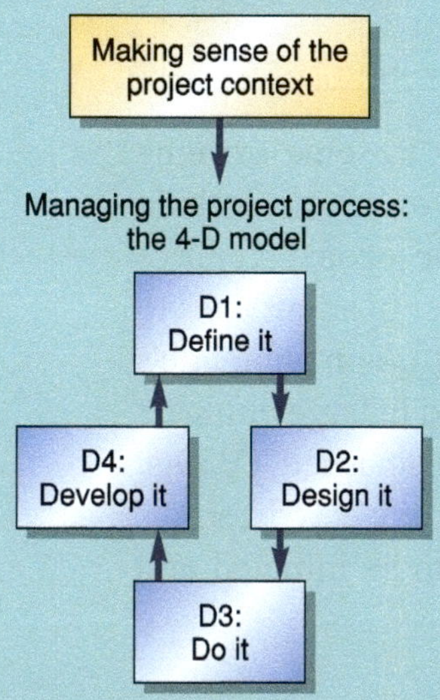

Get the thinking right first. The rest is detail.

Principles

1. Structures and frameworks are necessary to enable us to construct mental models of complex systems of human activity.
2. Well-developed structures and frameworks exist that work well in making sense of projects.
3. The nature of the managerial task in projects can usefully be described by assessing the complexity of that task.

Learning objectives

By the time you have completed this chapter, you should be able to:

- → describe the environment that a project operates in and some of the challenges facing project managers
- → use a basic framework to identify elements of a project
- → assess the managerial complexity of a project and the implications of this for the project manager and the organisation.

Contents

Source: Lightly Salted/Alamy

The European launch of Nintendo's seventh generation of gaming console, the Wii, was an eagerly anticipated event. It was also pivotal in the future of the company – there was much riding on the success of the product. So, launching a new gaming product for an established company which has done this many times before in the past 25 years. How difficult can it be?

As a development project, it had significant complexity. This was a new concept of gaming that for the first time claimed to involve the whole family. Herein lay some new challenges. When first released in Europe, it was so popular that demand totally outstripped supply. Customers, key stakeholders in the project, were disappointed and went to some extreme lengths to get hold of their consoles. But the stakeholders of the Wii launch didn't just include customers. Using the Wii turned out to be a dangerous pursuit for some people. Injuries sustained by people not used to exercising had a major impact on the number of admissions to A&E units over the Christmas period. A&E departments probably didn't figure on Nintendo's list of likely stakeholders. Also, games including a boxing simulation resulted in large numbers of insurance claims, as the controllers flew out of competitors' hands and smashed TV sets. Insurance companies became an unwitting stakeholder to the project. The fitting of wrist straps to the controllers helped reduce this but that required a retro-fit project to be initiated and thousands of straps to be distributed.

Introduction

Nintendo launching the Wii was a significant moment in the company's history. Considering launching the product as a project, one might expect the technical challenges to provide the greatest complexity for the project manager. As it turned out, these were not what caused Nintendo the greatest headaches. The company's customers' buying patterns and usage of the device were not 'as planned'. This is a good lesson for project managers and managing **stakeholders** (anyone with an interest in the project or its outcome) is a significant role for project managers and consumes a considerable portion of many project managers' time. Indeed, producing the immediate product is usually far simpler than making sure that all the necessary stakeholders are still happy at the end of the project.

Getting the thinking right on many projects is a real challenge. Chapter 6 provided a number of ways of looking at projects. Talk to many project managers and they have had to make sense of considerable complexity in order to deliver. Without this **sense-making** process, project activities can appear to be 'too difficult' and the project nothing more than an apparently random series of actions.

This chapter starts with a basic model of the project environment. It then considers the **issues** that project managers will face using the 7-S framework. How each of these issues is developed is determined by the project environment (one aspect of which is the project complexity) and these are the next two issues considered. It will be shown that the nature of the project management task is determined by this **complexity**.

As described in Chapter 6, important developments in the subject of project management in recent years have included the provision of documented 'Bodies of Knowledge' by the professional institutes. These are outlined and points of reference with this book are identified.

7.1 Describing the project context: high-level frameworks

The project environment

There is the view that 'work can be done almost anywhere'. The Mazda MX5 (Miata) car, for example, was designed in California, financed in Tokyo and New York, tested in the UK, assembled in Michigan and Mexico using components designed in America and made in Japan. Shipbuilding – a predominantly project-based environment – has faced competition from parts of the world that 20 years ago had little or no capability in this area. Traditional not-for-profit organisations (including many health services) are now required to meet performance targets and individual activities are being subjected to previously unthinkable commercial constraints.

Within the expanding European Union and World Trade Organization, trade barriers have fallen, the number of international collaborative ventures has increased and globalisation has had a considerable impact on the nature of work carried out. It is more likely then that project work will be undertaken internationally, possibly involving *virtual teams* (where the team members are geographically dispersed). In addition to this increase in organisational complexity, projects have become more complex as:

- generally the simplest ideas have been exploited first – it is becoming more difficult but more vital to be innovative;
- businesses are becoming more complex – it is less likely for a company to provide a commodity, product or service but to provide a 'package' which meets an entire need rather than just part of that need;[1]
- projects are being delivered through turnkey contracts – where the end-user does none of the interfacing between the different parts of the system but deals with a single supplier in the provision of an entire system, or through complex financing arrangements (e.g. the financing on public projects through public private partnerships or private finance initiative arrangements in the UK).

Source: Motoring Picture Library/Alamy

In addition:

- effective quality management has been shown to be the basis of many organisations obtaining a competitive advantage. A quality system carrying a recognised certification (such as BS-EN-ISO 9000) is a requirement for supplying goods or services into many markets – not just aerospace and defence where the standards originated.

The change in the competitive environment in which the majority of organisations operate has necessitated a major rethink of the way in which projects are managed. The effects of the changes on projects and their managers include the following:

- Time has become a major source of competitive advantage, whether it be in the construction of a road or the development of a new product.
- Human resource management has moved from considering that members of a project team should be treated as anonymous cogs in the machine to the idea that individual creativity can be harnessed. The concept is often heard expressed in the form 'with every pair of hands you get a free brain'.
- Rates of change in technology and methods have increased – not only is the change continuing, but the speed at which changes are occurring is increasing.
- Organisations are having to become customer focused and aspire to exceed rather than just meet customer requirements. Customer expectations of the way products and services are delivered are increasing all the time.
- There is a trend towards integration and openness between customers and suppliers. Company information that would previously have been a closely guarded secret is often shared in a move towards partnership rather than adversarial relationships.
- The most fundamental change in management has occurred through the investigation of the Toyota production system.[2] Toyota was seen to have achieved significant competitive advantage in the automotive market through its management philosophy and the application of associated tools and techniques. The principles have been taken and applied in many unrelated business areas with considerable benefits.
- The service sector has been the biggest growth area in most first world countries in the past ten years. The economy of the majority of European Union countries has had to cease its dependence on manufacturing and rely on the growth of the service sector to provide employment and economic growth.[3]

A further pressure on the project environment is the search for competitiveness. Many firms have gone a long way in improving their repetitive operations. As a result, the opportunities for improvement in performance in these systems without significant investment are declining. Projects are therefore a major source of competitiveness that many organisations have yet to realise.

The environment in which projects operate may be summarised by the **5 Cs.** These are:

- *Context* – the external general influences on the organisation in which the project is taking place;
- *Complexity* – the level of difficulty or complication of a piece of work called 'a project';
- *Completeness* – how much of the end requirement a project will deliver;
- *Competitiveness* – how many other organisations will be competing to deliver that work;
- *Customer focus* – the expectation that customers will have their needs met by the project.

These are shown in Figure 7.1. Complexity is more fully described later in this chapter.

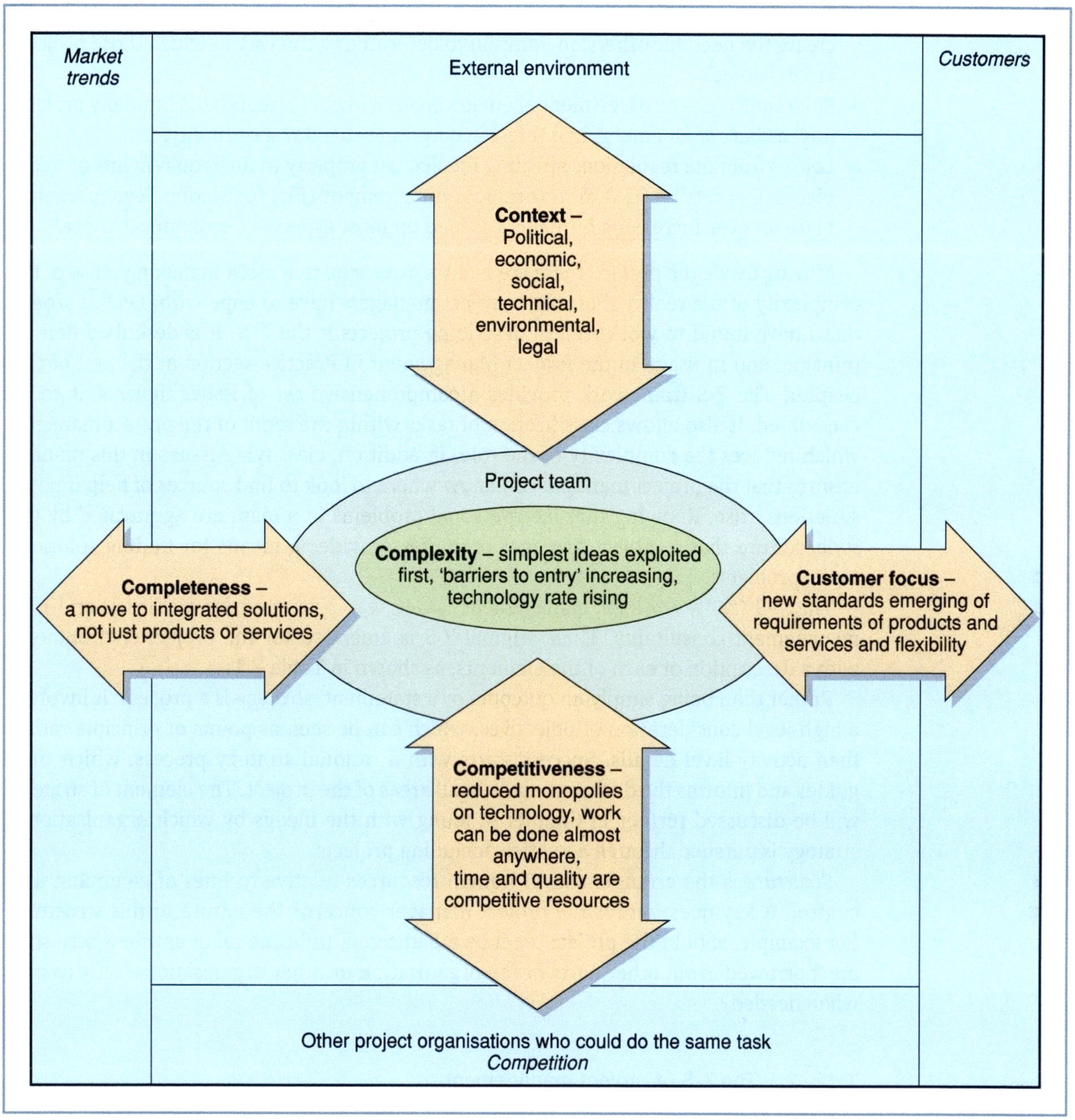

Figure 7.1 Describing the project environment: the 5-C model

The **context** can be described in many ways. One acronym that is widely used to describe context is **PESTEL**:

- *Political influence* – in government organisations this may be Political (capital P), where, for instance, a change in policy or the party in power, may have significant ramifications for what government does, what it funds and, just as importantly, what it decides not to continue funding.
- *Economic* – the influence of general and local economics. For instance, during a period of economic 'boom', there may be challenges recruiting staff or obtaining contractors to even bid for work. During economic 'bust' times, the picture changes radically.
- *Social* – the influence of social changes on the project environment, for instance on methods of communication, needs consideration.

- *Technical* – changes in technology will challenge the viability of some projects and create the need for others, in addition to determining the way in which those projects are delivered.
- *Environmental* – an assessment of environmental impact is mandated for many projects now as part of an emerging interest in corporate social responsibility.
- *Legal* – from the regulations affecting intellectual property to the requirements of major pieces of anti-trust (US) or government procurement (EU) legislation, legal pressures place an ever-increasing bureaucratic load on most aspects of economic activity.

Moving inside the project, there are many **structures** that assist in making sense of the complexity of the reality that many project managers have to cope with. One approach that I have found to work well in describing projects is the **7-S**. It is described here in principle and in usage in the Project Management in Practice section at the end of this chapter. The 7-S framework provides a comprehensive set of issues that needs to be considered. It also allows classification of tasks within the remit of the project manager, which reduces the complexity of the role. In addition, classifying issues in this manner ensures that the project manager will know where to look to find sources of help if novel situations arise. Knowing that interpersonal problems in a team are aggravated by the style/culture that a project manager promotes provides a means for finding solutions to the problems.

The 7-S **framework** of management issues was promoted by McKinsey and Co., management consultants. Their original 7-S is amended for the project environment, with a description of each of the elements, as shown in Table 7.1.

Rather than being simply an outcome or a statement, *strategy* is a process. It involves a high-level consideration of objectives, which can be seen as points of principle rather than activity-level details. Success starts with a rational strategy process, which then guides and informs the decisions made in all areas of the project. The element of strategy will be discussed further in Chapter 4, along with the means by which organisational strategy is pursued through activities, including projects.

Structure is the arrangement of human resources relative to lines of command and control. A key question for the project manager concerns the nature of this structure. For example, should the project team be a dedicated, full-time team or one where staff are 'borrowed' from other parts of the organisation or other organisations, only as and when needed?.

Table 7.1 The 7-S of project management

Element	*Description*
Strategy	The high-level requirements of the project and the means to achieve them
Structure	The organisational arrangement that will be used to carry out the project
Systems	The methods for work to be designed, monitored and controlled
Staff	The selection, recruitment, management and leadership of those working on the project
Skills	The managerial and technical tools available to the project manager and the staff, and how these are developed
Style/culture	The underlying way of working and inter-relating within the work team or organisation
Stakeholders	Individuals and groups with an interest in the project process or outcome

Systems are 'the way we work'. Both formal and informal systems will need to be designed or at least recognised for key tasks, including communication and quality assurance. Formal systems can be demonstrated through statements of procedure – simply put, 'under these conditions, we carry out this action'. Informal systems, particularly for information transfer, are far less easy to describe and control. It is normal, however, for these to be the main mode of communication within groups. A theme within the systems element is the focus of the systems on 'process'. That is, ensuring that all activities carried out are contributing to the end objective of the project in a constructive manner. Systems are a recurring theme throughout this text.

Staff need to be selected, recruited and then managed. How they respond to their treatment will have a large impact on the success or otherwise of the project. Yet this element has traditionally been neglected by texts on project management. In addition to a consideration of the *skills* they require.

Style/culture is part of the 'soft' side of management. Indeed, it cannot be managed in the short term in the same way that the finances of a project, for example, can be managed.

Stakeholders are an important consideration for project managers. Their importance has only recently been realised and methods for the management of expectations and perceptions developed. Issues concerned with stakeholders are considered further in Chapters 14.

These 7-S headings cover the issues that project managers will be faced with.

7.2 Describing the project process: activity models

'Improve constantly and forever every activity in the company, to improve quality and productivity and thus constantly decrease costs.' (Dr W. Edwards Deming)[4]

Making sense of the project as a system: the ICOM model

For many years, the most basic **model** of any operating system has been the input–output model.[5] This applies well here as the basic unit of analysis of project activities and follows process-based thinking, identified in Chapter 6.

The project is viewed as a conversion or transformation of input into output, under a set of constraints and utilising a set of mechanisms to make the project happen. As Figure 7.2 shows, the inputs include some form of want or need which is to be satisfied through the process. The project will take place under a set of controls or constraints including any assumptions or limitations placed on the project. The mechanisms are those resources that make the transformation process possible.

Inputs

The desire to develop a new bagless vacuum cleaner was the starting point for James Dyson's highly successful product range. The project did not start with any formalisation, just the want to develop a product that would not suffer from the drawbacks associated with a paper bag being the filter for particles passing through a vacuum cleaner.[6]

For many organisations there has to be a limit to the number of projects that are started and this need will be encapsulated into a *brief* – a document describing the nature of the work to be undertaken – before the resources will be released to do even the most

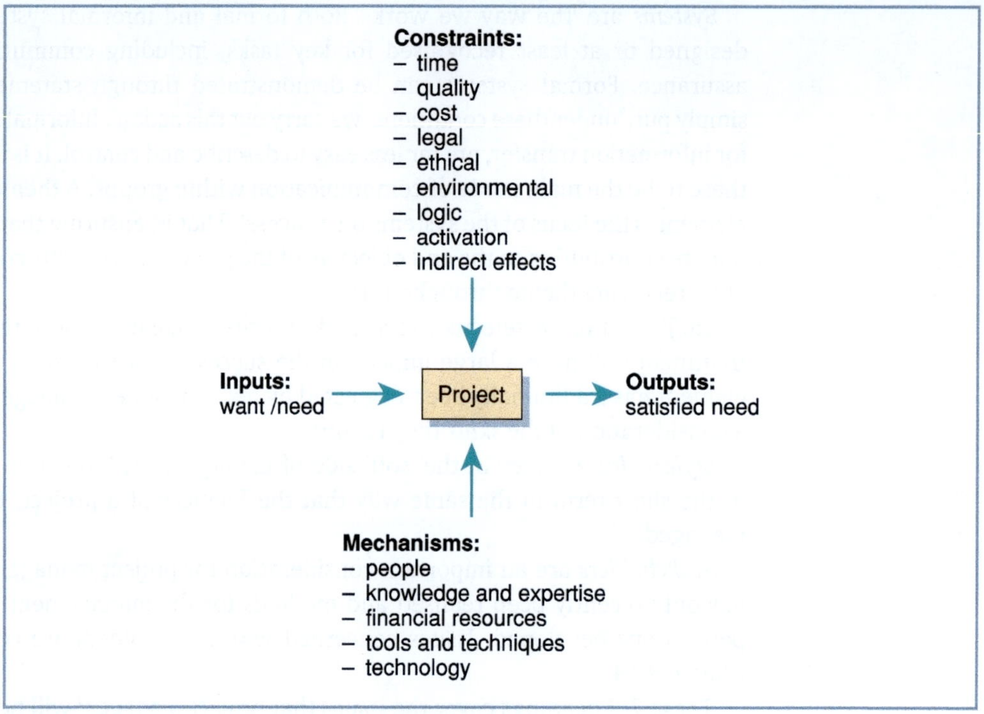

Figure 7.2 The project as a conversion process

preliminary work. For the project manager, there will be both explicitly stated requirements (original needs) and those that emerge during the course of the project due to the customer's changing needs or perceptions (emergent needs).

Constraints

The brief will also set out the constraints, which principally focus on time, cost and quality, but will also have a wider range of issues for the project manager to reconcile with the wants or needs. The main constraints are:

- *time* – all projects by definition have a time constraint. In practice, it is often found to be the most challenging to meet;
- *cost* – the value and timing of financial resources required to carry out the project work;
- *quality* – the standards by which both the product (the output of the process) and the process itself will be judged.

In addition to these three, the following constraints can prove limiting on the project:

- legal – this may not be explicitly stated but there will be legal constraints, e.g. a building may not be constructed unless the planning permission for it has been obtained;
- ethical – a major area for many organisations today, particularly those where the ethics of their organisational policies has been questioned in the past (e.g. Shell and Nike);
- environmental – the deluge of environmental legislation that has been generated by governments has changed the role of environmental control from a subsidiary issue to one which is at the forefront of management thinking in many sectors;
- logic – the need for certain activities to have been completed before a project can start;
- activation – actions to show when a project or activity can begin;
- indirect effects – it is practically impossible for any change to take place in isolation. There will be ripple effects, which will need to be taken into account at the outset.

Outputs

Figure 7.2 describes the output as a 'satisfied need'. This will usually be in the form of:

- converted information, e.g. a set of specifications for a new product;
- a tangible product, e.g. a building;
- changed people, e.g. through a training project, the participants have received new knowledge and so are part of the transformation process as well as being a product of it.

Mechanisms

The means or mechanisms by which the output is achieved are as follows:

- people – those involved both directly and indirectly in the project;
- knowledge and expertise – brought to the project by the participants and outside recruited help (e.g. consultants) of both technical specialisms and management processes;
- financial resources;
- tools and techniques – the methods for organising the potential work with the available resources;
- technology – the available physical assets that will be performing part or all of the conversion process.

From this Inputs, Outputs, Constraints and Mechanisms (**ICOM**) model one of the major roles of project managers becomes apparent. They are required to be the **integrator** of the elements of the project – the need or want with the available mechanisms or resources under the conditions imposed by the constraints. This is a key skill of the project manager. The nature of this task will change during the life of a project, and this will be described in the following section.

Continuously improving the system: the 4-D model

Two parties to a contract, a county council and a construction contractor, ended up taking their claims[7] and counter-claims to court following the construction of a new leisure centre. Seven years later, the same two parties were in court again, to settle their claims and counter-claims, following the construction of an almost identical facility and very similar claims being made. How did this happen? Why had the parties not learned from their earlier, expensive mistakes? The only people with an interest in this kind of process are the lawyers.

This is depressingly common in many organisations (particularly those that use a large proportion of contract staff who leave once the project is completed) and is termed *hedgehog syndrome*.[8]

We see this problem regularly on our roads, where the unsuspecting hedgehog encounters a car and the result is fairly predictable. Worse, as long as there are hedgehogs, roads and cars, we will continue to find our little flat friends. Why, then, don't hedgehogs learn from this? The reason is that there is no feedback to hedgehog-kind of the knowledge that the road is a dangerous place for them to be, so that they can amend their behaviour accordingly. All too often the same applies to projects – the same mistakes are repeated again and again. Unless there is an opportunity to develop the project processes and provide the feedback to the organisation, the knowledge is lost.

Organisations such as Hewlett-Packard, however, use previous projects and their reviews as the starting point for new projects. Their focus on the lessons from both good and bad experiences means that there is some path for continuous improvement in projects. It is a real challenge for project managers to get this learning transferred. One recently noted that his organisation had stopped calling the last phase the 'lessons

Hedgehog syndrome

learned review' and had instead decided to call it 'the lessons identified review'. Because, as he noted, 'we don't learn'. However, while that shows that such a learning process is challenging, that does not alter the objective that the approach to future projects should be based on the opportunity to learn from previous projects.

One approach is to consider a project as being structured into four identifiable phases. These were shown in Chapter 6; they provide the basic structure for this book and are repeated here in Figure 7.3.

The four phases are described in more detail in Table 7.2, but before continuing there are three points worth noting.

1 Projects involve a lot of pre-project work to be done to justify resources, prepare documents, evaluate options, and there is considerable diversity of opinion as to whether this work should be included in 'the project'.
2 Projects are terminated prior to completion for all sorts of reasons. For instance, a project to move a bank to new and larger premises was scrapped as a result of an economic downturn. The project was going well but the additional costs and facilities were suddenly deemed unnecessary.
3 There are often many stages within each of these main phases. Indeed, for large projects, the project lifecycle can be replicated within each phase, as each of them becomes a mini-project in its own right. This cycles-within-cycles is common to many other project processes. Such an approach does represent the reality of many projects well, as they are more akin to cycles of activities rather than the linear progression indicated by Figure 7.3. The real world is rarely so well defined!

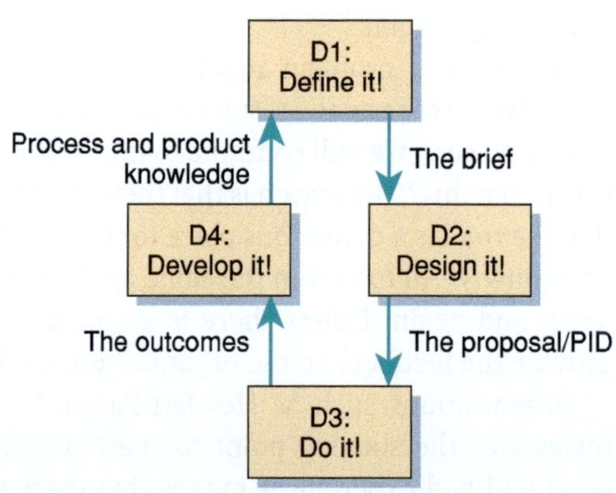

Figure 7.3 Four phases of project lifecycle

Table 7.2 The four phases of project management

Phase	*Key issues*	*Fundamental questions*
Define the project	Project and organisational strategy, goal definition	What is to be done? Why is it to be done?
Design the project process	Modelling and planning, estimating, resource analysis, conflict resolution and justification	How will it be done? Who will be involved in each part? When can it start and finish?
Deliver the project (Do it!)	Organisation, control, leadership, decision-making and problem-solving	How should the project be managed on a day-to-day basis?
Develop the process	Assessment of process and outcomes of the project, evaluation, changes for the future	How can the process be continually improved?

The **4-D** structure is as follows:

- *Define the project* – this is the time when it is determined what the project is about, its reasons for existence and the intentions that it intends to progress. It is a time to explore the possibilities, find alternatives to the problems presented.
- *Design the project process* – construct models to show how the needs will be developed, evaluate these to determine the optimum process for the task and minimise risk.
- *Do It! or Deliver the project* – carry out the project in line with the models or plans generated above.
- *Develop the process* – improve the products and processes in the light of the experience gained from the project.

There are a number of tasks and issues to be addressed in each phase. This provides a degree of complexity for the project manager and is one reason that there are few truly excellent examples of project management available. Taking the analogy of the project as a *chain*, it is important that there is general competence across the phases. This is preferable to there being excellence in one area, with other areas falling down.[9]

The generic lifecycle for a project involves consideration of how the level of activity varies with time. This is illustrated in Figure 7.4 and shows how the level of activity is

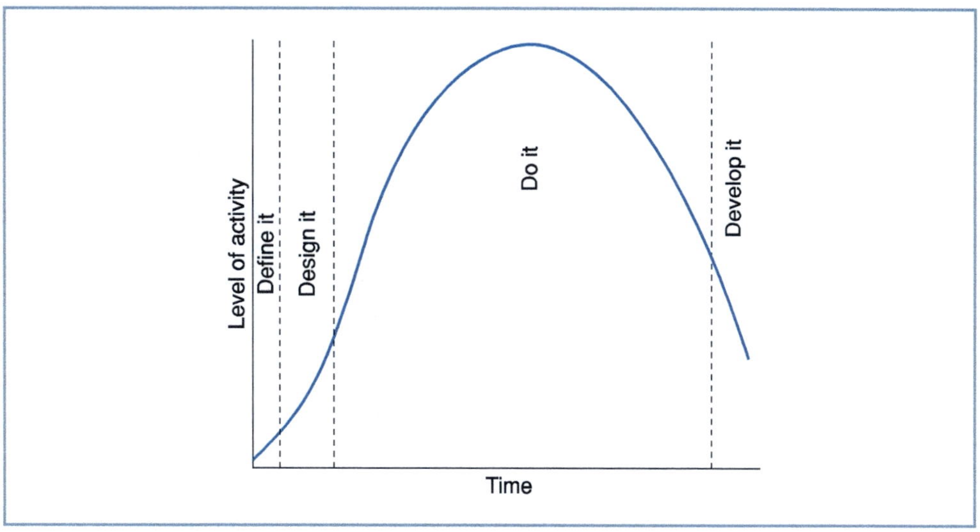

Figure 7.4 Graph showing how level of activity varies with time

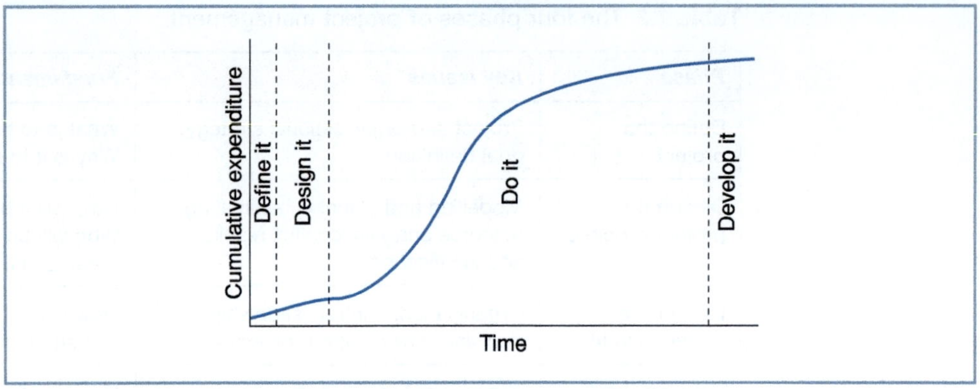

Figure 7.5 Graph of cumulative expenditure against time

relatively low during the early phases, increases through the doing phase when the major volume of work is done, and decreases through the development phase.

This pattern is reflected in the graph of cumulative expenditure against time (Figure 7.5). Outgoings are generally low in the early stages but grow rapidly during the execution phase. The graph also demonstrates why the develop it phase is so vital – by the time the majority of the doing phase is completed, the probability is that in excess of 98 per cent of the total project expenditure will have been incurred. The last phase is the time when the project team themselves can benefit from the process and ensure that lessons (good and bad) are applied in the future. The excuse is often used that organisations cannot review projects because there is no budget for the review work. Given that mistakes are observed to occur repeatedly (hedgehog syndrome), organisations seem perfectly prepared to pay when things inevitably go wrong. This last phase is therefore an investment in future performance, just as spending money on a new piece of equipment would be.

The lifecycle may be further broken down as shown in Table 7.3. Key additional features include some explicit analysis of the idea during the definition stage, and the focus on a business case being prepared for the project right from the outset. This is expanded during the justification activities of the second-stage processes.

This is still generic, however, and the practice of phasing the project is best illustrated by an application. Table 7.4 shows how a new management information system was supplied to a hospital through a software company with the description of how the project was broken down and the activities that were undertaken in each phase. It illustrates the early structuring that took place within the project. This had a number of plus-points for both the hospital and the IT firm, not least in the clarity that the phasing presented to each side. At a high level, the activities could be tracked to see progress (or lack of it).

The four phases each have different characteristics and different management requirements. Some points are of note here. The first is that many project managers will not be involved in the early stages and will be handed a brief for the project after the initial definition work has been done by another party. There are many reasons why this causes problems, not least because the project manager cannot be involved in problem-avoidance measures at the early stage.

A further example of a lifecycle comes from the UK Ministry of Defence, which uses the CADMID cycle as shown in Figure 7.6[10] for equipment procurement.

In the figure, the relationship between the 4D and CADMID is shown. 'Gates' are decision points in the process where it is decided whether the project continues. It should

Table 7.3 Development of the project lifecycle

Stage in project lifecycle	*Activity*	*Description*
Define the project	Conceptualisation	Generate explicit statement of needs
	Analysis	Identify what has to be provided to meet those needs – is it likely to be feasible?
Design the project process	Proposal	Show how those needs will be met through the project activities
	Justification	Prepare and evaluate financial costs and benefits from the project
	Agreement	Point at which go-ahead is agreed by project sponsor
Deliver the project (do it!)	Start-up	Gather resources, assemble project teams
	Execution	Carry out defined activities
	Completion	Time/money constraint reached or activity series completed
	Handover	Output of project passed to client/user
Develop the process	Review	Identify the outcomes for all stakeholders
	Feedback	Put in place improvements to procedures, fill gaps in knowledge, document lessons for the future

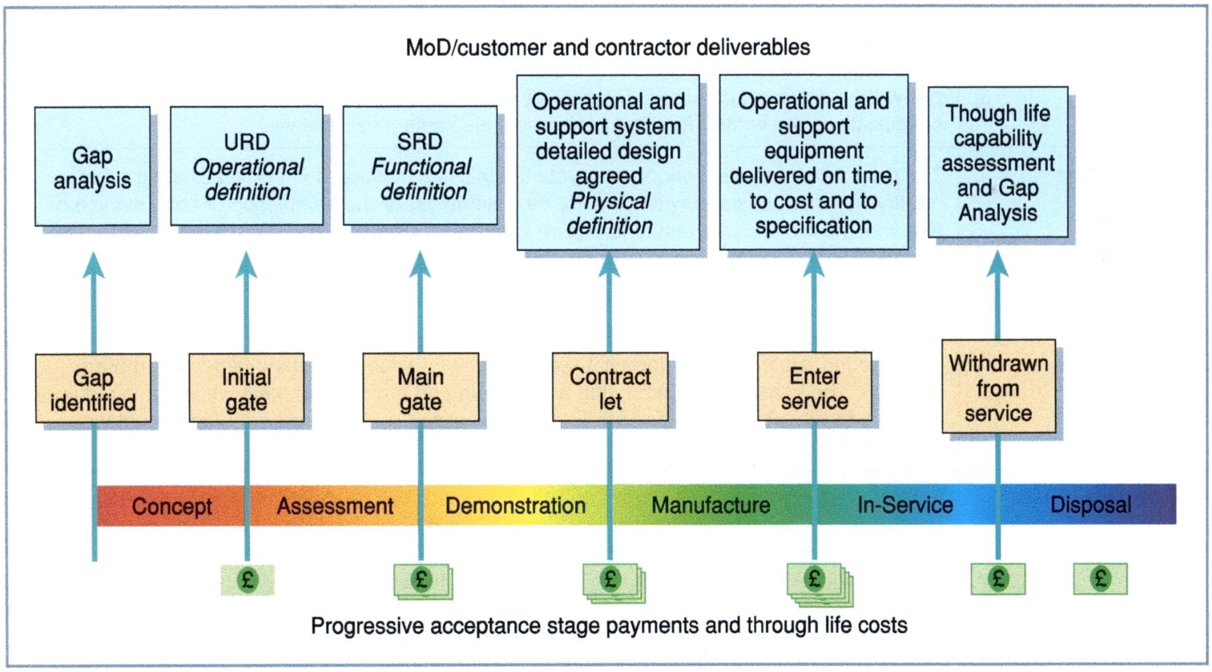

Figure 7.6 Project and product lifecycle in UK MoD procurement

Source: Ministry of Defence (MOD), www.mod.uk. Reproduced with permission.

be noted that in project terms, the development project ends when the equipment goes into service. There will be many projects thereafter to maintain and upgrade the equipment as it goes through its life. This shows that, as discussed in Chapter 6, the **lifecycle of a project** is generally considered to be different to the **lifecycle of a product**.

Table 7.4 Supply of a management information system to a hospital project

Sub-phase of project	*Activities*
D1 – Conceptualisation	Software house receives an outline from the management information system (MIS) department of the hospital; various pieces of information and points of clarification are requested.
D1 – Analysis	The concept is converted into the terminology of the software house (every organisation has its own jargon). An initial feasibility check is carried out to see what could be achieved at what cost. Objectives are set for the system to be developed and the interfaces with other systems studied. The analysis phase is completed by an appraisal of the capability of the company to provide what was being asked for by the client.
D2 – Proposal	The proposal document is submitted for approval by the client's MIS department in terms of whether or not it would meet the requirements set out in the initial request. The client organisation is offered the opportunity to visit the software house's premises and existing clients to view their systems.
D2 – Justification	There are two parts to this process. First, the software house carries out a financial analysis to show whether or not it is feasible for it to undertake the project. Second, the MIS people at the hospital need to provide evidence that the new system will provide a return. This has to be agreed by the financial managers.
D2 – Agreement	After the justification has been prepared by both sides, the formal act of preparation and signing of contracts can take place. This is the basis of the agreement between supplier and customer. The terms and conditions will have to go through each of the party's legal advisers.
D3 – Start-up	The software house starts to gather resources as soon as the contract looks likely to go ahead. Formal commitments are not made until the deal is formally signed. A project manager within the company is allocated to provide a single point of contact for the customer. The project team is gathered, external programmers hired and resources (development computers, pre-written software) procured. The project elements are allocated to individuals and specifications are written for what each of the elements must achieve.
D3 – Execution	The project team starts work on the system – this is a mixture of importing existing code, modifying other parts and writing totally new elements. At the completion of each section of the work the modules are tested to ensure integration. Gradually the system is pieced together and debugged. The client is involved in the process, with modules being demonstrated as they are completed, so that amendments are made at the time rather than at the end of the entire process.
D3 – Completion	Towards the end of the development the units being tested are getting larger and more complex. The in-house specialist staff are kept on and the programmers who were hired in continue to other jobs. The major task to be completed at this stage is the documentation of the system.
D3 – Handover	The software is transported to the user's site and installed on the machines. The software specialists are on hand to see that any problems can be resolved quickly. Staff are trained in the usage of the system and the MIS staff are taught to deal with its maintenance and support. Ongoing support is to be provided by the software house.
D4 – Review	The way in which each of the modules was developed is documented to provide a rich picture of the process. Mistakes and good practice are identified and customer perceptions of the system are canvassed. The results to the company in financial terms are compared with the proposal.
D4 – Feedback	Where deficiencies were highlighted, e.g. in the documentation of the system, the company puts in place new procedures and practices that will ensure (a) that the problem for the customer is resolved in this case and (b) that it does not occur in subsequent projects.

7.3 Describing the project management challenge: managerial complexity

The range of tasks called 'projects' has already been shown to be very wide and as you would expect, not all tools, techniques and management ideas are universally applicable across this range. The examples below illustrate two very different projects, how we can describe their **complexity** and hence the **managerial challenge** associated with each.

> **Book launch**
>
> As one of the few remaining privately owned bookstores, book launches were a major occasion. David Smith, the owner of the store, took charge of them personally so that he could maintain contact with both authors and his regular customers. Looking ahead to his next launch, he described it as 'a project of the utmost importance'. He had started planning this one six months in advance. He would need to liaise between the publishers, the author's agent and his own team to generate interest in the event and to use it to turn that interest into much-needed sales.

> **Scientific research project**
>
> A Nobel prize-winning scientist from a world-renowned institution, the Karolinska Institutet in Sweden, was considering how he would manage a major new research grant for which he was the principal investigator. The grant funded a network of scientists to pursue work that would assist in the understanding of major diseases, was worth many million euros per year and involved no less than 24 partners from all over Europe. The legal agreements between the parties alone ran to hundreds of pages, and that was before the discussions about the science even started. Managing groups of academics has been described as 'like herding feral cats' and this is before you add in any international dimensions, or that many will know little or nothing about managing a project.

In each case, how would you approach the project? The book launch has little complexity and some basic plans and documentation would be appropriate. This could be well achieved with a small number of written pages and would be unlikely to require professional project management assistance. The manager has done this before anyway and is confident of handling the requirements of this project. In the scientific research project, the financial and legal aspects of that work on their own are likely to keep not just the scientist but a small team of project support people busy for some time before, during and after the project. It is clearly of much higher complexity and would require a more structured and formalised approach to its management.

In order to provide meaningful consideration of the function of management in such a variety of settings, a classification of the complexity will be applied. In general, there will be a high correlation between the level of complexity of a project and the amount of resources required to manage it.

Recent research[11] has shown that the level of **structural complexity** of an activity is a function of five elements – giving the MODeST acronym: **M**ission, **O**rganisation, **De**livery **S**takeholders and **T**eam. Examples of each element are given in Table 7.5.

Table 7.5 The MODeST framework

Element of complexity	***Examples of issues that make management complex***
Mission	Lack of clarity of requirements Large scale, high value, high importance, high urgency Large number of constraints – legal, health and safety, security High level of interaction and interdependency with other projects High level of uncertainty – novelty, implications and side effects
Organisation	Multiple time zones project team members operating in Lack of collocation of project team Linguistic differences between team members Lack of appropriate organisational structure used in the project High level of change that the project produces in the organisation
Delivery	Lack of common or appropriate project management method Inappropriate human, financial or other resources Problematic communications in the project team Lack of clear or timely decision-making Lack of flexibility for the project manager to respond to changes
Stakeholders	Large number of stakeholders with differing requirements Lack of commitment to the project by key stakeholders Interference in the project by key stakeholders Lack of relationships with key stakeholders Problematic inter-relations between stakeholders
Team	Lack of leadership shown by project manager Cultural and other differences between team members Low level of motivation of team Lack of project, technical and business experience in the team Lack of appropriate training for team members

Using this framework and the examples of issues allows us to compare the book launch (labelled A in Table 7.6) and the scientific research project (labelled B). The results of this assessment are shown in Table 7.6, with issues that are expected to make the project complex to manage ticked or crossed.

It is clear that the projects are of different orders of complexity and that the project manager for the scientific research project will have to take measures to deal with the specific complexities that are identified here. For instance, the 'high level of interaction and interdependency with other projects' was identified. In response, it would be appropriate to put in place a system for monitoring those other projects to ensure that the impact of changes in those projects is known. Similarly, the 'large number of stakeholders with differing requirements' will require an approach to handling such diversity of requirements. Later chapters in this book will demonstrate (or provide pointers to) mechanisms for doing this. It is a core skill of a professional project manager that they have a range of responses to such complexities.

A complexity profile is a useful framework if used at the outset and then at various times during the project to identify particular difficulties and formulate a response to them. When considering these elements of complexity, it is worth considering their *interdependence* – for instance, the impact of organisational aspects on team aspects, and

Table 7.6 Assessing project complexity

Element of complexity	*Examples of issues that make management complex*	*A*	*B*
Mission	Lack of clarity of requirements	✗	✗
	Large scale, high value, high importance, high urgency	✗	✓
	Large number of constraints – legal, health and safety, security	✗	✓
	High level of interaction and interdependency with other projects	✗	✓
	High level of uncertainty – novelty, implications and side effects	✗	✓
Organisation	Multiple time zones project team members operating in	✗	✓
	Lack of collocation of project team	✗	✓
	Linguistic differences between team members	✗	✓
	Lack of appropriate organisational structure used in the project	✗	✓
	High level of change that the project produces in the organisation	✗	✗
Delivery	Lack of common or appropriate project management method	✗	✗
	Inappropriate human, financial or other resources	✗	✓
	Problematic communications in the project team	✗	✓
	Lack of clear or timely decision-making	✗	✓
	Lack of flexibility for the project manager to respond to changes	✗	✓
Stakeholders	Large number of stakeholders with differing requirements	✗	✓
	Lack of commitment to the project by key stakeholders	✗	✗
	Interference in the project by key stakeholders	✗	✗
	Lack of relationships with key stakeholders	✗	✗
	Problematic inter-relations between stakeholders	✗	✓
Team	Lack of leadership shown by project manager	✗	✗
	Cultural and other differences between team members	✗	✓
	Low level of motivation of team	✗	✗
	Lack of project, technical and business experience in the team	✗	✓
	Lack of appropriate training for team members	✗	✓

that the individual elements can change over time. That is, they may also have *dynamic* properties. Changes can of course be positive (e.g. the cancellation or delay of another project releases resources which can be used to speed up your own work), but organising to deploy those additional resources usefully does, at least temporarily, increase the complexity faced.

Summary

- The world in which projects operate grows in complexity. This places additional challenges on project managers in delivering and at the same time has increased expectations about delivery. It is no wonder, perhaps, that stories of 'failed projects' seem to have such presence in the media. Having frameworks or mental models enables us to make sense of complexity. This is not to say that we can ever completely describe something that is very complex, just in the words of Dr W. Edwards Deming: 'All models are wrong. Some are useful.' It is the utility that this chapter has sought to deliver in an attempt to facilitate the objective identified at the start – *get the thinking right*.

Key terms

4-D	ICOM	project/product lifecycle
5 Cs	integrator	sense-making
7-S	issues	stakeholders
complexity	managerial challenge	structural complexity
context	models	structures
framework	PESTEL	

Relevant areas of the Bodies of Knowledge

The two Bodies of Knowledge are included as they are used by many organisations as the basis for their own project management systems and as a skills base for their people. They do not set out to be comprehensive about everything that is known about project management; rather they provide guidance on some of the common ground between projects. For the PMI version, the guide is relatively extensive compared with the APM version, but neither is intended to be a text or a standard for operation. Another aspect as a result of their derivation is that they tend to be focused on aspects of first-time projects (see Chapter 6) rather than the vast majority of project management activity that takes place in as . . . but . . . and painting by numbers projects. They also assume that the relationship between the party carrying out the project and the 'customer' is contractual. Many projects are not 'direct revenue earners', instead being change projects (reorganising a firm, a merger or acquisition, or an individual undertaking a course of study, for instance). As a result of these factors, the application of the Bodies of Knowledge is a long way from universal. However, both are associated with professional qualifications and the contribution of these to the practice of project management globally is significant.

This section presents an overview of the Bodies of Knowledge. These provide points of reference to the approach and identify some of the areas of overlap with the content of this text. As Tables 7.7 and 7.8 show, the format of the APM document is rather different from that of the PMI, with the themes arranged into sections, and specific sub-sections within each covering particular topics. The guide does far less by way of description or definition, instead acting as a point of referral, with many sections simply containing lists of references to other texts on the area. The references are dominated by the construction and engineering industries, which limits the application of this work significantly. There is also little indication of how to determine 'what works where' from this document.

Table 7.7 The APM Body of Knowledge (2005)[12] and the relationship with topic coverage in this text

Section	***Title***	***Topics covered***	***Relevant chapters***
1	Project Management in Context	The definition referred to is as BS 6079[13] and the basic model of projects is as described in this chapter using the ICOMs model. Programmes and portfolios of projects are introduced and differentiated and management roles defined.	1,2
2	Planning the Strategy	The strategy referred to here is the integrating framework for the project, rather than corporate strategy. The topics covered include stakeholders, benefits, discussion of what constitutes a plan, and planning for value, risk and quality, health, safety and environmental considerations.	3,4

Table 7.7 continued

Section	*Title*	*Topics covered*	*Relevant chapters*
3	Executing the Strategy	Covering the detailed technical areas of project management, from identifying deliverables, through to scheduling, budgeting, resource management, scope and scope change management, use of earned value and the role of information management.	4,5,6
4	Techniques	This section is an extension of the previous one, pointing to a number of techniques that enable the technical tasks identified above. For instance, estimating is covered for use in scheduling and requirements management as a means to manage deliverables.	8,9,10,13
5	Business and Commercial	This covers the *raison d'être* of a large proportion of projects – that of generating a financial return. It considers the interfaces with other commercial functions, including marketing and sales, finance, procurement and legal.	1,4,8
6	Organisation and Governance	Describes the organisational structures that people work in. Structures include the definition of the basic organisational roles with respect to a project, including the sponsor, programme and project managers and the role of a project support office.	3,11
7	People and the Profession	Covers some of the 'soft issues' surrounding projects – including communications, teamwork, leadership, conflict management, negotiation and personnel management, as well as learning.	1,4,11,12,16

Table 7.8 The PMI Body of Knowledge[14] and the relationship with topic coverage in this text

Section	*Title*	*Summary*	*Relevant chapters*
1	Introduction	Sets out the purpose of the guide and the definitions of projects and project management, project lifecycle and the role of the project in organisations.	1,2,3
2	Project Life Cycle and Organization	This outlines a project lifecycle that broadly maps to the 4-D model. The influences of the organisation on the project are considered and the structures that people work in.	2,4,11
3	Project Management Processes for a Project	The guide identifies 42 processes within the five groups of initiating, planning, executing, monitoring and controlling, and closing activities. These are mapped to nine key areas of the Body of Knowledge – the subjects of the next nine chapters in the Body of Knowledge.	5
4	Project Integration Management	Integration management refers to bringing together the different aspects of a project in a coordinated way. Further, it recognises that there will be trade-offs in the decisions that project managers make and that the task of management is complex.	2,5
5	Project Scope Management	The scope of the project is defined in terms of a written statement of what is to be included in the project and what is specifically excluded. The main scoping work is carried out in the first two phases of the project and PMI includes a specific element of *scope verification* as a check on what is being agreed. *Scope change control* is also identified as a specific item, separate but linked to other aspects of change control.	5,6,10,13
6	Project Time Management	As the guide states: 'Project Time Management includes the processes required to ensure timely completion of the project.' Activities identified during scope management processes are compiled into an activity list, sequenced and times assigned to each activity. This then leads to the schedule for these activities – the times at which each must be completed to ensure the project as a whole finishes on time.	6,13

→

Table 7.8 continued

Section	*Title*	*Summary*	*Relevant chapters*
7	Project Cost Management	Similar to the process for time management, each of the activities is associated with a cost. This becomes the budget for each activity and there will need to be control measures to ensure that deviations from 'the plan' as a result of project problems and customer changes are 'managed'. Measures including *earned value* are suggested.	8,13
8	Project Quality Management	The focus on the carrying out of planning, assurance and control is comparable in many ways to the intention of ISO 9000[15] – that of providing *conformance*. (As for time and cost, in this text it is considered that conformance is only the minimum requirement of a project and that the current commercial environment for many organisations requires *performance* above and beyond these minimum standards.)	9,13
9	Project Human Resource Management	The main areas here are planning the organisational structure in which people will work, documenting their roles and reporting relationships, identifying the necessary individuals and developing the team. Requirements include performance appraisal of teams and individuals, and managing health and safety.	11,12
10	Project Communications Management	There are four aspects to this area: communications planning, information distribution, performance reporting and managing stakeholders. The guide provides a set of practices that are applicable to most projects.	4,9
11	Project Risk Management	Contains a broad description of risk management processes, from planning to identification to monitoring and control actions. Focus is on administrating the process.	10,13
12	Project Procurement Management	Covers a wide range of contract administration issues from the perspective of both buyer and seller of products or services.	14

For other publications related to this Body of Knowledge, see www.pmi.org.

PROJECT MANAGEMENT IN PRACTICE

The rescue of the Baghdad Zoo[16]

As the political head of steam that led to the invasion of Iraq in 2003 was building, there was much to consider in this project. One aspect that had escaped the attention of the invading forces was what would happen to the 600-plus captive animals of the Baghdad Zoo, one of the finest in the region.

Lawrence Anthony is a South African game reserve owner, who left home just as the US declared 'the war is over' in Iraq. His mission was to get into Baghdad as soon as was humanly possible after the initial push by the invading armies to see which animals he could rescue. Securing the necessary permission to attempt the mission was no small achievement, and this level of personal intervention and commitment was required throughout the mission. Compiling the necessary equipment to make the journey into Iraq from Kuwait was the next challenge, as was actually getting to Baghdad without getting killed by the various forces still engaged in combat. And that was before he even arrived in Baghdad.

This is an unusual project and one that is very different from the type of activity that project managers usually have to get involved in. There are lessons to be learned here for anyone associated with PM. Specifically, the project itself had relatively little structural complexity according to most of the elements of the MODeST framework. So how come it was so incredibly difficult?

Points for discussion

1 Rate this project using the MODeST framework. Why, then, was it so difficult to manage?

2 What are the characteristics of the kind of project manager that you need in such an environment?

3 For what kind of project would you not use such a person?

PROJECT MANAGEMENT IN PRACTICE
Using the 7-S approach in the review of a real project[17]

The Arson Task Force (ATF) was the name given to a 24-month project to reduce the incidence of arson in one area. During the project, the incidence of arson in the area declined and the team built an extensive knowledge base of cases of arson, its impact, effects and, most importantly, the causes and patterns of occurrence.

Source: Courtesy of Avon Fire & Rescue Service

This report considers the process by which the project has been managed for the purposes of identifying areas of good practice and improvement. Specific findings are that the project has been a success due to the team that has been put in place, the funding arrangements, flexible and adaptive management and considerable goodwill towards the project. Areas for improvement that have been identified include the project governance structure, project systems, staffing, skills and the management of stakeholders in the project.

Terms of reference

This report has been prepared to evaluate the project management practices used by the ATF during the bidding and execution of the project. The baseline for comparison of the processes and practices used is a combination of elements of PRINCE 2 2009 and the PMI Body of Knowledge.

Overview of the project

The ATF is an alliance between two fire and rescue services and an area police force. The task force comprises eight full-time staff with the following key objectives:

- To work in partnership with other agencies and private businesses to effect a sustainable reduction in the number of arson incidents.
- To increase the percentage of arson that is successfully detected.
- To reduce the number of arson incidents in schools and other educational premises.
- To produce and deliver educational programmes aimed at addressing the behaviour and attitudes of 7–16 year olds towards fire setting.
- To reduce the incidence of re-offending by working with Youth Offending Teams and developing intervention schemes for young offenders.

The framework for analysis

The 7-S framework will be used in this report. Under each heading, a statement of the understanding of relevant or illuminating events will be included with relevant elements of process. Where appropriate, suggestions will be made for improving the process of running future projects.

Strategy

Two aspects of strategy will be considered:

1 Project success measures – how are they defined?
2 Project strategy – the stated goals and priorities of the project.

Project success measures

The main measure for the success of the project is the reduction in arson in the region. This is an *outcome* measure that the work of the team will predominantly influence through indirect means. The team cannot stop acts of arson directly – they are working to influence the behaviour of those who may be or become arsonists. This outcome measure does little to allow the process that the team have gone through to be evaluated and could easily be influenced by events outside the control of the team (social disorder, for instance, causing a surge in the figures). In order to provide meaningful measures, it would also be appropriate to measure the *process* of the work, e.g. the number of workshops carried out or long-term initiatives established.

Project strategy

The project has a fixed time and budget. Any issues in the project would therefore be expected to affect the 'quality' (outcomes, achievements, etc.) of the project. As part of the bidding documentation for the project the high-level objectives for the project were established. These were sufficiently explicit to provide a focused framework for activities and yet still allowed considerable flexibility for dealing with issues that emerged as the research into incidents of arson progressed. There was no priority attached to these objectives however, and no allowance or process for change and assessing the impact of changes on quality.

Structure

The structure of a dedicated project team with permanently committed resources is an entirely appropriate arrangement. However, there are a number of issues.

Location

Co-locating the team was entirely appropriate for this kind of cross-agency working. Indeed, given the need for knowledge-sharing in the team, this kind of arrangement is to be encouraged.

Role of the project management board

The board, meeting quarterly, provided useful and informed views from a wide range of stakeholder groups. Its role was entirely advisory however, and there appears to have been minimal input to the management of the project by this board. The monitoring of progress by this board was not achieved – other than commenting on major milestones. In addition, it was noted that there were no terms of reference for the members of the board. It would be consistent with the declared intention to run the project using the PRINCE 2 2009 approach that a managerial board was put in place.

Authority structure

The project had two project managers who operated 'side by side'. This is very unusual, particularly when they come from different agencies. In reality, there were two team leaders, rather than project managers, who retained their line reporting from their own organisations. However, the arrangement appears to have worked. Whilst no single individual had overall responsibility or authority for the project, the shared goals and the efforts of the two individuals concerned have carried this. This practice should be reviewed for future projects as such a structure is more likely to be associated with project failure than success.

Systems

In PM terms, there are not a lot of project systems to report on. The effect of such a low level of systematisation is that the management has been able to be very flexible, unconstrained in many ways by incumbent plans. However, this does have an impact on the repeatability of such a project and does not provide any evidence for future time or resource planning. Indeed, if the project is to be an exemplar for other such projects in other areas in the future (as the organisations involved had hoped), some 'retrospective planning' would be worthwhile – for instance, recording at a high level basic timelines (using a Gantt Chart) indicating the phases of the project and key deliverables in each phase, identification of basic resource requirements (typical activities, time main activities take, job/role descriptions). Such a piece of documentation would add to the utility of the project outputs.

Planning and control

The objectives of the project were very well defined and provided a good basis for the broad categories of work that were followed. However, there was little by way of planning as would conventionally be expected, even in such a project. The effects of this 'it's all in my head' approach appear limited. In the event of the project not having been such a success, the management of the project, and in particular the planning and control, could be viewed unfavourably. Further, the project was unnecessarily 'at risk' from loss of one of the project managers.

In order to enhance the level of performance obtained through the existing approach and provide a level of management consistent with the context, there are a number of devices that could be applied. At the strategic level, these include the provision of basic work breakdown structures linked to stages and gates as an overview plan. These provide a basis for planning and resource allocation, without adding significantly to the bureaucratic workload. In addition, it would help with scoping activities (deciding what is in and what is outside the project) given resource availability and with communicating with the team and other stakeholders the plan for and progress of the project. Basic analysis of the work content of the project could be carried out and likely problems or opportunities identified proactively.

PRINCE 2 2009

According to the project proposal, ATF was going to be planned and managed using PRINCE 2 2009. Whilst this would have had to have been a selective application, there is no evidence that this standard was used. Unless mandated by the funding authority, it would be worth removing this requirement from future bids and developing basic project strategies, systems, structures etc. that are appropriate to the specific context and complexity.

Staff

Succession planning and knowledge management

There was no succession planning (what is to happen in the event of a team member leaving the team for whatever reason) in place at an organisational level. When a key member of staff was promoted out of the team, a core resource was removed. More importantly for the project was the loss of considerable knowledge as a result of this move, and instability for the team.

Teambuilding and team roles

Teambuilding did not appear as a specific activity in the project and would be worth including in the future. In addition, some personality profiling, as part of the ongoing teambuilding/staff development process, would help.

→

Recruitment

Recruitment and retention of team members is always going to be a challenge where there are uncertainties over funding beyond the life of the project. The approach taken here appears to have been highly pragmatic, with the scale and scope of work being flexible depending on resource availability. In future, it is likely that more specific task identification will be required and in such a case appropriate allowances must be made in the plans for the challenges of recruiting team members into specific roles and retaining them.

Skills

Not training the project managers in PRINCE 2 2009 until well into the execution phase of the project was a major oversight. In addition, there was no oversight of the management tasks being undertaken. In this case, it does not appear to have been detrimental to the performance of the project, although it does represent an unnecessary risk.

Style/culture

From the comments of the interviewees, the can-do culture of the team appeared to be entirely consistent with the goals of the project and has been encouraged by the team leaders.

Stakeholders

Managing stakeholders, particularly those who have an influence in the outcome of the project and the future of the team, is widely recognised as a core task for a project manager.

Stakeholders include:

- funders – Arson Control Forum (ACF) (central government, which would also fund any future work including continuation of the ATF);
- each of the partner organisations;
- local authorities;
- the project team;
- the project board;
- local businesses and residents;
- insurance companies (hoping to get reduced exposure to the risk of arson fires);
- other organisations looking to use the approach in their areas in the future.

There was no evidence that a communications plan/strategy was in place and this should form an integral part of the work packages in such a project. Marketing the project to stakeholder groups is again part of the role of a PM, particularly in a case such as this, where ongoing funding is required.

Points for discussion

1. How useful is the 7-S framework in the evaluation of this case?
2. How else could you review the management of such a project?
3. How complex is the ATF project?
4. The ATF received funding for a further two years. What would you recommend that the management of the ATF does to ensure success?

Topics for discussion

1 Identify a personal project that you have completed in the recent past – this may be a piece of coursework, a DIY project, etc. Consider the way in which the project was planned, carried out, the results analysed and then acted upon. What would you do differently if you were doing it all over again?

2 Taking the example of a personal project that you have recently completed (as for question 1), identify the inputs, outputs, constraints and mechanisms for the project. What is the importance of defining the nature of constraints on a project prior to starting work on it?

3 How would you describe the competitive environment of the following organisations?

- automotive industry;
- construction industry;
- banking;
- further/higher education.

What constraints does this place on projects being carried out in such an environment?

4 Why is it necessary to define the complexity of a project?

5 Identify the likely complexity of the following projects:

- the development of a new office block;
- the development of a new office complex where a radical new design is proposed;
- a project to put a new telescope in space by the European Space Agency;
- implementing a robotised assembly line in a manufacturing company.

6 Why is it necessary to consider the continuous improvement of the processes by which projects are carried out?

7 Identify the criteria for success or failure of the projects that you discussed in question 1 and question 2.

8 Show how developing a new product, for example a new range of vehicle engines, could benefit through the analysis of previous development projects.

9 Write a commentary on the Bodies of Knowledge, and how they could relate to your own work environment both now and in the future.

10 Explore the possibilities for gaining professional qualification and recognition in project management, through both APM and PMI. How well would these fit with your own intentions regarding your profession?

Further information

Caupin, G., Knöpfel, H., Morris, P.G.W., Motzel, E. and Pannebäcker, O. (eds) (1999) *IPMA Competence Baseline*, IPMA, Nijkerk, NL.

Checkland, P. and Poulter, J. (2006) *Learning for Action: A Short Definitive Guide to Soft Systems Methodology and Its Use for Practitioners, Students and Teachers*, John Wiley and Sons, Chichester.

Cicmil, S. and Marshall, D. (2005) 'Insights into Collaboration at the Project Level: Complexity, Social Interaction and Procurement Mechanisms', *Building Research and Information*, Vol. 33, No. 6, pp. 523–535.

Cooke-Davies, T., Cicmil, S., Crawford, L. and Richardson, K. (2007) 'We're Not in Kansas Anymore, Toto: Mapping the Strange Landscape of Complexity Theory, and Its Relationship to Project Management', *Project Management Journal*, Vol. 38, No. 2, pp. 50–61.

Lidow, D. (1999) 'Duck Alignment Theory: Going Beyond Classic Project Management to Maximise Project Success', *Project Management Journal*, Vol. 30, No. 4, pp. 8–14.

Söderlund, J. (2005) 'What Project Management Really Is About: Alternative Perspectives on the Role and Practice of Project Management', *International Journal of Technology Management*, Vol. 32, No. 3/4, pp. 371–387.

Stewart, T.A. (1995) 'The Corporate Jungle Spawns a New Species', *Fortune*, 10 July, pp. 121–122.

Weick, K., Sutcliffe, K. and Obstfeld, D. (2005) 'Organizing and the Process of Sensemaking', *Organisation Science*, Vol. 16, No. 4, pp. 409–421.

Weiss, A. and Hambleton, K. (2005) *Conquering Complexity: Lessons for Defence Systems Acquisition*, The Stationery Office, Norwich.

Williams, T. (2002) *Modelling Complex Projects*, Wiley, Chichester.

Xia, W. and Lee, G. (2004) 'Grasping the Complexity of IS Development Projects', *Communications of the ACM*, Vol. 47, No. 5, pp. 69–74.

Websites

www.mindtools.com/pages/article/newSTR_91.htm

www.themanager.org/models/7S%20Model.htm

Also see www.defence.gov.au/dmo/proj_man/Complex_PM_v2.0.pdf – this is a relatively recent development which, in addition to the regular project management professional institutes, describes the approach being taken by the International Centre for Complex Project Management.

References

1 Baines, T.S. et al. (2007) 'State of the Art in Product-Service Systems, *Proceedings of the Institution of Mechanical Engineers – Part B – Engineering Manufacture*, Vol. 221, No. 10, pp. 1543–1552.

2 Womack, J., Jones, D. and Roos, J. (1990) *The Machine That Changed The World*, Rawson Associates, New York.

3 Johnson, M. and Mena, C. (2008) 'Supply Chain Management For Servitised Products: A Multi-Industry Case Study', *International Journal of Production Economics*, Vol. 114, No. 1, pp. 27–39.

4 See Deming, W.E. (1986) *Out of the Crisis – Quality Productivity and Competitive Position*, MIT Center for Advanced Engineering Study, Cambridge, MA.

5 A further discussion of the use of such models in operations management can be found in Slack, N., Chambers, S. and Johnston, R. (2008) *Operations Management*, 5th edition, Financial Times Prentice Hall, Harlow.

6 For a further description of this development see Dyson, J. (2000) *Against the Odds*, Taxere Publishing, London.

7 It is the usual practice in some industries to have a period of claims following a contract completion. In the case of a building, there may be additional work as a result of clients changing specifications during the project or where there were unknowns (for instance, ground conditions) that were the risk of the client, not the contractor. Where these cannot be resolved amicably, a regular occurrence is the trip to court at the end of the project.

8 If not native to you, replace with any other animal that is more likely to be roadkill where you are.

9 This is supported by, among others, the findings of Clark and Fujimoto's study of excellence in the world automotive industry – see Clark, K.B. and Fujimoto, T. (1991) *Product Development Performance: Strategy, Organisation and Management in the World Automotive Industry*, Harvard Business School Press, Boston, MA.

10 See www.ams.mod.uk.

11 See Maylor, H., Vidgen, R. and Carver, S. (2008) 'What Makes a Project Complex to Manage?', *Project Management Journal*, Vol. 39, No. S1, pp. 15–26.

12 APM (2005) *Project Management Body of Knowledge*, Association for Project Management, High Wycombe.

13 BS 6079-1 (2002) *Project Management. Guide to Project Management*, British Standards Institute, London.

14 PMI (2008) *A Guide to the Project Management Body of Knowledge (PMBOK© Guide)*, 4th edition, Project Management Institute, Newtown Square, PA.

15 BS-EN-ISO 9000 (2005) *Quality Management Systems. Fundamentals and Vocabulary*, British Standards Institute, London.

16 See Anthony, L. and Grayham, S. (2007) *Babylon's Ark; The Incredible Wartime Rescue of the Baghdad Zoo*, Thomas Dunne Books, New York, NY.

17 This is not intended to illustrate good or bad practice or a good/bad report. The purpose is to show how such a framework is useful in providing a relatively straightforward but comprehensive review in practice. It is a synopsis of a longer report.

CHAPTER 8
Initiation - Macro Situational Analysis

LEARNING OUTCOMES

When you have worked through this chapter, you will be able to:

- explain why it is important to study the environment of the organisation;
- outline the main environmental influences on the organisation and relate the degree of change to prescriptive and emergent strategic approaches;
- undertake a PESTEL analysis of the general influences on the organisation;
- understand the implications of market growth and market cyclicality for strategic management;
- identify the key factors for success in an industry;
- carry out a Five Forces Analysis of the specific influences on the organisation;
- develop a Four Links Analysis of the organisation's co-operators;
- undertake a competitor profile and identify the competitor's advantages;
- explore the relationship between the organisation and its customers.

INTRODUCTION

In recent years, the term 'environment' has taken on a rather specialised meaning: it involves 'green' issues and the poisoning of our planet by human activity. These concerns are certainly part of our considerations in this book, but we use the term 'environment' in a much broader sense to describe everything and everyone outside the organisation. This includes customers, competitors, suppliers, distributors, government and social institutions. The important topic of green strategy and sustainability deserves a separate chapter.

As the starting point in the development of both prescriptive and emergent strategy, it is useful to begin by exploring the nine basic analytical tools of the environment that will influence the organisation's strategy (see Figure 8.1). Elements of the environment can change so the organisation needs to adjust its strategy accordingly. Prescriptive strategies will want to anticipate how the environment will change in the future in order to meet future needs ahead of competing organisations. Emergent strategies will be content with an understanding of the environment.

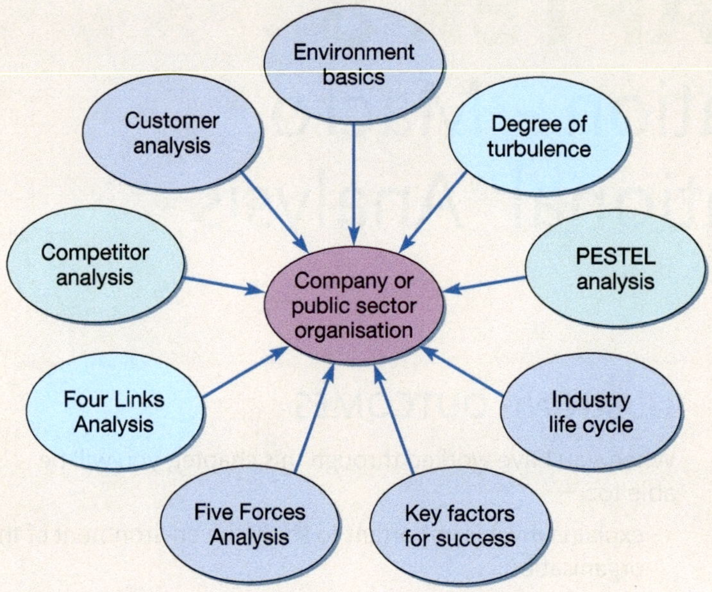

Figure 8.1 Analysing the strategic environment - the nine basic analytical tools

CASE STUDY 8.1

Ryanair™: why it has not (yet) moved into long-haul flights[1]

Although long-haul flights - such as those across the Atlantic - have higher profit margins, only two airlines have launched low-cost versions so far. Other airlines were not convinced about this strategy, which challenged the low-cost/low-price business model used in Europe. The doubters included Europe's leading low-cost airline, the bold and focused Ryanair. This case explores the reasons for Ryanair's caution. It raises the prospect of a new competitive battle between Europe's (and possibly the world's) leading airlines.

From its first flights in 1985, Ryanair has grown to become Europe's largest airline.
© Andrew Walters/Alamy

Early days for long-haul, low-cost airlines

Launched in 2014, Norwegian® Airlines was the first major European carrier to offer cheap flights from Europe to the USA. It was followed in 2015 by Eurowings®, with similar flights. Norwegian is a separate company but Eurowings is a wholly-owned subsidiary of one of Europe's leading airlines, the German carrier Lufthansa®.

In 2017, IAG™ then entered the fray: the company is the owner of British Airways™, Iberia® (Spain) and Aer Lingus™ (Ireland). These are full-cost carriers but IAG also owns the Spanish low-cost airline Vueling™. The company created another new company with the brand name Level to launch its new, low-cost, long-haul services. Level® would operate from Barcelona to Los Angeles, Oakland near San Francisco, Punta Cana in the Dominican Republic and Buenos Aires in Argentina. Willie Walsh, IAG's chief executive, explained that the initial operations from Barcelona were 'just the start'. 'We're really excited about the opportunities for expansion and we plan to bring Level to other European destinations.'

Level was initially planning to use two Airbus® A330 aircraft fitted with 293 economy and 21 premium economy seats. It would be painted in Level's own livery and, initially at least, use crews from Iberia, the Spanish flag carrier that is IAG's second-largest airline by revenue. Fares were priced from €99 or $149 one way. But, if the other low-cost, long-haul airlines were any guide, these prices would only be available for a limited number of seats. Moreover, there would be extra charges for food, luggage and other extras. For example, Norwegian was already charging around €90 on its long-haul flights to carry a suitcase. Hence, it was likely that such additional items would not be cheap.

Business model for long-haul, low-cost airlines

Like the existing similar low-cost European airlines, the new companies were operating on a similar model for the longer distances. The business model for these routes involved seeking the lowest possible costs, for example by having high load factors - selling every available seat - and charging for food, luggage and other items. They would also avoid the high landing fees of popular airports like JFK in New York and fly to cheaper destinations. In addition, to make costs even lower, Norwegian had purchased new aircraft that were more fuel-efficient: fuel still accounted for some 25 per cent of total airline costs. There would be no reserved seating but there would be some premium seating.

All this new strategic activity raises an intriguing strategy question: why was it that two of Europe's leading low-cost airlines, Ryanair and easyJet®, had not followed the same strategy? What was it about the business model above that did not hold together for these highly experienced airlines? Particularly because many new European routes had now been opened up: there were fewer opportunities than in the past for totally new routes in Europe.

Over the last few years, Ryanair was reported at various times as being about to launch new routes from Europe to the USA. The problem for the company was that its ultra-low-cost business model was more than just low landing fees, extra seats and charging for food and luggage. For example, Ryanair sought rapid turn-around times in each airport to reduce costs. It only operated point-to-point flights, thus making the whole booking process simple. This also allowed the company to work with simple flight schedules that did not involve matching with internal flights in another country. It had just a few major bases across Europe to maintain its aircraft. It could rapidly switch aircraft if there was a mechanical problem. This extreme focus on reducing the costs of its operations would be more complex if it had to operate flights much further from its existing operations. Its business model would need to change.

Opportunity and risk for Europe's leading airlines

Over the last few years, Ryanair, easyJet and other low-cost airlines had become the way forward in Europe. At the time of writing this case, British Airways had effectively acknowledged this reality by cutting back on free food and other items on its European flights: it was slowly turning itself from a full-cost into a low-cost European airline. Other leading European airlines were thinking about a similar strategy. But this was a catch-up strategy with Ryanair and the other low-cost airlines. In this sense, it was a strategy of survival amongst the flag carriers like British Airways rather than a growth strategy.

But there were still a number of European airlines that had not fully engaged in such a strategy for a variety of reasons: resistance by unions, government policy for a flag carrier and so on. Ryanair and the other low-cost airlines were reported to view such airlines as still being vulnerable to further attack. The low-cost model inside Europe would still present further opportunities if this was correct. It would explain, at least in part, why Ryanair and easyJet had still not moved into the long-haul market.

However, at the same time, there was an obvious risk for Ryanair, easyJet and others. If these companies ignored the potential business to be derived from new long-haul, low-cost routes, they may never be able to recover those opportunities and grow their business beyond Europe. And, without question, the European airline market was beginning to slow down for a variety of reasons.

Case questions

1 What are the competitive advantages of the existing European low-cost airlines? Are these under threat? Are such advantages therefore sustainable in the long term?

2 Where does the balance rest between opportunity and risk as the existing low-cost airlines, like Ryanair, decide whether to launch long-haul operations? What strategy would you recommend to Ryanair with regard to launching new long-haul flights?

Sources: see endnote 1.

On the website

On the book's free website: www.pearsoned.co.uk/lynch there is comprehensive case study: *Europe's leading airlines: low-cost strategy or bust?*

8.1 EXPLORING THE COMPETITIVE ENVIRONMENT

8.1.1 Why studying the competitive environment is important

Definition ▶ **In strategy, the environment means everything and everyone outside the organisation: competitors, customers, suppliers plus other influential institutions such as local and national governments.** Strategists are agreed that an understanding of the competitive environment is an essential element of the development of strategic management. It is important to study the environment surrounding the organisation for three main reasons. First, most organisations compete against others – for example, films like *Lord of the Rings* compete against other films for finance from the film studios – see Case 8.4. Hence a study of the environment will provide information on the nature of competition as a step to developing *sustainable competitive advantage.*[2] Sustainable competitive advantage is an advantage over competitors that cannot easily be imitated. Second, most organisations will perceive *opportunities* that might be explored and *threats* that need to be contained.[3] For example, the *Lord of the Rings* trilogy was seen by some film backers to have more threats than opportunities. Such opportunities and threats may come not just from competitors but also from government decisions, changes in technology and social developments and many other factors. Third, there are opportunities for networks and other linkages, which lead to sustainable co-operation. For example, Peter Jackson met his old friend Mark Ordesky® when needing some help in the final negotiations to finance *Lord of the Rings*. Such linkages with others may strengthen an organisation in its environment by providing mutual support. By contrast, Ryanair – see Case 8.1 – shows that linkages like the need for a network of airport landing slots takes time to develop and may not always be profitable.

However, there are three difficulties in determining the connection between the organisation's strategic management and its environment.

1 *The prescriptive versus emergent debate.* The first problem arises from the fundamental disagreement about the strategic management processes that were explored in Part 1 of this book. Some prescriptive strategists take the view that, in spite of the various uncertainties, the environment can usefully be predicted for many markets. Some (but not all) emergent strategists believe that the environment is so turbulent and chaotic that prediction is likely to be inaccurate and serve no useful purpose. Each of these interpretations implies a quite different status for the same basic topic. This difficulty is explored further in Section 8.2.

2 *The uncertainty.* Whatever view is taken about prediction, all strategists regard the environment as uncertain. New strategies have to be undertaken against a backdrop that cannot be guaranteed and this difficulty must be addressed as strategies are developed. For example, Case 8.4 shows that the risks were so high in financing the film *Lord of the Rings* that nearly every studio declined to finance it. Uncertainty remained high at Ryanair over long-haul flights at the time of writing this text – see Case 8.1.

3 *The range of influences.* It is conceivable, at least in theory, that every element of an organisation's environment may influence strategic management. One solution to the problem posed by such a wide range of factors might be to produce a list of every element. This would be a strategic mistake, however, because organisations and individuals would find it difficult to develop and manage every item. In strategic management, the production of comprehensive lists that include every major eventuality and have no priorities has no value. A better solution is to identify the key factors for success in the industry and then to direct the environmental analysis towards these factors. This is considered later in this chapter in Section 8.6.

8.1.2 The main elements of environmental analysis

To analyse an organisation's environment, while at the same time addressing the three difficulties outlined in Section 8.1.1, certain basic analytical procedures can be undertaken (see Table 8.1).

Table 8.1 Nine basic stages in environmental analysis

Stage	Techniques	Outcome of stage
1 Environment basics - an opening evaluation to define and explore basic characteristics of the environment (*see* Section 8.2)	Estimates of some basic factors surrounding the environment: • Market definition and size • Market growth • Market share	Basic strategic analysis: • Scope the strategic opportunity • Establish future growth prospects • Begin to structure market competition
2 Consideration of the degree of turbulence in the environment (*see* Section 8.3)	General considerations: • Change: fast or slow? • Repetitive or surprising future? • Forecastable or unpredictable? • Complex or simple influences on the organisation?	Guidance on initial questions: • Is the environment too turbulent to undertake useful predictions? • What are the opportunities and threats for the organisation?
3 Background factors that influence the competitive environment (*see* Section 8.4)	PESTEL analysis, Institutional Analysis and scenarios	• Identify key influences • Predict, if possible • Understand interconnections between events
4 Analysis of stages of market growth (*see* Section 8.5)	Industry life cycle	• Identify growth stage • Consider implications for strategy • Identify maturity, over-production and cyclicality issues
5 Factors specific to the industry: what delivers success? (*see* Section 8.6)	Key factors for success analysis	• Identify factors relevant to strategy • Focus strategic analysis and development
6 Factors specific to the competitive balance of power in the industry (*see* Section 8.7)	Five Forces Analysis	• Static and descriptive analysis of competitive forces
7 Factors specific to co-operation in the industry (*see* Section 8.8)	Four Links Analysis	• Analysis of current and future organisations with whom co-operation is possible • Network analysis
8 Factors specific to immediate competitors (*see* Section 8.9)	Competitor analysis and product portfolio analysis	• Competitor profile • Analysis of relative market strengths
9 Customer analysis (*see* Section 8.10)	Market and segmentation studies	• Strategy targeted at existing and potential customers • Market segmentation and positioning within segment

8.1.3 The distinction between proactive and reactive outcomes

When analysing the environment, it is useful to draw a distinction between two types of results from the analysis:

1 *Proactive outcomes.* The environmental analysis will identify positive opportunities or negative threats. The organisation will then develop proactive strategies to exploit or cope with the situation. For example, film producers might develop cross-financing co-operation as a result of identifying new market opportunities.

2 *Reactive outcomes.* The environmental analysis will highlight important strategic changes over which the organisation has no control but to which, if they happen, it will need to be able to react. For example, new EU legislation on cultural content and investment might influence strategic activity in the European film industry.

In both cases, the environment will need to be analysed but the strategic implications are very different.

KEY STRATEGIC PRINCIPLES

- Environmental analysis is important because it helps in developing sustainable competitive advantage, identifies opportunities and threats and may provide opportunities for productive co-operation with other organisations.
- There are three difficulties in studying the environment: the use to which the analysis will be put; uncertainty in the topic; coping with the wide range of environmental influences.
- Environmental analysis can be used to provide a *proactive* strategy outcome or highlight a *reactive* strategic situation that will need to be monitored.

On the website

On the book's free website, there is a case that examines the strategic environment: *The Rise and Fall of Blockbuster® Video Stores*. In addition to the case and linked questions, the website also has some *indicative answers* to the case questions. These should prove helpful if you want to see how to tackle strategy cases.
Go to: www.pearsoned.co.uk/lynch

8.2 STRATEGIC ENVIRONMENT – THE BASICS

In order to begin the environmental analysis, it is useful to start with some basic factors that are sometimes forgotten in the academic concepts but contribute to the strategic analysis of the environment.[4] We can divide the basics into three areas:

1 Market definition and size;

2 Market growth;

3 Market share.

8.2.1 Market definition and size[5]

In analysing the strategic environment, most organisations will want an answer to the basic question – 'What is the size of the market?' This is important because it will assist in defining the strategic task. Markets are usually described in terms of annual sales. From a strategy perspective, a 'large' market may be more attractive than a 'small' market. The words 'large' and 'small' need to be defined carefully – for example, a 'large' opportunity to Peter Jackson who directed the major film trilogy *Lord of the Rings* might be $200 million – see Case 8.4 later in this chapter. However, a 'large' opportunity to Warner Brothers® who ultimately funded the film and have much broader film interests might be \$1 billion. Despite such problems, it is a useful starting point to attempt to assess the strategic opportunity (or the lack of it).

Measuring market size raises a related problem – how to define the 'market'. For example, is the annual market for the film trilogy *Lord of the Rings* (LOTR) defined as *fantasy films* only – worth, say, \$500 million? Or is the annual LOTR market *all adventure films*, including *Lord of the Rings* but also covering others from James Bond films to those starring Clint Eastwood – worth, say, \$10 billion? The answer will depend on the customers and the extent to which other products are a real substitute. Although some market definitions may seem obvious – for example, 'the ice cream market' would seem to be clearly defined – they need to be treated with care: perhaps another snack will substitute for ice cream and should be included within the definition?

8.2.2 Market growth

In establishing the size of the market, it is also common practice to estimate how much the market has grown over the previous period – usually the previous year. From a strategy perspective, the importance of growth relates to the organisation's objectives. An organisation wishing to grow rapidly might be more attracted to a market growing rapidly. Clearly any such estimate also needs to take into account the argument about market definition made above.

8.2.3 Market share

Although some strategists disagree, a large share of a market is usually regarded as being strategically beneficial.[6] The reason is that a large share may make it possible to influence prices and may also reduce costs through scope for economies of scale, thereby increasing profitability.[7] Clearly, there are definitional problems here – see Section 8.2.1 above – but some estimate of market share is desirable from a strategy perspective. In practice, it may be difficult to establish a precise market share – for example, the share of the film market taken by *Lord of the Rings* in 2002 will depend on the fact that it had a high share during the few weeks after its general release and greatest popularity – but this may not matter. From a strategy perspective, the important point is that *Lord of the Rings* took a significant share of the *fragmented* film market during that year. Equally, there will be other strategic circumstances where a *dominant* share may be identified – for example, the market share held by companies supplying domestic water to households – without necessarily being able to measure the precise share.

KEY STRATEGIC PRINCIPLES

- Environmental analysis can usefully begin with a basic assessment of the market definition and size, the market growth and the market share.
- Market definition is important because it will determine the size and scope of the strategic opportunity. Market definition will be defined by a consideration of customers and the availability of substitute products.
- Market growth is commonly estimated early in any strategic analysis because of its importance with regard to the growth objectives of an organisation.
- A basic estimate of market share can be used to estimate whether an organisation has a significant share of a market as a starting point in exploring the strategic implications.

8.3 DEGREE OF TURBULENCE IN THE ENVIRONMENT[8]

At the general level of environmental analysis, it is important to consider the basic conditions surrounding the organisation. Special attention needs to be directed to the nature and strength of the forces driving strategic change – the *dynamics* of the environment. One reason for this consideration is that, if the forces are exceptionally turbulent, they may make it difficult to use some of the analytical techniques – like Porter's 'Five Forces', discussed later in this chapter. Another reason is that the nature of the environment may influence the way that the organisation is structured to cope with such changes.

The environmental forces surrounding the organisation can be assessed according to two main measures:

Definition ▶ 1 **Changeability – the degree to which the environment is likely to change.** For example, there is low changeability in the liquid milk market and high changeability in the various internet markets.

Definition ▶ 2 **Predictability – the degree to which such changes can be predicted.** For example, changes can be predicted with some certainty in the mobile telephone market but remain largely unknown in biogenetics.

These measures can each be subdivided further. Changeability comprises:

- *Complexity* – the degree to which the organisation's environment is affected by factors such as internationalisation and technological, social and political complications.
- *Novelty* – the degree to which the environment presents the organisation with new situations.

Predictability can be further subdivided into:

- *rate of change* of the environment (from slow to fast);
- *visibility of the future* in terms of the availability and usefulness of the information used to predict the future.

Using these factors as a basis, it is then possible to build a spectrum that categorises the environment and provides a rating for its *degree of turbulence* (see Table 8.2).

When turbulence is low, it may be possible to predict the future with confidence. For example, film companies like Warner Brothers might be able to use data on their film customers around the world, along with international economic data, to predict future demand for different types of films.

When turbulence is higher, such predictions may have little meaning. The changeability elements influencing the organisation may contain *many* and *complex* items and the *novelty* being introduced into the market place may be high. For example, new services, new suppliers, new ideas, new software and new payment systems were all being launched for the internet at the same time. Turbulence was high. Predicting the specific outcome of such developments was virtually impossible.

If the level of turbulence is high – called *hypercompetition*[9] by some strategists – and as a result the environment is difficult to study, the analysis recommended in some of the sections that follow may

Table 8.2 Assessing the dynamics of the environment

	Environmental turbulence	Repetitive	Expanding	Changing	Discontinuous	Surprising
Changeability	*Complexity*	National	National	Regional Technological	Regional Socio-political	Global Economic
	Familiarity of events	Familiar	Extrapolatable		Discontinuous Familiar	Discontinuous Novel
Predictability	*Rapidity of change*	Slower than response		Comparable to response		Faster than response
	Visibility of future	Recurring	Forecastable	Predictable	Partially predictable	Unpredictable surprises
	Turbulence level	*Low* 1	2	3	4	5 *High*

Source: Ansoff, I and McDonnell, E (1990) *Implanting Strategic Management*, FT Prentice-Hall. With permission.

need to be treated with some caution. However, for most fast-growing situations, including the internet, there is merit in at least attempting to understand the main areas of the environment influencing the organisation. It may not be possible to undertake formal predictions, but it will certainly be possible to identify the most important elements.

KEY STRATEGIC PRINCIPLES

- It is important to begin an analysis of the environment with a general consideration of the degree of turbulence in that environment. If it is high, then this will make prediction difficult and impact on prescriptive approaches to strategy development.
- There are two measures of turbulence: changeability, i.e. the degree to which the environment is likely to change; and predictability, i.e. the degree to which such change can be predicted.
- Each of the two measures can then be further subdivided: changeability can be split into complexity and novelty; predictability can be divided into rate of change and visibility of the future. All these elements can then be used to explore turbulence.

8.4 ANALYSING THE GENERAL ENVIRONMENT

In any consideration of the factors surrounding the organisation, three techniques can be used to explore the general environment: these are (1) the PESTEL checklist, (2) the institutional environment and (3) scenarios.

8.4.1 PESTEL checklist

It is already clear that there are no simple rules governing an analysis of the organisation. Each analysis needs to be guided by what is relevant for that particular organisation. However, it may be useful to begin the process with **the PESTEL checklist, which consists of the Political, Economic, Socio-cultural, Technological, Environmental and Legal aspects of the environment.**

Definition ▶

Exhibit 8.1 presents some of the main items that might be considered when undertaking a PESTEL analysis.

Comment

Importantly, there is no underpinning logic to a PESTEL checklist, unlike many other strategy environmental concepts, such as the degree of turbulence or the market share and growth analysis explored above. PESTEL is purely a reminder checklist and should be used selectively.

Like all checklists, a PESTEL analysis is really only as good as the individual or group preparing it. Listing every conceivable item has little value and betrays a lack of serious consideration and logic in the strategic management process. Better to have three or four well-thought-out items that are explored and justified with evidence than a lengthy 'laundry list' of items. This is why this book does not recommend simple + and – signs and accompanying short bullet points, although these might provide a useful summary.

To the prescriptive strategists, although the items in a PESTEL analysis rely on *past* events and experience, the analysis can be used as a *forecast of the future*. The past is history and strategic management is concerned with future action, but the best evidence about the future *may* derive from what happened in the past. Prescriptive strategists would suggest that it is worth attempting the task because major new investments make this hidden assumption anyway. For example, when Warner Brothers invested several hundred million dollars in the first *Harry Potter*® film, it was making an assumption that the fantasy film market would remain attractive; it might as well *formalise* this through a structured PESTEL analysis, even if the outcome is difficult to predict.

EXHIBIT 8.1

Checklist for a PESTEL analysis

Political future

- Political parties and alignments at local, national and European or regional trading-block level
- Legislation, e.g. on taxation and employment law
- Relations between government and the organisation (possibly influencing the preceding items in a major way and forming a part of future strategic management)
- Government ownership of industry and attitude to monopolies and competition

Socio-cultural future

- Shifts in values and culture
- Change in lifestyle
- Attitudes to work and leisure
- 'Green' environmental issues
- Education and health
- Demographic changes
- Distribution of income

Economic future

- Total GDP and GDP per head
- Inflation
- Consumer expenditure and disposable income
- Interest rates
- Currency fluctuations and exchange rates
- Investment - by the state, private enterprise and foreign companies
- Cyclicality
- Unemployment
- Energy costs, transport costs, communications costs, raw materials costs

Technological future

- Government and EU investment policy
- Identified new research initiatives
- New patents and products
- Speed of change and adoption of new technology
- Level of expenditure on R&D by organisation's rivals
- Developments in nominally unrelated industries that might be applicable

Environmental future

- 'Green' issues that affect the environment and impact on the company
- Level and type of energy consumed - renewable energy?
- Rubbish, waste and its disposal

Legal future

- Competition law and government policy
- Employment and safety law
- Product safety issues

The emergent corporate strategists may well comment that the future is so uncertain that prediction is useless. If this view is held, a PESTEL analysis will fulfil a different role in *interpreting* past events and their interrelationships. In practice, some emergent strategists may give words of caution but still be tempted to predict the future. For example, one prominent strategist, Herbert Simon, wrote a rather rash article in 1960 predicting that, 'We will have the technical ability, by 1985, to run corporations by machine.'[10] The emergent strategists are correct in suggesting that prediction in some fast-moving markets may have little value. Overall, when used wisely, the PESTEL checklist has a role in strategic management.

On the website

On the book's free website: www.pearsoned.co.uk
Analysing the role of government from a strategy perspective.

8.4.2 Analysing the institutional environment: the '5P' Framework

Some strategists regard the PESTEL analysis as being rather crude: it requires judgement and guesswork and has limited underpinning logic. An alternative approach that offers more structure and has a logical framework based on knowledge and innovation is the *5P Framework*. This is grounded in

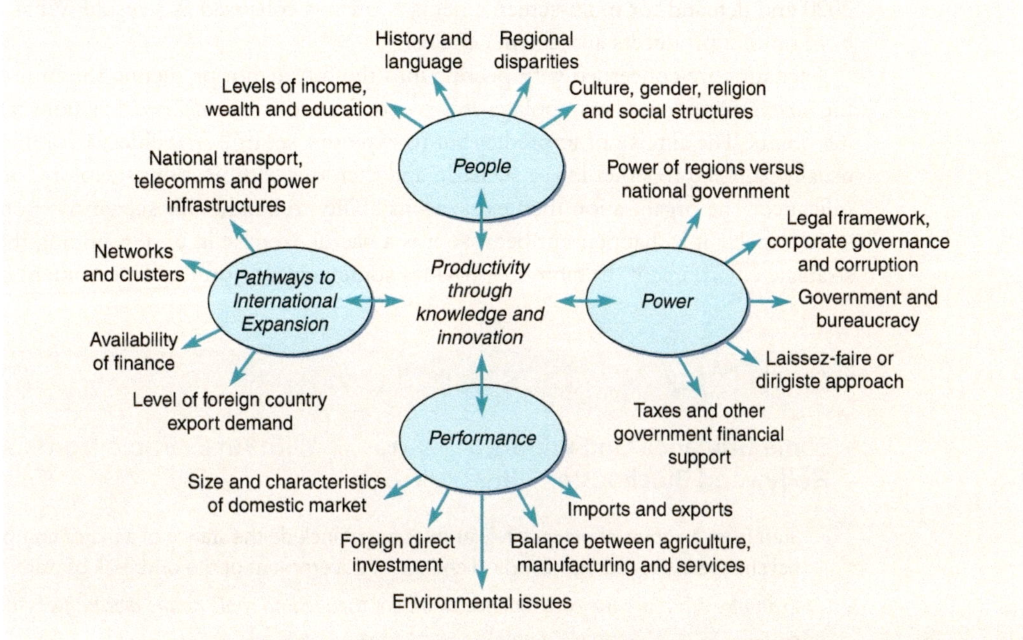

Figure 8.2 The '5P' Framework

Source: Lynch, R and Jin, Z (2016) 'Exploring the institutional perspective on international business expansion: tTowards a more detailed conceptual framework', Journal of Innovation & Knowledge, (2016) 1(2), 117–124. http://dx.doi.org/10.1016/j.jik.2016.01.001

three basic principles. The first is the *Institutional Perspective* on strategy development.[11] This theory explores the governmental, social and cultural institutions of a country. It includes both the formal rules, such as its constitution and legal framework, and the informal constraints, such as customs and self-imposed rules of conduct, which need to be understood in the assessment of its business potential. The second basic principle underpinning the Framework is that of *International Business Strategy*, especially from an economic perspective.[12] The third basic principle of the Framework is that the exchange process between the various elements will be governed, at least in part, by *Knowledge and Innovation*.[13]

Five fundamental elements then structure the Institutional Perspective. There are four principle elements in the paradigm: namely, *people*, *power*, *performance* and *pathways*. These four items have background influencing factors – see Figure 8.2. The outcome of these four elements then delivers the *productivity* impact of a country's institutions, defined in terms the increased knowledge and new innovation at both the level of the industry and of individual companies: the fifth 'P' of the paradigm. The central core of the Framework from a strategy perspective is that the basic strategic objectives of value-added and sustainable competitive advantage will be influenced by the 5P background factors. All the elements interact with each other. Some elements will be more dominant in some countries and in some contexts than others. Moreover, the balance will change over time and in relation to events outside the individual country. Because of these inter-relationships, the various elements are not simply a possible list of pointers but form a *paradigm* of factors that work together in various ways. From this perspective, they provide a useful alternative to the widely-used PESTEL analysis.

8.4.3 Scenario-based analysis

In the context of a scenario-based analysis, a scenario is a model of a possible future environment for the organisation, whose strategic implications can then be investigated. For example, a scenario might be developed to explore the question: 'What would happen if broadband allowed *every* film (and not just those offered by companies like Netflix and Sky) to be delivered in-home by the year

2020 and demand for multi-screen cinema showings collapsed as a result? What impact would this have on film producers and cinema chains?'

Scenarios are concerned with peering into the future, not predicting the future. Prediction takes the *current* situation and extrapolates it forward. Scenarios take *different* situations with *alternative* starting points. The aim is not to predict but to explore a set of possibilities; a combination of events is usually gathered together into a scenario and then this combination is explored for its strategic significance. The organisation then explores its ability to handle this scenario – not because it necessarily expects it to happen but because it is a useful exercise in understanding the dynamics of the strategic environment. Exhibit 8.2 provides some guidance on the development of scenarios.

EXHIBIT 8.2

Some Guidance On Building Scenarios . . . With An Example from Case 8.4 On Hollywood Blockbuster Films

- Start from an *unusual viewpoint*. Examples might include the stance of a major competitor, a substantial change in technology, a radical change of government or the outbreak of war.

  Example: What are the consequences if one of the leading male actors dies halfway through filming?

- Develop a *qualitative description* of a group of possible events or a *narrative* that shows how events will unfold. It is unlikely that this will involve a quantitative projection.

  Example: The actor dies on day 45 (out of a 90-day shoot). The press are informed the same day. The producers then need to find another actor but also face problems over what they do about existing film footage: Do they re-shoot? Do they change the story? Do they invent another character?

- Explore the *outcomes* of this description or narrative of events by building two or three scenarios of what might happen. It is usually difficult to handle more than three scenarios. Two scenarios often lend themselves to a 'most optimistic outcome' and a 'worst possible outcome'.

  Example: Scenario 1 - the worst possible outcome is a total re-shoot including the withdrawal of other stars because they have other film commitments. Scenario 2 - change the storyline to fit the new situation with costs in terms of reworking the script, hiring another actor, perhaps re-shooting some scenes. The financial consequences of each of these scenarios (and more) can be calculated - what does it cost to hire script writers? Etc.

- Include the inevitable *uncertainty* in each scenario and explore the *consequences* of this uncertainty for the organisation concerned - for example, 'What would happen if the most optimistic outcome was achieved?' The PESTEL factors may provide some clues here.

  Example: Scenario 1 - When precisely will other actors need to leave - after all, we still have another 45 days of contractual shooting? What does this really mean for the shoot? Surely we can do some rewrite that will help? Perhaps scenario 1 is actually too pessimistic?

- Test the usefulness of the scenario by the extent to which it leads to *new strategic thinking* rather than merely the continuance of existing strategy.

  Example: Importantly in terms of radical thinking: if the actor was so important in the first place, why didn't we take out special insurance against his life on the possibility of such an event before filming began?

- Recall that the objective of scenario building is to develop strategies to cope with uncertainty, *not* to predict the future.

  Example: No one wants a leading actor to die but imaginative scenarios help protect against uncertainties and unusual consequences.

On the website

Two extra items on the book's free website: www.pearsoned.co.uk/lynch

1 *Six political and economic trends that have affected strategic management.*

2 *Non-market strategies: what are they and why are they important?*

KEY STRATEGIC PRINCIPLES

- The PESTEL checklist - the study of Political, Economic, Socio-cultural, Technological, Environmental and Legal factors - provides a useful starting point to any analysis of the general environment surrounding an organisation. It is vital to select among the items from such a generalised list and explore the chosen areas in depth; long lists of items are usually of no use.
- Prescriptive and emergent strategists take different views on the merits of projecting forward the main elements of the PESTEL checklist. The prescriptive approach favours the development of projections because they are often implied in major strategic decisions in any event. Emergent strategists believe the turbulence of the environment makes projections of limited value.
- In analysing the institutional environment, the 5P Framework - People, Power, Pathways, Performance and Productivity (as measured by knowledge and innovation) - can form a useful structure for this purpose. These background factors may form an important element of strategy.
- A scenario is a picture of a possible future environment for the organisation, whose strategic implications can then be investigated. It is less concerned with prediction and more involved with developing different perspectives on the future. The aim is to stimulate new strategic thought about the possible consequences of events, rather than make an accurate prediction of the future.

CASE STUDY 8.2

Life cycle impact on strategy in the European ice cream market

During the period up to year 2004, the European ice cream market underwent significant change: some segments were relatively mature while some were experiencing strong growth. The North American market was more mature and fragmented with stronger regional brands. This case shows how the positions of the main European segments can be plotted in terms of the industry evolution (see Figure 8.3) and how strategies vary from one segment to another.

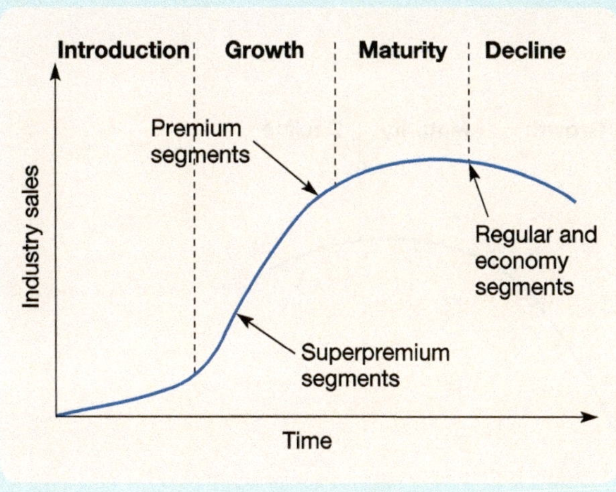

Figure 8.3 Industry evolution in the European ice cream market

The market can be divided into four distinct segments:

1 The *superpremium segment*, typified by Häagen-Dazs®, was still in the early stages of its growth at this time. New companies were still entering the segment, for example Ben and Jerry's from the USA had been acquired by Unilever, but it had yet to be launched in some parts of continental Europe. New products were being tried using new methods of carton presentation and new high prices.

2 The *premium segment* had developed significantly in 1989 with the introduction of premium-priced Mars® ice cream. By the year 2000, there were few new companies entering the market. The basic product ranges had become established among the leading players; the strategic battle was for distribution and branding.

3 The *regular* and 4 *economy segments* were typified by Unilever's™ bulk packs, sold under the name Carte d'Or™

Some ice cream products - like traditional tubs - need little strategic investment. Others - like premium ice creams from Häagen-Dazs and Ben & Jerry's - need investment to support their high price/strong market position.

across much of Europe. These had existed for many years but were still growing at around 5-6 per cent per annum (still regarded as a growth market according to some definitions). The segment also had a large number of other suppliers, not all of whom were national, let alone European. There was keen competition on price and with own-label products from grocery retailers. There was relatively little product innovation.

Case questions

1 What strategies are suggested for each segment of the market from the conventional view of the industry life cycle? (Refer to Table 8.3.)

2 Thinking of strategy as doing the unconventional, how might you modify the strategies identified in Question 1?

8.5 ANALYSING THE STAGES OF MARKET GROWTH

The well-known strategy writer, Professor Michael Porter from Harvard University Business School, has described the *industry life cycle* as 'the grandfather of concepts for predicting industry evolution'. The basic hypothesis is that an industry – or a market segment within an industry – goes through four basic phases of development, each of which has implications for strategy – see Case 8.2 for an example. **The four main phases of the industry life cycle are usually identified as introduction, growth, maturity and decline** and are shown in Figure 8.4.

Definition ▶

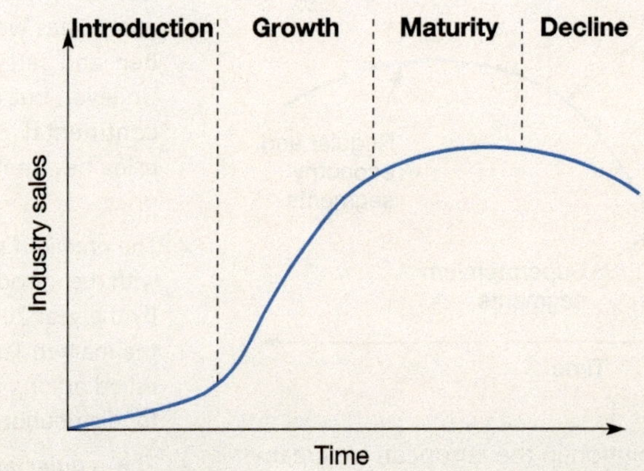

Figure 8.4 Stages of the industry life cycle

8.5.1 Industry life cycle

The nature of strategic management will change as industries move along the life cycle. In the *introductory* phase, organisations attempt to develop interest in the product. As the industry moves towards *growth*, competitors are attracted by its potential and enter the market: from a strategic perspective, competition increases. As all the available customers are satisfied by the product, growth slows down and the market becomes *mature*. Although growth has slowed, new competitors may still be attracted into the market: each company then has to compete harder for its market share, which becomes more fragmented – that is, the market share is broken down into smaller parts. Sales enter a period of *decline*.

To explore the strategic implications, it is useful to start by identifying what stage an industry has reached in terms of its development. For each stage in the cycle there are a number of commonly accepted strategies (see Table 8.3). In the case of ice cream customers in Case 8.2, the *introduction* phase will be used to present the product or service to new customers – perhaps a premium ice cream flavour to those who have never tasted it. By contrast, the *maturity* phase assumes that most customers are aware of the product and little new trial is required – perhaps a small tub of traditional chocolate ice cream.

As in other areas of strategic management, there are differing views regarding the choice of appropriate strategies for each phase of the industry life cycle. Table 8.3 represents the *conventional* view of the appropriate strategy for a particular stage in the industry's evolution. In strategic management, however, there are often good arguments for doing the *unconventional*, so this list would be seen as a starting point for analysing the dynamics of an industry. The most innovative strategy might well come by doing something different and breaking the mould.

As an example of the conventional view of such an analysis, the industry life cycle suggests that in the *early stages* of an industry's development there may be more opportunities for new and

Table 8.3 The industry life cycle and its strategy implications - a conventional view

	Introduction phase	Growth phase	Maturity phase	Decline phase
Customer strategy	• Early customers may experiment with product and will accept some unreliability • Need to explain nature of innovation	• Growing group of customers • Quality and reliability important for growth	• Mass market • Little new trial of product or service • Brand switching	• Know the product well • Select on basis of price rather than innovation
R&D strategy	• High	• Seek extensions before competition	• Low	
Company strategy	• Seek to dominate market • R&D and production particularly important to ensure product quality	• React to competition with marketing expenditure and initiatives	• Expensive to increase market share if not already market leader • Seek cost reductions	• Cost control particularly important
Impact on profitability	• High price, but probably making a loss due to investment in new category	• Profits should emerge here, but prices may well decline as competitors enter market	• Profits under pressure from need for continuing investment coupled with continued distributor and competitive pressure	• Price competition and low growth may lead to losses or need to cut costs drastically to maintain profitability
Competitor strategy	• Keen interest in new category • Attempt to replicate new product	• Market entry (if not before) • Attempt to innovate and invest in category	• Competition largely on advertising and quality • Lower product differentiation • Lower product change	• Competition based primarily on price • Some companies may seek to exit the industry

radical R&D. When an industry is more *mature*, rather less investment is needed in R&D.[14] However, the unconventional view argues that it is the mature industry that requires new growth and therefore

R&D or some other strategic initiative. In the ice cream case, a market leader in traditional ice cream might benefit from investment in more modern facilities to reduce costs further. This suggests that, even in the mature phase of a market, heavy investment is often necessary to remain competitive in the market. It is for this reason that the life cycle concept can best be seen as a starting point for growth analysis.

It is important to note in the development of strategy the two consequences of the industry life cycle that can have a significant impact on industries:

1 *Advantages of early entry.* There is substantial empirical evidence that the first company into a new market has the most substantial strategic advantage. For example, Aaker[15] quotes a study of 500 mature industrial businesses showing that pioneer firms average a market share of 29 per cent, early followers 21 per cent and the late entrants 15 per cent. Although there are clearly risks in early market entry, there may also be long-term advantages that deserve careful consideration in strategic development.
2 *Industry market share fragmentation.* In the early years, markets that are growing fast attract new entrants. This is both natural and inevitable. The consequence as markets reach maturity is that each new company is fighting for market share and the market becomes more fragmented. Again, this has important implications for strategy because it suggests that mature markets need revised strategies – perhaps associated with a segment of the market (see Section 8.10 later in this chapter.)

For strategic purposes, it may be better to examine different *segments* of an industry, rather than the market *as a whole*, as different segments may be at different stages of the industry life cycle and may require different strategies (see the European ice cream industry example in Case 8.2). For example, it is possible to take a totally different industry such as the global travel industry and apply the same thinking: in recent years, some special-interest holidays, such as wildlife and photography, were still growing strongly whereas standard beach-and-sun holidays were in the mature stage of the life cycle.

8.5.2 Critical comment on the industry life cycle

The concept of the industry life cycle has both supporters and critics. Smallwood[16] and Baker[17] defend its usefulness and offer empirical support for the basic concept. Dhalla and Yuspeh[18] have led the criticisms, some of which certainly have a degree of validity (see Exhibit 8.3).

EXHIBIT 8.3

Criticisms of the industry life cycle

1 It is *difficult to determine the duration* of some life cycles and to identify the precise stage an industry has reached. For example, the Mars Bar was launched in the 1930s and is certainly not in decline - but is it in the growth or mature phase?
2 Some industries miss stages or *cannot be clearly identified* in their stages, particularly as a result of technological change. For example, has the bicycle reached the mature phase or has it reached a new lease of life as the petrol-driven car pollutes city atmospheres?
3 Companies themselves can instigate change in their products and can, as a result, *alter the shape of the curve.* For example, new life has been brought into the camera industry by the introduction of miniaturisation and, more recently, by the use of electronic storage in place of film.

There are certainly some difficulties with the industry life cycle approach, but the reason for such an analysis is to identify the *dynamic factors that are shaping the industry's evolution.* The industry life cycle helps us to do this; it will then be possible to compare the organisation's own strategy with this analysis.

KEY STRATEGIC PRINCIPLES

- The industry life cycle - charting the development of a market from introduction, through growth and maturity to decline - is useful to identify the dynamic factors shaping the industry's evolution, although there are criticisms of its use.
- It also helps to specify the conventional view of the strategies that are appropriate to each stage of the cycle, even if these are then changed for logical reasons.
- Aspects of life cycle analysis that are worthy of special consideration include: the advantages of early entry, the fragmentation of market share as markets mature, the incidence of cyclicality and its effect on demand in mature markets.

CASE STUDY 8.3

Bajaj Motorcycles™: should the company move into cars?

One of India's largest motorcycle manufacturers, Bajaj Motorcycles, faces a major strategic decision over the next few years - whether to move into the Indian car market and, if so, with what model. This case explores the issues.

Bajaj Motorcycles is one of India's leading companies. It faces a major strategic decision - whether or not to move into the fast-growing Indian car market.
© Richard Lynch

Background

Unlike Western countries, where motorcycles are a minority form of transport, the Indian transport market is dominated by motorcycles, scooters and three-wheelers. Over 7 million such vehicles were sold in 2010, rising to 16 million in 2013. Indian markets were growing at 5 per cent per year in 2010 but were virtually static by 2013 mainly because of national government economic policies. Their engine sizes are quite small by international standards - typically 120cc machines in India versus 400cc ones in the West - and relatively cheap in India with prices around $2,000 compared with $8,000 in more wealthy Western countries. In addition, motorcycles are family transport in India - two children on the handlebars and mother side-saddle on the back behind the father - whereas motorcycles are largely for individuals in Western countries. All this reflects the fact that family incomes are substantially lower on average in India than in the West - typically, $5,000 per year versus anything up to $25-$30,000 in the West. But typical Indian customers are becoming more wealthy and there is a growing middle class with significantly higher incomes - hence the possible scope for a small family car.

Strategy at Bajaj for motorcycles and three-wheelers

In 1998, Bajaj sold 1.4 million vehicles. By 2013, the company's annual sales had grown to almost 3.8 million of which nearly 1 million were exported. Its major product area was motorcycles which accounted for around 90 per cent of the above sales.

In addition, the company had another important line of vehicles: Bajaj was the leading company in the Indian three-wheeler market and had a profitable revenue stream from this market segment. Three-wheelers are unusual in Western markets but form a major part of many Asian markets, including

Indonesia and the Philippines. They are open at the sides and often have no doors. They can be used as passenger carriers and also as goods carriers. Bajaj was the market leader in this market with 480,000 unit sales in 2013 and a dominant 57 per cent market share of the Indian domestic market.

In order to develop its early motorcycle business, Bajaj signed an agreement with the Japanese motorcycle company Kawasaki® back in the early 1990s to employ Kawasaki's technology. In the early years, Bajaj was motorcycle market leader in India. However, Bajaj Auto lost its market leadership in motorcycles to a rival company, Hero Honda™, over the years. The Bajaj market share was a steady 31 per cent in 2014. It had declined slightly in 2009 and 2010 because the company had limited success in launching successful models into the fast-growing executive segment of the Indian motorcycle market, where its major rival, Hero Honda, had established market leadership. Table 8.4 gives examples of models and prices.

Bajaj Auto was well established in 2013 as a major motorcycle and three-wheeler manufacturer in India. It had created three major manufacturing facilities for motorcycles and three- wheelers. It had also developed a strong distribution and service network and an important R&D facility, which had led to the introduction of new Digital Twin Spark Ignition Technology. The company had also become a major exporter of motorcycles in the Asian region and had set up a manufacturing facility in Indonesia.

To refresh its market position in motorcycles, Bajaj developed three major strategies:

1 *New 'executive' top of the range machines.* This was the fastest- growing market segment in India. The company had set up a new R&D facility at its main manufacturing plant in Pune to deliver new technology. Importantly, it was the executive segment that had the highest profit margins as a result of a premium pricing strategy associated with the top of the range.

2 *Cost reduction.* Bajaj had in its early years some 900 suppliers of parts for its motorcycles. This large number meant that its suppliers were fragmented and unable to gain true economies of scale in production. Bajaj therefore spent considerable effort over the 10 years 1998 to 2007 reducing the numbers of suppliers back to around 80 and, at the same time, locating them closer to its assembly lines - similar to Toyota's 'just-in-time' delivery systems described in the free web-based case (Toyota®: does it rely too heavily on production for world leadership?) outlined in the Global Cars case on the free website of this book. Low costs were particularly important in the smaller motorcycle segment where price competition was particularly fierce and profit margins low.

3 *Exports and overseas production.* Bajaj promoted overseas sales from its three factories. By 2010, the company was selling over 800,000 motorcycles and three-wheelers annually to countries such as Sri Lanka, Nepal, Columbia, Bangladesh, Mexico, Peru and Egypt.

Table 8.4 Indian motorcycle market 2007

Company	Examples of models	Pricing
Hero Honda	CDDeLuxe (97cc), Splendor (125cc), Passion (125cc), Hunk, CBZ Xtreme	CD DeLuxe - $3,000 Hunk - $3,800
Bajaj	Platina (100cc), XCD, Pulsar (150 and 220cc), Discover	Pulsar 150 - $2,800 Pulsar 200 - $3,200
TVS®	TVS Victor, Flame	
Yamaha	Gladiator (125cc)	Gladiator $2,000
Other manufacturers include Honda Japan and Suzuki® Japan		

Source: Richard Lynch, direct visits to Indian and Nepali motorcycle stores November 2007 with some updating thereafter.

The one lakh car - a new threat or an opportunity for Bajaj?

Up to 2008, the annual market for cars in India was substantially smaller than motorcycles - nearly 2 million cars versus around 7 million motorcycles. The main reason was that typical car prices were $5,000 and upwards - affordable only to the more wealthy middle-class Indian family and substantially higher than motorcycle prices. (The detailed and latest figures are given in the full case on Tata Motors, India, on the book's free website.)

Then along came one of India's most famous companies, the Tata Group, with a sensational new car launch in January 2008. Its brand name was the *Nano*™ and it was marketed as the 'One Lakh Car' being priced at 100,000 Indian rupees - 100,000 being called 'one lakh' in the Indian numbering system. Tata had produced the cheapest car in the world - one lakh was equivalent to around $2,500. The company had spent years working on a clever new car design that combined space, economy and simplicity. The on-road price would be somewhat higher - probably around 1.3 million lakh or $3,250 - but it would still be competitive with the top-of-the-range motorcycles. And this was the new threat and opportunity for Bajaj.

Initially, Tata Motors was planning to introduce the first prototypes from their new production line in June 2008 with full production in October 2008. The company planned to manufacture 250,000 Nano cars in the first year but expected this to rise towards 1 million cars after several years. The response to the new car was highly favourable. 'Nano is expected to change the automobile market in India. It would cater to a typical middle-income Indian family of four who want to avoid rain, wind and dust. It's freedom for four,' commented Dilip Chenoy of the Society of Indian Motor Manufacturers.

Even motorcycle manufacturers were impressed: 'It's a nice car and, as an Indian, I am proud of the product. I really liked it but I don't feel that it will impact two-wheelers very much. There is a huge market for two-wheelers and we are not worried about any market erosion.' That was the view of Pawan Munjal, the Managing Director of Hero Honda. But Tata was taking a different line: it argued that the Nano was far safer than a motorcycle and, if only 10 per cent of the motorcycle market switched to the Nano, then this would give Tata annual sales of 700,000 vehicles. It would bring down the cost of car ownership in India by at least 30 per cent and make cars affordable to many more people.

As the Tata case on the book's website explains in more detail, the Nano did not sell in the numbers originally predicted. By 2013, Tata was selling only around 50-60,000 Nanos per year - far short of the initial projections.

Implications for Bajaj strategy

Up to 2013, the sales of the Nano had no impact on the Indian motorcycle market. But companies like Bajaj were aware that the car's competitive price was much the same as its profitable executive model, the 'Pulsar™'. They would have read the comment in the Indian press of one Bajaj Pulsar user: 'I would definitely consider buying the Nano as the cost of the car fits my pocket and above all it has good mileage.' However, the company was also aware of the widely publicised weaker sales of the Nano from 2013 onwards.

Tata acknowledged that its own ideas for the Nano would help other manufacturers. 'It is not our god-given domain,' explained Rajan Tata, the Chairman of the Tata Group, when introducing the Nano. 'It will be an easier task for them than it was for us.' However, even allowing for this, it would be no easy task for Bajaj Group or any other company.

Back in 2008, Bajaj had discussions with the French car company Renault® about the possibility of a joint venture in the Indian car market. This led to an outline joint agreement to produce an ultra low-cost car (code-named the ULC) for the Indian market similar to the Nano.

Subsequently, there were two changes in strategic thinking. First, Renault decided that it would like to enter the Indian domestic market with its own range and therefore began planning this for launch around 2013-2014. This meant that it was less interested in the ULC - possibly supported by the relatively poor sales of the Nano. Second, Bajaj itself became increasingly doubtful about the market demand for the ULC. As an alternative, it was actively examining the possibility of dropping the ULC and developing an extended version of its three-wheeler vehicles - one with four wheels - but with the open design body work of the three-wheeler with no doors, rather than the closed design of a car body.

Bajaj strategic decision: stay within its existing range

Over time, Bajaj clearly had some major strategic decisions to take: should it make a ULC car like the Nano? Should it make a four-wheeler to complement its existing three-wheel range? Or should it just stay with motorcycles? Over the period to 2015, the company decided to stick with its existing range of motorcycles and three-wheelers. It argued that it knew these markets well and the increased competition of major international companies entering the car market made any such move highly risky. But this still raises the question of whether the company should have adopted a bolder strategy. Perhaps a joint venture with an incoming international company would have transformed Bajaj over time.

Green strategy

According to its 2015 annual report, the company has clearly designed policies, including an extensive contribution in the related areas of education and health activities.

 This case was written by Richard Lynch from published data only.[19] Richard Lynch is grateful to Binod Rai in Kathmandu, Nepal, for helping him initially understand the Indian and Nepali motorcycle markets. The original concept for this case came from a brief comment from a fellow professor when the author was lecturing in Delhi in November 2007. Unfortunately, he did not make a note of the professor's name at the time but would like to acknowledge this source.

Case questions

1 Why did Bajaj lose market share and how did it respond?

2 What are the most profitable segments of the Indian motorcycle market? Why were they threatened initially by the Nano?

3 Should Bajaj have moved into car manufacture? What are the arguments in favour and what against? What would you have recommended?

On the website

On the book's free website: www.pearsoned.co.uk/lynch
Case study: *Can the World's Regional Steel Companies Develop Truly Global Strategies?* This case includes indicative answers that may help in examination questions.

8.6 KEY FACTORS FOR SUCCESS IN AN INDUSTRY

In a strategic analysis of the environment, there is an immense range of issues that can potentially be explored, creating a problem for most organisations, which have neither the time nor the resources to cope with such an open-ended task. The Japanese strategist Kenichi Ohmae,[20] the former head of the management consultants McKinsey, in Japan, has suggested a way of tackling this matter by identifying *the key factors for success (KFS)* that are *likely* to deliver the company's objectives. These can then be used to focus the analysis on particularly important industry matters.

Definition ▶ **Key factors for success in an industry are those resources, skills and attributes of the organisations in an industry that are essential to deliver success in the market place.** Ohmae argued that, when resources of capital, labour and time are scarce, it is important that they should be *concentrated* on the key activities of the business – that is, those most important to the delivery of whatever the organisation regards as success.

This concept of key factors for success is also consistent with Porter's view[21] that there are factors that determine the relative competitive positions of companies within an industry. Moreover, the foundation of Kay's approach[22] is that it is important to concentrate resources on the specific areas of the business that are most likely to prove successful. Amit and Schoemaker[23] provide a more extended theoretical framework for the same topic, but call their treatment 'Strategic Industry Factors'. All the above have said that identifying the key factors is not an easy task.

KFS are common to all the major organisations in the industry and do not differentiate one company from another. For example, in Case 8.3, the factors mentioned – low labour costs, servicing centres, parts suppliers of motorbikes, etc. – are common to other similar companies to Bajaj. Such factors will vary from one industry to another. For example, by contrast, in the perfume and cosmetics industry the factors will include branding, product distribution and product performance, but they are unlikely to include labour costs.

When undertaking a strategic analysis of the environment, the identification of the KFS for an industry may provide a useful starting point. For example, the motorbike KFS item of 'low labour costs' would suggest an environmental analysis of the following areas:

- general wage levels in the country;
- government regulations and attitudes to worker redundancy, because high wage costs could be reduced by sacking employees;
- trade union strength to fight labour force redundancies.

In the Indian motorbike industry, these elements of the environment would benefit from careful study, whereas, in the cosmetics and perfume industry, they might have some relevance but would be far less important than other areas.

8.6.1 Identifying the key factors for success in the industry

Key factors concern not only the resources of organisations in the industry but also the *competitive environment* in which organisations operate. There are three principal areas that need to be analysed – Ohmae's *three Cs*.[24]

1 *Customers.* What do customers really want? What are the segments in the market place? Can we direct our strategy towards a group?

2 *Competition.* How can the organisation beat or at least survive against competition? What resources and customers does it have that make it particularly successful? How does the organisation compare on price, quality, etc.? Does the organisation have a stronger distributive network than its competitors?

3 *Corporation.* What special resources does the company itself possess and how do they compare with those of competitors? How does the company compare on costs with its rivals? And on technologies? Skills? Organisational ability? Marketing?

Exhibit 8.4 sets out some key questions in more detail. No single area is more important than another.

8.6.2 Critical comment on the concept

Criticism of the key factors for success has concentrated on four issues:[25]

1 *Identification.* It is difficult to pick out the important factors.

2 *Causality of relationships.* Even though they have been identified, it may not be clear *how* they operate or interact.

3 *Dangers of generalising.* The competitive advantage of a single organisation, by definition, cannot be obtained by seeking what is commonly accepted as bringing success to all organisations in an industry.

4 *Disregard of emergent perspectives.* Success may come from change in an industry, rather than the identification of the current key factors for success.

Beyond these specific criticisms, some strategists have a more general concern about industry analysis (this is explored in the next section). Some of the criticisms can be countered if key factors for success are regarded as *guidelines* for directing strategy development, rather than rigid rules. But the criticisms suggest that key factors for success should be explored with caution. They are only a starting point in strategy analysis – the 'best' strategy may be to reject the key factors and do something completely different!

EXHIBIT 8.4

Identifying Key Factors for Success in An Industry

Note that key factors for success are directed at *all companies in an industry*, not just the target company for strategy development.

1 Customers

Who are the customers? Who are the potential customers? Are there any special segments? Why do customers buy from us? And from our competitors?

- *Price.* Is the market segmented by high, medium and economy pricing? For example, the market for European ice cream.
- *Service.* Do some customers value service while others simply want to buy the product? For example, top-class fashion retailers versus standard clothing shops.
- *Product or service reliability.* Is product performance crucial to the customer or is reliability useful but not really important? For example, heart pacemakers and pharmaceuticals.
- *Quality.* Some customers will pay higher prices for actual or perceived quality differences. Does this provide a route to success? For example, organic vegetables.
- *Technical specifications.* In some industrial and financial services, technical details will provide major attractions for some customers. Is this relevant in this industry? For example, specialist financial bond dealers.
- *Branding.* How important is branding for the customer? For example, Coca-Cola and Pepsi Cola.

2 Competition

Who are the main competitors? What are the main factors in the market that influence competition? How intense is competition? What is necessary to achieve market superiority? What resources do competitors possess that we lack and vice versa?

- *Cost comparisons.* Which companies have the lowest costs? Why? For example, Toyota until the mid-1990s.
- *Price comparisons.* Which companies have high prices? For example, Daimler-Benz does not make cheap cars.
- *Quality issues.* Which companies have the highest quality? Why? How? For example, Xerox™ (USA) in the light of fierce competition from Japanese companies such as Canon.
- *Market dominance.* Which companies dominate the market? For example, Nestlé, with the strongest coffee product range in the world and the largest market share.

- *Service*. Are there companies in the industry that offer superior service levels? For example, industrial markets, such as those served by Asea Brown Boveri™, which need high levels of service to operate and maintain sophisticated equipment.
- *Distributors*. Which companies have the best distributive network? Lowest costs? Fastest delivery? Competent distributors that really know the product or service? For example, major glass companies such as St Gobain (France)® and Pilkington® (UK).

3 Corporation

What are our key resources and those of our competitors? What do they deliver to customers? Where are the majority of the industry costs concentrated? A small percentage reduction to a large part of the total costs will deliver more than a large percentage reduction in an area of lower total costs.

- *Low-cost operations*. Are low-cost operations important for ourselves or our competitors? For example, Aldi (Germany)™ and Tesco (UK) are both low-cost supermarket operators.
- *Economies of scale*. Do these exist in the industry? How important are they? For example, large-scale petroleum chemical refinery operations such as those operated by Royal Dutch®/Shell.
- *Labour costs*. Does our industry rely heavily on low labour costs for competitive operations? For example, Philips® (Netherlands) has moved its production to Singapore and Malaysia to lower labour costs.
- *Production output levels*. Does our industry need full utilisation of plant capacity? For example, European paper and packaging companies.
- *Quality operations*. Do customers need consistent and reliable quality? How do we compare with others in the industry? For example, McDonald's has applied the same standards around the world in its restaurants.
- *Innovative ability*. Does our industry place a high reliance on our ability to produce a constant stream of new innovations? For example, computer hardware and software companies such as Apple, Epson® and Microsoft.
- *Labour/management relations*. Is our industry heavily reliant on good relations? Are there real problems if disputes arise? For example, European large-scale steel production, at companies such as Usinor/Arbed™.
- *Technologies and copyright*. Does the industry rely on specialist technologies, especially those that are patented and provide a real competitive advantage? For example, News International® (Australia), which has exclusive global control over some forms of decoder cards for satellite television.
- *Skills*. Do organisations in the industry possess exceptional human skills and people? What are such skills? For example, advertising agencies and leading consultancy companies.

On the website

On the book's free website: www.pearsoned.co.uk/lynch
Ten more questions to help identify key factors for success in an industry.

KEY STRATEGIC PRINCIPLES

- Identifying the key factors for success shapes the key areas of strategic analysis.
- Such factors can conveniently be considered under three headings: customers, competition and corporation. By 'corporation' is meant the resources of the organisation.
- Key factors can be found in any area of the organisation and relate to skills, competitive advantage, competitive resources of an organisation in the industry, special technologies or customer contacts.
- Four criticisms of key factors have been made: identification, causality of relationships, dangers of generalising, and disregard of emergent perspectives. Caution is therefore needed in their application.

On the website

On the book's free website: www.pearsoned.co.uk
Some background on Porter's work: the nature and intensity of competition in an industry.

CASE STUDY 8.4

Strategic bargaining to film *Lord of the Rings*

FT

In the highly competitive and risky environment of Hollywood film-making, it is essential to analyse those who have the power to make things happen. This case explores the strategic environment surrounding one of the most profitable films ever made – and how the deal and the movie almost failed.

Background

It was one of the biggest gambles in movie history – handing $300 million to shoot an epic trilogy in one take to a virtually unknown director with no record of big-budget Hollywood pictures. And letting him do it 7,000 miles away, so that studio executives had little control over what actually happened on the set.

There were plenty of recent examples of how a huge investment in what seemed a sure-fire blockbuster had backfired, leaving massive dents in the studio's finances – *Waterworld*, *Heaven's Gate* and so on. Somehow, though, *Lord of the Rings* did get made and took over $500 million in its first year as well as winning four Oscars. It is easy to forget the scale of the risk involved and the convoluted strategic bargaining that was necessary before a single scene was shot.

For Peter Jackson, the film's New Zealand-born director, and his agent, Ken Kamins from ICM®, the story behind *Lord of the Rings* is one of a project that very nearly failed to see the light of day.

Competitive environment

When Jackson and Kamins set out to make the film in 1995, they first had to secure the rights to JRR Tolkien's novels, *The Fellowship of the Ring*, *The Two Towers* and *The Return of the King*. Producer Saul Zaentz had bought the rights from Professor Tolkien for a rumoured $15,000 30 years earlier and he had no intention of selling them. Up to that point, Jackson was known only for low-budget horror movies such as *Braindead*. However, an Oscar nomination in 1995 for the screenplay of his $3.5 million arthouse drama *Heavenly Creatures* had earned him a first-look deal with Harvey Goldstein, head of Miramax®, the independent studio allied to Disney®. So Jackson and Kamins approached Weinstein that year with the idea for a *Lord of the Rings* adaptation.

'When we told Harvey that Saul held the rights, he was immediately enthusiastic,' says Kamins, 'as he had just helped Saul on *The English Patient* [Miramax had stepped in to pick up the film after Fox®, part of News Corporation, dropped it on the eve of production]. That created the moral window by which Harvey could ask. But this wasn't charity either. Saul had Harvey pay a pretty penny – I've been told somewhere in the $3 million range.'

New bargaining problems

Having secured the film rights, the Miramax boss sent Jackson and his partner, Fran Walsh, off to write the scripts for a two-part adaptation, with both parts being filmed one after the other. Production research was also to begin in New Zealand. Just when things seemed to be going smoothly, the next wave of problems emerged. 'It soon became clear to Miramax that it

Outdoor advertising in Hollywood, USA. Even after the strategy was negotiated and implemented, it was important to promote the film.
© Richard Lynch

was going to be a very expensive proposition,' says Kamins, 'maybe more expensive than their brief as defined by Disney allowed them to get involved in. Harvey then went to Disney and asked whether they would want a partner in the project. When Disney said no, Miramax got concerned about the cost. And of course [started] asking obvious questions: what happens if the first movie doesn't work?'

Faced with such a risky and expensive project, Weinstein asked Jackson to make the trilogy as one film of no more than three hours. Jackson declined, and, instead, he and Kamins asked to take the project to another studio. Weinstein agreed, although he imposed very tough conditions. Says Kamins: 'We had three weeks to set it up somewhere else. Harvey also demanded that the $12 million that Miramax had already spent in development had to be repaid within 72 hours of the agreement being signed. Now this is highly unusual in the movie business. Normally, a studio would simply pay the former studio a 10 per cent option or they would work out a deal in the budget of the film once the movie got made. Most importantly, he and a partner insisted on 5 per cent of the gross, whether there was one movie, two movies or eight.'

The deal hangs on a knife-edge

With three weeks to find another studio, Jackson and Kamins decided to do two things. While Kamins started submitting the screenplays for the two-part adaptation to every studio in Hollywood, Jackson flew to New Zealand to produce a 35-minute documentary with $50,000 of his own money. The idea was that, if any of the studios was interested, the documentary would show them where Miramax's $12 million had gone, and, most importantly, why Jackson was the right director. But Kamins had little success – every studio said no, except two, Polygram™ and New Line®, which was owned by Warner Brothers. Then Polygram pulled out at the last minute: 'So we went to New Line realising that they were the last Popsicle stand in the desert, and them not knowing that,' said Kamins.

But at New Line, they had some luck. Jackson's old friend, Mark Ordesky, turned out to be one of those making the decision. New Line then asked: 'Why are you making two movies? It's three books, so it's three movies.' Negotiations started the next day. Many in the business doubted the sanity of the decision, especially making three rather than two films. 'But Peter's presentation made it clear that he had an absolutely commanding vision for the film . . . You would be surprised how, in the movie business, some of these commitments are made on far less sturdy ground.'

By 2002, AOL Time Warner® was estimated to have one of the biggest money-spinners in entertainment history on its hands. New Line and its distribution partners had turned *Lord of the Rings* into a worldwide franchise in the *Star Wars*® mould, and were exploiting the brand name across a huge range of platforms – DVD, video games, the internet, merchandise of every sort. The gamble was starting to pay.

Source: Heavily adapted by Richard Lynch from an article by Katja Hofmann in *FT Creative Business*, 19 March 2002, p 10. Richard Lynch is solely responsible for providing this adapted version of the original article and the Financial Times Limited does not accept any liability for the accuracy or quality of the adapted version.

Case questions

1 Who has the bargaining power in this strategic environment? And who has the co-operating power? Identify and analyse the players – use the concepts from Sections 8.6 and 8.7 to help you.

2 What useful strategic concepts, if any, from this chapter can be used in analysing the strategic environment? And what cannot be used? Why?

3 If risk and judgement are important in business decisions, can prescriptive strategic analysis be usefully employed?

8.7 ANALYSING THE COMPETITIVE INDUSTRY ENVIRONMENT – THE CONTRIBUTION OF PORTER

An industry analysis usually begins with a general examination of the forces influencing the organisation. The objective of such a study is to use this to develop the *competitive advantage* of the organisation to enable it to defeat its rival companies. Much of this analysis was structured and presented by Michael Porter.[26] His contribution to our understanding of the competitive environment of the firm has wide implications for many organisations in both the private and public sectors.

This type of analysis is often undertaken using the structure proposed by Porter; his basic model is illustrated in Figure 8.5. This is often called *Porter's Five Forces Model* because he identifies five basic forces that can act on the organisation:

1 the bargaining power of suppliers;

2 the bargaining power of buyers;

3 the threat of potential new entrants;

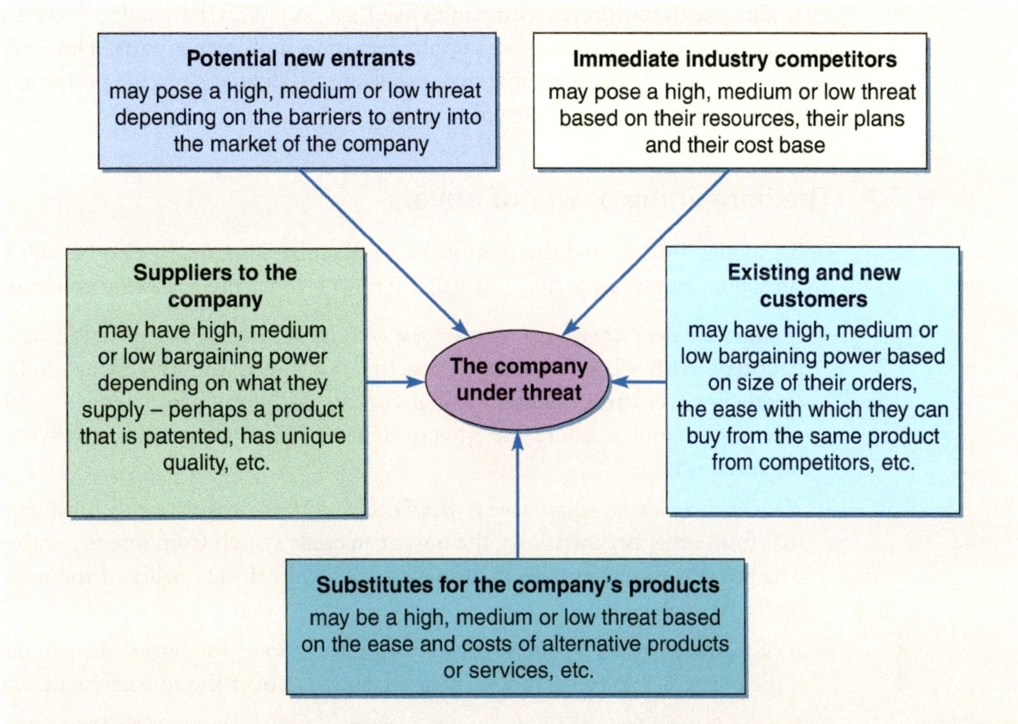

Figure 8.5 How to analyse five possible competitive forces in an industry or market

4 the threat of substitutes;
5 the extent of competitive rivalry.

The objective of such an analysis is to investigate how the organisation needs to form its strategy in order to develop opportunities in its environment and protect itself against competition and other threats. Porter himself cautiously described[27] his analysis as being concerned with the 'forces driving industry competition'. However, the general principles can perhaps be applied to public service and not-for-profit organisations where they compete for resources, such as government funding or charitable donations.

8.7.1 The bargaining power of suppliers

Virtually every organisation has suppliers of raw materials or services which are used to produce the final goods or services. Porter suggested that suppliers are more powerful under the following conditions:

- *If there are only a few suppliers.* This means that it is difficult to switch from one to another if a supplier starts to exert its power.
- *If there are no substitutes for the supplies they offer.* This is especially the case if the supplies are important for technical reasons – perhaps they form a crucial ingredient in a production process or the service they offer is vital to smooth production.
- *If suppliers' prices form a large part of the total costs of the organisation.* Any increase in price would hit value added unless the organisation was able to raise its own prices in compensation.
- *If a supplier can potentially undertake the value-added process of the organisation.* Occasionally a supplier will have power if it is able to integrate forward and undertake the value-added process undertaken by the organisation; this could pose a real threat to the survival of the organisation.

In the case of motorcycle companies like Bajaj, suppliers' bargaining powers are in some respects low. There are many sources of supply for some motorcycle parts. However, in terms of more sophisticated electronic parts that make a substantial difference to the performance of the machines, suppliers may have higher bargaining power.

8.7.2 The bargaining power of buyers

In his model, Porter used the term *buyers* to describe what might also be called the *customers* of the organisation. Buyers have more bargaining power under the following conditions:

- *If buyers are concentrated and there are few of them.* When the organisation has little option but to negotiate with a buyer because there are few alternative buyers around, the organisation is clearly in a weak position: national government contracts in defence, health and education are obvious examples where the government can, in theory at least, drive a hard bargain with organisations.
- *If the product from the organisation is undifferentiated.* If an organisation's product is much the same as that from other organisations, the buyer can easily switch from one to another without problems. The buyer is even more likely to make such a shift if the quality of the buyer's product is unaffected by such a change.
- *If backward integration is possible.* As with suppliers above, the buyer's bargaining power is increased if the buyer is able to backward-integrate and take over the role of the organisation.
- *If the selling price from the organisation is unimportant to the total costs of the buyer.*

In the case of Indian motorcycle customers, private buyers are unlikely to have much bargaining power with companies of the size of Bajaj; a letter from an individual customer, threatening to switch from its motorcycle purchase to Hero Honda, is unlikely to have much impact – the threat is low. For the sake of clarity, this reasoning does not imply that Bajaj would ignore a letter from an individual customer – just that the bargaining power of that individual is not high according to Porter's theory. However, if a large purchaser of motorcycles like a police authority were to make such a threat, then it would clearly have to be taken more seriously because of the potential impact on sales. In this latter case, the threat is high.

8.7.3 The threat of potential new entrants

New entrants come into a market place when the profit margins are attractive and the barriers to entry are low. The allure of high profitability is clear and so the major strategic issue is that of barriers to entry into a market.

Porter argued that there were seven[28] major sources of barriers to entry:

1. *Economies of scale.* Unit costs of production may be reduced as the absolute volume per period is increased. Such cost reductions occur in many industries and present barriers because they mean that any new entrant has to come in on a large scale in order to achieve the low cost levels of those already present: such a scale is risky. We have already examined the computer and motorcycle industries where such cost reductions are vital.
2. *Product differentiation.* Branding, customer knowledge, special levels of service and many other aspects may create barriers by forcing new entrants to spend extra funds or simply take longer to become established in the market. Real barriers to entry can be created in strategic terms by long-established companies with such strengths in a market. Retailers such as IKEA® with strong branding and specialist product lines and expertise are examples of companies with differentiated products.
3. *Capital requirements.* Entry into some markets may involve major investment in technology, plant, distribution, service outlets and other areas. The ability to raise such finance and the risks

associated with such outlays of capital will deter some companies – for example, the high capital cost of investing in new motorcycle production capacity in Case 8.3 earlier in this chapter.

4 *Switching costs.* When a buyer is satisfied with the existing product or service, it is naturally difficult to switch that buyer to a new entrant. The cost of making the switch would naturally fall to the new entrant and will represent a barrier to entry. Persuading buyers to switch their purchases of computer software from Microsoft Windows to Apple has an obvious cost and inconvenience to many companies that would need to be overcome. In addition to the costs of persuading customers to switch, organisations should expect that existing companies will retaliate with further actions designed to drive out new entrants. For example, Microsoft has not hesitated to upgrade its products and reduce its prices to retain customers that might otherwise switch.

5 *Access to distribution channels.* It is not enough to produce a quality product; it must be distributed to the customer through channels that may be controlled by companies already in the market. For many years, the leading petrol companies have owned their own retail petrol sites to ensure that they have access to retail customers.

6 *Cost disadvantages independent of scale.* Where an established company knows the market well, has the confidence of major buyers, has invested heavily in infrastructure to service the market and has specialist expertise, it becomes a daunting task for new entrants to gain a foothold in the market. Korean and Malaysian car companies are attempting to enter the European and American car markets and face these barriers created by well-entrenched companies such as Ford™, Volkswagen® and Renault.

7 *Government policy.* For many years, governments have enacted legislation to protect companies and industries: monopolies in telecommunications, health authorities, utilities such as gas and electricity are examples where entry has been difficult if not impossible. The European Commission has been working alongside European governments to remove some but not all such barriers over the past few years. The Chinese government will not allow foreign steel companies to take a controlling interest in Chinese steel companies.

8.7.4 The threat of substitutes

Occasionally, substitutes render a product in an industry redundant. For example, SmithKline™ Beecham lost sales from its product Tagamet® for the treatment of ulcers, due to the introduction of more effective products – first the introduction of Zantac® from Glaxo™ in the 1980s and then, in the 1990s, Losec™ from the Swedish company Astra™. Tagamet is still on sale as an over-the-counter remedy, but its major public health sales have largely ceased. More recently, Losec sales have also suffered as the drug patents protecting prices have come to an end and cheaper low-price substitutes have been launched by rival companies – the so-called 'generic' drugs, sourced from countries like India.

More often, substitutes do not entirely replace existing products but introduce new technology or reduce the costs of producing the same product. Effectively, substitutes may limit the profits in an industry by keeping prices down.

From a strategy viewpoint, the key issues to be analysed are:

- the possible threat of obsolescence;
- the ability of customers to switch to the substitute;
- the costs of providing some extra aspect of the service that will prevent switching;
- the likely reduction in profit margin if prices come down or are held.

In the motorcycle market, there is the possibility of substituting cars and three-wheelers depending on the price and usage. The threat of substitution may therefore be high, but this depends on the technology and end-use.

8.7.5 The extent of competitive rivalry

Some markets are more competitive than others. Higher competitive rivalry may occur in the following circumstances:

- *When competitors are roughly of equal size and one competitor decides to gain share over the others*, then rivalry increases significantly and profits fall. In a market with a dominant company, there may be less rivalry because the larger company is often able to stop quickly any move by its smaller competitors. In the UK market for electricity supply, there are only six major suppliers each with roughly equal market shares. If one was to bid for a major increase in share, then the others would have to follow.
- *If a market is growing slowly and a company wishes to gain dominance*, then by definition it must take its sales from its competitors – increasing rivalry.
- *Where fixed costs or the costs of storing finished products in an industry are high*, then companies may attempt to gain market share in order to achieve break-even or higher levels of profitability. Paper making, steel manufacture and car production are all examples of industries where there is a real case for cutting prices to achieve basic sales volumes – thus increasing rivalry.
- *If extra production capacity in an industry comes in large increments*, then companies may be tempted to fill that capacity by reducing prices, at least temporarily. For example, the bulk chemicals industry usually has to build major new plants and cannot simply add small increments of capacity. In the steel and oil industries, it is not possible to half-build a new processing plant: either it is built or not.
- *If it is difficult to differentiate products or services*, then competition is essentially price-based and it is difficult to ensure customer loyalty. Markets in basic pharmaceutical products such as aspirin have become increasingly subject to such pressures. In the steel market, flat-rolled steel from one manufacturer is much the same as that of another, so competition is price-based. However, where specialist steels are made with unique performance characteristics, the products are differentiated on performance and price rivalry is lower.
- *When it is difficult or expensive to exit from an industry* (perhaps due to legislation on redundancy costs or the cost of closing dirty plant), there is likely to be excess production capacity in the industry and increased rivalry. The steel industry has suffered from problems in this area during the past few years.
- *If entrants have expressed a determination to achieve a strategic stake in that market*, the costs of such an entry would be relatively unimportant when related to the total costs of the company concerned and the long-term advantages of a presence in the market. Japanese car manufacturing in the EU has advantages for Toyota and Nissan® beyond the short-term costs of building plant, as EU car markets were opened to full Japanese competition around the year 2000.

8.7.6 Strategy implications from the general industry and competitive analysis

In strategic management, it is not enough just to produce an analysis; it is important to consider the implications for the organisation's future strategy. Some issues that might arise from the above include:

- *Is there a case for changing the strategic relationships with suppliers?* Could more be gained by moving into close partnership with selected suppliers rather than regarding them as rivals? The Japanese car industry has sought to obtain much closer co-operation with suppliers and mutual cost reduction as a result.[29] (See Case on the website – *Prescriptive and emergent strategy: global car markets and the battle between the world's top car companies.*)
- *Is there a case for forming a new relationship with large buyers?* Manufacture of own-label products for large customers in the retail industry may be undertaken at lower margins than branded business but has proved a highly successful strategy for some leading European companies.[30]

- *What are the key factors for success that drive an industry and influence its strategic development?* What are the lessons for the future that need to be built into the organisation's strategic management? We looked at these questions in Section 8.6.
- *Are there any major technical developments that rivals are working on that could fundamentally alter the nature of the environment?* What is the timespan and level of investment for such activity? What action should we take, if any?

8.7.7 Critical comment on the Five Forces Model

Porter's Five Forces Model is a useful early step in analysing the environment, but it has been the subject of some critical comment:

- The analytical framework is essentially *static*, whereas the competitive environment in practice is constantly changing. Forces may move from high to low, or vice versa, rather more rapidly than the model can show.
- It assumes that the organisation's own interests come first; for some charitable institutions and government bodies, this assumption may be incorrect.
- It assumes that buyers (called customers elsewhere in this book) have no greater importance than any other aspect of the micro-environment. Other commentators such as Aaker,[31] Baker[32] and Harvey-Jones[33] would fundamentally disagree on this point: they argue that the customer is more important than other aspects of strategy development and is not to be treated as an equal aspect of such an analysis.
- In general, its starting point is that the environment poses a threat to the organisation – leading to the consideration of suppliers and buyers as threats that need to be tackled. As pointed out above, some companies have found it useful to engage in closer *co-operation* with suppliers; such a strategy may be excluded if they are regarded purely as threats. This is explained more fully in Section 8.8.
- Porter's strategic analysis largely ignores the human resource aspects of strategy: it makes little attempt to recognise, let alone resolve, aspects of the micro-environment that might connect people to their own and other organisations. For example, it considers neither the country cultures, nor the management skills aspects of strategic management.
- Porter's analysis proceeds on the basis that, once such an analysis has been undertaken, then the organisation can formulate a strategy to handle the results: *prescriptive* rather than *emergent*. Some commentators would challenge this basic assessment.

In spite of these critical comments, the approach taken in this book is that Porter's model provides a very useful starting point in the analysis of the environment. It has real merit because of the issues it raises in a logical and structured framework. It is therefore recommended as a useful first step in strategy development.

Porter presented his Five Forces Model as an early stage in strategic analysis and development. He followed it with two further analyses: an analysis of *industry evolution* – the extent to which the micro-environment is still growing or has reached maturity[34] – and the study of *strategic groups* within a market.

KEY STRATEGIC PRINCIPLES

- The purpose of industry and competitive strategic analysis is to enable the organisation to develop competitive advantage.
- Porter's Five Forces Model provides a useful starting point for such an analysis.
- Suppliers are particularly strong when they can command a price premium for their products and when their delivery schedules or quality can affect the final product.
- Buyers (or customers) are strong when they have substantial negotiating power or other leverage points associated with price, quality and service.

- New entrants pose a substantial threat when they are easily able to enter a market and when they are able to compete strongly through lower costs or other means.
- Substitutes usually pose a threat as a result of a technological or low-cost breakthrough.
- Competitive rivalry is the essence of such an analysis. It is necessary to build defences against competitive threat.
- The model has been the subject of some critical comment, but it remains a useful starting point for competitive strategic analysis.

8.8 ANALYSING THE CO-OPERATIVE ENVIRONMENT

8.8.1 The Four Links Model

As well as competing with rivals, most organisations also co-operate with others, for example through informal supply relationships or through formal and legally binding joint ventures. Until recently, such links were rarely analysed in strategy development – the analysis stopped at Porter's Five Forces and some in-depth studies of one or two competitors (see Section 8.9). However, it is now becoming increasingly clear that *co-operation* between the organisation and others in its environment is also important as:

- it may help in the achievement of sustainable competitive advantage;
- it may open up new markets and increase business opportunities;
- it may produce lower costs;
- it may deliver more sustainable relationships with those outside the organisation.

It should be noted that an extreme form of co-operation – collusion between competitors to rig markets – is illegal in most countries and is not explored further here. But there are many other forms of co-operation that are highly beneficial and should form part of any analysis of the environment. For example, European steel companies have formed joint ventures with Brazilian steel companies for the benefit of both parties, and Krupp Thyssen Stahl™ is co-operating with its energy suppliers to reduce costs. Moreover, all the main European steel companies are co-operating with the government of the EU on policy matters affecting the industry. Equally, North American steel companies are co-operating with federal and state governments for the benefit of the industry.

The basic co-operative linkages between the organisation and its environment can usefully be explored under four headings:

1. informal co-operative links and networks
2. formal co-operative links
3. complementors
4. government links and networks.

The objective of such an analysis is to establish the strength and nature of the co-operation that exists between the organisation and its environment. It can be conducted through the *Four Links Model* – see Figure 8.6.

8.8.2 Opportunities and threats from informal co-operative links and networks

Informal co-operative links and networks are the occasions when organisations link together for a mutual or common purpose *without* a legally binding contractual relationship. They have long been recognised as providing an important means of understanding the strategy of the firm.[35] By their nature, they may well occur by accident as well as by design. They will include many forms of

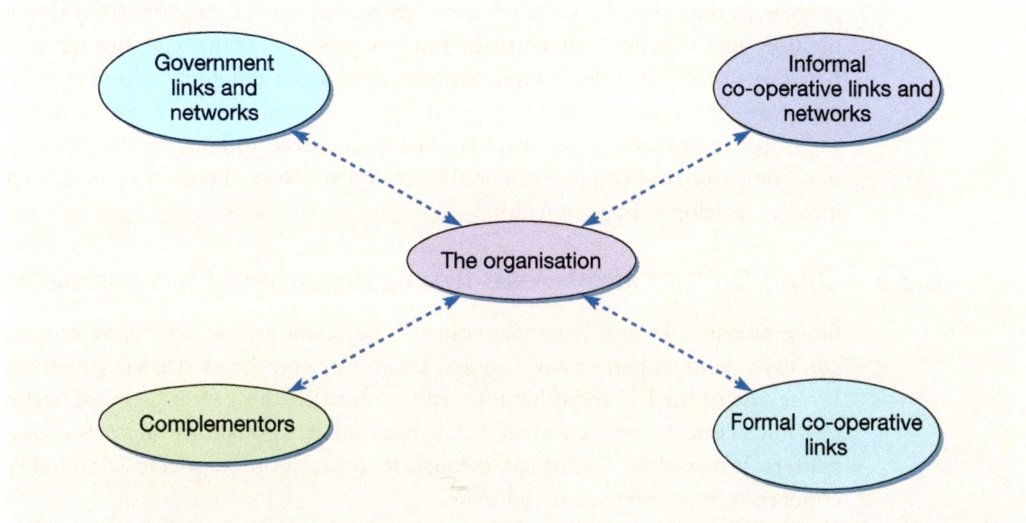

Figure 8.6 Analysing co-operation: the Four Links Model

contact, ranging from formal industry bodies that represent industry matters with other interested parties – for example, the European Confederation of Iron and Steel Industries – to informal contacts that take place when like-minded individuals from a variety of industries meet at a social function – for example, a local Chamber of Commerce meeting.

The analysis will need to assess the opportunities that such links and networks present. Occasionally, there may also be threats from arrangements. In analysing them, it is the *strength or weakness* of the relationship that matters. For example, in some parts of the world such as Japan and Korea, the networks are called *keiretsu* and *chaebol*, respectively, and have provided strong mutual support to those companies that belong to them. In some services, such as international banking, it is the strength of the network that provides the competitive advantage for those involved in it and excludes those that are not.[36]

8.8.3 Opportunities and threats from formal co-operative linkages

Formal co-operative linkages can take many business forms but are usually bound together by some form of legal contract. They differ from the networks described above in the higher degree of formality and permanence of the link with the organisation. They are shown in alliances, joint ventures, joint shareholdings and many other deals that exist to provide competitive advantage and mutual support over many years. The benefits and problems of such linkages are explored. Some companies like the UK retailer Marks & Spencer™, the Japanese car manufacturer Toyota and the Italian clothing company Benetton® have developed such linkages into vital contributors to the uniqueness of their strategies. Suppliers, distributors and other formal co-operators with such companies provide essential products and services at lower prices and higher service levels than those offered to others in the industry. Essentially, formal co-operative linkages develop out of many years of discussion and understanding. They are very difficult for other companies to copy.[37] The *strengths and weaknesses* of such linkages should therefore be measured in terms of their depth, longevity and degree of mutual trust. Although the main interest may come from opportunities offered by such formal linkages, threats may arise from those developed by competitors.

8.8.4 The opportunities and threats presented by complementors

Definition ▶ **Complementors are those companies whose products add more value to the products of the base organisation than they would derive from their own products by themselves.**[38] For example, computer hardware companies are worth little without the software that goes with them – one product *complements* the other. In strategic terms, there may be real benefits from developing new complementor opportunities that enhance both parties and contribute further to the links that exist between them. Typically, complementors come from different industries with different resources and skills that work together to present new and sustainable *joint offerings* to customers. Again, it is the *strengths and weaknesses* of the relationship that need to be analysed. Although the main interest may come from opportunities offered by complementors, threats may arise from the complementor linkages developed by competitors.

8.8.5 Opportunities and threats from government links and networks

Government links and networks concern the relationships that many organisations have with a country's national parliament, regional assemblies and the associated government administrations. In the case of the EU and other international treaties, these clearly extend beyond national boundaries. Such contact may be formal, through business negotiations on investment, legal issues and tax matters. It may also be informal, through representation on government/industry organisations in connection with investment and trade.

Government links and networks can be vital in tax and legal matters, such as the interpretation of competition law. Equally, governments can be important customers of organisations, for example in defence equipment and pharmaceuticals. Many organisations have come to devote significant time and effort to developing and cultivating such relationships through lobbying and other related activities. Because of the nature and role of government, it may need to remain relatively remote in its legislative and regulatory dealings with outside organisations. However, it is appropriate to evaluate the degree of co-operation or hostility between government and outside bodies. Thus outside organisations will wish to consider the *opportunities and threats* posed by government activities. These may form a significant part of their corporate strategic development, especially at very senior levels within an organisation.

8.8.6 Critical comment on Four Links Model

At least in part, such a model may not have the precision and clarity of the Five Forces Model and other competitor analyses: networks come and go, complementors may come to disagree, alliances may fall apart and democratic governments fail to be re-elected. All linkage relationships lack the simplicity of the bargaining power and competitive threat analyses of the Five Forces Model. However, the Four Links Model is essentially concerned with co-operation between organisations (see Figure 8.6). This will have many facets that go beyond simple bargaining relationships.

Developing such links is likely to involve, at least in part, an emergent approach to strategy development. Linkages may provide opportunities to experiment and develop new and original strategies. They may allow an unusual move in strategy development that will deliver sustainable competitive advantage. Hence, even though they may be imprecise and lacking in the simplicities of economic logic, such linkages deserve careful analysis.

Beyond the analysis of co-operation, companies have now come to recognise that co-operation provides new strategic opportunities. Strategic alliances, joint ventures and other forms of co-operation have been identified as possibilities for strategy development.

KEY STRATEGIC PRINCIPLES

- In addition to competing against rivals, most organisations also co-operate with other organisations. Such co-operation can deliver sustainable competitive advantage.
- The main elements that need to be analysed for co-operation are captured in the *Four Links Model*: informal co-operative links and networks, formal co-operative links, complementors and government links and networks.

- *Informal co-operative links and networks* are the range of contacts that arise from organisations joining together informally for a common purpose. *Formal co-operative linkages* are usually bound by some form of legal contract - examples include alliances and joint ventures. *Complementors* are those companies whose products add more value to the products of the base organisation than they would derive from their own products by themselves. *Government links and networks* concern the relationships that exist between national and international governments and organisations, including those concerning tax, legislation and formal government purchasing.
- Such relationships can be measured by the strength of the linkage in the case of the first three. In the case of government, they may be better measured by considering the opportunities and threats posed by the relationship. All such links are often less structured and formalised than those involving competitor analysis but may represent significant areas of long-term competitive advantage.

8.9 ANALYSING ONE OR MORE IMMEDIATE COMPETITORS IN DEPTH

In any analysis of competitors and their relationship to the organisation, it is useful to analyse some immediate and close competitors: this is often called competitor profiling. The purpose is to identify the competitive advantages (and disadvantages) of the organisation against its competitors.

8.9.1 What are the sustainable competitive advantages of our competitors?

Definition ▶ **Sustainable competitive advantage is an advantage over competitors that cannot easily be imitated.** Broad surveys of competitive forces are useful in strategy analysis. But it is normal to select one or two companies for more detailed examination to identify the competitive advantage of our company against one or two rivals. The reason is that sustainable competitive advantage becomes more precise and meaningful when we make a specific analysis of our competitors. Some rival companies will have competitive advantages that make them formidable opponents; for example, well-respected brand names like Coca-Cola and Volkswagen, specialist technologies such as laser printer production at the Japanese company Canon, and unique locations of hotels and restaurants, such as those owned by McDonald's. We focus in this section on analysing the competitive advantages of our competitors in the strategic environment.

8.9.2 Competitor profiling

As a starting point, it is useful to undertake competitor profiling – that is, the basic analysis of a leading competitor, covering its objectives, resources, market strength and current strategies.

In many markets, there will be more than one competitor and it will not be possible to analyse them all. It will be necessary to make a choice – usually the one or two that represent the most direct threat. In public service organisations where the competition may be for *resources* rather than for *customers*, the same principle can be adopted, with the choice being made among the agencies competing for funds. In small businesses, the need to understand competitors is just as great, although here it may be more difficult to identify which company will pose the most direct threat; a *typical* competitor may be selected in these circumstances. Once the choice has been made, the following aspects of the competitor's organisation need to be explored:

- *Objectives.* If the competitor is seeking sales growth or market share growth, this may involve an aggressive stance in the market place. If the company is seeking profit growth, it may choose to achieve this by investing in new plant or by some other means that might take time to implement. If this is the case, there will be less of an immediate impact on others in the market place, but new plant may mean lower costs and a longer-term impact on prices. Company annual reports and press statements may be helpful here in defining what the competitor says it wants to do. These need to be treated with some caution, however, since the company may be bluffing or using some other competitive technique.

- *Resources.* The scale and size of the company's resources are an important indicator of its competitive threat – perhaps it has superior or inferior technology, perhaps over-manning at its plants, perhaps financial problems.
- *Past record of performance.* Although this may be a poor guide to the future, it is direct evidence that is publicly available through financial statements and stockbrokers' reports.
- *Current products and services.* Many companies buy competing products or services for the sole purpose of tearing them apart. They analyse customers, quality, performance, after-sales service, promotional material and some will even interview former employees – unethical perhaps, but it does happen.
- *Links with other organisations.* Joint members, alliances and other forms of co-operation may deliver significant competitive advantage.
- *Present strategies.* Attitudes to subjects such as innovation, leading customers, finance and investment, human resource management, market share, cost reduction, product range, pricing and branding all deserve investigation.

Competitor profiling is time-consuming but vital to the development of strategic management. Some larger companies employ whole departments whose sole task is to monitor leading competitors. Small businesses also often have an acute awareness of their competitors, although this may be derived more informally at trade meetings, social occasions, exhibitions and so on. In strategic management, it is vital to gain a 'feel' for competitors.

8.9.3 Emergent perspectives on competition

One of the main dangers of competitive profiling is that it will be seen as essentially static. In practice, all organisations are changing all the time. Moreover, the competitive profiling process should be regarded as one of discovery and one that never finishes. Emergent perspectives on competitor analysis, which emphasise this changing nature, will deliver useful insights, especially where the environment is changing rapidly. For example, emergent perspectives are *essential* when analysing internet competitors in the recorded music industry.

8.9.4 Outcome of competitor profiling

However imprecisely, it is important to draw up a clear statement of the competitive advantages held by a rival organisation compared to ourselves. A useful means of summarising this is the SWOT analysis.

KEY STRATEGIC PRINCIPLES

- An environmental analysis needs to identify the competitive advantages of rival companies. This is undertaken using competitor profiling. It will seek to identify the competitive advantages by focusing on one or two rival companies in depth.
- More generally, it will explore the objectives, resources, past performance, current products and services, and present strategies of one or two competitors.
- Competitor profiling should be regarded as an ongoing task. Its emergent nature is particularly important in fast-moving markets.

8.10 ANALYSING THE CUSTOMER AND MARKET SEGMENTATION

Since customers generate the revenues that keep the organisation in existence and deliver its profits, customers are crucial in strategic management. In this context it is perhaps surprising that much greater emphasis has been given in some aspects of strategic development to *competition* rather than to the customer.[39] The reason is that the focus of the purchase decision for the customer is a competitive selection between the different products or services on offer. While this is undoubtedly true, it is easy to lose sight of the direct strategic importance of the customer.

There are three useful dimensions to an analysis of the customer:

1 identification of the customer and the market;

2 market segmentation and its strategic implications;

3 market positioning usually within a segment.

8.10.1 Identification of the customer and the market

Back in the 1960s, Levitt[40] wrote a famous article that argued that the main reason some organisations were in decline was because they had become too heavily product-oriented, and were not sufficiently customer-oriented. As a result, they defined their customer base too narrowly. To help this process, a useful distinction can be made between:[41]

- *immediate customer base* – for example, those travelling on railways; and
- *wider customer franchise* – for example, those travelling by public transport, including railways, aircraft and buses.

In order to define accurately this aspect of the environment it is important to develop strategies that identify customers and competitors. Ultimately, if the market environment is incorrectly defined, then competitors may creep up and steal customers without the company realising it until it is too late. Furthermore, it is vital to analyse *future* customers as well as the *current* customer profile.

On the website

On the book's free website: www.pearsoned.co.uk/lynch
Case study: *Two Methods of Segmenting Products in the European Ice Cream Market.*

8.10.2 Market segmentation

For many markets, customer analysis needs to move beyond the consideration of basic markets to an analysis of specific parts of a market – *market segmentation* – and to the competitive stance of organisations within the segment – their *market positioning*, which is explored in the next section.

Definition ► **Market segmentation is the identification of specific groups (or segments) of customers who respond to competitive strategies differently from other groups.**

The basic sequence for exploring the approach is shown in Figure 8.7. It employs a *prescriptive* approach as a first step in order to explore the elements. In practice, the sequence is likely to be more experimental and, in this sense, *emergent*, because it is often necessary to explore a number of positioning areas: this is also outlined in Figure 8.7.

The three prescriptive stages are:

1 *Identify market segment(s).* Identification of specialist needs of segments will lead to customer profiles of those in the segments.

2 *Evaluate segment(s).* Some segments are likely to be more attractive than others. They need to be identified and targeted.

3 *Position within market segment.* Within the segment, companies will then need to develop a differential advantage over competitors. See the example in Figure 8.8.

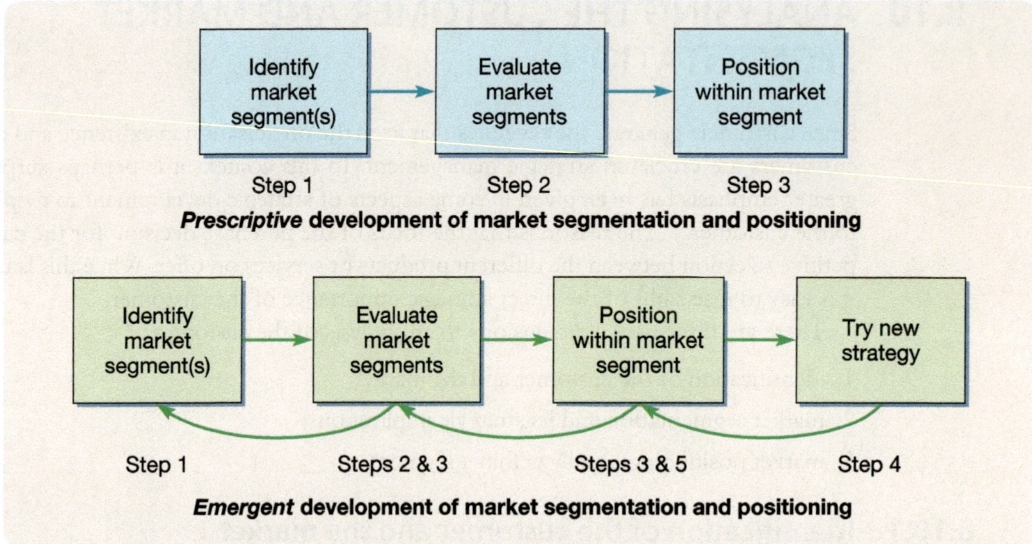

Figure 8.7 Market segmentation and position

In the development of customer strategy, customer analysis will often move rapidly to an examination of market segmentation.[42] Market segmentation may be defined as the identification of specific groups (or segments) of customers who respond differently from other groups to competitive strategies. The advantages of identifying a market segment include:

- Strength in (and possibly dominance of) a group, even though the overall market is large. It may be more profitable to have a large share of a group than a small share of the main market. Thus competitive advantage may be stronger in a segment than in the broader market.
- Closer matching of customer needs and the organisation's resources through targeting the segment. This will enhance sustainable competitive advantage.
- Concentration of effort on a smaller area, so that the company's resources can be employed more effectively.

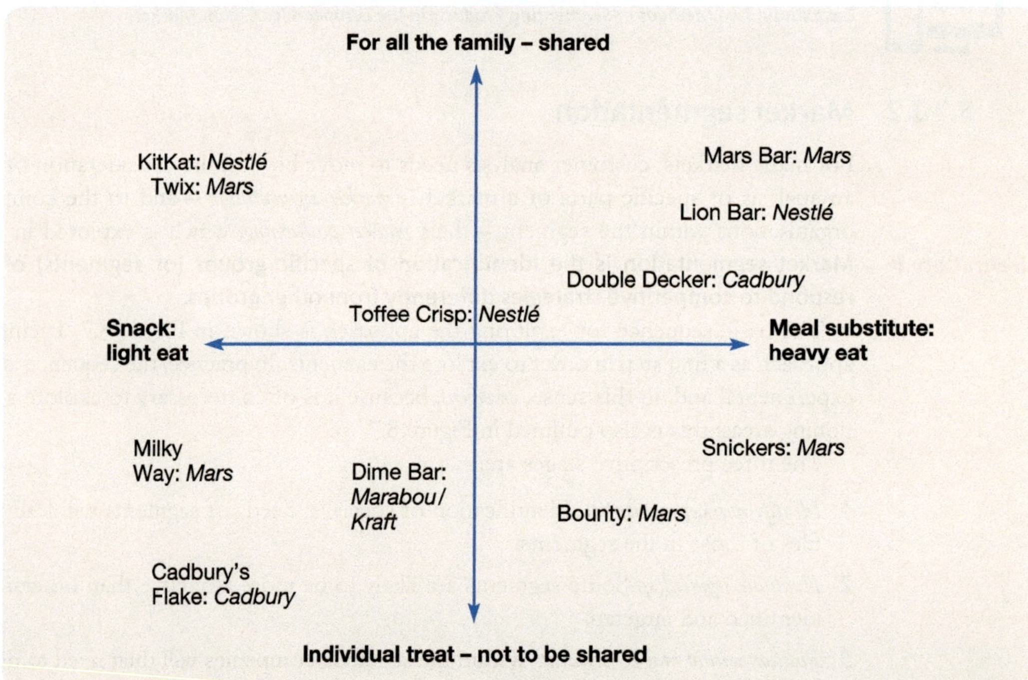

Figure 8.8 An example of market positioning – chocolate countlines

Table 8.5 Typical bases for market segmentation

Consumer products	Industrial products
• Geographic • Demographic (age, sex, education, etc.) • Socio-economic and income • Ethnic group • Benefits sought • Usage rate and brand loyalty • Attitudes • Lifestyle • Situation (where the consumption takes place)	• Area or region of country • End-use • Customer business • Buying situation • Market served • Value added by customer • Source of competitive advantage (price, service, etc.) • Emphasis on R&D and innovation • Professional membership

Hence, from a strategic viewpoint, the key advantage of market segmentation is probably the ability to dominate a sector of a market and then target benefits that will sustain this position, as in the case of Dyson's® domination of the premium-priced vacuum cleaner segment.

Typical bases for segmentation in consumer and industrial markets are listed in Table 8.5. However, markets can be segmented by any criteria that prove helpful and do not necessarily need to conform to this list.

Having established the segments, strategic customer analysis then proceeds to evaluate the *usefulness* of each segment: Step 2 in Figure 8.7. It is not enough for a segment to be different. There are four important characteristics of any segment if it is to be useful in strategic customer analysis. It must be:

1. *Distinguishable.* Customers must be distinguishable so that they can be isolated in some way.
2. *Relevant to purchasing.* The distinguishing criteria must relate to differences in market demand. For example, they may pay higher prices for higher quality.
3. *Sufficiently large.* If the segment is too small, then it will not justify the resources needed to reach it.
4. *Reachable.* It must be possible to direct the strategy to that segment.

It is also important to assess the future growth prospects of the segment.

KEY STRATEGIC PRINCIPLES

- There are three prescriptive stages in developing market segmentation and positioning: identify potential segments, evaluate and select segment(s), and position within segment(s).
- Market segmentation is the identification of specific groups of customers who respond differently from other groups to competitive strategies. They can be important in strategy development because they provide the opportunity to dominate part of the market.
- Identification of gaps in segment provision may provide the basis of new strategic opportunities.

8.10.3 Competitive Positioning[43]

Although a useful segment has been identified, this does not in itself resolve the organisation's strategy. The competitive position within the segment then needs to be explored, because only this will show how the organisation will compete within the segment. **Competitive positioning is the choice of differential advantage possessed by an organisation that allows it to compete and survive in a market place or in a segment of a market place.** A typical example of positioning is shown in Figure 8.8.

Definition ▶

For example, both the Mars Company (USA) and Nestlé® (Switzerland) compete in the market for chocolate products. However, the Mars' product Snickers® is positioned as a 'meal substitute' – it can be eaten in place of a meal, whereas the Nestlé product KitKat® is positioned as a 'snack' – it can be eaten as a break but is not substantial enough to be a substitute for a meal. Competitive positioning is thus the choice of differential advantage that the product or service will possess against its competitors. To develop positioning, it is useful to follow a two-stage process – first identify the segment gaps, second identify positioning within segments.

Stage 1: Identification of segmentation gaps and their competitive positioning implications

From a strategy viewpoint, the most useful strategic analysis often emerges by exploring where there are *gaps* in the segments of an industry: amongst others, Porter[44] and Ohmae[45] recommend this route. The starting point for such work is to map out the current segmentation position and then place companies and their products into the segments: it should then become clear where segments exist that are not served or are poorly served by current products. This is shown in Exhibit 8.5 using the European ice cream case as an example.

EXHIBIT 8.5

New or Under-Utilised Segment Gaps: Unilever's Presence in the European Ice Cream Market, Early 2000s

Market basis for possible segmentation

	Buyer type 1	Buyer type 2	Buyer type 3, etc.
Product variety 1			
Product variety 2			
Product variety 3, etc.			

Step 1: Existing segments with Unilever's European presence shown

	Grocery supermarkets	Small grocery stores	Restaurants and takeaways	Newsagents and leisure facilities
Superpremium	✓ market test only			✓ few
Premium	✓	✓		✓ most
Regular	✓			
Economy	✓	✓ some		

Step 2: Some possible new segments in addition to the above

	Garages	Temporary facilities at sporting and cultural events	Factory canteens and restaurants: contract catering
Superpremium		✓	
Premium	✓		
Regular			✓
Economy			✓

Note: For the sake of clarity, only Unilever's presence is shown in the above. Moreover, the example is *illustrative only* and may not represent the actual practice of the Unilever subsidiaries in each country. Further segmentation analyses based on criteria such as the geographical country might also produce some useful additional information.

Comment: It will be evident that there are some gaps in the existing coverage of the market. The segmentation criteria outlined in the text above could be used to assess whether it would be worthwhile filling the gaps. One obvious area where Unilever could take action was in the superpremium sector.

Stage 2: Identifying the positioning within the segment[46]

From a strategy perspective, some gaps may be more attractive than others. For example, they may have limited competition or poorly supported products. In addition, some gaps may possess a clear advantage in terms of competitive positioning. Others may not. To explore the development of positioning, we can return to our earlier example of two chocolate countlines from Nestlé and Mars. The full positioning map for the range of such products was shown earlier in the chapter in Figure 8.8.

The process of developing positioning of chocolate countlines runs as follows:

1 *Perceptual mapping* – in-depth qualitative research on actual and prospective customers on the way that they make their decisions in the market place, for example, strong versus weak, cheap versus expensive, modern versus traditional. In the case of chocolate the dimensions of meal/snack and family/individual were established.

2 *Positioning.* Brands or products are then placed on the map using the research dimensions. Figure 8.8 presents the existing configuration.

3 *Options development.* Take existing and new products and use their existing strengths and weaknesses to devise possible new positions on the map. Figure 8.8 shows some gaps for some companies and some products that have an unclear position – Toffee Crisp® at the time of the research.

4 *Testing* – first with simple statements with customers, then at a later stage in the market place.

It will be evident that this is essentially an emergent rather than a prescriptive process, involving experimentation with actual and potential customers.

KEY STRATEGIC PRINCIPLES

- Competitive positioning is the choice of differential advantage that the product or service will possess against its competitors.
- The sequence for developing competitive positioning has four main steps: perceptual mapping, positioning, options development and testing. The process is essentially emergent rather than prescriptive.

On the website

On the book's free website: www.pearsoned.co.uk
Conclusion: the danger of over-relying on strategic environmental analysis.

CASE STUDY 8.5

Arçelik® aims for Europe

When Arçelik's home market demand declined in 2000, Turkey's leading domestic appliance company aimed its export strategy at Europe. This case explains its four main strategies and how they made the company the third largest in Europe.

Background: domestic strength in the 1990s

Arçelik has been making domestic appliances - washing machines, refrigerators, freezers and ovens - since the 1950s. It is controlled by one of Turkey's leading and most respected industrial groups, Koç® Holdings. The holding company had sales of $43 billion in 2010 and, within this, Arçelik had sales of $3.5 billion - by any standards, an important company.

Back in the 1990s, Arçelik's domestic appliance business had been steadily expanded to dominate its Turkish home

Arçelik's strategy in Turkey relies on distribution through its own retail stores. But this retail strategy would take too long and be too expensive to set up across Europe.
© Richard Lynch

market. The country itself had a population of over 70 million with rapidly rising wealth. Arçelik's nearest competitor was another Turkish company called Vestel™. But Arçelik's strategies were so successful that it had almost four times the sales of its rival. There were four key strategies:

1 branding under the Arçelik and Beko® brand names;
2 quality-driven products;
3 efficient low-cost production;
4 extensive and dominant distribution outlets in all the main Turkish towns.

Change in the strategic environment: Turkey's economy takes a downturn

Around year 2000, Turkey's economy took a severe downturn. Arçelik was already exporting its domestic appliances outside Turkey in small quantities, but this only amounted to 15 per cent of its business. Suddenly, the company was faced with a serious profit problem. Economies of scale are a key factor for success in the domestic appliance business, but the local Turkish market was in decline. The company decided to export more of its products. But which countries and with what strategies?

Arçelik's export strategies in year 2000

Western European markets for domestic appliances - like Germany, the UK and France - were large but relatively mature. The lack of growth made it more difficult for new companies to enter, especially those from outside the European Union (EU). However, the EU had agreed to reduce its trade barriers with Turkey back in 1996, so EU markets were at least open to Arçelik in 2000. The problem was rather different in Eastern Europe. Markets were just beginning to open up after the fall of communism. Wealth and demand for consumer products was rising, but there were few good manufacturers.

As a result of these differences, Arçelik decided on a two-pronged strategy. In Western Europe, it would export domestic appliances from its Turkish factories and acquire some European brand names. In the east, it would also export but would also set up factories that would serve regional markets. The outcome was a significant increase in international sales - see Figure 8.9. Much of this increase was founded on the four home strategies outlined above. However, there was one difference. Arçelik judged that it would take too long and be too expensive to copy the home market competitive advantage of its own shops and distribution outlets. It would simply sell Arçelik products through existing stores.

Arçelik's strategies in Western Europe

In order to gain a rapid foothold, Arçelik bought a series of small companies in France, Germany and the UK. These acquisitions were not wholly successful because the company needed to manufacture its products from its efficient plants in Turkey so it was really only buying brand names and reputations such as its purchases of the Flavel® brand in the UK and the Grundig® name in Germany. There were also reported to be other brand and company acquisitions, for example Arctic® in Romania, Blomberg® in Germany and Elektra Bregenz® in Austria with most of these becoming sales and service companies for the Arçelik/Beko range. In addition to its acquisitions, Arçelik had to make another strategic decision: whether to make OEM goods or sell branded products.

Original equipment manufacture (OEM) refers to products that are made by one manufacturer and then sold to a second company who will re-brand them with the name of the second company. For example, Arçelik had the opportunity to make washing machines which were then sold in the UK under the brand name of a well-known retailer such as Tesco™. The problem with OEM is that such contracts

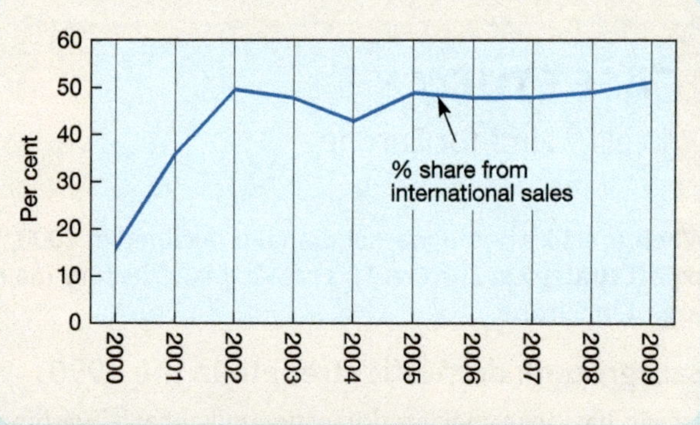

Figure 8.9 The outcome of Arçelik's export strategy

Source: Richard Lynch from Koç holding company report and accounts and research by Dr Tanses Gulsoy of Beykent University.

depend largely on price. Customers can switch over time to rivals offering lower prices. Competitive advantage is therefore low. By contrast, branding is initially more expensive in terms with, for example, the costs of advertising and sponsorship. However, it has several advantages. It allows companies like Arçelik to develop innovative and patented products and to develop a widely respected brand name over time. Importantly, branding and quality products were closer to Arçelik's core competencies back in its home country and thus familiar strategies for this company to develop and manage.

Initially, Arçelik undertook some OEM contracts. But its main strategy in Western Europe was brand building with the *Beko* brand name: the Turkish name Arçelik had some problems in terms of spelling the specialist Turkish letter ç and pronunciation in Western markets. Its acquisitions were supported but the main strategic effort was put behind the brand name Beko. Arguably, the acquisitions were expensive and unnecessary in the long term. Moreover, Arçelik had registered over 130 patents across Europe in a range of domestic appliance applications, thus delivering potential competitive advantages for its Beko branded product range.

Over the years from 2001, Beko slowly built its branded sales in some Western European countries. By 2010, it had become the second largest brand in the UK using advertising and sponsorship, strong retail distribution, good design and relatively low prices. It was less successful in Europe's biggest market, Germany, where the international and local brand competition was particularly strong. International brands included Electrolux® and domestic brands included the German companies Bosch® and Miele®.

Arçelik in Eastern Europe and beyond

Given the low labour costs and potential for higher growth in Eastern Europe, Arçelik's strategy in this area was different. There were no acquisitions because there were no attractive companies. However, there were some opportunities, to set up new factories and build brands. As a result, by 2010, Arçelik had set up new plant in Romania and Russia and its brands held 35 per cent of the Romanian market and nearly 10 per cent of the Polish market.

Back in 2000, Arçelik opened up a sales office in China. Market demand was such that the company decided to expand its operations in 2007 by opening up its first factory in that country. It then followed this with a small number of Chinese domestic appliance stores - similar to those back in Turkey.

Arçelik's profit record

Although the company made major advances in Europe in the period to 2010, it also suffered a dip in profits over this time - see Figure 8.10. In 2008, its profits were still based largely on its Turkish production plants and had declined by 25 per cent compared with two years earlier. This was primarily due to a drop in sales as European market demand declined as a result

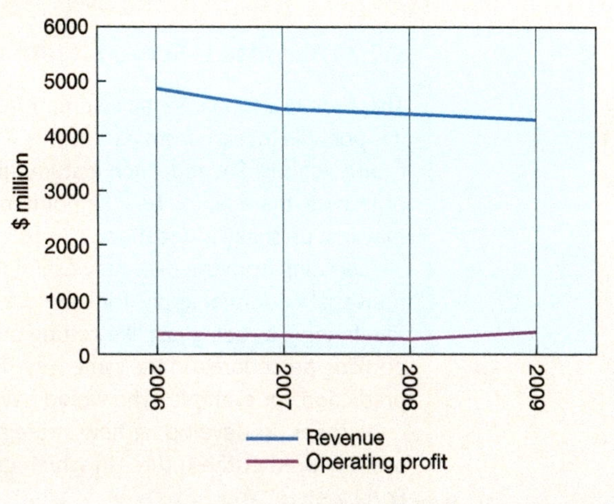

Figure 8.10 Arçelik's profit downturn with declining national economies

Source: Richard Lynch from Koç holding company report and accounts.

of international economic pressures: economies of scale can be affected disproportionately by declines in sales. Arçelik reacted by new cost cutting and efficiency strategies inside the company: better inventory management and improved stock turnover resulting in lower working capital. By 2011, Arçelik had become the third largest domestic appliance brand in Western Europe behind Electrolux from Sweden and Indesit™ from Italy.

Green strategy **Arçelik has been using its R&D facilities to develop new, greener domestic appliances. The Koç group has a strong record of sustainability projects.**

 However, he acknowledges the considerable help in preparing this case from his co-research colleagues, Dr Tanses Gulsoy of Beykent University, Istanbul and Professor Dr Ozlem Ozkanli of Ankara University, Ankara.

Case questions

1 What strategic environmental factors have influenced Arçelik's strategic decisions? And with what outcomes?

2 What were Arçelik's competitive advantages? Why was OEM inconsistent with these? Given its profit problems in 2008, would you have advised Arçelik to change strategy and pursue some OEM contracts?

3 Thinking about the various possible growth markets around the world, would you advise Arçelik to open up more country markets as part of its growth strategy? Or should the company concentrate primarily on its existing countries? You can assume that Arçelik is typical of many companies with only a limited amount of resources - both financial and human - to undertake further expansion.

CRITICAL REFLECTION

What Purpose is Served By Analysing the Strategic Environment?

There are two fundamental assumptions that underpin this chapter. First, strategic analysis assumes that it is possible to learn from past events. This assumption is important because strategy is essentially about future actions. Second, such a study implicitly assumes that the future is predictable in some way – otherwise, there would be little point in drawing any lessons from the analysis. Both these assumptions may rest on shaky foundations.

'Learning from the past' may examine a strategic environment with strategic perceptions and definitions that no longer apply: for example, the traditional market for air travel has been revolutionised by redefining it as being just like getting on a bus where aircraft seats are readily available without lengthy booking procedures. In the same way, 'Predicting the future' always runs the risk of making an incorrect prediction: for example, who would have predicted 18 years ago how the internet would develop?

Perhaps, in developing new strategies, we cannot learn much from the past. Perhaps we cannot usefully predict the future. In which case, what purpose is served by PESTEL Analysis, Porter's Five Forces, etc.?

SUMMARY

In analysing the environment surrounding the organisation, ten main factors were identified.

- *Environmental analysis can usefully begin with a basic assessment of the market definition and size, the market growth and the market share.* Market definition is important because it will determine the size and scope of the strategic opportunity. Market growth is commonly estimated early in any strategic analysis because of its importance with regard to the growth objectives of an organisation. A basic estimate of market share can be used to estimate whether an organisation has a significant share of a market as a starting point in exploring the strategic implications.
- *A general consideration of the nature of the environment and, in particular, the degree of turbulence.* When events are particularly uncertain and prone to sudden and significant change, strategic management needs to become more flexible and organise its procedures to cope with the situation.
- *A general analysis of the factors that will affect many industries.* This can be undertaken by two procedures: the PESTEL analysis and scenarios. The PESTEL analysis explores political, economic, socio-cultural, technological, environmental and legal influences on the organisation. It is important when undertaking such an analysis to develop a shortlist of only the most important items, not a long list under every heading. In analysing the institutional environment, the *5P Framework* – People, Power, Pathways, Performance and Productivity (as measured by knowledge and innovation) – can form a useful structure for this purpose. These background factors may form an important element of strategy
- *Growth characteristics.* These can be explored using the industry life cycle concept. Markets are divided into a series of development stages: introduction, growth, maturity and decline. In addition, the maturity stage may be subject to the cyclical variations associated with general economic or other factors over which the company has little control.
- *Different stages of the life cycle demand different corporate strategies.* The early stages probably require greater investment in R&D and marketing to develop and explain the product. The later stages should be more profitable on a conventional view of the life cycle. However, there is an argument that takes a more unconventional stance: it suggests that it is during the mature phase that investment should increase in order to restore growth.
- *Key factors for success in an industry.* Identifying these can help focus strategy development on those areas that really matter. They can conveniently be considered under three headings: customers, competition and corporation. By 'corporation' is meant the resources of the organisation. Key factors can be found in any area of the organisation and relate to skills, competitive advantage,

competitive resources of an organisation in the industry, special technologies or customer contacts. Four criticisms of key factors have been made: identification, causality of relationships, dangers of generalising, and disregard of emergent perspectives. Caution is therefore needed in their application.

- *A Five Forces Analysis.* This will involve an examination of buyers, suppliers, new entrants, substitutes and the competition in the industry. The aim is to analyse the balance of power between each force and the organisation in the industry.
- *A Four Links Analysis.* This is the analysis of those outside bodies co-operating with the organisation. This will include a study of the complementors, networks and legal links that the organisation has with its environment. The purpose is to analyse the relative strengths of such links and their ability to enhance the competitive advantages of the organisation.
- *A study of selected direct competitors.* An environmental analysis needs to identify the competitive advantages of rival companies. This is undertaken using competitor profiling. It will seek to identify the competitive advantages by focusing on one or two rival companies in depth. More generally, it will explore the objectives, resources, past performance, current products and services, and present strategies of one or two competitors. Such a study needs to recognise the fluid and changing nature of competitors and their resources.
- *A study of customers, market segmentation and positioning.* The final area of analysis is concerned with actual and potential customers and their importance to the organisation. Segmentation of markets derives from customer analysis and plays an important role in strategic management development. Positioning then determines how products will compete to attract customers in a particular part of the market.

QUESTIONS

1 Using Case 8.4 and your judgement, determine the degree of turbulence in the Hollywood film industry. Give reasons for your views.

2 Undertake a general environmental analysis of an industry of your choice, using both the PESTEL format and scenarios to draw out the major strategic issues.

3 Develop and compare the key factors for success in the following three industries: the computer industry (see companies like Acer® and Hewlett-Packard identified at the end of Part 3 on the web), the ice cream industry and the Indian motorcycle industry (Chapter 8).

4 For the Indian motorcycle industry, analyse the competitive forces within the industry using the Five Forces Model. Identify also any forms of co-operation in the industry using a Four Links Analysis.

5 Based on your answers to the previous questions, what strategic advice would you offer Bajaj? Use Section 8.7.6 to assist you.

6 Undertake a life cycle analysis of an industry of your choice. What strategic conclusions would you draw for organisations in the industry, if any? Comment specifically on the difficulties of this approach.

7 Prepare a full environmental analysis for an industry of your choice and make recommendations on its future strategic management.

8 Undertake a customer analysis for your own organisation. What segments can you identify? What role is played by customer service and quality? What strategic conclusions can you draw?

9 Do you agree with the statement that stable environments favour prescriptive approaches to strategy whereas turbulent environments demand emergent strategies? Consider carefully the impact technology may have on a stable environment and the problem of long-term investment, even in turbulent industries - remember the caution of Ryanair at the beginning of this chapter.

10 To what extent can competitive analytical techniques be applied to the public sector and charitable institutions?

FURTHER READING

M E Porter's *Competitive Strategy: Techniques for Analysing Industries and Competitors* (The Free Press, Harvard, MA, 1980) has careful and detailed studies for analysis of the immediate competitive environment. Mona Makhija's paper (2003) 'Comparing the resource-based and market-based views of the firm: empirical evidence from Czech privatisation', *Strategic Management Journal,*

Vol 24, pp 433–451 presents some useful comments on the Porter approach as well as a more general comparison that is also relevant.

Porter's article, 'How competitive forces shape strategy' (1979) *Harvard Business Review*, March–April, pp 136–145, is probably the classic short analysis here, but note that it says little or nothing about the importance of co-operation.

Finally, for a comprehensive review of the underpinning economic theory, read Séan Rickard's entitled 'Industrial Organisation Economics Perspective' in the edited text: Mark Jenkins and Veronique Ambrosini with Nardine Collier (2007) *Advanced Strategic Management*, 2nd edn, Palgrave Macmillan, Basingstoke, pp 61–82.

NOTES AND REFERENCES

1 Sources for Ryanair case: *Financial Times*, Robert Wright, 17 March 2017, 'British Airways' owner to launch low cost airline'; *Guardian*: Gwyn Topham, 25 February 2017, 'Norwegian plans New York flights for under £60'; *Sourced from the web* on 3 April 2017 at http://crankyflier.com/2017/01/03/ryanair-hopes-to-feed-norwegian-long-haul-soon-but-thats-just-the-beginning/.

2 Porter, M E (1980) *Competitive Strategy*, The Free Press, New York.

3 Andrews, K (1987) *The Concept of Corporate Strategy*, Irwin, Homewood, IL.

4 Many strategy texts (including previous editions of this one!) set out in great depth various environmental concepts and forget that it is useful to begin with some basic data.

5 Levitt, T (1960) 'Marketing myopia', *Harvard Business Review*, July–August, pp 45–56. Levitt's paper challenged the traditional definitions of the market.

6 There may be tautological problems here, but it is not appropriate to explore these at this early stage in strategy analysis. Suffice to say that it is possible to pursue this academic debate by starting with the well-known text by Buzzell, R D and Gale, B T (1987) *The PIMS Principles*, The Free Press, London. Follow this up with Baker, M (1993) *Marketing Strategy and Management*, 2nd edn, Macmillan, London.

7 Porter, M E (1980) Op. cit., Ch 2.

8 The early part of this section is based on Ansoff, I and MacDonnell, E (1990) *Implanting Strategic Management*, 2nd edn, Prentice Hall, Englewood Cliffs, NJ.

9 D'Aveni, R (1994) *Hypercompetitive Rivalries*, Free Press, New York.

10 Simon, H 'The corporation: will it be managed by machine?', in Leavitt, H and Pondy, L (eds) (1964) *Readings in Managerial Psychology*, University of Chicago Press, Chicago, IL, pp 592–617.

11 Institutional theory at the macro level has been well established for many years, particularly since the work of North, D C (1990, 1994, 2005) and Scott, W R (1995, 2001). See, for example, North, D C, (1990) *Institutions, Institutional Change and Economic Performance*, Cambridge University Press, Cambridge; (1994) 'Economic performance through time', *American Economic Review*, 84(3), 359–368; (2005) *Understanding the Process of Economic Change*, Princeton University Press, Princeton, NJ; Scott, W R, (1995) 'Introduction: institutional theory and organizations', in W R Scott and S Christensen (eds), *The Institutional Construction of Organizations*, pp xi–xxiii, Sage Publications, Thousand Oaks, CA; (2001) *Institutions and Organizations*, Sage Publications, Thousand Oaks, CA.

12 There has been extensive study of this topic over recent years. Two sources provide useful reviews: Dunning J H and Lundan S M (2008) *Multinational Enterprises and the Global Economy*, 2nd edn, Edward Elgar, Cheltenham, UK; Peng, M, Wang, D Y L and Yi, J (2008) 'An institution-based view of international business strategy: a focus on emerging economies', *Journal of International Business Studies*, 39, pp 920–936.

13 Knowledge and innovation are explicated and reviewed in the following selected papers. Damanpour, F, Walker, R, and Avellaneda, C (2009) 'Combinative effects of innovation types and organizational performance: a longitudinal study of service organizations', *Journal of Management Studies*, 46(4), pp 650–675; Grant, R (1996) 'Toward a knowledge-based theory of the firm', *Strategic Management Journal*, 17, pp 109–122; Leonard, D (1995) *Wellsprings of Knowledge*, Harvard Business School Press, Boston, MA; Nonaka, I and Takeuchi, H (1995) *The Knowledge-Creating Company*, Oxford University Press, Oxford.

14 Baden-Fuller, C and Stopford, J (1992) *Rejuvenating the Mature Business*, Routledge, Ch 2.

15 Aaker, D R (1992) *Strategic Marketing Management*, 3rd edn, Wiley, New York, p 236.

16 Smallwood, J E (1973) 'The product life cycle: a key to strategic marketing planning', *MSU Business Topics*, Winter, pp 29–35.

17 Baker, M (1993) *Marketing Strategy and Management*, 2nd edn, Macmillan, London, p 100 *et seq*. presents a short defence and interesting discussion of the main areas.

18 Dallah, N Y and Yuspeh, S (1976) 'Forget the product life cycle concept', *Harvard Business Review*, January–February, p 101 *et seq*.

19 Sources for the Bajaj case: *Financial Times*: 12 May 1999, p 31; 4 September 2007, p 14; 9 January 2008, p 30. *DNA Money Mumbai*: 24 November 2007, p 27; 26 November 2007, p 25. *The Economist*, 10 January 2008. *Economic Times*, 11 January 2008 – extracted from the *Times of India* website. Websites: www.bajaj.com and www.herohonda.com. Bajaj Auto annual report and accounts 2010: all the market data is sourced from this well-presented and clearly written document.

20 Ohmae, K (1983) *The Mind of the Strategist*, Penguin, Harmondsworth, Ch 3.

21 Porter, M E (1985) *Competitive Advantage*, The Free Press, New York, Ch 7.

22 Kay, J (1993) *Foundations of Corporate Success*, Oxford University Press, Oxford, Chs 5 to 8.
23 Amit, R and Schoemaker, P (1993) 'Strategic assets and organizational rent', *Strategic Management Journal*, Vol 14, pp 33–46.
24 Ohmae, K (1983) Op. cit., p 96.
25 Ghemawat, P (1991) *Commitment*, The Free Press, New York.
26 Porter, M E (1980) Op. cit. Note that Porter's work owes much to the writings of Joel Bain and others in the 1950s on industrial economies. However, it was Porter who gave this earlier material its strategic focus. See also Porter's article, 'How competitive forces shape strategy' (1979) *Harvard Business Review*, March–April, pp 136–145, which is a useful summary of the main points from the early part of his book.
27 Op. cit., p 4.
28 Porter (1980) actually refers in his book to 'six' areas and then goes on to list seven!
29 Cusumano, M and Takeishi, A (1991) 'Supplier relations and management: a survey of Japanese, Japanese transplant and US auto plants', *Strategic Management Journal*, Vol 12, pp 563–588.
30 Nielsen, A C (1988) *International Food and Drug Store Trends*, Nielsen, Oxford.
31 Aaker, D (1992) Op. cit.
32 Baker, M (1993) Op. cit
33 Harvey-Jones, J (1991) *Getting it Together*, Heinemann, London, Ch 14.
34 Porter (1980) Op. cit., Chs 7 and 8.
35 Reve, T (1990) 'The firm as a nexus of internal and external contracts', *The Firm as a Nexus of Treaties*, Aoki, M, Gustafson, M and Williamson, O E (eds), Sage, London. See also Kay, J (1993) *The Foundations of Corporate Success*, Oxford University Press, Oxford, Ch 5.
36 Kay, J (1993) Op. cit., p 80.
37 Kay, J (1993) Op. cit.: Ch 5 on architecture explores this topic in depth.
38 Nalebuff, B J and Brandenburger, A M (1997) *Coopetition*, HarperCollins Business, London.
39 For example, Porter, M E (1980) Op. cit.
40 Levitt, T (1960) 'Marketing myopia', *Harvard Business Review*, July–August, p 45.
41 Davidson, H (1987) *Offensive Marketing*, Penguin, Harmondsworth.
42 Aaker, D (1992) Op. cit., p 48.
43 It should be noted that, in theory at least, it is not necessary to segment a market before exploring its competitive positioning. However, it is usual and much easier to select part of a market before undertaking positioning. Many marketing strategy texts do not make this clear.
44 Porter, M E (1985) *Competitive Advantage*, The Free Press, New York, p 233.
45 Ohmae, K (1983) *The Mind of the Strategist*, Penguin, Harmondsworth, p 103.
46 Probably the best-known text exploring positioning issues in depth is: Hooley, G J and Saunders, J (1999) *Competitive Positioning*, Prentice Hall, Hemel Hempstead.

9 Initiation - Micro Problem Identification

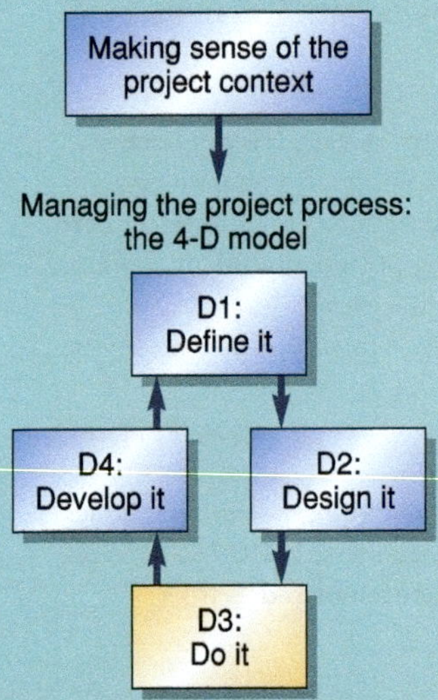

Principles

1. It happens. What matters is how you deal with it.
2. Complex situations benefit from basic tools to help with sense-making.
3. Establishing basic principles and 'rules of thumb' dramatically improves the success of decision-making processes.

Learning objectives

By the time you have completed this chapter, you should be able to:

→ provide a structure for the identification, definition and solution of problems

→ identify appropriate tools which can be brought to bear at different stages of the problem-solving process

→ show the implications of some of the changes in modern management thinking in the area of decision-making.

Contents

Houston – we have a problem . . .

Source: GNU Free Documentation License

The construction of the Heathrow Express, a new rail service linking central London to Heathrow Airport, was running behind schedule. Tunnelling work was continuing under the existing airport when on 20 October 1994, on the night shift, an attempt to 'fix' cracking in the concrete lining of the tunnel resulted in its structural integrity being compromised. It soon became clear that a full-scale collapse was under way and the tunnel was evacuated. Nobody was hurt, but work was delayed for a further six months while what remained of the tunnel was filled with concrete and a new tunnel route prepared. Costs of the collapse were in the region of £150 million.

Introduction

During the execution phase of a project, the project manager will be faced with the need to solve problems and make decisions rapidly and effectively. Fortunately, the consequences of these on the whole will not be as severe as the Heathrow Tunnel collapse described above. As it will not be possible to pre-plan all eventualities, the objective of this chapter is to show how such situations can be handled. Some of the techniques are simple enough to be used by almost anyone, though some are considerably more involved. Decision-making is considered as part of a generic problem-solving process.

Price (1984) describes one of the challenges for managers:

> *Business is a risky undertaking. According to those who have devoted their lives to the proper study of mankind, Man is a risk-evasive animal. From what I have seen, risk addicted seems closer to the norm. There is excitement in taking risky decisions and it is possible to get hooked on it; it makes you feel good.*
>
> *Risk, unnecessary risks, are taken by the thousand every day. Often they are unnecessary simply because they are made in the light of inadequate knowledge, but it boosts somebody's self-esteem to make them with an air of omniscience, which is one of the reasons why we are on the whole, such poor quality performers.*

There is another view, namely that the modern project manager is overloaded with data rather than information; the information revolution has provided the means to access large quantities of numbers quickly, often without the means to assimilate them. Handling such volume complexity without succumbing to 'data paralysis' is a significant task and one of the value-adding roles that management can play.

The project manager should have the option either to try to provide a structure for making 'rational' decisions or rely on gut-feel and experience and hope that this is appropriate.

9.1 Structuring problems

One of the key roles of a manager is to handle problems that challenge them in their own role, as well as being a resource for members of the project team to turn to for help. Problem-solving is a core management skill but, like leadership, one that too often is assumed to be an inbred attribute rather than an acquired skill.

For the purposes of this discussion, a problem is defined as:

The gap between an actual situation or the perception of it and the required or expected situation.

The two properties, expectation and perception, are subjective and based on the viewpoint of the individual. Many issues presented to managers fail this definition; people perceive that there is a problem without identifying the gap. Clarifying the reality of the situation with objective measures is a precursor to the problem-solving process. Part of the role of the project manager in this process is the gathering of the possible worldviews. This requires the skill of being involved yet objective.

The nature of the problem determines the point of departure for the manager. This can be categorised as:

- *requiring an immediate reaction* – the timescale of a decision requires a 'conditioned reflex' rather than a 'considered response'. Such a situation would include the threatening of the wellbeing of an individual;
- *response to a crisis* – the problem can be considered within a relatively short time period, i.e. an undesirable state of affairs has occurred – you need to do something about it soon;
- *emerging problem* – some undesirable state of affairs appears likely to happen – what are you going to do to resolve it?
- *response to an opportunity* – speculative problem-solving or avoidance in advance of an undesirable situation (missed opportunity);
- *strategy formulation* – the plotting of a course to a desired situation over a period of years.

The time period of the first kind of problem means that the response or intended solution must be either instinctive (such as to run away) or ingrained through training (to remove the source of potential danger). There is scope in the latter for a major component of any discussion on problem-solving, that of proceduralisation. This is not restricted to emergency situations but is a major component of any work situation today. This proceduralisation or systematisation can be defined as:

The enaction of a predetermined response to a given set of conditions.

The systematisation of problem resolution depends on identifying the situation. The **programmed response** is then initiated, as shown in Figure 9.1.

The preprogramming of actions has a number of advantages:

- once a method has been defined for resolving a situation, it can be refined and improved;
- by removing thought processes from the actions they are, to a great extent, independent of the individual carrying them out;
- if a predetermined procedure is followed, actions are traceable back to the people who carried them out;
- the actions are then the responsibility of the organisation rather than the individual;
- should the procedure fail, the identification of the fail-point is considerably helped, as the steps can be retraced.

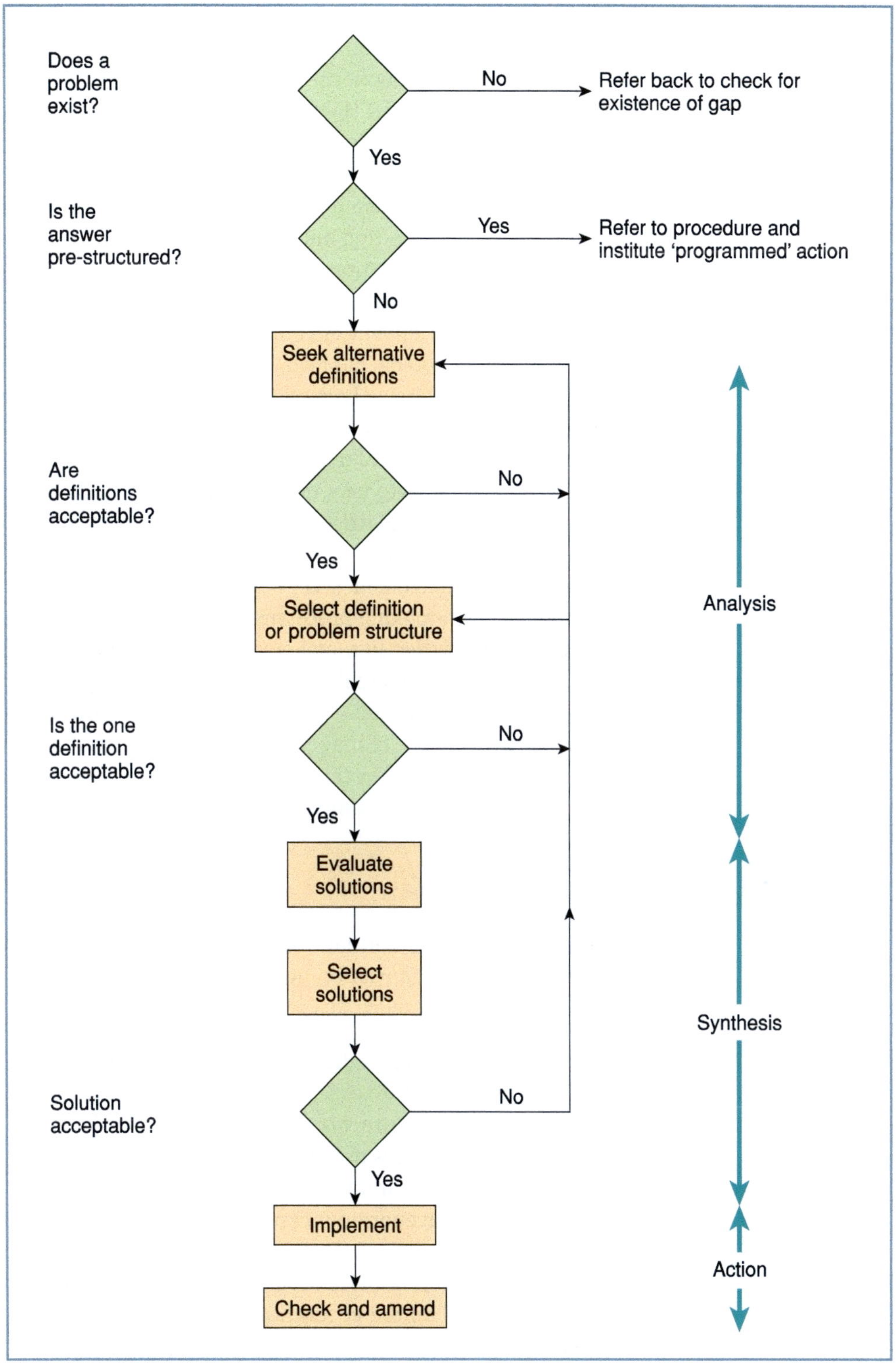

Figure 9.1 Systematic problem-solving model

The alternative is that the **problem-solving cycle** is invoked. As for the planning process, the cycle is iterative (involves repetition of steps if the output does not meet recognised or emerging conditions). The remainder of this chapter will consider the possible approaches to problems with a degree of novelty – those that are being solved for the first time and those that are being considered for proceduralisation. There is a downside, not least of which is the removal of the individualism in the performance of that part of the task. No one has yet achieved an effective procedural description for carrying out the job 'as if you cared personally about the outcome'.

The problem-solving model (Figure 9.1) shows the process moving from determining whether a standard procedure exists, to choosing a definition for the problem. Classical problem-solving focuses very heavily on providing a definition for the problem – indeed, it is often stated that 'if you can define the problem you are working with, you are half-way to a solution'. The definition must include the statement of the gap between the two states: actual/perceived situation and desired/expected situation. Without these two, the **problem** is said to be '**unbounded**' and, to all practical purposes, is not amenable to 'problem solving' in the conventional manner.[1]

However, once the problem has been defined, the process can move on to the next stage – the construction of various alternatives. At this point the process leaves the **analysis** of the problem, at least temporarily, and moves to the **synthesis** phase. This transition involves the first major piece of decision-making. The logic of the process is fairly simple at this point – there needs to be a decision made only if there is a choice of definitions or solutions. Where only one exists the implications need to be considered, but without wasting time on non-decisions.

The extremes of management style were identified as 'coercive' and 'cooperative'. The natures of the decision-making processes are different. For the former, the project manager would be the key decision-maker. In the latter, many of the decisions would be devolved, either to the individual with the most knowledge or responsibility for this part of the project or to the group as a whole. This devolution removes a large part of the decision-making role of the manager. Part of the process of devolution involves seeking ideas from others. This ensures that the set of possible solutions can bridge the problem gap – and includes '**brainstorming**'.

Brainstorming

Taking a group out of their normal work situation to ponder a problem can be immensely beneficial to both the organisation and the group. The dynamics of the brainstorming process are aided by adherence to a few rules:

- Provide a basic structure to the task of decision-making – groups are generally very bad at looking for structure or logic in decisions.
- The benefit is from the extraction and combination of ideas from a variety of people – the object of the exercise is therefore to facilitate this.
- Give people the opportunity to do some pre-thinking on the problem – the sub-conscious mind has an enormous capacity and can provide solutions without the input of conscious effort.
- At the start of the meeting an ice-breaking exercise will help people to relax and provide a 'safe environment' for the generation of ideas.
- All ideas must be written down – use whiteboards and 3M's Post-it notes, for example.
- Express ideas as the participants state them – paraphrasing removes the original meaning and adds a slant of your own. If in doubt as to the veracity of the point being made, seek clarification.
- Do not allow any criticism of ideas put forward – this will destroy the credibility of that person and you will be unlikely to gain much more from them.
- Do not permit one or a small group of individuals to dominate the proceedings – this will exclude potentially valuable input from others.

- Summarise and record the outcome of the brainstorming session and then circulate it to all those concerned – the after-meeting feedback is a further source of solutions and ideas, as people think of all the things that they would like to have contributed during the session.

Decision-making as a process is the period involving the seeking of alternatives through to the end of the comparative evaluation stage. The inputs to this process are:

- strategic – in order for an organisation to retain coherence the decisions made in the projects that it undertakes need to fit with the overall strategy outlined for the organisation;
- fundamental/political – each person brings their own viewpoint to the decision-making process. This will range in form from bias (often undeclared) to a forthright statement of personal beliefs;
- quantitative modelling;
- subconscious elements – obtaining people's legitimate reservations about a decision can be a preventor of 'group-think' provided that an atmosphere can be created in which people feel free to try to elucidate such thoughts.

The nature of the decision-making process depends on the system that the decision concerns. A basic overview of systems was given which showed the application of the input/ output/ constraints and mechanisms model to a project system. Further examination of this is needed to determine whether it is:

- an open system – having interaction with systems outside through the flows of material or information;
- a closed system – being self-sustaining in informational and material terms, operating in isolation.

It is tempting when considering systems to look for the closed-system model. If this is possible, the modelling process involves defining variables from within the system and then optimising these. In most projects, however, this leads to inappropriate models of behaviour being constructed, as they do not show the dynamic nature of the interchange between the systems and their external environments, i.e. they are open systems.

The use of open-system models is not as attractive, however, as by definition they require the variables from external factors to be continuously introduced and the nature of the environment to be dynamic and inherently unstable. This instability is reflected in a tendency for the behaviour of the system to be unpredictable, and hence the need for the risk and uncertainty management practices developed in previous chapters.

Modelling systems for decision-making

A study published over 50 years ago[2] identified the reasons for poor decision-making as being:

- data not properly ordered or structured;
- too much time spent developing answers to problems rather than the statement of the problem;
- an inability on the part of the decision-makers to consider all the variables/factors involved;
- an inability to evaluate the impact of extraneous factors.

Given the problems faced by many project managers and the evidence from the case studies covered so far, it appears that not much has changed over this time. While the growth of the power and usage of personal computers and the availability of a great range of highly capable software mean that there exists relatively cheap means of processing large quantities of data, the volume of data that the modern organisation can generate has increased accordingly. While there appears to be little excuse now for the data not to be properly ordered or structured (the ease of preparation of graphs and other graphical techniques should have removed this as a cause) the sheer complexity of the data that many programme and project managers have to handle can be literally overwhelming. One programme manager interviewed recently had so much data coming in from the projects he was overseeing, he spent 3 days each week making sense of it and reporting summaries of it up to his senior management team.

The same argument could also be applied to the third of Drucker's points, as the ability to build more data into decision-making models has been greatly enhanced. The second and fourth of the factors are procedurally linked to the decision-making process and are only removed by:

- increased awareness of the potential of both of these to affect the process;
- focus on the removal of the damaging effects of poor decisions, i.e. make the decisions more robust.

There has been a considerable growth in the use of sophisticated models in decision-making. The application of scientific models to the solving of management problems has developed into a specialist branch of management known as '**management science**' or '**operational research**'. The temptation is to view the output of management science analysis as having a high degree of truth, because the mathematical models that are used are very difficult for a lay person to dispute. In reality, management science is one of the tools that can be employed in decision-making, rather than being the totality of the process.

The model of the system may take on one of many forms, including:

- a descriptive model – using words or graphical means to describe the action or performance of a system, e.g. systemigrams;
- a geometric model – expressing an object in a mathematical form (as used in computer-aided design systems);
- a mechanistic model – determining the inputs to and outputs from a system;
- static predictive – taking a limited picture of the state of a system at a particular point in time and using various mathematical techniques to predict the future performance;
- a dynamic predictive model – a 'real-time system' which takes a constant review of the inputs to a system, providing the most up-to-date forecast of future performance.

Taking a generic view of the modelling process, a model of a system is defined as:

A system which is constructed under controlled conditions, whose behaviour mimics that of another system where it would not be possible for those conditions to be controlled (economically or physically).

The benefits of using modelling during projects are:[3]

- time contraction – it is often possible to speed up events to show the effects of time on a system and use it in the prediction as to what will happen after a period of time, without necessarily waiting that long;

- **what-if** – the decision-makers have the option to manipulate a model and determine a range of scenarios based on their own individual predictions of the conditions as to what the external environment for the system will be;
- error avoidance/detection – there are many systems that can shadow the decisions made by others and act as a coarse filter for marginal decisions or ones where there has been an error. Such systems are often used both in mechanical design and stock-market trading.

In addition:

- it is possible to examine the fundamental assumptions on which a model was based;
- parameters can be optimised without the need for potentially expensive trial and error with reality;
- the sensitivity to external effects can be measured.

Modelling involves a cycle of activities as used in the project planning cycle – that is, the model is designed, built, tested and then amended based on the comparison of the performance of the real system and the model. The model is then updated based on this performance. The process itself involves:

- making assumptions about the behaviour of systems;
- simplification of the system parameters;
- estimation of the likely values of unrelated variables.

A Gantt Chart is one model of a project system. Properly constructed, it presents one view of the project. A risk analysis is another view. A cost-benefit model another. A systems diagram, another. All of these are valid and potentially useful models for understanding projects, but each is incomplete. For instance, showed how the failure to include uncertainty in a basic project plan resulted in instability in the schedule. As a model of a project system, the plan is incomplete. It is ONE view – it must not be THE view. Work carried out following on from the Rethinking Project Management network (Chapter 6) has demonstrated the benefits of using *multiple perspectives* on projects – that is, to take not just a planning view, but also to consider wider issues – stakeholders, politics, team interactions, processes, strategy and more.[4] A strategic approach to modelling is therefore part of the skillset of the modern project manager.

9.2 Problem analysis

Uncertainty

There are two approaches to handling uncertainty – dealing with the cause and dealing with the effects. Risk and opportunities management in projects is deliberately structured to take advantage of both of these approaches.

As an example, a company is about to launch a new product onto a market in which it has previously operated. It feels that there is a considerable degree of uncertainty as to whether the new product will be a success. There are a number of possible routes open to it:

- first, analyse the causes of the uncertainty and minimise this, and using the best data available, suggest possible sales scenarios for this product;
- second, look for options for how to respond to the given various scenarios – both good and bad.

Table 9.1 The use of mathematical modelling techniques

Technique	*Description*
Simulation	Computer modelling of a scenario
Linear programming	Optimal allocation of restricted resources to maximise or minimise a variable (such as price or cost)
Network analysis through CPM or PERT	Obtaining the logic of both precedence relationships and time requirements in a project environment through graphical means (see Chapter 15)
Queuing theory	Shows how a system reacts when faced with a random (stochastic) customer who demands the services of that system
Decision trees	Graphical method for describing the flow of decisions depending on the possibilities available at each juncture. May be pursued as a statement of possibilities or with statistical analysis

The scenarios generated are not 'the picture' – they simply paint 'a number of possible pictures' which the organisation may find themselves in. The first looks at handling the cause of a problem, the uncertainty inherent with product volume forecasting, and tries to remove it. The second accepts that variability exists and focuses on the task of pre-evaluating various management strategies given various sets of conditions. The point is that the modelling activity is only the first part of a process of decision-making. As will be shown, there are a number of well-developed techniques to support this activity.

Mathematical modelling techniques

The use of mathematical models in decision-making is widespread, ranging from basic spreadsheet calculations to the most advanced statistical techniques. Table 9.1 indicates the most-used techniques and a description of their usage. Each of these techniques requires a different level of mathematical skill to use effectively and each would justify a chapter to itself.[5]

Problem-solving tools

The basic problem-solving tools of the project manager include **Pareto analysis** and **Ishikawa/fishbone diagrams**.

Pareto analysis

Vilfredo Pareto was an economist who in 1906 published his finding that 80 per cent of the wealth of Milan was held by 20 per cent of the people. This 80/20 'rule' often recurs – many companies find that 80 per cent of their profits are generated by 20 per cent of their products or services (see Figure 9.2) or that 20 per cent of their clients provide 80 per cent of their business. The Pareto principle applied to problem-solving means that part of the initial analysis is to discover which 20 per cent of causes are causing 80 per cent of the problems. The effort of the problem-solvers can then be focused on establishing solutions to the major factors. Over time, the 80 per cent of problems has been removed, but the principle is still valid, stated simply – apply effort where it is going to yield the greatest result.

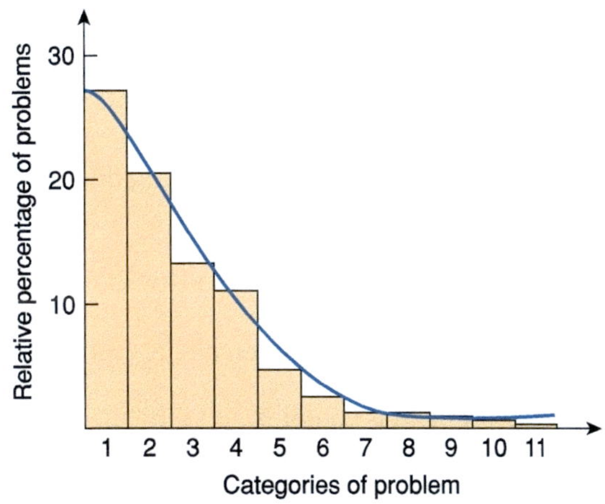

Figure 9.2 Pareto analysis

Ishikawa/fishbone diagrams

The fishbone diagram is a simple graphical technique which can help to structure a problem and guide a team into seeking further information about the nature of the system under consideration. The effect is shown on the right-hand end of Figure 9.3. The causes are then broken down into categories and these are then further deconstructed to show what contributes to that problem from those categories.

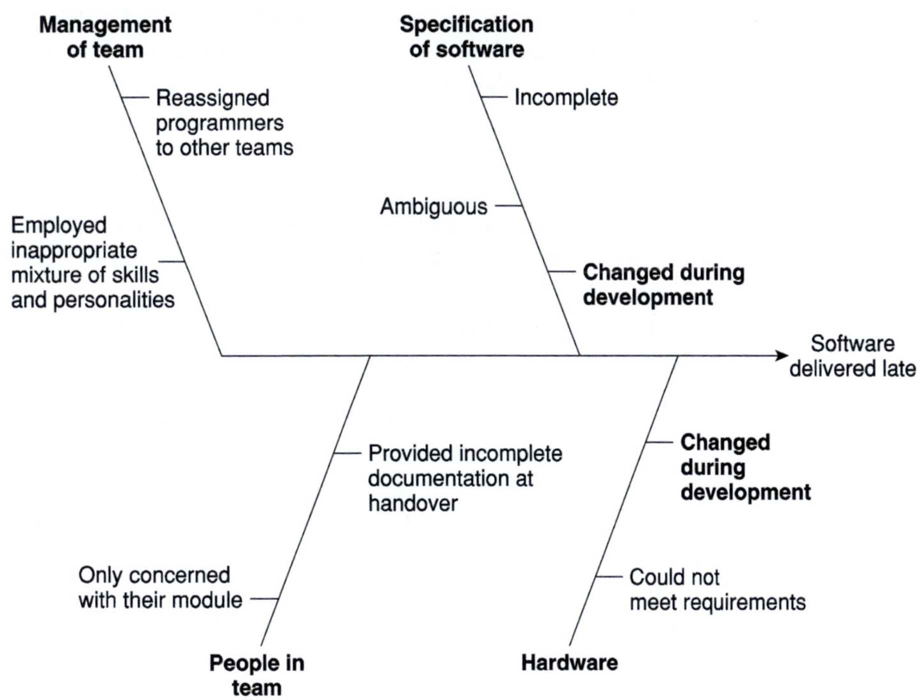

Figure 9.3 Ishikawa/fishbone diagram applied to late delivery problem

The problem of late delivery of software to clients is considered in the example shown in Figure 9.3. The problem is broken down into four main subject areas – management of the team, specification of the software, the people in the development team and the hardware on which they are working. Each of these is then broken down further. The predominant cause is shown by highlighting the particular area – in this case it is the changing of the specification during development.[6]

Cause–effect–cause analysis

Several challenges frequently emerge during the problem-solving process:

- the problem is complex and difficult to structure;
- people enter the discussions with solutions in mind rather than the analysis of the problem itself.

This leads either to stagnation in the process due to the inability to handle the complexity or to inappropriate solutions being given lengthy discussion time. Neither of these is likely to promote good decision-making. Among the problem-solving techniques that have sought to overcome these challenges is **cause–effect–cause analysis**. This is appropriate where:

- a trained, literate and skilful facilitator is available;
- the group is open to consideration of new problem-solving methods.

The objective is to analyse what the group states to be the undesirable effects of the problem (the gap) to find the root cause or causes. These can then be systematically addressed, rather than attention being focused on the effects. This is an excellent way to bound a problem and come up with a detailed description of its nature. Used as above it can be very powerful. It has been found from experience to be less useful for solving tactical problems than for strategic ones, due to the level of input required from team members to keep the logic strong.

One technique inherited from Japanese quality control techniques asks why a problem occurs five times (the five whys). This gets close to the root of the problem, though it is likely to suggest a single root cause rather than, as often happens, several. The process is similar for constructing cause–effect–cause analysis – for the tool to work, the logic has to be preserved in both the reality of the effects listed (do they exist?) and for the linking of causes to effects.

The task order should be completed as follows. It looks odd to start with but, like the construction of network diagrams, will become clear once you have practised using it.

- List the effects of the problem you are tackling – development projects are always delivered late, for example. These must all be real entities, i.e. it must be agreed that these do exist as statements in their own right.
- Start with this as one bubble in the middle of a page (see Figure 9.4).
- Select another of the effects and show how this relates to the first – either as a cause or an effect. Show the result as in Figure 9.5. This should then be read as: IF A THEN B, e.g. IF [it rains tomorrow] THEN [we will not be able to complete the site testing].
- Select other effects and build these round the first two. Many will be interlinked, though at first sight they appeared unrelated. Go as far as you can, again each time checking the links you have made to ensure that the logic is followed.

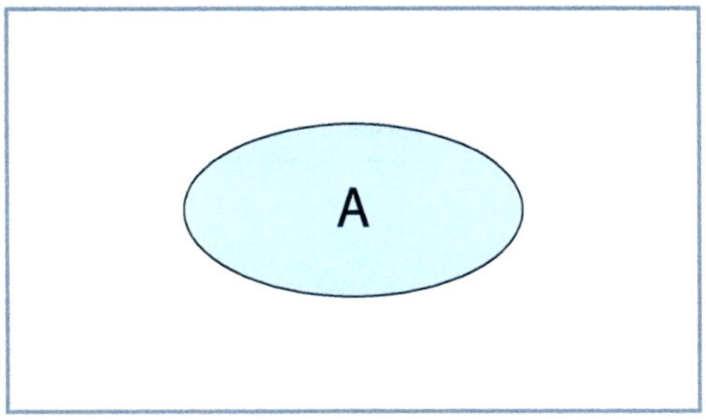

Figure 9.4 Entity A

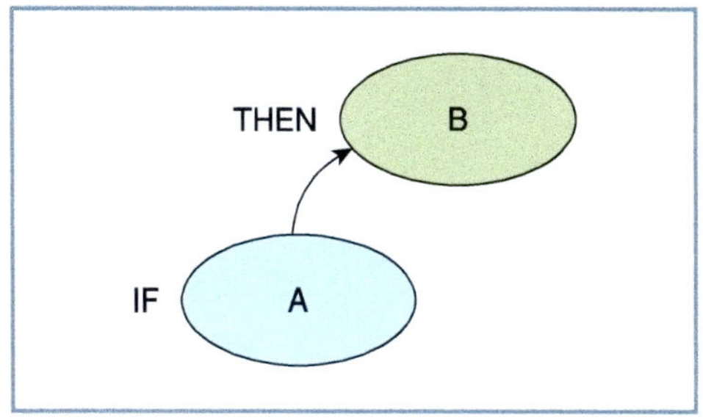

Figure 9.5 IF A THEN B

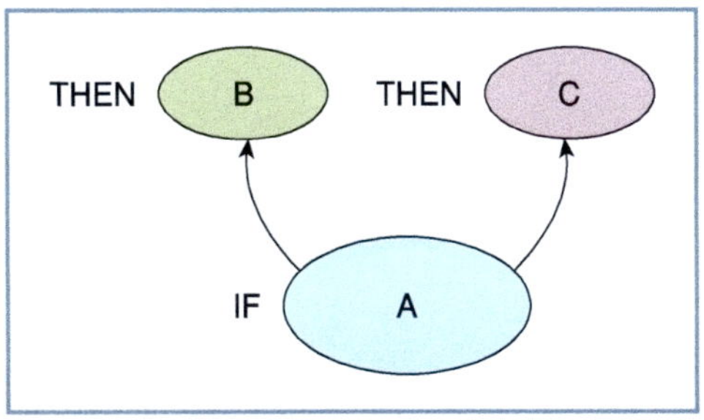

Figure 9.6 IF A THEN B AND C

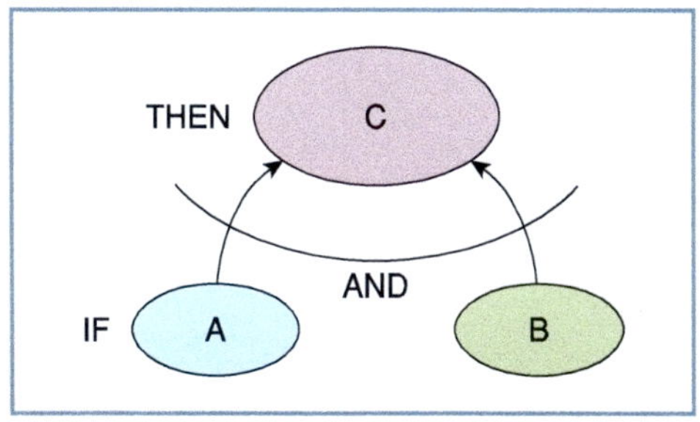

Figure 9.7 IF A AND B THEN C

- Where one cause has a number of effects, this should be drawn as in Figure 9.6.
- Where there is more than one cause linked to an effect, this should be as Figure 9.7, if there is dependency on both of them, i.e. IF [A] AND [B] THEN [C]. If the dependency is on either [A] OR [B] for [C] to exist, this is drawn without the 'banana' linking the two.

It is often necessary during the course of constructing the diagrams both to amend the entities and to add others, e.g. in the example that follows the link between [doesn't allocate time well] and [permanently tired] is not entirely logical. The additional entity [goes to bed late] was added to keep the logic flow. It was obviously necessary to check, as before, that this entity was real. The example shows how a problem concerning the poor performance of a person was analysed. The limited set of effects was listed as:

[Bill's work performance is poor]
[He works slower]
[He has a bad attitude to work]
[He is often late]
[He is permanently tired at work]
[He appears more interested in fishing]
[He does not allocate his time well]

These are then formed into the diagram shown in Figure 9.8. The additional entities and logic links are a matter of opinion to some degree. A further example of how this technique can be used to structure problems is included at the end of this chapter.[7]

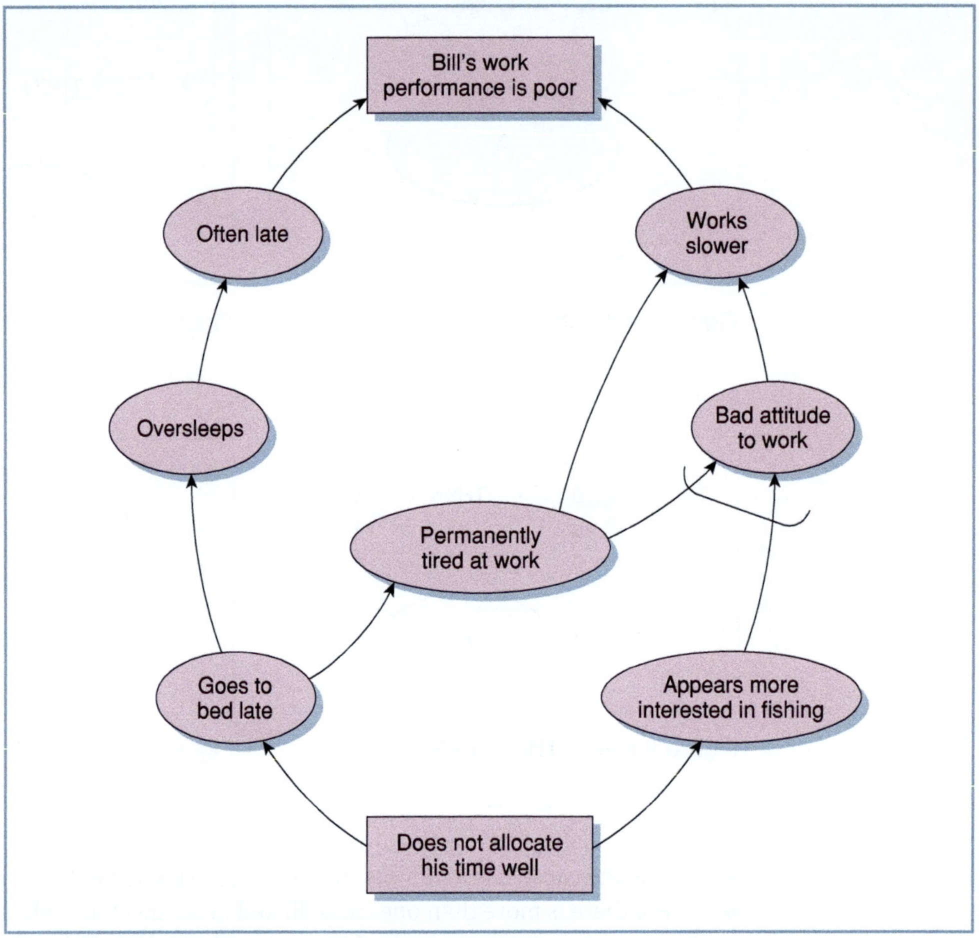

Figure 9.8 Logic diagram for Bill's performance

9.3 Decision support

Decision trees

A technique similar in format to the cause–effect–cause analysis, **decision trees** can be treated at a simple qualitative level or by detailed consideration through the addition of probabilities/distributions to each of the events. A basic format for constructing decision trees is shown in Figure 9.9.

The decision points are shown as squares while possible outcomes are shown as circles. The possibilities and implications of decisions are therefore clearly identified provided that all the decision points are shown. The qualitative treatment of the structure has merit in its simplicity and speed of construction. Further analysis of the probabilities of the chance events occurring can be made, providing a means for assessing the likelihood of needing contingency plans. The use of 'expected value' measurements can be both derived from and applied to this tool. The likelihood of the outcome of an event is assessed, and the cost/benefit in monetary terms calculated based on this outcome. The expected value of the branches can then be calculated from the sum of the subsequent expected values.

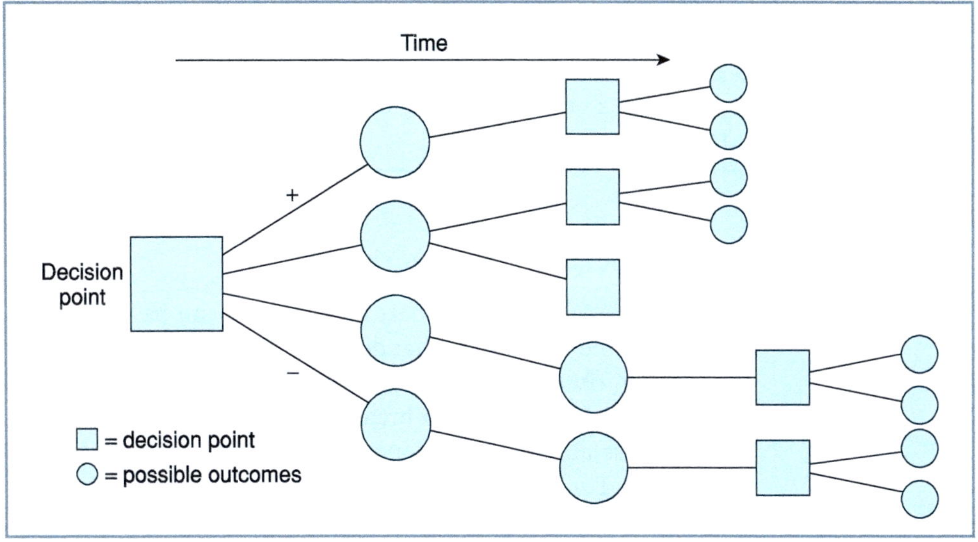

Figure 9.9 Decision trees[8]

Source: Greenwood, W.T. (1969) *Decision Theory and Information Systems*, South Western, pp. 83–104. Reproduced with permission.

Example

A decision has to be made on whether to fund project X or project Y. Each has two possible outcomes. For X, it has a 75 per cent chance of yielding £100 000 but a 25 per cent chance of yielding only £20 000. For Y, it has a 50 per cent chance of yielding £200 000 and a 50 per cent chance that there will be no yield. The decision tree in Figure 9.10 illustrates the problem.

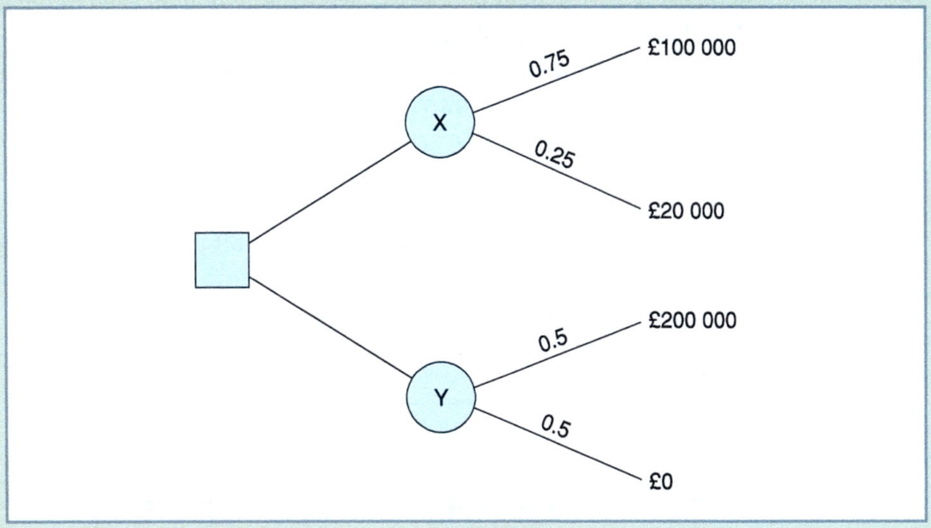

Figure 9.10 Decision tree: project X versus project Y

The financial decision is based on the sum of the expected values of the yields of each branch of the decision tree:

For project X – expected value = (0.75 × 100 000) + (0.25 × 20 000) = 80 000
For project Y – expected value = (0.5 × 200 000) + (0.5 × 0) = 100 000.

The assumption is that we wish to maximise the yield, therefore project Y should be pursued.

→

This method is attractive in that relatively complex models can be constructed and evaluated quickly. The figures for probabilities and values of return are both a matter of prediction, so the outcome will be determined by the quality of the data with which the model is provided.

Simple decision frameworks

Many complex decisions are best made if they can be broken down into the desirable elements of the outcome of that decision. Techniques for aiding in this process include the use of **attribute analysis** and **force-field analysis**.

Attribute analysis involves breaking down the decision into a set of desirable outcomes. These are then placed alongside the choices in the decision process and rated accordingly. For example, a company wishes to choose a supplier for a project. There are five alternative suppliers (A to E) which are arranged across the top of the table, as shown in Table 9.2. The desirable outcomes are arranged down the table (knowledge and experience, reputation, etc.). The manager of the team can then rate the individual suppliers on their perception of how they will perform on each of those outcomes/attributes. The rating is given out of ten (where 1 = very bad, 10 = excellent), and then totalled for each supplier.

This form of attribute analysis assumes that each of the attributes is of equal importance. Where one is considerably more important than another (e.g. reliability of delivery times may be vital if this is a critical path activity), it can be given an increased weighting, making the score out of 30, say, for that attribute. The totals are viewed in the same way as before. This is clearly a fairly arbitrary means of arriving at the decision, however it is simple to construct and allows a degree of traceability back to how a decision was made. It also enables people to have a discussion on each of the attributes and come up with some relatively objective measure.

Force-field analysis examines the strengths of different influences on a decision. This is best illustrated through the following example (see Figure 9.11). The decision to stand for election to a representative body (student's union council, parish or town council, club committee, etc.) has a number of implications. First, the time input to get elected may be substantial and the fear of losing the election significant. There is an opportunity cost – other work has to be put off until after the project is complete (which

Table 9.2 Supplier selection using unweighted attributes

Attribute	*A*	*B*	*C*	*D*	*E*
Knowledge and experience	6	7	7	9	8
Reputation	6	6	7	9	10
Prone to strikes/bankruptcy	4	6	9	9	9
Significance of their support	4	8	7	9	9
Design appreciation and conformance	7	7	8	8	9
QA system	5	6	8	9	9
Defects and warranty claims to date	7	6	8	9	10
Reliability of delivery times	6	6	6	9	10
Cost control	7	6	7	6	6
Service level	8	7	8	8	10
Total	60	65	75	85	90

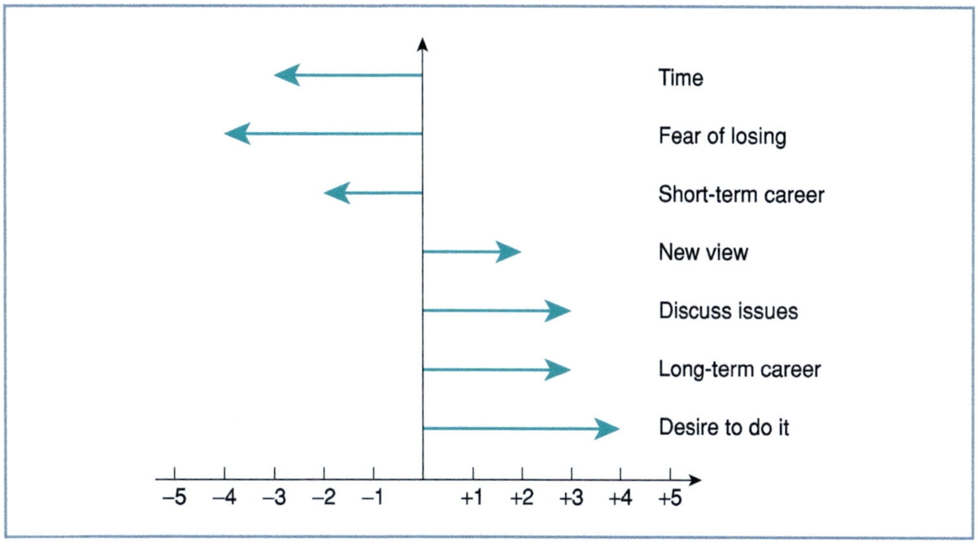

Figure 9.11 **Force-field analysis on standing for election**

generally proves to be a poor career move, at least in the short term). There are benefits, such as the requirement to take a new view on a subject and to discuss issues that affect your life. It may improve your CV and career prospects. A major consideration is also whether you want to be elected. These influences can then be rated on a 0–5 scale as being positive (stand for election) or negative (find something better to do). The influences with some numbers assigned are shown in Figure 9.11. As can be seen by summing the positive (+12) and negative (–9) influences and subtracting the negative from the positive, the decision was positive.

Decision-support systems

The principle which **decision-support systems** embrace is that there is sufficient knowledge existing for the subject to be considered complex, and therefore can be better interpreted through the abilities of computers to deal with large amounts of information. The knowledge must exist within the system, and this is provided through the contribution of experts in the relevant subjects.

The most basic form of decision-support system is a database. The data is structured in 'fields' which the database system can manipulate and structure as required. One example from the UK is the database of poisons held at Llandough Hospital in Cardiff – the effects of the poison, and its antidote or appropriate treatment, are held on a central computer which other hospitals can access remotely or by telephone. The decision on the appropriate form of treatment is taken without the need for guesswork by the treating doctor. Another use of the information on that database is to track back from the symptoms to the nature of the poison.

A further development of the database is the **expert system** – otherwise known as **artificial intelligence**. The expert system takes the expert knowledge, usually gained from an individual or a number of individuals over a period of time.

An expert system typically:[9]

- incorporates expert knowledge in a particular subject area, usually by storing and representing this as rules or other representative forms (knowledge base);
- separates the general knowledge from the details of a particular case under consideration to which the knowledge base is applied (particular context);

- clearly distinguishes the knowledge from the mechanism of reasoning (inference engine);
- possesses an interactive user interface for providing explanations, justifications and questions to the user;
- provides, as its output, advice or decisions in the area of expertise.

The logic IF [A] THEN [B] is simple for computers to handle. Decision-taking far more often involves the logic IF to a certain extent [A] THEN to a certain extent [B]. This is known as 'fuzzy logic' and needs further examination before it is amenable to computer analysis.

This system of rules can be modelled directly as a system, although for people who do not have this level of programming skills, the use of an expert system 'shell' is likely to be the most beneficial.

Summary

■ Problems will arise during projects – that is one certainty that you can rely on! As for other project issues, some structure to the thinking and some tools for the process greatly help the project manager in managing towards a successful conclusion. The first stage in this is to define the issue. We defined a problem as the gap between perceptions of an actual situation and that of the expected or required situation. Furthermore, problems may be categorised according to the required reaction time and the nature of the response required – for instance, responses may be predetermined through procedures or reasoned through the problem-solving cycle.

■ To assist the process, a model may be constructed either qualitatively (through descriptive modelling) or quantitatively (through mathematical modelling) to provide one representation of reality which can be tested under controlled conditions. As we saw during the discussion of risk, uncertainty can be handled either through statistical means, calculating the most likely set of events, or through managerial action to make the system more robust to the effects of uncertainty. Various mathematical tools can be employed to take away the need for subjective decision-making in some areas, while providing decision support in others. Other methods to help in the problem-solving process include the following:

- Ishikawa/fishbone diagrams provide a graphical method for structuring problems; Pareto analysis provides a guide as to which problems to tackle first.
- Cause–effect–cause analysis provides a graphical technique for finding the 'root' of a problem through structuring the logic of the situation.
- Decision trees where the route that actions take can be graphically evaluated and probabilities then assigned to each route if required.

■ Decision-support systems are normally computer-based and allow expert knowledge to be expressed as a series of rules which are then interpreted by the system. These do not eliminate the need for gut-feel and experience, however – indeed they should be better at capturing these elements. They have a vital role to play in decision-making – an area that is central to the discussion of 'what managers do'. Moreover, the increase in the availability of data and sophisticated modelling systems doesn't appear to have made the job of managing projects any easier, or any more successful. Perhaps this is because a modelling process will usually only focus on one viewpoint of a project. The core skill in decision-making is in acquiring multiple viewpoints on an issue – not relying on a single view.

Key terms

analysis
attribute analysis
brainstorming
cause–effect–cause analysis
decision frameworks
decision-support systems
decision trees
expert system/artificial intelligence
force-field analysis
Ishikawa/fishbone diagrams
management science/operational research
Pareto analysis
problem-solving cycle
programmed response
synthesis
unbounded problem
what-if

Relevant areas of the Bodies of Knowledge

While both Bodies of Knowledge refer to decision-making, neither actively recognises the need for the problem-solving process. To some extent, this is dealt with procedurally through the risk and quality management processes that have been described elsewhere, but there are no specific sections on either of these topics.

PROJECT MANAGEMENT IN PRACTICE
The use of cause–effect–cause analysis

A board meeting was held at the Mighty Sealing Company. There was growing concern about the competitive environment in which the company was operating. Board members were asked to state what they felt the major problems were. They highlighted eight issues. These were:

1 existing market is in decline;
2 sales people do not sell effectively;
3 we have insufficient sales support material;
4 we have an inadequate entry barrier (to the markets in which we operate);
5 we are confused as to which products we should sell;
6 we are unable to exploit new markets;
7 we do not really understand our market environment;
8 there is increasing competition.

These problems or 'undesirable effects' (UDEs) provided the basis for constructing the logic diagram (the 'current reality tree'). Other entities (or logic elements) were introduced to the tree to clarify the logic (see Figure 9.12). The current reality tree shows that there are many effects (including the most significant – the decline in sales volume), but that there is one major cause over which the company has some control – UDE no. 7 [we do not really understand our market environment]. This finding provided the basis for the next steps.

In order to start to resolve the issues faced, the same form of logic diagramming was used. The result: the 'future reality tree' where the root causes are put in place to result in a particular desired effect (in this case sales volume grows). This is shown in Figure 9.13.

→

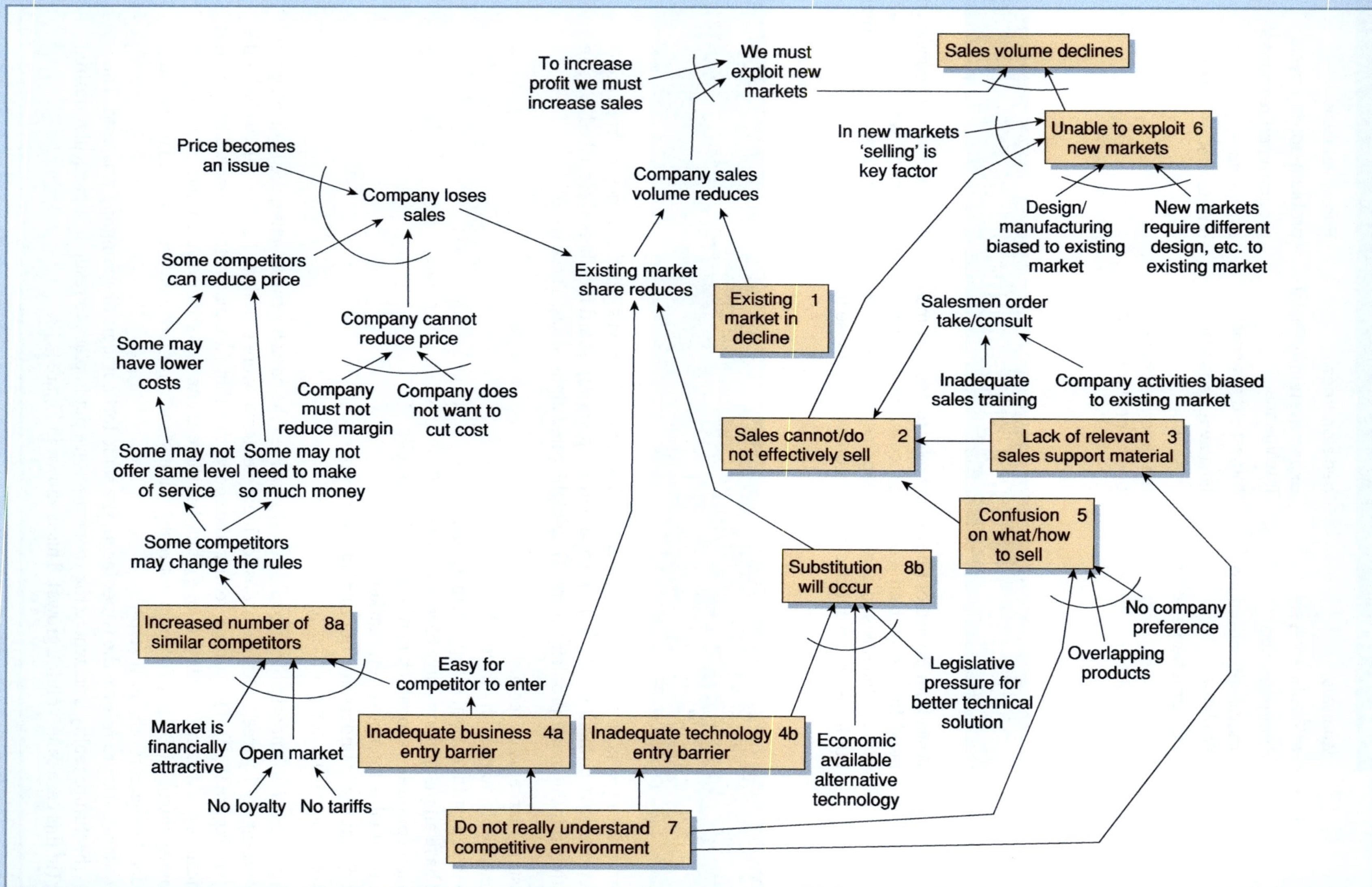

Figure 9.12 Current reality tree

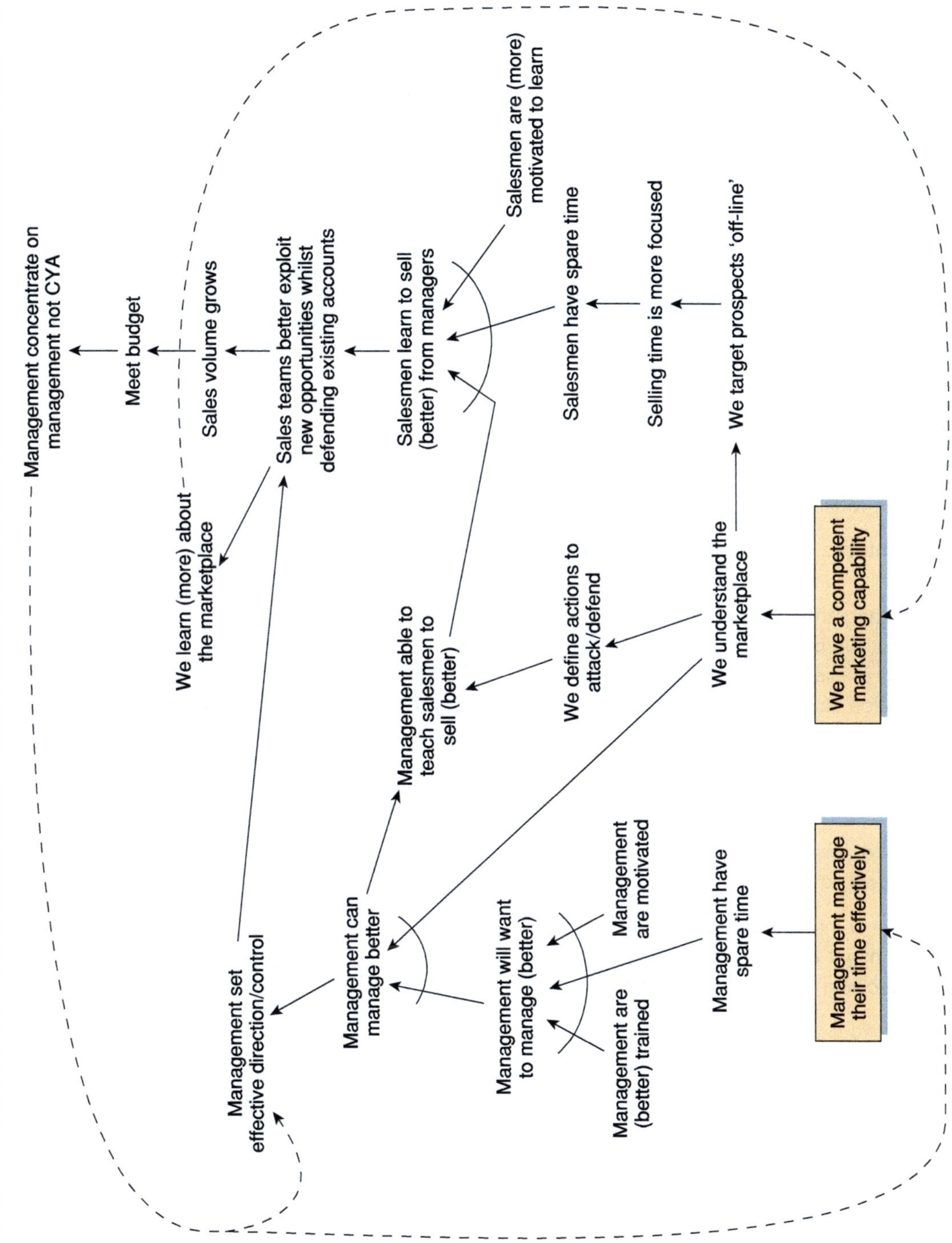

Figure 9.13 Future reality tree: selling effectiveness

The method shown allowed a complex problem to be addressed in a systematic way, and initiatives put in place to help understand the processes that were taking place. How these would contribute to the desired objective could then be mapped.[10]

Points for discussion

1 What is the benefit of constructing a 'current reality tree'?

2 Why is it necessary to insert additional elements into the tree?

3 Why would focusing on 'selling effectiveness' lead to a better understanding of the market?

4 Evaluate the 'future reality tree' – does it resolve the UDEs listed at the start of the exercise?

Topics for discussion

1 Discuss the statement made by Price in the introduction to this chapter that 'Man is a risk-addicted animal'.

2 How might the tools outlined in this chapter reduce the risk in decision-making?

3 Show the advantages of having preprogrammed actions:

(a) as part of a health and safety policy – for example, in the event of a fire
(b) in the handling of client enquiries
(c) for the installation of new work procedures.

4 Show the effect of time on problem-solving and give practical examples of each of the different timescales.

5 What is the role of 'brainstorming' and how might it be used to greatest effect?

6 What are the major inputs to the decision-making process and how might these be best harnessed to ensure that the decision-making process is effective?

7 What are the basic forms of systems model? Give an example of each and their role in a project environment.

8 As a project manager in a development activity for a new range of computer software, discuss how uncertainty may be handled.

9 You are the coordinator of a moderately complex project. The following problems have arisen during the execution phase of previous projects with the resulting delays as shown. Use an appropriate technique to show which of the problems you would focus your attention on and show the results of your analysis graphically.

	Problem	*Delay (days)*
A	Late delivery from suppliers	36
B	Last-minute redesign of assembly due to customer change of specification	7
C	Suppliers fail to meet the quality levels required in goods supplied	41
D	Schedule did not leave enough time for testing	5
E	Components did not fit together when assembled	6
F	Customer rejected initial trial system	12
G	Engineer left team during the project	16
H	Office move was scheduled for during the completion phase	5
J	Hauliers' firm sacked by customer due to dispute over delivery times	3

10 Select a problem with which you have been involved, and use the Ishikawa/fishbone diagram to structure the causes of the problem. Indicate what you feel to be the biggest causal factor.

Further information

Adair, J. (2009) *Effective Decision Making: The Essential Guide to Thinking for Management Success*, Pan Books, London.

Cooke, S. and Slack, N. (1991) *Making Management Decisions*, 2nd edition, Prentice Hall International, Hemel Hempstead.

Goldratt, E. (1995) *It's Not Luck*, North River Press, New York.

Goodwin, P. and Wright, P. (2003) *Decision Analysis for Management Judgement*, John Wiley & Sons, Chichester.

Littlechild, S.C. and Shutler, M.F. (eds) (1991) *Operations Research in Management*, Prentice Hall, Englewood Cliffs, NJ.

Nutt, P. and Wilson, D. (2009) *Handbook of Decision Making*, Blackwell, Oxford.

Price, F. (1984) *Right First Time*, Wildwood House, London, p. 66.

Rivett, P. (1994) *The Craft of Decision Modelling*, Wiley, Chichester.

References

1 Hancock, D.J. (2004) 'What New Skills Must Project Managers Master to Deliver Successful Project Outcomes for the Future?', Engineering Management Conference 2004, *IEEE International*, Vol. 3, pp. 944–948.

2 Drucker, P. (1956) 'How to Make a Business Decision', *Nation's Business*, The Chamber of Commerce of the US.

3 Jennings, D. and Wattam, S. (1994) *Decision-Making: An Integrated Approach*, Pitman Publishing, London.

4 Winter, M. and Sczepanek, A. (2009) *Images of Projects*, Gower Publishing, Aldershot.

5 For a detailed discussion of linear and integer programming, and queueing theory, see for example Anderson, D.R., Sweeney, D.J. and Williams, T.A. (2007) *Quantitative Methods for Business*, Southwestern Publishing, St Paul, MN.

6 Further problem-solving tools may be found in Bicheno, J. (1998) *The Quality 60*, Picsie Books, Buckingham and Mizuno, S. (ed) (1988) *Management for Quality Improvement: The 7 New QC Tools*, Productivity Press, New York.

7 For further developments of this technique see Goldratt, E. (1993) *Theory of Constraints*, North River Press, New York.

8 Greenwood, W.T. (1969) *Decision Theory and Information Systems*, South Western, Mason, OH, pp. 83–104.

9 Curtis, G. and Cobham, D. (2004) *Business Information Systems*, 5th edition, FT Prentice Hall, Harlow.

10 For further discussion and elaboration of these techniques see Scheinkopf, L. (2003) *Thinking for a Change*, St Lucie Press, Boca Raton, FL.

Chapter 10

Developing a Solution - Research Methods

Learning outcomes

By the end of this chapter you should be able to:

- understand the importance of your decisions when designing research and the need to achieve methodological coherence throughout your research design;
- explain the differences between quantitative, qualitative and mixed methods research designs and choose between these;
- explain the differences between exploratory, descriptive, explanatory and evaluative research;
- identify the main research strategies and choose from among these to achieve coherence throughout your research design;
- consider the implications of the time frames required for different research designs;
- consider some of the main ethical issues implied by your research design;
- understand criteria to evaluate research quality and consider these when designing your research;
- consider the constraints of your role as researcher when designing your research.

10.1 Introduction

We introduced the research onion as a way of depicting the issues underlying your choice of data collection method or methods and peeled away the outer two layers – research philosophy and approach to theory development. In this chapter we uncover the next three layers: methodological choice, research strategy or strategies and choosing the time horizon for your research. The way you answer your research question will be influenced by your research philosophy and approach to theory development. Your research philosophy and approach to theory development, whether this is deliberate or by default, will subsequently influence your selections shown in the next three layers of the research onion

(Figure 10.1). These three layers can be thought of as focusing on the process of research design, which is the way you turn your research question into a research project. The key to these selections will be to achieve coherence all the way through your research design.

10.2 Choice and coherence in research design

Your **research design** is the general plan of how you will go about answering your research question(s) (the importance of clearly defining the research question cannot be overemphasised). It will contain clear objectives derived from your research question(s), specify the sources from which you intend to collect data, how you propose to collect and analyse these, and discuss

Travelling downriver
Source: © Jan Thornhill 2015

The cover photographs of recent editions of this book have indicated that the research process is like a journey – a journey along a road with you as the driver of the vehicle. Like many such journeys, there is generally a choice of roads to travel along. When you are thinking about setting out on a new journey of some distance, you will probably find a road map and look at the options to get to your destination. A number of factors may influence your decision about which route to take, including speed, time, cost and your preference between taking the shortest route or staying on the motorway network and main roads. The route you plan is likely to be as coherent as you can work out from the map in front of you given your travel criteria. As you actually undertake your journey you will find yourself interacting with the reality of your planned route. Some parts of the journey will go according to plan; other parts may not and you may need to alter your route. You may change your route because a better option presents itself as you travel along. In many ways, designing research is like planning a journey. Formulating the most appropriate way to address your research question is similar to planning the route to your destination, your research objectives are a little like your planning criteria, the need for coherence is the same in each situation and the journey itself, like the research process, will necessarily prove to be an interactive experience.

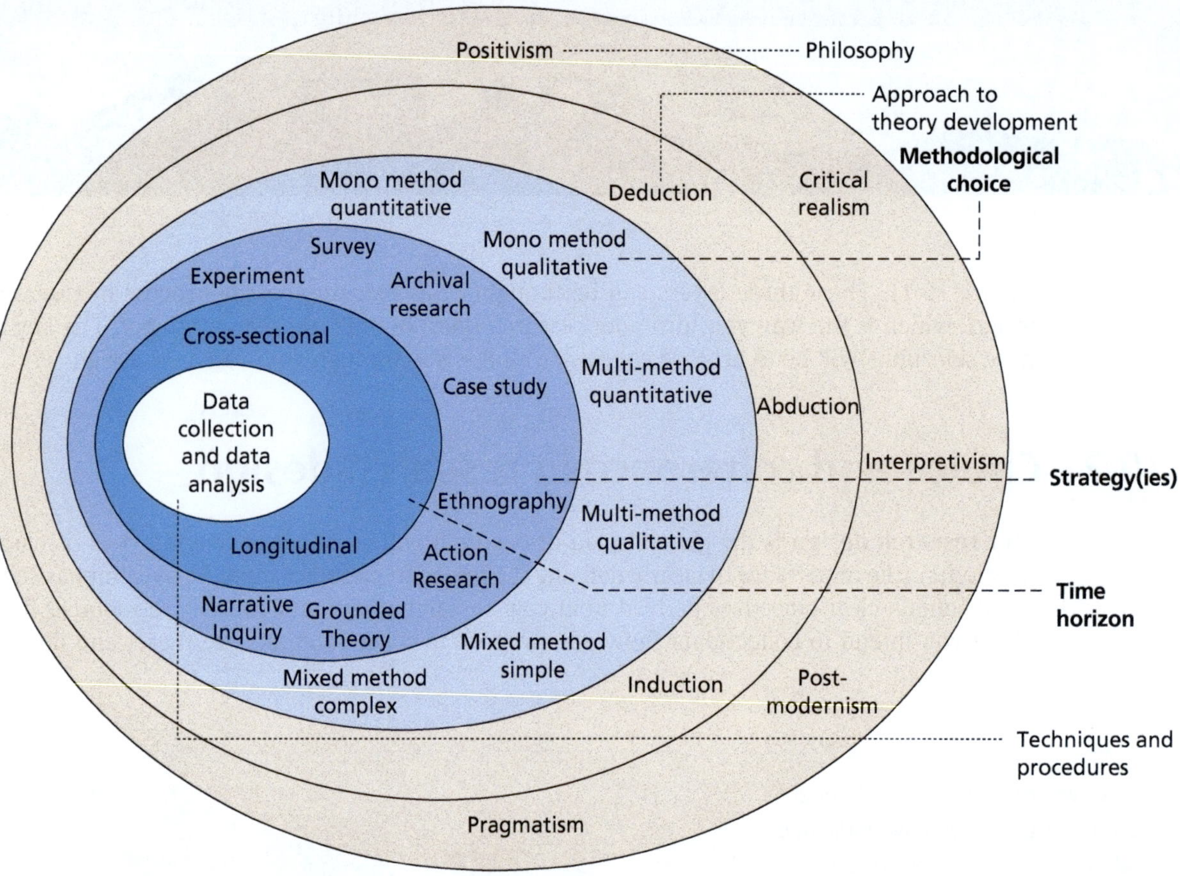

Figure 10.1 The research onion

Source: © 2015 Mark Saunders, Philip Lewis and Adrian Thornhill

ethical issues and the constraints you will inevitably encounter (e.g. access to data, time, location and money). Crucially, it should demonstrate that you have thought through the elements of your particular research design.

The first methodological choice is whether you follow a quantitative, qualitative or mixed methods research design. Each of these options is likely to call for a different mix of elements to achieve coherence in your research design. We return to consider what this involves in Section 10.3. The nature of your research project will also be either exploratory, descriptive, explanatory, evaluative or a combination of these, and we discuss the role of these in your research design in Section 10.4. Within your research design you will need to use one or more research strategies, to ensure coherence within your research project. We discuss research strategies, their fit to research philosophy and to quantitative, qualitative or mixed methods methodological choices in Section 10.5. Your methodological choice and related strategies will also influence the selection of an appropriate time horizon, and we consider this in Section 10.6. Each research design will lead to potential ethical concerns and it will be important to consider these, in order to minimise or overcome them. We briefly consider ethical issues related to research designs in Section 10.7. It is also important to establish the quality of your research design, and we discuss the ways in which this may be considered in Section 10.8. Finally, we recognise that practical constraints will affect research design, especially the nature of your own role as researcher, and briefly consider this in Section 10.9.

These aspects of your research design are vital to understand what you wish to achieve and how you intend to do so, even if your design changes subsequently. You are likely to be assessed at this stage of your research project by your university or examining institution and your research design will need to achieve a pass standard before you are allowed to proceed. You therefore need to have a clear design with valid reasons for each of your research design decisions. Your justification for each element should be based on the nature of your research question(s) and objectives, show consistency with your research philosophy and demonstrate coherence across your research design.

It is useful at this point to recognise a distinction between design and tactics. Design is concerned with the overall plan for your research project; tactics are about the finer details of data collection and analysis – the centre of the research onion. Decisions about tactics will involve you being clear about the different quantitative and qualitative data collection techniques (e.g. questionnaires, interviews, focus groups and secondary data) and subsequent quantitative and qualitative data analysis procedures, which are discussed in later chapters.

We first outline the nature of quantitative, qualitative and mixed methods research and how these may be combined to help you to choose and design your research.

10.3 Methodological choice: the use of a quantitative, qualitative or mixed methods research design

One way of differentiating quantitative research from qualitative research is to distinguish between numeric data (numbers) and non-numeric data (words, images, video clips and other similar material). In this way, 'quantitative' is often used as a synonym for any data collection technique (such as a questionnaire) or data analysis procedure (such as graphs or statistics) that generates or uses numerical data. In contrast, 'qualitative' is often used as a synonym for any data collection technique (such as an interview) or data analysis procedure (such as categorising data) that generates or uses non-numerical data. This is an important way to differentiate this methodological choice; however, this distinction is both problematic and narrow.

It is problematic because, in reality, many business and management research designs are likely to combine quantitative and qualitative elements. This may be for a number of reasons. For example, a research design may use a questionnaire but it may be necessary to ask respondents to answer some 'open' questions in their own words rather than ticking the appropriate box, or it may be necessary to conduct follow-up interviews to seek to explain findings from the questionnaire. Equally, some qualitative research data may be analysed quantitatively, or be used to inform the design of a subsequent questionnaire. In this way, quantitative and qualitative research may be viewed as two ends of a continuum, which in practice are often mixed. A research design may therefore mix methods in a number of ways, which we discuss later.

The distinction drawn earlier between quantitative research and qualitative research is also narrow. Given the way in which your philosophical assumptions inform your methodological choice, the initial distinction drawn earlier between numeric and non-numeric data appears insufficient for the purpose of designing research. From this broader perspective, we can reinterpret quantitative and qualitative methodologies through their associations to philosophical assumptions and also to research approaches and strategies. This will help you to decide how you might use these in a coherent way to address your research question. We now briefly outline some of these key associations.

Quantitative research design

Research philosophy

Quantitative research is generally associated with positivism, especially when used with predetermined and highly structured data collection techniques. However, a distinction needs to be drawn between data about the attributes of people, organisations or other things and data based on opinions, sometimes referred to as 'qualitative' numbers (Box 10.1). In this way, some survey research, while conducted quantitatively, may be seen to fit partly within an interpretivist philosophy. Quantitative research may also be used within the realist and pragmatist philosophies (see 'Mixed methods research design' later).

Approach to theory development

Quantitative research is usually associated with a deductive approach, where the focus is on using data to test theory. However, it may also incorporate an inductive approach, where data are used to develop theory.

Characteristics

Quantitative research examines relationships between variables, which are measured numerically and analysed using a range of statistical and graphical techniques. It often incorporates controls to ensure the validity of data, as in an experimental design. Because data are collected in a standard manner, it is important to ensure that questions are expressed clearly so they are understood in the same way by each participant. This methodology often uses probability sampling techniques to ensure generalisability. The researcher is seen as independent from those being researched, who are usually called respondents.

A quantitative research design may use a single data collection technique, such as a questionnaire, and corresponding quantitative analytical procedure. This is known as a **mono method quantitative study** (Figures 10.1 and 10.2). A quantitative research design may also use more than one quantitative data collection technique and corresponding analytical procedure. This is known as a **multi-method quantitative study** (Figures 10.1 and 10.2). You might, for example, decide to collect quantitative data using both questionnaires and structured observation, analysing these data using statistical (quantitative) procedures. **Multi-method** is the branch of **multiple methods** research that uses more than one quantitative or qualitative method but does not mix the two (Figure 10.2).

Use of multiple methods has been advocated within business and management research (Bryman 2006) because it is likely to overcome weaknesses associated with using only a single or mono method, as well as providing scope for a richer approach to data collection, analysis and interpretation.

Box 10.1 Research in the news

Middle-aged are so downbeat about money

By Norma Cohen

The 45 to 54-year-old cohort have high but increasingly unrealistic expectations and struggle to make sense of their financial futures, reports *Norma Cohen*.

Early middle age, it seems, is the new winter of our discontent.

According to a new study from fund managers BlackRock, people aged 45 to 54 are the most negative about their financial future and the least confident about their ability to control their finances, pay for their children's education or make the right decisions about investments.

That is not what you might expect. The young, embarking on their careers while saddled with heavy debts, and facing a struggle to get on the housing ladder, are more optimistic and in some ways better prepared. Those closest to retirement are content with their lot. But the group who appear to have the best odds of managing their way out of tough times and into a reasonable retirement are thoroughly miserable – in the UK and in other countries.

A close look at data from Britain's Office for National Statistics backs up the hunch that this group is doing fine. On average, wealth is highest among the 45 to 64-year-old age group, remains relatively high among the 65-plus age group, but is lower for households with adults aged 25 to 44 in which children or young adults live, the ONS says in its latest report on household wealth. Roughly a quarter of 45 to 54-year-olds have total household wealth of between £500,000 and £1m – and a further fifth have wealth of more than £1m. That is much higher than younger age groups – and not much lower than for over-65s.

Neither has this group suffered from unemployment; the unemployment rate for those aged 35 to 49 and those aged 50 to 64 has straddled 5 per cent against a national average of 7.7–8.0 per cent. And of the younger group, 92 per cent are participating in work. But this group is much less satisfied with its income than those aged 60 and over, although marginally happier with it than are younger groups. The ONS found they are much more likely to describe their financial situation as "quite or very difficult" than those aged over 55.

Greg Davies, head of behavioural finance at Barclays Wealth, says that the reason the 45 to 54-year-old age group might feel miserable and gloomy may not be because objectively, its finances are deteriorating. Rather, it is just a tough age to be generally.

"This is a pattern we see globally," Mr Davies says, noting that this age group appears glum in happiness surveys in many countries (as it did in the BlackRock one). "There is a U-shaped curve in happiness. It may have nothing to do with their finances."

Source of extracts: Cohen, N. (2013) 'Middle aged Britons are so downbeat about money', *Financial Times*, 02 November.

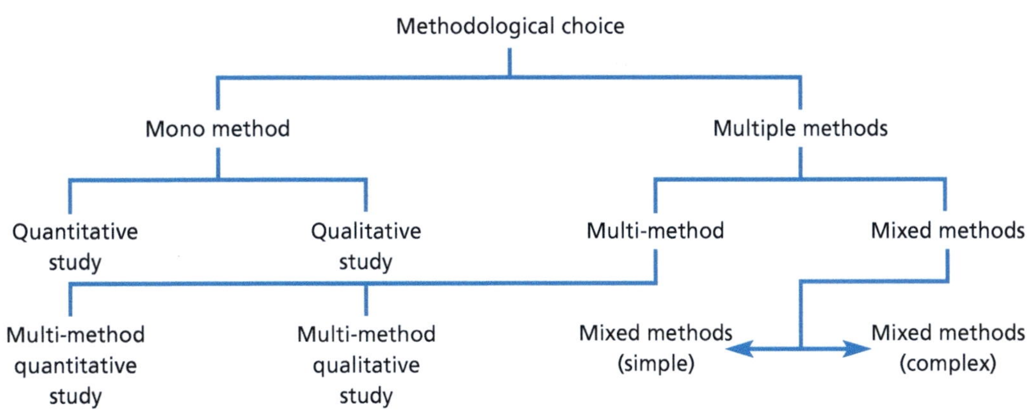

Figure 10.2 Methodological choice

Research strategies

Quantitative research is principally associated with experimental and survey research strategies, which we discuss in Section 10.5. In quantitative research, a survey research strategy is normally conducted through the use of questionnaires or structured interviews or, possibly, structured observation. Techniques associated with the use of these particular methods are considered in Chapter 11.

Qualitative research design

Research philosophy

Qualitative research is often associated with an interpretive philosophy (Denzin and Lincoln 2011). It is interpretive because researchers need to make sense of the subjective and socially constructed meanings expressed about the phenomenon being studied. Such research is sometimes referred to as naturalistic since researchers need to operate within a natural setting, or research context, in order to establish trust, participation, access to meanings and in-depth understanding. Like quantitative research, qualitative research may also be used within realist and pragmatist philosophies (see 'Mixed methods research design' later).

Approach to theory development

Many varieties of qualitative research commence with an inductive approach to theory development, where a naturalistic and emergent research design is used to build theory or to develop a richer theoretical perspective than already exists in the literature. However, some qualitative research strategies start with a deductive approach, to test an existing theory using qualitative procedures (Yin 2014). In practice, much qualitative research uses an abductive approach to theory development where inductive inferences are developed and deductive ones are tested iteratively throughout the research.

Characteristics

Qualitative research studies participants' meanings and the relationships between them, using a variety of data collection techniques and analytical procedures, to develop a conceptual framework and theoretical contribution. Bansal and Corley (2011) point out that while qualitative research is characterised by methodological variations, it remains vital irrespective of the method used to demonstrate methodological rigour and theoretical contribution.

Data collection is non-standardised so that questions and procedures may alter and emerge during a research process that is both naturalistic and interactive. It is likely to use non-probability sampling techniques. The success of the researcher's role is dependent not only on gaining physical access to participants but also building rapport and demonstrating sensitivity to gain cognitive access to their data.

A qualitative research design may use a single data collection technique, such as semi-structured interviews, and corresponding qualitative analytical procedure. This is known as a **mono method qualitative study** (Figures 10.1 and 10.2). A qualitative research design may also use more than one qualitative data collection technique and corresponding analytical procedure. This is known as a **multi-method qualitative study** (Figures 10.1 and 10.2). You might, for example, decide to collect qualitative data using in-depth interviews and diary accounts, analysing these data using qualitative procedures. Box 10.2 provides an example of a multi-method qualitative study.

Box 10.2 Focus on student research

Multi-method qualitative study

Harry wanted to establish how new supervisors learned to do their job. In order to do this he thought it essential that he should have the clearest possible grasp of what the supervisor's job entailed.

This involved him in:

- shadowing a new supervisor for a week (qualitative data);
- interviewing a day and a night shift supervisor to establish any differences in approach (qualitative data);
- interviewing the managers to whom these two supervisors reported (qualitative data).

This gave Harry a much better grasp of the content of the supervisor's job. It also did much to enhance his credibility in the eyes of the supervisors. He was then able to draw on the valuable data he had collected to complete his main research task: interviewing new supervisors to discover how they learned to do the job. This provided further qualitative data.

Research strategies

Qualitative research is associated with a variety of strategies. While these share ontological and epistemological roots and common characteristics, each strategy has a specific emphasis and scope as well as a particular set of procedures. Some of the principal strategies used with qualitative research are: action research, case study research, ethnography, Grounded Theory and narrative research. These are discussed in Section 10.5. Some of these strategies can also be used in a quantitative research design such as a case study strategy, or used in a mixed methods research design as we now discuss. Techniques associated with the use of particular methods are considered in Chapter 11.

Mixed methods research design

Research philosophy

We consider two philosophical positions that often lead to mixed methods research designs. **Mixed methods** research is the branch of multiple methods research that combines the use of quantitative and qualitative data collection techniques and analytical procedures (Figure 10.2).

The philosophical position of realism and in particular that of the critical realists. They believe that while there is an external, objective reality to the world in which we live, the way in which each of us interprets and understands it will be affected by our particular social conditioning. To accommodate this realist ontology and interpretivist epistemology (Tashakkori and Teddlie 2010), researchers may, for example, use quantitative analysis of officially published data followed by qualitative research methods to explore perceptions.

Pragmatism may also be likely to influence a mixed methods research design. Pragmatists view the exclusive adoption of one philosophical position as unhelpful and choose instead to see these as either end of a continuum, allowing a choice of whichever position or mixture of positions will help them to undertake their research (Tashakkori and Teddlie 2010). For pragmatists, the nature of the research question, the research context and likely research consequences are driving forces determining the most appropriate methodological choice (Nastasi et al. 2010). Both quantitative and qualitative research are valued by pragmatists and the exact choice will be contingent on the particular nature of the research.

Approach to theory development

A mixed methods research design may use a deductive, inductive or abductive approach to theory development. For example, quantitative or qualitative research may be used to test a theoretical proposition or propositions, followed by further quantitative or qualitative research to develop a richer theoretical understanding. Theory may also be used to provide direction for the research. In this way a particular theory may be used to provide a focus for the research and to limit its scope (Tashakkori and Teddlie 2010).

Characteristics

In mixed methods research quantitative and qualitative techniques are combined in a variety of ways that range from simple, concurrent forms to more complex and sequential forms (Figure 10.2). The ways in which quantitative and qualitative research may be combined, as well as the extent to which this may occur, have led to the identification of a number of variations of mixed methods research (Creswell and Plano Clark 2011; Nastasi et al. 2010). We now briefly consider these.

Concurrent mixed methods research involves the separate use of quantitative and qualitative methods within a single phase of data collection and analysis (a **single-phase research design**) (Figure 10.3). This allows both sets of results to be interpreted together to provide a richer and more comprehensive response to the research question in comparison to the use of a mono method design. Where you collect qualitative and quantitative data in the same phase of research in order to compare how these data sets support one another, you will be using a **concurrent triangulation design**.

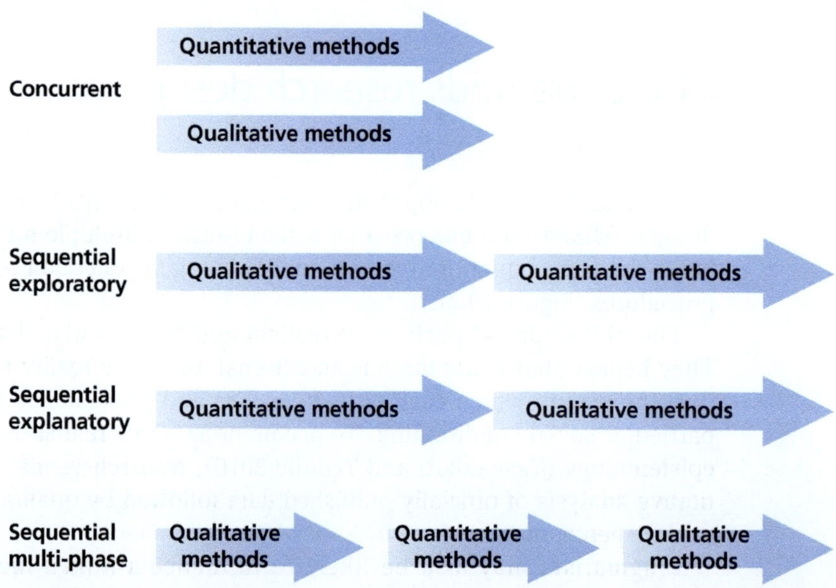

Figure 10.3 Mixed methods research designs

Using a concurrent mixed methods design should provide richer data than a mono method design and be shorter in timescale as well as more practical to undertake than a sequential mixed methods design.

Sequential mixed methods research involves more than one phase of data collection and analysis (Figure 10.3). In this design, the researcher will follow the use of one method with another in order to expand or elaborate on the initial set of findings. In a **double-phase research design** this leads to two alternative mixed methods research strategies, either a **sequential exploratory research design** (qualitative followed by quantitative) or a **sequential explanatory research design** (quantitative followed by qualitative). In a more complex, sequential, **multi-phase design**, mixed methods research will involve multiple phases of data collection and analysis (e.g. qualitative followed by quantitative, then by a further phase of qualitative) (Box 10.3).

Using a double-phase or multi-phase research design suggests a dynamic approach to the research process which recognises that mixed methods research is both interactive and iterative, where one phase subsequently informs and directs the next phase of data collection and analysis. The exact nature of this interaction and iteration in a particular research project may shape the way in which qualitative and quantitative methods are chosen and integrated at each phase of the research (Greene 2007; Nastasi et al. 2010; Ridenour and Newman 2008; Teddlie and Tashakkori 2009).

Where you mix quantitative and qualitative methods at every stage of your research (design, data collection and analysis, interpretation and presentation of the research), you will be using a **fully integrated mixed methods research** design. Where you use

Box 10.3 Focus on student research

Mixed methods research

Andreas conducted research into organisational change in an IT company, using a mixed methods research design. This was designed as a sequential mixed methods research project and consisted of four stages:

1. *Initial exploratory discussions* were held with key senior managers, which combined the purpose of helping to negotiate access, agree the scope of the project and gain essential contextual data. These data were analysed qualitatively in order to get a picture of important internal and external organisational issues.
2. *Individual in-depth interviews* were held with 28 directly employed staff (excluding contractor staff), who formed a sample representing the organisation across its departments and throughout its grade structure. These data were also analysed qualitatively. This was to establish the issues that were important to staff, to help to inform the content of the questionnaire.
3. *A questionnaire* was designed, pilot-tested, amended and then administered to a representative sample of directly employed staff, producing a 42 per cent response rate. The quantitative data produced were analysed statistically to allow the views of employee groups to be compared for differences by age, gender, length of service, occupation and grade. The subsequent production of summary data based on these findings was particularly important to the IT company.
4. A fourth stage consisted of *presentations to groups of employees*. This allowed employees' questions to be answered with care, while continuing to ensure anonymity. It also allowed discussion to occur to clarify the content of some of the questionnaire results. Notes from these presentations were analysed quantitatively.

quantitative and qualitative methods at only one stage or particular stages of your research, you will be using a **partially integrated mixed methods research** approach (Nastasi et al. 2010; Teddlie and Tashakkori 2009, 2011).

Quantitative and qualitative methods may also be 'merged' so that qualitative data are '**quantitised**' (e.g. specific events in the data are counted as frequencies and numerically coded for statistical analysis) and quantitative data are '**qualitised**' (e.g. frequencies are turned into text, although this is extremely rare in practice). Both types of data may also be presented together on a matrix, qualitative data may be presented diagrammatically (Box 11.15) and quantitative data presented using categorisation. This approach to mixing methods may be risky, since there is a danger that the respective value of each form of data may be diluted; for example, excessively 'quantitising' qualitative data may lead to loss of its exploratory or explanatory richness.

Mixed methods research may use quantitative research and qualitative research equally or unequally (Creswell and Plano Clark 2011). In this way, the priority or weight given to either quantitative or qualitative research may vary, so that one methodology has a dominant role, while the other plays a supporting role, depending on the purpose of the research project. This prioritisation may also reflect the preferences of the researcher or the expectations of those who commission the research (such as your project tutor or the managers in an organisation).

The purpose of the research may emphasise the initial use and prioritisation of qualitative research (as in an exploratory study, where qualitative precedes quantitative) or the initial use and prioritisation of quantitative research (as in a descriptive study, before the possible use of supporting qualitative research to explain particular findings further). The overall purpose of the research may also emphasise the dominance of either quantitative or qualitative research (e.g. as in a sequential project which commences with a qualitative, exploratory phase, followed by a quantitative, descriptive phase and which is completed by a further qualitative, explanatory phase). The purpose of other research projects may lead to the more equal use of quantitative and qualitative research methods. The research approach may also lead to the relative prioritisation of either quantitative or qualitative methods. In this way, an inductive approach designed to generate theoretical concepts and to build theory may lead to a greater emphasis on the use of qualitative methods.

Embedded mixed methods research is the term given to the situation where one methodology supports the other (Creswell and Plano Clark 2011). During data collection, this may occur in a number of ways. One methodology may be embedded within the other during a single means to collect data (e.g. some quantitative questions are included in an interview schedule, or some questions within a questionnaire require a qualitative response). This is known as a **concurrent embedded design**. Alternatively, a single-phase research design may use both quantitative and qualitative methods concurrently but collect these separately, one of which will be analysed to support the other. Within a double-phase, sequential research design, both quantitative and qualitative methods will be collected and analysed, one after the other, with one being used in a supporting role.

The characteristics that help to define mixed methods research highlight how quantitative and qualitative methods may be combined in a number of ways to provide you with better opportunities to answer your research question (Tashakkori and Teddlie 2010). Table 10.1 outlines a number of reasons for and advantages of using a mixed methods design. The specific nature of your mixed methods design will be related to particular reasons and advantages.

Box 10.4 summarises how mixed methods have been used in management research.

Table 10.1 Reasons for using a mixed methods design

Reason	Explanation
Initiation	Initial use of a qualitative or quantitative methodology may be used to define the nature and scope of sequential quantitative or qualitative research. May also be used to provide contextual background and to better understand the research problem (e.g. Box 5.3). May also help in the formulation or redrafting of research questions, interview questions and questionnaire items and the selection of samples, cases and participants
Facilitation	During the course of the research, one method may lead to the discovery of new insights which inform and are followed up through the use of the other method
Complementarity	Use of mixed methods may allow meanings and findings to be elaborated, enhanced, clarified, confirmed, illustrated or linked
Interpretation	One method (e.g. qualitative) may be used to help to explain relationships between variables emerging from the other (e.g. quantitative)
Generalisability	Use of mixed methods may help to establish the generalisability of a study or its relative importance. In a similar way the use of mixed methods may help to establish the credibility of a study or to produce more complete knowledge (Section 5.8)
Diversity	Use of mixed methods may allow for a greater diversity of views to inform and be reflected in the study
Problem solving	Use of an alternative method may help when the initial method reveals unexplainable results or insufficient data
Focus	One method may be used to focus on one attribute (e.g. quantitative on macro aspects), while the other method may be used to focus on another attribute (e.g. qualitative on micro aspects)
Triangulation	Mixed methods may be used in order to combine data to ascertain if the findings from one method mutually corroborate the findings from the other method (Section 5.8)
Confidence	Findings may be affected by the method used. Use of a single method will make it impossible to ascertain the nature of that effect. To seek to cancel out this 'method effect', it is advisable to use mixed methods. This should lead to greater confidence in your conclusions

Source: Developed from Bryman (2006), Greene et al. (1989), Molina-Azorin (2011) and authors' experience

Research design

As we have just discussed, different combinations of mixed methods research characteristics lead to various research designs. The principal mixed methods research designs summarised earlier in this section are: concurrent triangulation design, concurrent embedded design, sequential exploratory design, sequential explanatory design (Creswell 2009; Creswell and Plano Clark 2011) and sequential, multi-phase design. Quantitative

Box 10.4 Focus on management research

Use of mixed methods in strategic management research

It is interesting to note the findings of Molina-Azorin (2012), who analysed the methodologies used in articles published in the *Strategic Management Journal* from 1980 to 2006. Out of 1086 empirical articles published in this journal during this period, 165 used a mixed methods approach (15.2%). Of these, one method was used in a dominant role in just over 80 per cent (134) of these mixed methods-based articles. Quantitative methods dominated in 129 of these 134 cases. A sequential research design also dominated over the use of a concurrent research design, used in 150 of these 165 articles (90%). It is interesting to speculate how the use of mixed methods research may vary in other business and management subject areas.

Molina-Azorin (2012) also found that these mixed methods articles attracted more citations in subsequent publications than a comparison group of mono method-based articles. He believes this may be explained by the enhanced value of mixed methods research. The use of qualitative as well as quantitative methods may enhance theory development, allow the research context to be better understood, permit case-specific variables to be better identified and encourage the research process to produce analytical outcomes to a greater extent than might be the case with a mono method design (Molina-Azorin 2012).

data collection techniques and analysis procedures that may be used as part of mixed methods research are considered in Chapter 11 and qualitative techniques and procedures that may be used as part of mixed methods research are considered in Chapter 11.

10.4 Recognising the purpose of your research design

In Section 10.3 we referred to your research following an exploratory or explanatory purpose. Research can be designed to fulfil either an exploratory, descriptive, explanatory or evaluative purpose, or some combination of these. We encouraged you to think about your research project in terms of the question you wish to answer and your research objectives. The way in which you ask your research question will inevitably involve you in exploratory, descriptive, explanatory or evaluative research. The purpose of your research may also change over time.

In this section we discuss each purpose in more detail to help you to choose which of these is appropriate to the nature of your research project.

Exploratory studies

An **exploratory study** is a valuable means to ask open questions to discover what is happening and gain insights about a topic of interest. Research questions that are exploratory are likely to begin with 'What' or 'How'. Questions that you ask during data collection to explore an issue, problem or phenomenon will also be likely to start with 'What' or 'How'. An exploratory study is particularly useful if you wish to clarify your understanding of an issue, problem or phenomenon, such as if you are unsure of its precise nature. It may be that time is well spent on exploratory research, as it might show that the research is not worth pursuing!

There are a number of ways to conduct exploratory research. These include a search of the literature; interviewing 'experts' in the subject; conducting in-depth individual interviews or conducting focus group interviews. Because of their exploratory nature, these interviews are likely to be relatively unstructured and to rely on the quality of the contributions from those who participate to help guide the subsequent stage of your research.

Exploratory research has the advantage that it is flexible and adaptable to change. If you are conducting exploratory research you must be willing to change your direction as a result of new data that appear and new insights that occur to you. A quotation from the travel writer V.S. Naipaul (1989: 222) illustrates this point beautifully:

> I had been concerned, at the start of my own journey, to establish some lines of enquiry, to define a theme. The approach had its difficulties. At the back of my mind was always a worry that I would come to a place and all contacts would break down . . . If you travel on a theme the theme has to develop with the travel. At the beginning your interests can be broad and scattered. But then they must be more focused; the different stages of a journey cannot simply be versions of one another. And . . . this kind of travel depended on luck. It depended on the people you met, the little illuminations you had. As with the next day's issue of fast-moving daily newspapers, the shape of the character in hand was continually being changed by accidents along the way.

Exploratory research may commence with a broad focus but this will become narrower as the research progresses.

Descriptive studies

The purpose of **descriptive research** is to gain an accurate profile of events, persons or situations. Research questions that are descriptive are likely to begin with, or include, either 'Who', 'What', 'Where', 'When' or 'How'. Questions that you ask during data collection to gain a description of events, persons or situations will also be likely to start with, or include, 'Who', 'What', 'Where', 'When' or 'How'. Descriptive research may be an extension of a piece of exploratory research or a forerunner to a piece of explanatory research. It is necessary to have a clear picture of the phenomenon on which you wish to collect data prior to the collection of the data. One of the earliest well-known examples of a descriptive survey is the *Domesday Book*, which described the population of England in 1085.

Often project tutors are rather wary of work that is too descriptive. There is a danger of their saying 'That's very interesting . . . but so what?' They will want you to go further and draw conclusions from the data you are describing. They will encourage you to develop the skills of evaluating data and synthesising ideas. These are higher-order skills than those of accurate description. Description in business and management research has a very clear place. However, it should be thought of as a means to an end rather than an end in itself. This means that if your research project utilises description it is likely to be a precursor to explanation. Such studies are known as **descripto-explanatory** studies.

Explanatory studies

Studies that establish causal relationships between variables may be termed **explanatory research**. Research questions that seek explanatory answers are likely to begin with, or include, 'Why' or 'How'. Questions that you ask during data collection to gain an explanatory response will also be likely to start with, or include, 'Why' or 'How'.

The emphasis in explanatory research is to study a situation or a problem in order to explain the relationships between variables. You may find, for example, that a cursory analysis of quantitative data on manufacturing scrap rates shows a relationship between scrap rates and the age of the machine being operated. You could go ahead and subject the data to statistical tests such as correlation in order to get a clearer view of the relationship. As an alternative example, you might collect qualitative data to explain the reasons why customers of your company rarely pay their bills according to the prescribed payment terms.

Evaluative studies

The purpose of **evaluative research** is to find out how well something works. Research questions that seek to evaluate answers are likely to begin with 'How', or include 'What', in the form of 'To what extent'. Evaluative research in business and management is likely to be concerned with assessing the effectiveness of an organisational or business strategy, policy, programme, initiative or process. This may relate to any area of the organisation or business: for example, evaluating a marketing campaign, a personnel policy, a costing strategy, the delivery of a support service.

Questions that you ask during data collection to seek an evaluative understanding will be likely to start with, or include, 'What', 'How' or 'Why'. As part of your evaluative study you may also be interested to make comparisons between events, situations, groups, places or periods, so that you are interested to ask questions that include 'Which', 'When', 'Who' or 'Where'. Asking such questions would help you to compare the effectiveness of, say, an advertising campaign in different locations or between different groups of consumers. In this way, evaluative research allows you assess performance and to compare this. An evaluative study may produce a theoretical contribution where emphasis is placed on understanding not only 'how effective' something is, but also 'why', and then comparing this explanation to existing theory.

Combined studies

A research study may combine more than one purpose in its design. This may be achieved by the use of mixed methods in the research design (Section 10.3), to facilitate some combination of exploratory, descriptive, explanatory or evaluative research. Alternatively a single method research design may be used in a way that provides scope to facilitate more than one purpose. Box 10.5 describes a qualitative study that used relatively unstructured interviews to facilitate collection of data that were exploratory, descriptive and explanatory.

Box 10.5 Focus on management research

Demonstrating an exploratory, descriptive and explanatory purpose in a study about workplace bullying

Jenkins and colleagues (2012) undertook an unusual study into workplace bullying which focused on the perspective of those accused of this behaviour. Their study published in the *British Journal of Management* is based on an analysis of interviews conducted with 24 managers accused of workplace bullying. They describe how many of these accused managers reported that their places of work were highly stressful, and marked by staff shortages, unclear roles, conflict and wide-ranging improper workplace behaviours.

Jenkins et al. (2012: 491) commenced their research with a stated aim and two research questions. Their research aim was 'to elicit the views, perceptions and attributions of the alleged perpetrator, helping to bridge the gap between perpetrator- and target-orientated approaches to examining workplace bullying'. Their research questions were: '(1) What behaviours have the accused bullies been accused of? Do these behaviours fit the recognised definitions of workplace bullying? (2) How do the accused bullies describe the complainants' behaviour?' They describe their study as being exploratory, in order to seek to understand the perceptions and experiences of those accused of workplace bullying. However, the article demonstrates that the scope of their research project was not only exploratory but also descriptive and explanatory. To understand this phenomenon they used semi-structured interviews that allowed (from the perspective of an alleged perpetrator) behaviours to be described and workplace factors to be discussed. These led to explanation building for some aspects of these behaviours during the analysis of the data collected.

Jenkins et al. describe how they used an analytical approach that identified themes in their data and then examined how these related to existing theory in relevant literature. In this way, the results from their study confirmed the importance of organisational climate and workplace pressures as contributory, if not causal, factors in the incidence of workplace bullying – a relationship also identified from research on workplace bullying that focuses on the perspective of those being bullied. However, Jenkins et al. report that the results of their study may raise doubts about some accepted relationships about workplace bullying: notably that workplace bullying is necessarily downward (they report descriptions of upward bullying) and that the demarcation between being a perpetrator and a target of bullying may in some cases be ill defined.

The study demonstrates how a combination of exploratory, descriptive and explanatory research helps to generate a theoretical contribution.

10.5 Choosing a research strategy or strategies

The different research strategies

In this section we turn our attention to your choice of **research strategy** (Figure 10.1). In general terms, a strategy is a plan of action to achieve a goal. A research strategy may therefore be defined as a plan of how a researcher will go about answering her or his research question. It is the methodological link between your philosophy and subsequent choice of methods to collect and analyse data (Denzin and Lincoln 2011).

Different research traditions have led to a number of possible research strategies, as we outlined earlier. In Section 10.3 we outlined the research strategies that are principally linked with quantitative, qualitative and mixed methods research designs, respectively. Particular research strategies may be associated with one of the philosophies and also a deductive or inductive approach; however, we also recognised in Section 10.3 that there are often open boundaries between research philosophies, research approaches and research strategies. In a similar way, a particular research strategy should not be seen as inherently superior or inferior to any other. Consequently, we believe that what is most important is not attaching labels for their own sake, or linking research elements to try to be methodologically aloof. For us, the key to your choice of research strategy or strategies is that you achieve a reasonable level of coherence throughout your research design which will enable you to answer your particular research question(s) and meet your objectives. Your choice of research strategy will therefore be guided by your research question(s) and objectives, the coherence with which these link to your philosophy, research approach and purpose, and also to more pragmatic concerns including the extent of existing knowledge, the amount of time and other resources you have available and access to potential participants and to other sources of data. Finally, it must be remembered that these strategies should not be thought of as being mutually exclusive. For example, it is quite possible to use the survey strategy within a case study, or combine a number of different strategies within mixed methods.

The first two research strategies in the list below that we consider in this section are principally or exclusively linked to a quantitative research design. The next two may involve quantitative or qualitative research, or a mixed design combining both. The final four strategies are principally or exclusively linked to a qualitative research design.

In our experience it is the choice between qualitative research strategies that is likely to cause the greatest confusion. Such confusion is often justified given the diversity of qualitative strategies (many more than those we consider), with their conflicting tensions and 'blurred genres' (Denzin and Lincoln 2011: 3). In our discussion we draw out the distinctions between these strategies to allow you to make an informed choice between qualitative strategies (as between or across quantitative and qualitative strategies). This is intended to help you avoid the vague assertion that you are 'doing qualitative research', without any further qualification! The strategies we discuss are:

- Experiment;
- Survey;
- Archival and Documentary Research;
- Case Study;
- Ethnography;
- Action Research;
- Grounded Theory;
- Narrative Inquiry.

Experiment

We start with discussion of the experiment strategy because its roots in natural science, laboratory-based research and the precision required to conduct it mean that the 'experiment' is often seen as the 'gold standard' against which the rigour of other strategies is assessed. **Experiment** is a form of research that owes much to the natural sciences, although it features strongly in psychological and social science research. The purpose of an experiment is to study the probability of a change in an **independent variable** causing a change in another, **dependent variable**. Table 10.2 provides a description of types of variable. An experiment uses predictions, known as hypotheses, rather than research questions. This is because the researcher anticipates whether or not a relationship will exist between

Table 10.2 Types of variable

Variable	Meaning
Independent (IV)	Variable that is being manipulated or changed to measure its impact on a dependent variable
Dependent (DV)	Variable that may change in response to changes in other variables; observed outcome or result from manipulation of another variable
Mediating (MV)	A variable located between the independent and dependent variables, which explains the relationship between them (IV → MV → DV)
Moderator	A new variable that is introduced which will affect the nature of the relationship between the IV and DV
Control	Additional observable and measurable variables that need to be kept constant to avoid them influencing the effect of the IV on the DV
Confounding	Extraneous but difficult to observe or measure variables that can potentially undermine the inferences drawn between the IV and DV. Need to be considered when discussing results, to avoid spurious conclusions

the variables. Two types of (opposing) hypothesis are formulated in a standard experiment: the **null hypothesis** and the **alternative hypothesis** (often referred to as the **hypothesis**). The null hypothesis predicts that there will not be a significant difference or relationship between the variables. An example of a null hypothesis might be that:

> customer services training of IT telephone support staff will not lead to a significant improvement in users' satisfaction feedback.

The alternative hypothesis predicts that there may be a significant difference or relationship between the variables. An example of a (directional) alternative hypothesis might be that:

> customer services training of IT telephone support staff will lead to a significant improvement in users' satisfaction feedback.

In an experiment, it is the null hypothesis that is tested statistically. Where the probability of there being no statistical difference is greater than a prescribed value (usually 0.05), the null hypothesis is accepted and the alternative hypothesis is rejected. Where the probability is less than or equal to the prescribed value (usually 0.05), this indicates that the alternative hypothesis is likely to be true. The simplest experiments are concerned with whether there is a link between two variables. More complex experiments also consider the size of the change and the relative importance of two or more independent variables. Experiments therefore tend to be used in exploratory and explanatory research to answer 'what', 'how' and 'why' questions.

Different experimental designs may be used, each with different advantages and disadvantages, particularly in relation to **control variables** and **confounding variables** (Table 10.2). Experimental designs include classical experiments, quasi-experiments and within-subject designs. In a **classical experiment**, a sample of participants is selected and then randomly assigned to either an experimental group or to the control group. In the **experimental group**, some form of planned intervention or manipulation will be tested. In the **control group**, no such intervention is made. Random assignment means each group should be similar in all aspects relevant to the research other than whether or not they are exposed to the planned intervention or manipulation. In assigning the members to the control and experimental groups at random and using a control group, you try to control (that is, remove) the possible effects of an alternative explanation to the planned intervention (manipulation) and eliminate threats to internal validity. This is because the control group is subject to exactly the same external influences as the experimental group other than the planned intervention and, consequently, this intervention is the only explanation for any changes to the dependent variable.

A **quasi-experiment** will still use an experimental group(s) and a control group, but the researcher will not randomly assign participants to each group, perhaps because participants are only available in pre-formed groups (e.g. existing work groups). Differences in participants between groups may be minimised by the use of matched pairs. **Matched pair analysis** leads to a participant in an experimental group being paired with a participant in the control group based on matching factors such as age, gender, occupation, length of service, grade etc., to try to minimise the effect of extraneous variables on the experiment's outcomes. Those factors relevant to the nature of the experiment will need to be matched.

The basic experimental procedure in classical and quasi-experiments is the same (Figure 10.4), with the exception of random assignment, and we illustrate this procedure with an example related to the introduction of a sales promotion. The dependent variable in this example, purchasing behaviour, is measured for members of both the experimental group and control group before any intervention occurs. This provides a **pre-test** measure of purchasing behaviour. A planned intervention is then made to members of the experimental group in the form of a 'buy two, get one free' promotion. In the control group, no such intervention is made. The dependent variable, purchasing behaviour, is measured after the manipulation of the independent variable (the use of the 'buy two, get one free' promotion) for both the experimental group and the control group, so that a pre-test and **post-test** comparison can be made. On the basis of this comparison, any difference between the experimental and control groups for the dependent variable (purchasing behaviour) is attributed to the intervention of the 'buy two, get one free' promotion. This experimental approach is known as a **between-subjects design**, where participants belong to either the experimental group or control group but not both. In a between-subjects design, if more than one intervention or manipulation is to be tested, a separate experimental group will be required for each test (known as **independent measures**). For example, if the experiment was designed to compare two separate interventions, such as a 'buy one, get one free' as well as the 'buy two, get one free' manipulation, two experimental groups would be required alongside the control group.

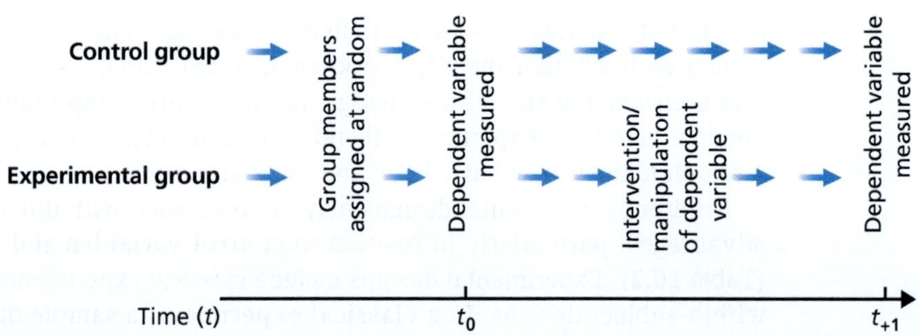

Figure 10.4 A Classical experiment strategy

In a **within-subjects design**, or within-group design, there will be only a single group, rather than a separation into an experimental group and a control group. In this approach every participant is exposed to the planned intervention or series of interventions. For this reason, this approach is known as **repeated measures**. The procedure involves a pre-intervention observation or measurement, to establish a baseline (or control for the dependent variable). This is followed by a planned intervention (independent variable) and subsequent observation and measurement (related to the dependent variable). Following the withdrawal of the intervention and a period of 'reversal', to allow a return to the baseline, a further planned intervention may be attempted followed by subsequent observation and measurement. A within-subject design may be more practical than a between-subjects design because it requires fewer participants, but it may lead to carryover effects where familiarity or fatigue with the process distorts the validity of the findings. This may lead to a counterbalanced design, where some of the participants undertake tasks in a different order to see if familiarity or fatigue affects the outcomes.

Often experiments, including those in disciplines closely associated with business and management such as organisational psychology, are conducted in laboratories rather than in the field. This means that you have greater control over aspects of the research process such as sample selection and the context within which the experiment occurs. However, while this improves the **internal validity** of the experiment, that is, the extent to which the findings can be attributed to the interventions rather than any flaws in your research design, **external validity** is likely to be more difficult to establish (we discuss issues of validity in Section 10.8). Laboratory settings, by their very nature, are unlikely to be related to the real world of organisations. As a consequence, the extent to which the findings from a laboratory experiment are able to be generalised to all organisations is likely to be lower than for a field-(organisation-) based experiment.

The feasibility of using an experimental strategy will depend on the nature of your research question. As we noted, an experiment uses predictive hypotheses rather than open research questions. It may be appropriate to turn your question into hypotheses where you wish to test for expected relationships between variables. However, most business and management research questions will be designed to inquire into the relationships between variables, rather than to test a predicted relationship. This indicates the difference between experiments and other research strategies. Within quantitative research designs, it highlights a key difference between an experimental strategy and a survey strategy.

Survey

The **survey** strategy is usually associated with a deductive research approach. It is a popular and common strategy in business and management research and is most frequently used to answer 'what', 'who', 'where', 'how much' and 'how many' questions. It therefore tends to be used for exploratory and descriptive research. Survey strategies using questionnaires are popular as they allow the collection of standardised data from a sizeable population in a highly economical way, allowing easy comparison. In addition, the survey strategy is perceived as authoritative by people in general and is comparatively easy both to explain and to understand. Every day a news bulletin, news website or newspaper reports the results of a new survey that is designed to find out how a population thinks or behaves in relation to a particular issue (Box 10.6).

Box 10.6 Focus on research in the news

Shoppers turn to web for deals

By Scheherazade Daneshkhu

Consumers with Internet access in developing countries are just as likely to search for money-saving grocery deals to beat food price inflation as those in the developed world, according to a new report.

The online survey of 29,000 shoppers in 58 countries conducted by Nielsen, the global information company, showed many similarities in behaviour no matter where the consumer lives – but also striking differences.

In the US, half of those who responded said they would stock up on sale items as a way of beating inflation compared to one-third in the Asia-Pacific region, possibly reflecting space and transport differences.

But social media plays a bigger role in developing countries. In South Africa and South Korea, 43 per cent said they would use social media to find online deals compared to 20 per cent in the US and 24 per cent in Canada.

Overall, 32 per cent of shoppers in developing countries said they would turn to the internet as a tool to beat food price inflation, only fractionally below the 33 per cent in developed economies.

Since the survey was based on respondents with online access, Nielsen said the results indicated that "consumers in developing regions actually outperformed those in developed markets for their intention to use online sources to search for deals".

FT *Source of extract:* Daneshkhu, S. and Consumer Industries Editor (2013) 'Emerging markets shoppers turn to web for deals', *Financial Times*, 13 October. Copyright The Financial Times Limited

The survey strategy allows you to collect quantitative data which you can analyse quantitatively using descriptive and inferential statistics. In addition, data collected using a survey strategy can be used to suggest possible reasons for particular relationships between variables and to produce models of these relationships. Using a survey strategy should give you more control over the research process and, when probability sampling is used, it is possible to generate findings that are statistically representative of the whole population at a lower cost than collecting the data for the whole population. You will need to spend time ensuring that your sample is representative, designing and piloting your data collection instrument and trying to ensure a good response rate. Preparing and analysing the data will also be time consuming, even with readily available analysis software. However, it will be your time and, once you have collected your data, you will be independent. Many researchers complain that their progress is delayed by their dependence on others for information.

The data collected using a survey strategy is unlikely to be as wide ranging as those collected by other research strategies. For example, there is a limit to the number of questions that any questionnaire can contain if the goodwill of the respondent is not to be presumed on too much. Despite this, perhaps the biggest drawback with using a questionnaire as part of a survey strategy is the capacity to do it badly!

The questionnaire, however, is not the only data collection technique that belongs to the survey strategy. Structured observation, of the type most frequently associated with organisation and methods (O&M) research, and structured interviews, where standardised questions are asked of all interviewees, also often fall into this strategy.

Archival and documentary research

The digitalisation of data and the creation of online archives have increased the scope for you to use an archival or documentary research strategy. Because of the Internet and the digitalisation of university-based, governmental, organisational and media documents and other data, it is now possible to access such sources from around the world. This potentially provides you with considerable scope to design a research project that capitalises on a wide range of available data sources. There are limitations in attempting to use this strategy and we briefly consider these after outlining types of documentary sources and discussing their attributes.

It is difficult to describe adequately the range of archival and documentary sources potentially available. Lee (2012: 391) suggests that 'a document is a durable repository for textual, visual and audio representations'. This illustrates the wide range of sources encompassed by this definition. Categories of textual documents include:

- communications between individuals or within groups such as email, letters, social media and blog postings;
- individual records such as diaries, electronic calendars and notes;
- organisational sources such as administrative records, agendas and minutes of meetings, agreements, contracts, memos, personnel records, plans, policy statements, press releases, reports and strategy documents;
- government sources such as publications, reports and national statistics;
- media sources including printed and online articles and other data.

Visual and audio sources include advertising posters, artefacts, audio recordings, audio-visual corporate communications, digital recordings, DVDs, films, photographs, products, promotional advertisements and recordings, television and radio programmes and web images.

Many types of archival and documentary sources may be accessed online. Organisations' websites may provide access to certain types of documentary sources such as annual reports, company results, financial highlights, press releases and regulatory news. Media websites also provide facilities to search for articles about organisations and business and management topics. Other internal organisational documents are less likely to be available online and you would need to contact an organisation to seek access, providing these were not considered to be commercially sensitive. Some documents created by individuals may be accessible through data archives (e.g. a collection of papers of a notable business person) but use of recently created materials will probably require you to contact a potential participant to negotiate access, where these are not considered to be private or commercially sensitive.

Documents used for research are considered secondary sources because they were originally created for a different purpose (see the earlier bullet-point list). Researchers using an archival or documentary research strategy therefore need to be sensitive to the fact that the documents they use were not originally created for a research purpose. However, we would like to stress the difference between a secondary data analysis that re-analyses data originally collected for a research purpose and using secondary sources in an archival or documentary research strategy. Where original research data are re-analysed for a different purpose in a secondary data analysis, you should assess the quality of the original research data – i.e. were these data drawn from a representative sample; was the original research designed to overcome threats to reliability and validity (Section 10.9). In contrast, where documents are used as secondary sources in an archival or documentary research strategy, their original purpose had nothing to do with research and so as a researcher using this strategy, you will need to be sensitive to the nature and original purpose of the documents you select, the way in which you analyse them and the generalisations that you can draw (Hakim 2000).

While great care needs to be taken when using documents for research purposes, they potentially offer a rich source of data for you to analyse. The data they provide may be quantitative, qualitative or both. Using qualitative documents may allow you to generate a rich or 'thick' description of key events, the context within which these events occurred, the roles of the actors involved, the influence of external influences such as economic or commercial pressures, as well as outcomes. Your scope to achieve such an outcome will of course depend on the nature of your research question and whether you find suitable documents. Documents may, for example, allow you to analyse critical incidents or decision-making processes, or evaluate different policy positions or strategies. Using quantitative data in documents such as annual or financial reports will provide you with access to actual data that may, for example, facilitate comparisons between organisations or across reporting periods. Prior (2007) points out that documents can also be analysed to reveal:

- not only what they contain but what is omitted;
- which facts are used and why these might be emphasised while others are not used;
- how they are used in an organisation and how they are circulated and to whom.

Archival or documentary research may be an effective and efficient strategy to use but this will depend on its appropriateness to your research question and being able to gain access to sufficient numbers of suitable documents. You may be refused access to use documents, or find that some data are restricted for confidentiality reasons. You may also find that the documents you locate vary in quality, especially where they come from different sources. Some data may be missing or not presented in a consistent way, making comparison difficult or potentially leaving gaps in your analysis. Using an archival research strategy may therefore necessitate you establishing what documents are available and designing your research to make the most of these. This may mean combining this research strategy with another. This could be undertaken in a number of ways, so that, for example, you conduct documentary research alongside a Grounded Theory strategy based on qualitative interviews and use a similar procedure to analyse both sets of data. Another example could involve using documentary research within a case study strategy.

Case study

A **case study** is an in-depth inquiry into a topic or phenomenon within its real-life setting (Yin 2014). The 'case' in case study research may refer to a person (e.g. a manager), a group (e.g. a work team), an organisation (e.g. a business), an association (e.g. a joint venture), a change process (e.g. restructuring a company), an event (e.g. an annual general meeting) as well as many other types of case subject. Choosing the case to be studied and determining the boundaries of the study is a key factor in defining a case study (Flyvberg 2011). Once defined, case study research sets out to understand the dynamics of the topic being studied within its setting or context (Eisenhardt 1989; Eisenhardt and Graebner 2007). 'Understanding the dynamics of the topic' refers to the interactions between the subject of the case and its context.

The study of a case within its real-life setting or context helps to distinguish this research strategy from others. In an experimental strategy, outlined earlier, contextual variables are highly controlled as they are seen as a potential threat to the validity of the results. In a survey strategy, research is undertaken in a real-life setting, but the ability to understand the impact of this context is limited by the number of variables for which data can be collected. In contrast, case study research is often used when the boundaries between the phenomenon being studied and the context within which it is being studied are not always apparent (Yin 2014). Understanding context is fundamental to case study research.

A case study strategy has the capacity to generate insights from intensive and in-depth research into the study of a phenomenon in its real-life context, leading to rich, empirical descriptions and the development of theory (Dubois and Gadde 2002; Eisenhardt 1989; Eisenhardt and Graebner 2007; Ridder et al. 2014; Yin 2014). Dubois and Gadde (2002: 554) make the point that, 'the interaction between a phenomenon and its context is best understood through in-depth case studies'. An in-depth inquiry can be designed to identify what is happening and why, and perhaps to understand the effects of the situation and implications for action. To achieve such insights, case study research draws on quantitative or qualitative research and frequently uses a mixed methods approach, to understand fully the dynamics of the case.

Flyvberg (2011) refers to the paradox of case study research: case studies have been widely used over a long period, including in business and management, but have been criticised by some as a research strategy because of 'misunderstandings' about their ability to produce generalisable, reliable and theoretical contributions to knowledge. This is largely based on positivist criticisms of using small samples and more generally about using interpretive, qualitative research. This type of criticism has been countered in many works (e.g. Buchanan 2012; Flyvberg 2011) and is generally losing favour as the value of qualitative and mixed methods research is being recognised much more widely (e.g. Bansal and Corley 2011; Denzin and Lincoln 2011). We return to consider how the quality of both quantitative and qualitative research may be recognised in Section 10.8.

The long and widespread use of case studies has resulted in them being designed in different ways and for different purposes. They have been used by 'positivist' as well as 'interpretivist' researchers; deductively as well as inductively; and for descriptive, exploratory or explanatory purposes. Some positivist researchers have advocated using case studies inductively to build theory and develop theoretical hypotheses, which can be tested subsequently. In this way, the use of the case study is advocated in the early, exploratory stage of research as a complement to deductive research (Eisenhardt 1989; Eisenhardt and Graebner 2007). This approach has been called 'indicative case study research', designed to reveal 'specific attributes' rather than rich description (Ridder et al. 2014: 374). Yin (2014) recognises that case studies may be used not only for exploratory but also descriptive and explanatory purposes. An explanatory case study is likely to use a deductive approach, using theoretical propositions to test their applicability in the case study, to build and verify an explanation (Chapter 11). Interpretivist researchers are more interested, at least initially, to develop richly detailed and nuanced descriptions of their case study research (Ridder et al. 2014). For some interpretivists, making comparisons with existing theory is unnecessary. Stake (2005) says that many interpretivist researchers prefer to describe their case study in ample detail, allowing readers to make their own links to existing theory. Other interpretivist researchers will work inductively, analysing their data, identifying themes and patterns in these data, and at some point locating this in existing literature in order to refine, extend or generate theory (Ridder et al. 2014; Chapter 11). Where you work as an interpretivist, it is highly likely that you will need to follow this second route and provide a clear link to theory!

The existence of these various approaches to case study research potentially provides you with opportunities to use this strategy, as well as challenges when using it. Where you are considering using a case study strategy, you may be able to find earlier work in the social sciences if not specifically in business and management, which provides guidance in an approach that logically fits your research idea and question (deductive or inductive, exploratory or explanatory etc.). To achieve an in-depth inquiry and a rich, detailed flow of analytical data, a case study strategy can offer you the opportunity to use a mixed methods research design (although case studies may rely on a mono or multi-method choice). Case study research may beneficially use some combination of archival records and documentation, different forms of observation, ethnography (discussed later in this section), interviews and focus groups, questionnaires, reflection and the use of research diaries and other research aids (Chapter 11). Case study research is likely to prove to be challenging because of its intensive and in-depth nature and your need to be able to identify, define and gain access to a case study setting.

You will also need to identify the nature of your case study strategy and we conclude our discussion of this by considering ways in which your case study research may be structured. Yin (2014) distinguishes between four case study strategies based upon two discrete dimensions:

- single case versus multiple cases;
- holistic case versus embedded case.

A single case is often used where it represents a critical case or, alternatively, an extreme or unique case. Conversely, a single case may be selected purposively because it is typical or because it provides you with an opportunity to observe and analyse a phenomenon that few have considered before. Inevitably, an important aspect of using a single case is defining the actual case. For many part-time students this is the organisation for which they work (Box 10.7). The key here will be to ensure that this approach is suitable for the nature of your research question and objectives.

Box 10.7 Focus on student research

Using a single organisation as a case study

Simon was interested in discovering how colleagues within his organisation were using a recently introduced financial costing model in their day-to-day work. In discussion with his project tutor, he highlighted that he was interested in finding out how it was actually being used in his organisation as a whole, as well as seeing if the use of the financial costing model differed between senior managers, departmental managers and front-line operatives. Simon's project tutor suggested that he adopt a case study strategy, using his organisation as a single case within which the senior managers', departmental managers' and front-line operatives' groups were embedded cases. He also highlighted that, given the different numbers of people in each of the embedded cases, Simon would be likely to need to use different data collection techniques with each.

A case study strategy can also incorporate multiple cases, that is, more than one case. The rationale for using multiple cases focuses on whether findings can be replicated across cases. Cases will be carefully chosen on the basis that similar results are predicted to be produced from each one. Where this is realised, Yin (2014) terms this **literal replication**. Another set of cases may be chosen where a contextual factor is deliberately different. The impact of this difference on the anticipated findings is predicted by the researcher. Where this predicted variation is realised, Yin terms this a **theoretical replication**. Yin (2014) proposes that a multiple case study strategy may combine a small number of cases chosen to predict literal replication and a second small number chosen to predict theoretical replication. Where all of the findings from these cases are as predicted, this would clearly produce very strong support for the theoretical propositions on which these predictions were based. This particular approach to case study strategy therefore commences deductively, based on theoretical propositions and theory testing, before possibly incorporating an inductive or abductive approach. Where the findings are in some way contrary to the predictions in the theoretical propositions being tested, it would be necessary to reframe these propositions and choose another set of cases to test them.

Yin's second dimension, holistic versus embedded, refers to the unit of analysis. For example, you may have chosen to use an organisation in which you have been employed or are currently employed as your case. If your research is concerned only with the organisation as a whole then you are treating the organisation as a holistic case study. Conversely, even if you are only researching within a single organisation, you may wish to examine a number of logical sub-units within the organisation, such as departments or work groups. Your case will inevitably involve more than one unit of analysis and, whichever way you select these units, would be called an embedded case study (Box 10.7).

As a student you are likely to find a single case study strategy to be more manageable. Alternatively, you may be able to develop a research design based on two to three cases, where you seek to achieve a literal replication. However, as we have indicated earlier, choosing between a single or multiple case study is not simply related to producing more evidence. While a multiple case study is likely to produce more evidence, the purpose of each approach is different. A single case study approach is chosen because of the nature of the case (i.e. because it is a critical, unique or typical case etc.). A multiple case study approach is chosen to allow replication. Where you are interested in using this strategy, you will therefore need to ensure that the approach chosen is suitable for the nature of your research question and objectives.

Ethnography

Ethnography is used to study the culture or social world of a group. Ethnography literally means a written account of a people or ethnic group. It is the earliest qualitative research strategy, with its origins in colonial anthropology. From the 1700s to the early 1900s, ethnography was developed to study cultures in so-called 'primitive' societies that had been brought under the rule of a colonial power, to facilitate imperialist control and administration. Early anthropologists treated those among whom they lived and conducted their fieldwork as subjects and approached their ethnography in a detached way, believing that they were using a scientific approach, reminiscent of a positivism, to produce monographs that were meant to be accurate and timeless accounts of different cultures (Denzin and Lincoln 2005; Tedlock 2005). From the 1920s the use of ethnography changed through the work of the Chicago School (University of Chicago), which used ethnographic methods to study social and urban problems within cultural groups in the

USA. A seminal example of this work is Whyte's 'Street Corner Society' published in 1943, which examined the lives of street gangs in Boston. This approach to ethnography involved researchers living among those whom they studied, to observe and talk to them in order to produce detailed cultural accounts of their shared beliefs, behaviours, interactions, language, rituals and the events that shaped their lives (Cunliffe 2010). This use of ethnography adopted a more interpretive and naturalistic focus by using the language of those being studied in writing up cultural accounts. However, the researcher remained the arbiter of how to tell the story and what to include, leading many to question how the socialisation and values of this person might affect the account being written (Geertz 1988).

This problem of 'representation' (Denzin and Lincoln 2011) meant that ethnography, as well as qualitative research more generally, was still in a fluid developmental state. Researchers developed a 'bewildering array' (Cunliffe 2010: 230) of qualitative research strategies in the second half of the twentieth century, associated with a great deal of 'blurring' across these strategies (Denzin and Lincoln 2011). We go on to discuss some of these new strategies (action research, grounded theory and narrative inquiry) in this section. As we shall see, these other strategies were designed for a different research focus to that of ethnography. Ethnographers study people in groups, who interact with one another and share the same space, whether this is at street level, within a work group, in an organisation or within a society. Conflict about how best to achieve this focus led to a range of ethnographic strategies of which Cunliffe (2010) outlines three: Realist Ethnography, Impressionist or Interpretive Ethnography and Critical Ethnography.

Realist Ethnography is the closest to the ethnographic strategy described earlier. The realist ethnographer believes in objectivity, factual reporting and identifying 'true' meanings. She or he will report the situation observed through facts or data about structures and processes, practices and customs, routines and norms, artefacts and symbols. Such reporting is likely to use standardised categories that produce quantitative data from observations. The realist ethnographer will write up her or his account in the third person, portraying their role as the impersonal reporter of facts. This account will present a detailed contextual background and the nature of the cultural interactions observed, and identify patterns of behaviour and social processes. It will use edited quotations in a dispassionate way without personal bias or seeking to act as an agent for change. The realist ethnographer's final written account is his or her representation of what he or she has observed and heard.

In contrast, **Interpretive Ethnography** places much greater stress on subjective impressions than on objectivity. The interpretive ethnographer believes in the likelihood of multiple meanings rather than being able to identify a single, true meaning. Multiple meanings will be located in the socially constructed interpretations of the different participants. This suggests a more pluralistic approach, in which the interpretive ethnographer focuses on understanding meanings, with those being observed treated as participants rather than subjects. This requires an ethnographic researcher to engage in continuous reflexivity to try to ensure reliability and validity in this research process (Delamont 2007). The research report will reflect the participation of both the ethnographer (writing in the first person, editing herself into the text, rather than out of it) and those being observed, through devices such as personalisation, use of dialogue and quotations, dramatisation and presentation of different perspectives as well as contextualisation, orderly and progressive description, factual reporting, analysis and evaluation.

Critical Ethnography has a radical purpose, designed to explore and explain the impact of power, privilege and authority on those who are subject to these influences or marginalised by them. You may therefore ask if it can have any appeal to business and management research that is dependent on achieving organisational access. Critical ethnographers often adopt an advocacy role in their work to try to bring about change. You may adopt a constrained or bounded version of Critical Ethnography to explore the impact of a problematic issue within an organisation or work group with a view to advocating internal or external change. Such an issue might be concerned with strategy, decision-making procedures, regulation, governance, organisational treatment, reward and promotion, communication and involvement and so forth.

We have partly presented our discussion of ethnography as a developmental account because it would be misleading to suggest that ideas about this strategy are unified. While ethnography is a demanding strategy to use because you would need to develop some grounding in this approach and because of the time scale and intensity involved, it may be relevant to you. If you are currently working in an organisation, there may be scope to undertake participant observation of your workgroup or another group in the organisation. Alternatively, where you have recently undertaken a work placement, you will be familiar with the context and complexity of this workplace and you may be able to negotiate access based on your credibility to undertake an ethnographic study related to a work group.

Ethnography is relevant for modern organisations. For example, in market research ethnography is a useful technique when companies wish to gain an in-depth understanding of their markets and the experiences of their consumers (Cayla and Arnould 2013; IJMR 2007) (Box 10.8). If you are interested in undertaking your research in the field of marketing, the use of an ethnographic research strategy may be relevant to you. Likewise, use of this research strategy may well be relevant in other business and management subject areas.

Being successful with this strategy is likely to include making sure that the scale or scope of your proposed ethnographic research project is achievable. This will relate to your research question and objectives, which you should discuss with your project tutor. When undertaking 'fieldwork' you will need to make detailed notes of everything you observe and spend as much time as you can reflecting on what you have observed. You will also need to make additional notes to elaborate on these and supplement the process of observation by conducting informal discussions and interviews to explore what you have observed, and collect any documentation that supports your data collection (Delamont 2007). This should help you to collect a sufficient set of data to analyse to answer your research question and fulfil your objectives.

Where an ethnographic strategy is appropriate to you and proves to be feasible, you will need to consider which ethnographic approach relates to the nature of your research question. You should then be in position to build trust and commence fieldwork to be able to undertake this approach successfully.

Action Research

Lewin first used the term **Action Research** in 1946. It has been interpreted subsequently by management researchers in a variety of ways, but a number of common and related themes have been identified within the literature. In essence, Action Research is an emergent and iterative process of inquiry that is designed to develop solutions to real organisational problems through a participative and collaborative approach, which uses different forms of knowledge, and which will have implications for participants and the organisation beyond the research project (Coghlan 2011; Coghlan and Brannick 2014). Our definition identifies five themes, which we briefly consider in the following order: purpose, process, participation, knowledge and implications.

Box 10.8 Focus on management research

How companies use ethnographic stories in their market research and market learning

Cayla and Arnould (2013) explore how companies use a combination of ethnographic investigation and narrative presentation in their market research, in an article published in the *Journal of Marketing*.

Cayla and Arnould conducted semi-structured interviews with 35 participants. These participants worked either as managers in companies who commissioned ethnographic market research, or as corporate ethnographers providing this service. Some of these ethnographic researchers were directly employed by a commissioning company whereas others were external consultants. The aim of Cayla and Arnould's research was to understand how companies use ethnography in strategic marketing decision making. They developed four research questions and interview themes. (1) How do companies use ethnography in marketing decision making? (2) What is the scope of ethnography's application? (3) What are the benefits of using ethnography? (4) What are the challenges of using ethnography, including ethical ones?

While quantitative research and analysis generates broad generalisations, the use of corporate ethnography was found to be effective in understanding the detailed nature and complexity of human behaviour in relation to perceptions about products, purchasing decisions, use of products and so forth. Ethnographic research involves corporate ethnographers getting to know consumers by spending time with them in their homes and in their cars, talking and listening to them, and noting their conversations, stories and reflections to understand how they feel about and use the product(s) being researched. The ethnographers who participated in Cayla and Arnould's study undertook ethnographic investigations into a range of products including alcoholic drinks, consumer goods, mobile phones, electronic devices, cars, banking services and health products. Cayla and Arnould found that visually recording these observations was a critical part of the corporate ethnographic research process. The use of video-recording allows corporate ethnographers to record and edit their observations of consumers into stories that provide a powerful way of presenting a coherent and insightful account of consumer experiences. Cayla and Arnould refer to these accounts as ethnographic stories, helping corporate ethnographers make sense of reality and construct meaning.

They discuss a number of advantages of using a narrative form to present the key points from corporate ethnographic research. Creating a story from the pre-edited observations of a consumer allows that consumer's experiences to be sequenced and structured around a revelatory incident that incorporates sufficient detail and emotional content to make the resulting account meaningful for the company managers who commissioned the research. Cayla and Arnould emphasise how using this narrative approach has the potential to allow strategic marketing decision-makers to better understand their company's product market; better understand their company's consumers and how they relate to the company's products; and to revise and develop their marketing strategies.

Cayla and Arnould's article demonstrates how combining ethnographic investigation and narrative presentation forms a powerful strategy to stimulate managerial action. Ethnographic stories facilitate market learning because of the way they illuminate consumer behaviour and provide memorable accounts of their experiences that point to the potential for managerial action.

The purpose of an Action Research strategy is to promote organisational learning to produce practical outcomes through identifying issues, planning action, taking action and evaluating action. Coghlan and Brannick (2014: 4) state that Action Research is about 'research in action rather than research about action'. This is because Action Research focuses on 'addressing worthwhile practical purposes' (Reason 2006: 188) and resolving real organisational issues (Shani and Pasmore 1985).

The process of Action Research is both emergent and iterative. An Action Research strategy commences within a specific context and with a research question but because it works through several stages or iterations the focus of the question may change as the research develops. Each stage of the research involves a process of diagnosing or constructing issues, planning action, taking action and evaluating action (Figure 10.5). Diagnosing or constructing issues, sometimes referred to as fact finding and analysis, is undertaken to enable action planning and a decision about the actions to be taken. These are then taken and the actions evaluated (cycle 1). This evaluation provides a direction and focus for the next stage of diagnosing or constructing issues, planning action, taking action and evaluating action (cycle 2), demonstrating the iterative nature of the process. Subsequent cycles (cycle 3 and possibly beyond) involve further diagnosing or constructing of issues, taking into account previous evaluations, planning further actions, taking these actions and evaluating them. In this way, Action Research differs from other research strategies because of its explicit focus on action related to multiple stages, to explore and evaluate solutions to organisational issues and to promote change within the organisation.

Participation is a critical component of Action Research. Greenwood and Levin (2007) emphasise that Action Research is a social process in which an action researcher works with members in an organisation, as a facilitator and teacher, to

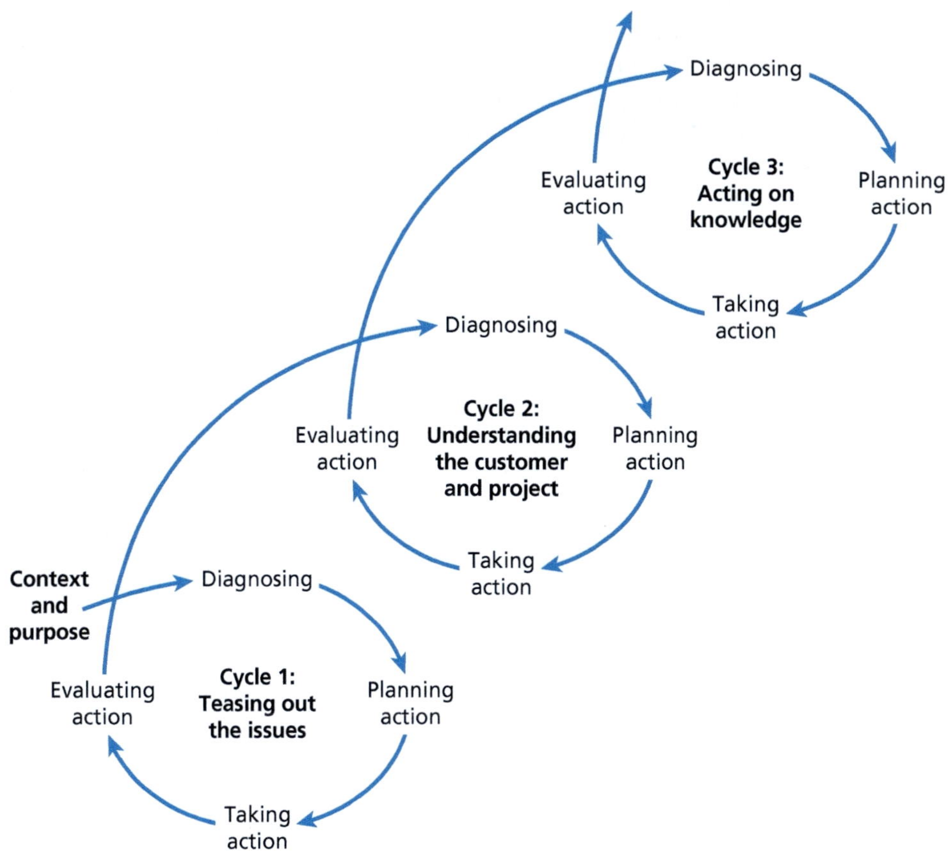

Figure 10.5 The three cycles of the Action Research spiral

improve the situation for these participants and their organisation. For Greenwood and Levin, a process can only be called Action Research if research, action and participation are all present. Participation by organisational members may take a number of forms. Firstly, organisational members need to cooperate with the researcher to allow their existing work practices to be studied. The process of Action Research then requires participation in the form of collaboration through its iterative cycles (as we described earlier) to facilitate the improvement of organisational practices. Collaboration means building a democratic approach to communication and decision making when constructing, planning, taking and evaluating each Action Research stage or cycle. The researcher passes on her or his skills and capabilities to participants so that they effectively become co-researchers in the Action Research process. Without such participation, this approach simply would not be viable, although creating such participation is likely to be difficult in practice and to meet with resistance at various levels (Reason 2006).

How then may this form of participation be developed? Eden and Huxham (1996: 75) argue that the participation of organisational members results from their involvement in 'a matter which is of genuine concern to them'. Schein (1999) emphasises that members of an organisation are more likely to implement change they have helped to create. Once the members of an organisation have identified a need for change and have widely shared this need, it becomes difficult to ignore, and the pressure for change comes from within the organisation. In this way, an Action Research strategy combines both data gathering and the facilitation of change.

The nature of Action Research means that it will also be able to incorporate different forms of knowledge. Action Research will not only be informed by abstract theoretical knowledge, known as propositional knowledge, but also by participants' everyday lived experiences (their experiential knowledge) and knowing-in-action (knowledge that comes from practical application) (Reason 2006). These forms of knowledge will inform and be incorporated into each stage or cycle of the Action Research process, encouraged by the collaborative approach that underpins this strategy. Incorporating these forms leads to 'actionable knowledge' that has the potential to be useful to organisational practitioners as well as being academically robust (Coghlan 2011: 79). Coghlan believes that Action Research not only affects 'what we know' but emphasises understanding of 'how we know'.

Action Research also has implications beyond the research project. Participants in an organisation where action research takes place are likely to have their expectations about future treatment and involvement in decision making raised (Greenwood and Levin 2007). There are also likely to be consequences for organisational development and culture change. Implications from the process may be used to inform other contexts. Academics will use the results from undertaking Action Research to develop theory that can be applied more widely. Consultants will transfer knowledge gained to inform their work in other contexts. Such use of knowledge to inform, we believe, also applies to others undertaking Action Research, such as students undertaking research in their own organisations.

Where you think about using Action Research there will be a number of practical concerns to consider. Identifying an accommodating context, the emergent nature of this strategy, the need to engender participation and collaboration, the researcher's role as facilitator, and the stages or iterations involved are some of the reasons that make Action Research a demanding strategy in terms of the intensity involved and the resources and time required. As we have indicated, Action Research can be suited to part-time students who undertake research in their own organisation. The longitudinal nature of this strategy means that it is more appropriate for medium- or long-term research projects rather than short-term ones. There is the related issue of deciding how many Action Research cycles are sufficient. Where these practical as well as political concerns have been properly anticipated and evaluated in terms of a feasible design, Action Research has the potential to offer a worthwhile and rich experience for those involved.

Grounded Theory

'**Grounded theory**' can be used to refer to a methodological approach, a method of inquiry and the result of a research process (Bryant and Charmaz 2007; Charmaz 2011; Corbin and Strauss 2008). 'Grounded theory methodology' refers to the researcher's choice of this strategy as a way to conduct research. '**Grounded theory method**' refers to the data collection techniques and analytic procedures that it uses (discussed in Chapter 11). 'Grounded theory' may be used loosely to incorporate methodology and method but more specifically it refers to a theory that is grounded in or developed inductively from a set of data. In this section we refer to 'Grounded Theory' (i.e. as a proper noun), to indicate its use as a research strategy and to distinguish this from 'a grounded theory' (no capital letters).

Grounded Theory was developed by Glaser and Strauss (1967) as a response to the 'extreme positivism' of much social research at that time (Suddaby 2006: 633). They disputed the view that social research should use a paradigm based on a premise that theory will reveal a pre-existing reality. In positivism, reality is seen as existing independently and externally (to human cognition). While positivism is suited to research in the natural sciences, they believed that social research should use a different philosophy. By adopting interpretivism in social research, 'reality' is seen as being socially constructed through the meanings that social actors ascribe to their experiences. Grounded Theory was therefore developed as a process to analyse, interpret and explain the meanings that social actors construct to make sense of their everyday experiences in specific situations (Charmaz 2006; Glaser and Strauss 1967; Suddaby 2006).

Grounded Theory is used to develop theoretical explanations of social interactions and processes in a wide range of contexts, including business and management. As much of business and management is about people's behaviours, for example consumers' or employees', a Grounded Theory strategy can be used to explore a wide range of business and management issues. As the title of Glaser and Strauss's (1967) book *The Discovery of Grounded Theory* indicates, the aim is to 'discover' or generate theory grounded in the data produced from the accounts of social actors.

We now briefly outline the key elements of Grounded Theory to enable you to assess whether it may be appropriate for the nature of your proposed research project, before evaluating its use in practice. Grounded Theory provides a systematic approach to collect and analyse qualitative data. Its use is often well suited to the nature of qualitative research. Whereas in quantitative research it is usual to collect a complete set of data and then analyse these, in qualitative data it is often useful to analyse data as you collect them (e.g. you conduct an interview and analyse it before conducting the next one). Grounded Theory is designed to allow you to achieve this. In this way, Grounded Theory provides you with a systematic and emergent strategy to undertake qualitative research.

Grounded Theory is usually referred to as taking an inductive approach, although, as we discuss later, it may be more appropriate to think of it as abductive, moving between induction and deduction (Charmaz 2011; Strauss and Corbin 1998; Suddaby 2006). The researcher collects and analyses data simultaneously, developing analytical codes as these emerge from the data in order to reorganise (fragment) these data into categories. In the Grounded Theory strategy of Strauss and Corbin (1998) there are three coding stages: the reorganisation of data into categories is called **open coding**, the process of recognising relationships between categories is referred to as **axial coding** and the integration of categories to produce a theory is labelled **selective coding**. Charmaz (2006) simplifies this to two principal stages: **initial coding** and **focused coding**, supported by sufficient stages of sampling (Section 11.7). More recently, Corbin has altered the approach in Corbin and Strauss (2008), with axial coding being combined within open coding and selective coding simply becoming 'integration'. We expand on analytical coding in some detail in Section 11.9; needless to say here that coding is a key element of Grounded Theory.

Underpinning coding is the process of **constant comparison**. Each item of data collected is compared with others, as well as against the codes being used to categorise data. This is to check for similarities and differences, to promote consistency when coding data and to aid the process of analysis. Where appropriate, new codes are created and existing codes reanalysed as new data are collected. Constant comparison promotes the higher levels of analytical coding we referred to earlier because it involves moving between inductive and deductive thinking. As the researcher codes data into categories, a relationship may begin to suggest itself between specific codes (here, the researcher is using inductive thinking because she or he will be linking specific codes to form a general proposition). This emerging interpretation will need to be 'tested' through collecting data from new cases (here, the researcher will use deductive thinking to 'test' this abstract generalisation back to a new set of specific cases, to see if it stands up as an explanatory relationship to form a higher-level code) (Strauss and Corbin 1998). The process of gaining insights to create new conceptual possibilities which are then examined is termed abduction (Charmaz 2011; Reichertz 2007; Suddaby 2006).

Another key element that aids the development of grounded theory is **memo writing** (Section 11.5). Memos are created throughout a research project to define or make notes about:

- the codes being used;
- how codes change through the research process;
- how codes might be related, leading to the identification of theoretical relationships and the emergence of higher-level codes and categories;
- any other ideas that occur to the researcher that help her or him to develop the research process and analyse the data.

Where you use a Grounded Theory strategy, your collection of self-memos will provide you with a chronological record of the development of your ideas and your project, and show how you arrived at your grounded theory.

When using Grounded Theory you will also need to decide how to select cases for your research. As you analyse data, the categories being developed will indicate the type of new cases (e.g. new participants) to select for further data collection. The purpose of sampling is therefore to pursue theoretical lines of enquiry rather than to achieve population representativeness. As you identify a core theme, relationship or process around which to focus the research, a particular focus will be provided from which to select new cases to collect and analyse further data. This approach is a special form of purposive sampling, known as **theoretical sampling**, which continues until **theoretical saturation** is reached. This occurs when data collection ceases to reveal any new properties that are relevant to a category, where categories have become well developed and understood and relationships between categories have been verified (Strauss and Corbin 1998). This is also referred to as achieving conceptual density (Glaser 1992) or conceptual saturation (Strauss and Corbin 2008). Using these elements of Grounded Theory means that the process of data collection and analysis becomes increasingly focused, leading to the generation of a contextually based theoretical explanation (Bryant and Charmaz 2007).

Grounded Theory is a useful and widely recognised research strategy and yet it has been the subject of much evaluation, criticism and even misunderstanding (Box 10.9). This is partly due to the development of different approaches to grounded theory method. Glaser and Strauss, who developed Grounded Theory, each went on to develop different approaches to its use. Strauss has become associated with the development of a particularly prescriptive approach to grounded theory method (e.g. Corbin and Strauss 2008; Strauss and Corbin 1998).

A further difference has been revealed by Charmaz (2006: 130–31), who makes a distinction between 'objectivist grounded theory' and 'constructivist grounded theory'. Charmaz views the approach of Glaser, Strauss and Corbin to grounded theory as being 'objectivist', which assumes that data have an external reality, just waiting to be 'discovered'. She considers that, 'objectivist grounded theory resides in the positivist tradition' (Charmaz 2006: 131). According to this view, it is only 'constructivist' grounded theory that is truly based on an interpretive approach (Section 10.3), because it recognises that the researcher's role in interpreting the data will affect the development of a grounded theory. In this approach, grounded theories are 'constructed', not discovered. This might seem a rather abstract difference, but because Charmaz advocates a 'constructivist' approach she also promotes a more flexible approach to grounded theory method (Section 11.9).

Adopting a Grounded Theory strategy leads to other issues and implications. These concern the collection of data; the use of existing theory; identifying a core category or categories around which to focus the research; the emergence of theory; and the time required to undertake this strategy. We briefly consider each of these.

In Grounded Theory, data collection may start as soon as the research idea has been developed and the initial research participants have agreed to take part (or the first set of documents have been identified). Using this strategy places an obligation on you to make sure you are interested in and committed to your research idea.

There is sometimes confusion about the role of published theory in a Grounded Theory research project. Grounded Theorists may use published theory before and during their research project (Box 10.9). The idea for such a research project may come from existing theory and your understanding of the theoretical background to your research topic may help to inform the project in general terms. Where existing theory should not be allowed to influence the conduct of your Grounded Theory project is in relation to the way you code your data, decide on new cases and conduct your analysis, as we have discussed in this section. Grounded Theory is an emergent strategy and researchers wish to be guided by concepts emerging from the data they collect rather than being sensitised by concepts in existing theory. Using this strategy will mean you should avoid being overly sensitised to pre-existing theoretical concepts, to allow yourself to make sense of participants' meanings in the data to guide your research. This is known as **theoretical sensitivity**, where you focus on interpreting meanings by using *in vivo* and researcher generated rather than *a priori* codes (explained in Section 11.6) to analyse your data and construct a grounded theory (Glaser 1978). Theoretical sensitivity means that you must be sensitive to meanings in your data and orientated towards generating a grounded theory from these data. You will, however, need to allow yourself sufficient time later on to link your grounded theory to published theories as you write your research report!

Box 10.9 Focus on management research

Using Grounded Theory, or not!

Bryant and Charmaz (2007) in *The Sage Handbook of Grounded Theory* report that this strategy has, for the last couple of decades, been the qualitative research method used most widely across a range of subjects. They cite Titscher et al. (2000), who reported that out of 4134 citations for all types of research methods in the Social Science Citation Index between 1991 and 1998, Grounded Theory accounted for 2622 of these. However, Titscher et al. (2000, cited in Bryant and Charmaz 2007) question whether the ascendancy of Grounded Theory is as dominant as these data appear to suggest. Bryant and Charmaz (2007: 2) reflect back to Lee and Fielding (1996) in concluding that 'the discrepancy between claiming use of [Grounded Theory] and actual evidence of this continues today'. Lee and Fielding (1996:3.1) had stated in their *Sociological Research Online comment* that, 'When qualitative researchers are challenged to describe their approach, reference to "grounded theory" has the highest recognition value. But the very looseness and variety of researchers' schooling in the approach means that the tag may well mean something different to each researcher. A detailed examination of work claiming the label may deviate sharply from what Glaser and Strauss had in mind'.

More recently, O'Reilly et al. (2012) report a search using Business Source Premier to find out how Grounded Theory was being used in practice. This search revealed 126 journal articles that used 'grounded theory' in their titles over a recent 5-year period, of which 46 reported using Grounded Theory Method. However, of these just 16 reported using more than one element of Grounded Theory, with the considerable majority only reporting the use of its coding procedures.

Suddaby (2006) published an excellent article in the *Academy of Management Journal* based on reviewing pre-publication management research manuscripts claiming to use Grounded Theory. He identifies six common misconceptions about Grounded Theory. We briefly summarise these, but where you are thinking about using Grounded Theory we would advise you to read Suddaby's article as we believe that it will help you to understand this approach and avoid these common misunderstandings:

1 Ignoring literature until late in the research project. It is a mistake to ignore existing literature before and during undertaking Grounded Theory.
2 Presenting raw data. Grounded Theory should never present unanalysed data. This is to ignore the essence of Grounded Theory, which is a conceptual process to develop a theory from the data.
3 Using inappropriate philosophical assumptions and testing theory rather than developing theory. Avoid methodological confusions or 'slurring' such as starting with positivist assumptions or commencing with interpretive assumptions but then proceeding to use objectivist rather than Grounded Theory methods.
4 Mechanically following Grounded Theory procedures without sufficient creative insight. The use of Grounded Theory procedures and techniques needs to be accompanied by creative insights and theoretical sensitivity to infer meanings in the data, to progress the research and in writing it up.
5 Following Grounded Theory procedures rigidly. In practice Grounded Theory procedures are 'messy' and require researchers to develop a tacit feel for their research to make judgements about issues such as deciding when theoretical saturation is achieved.
6 Grounded Theory is methodologically simple. Instead, it requires practice, dedication, creativity and sometimes good luck. Using it is also not an excuse to avoid developing a clear methodology based on the core principles and procedures of coding, constant comparison, theoretical sensitivity, theoretical sampling and theoretical saturation.

Because Grounded Theory is emergent, you will need at some point to identify a core category or categories around which to focus your research and develop a grounded theory to explain the relationships you identify. This will require rigorous use of coding, constant comparison, theoretical sampling, theoretical saturation and theoretical sensitivity to develop a theoretical explanation. Use of this strategy is also associated with a concern that either little of significance will emerge at the end of the research process, or that what emerges is simply descriptive.

Using Grounded Theory is time consuming, intensive and reflective. Before committing yourself to this strategy, you need to consider the time that you have to conduct your research, the level of competence you will need, your access to data, and the logistical implications of immersing yourself in an intensive approach to research. Kenealy (2012) advises novice Grounded Theory researchers to identify one approach to grounded theory method and follow it without too much adaptation. He also advises researchers to focus on identifying 'ideas that fit and work' from their data to develop a grounded theory (Kenealy 2012: 423). Kenealy recognises that using Grounded Theory requires experience but says that the only way to build this is to practise the use of grounded theory method!

In summary, while some Grounded Theory authors produce prescriptive accounts of grounded theory method and others offer more flexible accounts, all appear to be agreed on the key elements we discussed earlier:

- Early commencement of data collection;
- Concurrent collection and analysis of data;
- Developing codes and categories from the data as these are collected and analysed;
- Use of constant comparison and writing of self-memos to develop conceptualisation and build a theory;
- Use of theoretical sampling and theoretical saturation aimed at building theory rather than achieving (population) representativeness;
- Use of an abductive approach that seeks to gain insights to create new conceptual possibilities which are then examined;
- Initial use of literature as a complementary source to the categories and concepts emerging in the data, rather than as the source to categorise these data. Later use to review the place of the grounded theory in relation to existing, published theories;
- Development of a theory that is grounded in the data.

Narrative Inquiry

A narrative is a story; a personal account which interprets an event or sequence of events (Box 10.8). Using the term 'narrative' requires a distinction to be drawn between its general meaning and the specific meaning used here. A qualitative research interview inevitably involves a participant in storytelling. In this way, the term 'narrative' can be applied generally to describe the nature or outcome of a qualitative interview. As a research strategy, however, **Narrative Inquiry** has a more specific meaning and purpose. There will be research contexts where the researcher believes that the experiences of her or his participants can best be accessed by collecting and analysing these as complete stories, rather than collecting them as bits of data that flow from specific interview questions and which are then fragmented during data analysis. Chase (2011) distinguishes between asking participants to generalise when answering questions in more structured types of qualitative research and being invited to provide a complete narrative of their experience. This contrasts with the approach to Grounded Theory which we discussed earlier.

Narrative Inquiry seeks to preserve chronological connections and the sequencing of events as told by the narrator (participant) to enrich understanding and aid analysis. Chase (2011: 421) refers to this strategy as providing the opportunity to connect events, actions and their consequences over time into a 'meaningful whole'. Through storytelling the narrator will also provide his or her interpretation of these events, allowing the narrative researcher to analyse the meanings which the narrator places on events. Where there is more than one participant providing a personal account of a given context, the narrative researcher will also be able to compare and to triangulate or contrast these narratives.

The depth of this process is also likely to produce 'thick descriptions' of contextual detail and social relations. Gabriel and Griffiths (2004: 114) believe that using this strategy may allow researchers to 'gain access to deeper organisational realities, closely linked to their members' experiences'. A **narrative** may therefore be defined as an account of an experience that is told in a sequenced way, indicating a flow of related events that, taken together, are significant for the narrator and which convey meaning to the researcher (Coffey and Atkinson 1996).

In Narrative Inquiry, the participant is the narrator, with the researcher adopting the role of a listener facilitating the process of narration (Box 10.10). The narrative provided may be a short story about a specific event; a more extended story (for example, about a work project, managing or setting up a business, or an organisational change programme); or a complete life history (e.g. Chase 2011; Maitlis 2012). While in-depth interviews are the primary method to collect stories, other methods may be used by the narrative researcher to record stories as they occur naturally, such as participant observation in the research setting (Coffey and Atkinson 1996; Gabriel and Griffiths 2004). Other sources of narratives include autobiographies, authored biographies, diaries, documentation (see our earlier discussion of this strategy) and informal discussions (Chase 2011; Maitlis 2012). This raises the issue of the Narrative Researcher adopting the role of narrator in particular circumstances, which we will consider further later. It is also important to note that Narrative Inquiry may be used as the sole research strategy, or it may be used in conjunction with another strategy as a complementary approach (Musson 2004).

Narrative Inquiry may be used in different ways. It may be used with a very small number of participants (one, two or three), where these are selected because they are judged as being typical of a much larger culture-sharing population (Chase 2011). As an example, you may decide to interview a small number of accountants or marketing managers who are typical of their occupational population (Box 10.10). It may also be used with a very small sample because those selected are judged as being critical cases or extreme cases, from whom much may be learnt. In this context, in-depth narrative interviews with a small sample of company founders or entrepreneurs may prove to be valuable (Musson 2004). Narrative Inquiry may also be used with slightly larger samples, where, for example, narrative interviews are conducted with, or observations made of, participants from across an organisation, to be able to analyse how narratives are constructed around an event or series of events and to be able to compare how accounts differ, such as between departments, occupational groups, genders and/or grades.

This strategy is generally associated with small, purposive samples because of its intensive and time-consuming nature. It is likely to generate large amounts of data in the form of interview transcripts or observational notes. The narratives that emerge may not do so in an easy-to-use structural and coherent form (Gabriel and

Box 10.10 Focus on student research

Using narrative inquiry to explore a marketing strategy

Kasia was undertaking a marketing degree and, because of her longstanding interest in fashion and textiles, she hoped to find a job in that sector. Kasia's interests led her to focus her research project on factors that affected the success of marketing strategies in a small sample of fashion companies. After considering her choice of research strategy and discussing this with her project tutor, she decided to use a narrative inquiry strategy, using in-depth interviews with senior managers in a sample of carefully selected companies. She negotiated access to conduct interviews with the marketing directors or managers of three medium-sized fashion companies. Kasia realised that the outcome of her research would very much depend on the quality of these three in-depth interviews and the ways in which her interviewees responded to her request to participate in this narrative approach. She decided to send each of these three managers a letter very briefly outlining this approach and a list of the structural elements of narrative inquiry she had read about.

She was nervous going to the first interview and realised that her participant, Hetal, sensed this. Hetal had read Kasia's letter and knew a little about narrative inquiry from her own degree studies. Hetal provided Kasia with a full and useful narrative of the factors affecting the outcomes of her employer's marketing strategy over the past year. However, after the interview Kasia realised that she had interrupted Hetal unnecessarily with interview questions on several occasions, interrupting the flow of Hetal's narrative account. Kasia wrote and thanked Hetal for her very useful narrative account and resolved to read more about conducting this type of in-depth interview before conducting the second one. She read Czarniawska's (1997) book, *Narrating the Organization*, and learnt that she would need to move from the interviewer's standard role of asking questions and instead allow her interviewees to act as narrators, using their own voices to tell their stories.

Kasia contacted her next participant and went to the interview with a list of elements and themes in which she was interested but resolved that her second participant, Jorg, should be allowed to use his own voice. Jorg provided Kasia with another full and useful narrative, with Kasia acting as listener rather than traditional interviewer, only seeking clarification occasionally, after explaining the nature and purpose of the process as they started. Kasia left this second interview feeling very pleased, and looked forward to the next one.

Griffiths 2004). Coffey and Atkinson (1996) recognise this, drawing on previous research to outline the structural elements that are useful to facilitate analysis of narratives:

- What is the story about?
- What happened, to whom, whereabouts and why?
- What consequences arose from this?
- What is the significance of these events?
- What was the final outcome?

To achieve such analytical coherence in a narrative account may involve the narrative researcher in (re)constructing the story from the strands that emerge from conducting a number of in-depth interviews with one participant or with different participants (Box 10.8). As we recognised earlier, this action places the narrative researcher in a central role in telling the story. Decisions will need to be taken about what to include and what to leave out, and how to connect parts of the account. We consider issues of narrative analysis further in Section 11.10.

Where your research question and objectives suggest the use of an interpretive and qualitative strategy, Narrative Inquiry may be suitable for you to use. Narrative Inquiry will allow you to analyse the linkages, relationships and socially constructed explanations that occur naturally within narrative accounts in order 'to understand the complex processes which people use in making sense of their organisational realities' (Musson 2004: 42). The purpose of Narrative Inquiry is to derive theoretical explanations from narrative accounts while maintaining their integrity. While analysis in Narrative Inquiry does not use the analytical fragmentation of Grounded Theory, neither does it offer a well-developed set of analytical procedures comparable to those used by grounded theorists. Despite this, analytical rigour is still important in order to derive constructs and concepts to develop theoretical explanations. While narrative researchers may believe that predefined analytical procedures are neither advisable nor desirable, this may make the task of analysis more demanding for you. We return in Section 11.10 to consider some of the approaches that narrative researchers have used to analyse their data.

10.6 Choosing a time horizon

An important question to be asked in designing your research is, 'Do I want my research to be a "snapshot" taken at a particular time or do I want it to be more akin to a diary or a series of snapshots and be a representation of events over a given period?' This will, of course, depend on your research question. The 'snapshot' time horizon we call **cross-sectional**, while the 'diary' perspective we call **longitudinal**.

Cross-sectional studies

It is probable that your research will be cross-sectional, involving the study of a particular phenomenon (or phenomena) at a particular time. We say this because we recognise that most research projects undertaken for academic courses are necessarily time constrained. However, the time horizons on many courses do allow sufficient time for a longitudinal study, provided, of course, that you start your research early!

Cross-sectional studies often employ the survey strategy. They may be seeking to describe the incidence of a phenomenon (for example, the IT skills possessed by managers in one organisation at a given point in time) or to explain how factors are related in different organisations (e.g. the relationship between expenditure on customer care training for sales assistants and sales revenue). However, they may also use qualitative or mixed methods research strategies. For example, many case studies are based on interviews conducted over a short period of time.

Longitudinal studies

The main strength of longitudinal research is its capacity to study change and development. This type of study may also provide you with a measure of control over some of the variables being studied. One of the best-known examples of this type of research comes from outside the world of business. It is the long-running UK television series, 'Seven Up'. This has charted the progress of a cohort of people every seven years of their life. Not only is this fascinating television, it has also provided the social scientist with a rich source of data on which to test and develop theories of human development.

Even with time constraints it is possible to introduce a longitudinal element to your research. There is a massive amount of published data collected over time just waiting to be reanalysed! An example is the Workplace Employment Relations Study, conducted in 1980, 1984, 1990, 1998, 2004 and 2011 (Department for Business, Innovation and Skills 2013). From these surveys you would be able to gain valuable secondary data, which would give you a powerful insight into developments in human resource management and employee relations over a period of wide-ranging change.

10.7 Establishing the ethics of the research design

Research ethics are a critical part of formulating your research design. Here we introduce two ethical issues that you need to consider when starting to design your research.

Your choice of topic will be governed by ethical considerations. You may be particularly interested to study the consumer decision to buy flower bouquets. Although this may provide some interesting data collection challenges (who buys, for whom and why), there are not the same ethical difficulties as will be involved in studying, say, the funeral purchasing decision. Your research design in this case may have to concentrate on data collection from the undertaker and, possibly, the purchaser at a time as close to the death as delicacy permits. The ideal population, of course, may be the purchaser at a time as near as possible to the death. It is a matter of judgement as to whether the strategy and data collection method(s) suggested by ethical considerations will yield data that are valid. The general ethical issue here is that the research design should not subject those you are researching to the risk of embarrassment, pain, harm or any other material disadvantage.

Your research design may need to consider whether you should collect data if those you are researching are unaware they are the subject of research and so have not consented. There was a dispute between solicitors and the Consumers' Association (CA). Telephone enquiries were conducted by the CA with a sample of solicitors for the purpose of assessing the accuracy of legal advice given and the cost of specified work. The calls were, allegedly, made without the CA's identity or the purpose of the research being disclosed (Gibb 1995). Although it is for you to decide whether a similar covert research design for your project would be ethical, it is worth emphasising that many university research ethics procedures preclude the use of covert research.

10.8 Establishing the quality of the research design

Underpinning our discussion of research design is the issue of the quality of the research and its findings. This is neatly expressed by Raimond (1993: 55) when he subjects findings to the 'how do I know?' test, 'Will the evidence and my conclusions stand up to the closest scrutiny?' For example, how do you know that the advertising campaign for a new product has resulted in enhanced sales? How do you know that manual employees in an electronics factory have more negative feelings towards their employer than their clerical counterparts? The answer, of course, is that, in the literal sense of the question, you cannot know. All you can do is reduce the possibility of getting the answer wrong. This is why good research design is important. This is aptly summarised by Rogers (1961; cited by Raimond 1993: 55): 'scientific methodology needs to be seen for what it truly is, a way of preventing me from deceiving myself in regard to my creatively formed subjective hunches which have developed out of the relationship between me and my material'.

A split often occurs at this point between positivist and interpretivist researchers. The former will use the 'canons of scientific inquiry' related to reliability and validity to assess the quality of their research or, perhaps more pertinently, that of others. The latter either seek to adapt these terms to assess their research, or reject them as inappropriate to interpretivist studies (Guba and Lincoln 1989, 2005; Lincoln and Guba 1985; Lincoln et al. 2011). We briefly discuss each of these approaches to establish and assess research quality.

Scientific canons of inquiry: reliability and validity

Reliability and validity are central to judgements about the quality of research in the natural sciences and quantitative research in the social sciences. Their role in relation to qualitative research is contested, as we discuss later. **Reliability** refers to replication and consistency. If a researcher is able to replicate an earlier research design and achieve the same findings, then that research would be seen as being reliable. In essence, **validity** refers to the appropriateness of the measures used, accuracy of the analysis of the results and generalisability of the findings:

1. Do the measures being used in the research to assess the phenomenon being studied actually measure what they are intended to – are they appropriate for their intended purpose?
2. Are the analysis of the results and the relationships being advanced accurate?
3. What do the research findings represent: does the claim about how generalisable they are stand up?

This first aspect of validity is sometimes termed **measurement validity** and is associated with different types of validity designed to assess this intention. These include face validity, construct validity, content validity and predictive validity. The second aspect of validity refers to internal validity and the third aspect to external validity, both discussed later in this section.

When considering reliability, sometimes a distinction is made between internal reliability and external reliability. Internal reliability refers to ensuring consistency during a research project. This may be achieved, where possible, by using more than one researcher within a research project to conduct interviews or observations and to analyse data to be able to evaluate the extent to which they agree about the data and its analysis. You may seek to ensure consistency through the stages of your research project by writing memos to promote stability in the way you code your data, and analyse and interpret it. External reliability refers to whether your data collection techniques and analytic procedures would produce consistent findings if they were repeated by you on another occasion or if they were replicated by a different researcher. Ensuring reliability is not necessarily easy and a number of threats to reliability are described in Table 10.3. Research that is unreliable will also prove to be invalid since any error or bias will affect

Table 10.3 Threats to reliability

Threat	Definition and explanation
Participant error	Any factor which adversely alters the way in which a participant performs. For example, asking a participant to complete a questionnaire just before a lunch break may affect the way they respond compared to choosing a less sensitive time (i.e. they may not take care and hurry to complete it)
Participant bias	Any factor which induces a false response. For example, conducting an interview in an open space may lead participants to provide falsely positive answers where they fear they are being overheard, rather than retaining their anonymity
Researcher error	Any factor which alters the researcher's interpretation. For example, a researcher may be tired or not sufficiently prepared and misunderstand some of the more subtle meanings of his or her interviewees
Researcher bias	Any factor which induces bias in the researcher's recording of responses. For example, a researcher may allow her or his own subjective view or disposition to get in the way of fairly and accurately recording and interpreting participants' responses

the results and subsequent interpretation, and possibly cast doubt on the means to measure the phenomenon being studied.

These threats imply that you will need to be methodologically rigorous in the way you devise and carry out your research to seek to avoid threatening the reliability of your findings and conclusions. More specific advice appears in other chapters but one key aspect is to ensure that your research process is clearly thought through and evaluated and does not contain 'logic leaps and false assumptions'. You will need to report each part of your work in a fully transparent way to allow others to judge for themselves and to replicate your study if they wished to do so.

Reliability is a key characteristic of research quality; however, while it is necessary, it is not sufficient by itself to ensure good-quality research. As indicated earlier, the quality of research depends not only on its reliability but also its validity. **Internal validity** is established when your research accurately demonstrates a **causal relationship** between two variables. For example, in an experiment internal validity would be established where an intervention can be shown statistically to lead to an outcome. In a questionnaire-based survey, internal validity would be established where a set of questions can be shown statistically to be associated with an analytical factor or outcome. This concept is associated with positivist and quantitative research: it can be applied to causal or explanatory studies, but not to exploratory or purely descriptive studies.

Your research findings would be seen as invalid when a finding has been arrived at falsely or when a reported relationship is inaccurate. There are a number of reasons that might threaten the internal validity of your research (Cook and Campbell 1979). We offer definitions and examples of the most frequent in Table 10.4. Research that produces invalid results and conclusions will also adversely affect its reliability since it will be highly unlikely for a subsequent study to find the same false results and statistical relationships.

Table 10.4 Threats to internal validity

Threat	Definition and explanation
Past or recent events	An event which changes participants' perceptions. For example, a vehicle maker recalling its cars for safety modifications may affect its customers' views about product quality and have an unforeseen effect on a planned study (unless the objective of the research is to find out about post-product recall opinions)
Testing	The impact of testing on participants' views or actions. For example, informing participants about a research project may alter their work behaviour or responses during the research if they believe it might lead to future consequences for them
Instrumentation	The impact of a change in a research instrument between different stages of a research project affecting the comparability of results. For example, in structured observational research on call centre operations, the definitions of behaviours being observed may be changed between stages of the research, making comparison difficult
Mortality	The impact of participants withdrawing from studies. Often participants leave their job or gain a promotion during a study
Maturation	The impact of a change in participants outside of the influence of the study that affects their attitudes or behaviours etc. For example, management training may make participants revise their responses during a subsequent research stage
Ambiguity about causal direction	Lack of clarity about cause and effect. For example, during a study, it was difficult to say if poor performance ratings were caused by negative attitudes to appraisal or if negative attitudes to appraisal were caused by poor performance ratings

External validity is concerned with the question: can a study's research findings be generalised to other relevant settings or groups? For example, a corporate manager may ask, 'Can the findings from the research study in one organisation in our corporation also be used to inform policy and practice in other organisations in the group?' The chief executive of a county council may ask, 'Are the findings from the survey in the Finance and Resources Department applicable to other departments in the Council?' Just as researchers take great care when selecting a sample from within a population to make sure that it represents that population, researchers and their clients are often concerned to establish the generalisability of their findings to other contexts. Even in such cases, however, it will be necessary to replicate the study in that other context, or contexts, to be able to establish such statistical generalisability.

Alternative criteria to assess the quality of research inquiry

All researchers take issues of research quality seriously if they wish others to accept their research as credible. However, while types of measurement validity are appropriate to assess quantitative research based on positivist assumptions, they are often considered as philosophically and technically inappropriate in relation to qualitative research based on interpretive assumptions, where reality is regarded as being socially constructed and multifaceted. If good-quality research is judged against the criteria of reliability and validity, but these concepts are applied in a rigid way that is inappropriate to qualitative research, it becomes difficult for qualitative researchers to demonstrate that their research is of high quality and credible.

Three types of response to this are evident. Firstly, there are those who continue to use the concepts of reliability and validity, adapting them to qualitative research. Those who adopt this response generally believe that since all research needs to be reliable and valid, using these terms is important to be able to demonstrate the quality and comparable status of qualitative research. Qualitative research is not necessarily intended to be replicated because it will reflect the socially constructed interpretations of participants in a particular setting at the time it is conducted. However, rigorous description of the research design, context and methods may help others to replicate similar studies. Where possible, use of more than one interviewer, observer and data analyst will also improve the quality of the research, referred to as its internal reliability. The adaptation of the concept of internal validity to qualitative research is generally not seen as a problem since the in-depth nature of qualitative methods means that the theoretical relationships that are proposed can be shown to be well grounded in a rich collection of data. The adaptation of external validity to qualitative research has been questioned because small samples limit the generalisability of such studies. However, qualitative researchers have pointed to other forms of generalisability that demonstrate the quality and value of qualitative research. For example, findings from one qualitative research setting may lead to generalisations across other settings, where, for example, characteristics of the research setting are similar, or where learning from the research setting can be applied in other settings (Buchanan 2012).

Secondly, there are those who have developed parallel versions of reliability, internal validity and external validity, with distinct names, that recognise the nature of qualitative research. In this regard, Lincoln and Guba (1985) formulated 'dependability' for 'reliability', 'credibility' for 'internal validity' and 'transferability' for 'external validity' (Table 10.5). Thirdly, there are those who have moved further away from the concepts of reliability and validity and have sought to develop new concepts through which to ensure and judge the quality of qualitative research. In this regard, Guba and Lincoln (1989, 2005; Lincoln et al. 2011) have developed 'authenticity criteria' as an alternative to validity (Table 10.5).

A key concern in designing your research will be to familiarise yourself with the criteria to be used to assess your research project. These assessment criteria might state that your research design and report has to consider issues of reliability/dependability and validity/credibility/authenticity. Other assessment criteria will be generic, related to analytical and evaluative abilities, only implicitly recognising the need for reliable/dependable and valid/credible/authentic research in assessing your research design and outcomes. Familiarising yourself with the assessment criteria to be used will help you to decide how you should approach the way you describe and discuss the quality of your research.

Validation

In our discussion about assessing quality and alternative criteria to evaluate it (i.e. reliability/dependability and validity/credibility/authenticity) we have already referred to techniques of validation (e.g. measurement validity, checking data with participants),

Table 10.5 Alternative quality criteria

Criterion	Definition and techniques to achieve each criterion
Dependability	This is the parallel criterion to reliability. In interpretivist research, the research focus is likely to be modified as the research progresses. Dependability in this context means recording all of the changes to produce a reliable/dependable account of the emerging research focus that may be understood and evaluated by others
Credibility	This is the parallel criterion to internal validity. Emphasis is placed on ensuring that the representations of the research participants' socially constructed realities actually match what the participants intended. A range of techniques to ensure this match include: • lengthy research involvement to build trust and rapport and to collect sufficient data; • use of reflection using a different person to discuss ideas and test out findings etc.; • developing a thorough analysis that accounts for negative cases by refining the analysis in order to produce the best possible explanation of the phenomenon being studied; • checking data, analysis and interpretations with participants; • making sure that the researchers' preconceived expectations about what the research will reveal are not privileged over the social constructions of the participant by regularly recording these and challenging them during analysis of the data
Transferability	This is the parallel criterion to external validity or generalisability. By providing a full description of the research questions, design, context, findings and interpretations, the researcher provides the reader with the opportunity to judge the transferability of the study to another setting in which the reader is interested to research
Authenticity criteria	These were not conceived as parallel criteria but as criteria that are specifically designed for the nature of constructivist/interpretivist research. Guba and Lincoln (1989) devised 'fairness', 'ontological', 'educative', 'catalytic' and 'tactical' authenticity criteria. These are designed to promote fairness by representing all views in the research; raise awareness and generate learning; and bring about change

Sources: Developed from Guba and Lincoln 1989; Lincoln and Guba 1985; Lincoln et al. 2011

without using this term. **Validation** is the process of verifying research data, analysis and interpretation to establish their validity/credibility/authenticity. We now discuss two validation techniques which may help you to establish the quality of your research:

- triangulation;
- participant or member validation.

Triangulation involves using more than one source of data and method of collection to confirm the validity/credibility/authenticity of research data, analysis and interpretation. This will necessitate you using a multi-method quantitative study, multi-method qualitative study or a mixed methods study (Section 10.3). The purpose is to use two or more independent sources of data and methods of collection within one study to ensure that the data are telling you what you think they are telling you. In a research study based on positivist assumptions, this will help to reveal the 'reality' in the data. Interpretivist researchers challenge this outcome as they consider that in relation to studies involving people's beliefs, attitudes and interpretations, 'reality' is socially constructed and multifaceted. For interpretivists, the value of using triangulation is that it adds depth, breadth, complexity and richness to their research (Denzin 2012; Denzin and Lincoln 2011).

Participant or **member validation** involves taking or sending research data back to participants to allow them to confirm its accuracy, by permitting them to comment on and correct it to validate it. This may take the form of showing them interview transcripts, observation or other notes, storied accounts as well as researcher interpretations of participants' data (e.g. Cayla and Arnould 2013). Participant collaboration is essential in some qualitative research strategies such as Action Research, while forms of collaboration such as member validation will be important in other qualitative research strategies and in mixed methods research. While the nature of quantitative data may preclude member validation, where you use a survey strategy you may still find it useful to discuss the results from your quantitative analysis with a sample of your respondents to help you to explain and interpret these data. Member validation may be problematic when a participant wishes to withdraw some of the data shared with you. You will need to differentiate between cases where participants correct your interpretation of the data they shared with you and cases where they simply change their attitude. The latter scenario may relate to an ethical concern and you will need to reflect on the extent to which you should alter the original data.

Logic leaps and false assumptions

So far in this chapter we have shown that there are a host of research design decisions to be made in order that your research project can yield sufficient good-quality data. These decisions will necessitate careful thought. Your research design will need to be logical and, along with any assumptions you make, to stand up to careful scrutiny. Raimond (1993: 128) advises you to 'stand back from your research [design] and take a critical, objective view of it, as though you were a detached observer'. This will allow you to see your design as others might, so that you can examine the logic of the research steps you propose to take to see if they will stand up to rigorous scrutiny.

10.9 Taking into account your role as researcher

This chapter has discussed the decisions you will need to take to formulate your research design. You need to choose between quantitative, qualitative or mixed methods; between research strategies; and between time frames. Each decision will have implications for the nature of your design (between an exploratory, descriptive, explanatory or evaluative purpose, or some combination of these). Each decision also has implications for the ways in which you seek to establish a quality research design that is ethical. As you have read through this chapter, you have probably been evaluating each of these decisions in relation to practical constraints as well as personal preferences. We have alluded to practical constraints in a number of places in the chapter in terms of the way they may affect each choice. An important practical consideration in deciding how to formulate a research design is related to your role as researcher.

The role of the external researcher

If you are a full-time student you are likely to adopt the role of an **external researcher**, as you need to identify an organisation within which to conduct your research. In such cases you will need to negotiate access to the organisation and to those from whom you would like to collect data. Having achieved this you will need to gain their trust so that they will participate meaningfully to allow you to collect these data. You will need to take these practical factors into account when formulating your research question and your research design.

The role of the internal researcher or practitioner researcher

If you are currently working in an organisation, you may choose to undertake your research project within that organisation, adopting the role of an **internal researcher** or **practitioner researcher**. As a part-time student, you will be surrounded by numerous opportunities to pursue business and management research. You are unlikely to encounter one of the most difficult hurdles that an external researcher has to overcome: that of negotiating research access. Indeed, like many people in such a position, you may be asked to research a particular problem by your employer.

As an internal researcher, another advantage for you will be your knowledge of the organisation and all this implies about understanding the complexity of what goes on in that organisation. It will not be necessary to spend a great deal of time 'learning the context' in the same way as an external researcher will need to do. However, this advantage carries with it a significant disadvantage. You must be very conscious of the assumptions and preconceptions that you carry around with you. This is an inevitable consequence of knowing the organisation well and can prevent you from exploring issues that would enrich the research.

Familiarity may create other problems for the internal researcher. When we were doing case study work in a manufacturing company, we found it very useful to ask 'basic' questions revealing our ignorance about the industry and the organisation. These 'basic' questions are ones that as a practitioner researcher you would be less likely to ask because you, and your respondents, would feel that you should know the answers already. There is also the problem of status. If you are a junior employee you may feel that working with more senior colleagues inhibits your interactions as researcher practitioner. The same may be true if you are more senior than your colleagues.

A more practical problem is that of time. Combining two roles at work is obviously very demanding, particularly as it may involve you in much data recording 'after hours'. This activity is hidden from those who determine your workload. They may not appreciate the demands that your researcher role is making on you. For this reason, practitioner researchers may need to negotiate a proportion of their 'work time' to devote to their research. There are no easy answers to these problems. All you can do is be aware of the possible impact on your research of being too close to your research setting.

Tietze (2012) offers some guidance for internal researchers. These include reflecting on your role as internal researcher so that you may recognise how this affects the way you design and conduct your research (where you have scope to influence what you are going to research). The research you undertake and the report you produce of it may have implications for those you work with and you will therefore need to consider the implications of how you research and what you report. You will need to consider your emotions and to manage these during this process of being an internal researcher. The process of analysing, interpreting and theorising about the research data you collect may have the effect of making 'strange the all-too-familiar' (Tietze 2012: 68) and you will need to cope with the degree of detachment that this may produce as you re-evaluate the way in which you view the organisation.

10.10 Summary

- Research design is the way a research question and objectives are operationalised into a research project. The research design process involves a series of decisions that need to combine into a coherent research project.
- Research design will be informed by your research philosophy.
- A choice has to be made to use quantitative or qualitative methods, or both, to create a mono method, multi-method or mixed methods research design.
- The focus of your research will be exploratory, descriptive, explanatory, evaluative or a combination of these.
- A decision will be made to use one or more research strategies, related to the nature of the research question and objectives and to ensure coherence with the other elements of your research design.
- Possible research strategies include: Experiment; Survey; Archival and Documentary Research; Case Study; Ethnography; Action Research; Grounded Theory and Narrative Inquiry.
- Choice of research strategy or strategies will be related to use of an appropriate time horizon.
- Research ethics play a critical part in formulating a research design.
- Establishing the quality of research is also a critical part of formulating a research design. Researchers from different research traditions have developed different criteria to judge and ensure the quality of research.
- Practical considerations will also affect research design, including the role of the researcher.

Self-check questions

Answers to these questions are available at the end of the chapter.

10.1 You wish to study the reasons why car owners join manufacturer-sponsored owners' clubs. You choose to use a qualitative methodology and narrative inquiry research strategy involving unstructured 'discussions' with some members of these owners' clubs. You are asked by a small group of marketing managers to explain why your chosen research design is as valid as a quantitative methodology, survey strategy that uses a questionnaire. What would be your answer?

10.2 You are working in an organisation that has branches throughout the country. The managing director is mindful of the fact that managers of the branches need to talk over common problems on a regular basis. That is why there have always been monthly meetings. However, she is becoming increasingly concerned that these meetings are not cost-effective. Too many managers see them as an unwelcome intrusion. They feel that their time would be better spent pursuing their principal job objectives. Other managers see it as a 'day off': an opportunity to recharge the batteries.

She has asked you to carry out some research on the cost effectiveness of the monthly meetings. You have defined the research question you are seeking to answer as 'What are the managers' opinions of the value of their monthly meetings?'

Your principal research strategy will be a survey using a questionnaire to all managers who attend the monthly meetings. However, you are keen to triangulate your findings. How might you do this?

10.3 You have started conducting interviews in a university with the non-academic employees (such as administrative and other support staff). The research objective is to establish the extent to which those employees feel a sense of 'belonging' to the university. You have negotiated access to your interviewees through the head of each of the appropriate departments. In each case you have been presented with a list of interviewees.

It soon becomes apparent to you that you are getting a rather rosier picture than you expected. The interviewees are all very positive about their jobs, their managers and the university. This makes you suspicious. Are all the non-academic staff as positive as this? Are you being given only the employees who can be relied on to tell the 'good news'? Have they been 'got at' by their manager?

There is a great risk that your results will not be valid. What can you do?

10.4 You are about to embark on a year-long study of customer service training for sales assistants in two national supermarket companies. The purpose of the research is to compare the way in which the training develops and its effectiveness. What measures would you need to take in the research design stage to ensure that your results were valid?

Review and discussion questions

10.5 Agree with a friend to watch the same television documentary.

a Does the documentary use a quantitative, qualitative or mixed methods research methodology?

b To what extent is the nature of the documentary exploratory, descriptive, explanatory, evaluative or a combination of these?

c What other observations can you make about the research strategy or strategies the documentary makers have used in their programme?

Do not forget to make notes regarding your reasons for your answers to each of these questions and to discuss these answers with your friend.

10.6 Use the search facilities of an online database to search for scholarly (peer-reviewed) articles which have used firstly a case study, secondly Action Research and thirdly experiment research strategy in an area of interest to you. Download a copy of each article. What reasons do the articles' authors give for the choice of strategy?

10.7 Visit the online gateway to the European Union website (http://europa.eu/) and click on the link in your own language. Discuss with a friend how you might use the data available via links from this web page in archival research. In particular, you should concentrate on the research questions you might be able to answer using these data to represent part of the reality you would be researching.

Progressing your research project

Deciding on your research design

- Review your research question and objectives. Make notes on your philosophy and how it will impact on your research (which philosophy and the likely impact).
- Do your research question and objectives and philosophy support using mono method quantitative or qualitative, multi-method quantitative or qualitative, or mixed methods research design? Make notes for and against using each methodological choice. Decide which one is most appropriate.
- Based on the decisions you have made so far, create a shortlist of research strategies which may be appropriate to conduct your research, together with the advantages and disadvantages of each. Set this shortlist aside. Search for studies in the literature that are similar to your own. Use these to note which strategies have been used. What explanations do the researchers give for their choice of strategy? Evaluate your shortlist against the notes from your search of studies in the literature. Use this evaluation to decide which strategy or combination of strategies would be most appropriate for your own research.
- Decide on the time frame to conduct your proposed research.
- Ask yourself, 'What are the practical constraints on my proposed design?' Use this question to review your decisions above and if necessary make changes. Repeat this step until you are satisfied your proposals are practical.
- Use your draft research design to list (1) potential threats to research quality and (2) ethical issues in your design and make notes about how you propose to deal with each. Where necessary, make further changes to the decisions in the steps above until you are satisfied with your research design.
- You should now be ready to discuss your proposed research design with your project tutor.
- Use the questions to guide your reflective diary entry.

References

Bansal, P. and Corley, K. (2011) 'The coming of age for qualitative research: Embracing the diversity of qualitative methods', *Academy of Management Review*, Vol. 54, No. 2, pp. 233–7.

Bryant, A. and Charmaz, K. (2007) *The Sage Handbook of Grounded Theory*. London: Sage.

Bryman, A. (2006) 'Integrating quantitative and qualitative research: How is it done?', *Qualitative Research*, Vol. 6, No. 1, pp. 97–113.

Buchanan, D.A. (2012) 'Case studies in organizational research', in G. Symon and C. Cassell (eds) *Qualitative Organisational Research Core Methods and Current Challenges*. London: Sage, pp. 351–70.

Cayla, J. and Arnould, E. (2013) 'Ethnographic stories for market learning', *Journal of Marketing*, Vol. 77, July, pp. 1–16.

Charmaz, K. (2006) *Constructing Grounded Theory*. London: Sage.

Charmaz, K. (2011) 'Grounded theory methods in social justice research', in N.K. Denzin and Y.S. Lincoln (eds) *The Sage Handbook of Qualitative Research* (4th edn). London: Sage, pp. 359–80.

Chase, S.E. (2011) 'Narrative Inquiry: Still a field in the making', in N.K. Denzin and Y.S. Lincoln (eds) *The Sage Handbook of Qualitative Research* (4th edn). London: Sage, pp. 421–34.

Coffey, A. and Atkinson, P. (1996) *Making Sense of Qualitative Data*. London: Sage.

Coghlan, D. (2011) 'Action Research: Exploring perspectives on a philosophy of practical knowing', *The Academy of Management Annals*, Vol. 5, No. 1, pp. 53–87.

Coghlan, D. and Brannick, T. (2014) *Doing Action Research in Your Own Organisation* (4th edn). London: Sage.

Cook, T.D. and Campbell, D.T. (1979) *Quasi-experimentation: Design and Analysis Issues for Field Settings*. Chicago: Rand McNally.

Corbin, J. and Strauss, A. (2008) *Basics of Qualitative Research* (3rd edn). London: Sage.

Creswell, J.W. (2009) 'Mapping the field of mixed methods research', *Journal of Mixed Methods Research*, Vol. 3, No. 2, pp. 95–108.

Creswell, J.W. and Plano Clark, V.L. (2011) *Designing and Conducting Mixed Methods Research* (2nd edn). Thousand Oaks, CA: Sage.

Cunliffe, A.L. (2010) 'Retelling tales of the field: In search of organisational ethnography 20 years on', *Organizational Research Methods*, Vol. 13, No. 2, pp. 224–39.

Czarniawska, B. (1997) *Narrating the Organization: Dramas of Institutional Identity*. Chicago: University of Chicago Press.

Daneshkhu, S .and Consumer Industries Editor (2013) 'Emerging markets shoppers turn to web for deals', *Financial Times*, 13 October.

Delamont, S. (2007) 'Ethnography and participant observation', in C. Seale, G. Gobo, J.F. Gubrium and D. Silverman (eds) *Qualitative Research Practice*. London: Sage, pp. 205–17.

Denzin, N.K. (2012) 'Triangulation 2.0', *Journal of Mixed Methods Research*, Vol. 6, No. 2, pp. 80–8.

Denzin, N.K. and Lincoln, Y.S. (2005) *The Sage Handbook of Qualitative Research* (3rd edn). London: Sage.

Denzin, N.K. and Lincoln, Y.S. (2011) 'Introduction: The discipline and practice of qualitative research', in N.K. Denzin and Y.S. Lincoln (eds) *The Sage Handbook of Qualitative Research* (4th edn). London: Sage, pp. 1–19.

Department for Business, Innovation and Skills (2013) *Workplace employment relations study (WERS)*. Available at: https://www.gov.uk/government/collections/workplace-employment-relations-study-wers [Accessed 10 March 2014].

Dubois, A. and Gadde, L-E. (2002) 'Systematic combining: An abductive approach to case research', *Journal of Business Research*, Vol. 55, pp. 553–60.

Eden, C. and Huxham, C. (1996) 'Action research for management research', *British Journal of Management*, Vol. 7, No. 1, pp. 75–86.

Eisenhardt, K.M. (1989) 'Building theories from case study research', *Academy of Management Review*, Vol. 14, No. 4, pp. 532–50.

Eisenhardt, K.M. and Graebner, M.E. (2007) 'Theory building from cases: Opportunities and challenges', *Academy of Management Journal*, Vol. 50, No. 1, pp. 25–32.

Flyvberg, B. (2011) 'Case study', in N.K. Denzin and Y.S. Lincoln (eds) *The Sage Handbook of Qualitative Research* (4th edn). London: Sage, pp. 301–16.

Gabriel, Y. and Griffiths, D.S. (2004) 'Stories in organizational research', in C. Cassell and G. Symon (eds) *Essential Guide to Qualitative Methods in Organizational Research*. London: Sage, pp. 114–26.

Geertz, C. (1988) *Works and Lives: The Anthropologist as Author*. Stanford, CA: Stanford University Press.

Gibb, F. (1995) 'Consumer group accuses lawyers of shoddy service', *The Times*, 5 October.

Glaser, B. and Strauss, A. (1967) *The Discovery of Grounded Theory*. Chicago, IL: Aldine.

Glaser, B.G. (1978) *Theoretical Sensitivity: Advances in the Methodology of Grounded Theory*. Mill Valley, CA: Sociology Press.

Glaser, B.G. (1992) *Basics of Grounded Theory*. Mill Valley, CA: Sociology Press.

Greene, J.C. (2007) *Mixed Methods in Social Inquiry*. San Francisco, CA: Jossey-Bass.

Greene, J.C., Caracelli, V.J. and Graham, W.F. (1989) 'Towards a conceptual framework for mixed-method evaluation designs', *Educational Evaluation and Policy Analysis*, Vol. 11, No. 3, pp. 255–74.

Greenwood, D.J. and Levin. M. (2007) *Introduction to Action Research* (2nd edn). London: Sage.

Guba, E.G. and Lincoln, Y.S. (1989) *Fourth Generation Evaluation*. Newbury Park, CA: Sage.

Hakim, C. (2000) *Research Design: Successful Designs for Social and Economic Research* (2nd edn). London: Routledge.

IJMR (2007) 'Special Issue on Ethnography', *International Journal of Market Research*, Vol. 49, No. 6, pp. 681–778.

Jenkins, M.F., Zapf, D., Winefield, H. and Sarris, A. (2012) 'Bullying allegations from the accused bully's perspective', *British Journal of Management*, Vol. 23, No. 4, pp. 489–501.

Kenealy, G.J.J. (2012) 'Grounded Theory: A theory building approach', in G. Symon and C. Cassell (eds) *Qualitative Organisational Research Core Methods and Current Challenges*. London: Sage, pp. 408–25.

Lee, B. (2012) 'Using documents in organizational research', in G. Symon and C. Cassell (eds) *Qualitative Organisational Research Core Methods and Current Challenges*. London: Sage, pp. 389–407.

Lee, R.M. and Fielding, N. (1996) 'Qualitative data analysis: Representations of a technology', *Sociological Research Online*, Vol. 1, No. 4. Available at: http://www.socresonline.org.uk/1/4/lf.html [Accessed 11 October 2011].

Lincoln, Y.S. and Guba, E.G. (1985) *Naturalistic Inquiry*. Beverly Hills, CA: Sage.

Lincoln, Y.S., Lynham, S.A. and Guba, E.G. (2011) 'Paradigmatic controversies, contradictions, and emerging confluences, revisited', in N.K. Denzin and Y.S. Lincoln (eds) *The Sage Handbook of Qualitative Research* (4th edn). London: Sage, pp. 97–128.

Maitlis, S. (2012) 'Narrative analysis', in G. Symon and C. Cassell (eds) *Qualitative Organisational Research Core Methods and Current Challenges*. London: Sage, pp. 492–511.

Molina-Azorin, J.F. (2011) 'The use and added value of mixed methods in management research', *Journal of Mixed Methods Research*, Vol. 5, No. 1, pp. 7–24.

Molina-Azorin, J.F. (2012) 'Mixed methods research in strategic management: Impact and applications', *Organizational Research Methods*, Vol. 15, No. 1, pp. 33–56.

Musson, G. (2004) 'Life histories', in C. Cassell and G. Symon (eds) *Essential Guide to Qualitative Methods in Organizational Research*. London: Sage, pp. 34–46.

Naipaul, V.S. (1989) *A Turn in the South*. London: Penguin.

Nastasi, B.K., Hitchcock, J.H. and Brown, L.M. (2010) 'An inclusive framework for conceptualising mixed methods typologies', in A. Tashakkori and C. Teddlie (eds) *The Sage Handbook of Mixed Methods in Social and Behavioural Research* (2nd edn). Thousand Oaks, CA: Sage.

O'Reilley, K., Paper, D. and Marx, S. (2012) 'Demystifying Grounded Theory for business research', *Organizational Research Methods*, Vol. 15, No. 2, pp. 247–62.

Prior, L. (2007) 'Documents', in C. Seale, G. Gobo, J.F. Gubrium and D. Silverman (eds) *Qualitative Research Practice*. London: Sage, 345–60.

Raimond, P. (1993) *Management Projects*. London: Chapman & Hall.

Reason, P. (2006) 'Choice and quality in action research practice', *Journal of Management Inquiry*, Vol. 15, No. 2, pp. 187–202.

Reason, P. and Bradbury, H. (2008) *Handbook of Action Research* (2nd edn). London: Sage.

Reichertz, J. (2007) Abduction: The logic of discovery of grounded theory', in A. Bryant and K.Charmaz (eds) *The Sage Handbook of Grounded Theory*. London: Sage.

Ridder, H-G., Hoon, C. and McCandless Baluch, A. (2014) 'Entering a dialogue: Positioning case study findings towards theory', *British Journal of Management*, Vol. 25, No. 2, pp. 373–87.

Ridenour, C.S. and Newman, I. (2008) *Mixed Methods Research: Exploring the Interactive Continuum*. Carbondale, IL: South Illinois University Press.

Rogers, C.R. (1961) *On Becoming a Person*. London: Constable.

Schein, E. (1999) *Process Consultation Revisited: Building the Helping Relationship*. Reading, MA: Addison-Wesley.

Shani, A.B. and Pasmore, W.A. (1985) 'Organization inquiry: Towards a new model of the action research process', in D.D. Warrick (ed.) *Contemporary Organization Development*. Glenview, IL: Scott Foresman, pp. 438–48.

Stake, R.E. (2005) 'Qualitative case studies', in N.K. Denzin and Y.S. Lincoln (eds) *The Sage Handbook of Qualitative Research* (3rd edn). London: Sage, pp. 443–65.

Strauss, A. and Corbin, J. (1998) *Basics of Qualitative Research* (2nd edn). London: Sage.

Suddaby, R. (2006) 'From the editors: What grounded theory is not', *Academy of Management Journal*, Vol. 49, No. 4, pp. 633–42.

Tashakkori, A. and Teddlie, C. (eds) (2010) *The Sage Handbook of Mixed Methods in Social and Behavioural Research* (2nd edn). Thousand Oaks, CA: Sage.

Teddlie, C. and Tashakkori, A. (2009) *Foundations of Mixed Methods Research: Integrating Quantitative and Qualitative Approaches in the Social and Behavioral Sciences*. Thousand Oaks, CA: Sage.

Teddlie, C. and Tashakkori, A. (2011) 'Mixed methods research: Contemporary issues in an emerging field', in N.K. Denzin and Y.S. Lincoln (eds) *The Sage Handbook of Qualitative Research* (4th edn). London: Sage, pp. 285–99.

Tedlock, B. (2005) 'The observation of participation and the emergence of public ethnography', in N.K. Denzin and Y.S. Lincoln (eds) *The Sage Handbook of Qualitative Research* (3rd edn). London: Sage.

Tietze, S. (2012) 'Researching your own organization', in G. Symon and C. Cassell (eds) *Qualitative Organisational Research Core Methods and Current Challenges*. London: Sage, pp. 53–71.

Titscher, S., Meyer, M., Wodak, R. and Vetter, E. (2000) *Methods of Text and Discourse Analysis*. London: Sage, pp. 467–82.

Whyte, W.F. (1993) *Street Corner Society: The Social Structure of an Italian Slum* (4th edn). Chicago, IL: University of Chicago Press.

Yin, R.K. (2014) *Case Study Research: Design and Method* (5th edn). London: Sage.

Further reading

Charmaz, K. (2006) *Constructing Grounded Theory*. London: Sage. Useful for Grounded Theory strategy.

Coghlan, D. and Brannick, T. (2014). *Doing Action Research in Your Own Organisation* (4th edn). London: Sage. Useful for Action Research strategy.

Cunliffe, A.L. (2010) 'Retelling tales of the field: In search of organisational ethnography 20 years on', *Organizational Research Methods*, Vol. 13, No. 2, pp. 224–39. Useful for Organisational Ethnography.

deVaus, D.A. (2014) *Surveys in Social Research* (6th edn). Abingdon: Routledge. Useful for Survey strategy.

Hakim, C. (2000) *Research Design: Successful Designs for Social and Economic Research* (2nd edn). London: Routledge. Chapter 9 is useful for Experiment strategy.

Symon, G. and Cassell, C. (eds) (2012) *Qualitative Organisational Research Core Methods and Current Challenges*. London: Sage. Useful for several research strategies including Action Research, Case Study, Documentary research, Ethnography, Grounded Theory and Narrative Inquiry.

Yin, R.K. (2014) *Case Study Research: Design and Method* (5th edn). London: Sage. Useful for Case Study strategy.

Case 5
Managers' challenges when dealing with change

Ying was struck when one of the lecturers on her postgraduate module talked about how managers often struggle when companies undergo changes such as mergers, and how they often fail to address their own difficulties. Since it was time for her to start thinking about her postgraduate research project, she thought that understanding the challenges managers face in looking after the organisation and its employees during change processes would be a worthwhile and fulfilling research aim for her project and that maybe she could use her findings to help people cope with organisational change in future. As Ying filled out the form that would help her department assign her project tutor, she started to think about how she could design a project like this. She recalled several different methodologies from her research methods module, including quantitative and more qualitative research designs. She vaguely remembered that qualitative methods were better for understanding people so that was what she put down.

Soon after she was assigned her research project tutor, Mikael, they sat down together and discussed the best method. Mikael agreed that qualitative methods would be well suited and suggested that Ying could start reading around what methods there were and the analysis that she would be doing. Soon after starting to read about qualitative methods in more detail, she ruled out interviews. These she reasoned would not allow her to follow what was actually going on 'live' in the organisation (Van Maanen, 2011). She was convinced that the challenges that managers face in a change process could only really be understood by observing what they were actually doing and understanding the context in which this was happening. Consequently Ying decided that an ethnographic research design would most suit her research goal, which was to understand the challenges that managers face when dealing with change (Stahl et al., 2013) and understand aspects such as emotions experienced by managers themselves, making sense of what is happening around them and dealing with their own workload (Hammersley and Atkinson, 2003).

On reading further about ethnography, Ying realised that she needed to further refine her research design and think about her underlying research philosophy. From her reading she identified three common approaches to ethnography: critical, realist and interpretive. Each of these would mean something different for the way she would gather data in her ethnography. She immediately decided that the critical approach to ethnography might not fit since she was not interested in the power relations in the organisation. She felt it was difficult to decide between the realist and interpretive approaches on her own. The realist approach would give her insights into how managers deal with change by focusing on the objective decisions and actions they take, but it would not allow her to gain insight into how they actually make sense of and interpret change. Interpretive ethnography might give her a richer understanding of how managers deal with change, but she was concerned that interpretive ethnography was rather unscientific as, unlike the realist stance, it involved her own interpretation of the data. For this reason, she felt that realist ethnography might help her to gain better data. After having mulled it over for a couple of days she decided, slightly reluctantly, to ask Mikael for help. Soon after the two of them met and discussed which stance would be more appropriate. Mikael told her that the realist and interpretive approaches were equally accepted methods. He questioned whether taking a realist stance would really let her find out what motivated managerial actions during change. He felt that interpretive ethnography might be most appropriate for Ying's study as she wanted to look at how managers deal and cope with change beyond what they say and do. He advised her that it was important to acknowledge that the researcher is part of the creation of knowledge, but that this is an accepted means of uncovering the rich insights that will come from interpretive work. Consequently Ying felt more comfortable taking an interpretive stance.

Having decided on her philosophical position, Ying started thinking about some other aspects of her research design – how many cases she was going to study and for how long. She remembered that it was acceptable to carry out a single case study but that using multiple cases would allow her to make comparisons between different situations. Upon reflecting on the amount of work that goes into an ethnography and reading some articles that used ethnography, she realised that one case was all that she would be able to manage since she only really had a couple of months for gathering data. However, she realised that in order to understand the managers and how they dealt with change she would have to study the company for as long as possible. Therefore she decided that she would use the entire two months that she had available for data collection, which seemed like a good amount of time since she found that other researchers had spent similar amounts of time in their research setting.

Ying stepped back and thought about her decisions. She was very happy with every aspect of her research design so far and was already looking forward to the next step – finding access to a company to help her work out who she would talk to and observe. She knew getting access was not going to be easy but she was ready for the challenge.

References

Hammersley, M. and Atkinson, P. (2003). *Ethnography, Principles in Practice*. London: Routledge.

Stahl, G.K., Angwin, D.N., Very, P. Gomes, E., Weber, Y. et al. (2013) 'Sociocultural integration in mergers and acquisitions: Unresolved paradoxes and directions for future research', *Thunderbird International Business Review*, Vol. 55, No. 4, pp. 333–56.

Van Maanen, J. (2011) *Tales of the Field: On Writing Ethnography* (2nd edn). Chicago: Chicago Guides to Writing, Editing and Publishing.

Questions

1 a Do you agree with Ying's choice of an interpretive ethnographic strategy?
  b What would the choice of another strategy such as a survey have meant for the kind of insights she would have gained?
  c Would these have been different from the insights gained through the ethnographic research design?

2 Ying chose a single case study. Do you think she could have chosen to do multiple case studies in the time frame that she had? What difference would that have made to her study?
3 Was Ying right to seek help with deciding what type of ethnography to use? What might have happened if she had not sought help?
4 What can you learn about ethnographic methods from Ying's case?

Additional case studies relating to material covered in this chapter are available via the book's companion website: **www.pearsoned.co.uk/saunders**.

They are:

- The effectiveness of computer-based training at Falcon Insurance Company.
- Embedded quality at Zarlink Semi-conductor.
- The international marketing management decisions of UK ski tour operators.
- Managing the acquisition from the middle.
- Sangita's career.

Self-check answers

10.1 You would need to stress here that your principal interest would be in getting a deep understanding of why car owners join manufacturer-sponsored owners' clubs. You would discover why the owners joined these clubs and what they thought of them. In other words, you would establish what you set out to establish and, no doubt, a good deal besides. There is no reason why your discussions with owners should not be as valid as a survey questionnaire. Your initial briefing should be skilful enough to elicit rich responses from your interviewees (Chapter 10) and you may also use prompts to focus on themes that emerge in the narratives of your participants.

Of course, you may alleviate any fears about 'validity' by using a mixed methods research methodology and delivering a questionnaire as well, so that your findings may be triangulated!

10.2 The questionnaire will undoubtedly perform a valuable function in obtaining a comprehensive amount of data that can be compared easily, say, by district or age and gender. However, you would add to the understanding of the problem if you observed managers' meetings. Who does most of the talking? What are the non-verbal behaviour patterns displayed by managers? Who turns up late, or does not turn up at all? You could also consider talking to managers in groups or individually. Your decision here would be whether to talk to them before or after the questionnaire, or both. In addition, you could study the minutes of the meetings to discover who contributed the most. Who initiated the most discussions? What were the attendance patterns?

10.3 There is no easy answer to this question! You have to remember that access to organisations to research is an act of goodwill on the part of managers, and they do like to retain a certain amount of control. Selecting whom researchers may interview is a classic way of managers doing this. If this is the motive of the managers concerned then they are unlikely to let you have free access to their employees.

What you could do is ask to see all the employees in a particular department rather than a sample of employees. Alternatively, you could explain that your research was still uncovering new patterns of information and more interviews were necessary. This way you would penetrate deeper into the core of the employee group and might start seeing those who were rather less positive. All this assumes that you have the time to do this!

You could also be perfectly honest with the managers and confess your concern. If you did a sound job at the start of the research in convincing them that you are purely interested in academic research, and that all data will be anonymous, then you may have less of a problem.

Of course, there is always the possibility that the employees generally are positive and feel as if they really do 'belong'!

10.4 This would be a longitudinal study. Therefore, the potential of some of the threats to internal validity explained in Section 10.8 is greater simply because they have longer to develop. You would need to make sure that most of these threats were controlled as much as possible. For example, you would need to:

- account for the possibility of a major event during the period of the research (wide-scale redundancies, which might affect employee attitudes) in one of the companies but not the other;
- ensure that you used the same data collection devices in both companies;
- be aware of the 'mortality' problem. Some of the sales assistants will leave. You would be advised to replace them with assistants with similar characteristics, as far as possible.

Get ahead using resources on the companion website at: **www.pearsoned.co.uk/saunders**.

- Improve your IBM SPSS for Windows and NVivo research analysis with practice tutorials.
- Save time researching on the Internet with the Smarter Online Searching Guide.
- Test your progress using self-assessment questions.
- Follow live links to useful websites.

Chapter 11

Developing a Solution - Data Collection and Information Analysis

Learning outcomes

By the end of this chapter, you should be able to:

- identify the main issues that you need to consider when preparing quantitative data for analysis and when analysing these data by computer;
- recognise different types of data and understand the implications of data type for subsequent analyses;
- create a data matrix and code data for analysis by computer;
- select the most appropriate tables and graphs to explore and illustrate different aspects of your data;
- select the most appropriate statistics to describe individual variables and to examine relationships between variables and trends in your data;
- interpret the tables, graphs and statistics that you use correctly.

11.1 Introduction

Quantitative data in a raw form, that is, before these data have been processed and analysed, convey very little meaning to most people. These data, therefore, need to be processed to make them useful, that is, to turn them into information. Quantitative analysis techniques such as tables, graphs and statistics allow us to do this, helping us to explore, present, describe and examine relationships and trends within our data.

Virtually any business and management research you undertake is likely to involve some numerical data or contain data that could usefully be quantified to help you answer your research question(s) and to meet your objectives. Quantitative data refer to all such primary and secondary data and can range from simple counts such as the frequency of occurrences to more complex data such as test scores, prices or rental costs. To be useful these data need to be analysed and interpreted. Quantitative analysis techniques assist you in this process. They range from creating simple tables or graphs that show the frequency of occurrence and using statistics such as indices to enable comparisons, through establishing statistical relationships between variables to complex statistical modelling.

Within quantitative analysis, calculations and chart drawing are undertaken using analysis software ranging from spreadsheets such as Excel™ to more advanced data management and statistical analysis software packages such as Minitab™, SAS™, IBM SPSS Statistics™ and Statview™. You might also use more specialised survey design and analysis packages such as Qualtrics™ or

The Big Mac Index is published biannually by *The Economist* to provide a simple way of measuring differences in purchasing power between currencies. The index provides an idea of the extent to which currency exchange rates actually result in goods costing the same in different countries. Obviously the index does not take into account that Big Mac hamburgers are not precisely the same in every country; nutritional values, weights and sizes often differ. Similarly it does not allow for prices within a country differing between McDonald's restaurants, McDonald's providing *The Economist* with a single price for each country. However, it does provide an indication of whether purchasing power parity exists between different currencies.

The Big Mac Index is calculated by first converting the country price of a Big Mac (in the local currency) to US dollars using the current exchange rate. Using Big Mac Index figures available on the Internet (bigmacindex.org 2014), the British price of a Big Mac was £2.89 in July 2014. Using the exchange rate at that time of £1 equals $1.69, this converts to $4.93. At this time, the price of a Big Mac in the USA was $4.80, only 13 cents less than was charged in Britain. This means theoretically you could buy a Big Mac in the USA for $4.80 and sell it in the USA for $4.93, a profit of 13 cents. Unlike most index numbers which use the value 100 to express parity, the difference between the country price and the USA price is expressed as a percentage in the Big Mac Index. Consequently, as the British price for a Big Mac was 13 cents more than the USA price, the value of the index was −1.7 per cent. This indicates that purchasing power of the British pound was very slightly less than the US dollar, suggesting the currencies were valued about the same. According to the July 2014 index, one of the currencies with the greatest difference in purchasing power to the US dollar was the Ukrainian hryvnia; a Big Mac cost the equivalent of $1.63, less than a third of the price in the USA (with a Big Mac index value of +195 per cent). This suggests the currency was overvalued. In contrast, the Norwegian kroner could be considered undervalued; a Big Mac costing the equivalent of $7.60, over one and a half times the price in the USA (with a Big Mac Index value of −38 per cent). Where there is a parity of purchasing power, the index value is zero. This allows for easy comparisons between countries.

statistical shareware such as the R Project for Statistical Computing. However, while this means you do not have to be able to draw charts by hand or undertake calculations manually, if your analyses are to be straightforward and of any value you need to:

- have prepared your data with quantitative analyses in mind;
- be aware of and know when to use different graphing and statistical techniques.

This is not to say that there is only one possible technique for any analysis situation. As we will see, a range of factors need to be taken into account when selecting the most appropriate tables, graphs and statistics. Consequently, if you are unsure about which of these to use, you need to seek advice.

This chapter builds on the ideas outlined in earlier chapters about secondary data and primary data collection, including issues of sample size. It assumes that you will use a computer (with at least a spreadsheet) to undertake all but the simplest quantitative analyses. Although it does not focus on one particular piece of analysis software, you will notice in the Focus on student research boxes that many of the analyses were undertaken using widely available software such as Excel and IBM SPSS Statistics. If you wish to develop your skills in either of these software packages, self-teach packages are available via our companion website. In addition, there are numerous statistics books already published that concentrate on specific software packages. These include Dancey and Reidy (2011), Field (2013) or Pallant (2013) on IBM SPSS Statistics, Swift and Piff (2014) on IBM SPSS Statistics and Excel, and Scherbaum and Shockley (2015) on Excel. Likewise, this chapter does not attempt to provide an in-depth discussion of the wide range of graphical and statistical techniques available or to cover more complex statistical modelling, as these are already covered elsewhere (e.g. Dancey and Reidy 2011; Everitt and Dunn 2001; Hair et al. 2013; Hays 1994). Rather it discusses issues that need to be considered at the planning and analysis stages of your research project, and outlines analytical techniques that our students have found to be of most use. In particular, the chapter is concerned with:

- preparing, entering into a computer and checking your data (Section 11.2);
- selecting appropriate tables and graphs to explore and present your data (Section 11.3);
- selecting appropriate statistics to describe your data (Section 11.4);
- selecting appropriate statistics to examine relationships and trends in your data (Section 11.5).

11.2 Preparing, entering and checking data

If you intend to undertake quantitative analysis we recommend that you consider the:

- number of cases of data, that is the sample size (already discussed in Section 7.2);
- type or types of data (scale of measurement);
- data layout and format required by the analysis software;
- impact of data coding on subsequent analyses (for different types of data);
- process of entering (or inputting) data;
- need to weight cases;
- process of checking the data for errors.

Ideally, all of these should be considered before obtaining your data. This is equally important for both primary and secondary data analysis, although you obviously have far greater control over the type, format and coding of primary data. We shall now consider each of these.

Types of data

Many business statistics textbooks classify quantitative data into *data types* using a hierarchy of measurement, often in ascending order of numerical precision (Berman Brown and Saunders 2008; Dancey and Reidy 2011). These different levels of numerical measurement dictate the range of techniques available to you for the presentation, summary and analysis of your data. They are discussed in more detail in subsequent sections of this chapter.

Quantitative data can be divided into two distinct groups: categorical and numerical (Figure 11.1). **Categorical data** refer to data whose values cannot be measured

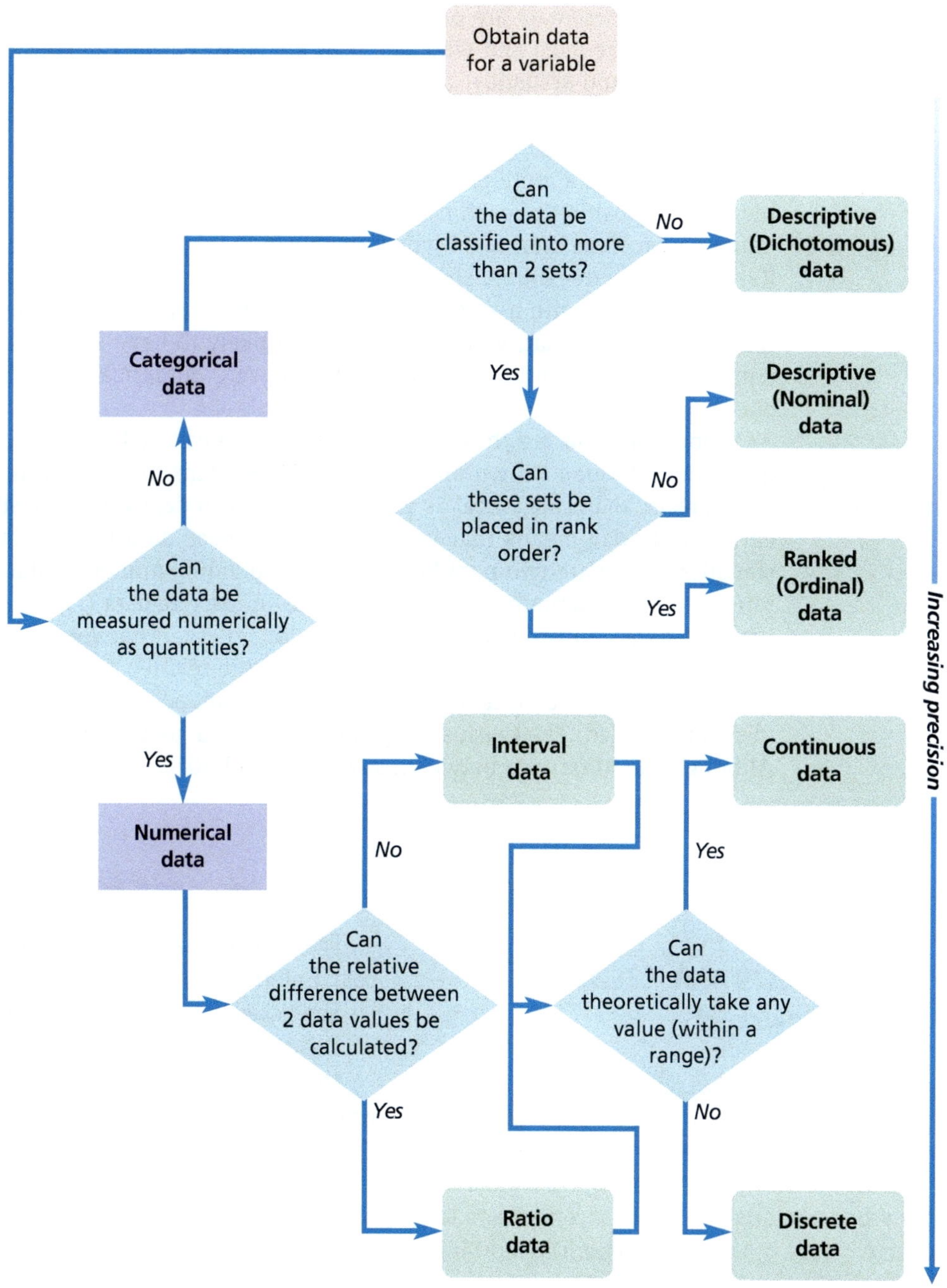

Figure 11.1 Defining the data type

numerically but can be either classified into sets (categories) according to the characteristics that identify or describe the variable or placed in rank order (Berman Brown and Saunders 2008). They can be further subdivided into descriptive and ranked. A car manufacturer might categorise the types of cars it produces as hatchback, saloon and estate. These are known as **descriptive data** or **nominal data** as it is impossible to define the category numerically or to rank it. Rather, these data simply count the number of occurrences in each category of a variable. For virtually all analyses the categories should be unambiguous and discrete; in other words, having one particular feature, such as a car being a hatchback, excludes all other features for that variable. This prevents questions arising regarding which category an individual case belongs to. Although these data are purely descriptive, you can count them to establish which category has the most and whether cases are spread evenly between categories. Some statisticians (and statistics) also separate descriptive data where there are only two categories. These are known as **dichotomous data**, as the variable is divided into two categories, such as the variable gender being divided into female and male. **Ranked** (or **ordinal**) **data** are a more precise form of categorical data. In such instances you know the relative position of each case within your data set, although the actual numerical measures (such as scores) on which the position is based are not recorded (Box 11.1). Rating or scale questions, such as where a respondent is asked to rate how strongly she or he agrees with a statement, collect ranked (ordinal) data. Despite this, some researchers argue that, where such data are likely to have similar size gaps between data values, they can be analysed as if they were numerical interval data (Blumberg et al. 2014).

Numerical data are those whose values are measured or counted numerically as quantities (Berman Brown and Saunders 2008). This means that numerical data are more precise than categorical as you can assign each data value a position on a numerical scale. It also means that you can analyse these data using a far wider range of statistics. There are two possible ways of subdividing numerical data: into interval or ratio data and, alternatively, into continuous or discrete data (Figure 11.1). If you have **interval data** you can state the difference or 'interval' between any two data values for a particular variable, but you cannot state the relative difference. This means that values on an interval scale can meaningfully be added and subtracted, but not multiplied and divided. The Celsius temperature scale is a good example of an interval scale. Although the difference between, say, 20°C and 30°C is 10°C it does not mean that

Box 11.1 Focus on student research

Scales of measurement

As part of a marketing questionnaire, Rashid asked individual customers to rank up to five features of a new product in order of importance to them. Data collected were, therefore, categorical and ranked (ordinal). Initial analyses made use of these ranked data. Unfortunately, a substantial minority of customers had ticked, rather than ranked, those features of importance to them.

All responses that had been ranked originally were therefore re-coded to 'of some importance'. This reduced the precision of measurement from ranked (ordinal) to descriptive (nominal) but enabled Rashid to use all responses in the subsequent analyses.

30°C is one and a half times as warm. This is because 0°C does not represent a true zero. When it is 0°C outside, there is still some warmth, rather than none at all! In contrast, for **ratio data**, you can also calculate the relative difference or ratio between any two data values for a variable. Consequently, if a multinational company makes a profit of $1,000,000,000 in one year and $2,000,000,000 the following year, we can say that profits have doubled.

Continuous data are those whose values can theoretically take any value (sometimes within a restricted range) provided that you can measure them accurately enough (Dancey and Reidy 2011). Data such as furnace temperature, delivery distance and length of service are therefore continuous data. **Discrete data** can, by contrast, be measured precisely. Each case takes one of a finite number of values from a scale that measures changes in discrete units. These data are often whole numbers (**integers**) such as the number of mobile telephones manufactured or customers served. However, in some instances (e.g. UK shoe size) discrete data will include non-integer values. Definitions of discrete and continuous data are, in reality, dependent on how your data values are measured. The number of customers served by a large organisation is strictly a discrete datum as you are unlikely to get a part customer! However, for a large organisation with many customers you might treat this as a continuous datum, as the discrete measuring units are exceedingly small compared with the total number being measured.

Understanding differences between types of data is extremely important when analysing your data quantitatively, for two reasons. Firstly, it is extremely easy with analysis software to generate statistics from your data that are inappropriate for the data type and are consequently of little value (Box 11.2). Secondly, as we will see in Sections 11.4 and 11.5, the more precise the scale of measurement, the greater the range of analytical techniques available to you. Data that have been collected and coded using a precise numerical scale of measurement can also be regrouped to a less precise level where they can also be analysed (Box 11.1). For example, a student's score in a test could be recorded as the actual mark (discrete data) or as the position in their class (ranked data). By contrast, less precise data cannot be made more precise. Therefore, if you are not sure about the scale of measurement you require, it is usually better to collect data at the highest level of precision possible and to regroup them if necessary.

Data layout

Some primary data collection methods, such as computer-aided personal interviewing (CAPI), computer-aided telephone interviewing (CATI) and Internet questionnaires, automatically enter and save data to a computer file at the time of collection, normally using predefined codes. These data can subsequently be exported in a range of formats to ensure they are compatible with different analysis software. Survey design and analysis software such as Qualtrics™ and SurveyMonkey™ goes one stage further and integrates the analysis software in the same package as the questionnaire design/data entry software (Qualtrics 2014; SurveyMonkey 2014). Alternatively, secondary data downloaded from the Internet can be saved to a file, removing the need for re-entering. For such data, it is often possible to specify a data layout compatible with your analysis software. For other data collection methods, you will have to prepare and enter your data for computer analysis. You therefore need to be clear about the precise data layout requirements of your analysis software.

Box 11.2 Focus on student research

The implications of data types for analysis

Pierre's research was concerned with customers' satisfaction for a small hotel group of six hotels. In collecting the data he had asked 760 customers to indicate the hotel at which they were staying when they completed their Internet questionnaires. When he downloaded his data, the Internet questionnaire software automatically allocated a numerical code to represent the hotel and named the variable. The codes allocated for the hotels were:

Hotel	Code
Amsterdam	1
Antwerp	2
Eindhoven	3
Nijmegen	4
Rotterdam	5
Tilburg	6

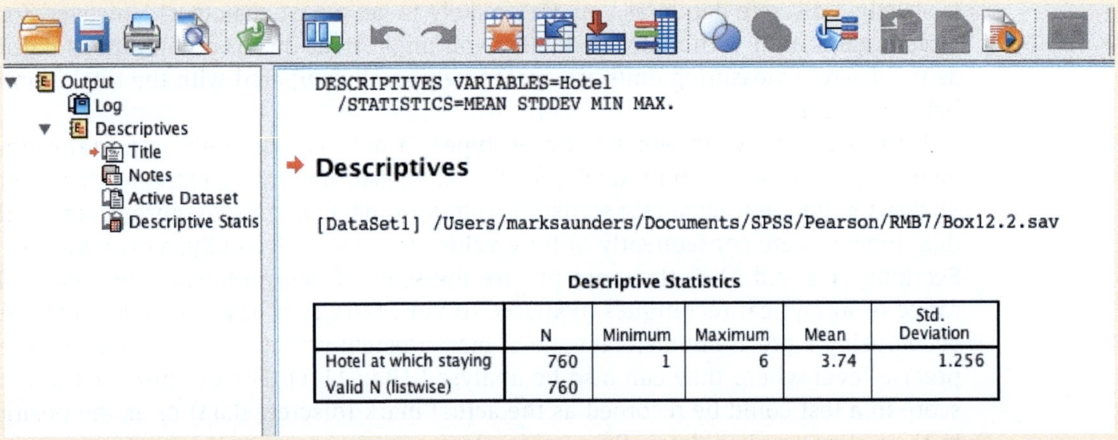

	N	Minimum	Maximum	Mean	Std. Deviation
Hotel at which staying	760	1	6	3.74	1.256
Valid N (listwise)	760				

In his initial analysis, Pierre used the analysis software to calculate descriptive statistics for every data variable, including the variable 'Hotel'. These included the minimum value (the code for Amsterdam), the maximum value (the code for Tilburg), the mean and the standard deviation. Looking at his computer screen, Pierre noted that the mean (average) was 3.74 and the standard deviation was 1.256. He had forgotten that the data for this variable were categorical and, consequently, the descriptive statistics he had chosen were inappropriate.

Virtually all analysis software will accept your data if they are entered in table format. This table is called a **data matrix** (Table 11.1). Once data have been entered into your analysis software, it is usually possible to save them in a format that can be read by other software. Within a data matrix, each column usually represents a separate **variable** for which you have obtained data. Each matrix row contains the variables for an individual **case**, that is, an individual unit for which data have been obtained. If your data have been collected using a questionnaire, each row will contain the data from one completed questionnaire. Secondary data that have already been stored in a data file are almost always held as a large data matrix. For such data sets you usually select the subset of variables and cases you require and save these

Table 11.1 A simple data matrix

	Id	Variable 1	Variable 2	Variable 3	Variable 4
Case 1	1	27	1	2	1
Case 2	2	19	2	1	2
Case 3	3	24	2	3	1

as a separate matrix. If you are entering your own data, they are typed directly into your chosen analysis software one case (row) at a time using codes to record the data (Box 11.3). Larger data sets with more data variables and cases are recorded using larger data matrices. Although data matrices store data using one column for each variable, this may not be the same as one column for each question for data collected using surveys.

We strongly recommend that you save your data regularly as you are entering it, to minimise the chances of deleting it all by accident! In addition, you should save a backup or security copy on your MP3 player or other mass storage device, the cloud and email it to yourself.

Box 11.3 Focus on student research

An Excel data matrix

Lucy's data related to employees who were working or had worked for a large public-sector organisation. In her Excel spreadsheet, the first variable (id) was the *survey form identifier*. This meant that she could link data for each case (row) in her matrix to the survey form when checking for errors (discussed later). The second variable (age) contained numerical data, the age of each respondent (case) at the time her questionnaire was administered. Subsequent variables contained the remaining data: the third (gender) recorded this dichotomous data using code 1 for male and 2 for female; the fourth (service) recorded numerical data about each case's length of service to the nearest year in the organisation. The final dichotomous variable (employed) recorded whether each respondent was (code 1) or was not (code 2) employed by the organisation at the time the data were collected. The codes used by Lucy, therefore, had different meanings for different variables.

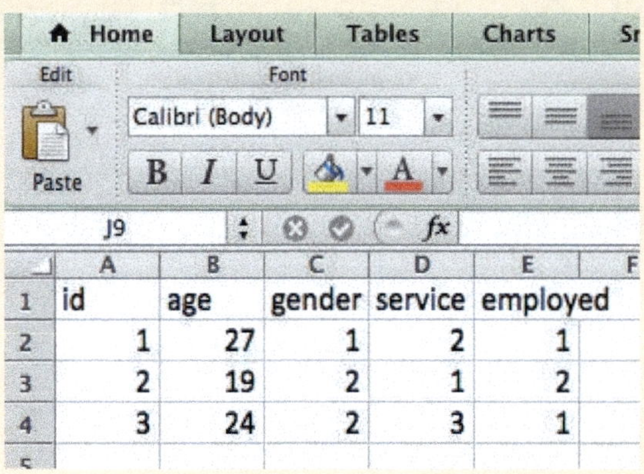

id	age	gender	service	employed
1	27	1	2	1
2	19	2	1	2
3	24	2	3	1

If you intend to enter data into a spreadsheet, the first variable is in Column A, the second in Column B and so on. Each cell in the first row (1) should contain a short variable name to enable you to identify each variable. Subsequent rows (2 onwards) will each contain the data for one case (Box 11.3). Statistical analysis software follows the same logic, although the variable names are usually displayed 'above' the first row (Box 11.4).

Box 11.4 Focus on student research

Data coding

As part of a market research interview survey, Zack needed to discover which of four products (tomato ketchup, brown sauce, soy sauce, vinegar) had been purchased within the last month by consumers. He therefore needed to collect four data items from each respondent:

- Tomato ketchup purchased within the last month? Yes/No
- Brown sauce purchased within the last month? Yes/No
- Soy sauce purchased within the last month? Yes/No
- Mayonnaise purchased within the last month? Yes/No

Each of these data items is a separate variable. However, the data were collected using one question:

1 Which of the following items have you purchased within the last month?

Item	Purchased	Not purchased	Not sure
Tomato ketchup	$\square_1$	$\square_2$	$\square_3$
Brown sauce	$\square_1$	$\square_2$	$\square_3$
Soy sauce	$\square_1$	$\square_2$	$\square_3$
Mayonnaise	$\square_1$	$\square_2$	$\square_3$

The data Zack collected from each respondent formed four separate variables in the data matrix using numerical codes (1 = purchased, 2 = not purchased, 3 = not sure). This is known as multiple-dichotomy coding.

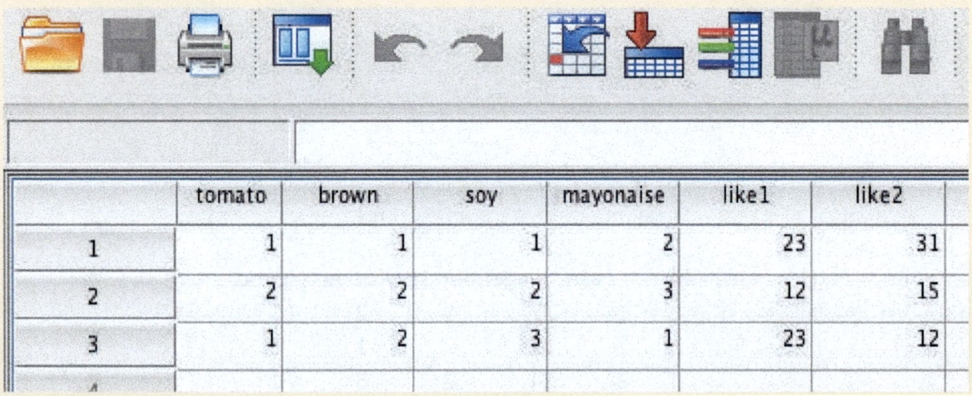

	tomato	brown	soy	mayonaise	like1	like2
1	1	1	1	2	23	31
2	2	2	2	3	12	15
3	1	2	3	1	23	12
4						

Zack also included a question (question 2 below) that could theoretically have millions of possible responses for each of the 'things'. For such questions, the number that each respondent mentions may also vary. Our experience suggests that virtually all respondents will select five or fewer. Zack therefore left space to code up to five responses after data had been collected.

For office use only

2 List up to five things you like about tomato ketchup .... □ □ □ □
.... □ □ □ □
.... □ □ □ □
.... □ □ □ □
.... □ □ □ □

The **multiple-response method** of coding uses the same number of variables as the maximum number of different responses from any one case. For Question 2 these were named 'like1', 'like2', 'like3', 'like4' and 'like5' (Box 11.4). Each of these variables would use the same codes and could include any of the responses as a category. Statistical analysis software often contains special multiple-response procedures to analyse such data. The alternative, the **multiple-dichotomy method** of coding, uses a separate variable for each different answer (Box 11.4). For Question 2 (Box 11.4) a separate variable could have been used for each 'thing' listed: for example, flavour, consistency, bottle shape, smell, price and so on. You subsequently would code each variable as 'listed' or 'not listed' for each case. This makes it easy to calculate the number of responses for each 'thing' (De Vaus 2014).

Coding

All data types should, with few exceptions, be recorded using numerical codes. This enables you to enter the data quickly using the numeric keypad and with fewer errors. It also makes subsequent analyses, in particular those that require re-coding of data to create new variables, more straightforward. Unfortunately, meaningless analyses are also easier, such as calculating a mean (average) gender from codes 1 and 2, or the mean hotel location (Box 11.2)! A common exception to using a numerical code for categorical data is where a postcode or zip code is used as the code for a geographical reference. If you are using a spreadsheet, you will need to keep a list of codes for each variable. Statistical analysis software can store these so that each code is automatically labelled.

Coding numerical data

Actual numbers are often used as codes for numerical data, even though this level of precision may not be required. Once you have entered your data as a matrix, you can use analysis software to group or combine data to form additional variables with less detailed categories. This process is referred to as **re-coding**. For example, a Republic of Ireland employee's salary could be coded to the nearest euro and entered into the matrix as 53543 (numerical discrete data). Later, re-coding could be used to place it in a group of similar salaries, from €50,000 to €59,999 (categorical ranked data).

Coding categorical data

Codes are often applied to categorical data with little thought, although you can design a coding scheme that will make subsequent analyses far simpler. For many secondary data sources (such as government surveys), a suitable coding scheme will have already been devised when the data were first collected. However, for some secondary and all primary data you will need to decide on a coding scheme. Prior to this, you need to establish the highest level of precision required by your analyses (Figure 11.1).

Existing coding schemes can be used for many variables. These include industrial classification (Prosser 2009), occupation (Office for National Statistics nd a), social class and socioeconomic classification (Office for National Statistics nd b) and ethnic group (Office for National Statistics nd c) as well as social attitude variables (Park et al. 2013). Wherever possible, we recommend you use these as they:

- save time;
- are normally well tested;
- allow comparisons of your results with other (often larger) surveys.

Where possible these codes should be included on your data collection form or online survey software as **pre-set codes** provided that there are a limited number of categories. Even if you decide not to use an existing coding scheme, perhaps because of a lack of detail, you should ensure that your codes are still compatible. This means that you will be able to compare your data with those already collected.

Coding at data collection usually occurs when there is a limited range of well-established categories into which the data can be placed. These are either included on your data collection form, the person filling in the form selecting the correct category, or can be undertaken automatically by your Internet questionnaire software.

Coding after data collection is necessary when you are unclear as to the likely responses or there are a large number of possible responses in the coding scheme. To ensure that the coding scheme captures the variety in responses (and that it will work!) it is better to wait until data from the first 50 to 100 cases are available and then develop the coding scheme. This is called the **codebook** (Box 11.5). As when designing your data collection method(s), it is essential to be clear about the intended analyses, in particular:

- the level of precision required;
- the coding schemes used by surveys with which comparisons are to be made.

To create your codebook for each variable you:

1. examine the data and establish broad groupings;
2. subdivide the broad groupings into increasingly specific subgroups dependent on your intended analyses;
3. allocate codes to all categories at the most precise level of detail required;
4. note the actual responses that are allocated to each category and produce a codebook;
5. ensure that those categories that may need to be aggregated are given adjacent codes to facilitate re-coding.

Coding missing data

Each variable for each case in your data set should have a code, even if no data have been collected. The choice of code is up to you, although some statistical analysis software has a code that is used by default. A missing data code is used to indicate why data are missing. Missing data are important as they may affect whether the data you have collected are representative of the population. If missing data follow some form of pattern, such as occurring for particular questions or for a subgroup of the population, then your results are unlikely to be representative of the population and so you should not ignore the fact they are missing. However, if data are missing at random, then it is unlikely that this will affect your results being representative of the

Box 11.5 Focus on student research

Creating a codebook, coding multiple responses and entering data

As part of his research project, Amil used a questionnaire to collect data from the customers of a local themed restaurant. The questionnaire included an open question which asked 'List up to three things you like about this restaurant'. The answers included over 50 different 'things' that the 186 customers responding liked about the restaurant, although the maximum number mentioned by any one customer was three.

Once data had been collected, Amil devised a hierarchical coding scheme based on what the customers liked about the restaurant. Codes were allocated to each 'thing' a customer liked, as shown in the extract below.

Codes were entered into three (the maximum number customers were asked to list) variables, like1, like2 and like3, in the data matrix using the multiple-response method for coding. This meant that any response could appear in any of the three variables. When there were fewer than three responses given, the code '.' was entered automatically by the software into empty cells in the remaining outlet variables, signifying missing data. The first customer in the extract below listed 'things' coded 11, 21 and 42, the next 3 and 21 and so on. No significance was attached to the order of variables to which responses were coded.

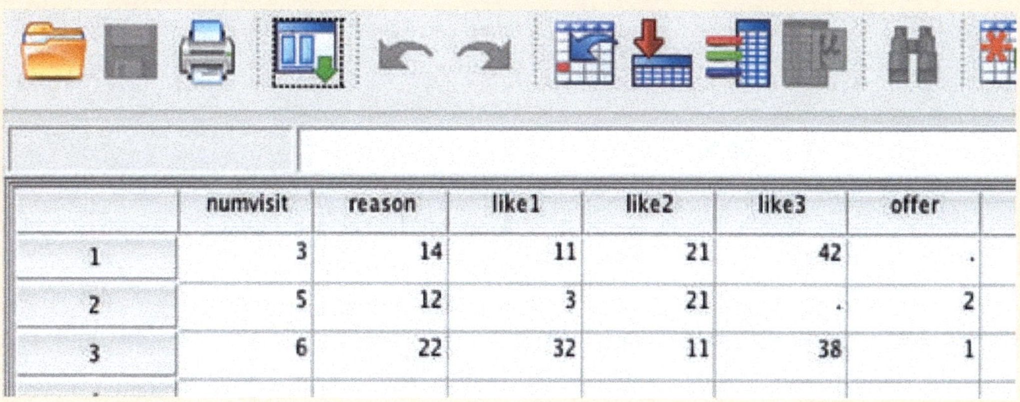

	numvisit	reason	like1	like2	like3	offer
1	3	14	11	21	42	.
2	5	12	3	21	.	2
3	6	22	32	11	38	1

Box 11.5 Focus on student research (*continued*)

Creating a codebook, coding multiple responses and entering data

Extract from coding scheme used to classify responses

Grouping	Subgrouping	Response	Code
Physical surroundings			1–9
		Decoration	1
		Use of colour	2
		Comfort of seating	3
Dining experience	*Menu*		10–19
		Choice	11
		Regularly changed	12
	Food		20–29
		Freshly prepared	21
		Organic	22
		Served at correct temperature	23
	Staff attitude		30–39
		Knowledgeable	31
		Greet by name	32
		Know what diners prefer	33
		Discreet	34
		Do not hassle	35
		Good service	36
		Friendly	37
		Have a sense of humour	38
	Drinks		40–49
		Value for money	41
		Good selection of wines	42
		Good selection of beers	43
		Served at correct temperature	44

The hierarchical coding scheme meant that individual responses could subsequently be re-coded into subgroupings and groupings such as those indicated earlier to facilitate a range of different analyses. These were undertaken using statistical analysis software.

population (Little and Rubin 2002). Four main reasons for missing data are identified by De Vaus (2014):

- The data were not required from the respondent, perhaps because of a skip generated by a filter question in a survey.
- The respondent refused to answer the question (a **non-response**).
- The respondent did not know the answer or did not have an opinion. Sometimes this is treated as implying an answer; on other occasions it is treated as missing data.
- The respondent may have missed a question by mistake, or the respondent's answer may be unclear.

In addition, it may be that:

- leaving part of a question in a survey blank implies an answer; in such cases the data are not classified as missing.

Statistical analysis software often reserves a special code for missing data. Cases with missing data can then be excluded from subsequent analyses when necessary (Box 11.5). For some analyses it may be necessary to distinguish between reasons for missing data using different codes.

Entering and saving data

If you have downloaded secondary data as a file, or have used Internet questionnaire software, your data will already have been entered (input) and saved. However, often you will need to enter and save the data as a file on your computer. Although some data analysis software contains algorithms that check the data for obvious errors as it is entered, it is essential that you take considerable care to ensure that your data are entered correctly and save the file regularly. We have found it helpful to include the word data in the filename. When entering data the well-known maxim 'rubbish in, rubbish out' certainly applies! More sophisticated analysis software allows you to attach individual labels to each variable and the codes associated with each of them. If this is feasible, we strongly recommend that you do this. By ensuring the labels replicate the exact words used in the data collection, you will reduce the number of opportunities for misinterpretation when analysing your data. Taking this advice for the variable 'like1' in Box 11.5 would result in the variable label 'List up to three things you like about this restaurant', each value being labelled with the actual response in the coding scheme.

Checking for errors

No matter how carefully you code and subsequently enter data there will always be some errors. The main methods to check data for errors are as follows:

- Look for illegitimate codes. In any coding scheme, only certain numbers are allocated. Other numbers are, therefore, errors. Common errors are the inclusion of letters O and o instead of zero, letters l or I instead of 1, and number 7 instead of 1.
- Look for illogical relationships. For example, if a person is coded to the 'higher managerial occupations' socioeconomic classification category and she describes her work as 'manual', it is likely an error has occurred.
- Check that rules in filter questions are followed. Certain responses to filter questions mean that other variables should be coded as missing values. If this has not happened, there has been an error.

For each possible error, you need to discover whether it occurred at coding or data entry and then correct it. By giving each case a unique identifier (normally a number), it is possible to link the matrix to the original data. You must, however, remember to ensure the identifier is on the data collection form and entered along with the other data into the matrix.

Data checking is very time consuming and so is often not undertaken. Beware: not doing it is very dangerous and can result in incorrect results from which false conclusions are drawn!

Weighting cases

Most data you use will be a sample. For some forms of probability sampling, such as stratified random sampling, you may have used a different sampling fraction for each stratum. Alternatively, you may have obtained a different response rate for each of the strata. To obtain an accurate overall picture you will need to take account of these differences in response rates between strata. A common method of achieving this is to use cases from those strata that have lower proportions of responses to represent more than one case in your analysis (Box 11.6). Most statistical analysis software allows you to do this by **weighting** cases. To weight the cases you:

1 Calculate the percentage of the population responding for each stratum.
2 Establish which stratum had the highest percentage of the population responding.
3 Calculate the weight for each stratum using the following formula:

$$\text{Weight} = \frac{\text{highest proportion of population responding for any stratum}}{\text{proportion of population responding in stratum for which calculating weight}}$$

(Note: if your calculations are correct this will always result in the weight for the stratum with the highest proportion of the population responding being 1.)

4 Apply the appropriate weight to each case.

Box 11.6 Focus on student research

Weighting cases

Doris had used stratified random sampling to select her sample. The percentage of each stratum's population that responded is given below:

- Upper stratum: 90%
- Lower stratum: 65%

To account for the differences in the response rates between strata she decided to weight the cases prior to analysis.

The weight for the upper stratum was: $\frac{90}{90} = 1$

This meant that each case in the upper stratum counted as 1 case in her analysis.

The weight for the lower stratum was: $\frac{90}{65} = 1.38$

This meant that each case in the lower stratum counted for 1.38 cases in her analysis.

Doris entered these as a separate variable in her data set and used the statistical analysis software to apply the weights.

Beware: many authors (for example, Hays 1994) question the validity of using statistics to make inferences from your sample if you have weighted cases.

11.3 Exploring and presenting data

Once your data have been entered and checked for errors, you are ready to start your analysis. We have found Tukey's (1977) **Exploratory Data Analysis (EDA)** approach useful in these initial stages. This approach emphasises the use of graphs to explore and understand your data. Although within data analysis the term graph has a specific meaning: '. . . a visual display that illustrates one or more relationships among numbers' (Kosslyn 2006: 4), it is often used interchangeably with the term 'chart'. Consequently, while some authors (and data analysis software) use the term bar graphs, others use the term bar charts. Even more confusingly, what are referred to as 'pie charts' are actually graphs! Tukey (1977) also emphasises the importance of using your data to guide your choice of analysis techniques. As you would expect, we believe that it is important to keep your research question(s) and objectives in mind when exploring your data. However, the Exploratory Data Analysis approach allows you flexibility to introduce previously unplanned analyses to respond to new findings. It therefore formalises the common practice of looking for other relationships in data, which your research was not initially designed to test. This should not be discounted, as it may suggest other fruitful avenues for analysis. In addition, computers make this relatively easy and quick.

Even at this stage it is important that you structure and label clearly each graph and table to avoid possible misinterpretation. Box 11.7 provides a summary checklist of the points to remember when designing a graph or table.

We have found it best to begin exploratory analysis by looking at individual variables and their components. The key aspects you may need to consider will be guided by your

Box 11.7 Checklist

Designing your graphs and tables

For both graphs and tables

- ✔ Does it have a brief but clear and descriptive title?
- ✔ Are the units of measurement used stated clearly?
- ✔ Are the sources of data used stated clearly?
- ✔ Are there notes to explain abbreviations and unusual terminology?
- ✔ Does it state the size of the sample on which the values in the table are based?

For graphs

- ✔ Does it have clear axis labels?
- ✔ Are bars and their components in the same logical sequence?
- ✔ Is more dense shading used for smaller areas?
- ✔ Have you avoided misrepresenting or distorting the data?
- ✔ Is a key or legend included (where necessary)?

For tables

- ✔ Does it have clear column and row headings?
- ✔ Are columns and rows in a logical sequence?

research question(s) and objectives, and are likely to include (Kosslyn 2006) for single variables:

- specific amounts represented by individual data values;
- relative amounts such as:
  - highest and lowest data values;
  - trends in data values;
  - proportions and percentages for data values;
  - distributions of data values.

Once you have explored these, you can then begin to compare variables and interdependences between variables, by (Kosslyn 2006):

- comparing intersections between the data values for two or more variables;
- comparing cumulative totals for data values and variables;
- looking for interdependences between cases for variables.

These are summarised in Table 11.2. Most analysis software contains procedures to create tables and graphs. Your choice will depend on those aspects of the data to which you wish to direct your readers' attention and the scale of measurement at which the data were recorded. This section is concerned only with tables and two-dimensional graphs, including pictograms, available on most spreadsheets (Table 11.2). Three-dimensional graphs are not discussed, as these can often mislead or hinder interpretation (Kosslyn 2006). Those tables and graphs most pertinent to your research question(s) and objectives will eventually appear in your research report to support your arguments. You should therefore save an electronic copy of all tables and graphs you create.

Exploring and presenting individual variables

To show specific amounts

The simplest way of summarising data for individual variables so that specific amount can be read is to use a **table (frequency distribution)**. For categorical data, the table summarises the number of cases (frequency) in each category. For variables where there are likely to be a large number of categories (or values for numerical data), you will need to group the data into categories that reflect your research question(s) and objectives.

To show the highest and lowest values

Tables attach no visual significance to highest or lowest data values unless emphasised by alternative fonts. Graphs can provide visual clues, although both categorical and numerical data may need grouping. For categorical and discrete data, bar graphs and pictograms are both suitable. Generally, bar graphs provide a more accurate representation and should be used for research reports, whereas pictograms convey a general impression and can be used to gain an audience's attention. In a **bar graph**, also often known as **a bar chart**, the height or length of each bar represents the frequency of occurrence. Bars are separated by gaps, usually half the width of the bars. Bar graphs where the bars are vertical (as in Figure 11.2) are sometimes called bar or column charts. This bar graph emphasises that the European Union member state with the highest total carbon dioxide emissions in 2011 was Germany, while either Latvia, Luxembourg or Malta had the lowest total carbon dioxide emissions.

Table 11.2 Data presentation by data type: A summary

	Categorical		Numerical	
	Descriptive	**Ranked**	**Continuous**	**Discrete**
To show one variable so that any *specific amount* can be read easily	Table/frequency distribution (data often grouped)			
To show the relative amount for categories or values for one variable so that *highest* and *lowest* are clear	Bar graph/chart or pictogram (data may need grouping)		Histogram or frequency polygon (data must be grouped)	Bar graph/chart or pictogram (data may need grouping)
To show the *trend* for a variable		Line graph or bar graph/chart	Line graph or histogram	Line graph or bar graph/chart
To show the *proportion* or *percentage* of occurrences of categories or values for one variable	Pie chart or bar graph/chart (data may need grouping)		Histogram or pie chart (data must be grouped)	Pie chart or bar graph/chart (data may need grouping)
To show the *distribution* of values for one variable			Frequency polygon, histogram (data must be grouped) or box plot	Frequency polygon, bar graph/chart (data may need grouping) or box plot
To show the *interdependence* between two or more variables so that any *specific* amount can be read easily	Contingency table/cross-tabulation (data often grouped)			
To compare the relative amount for categories or values for two or more variables so that *highest* and *lowest* are clear	Multiple bar graph/chart (continuous data must be grouped, other data may need grouping)			
To compare the *proportions* or *percentages* of occurrences of categories or values for two or more variables	Comparative pie charts or percentage component bar graph/chart (continuous data must be grouped, other data may need grouping)			
To compare the *distribution* of values for two or more variables			Multiple box plot	
To compare the *trends* for two or more variables so that *intersections* are clear		Multiple line graph or multiple bar graph/chart		
To compare the frequency of occurrences of categories or values for two or more variables so that *cumulative totals* are clear	Stacked bar graph/chart (continuous data must be grouped, other data may need grouping)			
To compare the *proportions* and *cumulative totals* of occurrences of categories or values for two or more variables	Comparative proportional pie charts (continuous data must be grouped, other data may need grouping)			
To show the *interdependence* between cases for two variables		Scatter graph/scatter plot		

Source: © Mark Saunders, Philip Lewis and Adrian Thornhill 2015

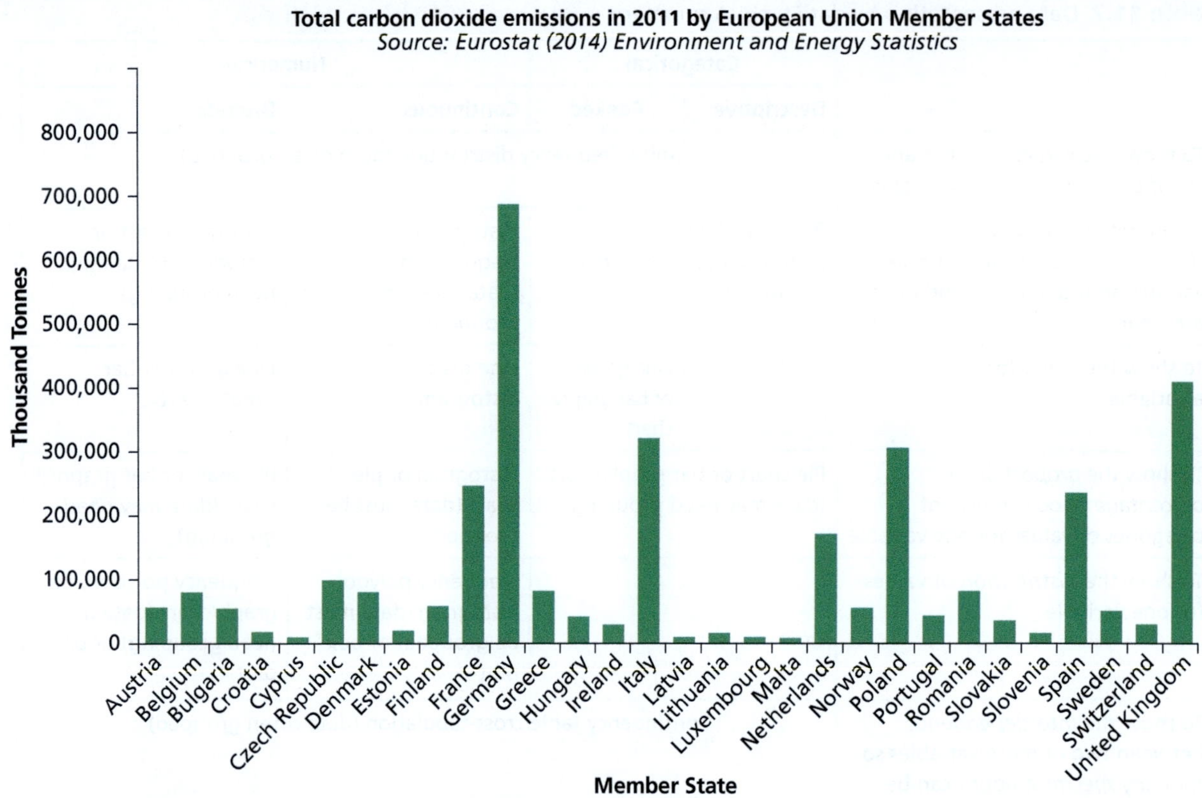

Figure 11.2 Bar graph

Source: Adapted from Eurostat (2014) © European Communities, 2014. Reproduced with permission

To emphasise the relative values represented by each of the bars in a bar graph, the bars may be reordered in either descending or ascending order of the frequency of occurrence represented by each bar (Figure 11.3). It is now from the order of the bars that Malta has the lowest greenhouse gas emissions.

Most researchers use a histogram to show highest and lowest values for continuous data. Prior to being drawn, data will often need to be grouped into class intervals. In a **histogram**, the area of each bar represents the frequency of occurrence and the continuous nature of the data is emphasised by the absence of gaps between the bars. For equal width class intervals, the height of your bar still represents the frequency of occurrences (Figure 11.4) and so the highest and lowest values are easy to distinguish. For histograms with unequal class interval widths, this is not the case. In Figure 11.4 the histogram emphasises that the highest number of Harley-Davidson motorcycles shipped worldwide was in 2006, and the lowest number in 2000.

Analysis software treats histograms for data of equal width class intervals as a variation of a bar chart. Unfortunately, few spreadsheets will cope automatically with the calculations required to draw histograms for unequal class intervals. Consequently, you may have to use a bar chart owing to the limitations of your analysis software.

In a **pictogram**, each bar is replaced by a picture or series of pictures chosen to represent the data. To illustrate the impact of doing this, we have used data of worldwide Harley-Davidson motorcycle shipments to generate both a histogram (Figure 11.4) and a pictogram

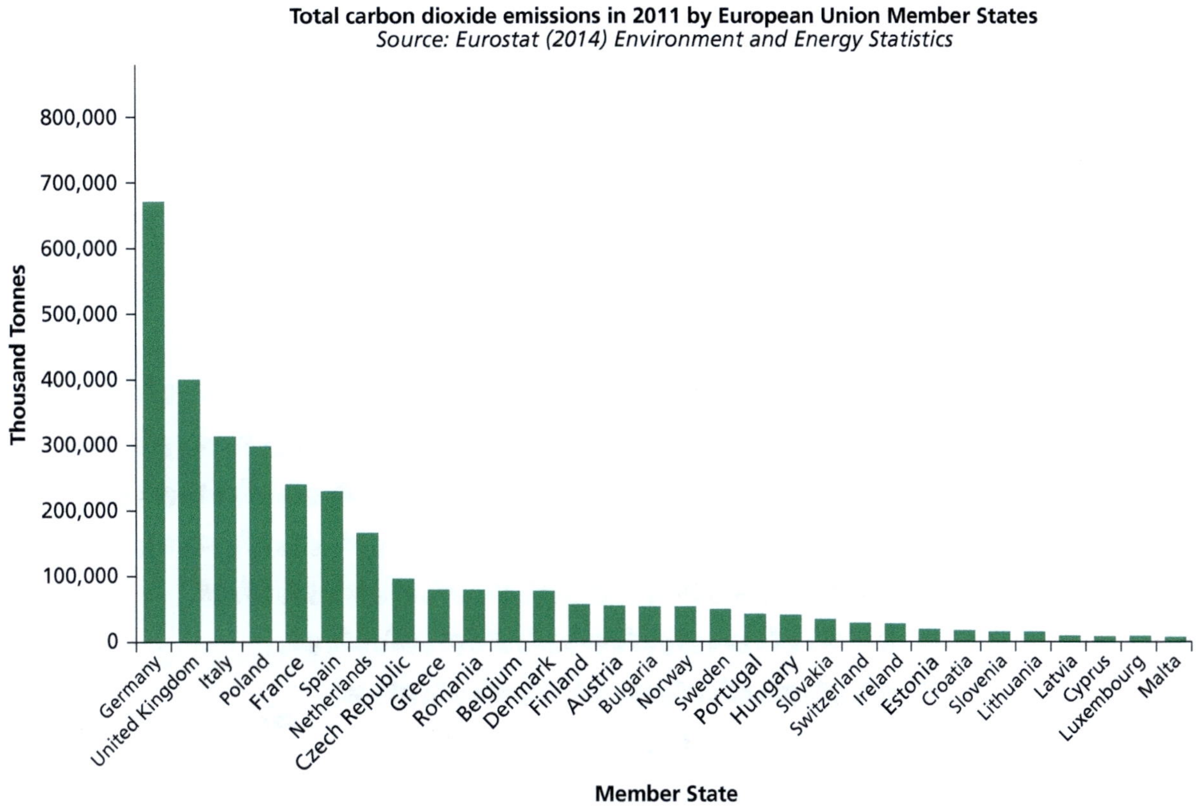

Figure 11.3 Bar graph (data reordered)

Source: Adapted from Eurostat (2014) © European Communities, 2014. Reproduced with permission

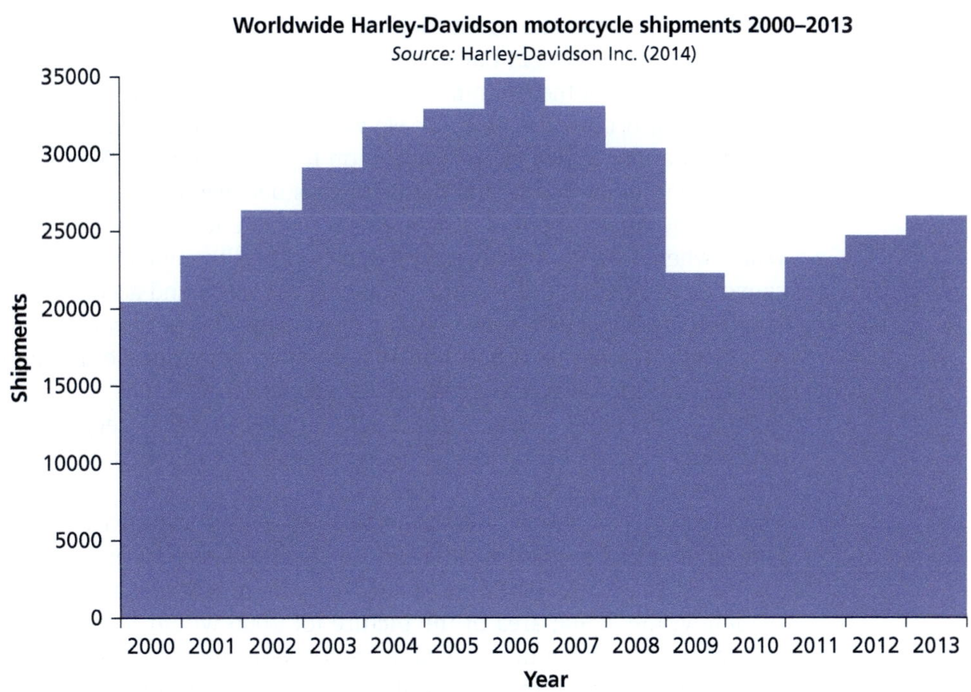

Figure 11.4 Histogram

Source: Adapted from Harley-Davidson Inc. (2014)

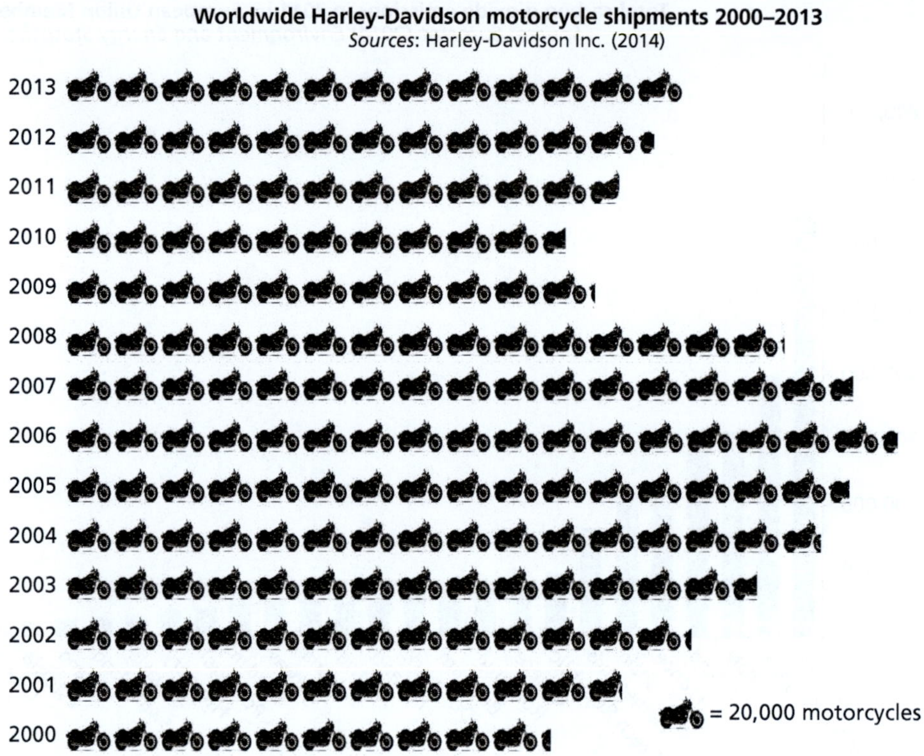

Figure 11.5 Pictogram
Source: Adapted from Harley-Davidson Inc. (2014)

(Figure 11.5). In the pictogram each picture represents 20,000 motorcycles. Pictures in pictograms can, like bars in bar graphs and histograms, be shown in columns or horizontally. The height of the column or length of the bar made up by the pictures represents the frequency of occurrence. In this case we felt it was more logical to group the pictures as a horizontal bar rather than vertically on top of each other. You will have probably also noticed that, in the pictogram, there are gaps between the bars. While this normally signifies discrete categories of data, it is also acceptable to do this for continuous data (such as years) when drawing a pictogram, to aid clarity. Although analysis software allows you to convert a bar graph or histogram to a pictogram easily and accurately, it is more difficult to establish the actual data values from a pictogram. This is because the number of units part of a picture represents is not immediately clear. For example, in Figure 11.5, how many motorcycles shipped would a rear wheel represent?

Pictograms have a further drawback, namely that it is very easy to misrepresent the data. Both Figures 11.4 and 11.5 show that shipments of Harley-Davidson motorcycles grew between 2006 and 2010. Using our analysis software, this could have been represented using a picture of a motorcycle in 2006 that was nearly one and a half times as long as the picture in 2010. However, in order to keep the proportions of the motorcycle accurate, the picture would have needed to be nearly one and a half times as tall. Consequently, the actual area of the picture for 2006 would have been over twice as great and would have been interpreted as motorcycle shipments being twice as large in 2006 and 2010! Because of this we would recommend that, if you are using a pictogram, you decide on a standard value for each picture and do not alter its size. In addition, you should include a key or note to indicate the value each picture represents.

Frequency polygons are used less often to illustrate limits. Most analysis software treats them as a version of a line graph (Figure 11.6) in which the lines are extended to meet the horizontal axis, provided that class widths are equal.

To show a trend

Trends can only be presented for variables containing numerical (and occasionally ranked) longitudinal data. The most suitable diagram for exploring the trend is a **line graph** (Kosslyn 2006) in which your data values for each time period are joined with a line to represent the trend (Figure 11.6). In Figure 11.6 the line graph reveals the rise and decline in the number of Harley-Davidson motorcycles shipped worldwide between 2000 and 2013. You can also use histograms (Figure 11.4) to show trends over continuous time periods and bar graphs (Figure 11.2) to show trends between discrete time periods. The trend can also be calculated using time-series analysis.

To show proportions or percentages

Research has shown that the most frequently used diagram to emphasise the proportion or share of occurrences is the pie chart, although bar charts have been shown to give equally good results (Anderson et al. 2014). A **pie chart** is divided into proportional segments according to the share each has of the total value and the total value represented by the pie is noted (Box 11.8). For numerical and some categorical data you will need to group data prior to drawing the pie chart, as it is difficult to interpret pie charts with more than six segments (Keen 2010).

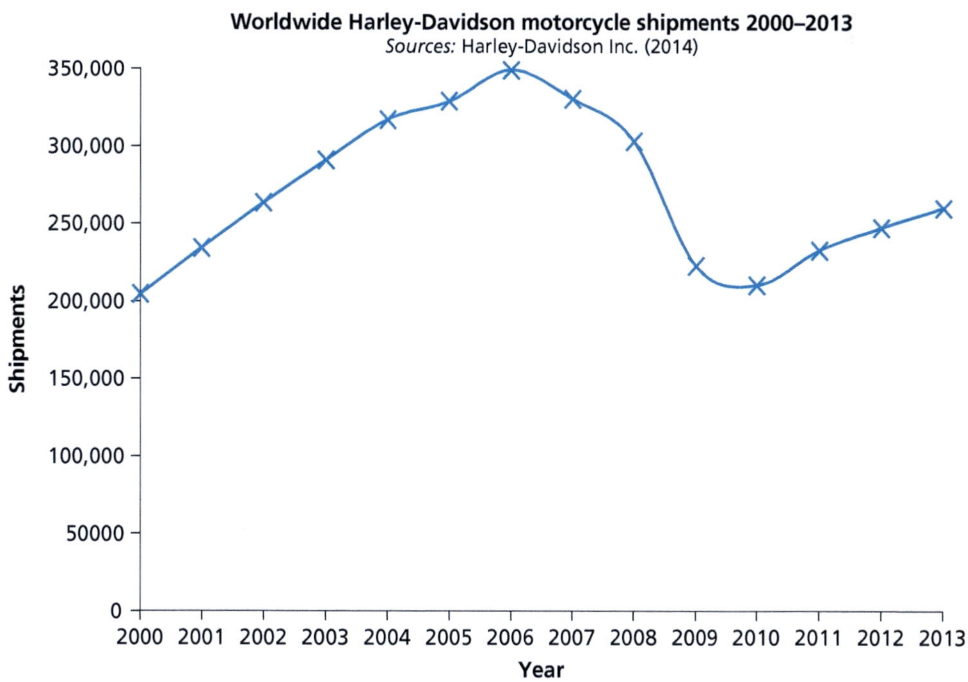

Figure 11.6 Line graph
Source: Adapted from Harley-Davidson Inc. (2014)

Box 11.8 Focus on research in the news

Pie chart

November 6, 2014 2:50 pm

Chart that tells a story – tax summaries

Adam Palin Author alerts

How your tax was (really) spent in 2013-14

% of total tax paid

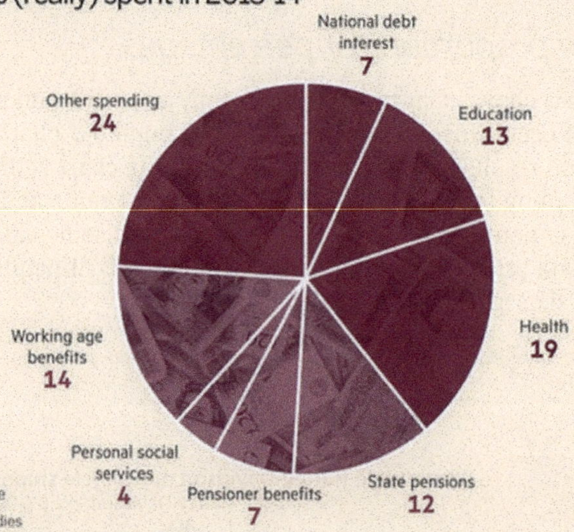

FT graphic Photo: Dreamstime

Source: Institute for Fiscal Studies

What does this show?

This chart illustrates a simplified breakdown of the main areas of UK government spending – £686bn – in 2013-14.

To show the distribution of values

Prior to using many statistical tests it is necessary to establish the distribution of values for variables containing numerical data (Sections 11.4, 11.5). This can be seen by plotting either a frequency polygon or a histogram (Figure 11.4) for continuous data or a frequency polygon or bar graph for discrete data. If your graph shows a bunching to the left and a long tail to the right the data are **positively skewed** (Figure 11.7). If the converse is true, the data are **negatively skewed** (Figure 11.7). If your data are equally distributed either side of the highest frequency then they are **symmetrically distributed**. A special form of the symmetric distribution, in which the data can be plotted as a bell-shaped curve, is known as **normal distribution** (Figure 11.7).

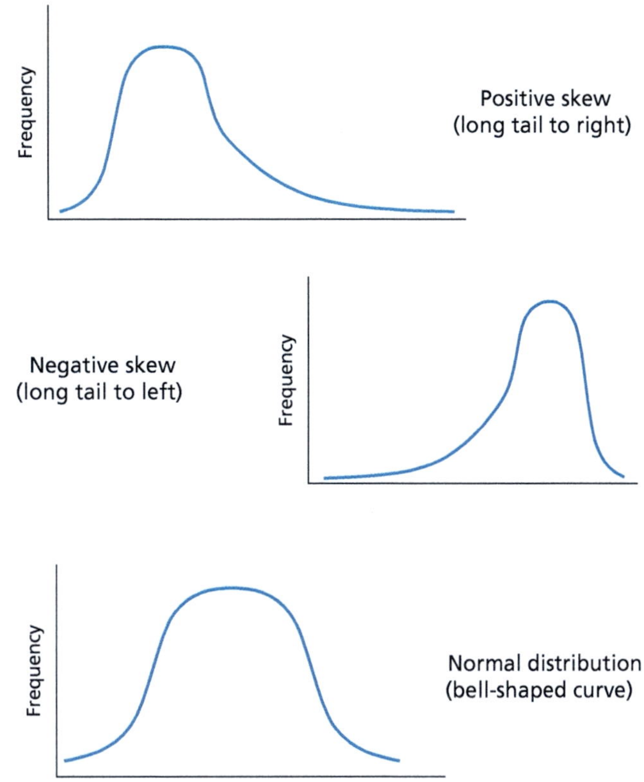

Figure 11.7 Distributions of values

The other indicator of the distribution's shape is **kurtosis** - the pointedness or flatness of the distribution compared with normal distribution. If a distribution is more pointed or peaked, it is said to be leptokurtic and the kurtosis value is positive. If a distribution is flatter, it is said to be platykurtic and the kurtosis value is negative. A distribution that is between the extremes of peakedness and flatness is said to be mesokurtic and has a kurtosis value of zero (Dancey and Reidy 2011).

An alternative often included in more advanced statistical analysis software is the **box plot** (Figure 11.8). This provides a pictorial representation of the distribution of the data for a variable. The plot shows where the middle value or median is, how this relates to the middle 50 per cent of the data or inter-quartile range, and highest and lowest values or *extremes* (Section 11.4). It also highlights outliers, those values that are very different from the data. In Figure 11.8 the two outliers might be due to mistakes in data entry. Alternatively, they may be correct and emphasise that sales for these two cases (93 and 88) are far higher. In this example we can see that the data values for the variable are positively skewed as there is a long tail to the right.

Comparing variables

To show interdependence and specific amounts

As with individual variables, the best method of showing interdependence between variables so that any specific amount can be discerned easily is a table. This is known as a

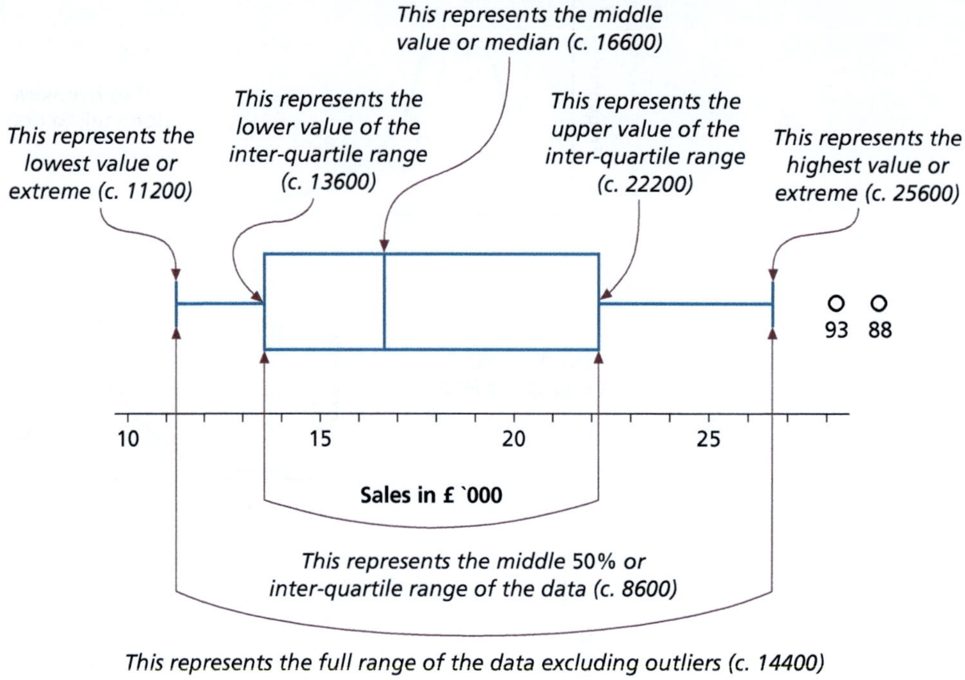

Figure 11.8 Annotated box plot

contingency table or as a **cross-tabulation** (Table 11.3). For variables where there are likely to be a large number of categories (or values for numerical data), you may need to group the data to prevent the table from becoming too large.

Most statistical analysis software allows you to add totals, and row and column percentages when designing your table. Statistical analyses such as chi square can also be undertaken at the same time (Section 11.5).

To compare the highest and lowest values

Comparisons of variables that emphasise the highest and lowest rather than precise values are best explored using a **multiple bar graph**, also known as a **multiple bar chart**

Table 11.3 Contingency table: Number of insurance claims by gender, 2015

Number of claims*	Male	Female	Total
0	10032	13478	23510
1	2156	1430	3586
2	120	25	145
3	13	4	17
Total	12321	14937	27258

*No clients had more than three claims
Source: PJ Insurance Services

Box 11.9 Focus on student research

Exploring and presenting data for individual variables

As part of audience research for his dissertation, Valentin asked people attending a play at a provincial theatre to complete a short questionnaire. This collected responses to 25 questions including:

3 How many plays (including this one) have you seen at this theatre in the past year?

11 This play is good value for money

strongly disagree □$_1$ disagree □$_2$
agree □$_3$ strongly agree □$_4$

24 How old are you?

Under 18 □$_1$ 18 to 34 □$_2$
35 to 64 □$_3$ 65 and over □$_4$

Exploratory analyses were undertaken using analysis software and diagrams and tables generated. For Question 3, which collected discrete data, the aspects that were most important were the distribution of values and the highest and lowest numbers of plays seen. A bar graph, therefore, was drawn:

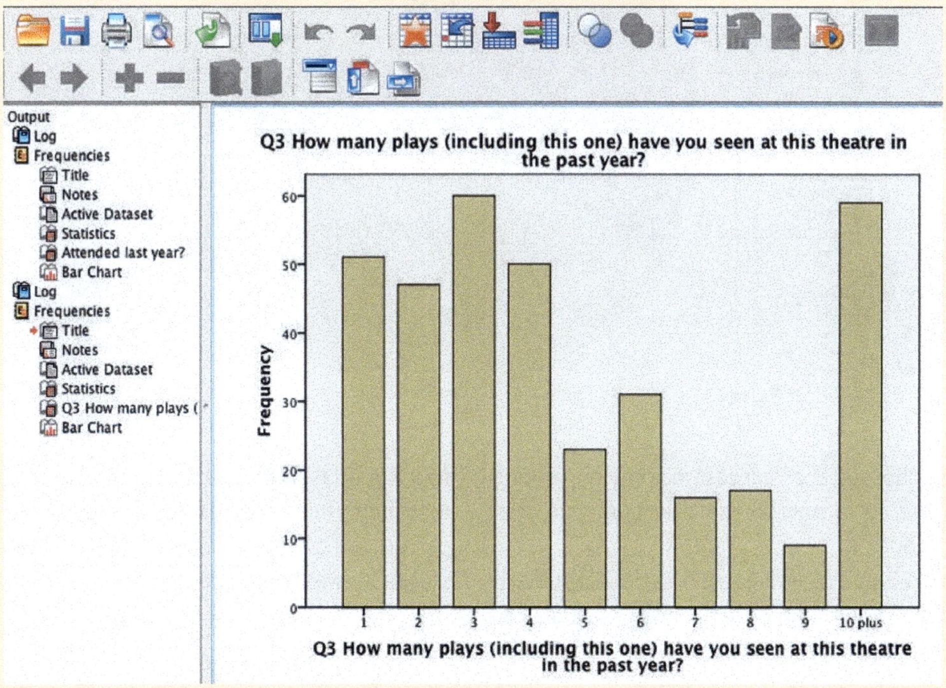

This emphasised that the most frequent number of plays seen by respondents was three and the least frequent number of plays seen by the respondents was either nine or probably some larger number. It also suggested that the distribution was positively skewed towards lower numbers of plays seen.

For Question 11 (categorical data), the most important aspect was the proportion of people agreeing and disagreeing with the statement. A pie chart was therefore drawn, although unfortunately the shadings were not similar for the two agree categories and for the two disagree categories.

Box 11.9
Focus on student research (*continued*)

Exploring and presenting data for individual variables

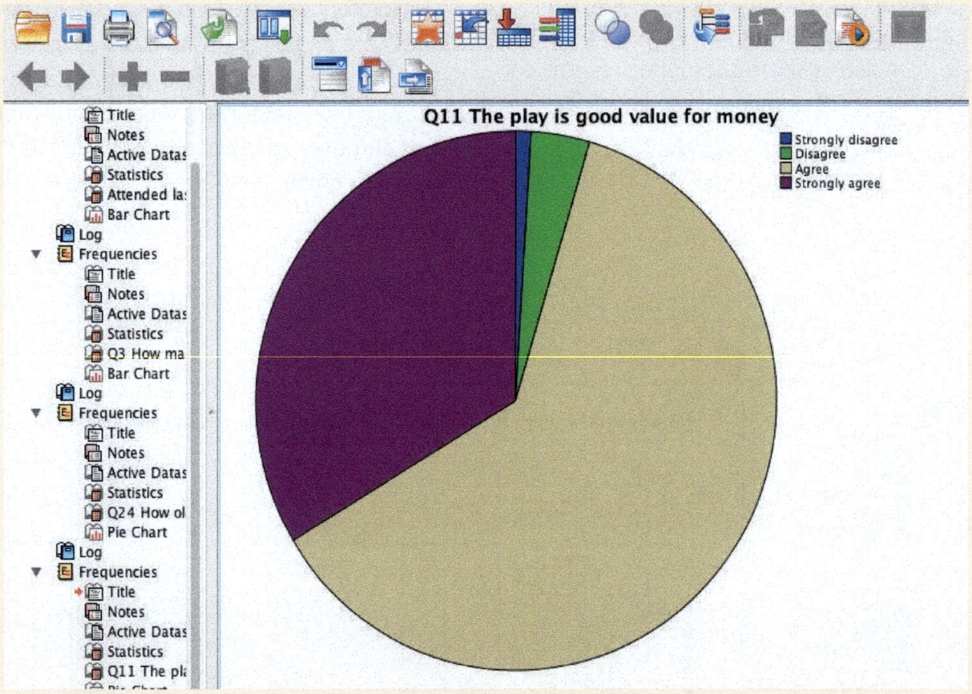

This emphasised that the vast majority of respondents (95 per cent) agreed that the play was good value for money.

Question 24 collected data on each respondent's age. This question had grouped continuous data into four unequal-width age groups. For this analysis, the most important aspects were the specific number and percentage of respondents in each age category and so a table was constructed.

Q24 How old are you?

		Frequency	Percent	Valid Percent	Cumulative Percent
Valid	Under 18	30	4.4	4.4	4.4
	18 to 34	144	20.9	21.0	25.4
	35 to 64	366	53.2	53.4	78.8
	65 plus	145	21.1	21.2	100.0
	Total	685	99.6	100.0	
Missing	System	3	.4		
Total		688	100.0		

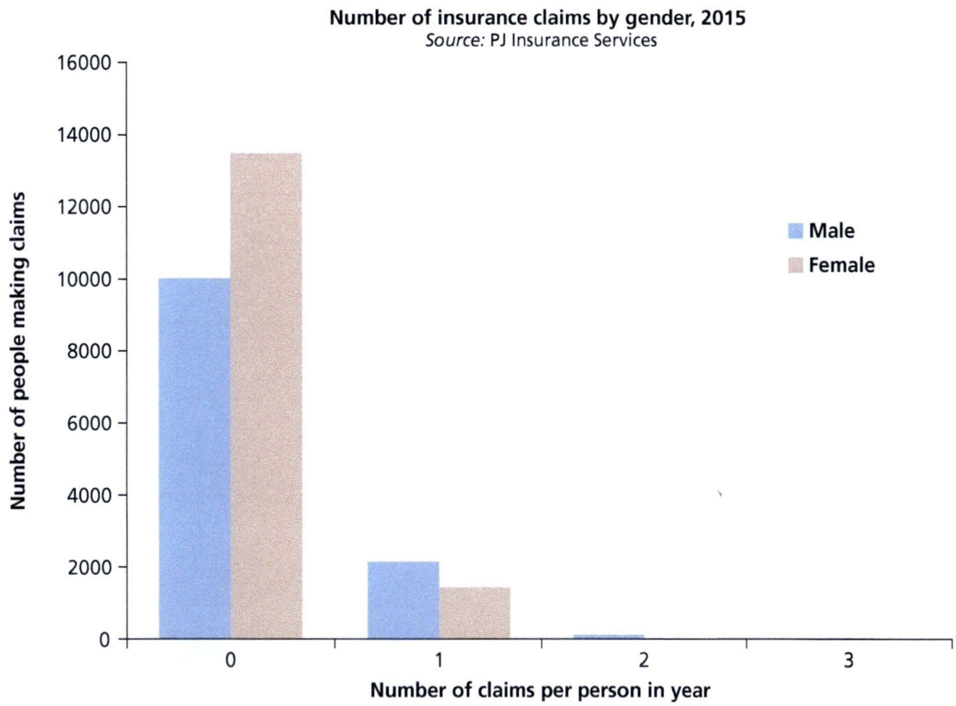

Figure 11.9 Multiple bar graph

(Kosslyn 2006), alternatively known as a **compound bar graph** or **compound bar chart**. As for a bar graph, continuous data – or data where there are many values or categories – need to be grouped. Within any multiple bar graph you are likely to find it easiest to compare between adjacent bars. The multiple bar graph (Figure 11.9) has therefore been drawn to emphasise comparisons between males and females rather than between numbers of claims.

To compare proportions or percentages

Comparison of proportions between variables uses either a **percentage component bar graph** (**percentage component bar chart** also known as a divided bar chart) or two or more pie charts. Either type of diagram can be used for all data types, provided that continuous data, and data where there are more than six values or categories, are grouped. Percentage component bar graphs are more straightforward to draw than comparative pie charts when using most spreadsheets. Within your percentage component bar graphs, comparisons will be easiest between adjacent bars. The chart in Figure 11.10 has been drawn to emphasise the proportions of males and females for each number of insurance claims in the year. Males and females, therefore, form a single bar.

To compare trends so the intersections are clear

The most suitable diagram to compare trends for two or more numerical (or occasionally ranked) variables is a **multiple line graph** where one line represents each variable

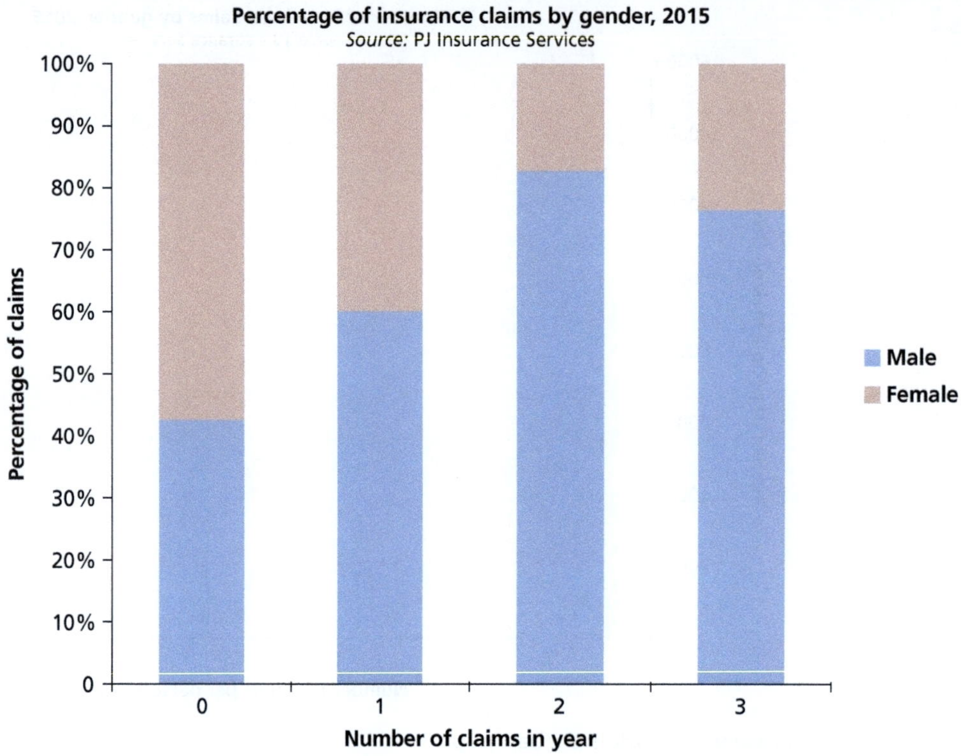

Figure 11.10 Percentage component bar graph

(Kosslyn 2006). You can also use multiple bar graphs (Box 11.10) in which bars for the same time period are placed adjacent to each other.

Conjunctions in trends – that is, where values for two or more variables intersect – are shown by the place where the lines on a multiple line graph cross.

Box 11.10 Focus on student research

Comparing variables

Francis was asked by his uncle, an independent ice cream manufacturer, to examine the records of monthly sales of ice cream for 2013 and 2014. In addition, his uncle had obtained longitudinal data on average (mean) daily hours of sunshine for each month for the same time period from their local weather station. Francis decided to explore data on sales of the three best-selling flavours (vanilla, strawberry and chocolate), paying particular attention to:

- comparative trends in sales;
- the relationship between sales and amount of sunshine.

To compare trends in sales between the three flavours he plotted a multiple line graph using a spreadsheet.

This indicated that sales for all flavours of ice cream were following a seasonal pattern but with an overall upward trend. It also showed that sales of vanilla ice cream were highest, and that those of chocolate had overtaken strawberry. The multiple line graph highlighted the intersection when sales of chocolate first exceeded strawberry, September 2014.

To show interdependence between sales and amount of sunshine Francis plotted scatter graphs for sales of each ice cream flavour against average (mean) daily hours of sunshine for each month. He plotted sales on the vertical axis, as he presumed that these were dependent on the amount of sunshine (see below).

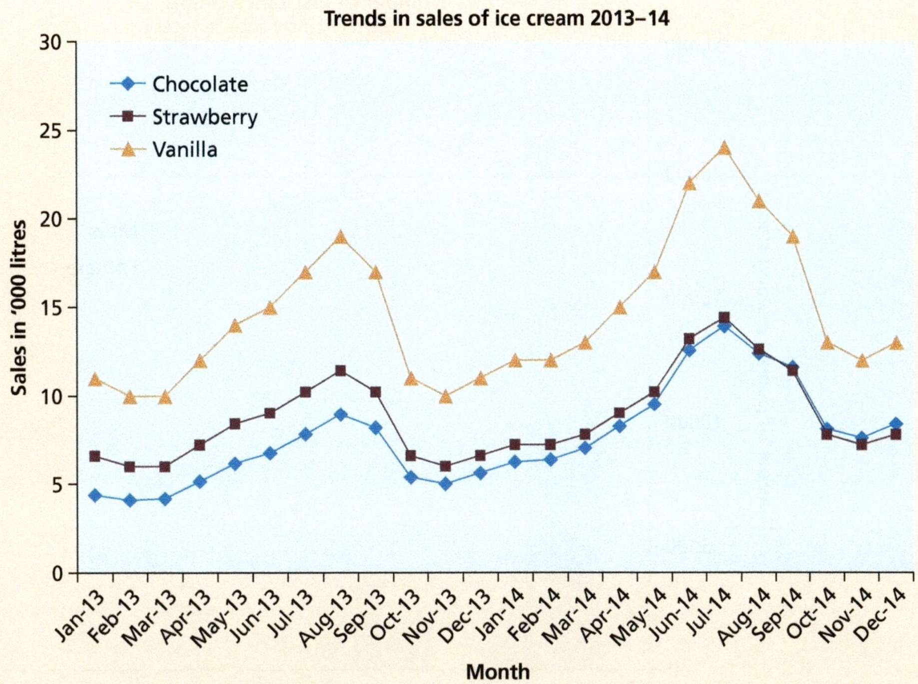

The scatter graph showed that there was a positive relationship between the amount of sunshine and sales of vanilla flavour ice cream. Subsequent scatter plots revealed similar relationships for strawberry and chocolate flavours.

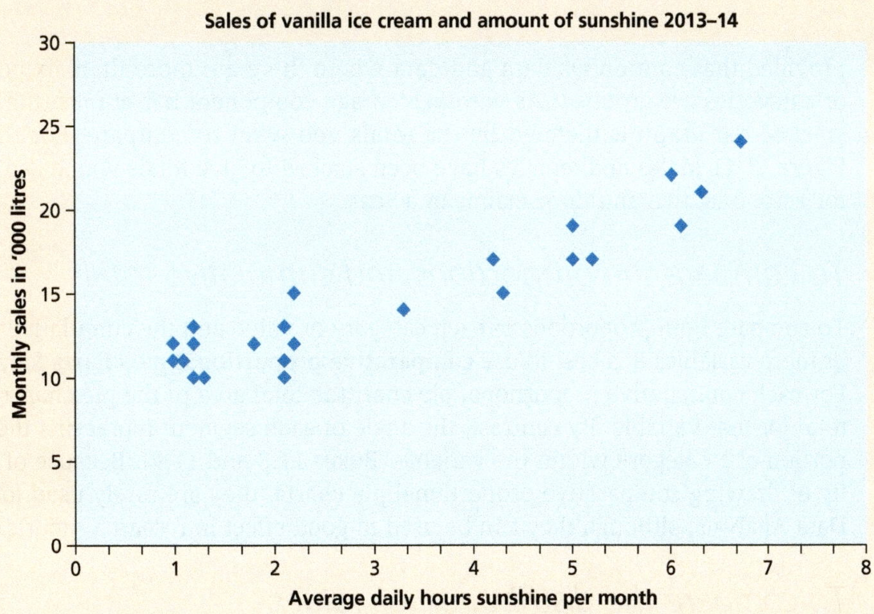

To compare the cumulative totals

Comparison of cumulative totals between variables uses a variation of the bar chart. A **stacked bar graph**, also known as a **stacked bar chart**, can be used for all data types

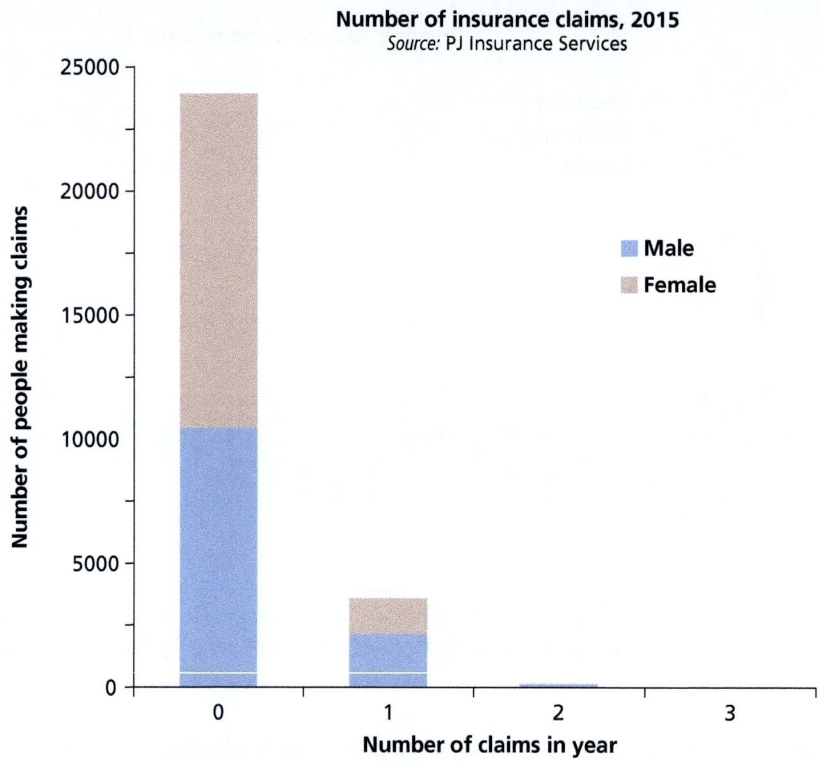

Figure 11.11 Stacked bar graph

provided that continuous data and data where there are more than six possible values or categories are grouped. As with percentage component bar graphs, the design of the stacked bar graph is dictated by the totals you want to compare. For this reason, in Figure 11.11 males and females have been stacked to give totals which can be compared for zero, one, two and three claims in a year.

To compare the proportions and cumulative totals

To compare both proportions of each category or value and the cumulative totals for two or more variables it is best to use **comparative proportional pie charts** for all data types. For each comparative proportional pie chart the total area of the pie chart represents the total for that variable. By contrast, the angle of each segment represents the relative proportion of a category within the variable (Boxes 11.8 and 11.9). Because of the complexity of drawing comparative proportional pie charts, they are rarely used for Exploratory Data Analysis, although they can be used to good effect in research reports.

To compare the distribution of values

Often it is useful to compare the distribution of values for two or more variables. Plotting multiple frequency polygons (Box 11.10) or bar graphs will enable you to compare distributions for up to three or four variables. After this your diagram is likely just to look a mess! An alternative is to use a diagram of multiple box plots, similar to the one in Figure 11.8. This provides a pictorial representation of the distribution of the data for the

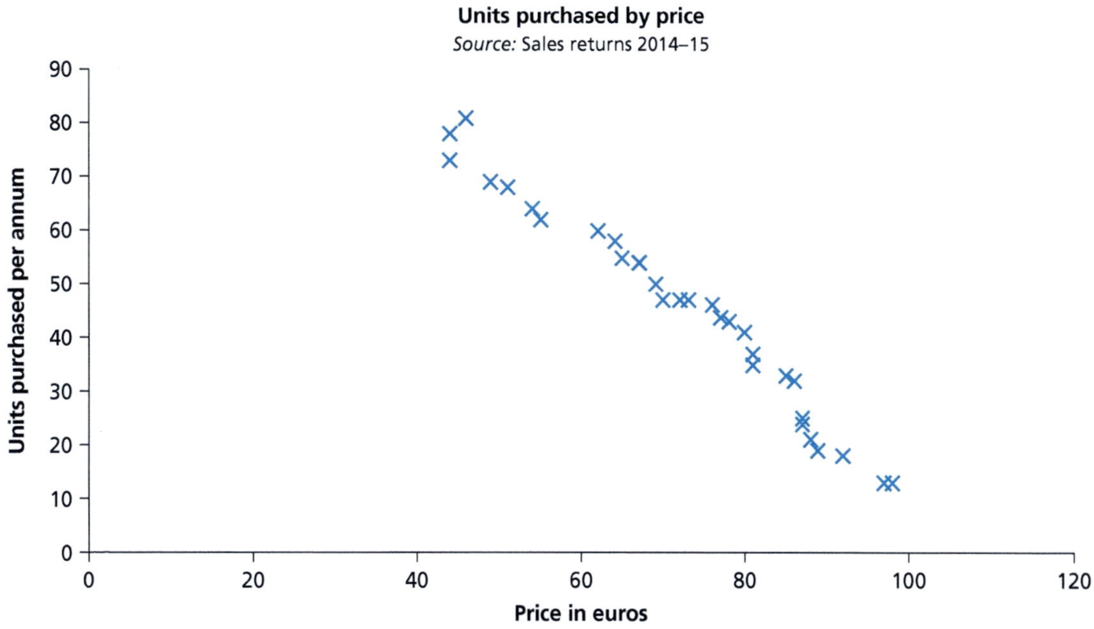

Figure 11.12 Scatter graph

variables in which you are interested. These plots can be compared and are interpreted in the same way as the single box plot.

To show the interdependence between cases for variables

You can explore possible interdependence between ranked and numerical data variables by plotting one variable against another. This is called a **scatter graph** (also known as a **scatter plot**), and each cross (point) represents the values for one case (Figure 11.12). Convention dictates that you plot the **dependent variable** – that is, the variable that changes in response to changes in the other **(independent) variable** – against the vertical axis. The strength of the interdependence or relationship is indicated by the closeness of the points to an imaginary straight line. If as the values for one variable increase so do those for the other then you have a positive relationship. If as the values for one variable decrease those for the other variable increase then you have a negative relationship. Thus, in Figure 11.12 there is a negative relationship between the two variables. The strength of this relationship can be assessed statistically using techniques such as correlation or regression (Section 11.5).

11.4 Describing data using statistics

The Exploratory Data Analysis approach (Section 11.3) emphasised the use of diagrams to understand your data. **Descriptive statistics** enable you to describe (and compare) variables numerically. Your research question(s) and objectives, although limited by the type of data (Table 11.4), should guide your choice of statistics. Statistics to describe a variable focus on two aspects:

- the central tendency;
- the dispersion.

Table 11.4 Descriptive statistics by data type: a summary

To calculate a measure of:		Categorical		Numerical	
		Descriptive	**Ranked**	**Continuous**	**Discrete**
Central tendency that . . .	. . . represents the value that occurs most frequently	Mode			
	. . . represents the middle value			Median	
	. . . includes all data values (average)			Mean	
	. . . includes all data values other than those at the extremes of the distribution			Trimmed mean	
Dispersion that . . .	. . . states the difference between the highest and lowest values			Range (data need not be normally distributed but must be placed in rank order)	
	. . . states the difference within the middle 50% of values			Inter-quartile range (data need not be normally distributed but must be placed in rank order)	
	. . . states the difference within another fraction of the values			Deciles or percentiles (data need not be normally distributed but must be placed in rank order)	
	. . . describes the extent to which data values differ from the mean			Variance, or more usually, the standard deviation (data should be normally distributed)	
	. . . compares the extent to which data values differ from the mean between variables			Coefficient of variation (data should be normally distributed)	
	. . . allows the relative extent that data values differ to be compared			Index numbers	

Source: © Mark Saunders, Philip Lewis and Adrian Thornhill 2015

These are summarised in Table 11.4. Those most pertinent to your research question(s) and objectives will eventually be quoted in your project report as support for your arguments.

Describing the central tendency

When describing data for both samples and populations quantitatively it is usual to provide some general impression of values that could be seen as common, middling or average. These are termed measures of **central tendency** and are discussed in virtually all statistics textbooks. The three main ways of measuring the central tendency most used in business research are the:

- value that occurs most frequently (mode);
- middle value or mid-point after the data have been ranked (median);
- value, often known as the average, that includes all data values in its calculation (mean).

However, as we saw in Box 11.2, beware: if you have used numerical codes, most analysis software can calculate all three measures whether or not they are appropriate!

To represent the value that occurs most frequently

The **mode** is the value that occurs most frequently. For descriptive data, the mode is the only measure of central tendency that can be interpreted sensibly. You might read in a report that the most common (modal) colour of motor cars sold last year was silver, or that the two equally most popular makes of motorcycle in response to a questionnaire were Honda and Yamaha. In such cases where two categories occur equally most frequently, this is termed bi-modal. The mode can be calculated for variables where there are likely to be a large number of categories (or values for numerical data), although it may be less useful. One solution is to group the data into suitable categories and to quote the most frequently occurring or **modal group**.

To represent the middle value

If you have quantitative data it is also possible to calculate the middle or **median** value by ranking all the values in ascending order and finding the mid-point (or **50th percentile**) in the distribution. For variables that have an even number of data values the median will occur halfway between the two middle data values. The median has the advantage that it is not affected by extreme values in the distribution (Box 11.11).

To include all data values

The most frequently used measure of central tendency is the **mean** (average in everyday language), which includes all data values in its calculation. However, it is usually only possible to calculate a meaningful mean using numerical data.

The value of your mean is unduly influenced by extreme data values in skewed distributions (Section 11.3). In such distributions the mean tends to get drawn towards the long tail of extreme data values and may be less representative of the central tendency. For this and other reasons Anderson et al. (2014) suggest that the median may be a more useful descriptive statistic. Alternatively, where the mean is affected by extreme data values (outliers) these may be excluded and a **trimmed mean** calculated. This excludes a certain proportion (for example 5 per cent) of the data from both ends of the distribution, where the outliers are located. Because the mean is the building block for many of the statistical tests used to explore relationships (Section 11.5), it is usual to include it as at least one of the measures of central tendency for numerical data in your report. This is, of course, provided that it makes sense!

Describing the dispersion

As well as describing the central tendency for a variable, it is important to describe how the data values are dispersed around the central tendency. As you can see from

Box 11.11 Focus on student research

Measuring the central tendency

As part of her research project, Kylie had obtained secondary data from the service department of her organisation on the length of time for which their customers had held service contracts:

Length of time held contract	Number of customers
< 3 months	50
3 to < 6 months	44
6 months to < 1 year	71
1 to < 2 years	105
2 to < 3 years	74
3 to < 4 years	35
4 to < 5 years	27
5+ years	11

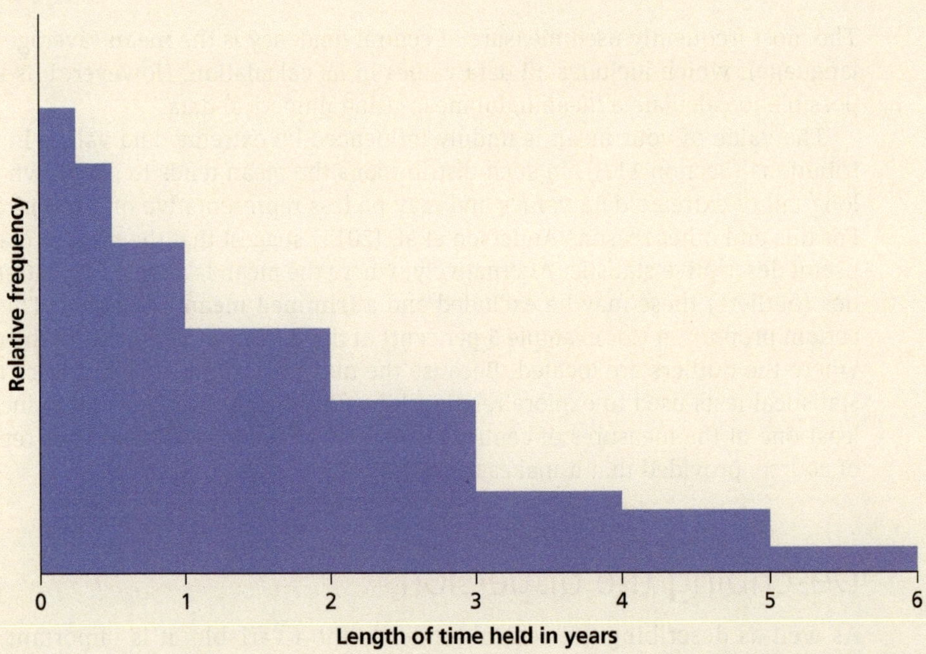

Her exploratory analysis revealed a positively skewed distribution (long tail to the right).

From the table, the largest single group of customers were those who had contracts for 1 to 2 years. This was the modal time period (most commonly occurring). However, the usefulness of this statistic is limited owing to the variety of class widths. By definition, half of the organisation's customers will have held contracts below the median time period (approximately 1 year 5 months) and half above it. As there are 11 customers who have held service contracts for over 5 years, the mean time period (approximately 1 year 9 months) is pulled towards longer times. This is represented by the skewed shape of the distribution.

Kylie needed to decide which of these measures of central tendency to include in her research report. As the mode made little sense she quoted the median and mean when interpreting her data:

> The length of time for which customers have held service contracts is positively skewed. Although mean length of time is approximately 1 year 9 months, half of customers have held service contracts for less than 1 year 5 months (median). Grouping of these data means that it is not possible to calculate a meaningful mode.

Table 11.4, this is only possible for numerical data. Two of the most frequently used ways of describing the dispersion are the:

- difference within the middle 50 per cent of values (inter-quartile range);
- extent to which values differ from the mean (standard deviation).

Although these **dispersion measures** are suitable only for numerical data, most statistical analysis software will also calculate them for categorical data if you have used numerical codes!

To state the difference between values

In order to get a quick impression of the distribution of data values for a variable you could simply calculate the difference between the lowest and the highest values - that is, the **range**. However, this statistic is rarely used in research reports as it represents only the extreme values.

A more frequently used statistic is the **inter-quartile range**. As we discussed earlier, the median divides the range into two. The range can be further divided into four equal sections called **quartiles**. The **lower quartile** is the value below which a quarter of your data values will fall; the **upper quartile** is the value above which a quarter of your data values will fall. As you would expect, the remaining half of your data values will fall between the lower and upper quartiles. The difference between the upper and lower quartiles is the inter-quartile range (Anderson et al. 2014). As a consequence, it is concerned only with the middle 50 per cent of data values and ignores extreme values.

You can also calculate the range for other fractions of a variable's distribution. One alternative is to divide your distribution using **percentiles**. These split your distribution into 100 equal parts. Obviously the lower quartile is the 25th percentile and the upper quartile the 75th percentile. However, you could calculate a range between the 10th and 90th percentiles so as to include 80 per cent of your data values. Another alternative is to divide the range into 10 equal parts called **deciles**.

To describe and compare the extent by which values differ from the mean

Conceptually and statistically in research it is important to look at the extent to which the data values for a variable are spread around their mean, as this is what you need to know to assess its usefulness as a typical value for the distribution. If your data values are all close to the mean, then the mean is more typical than if they vary widely. To describe the extent of spread of numerical data you use the **standard deviation**. If your data are a sample, this is calculated using a slightly different formula than if your data are a population, although if your sample is larger than about 30 cases there is little difference in the two statistics.

You may need to compare the relative spread of data between distributions of different magnitudes (e.g. one may be measured in hundreds of tonnes, the other in billions of tonnes). To make a meaningful comparison you will need to take account of these different magnitudes. A common way of doing this is:

1. to divide the standard deviation by the mean;
2. then to multiply your answer by 100.

This results in a statistic called the **coefficient of variation** (Black 2009). The values of this statistic can then be compared. The distribution with the largest coefficient of variation has the largest relative spread of data (Box 11.12).

Box 11.12 Focus on student research

Describing variables and comparing their dispersion

Cathy was interested in the total value of transactions at the main and sub-branches of a major bank. The mean value of total transactions at the main branches was approximately five times as high as that for the sub-branches. This made it difficult to compare the relative spread in total value of transactions between the two types of branches. By calculating the coefficients of variation Cathy found that there was relatively more variation in the total value of transactions at the main branches than at the sub-branches. This is because the coefficient of variation for the main branches was larger (23.62) than the coefficient for the sub-branches (18.08).

	A	B	C	D
1	Branch type	Mean total transaction value	Standard deviation	Coefficient of variation
2	Main	£6,000,000	£1,417,000	23.62
3	Sub	£1,200,000	£217,000	18.08

Alternatively, as discussed in the introduction in relation to the cost of Big Mac hamburgers in different countries, you may wish to compare the relative extent to which data values differ. One way of doing this is to use **index numbers** and consider the relative differences rather than actual data values. Such indices compare each data value against a base value that is normally given the value of 100, differences being calculated relative to this value. An index number greater than 100 represents a larger or higher data value relative to the base value and an index less than 100, a smaller or lower data value.

To calculate an index number for each case for a data variable you use the following formula:

$$\text{Index number for case} = \frac{\text{data value for case}}{\text{base data value}} \times 100$$

11.5 Examining relationships, differences and trends using statistics

One of the questions you are most likely to ask in your analysis is: 'How does a variable relate to another variable?' In statistical analysis you answer this question by testing the likelihood of a relationship (or one more extreme) occurring by chance alone, if there really was no difference in the population from which the sample was drawn (Robson 2011). This process is known as significance or hypothesis testing as, in effect, you are comparing the data you have collected with what you would theoretically expect to happen. Significance testing can therefore be thought of as helping to rule out the possibility that your result could be due to random variation in your sample.

There are two main groups of statistical significance tests: non-parametric and parametric. **Non-parametric statistics** are designed to be used when your data are not normally distributed. Not surprisingly, this most often means they are used with categorical data. In contrast, **parametric statistics** are used with numerical data. Although parametric statistics are considered more powerful because they use numerical data, a number of assumptions about the actual data being used need to be satisfied if they are not to produce spurious results (Blumberg et al. 2014). These include:

- the data cases selected for the sample should be independent – in other words the selection of any one case for your sample should not affect the probability of any other case being included in the same sample;
- the data cases should be drawn from normally distributed populations (Section 11.3 and later in Section 11.5);
- the populations from which the data cases are drawn should have equal variances (don't worry, the term variance is explained later in Section 11.5);
- the data used should be numerical.

In addition, as we will discuss later, you need to ensure that your sample size is sufficiently large to meet the requirements of the statistic you are using. If the assumptions are not satisfied, it is often still possible to use non-parametric statistics.

The way in which this significance is tested using both non-parametric and parametric statistics can be thought of as answering one from a series of questions, dependent on the data type:

- Is the independence or association statistically significant?
- Are the differences statistically significant?
- What is the strength of the relationship, and is it statistically significant?
- Are the predicted values statistically significant?

These are summarised in Table 11.5 along with statistics used to help examine trends.

Testing for normality

As we have already noted, parametric tests assume that the numerical data cases in your sample are drawn from normally distributed populations. This means that the data values for each quantitative variable should also be normally distributed, being clustered around the variable's mean in a symmetrical pattern forming a bell-shaped frequency distribution. Fortunately, it is relatively easy to check if data values for a particular variable are distributed normally, both using graphs and statistically.

In Section 11.3 we looked at a number of different types of graphs including histograms (Figure 11.4), box plots (Figure 11.8) and frequency polygons (Figure 11.13). All of these can be used to assess visually whether the data values for a particular numerical variable are clustered around the mean in a symmetrical pattern, and so normally distributed. For normally distributed data, the value of the mean, median and mode are also likely to be the same.

Table 11.5 Statistics to examine relationships, differences and trends by data type: A summary

	Categorical		Numerical	
	Descriptive	**Ranked**	**Continuous**	**Discrete**
To test normality of a distribution			Kolmogorov–Smirnov test, Shapiro–Wilk test	
To test whether two variables are independent	Chi square (data may need grouping)		Chi square if variable grouped into discrete classes	
To test whether two variables are associated	Cramer's V and Phi (both variables must be dichotomous)			
To test whether two groups (categories) are different		Kolmogorov–Smirnov (data may need grouping) or Mann–Whitney *U* test	Independent *t*-test or paired *t*-test (often used to test for changes over time) or Mann–Whitney *U* test (where data skewed or a small sample)	
To test whether three or more groups (categories) are different			Analysis of variance (ANOVA)	
To assess the strength of relationship between two variables		Spearman's rank correlation coefficient (Spearman's rho) or Kendall's rank order correlation coefficient (Kendall's tau)	Pearson's product moment correlation coefficient (PMCC)	
To assess the strength of a relationship between one dependent and one independent variable			Coefficient of determination	
To assess the strength of a relationship between one dependent and two or more independent variables			Coefficient of multiple determination	
To predict the value of a dependent variable from one or more independent variables			Regression equation	
To explore relative change (trend) over time			Index numbers	
To compare relative changes (trends) over time			Index numbers	
To determine the trend over time of a series of data			Time series: moving averages or regression equation (regression analysis)	

Source: © Mark Saunders, Philip Lewis and Adrian Thornhill 2015

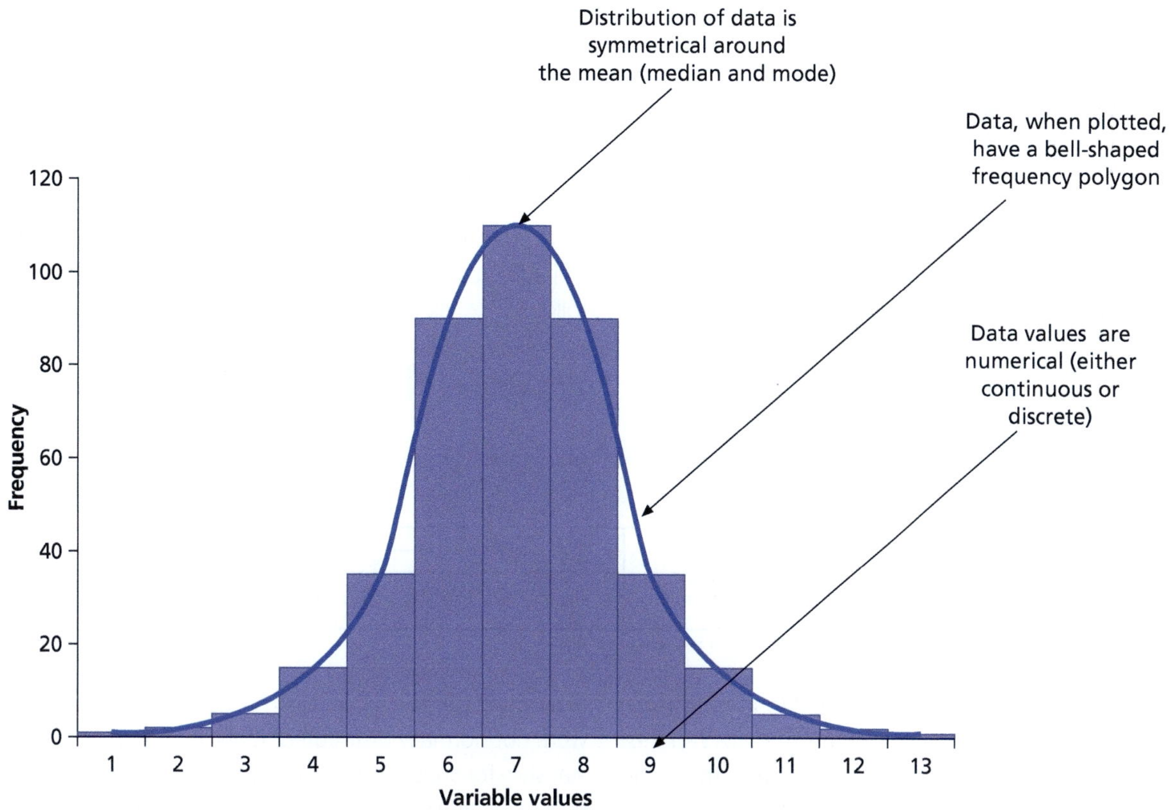

Figure 11.13 Annotated frequency polygon showing a normal distribution

Another way of testing for normality is to use statistics to establish whether the distribution as a whole for a variable differs significantly from a comparable normal distribution. Fortunately, this is relatively easy to do in statistical software such as IBM SPSS Statistics using the **Kolmogorov–Smirnov test** and the **Shapiro–Wilk test** (Box 11.13), as the software also calculates a comparable normal distribution automatically. For both these tests the calculation consists of the test statistic (labelled *D* and *W* respectively), the degrees of freedom[1] (*df*) and, based on this, the probability (*p*-value) that the data for your variable differ by chance from a comparable normal distribution for that variable. For either statistic, a probability of 0.05 means there is only a 5 per cent likelihood of the actual data distribution differing from a comparable normal distribution by chance alone. Therefore a probability of 0.05 or lower[2] for either statistic means that these data are not normally distributed. When interpreting probabilities from software packages, beware: owing to statistical rounding of numbers a probability of 0.000 does not mean zero, but that it is less than 0.001 (Box 11.13). If the probability

[1]Degrees of freedom are the number of values free to vary when computing a statistic. The number of degrees of freedom for a contingency table of at least 2 rows and 2 columns of data is calculated from: (number of rows in the table − 1) × (number of columns in the table - 1).

[2]A probability of 0.05 means that the probability of your test result or one more extreme occurring by chance alone, if there really was no difference, is 5 in 100, that is 1 in 20.

Box 11.13 Focus on student research

Testing for normality

As part of his research project, Osama had collected quantitative data about music piracy and illegal downloading of music from a number of student respondents. Before undertaking his statistical analysis Osama decided to test his quantitative variables for normality using the Kolmogorov–Smirnov test and the Shapiro–Wilk test. The output from IBM SPSS Statistics for one of his data variables, 'number of legal music downloads made in the past month', follows:

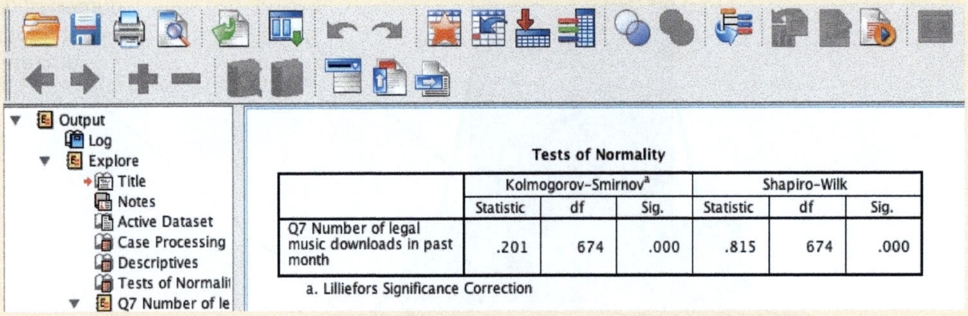

Tests of Normality

	Kolmogorov–Smirnov[a]			Shapiro–Wilk		
	Statistic	df	Sig.	Statistic	df	Sig.
Q7 Number of legal music downloads in past month	.201	674	.000	.815	674	.000

a. Lilliefors Significance Correction

This calculated the significance (Sig.) for both the Kolmogorov–Smirnov test and the Shapiro–Wilk test as '000', meaning that for this variable the likelihood of the actual distribution differing from a normal distribution occurring by chance alone was less than 0.001. Consequently the data values for variable 'Number of legal music downloads in past month' were not normally distributed, reducing his choice of statistics for subsequent analyses. This was confirmed by a bar chart showing the distribution of the data for the variable:

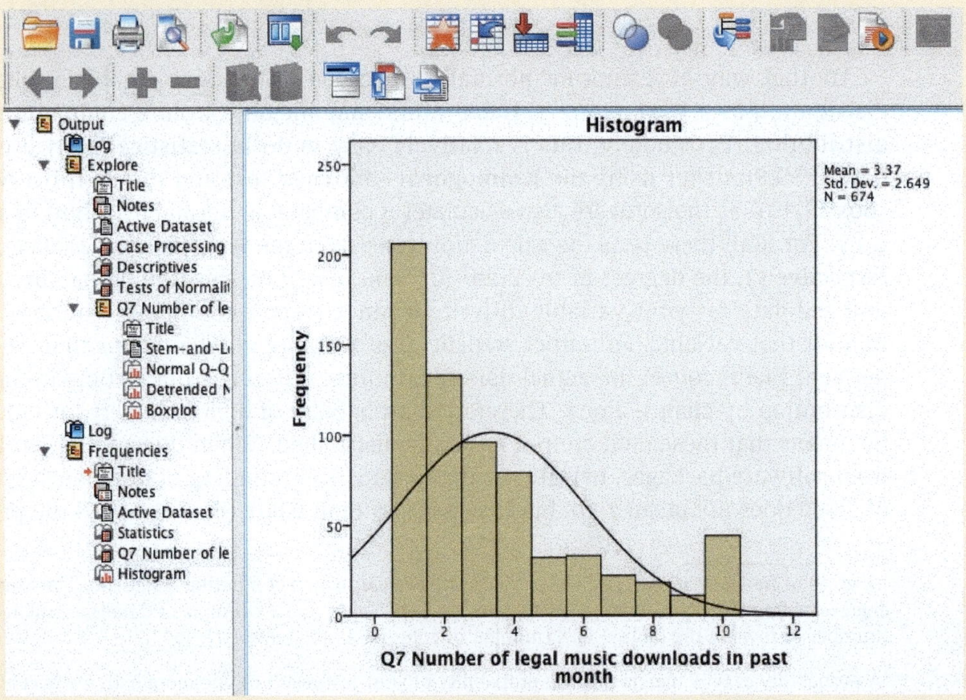

Osama reported the outcome of this analysis in his project report, quoting the test statistics '*D*' and '*W*' and their associated degrees of freedom '*df*' and probabilities '*p*' in brackets:

Tests for normality revealed that data for the variable 'number of legal music downloads in the past month' were not normally distributed [$D = 0.201$, $df = 674$, $p < 0.001$; $W = 0.815$, $df = 674$, $p < 0.001$].

is greater than 0.05, then the data are considered to be normally distributed. However, you need to be careful. With very large samples it is easy to get significant differences between a sample variable and a comparable normal distribution when actual differences are quite small. For this reason it is often helpful to also use a graph to make an informed decision.

Testing for significant relationships and differences

Testing the probability of a pattern or hypothesis such as a relationship between variables occurring by chance alone is known as **significance testing** (Berman Brown and Saunders 2008). As part of your research project, you might have collected sample data to examine the relationship between two variables. Once you have entered data into the analysis software, chosen the statistic and clicked on the appropriate icon, an answer will appear as if by magic! With most statistical analysis software this consists of a test statistic, the degrees of freedom (*df*) and, based on these, the probability (*p*-value) of your test result or one more extreme occurring by chance alone. If the probability of your test statistic or one more extreme having occurred by chance alone is very low (usually $p < 0.05$ or lower[3]), then you have a statistically significant relationship. Statisticians refer to this as rejecting the null hypothesis and accepting the hypothesis, often abbreviating the terms null hypothesis to H_0 and hypothesis to H_1. Consequently, rejecting a null hypothesis will mean rejecting a testable statement something like 'there is no difference between . . .' and accepting a testable statement something like 'there is a difference between . . .'. If the probability of obtaining the test statistic or one more extreme by chance alone is higher than 0.05, then you conclude that the relationship is not statistically significant. Statisticians refer to this as failing to reject the null hypothesis. There may still be a relationship between the variables under such circumstances, but you cannot make the conclusion with any certainty. Remember, when interpreting probabilities from software packages, beware: owing to statistical rounding of numbers a probability of 0.000 does not mean zero, but that it is less than 0.001 (Box 11.14).

The hypothesis and null hypothesis we have just stated are often termed **non-directional**. This is because they refer to a difference rather than also including the nature of the difference. A **directional hypothesis** includes within the testable statement the direction of the difference, for example 'larger'. This is important when interpreting the probability of obtaining the test result, or one more extreme, by chance. Statistical software (Box 11.17) often states whether this probability is one-tailed or two-tailed. Where you have a directional hypothesis such as when the direction of the difference is larger, you should use the one-tailed probability. Where you have a non-directional hypothesis and are only interested in the difference you should use the two-tailed probability.

[3]A probability of 0.05 means that the probability of your test result or one more extreme occurring by chance alone, if there really was no difference in the population from which the sample was drawn (in other words if the null hypothesis was true), is 5 in 100, that is 1 in 20.

Despite our discussion of hypothesis testing, albeit briefly, it is worth mentioning that a great deal of quantitative analysis, when written up, does not specify actual hypotheses. Rather, the theoretical underpinnings of the research and the research questions provide the context within which the probability of relationships between variables occurring by chance alone is tested. Thus, although hypothesis testing has taken place, it is often only discussed in terms of statistical significance.

The statistical significance of the relationship indicated by a test statistic is determined in part by your sample size. One consequence of this is that it is very difficult to obtain a significant test statistic with a small sample. Conversely, by increasing your sample size, less obvious relationships and differences will be found to be statistically significant until, with extremely large samples, almost any relationship or difference will be significant (Anderson 2003). This is inevitable as your sample is becoming closer in size to the population from which it was selected. You therefore need to remember that small populations can make statistical tests insensitive, while very large samples can make statistical tests overly sensitive. There are two consequences to this:

- If you expect a difference, relationship or association will be small, you need to have a larger sample size.
- If you have a large sample and the difference, relationship or association is significant, you need to assess the practical significance of this relationship by calculating an effect size index such as Cohen's *d*. An excellent discussion of these can be found in Ellis (2010).

Type I and Type II errors

Inevitably, errors can occur when making inferences from samples. Statisticians refer to these as Type I and Type II errors. Blumberg et al. (2014) use the analogy of legal decisions to explain Type I and Type II errors. In their analogy they equate a Type I error to a person who is innocent being unjustly convicted and a Type II error to a person who is guilty of a crime being unjustly acquitted. In business and management research we would say that an error made by wrongly rejecting a null hypothesis and therefore accepting the hypothesis is a **Type I error**. Type I errors might involve you concluding that two variables are related when they are not, or incorrectly concluding that a sample statistic exceeds the value that would be expected by chance alone. This means you are rejecting your null hypothesis when you should not. The term '**statistical significance**' discussed earlier therefore refers to the probability of making a Type I error. A **Type II error** involves the opposite occurring. In other words, you fail to reject your null hypothesis when it should be rejected. This means that Type II errors might involve you in concluding that two variables are not related when they are, or that a sample statistic does not exceed the value that would be expected by chance alone.

Given that a Type II error is the inverse of a Type I error, it follows that if we reduce our likelihood of making a Type I error by setting the significance level to 0.01 rather than 0.05, we increase our likelihood of making a Type II error by a corresponding amount. This is not an insurmountable problem, as researchers usually consider Type I errors more serious and prefer to take a small likelihood of saying something is true when it is not (Figure 11.14). It is therefore generally more important to minimise Type I than Type II errors.

To test whether two variables are independent or associated

Often descriptive or numerical data will be summarised as a two-way contingency table (such as Table 11.3). The **chi square test** enables you to find out how likely it is that

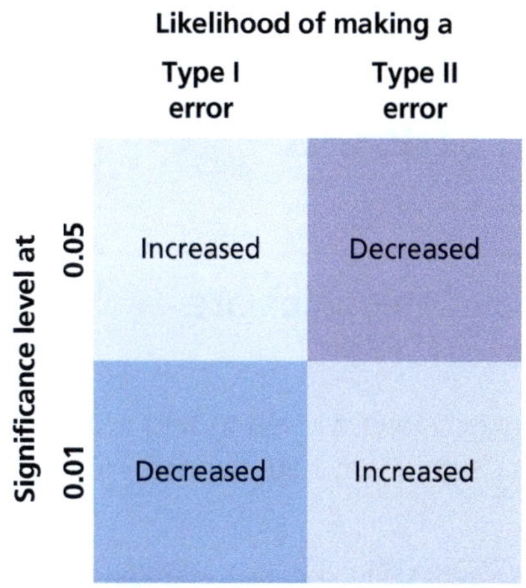

Figure 11.14 Type I and Type II errors

the two variables are independent. It is based on a comparison of the observed values in the table with what might be expected if the two distributions were entirely independent. Therefore you are assessing the likelihood of the data in your table, or data more extreme, occurring by chance alone by comparing it with what you would expect if the two variables were independent of each other. This could be phrased as the null hypothesis: 'there is no dependence . . .'.

The test relies on:

- the categories used in the contingency table being mutually exclusive, so that each observation falls into only one category or class interval;
- no more than 25 per cent of the cells in the table having expected values of less than 5. For contingency tables of two rows and two columns, no expected values of less than 10 are preferable (Dancey and Reidy 2011).

If the latter assumption is not met, the accepted solution is to combine rows and columns where this produces meaningful data.

The chi square (χ^2) test calculates the probability that the data in your table, or data more extreme, could occur by chance alone. Most statistical analysis software does this automatically. However, if you are using a spreadsheet you will usually need to look up the probability in a 'critical values of chi square' table using your calculated chi square value and the degrees of freedom.[4] There are numerous copies of this table online. A probability of 0.05 means that there is only a 5 per cent likelihood of the data in your table occurring by chance alone, and is termed statistically significant. Therefore, a probability of 0.05 or smaller means you can be at least 95 per cent certain that the dependence between your two variables represented by the data in the table could not have occurred by chance factors alone.

Some software packages, such as IBM SPSS Statistics, calculate the statistic **Cramer's V** alongside the chi square statistic (Box 11.14). If you include the value of Cramer's V in your research report, it is usual to do so in addition to the chi square statistic. Whereas

[4]Degrees of freedom are the number of values free to vary when computing a statistic. The number of degrees of freedom for a contingency table of at least two rows and two columns of data is calculated from (number of rows in the table − 1) × (number of columns in the table − 1).

Box 11.14 Focus on student research

Testing whether two variables are independent or associated

As part of his research project, John wanted to find out whether there was a significant dependence between salary grade of respondent and gender. Earlier analysis using IBM SPSS Statistics had indicated that there were 385 respondents in his sample with no missing data for either variable. However, it had also highlighted there were only 14 respondents in the five highest salary grades (GC01 to GC05).

Bearing in mind the assumptions of the chi square test, John decided to combine salary grades GC01 through GC05 to create a combined grade GC01–5 using IBM SPSS Statistics:

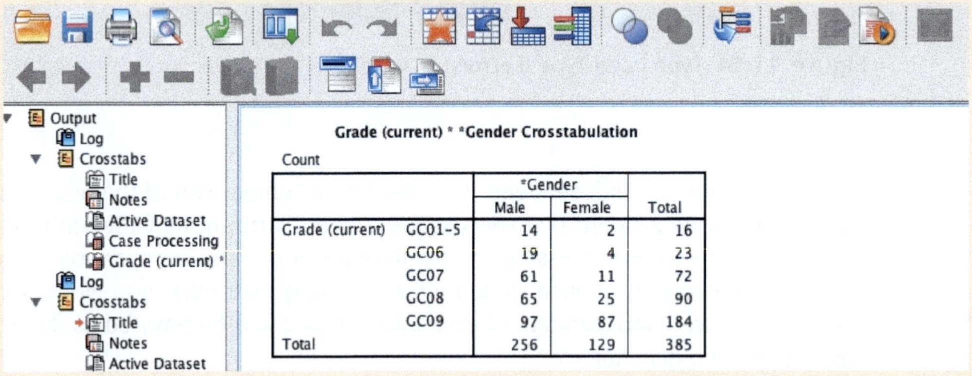

Grade (current) * *Gender Crosstabulation

Count

		*Gender		Total
		Male	Female	
Grade (current)	GC01-5	14	2	16
	GC06	19	4	23
	GC07	61	11	72
	GC08	65	25	90
	GC09	97	87	184
Total		256	129	385

He then used his analysis software to undertake a chi square test and calculate Cramer's V.

As can be seen, this resulted in an overall chi square value of 33.59 with 4 degrees of freedom (*df*).

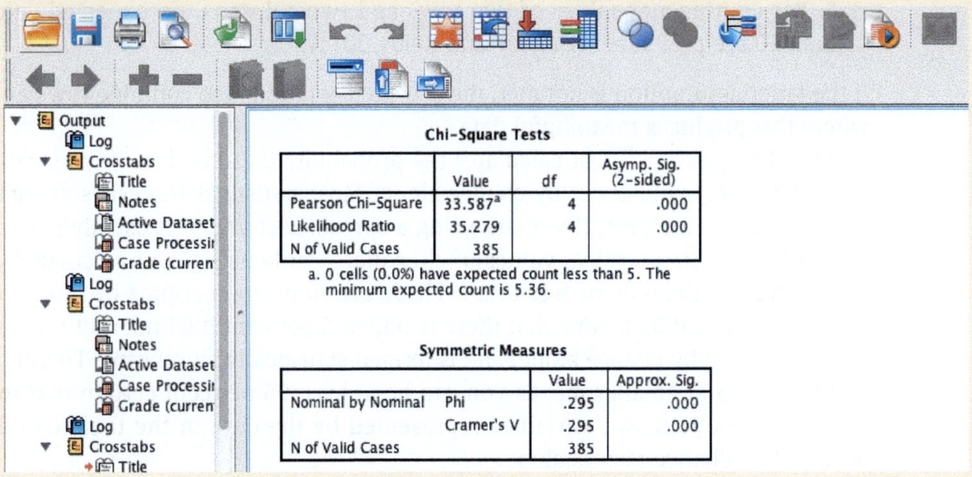

Chi-Square Tests

	Value	df	Asymp. Sig. (2-sided)
Pearson Chi-Square	33.587[a]	4	.000
Likelihood Ratio	35.279	4	.000
N of Valid Cases	385		

a. 0 cells (0.0%) have expected count less than 5. The minimum expected count is 5.36.

Symmetric Measures

		Value	Approx. Sig.
Nominal by Nominal	Phi	.295	.000
	Cramer's V	.295	.000
N of Valid Cases		385	

The significance of .000 (Asymp. Sig. – two sided) meant that the probability of the values in his table occurring by chance alone was less than 0.001. He therefore concluded that the gender and grade were extremely unlikely to be independent and quoted the statistic in his project report:

$[x^2 = 33.59, df = 4, p < 0.001]$*

The Cramer's V value of .295, significant at the <.001 level (Approx. Sig.), showed that the association between gender and salary grade, although weak, was positive. This meant that men (coded 1 whereas females were coded 2) were more likely to be employed at higher salary grades GC01–5 (coded using lower numbers). John also quoted this statistic in his project report:

$$[V_c = 0.295, p < 0.001]$$

To explore this association further, John examined the cell values in relation to the row and column totals. Of males, 5 per cent were in higher salary grades (GC01–5) compared to less than 2 per cent of females. In contrast, only 38 per cent of males were in the lowest salary grade (GC09) compared with 67 per cent of females.

*You will have noticed that the computer printout in this box does not have a zero before the decimal point. This is because most software packages follow the North American convention, in contrast to the UK convention of placing a zero before the decimal point.

the chi square statistic gives the probability that data in a table, or data more extreme, could occur by chance alone, Cramer's V measures the association between the two variables within the table on a scale where 0 represents no association and 1 represents perfect association. Because the value of Cramer's V is always between 0 and 1, the relative strengths of significant associations between different pairs of variables can be compared.

An alternative statistic used to measure the association between two variables is **Phi**. This statistic measures the association on a scale between −1 (perfect negative association), through 0 (no association) to 1 (perfect association). However, unlike Cramer's V, using Phi to compare the relative strengths of significant associations between pairs of variables can be problematic. This is because, although values of Phi will only range between −1 and 1 when measuring the association between two dichotomous variables, they may exceed these extremes when measuring the association for categorical variables where at least one of these variables has more than two categories. For this reason, we recommend that you use Phi only when comparing pairs of dichotomous variables.

To test whether two groups are different

Ranked data

Sometimes it is necessary to see whether the distribution of an observed set of values for each category of a variable differs from a specified distribution other than the normal distribution, for example whether your sample differs from the population from which it was selected. The **Kolmogorov–Smirnov test** enables you to establish this for ranked data (Kanji 2006). It is based on a comparison of the cumulative proportions of the observed values in each category with the cumulative proportions in the same categories for the specified population. Therefore you are testing the likelihood of the distribution of your observed data differing from that of the specified population by chance alone.

The Kolmogorov–Smirnov test calculates a D statistic to work out the probability of the two distributions differing by chance alone. Although the test statistic is not often found in analysis software other than for comparisons with a normal distribution (discussed earlier), it is relatively straightforward to calculate using a spreadsheet (Box 11.15). A reasonably clear description of this can be found in Cohen and Holliday (1996). Once calculated, you will need to look up the significance of your *D* value in a 'critical values of *D* for the Kolmogorov–Smirnov test' table. A probability of 0.05 means that there is only a 5 per cent likelihood that the two distributions differ by chance alone, and is termed statistically significant. Therefore a probability of 0.05 or smaller means you can be at least 95 per cent certain that the difference between your two distributions cannot be explained by chance factors alone.

Numerical data

If a numerical variable can be divided into two distinct groups using a descriptive variable, you can assess the likelihood of these groups being different using an **independent**

Box 11.15 Focus on student research

Testing the representativeness of a sample

Benson's research question was, 'To what extent do the espoused values of an organisation match the underlying cultural assumptions?' As part of his research, he emailed a link to a Web questionnaire to the 150 employees in the organisation where he worked and 97 of these responded. The responses from each category of employee in terms of their seniority within the organisation's hierarchy were as shown in the spreadsheet below.

The maximum difference between his observed cumulative proportion (that for respondents) and his specified cumulative proportion (that for total employees) was 0.034. This was the value of his *D* statistic. Consulting a 'critical values of *D* for the Kolmogorov–Smirnov test' table online for a sample size of 97 revealed the probability that the two distributions did not differ by chance alone was less than 0.01, in other words, less than 1 per cent. He concluded that those employees who responded did not differ significantly from the total population in terms of their seniority within the organisation's hierarchy. This was stated in his research report:

> Statistical analysis showed the sample selected did not differ significantly from all employees in terms of their seniority within the organisation's hierarchy [D=.034, p=.014].

	A	B	C	D	E	F	G	H
1			Shop floor workers	Technicians	Supervisors	Quality managers	Management team	Total
2	Respondents	Number	49	15	21	8	4	97
3		Cumulative proportion	0.505	0.660	0.876	0.959	1.000	
4	Total Employees	Number	73	31	24	17	5	150
5		Cumulative proportion	0.487	0.693	0.853	0.967	1.000	
6	*Difference*		0.018	0.034	0.023	0.008	0.000	

groups *t*-test. This compares the difference in the means of the two groups using a measure of the spread of the scores. If the likelihood of any difference between these two groups occurring by chance alone is low, this will be represented by a large t statistic with a probability less than 0.05. This is termed statistically significant.

Alternatively, you might have numerical data for two variables that measure the same feature but under different conditions. Your research could focus on the effects of an intervention such as employee counselling. As a consequence, you would have pairs of data that measure work performance before and after counselling for each case. To assess the likelihood of any difference between your two variables (each half of the pair) occurring by chance alone, you would use a **paired *t*-test** (Box 11.16). Although the calculation of this is slightly different, your interpretation would be the same as for the independent groups *t*-test.

Although the *t*-test assumes that the data are normally distributed (discussed earlier and Section 11.3), this can be ignored without too many problems even with sample sizes of less than 30 (Hays 1994). The assumption that the data for the two groups have the same variance (standard deviation squared) can also be ignored provided that the two samples are of similar size (Hays 1994). If the data are skewed or the sample size is small, the most appropriate statistical test is the Mann–Whitney *U* Test. This test is the non-parametric equivalent of the independent groups *t*-test (Dancey and Reidy 2011). Consequently, if the likelihood of any difference between these two groups occurring by

Box 11.16 Focus on management research

Testing whether groups are different

Behavioural ethics research has traditionally viewed ethical decision making as rational and deliberate. However, more recently research has argued it comprises both conscious and subconscious components. Welsh and Ordóñez's (2014) article in the *Academy of Management Journal* explores the extent to which subconscious processes can influence ethical behaviour, particularly in relation to performance goals. Their research comprised three studies, including an experiment using 291 US residents recruited online using Amazon mTurk. These participants were randomly assigned to one of six conditions relating to all possible combinations of the subconscious and conscious components of their ethical standards. These were the two independent variables in the study:

- initial subconscious activation of ethical standards. Here participants were divided into three groups and primed by an exercise involving either (1) ethical, (2) unethical or (3) neutral sentences. These three groups were referred to as the three subconscious activation conditions ethical, unethical and neutral;
- subsequent conscious activation of ethical standards. Participants in each of the three subconscious groups were next divided into two groups and asked to complete either (1) a 1 neutral recall task or (2) a recall task designed to activate their moral standards. These two groups were referred to as the two conscious activation conditions, neutral and activated;

and one dependent variable:

- reported unethical behaviour, in which participants in each of the six groups read a scenario describing a manager who had an opportunity to behave unethically and indicate how likely they would be to behave unethically on a seven-point scale. This ranged from 1 = not likely to 7 = very likely.

Box 11.16 Focus on management research (*continued*)

Testing whether groups are different

Welsh and Ordóñez (2014) found that participants whose initial subconscious ethical standards had not been activated (the neutral subconscious activation condition) and who had also not subsequently had their ethical standards consciously activated (the neutral conscious activation condition) were significantly more likely to engage in unethical behaviour than those whose ethical standards had been activated. They reported these results in their article, quoting both the mean score for the likelihood of unethical behaviour and the value of the *t*-test for the neutral subconscious activation condition, writing (Welsh and Ordóñez 2014: 732): 'the mean unethical behaviour likelihood (3.59) was significantly higher than in the conscious activation condition (mean = 2.61, $t\,(95) = 2.18$, $p < 0.05$), the subconscious activation condition (mean = 2.84, $t\,(140) = 2.06$, $p < .05$), and the conscious-subconscious activation condition (mean = 2.84, $t\,(141) = 2.00$, $p < 0.05$)'. Based upon this they noted that subconscious priming produces unethical behaviour through the activation of moral standards.

chance alone is low, this will be represented by a large *U* statistic with a probability less than 0.05. This is termed statistically significant.

To test whether three or more groups are different

If a numerical variable is divided into three or more distinct groups using a descriptive variable, you can assess the likelihood of these groups being different occurring by chance alone by using **one-way analysis of variance** or one-way **ANOVA** (Table 11.5). As you can gather from its name, ANOVA analyses the **variance**, that is, the spread of data values, within and between groups of data by comparing means. The *F* ratio or *F* statistic represents these differences. If the likelihood of any difference between groups occurring by chance alone is low, this will be represented by a large *F* ratio with a probability of less than 0.05. This is termed statistically significant.

The following assumptions need to be met before using one-way ANOVA. More detailed discussion is available in Hays (1994) and Dancey and Reidy (2011).

- Each data value is independent and does not relate to any of the other data values. This means that you should not use one-way ANOVA where data values are related in some way, such as the same case being tested repeatedly.
- The data for each group are normally distributed (discussed earlier and Section 11.3). This assumption is not particularly important provided that the number of cases in each group is large (30 or more).
- The data for each group have the same variance (standard deviation squared). However, provided that the number of cases in the largest group is not more than 1.5 times that of the smallest group, this appears to have very little effect on the test results.

Assessing the strength of relationship

If your data set contains ranked or numerical data, it is likely that, as part of your Exploratory Data Analysis, you will already have plotted the relationship between cases for these ranked or numerical variables using a scatter graph (Figure 11.12). Such relationships might include those between weekly sales of a new product and those of a similar established product, or age of employees and their length of service with the company. These examples emphasise the fact that your data can contain two sorts of relationship:

- those where a change in one variable is accompanied by a change in another variable but it is not clear which variable caused the other to change, a **correlation**;
- those where a change in one or more (independent) variables causes a change in another (dependent) variable, a cause-and-effect relationship.

To assess the strength of relationship between pairs of variables

A **correlation coefficient** enables you to quantify the strength of the linear relationship between two ranked or numerical variables. This coefficient (usually represented by the letter *r*) can take on any value between $+1$ and -1 (Figure 11.15). A value of $+1$ represents a perfect **positive correlation**. This means that the two variables are precisely related and that as values of one variable increase, values of the other variable will increase. By contrast, a value of -1 represents a perfect **negative correlation**. Again, this means that the two variables are precisely related; however, as the values of one variable increase those of the other decrease. Correlation coefficients between $+1$ and -1 represent weaker positive and negative correlations, a value of 0 meaning the variables are perfectly independent. Within business research it is extremely unusual to obtain perfect correlations.

For data collected from a sample you will need to know the probability of your correlation coefficient having occurred by chance alone. Most analysis software calculates this probability automatically (Box 11.17). As outlined earlier, if this probability is very low (usually less than 0.05) then it is considered statistically significant. If the probability is greater than 0.05 then your relationship is usually considered not statistically significant.

If both your variables contain numerical data you should use **Pearson's product moment correlation coefficient** (PMCC) to assess the strength of relationship (Table 11.5). Where these data are from a sample then the sample should have been selected at random and the data should be normally distributed. However, if one or both of your variables contain ranked data you cannot use PMCC, but will need to use a correlation coefficient that is calculated using ranked data. Such rank correlation coefficients represent the degree of agreement between the two sets of rankings. Before calculating the rank correlation coefficient, you will need to ensure that the data for both variables are ranked. Where one of the variables is numerical this will necessitate converting these data to ranked data. Subsequently, you have a choice of rank correlation coefficients. The two used most widely in business and management research are

Figure 11.15 Values of the correlation coefficient
Sources: Developed from earlier editions; Hair et al. (2006)

Box 11.17 Focus on student research

Assessing the strength of relationship between pairs of variables

As part of his research project, Hassan obtained data from a company on the number of television advertisements, number of enquiries and number of sales of their product. These data were entered into the statistical analysis software. He wished to discover whether there were any relationships between the following pairs of these variables:

- number of television advertisements and number of enquiries;
- number of television advertisements and number of sales;
- number of enquiries and number of sales.

As the data were numerical, he used the statistical analysis software to calculate Pearson's product moment correlation coefficients for all pairs of variables. The output was a correlation matrix below.

Hassan's matrix is symmetrical because correlation implies only a relationship rather than a cause-and-effect relationship. The value in each cell of the matrix is the correlation coefficient. Thus, the correlation between the number of advertisements and the number of enquiries is 0.362. This coefficient shows that there is a weak to moderate positive relationship between the number of television advertisements and the number of enquiries. The (**) highlights that the probability of this correlation coefficient occurring by chance alone is less than or equal to 0.01 (1 per cent). This correlation coefficient is therefore statistically significant. A two-tailed significance for each correlation, rather than a one-tailed significance, is used as correlation does not test the direction of a relationship, just whether they are related.

Using the data in this matrix Hassan concluded that:

> There is a statistically significant strong positive relationship between the number of enquiries and the number of sales ($r=.726$, $p<0.001$) and a statistically significant but weak to moderate relationship between the number of television advertisements and the number of enquiries ($r=.362$, $p=0.006$). However, there is no statistically significant relationship between the number of television advertisements and the number of sales ($r=.204$, $p=0.131$).

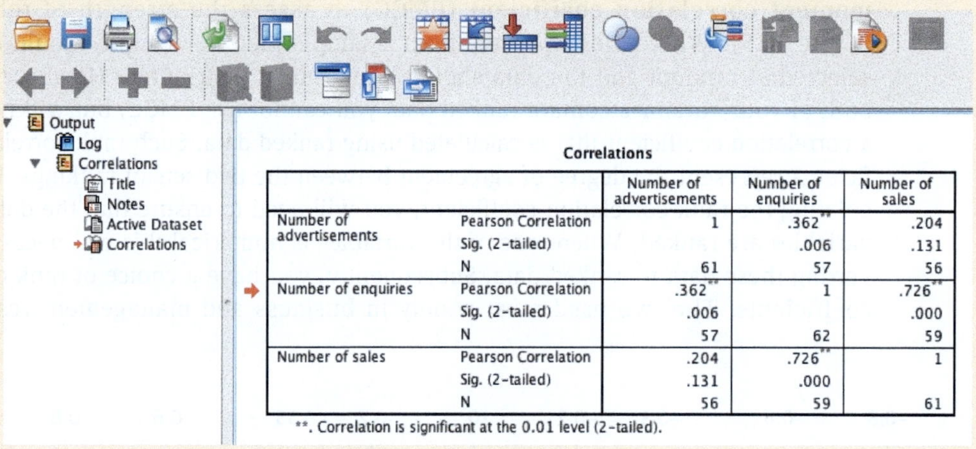

Correlations

		Number of advertisements	Number of enquiries	Number of sales
Number of advertisements	Pearson Correlation	1	.362**	.204
	Sig. (2-tailed)		.006	.131
	N	61	57	56
Number of enquiries	Pearson Correlation	.362**	1	.726**
	Sig. (2-tailed)	.006		.000
	N	57	62	59
Number of sales	Pearson Correlation	.204	.726**	1
	Sig. (2-tailed)	.131	.000	
	N	56	59	61

**. Correlation is significant at the 0.01 level (2-tailed).

Spearman's rank correlation coefficient (Spearman's ρ, the Greek letter rho) and **Kendall's rank correlation coefficient** (Kendall's τ, the Greek letter tau). Where data are being used from a sample, both these rank correlation coefficients assume that the sample is selected at random and the data are ranked (ordinal). Given this, it is not surprising that whenever you can use Spearman's rank correlation coefficient you can also use Kendall's rank correlation coefficient. However, if your data for a variable contain tied ranks, Kendall's rank correlation coefficient is generally considered to be the more appropriate of these coefficients to use. Although each of the correlation coefficients discussed uses a different formula in its calculation, the resulting coefficient is interpreted in the same way as PMCC.

To assess the strength of a cause-and-effect relationship between dependent and independent variables

In contrast to the correlation coefficient, the **coefficient of determination** enables you to assess the strength of relationship between a numerical dependent variable and one numerical independent variable and the **coefficient of multiple determination** enables you to assess the strength of relationship between a numerical dependent variable and two or more independent variables. Once again, where these data have been selected from a sample, the sample must have been selected at random. For a dependent variable and one (or perhaps two) independent variables you will have probably already plotted this relationship on a scatter graph. If you have more than two independent variables this is unlikely as it is very difficult to represent four or more scatter graph axes visually!

The coefficient of determination (represented by r^2) and the coefficient of multiple determination (represented by R^2) can both take on any value between 0 and +1. They measure the proportion of the variation in a dependent variable (amount of sales) that can be explained statistically by the independent variable (marketing expenditure) or variables (marketing expenditure, number of sales staff, etc.). This means that if all the variation in amount of sales can be explained by the marketing expenditure and the number of sales staff, the coefficient of multiple determination will be 1. If 50 per cent of the variation can be explained, the coefficient of multiple determination will be 0.5, and if none of the variation can be explained, the coefficient will be 0 (Box 11.18). Within our research we have rarely obtained a coefficient above 0.8.

For a dependent variable and two or more independent variables you will have probably already plotted this relationship on a scatter graph.

The process of calculating the coefficient of determination and regression equation using one independent variable is normally termed **regression analysis**. Calculating a coefficient of multiple determination and regression equation using two or more independent variables is termed **multiple regression analysis**. The calculations and interpretation required by multiple regression are relatively complicated, and we advise you to use

Box 11.18 Focus on student research

Assessing a cause-and-effect relationship

As part of her research project, Arethea wanted to assess the relationship between all the employees' annual salaries and the number of years each had been employed by an organisation. She believed that an employee's annual salary would be dependent on the number of years for which she or he had been employed (the independent variable). Arethea entered these data into her analysis software and calculated a coefficient of determination (r^2) of 0.37.

As she was using data for all employees of the firm (the total population) rather than a sample, the probability of her coefficient occurring by chance alone was 0. She therefore concluded that 37 per cent of the variation in current employees' salary could be explained by the number of years they had been employed by the organisation.

statistical analysis software and consult a detailed statistics textbook that also explains how to use the software, such as Field (2013). Most statistical analysis software will automatically calculate the significance of the coefficient of multiple determination for sample data. A very low significance value (usually less than 0.05) means that your coefficient is unlikely to have occurred by chance alone. A value greater than 0.05 means you can conclude that your coefficient of multiple determination could have occurred by chance alone.

To predict the value of a variable from one or more other variables

Regression analysis can also be used to predict the values of a dependent variable given the values of one or more independent variables by calculating a **regression equation** (Box 11.19). You may wish to predict the amount of sales for a specified marketing expenditure and number of sales staff. You would represent this as a regression equation:

$$AoS_i + \alpha + \beta_1 ME_i + \beta_2 NSS_i$$

where:
AoS is the amount of sales
ME is the marketing expenditure
NSS is the number of sales staff
α is the regression constant
β_1 and β_2 are the beta coefficients

This equation can be translated as stating:

$$Amount\ of\ sales_i = value + (\beta_1{}^*\ Marketing\ expenditure_i) + (\beta_2{}^*\ Number\ of\ sales\ staff_i)$$

Using regression analysis you would calculate the values of the constant coefficient α and the slope coefficients β_1 and β_2 from data you had already collected on amount of sales, marketing expenditure and number of sales staff. A specified marketing expenditure and number of sales staff could then be substituted into the regression equation to predict the amount of sales that would be generated. When calculating a regression equation you need to ensure the following assumptions are met:

- The relationship between dependent and independent variables is linear. **Linearity** refers to the degree to which the change in the dependent variable is related to the change in the independent variables. Linearity can easily be examined through residual plots (these are usually drawn by the analysis software). Two things may influence the linearity. First, individual cases with extreme values on one or more variables (outliers) may violate the assumption of linearity. It is, therefore, important to identify these outliers and, if appropriate, exclude them from the analysis. Second, the values for one or more variables may violate the assumption of linearity. For these variables the data values may need to be transformed. Techniques for this can be found in other, more specialised books on multivariate data analysis, for example Hair et al. (2013).
- The extent to which the data values for the dependent and independent variables have equal variances (this term was explained earlier in Section 11.4), also known as **homoscedasticity**. Again, analysis software usually contains statistical tests for equal variance. For example, the Levene test for homogeneity of variance measures the equality of variances for a single pair of variables. If **heteroscedasticity** (that is, unequal variances) exists, it may still be possible to carry out your analysis. Further details of this can again be found in more specialised books on multivariate analysis, such as Hair et al. (2013).
- Absence of correlation between two or more independent variables (**collinearity** or **multicollinearity**), as this makes it difficult to determine the separate effects of individual variables. The simplest diagnostic is to use the correlation coefficients, extreme

collinearity being represented by a correlation coefficient of 1. The rule of thumb is that the presence of high correlations (generally 0.90 and above) indicates substantial collinearity (Hair et al. 2013). Other common measures include the tolerance value and its inverse – the **variance inflation factor** (VIF). Hair et al. (2013) recommend that a very small tolerance value (0.10 or below) or a large VIF value (10 or above) indicates high collinearity.

- The data for the independent variables and dependent variable are normally distributed (discussed earlier in this section and Section 11.3).

The coefficient of determination, r^2 (discussed earlier), can be used as a measure of how good a predictor your regression equation is likely to be. If your equation is a perfect predictor then the coefficient of determination will be 1. If the equation can predict only 50 per cent of the variation, then the coefficient of determination will be 0.5, and if the equation predicts none of the variation, the coefficient will be 0. The coefficient of multiple

Box 11.19 Focus on student research

Forecasting the number of road injury accidents

As part of her research project, Nimmi had obtained data on the number of road injury accidents and the number of drivers breath tested for alcohol in 39 police force areas. In addition, she obtained data on the total population (in thousands) for each of these areas from the most recent census. Nimmi wished to find out if it was possible to predict the number of road injury accidents (*RIA*) in each police area (her dependent variable) using the number of drivers breath tested (*BT*) and the total population in thousands (*POP*) for each of the police force areas (independent variables). This she represented as an equation:

$$RIA_i + \alpha + \beta_1 BT_i + \beta_2 POP_i$$

Nimmi entered her data into the analysis software and undertook a multiple regression analysis. She scrolled down the output file and found the

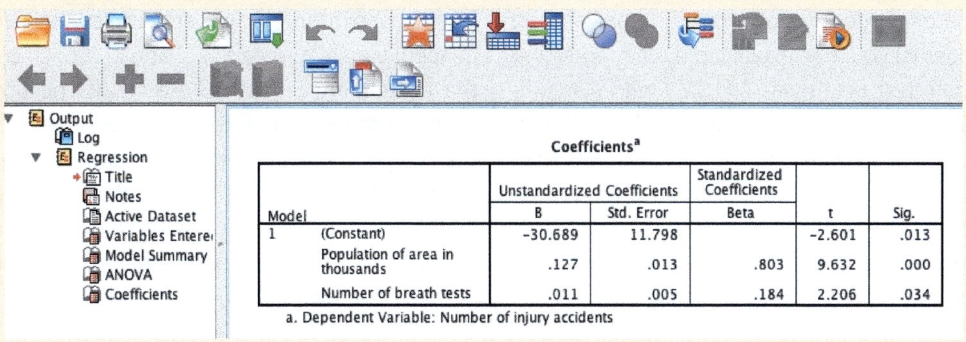

Coefficients[a]

Model		Unstandardized Coefficients B	Unstandardized Coefficients Std. Error	Standardized Coefficients Beta	t	Sig.
1	(Constant)	-30.689	11.798		-2.601	.013
	Population of area in thousands	.127	.013	.803	9.632	.000
	Number of breath tests	.011	.005	.184	2.206	.034

a. Dependent Variable: Number of injury accidents

table headed 'Coefficients'. Nimmi substituted the 'unstandardized coefficients' into her regression equation (after rounding the values):

$$RIA_i = -30.689 + 0.011\ BT_i + 0.127\ POP_i$$

This meant she could now predict the number of road injury accidents for a police area of different populations for different numbers of drivers breath tested for alcohol. For example, the number of road injury accidents for an area of 500,000 population in which 10,000 drivers were breath tested for alcohol can now be estimated:

$$-30.689 + (0.011 \times 10000) + (0.127 \times 500)$$
$$= -30.689 + 110 + 49 + 63.5$$
$$= 81.8$$

Box 11.19
Focus on student research (*continued*)

Forecasting the number of road injury accidents

In order to check the usefulness of these estimates, Nimmi scrolled back up her output and looked at the results of R^2, *t*-test and *F*-test:

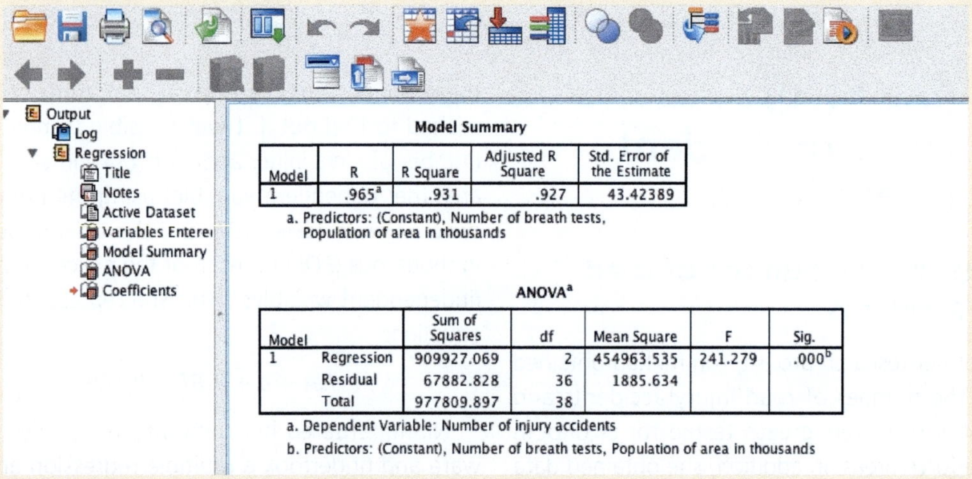

Model Summary

Model	R	R Square	Adjusted R Square	Std. Error of the Estimate
1	.965[a]	.931	.927	43.42389

a. Predictors: (Constant), Number of breath tests, Population of area in thousands

ANOVA[a]

Model		Sum of Squares	df	Mean Square	F	Sig.
1	Regression	909927.069	2	454963.535	241.279	.000[b]
	Residual	67882.828	36	1885.634		
	Total	977809.897	38			

a. Dependent Variable: Number of injury accidents

b. Predictors: (Constant), Number of breath tests, Population of area in thousands

The R^2 and adjusted R^2 values of 0.965 and 0.931 respectively both indicated that there was a high degree of goodness of fit of her regression model. It also meant that over 90 per cent of variance in the dependent variable (the number of road injury accidents) could be explained by the regression model. The *F*-test result was 241.279 with a significance ('Sig.') of .000. This meant that the probability of these results occurring by chance was less than 0.001. Therefore, a significant relationship was present between the number of road injury accidents in an area and the population of the area, and the number of drivers breath tested for alcohol.

The *t*-test results for the individual regression coefficients (shown in the first extract) for the two independent variables were 9.632 and 2.206. Once again, the probability of both these results occurring by chance was less than 0.05, being less than 0.001 for the independent variable population of area in thousands and 0.034 for the independent variable number of breath tests. This means that the regression coefficients for these variables were both statistically significant at the $p < 0.05$ level.

determination (R^2) indicates the degree of the goodness of fit for your estimated multiple regression equation. It can be interpreted as how good a predictor your multiple regression equation is likely to be. It represents the proportion of the variability in the dependent variable that can be explained by your multiple regression equation. This means that when multiplied by 100, the coefficient of multiple determination can be interpreted as the percentage of variation in the dependent variable that can be explained by the estimated regression equation. The adjusted R^2 statistic (which takes into account the number of independent variables in your regression equation) is preferred by some researchers as it helps avoid overestimating the impact of adding an independent variable on the amount of variability explained by the estimated regression equation.

The t-test and F-test are used to work out the probability of the relationship represented by your regression analysis having occurred by chance. In simple linear regression (with one independent and one dependent variable), the t-test and F-test will give you the same answer. However, in multiple regression, the t-test is used to find out the probability of the relationship between each of the individual independent variables and the dependent variable occurring by chance. In contrast, the F-test is used to find out the overall probability of the relationship between the dependent variable and all the independent variables occurring by chance. The t distribution table and the F distribution table are used to determine whether a t-test or an F-test is significant by comparing the results with the t distribution and F distribution respectively, given the degrees of freedom and the predefined significance level.

Examining trends

When examining longitudinal data the first thing we recommend you do is to draw a line graph to obtain a visual representation of the trend (Figure 11.6). Subsequent to this, statistical analyses can be undertaken. Three of the more common uses of such analyses are:

- to explore the trend or relative change for a single variable over time;
- to compare trends or the relative change for variables measured in different units or of different magnitudes;
- to determine the long-term trend and forecast future values for a variable.

These were summarised earlier in Table 11.5.

To explore the trend

To answer some research question(s) and meet some objectives you may need to explore the trend for one variable. One way of doing this is to use **index numbers** to compare the relative magnitude for each data value (case) over time rather than using the actual data value. Index numbers are also widely used in business publications and by organisations. Various share indices (Box 11.20), such as the *Financial Times* FTSE 100, and the UK's Consumer Prices Index are well-known examples.

Although such indices can involve quite complex calculations, they all compare change over time against a base period. The **base period** is normally given the value of 100 (or 1000 in the case of many share indices, including the FTSE 100), and change is calculated relative to this. Thus a value greater than 100 would represent an increase relative to the base period, and a value less than 100 a decrease.

To calculate simple index numbers for each case of a longitudinal variable you use the following formula:

$$\text{Data value for case index number of a case} = \frac{\text{data value for case}}{\text{data value for base period}} \times 100$$

Thus, if a company's sales were 125,000 units in 2014 (base period) and 150,000 units in 2015, the index number for 2014 would be 100 and for 2015 it would be 120.

To compare trends

To answer some other research question(s) and to meet the associated objectives you may need to compare trends between two or more variables measured in different units or at different magnitudes. For example, to compare changes in prices of fuel oil and coal over time is difficult as the prices are recorded for different units (litres and tonnes). One way of overcoming this is to use index numbers (Section 11.4) and compare the relative changes in the value of the index rather than actual figures. The index numbers for each variable are calculated in the same way as outlined earlier.

Box 11.20 Focus on research in the news

Global overview US: Advance continues as German data and M&A buoy sentiment

By Dave Shellock

Chinese equities respond positively to central bank interest rate cut and prospect of further easing in the pipeline. US stocks were heading for yet another record breaking session as a flurry of merger and acquisition activity and some encouraging German economic data added to the afterglow from Friday's bout of global central bank dovishness.

By midday in New York, the S&P 500 equity benchmark was up 0.2 per cent at 2,068, putting it on track for a third successive record close although it failed to break above Friday's intraday all time peak of 2,071.46.

The FTSE Eurofirst 300 pared its early advance but still ended 0.1 per cent higher at a two month peak. BT shares rose 3.7 per cent after the telecoms group confirmed talks to acquire mobile businesses of EE or Telefónica. Chinese equities got their first chance to respond to the unexpected cut in interest rates by the People's Bank of China as well as reports that further easing could be in the pipeline. The Shanghai Composite index rose 1.9 per cent to a three year high while, in Hong Kong, the Hang Seng China Enterprises Index of "H" shares climbed 3.8 per cent, its biggest one day gain in a year. Tokyo was closed for a holiday.

According to media reports, the central bank was ready to cut rates further to head off slowing inflation. "Needless to say anytime the market gets a sense the Chinese government and central bank are poised to apply more muscle to stabilising and boosting growth you are going to see a strong rally in regional shares," said Adrian Miller at GMP Securities. Divyang Shah, a global strategist at IFR Markets, said further monetary stimulus in the form of rate and reserve ratio requirement cuts, and "smart" fiscal stimulus were likely in the first half of next year as policy makers deal with slower growth with greater urgency. "The shift from targeted easing should not be seen as a return to the old days of prizing growth above anything else the emphasis on reforms and responsible lending will remain in play," Mr Shah said. "Instead, officials are uneasy at the pace of structural reforms and want to slow things down a touch to keep growth from falling below 7 per cent."

Meanwhile, the outlook for the Eurozone economy, another thorny subject for the markets, appeared to improve as Germany's Ifo index of business confidence rose for the first time in seven months. November's reading came in at 103.2, up from 104.7, defying expectations for a fall.

"Finally, stabilisation," said Carsten Brzeski, an economist at ING. "In our view, the Ifo index is currently the best single leading indicator for the German economy. Therefore, today's Ifo reading gives clear comfort for our view of an accelerating economy in the final quarter of the year."

FT *Source:* Abridged from 'Resource stocks set to skew FTSE 100', Dave Shellock (2014) *Financial Times*, 25 Nov.

To determine the trend and forecasting

The trend can be estimated by drawing a freehand line through the data on a line graph. However, these data are often subject to variations such as seasonal fluctuations, and so this method is not very accurate. A straightforward way of overcoming this is to calculate a moving average for the time series of data values. Calculating a **moving average** involves replacing each value in the time series with the mean of that value and those values directly preceding and following it (Anderson et al. 2014). This smoothes out the variation in the data so that you can see the trend more clearly. The calculation of a moving average is relatively straightforward using either a spreadsheet or statistical analysis software.

Once the trend has been established, it is possible to forecast future values by continuing the trend forward for time periods for which data have not been collected. This involves calculating the **long-term trend** - that is, the amount by which values are changing in each time period after variations have been smoothed out. Once again, this is relatively straightforward to calculate using analysis software. Forecasting can also be undertaken using other statistical methods, including regression analysis.

If you are using regression for your time-series analysis, the **Durbin–Watson statistic** can be used to discover whether the value of your dependent variable at time t is related to its value at the previous time period, commonly referred to as $t - 1$. This situation, known as **autocorrelation** or **serial correlation**, is important as it means that the results of your regression analysis are less likely to be reliable. The Durbin–Watson statistic ranges in value from zero to 4. A value of 2 indicates no autocorrelation. A value towards zero indicates positive autocorrelation. Conversely, a value towards 4 indicates negative autocorrelation. More detailed discussion of the Durbin–Watson test can be found in other, more specialised books on multivariate data analysis, for example Hair et al. (2013).

11.6 Summary

- Data for quantitative analysis can be collected and subsequently coded at different scales of measurement. The data type (precision of measurement) will constrain the data presentation, summary and analysis techniques you can use.
- Data are entered for computer analysis as a data matrix in which each column usually represents a variable and each row a case. Your first variable should be a unique identifier to facilitate error checking.
- All data should, with few exceptions, be recorded using numerical codes to facilitate analyses.
- Where possible, you should use existing coding schemes to enable comparisons.
- For primary data you should include pre-set codes on the data collection form to minimise coding after collection. For variables where responses are not known, you will need to develop a codebook after data have been collected for the first 50 to 100 cases.
- You should enter codes for all data values, including missing data.
- Your data matrix must be checked for errors.
- Your initial analysis should explore data using both tables and graphs. Your choice of table or graph will be influenced by your research question(s) and objectives, the aspects of the data you wish to emphasise, and the measurement precision with which the data were recorded. This may involve using:
  - tables to show specific amounts;
  - bar graphs, multiple bar graphs, histograms and, occasionally, pictograms to show (and compare) highest and lowest amounts;
  - line graphs to show trends;
  - pie charts and percentage component bar graphs to show proportions or percentages;
  - box plots to show distributions;
  - multiple line graphs to compare trends and show intersections
  - scatter graphs to show interdependence between variables.
- Subsequent analyses will involve describing your data and exploring relationships using statistics and testing for significance. Your choice of statistics will be influenced by your research question(s) and objectives, your sample size the measurement precision at which the data

were recorded and whether the data are normally distributed. Your analysis may involve using statistics such as:
- the mean, median and mode to describe the central tendency;
- the inter-quartile range and the standard deviation to describe the dispersion;
- chi square to test whether two variables are independent;
- Cramer's V and Phi to test whether two variables are associated;
- Kolmogorov–Smirnov to test whether the values differ from a specified population;
- *t*-tests and ANOVA to test whether groups are different;
- correlation and regression to assess the strength of relationships between variables;
- regression analysis to predict values.

- Longitudinal data may necessitate selecting different statistical techniques such as:
  - index numbers to establish a trend or to compare trends between two or more variables measured in different units or at different magnitudes;
  - moving averages and regression analysis to determine the trend and forecast.

Self-check questions

Help with these questions is available at the end of the chapter.

11.1 The following secondary data have been obtained from the Park Trading Company's audited annual accounts:

Year end	Income	Expenditure
2007	11000000	9500000
2008	15200000	12900000
2009	17050000	14000000
2010	17900000	14900000
2011	19000000	16100000
2012	18700000	17200000
2013	17100000	18100000
2014	17700000	19500000
2015	19900000	20000000

a Which are the variables and which are the cases?

b Sketch a possible data matrix for these data for entering into a spreadsheet.

11.2 **a** How many variables will be generated from the following request?

Please tell me up to five things you like about this film. For office use

.... ❒ ❒ ❒

.... ❒ ❒ ❒

.... ❒ ❒ ❒

.... ❒ ❒ ❒

.... ❒ ❒ ❒

b How would you go about devising a coding scheme for these variables from a survey of 500 cinema patrons?

11.3 **a** Illustrate the data from the Park Trading Company's audited annual accounts (Question 11.1) to show trends in income and expenditure.

b What does your diagram emphasise?

c What diagram would you use to emphasise the years with the lowest and highest income?

11.4 As part of research into the impact of television advertising on donations by credit card to a major disaster appeal, data have been collected on the number of viewers reached and the number of donations each day for the past two weeks.

a Which diagram or diagrams would you use to explore these data?

b Give reasons for your choice.

11.5 **a** Which measures of central tendency and dispersion would you choose to describe the Park Trading Company's income (Question 11.1) over the period 2007–15?

b Give reasons for your choice.

11.6 A colleague has collected data from a sample of 74 students. He presents you with the following output from the statistical analysis software:

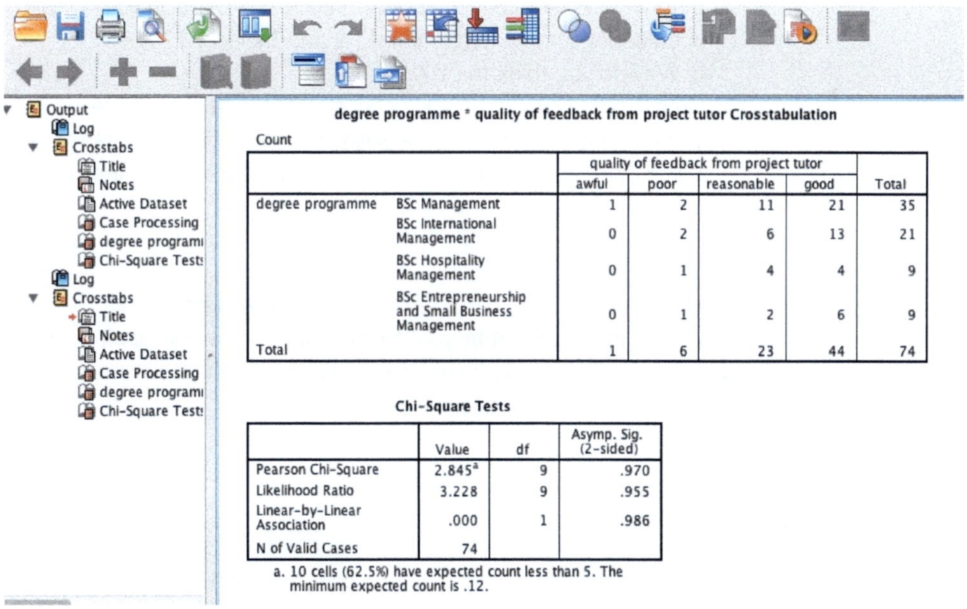

degree programme * quality of feedback from project tutor Crosstabulation

Count

		quality of feedback from project tutor: awful	poor	reasonable	good	Total
degree programme	BSc Management	1	2	11	21	35
	BSc International Management	0	2	6	13	21
	BSc Hospitality Management	0	1	4	4	9
	BSc Entrepreneurship and Small Business Management	0	1	2	6	9
Total		1	6	23	44	74

Chi-Square Tests

	Value	df	Asymp. Sig. (2-sided)
Pearson Chi-Square	2.845[a]	9	.970
Likelihood Ratio	3.228	9	.955
Linear-by-Linear Association	.000	1	.986
N of Valid Cases	74		

a. 10 cells (62.5%) have expected count less than 5. The minimum expected count is .12.

Explain what this tells you about students' opinions about feedback from their project tutor.

11.7 Briefly describe when you would use regression analysis and correlation analysis, using examples to illustrate your answer.

11.8 **a** Use an appropriate technique to compare the following data on share prices for two financial service companies over the past six months, using the period six months ago as the base period:

	EJ Investment Holdings	AE Financial Services
Price 6 months ago	€10	€587
Price 4 months ago	€12	€613
Price 2 months ago	€13	€658
Current price	€14	€690

b Which company's share prices have increased most in the last six months? (Note: you should quote relevant statistics to justify your answer.)

Review and discussion questions

11.9 Use a search engine to discover coding schemes that already exist for ethnic group, family expenditure, industry group, socio-economic class and the like. To do this you will probably find it best to type the phrase 'coding ethnic group' into the search box.

a Discuss how credible you think each coding scheme is with a friend. To come to an agreed answer pay particular attention to:

- the organisation (or person) that is responsible for the coding scheme;
- any explanations regarding the coding scheme's design;
- use of the coding scheme to date.

b Widen your search to include coding schemes that may be of use for your research project. Make a note of the web address of any that are of interest.

11.10 With a friend, choose a large company in which you are interested. Obtain a copy of the annual report for this company. Examine the use of tables, graphs and charts in your chosen company's report.

a To what extent does the use of graphs and charts in your chosen report follow the guidance summarised in Box 11.8 and Table 11.2?

b Why do you think this is?

11.11 With a group of friends, each choose a different share price index. Well-known indices you might choose include the Nasdaq Composite Index, France's CAC 40, Germany's Dax, Hong Kong's Hang Seng Index (HSI), Japan's Nikkei Index, the UK's FTSE 100 and the USA's Dow Jones Industrial Average Index.

a For each of the indices, find out how it is calculated and note down its daily values for a one-week period.

b Compare your findings regarding the calculation of your chosen index with those for the indices chosen by your friends, noting down similarities and differences.

c To what extent do the indices differ in the changes in share prices they show? Why do you think this is?

Progressing your research project

Analysing your data quantitatively

- Examine the technique(s) you are proposing to use to collect data to answer your research question. You need to decide whether you are collecting any data that could usefully be analysed quantitatively.
- If you decide that your data should be analysed quantitatively, you must ensure that the data collection methods you intend to use have been designed to make analysis by computer as straightforward as possible. In particular, you need to pay attention to the coding scheme for each variable and the layout of your data matrix.
- Once your data have been entered into a computer and the data set opened in your analysis software, you will need to explore and present them. Bearing your research question in mind, you should select the most appropriate diagrams and tables after considering the suitability of all possible techniques. Remember to label your diagrams clearly and to keep an electronic copy, as they may form part of your research report.
- Once you are familiar with your data, describe and explore relationships using those statistical techniques that best help you to answer your research questions and are suitable for the data type. Remember to keep an annotated copy of your analyses, as you will need to quote statistics to justify statements you make in the findings section of your research report.
- Use the questions in Box 1.4 to guide you in your reflective diary entry.

11.12 Find out whether your university provides you with access to IBM SPSS Statistics. If it does, visit this book's companion website and download the self-teach package and associated data sets. Work through this to explore the features of IBM SPSS Statistics.

References

Anderson, D.R., Sweeney, D.J., Williams, T.A., Freeman, J. and Shoesmith E. (2014) *Statistics for Business and Economics* (3rd edn). Andover: Cengage Learning.

Anderson, T.W. (2003) *An Introduction to Multivariate Statistical Analysis*. New York: John Wiley.

Berman Brown, R. and Saunders, M. (2008) *Dealing with Statistics: What You Need to Know*. Maidenhead: McGraw-Hill Open University Press.

Bigmacindex.org (2014) *Big Mac Index 2014: Historical Data from the BIG Mac Index*. Available at http://bigmacindex.org/ [Accessed 17 November 2014].

Black, K. (2009) *Business Statistics* (6th edn). Hoboken, NJ: Wiley.

Blumberg, B., Cooper, D.R. and Schindler, D.S. (2014) *Business Research Methods* (4th edn). Maidenhead: McGraw-Hill.

Cohen, L. and Holliday, M. (1996) *Practical Statistics for Students*. London: Paul Chapman.

Dancey, C.P. and Reidy, J. (2011) *Statistics Without Maths for Psychology: Using SPSS for Windows* (5th edn). Harlow: Prentice Hall.

De Vaus, D.A. (2014) *Surveys in Social Research* (6th edn). Abingdon: Routledge.

Ellis, P. (2010) *The Essential Guide to Effect Sizes*. Cambridge: Cambridge University Press.

Eurostat (2014) Environment and energy statistics – air emissions accounts by industry and households (NACE Rev. 2) carbon dioxide. Available at http://appsso.eurostat.ec.europa.eu/nui/show.do?dataset=env_ac_ainah_r2&lang=en [Accessed 17 November 2014].

Everitt, B.S. and Dunn, G. (2001) *Applied Multivariate Data Analysis* (2nd edn). London: Arnold.

Field, A. (2013) *Discovering Statistics Using SPSS* (4th edn). London: Sage.

Hair, J.F., Black, B., Babin, B., Anderson, R.E. and Tatham, R.L. (2013) *Multivariate Data Analysis* (7th edn). Harlow: Pearson.

Harley-Davidson Inc. (2014) *Harley-Davidson Inc. Investor Relations: Motorcycle Shipments* Available at http://investor.harley-davidson.com/phoenix.zhtml?c=87981&p=irol-shipments [Accessed 10 September 2014].

Hays, W.L. (1994) *Statistics* (4th edn). London: Holt-Saunders.

Kanji, G.K. (2006) *100 Statistical Tests* (3rd edn). London: Sage.

Keen, K.J. (2010) *Graphics for Statistics and Data Analysis with R*. Boca Raton, FL: Chapman and Hall.

Kosslyn, S.M. (2006) *Graph Design for the Eye and Mind*. New York: Oxford University Press.

Little, R. and Rubin, D. (2002) *Statistical Analysis with Missing Data* (2nd edn). New York: John Wiley.

Office for National Statistics (2005) *The National Statistics Socio-Economic Classification User Manual*. Basingstoke: Palgrave Macmillan.

Office for National Statistics (no date a) *Standard Occupation Classification 2010 (SOC2010)* Available at http://www.ons.gov.uk/ons/guide-method/classifications/current-standard-classifications/soc2010/index.html [Accessed 27 November 2014].

Office for National Statistics (no date b) *The National Statistics Socio-economic Classification (NS-SEC rebased on the SOC2010)*. Available at http://www.ons.gov.uk/ons/guide-method/classifications/current-standard-classifications/soc2010/soc2010-volume-3-ns-sec–rebased-on-soc2010–user-manual/index.html [Accessed 27 November 2014].

Office for National Statistics (no date c) *Ethnic Group*. Available at http://www.ons.gov.uk/ons/guide-method/measuring-equality/equality/ethnic-nat-identity-religion/ethnic-group/index.html [Accessed 27 November 2014].

Pallant, J. (2013) *SPSS Survival Manual: A Step-by-Step Guide to Data Analysis Using IBM SPSS* (5th edn). Maidenhead: McGraw-Hill.

Park, A., Bryson, C., Clery, E., Curtice, J. and Phillips, M. (2013) *British Social Attitudes: The 30th Report*. London: NatCen Social Research. Available at http://www.bsa-30.natcen.ac.uk/media/37580/bsa30_full_report_final.pdf [Accessed 27 November 2014]

Prosser, L. (2009) *Office for National Statistics UK Standard Industrial Classification of Activities 2007 (SIC 2007)*. Basingstoke: Palgrave Macmillan. Available at http://www.ons.gov.uk/ons/guide-method/classifications/current-standard-classifications/standard-industrial-classification/index.html [Accessed 27 November 2014].

Qualtrics (2014) *Qualtrics Research Suite: Sophisticated online surveys made simple*. Available at http://www.qualtrics.com/research-suite/ [Accessed 17 November 2014]

Robson, C. (2011) *Real World Research: A Resource for Users of Social Research Methods in Applied Settings* (3rd edn). Chichester: John Wiley.

Sherbaum, C. and Shockley, K. (2015) *Analysing Quantitative Data for Business and Management Students*. London: Sage.

SurveyMonkey (2014) SurveyMonkey home page. https://www.surveymonkey.com/ [Accessed 17 November 2014].

Swift, L. and Piff, S. (2014) *Quantitative Methods for Business, Management and Finance* (4th edn). Basingstoke: Palgrave Macmillan.

Tukey, J.W. (1977) *Exploratory Data Analysis*. Reading, MA: Addison-Wesley.

Welsh, D.T. and Ordóñez, L.D. (2014) 'Conscience without cognition: The effects of subconscious priming on ethical behaviour', *Academy of Management Journal*, Vol. 57, No. 3, pp. 723–42.

Further reading

Berman Brown, R. and Saunders, M. (2008) *Dealing with Statistics: What You Need to Know*. Maidenhead: McGraw Hill Open University Press. This is a statistics book that assumes virtually no statistical knowledge, focusing upon which test or graph, when to use it and why. It is written for people who are fearful and anxious about statistics and do not think they can understand numbers!

De Vaus, D.A. (2013) *Surveys in Social Research* (6th edn). London: Routledge. Chapters 9 and 10 contain an excellent discussion about coding data and preparing data for analysis. Part IV (Chapters 12–18) provides a detailed discussion of how to analyse survey data.

Field, A. (2013) *Discovering Statistics Using SPSS* (4th edn). London: Sage. This book offers a clearly explained guide to statistics and using SPSS. It is divided into four levels, the lowest of which assumes no familiarity with the data analysis software and very little with statistics. It covers entering data and how to generate and interpret a wide range of tables, diagrams and statistics using SPSS versions 20 and 21. If you are using an earlier version of SPSS, particularly pre-version 9, be sure to use a book written specifically for that version as there are a number of changes between versions.

Hair, J.F., Black, B., Babin, B., Anderson, R.E. and Tatham, R.L. (2013) *Multivariate Data Analysis* (7th edn). Harlow: Pearson. This book provides detailed information on statistical concepts and techniques. Issues pertinent to design, assumptions, estimation and interpretation are systematically explained for users of more advanced statistical techniques.

Case 11.1
Predicting work performance

As an MSc student in Human Resource Management in the later stages of his programme, Vishal had started thinking about his final research project. Owing to his good grades, he had been able to secure a 'company project' – these were offered by local organisations keen to get involved with his university. Vishal felt very lucky to have been allocated a project relating to performance management, an area he had become really interested in during his MSc studies. His project was with an insurance provider, 'Walker & Moore'. The company was interested in establishing how well indices they routinely drew on to select new employees could predict subsequent on-the-job performance of successful job applicants. They had gathered data already, which included applicants' scores on online ability and personality tests, as well as other information they often took into account in their recruitment and selection decisions, namely applicants' amount of work experience and their level of education. As part of their annual performance reviews, Walker & Moore also routinely collected data about their employees' performance; this consisted of supervisor ratings on four aspects of performance relating to 'completing tasks', 'dealing with colleagues and customers', 'thinking ahead/strategically' and 'avoiding counterproductive behaviours'. An overall performance rating was also available.

Walker & Moore had provided Vishal with anonymised data for 162 employees (75 men, 87 women) for which information on both the predictor variables (i.e. the results of the online tests, amount of work experience and educational level), as well as for individuals' performance ratings, in other words the criterion variable, was available (see Figure 11.C1).

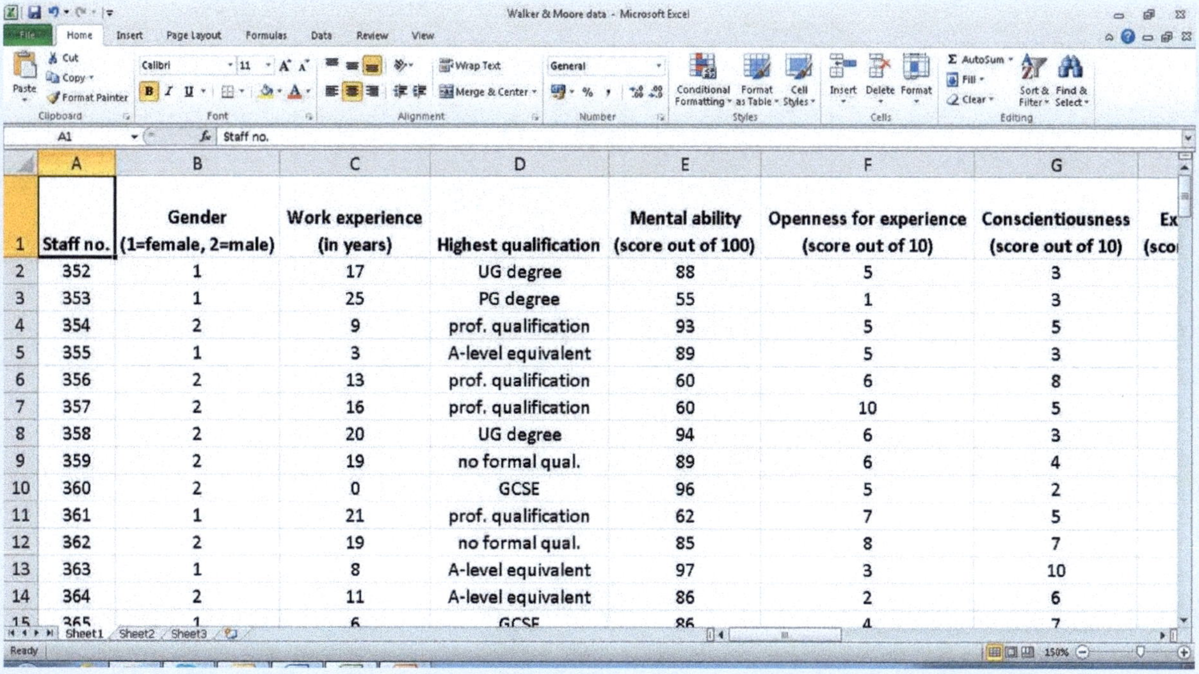

	A	B	C	D	E	F	G	
1	Staff no.	Gender (1=female, 2=male)	Work experience (in years)	Highest qualification	Mental ability (score out of 100)	Openness for experience (score out of 10)	Conscientiousness (score out of 10)	Ex (sco
2	352	1	17	UG degree	88	5	3	
3	353	1	25	PG degree	55	1	3	
4	354	2	9	prof. qualification	93	5	5	
5	355	1	3	A-level equivalent	89	5	3	
6	356	2	13	prof. qualification	60	6	8	
7	357	2	16	prof. qualification	60	10	5	
8	358	2	20	UG degree	94	6	3	
9	359	2	19	no formal qual.	89	6	4	
10	360	2	0	GCSE	96	5	2	
11	361	1	21	prof. qualification	62	7	5	
12	362	2	19	no formal qual.	85	8	7	
13	363	1	8	A-level equivalent	97	3	10	
14	364	2	11	A-level equivalent	86	2	6	
15	365	1	6	GCSE	86	4	7	

Figure 11.C1 Extract from Vishal's spreadsheet

In addition to understanding whether or not the information gathered from applicants could forecast subsequent performance in the job, Walker & Moore had asked Vishal to determine whether or not there are any gender differences in terms of how well employees' performance can be predicted using the information available upon their entry into the organisation.

Vishal had been emailed the data in a spreadsheet and it was now time for him to consider how he would address Walker & Moore's brief. Having already reviewed literature on individual work performance (e.g. Arvey and Murphy 1998; Latham, Almost, Mann and Moore 2005), he decided to start out by formulating a series of hypotheses in relation to the data he had access to; among others, he hypothesised the following:

- Hypothesis 1 (H_1): There is a positive association between individuals' ability scores and their subsequent performance ratings.
- Hypothesis 2 (H_2): There is no difference between males and females regarding the effectiveness of predictor variables.

Vishal had been introduced to the software IBM SPSS Statistics in his research methods module and figured that it would be best to import the data from Walker & Moore into this program for quantitative analysis. Having done this, he then came up with the following four-stage analysis plan:

He would first check his data for errors, which would entail his looking at the values to determine if they looked regular (i.e. no apparent data entering mistakes?), how much missing data there might be and what the minimum/maximum values for his predictor and criterion variables are. Vishal hoped that this initial check would give him a 'feel for' his data set.

Next, he would undertake a series of descriptive analyses to describe and summarise his data; this would involve obtaining statistics of central tendency (such as the arithmetic mean) and dispersion (or spread) (such as the standard deviation) and also getting IBM SPSS Statistics to create graphs to visually represent his data. A histogram with normal distribution curve for example (such as the one in Figure 11.C2) would tell him about the distribution of his data and

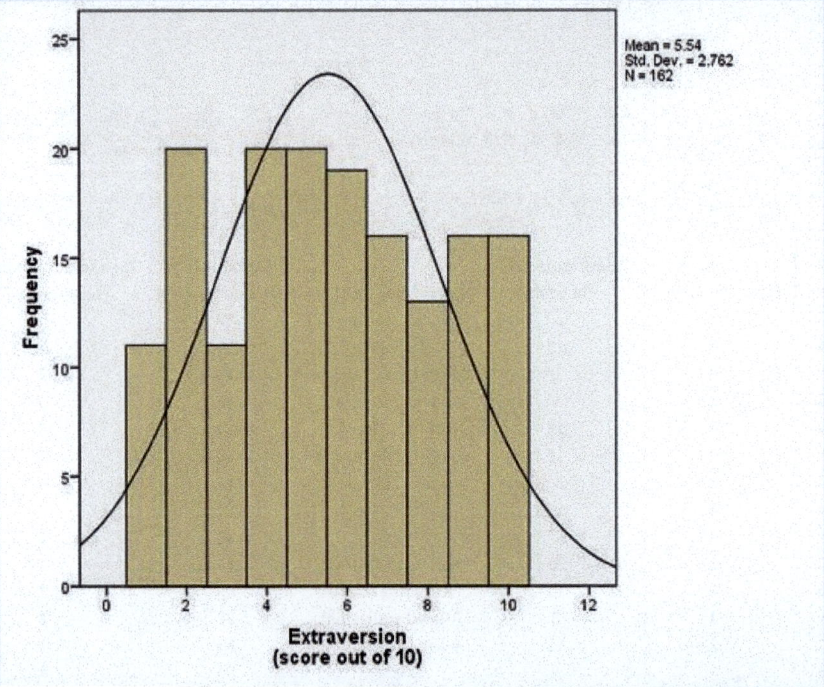

Figure 11.C2 Histogram of 'Extraversion'

whether or not this was likely to be normal. He would also determine the levels of numerical measurement of his variables, as this would have a direct impact on what analyses he would be able to run. For example, he thought it was likely the performance data might be ordinal or interval level data, while categorical variables such as gender or level of education would be classified as nominal (descriptive) level data, thus requiring different types of statistical tests.

Afterwards, Vishal would conduct correlation analyses to determine whether or not any of the predictor variables were significantly associated – either positively or negatively – with performance, including both the overall performance rating and the four more specific performance aspects that Walker& Moore appraised. Examining the resulting correlation coefficients would also enable him to say how strong the links were, if any, between the predictor and criterion variables. Vishal anticipated he would be using Pearson's r for this analysis, but he knew that it would depend on his data; if, for example, the available performance data had been expressed as ranks, he acknowledged it would be more appropriate to instead use Spearman's rank correlation coefficient.

Finally, Vishal was aware that while the correlations would tell him about any relationships between his variables, this would not allow any statements to be made regarding the prediction of performance – which was what Walker and Moore wanted him to find out about. Therefore, he would have to undertake regression analyses to examine the extent to which his predictor variables could forecast performance. In order to indicate whether some predictors might work better for females than for males – or vice versa – he decided he could run the regressions twice, once for women and once for men, and compare the results for both groups.

Vishal felt confident that by undertaking the above analyses, he would be able to address Walker& Moore's brief. Yet, before actually embarking on the statistical analysis, he asked for a meeting with his project tutor to double check if his ideas were going in the right direction.

Questions

1 Do you think Vishal is on the right track with his ideas for statistical analysis? What, if anything, might you do differently or in addition to what Vishal has suggested when it comes to addressing Walker & Moore's brief?

2 Besides histograms, what other types of graphs might Vishal like to use to provide a visual representation of his data?

3 What might be the limitations of Vishal's suggested four-stage analysis plan?

References

Arvey, R.D. and Murphy, K.R. (1998) 'Performance evaluation in work settings', *Annual Review of Psychology*, Vol. 49, pp. 141–68.

Field, A. (2013) *Discovering Statistics Using IBM SPSS Statistics* (4th edn). London: Sage.

Latham, G.P., Almost, J., Mann, S. and Moore, C. (2005) 'New developments in performance management', *Organizational Dynamics*, Vol. 34, pp. 77–87.

Additional case studies relating to material covered in this chapter are available via the book's companion website: **www.pearsoned.co.uk/saunders**.

They are:

- The marketing of arts festivals.
- Marketing a golf course.
- The impact of family ownership on financial performance.
- Small business owner-managers' skill sets.
- Food miles, carbon footprints and supply chains.

Self-check answers

11.1 a The variables are 'income', 'expenditure' and 'year'. There is no real need for a separate case identifier as the variable 'year' can also fulfil this function. Each case (year) is represented by one row of data.

b When the data are entered into a spreadsheet the first column will be the case identifier, for these data the year. Income and expenditure should not be entered with the £ sign as this can be formatted subsequently using the spreadsheet:

	A	B	C
1	Year	Income (£)	Expenditure (£)
2	2007	11000000	9500000
3	2008	15200000	12900000
4	2009	17050000	14000000
5	2010	17900000	14900000
6	2011	19000000	16100000
7	2012	18700000	17200000
8	2013	17100000	18100000
9	2014	17700000	19500000
10	2015	19900000	20000000
11			

11.2 a There is no one correct answer to this question as the number of variables will depend on the method used to code these descriptive data. If you choose the multiple-response method, five variables will be generated. If the multiple-dichotomy method is used, the number of variables will depend on the number of different responses.

b Your first priority is to decide on the level of detail of your intended analyses. Your coding scheme should, if possible, be based on an existing coding scheme. If this is of insufficient detail then it should be designed to be compatible to allow comparisons. To design the coding scheme you need to take the responses from the first 50–100 cases and establish broad groupings. These can be subdivided into increasingly specific subgroups until the detail is sufficient for the intended analysis. Codes can then be allocated to these subgroups. If you ensure that similar responses receive adjacent codes, this will make any subsequent grouping easier. The actual responses that correspond to each code should be noted in a codebook. Codes should be allocated to data on the data collection form in the 'For office use' box. These codes need to include missing data, such as when four or fewer 'things' have been mentioned.

11.3 a Park Trading Company – Income and Expenditure 2007–15.

b Your diagram (it is hoped) emphasises the upward trends of expenditure and (to a lesser extent) income. It also highlights the conjunction where income falls below expenditure in 2013.

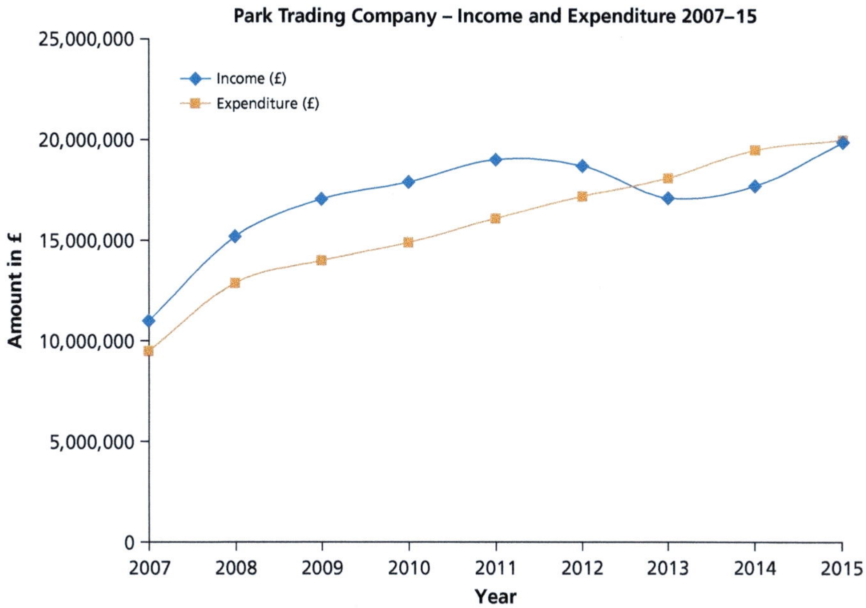

c To emphasise the years with the lowest and highest income, you would probably use a histogram because the data are continuous. A frequency polygon would also be suitable.

11.4 a You would probably use a scatter graph in which number of donations would be the dependent variable and number of viewers reached by the advertisement the independent variable.

b This would enable you to see whether there was any relationship between number of viewers reached and number of donations.

11.5 a The first thing you need to do is to establish the data type. As it is numerical, you could theoretically use all three measures of central tendency and both the standard deviation and inter-quartile range. However, you would probably calculate the mean and perhaps the median as measures of central tendency and the standard deviation and perhaps the inter-quartile range as measures of dispersion.

b The mean would be chosen because it includes all data values. The median might be chosen to represent the middle income over the 2007–15 period. The mode would be of little use for these data as each year has different income values.

If you had chosen the mean you would probably choose the standard deviation, as this describes the dispersion of data values around the mean. The inter-quartile range is normally chosen where there are extreme data values that need to be ignored. This is not the case for these data.

11.6 The probability of a chi square value of 2.845 with 9 degrees of freedom occurring by chance alone for these data is 0.970. This means that statistically the interdependence between students' degree programmes and their opinion of the quality of feedback from project tutors is extremely likely to be explained by chance alone. In addition, the assumption of the chi square test that no more than 20 per cent of expected values should be less than 5 has not been satisfied.

To explore this lack of interdependence further, you examine the cell values in relation to the row and column totals. For all programmes, over 80 per cent of respondents thought the quality of feedback from their project tutor was reasonable or good.

11.7 Your answer needs to emphasise that correlation analysis is used to establish whether a change in one variable is accompanied by a change in another. In contrast, regression analysis is used to establish whether a change in a dependent variable is caused by changes in one or more independent variables – in other words, a cause-and-effect relationship. Although it is impossible to list all the examples you might use to illustrate your answer, you should make sure that your examples for regression illustrate a dependent and one or more independent variables.

11.8 a These quantitative data are of different magnitudes. Therefore, the most appropriate technique to compare these data is index numbers. The index numbers for the two companies are:

	EJ Investment Holdings	AE Financial Services
Price 6 months ago	100	100.0
Price 4 months ago	120	104.4
Price 2 months ago	130	112.1
Current price	140	117.5

b The price of AE Financial Services' shares has increased by €103 compared with an increase of €4 for EJ Investment Holdings' share price. However, the proportional increase in prices has been greatest for EJ Investment Holdings. Using six months ago as the base period (with a base index number of 100), the index for EJ Investment Holdings' share price is now 140 while the index for AE Financial Services' share price is 117.5.

Get ahead using resources on the companion website at: **www.pearsoned.co.uk/saunders**.

- Improve your IBM SPSS Statistics and NVivo research analysis with practice tutorials.
- Save time researching on the Internet with the Smarter Online Searching Guide.
- Test your progress using self-assessment questions.
- Follow live links to useful websites.

Learning outcomes

By the end of this chapter you should be:

- able to understand the nature of qualitative data and appreciate the implications of this for their analysis;
- able to evaluate different approaches to analyse your qualitative data;
- able to identify the main issues that you need to consider when preparing your qualitative data for analysis including preparation to use computer-aided qualitative data analysis software (CAQDAS);
- able to transcribe a recorded interview or notes of an interview or observation and create a data file for analysis by computer;
- aware of different analytical aids to help you to analyse your qualitative data, including keeping a reflective or reflexive journal;
- able to select an appropriate analytical technique for your research project to undertake qualitative data analysis;
- able to identify the common functions of CAQDAS and describe the issues associated with its use.

11.7 Introduction

This chapter is designed to help you analyse qualitative data. The nature of qualitative data is discussed in Section 11.8. Following this we discuss two important aspects related to the nature of qualitative analysis in Section 11.9. The first of these relates to whether you approach your qualitative data analysis from a deductive or inductive perspective. The second relates to the interactive nature of qualitative data collection and analysis. As you read through the sections of this chapter you will recognise the interrelated and interactive nature of qualitative data collection and analysis. Because of this it will be necessary to plan your qualitative research as an interconnected process where you collect and begin to analyse and interpret data as you undertake each interview or observation.

In Section 11.10 we discuss the preparation of your data for analysis and in Section 11.11 we outline a number of aids that will help you analyse these data and record your ideas about how to progress your research.

Sections 11.12–11.19 discuss different analytical techniques to analyse your qualitative data. These are Thematic Analysis (Section 11.12), Template Analysis (Section 11.13), Explanation Building and Testing (Section 11.14), Grounded Theory Method (Section 11.15), Narrative Analysis (Section 11.16), Discourse Analysis (Section 11.17), Content Analysis (Section 11.18) and Data Display and Analysis (Section 11.19).

Source: © Mark Saunders, 2015

Nearly all of us have, at some time in our lives, completed a jigsaw puzzle. As children we may have played with jigsaw puzzles and, as we grew older, those we were able to complete became more complex. In some ways, qualitative data analysis can be likened to the process of completing a jigsaw puzzle in which the pieces represent data. These pieces of data and the relationships between them help us as researchers to create a picture of what we think the data are telling us!

When trying to complete a jigsaw puzzle, most of us begin by looking at the picture on the lid of our puzzle's box. A puzzle for which there is no picture is usually more challenging as we have no idea how the pieces fit together or what the picture will be! Similarly, we may not be clear about how, or even if, the data we have collected can form a clear picture.

Perhaps you haven't tried to complete a jigsaw puzzle for many years but you might find the following useful as well as entertaining! Get a friend to give you the contents of a jigsaw in a bag without the box (since this normally shows the picture of what it is!). Turn all of the pieces picture side up. Think about how you will categorise these data that lie in front of you. What do they mean? You will be likely to group pieces with similar features such as those of a particular colour together. Normally you might then try to fit these similar pieces together to begin to reveal the picture that the fitted pieces are designed to show. Perhaps completing jigsaws reinforces a sense of there being an external reality 'out there', so all we need to do is reveal it! However, for many qualitative researchers, the picture that our pieces of data reveal will depend on the nature of our research question and the concepts we use to make sense of what we see!

A range of computer-aided qualitative data analysis software (CAQDAS) now exists, which we consider in Section 11.20. Consequently, although you need to understand which analytical technique, or combination of techniques, is suitable for the nature of your qualitative or mixed methods research project to be able to make an informed choice about how to analyse your data, it may no longer be necessary for you to undertake routine qualitative data management tasks manually, such as coding your data and sorting these into categories. However, we do not assume that use of CAQDAS is automatic, for two reasons. Firstly, you may not have access to CAQDAS, or at least to software that is suitable for the nature of your research project. Secondly, qualitative data analysis is, as we noted, an interactive and iterative process, a gradual process and a thoughtful and reflective rather than a mechanical process, so using CAQDAS isn't a quick fix. On the other hand, using CAQDAS helps the management and organisation of data, helping to facilitate analysis, where you are able to use a suitable program for your research project.

Consequently, although we make reference to, and include screenshots of, different software packages in some worked examples, these are used to illustrate generic issues associated with analysis rather than imply that you must use such software. If you wish to develop your skills in one of the more widely used CAQDAS packages, called NVivo™, a self-teach package is available via our companion website.

11.8 The nature of qualitative data

It is helpful to commence our discussion by understanding what we mean by qualitative data. Understanding **qualitative data** will help you to analyse these meaningfully. We recognised that qualitative research is often associated with an interpretivist philosophy because researchers need to make sense of the subjective and socially constructed meanings expressed by those who take part in research about the phenomenon being studied. **Social constructionism** indicates that partially shared meanings and realities are dependent on people's interpretation of the events that occur around them. Since meanings in qualitative research depend on social interaction, qualitative data are likely to be more varied, elastic and complex than quantitative data. Analysis and understanding of these data therefore need to be sensitive to these characteristics to be meaningful.

Qualitative data are likely to be characterised by their richness and fullness, based on your opportunity to explore a subject in as real a manner as is possible. A contrast can thus be drawn between the 'thin' abstraction or description that principally results from quantitative data collection and the 'thick' or 'thorough' abstraction or description associated with qualitative data (Brekhus et al. 2005; Dey 1993).

A further way to understand qualitative data is to distinguish them from quantitative data. Table 11.6 highlights three distinct differences between quantitative and qualitative data.

In qualitative research, meanings are principally derived from words and images, not numbers. Since words and images may have multiple meanings as well as unclear meanings, it is necessary to explore and clarify these with great care. This indicates that the quality of qualitative research depends on the interaction between data collection and data analysis to allow meanings to be explored and clarified. This aspect permeates much of the discussion in this chapter.

The nature of qualitative data has further implications for their analysis. These non-standardised data will be likely to be large in volume and complex in nature. You will therefore be confronted by ether a mass of paper, still images, visual recordings or electronic files that you will need to explore, analyse, synthesise and transform in order to

Table 11.6 Distinctions between quantitative and qualitative data

Quantitative data	Qualitative data
Based on meanings derived from numbers	Based on meanings expressed through words (spoken and textual) and images
Collection results in numerical and standardised data	Collection results in non-standardised data requiring classification into categories
Analysis conducted through the use of diagrams and statistics	Analysis conducted through the use of conceptualisation

address your research objectives and answer your research question. In making use of many techniques discussed later, this will involve you in processes where you summarise some parts of your data to condense them, code and categorise data in order to group them according to themes that begin to make sense of these data, and then to link these categories and themes in ways that provide you with a structure or structures to answer your research question. Without undertaking one or more of these processes, the most that may result may be an impressionistic view of what these qualitative data mean.

While it might be possible to make some use of diagrams and statistics at this stage, such as the frequency of occurrence of certain categories of data (Sections 11.3, 11.4 and Section 11.12), the way in which you are likely to analyse the qualitative data that you collect is through the development of research-specific concepts that you may then link into a conceptual framework. This framework may be developed before, during or after your data collection and then refined as your research progresses. These analytical processes are discussed in much greater detail in Sections 11.12–11.19.

11.9 The nature of qualitative analysis

As we noted earlier, it is important to understand the nature of qualitative analysis before embarking on its use. In this section we consider two aspects related to the nature of qualitative analysis: your approach to analysis and the interactive nature of qualitative research.

Deciding on your approach to analysis

Research commences from either a deductive or an inductive approach. Where you commence your research project using a deductive approach you will seek to use existing theory to shape the qualitative research process and aspects of data analysis. Where you commence your research project using an inductive approach you will seek to build up a theory that is adequately grounded in your data. In this section we discuss the difference between using theory at the start of your research to analyse qualitative data and commencing your research by collecting and exploring your data without a predetermined theoretical or descriptive framework.

Using a deductive approach

Yin (2014) suggests that, where you have made use of existing theory to formulate your research question and objectives, you may also use the theoretical propositions that helped you do this as a means to devise a framework to help you to organise and direct

> **Box 11.21**
> **Focus on student research**
>
> **Incorporating an inductive approach**
>
> Phil commenced a research project by adopting a deductive approach, but found that the theoretical framework he adopted did not yield a sufficiently convincing answer to his research questions and objectives. He therefore decided to reanalyse his data inductively. This revealed themes that had not figured prominently in the deductive analysis. A combination of the two approaches generated a more convincing answer to Phil's research questions and objectives.

your data analysis. There is debate about this approach when applied to qualitative analysis because this theoretical framework may be too restrictive in relation to the issues revealed in the data and fail to allow the meanings expressed by research participants to be explored adequately. If this occurs when you use a theoretical framework to design and analyse your research, you will need to adapt your approach (Box 11.21).

Even though you may incorporate an inductive approach in your research, commencing your work from a theoretical perspective may have certain advantages. It will link your research into the existing body of knowledge in your subject area, help you to get started and provide you with an initial analytical framework.

To devise a theoretical or descriptive framework you need to identify the main variables, components, themes and issues in your research project and the predicted or presumed relationships between them. A descriptive framework will rely more on your prior experience and what you expect to occur, although it is of course possible to develop an explanatory framework based on a mixture of theory derived from the literature you used and your own expectations. You will use this framework as the means to start and direct the analysis of your data.

Using an inductive approach

The alternative to a deductive approach is to start to collect data and then explore them to see which themes or issues to follow up and concentrate on. An inductive approach may be a difficult strategy to follow and may not lead to success for someone who is an inexperienced researcher. This is likely to happen where you simply go ahead and collect data without examining them to assess which themes are emerging from the data as you progress. Where you commence your data collection with this type of approach – related initially to an exploratory purpose – you should analyse the data as you collect them and develop a conceptual framework to guide your subsequent work. This is also referred to as a grounded approach because of the nature of the theory or explanation that emerges as a result of the research process. In this approach:

- you do not commence such a study with a clearly defined theoretical framework;
- instead you identify relationships between your data and develop questions and hypotheses or research propositions to test these;
- theory emerges from the process of data collection, analysis and interpretation.

You will need to commence this approach with a clear research purpose and careful preparation before embarking on data collection and analysis. Researchers who use an inductive approach develop a competent level of knowledge about their research topic. Their research generally commences with a clearly defined research question and objectives, even though these may be amended by the data they subsequently collect.

Not using a predetermined theoretical framework in an inductive approach is related to the desire to avoid being sensitised by existing theoretical constructs. Instead, researchers using an inductive approach aim to search for and recognise meanings in the data and to understand the social context and perceptions of research participants. The use of an inductive approach should allow a good 'fit' to develop between the social reality of the research participants and the theory that emerges – it will be 'grounded' in that reality. You will need to compare your grounded theory with existing theory contained in the literature once you have developed this.

The use of an inductive approach may involve you in a lengthy period of concurrent data collection and analysis in order to research an issue or topic adequately or to derive a well-grounded theory. Corbin and Strauss (2008) suggest that this type of approach may take months to complete. This is an important consideration if, like many of our students, your research project is time-constrained by a submission date. It is also likely that this approach will combine some elements of a deductive approach as you develop theoretical propositions and then test their applicability through subsequent data collection and analysis. Consequently, while you may commence with either an inductive or a deductive approach, in practice your research is likely to combine elements of both.

The interactive nature of the process

Data collection, data analysis and the development and verification of propositions are very much an interrelated and interactive set of processes in qualitative research. Analysis is undertaken during the collection of data as well as after it. This analysis helps to shape the direction of data collection, especially where you are following a more inductive, grounded approach. The research propositions that emerge from your data in an inductive approach or those you commenced with at the start of your data collection in a deductive approach will be tested as you compare them with the data in your study. The key point here is the relative flexibility that this type of process permits you.

The interactive nature of data collection and analysis allows you to recognise important themes, patterns and relationships as you collect data: in other words, to allow these to emerge from the process of data collection and analysis. As part of this you will need to re-categorise and re-code your existing data to see whether emergent themes, patterns and relationships are present in the cases where you have already collected data. You will also be able to adjust your future data collection to see whether related data exist in cases where you intend to conduct your research (Corbin and Strauss 2008).

The concurrent process of data collection and analysis also has implications for the way in which you manage your time and organise your data and related documentation. It will be necessary to arrange interviews or observations with enough space between them to allow yourself sufficient time to write up or word process a transcript or set of notes, and to analyse this before proceeding to your next data collection session. Where you conduct a small number of interviews in one day, you will need time during the evening to undertake some initial analysis on these before carrying out further interviews. You may also be able to find a little time between interviews to carry out a cursory level of analysis. As part of this we have found it extremely helpful to listen to audio-recordings of interviews while travelling to and from the university.

There is a clear limit to the value of continuing to undertake interviews or observations without properly analysing these in this way. There is a danger of data overload where you continue to collect data without sufficiently analysing these. This will be associated with a lost opportunity to understand what your data reveal in relation to your research question and the directions that might be worth pursuing for your research. Important ideas that occur to you as you undertake an interview, conduct an observation, read a document, listen to an audio-recording, or view a set of images or a visual-recording may be lost if you do not record these because you are focused on collecting data without interacting with and analysing these.

11.10 Preparing your data for analysis

As we have seen in Chapter 10, qualitative data can be generated in many forms. In Chapter 10, when we considered archival and documentary research, and when we considered secondary data, we highlighted how documentary data were available in a range of written and non-written forms. We considered how observation may be video-recorded, in addition to being recorded using an observation schedule or by taking notes. Finally, although focusing on collecting data that will be quantified, noted that open questions may be used to collect qualitative data from respondents, which are recorded in writing by either the respondent or an interviewer.

It is important to emphasise the importance of copying any recordings you make and transcribing both these and your notes to ensure data are not lost. In this section we focus upon the conversion of qualitative data from oral or handwritten form to word-processed text, as this is the way that you are most likely to use these in your analysis. As part of this, we discuss the general requirements of CAQDAS packages.

Transcribing qualitative data

We emphasised that, in qualitative research interviews, the interview is often audio-recorded and subsequently **transcribed**, that is, reproduced verbatim as a word-processed account. We also emphasised that, as an interviewer, you would be interested not only in what participants said, but in the way they said it as well. This means that the task of transcribing audio-recorded interviews is likely to be time-consuming as you will need not only to record exactly what was said and by whom, but also try to give an indication of the tone in which it was said and the participants' non-verbal communications. Without this additional contextual information, important incidents that affect the conduct of your interview or observation may be missed (e.g. see Box 11.24). You also need to ensure it can be linked to the contextual information that locates the interview.

Even if you are a touch-typist, you will find the task of transcribing an audio-recording extremely time-consuming. Most research methods texts suggest that it takes a touch-typist between 6 and 10 hours to transcribe every hour of audio-recording. Consequently, it is helpful if your interviews are transcribed as soon as possible after they are undertaken in order to avoid a build-up of audio-recordings and associated transcription work. Fortunately, there are a number of possible ways of reducing the vast amount of personal time needed to transcribe interviews verbatim. These are summarised in Table 11.7 along with some of the associated potential problems. As you will see in Table 11.7, one problem, however you choose to transcribe the data, is making sure that the transcription is accurate by correcting any transcription errors. This process is known as data cleaning. Once this has been done, some researchers send a copy of the transcript to the participant for final checking. While this can be helpful for ensuring factual accuracy, we have found that interviewees often want to correct their own grammar and use of language as well! This is

Table 11.7 Alternative ways of reducing the time needed to transcribe audio-recordings

Alternative	Potential problems
Pay a touch-typist to transcribe your audio-recordings	• Expense of paying someone else • Important data such as pauses, coughs, sighs and the like may not be included • You will not be familiarising yourself with the data as you are not transcribing them yourself • The transcription will still require careful checking as errors can creep in
Borrow a transcription machine with a foot-operated play–pause–rewind–fast forward mechanism and software to control the audio speed	• Although this will allow you to control the audio-recorder more easily, the speed of transcription will still be dependent upon your typing ability • The transcription will still require careful checking • You may not be able to gain access to a transcription machine
'Dictate' your audio-recordings to your computer using voice-recognition software	• You will need to discover which voice-recognition software works best with your voice • You will also need to discover which voice-recognition software is suited to the needs of your research project • You will need to 'teach' the voice-recognition software to understand your voice • You will need to listen to and dictate the entire audio-recording • The transcription will still require careful checking as the software is not entirely accurate
Only transcribe those sections of each audio-recording that are pertinent to your research **(data sampling)**	• You will need to listen to the entire recording carefully first, at least twice • You may miss certain things, meaning you will have to go back to the audio-recording later • Those sections you transcribe will still require careful checking

because spoken and written language are very different. For this reason, you need to think carefully before offering to provide each interviewee with a full copy of their transcript.

Each interview you transcribe should be saved as a separate word-processed file. As part of this we recommend that you use a filename that maintains confidentiality and preserves anonymity but that you can easily recognise and which codifies important information. When doing this Mark always starts his transcription filenames with the interview number and saves the word-processed transcripts for each research project in a separate subdirectory. Subsequent parts of the filename provide more detail. Thus the file '26MPOrg1.docx' is the transcript of the **26**th interview, **M**ale, **P**rofessional, undertaken at **Org**anisation**1**. As some CAQDAS programs require filenames of eight or fewer characters, you may need to limit your filenames to this length.

When transcribing interviews and group interviews, you need to be able to distinguish between the interviewer and the participant or participants. This means you need to have clear speaker identifiers such as '17FA' for the 17th interviewee who is a female administrator. This tends to be more visible in the transcript if they are in capitals (Box 11.22). Similarly, you need to be able to distinguish between any topic headings you use, questions and responses. One way of doing this, dependent upon the precise requirements of

Box 11.22 Focus on student research

Extract from an interview transcript

Martin had decided to use the code IV to represent himself in the transcripts of his in-depth interviews and 01FS to represent his first interviewee, a female student. By using capital letters to identify both himself and the interviewee Martin could identify clearly where questions and responses started. In addition, it reduced the chance of a mistype in the transcription as identifiers were always a combination of capital letters and numbers. Martin used transcription symbols such as '(.)' to represent a brief pause and '.hhh' to represent an in-breath. He also included brief comments relating to a respondent's actions in the interview transcript. These he enclosed with double parentheses (()). A brief extract from a transcript follows:

IV: So tell me, why do you use the Student Union Bar?

01FS: Well,.hhh (.), a lot of my friends go there for the final drink of the evening (.) there is an atmosphere and the drinks are cheap. I don't feel embarrassed to walk in on my own and there's always someone to talk to and scrounge a fag off ((laughs))

your CAQDAS, is to put topic headings in CAPITALS, questions in *italics* and responses in normal font. The most important thing is to be consistent within and across all your transcriptions. Some authors also recommend the use of specific transcription symbols to record intakes of breath, overlapping talk and changes in intonation. A useful list of transcription symbols is provided as an appendix by Silverman (2013).

In a transcription of a more structured interview, you also need to include the question number and the question in your transcription. For example, by including the question number 'Q27' at the start of the question you will be able to search for and find question 27 quickly. In addition, by having the full question in your transcript you will be far less likely to misinterpret the question your respondent is answering.

When transcribing audio-recordings or your own notes you need to plan in advance how you intend to analyse your transcriptions. If you only have access to a black and white printer, there is little point in using different coloured fonts to distinguish between participants in a group interview or to distinguish non-verbal responses such as nervous laughter in your transcripts as these will be difficult to discern when working from the paper copies. You also need to be careful about using these and other word-processing software features if you are going to analyse the data using CAQDAS. These programs often have precise file formats which can mean that word-processing software features such as *bold* and *italics* generated by your word-processing software will disappear when your data file is imported (Lewins and Silver 2009). For example, although you may transcribe your interviews using a word processor such as Microsoft Word, your chosen CAQDAS package may require this textual data to be saved as a text-only file (.txt) or using rich text format (.rtf), resulting in the loss of some of these features. These are summarised as a checklist in Box 11.23.

Using electronic textual data including scanned documents

For some forms of textual data such as, for example, email interviews or electronic versions of documents, including organisational emails, blogs and web-based reports, your data may already be in electronic format. Although these data have already been captured electronically, you are still likely to need to spend some

Box 11.23 Checklist

Transcribing your interviews

- ✔ Have you thought about how you intend to analyse your data and made sure that your transcription will facilitate this?
- ✔ Have you chosen clear interviewer and respondent identifiers and used them consistently?
- ✔ Have you included the interview questions in full in your transcription?
- ✔ Have you saved your transcribed data using a separate file for each interview?
- ✔ Does your filename maintain confidentiality and preserve anonymity while still allowing you to recognise important information easily?
- ✔ Have you checked your transcript for accuracy and, where necessary, 'cleaned up' the data?
- ✔ (If you intend to use CAQDAS) Will the package you are going to use help you to manage and analyse your data effectively? In other words, will it do what you need it to do?
- ✔ (If you intend to use CAQDAS) Are your saved transcriptions compatible with the CAQDAS package you intend to use, so you will not lose any features from your word-processed document when you import the data?
- ✔ (If you intend to use CAQDAS) Have you checked your transcript for accuracy and 'cleaned up' the data prior to importing into your chosen CAQDAS package?
- ✔ Have you stored a separate backup or security copy of each data file on your USB mass storage device?

time preparing them for analysis. This is likely to involve you in ensuring that, where necessary, the data are:

- suitably anonymised, such as by using separate codes for yourself and different participants;
- appropriately stored for analysis, for example one file for each interview, each meeting's minutes or each organisational policy;
- free of typographical errors that you may have introduced, and, where these occurred, they have been 'cleaned up'.

Consequently, you are likely to find much of the checklist in Box 11.23 helpful. If you intend to use CAQDAS to help you to manage and analyse documents which are not available electronically, you will need to scan these into your word-processing software and ensure they are in a format compatible with your chosen CAQDAS.

11.11 Aids to help your analysis

In addition to transcribing your notes and audio or digital recordings, it will also help your analysis if you record contextual information about the interviews or observations that you conduct. This will help you to recall the context and content of each interview or observation as well as informing your interpretation as you will be more likely to remember the precise circumstances of your data collection. Various researchers have suggested ways of recording information and developing reflective ideas to supplement your written-up notes or transcripts and your categorised data (e.g. Brinkmann and Kvale 2015; Gerstl-Pepin and Patrizio 2009). These include:

- interim or progress summaries;
- transcript summaries;
- document summaries;

- self-memos;
- a research notebook;
- a reflective diary or journal.

The way in which you use these analytical aids should be dependent on your preferred approach to recording your ideas and reflections, and the context of your research. You may, for example, develop a preference for using either interim summaries or self-memos or a research notebook. You may decide to use more than one of these aids. Where you produce transcripts of interviews or observations, it will be helpful to write a transcript summary for each one; similarly where you use documents, it will be helpful to write document summaries. Your university or awarding body may require you to keep a reflective diary, although you may also find it helpful to write interim summaries, self-memos or a research notebook to produce this. We recommend using these analytical aids to help you with your research project, although choice of which to use is partly a matter of personal preference.

Interim or progress summaries

As your analysis progresses you may wish to write an **interim summary** of your progress to date. You may decide to write an interim summary after each interview or observation, or after a set of related interviews or observations. Similarly, you may wish to write an interim summary after a period of using secondary data or conducting a search of the literature. In this way, you may write up a number of summaries that detail the development of your thoughts to aid your analysis and the direction of your data collection. Alternatively, your interim summary may become a unified working document that you modify and continue to refer to, as your research project progresses. The way in which you use this analytical aid should suit your preferred approach. An interim summary may include:

- what you have found so far;
- what level of confidence you have in your findings and explanations to date;
- what you need to do in order to improve the quality of your data and/or to seek to substantiate your apparent explanations, or to seek alternative explanations;
- how you will seek to achieve the needs identified by the interim analysis.

Transcript summaries

After you have written up your notes, or produced a transcript, of an interview or observation session, you can also produce a summary of the key points that have emerged from undertaking this activity. A **transcript summary** compresses long statements into briefer ones in which the main sense of what has been said or observed is rephrased in a few words. Through summarising you will become conversant with the principal themes that have emerged from each interview or observation. You may be able to identify apparent relationships between themes that you wish to note down so that you can return to these to seek to establish their validity. It will also be useful to make some comments about the person(s) you interviewed or observed, the setting in which this occurred and whether anything occurred during the interview or observation which might have affected the nature of the data that you collected (Box 11.24).

Once you have produced a summary of the key points that emerge from the interview or observation and its context, you should attach a copy to the file of your written-up notes or transcript for further reference.

Box 11.24 Focus on student research

Noting an event that affected the nature of data collection

Birjit was facilitating a focus group whose participants were the customers of a large department store. Approximately halfway through the allotted time, an additional participant joined the group. This person almost immediately took control of the discussion, two other participants appearing to become reticent and withdrawing from the group's discussion. Despite this, all Birjit's questions were answered fully and she felt the data she had obtained was valuable. However, she recorded the point at which the new participant joined the group in a post-transcript summary in case any divergence was apparent between the nature of the data in the two parts of the focus group.

Document summaries

Where you use any sort of documentation it is helpful to produce a **document summary**. A document summary may fulfil two purposes. It may be used to summarise and list the document's key points for your research. These points become part of your data set. Secondly, you may use it to describe the purpose of the document, how it relates to your work and why it is significant.

This type of summary is likely to be useful as you continue to conduct your analysis. You will be able to return to a document summary to look again at the data you drew from the document, to see how you coded and categorised these data, and to be able to re-read your notes about its relevance to your research. As a research project progresses, there is a likelihood that you will forgot some of your thoughts about your previous data collection and analysis, so that a document summary, like other analytical aids discussed in this sub-section, will act as a reminder of your earlier ideas.

Self-memos

Self-memos allow you to record ideas that occur to you about any aspect of your research, as you think of them. Where you omit to record any idea as it occurs to you it may well be forgotten. The occasions when you are likely to want to write a memo include:

- when you are writing up interview or observation notes, or producing a transcript of this event;
- when you are coding and categorising data;
- as you continue to categorise, analyse and interpret these data;
- when you are constructing a narrative;
- when you engage in writing your research project.

Most CAQDAS programs include some form of writing tool that allows you make notes, add comments or write self-memos as you are analysing your data (Lewins and Silver 2009). This facility is very helpful and, as your self-memos are automatically dated, you can also trace the development of your ideas.

Ideas may also occur as you engage in an interview or observation session. In this case you may record the idea very briefly as a margin note and write it as a memo to yourself after the event. Similarly, ideas may occur as you work through a documentary source.

It may be useful to carry a reporter's notebook or an e-notebook in order to be able to record your ideas, whenever and wherever they occur. When you are undertaking the production of notes, or a transcript, or any aspect of qualitative analysis, the notebook will be available for you to record your ideas.

Self-memos may vary in length from a few words to one or more pages. They can be written as simple notes – they do not need to be set out formally. It will be useful to date them and to provide cross-references to appropriate places in your written-up notes or transcripts, where appropriate. Alternatively, an idea that is not grounded in any data (which may nevertheless prove to be useful) should be recorded as such. Memos should be filed together, not with notes or transcripts, and may themselves be categorised where this will help you to undertake later stages of your qualitative analysis. Memos may also be updated as your research progresses, so that your bank of ideas continues to have currency and relevance.

Research notebook

An alternative approach to recording your ideas about your research is to keep a **research notebook**. You may of course keep such a notebook alongside the creation of self-memos. Its purpose will be similar to the creation of self-memos: to record your ideas and reflections, and to act as an aide-mémoire about your intentions for the direction of your research. Using a chronological format may help you to identify the development of certain ideas (such as data categories, propositions or hypotheses) and the way in which your research has progressed, as well as providing an approach that suits the way in which you like to think.

Reflective diary or journal

We recommended you also keep a reflective diary or journal. This is devoted to reflections about your experiences of undertaking research, what you have learnt from these experiences, how you will seek to apply this learning as your research progresses and what you will need to do to develop your competence to further your research. Universities generally require students to reflect on their research as part of their project reports to be able to evaluate their learning from the research process. We talked about keeping a reflective diary and provided you with a checklist.

Reflection may occur in a number of ways. It may occur during an event, so that you reflect on your approach while you conducting an activity. This type of reflection may occur, for example, while you are interviewing or observing. Reflection may also occur after an activity has taken place so that you reflect on what occurred and how you might be able to do better next time. A more fundamental type of reflection, known as reflexivity, involves you in monitoring and reflecting on all aspects of the research project from initial ideas to submission of the project report. It includes examining your reactions to what is being researched, the nature of your relationship with those who take part in the research and evaluating the way in which you interpret data to construct knowledge (Haynes 2012). Given its interpretivist nature, Finlay (2002: 211) says that reflexivity is 'now the defining feature of qualitative research'. Your reactions, your interactions with those taking part and your attitudes and beliefs may each impact on your interpretation of the data that are shared with you. Engaging in forms of reflexivity may enable you to develop greater insights as you explore and analyse these data. Developing a reflexive focus in your reflective diary may therefore prove to be a valuable aid to further your research.

11.12 Thematic Analysis

Introduction

We start by outlining **Thematic Analysis** as this is often thought of as a generic approach to analysing qualitative data. Braun and Clarke (2006: 78) refer to Thematic Analysis as a 'foundational method for qualitative analysis'. The process of Thematic Analysis is found in other approaches to qualitative analysis, albeit in more particularised ways, as we outline in the following sections. The essential purpose of this approach is to search for themes, or patterns, that occur across a data set (such as a series of interviews, observations, documents or websites being analysed). Thematic Analysis involves a researcher coding her or his qualitative data to identify themes or patterns for further analysis, related to his or her research question. We discuss procedures to undertake analysis in the next part of this section.

Thematic Analysis offers a systematic yet flexible and accessible approach to analyse qualitative data (Braun and Clarke 2006). It is systematic as it provides an orderly and logical way to analyse qualitative data. In this way, Thematic Analysis can be used to analyse large qualitative data sets, as well as smaller ones, leading to rich descriptions, explanations and theorising. Thematic Analysis can be used to help you:

1 comprehend often large and disparate amounts of qualitative data;
2 integrate related data drawn from different transcripts and notes;
3 identify key themes or patterns from a data set for further exploration;
4 produce a thematic description of these data; and/or
5 develop and test explanations and theories based on apparent thematic patterns or relationships;
6 draw and verify conclusions.

Thematic Analysis is flexible as it is not tied to a particular philosophical position. You may use Thematic Analysis irrespective of whether you are adopting an objectivist or subjectivist position. Your assumptions will, however, affect how you use it to interpret your data (which is why you should be explicit about your philosophical assumptions and remain reflexive through your research project). You may use Thematic Analysis in a realist study that seeks to understand factors underpinning human attitudes and actions. You may also use Thematic Analysis in an interpretivist study to explore different interpretations of a phenomenon. The reason why you may use Thematic Analysis irrespective of your position relates to its development as a standalone analytical technique or process, rather than being part of a theoretically mounted methodological approach.

For the same reason, Thematic Analysis may be used irrespective of whether you adopt a deductive or inductive approach. In a deductive approach, the themes you wish to examine would be linked to existing theory. Your research question is also more likely to be firmly established and this and your research objectives may be used to derive themes to examine in your data. This may lead you to focus on parts of your data set rather than seek to analyse it all in an undiscriminating way. In an inductive approach, themes will be derived from the data. You will search for themes to explore related to your research interest but will not impose a framework of themes to examine your data set based on existing theory. Depending on which themes you decide to explore in an inductive approach, you may also modify your research question. Initially you will be likely to explore the whole data set looking for the occurrence and reoccurrence of themes. You may also use a combination of a deductive and inductive approach, commencing analysis with theoretically-derived themes which you then modify or add to as you explore your data set (Box 11.21).

The nature and flexibility of Thematic Analysis mean that it is fairly straightforward to use in comparison to some of the techniques discussed later. Where you use Thematic Analysis, your energy can be invested in making sure your analysis is rigorous, rather than spending lots of time checking you are applying a more particularised approach to qualitative analysis according to strict rules advocated for its use. In practice, your choice of analytical method will be influenced by the nature of your research question and philosophical position, approach and research strategy, although Thematic Analysis may offer you an effective technique to analyse your qualitative data set. We now outline the procedures used in Thematic Analysis.

Procedure

The following procedures provide a set of guidelines to undertake Thematic Analysis. In practice, these procedures do not occur in a simple linear progression. Instead they are often concurrent and recursive, involving you analysing data as you collect them and going back over earlier data and analysis as you refine the way in which you code and categorise newly collected data and search for analytical themes.

The procedures outlined here involve: becoming familiar with your data; coding your data; searching for themes and recognising relationships; refining themes and testing propositions. We now consider each of these.

Becoming familiar with your data

You will start to become familiar with your data as you produce transcripts of the interviews or observations you conduct. The act of transcribing a data item yourself, although laborious, allows you to develop familiarity. This should also prompt you to generate summaries, self-memos or entries in your notebook or diary that aid your analysis.

Familiarisation with your data involves a process of immersion that continues throughout your research project. You will need to read and re-read your data during your analysis. You will be interested to look for meanings, recurring themes and patterns in your data. Without familiarity, you will not be able to engage in the analytical procedures that follow. Producing transcripts and data familiarisation are therefore important elements in analysing data.

Coding your data

Coding is used to categorise data with similar meanings. **Coding** involves labelling each unit of data within a data item (such as a transcript or document) with a code that symbolises or summarises that extract's meaning. Your purpose in undertaking this process is to make each piece of data in which you are interested accessible for further analysis. Qualitative data sets are frequently large and their content complex. A qualitative data set may include references to actions, behaviours, beliefs, conditions, events, ideas, interactions, outcomes, policies, relationships, strategies, etc. Without coding these data you may struggle to comprehend all of the meanings in your data in which you are interested. Coding is therefore an important means to manage your data so that you may rearrange and retrieve it under relevant codes. It is also an important element in data analysis, as we discuss later.

A **code** is a single word or a short phrase, which may also be abbreviated in use (Box 11.25). A coded extract of data is referred to as a unit of data. A **unit of data** may be a number of words, a line of a transcript, a sentence, a number of sentences, a complete paragraph, other chunk of textual data, or visual image that is summed up by a particular code (Boxes 11.25 and 11.26). The exact size of a unit of data will be determined by its meaning. Some units of data will overlap and some with be coded using more than one code (Box 11.26).

Box 11.25 Focus on student research

Interview extract with categories attached

Adrian's research project was concerned with how human resource management professionals managed a downsizing process in their own organisations. He derived initial codes from existing theory in the academic literature and attached them to appropriate units of data in each transcript. His initial categories were hierarchical; the codes he used being shown in brackets:

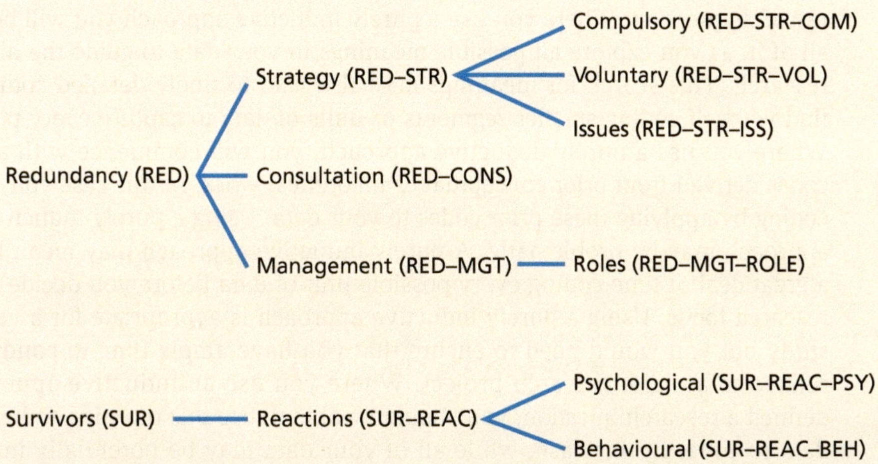

These were then attached to the interview transcript, using sentences as units of data. Like our jigsaw example at the start of this chapter, those units of data that were coded with more than one category suggested interrelationships:

RED–CONS	27MM The first stage is to find out what particular employees
	want for themselves and how they want this to happen. Staff are
	seen by their line manager and/or a member of personnel.
RED–MGT–ROLE	Employees might want to talk to someone from personnel rather
	than talk with their line manager – well, you know, for obvious
	reasons, at least as they see it – and this would be acceptable to the
RED–STR–VOL	organisation. This meeting provides them with the opportunity to
	opt for voluntary redundancy. We do not categorise employees
RED–STR–ISS	into anything like core or non-core, although we will tell a group
RED–CONS	of employees something like 'there are four of you in this
	particular function and we only need two of you, so you think
RED–CONS	about what should happen'. Sometimes when we attempt to give
	employees a choice about who might leave, they actually ask us to
	make the choice. This is one such situation where a compulsory
RED–STR–COM	selection will occur. We prefer to avoid this compulsory selection
SUR–REAC–PSY	because of the impact on those who survive – negative feelings,
	guilt and so on.

If you think that a new piece of data has a similar meaning to a previously coded unit of data, it should be labelled with the same code. If you think that a new piece of data does not have a similar meaning to a previously coded unit of data, you will need to devise a new code for it. Throughout the process of coding it will be important to keep a list of codes you are using and a working definition for each, to ensure consistency (Box 11.26).

At this point you may be asking two questions. How much of my data should I code - all or only some of it? Where should my codes come from? Both of these questions are related to your research approach and also to your research question - whether you are setting out to use an inductive or deductive approach and how well you have defined your research question. We now answer each of these questions in turn.

How much of your data you code will depend upon your research approach and research question. Where you use a purely inductive approach you will be likely to code all of it, as you explore all possible meanings in your data to guide the direction of your research. This search for meanings may also lead to finely detailed coding, where you find yourself coding smaller segments or units of data to capture every possible nuance. Where you use a purely deductive approach, you will commence with a framework of codes derived from prior conceptual or theoretical work. In this case you will commence coding by applying these prior codes to your data. Using a purely inductive or deductive approach may be problematic. A purely inductive approach may mean that you spend a great deal of time coding every possible unit of data before you decide on a particular research focus. Using a purely inductive approach is appropriate for a very exploratory study but you would need to ensure that you have ample time to conduct it, perhaps related to a major research project. Where you use an inductive approach and have defined a research question, you should be able to use this question to help select which data to code. In this case, while all of your data may be potentially interesting, your research question will help you focus on which data to code. Using a purely deductive approach may lead you to conclude that your list of prior codes is inadequate and that you need to devise other codes in order to be able to code your data adequately to begin to answer your research question and address your research objectives.

This discussion indicates where your codes may come from. There are three main sources of codes:

- They may be based on the actual terms used by your participants, recorded in your data. These are often referred to as 'in vivo' codes.
- They may be labels you develop which you think best describe a unit of data you wish to code.
- They may be derived from terms used in existing theory and the literature. These are often referred to as 'a priori' codes.

These sources of codes are shown in Figure 11.16 to illustrate their relationship.

Coding is a simple but versatile and valuable tool. The process of coding allows you to link units of data that refer to the same aspect or meaning, or to link aspects or meanings that you want to compare and contrast. It allows you to rearrange your original data into groupings for the next stage of analysis. Any unit of data may be coded with as many different codes as you think is appropriate, creating a web of connections to aid your analysis (Box 11.26). It is often important to understand the context of the data you are analysing. Where it is important to include some contextual background, you can code larger units of data such as whole paragraphs, as opposed to smaller units such as a few words or single sentences (Box 11.26). (Note in Box 11.26 that codes are referred to as categories. These terms are sometimes used interchangeably and sometimes to refer to different aspects of the analytical process - see the next sub-section.)

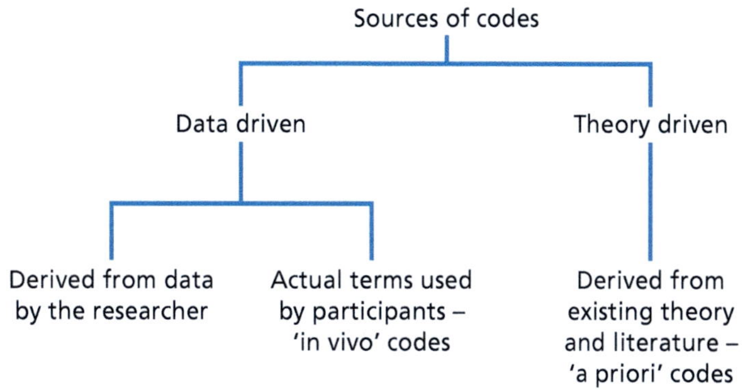

Figure 11.16 Sources and types of codes

Your approach to coding will be guided by the purpose of your research as expressed through your research question and objectives. Another researcher with different objectives to you may derive different codes from the same data. You will be likely to develop new codes as you conduct more interviews or observations and expand your data set. You will also be likely to gain new insights from existing codes that suggest new ones during the process of analysis. This will require you to re-read all of your earlier data transcripts to re-code them according to your current list of codes. This process is termed constant comparison and is undertaken to ensure consistency in the way you code and analyse your data set.

Your codes will show the occurrence or non-occurrence of a phenomenon and the strength of opinion in some instances. Some codes may attract large numbers of units of data. Some of these may prove to be too broad for further analysis without being subdivided. For example, Adrian undertook a research project where some codes had large amounts of data attached to them, while others attracted relatively small amounts of data. This led to the large codes being subdivided into further codes, which was helpful in pursuing the analysis (Box 11.25). Codes attracting small numbers of units of data may be merged with similar ones, or retained until later in the process of analysis in case they prove to be more important than they appear initially.

Box 11.26 Focus on management research

Assigning data to and developing categories

'After each interview, I transcribed the interview verbatim and filed its material according to the categorisation then in use. The material was typically in the form of paragraphs [that] were cross-classified to several categories. As I filed each statement, I compared it with previous statements in that category and kept running notes on the content of the category. The categories changed over time; some disappeared and were merged under more general titles. Some emerged out of previous categories that became too heterogeneous. Some categories became parts of matched pairs or triads in which any given comment would typically be filed in each constituent category. For example, comments [that] described instances of lax work or bad workmanship also typically mentioned abusive management. Similarly, statements that described devising one's own procedures also typically included statements of satisfaction with the autonomy that provided. This helped to reveal connections between categories.'

Source: Hodson (1991), cited in Erlandson *et al.* (1993: 119) *Journal of Contemporary Ethnography*. Copyright © 1991 by Sage Publications, Inc. Reprinted by permission

You may use CAQDAS to help you to code your data (Section 11.34) or you may use a manual approach. Where you use the second approach, you can label a unit of data with the appropriate code (or codes) in the margin of your transcript or set of notes (Box 11.26). This may then be copied, cut up and stuck onto a data card, or otherwise transferred, and filed so that you end up with piles of related units of data. When doing this, it is essential to label each unit of data carefully so that you know its precise source (Section 11.10). An alternative is to index codes by recording precisely where they occur in your transcripts or notes (e.g. interview 7, page 2, line 16) on cards headed with particular codes. Undertaking this stage of the analytic process means that you are engaging in a selective process, guided by the aim of your research and your research objectives, which has the effect of reducing and rearranging your data into a more manageable and comprehensible form.

One way of achieving this reduction and rearrangement of your data, depending on its suitability, is to use one or more of the analytical techniques described by Miles et al. (2014). These are considered later in Section 11.10.

Searching for themes and recognising relationships

This is seen as a distinct stage of analysis that follows coding, although in practice you will be searching for themes, patterns and relationships in your data as you collect and code them. Producing progress summaries, transcript summaries, document summaries, self-memos and/or entries in your research notebook and reflective diary will help you to record your ideas about possible themes, patterns and relationships in your data.

The search for themes fully begins when you have coded all of your data set. At this point you will have a long list of codes that you have created to make sense of and draw meaning from your data. Advice about the number of codes you might be working with at this point varies considerably. Some advice refers to working with up to 30 codes. Other advice refers to creating as many codes as you require to interpret every distinct meaning in your data. This may mean creating up to a couple of hundred codes, or possibly more. Our view is that data should not be forced into a particular number of codes. The number of codes you create will be related to the meanings you wish to explore in your data set, the nature of your research approach and the focus of your research question. However, where you find yourself creating very large numbers of codes you will need to evaluate whether your coding is too detailed or whether you are trying to analyse too much data for your project. Always refer back to your research question, research aim and research objectives to focus your approach to data analysis.

This stage of analysis involves you searching for patterns and relationships in your long list of codes to create a short list of themes that relate to your research question. A **theme** is a broad category incorporating several codes that appear to be related to one another and which indicates an idea that is important to your research question. A theme may also be a single code which indicates an idea that assumes general importance to your research question and is therefore elevated to become a theme. Searching for themes is part of the overall process of condensing your raw data, firstly by coding them and then grouping these coded data into analytic categories.

Searching for themes involves you making judgements about your data and immersing yourself in them. You will be looking to see how the codes you have created might fit together to allow you to further your analysis. As you search these codes, some initial questions you may ask include:

- What are the key concepts in these codes?
- What, if anything, seems to be recurring in these codes?
- What seems to be important, whether it recurs often or not?

- What patterns and/or trends are evident in the coded data?
- Which codes appear to be related?
- How do a particular set of codes appear to be related?

As you start to decide on themes to analyse your data further, some additional questions you may ask include:

- What is the essence of each apparent theme?
- How might themes be related to each other?
- Which themes appear to be main themes and which appear to be sub-themes (related to a main theme)?
- How may the relationship between themes be represented (as a hierarchy or a network) to produce a thematic map?
- Is there an overarching theme (or more than one) that unites your analysis?

You should not expect this process to be unproblematic. In attempting to achieve a thorough understanding of your data set, some further questions you may ask include:

- How well does this initial thematic map represent the relationships between themes?
- Which themes, if any, do not fit within this thematic representation?
- Does the way the data have been coded need to be revised; if so which data and how?
- Which themes need to be refined, discarded or newly introduced?
- How may the thematic representation be modified to represent my data better?

In the first set of questions, you begin to decide on themes to further your analysis. In the second set of questions, you begin to define your themes and the relationships between them (Box 11.25). Some themes will become main themes; some may become secondary-level themes, linked to a main theme; yet others may be tertiary-level themes, linked to a secondary-level theme. In the third set of questions, you evaluate your themes and the relationships between them. This will mean refining your themes and testing proposed relationships, as we discuss further in the next sub-section.

Refining themes and testing propositions

Refining themes and the relationships between them is likely to be an important part of your analytical process. The themes that you devise need to be part of a coherent set so that they provide you with a well-structured analytical framework to pursue your analysis. As you develop themes you should reorganise your coded data extracts under the relevant theme or sub-theme. This will help you to evaluate whether these coded data are meaningful to one another within their theme and whether (and how) themes are meaningful in relation to one another and in relation to your data set. This is likely to be a developmental process, as you re-read and reorganise your data. As you continue to examine your data set, the codes you have used and the themes you devise to organise your coded data to answer your research question, you will be likely to refine these themes.

You may decide that some of your initial themes should be combined to make a new theme while others should be separated into different themes. You may also decide that some of your initial themes should be discarded. Your decisions to make these changes will be based on re-reading the coded data that you have reorganised under each relevant theme. By reading the coded data attached to a possible theme, you will be able to evaluate whether these data support the continuation of the theme, or whether there is insufficient data to sustain it. This will allow you to decide whether these data are too dissimilar so that it should be separated into more than one theme. It will also allow you to decide whether two or more themes contain similar meanings and so should be collapsed into a single theme. As you refine your themes in this way you will also be able to revise the relationships between them.

Box 11.27 Focus on student research

Research propositions

During the process of qualitative data analysis a student evaluating the growth of online retailing formulated the following proposition:

Customers' willingness to trust online retailers depends on the ease of use of their website.

A student exploring mortgage borrowers' decision making drew up this proposition:

Potential mortgage borrowers' choice of lending institution is strongly affected by the level of customer service that they receive during the initial inquiry stage.

Another student investigating cause-related marketing formulated the following proposition:

Companies engaging in cause-related marketing are motivated principally by altruism.

A relationship is evident in each of these propositions. Each was tested using the data that had been collected.

As you seek to reveal patterns within your data and to recognise relationships between themes, you will be able to develop testable propositions (Box 11.27). The appearance of an apparent relationship or connection between themes will need to be tested if you are to be able to conclude that there is an actual relationship. However, while this is sometimes referred to as 'testing a hypothesis', it is not the same as the statistical hypothesis or significance testing we discussed in relation to quantitative analysis in Section 11.5.

It is important to test the propositions that emerge inductively from the data by seeking alternative explanations and negative examples that do not conform to the pattern or relationship being tested. Alternative explanations frequently exist, and only by testing the propositions that you identify will you be able to move towards formulating valid conclusions and an explanatory theory, even a simple one (Miles et al. 2014). Dey (1993: 48) points out that 'the association of one variable with another is not sufficient ground for inferring a causal or any other connection between them'. The existence of an intervening variable may offer a more valid explanation of an association that is apparent in your data (Box 11.28).

By rigorously testing your propositions against your data, looking for alternative explanations and seeking to explain why negative cases occur, you will be able to move towards the development of valid and well-grounded conclusions. The validity of your conclusions needs to be verified by their ability to withstand alternative explanations and the nature of negative cases. **Negative cases** are those that do not support your explanations and the induction of your grounded theory. Finding cases that do not fit with your analysis should be seen positively as these will help to refine your explanations and direct the selection of further cases to collect and analyse data.

This will help you to avoid interpretations that prove to be unreliable because you only notice evidence that supports your own opinions. It relates to our discussion of reflexivity in Section 11.11. As a researcher you need to recognise your own attitudes and beliefs about the topic being researched, perhaps by writing about these to make them explicit, in order to understand how this affects your judgement about what the research data might mean and to gain greater insights while analysing these data. Brinkmann and Kvale (2015: 278) refer to this process as seeking to achieve 'reflexive objectivity'.

Box 11.28 Focus on student research

The impact of an intervening variable

Kevin's research project involved looking at the use of subcontractors by an organisation. A relationship appeared to emerge between the total value of contracts a particular subcontractor had been awarded and the size of that contractor in terms of number of employees; in particular, those contractors with larger numbers of employees had a larger total value of contracts. This could have led Kevin to conclude that the value of work undertaken by a particular subcontractor was related to that organisation's size and that, in particular, the organisation tended to use subcontractors with large numbers of employees.

Reality was not so simple. The organisation had originally used over 2500 subcontractors but had found this exceedingly difficult to manage. To address this issue the organisation had introduced a system of preferred contractors. All 2500 subcontractors had been graded according to the quality of their work, with those whose work had been consistently of high quality being awarded preferred contractor status. This meant that they were invited by the organisation Kevin was researching to tender for all relevant contracts. The intervening variable was therefore the introduction of preferred contractor status dependent upon the quality of work previously undertaken. The fact that the majority of these subcontractors also had relatively large numbers of employees was not the reason why the organisation had awarded them contracts.

Evaluation

Thematic Analysis offers a systematic approach to qualitative data analysis that is accessible and flexible. Compared to some qualitative approaches, it is not overly prescriptive about the application of its analytical procedures. As a generic approach to qualitative data analysis it is suitable to use with several qualitative research strategies, where you are not following a named version of a strategy that prescribes precise analytic procedures, as in Grounded Theory Method.

Thematic Analysis may be used to induce theory in a similar way to Grounded Theory Method, but without following its prescribed approach to coding (Section 11.15). It may also be used to produce descriptive or explanatory accounts that fall short of generating a grounded theory.

Thematic Analysis is more adaptable, so that if the research strategy you are using requires you to search for particular themes you may consider using it. The process of searching for themes is common to other analytical approaches, as we consider in the following sections of this chapter.

Thematic Analysis may also be used in relation to deductive and inductive research approaches. Using a purely deductive or inductive research approach may be problematic, affecting the scope of the analysis. Thematic Analysis allows the researcher to move between these approaches.

11.13 Template Analysis

Introduction

Template Analysis is a type of Thematic Analysis, with a few key differences. In Thematic Analysis all data items (transcripts or other text) are coded first before the search for themes fully begins. In Template Analysis a researcher only codes a proportion of the data items before developing an initial list of codes and themes, known as a coding template (King 2012).

This **coding template** is the hierarchical list of codes and themes, which is used as the central analytical tool in Template Analysis. A researcher using Template Analysis will start by coding a sufficient part of their data to develop an initial coding template (Box 11.29). This may mean coding the first interview or observation transcript, or a number of these, in order to be able to develop a set of initial codes. These codes are then arranged and rearranged until a satisfactory initial template is developed. Subsequent transcripts are then coded using the codes in this initial template, which is modified as new data suggests deficiencies in the codes being used, leading eventually to the development of a final coding template. We provide further information on the procedures involved in this approach in the next sub-section.

Like Thematic Analysis, Template Analysis is a standalone analytical technique, rather than being part of a wider methodological approach. As a consequence it may be used irrespective of whether you are adopting an objectivist or subjectivist position or whether you adopt a deductive or inductive research approach (see Section 11.12, Introduction, for further explanation of this point). Template Analysis may commence with a number of a priori codes which are then supplemented by the use of in vivo codes, as we discussed earlier.

Procedure

The initial procedure of Template Analysis reflects that of Thematic Analysis. You will need to become familiar with the data you collect by transcribing this and reading it carefully. The initial transcript or transcripts will be coded as described in Section 11.12. Prior codes may be used where appropriate and these will be supplemented by the development of in vivo codes.

At an appropriate point in this process you reflect on the coding you have undertaken and begin to develop an initial coding template. The development of an initial coding template will be an exploratory process involving the arrangement and rearrangement of the codes you have used until you devise themes that appear to represent key ideas and relationships in your data. The resulting coding template will be able to show relationships between themes hierarchically and also laterally if you wish (King 2012).

Box 11.29 provides an example of an initial coding template, with a hierarchical relationship shown between the codes listed. In this example, three levels of codes or themes have been used. The highest level codes or themes are shown in capital letters (e.g. CONTEXTUAL FACTORS). The numbering system and placing of lower-level codes towards the right-hand side also helps to indicate the hierarchical relationships in this coding template. Codes are also grouped together in levels 2 and 3 to show how higher-order themes are constituted.

As data collection proceeds, your template will be subject to modification. The process of analysing interview transcripts or observation notes will lead to some of the codes being revised and even changes to their level or place in the template hierarchy. Where you consider introducing a new code or altering the level of an existing code in the template, you need to verify this action and explore its implications in relation to your previous coding activity. This is usually more straightforward using CAQDAS (Lewins and Silver 2009). As part of this, it is helpful to use self-memos to note the reasons for these changes.

King (2012) outlines five principal ways in which a template may be reorganised and revised:

- insertion of a new code into the hierarchy as the result of a relevant issue being identified through data collection for which there is no existing code;
- deletion of a code from the hierarchy if it is not needed;
- merging codes that were originally considered distinctive;
- altering the classification of codes/themes, so that some are promoted to a higher level in the coding template, while others may be demoted;
- changing the scope of a code. Inserted, deleted, merged and altered codes may have implications for other related codes. This may result in the need to move a code within the coding template, change its purpose or split it into two or more new codes.

Box 11.29 Focus on student research

Part of an initial template to analyse an advertising campaign's impact

Joss was asked to gather and analyse perceptions from a range of professionals in an organisation about a recent advertising campaign it had commissioned. Using her interview topic guide, she used the main questions to set higher-order codes or themes (shown in CAPITALS). Subsidiary questions and probes were used to generate lower-order codes, shown in lower case and italic script. An extract of her initial template follows:

1 CONTEXTUAL FACTORS
- **1.1** Reasons for campaign
- **1.2** Environment
  - **1.2.1** *Political*
  - **1.2.2** *Economic*
  - **1.2.3** *Socio-cultural*
  - **1.2.4** *Technological*
  - **1.2.5** *Legal*
- **1.3** Nature of the product
  - **1.3.1** *Cost*
  - **1.3.2** *Features*
  - **1.3.3** *Target groups*

2 NATURE OF THE CAMPAIGN
- **2.1** Media
- **2.2** Coverage

3 AWARENESS BY TARGET GROUPS AND OTHERS
- **3.1** Those in target groups
- **3.2** Others

Box 11.30 shows how the codes in the initial coding template in Box 11.29 were altered as the process of data collection and analysis progressed. Several codes have been deleted and new ones inserted that better reflect the terms used in the data by participants. Some initial codes have been merged. For example, the original, second-level code, 'Reasons for campaign' has been merged with the first-level code 'Contextual factors' to form a new first-level code, 'Perceiving the need for the campaign'. The original second-level codes, 'Media' and 'Coverage' have both been reclassified to become first-level codes. As a result of this reclassification, the scope of these themes has been enlarged and new subsidiary codes created to encompass this.

The template may continue to be revised until all of the data collected have been coded and analysed carefully. It therefore serves as an analytical device through which to devise an initial conceptual framework, which is subsequently revised and then finalised as a means to represent and explore key themes and relationships in your data. Using a template will also help you to select key themes to explore and to identify emergent issues that arise through the process of data collection and analysis that you may not have intended to focus on as you commenced your research project (King 2012).

Evaluation

Like Thematic Analysis, Template Analysis offers a systematic, flexible and accessible approach to analyse qualitative data. It adopts a higher level of structure earlier on than Thematic Analysis through the development of an initial coding template. This may be preferred by some who like the idea of developing a very structured approach to analysing their data early on. Others may prefer to code all of their data first before playing around with analytical structures.

The flexibility of developing a coding template early on and then revising this in relation to each subsequent data item allows a researcher to undertake the stages of analysis (e.g. coding, devising and linking themes, exploring relationships, sense-making) in a more holistic way. However, some researchers may feel constrained by using a template

Box 11.30 Focus on student research

Part of a final template to analyse an advertising campaign's impact

As Joss continued to collect data she used her coding template to conduct analysis. The coding template was revised as these data were analysed. An extract of her final template follows:

1 PERCEIVING THE NEED FOR THE CAMPAIGN
  1.1 Market changes
    1.1.1 *Globalisation*
    1.1.2 *Competition*
    1.1.3 *Segmentation*
    1.1.4 *Technological convergence*
    1.1.5 *Compliance*
  1.2 Product promotion
    1.2.1 *Product awareness*
    1.2.2 *Product differentiation*
    1.2.3 *Product upgrades*
2 EVALUATING MEDIA
  2.1 Social media
  2.2 Television
  2.3 Radio
  2.4 Newspapers
3 EXPLORING COVERAGE
  3.1 National
  3.2 Regional/Local
  3.3 Market segments

while working though transcripts and may become too focused on applying the template to the data rather than using the data to develop the template (King 2012).

11.14 Explanation Building and Testing

In this section we outline three techniques where the nature of reaching an explanation and theorising may be differentiated from both Thematic Analysis and Template Analysis. In these three techniques the emphasis is on building (or predicting) and testing an explanation. These techniques are Analytic Induction, Deductive Explanation Building and Pattern Matching. We discuss each of these in turn.

Analytic Induction

Introduction

Analytic Induction is an inductive version of Explanation Building. A key characteristic of this technique is that it uses an incremental approach to build and test an explanation or theory. **Analytic Induction** seeks to develop and test an explanation by intensively examining the phenomenon being explored through the successive selection of purposive cases. This means that the process of collecting and analysing data will be composed of a number of repeated steps to find a valid explanation of the phenomenon being studied. Johnson (2004: 165) defines Analytic Induction as 'the intensive examination of a strategically selected number of cases so as to empirically establish the causes of a specific phenomenon'. Analytic Induction emphasises a cycle of developing and testing propositions that are inductively grounded in participants' data rather than using existing knowledge and theory. Its analytical procedures are not highly developed or formalised. As a result, where you use Analytic Induction, you may also find the generic procedures outlined for Thematic Analysis in Section 11.12 helpful to guide your analysis within each case you examine.

Procedure

Data will need to be collected from an initial purposive case study, usually by conducting exploratory interviews or observations. These data should be analysed to devise codes and themes, and to recognise relationships between them to develop an initial definition of a proposition that seeks to explain the phenomenon being studied. This initial proposition is then tested through the purposive selection of a second, related case study, involving further exploratory interviews or observations.

Given the loosely defined nature of this initial proposition, it is likely that it will either need to be redefined or that the scope of the phenomenon to be explained will need to be narrowed. Redefining the proposition leads to a third iteration or step in the Analytic Induction process, involving the purposive selection of a third case study to explore the phenomenon and test this redefined proposition. If at this stage your redefined proposition appears to explain the phenomenon, you may either cease data collection on the basis that you believe you have found a valid explanation or seek to test the explanation in other purposively selected cases to see whether it is still valid.

You will be likely to encounter one or more cases where your proposition is not adequate to explain the phenomenon you are studying. These are referred to as negative or deviant cases. When you encounter a negative case you will need to redefine the proposition you are testing and to test this in the context of another purposively selected case. This process may continue until a redefined proposition is generated that reasonably explains the phenomenon in relevant cases where you have collected and analysed data. In practice several redefinitions of the proposition may be necessary to develop a valid explanation of the phenomenon being studied.

Evaluation

As an inductive and incremental way of collecting and analysing data qualitatively this technique has the capability to lead to the development of well-grounded explanations. Analytic Induction encourages the collection of data that are thorough and rich by exploring the actions and meanings of those who participate in this process, through in-depth interviews or observation, or some combination of these methods.

However, like each of the techniques in this section, it should not be thought of as a quick or easy approach to conducting qualitative analysis. While it may lead to a well-grounded and unassailable explanation, where all negative cases are either accounted for by the final revised explanation or excluded by redefining the phenomenon being studied, this outcome is only likely to occur as the result of using this technique in a thorough and rigorous way. This will involve a search for cases that are related to the phenomenon being studied, the in-depth collection of data within each case and the rigorous analysis of these data to devise a final revised proposition that explains the phenomenon being studied throughout these cases.

Analytic Induction may be criticised because of issues about its limited representativeness and generalisability. Because the final explanation of the research phenomenon will be completely grounded in the cases that give rise to it, this explanation may be without the ability to predict what may be found in other cases, even those containing the same characteristics or conditions. This is similar to criticism which is often made about other inductive research.

Two points may be made in response to such criticism. First, this type of criticism misses the point of inductive research, which is to find explanations that are well grounded in the context being researched. These explanations will exhibit high levels of reliability and internal validity. Others may subsequently seek to test these explanations in other settings. Secondly, such criticism may also be made in relation to much survey research. While survey research will be representative of a wider population, the nature of that population may be restricted to a particular case or number of cases.

In relation to Analytic Induction, you will need to select your sample of cases with care to be able to demonstrate how they relate to the phenomenon you are studying. Selecting diverse cases related to the phenomenon being studied may also help to overcome issues related to theoretical generalisability. For example, if you were seeking to explain how small enterprises respond to regulatory change you could select a sample of cases (organisations) from different business sectors and in relation to a range of regulatory changes, where feasible.

Deductive Explanation Building

Introduction

This version of Explanation Building uses a deductive approach (Yin 2014). It involves an incremental attempt to build an explanation by testing and refining a predetermined theoretical proposition. As with Analytic Induction, the process of collecting and analysing data to understand the research topic or phenomenon will be composed of a number of repeated steps to find a valid explanation.

Procedure

This explanation-building procedure follows these steps (Yin 2014):

1 Devise a theoretically based proposition, which you will then seek to test.
2 Undertake data collection through an initial, purposive case study in order to be able to compare the findings from this in relation to your theoretically based proposition.
3 Where necessary, amend the theoretically based proposition in the light of the findings from the initial case study.
4 Select a further, purposive case study to undertake a further round of data collection in order to compare the findings from this in relation to the revised proposition.
5 Where necessary, further amend the revised proposition in the light of the findings from the second case study.
6 Undertake further iterations of this process until a satisfactory explanation is derived.

Evaluation

This technique and the one discussed next, Pattern Matching, use a deductive approach involving the testing of a theoretical proposition or prediction. Where you are able to utilise existing theory to produce such a proposition or prediction (as in Pattern Matching) this may make the process of explaining the phenomenon being studied less onerous than using Analytic Induction, although use of these techniques may be just as demanding. Given the commonality of using a deductive approach in both of these techniques, we evaluate them together after outlining Pattern Matching, next.

Pattern Matching

Introduction

Pattern Matching involves predicting a pattern of outcomes based on theoretical propositions to explain what you expect to find from analysing your data (Yin 2014). Using this approach, you will need to develop a conceptual or analytical framework, utilising existing theory, and then test the adequacy of the framework deductively as a means to explain your findings. If the pattern of your data matches that which has been predicted through the conceptual framework you will have found an explanation, where possible threats to the validity of your conclusions can be discounted. We discuss examples related to two uses of this procedure that depend on whether you are matching patterns for the dependent or for the independent variables.

Procedure

The first use is matching patterns for dependent variables arising from another, independent variable. For example, based on theoretical propositions drawn from appropriate literature you specify a number of related outcomes (dependent variables) that you expect to find as a result of the implementation of a particular change management programme (independent variable) in an organisation where you intend to undertake research. Having specified these expected outcomes, you then engage in the process of data collection and analysis. Where your predicted outcomes are found, it is likely that your theoretically based explanation is appropriate to explain your findings. If, however, you reveal one or more outcomes that have not been predicted by your explanation, you will need to seek an alternative one (Yin 2014).

The second use is matching patterns for variables that are independent of each other. In this case you would identify two or more alternative explanations to explain the pattern of outcomes that you expect to find (Box 11.31). As a consequence, only one of these predicted explanations may be valid. If one explanation is found to explain your findings then the others may be discarded. Where you find a match between one of these predicted explanations and the data you have collected and analysed, you will have evidence to suggest that this is indeed an explanation for your findings. Further evidence that this is a correct explanation will flow from finding the same pattern of outcomes in other similar cases (Yin 2014).

Evaluation

In relation to Pattern Matching and Explanation Building, you will still be able to follow the generic processes outlined earlier for analysing qualitative data (Section 11.12), with some modification. First, you will be in a position to commence your data collection with a well-defined research question and set of objectives, and a clear framework and propositions, derived from the theory that you have used. Second, with regard to sampling,

Box 11.31 Focus on student research

Alternative predicted explanations

The objective of Linzi's research project was to explain why productivity had increased in a case study organisation even though a number of factors had been held constant (technology, numbers of staff employed, pay rates and bonuses, and the order book) during the period of the increase in productivity. She developed two alternative explanations based on different theoretical propositions to explain why this increase in productivity had occurred in the organisation. Her explanations were related to the following propositions:

1 the productivity increase is due to better management, which has been able to generate greater employee engagement, where this proposition is based on theory related to strategic human resource management;
2 the productivity increase is due to fears about change and uncertainty in the future, where this proposition is based on theory related to organisational behaviour and the management of change.

These propositions offered her two possible and exclusive reasons why the described phenomenon had occurred, so that where evidence could be found to support one of these, the other, which did not match her outcomes, could be discounted.

you will be in a position to identify the number and type of organisations to which you wish to gain access in order to undertake data collection. You should select sufficient cases to test the propositions that have been advanced and to answer your research question and meet your objectives. Third, the literature that you used and the theory within it should help to shape the data collection questions that you ask those who participate in your research project. It is also to be expected that codes for analysis will emerge from the nature of your interview questions. Therefore you will be able to commence data collection with an initial set of codes derived from your theoretical propositions and conceptual framework, linked to your research question and objectives.

Of course, these codes will be subject to change (insertions, deletions and merging) depending on their appropriateness for the data that your participants provide. However, where your predicted theoretical explanations appear to fit the data being revealed, your predetermined codes may prove to be useful, subject to some revision and development.

Your use of this deductive approach will also provide you with key themes and patterns to search for in your data. For example, as you collect data and analyse these by attaching units of data to codes, and examine these for emergent patterns, your analysis will be guided by the theoretical propositions and explanations with which you commenced. Your propositions will still need to be tested with rigour - associated with the thoroughness with which you carry out this analytical process and by seeking negative examples and alternative explanations that do not conform to the pattern or association being tested for.

The use of predicted explanations should mean that the pathway to an answer to your research question and objectives is reasonably defined. The extent to which this is the case will depend on two factors:

- your level of thoroughness in using existing theory to define clearly the theoretical propositions and conceptual framework that will guide your research project;
- the appropriateness of these theoretical propositions and the conceptual framework for the data that you reveal.

The use of a deductive approach is underpinned by the need to specify theoretical propositions before the commencement of data collection and analysis. Even in Explanation Building, a theoretically based proposition is suggested initially, although this may be revised through the iterative stages of the process involved. The general processes outlined earlier for analysing qualitative data will be useful to you in carrying out these deductive analytical procedures. In particular, the stages of the process related to devising codes and identifying themes and patterns are likely to be more apparent, at least initially, because this approach is based on existing theory.

11.15 Grounded Theory Method

Introduction

Grounded Theory Method is part of a wider methodological approach. Grounded Theory is an emergent and systematic research strategy. It avoids using a priori codes (Section 11.12) derived from existing theory and commences inductively, by developing codes from the data. The development of an emergent idea or theory from these data informs the direction of a Grounded Theory study. Grounded Theory is seen as systematic, or even prescriptive, because it sets out a number of tenets or elements that should be followed. Its use in practice is criticised when researchers only implement some of these elements, not all.

Grounded Theory is not as flexible as Thematic Analysis or Template Analysis. In Sections 11.12 and 11.13 we discussed how both Thematic Analysis and Template Analysis are not tied to a particular philosophical position or research approach. Both are standalone analytical techniques, rather than being part of a wider strategy. As a consequence, either may be used irrespective of whether you are adopting a realist or interpretivist position or whether you adopt a deductive or inductive research approach. Such flexibility offered by these analytical approaches may suit your choice of research strategy.

Alternatively, the existence and clarity of the elements and procedures developed for Grounded Theory may suit your approach. As a strategy and a method, Grounded Theory may provide you with a holistic approach to your research project that guides you from inception through the processes of data collection and analysis to completion.

We discussed the elements of Grounded Theory as a research strategy. These include the early commencement of data collection, concurrent collection and analysis of data, development of codes from the data, and the use of constant comparison, self-memos, theoretical sampling, theoretical saturation and theoretical sensitivity, leading to the development of a theory that is grounded in the data. We suggest re-reading about these elements of Grounded Theory before reading further in this section.

Grounded Theory Method is associated with a number of defined procedures to collect and analyse data. An issue arises in that the exact nature of these procedures varies between sources that outline Grounded Theory Method (e.g. Bryant and Charmaz 2007; Charmaz 2006; Corbin and Strauss 2008; Glaser and Strauss 1967) and even between editions of the same book (Corbin and Strauss 2008; Strauss and Corbin 1998). For example, the Grounded Theory Method of Strauss and Corbin (1998) and Corbin and Strauss (2008) is highly structured and systematic, with set procedures to follow at each stage of analysis. However, between the two editions of this book, advice about some of these analytical procedures changed. In the Grounded Theory Method of Strauss and Corbin (1998) the disaggregation of data into units is called open coding, the process of recognising relationships between categories is referred to as axial coding, and the integration of categories around a core category to develop a grounded theory is labelled selective coding. In the 2008 edition, open coding and axial coding have been merged and selective coding has been relabelled as integration. Alternatively, the more flexible approach to Grounded Theory Method of Charmaz (2006) consists of two major phases of coding: initial coding and focused coding, while she also discusses and evaluates axial coding (Strauss and Corbin 1998) and the theoretical coding approach developed by Glaser (1978, 1998).

As an introduction to the analytical procedures associated with using Grounded Theory Method, we focus on those of Strauss and Corbin (1998) and Charmaz (2006) (Figure 11.17). Where you decide to use a Grounded Theory strategy you may find it useful to consult not only these two books but also the others to which we have referred. However, the key to the success of using Grounded Theory Method is choosing one approach to this method with which you are comfortable, undertaking this without too much adaptation, and to develop your appreciation of and skills in using this method (Kenealy 2012). We would advise you to discuss this choice with your project tutor.

Procedure

Because we outlined the elements of Grounded Theory, we concentrate here on discussing the procedures used to code data. It is important, however, to recognise that all of these elements are used in combination throughout a Grounded Theory

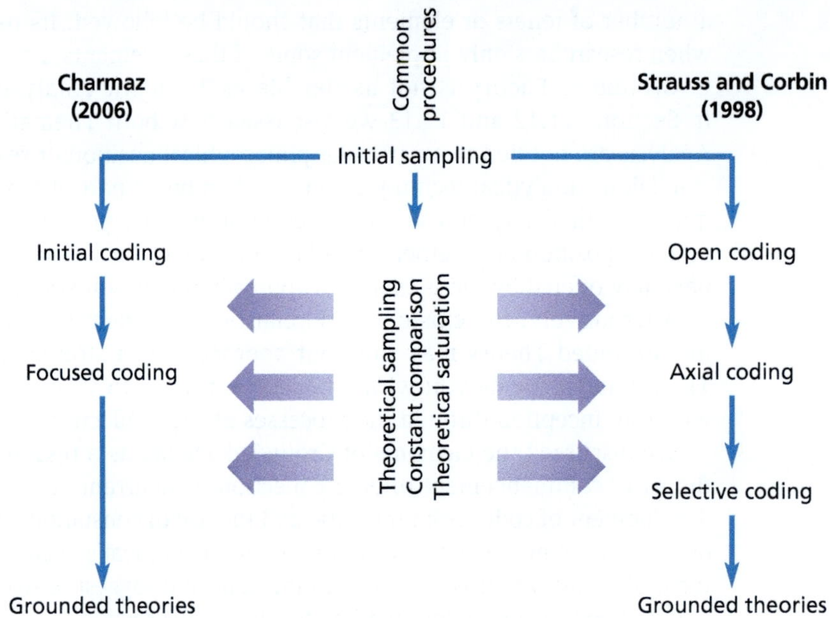

Figure 11.17 Comparing approaches to Grounded Theory Method
Source: © Mark Saunders, Philip Lewis and Adrian Thornhill 2015

study. Theoretical sampling is used to choose pertinent cases at each phase of data collection and analysis. An initial sample will be chosen that relates to your research question or topic. Each further case will be selected to explore analytical ideas and categories emerging from coding data in the previous case or cases. The purpose of this will be to further the development of your codes and analytical categories to be able to explore relationships between these to develop a grounded theory. Underpinning this is the process of constantly comparing the data being collected with the codes and categories being used, so as to aid the process of developing an emerging theory that will be thoroughly grounded in these data. Memo writing throughout your Grounded Theory study allows you to sum up, clarify and develop ideas that relate to the codes you develop, the categories you derive, the relationships between these, the emergence of theory and other aspects related to the conduct of your study. Theoretical sampling continues until theoretical saturation is reached. This will occur when data collection ceases to reveal new data that are relevant to a category, where the properties or dimensions of categories have become well developed and understood, and relationships between categories have been verified (Figure 11.17).

Having recognised the interrelated nature of the procedures of Grounded Theory Method we discuss coding and differences in approaches to this.

Initial coding or open coding

Initial coding or **open coding** is similar to the coding procedure outlined in Section 11.12. The data that you collect will be disaggregated into conceptual units and provided with a label. The same label or name will be given to similar units of data. However, because this research process commences without an explicit basis in existing theory, the result may be the creation of a multitude of conceptual labels related to the lower level of focus and structure with which you commence your research (Box 11.32). The emphasis in Grounded Theory Method is to derive meaning from the activities, subjects and settings being studied. In this way you will use in vivo codes (Section 11.12) to code your data.

Box 11.32 Focus on student research

Using open coding

James's research was concerned with the micro-strategising activities of individuals in small enterprises. He was particularly interested in how 'firm-level' strategy might evolve from 'day-to-day' mundane and routine activities. He undertook a series of semi-structured interviews with owner-managers of small enterprises. The audio-recordings of each interview were subsequently transcribed into a text file and imported into the CAQDAS package NVivo™. Open codes such as 'sharing knowledge' and 'formal strategy' and 'strategy as lived' were then applied to each transcript as illustrated in the extract.

Based upon analysis using his codes James noticed that these small organisations all seemed to have at least one individual (Karen in the extract) who was performing at least some micro-strategising activities (indicated by her strategic vision 'concerning what we might do in the future'). He theorised that most small organisations performed at least some micro-strategising activities, although the accumulation of such actions into an explicit and disseminated strategy was not so prevalent. Taking the theoretical perspective of 'Strategy-as-Practice', James developed his analysis to argue that even those firms which did not believe they were indulging in strategic thinking were actually creating some of its precursors.

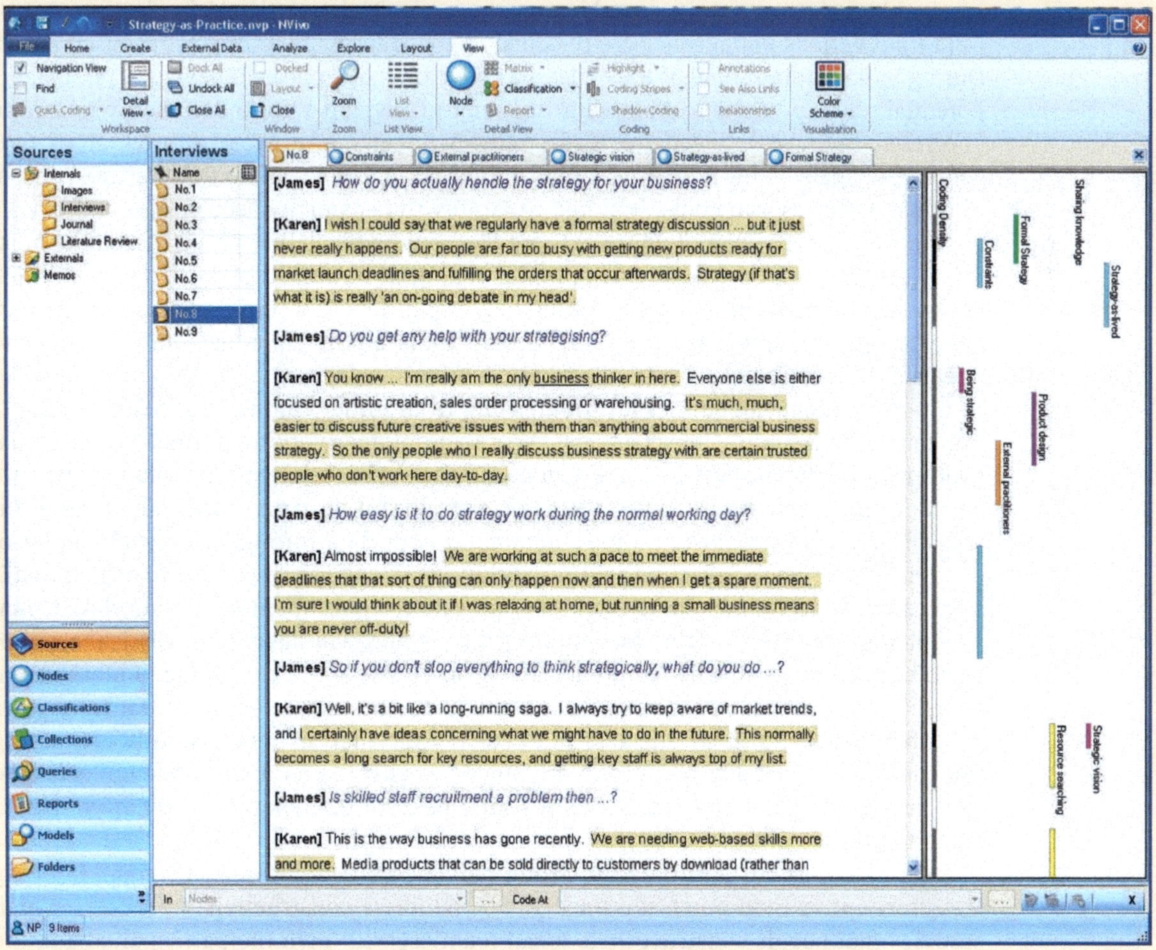

In Section 11.12 we stated that a unit of data might relate to a few words, a line, a sentence or number of sentences, or a paragraph. The need to understand meanings and to generate codes to encompass these in Grounded Theory Method is likely to lead you to conduct your early analysis by looking at smaller rather than larger units of data. The resulting multitude of code labels will therefore need to be compared and placed into broader, related groupings or categories. This will allow you to produce a more manageable and focused research project and to develop the analytical process. This is discussed in focused coding and axial coding.

Coding your data should lead you to identify analytical concepts and categories and help you to consider where data collection should be focused in the future (theoretical sampling). It may also help you to develop the focus of your research question. Using a Grounded Theory strategy may mean that your initial research question is broadly focused, although still within manageable exploratory confines. As you develop a narrower focus through this process, you will be able to refine and limit the scope of your research question.

Focused coding

In Charmaz's (2006) approach, **focused coding** involves deciding which of your initial codes to use to develop the analytic and explanatory focus of your coded data. This results in a smaller number of codes being attached to larger units of data and may be seen as serving the same purpose as searching for themes in Thematic Analysis (Section 11.12). Data from various initial codes are re-coded to a smaller number of more focused codes. During initial coding some of the codes you develop may appear to have greater analytic potential, to help you to explain your data and to develop a grounded theory related to you research question. Selecting these codes will lead you to work through all of your coded data again to see if they are suitable to begin to develop a more explanatory focus. Charmaz suggests that codes with the capability to become focused codes, and to able to categorise larger units of your data, are likely to be those that proved to be the most important or frequently used during initial coding. It is worth noting that codes which are frequently used during initial coding may not necessarily prove to have the greatest analytical potential, just as codes that become important may not have initially attracted large amounts of data.

Charmaz (2006) believes that progressing from initial coding to focused coding is unlikely to be a simple, linear process. Working out and working through which initial codes may be the best ones to use as focused codes may lead you to re-code your data and develop a new set of codes. If this occurs, do not despair: it will take time but it will allow you to get closer to and understand your data through the development of greater insight. Such reflection and re-working may occur irrespective of which qualitative analytic technique you choose. As you gain insights about what your data mean, you should use these insights to evaluate which codes will have the analytical capability to become focused codes to progress your analysis. These conceptually more useful focused codes should allow you to code and compare data across different interviews and observations. You will be able to develop your analysis by constantly comparing the codes you are using to categorise your data with the data you have collected, to gain further insights and work towards an emergent explanation of what your data mean to you.

Charmaz's (2006) approach to Grounded Theory Method may be seen as being less prescriptive than other approaches. She adopts a constructivist approach, which assumes that people construct their social realities, with both the participants' and the researcher's interpretations being socially constructed. Charmaz emphasises a Grounded

Theory Method that is interactive, flexible and less prescriptive. Analysis develops from constantly comparing data to codes and codes to data, codes with other codes, and data with other data to develop higher levels of abstraction rather than necessarily using axial coding or selective coding (discussed later). Analysis is shaped by the researcher's interaction with and interpretation of these constant comparisons. As a result, this approach to Grounded Theory Method does not follow the more tightly defined prescriptive procedures of other approaches.

For these reasons, Charmaz (2006) believes that axial coding (Strauss and Corbin 1998) may be too rigid for some Grounded Theory researchers. As we go on to describe, axial coding is a way of rearranging the data that were fragmented during open or initial coding into a new whole, based on a hierarchical structure. In some Grounded Theory Method prescriptions, this may involve identifying structural elements such as the situation involved, the issue at the centre of this situation, the interactions that took place and the outcomes or consequences of these actions to develop a hierarchical structure. Charmaz believes that this approach may be appropriate where you wish to use a prescribed analytical framework to develop your analysis. But she believes that some will find it to be too prescriptive and will prefer to use a simpler, more flexible approach. For these, axial coding as specified by Strauss and Corbin will not be useful. The use of initial coding and focused coding, combined with the use of theoretical sampling, constant comparison and theoretical saturation, will provide a more suitable and flexible approach (Figure 11.17). Where axial coding is still used in this more flexible Grounded Theory Method it is used in a less prescriptive and more flexible way.

We now describe Strauss and Corbin's (1998) approach to axial coding and the approach to selective coding of Strauss and Corbin (1998) and Corbin and Strauss (2008) (see also Figure 11.17).

Axial coding

Axial coding refers to the process of looking for relationships between the categories of data that have emerged from open coding. It indicates a process of theoretical development. As relationships between categories are recognised, they are rearranged into a hierarchical form, with the emergence of subcategories. The essence of this approach is to explore and explain a phenomenon (a subject of your research) by identifying what is happening and why, the environmental factors that affect this (such as economic, technological, political, legal, social and cultural), how it is being managed within the context being examined, and the outcomes of action that has been taken. Clearly, there will be a relationship between these aspects, or categories, and the purpose of your analysis will be to explain this.

Once these relationships have been recognised, you will then seek to verify them against actual data that you have collected. Strauss and Corbin (1998) recommend that you undertake this by formulating questions or statements, which can then be phrased as hypotheses, to test these apparent relationships. As you undertake this process you will be testing these hypotheses by looking for both supporting evidence and negative cases that demonstrate variations from these relationships.

Selective coding

Strauss and Corbin (1998) suggest that after a lengthy period of data collection, which may take several months, you will have developed a number of principal categories and related subcategories. The stage that follows is called **selective coding**. This is intended to identify one of these principal categories, which becomes known as the central or core category, in order to relate the other categories to this with the intention of integrating the research and developing a grounded theory (Corbin and Strauss 2008; Strauss and Corbin 1998). In the previous stage the emphasis was placed on recognising the relationships between categories and their subcategories. In this stage the emphasis is placed on recognising and developing the relationships between the principal categories that have emerged from this grounded approach in order to develop an explanatory theory.

Evaluation

A number of implications have emerged from this brief outline of the main procedures involved in the use of grounded theory. These may be summed up by saying that the use of Grounded Theory Method will involve you in processes that will be time-consuming, intensive and reflective.

Before you commit yourself to this method, you will need to consider the time that you have to conduct your research, the level of competence you will need, your access to data, and the logistical implications of immersing yourself in such an intensive approach to research. There may also be a concern that little of significance will emerge at the end of the research process, and this will be an important aspect for you to consider when determining the focus of your research if you use Grounded Theory Method.

Grounded Theory Method has the scope to provide you with a systematic analytical technique where you wish to use an emergent research approach that is part of a wider methodological strategy which you can follow to guide your research project from its inception, through the processes of data collection and analysis, to completion. The theory that you develop from using this approach should have the capacity to be well grounded in the meanings expressed by your participants and the context of the research setting. The successful application of this approach is likely to be related to making sure that you understand one or other of the published versions of Grounded Theory Method and your willingness to commit yourself to following its procedures.

11.16 Narrative Analysis

Introduction

We discussed Narrative Inquiry as a research strategy. Our discussion here focuses on the different ways in which narrative data may be analysed. Narrative Analysis is not a specific analytical technique, such as Thematic Analysis or Template Analysis (discussed earlier). Nor is Narrative Analysis part of a wider methodological approach, as with Grounded Theory Method. Instead **Narrative Analysis** is a collection of analytical approaches to analyse different aspects of narrative. These may be combined in practice, depending on your research question and purpose, and the nature of your data.

What these analytical approaches have in common is the preservation of the data's narrative form. Unlike Thematic Analysis, Template Analysis or Grounded Theory Method, where original data are fragmented by coding and then assigned to analytical categories, narrative data are preserved and analysed as a whole unit or narrative sequence. Categories, themes and facets of content may still be identified and coded but this occurs from within a narrative. In Narrative Analysis it is important to preserve data within their narrated context to maintain the sequential and structural elements of each case.

While a narrative tends to be analysed as a whole, the nature of what constitutes a narrative varies considerably. Textual narratives may vary from a segment of text or speech to a whole life story provided by a narrator. Within this range of possibilities, analysis may focus on extracts from interview transcripts, which each provide a short narrative about a related topic or incident in which the researcher is interested. These extracts will tend to be short stories that have a clear purpose, encompassing a situation, an action and an outcome, expressed in a structure containing a beginning, middle and end. Analysis may also focus on passages of speech or dialogue, where the purpose is to analyse how the narrative is constructed. In terms of extended narratives, analysis may focus on narrated accounts of life stories or organisational events, where emphasis is likely to be placed on sequential and structural elements. Analysis may also involve a researcher constructing a narrative from fragments of data collected from multiple sources, such as different documents or research interviews. A narrative may also be constructed from other narratives to provide a unified account to further analysis, sometimes referred to as re-storying.

Narrative Analysis may use a deductive or inductive research approach. In thematic narrative analysis, prior theory can be used to develop codes and categories to help to analyse each narrative. Codes and categories may also be allowed to emerge inductively from each narrative. As in some other qualitative approaches, analysis of narratives may combine the use of deductive and inductive approaches.

Because Narrative Analysis is a collection of analytical approaches, with variations evident in each approach in terms of the way they have been used in practice by researchers, it is not sensible to describe a procedural outline as we have done in earlier sections. Instead, we briefly outline two approaches used in Narrative Analysis. These are Thematic Narrative Analysis and Structural Narrative Analysis (Maitlis 2012; Riessman, 2008).

Outline

Thematic Narrative Analysis

The purpose of **Thematic Narrative Analysis** is to identify analytical themes within narratives. This approach to Narrative Analysis focuses on the content of a narrative, rather than on the way in which it is structured. In this approach the emphasis is therefore on 'what' the narrative is about rather than 'how' it is constructed.

Thematic Narrative Analysis can be used to analyse an individual narrative or multiple, related narratives. In either approach, you will need to pay attention to the chronological sequence and contextual background of the themes you identify. Understanding sequence and context is important to be able to develop a rich and full explanation when analysing an individual narrative. Analysis of multiple narratives can commence by analysing each narrative separately or by working across all of the narratives at the same time, as we go on to describe. Multiple narratives will be related by a common focus, such as an organisational event, with each narrative provided by a different person involved in this. In analysing multiple narratives separately, the initial emphasis will be on the in-depth analysis of each narrative before then comparing and contrasting findings across them. The reason why you may wish to analyse multiple narratives individually will be to illustrate how variations in context affect the actions taken and outcomes recorded, or; to illustrate how differences in the actions taken and outcomes recorded may vary in spite of contextual similarities and to explain why (Box 11.33).

Analysis of multiple narratives can also commence by searching for themes across these narratives, rather than concentrating on the in-depth analysis of each narrative in turn in the dataset. This difference in emphasis may be more suitable where you

Box 11.33 Focus on management research

Using Narrative Analysis to analyse acts of workplace courage

In an article published in *Academy of Management Journal*, Koerner (2014) analysed narratives relating to acts of workplace courage. Koerner defines courage as acting intentionally in spite of the risks associated with undertaking such an act. From the literature about courage she identifies three essential elements of a courageous act: 'a morally worthy goal, intentional action and perceived risks, threats or obstacles' (Koerner 2014: 65). Data collection resulted in 89 narrative accounts of workplace courage.

Koerner analysed these narratives using two complementary approaches. The first approach focused on the broad subject or storyline of each narrative, in order to be able to categorise (label) the act of courage told in the story. This involved analysing each narrative as a whole unit. The second approach focused on more detailed aspects of the content of the narratives, related to, for example, the occurrence of the three elements of a courageous act theorised in the literature. In this second approach the unit of analysis was a segment of data rather than the whole narrative. This second approach led to the text of each narrative being coded with a number of analytical categories.

The first approach led to the development of five storyline categories, from which Koerner was able to develop a typology of acts of courage in the workplace. These five types are: endurance of a difficult situation to achieve a worthy goal; reaction to a difficult situation to overcome it; opposition to a more powerful individual to remedy a problem; creation of a solution to remedy a problem in spite of risks; failure to act courageously in the face of a problem. This allowed each of the 89 narratives to be categorised into one of these five types of workplace courage (or lack of it).

The second approach led to the development of a number of categories to code data within and across these narratives, including how the three elements of a courageous act manifested themselves in each narrative. This approach allowed Koerner to analyse how these elements varied in relation to each type of courage. For example, narrators in her study associated enduring a difficult situation with the worthy goal of achieving an outcome, retaining a job or providing an income for families; whereas opposing a powerful person to remedy a problem was associated with the worthy goal of retaining integrity, being fair, or preventing harm.

commence your research approach deductively with a predetermined theoretical framework of analytical categories or themes for which to search. In this approach, you will be able to identify whether and which themes occur across the narratives in the dataset or parts of it, where variations occur and how contextual factors affect these. This should help you to develop an explanation that evaluates the application of prior theory to your data as well as being grounded in these data, while preserving the integrity of your narratives (Box 11.33).

Analysing narratives to identify themes while keeping each narrative intact can be achieved by adapting the method of coding we discussed earlier in this chapter. One adaptation you might use is to colour-code analytical themes in each narrative. By using a particular colour-code for a theme, you will be able to identify its occurrence across different narratives, without fragmenting these data. This simple procedure will allow you to compare different narrative accounts more easily as you read and reread each one. A further adaptation that you may find useful in order to keep your narratives intact is to make several copies of each set of narratives and to code a particular theme on one set of copies. A further tactic you may use is to read each narrative transcript several times to become familiar with its content to aid your analysis.

Structural Narrative Analysis

Structural Narrative Analysis analyses the way in which a narrative is constructed. This approach to Narrative Analysis examines use of language to understand how it affects a listener or an audience. In this approach the emphasis is therefore on 'how' the narrative is constructed and language is used rather than 'what' it is about.

While Thematic Narrative Analysis is likely to be easier to use and therefore to be used more often, the use of Structural Narrative Analysis is capable of adding a further level of insight when conducting Narrative Analysis. To use this approach you will need to develop some understanding of the socio-linguistic and cognitive theories that underpin it (see the discussion in Riessman 2008). These have led to methods to analyse the structures of spoken narratives. A key method to analyse the way narrative accounts are sequenced and structured is the technique developed by Labov and Waletzky (1967) and Labov (1972), which remains a standard approach today. In this approach a researcher analyses a narrative to look for the presence of six elements and the way these have been used. These are:

- an abstract (which states the point of the story);
- an orientation (which describes the situation including when and where it took place and who was involved);
- a complicating action (which describes the sequence of events including a critical point);
- an evaluation (where the narrator explains the meaning of the narrative);
- a resolution (how the issue is solved – the outcome); and
- a coda (which ends the narrative and relates it to the present).

This analytical structure provides a framework to evaluate narratives, since not every element may be present in a narrative and the nature and sequencing of these elements is likely to vary. It is, however, worth noting that the purpose of much of the research undertaken using this and other approaches to analyse the structure of narratives is not so much to form judgemental evaluations but to understand how people in different groups form narratives. This has been undertaken to fulfil different aims: sometimes to understand how acts of speech may lead to certain actions or to falsely negative perceptions; sometimes to change professional practice.

Where your research focuses on interactions between individuals or across those in different groups, where you have collected narrated accounts of these interactions, you may consider using Structural Narrative Analysis. This potentially encompasses a wide range of interactions; for example, between managers and other employees; across occupational groups; up and down organisational levels; across cultural and transnational boundaries, to understand the relationship between the way a narrative is constructed and the effect of this on the attitudes and subsequent actions of those who receive it. More generally, Structural Narrative Analysis may be suitable for you to analyse the narratives you collect through conducting interviews or recording naturally occurring conversations.

Evaluation

We noted that collecting data through narratives may be advantageous in certain circumstances. These include research contexts where the experiences of your participants can best be understood by collecting and analysing these as complete stories or narrative sequences. The ways in which events in a narrative are linked, the actions that follow and their implications are more likely to be revealed by encouraging a participant to narrate his or her experiences than asking them to respond to a series of pre-formed questions. Narrative Analysis allows chronological connections and the sequencing of events as told by the narrator to be preserved, with the potential to enrich understanding and aid analysis.

A number of the research strategies outlined may lead to the use of Narrative Analysis, not just the use of Narrative Inquiry. Narrative research is a case-centred approach and you may find that use of an Action Research, Case Study, Documentary, Ethnographic or Grounded Theory research strategy will lead to the collection of narrative sequences that draw you towards the use of Narrative Analysis. In this way, your data collection may lead you to use Narrative Analysis as a complementary method to analyse some data that you judge are best analysed in their narrative form, or as your primary method of analysis, depending on your research question and purpose, and nature of your data. In analysing data in narrative form, Narrative Analysis offers you a choice of analytical approaches to suit the purpose of your research. These approaches may be used individually or in combination. Where they are combined in practice, your analysis is likely to be richer in terms of the insights you will be able to produce from your data.

11.17 Discourse Analysis

Introduction

'Discourse Analysis' is a term covering a variety of approaches that analyse the social effects of the use of language. In general terms 'discourse' refers to the spoken or written use of language, often referred to as talk or text. In Discourse Analysis, the emphasis is not on studying the way in which language is used for its own sake. Use of language is a key way in which people make sense of their social world. In this more specific sense, 'discourse' describes how language is used to shape this meaning-making process, to construct social reality. A **discourse** is therefore not just seen as neutrally reflecting social practice or relations but as constructing these (although the notion of 'constructing' is contentious and we return to it later). In this way, **Discourse Analysis** explores how discourses construct or constitute social reality and social relations through creating meanings and perceptions.

This conceptualisation allows the complexity and diversity of social practice and relations to be recognised through the existence of different, often competing and sometimes conflicting discourses. For example, different discourses construct perceptions about organisations and organisational relations. It also follows that language (discourse) can be used intentionally to attempt to create ideologically mounted positions, intended to be in the interests of those who produce and disseminate them. A unitarist view would emphasise the commonality of interest within an organisation (or society) and use some means (focusing on discourse) to persuade its members of this approach. By contrast, a pluralist view would see an organisation (or society) as a collection of competing interests. Even within the pluralist view, some discourses may be seen to dominate while others are marginalised.

Discourse Analysis involves studying textual sources or passages of naturally occurring talk. Textual sources may be organisational documents such as those outlined in the discussion of documentary research. Discourse Analysis will often involve using multiple texts that are interrelated to understand the nature and development of a discourse. Phillips and Hardy (2002) point out that the (diffuse, interactional and often taken-for-granted) nature of a discourse means that although it cannot be explored comprehensively, by using a range of interrelated sources it should be possible to gain access to aspects of its formation, propagation and acceptance.

Transcripts of recordings of naturally occurring talk can also be used to explore a discourse. Such data may be collected through conducting and recording observation in an ethnographic study, or one incorporating ethnography. As discourse occurs through naturally occurring talk, it is preferred to contrived talk through interviewing where the intervention of the researcher in asking questions, eliciting responses and analysing the data is likely to affect the authenticity of the discourse being analysed (Hepburn and Potter 2007). There may of course be a use for interview data in a subsequent, supplementary capacity.

To be able to explore the relationship between discourse and social reality also means placing emphasis on contextual and social theoretical aspects. The way in which a discourse emerges and constructs social reality through influencing social relations and practices is likely to be rooted in a particular period or event, such as the foundation of an organisation or an organisational change. Discourse Analysis may therefore require an understanding of historical context to be able to understand the ways in which discourse develops and constructs social practices. Using a range of texts may help to reveal this historical contextual development. Some approaches to Discourse Analysis also draw on existing theoretical perspectives to explore the nature of a discourse and to contextualise its impact on social practice and relations. We consider this further in the following sub-section.

Outline

Discourse Analysis encompasses a range of approaches and unlike some of the techniques we discussed earlier does not specify a particular set of procedures to conduct analysis. For this reason we briefly outline some of the approaches used in Discourse Analysis in this sub-section. Approaches to Discourse Analysis can be differentiated according to their focus and philosophical assumptions. The focus of Discourse Analysis ranges from 'finely-grained' analysis of text or talk to grand theoretical abstractions about the nature of social practice.

A finely grained approach focuses on the analysis (deconstruction) of an individual text, or of a transcript of 'talk' that occurred during a social interaction located within a particular situation. The purpose of this type of close reading of a text (or passage of talk) is to understand how the use of language indicates meaning and to categorise the nature of this discourse. Hyatt (2005, 2013) provides advice about conducting this type of analysis. His 'Critical Literacy Analysis' (2005) and 'Critical Policy Discourse Analysis' (2013) include a range of criteria for analysing text. Although these analyses are devised within the context of education, the generic analytical criteria they include are transferable or translatable to other contexts. If you are considering using Discourse Analysis you may find it useful to consult these articles.

Further (and complementary) approaches include interdiscursive and intertextual analyses. **Interdiscursivity** refers to the way one discourse is introduced into another discourse. For example, discourses and practices associated with the private sector have been introduced into the public sector in some societies to justify change. Box 11.34 provides an example of this in the context of the UK's National Health Service where the discourse of 'privatisation', value for money and income generation now sit alongside its traditional discourse of public service. **Intertextuality** refers to the way a text or texts overtly or covertly borrow from and are informed by other texts. Overt borrowing from another text is acknowledged through use of quotations and citations. Covert borrowing involves adopting ideas or ideological positions and arguments from other texts without overtly

Box 11.34 Focus on research in the news

Health reform fails to lift private patient income

By Sarah Neville

The sums earned by the National Health Service from treating private patients have barely risen even though most foundation trust hospitals are struggling to make ends meet amid a historic budget squeeze.

Rules introduced last year allowed a far higher percentage of turnover to be raised from non-NHS work, leading to warnings by critics of health service "privatisation".

But research by the Foundation Trust Network (FTN), based on an analysis of hospital accounts, suggests some parts of the sector are finding it far easier than others to earn money in this way.

Big, specialist hospitals such as Moorfields Eye Hospital and the Royal Marsden, both in London, can use their equipment, expertise and internationally known brands to attract private patients and pursue cash-generating research.

Although district general hospitals have also entered into the non-NHS market, they must bear the costs of running a full range of services, including maternity and accident and emergency, for their local communities, making it harder for some to compete with independent providers able to focus on single specialities such as orthopaedics.

Underlining the importance of developing non-NHS income for overstretched hospitals, Chris Hopson, chief executive of the FTN, said it was "a crucial revenue stream . . . in the current financially challenging climate".

FT *Source:* Extract from 'Health reform fails to lift private patient income', Sarah Neville, Public Policy Editor (2014) *Financial Times*, 4 September. Copyright © The Financial Times Ltd

acknowledging this. The focus of these types of analysis in Discourse Analysis is to analyse how discourses and texts are used in the construction of other discourses and texts, to identify how discourses change and develop, and to understand how attempts are made to give credibility to such changes or developments. These approaches to analysis point to the importance of contextual knowledge, not only to understand how discourses develop and evolve, but also to appreciate the factors that bring about change – why change occurs. Using interdiscursive and intertextual analyses therefore involves using multiple texts.

Our discussion so far has emphasised the role of social constructionism in Discourse Analysis. By this we mean the assumption that the social world is socially constructed through discourse and that Discourse Analysis analyses how use of language constructs versions of social reality (including dominant, marginalised and competing discourses). However, the extent to which social reality is socially constructed is contested. To this end, Holstein and Gubrium (2011: 342) reflect a dictum of Karl Marx in saying 'that people actively construct their worlds but not completely on, or in, their own terms'. This points to the (ontological) distinction between objectivism and subjectivism. According to realist philosophical positions, objective entities exist that are external to social actors, which impact on their social constructions. It is therefore important to understand external factors that affect human attitudes and actions, whether or not social actors are aware of these influences on the ways in which they make sense of their social world.

A methodological approach to Discourse Analysis based on a realist epistemological view exists in the form of **Critical Discourse Analysis** (e.g. Fairclough, 1992, 2010). Critical Discourse Analysis adopts a critical realist approach, drawing a distinction between the natural world and the social world, with the implication that social actors' understanding of the latter is affected by the former and is not entirely socially constructed. Fairclough (2010: 4–5) captures this when he writes,

> The socially constructive effects of discourse are thus a central concern, but a distinction is drawn between construal and construction; the world is discursively construed (or represented) in many and various ways, but which construals come to have socially constructive effects depends upon a range of conditions which include for instance power relations but also properties of whatever parts or aspects of the world are being construed. We cannot transform the world in any old way we happen to construe it; the world is such that some transformations are possible and others are not. So CDA is a 'moderate' or 'contingent' form of social constructionism.

Critical Discourse Analysis examines relations between discourse and other objects in the world that are recognised as existing, including the exercise of power by those who control resources (power relations). In this approach, discourse is seen as being affected or conditioned by social reality, knowingly or unknowingly, as well as socially construing it. As a result it incorporates the need to not only analyse incidents of discourse (analysis of social interactions or text) but also to understand how wider discursive and social practices influence and are influenced by discourse. This approach, in which an incidence of discourse is 'simultaneously a piece of text, an instance of discursive practice, and an instance of social practice (Fairclough, 1992: 4), is outlined in Figure 11.18. This approach involves analysing discourse at the level of text or social inaction (discussed earlier in this sub-section), discursive practice (including the use of interdiscursive and intertextual analyses outlined earlier) and social practice (seen as requiring an interdisciplinary or transdisciplinary approach to analysis) in order to achieve an integrated and critical understanding.

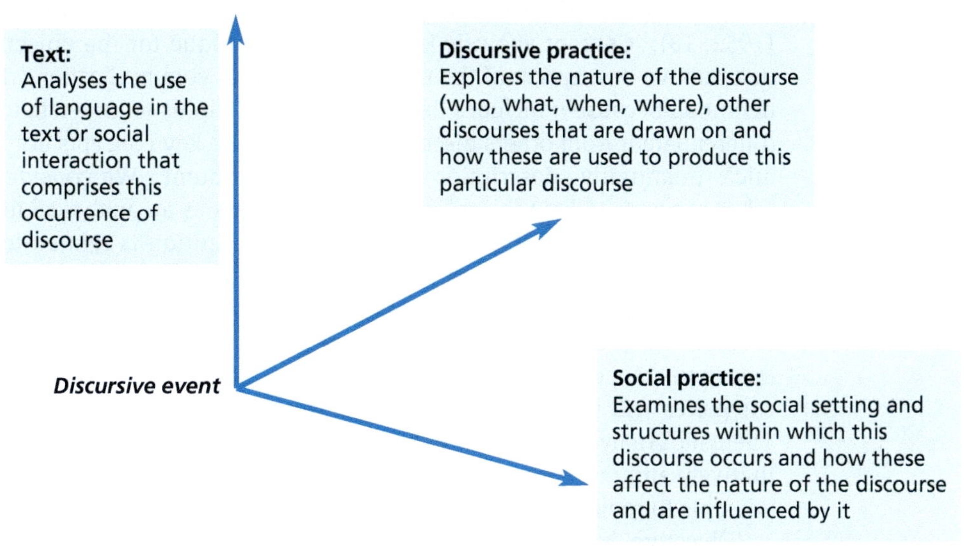

Figure 11.18 A three-dimensional analytical framework for Critical Discourse Analysis
Source: Developed from Fairclough (1992)

Evaluation

Discourse Analysis potentially provides you with a valuable analytical approach where your research involves social action and interaction within a particular setting such as an organisation. This analytical approach may be appropriate where your research is focused on a topic such as organisational communication, culture, decision making, governance, power, practices, processes, relations or trust. It may be an approach that provides you with an insightful means to analyse data resulting from the use, for example, of an Action Research, documentary or ethnographic strategy where you have transcripts relating to the use of language in discourse.

Where you consider using this approach as you formulate your research design, you will need to develop some level of familiarity with and understanding of approaches to Discourse Analysis. In particular you will need to be able to articulate your approach to Discourse Analysis and say why it is suitable for your research. Discourse Analysis, like some other analytical approaches, has developed to suit a number of purposes, incorporating different philosophical and theoretical assumptions suitable for different types of data and using different methods. Discourse Analysis can be used as your primary analytical technique, depending on your research question, research design and nature of your data, or in support of other analytical techniques where appropriate. Discourse Analysis therefore offers a potentially valuable research approach but consideration about using this approach will benefit from adequate and early preparation!

11.18 Content Analysis and quantifying qualitative data

Introduction

Content Analysis is an analytical technique that codes and categorises qualitative data in order to analyse them quantitatively. Content Analysis has a long history that illustrates its use as an approach spanning qualitative and quantitative methods. There are numerous definitions of Content Analysis, which often draw on an early definition by Berelson (1952: 18): 'Content analysis is a research technique for the objective, systematic and quantitative description of the manifest content of communication.' This is an important definition because it includes key concepts that help us to understand this technique and differentiate it from others discussed earlier. These key concepts are 'objective', 'systematic', 'quantitative description' and 'manifest content'. We consider each of these and other concepts to help to explore Content Analysis as an analytical technique.

Use of 'objective' and 'systematic' in the definition is related to the importance of defining explicit rules to code and categorise data in Content Analysis. These codes and categories are typically predetermined by a researcher before data collection begins. This is similar to structured observation, which uses predetermined categories and adopts a detached stance to quantify data. In some approaches to Content Analysis, analytical categories will be allowed to emerge during analysis, in a way that appears similar to Thematic Analysis discussed earlier, although the aim will still be to analyse data quantitatively and these categories will need to be explicitly reported to facilitate subsequent attempts to replicate the results.

'Objective' in the definition also extends to the researcher identifying 'factual' objects in the data and not relying on subjective judgement. These are objects which are seen as possessing an external reality to the researcher that do not rely on her or his interpretive opinion. Stress is laid on different researchers being able to replicate a Content Analysis by using explicit categories to produce an identical outcome. A research project may focus, for example, on attitudes towards an organisational policy and who holds these views. Content Analysis may be used to identify positive and negative attitudes towards the policy and who voices such views. Terms denoting negative or positive attitudes will be identified, typically being predetermined before analysis commences, so that the researcher, perhaps using an analytical software program (Section 11.20), is required to identify instances of these in the text or visual data being analysed. The researcher will also identify the characteristics of the holders of each of these attitudes – perhaps related to gender, age, occupation, work department and so forth. This example illustrates another aspect of Content Analysis, which stresses the importance of understanding the contextual use of the content being analysed (Krippendorff 2004).

'Systematic' in the definition also relates to the conduct of Content Analysis. Content Analysis should be conducted in a consistent, transparent and replicable way. This includes explicitly explaining how the data were categorised in a consistent and transparent way that can be understood and replicated by others (see next sub-section). Holsti (1969) advocates five general principles for the systematic development of analytical categories in Content Analysis. Categories should:

- link obviously to the scope and purpose of the research topic, not least so that the relationship of these categories to the research question(s) and objectives is evident ;
- be exhaustive so that every relevant unit of data may be placed into an analytical category;
- be mutually exclusive so that each unit of data may only be placed into one analytical category, rather than possibly fitting into more than one (this is different from the approach in qualitative analytical techniques discussed earlier);
- be independent so that units of data exhibiting related but not the same characteristics cannot be coded into the same category; and
- be developed from a single classification to avoid conceptual confusion.

'Quantitative description' in the definition makes apparent that the purpose of Content Analysis is to quantify and describe aspects of textual or visual data after coding and categorising them. These data are collected qualitatively (Section 11.8) or derived from existing, qualitative sources and then categorised in order to reduce them to a relatively small number of content categories for subsequent quantitative analysis. This analysis may vary from identifying frequencies to examining relationships between variables. Using our earlier example about attitudes towards an organisational policy and who holds these views, the frequencies of different attitudes may be measured and the relative importance of negative or positive ones identified; it would also be possible to examine relationships between these different attitudes and the characteristics of those who hold them. Depending on the nature of the research question, research purpose and research strategy, Content Analysis may be used as either the main or secondary method to produce this type of data analysis.

'**Manifest content**' in the definition makes clear that Content Analysis is concerned with analysing what is apparent in the data. In Berelson's definition 'objective' and 'manifest content' are linked, and we noted earlier that 'objective' refers to the researcher identifying 'factual' objects in the data, not relying on subjective judgement. The most manifest way to achieve this is to use words or phrases that are physically present in a data set as the basis of a system of categories to analyse its content. Returning to our example about attitudes towards an organisational policy, the occurrence of positive words such as 'enthusiastic', 'involved', 'trust' and negative words such as 'concerned', 'distrust', 'sceptical' may be coded and their frequencies counted and analysed in the data. Analysing 'manifest content' should increase the chance that analysis is conducted in a consistent, transparent and replicable way, thereby improving reliability.

Content Analysis may involve analysing data for other than just 'manifest content'. Greater latitude is often required to infer meanings in the data and to categorise these. This goes beyond simply coding particular words or phrases in the data. Interpreting meanings in order to code units of data such as sentences or paragraphs is referred to as '**latent content**'. Coding 'latent content' may reduce reliability in comparison to 'manifest content'. In order to ensure consistency and transparency, it will be necessary to define the properties of the categories devised for such latent content very clearly.

Choosing to use Content Analysis will depend on the nature of your research data and your research question. Where you have collected a large amount of qualitative data, Content Analysis may be suitable to analyse and describe some of its content, depending on your research question. Content Analysis may be suitable to use in relation to descriptive types of 'what', 'when', 'where', 'who' and 'how' questions. For example, it may help you to analyse what is included in the content (and what is not included by omission); when and where an issue is evident in the content; who is included in the content; how much or how many of a variable occurs in the content; how much something changes and what trends or patterns are evident across comparable data sources. Using Content Analysis to address these descriptive types of question may partially help to answer a research question with a wider exploratory, explanatory or evaluative purpose. As we have noted in our example about attitudes towards an organisational policy, Content Analysis will also provide you with a means to quantify given variables in your data in order to be able to statistically analyse relationships between these variables (Section 11.5).

Content Analysis may be applied in a wide variety of contexts. It has been used to analyse the content of newspapers and other media, including radio and television programmes. It can be used to analyse textual material, such as documents, and audio-visual material, including online media. In an organisational context, it can be used in the analysis of a wide range of documents, including agendas and minutes of meetings, briefing papers, contracts, diaries, email, letters, memos, plans, policy statements, press releases, reports and strategy documents. It may also be used to analyse textual material in corporate websites, social media websites and blog postings. In an organisational context, it can also be used in the analysis of a wide range of visual and audio sources including advertising posters, audio-visual corporate communications, digital recordings, promotional advertisements and recordings, and web images. In a broader context related to business and management it may be used to analyse other online material and government publications and reports. These potential sources of data to which Content Analysis may be applied have in common the fact that they existed before the research project was conducted – they were not created as data in response to a research project. This has a number of possible implications for the use of Content Analysis, which we consider later in our evaluation of this analytical technique.

Content Analysis may also be used to analyse the qualitative data you generate through conducting interviews or including open-ended questions in questionnaires, as we indicated in our example about attitudes towards an organisational policy. This would involve producing a transcript of each semi-structured or unstructured interview, or of the responses to open-ended questions included in questionnaires, in order to apply Content Analysis. Content Analysis may also be applied to data from conducting participant observation, where transcripts or recordings of these are available.

Procedure

Unlike the qualitative analytical techniques considered earlier, which tend to follow a concurrent and even recursive or circular approach to data sampling, collection and analysis, Content Analysis is more likely to follow a step-by-step or sequential process. For Content Analysis, this process involves sampling, devising analytical categories, defining the unit of analysis, conducting coding and undertaking quantitative analysis. We outline briefly each of these procedural steps.

Where you use existing textual or visual sources you may need to select a sample if the amount of material available is large, in order to conduct your research in a manageable way. Determining the amount of material that exists will depend on your research question and factors such as the existence of and access to suitable documents. Where it is necessary to select a sample, the sampling techniques should be reviewed to guide your choice of a sampling method that is appropriate for the purpose of your research. You may find that there is a shortage of suitable material and we consider this possibility further in our evaluation of Content Analysis in the next sub-section.

Devising analytical categories is a critical part of using Content Analysis. The categories you devise signify the essence of what you wish to record and analyse. We noted five general principles for the systematic development of analytical categories earlier whereby they should link to the scope and purpose of the research topic, be exhaustive, mutually exclusive, independent and developed from a single classification. Where the categories you devise are not clearly defined and do not fulfil these principles, it is likely that the validity and reliability of your Content Analysis will be flawed.

You will also need to define the unit of analysis you intend to use to record content. This will be determined by your research question and purpose. The unit of analysis may focus on individual words, based on identifying and counting particular words in the content of your sample, as in our example about attitudes towards an organisational policy. The unit of analysis may be larger than the word, related to the occurrence of particular phrases or to sentences or paragraphs. Larger units (sentences or paragraphs) may be used where it is important to contextualise content in order to be able to categorise its meaning. The distinction we highlighted earlier between manifest content and latent content is likely to be evident in the size of the unit of analysis used. Manifest content is likely to be reflected in the use of the word or phrase as the unit of analysis and latent content is likely to be reflected in the use of larger units of analysis. The unit of analysis may also focus on the characteristics of those involved, as in our example where gender, age, occupation, work department were recorded. It may also focus on other characteristics of the content that are relevant to record and analyse in your research. The unit of analysis in visual materials varies from individual images to visual sequences.

Coding involves you working through your data to code units of these data according to the categories you have devised. This will provide you with the opportunity to test your system of categories, where this is predetermined, on a sample of your data and to modify it if necessary before applying it across all of your data. An important way for you to assess whether your system of categories is transparent and capable of being applied consistently by others is for you and a friend to code the same sample of data separately using this system of categories and then to compare your results. This is known as inter-rater reliability and may be assessed by measuring the extent to which two coders agree using a measure known as Cohen's Kappa (which may be calculated using IBM SPSS Statistics).

Where categories are derived from the data rather than being predetermined, you will need to 'immerse' yourself in the data set you have collected. Initially you will need to read through your data very carefully, highlighting or noting key aspects that relate to the purpose of your research and your anticipated use of this technique. As this process continues you will need to identify analytical categories, define these and ensure that they fulfil the general principles for their systematic development (e.g. be exhaustive, mutually exclusive). You may also test the system of categories you devise in this way with a friend to assess inter-rater reliability on a sample of the data before applying it across all of your data. Once you have coded and categorised your data you will be able to undertake quantitative analysis.

Evaluation

Content Analysis potentially offers a number of advantages. It can provide a means to analyse large amounts of qualitative data where your aim is to describe these quantitatively. In addition to being able to count frequencies and examine relationships between variables in the data, use of this technique may also allow you to observe patterns, shifts and trends in documentary forms of data over time.

Combining Content Analysis and documentary research can provide you a means to undertake a longitudinal study relatively easily where this is appropriate to your research question and where suitable documentary sources are readily available. As we noted earlier, a wide range of documentary sources may be suitable, including those accessible online. Using pre-existing documentary or visual forms of data also has the advantage that their use is unobtrusive. This means that you can use these types of data without the creators of these documents being aware of their use. This avoids the possibility in face-to-face data collection of research participants reacting to the presence of the researcher affecting the reliability of the data being collected.

Content Analysis can also be used in combination with other qualitative analytical techniques discussed in this chapter. This allows Content Analysis to be used to support the exploratory and explanatory purposes of qualitative analytical techniques, by describing the quantitative aspects of qualitative data, where you are willing to analyse your data for each purpose.

While Content Analysis can be useful, it may also be problematic. Issues may arise when you seek to use Content Analysis in relation to documentary sources. In some situations, the documentary sources you wish to use for your data will be inaccessible, missing, incomplete, or unusable. This will mean that you will not be able to pursue your research unless you are able to source an alternative set of documentary sources. Even where you are able to pursue this research approach, some documents may be incomplete or unusable for your purpose and you will need to discard these. Because documentary sources have been created for another purpose, they may also prove to be partial and biased accounts. Consequently, while they are available to you to use, you will need to use these with care, in a qualified way, or to reject them, depending on the purpose of your research project.

Issues can also arise in relation to data you collect and your analysis of this. Earlier we discussed the need to devise analytical categories, define units of analysis and conduct coding systematically and objectively to ensure reliability. We discussed tactics related to inter-rater reliability. Coding all of your data consistently will also require you to exercise care, skill and concentration to avoid analytical 'drift', which will affect **intra-rater reliability** (which concerns the reliability of coding by a single researcher over time). We also noted the distinction earlier between manifest and latent forms of content. Coding latent content will necessitate a higher level of interpretation than that of manifest content, leading to a higher risk of making invalid inferences and producing unreliable results.

In analysing data, we noted that Content Analysis may be used to examine relationships between variables in the data. However, Content Analysis is not appropriate to assess causal relationships. In our earlier example about attitudes towards an organisational policy and who holds these views, we noted that it would be possible to examine relationships between different attitudes and the characteristics of those who hold them. However, it would not be possible to explain why particular groups tended to hold particular attitudes (e.g. those in particular occupational groups may hold much more positive attitudes to those in other groups). To understand why this would be the case requires in-depth analysis of the qualitative data that you have collected.

Box 11.35 Focus on student research

Using a data cloud to display the frequency of key terms

Luca undertook a research project evaluating types of pay structure. This involved him conducting interviews in organisations that each used a different pay structure. Luca wanted to understand the reasons why each had decided to adopt a particular structure and to evaluate perceptions about that structure's use in practice. He was interested to use different types of data analysis and this led him to code some of manifest content in his data to categorise key terms. To demonstrate the frequency of key terms used by his interview participants he thought it might be useful to produce a data cloud for each set of interviews exploring a particular pay structure. Since these data clouds would represent the actual terms used by his interview participants, they also helped Luca to demonstrate how he had derived the 'in vivo' codes he used in his Grounded Theory analytical approach. This data cloud represents the terms used by interview participants in an organisation that had implemented a Job Families pay structure:

This raises a general concern about the extent to which you should collect qualitative data in order to quantify them. As we have discussed, there are advantageous reasons why you may wish to code and categorise qualitative data in order to describe them quantitatively, but more generally there is limited purpose in collecting qualitative data if you intend to ignore the nature and value of these data by reducing most of them to a simplified form. In this way, Content Analysis may prove to be a main method when applied to documentary sources but a secondary method when applied to qualitative data you collect yourself (Box 11.35).

11.19 Data Display and Analysis

Introduction

The Data Display and Analysis approach is based on the work of Miles et al. (2014). For them, the process of analysis consists of three concurrent sub-processes:

- data condensation;
- data display;
- drawing and verifying conclusions.

We now outline each of these.

Procedural outline

As part of the process, **data condensation** includes summarising and simplifying the data collected and/or selectively focusing on some parts of this data. The aim of this process is to transform the data and to condense it. Miles et al. (2014) outline a number of methods for condensing data. These include the production of interview or observation summaries, document summaries, coding and categorising data and perhaps constructing a narrative.

Data display involves organising and assembling your data into summary diagrammatic or visual displays. Miles et al. (2014) describe a number of ways of displaying data, and refer to two main families of data display: matrices and networks. Matrices are generally tabular in form, with defined columns and rows, where data are entered selectively into the appropriate cells of such a matrix, to facilitate further data analysis (Box 11.36). A network is a collection of nodes or boxes that are joined or linked by lines, perhaps with arrows to indicate relationships. The boxes or nodes contain brief descriptions or labels to indicate variables or key points from the data.

Box 11.36 Focus on student research

Using CAQDAS to explore how key words are used in context

Marcus' research was concerned with how staff were responding to the managed changes in the organisation where he worked. He had collected his data using a Web questionnaire, which contained the open question: 'If there is anything further you would like to add in relation to the changes at OrgCo, please type your comment in the box'. Marcus downloaded the responses verbatim from the online survey tool as a data file and spellchecked them, correcting words that had been misspelled or used American spellings to the English spelling. This ensured he would pick up all occurrences of particular words such as 'staff' or 'OrgCo', the pseudonym he used to anonymise the organisation. He then loaded the spellchecked data into Provalis Research's text analysis software WordStat. These were displayed in a tabular form. During the next stage of his analysis Marcus wanted to see which respondents had mentioned staff or staffing in their responses to the question and the context in which the words had been used. He therefore searched for the keyword 'staff' within his data.

Scanning the responses suggested that those respondents who had answered this question often appeared to talk about how staff were treated at OrgCo. Marcus decided to investigate further.

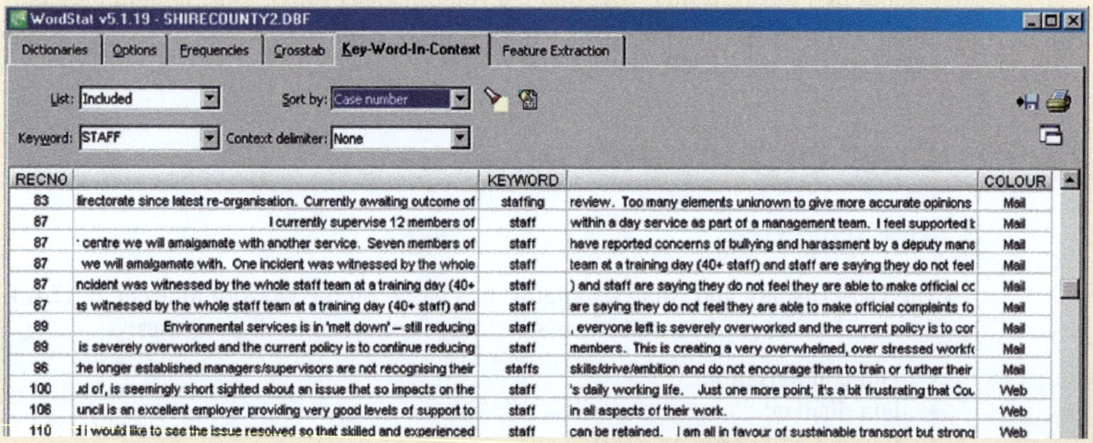

RECNO		KEYWORD		COLOUR
83	lirectorate since latest re-organisation. Currently awaiting outcome of	staffing	review. Too many elements unknown to give more accurate opinions	Mail
87	I currently supervise 12 members of	staff	within a day service as part of a management team. I feel supported t	Mail
87	· centre we will amalgamate with another service. Seven members of	staff	have reported concerns of bullying and harassment by a deputy mans	Mail
87	we will amalgamate with. One incident was witnessed by the whole	staff	team at a training day (40+ staff) and staff are saying they do not feel	Mail
87	ncident was witnessed by the whole staff team at a training day (40+	staff	) and staff are saying they do not feel they are able to make official cc	Mail
87	ıs witnessed by the whole staff team at a training day (40+ staff) and	staff	are saying they do not feel they are able to make official complaints fo	Mail
89	Environmental services is in 'melt down' – still reducing	staff	, everyone left is severely overworked and the current policy is to cor	Mail
89	is severely overworked and the current policy is to continue reducing	staff	members. This is creating a very overwhelmed, over stressed workfo	Mail
96	the longer established managers/supervisors are not recognising their	staffs	skills/drive/ambition and do not encourage them to train or further their	Mail
100	ıd of, is seemingly short sighted about an issue that so impacts on the	staff	's daily working life. Just one more point; it's a bit frustrating that Cou	Web
106	uncil is an excellent employer providing very good levels of support to	staff	in all aspects of their work.	Web
110	d i would like to see the issue resolved so that skilled and experienced	staff	can be retained. I am all in favour of sustainable transport but strong	Web

Recognising relationships and patterns in the data, as well as drawing conclusions and verifying these, is helped by the use of data displays. A display allows you to make comparisons between the elements of the data and to identify any relationships, key themes, patterns and trends that may be evident. These will be worthy of further exploration and analysis. In this way, the use of data displays can help you to interpret your data and to draw meaning from it.

Evaluation

Miles et al. (2014) believe there are a number of advantages associated with using forms of data display. Qualitative data collection tends to produce hours of audio-recorded interviews or extensive piles of notes. Once these have been transcribed or word processed, they are generally referred to as 'extended text'. Extended text is considered an unreduced form of display that is difficult to analyse because it is both extensive and poorly ordered. Based on the logic that 'you know what you display', the analysis of data and the drawing of conclusions from these will be helped by using matrices, networks or other visual forms to display reduced or selected data drawn from your extended text. These forms of display are relatively easy to generate, can be developed to fit your data specifically, and help you to develop your analytical thinking as you work through several iterations to develop a visual form that represents your data well.

Use of Data Display and Analysis can provide you with a set of procedures to analyse your qualitative data, or alternatively one or more of the techniques that Miles et al. (2014) outline can be useful as part of your approach to analysing this type of data. They describe the analysis of qualitative data as an interactive process, and in this sense their approach includes many aspects of analysis that complement the analytical techniques we discussed earlier. Their approach is a systematic and structured one, and they recognise that the procedures they outline are often associated with a fairly high level of formalisation. However, unlike grounded theory, the exact procedures to be followed within their framework of data reduction, display and conclusion drawing and verification are not specified. Miles et al. (2014) refer to their book as a 'sourcebook', and as such they offer a number of possible techniques that may be appropriate within your overall approach to analysis. If you intend to use their book we suggest you take care in identifying what is useful for you in the context of your own research question and objectives.

Data Display and Analysis is suited to an inductive strategy to analyse qualitative data, although it is also compatible with a deductive strategy. Miles et al.'s (2014) book is useful both for its overall discussion of the analysis of qualitative data and in relation to its many analytical tools.

11.20 Using CAQDAS

Introduction

CAQDAS (Computer Assisted Qualitative Data Analysis Software, sometimes abbreviated to QDAS) refers to programs containing a range of tools to facilitate the analysis of qualitative data. The use of CAQDAS offers a number of advantages in relation to the analytical procedures we have been discussing. In particular, when used systematically, it can aid continuity and increase both transparency and methodological rigour (Lewins and Silver 2009). These points were summarised by one of our students as 'it forces you to do your analysis properly!'

The literature that evaluates CAQDAS raises issues associated with its use. CAQDAS programs vary in relation to the type and style of facilities that they offer and, therefore, potentially in their usefulness for different analytic situations. Consequently, you need to develop some familiarity with a range of programs to be able to evaluate their applicability for the particular analyses you wish to undertake. However, attempting to use CAQDAS may be problematic if the program you wish to explore is not readily available, although it is worth noting that some programs that may be suitable for your purpose are available to download as freeware and software producers offer free downloads of trial versions. Lewins and Silver (2009: 1) summarise the problem you may experience in evaluating which programs to invest time in to explore their potential use in analysing the data you collect:

> It is not always easy to visualise exactly what a CAQDAS package offers when exploring it for the first time yourself. Equally when asking someone else for their opinion, it is not always easy to know which questions you should be asking. Most of the software packages we are aware of and discuss regularly are excellent products in several ways. Sometimes you choose a package that is already in situ and make good use of it – but if you have a choice about which software to purchase for your research project, you may be in some uncertainty about how to proceed.

Functions

Despite differences between CAQDAS programs, the basic ways in which they can facilitate your qualitative data analysis are similar. Lewins and Silver (2009) summarise these as:

- *Structure of work:* all data files can be stored in or linked through a project file created within the software, allowing access to all elements of the project.
- *Closeness to data and interactivity:* by bringing data files together rapid access to any aspect of these data will be facilitated, increasing closeness to and interactivity with the data.
- *Explore the data:* allows data to be explored prior to coding and text search tools enable individual, or collections of, words to be searched and retrieved within context.
- *Code and retrieve:* offers scope to devise a coding scheme that is appropriate to the research approach to generate codes and subsequently to be able to retrieve, reflect on, re-code and output data, and generate themes from initial coding.
- *Project management and data organisation:* provides the means to manage the research project throughout its progress by being able to import any relevant files that are supported by the software and organise the qualitative data collected to facilitate analysis.
- *Searching and interrogating:* facilitates searching and interrogating the data set for a range of purposes including exploring the content of the data, linking and grouping codes, conceptualising and mapping themes, developing relationships and representing explanations.
- *Writing memos, comments, notes, etc.:* allow thoughts about the data and the research process to be recorded systematically.
- *Output:* produces reports allowing you to view material in hard copy or to export it to other applications such as word-processing and spreadsheet programs, as well as producing tabular reports, charts and graphical representations.

What is not apparent from this list is that the functions contained in some CAQDAS packages are better at supporting certain types of qualitative data analysis procedures than others. A wide range of qualitative data exists and your research may involve collecting one particular type or some combination of these. Text makes up a major type of qualitative data but this comprises different types such as documents, narratives

Box 11.37 Checklist

Choosing a CAQDAS package

- ✔ How much data do you have that needs to be analysed qualitatively?
- ✔ How important are these qualitative data in relation to any other data you have collected for your research project and will you want to integrate any quantitative data into the qualitative software package you use?
- ✔ What type(s) of qualitative data do you need to analyse: audio, documentary, narratives, transcripts or visual?
- ✔ How much time do you have to learn how to use the package?
- ✔ What is the timeframe for your research project?
- ✔ How much support is available in your university to help you learn to use the package?
- ✔ What is the operating system of your computer?
- ✔ How much memory does your computer have?
- ✔ Do you want software that will allow you to take an inductive, deductive or combined approach to your analysis?
- ✔ Do you want a package that will help you manage your thinking and assist you in developing your own codes?
- ✔ Do you want a package that will allow you to explore the way language is used in your data?
- ✔ Do you want a package that allows you to display relationships within your data diagrammatically?
- ✔ Do you want a package that will allow you to quantitatively describe the content of your data?

and transcripts, affecting what you wish to achieve through analysis. Audio, still images and video sources are also important types of qualitative data. This means that you may need to experiment with more than one package before you find the CAQDAS that meets your needs. Your final choice of CAQDAS package will be dependent on a range of factors, including, not least, the relative benefits you will gain relative to the time you need to invest to learn a CAQDAS program. These factors are summarised in Box 11.37 as a checklist.

Where you decide to use a CAQDAS program and have selected a package, you will need to familiarise yourself with it before you start collecting your data. This will avoid the problem of trying to learn the features of the package at the same time as you analyse your data, although you will of course continue to learn about these as you conduct this analysis.

Exploring the latest versions of CAQDAS

Published information about CAQDAS programs is likely to become out of date fairly quickly. Fortunately, there is a wealth of up-to-date information available from the CAQDAS Networking Project's website hosted by the University of Surrey.[1] If you are considering using CAQDAS, we would strongly recommend a visit to this website which, in addition to a wealth of useful articles, also contains web links to commercial software producers' sites including downloadable demonstration versions of the software. We would also advise you to explore the Internet sites of CAQDAS producers to obtain details and demonstrations of the latest versions of these packages and the features that they offer. Some of those most widely used are listed in Table 11.8.

---

[1]The Internet address for the CAQDAS Networking Project is http://www.surrey.ac.uk/sociology/research/researchcentres/caqdas/.

Table 11.8 Internet addresses for a range of selected CAQDAS developers

Name	Internet address	Brief comments
ATLAS.ti	http://www.atlasti.com	Windows and MAC versions. Versatile and flexible. Supports multimedia
Dedoose	http://www.dedoose.com	Windows and MAC versions. Web-based application for analysis of mixed methods data by members of a research team in different locations
HyperRESEARCH	http://www.researchware.com	Windows and MAC versions. Simple to use. Case-based structure. Supports multimedia
Leximancer	https://www.leximancer.com	Windows and MAC versions. Content analysis software with a wide range of applications
MAXQDA	http://www.maxqda.com	Windows and MAC versions. Intuitive and easy to use. Mixed methods features. Supports multimedia. Content analysis features with addition of MAXDictio in MAXQDAplus
QSR NVivo	http://www.qsrinternational.com	Windows and MAC versions. Versatile with large range of searching possibilities. Supports multimedia
QDA Miner	http://www.provalisresearch.com	Windows and MAC versions. Mixed methods analytical capabilities. Supportive functionality. Content analysis features with addition of WordStat
Qualrus	http://www.qualrus.com	Windows version. May also run on MAC OS using a Windows virtual machine according to the www.ideaworks website. Uses artificial intelligence to offer suggestive coding based on learning from coding trends. Supports multimedia
Transana	http://www.transana.org	Windows and MAC versions. Specifically designed for qualitative analysis of audio, still image and video data. Ability to synchronise multiple video streams during playback and to synchronise playback with transcripts

Sources: Developed from QUIC Working Paper software reviews available from the CAQDAS Networking Project website hosted by the University of Surrey and/or software producers' websites. Each comment in this table only provides a very brief indication and is not intended to promote or discourage the use of a particular software program, or to advocate the use of one program over other compatible programs. You are advised to evaluate the features and applications of current versions of CAQDAS at the time of your project in relation to the requirements of research.

11.21 Summary

- Qualitative data are rich and full textual and/or visual data. They may also be characterised as non-standardised and as non-numerical data.
- A qualitative approach involves commencing your research from a deductive or inductive perspective.

- Data collection, analysis and interpretation are very much an interrelated and interactive set of processes in qualitative research. Analysis occurs during the collection of data as well as after it.
- Qualitative data need to be carefully prepared for manual or computer-assisted analysis, usually involving transcription where the spoken word is involved.
- There are a number of aids that you might use to help you through the process of qualitative analysis, including: interim summaries, event summaries, document summaries, self-memos, maintaining a research notebook and keeping a reflective diary or reflexive journal.
- There are several different approaches to analyse your qualitative data. In this chapter we discuss Thematic Analysis; Template Analysis; Explanation Building and Testing; Grounded Theory Method; Narrative Analysis; Discourse Analysis; Content Analysis; and Data Display and Analysis.
- The use of computer-assisted qualitative data analysis software (CAQDAS) can help you during qualitative analysis with regard to project management and data organisation, keeping close to your data, exploration, coding and retrieval of your data, searching and interrogating to build propositions and theorise, and recording your thoughts systematically.

Self-check questions

Help with these questions is available at the end of the chapter.

11.13 Why do we describe qualitative analysis as an 'interactive process'?

11.14 Which sorts of data will you need to retain and file while you are undertaking qualitative research?

11.15 How would you differentiate between a deductive and an inductive analytical approach?

11.16 What are the main implications of using a deductive analytical approach for the way in which you conduct the process of qualitative analysis?

11.17 What are the main implications of using an inductive analytical approach for the way in which you conduct the process of qualitative analysis?

Review and discussion questions

11.18 With a friend, use the extract of the interview transcript to undertake the following tasks.

- **a** Using the aim of the focus group stated, independently code the data in the extract.
- **b** Compare the results of your coding.
- **c** Identify where your coding is similar to and where it differs from that of your friend.
- **d** Where you identify differences in coding, discuss the assumptions you each made when you coded these data and why you made these.
- **e** By reflecting on your attempt at coding these data, which codes, if any, would you change and why?

11.19 Visit one of the CAQDAS websites listed in Table 11.8. Find and download a demonstration version of the CAQDAS package and explore its features. How useful do you think this will be for analysing your research data?

11.20 Find out whether your university provides you with access to the NVivo™ CAQDAS. If it does, visit this book's companion website and download the self-teach package and associated data sets. Work through this to explore the features of NVivo™.

Progressing your research project

Analysing your data qualitatively

- Undertake and audio-record an initial semi-structured or in-depth interview related to your research project, transcribe this interview, and make a few copies of your transcript. Alternatively obtain a copy of a relevant document.
- Decide whether it is most appropriate to summarise, categorise or develop a narrative using your data in order to answer your research question.
- Where a summary is most appropriate develop this, ensuring you also include contextual data.
- Where a narrative is most appropriate, develop this paying particular attention to the temporal order and the organisational and social contexts.
- Where categorising is most appropriate and your research project is based on a deductive approach, develop a provisional set of categories and codes from your research question and objectives, conceptual framework, research themes and initial propositions. Produce a description of each of these categories. Evaluate these categories to see whether they appear to form a coherent set in relation to the aim of your research.
- Using one of your transcripts, attempt to allocate units of data to appropriate categories by using CAQDAS or writing their code labels alongside the text in the left-hand margin. Again, evaluate this provisional set of categories and codes and modify any that appear to be inappropriate.
- Where categorising is most appropriate and your research project is based on an inductive approach, work through one of the transcript copies and seek to identify categories related to your research purpose. Allocate units of data to appropriate categories by using CAQDAS or writing appropriate code labels for these categories alongside the text in the left-hand margin. List these categories and their labels and produce a description for each of the categories that you have devised.
- Once you have allocated units of data to the set of categories, use the CAQDAS program to organise your data by different categories. Alternatively, cut out the units of data related to different categories and transfer them to an appropriately labelled index card (reference to the interview, location of the text in the transcript and the date and so forth). Read through the units of data within each category.
- Analyse these data by asking questions such as: What are the points of interest that emerge within each category? How will you seek to follow these up during your next data collection session? How does the material that has been revealed through this interview relate to any theoretical explanation or initial propositions with which you commenced your data collection? Are any connections evident between the categories?
- Produce a summary of the interview and attach it to a copy of the transcript. Memo any ideas that you have and file these.
- Repeat the procedures for the remaining qualitative data as appropriate and revise your ideas as necessary.
- Use the questions to guide your reflective diary entry.

References

Berelson, B. (1952) *Content Analysis in Communication Research*. Glencoe, IL: Free Press.

Braun, V. and Clarke, V. (2006) 'Using thematic analysis in psychology', *Qualitative Research in Psychology*, Vol. 3, No. 2, pp. 77–101.

Brekhus, W.H., Galliher, J.F. and Gubrium, J.F. (2005) 'The need for thin description', *Qualitative Inquiry*, Vol. 11, No. 6, pp. 861–79.

Brinkmann, S. and Kvale, S. (2015) *InterViews: Learning the Craft of Qualitative Research Interviewing* (3rd edn). London: Sage.

Bryant, A. and Charmaz, K. (2007) *The Sage Handbook of Grounded Theory*. London: Sage.

Charmaz, K. (2006) *Constructing Grounded Theory*. London: Sage.

Corbin, J. and Strauss, A. (2008) *Basics of Qualitative Research* (3rd edn). Thousand Oaks, CA: Sage.

Dey, I. (1993) *Qualitative Data Analysis*. London: Routledge.

Erlandson, D.A., Harris, E.L., Skipper, B.L. and Allen, S.D. (1993) *Doing Naturalistic Inquiry*. Newbury Park, CA: Sage.

Fairclough, N. (1992) *Discourse and Social Change*. Cambridge: Polity Press.

Fairclough, N. (2010) *Critical Discourse Analysis: The Critical Study of Language* (2nd edn). Harlow: Pearson Education.

Finlay, L. (2002) 'Negotiating the swamp: The opportunity and challenge of reflexivity in research practice', *Qualitative Research*, Vol. 2, No. 2, pp. 209–30.

Gerstl-Pepin, C. and Patrizio, K. (2009) 'Learning from Dumbledore's Pensieve: Metaphor as an aid in teaching reflexivity in qualitative research', *Qualitative Research*, Vol. 9, No. 3, pp. 299–308.

Glaser, B. and Strauss, A. (1967) *The Discovery of Grounded Theory*. Chicago, IL: Aldine.

Glaser, B.G. (1978) *Theoretical Sensitivity: Advances in the Methodology of Grounded Theory*. Mill Valley, CA: Sociology Press.

Glaser, B.G. (1998) *Doing Grounded Theory: Issues and Discussions*. Mill Valley, CA: Sociology Press.

Haynes, K. (2012) 'Reflexivity in qualitative research', in G. Symon and C. Cassell (eds) *Qualitative Organizational Research: Core Methods and Current Challenges*. London: Sage.

Hepburn, A. and Potter, J. (2007) 'Discourse analytic practice', in C. Seale, G. Gobo, J. F. Gubrium and D. Silverman (eds) *Qualitative Research Practice*. London: Sage.

Hodson, R. (1991) 'The active worker: Compliance and autonomy at the workplace', *Journal of Contemporary Ethnography*, Vol. 20, No. 1, pp. 47–8.

Holstein, J.A. and Gubrium, J.F. (2011) 'The constructionist analytics of interpretive practice', in N.K. Denzin and Y.S. Lincoln (eds) *The Sage Handbook of Qualitative Research*. London: Sage.

Holsti, O.R. (1969) *Content Analysis for the Social Sciences and Humanities*. Reading, MA: Addison-Wesley.

Hyatt, D. (2005) 'A critical literacy frame for UK secondary education contexts', *English in Education*, Vol. 39, No. 1, pp. 43–59.

Hyatt, D. (2013) 'The critical policy discourse analysis frame: Helping doctoral students engage with the educational policy analysis', *Teaching in Higher Education*, Vol. 18, No. 8, pp. 833–45.

Johnson, P. (2004) 'Analytic induction', in G. Symon and C. Cassell (eds) *Essential Guide to Qualitative Methods and Analysis in Organizational Research*. London: Sage, pp. 165–79.

Kenealy, G.J.J. (2012) 'Grounded theory: A theory building approach', in G. Symon and C. Cassell (eds) *Qualitative Organizational Research: Core Methods and Current Challenges*. London: Sage.

King, N. (2012) 'Doing template analysis', in G. Symon and C. Cassell (eds) *Qualitative Organizational Research: Core Methods and Current Challenges*. London: Sage, pp. 246–50.

Koerner, M.M. (2014) 'Courage as identity work: Accounts of workplace courage', *Academy of Management Journal*, Vol. 57, No. 1, pp. 63–93.

Krippendorff, K. (2004) *Content Analysis: An Introduction to its Methodology* (2nd edn). Thousand Oaks, CA: Sage.

Labov, W. (1972) *Language in the Inner City: Studies in the Black English Vernacular*. Philadelphia: University of Pennsylvania Press.

Labov, W. and Waletzky, J. (1967) 'Narrative analysis: Oral versions of personal experience', in J. Helm (ed.) *Essays on the Verbal and Visual Arts*. Seattle, WA: University of Washington Press.

Lewins, A. and Silver, C. (2009) 'Choosing a CAQDAS package – 6th edition', CAQDAS Networking Project Working Paper. Available at http://www.surrey.ac.uk/sociology/research/researchcentres/caqdas/files/2009ChoosingaCAQDASPackage.pdf [Accessed 30 June 2014].

Maitlis, S. (2012) 'Narrative analysis', in G. Symon and C. Cassell (eds) *Qualitative Organizational Research: Core Methods and Current Challenges*, London: Sage, pp. 492–511.

Miles, M.B., Huberman, A.M. and Saldana, J. (2014) *Qualitative Data Analysis: A Methods Sourcebook* (3rd edn). London: Sage.

Phillips, N. and Hardy, C. (2002) *Discourse Analysis: Investigating Processes of Social Construction*. London: Sage.

Riessman, C.K. (2008) *Narrative Methods for the Human Sciences*. London: Sage.

Silverman, D. (2013) *A Very Short, Fairly Interesting and Reasonably Cheap Book about Qualitative Research* (2nd edn.) London: Sage.

Strauss, A. and Corbin, J. (1998) *Basics of Qualitative Research* (2nd edn). Thousand Oaks, CA: Sage.

Yin, R.K. (2014) *Case Study Research: Design and Methods* (5th edn). Thousand Oaks, CA: Sage.

Further reading

Braun, V. and Clarke, V. (2006) 'Using thematic analysis in psychology', *Qualitative Research in Psychology*, Vol. 3, No. 2, pp. 77–101. This article provides a helpful discussion of Thematic Analysis.

Charmaz, K. (2006) *Constructing Grounded Theory*. London: Sage. This book provides an accessible discussion and evaluation of Grounded Theory and Grounded Theory Method.

Miles, M.B., Huberman, A.M. and Saldana, J. (2014) *Qualitative Data Analysis: A Methods Sourcebook* (3rd edn). London: Sage. This sourcebook presents a range of techniques for the analysis of qualitative data.

Riessman, C.K. (2008) *Narrative Methods for the Human Sciences*. London: Sage. This book provides a helpful discussion of approaches to Narrative Analysis.

Symon, G. and Cassell, C. (eds) (2012) *Qualitative Organizational Research: Core Methods and Current Challenges*. London: Sage. This edited book contains a range of chapters on qualitative analysis including Template Analysis, Grounded Theory, Narrative Analysis and Discourse Analysis.

Case 11.2
The impact of share announcements on market analysts' behaviour

Caitlin is studying for a master's degree in Finance and Banking. Before starting her course, Caitlin worked as a trainee accountant and also had an internship with a large merchant bank. During her time at the bank, Caitlin became particularly interested in the different factors that impacted upon the behaviour of financial market analysts. As part of her master's programme, Caitlin has to conduct her own research project, something that she is very much looking forward to. She is keen to bring her practical experience from the banking industry to her academic studies. Having learnt about the efficient market hypothesis as part of her postgraduate programme, Caitlin would like to conduct research about the impact of market share announcements on the behaviour of analysts. She is interested in some of the cognitive biases such as overconfidence and overreaction that she has read about in the behavioural finance literature. Given her background and undergraduate degree in accounting, Caitlin has always felt comfortable with using and analysing numbers. However, her interest in behavioural finance has led to her making a decision to take a qualitative approach to her research (see Humphrey and Lee 2004/2008). The aim is to interview market analysts about their views regarding the impact of share announcements on their own behaviour.

Caitlin had read the relevant literature in the area (e.g. Fenton O'Creevy et al. 2004; Willman et al. 2002) and has decided that it would be useful to study the impact of share announcements by the top ten companies in the FTSE (Financial Times Stock Exchange) index. She is in the lucky position that she has access to market analysts in the bank where she did her internship and they have agreed to be interviewed. Caitlin decides that she will use critical incident technique as a way of asking interviewees to talk about their views of the impact of the share announcements of those companies on their behaviour. Hence each announcement will be treated as a critical incident. From hearing how interviewees talk about these specific incidents she aims to generate insights into the perceptions of analysts which can further develop her understanding of the extent to which markets behave efficiently.

When planning her research project, Caitlin had realised that she needed to familiarise herself with different types of qualitative data analysis (Symon and Cassell 2012). This is the first time that Caitlin has conducted any qualitative data analysis and she is concerned to find an appropriate method that will enable her to draw some insightful conclusions from her interview study. Initially it all seemed a bit bewildering and she was unsure where to start. In her research methods training her tutor had talked about three different types of qualitative data analysis as examples of the variety of data analytic processes available. These were Content Analysis; Narrative Analysis; and Thematic Analysis using templates. Caitlin was unsure about which of these would be appropriate in her case.

Caitlin initially decided to use Content Analysis for her interview data. The idea of counting was particularly attractive to her given her background. She decided that the best way was to categorise reactions to each of the critical incidents – or share announcements – in one of three categories: positive, negative or neutral. She then went through the interview transcripts and categorised each incident accordingly. From a total of 51 critical incidents identified through the 10 interviews Caitlin found that 17 were categorised as positive, 7 as negative and 27 as neutral. However, on reflection, Caitlin was concerned that this form of analysis provided little rich detail about her research question. The interviews had generated a range of insightful comments from the analysts, yet she felt that this detail had been lost through the analytic process. Therefore she decided to try a different approach.

When reflecting upon the data she had generated from the interviews, Caitlin realised that the analysts talked about responding differently to different announcements as a result of a range of different contextual factors. Indeed one way of understanding the data was that they were telling her stories about the different announcements. These stories drew upon their previous experience of the company and their extensive knowledge of the market. After discussing these impressions with her supervisor, Caitlin decided that Narrative Analysis might be a more appropriate technique to use.

Using Narrative Analysis meant that Caitlin had to look at the data in a different way. Initially she looked at each individual transcript and focused upon the way the analysts talked about their different responses. For example, she identified that when talking about some of the incidents or share announcements, analysts would contextualise their responses by drawing upon the history of the company concerned and the extent to which the announcement followed the usual trend of that particular company. Therefore she identified a narrative throughout their accounts which she labelled as the *historical consistency* narrative in that analyst behaviour and decisions were influenced by how they interpreted the historical consistency of the share announcement. Another issue that Caitlin believed influenced how the analysts talked and behaved was informed by a shared or collective understanding among their colleagues about the relative performance of different companies. She labelled this as a *consensus* narrative, in that analysts would comment on the interpretations that others had of share announcements when they discussed their own evaluations and resultant behaviours. Through this Narrative Analysis, Caitlin felt that she had found an interesting way of addressing her research question. In identifying the narratives that the analysts drew upon to talk about their responses she could understand more about their resultant behaviours.

When Caitlin came to write up her research project she found herself in a bit of a dilemma. Although she felt that the Narrative Analysis was perhaps more insightful in enabling her to answer her research question, she was concerned about what she saw to be the somewhat subjective nature of her analysis and interpretations. Whereas incidents were real, narratives were constructed. Perhaps she should go back to the content analysis where she could comfortably allocate the different incidents to the different categories and do some basic statistical analysis of patterns. In discussion with her supervisor she was told to relax. What she was facing here was an ontological dilemma, and one that was quite easy to deal with.

References

Fenton O'Creevy, M.P., Nicholson, N., Soane, E. and Willman, P. (2004) *Traders: Managing Risks and Decisions in Financial Markets*. Oxford: Oxford University Press.

Humphrey, C. and Lee, B. (eds) (2004/2008) *The Real Life Guide to Accounting Research: A Behind the Scenes View of Qualitative Research Methods*. Oxford: Elsevier, particularly: Chapter 3 'Using case studies in finance research' by Greg Stoner and John Holland, pp. 37–56; Chapter 23 'Qualitative data analysis: Illuminating a process for transforming a "messy" but "attractive" "nuisance"' by Brendan O'Dwyer, pp. 391–407; and Chapter 30 'Qualitative dimensions in finance and risk management research' by Kevin Dowd, pp. 509–23.

Symon, G. and Cassell, C. (eds) (2012) *Qualitative Organizational Research: Core Methods and Current Challenges*, London: Sage, particularly: Chapter 24 'Doing template analysis' by Nigel King, pp. 426–50; and Chapter 27 'Narrative analysis' by Sally Maitlis, pp. 492–511.

Willman, P., Fenton-O'Creevy, M.P., Nicholson, N. and Soane, E. (2002) 'Traders, managers and loss aversion in investment banking: A field study', *Accounting, Organizations and Society*, Vol. 27, No. 1, pp. 85–98.

Questions

1 Which form of analysis do you think Caitlin should use in her dissertation write-up and why?
2 What does Caitlin's supervisor mean by her 'ontological dilemma'?
3 How can that ontological dilemma be addressed?

Additional case studies relating to material covered in this chapter are available via the book's companion website: **www.pearsoned.co.uk/saunders**.

They are:

- Creating environmentally friendly office spaces.
- Communicating bad news at Abco.
- Paying for competence at Investco.
- Internet abuse in universities.
- The influence of film on tourist decision making.
- Creating environmentally friendly office spaces.

Self-check answers

11.13 There are a number of reasons why we may describe qualitative analysis as an 'interactive process'. Analysis needs to occur during the collection of data as well as after it. This helps to shape the direction of data collection, especially where you are following a grounded theory approach. The interactive nature of data collection and analysis allows you to recognise important themes, patterns and relationships as you collect data. As a result, you will be able to re-code and re-categorise your existing data to see whether emergent themes, patterns and relationships are present in the cases you have previously analysed. In addition, you will be able to adjust your future data collection approach to see whether they exist in cases where you intend to conduct your research.

11.14 You will generate three sorts of data that you will need to retain and file as the result of undertaking qualitative research.

The first of these may be referred to as raw data files. A wide range of files potentially fit within this category. These include audio-visual recordings, documents, images, original notes, written up notes and transcripts you make or collect. Electronic and word-processed versions of these files may be contained in a computer-based project file.

The second of these is analytical files containing your coded and categorised data. Alternatively, this may contain your summary or your narrative. These may also be contained in a computerised project file.

The third of these may be referred to as a supporting file, or indeed it may be different files, containing working papers, self-memos, interim reports and so forth. Again, these may also be contained in a computerised project file. You are well advised to keep all of this until the end of your research project.

Eventually you will create a fourth type of file – containing your finished work!

11.15 A *deductive* analytical approach is one where you will seek to use existing theory to shape the approach that you adopt to the qualitative research process and to aspects of data analysis. An *inductive* analytical approach is one where you will seek to build up a theory that is adequately grounded in a number of relevant cases. The design of qualitative research requires you to recognise this choice and to choose an appropriate approach to guide your research project.

11.16 There are a number of implications of using a deductive analytical approach for the way in which you conduct the process of qualitative analysis:

- You will be in a position to commence your data collection with a well-defined research question and objectives and a clear framework and propositions, derived from the theory that you will have used.
- With regard to sampling, you will be in a position to identify the number and type of organisations to which you wish to gain access in order to undertake data collection to answer your research question and meet your objectives.
- The use of literature and the theory within it will shape the data collection questions that you wish to ask those who participate in your research project.
- You will be able to commence data collection with an initial set of categories and codes derived from your theoretical propositions/hypotheses and conceptual framework linked to your research question and objectives.
- This approach will provide you with key themes and patterns to search for in your data, and your analysis will be guided by the theoretical propositions and explanations with which you commenced.

11.17 The main implicatiosns of using an inductive analytical approach for the process of qualitative analysis are likely to be related to:

- managing and categorising a large number of code labels, which will probably emerge from the data that you collect;
- working with smaller rather than larger units of data;
- recognising significant themes and issues during early analysis to help you to consider where data collection should be focused in the future;
- recognising the relationships between categories and rearranging these into a hierarchical form, with the emergence of subcategories;
- seeking to verify apparent relationships against the actual data that you have collected;
- understanding how negative cases broaden (or threaten) your emerging explanation;
- recognising the relationships between the principal categories that have emerged from this grounded approach in order to develop an explanatory theory;
- being rigorous in your use of the procedures that are advocated in order to be able to produce a research report that contains findings that are sufficiently 'grounded' to substantiate the analysis or theory that you are seeking to advance.

Get ahead using resources on the companion website at: **www.pearsoned.co.uk/saunders**.

- Improve your IBM SPSS Statistics and NVivo research analysis with practice tutorials.
- Save time researching on the Internet with the Smarter Online Searching Guide.
- Test your progress using self-assessment questions.
- Follow live links to useful websites.

12 Choosing a Solution - Business Case, SAF, Cost-Benefit Analysis

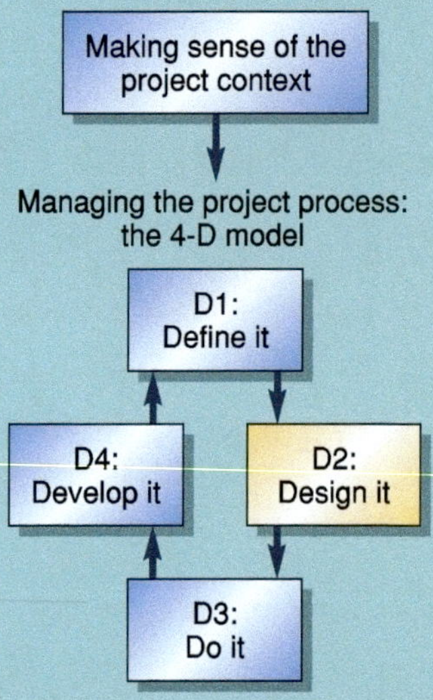

'The method I use to estimate costs, is think of a number and double it.' (Project Planner)

'The only people who give reliable estimates are depressed, or worse.' (Professor of Accounting)

Principles

1 In order to provide an assessment of plans it is vital to understand the costs associated with activities and projects and to have a realistic cost plan.

2 Costs should be justified in terms of payback or return on investment as part of a business case.

3 Determining the magnitude of the costs and benefits of projects needs to be carried out critically.

Learning objectives

By the time you have completed this chapter, you should be able to:

➔ identify elements of cost and a process for construction of cost plans

➔ recognise methods for the development of a business case

➔ identify causes of failure in cost and benefits analysis.

Contents

Source: Jeff J. Mitchell/Getty

The construction costs of Holyrood, the Scottish Parliament building, increased from a forecast £40 million when the project started, to in excess of £400 million by the time it was finished. As the Scotsman newspaper in August 2003 noted, *'it is now officially ranked as one of the worst building projects in the world for cost overruns'.* It continued: *'A spokesman for the Scottish Parliament said: "Clearly, we are not dealing with a fixed-price project, but the Presiding Officer is adamant that every penny will be clawed back where it is possible to do so." He added that: "The Auditor General did not recognise the figure of £40 million as a realistic initial estimate."'*

A report to the Scottish Parliament concluded that: *'It was not helpful that, from the outset of the project, a misunderstanding in the public mind should have been created (by the Scottish Office) about the full costs of this project (i.e. the construction costs plus dependent costs). It was unnecessary and wrong not to disclose the estimated full costs once they were available.'*[1]

Introduction

The example of the Holyrood Parliament Project demonstrates some of the challenges with cost estimating and the process of delivering to plan. It does show that such costing processes are rarely objective, due to the influence of stakeholders determining what is *politically acceptable* in the evaluation of costs and benefits. In this case, even when these began to be determined, as was stated, there was little political will to make them public. However, there is no such thing as the *perfect estimate*. The estimate is an attempt to predict the status of spend at some point in the future and as such is subject to that fundamental property of projects – uncertainty.

A fundamental principle of economics is that resources are scarce. In practice, this means that it is not possible to attempt every idea or opportunity that comes along, as, in any organisation or environment, there are insufficient resources to undertake them all. The implication of 'some can be done, some can't' is the need for choices to be made by organisations as to which projects are pursued and which are not. During the D1 phase of a project, it becomes necessary to evaluate the likely costs and benefits of the project – providing *an* input (but note – not *the* input) to the process of selection and then providing a baseline for the project if approved. Preparing a **business case** as a statement of predicted costs, benefits and risks is a process common to most large organisations and is a key role in the D2 phase for project managers.

The challenges for the business case include the estimation of costs and the identification of benefits. These are particularly challenging where the benefits may not be purely financial, as will be shown. For instance, the Holyrood building has provided a landmark that has been described as an emblem of Scottish independence and heritage (bamboo cladding and all). It is certainly a challenge to derive a monetary benefit from something iconic, whatever its costs.

This chapter considers the basics of obtaining an estimate of project costs, the preparation of the business case, and some challenges for the perceived wisdom in this area, including some of the issues raised by Holyrood and other cases. It is recognised that there are some projects that are completely inappropriate for a business case.

12.1 Basics of a cost planning process

As a **process**, **cost planning** resembles the iterative steps of the time planning process. It differs in that there is a further uncertainty with projects of several years' duration – we cannot know exactly what activities will be required that far into the project or how long they will take, but we also are susceptible to the vagaries of changes in costs over time as a result of currency fluctuations, inflation and base material costs. We also need to know the basis of the relationship between cost, price and profit in the project that we are undertaking. This will be determined by the context in which we are working.

The role of costing

The basic relationship between price, cost and profit can be expressed in a number of ways:

$$\left.\begin{array}{l}\text{price} = \text{cost} + \text{profit}\\ \text{cost} = \text{price} - \text{profit}\\ \text{profit} = \text{price} - \text{cost}\end{array}\right\}\ \text{same equation different meaning}$$

Which one applies depends on whether price, cost or profit is fixed first. These differences can be explained as follows:

- in the first case the price is fixed through legislation, for example, or in the case of a **target costing** system (see below), through market analysis;
- in the second the cost is fixed, generally through contract purchase which guarantees that goods will be supplied to you at a particular price. This fixes your costs while your selling price and profits can be varied;
- some agreements state the profit that a company is allowed to make through the system known as **cost-plus** or **reimbursable pricing**.

Target costing is being used increasingly in the automotive and aerospace industries, among others. The target price for a complete vehicle or aircraft is established that will give it competitiveness in the intended market and the margin determined by corporate decision. That leaves a figure of the target cost. Designers work back from that figure to the individual component or system costs. The main implication is for component suppliers, who are subsequently set target costs to achieve on their components or systems.

It was normal in the defence industry until a few years ago for everyone to work on a cost-plus basis. This required very detailed time and material cost estimates (and subsequently, records) for a project to be submitted to the purchaser for vetting. Should a supplier be awarded a contract it would be on the basis of direct costs plus a percentage towards overheads and profit. The procedures were lengthy, involved massive bureaucracy and, most importantly, did not encourage suppliers to improve their performance. If costs over-ran they would still be paid. The changes in the relationships between the various national military procurement agencies and their suppliers mean that contracts are now most likely to be awarded on the basis of competitive tendering with fixed costs for the delivery required. The supplier knows how much they will be paid if awarded the contracts, and has a vested interest in ensuring costs are minimised.

Not everyone welcomed the demise of cost-plus – as one veteran of the era said: 'When we worked to cost-plus, you would do the job properly and know you'd get paid for doing a proper job. Now we have to watch every bean. Previously, the engineers had control over these projects, now it's the accountants.' Reimbursable contracts are still in evidence in some sectors, particularly construction.

As stated at the outset, cost planning is an iterative process that will be refined during the D2 phase. Indeed, it is likely to be ongoing, as planned costs become baselines, budgets are turned into activities and outcomes, and requirements change as the project progresses. The elements of this process are unpacked in the discussion that follows.

Approaches to costing

There are two basic approaches to the preparation of costing information:

- **ground-up costing** – the estimates of each level in the work breakdown structure are compiled and added together by each level of supervision in the project hierarchy, as would be the case for reimbursable contracts;
- **top-down costing** – you are allocated a certain amount of money to complete the project activities and this has to be split between the sub-projects. The allocation is based on either senior management's estimates or the use of target costing.

The two systems are illustrated in Figure 12.1. The advantage of ground-up costing is that the estimates are prepared by the people who will carry out the activities or their supervisor. In principle, this may give some notion of commitment to achieving these figures if the costs are accepted unmodified by the project manager. In practice, some organisations find that it is common for costing proposals to be cut by project managers or other decision-makers. As a result, the activity level costs may become artificially inflated, as staff try to remove the effect of such cuts. The process consequently loses its apparently straightforward motives and purpose.

Top-down costing involves the allocation of the costs to the sub-activities. This creates a degree of competition between the supervisors of the activities for resources which many view as being beneficial.

Having determined the nature of the costing process it is now necessary to identify the elements of cost. The methods for putting numbers to these elements are then discussed, leading on to how they are accumulated into a final cost estimate.

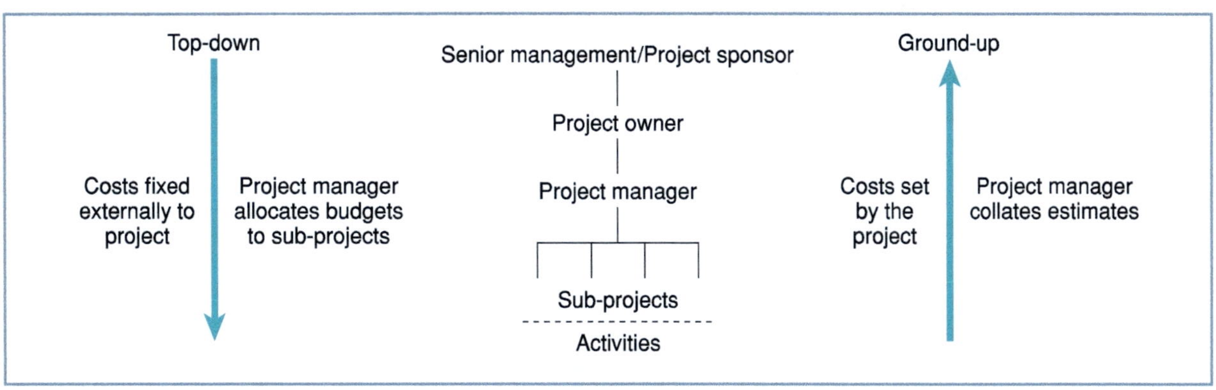

Figure 12.1 Top-down and ground-up approaches to costing

Elements of cost

The major elements of cost are:

- **time** – the direct input of labour into activities;
- **materials** – consumables and other items used in the process;
- **capital equipment** – the purchase of the means of providing the conversion process, or part of its cost, maintenance, running and depreciation offset against activities;
- **indirect expenses** – e.g. transportation, training;
- **overheads** – provision of an office, financial and legal support, managers and other non-direct staff;
- **contingency** margin/allowance.

Materials can be included in the costings, either at the cost to the company or with a margin added. Capital equipment may have to be purchased specially, in which case its entire cost, or part of it, will need to be offset against the project. Where the equipment will have potential further use after the project has finished with it, it may attract a residual value. Indirect expenses are those not directly related to the value-adding activities, but which are considered necessary to support the project. Overheads are carried by all organisations and include the running of the headquarters and the provision of central services.

In some industries, a margin is allowed for contingencies under the control of the project manager. A margin of 10 per cent of the budget is not unusual in such cases.

Estimating techniques

In the material covered so far, the approach has been to build up the costs from the elements of the WBS and to add to them the elements identified above. In addition to this ground-up approach, there are various techniques that are used. These include:

- **parametric estimating**;
- as . . . but . . . s;
- forecasts;
- **synthetic estimation**;
- using **learning curve** effects;
- **wishful thinking**.

Parametric estimating

This type of estimating works well where there is considerable experience of a particular type of project. The project is broken down into a unit that can be readily estimated – for instance, this could be lines of code in a computer program[2], hours of contact for a training programme or cost per mile of resurfacing a road, or relaying track in the rail sector. This provides a number to start from with your estimates as shown in the following illustration.

How much?

A builder was asked to provide a cost estimate for an extension to a house. The architect had estimated £30 000 for the building works. The builder worked on the basis of £1200 per square metre of additional ground area. The additional ground area was 60 square metres equating to a cost in the region of £72 000. For the customer, this difference was unacceptable for their purposes, and so they sought out another source for an estimate. In this instance, they turned to a quantity surveyor (QS). A QS is a specialist in providing such estimates, and had a much more detailed set of parametrics that they used. These included rates per square metre for walling, hours taken to dig foundations, and standard costs per metre for timber. The result was that the QS confirmed the builder's estimate, allowing the client to make a well-founded decision on whether to go ahead with the project or not.

Parametrics provide a means to estimate costs from knowledge of the work being undertaken and can be used at different levels in the product breakdown. In the above example, this was evident from the different approaches taken by the builder (from experience of previous projects) and simply based on floor area, and by the QS based on product and work breakdown. This recognises the principle described in Chapter 6, that projects are rarely totally unique and that at the lowest level of the WBS there is usually a high degree of repetition in activities.

As . . . but . . . s

As . . . but . . . s are where you or your organisation has experience of doing a similar job previously. The use of previous costs as a baseline for future estimation assumes that these were in some way validated by the previous experience. Given the statement made in Chapter 2 that so many projects are not reviewed in any meaningful way, this is an assumption worth challenging. Indeed, unless there is some method of tracking the actual costings and these are compared with the originals there is considerable doubt as to the validity of such records. Hedgehog syndrome will rule the day. Provided there is some logic to back the continued use of such estimates, they are a good basis from which to start.

Forecasts

In many instances, there will be a degree of uncertainty in cost elements and these can only be **forecast** – a real 'best guess'. In some instances parametrics or **proxies** can be used, as shown in the example below.

Forecasting a conference

The 8th International European Operations Management Association (EurOMA) conference was held in Bath, UK, on 3–5 June 2001. The budget on which the conference was based had been approved at the EurOMA board meeting in June 1999. It had been approved with all the income in euros and all the expenses in pounds. The conference organiser included some allowance for the variable number of delegates as it was not known until people registered exactly how many would attend. This created a problem in deciding the fixed-cost allocation (per head). Further risks to the budget included the potential for currency fluctuation.

What happened?

The euro depreciated by 17 per cent relative to the pound during the period. This was below the lower figures for the income per delegate allowed by the organiser, but more delegates than had been expected registered, and many late – incurring a late fee. In addition, more sponsors were found. The result was that the conference made a healthy surplus which was returned to EurOMA for developing its activities.

There are a number of issues in this case. The first is the difference between fixed and variable costs. In a case such as a conference, the fixed costs would include the venue and the administration – they will not change no matter what the number of delegates (within certain ranges). The variable costs include the food costs, which are usually charged per delegate.

Secondly, it was not possible to determine the numbers of delegates in advance – people rarely booked until a few weeks before the conference, yet the venue and facilities would need to be booked months in advance. Instead of this actual data, it had been noted in previous years that the number of delegates would be roughly the same as the number of abstracts (outlines of papers) that were submitted for the conference. This number provided a *proxy* – an indirect best guess of the final number of delegates.

Thirdly, there was another fundamental uncertainty – the exchange rate. In this case, there was no way to deal with such risk – it was simply necessary to provide a series of estimates and feed these into a spreadsheet model to see the impact of these on the budget. For very large projects it is not unknown for the organisation to become involved in currency speculation – either buying the necessary amount of currency when the rates appear favourable, or agreeing exchange deals at particular rates. Where key materials are commodities they may also take an interest in the relevant commodity market. Whatever the case, projects having a currency risk have to factor this into their risk analysis.

Synthetic estimation

Where there are considerable items of repetitive work in a project the times for people to carry out certain activities can be analysed to provide a generic set of actions and consequent timings. New activities can be deconstructed into these generic actions and the timings added accordingly. Little or no direct measurement of the workplace needs subsequently to be carried out. This is based on the practices of work measurement, and can be used with some reliability off-line to give indications of the scale of effort required to perform particular tasks.

Time estimation – learning curve effects

Watching a skilled craftsperson at work shows how a highly intricate task can be learned and carried out so that it is made to look easy. Gaining such a level of skill requires years of training and practice (and many mistakes). A project rarely has such an opportunity to gain advantage through repetition. There will, however, be repetitive elements to any project – and usually at the lowest levels of the WBS. Where these occur, the time taken each time the task is carried out will decrease as the person becomes familiar with the methods. Subsequent improvements in speed are seen to become smaller over time. This can be quantified using the following formula:

$$Y_x = Kx^n$$

where

x = the number of times the task has been carried out
Y_x = time taken to carry out the task the xth time
K = time taken to carry out the task the first time
n = log b/log 2 where b = learning rate

Learning curves and painting by numbers projects

A team is set up to carry out a quality audit of 10 departments. The first audit takes 4 days as the auditors are unfamiliar with the procedures. The second audit takes 3. After a period of time, the minimum audit time is reached, and very little further improvement is seen. We can plot this progression as shown in Figure 12.2.

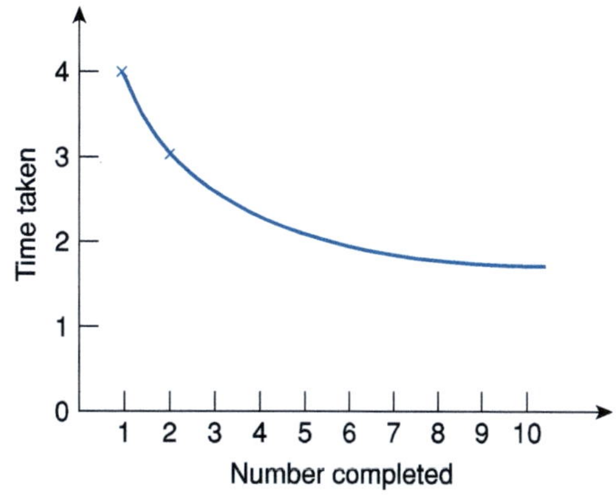

Figure 12.2 Learning curve effects on time taken

If we wish to find out how long the eighth audit will take we need to calculate the learning rate, *b*. The following values can be assigned from the above information:

x = the number of times the task has been carried out = 2
Y_x = time taken to carry out the task the xth time = 3
K = time taken to carry out the task the first time = 4

n can be calculated.

Putting these values in:

$$3 = 4(2)^n$$
$$2^n = 3/4$$
$$n \log 2 = \log(3/4)$$
$$n = -0.1249/0.4149$$
$$n = \log b/\log 2 = -0.4149$$
$$\log b = -0.1249$$
$$b = 0.75$$

From this we can say that the project has a 75 per cent learning curve.

This can also be seen intuitively, as another way of expressing the learning curve is to say that every time the total number of audits completed doubles the time taken for the last audit will be the learning percentage multiplied by the original time. In this case as the number of audits doubled from one to two, the time decreased from 4 to 3. The percentage is therefore 3/4 = 75 per cent. As the number of times the audit is done increases, the times taken will decrease as shown in Table 12.1.

Table 12.1 Improvement over time

Audit no.	*Time taken (days)*
1	4
2	3
3	2.54
4	2.25
5	2.05
6	1.90
7	1.78
8	1.69

To complete this example, the time figures can then be put into the kind of cost build-up calculations described in the following section.

Wishful thinking

You are unlikely to find this in any company procedure manual, but the instances of this occurring in practice are legion in most organisations. The prime causes for 'costing by wishful thinking' are:

- *optimism bias* – as will be demonstrated later in this chapter, a common activity in preparing and assessing estimates is to be over-optimistic in how much can be achieved in a project and how much or little it will cost;
- *politics* – for instance, in The Channel Tunnel project, the total cost escalated from £5 billion to £10 billion. Some of the people who worked on the estimating for that project always maintained that the costs would be £10 billion, but that such a figure was not politically acceptable on either side of The Channel. The need to have the fixed transport link was believed by some to be a key requirement of European integration. As for the Oresund Link in Chapter 14, sometimes that objective is placed above the costs. This issue is expanded in the next section;
- *improper use of estimates* – where 'ballpark figures' become official estimates without any checking or further development (what Eric Verzuh calls an 'on the way to the lift' estimate[3]). For instance, you are asked by a colleague how much time it would take to do a particular task just so they can do some preliminary costings. Without any further referral to you the original request is changed, but your figures are still used in preparing a detailed estimate. The latest version of the work is far more involved than you had been led to believe and it is too late to change the figures;
- *failure to be systematic about planning* – through either complacency or certainty that they will not actually be called on to do the work being discussed, people are vague and give an unqualified estimate to 'get the request off their desks'.

There are many other reasons for wishful thinking in costing. Various techniques have been demonstrated, with the objective of avoiding wishful thinking. However, as has been said many times already, the answers from even the best techniques are only estimates, and errors made at this stage can be multiplied many times.

Cost build-up

We decided to employ a researcher for 6 months to do some data collection and analysis. The direct cost of employing the person was calculated at £12 000. The expenses involved in carrying out the work were in the region of £5000. The total mini-project budget ended up at an incredible £52 000 by the time overheads, sundry expenses, administrative assistance and office space costs had been taken into account. How do we end up with the final cost? As this shows, relatively small pieces of work can look very expensive once they have been fully calculated. The elements of cost are added as shown in Figure 12.3.

The following example illustrates the cost build-up principle and the use of this in determining the level of benefits needed to make the project worthwhile.

Training course – how much should I charge?

A course coordinator wishes to advertise the course but needs to know how much will have to be charged in order to make a profit. The time estimates are made based on the proposed course length – determined by first considering what it could usefully achieve in

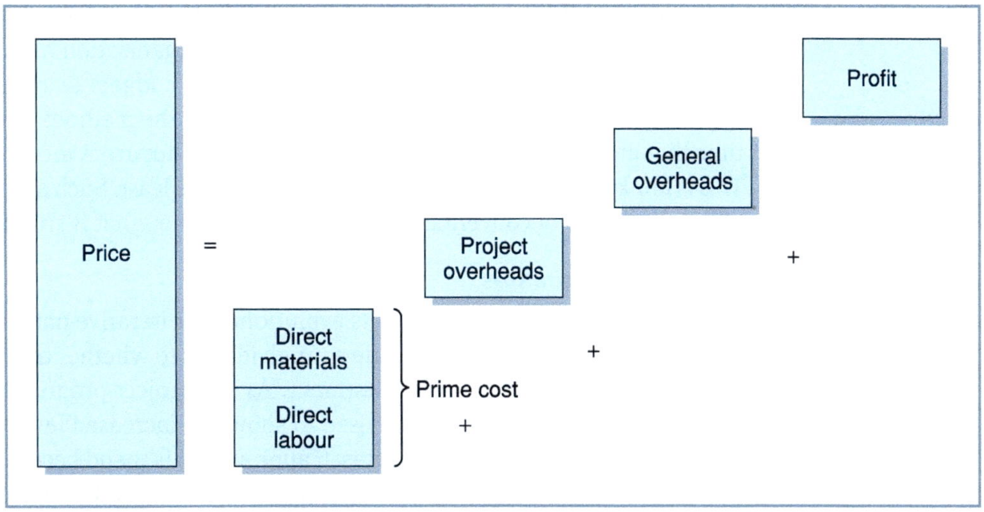

Figure 12.3 Elements of cost

given times. These are correlated with the necessary labour input to ascertain the direct cost. The programme requires a consultant to do three days' training which costs £250 per day, to be supported by an administrator, whose time is costed at £90 per day. The direct costs (fixed, i.e. regardless of how many delegates attend) are therefore £1020. The course requires the provision of printed materials and stationery, which are a variable cost (the more delegates, the greater the cost) of £60 per delegate. Assuming the course is fully subscribed and can accommodate 15 delegates, a further £900 needs to be added to the estimate. The total of these is the prime cost. Indirect labour and materials include administrative time arranging the course (say eight days at £90 per day), and general overheads would be the ongoing 'fixed costs' of providing the building, heating, lighting and functions such as finance to provide the funds, and procurement in raising the necessary purchase orders. The overhead is added to the total cost at a rate of 60 per cent.

The cost build-up is as Figure 12.4. This does not include the profit for the organisation. The minimum rate per delegate should be the total cost (£4224) divided by the number of delegates (15). This gives £281.60. To this should be added a profit margin and a contingency figure in case the course is undersubscribed.

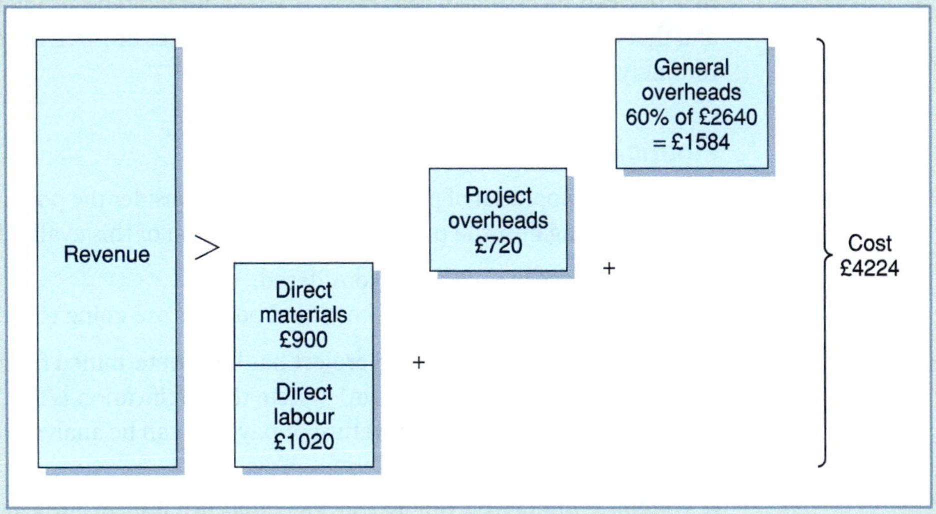

Figure 12.4 Cost build-up

Reliance on this form of allocating overheads does cause anomalies in costing, which can be very damaging to the profitability of the organisation as a whole. For instance, if a department has the overhead allocated to its budgets as revenue (income to that department) then there is little incentive to improve the methods or reduce the amount of time that an activity takes, as this would reduce the apparent income to that department. This is unlikely to encourage improvement, to say the least. Such anomalies raise questions about the merits of conventional cost accounting, though it is still the most-used system.

Use of cost estimates

A consistent theme in planning is its evolutionary or iterative nature. At the outset of the project initial cost plans will provide a rough idea as to whether the project is viable – that is, the returns will justify the investment. As the project progresses to detail planning, these estimates will have to be revised to show the increased level of consideration that has gone into compiling the estimates. If approved, this spend becomes the budget, though often not without being 'trimmed'. It is this budget that is the subject of the next section, and the basis for control – in particular through earned value.

12.2 Business case development

In contrast to the problems faced by Holyrood, the original plans for the building for the Welsh Assembly were scrapped, when it became clear that the estimates were hopelessly understated. This early recognition is a good example of the application of gated processes linked to costs and benefit analysis. The objective of this section is to demonstrate how such an analysis can be constructed and some of the challenges that such a supposedly 'objective process' can face.

APM defines the business case as:

> ***'. . . justification for undertaking a project, in terms of evaluating the benefits, cost and risk of alternative options and rationale for the preferred solution. Its purpose is to obtain management commitment and approval for investment in the project. The business case is owned by the sponsor.'***

The basic definition is useful, but assumes that there are always definable benefits, costs, that risk can be assessed, that there is a well understood problem that needs 'solution' and that there is a defined sponsor. Where processes are well developed and projects are routinely executed, this may indeed be the case.

Financial appraisal

The financial appraisal of project proposals will consider the potential rewards of carrying out a project against the predicted costs. The form of this evaluation will depend on:

- the size of the project being considered;
- the timespan over which the costs and benefits are going to be spread.

Once the cost of completing the project has been determined from the WBS (ground-up) or senior management (top-down) system the justification is that the return will at least exceed the amount spent. This return or payback can be analysed in a number of ways to determine feasibility or net benefit:

- **payback analysis** – simply considers the cash flow of costs and benefits;
- **discounted cash flow** – considers the 'time value' of cash flows;
- **internal rate of return** – sets basic return criteria on time value of money.

Payback

The most basic method of financial evaluation is simply to compare the income that will be generated with the initial investment. From this a payback period can be determined, i.e. the amount of time the revenue will need to be generated to cancel out the investment. For instance, an initial investment of £30 million will be paid back in 5 years if the revenue generated is £6 million per year. Many companies set this time period as a hurdle for projects. Some examples of payback times for various items are as follows:

Manufacturing company (Western) production hardware	5 years
Manufacturing company (Japanese) production hardware	10 years
Computer facilities	3 years
McDonald's franchise burger production	12 years

While this method has inherent simplicity it ignores:

- the total lifecycle cost of an item and only considers costs within the payback period (if there are major items outside this period to be considered, e.g. high disposal or decommissioning costs, the analysis does not provide a good financial model of reality);
- the time value of money (see below).

Discounted cash flow

Where the timespan extends over more than one financial period and certainly where it is over many years, this 'time value of money' will need to be taken into account, through techniques known as *discounting*. The basis of the technique is the comparison between the value of the return on an investment and the value of the same sum of money had it been deposited in a bank account at a given rate of interest for the same period. The technique therefore considers the opportunity cost of the project (i.e. the cost of not doing something else with the resources).

Example

A project proposal aims to spend £100 000 on information technology and £20 000 a year to maintain it for four years. The return is £50 000 per year in terms of labour savings and extra profit generated. Would the project be worth pursuing or should other options be considered?

The payback model shows that the project would generate £200 000 in revenue from an expenditure of £180 000, and so looks plausible. However, if the money was deposited in a bank account, at say 2 per cent interest p.a., the account would show a balance of £194 837 at the end of year 4 (see later work for how the calculation was carried out). It is clearly better to carry out the project than to leave the money in the bank.

The concept of discounting is applied to the cash flows (not just profits) to determine whether or not the projected costs and benefits are going to yield the necessary results and is called discounted cash flow.

Compound interest or 'to those that have shall be given . . .'

When a sum of money is left on deposit in a bank account it accrues interest. If the interest is paid into the account then in the following period there will be interest paid on the original amount plus interest on the first period's interest. As time progresses the amount on which interest is being paid grows, hence in the following period more interest is paid, and so on. This phenomenon is known as **compound interest** and was described by

Einstein as the eighth wonder of the modern world! If you are in a situation where you have money in the bank it is a great invention. Of course, the converse is also true, that if you borrow money, you will accrue interest charges not only on the capital amount but also on any unpaid interest levied on the amount.

Discounting is the opposite of compounding. All values are considered in today's terms – called the present value (PV). We can calculate the value of the sum that would have to be deposited at a given rate of interest for a certain period to yield a stated end value.

Example

If you wanted to have a final value of £2012 in 12 years' time with a rate of return (called the discount rate) of 6 per cent, the present value (the amount that would have to be deposited) is £1000. The calculation is done through:

$$PV = \frac{C_n}{(1 + i)^n}$$

where

C_n = future value of the investment n years hence
i = discounting rate

(Check the above example by putting $C_n = 2012$, $i = 0.06$ and $n = 12$.)

This basic calculation is applied to the benefits, which must then be offset against the costs. This figure is called the **net present value** (NPV):

Net present value = present value of benefits – present value of costs

Example

If a project requires the expenditure of £100 000 now and will yield £200 000 in 6 years, how will the manager evaluate whether or not this is viable (assuming a 10 per cent discount rate)?

$$\text{The PV of the benefits} = \frac{200\,000}{(1 + i)^n}$$

$$= \frac{200\,000}{(1 + 0.1)^6}$$

$$= 112\,800$$

The PV of the costs = 100 000
∴ the NPV = 112 800 – 100 000 = 12 800

The minimum criterion for project selection is that the NPV ≥ 0 at a given discounting rate. The project therefore meets this basic criterion and could be allowed to proceed.

The discounting rate can be taken as the interest rate which could be earned from a bank. It is more usual for the rate to be stated according to the type of project and allied to the cost of borrowing that money. A consequently higher rate than the normal bank rates is set, for example one manufacturing company had a discounting rate of 20 per cent. The effect was that it was correspondingly harder for projects to meet the minimum criterion of having an NPV of zero.

It is usual for the revenues and costs to be occurring over a period of years. More complex examples such as the following can be evaluated.

Example

You have been asked to evaluate the following proposal. Apply the technique of discounted cash flow to the figures to show whether or not this is worth pursuing. The applicable discount rate is 12 per cent.

	Now	*Year 1*	*Year 2*	*Year 3*
Start-up costs	£50 000			
Running costs (rent, rates, staffing, etc.)		£30 000	£45 000	£45 000
Revenues		£40 000	£50 000	£60 000
Sale of business				£70 000

NPV(project) = NPV(year 1) + NPV(year 2) + NPV(year 3)

$$= (-50\,000) + \frac{(-30\,000 + 40\,000)}{(1 + 0.12)^1} + \frac{(-45\,000 + 50\,000)}{(1 + 0.12)^2} + \frac{(-45\,000 + 60\,000 + 70\,000)}{(1 + 0.12)^3}$$

$$= -50\,000 + 8928 + 3986 + 60\,501 = £23\,415$$

The project on this basis is worth pursuing.

(*Note*: this does assume that there is no competition for this investment – that this is the only project being considered.)

Future value (FV)

The **future value** of an investment is the value of that money C if deposited for n years at an interest rate of i and is given by:

$$\mathrm{FV} = C(1 + i)^n$$

There is a 'rule of thumb' called the 'rule of 72'. If you invest at a per cent for b years, where $a \times b = 72$, your money will roughly double, e.g. if you invest £1000 at a fixed rate of 6 per cent for 12 years, the balance at the end of the 12th year ($6 \times 12 = 72$) will be roughly £2000 (actually £2012), and if the rate was 18 per cent and the term 4 years the balance would be the same (actually £1938).

The internal rate of return (IRR)

A related technique is to calculate the IRR of a project, i.e. the discount rate for which the NPV = 0. This can be done mathematically involving a number of iterations (working out the NPV with a variety of discount rates and gradually getting to the point where NPV = 0), or graphically. This does depend on the problem to solve being limited.

Example

A sum of £100 000 is invested over 6 years with a potential yield of £200 000 at the end of the sixth year. What is the IRR of the project? As a starting point, an arbitrary rate of 10 per cent is chosen.

$$\mathrm{NPV}_{10\%} = \frac{200\,000}{(1 + 0.1)^6} - 100\,000 = 112\,895 - 100\,000 = 12\,895$$

The discount rate in this case is clearly too low (the PV of the benefits is too high); try 14 per cent:

$$\mathrm{NPV}_{14\%} = \frac{200\,000}{(1 + 0.14)^6} - 100\,000 = -8883$$

→

This rate is too high (the PV of the benefits is too low). Having two points for the NPV, each on either side of the zero NPV target, the value must be somewhere between the two. This is shown graphically in Figure 12.5. As can be seen, the relationship within small changes in the discount rate can often be approximated to linear. Over a larger range, the change is as shown in Figure 12.6. As the number of benefit points and payout points increases, there will be multiple IRRs. This is shown in Figure 12.7, there being one change in direction of the curve (point of inflection) for each change in the sign (+ to –, or – to +) in the NPV analysis.

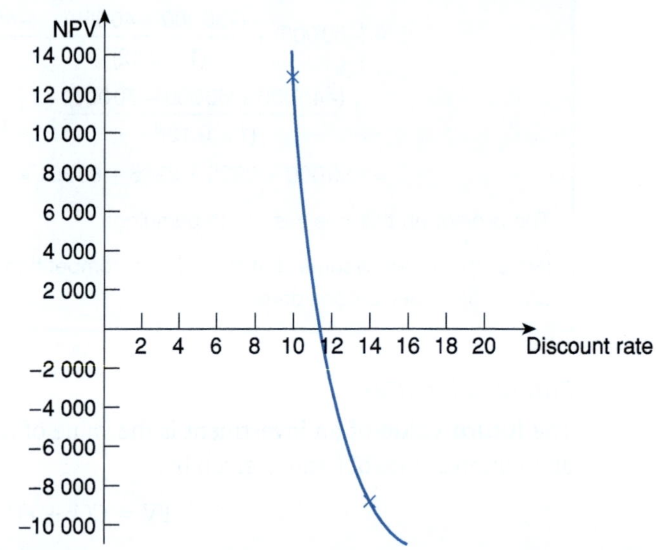

Figure 12.5 NPV profile

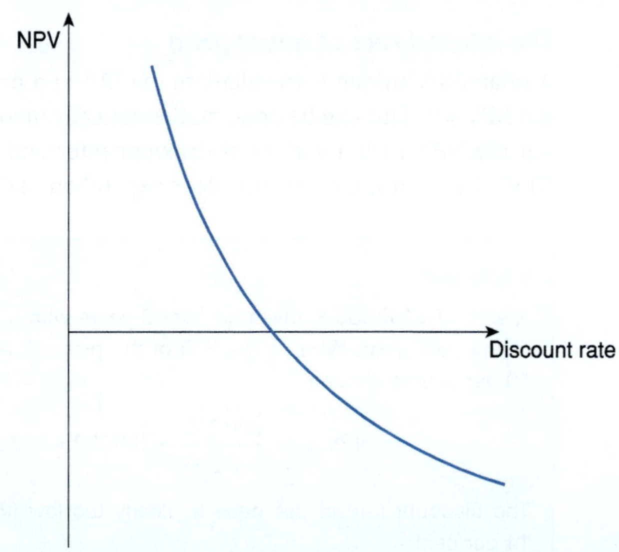

Figure 12.6 NPV profile: large discount rate range

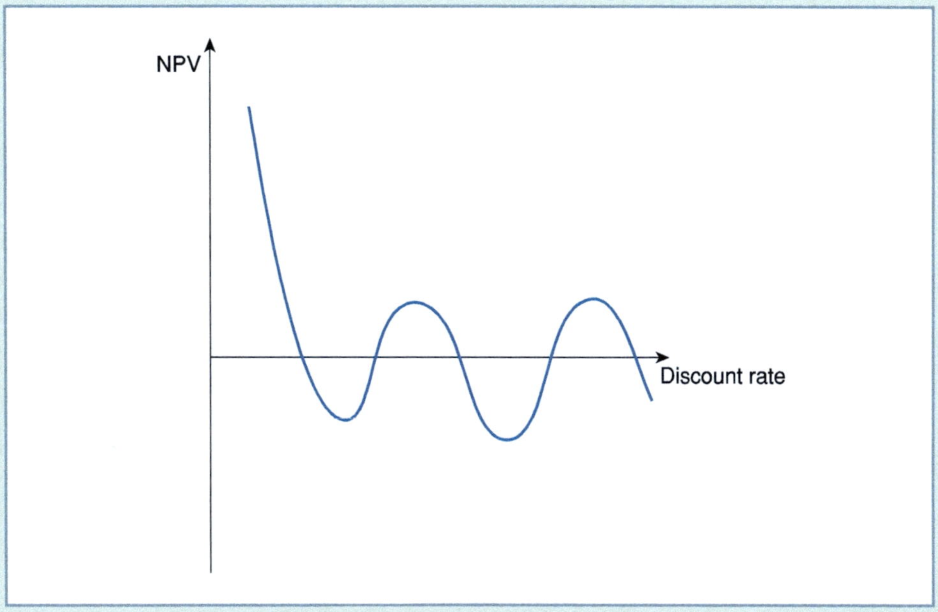

Figure 12.7 Multiple benefit and payment points

Using IRR

Using the percentage rate from an IRR calculation has a certain appeal. It also gets over the need to choose a discount rate for a project, which can save considerable debate. On the other hand, two projects may have the same IRR but yield very different NPVs, e.g. if two proposals have the same IRR but one has a much higher NPV, the one with the high NPV is clearly preferable (risk and availability of funds allowing). The IRR also cannot cope with changes in the discount rate over time. This would have been particularly problematic during periods such as the early 1990s, when rates changed rapidly and by over 10 per cent.

Using discounted cash flow (DCF)

Originally it was only accountants who would be given the knowledge for the use and application of DCF, and would be the ones to accept/reject projects. Its use is now widespread and built into most financial appraisal systems and there are powerful functions in most spreadsheets (including Lotus and Excel) to assist in this analysis (see Appendix at end of chapter). Almost anyone can run a project through the financial constraints without needing to submit a project plan formally. This has numerous benefits to the project manager, as they can build not only time-based models of the project but also financial ones. The use of financial models has similar benefits to written project plans:

- the model can be interpreted by a non-financial expert to make changes where necessary to components of the model and evaluate the impact of those changes;
- no third-party intervention is necessary until a well-developed plan has been constructed.

It does have certain limitations, however:

- how to determine the interest rate to use – as the late 1980s showed, just about anything can happen where this is concerned. In 4 years, interest rates have fluctuated by as much as 10 per cent;

- the process of forecasting cash flow years into the future involves a high degree of uncertainty;
- defining the **cash flows** – they are different from the data generally presented in a balance sheet – write-off values, for example, are treated very differently.

For many firms, this is an important area of intersection between the financial controllers, management accountants and project managers. In order for everyone to understand the process of financial evaluation of projects better, many organisations provide simple spreadsheet-based evaluation packages, available on intranets or online, that can be used by project managers for the purposes of doing initial financial evaluation to see if ideas are worth pursuing. Having such models readily available for people to try out ideas quickly and easily is one of the keys to innovation in both products and processes.

Determining cash flow figures for DCR and IRR calculations

In order to present the most accurate picture of the financial health or otherwise of the proposal the following rules should be applied:[4]

- cash flows, not profit figures, should be used;
- **sunk costs** (those already incurred) should be ignored;
- only **variable costs** arising directly from the project should be included (**fixed costs**, which would be incurred whether or not the project goes ahead, should be excluded);
- **opportunity costs** must be taken into account (developing one area of a business to the detriment of another).

Determining the discount rate

It is more usual for the project manager to have discount rates set as part of organisational policy. There are a number of methods for obtaining values for the discount rate – this one determines the risk adjusted discount rate (RADR).

There are three factors that determine the discount rate:

(a) = the rate charged for the use of the capital;
(b) = the rate due to inflation (so that the purchasing power is not reduced);
(c) = a premium factor due to the fact that the investor is taking a risk that the capital amount may never be repaid.

These are selected as follows:

$$(\text{overall rate}) = (1 + a)(1 + b)(1 + c)$$

Cash flow considerations

The rejection or deferral of a project proposal may have nothing to do with its intrinsic merit. The decision will be based on the availability or otherwise of the necessary cash in the context of an organisation that has to meet both its current liabilities and future investment requirements. A project is almost certain to be competing against others for scarce resources, and as the project manager will have to balance the trade-offs inherent in a project, so the project sponsor will have to balance the cost–benefit trade-offs of a number of proposals.

In large projects, the timing of payments may be critical for both the project organisation and its customers. For this reason it is necessary for both to know when expenditures are going to be made. In order to ease cash flow, projects may involve stage payments. This is common both in construction and large-scale engineering. While all the necessary credit checks can and should be carried out, it is still a matter of risk for both parties when large contracts are entered into.

12.3 Challenges for the perceived wisdom

So far, we have considered the relatively straightforward case, where there is a well-defined benefit for a well-defined investment. Reality is rarely so simple and while rational investment appraisal based on 'objective criteria' is often held up as an ideal, there are many instances where judgement as to the benefits of a project will have to be made on a qualitative basis. In particular, conventional approaches are problematic where:

- there is no guaranteed return;
- the benefit is made in terms of reduction of labour – some companies do not see this as being in line with their philosophy;
- the project is considered to be 'strategic' in nature;
- the organisation is in a not-for-profit sector – e.g. government or charity.

A good example of a *strategic investment* is in organisational change. Very often the justification will be made in terms of increased flexibility or capability of the organisation – both of which are very difficult to assign a monetary value to. Likewise, a new computer system may help speed the transfer of information and encourage an organisation to become more integrated, but will be challenged to show a cash return.

Some countries, particularly Germany and Japan, appear to set less demanding payback criteria where longer-term objectives are served by the investment. As Charles Handy commented:

> *'The Japanese put long-term growth above short- or even medium-term profits, indeed the profitability calculations hardly figure in some of their strategic decisions. To keep IBM at bay, Fujitsu won the computer contract for the water-distribution system of Hiroshima City with a bid of just one yen. The required rate of return for a 10-year R&D (research and development) project averages 8.7 per cent in Japan compared with 20.3 per cent in the US and 23.7 per cent in the UK. As a result, there is more investment in the future in Japan than in other countries.'*[5]

Also, some projects do have to have a 'leap of faith' attached to them – the founder of Kentucky Fried Chicken presented a proposal that was not attractive to hundreds of banks (over 600 said 'no'). There are many other pieces of business folklore that initially did not meet the conventional criteria. Indeed, as companies strive to find competitive advantage, conventional solutions are less likely to provide them. This is far more likely to be provided by those that challenge the limits of appraisal systems, though as the bursting of the dot-com bubble showed in the late 1990s, there is no getting around some business basics concerning expenditure and return.

When the organisation carrying out a project does not have the profit motive, assessing projects can be far more difficult. What is the financial benefit of a development project, for instance, which improves the quality of life of a group of people, or has an environmental benefit? How would you justify choosing a more expensive supplier because of their ethical stance despite making the project more expensive? Such questions are becoming more rather than less common for project managers, as the requirements of ethical and environmental policies produce considerable impacts for the context of their work.

Factoring for optimism bias

Another challenge for the organisation trying to assess the business case for a project is demonstrated by Flyvberg's work on **optimism bias**.[6] Headline findings from his work include the critique of project approval processes that:

> ***Understated costs + overstated benefits + understated environmental impact + overstated economic impact = project approval***

This is fairly condemning of the approach that has been outlined for assessing costs and benefits. Indeed, further work carried out for the UK Treasury[7] yielded the guidance shown in Table 12.2 for budget assessment of infrastructure projects.

Table 12.2 Recommended cost uplift for different project types

Category	*Types of projects*	*Applicable optimism bias uplifts*	
		50% percentile	*80% percentile*
Roads	Motorway trunk roads Local roads Bicycle facilities Pedestrian facilities Park and ride Bus lane schemes Guided buses on wheels	15%	32%
Rail	Metro Light rail Guided buses on tracks Conventional rail High-speed rail	40%	57%
Fixed links	Bridges Tunnels	23%	55%

Table 12.2 shows the levels of uplift (increase in the budget) of a project that would have to be added, for a given level of confidence. For instance, data collected from projects that have been completed shows that if the sponsor of a rail project wanted 50 per cent confidence in the budget being adhered to during the project, they would have to add 40 per cent to the original budget figure for that project. If it was a scheme costed at €200 million, then to have 50 per cent confidence that the budget would be achieved, an 'uplift' of 80 million would be required, making the project budget €280 million. 50 per cent is not usually a level of confidence that people are comfortable with, so figures are provided at the 80 per cent level, which is often seen to be the level at which people are more comfortable. From Table 12.2, that same €200 million project would need an uplift of 57 per cent, resulting in a 'real budget' of €314 million.

This demonstrates some key principles about business case analysis. Firstly, that experience shows that budgets are usually conservatively estimated. Secondly, that the results of the analysis will depend on the level of *risk* that the organisation is prepared to accept. Lastly, while there may be uplift on the cost side, a similarly critical approach should be taken to the benefits side.

Benefits realisation analysis

A study carried out by KPMG[8] demonstrated that of the projects it surveyed, 75 per cent had no business case; of those that did, 75 per cent did not meet the targets set out in the business case. Indeed, there is a real challenge in projects: the basis on which a business case will be assessed. When business cases for projects are aggregated (as should happen at a programme management level), the overall contribution of the projects being undertaken can be assessed. The case of Abbey in Chapter 3 included the statement from their commercial director that, when they first analysed their business back in 2001, the combined benefits claimed by their projects meant they were heading for 110 per cent of the retail mortgage market in the UK. Clearly simply adding together the benefits claimed by projects is not going to give the best overall picture – such projects rarely act in isolation, and are frequently subject to overstated benefits, as mentioned above.

The conclusion of this discussion of optimism bias in both costs and benefits should not necessarily be to dispense with the method of business case analysis altogether. The challenge for project managers and appraisers is to use the experience of similar projects to provide a critical approach to costs and benefits, and be aware of the levels of risk or uncertainty attached to either.

Summary

- For cost planning the issue here is to determine its importance, and through the iterative process outlined to come to some decisions as to the likely costs (and hence price and profit) on the project. This also determines the project viability. There are many techniques for cost estimation, although there is a 'wishful thinking' element to some estimates. Through the idea of cost build-up, all the elements are integrated and may become the budget against which your project will be assessed. Combined with the analysis of the benefits, starting qualitatively (as Chapter 14), and moving to a quantitative basis where possible, the business case can be developed. While there is an apparently rational process in operation here, there are considerable behavioural interventions in this process (e.g. optimism bias) that provide an added complication. Unless these are considered, they are likely to have a significant negative impact on the project as it progresses.

Key terms

- benefits realisation analysis
- business case
- capital equipment
- cash flows
- compound interest
- contingency
- cost planning process
- cost-plus
- discounted cash flow
- fixed/variable costs
- forecast
- indirect expenses
- internal rate of return
- learning curve
- materials
- net present/future value
- opportunity costs
- optimism bias
- overheads
- parametric estimating
- payback analysis
- proxies
- reimbursable pricing
- sunk costs
- synthetic estimation
- target costing
- time
- top-down and ground-up costing
- wishful thinking

Relevant areas of the Bodies of Knowledge

Table 12.3 Relevant area of the APM Body of Knowledge

Relevant section	*Title*	*Summary*
33	Budgeting and cost management	The role of the budget as the means by which a project is judged is outlined, along with some of the measures that are associated with the measuring conformance to this.

Table 12.4 Relevant areas of the PMI Body of Knowledge

Relevant section	*Title*	*Summary*
7.1	Project cost management – resource planning	Having determined the activities, how long they will take and other resource requirements, the resource planning stage pulls all this together prior to the start of cost estimating.
7.2	Project cost management – cost estimating	The inputs to the process include several elements not previously discussed – including estimating publications (containing cost rates for different tasks) and risks. Tools for estimating are identified, including *analogous estimating* (top-down) and use of computerised tools.

PROJECT MANAGEMENT IN PRACTICE
Justify IT!

IT investment

A report published in 2006 claimed that US and Canadian companies were spending 2 per cent of their turnover (median figure) on their IT provision. This is an increase from 1.7 per cent in the previous year.[9] Similarly, according to the UK's Department of Trade and Industry 2006 R&D scoreboard, spending on research and development in the UK rose to £19.2bn that year from around £17bn in 2005. One of the key growth areas is the software sector, which saw a 13 per cent increase in R&D spending. Other big growth areas include the aerospace and pharmaceutical industries. Some of the overall increase in spending is due to a number of companies revealing their R&D spending for the first time but a third of this increase is the result of a 4 per cent boost in spending from the UK's top 800 companies.[10]

Points for discussion

1. Identify the nature of the costs and benefits that might be derived from such significant investments in both IT and R&D.
2. What levels of risk might be attributed to both IT and R&D projects?
3. Given the potential for optimism bias in business case development, how might organisations respond to this?

Topics for discussion

1 Identify the different roles that cost, price and profit can play in determining project costs.

2 In costing proposals, discuss the differences between top-down and ground-up approaches.

3 Describe the major elements of cost in a proposal to:

(a) implement a new computer system for the administration of a college or university
(b) construct a new theme park
(c) introduce a new range of non-paracetamol headache tablets.

4 Identify the benefits and potential disadvantages of a budget system.

5 'Evans the Steam' has set up a new business and secured a contract to build 32 locomotives for mountain railways, which are being reopened as tourist attractions. The order is to be fulfilled in two batches of 16. The first locomotive takes 30 days to assemble with seven people working full time on it. The daily rate for a locomotive fitter is £80 and the overheads are estimated to be 50 per cent on top of the labour rate. Evans is confident that an 80 per cent learning curve is possible. The first batch has been priced with a labour estimate of £16 000 per locomotive and the last 16 with a labour cost of £10 000. Comment on the pricing of the labour content and show whether the rates per locomotive are sufficient to cover the likely actual costs.

6 Draw up a table of potential costing methods, and show where each might be appropriate, giving examples.

7 Evaluate, using discounting techniques, which option, lease or buy, is most financially beneficial in the scenario given in Table 12.5. You should consider the discount rate to be 10 per cent and the period of consideration to be five years.

Table 12.5

	Buy	*Lease*
Purchase/lease cost	£50 000	£10 000 per year
Annual operating cost	£4000 per year	£4000 per year
Maintenance cost	£2000 per year	Maintained by leasing co.
Salvage value at the end of five years	£20 000	not applicable

8 The purchase of new office furniture for a boardroom has caused conflict between two factions within a company. One faction argues that the company should buy modern furniture, which will cost £12 000, and can be scrapped (replaced with zero salvage costs) in six years' time. The other favours the purchase of antique furniture which costs £30 000, but can be sold for £30 000 in six years' time. The modern furniture will cost £500 in maintenance and the antique £1000. You have been asked to arbitrate the decision and resolve the conflict using financial methods (calculate the net present value of each scheme, using the company discount rate of 12 per cent).

9 Discuss the three main pricing strategies and indicate which one you feel provides the greatest benefits to customers and which to suppliers.

10 Holyrood (again). How did this project go so massively over its original budget? A cost over-run of 10 per cent, for instance, suggests that natural variation was present – it is not unreasonable. A cost over-run in excess of 900 per cent indicates some more fundamental issues with the whole costing process. Suggest where the process might have failed in this case given the material covered in this chapter.

Further information

Ashta, A. (2007) 'Behavioral Influences on the Calculation of Expectations in Project Appraisal', *The Icfai Journal of Behavioral Finance*, Vol. 4, No. 2, pp. 7–31.

Kahneman, D. and Lavallo, D. (2002) 'Timid Choices and Bold Forecasts: A Cognitive Perspectiveon Risk Taking' in Kahneman, D. and Tversky, A. (eds) (2002) *Choices, Values, and Frames*, Cambridge University Press, Cambridge, pp. 393–413.

Lovallo, D. and Kahneman, D. (2003) 'Delusions of Success – How Optimism Undermines Executives' Decisions', *Harvard Business Review*, July, pp. 56–63.

Lin, C. and Pervan, G. (2003) 'The Practice of IS/IT Benefits Management in Large Australian Organisations', *Information and Management*, Vol. 41, No. 1, pp. 13–24.

Mishan, E.J. and Quah, E. (2007) *Cost Benefit Analysis*, 5th edition, Routledge, Oxford.

Monden, Y. (1992) *Cost Management in the New Manufacturing Age*, Productivity Press, New York.

Ward, J. and Daniel, E. (2005) *Benefits Management: Delivering Value From IS & IT Investments*, Wiley, Chichester.

Websites

www.maxwideman.com/pmglossary/PMG_C11.htm – useful glossary of project cost management terms; wider in scope than this chapter.

www.lacity.org/pm/methodology/chapter11.doc – city of Los Angeles project cost process.

www.nehta.gov.au/component/option,com_docman/task,doc_view/gid,72/Itemid,139/ – statement of policy on how cost:benefit analysis is applied in ecommerce projects in the Australian Health Service.

http://flyvbjerg.plan.aau.dk/0406DfT-UK%20OptBiasASPUBL.pdf – report to UK government on optimism bias.

References

1 www.scottish.parliament.uk/nmCentre/news/news-comm-00/cau00-018.htm.
2 Brooks, F.P. (1995) *The Mythical Man-Month*, Addison Wesley Longman, Boston, MA.
3 Verzuh, E. (2003) *The Portable MBA in Project Management*, Wiley, Chichester.
4 Hogg, N. (1994) *Business Forecasting Using Financial Models*, Financial Times Pitman Publishing, London.
5 Handy, C. (1994) *The Empty Raincoat*, Hutchinson, London.
6 Flyvberg, B., Bruzelius, N. and Rothengatter, W. (2003) *Megaprojects and Risk: An Anatomy of Ambition*, Cambridge University Press, Cambridge.
7 www.hm-treasury.gov.uk/media/376/3A/Optimism%20Bias_Guidance%20Document_june04.pdf.
8 KPMG 2002.
9 17th Annual Computer Economics IT Spending and Staffing Study – www.computereconomics.com.
10 www.silicon.com/cxoextra/0,3800005416,39163695,00.htm.

APPENDIX
Present value of £1

Year	Discount rate												
	1%	*2%*	*3%*	*4%*	*5%*	*6%*	*7%*	*8%*	*9%*	*10%*	*12%*	*14%*	*15%*
1	0.990	0.980	0.971	0.962	0.952	0.943	0.935	0.926	0.917	0.909	0.893	0.877	0.870
2	0.980	0.961	0.943	0.925	0.907	0.890	0.873	0.857	0.842	0.826	0.797	0.769	0.756
3	0.971	0.942	0.915	0.889	0.864	0.840	0.816	0.794	0.772	0.751	0.712	0.675	0.658
4	0.961	0.924	0.889	0.855	0.823	0.792	0.763	0.735	0.708	0.683	0.636	0.592	0.572
5	0.951	0.906	0.863	0.822	0.784	0.747	0.713	0.681	0.650	0.621	0.567	0.519	0.497
6	0.942	0.888	0.838	0.790	0.746	0.705	0.666	0.630	0.596	0.564	0.507	0.456	0.432
7	0.933	0.871	0.813	0.760	0.711	0.665	0.623	0.583	0.547	0.513	0.452	0.400	0.376
8	0.923	0.853	0.789	0.731	0.677	0.627	0.582	0.540	0.502	0.467	0.404	0.351	0.327
9	0.914	0.837	0.766	0.703	0.645	0.592	0.544	0.500	0.460	0.424	0.361	0.308	0.284
10	0.905	0.820	0.744	0.676	0.614	0.558	0.508	0.463	0.422	0.386	0.322	0.270	0.247
11	0.896	0.804	0.722	0.650	0.585	0.527	0.475	0.429	0.388	0.350	0.287	0.237	0.215
12	0.887	0.788	0.701	0.625	0.557	0.497	0.444	0.397	0.356	0.319	0.257	0.208	0.187
13	0.879	0.773	0.681	0.601	0.530	0.469	0.415	0.368	0.326	0.290	0.229	0.182	0.163
14	0.870	0.758	0.661	0.577	0.505	0.442	0.388	0.340	0.299	0.263	0.205	0.160	0.141
15	0.861	0.743	0.642	0.555	0.481	0.417	0.362	0.315	0.275	0.239	0.183	0.140	0.123
16	0.853	0.728	0.623	0.534	0.458	0.394	0.339	0.292	0.252	0.218	0.163	0.123	0.107
17	0.844	0.714	0.605	0.513	0.436	0.371	0.317	0.270	0.231	0.198	0.146	0.108	0.093
18	0.836	0.700	0.587	0.494	0.416	0.350	0.296	0.250	0.212	0.180	0.130	0.095	0.081
19	0.828	0.686	0.570	0.475	0.396	0.331	0.276	0.232	0.194	0.164	0.116	0.083	0.070
20	0.820	0.673	0.554	0.456	0.377	0.312	0.258	0.215	0.178	0.149	0.104	0.073	0.061
25	0.780	0.610	0.478	0.375	0.295	0.233	0.184	0.146	0.116	0.092	0.059	0.038	0.030
30	0.742	0.552	0.412	0.308	0.231	0.174	0.131	0.099	0.075	0.057	0.033	0.020	0.015

Year	Discount rate												
	16%	18%	20%	24%	28%	32%	36%	40%	50%	60%	70%	80%	90%
1	0.862	0.847	0.833	0.806	0.781	0.758	0.735	0.714	0.667	0.625	0.588	0.556	0.526
2	0.743	0.718	0.694	0.650	0.610	0.574	0.541	0.510	0.444	0.391	0.346	0.309	0.277
3	0.641	0.609	0.579	0.524	0.477	0.435	0.398	0.364	0.296	0.244	0.204	0.171	0.146
4	0.552	0.516	0.482	0.423	0.373	0.329	0.292	0.260	0.198	0.153	0.120	0.095	0.077
5	0.476	0.437	0.402	0.341	0.291	0.250	0.215	0.186	0.132	0.095	0.070	0.053	0.040
6	0.410	0.370	0.335	0.275	0.227	0.189	0.158	0.133	0.088	0.060	0.041	0.029	0.021
7	0.354	0.314	0.279	0.222	0.178	0.143	0.116	0.095	0.059	0.037	0.024	0.016	0.011
8	0.305	0.266	0.233	0.179	0.139	0.108	0.085	0.068	0.039	0.023	0.014	0.009	0.006
9	0.263	0.226	0.194	0.144	0.108	0.082	0.063	0.048	0.026	0.015	0.008	0.005	0.003
10	0.227	0.191	0.162	0.116	0.085	0.062	0.046	0.035	0.017	0.009	0.005	0.003	0.002
11	0.195	0.162	0.135	0.094	0.066	0.047	0.034	0.025	0.012	0.006	0.003	0.002	0.001
12	0.168	0.137	0.112	0.076	0.052	0.036	0.025	0.018	0.008	0.004	0.002	0.001	0.001
13	0.145	0.116	0.093	0.061	0.040	0.027	0.018	0.013	0.005	0.002	0.001	0.001	0.000
14	0.125	0.099	0.078	0.049	0.032	0.021	0.014	0.009	0.003	0.001	0.001	0.000	0.000
15	0.108	0.084	0.065	0.040	0.025	0.016	0.010	0.006	0.002	0.001	0.000	0.000	0.000
16	0.093	0.071	0.054	0.032	0.019	0.012	0.007	0.005	0.002	0.001	0.000	0.000	
17	0.080	0.060	0.045	0.026	0.015	0.009	0.005	0.003	0.001	0.000	0.000		
18	0.069	0.051	0.038	0.021	0.012	0.007	0.004	0.002	0.001	0.000	0.000		
19	0.060	0.043	0.031	0.017	0.009	0.005	0.003	0.002	0.000	0.000			
20	0.051	0.037	0.026	0.014	0.007	0.004	0.002	0.001	0.000	0.000			
25	0.024	0.016	0.010	0.005	0.002	0.001	0.000	0.000					
30	0.012	0.007	0.004	0.002	0.001	0.000	0.000						

Project Selection and Portfolio Management

Chapter Outline

Chapter Objectives

After completing this chapter, you should be able to:

1. Explain six criteria for a useful project selection/screening model.
2. Understand how to employ checklists and simple scoring models to select projects.
3. Use more sophisticated scoring models, such as the Analytical Hierarchy Process.
4. Learn how to use financial concepts, such as the efficient frontier and risk/return models.
5. Employ financial analyses and options analysis to evaluate the potential for new project investments.
6. Recognize the challenges that arise in maintaining an optimal project portfolio for an organization.
7. Understand the three keys to successful project portfolio management.

PROJECT MANAGEMENT BODY OF KNOWLEDGE CORE CONCEPTS COVERED IN THIS CHAPTER

1. Portfolio Management (PMBoK sec. 1.4.2)

PROJECT PROFILE

Project Selection Procedures: A Cross-Industry Sampler

The art and science of selecting projects is one that organizations take extremely seriously. Firms in a variety of industries have developed highly sophisticated methods for project screening and selection to ensure that the projects they choose to fund offer the best promise of success. As part of this screening process, organizations often evolve their own particular methods, based on technical concerns, available data, and corporate culture and preferences. The following list gives you a sense of the lengths to which some organizations go with project selection:

- Hoechst AG, a pharmaceutical firm, uses a scoring portfolio model with 19 questions in five major categories when rating project opportunities. The five categories include probability of technical success, probability of commercial success, reward to the company, business strategy fit, and strategic leverage (ability of the project to employ and elevate company resources and skills). Within each of these factors are a number of specific questions, which are scored on a 1 to 10 scale by management.
- At German industrial giant Siemens, every business unit in each of the 190 countries in which the company operates uses a system entitled "PM@Siemens" for categorizing projects that employs a two-digit code. Each project is awarded a letter from A to F, indicating its significance to the company, and a number from 0 to 3, indicating its overall risk level. Larger or riskier projects (e.g., an "A0") require approval from Siemens's main board in Germany, but many of the lesser projects (e.g., an "F3") can be approved by local business units. Too many A0s in the portfolio can indicate mounting risks while too many F3 projects may signal a lack of economic value overall.
- The Royal Bank of Canada has developed a scoring model to rate its project opportunities. The criteria for the portfolio scoring include project importance (strategic importance, magnitude of impact, and economic benefits) and ease of doing (cost of development, project complexity, and resource availability). Expected annual expenditure and total project spending are then added to this rank-ordered list to prioritize the project options. Decision rules are used (e.g., projects of low importance that are difficult to execute get a "no-go" rating).
- The Weyerhaeuser corporate research and development (R&D) program has put processes in place to align and prioritize R&D projects. The program has three types of activities: technology assessment (changes in external environment and impact to the company), research (building knowledge bases and competencies in core technical areas), and development (development of specific commercial opportunities). Four key inputs are considered when establishing priorities: significant changes in the external environment; long-term future needs of lead customers; business strategies, priorities, and technology needs; and corporate strategic direction.
- Mobil Chemical uses six categories of projects to determine the right balance of projects that will enter its portfolio: (1) cost reductions and process improvements; (2) product improvements, product modifications, and customer satisfaction; (3) new products; (4) new platform projects and fundamental/breakthrough research projects; (5) plant support; and (6) technical support for customers. Senior management reviews all project proposals and determines the division of capital funding across these six project types. One of the key decision variables involves a comparison of "what is" with "what should be."
- The Texas Department of Transportation identifies several criteria in its project selection process. Infrastructure and building projects are selected by the Texas Transportation Commission based on the following criteria: safety, maintenance and preservation of the existing system, congestion relief, access and mobility, economic vitality, efficient system management and operations, and any additional transportation goals identified in the statewide long-range transportation plans. These projects must adhere to all department design standards as well as applicable state and federal law and regulations.[1]
- At 3M's Traffic Control Materials Division, during project screening and selection, management uses a project viability chart to score project alternatives. As part of the profile and scoring exercise, personnel must address how the project accomplishes strategic project objectives and critical business issues affecting a specific group within the target market. Projected project return on investment is always counterbalanced with riskiness of the project option.
- Exxon Chemical's management begins evaluating all new project proposals in light of the business unit's strategy and strategic priorities. Target spending is decided according to the overall project mix portfolio. As the year progresses, all projects are reprioritized using a scoring model. As significant differences between projected and actual spending are uncovered, the top management group makes adjustments for the next year's portfolio.[2]

INTRODUCTION

All organizations select projects they decide to pursue from among numerous opportunities. What criteria determine which projects should be supported? Obviously, this is no simple decision. The consequences of poor decisions can be enormously expensive. Recent research suggests that in the realm of information technology (IT), companies squander nearly $100 billion a year on projects that are created but never used by their intended clients. How do we make the most reasonable choices in selecting projects? What kind of information should we collect? Should decisions be based strictly on financial analysis, or should other criteria be considered? In this chapter, we will try to answer such questions as we take a closer look at the process of project selection.

We will examine a number of different approaches for evaluating and selecting potential projects. The various methods for project selection run along a continuum from highly qualitative, or judgment-based approaches to those that rely on quantitative analysis. Of course, each approach has its benefits and drawbacks, which must be considered in turn.

We will also discuss a number of issues related to the management of a **project portfolio**—the set of projects that an organization is considering/undertaking at any given time. For example, Rubbermaid, Inc., routinely undertakes hundreds of new product development projects simultaneously, always searching for opportunities with strong commercial prospects. When a firm is pursuing multiple projects, the challenges of strategic decision making, resource management, scheduling, and operational control are magnified.

12.4 PROJECT SELECTION

Firms are literally bombarded with opportunities, but no organization enjoys infinite resources with which to pursue every opportunity that presents itself. Choices must be made, and to best ensure that they select the most viable projects, many managers develop priority systems—guidelines for balancing the opportunities and costs entailed by each alternative. The goal is to balance the competing demands of time and advantage.[3] The pressures of time and money affect most major decisions, and decisions are usually more successful when they are made in a timely and efficient manner. For example, if your firm's sales department recognizes a commercial opportunity it can exploit, you need to generate alternative approaches to the project quickly to capitalize on the prospect. Time wasted is generally opportunity lost. On the other hand, you need to be careful: You want to be sure that, at least as far as possible, you are making the best choice among your options. Thus organizational decision makers develop guidelines—*selection models*—that permit them to save time and money while maximizing the likelihood of success.

A number of decision models are available to managers responsible for evaluating and selecting potential projects. As you will see, they run the gamut from qualitative to quantitative and simple to complex. All firms, however, try to develop a screening model (or set of models) that will allow them to make the best choices among alternatives within the usual constraints of time and money.

Suppose you were interested in developing a model that allowed you to effectively screen project alternatives. How might you ensure that the model was capable of picking potential "winners" from the large set of possible project choices? After much consideration, you decide to narrow the focus for your screening model and create one that will allow you to select only projects that have high potential payoffs. All other issues are ignored in favor of the sole criterion of commercial profitability. The question is: Would such a screening model be useful? Souder[4] identifies five important issues that managers should consider when evaluating screening models:

1. ***Realism:*** An effective model must reflect organizational objectives, including a firm's strategic goals and mission. Criteria must also be reasonable in light of such constraints on resources as money and personnel. Finally, the model must take into account both commercial risks and technical risks, including performance, cost, and time. That is: Will the project work as intended? Can we keep to the original budget or is there a high potential for escalating costs? Is there a strong risk of significant schedule slippage?
2. ***Capability:*** A model should be flexible enough to respond to changes in the conditions under which projects are carried out. For example, the model should allow the company to compare different types of projects (long-term versus short-term projects, projects of different technologies or capabilities, projects with different commercial objectives). It should be

robust enough to accommodate new criteria and constraints, suggesting that the screening model must allow the company to use it as widely as possible in order to cover the greatest possible range of project types.

3. *Flexibility:* The model should be easily modified if trial applications require changes. It must, for example, allow for adjustments due to changes in exchange rates, tax laws, building codes, and so forth.
4. *Ease of use:* A model must be simple enough to be used by people in all areas of the organization, both those in specific project roles and those in related functional positions. Further, the screening model that is applied, the choices made for project selection, and the reasons for those choices should be clear and easily understood by organizational members. The model should also be timely: It should generate the screening information rapidly, and people should be able to assimilate that information without any special training or skills.
5. *Cost:* The screening model should be cost-effective. A selection approach that is expensive to use in terms of either time or money is likely to have the worst possible effect: causing organizational members to avoid using it because of the excessive cost of employing it. The cost of obtaining selection information and generating optimal results should be low enough to encourage use of the models rather than diminish their applicability.

Let's add a sixth criterion for a successful selection model:

6. *Comparability:* The model must be broad enough to be applied to multiple projects. If a model is too narrowly focused, it may be useless in comparing potential projects or foster biases toward some over others. A useful model must support general comparisons of project alternatives.

Project selection models come in two general classes: numeric and nonnumeric.[5] **Numeric models** seek to use numbers as inputs for the decision process involved in selecting projects. These values can be derived either objectively or subjectively; that is, we may employ objective, external values ("The bridge's construction will require 800 cubic yards of cement") or subjective, internal values ("We will need to hire two code checkers to finish the software development within eight weeks"). Neither of these two input alternatives is necessarily wrong: An expert's opinion on an issue may be subjective but very accurate. On the other hand, an incorrectly calibrated surveyor's level can give objective but wrong data. The key is to remember that most selection processes for project screening involve a combination of subjective and objective data assessment and decision making. **Nonnumeric models**, on the other hand, do not employ numbers as decision inputs, relying instead on other data.

Companies spend great amounts of time and effort trying to make the best project selection decisions possible. These decisions are typically made with regard for the overall objectives that the company's senior management staff have developed and promoted based on their strategic plan. Such objectives can be quite complex and may reflect a number of external factors that can affect a firm's operations. For example, suppose the new head of Sylvania's Lighting Division mandated that the strategic objective of the organization was to be sales growth at all costs. Any new project opportunity would be evaluated against this key strategic imperative. Thus, a project offering the potential for opening new markets might be viewed more favorably than a competing project promising a higher potential rate of return.

The list of factors that can be considered when evaluating project alternatives is enormous. Table 12.6 provides only a partial list of the various elements that a company must address, organized into the general categories of risk and commercial factors, internal operating issues, and other factors. Although such a list can be long, in reality the strategic direction emphasized by top management often highlights certain criteria over others. In fact, if we apply Pareto's 80/20 principle, which states that a few issues (20%) are vital and many (80%) are trivial, it may be fairly argued that, for many projects, less than 20% of all possible decision criteria account for over 80% of the decision about whether to pursue the project.

This being said, we should reflect on two final points regarding the use of any decision-making approach to project selection. First, the most complete model in the world is still only a partial reflection of organizational reality. The potential list of inputs into any project selection decision is literally limitless—so much so, in fact, that we must recognize this truth before exploring project selection lest we erroneously assume that it is possible, given enough time and effort, to identify all relevant issues that play a role. Second, embedded in every decision model are both

TABLE 12.6 Issues in Project Screening and Selection

1. Risk—Factors that reflect elements of unpredictability to the firm, including:
   a. Technical risk—risks due to the development of new or untested technologies
   b. Financial risk—risks from the financial exposure caused by investing in the project
   c. Safety risk—risks to the well-being of users or developers of the project
   d. Quality risk—risks to the firm's goodwill or reputation due to the quality of the completed project
   e. Legal exposure—potential for lawsuits or legal obligation
2. Commercial—Factors that reflect the market potential of the project, including:
   a. Expected return on investment
   b. Payback period
   c. Potential market share
   d. Long-term market dominance
   e. Initial cash outlay
   f. Ability to generate future business/new markets
3. Internal operating issues—Factors that have an impact on internal operations of the firm, including:
   a. Need to develop/train employees
   b. Change in workforce size or composition
   c. Change in physical environment
   d. Change in manufacturing or service operations resulting from the project
4. Additional factors, including:
   a. Patent protection
   b. Impact on company's image
   c. Strategic fit

objective and subjective factors. We may form opinions based on objective data; we also may derive complex decision models from subjective inputs. Acknowledging that there exists a place for both subjective and objective inputs and decisions in any useful screening model is worthwhile.

12.5 APPROACHES TO PROJECT SCREENING AND SELECTION

A **project screening model** that generates useful information for project choices in a timely and useful fashion at an acceptable cost can serve as a valuable tool in helping an organization make optimal choices among numerous alternatives.[6] With these criteria in mind, let's consider some of the more common project selection techniques.

Method One: Checklist Model

The simplest method of project screening and selection is developing a **checklist**, or a list of criteria that pertain to our choice of projects, and then applying them to different possible projects. Let's say, for example, that in our company, the key selection criteria are cost and speed to market. Because of our strategic competitive model and the industry we are in, we favor low-cost projects that can be brought to the marketplace within one year. We would screen each possible project against these two criteria and select the project that best satisfies them. But depending on the type and size of our possible projects, we may have to consider literally dozens of relevant criteria. In deciding among several new product development opportunities, a firm must weigh a variety of issues, including the following:

- *Cost of development:* What is a reasonable cost estimate?
- *Potential return on investment:* What kind of return can we expect? What is the likely payback period?
- *Riskiness of the new venture:* Does the project entail the need to create new-generation technology? How risky is the venture in terms of achieving our anticipated specifications?
- *Stability of the development process:* Are both the parent organization and the project team stable? Can we expect this project to face funding cuts or the loss of key personnel, including senior management sponsors?
- *Governmental or stakeholder interference:* Is the project subject to levels of governmental oversight that could potentially interfere with its development? Might other stakeholders

oppose the project and attempt to block completion? For example, environmental groups, one of the "intervenor" stakeholders, have a long history of opposing natural resource development projects and may work in opposition to our project objectives.[7]

- ***Product durability and future market potential:*** Is this project a one-shot opportunity, or could it be the forerunner of future opportunities? A software development firm may, for example, develop an application for a client in hopes that successful performance on this project will lead to future business. On the other hand, the project may be simply a one-time opportunity with little potential for future work with the customer.

This is just a partial list of criteria that may be relevant when we are selecting among project alternatives. A checklist approach to the evaluation of project opportunities is a fairly simple device for recording opinions and encouraging discussion. Thus, checklists may be best used in a consensus-group setting, as a method for initiating conversation, stimulating discussion and the exchange of opinions, and highlighting the group's priorities.

EXAMPLE 12.1 Checklist

Let's assume that SAP Corporation, a leader in the business applications software industry, is interested in developing a new application package for inventory management and shipping control. It is trying to decide which project to select from a set of four potential alternatives. Based on past commercial experiences, the company feels that the most important selection criteria for its choice are *cost, profit potential, time to market,* and *development risks.* Table 12.7 shows a simple checklist model with only four project choices and the four decision criteria. In addition to developing the decision criteria, we create evaluative descriptors that reflect how well the project alternatives correspond to our key selection criteria. We evaluate each criterion (which is rated *high, medium,* or *low*) in order to see which project accumulates the highest checks—and thus may be regarded as the optimal choice.

SOLUTION

Based on this analysis, Project Gamma is the best alternative in terms of maximizing our key criteria—cost, profit potential, time to market, and development risks.

TABLE 12.7 Simplified Checklist Model for Project Selection

		Performance on Criteria		
Project	**Criteria**	**High**	**Medium**	**Low**
Project Alpha	Cost	X		
	Profit potential			X
	Time to market		X	
	Development risks			X
Project Beta	Cost		X	
	Profit potential		X	
	Time to market	X		
	Development risks		X	
Project Gamma	Cost	X		
	Profit potential	X		
	Time to market			X
	Development risks	X		
Project Delta	Cost			X
	Profit potential			X
	Time to market	X		
	Development risks		X	

The flaws in a model such as that shown in Table 12.7 include the subjective nature of the *high, medium,* and *low* ratings. These terms are inexact and subject to misinterpretation or misunderstanding. Checklist screening models also fail to resolve trade-off issues. What if our criteria are *differentially weighted*—that is, what if some criteria are more important than others? How will relative, or weighted, importance affect our final decision? Let's say, for instance, that we regard time to market as our paramount criterion. Is Project Gamma, which is rated low on this criterion, still "better" than Project Beta or Delta, both of which are rated high on time to market though lower on other, less important criteria? Are we willing to make a trade-off, accepting low time to market in order to get the highest benefits in cost, profit potential, and development risks?

Because the simple checklist model does not deal satisfactorily with such questions, let's turn next to a more complex screening model in which we distinguish more important from less important criteria by assigning each criterion a simple *weight.*

Method Two: Simplified Scoring Models

In the **simplified scoring model**, each criterion is ranked according to its relative importance. Our choice of projects will thus reflect our desire to maximize the impact of certain criteria on our decision. In order to score our simplified checklist, we assign a specific weight to each of our four criteria:

Criterion	Importance Weight
Time to market	3
Profit potential	2
Development risks	2
Cost	1

Now let's reconsider the decision that we made using the basic checklist approach illustrated in Table 12.7.

EXAMPLE 12.2 Scoring Models

SAP Corporation is attempting to determine the optimal project to fund using the criterion weighting values we developed above. As you can see in Table 12.8, although adding a scoring component to our simple checklist complicates our decision, it also gives us a more precise screening model—one that more closely reflects our desire to emphasize certain criteria over others.

SOLUTION

In Table 12.8, the numbers in the column labeled *Importance Weight* specify the numerical values that we have assigned to each criterion: *Time to market* always receives a value of *3*, *profit potential* a value of *2*, *development risk* a value of *2*, and *cost* a value of *1*. We then assign relative values to each of our four dimensions.

The numbers in the column labeled *Score* replace the Xs of Table 12.7 with their assigned score values:

High = *3*
Medium = *2*
Low = *1*

In Project Alpha, for example, the *High* rating given *Cost* becomes a *3* in Table 12.8 because *High* is here valued at *3*. Likewise, the *Medium* rating given *Time to market* in Table 12.7 becomes a *2*. But notice what happens when we calculate the numbers in the column labeled *Weighted Score*. When we multiply the numerical value of *Cost* (*1*) by its rating of *High* (*3*), we get a *Weighted Score* of *3*. But when we multiply the numerical value of *Time to market* (*3*) by its rating of *Medium* (*2*), we get a *Weighted Score* of *6*. Once we add the numbers in the *Weighted Score* column for each project in Table 12.8 and examine the totals, Project Beta (with a total score of *19*) is the best alternative, compared to the other options: Project Alpha (with a total score of *13*), Project Gamma (with a total score of *18*), and Project Delta (with a total score of *16*).

TABLE 12.8 Simple Scoring Model

		(A)	(B)	(A) × (B)
Project	**Criteria**	**Importance Weight**	**Score**	**Weighted Score**
Project Alpha				
	Cost	1	3	3
	Profit potential	2	1	2
	Development risk	2	1	2
	Time to market	3	2	6
	Total Score			**13**
Project Beta				
	Cost	1	2	2
	Profit potential	2	2	4
	Development risk	2	2	4
	Time to market	3	3	9
	Total Score			**19**
Project Gamma				
	Cost	1	3	3
	Profit potential	2	3	6
	Development risk	2	3	6
	Time to market	3	1	3
	Total Score			**18**
Project Delta				
	Cost	1	1	1
	Profit potential	2	1	2
	Development risk	2	2	4
	Time to market	3	3	9
	Total Score			**16**

Thus, the simple scoring model consists of the following steps:

- ***Assign importance weights to each criterion:*** The first step is to develop logic for differentiating among various levels of importance and to devise a system for assigning appropriate weights to each criterion. Relying on collective group judgment may help to validate the reasons for determining importance levels. The team may also designate some criteria as "must" items. Safety concerns, for example, may be stipulated as nonnegotiable. In other words, all projects must achieve an acceptable safety level or they will not be considered further.
- ***Assign score values to each criterion in terms of its rating (High = 3, Medium = 2, Low = 1):*** The logic of assigning score values is often an issue of scoring sensitivity—of making differences in scores distinct. Some teams, for example, prefer to widen the range of possible values—say, by using a 1-to-7 scale instead of a 1-to-3 scale—in order to ensure a clearer distinction among scores and, therefore, among project choices. Such decisions will vary according to the number of criteria being applied and, perhaps, the team members' experience with the accuracy of outcomes produced by a given approach to screening and selection.
- ***Multiply importance weights by scores to arrive at a weighted score for each criterion:*** The weighted score reflects both the value that the team assigns to each criterion and the ratings that the team gives each criterion for the project.
- ***Add the weighted scores to arrive at an overall project score:*** The final score for each project represents the sum of all its weighted criteria.

The pharmaceutical company Hoechst Marion Roussel uses a scoring model for selecting projects that identifies not only five main criteria—reward, business strategy fit, strategic leverage, probability of commercial success, and probability of technical success—but also a number of more specific subcriteria. Each of these 19 subcriteria is scored on a scale of 1 to 10. The score for each criterion is then calculated by averaging the scores for each criterion. The final project score is determined by adding the average score of each of the five subcategories. Hoechst has had great success with this scoring model, both in setting project priorities and in making go/no-go decisions.[8]

The simple scoring model has some useful advantages as a project selection device. First, it is easy to use in tying critical strategic goals for the company to various project alternatives. In the case of the pharmaceutical company Hoechst, the company has assigned several categories to strategic goals for its project options, including *business strategy fit* and *strategic leverage*. These strategic goals become a critical hurdle for all new project alternatives. Second, the simple scoring model is easy to comprehend and use. With a checklist of key criteria, evaluation options (high, medium, and low), and attendant scores, top managers can quickly grasp how to employ this technique.

Limitations of Scoring Models

The simple scoring model illustrated here is an abbreviated and unsophisticated version of the weighted-scoring approach. In general, scoring models try to impose some structure on the decision-making process while, at the same time, combining multiple criteria.

Most scoring models, however, share some important limitations. A scale from 1 to 3 may be intuitively appealing and easy to apply and understand, but it is not very accurate. From the perspective of mathematical scaling, it is simply wrong to treat evaluations on such a scale as real numbers that can be multiplied and summed. If *3* means *High* and *2* means *Medium*, we know that *3* is better than *2*, but we do not know by how much. Furthermore, we cannot assume that the difference between *3* and *2* is the same as the difference between *2* and *1*. Thus, in Table 12.8, if the score for Project Alpha is *13* and the score for Project Beta is *19*, may we assume that Beta is 46% better than Alpha? Unfortunately, no. Critics of scoring models argue that their ease of use may blind novice users to the false assumptions that sometimes underlie them.

From a managerial perspective, another drawback of scoring models is the fact that they depend on the relevance of the selected criteria and the accuracy of the weight given them. In other words, they do not ensure that there is a reasonable link between the selected and weighted criteria and the business objectives that prompted the project in the first place.

For example As a means of selecting projects, the Information Systems steering committee of a large bank has adopted three criteria: *contribution to quality*, *financial performance*, and *service*. The bank's strategy is focused on customer retention, but the criteria selected by the committee do not reflect this fact. As a result, a project aimed at improving service to potential *new* markets might score high on *service* even though it would not serve *existing* customers (the people whose business the bank wants to retain). Note, too, that the criteria of *quality* and *service* may overlap, leading managers to double-count and overestimate the value of some factors.[9] Thus, the bank has employed a project selection approach that neither achieves its desired ends nor matches its overall strategic goals.

Method Three: The Analytical Hierarchy Process

The **Analytical Hierarchy Process (AHP)** was developed by Dr. Thomas Saaty[10] to address many of the technical and managerial problems frequently associated with decision making through scoring models. An increasingly popular method for effective project selection, the AHP is a four-step process.

STRUCTURING THE HIERARCHY OF CRITERIA The first step consists of constructing a hierarchy of criteria and subcriteria. Let's assume, for example, that a firm's IT steering committee has selected three criteria for evaluating project alternatives: (1) *financial benefits*, (2) *contribution to strategy*, and (3) *contribution to IT infrastructure*. The *financial benefits* criterion, which focuses on the tangible benefits of the project, is further subdivided into long-term and short-term benefits. *Contribution to strategy*, an intangible factor, is subdivided into three subcriteria: (a) *increasing market share for product X*, (b) *retaining existing customers for product Y*, and (c) *improving cost management*.

TABLE 12.9 Hierarchy of Selection Criteria Choices

First Level	Second Level
1. Financial benefits	1A: Short-term
	1B: Long-term
2. Contribution to strategy	2A: Increasing market share for product X;
	2B: Retaining existing customers for product Y;
	2C: Improving cost management
3. Contribution to IT infrastructure	

Table 12.9 is a representational breakdown of all these criteria. Note that subdividing relevant criteria into a meaningful hierarchy gives managers a rational method for sorting among and ordering priorities. Higher-order challenges, such as *contribution to strategy,* can be broken down into discrete sets of supporting requirements, including *market share, customer retention,* and *cost management,* thus building a hierarchy of alternatives that simplifies matters. Because the hierarchy can reflect the structure of organizational strategy and critical success factors, it also provides a way to select and justify projects according to their consistency with business objectives.[11] This illustrates how we can use meaningful strategic issues and critical factors to establish logic for both the types of selection criteria and their relative weighting.

Recently, a large U.S. company used the AHP to rank more than a hundred project proposals worth millions of dollars. Because the first step in using the AHP is to establish clear criteria for selection, 10 managers from assorted disciplines, including finance, marketing, management information systems, and operations, spent a full day establishing the hierarchy of criteria. Their challenge was to determine the key success criteria that should be used to guide project selection, particularly as these diverse criteria related to each other (relative weighting). They found that, in addition to clearly defining and developing the criteria for evaluating projects, the process also produced a more coherent and unified vision of organizational strategy.

ALLOCATING WEIGHTS TO CRITERIA The second step in applying AHP consists of allocating weights to previously developed criteria and, where necessary, splitting overall criterion weight among subcriteria. Mian and Dai[12] and others have recommended the so-called **pairwise comparison approach** to weighting, in which every criterion is compared with every other criterion. This procedure, argue the researchers, permits more accurate weighting because it allows managers to focus on a series of relatively simple exchanges—namely, two criteria at a time.

The simplified hierarchy in Figure 12.8 shows the breakdown of criterion weights across the same three major criteria that we used in Table 12.9. As Figure 12.8 shows, *Finance* (that is, *financial benefits*) received a weighting value of 52%, which was split between *Short-term benefits* (30%) and *Long-term benefits* (70%). This configuration means that *long-term financial benefits* receives an overall weighting of $(0.52) \times (0.7) = 36.4\%$.

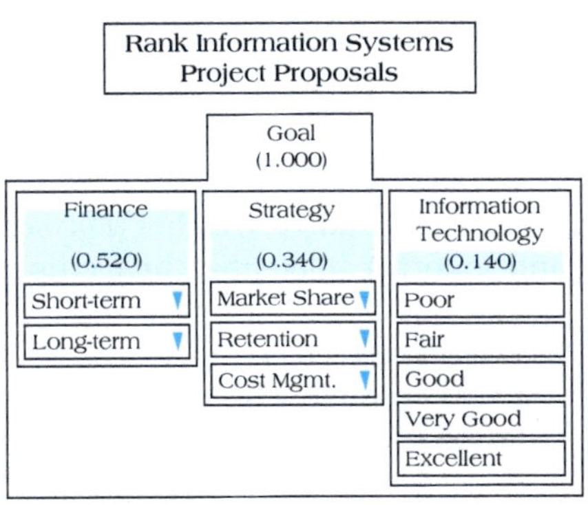

FIGURE 12.8 Sample AHP with Rankings for Salient Selection Criteria

Source: J. K. Pinto and I. Millet. (1999). *Successful Information System Implementation: The Human Side,* 2nd ed., figure on page 76. Newtown Square, PA: Project Management Institute. Copyright and all rights reserved. Material from this publication has been reproduced with the permission of PMI.

	Nominal	Priority	Bar Graph
Poor	0.00000	0.000	
Fair	0.10000	0.050	
Good	0.30000	0.150	
Very Good	0.60000	0.300	
Excellent	1.00000	0.500	
Total	2.00000	1.000	

FIGURE 12.9 Assigning Numerical Values to Labels

Source: J. K. Pinto and I. Millet. (1999). *Successful Information System Implementation: The Human Side,* 2nd ed., figure on page 77. Newtown Square, PA: Project Management Institute. Copyright and all rights reserved. Material from this publication has been reproduced with the permission of PMI.

The hierarchical allocation of criteria and splitting of weights resolves the problem of double counting in scoring models. In those models, criteria such as *service, quality,* and *customer satisfaction* may be either separate or overlapping factors, depending on the objectives of the organization. As a result, too little or too much weight may be assigned to a given criterion. With AHP, however, these factors are grouped as subcriteria and share the weight of a common higher-level criterion.

ASSIGNING NUMERICAL VALUES TO EVALUATION DIMENSIONS For the third step, once the hierarchy is established, we can use the pairwise comparison process to assign numerical values to the dimensions of our evaluation scale. Figure 12.9 is an evaluation scale with five dimensions: *Poor, Fair, Good, Very Good,* and *Excellent.* In this figure, for purposes of illustration, we have assigned the values of *0.0, 0.10, 0.30, 0.60,* and *1.00,* respectively, to these dimensions. Naturally, we can change these values as necessary. For example, if a company wants to indicate a greater discrepancy between *Poor* and *Fair,* managers may increase the range between these two dimensions. By adjusting values to suit specific purposes, managers avoid the fallacy of assuming that the differences between numbers on a scale of, say, 1 to 5 are equal—that is, assuming that the difference between 4 and 5 is the same as the difference between 3 and 4. With the AHP approach, the "best" outcome receives a perfect score of 1.00 and all other values represent some proportion relative to that score.

When necessary, project managers are encouraged to apply different scales for each criterion. Note, for example, that Figure 12.9 uses scale points ranging from *Poor* to *Excellent.* Suppose, however, that we were interviewing a candidate for our project team and one of the criterion items was "Education level." Clearly, using a scale ranging from *Poor* to *Excellent* makes no sense, so we would adjust the scales to make them meaningful; for example, using levels such as "High School," "Some College," "College Graduate," and so forth. Allocating weights across dimensions gives us a firmer understanding of both our goals and the methods by which we are comparing opportunities to achieve them.

EVALUATING PROJECT PROPOSALS In the final step, we multiply the numeric evaluation of the project by the weights assigned to the evaluation criteria and then add the results for all criteria. Figure 12.10 shows how five potential projects might be evaluated by an AHP program offered by Expert Choice, a maker of decision software.[13] Here's how to read the key features of the spreadsheet:

- The second row specifies the value assigned to each of five possible ratings (from *Poor* = *1* = *.000* to *Excellent* = *5* = *1.000*).
- The fourth row specifies the five decision criteria and their relative weights (*Finance/Short-Term* = .1560, *Strategy/Cost Management* = .0816, and so forth). (Note that three criteria have been broken down into six subcriteria.)
- The second column lists the five projects (*Perfect Project, Aligned,* etc.).
- The third column labeled "Total" gives a value for each alternative. This number is found by multiplying each evaluation by the appropriate criterion weight and summing the results across all criteria evaluations.

Finance	Short-term

Poor	Fair	Good	Very Good	Excellent
1 (.000)	2 (.100)	3 (.300)	4 (.600)	5 (1.000)

	Alternatives	Total	Finance		Strategy			Technology
			Short-Term	Long-Term	Market Share	Retention	Cost Management	
			.1560	.3640	.1020	.1564	.0816	.1400
1	Perfect Project	1.000	Excellent	Excellent	Excellent	Excellent	Excellent	Excellent
2	Aligned	0.762	Good	Excellent	Good	Excellent	Good	Excellent
3	Not Aligned	0.538	Excellent	Good	Excellent	Good	Excellent	Good
4	All Very Good	0.600	Very Good	Very Good	Very Good	Very Good	Very Good	Very Good
5	Mixed	0.284	Poor	Fair	Good	Very Good	Excellent	Good
6								
7								
8								
9								
10								

FIGURE 12.10 The Project Rating Spreadsheet

Source: J. K. Pinto and I. Millet. (1999). *Successful Information System Implementation: The Human Side,* 2nd ed., figure on page 78. Newtown Square, PA: Project Management Institute. Copyright and all rights reserved. Material from this publication has been reproduced with the permission of PMI.

To illustrate how the calculations are derived, let us take the *Aligned* project as an example. Remember that each rating (Excellent, Very Good, Good, etc.) carries with it a numerical score Figure 12.9. These scores, when multiplied by the evaluation criteria and then added together, yield:

$$(.1560)(.3) + (.3640)(1.0) + (.1020)(.3) + (.1564)(1.0) + (.0816)(.3) + (.1400)(1.0) = .762$$

The *Perfect Project,* as another example, was rated *Excellent* on all six dimensions and thus received a total score of 1.000. Also, compare the evaluations of the *Aligned* and *Not Aligned* project choices. Although both projects received an equal number of *Excellent* and *Good* rankings, the *Aligned* project was clearly preferable because it was rated higher on criteria viewed as more important and thus more heavily weighted.

Unlike the results of typical scoring models, the AHP scores are significant. The *Aligned* project, for example, which scored 0.762, is almost three times better than the *Mixed* project, with its score of 0.284. This feature—the ability to quantify superior project alternatives—allows project managers to use AHP scores as input to other calculations. We might, for example, sort projects by the ratios of AHP scores to total their development costs. Let's say that based on this ratio, we find that the *Not Aligned* project is much cheaper to initiate than the *Aligned* project. This finding may suggest that *from a cost/benefit perspective,* the *Not Aligned* project offers a better alternative than the *Aligned* project.

The AHP methodology can dramatically improve the process of developing project proposals. In firms that have incorporated AHP analysis, new project proposals must contain, as part of their core information, a sophisticated AHP breakdown listing the proposed project, alternatives, and projected outcomes. The Analytical Hierarchy Process offers a true advantage over traditional scoring models, primarily because it reduces many of the technical and managerial problems that plague such approaches.

The AHP does have some limitations, however. First, current research suggests that the model does not adequately account for "negative utility"; that is, the fact that certain choice options do not contribute positively to the decision goals but actually lead to negative results. For example, suppose that your company identified a strong project option that carried a prohibitively expensive price tag. As a result, selecting this project is really not an option because it would be just too high an investment. However, using the AHP, you would first need to weigh all positive elements, develop your screening score, and then compare this score against negative aspects, such as cost. The result can lead to bias in the project scoring calculations.[14] A second limitation is that the AHP requires that all criteria be fully exposed and accounted for at the beginning of the selection process. Powerful members of the organization with political agendas or pet projects they wish to pursue may resist such an open selection process.

Method Four: Profile Models

Profile models allow managers to plot **risk/return** options for various alternatives and then select the project that maximizes return while staying within a certain range of minimum acceptable risk. "Risk," of course, is a subjective assessment: It may be difficult to reach overall agreement on the level of risk associated with a given project. Nevertheless, the profile model offers another way of evaluating, screening, and comparing projects.[15]

Let's return to our example of project screening at SAP Corporation. Suppose that instead of the four project alternatives for the new software project we discussed earlier, the firm had identified six candidates for development. For simplicity's sake, managers chose to focus on the two criteria of *risk* and *reward.*

In Figure 12.11, the six project alternatives are plotted on a graph showing perceived *Risk* on the *y*-axis and potential *Return* on the *x*-axis. Because of the cost of capital to the firm, we will specify some minimum desired rate of return. All projects will be assigned some risk factor value and be plotted relative to the maximum risk that the firm is willing to assume. Figure 12.11, therefore, graphically represents each of our six alternatives on a profile model. (Risk values have been created here simply for illustrative purposes.) In our example, SAP can employ a variety of measures to assess the likely return offered by this project, including discounted cash flow analysis and internal rate of return expectations. Likewise, it is increasingly common for firms to quantify their risk assessment of various projects, enabling us to plot them along the *y*-axis. The key lies in employing identical evaluation criteria and quantification approaches across all projects to be profiled on the graph. Clearly, when project risks are unique or we have no way of comparing the relative risks from project to project, it is impossible to accurately plot project alternatives.

In Figure 12.11, we see that Project X_2 and Project X_3 have similar expected rates of return. Project X_3, however, represents a better selection choice. Why? Because SAP can achieve the same rate of return with Project X_3 as it can with Project X_2 but with less risk. Likewise, Project X_5 is a superior choice to X_4: Although they have similar risk levels, X_5 offers greater return as an investment. Finally, while Project X_6 offers the most potential return, it does so at the highest level of risk.

The profile model makes use of a concept most widely associated with financial management and investment analysis—the *efficient frontier.* In project management, the **efficient frontier** is the set of project portfolio options that offers either a maximum return for every given level of risk or the minimum risk for every level of return.[16] When we look at the profile model in Figure 12.11, we note that certain options (X_1, X_3, X_5, X_6) lie along an imaginary line balancing optimal risk and return combinations. Others (X_2 and X_4), however, are less desirable alternatives and would therefore be considered inferior choices. The efficient frontier serves as a decision-making guide by establishing the threshold level of risk/return options that all future project choices must be evaluated against.

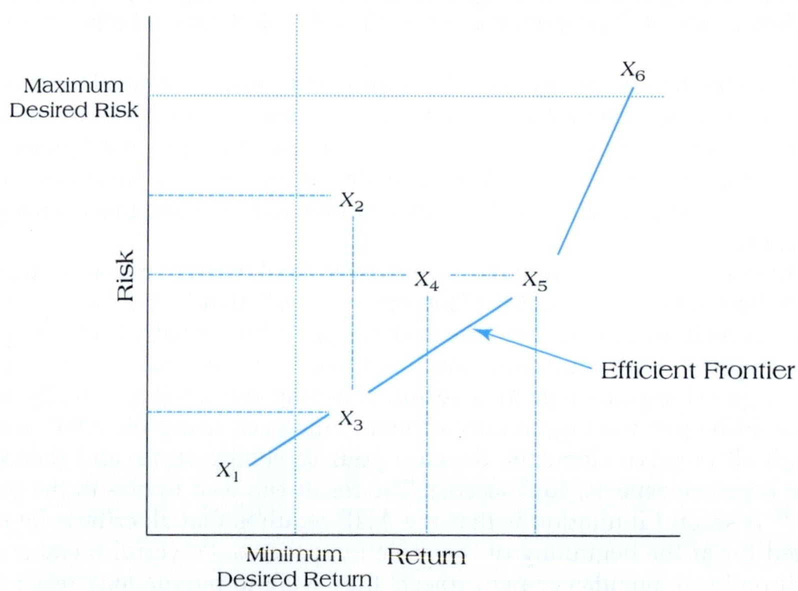

FIGURE 12.11 Profile Model

One advantage of the profile model is that it offers another method by which to compare project alternatives, this time in terms of the risk/return trade-off. Sometimes it is difficult to evaluate and compare projects on the basis of scoring models or other qualitative approaches. The profile model, however, gives managers a chance to map out potential returns while considering the risk that accompanies each choice. Thus, profile models give us a method for eliminating alternatives that either carry too much risk or promise too little return.

On the other hand, profile models also have disadvantages:

1. They limit decision criteria to just two—risk and return. Although an array of issues, including safety, quality, and reliability, can come under the heading of "risk," the approach still necessarily limits the decision maker to a small set of criteria.
2. In order to be evaluated in terms of an efficient frontier, some value must be attached to risk. Expected return is a measure that is naturally given to numerical estimate. But because risk may not be readily quantified, it may be misleading to designate "risk" artificially as a value for comparison among project choices.

EXAMPLE 12.3 Profile Model

Let's consider a simple example. Suppose that our company has identified two new project alternatives and we wish to use risk/return analysis to determine which of the two projects would fit best with our current project portfolio. We assess return in terms of the profit margin we expect to achieve on the projects. Risk is evaluated at our company in terms of four elements: (1) technical risk—the technical challenge of the project, (2) capital risk—the amount invested in the project, (3) safety risk—the risk of accidents or employee safety, and (4) goodwill risk—the risk of losing customers or diminishing our company's image. The magnitude of each of these types of risk is determined by applying a "low, medium, high" risk scale where 1 = low, 2 = medium, and 3 = high.

After conducting a review of the likely profitability for both of the projects and evaluating their riskiness, we conclude the following:

	Risk	Return Potential
Project Saturn	10	23%
Project Mercury	6	16%

Figure 12.12 shows our firm's efficient frontier for the current portfolio of projects. How would we evaluate the attractiveness of either Project Saturn or Project Mercury?

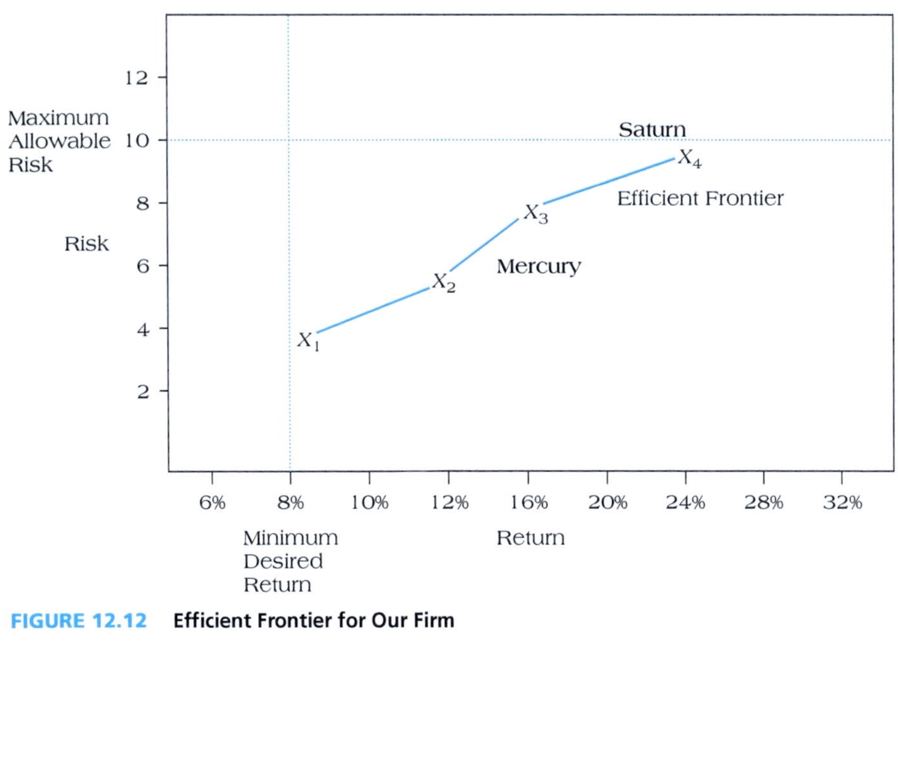

FIGURE 12.12 Efficient Frontier for Our Firm

SOLUTION

When we consider the two choices, Projects Saturn and Mercury, in terms of their projected risk and return, we can chart them on our profile model relative to other projects that we are undertaking. Figure 12.12 illustrates the placement of the two new project options. Note that Project Saturn, although within our maximum risk limit, does not perform as well as the other projects in our current portfolio (it has a higher risk rating for its projected return than other comparable projects). On the other hand, Project Mercury offers us a 16% rate of return for a lower level of risk than the current efficient frontier, suggesting that this project is an attractive option and a better alternative than Project Saturn.

12.6 FINANCIAL MODELS

Another important series of models rely on financial analysis to make project selection decisions. In this section, we will examine three commonly used financial models: *discounted cash flow analysis, net present value,* and *internal rate of return.*

Financial models are all predicated on the **time value of money** principle. The time value of money suggests that money earned today is worth more than money we expect to earn in the future. In other words, $100 that I receive four years from now is worth significantly less to me than if I were to receive that money today. In the simplest example, we can see that putting $100 in a bank account at 3% interest will grow the money at a compounded rate each year. Hence, at the end of year 1, the initial investment will be worth $103. After two years, it will have grown to $106.09, and so on. The principle also works in reverse: To calculate the *present value* of $100 that I expect to have in the bank in four years' time, I must first discount the amount by the same interest rate. Hence, assuming an interest rate of 3%, I need only invest $88.85 today to yield $100 in four years.

We expect future money to be worth less for two reasons: (1) the impact of inflation, and (2) the inability to invest the money. Inflation, as we know, causes prices to rise and hence erodes consumers' spending power. In 1900, for example, the average house may have cost a few thousand dollars to build. Today housing costs have soared. As a result, if I am to receive $100 in four years, its value will have decreased due to the negative effects of inflation. Further, not having that $100 today means that I cannot invest it and earn a return on my money for the next four years. Money that we cannot invest is money that earns no interest. In real terms, therefore, the **present value of money** must be discounted by some factor the farther out into the future I expect to receive it. When deciding among nearly identical project alternatives, if Project A will earn our firm $50,000 in two years and Project B will earn our company $50,000 in four years, Project A is the best choice because we will receive the money sooner.

Payback Period

The project **payback period** is the estimated amount of time that will be necessary to recoup the investment in a project, that is, how long will it take for the project to pay back its initial investment and begin to generate positive cash flow for the company. In determining the payback period for a project, we employ a discounted cash flow analysis, based on the principle of the time value of money. The goal of the **discounted cash flow (DCF) analysis** is to estimate cash outlays and expected cash inflows resulting from investment in a project. All potential costs of development (most of which are contained in the project budget) are assessed and projected prior to the decision to initiate the project. They are then compared with all expected sources of revenue from the project. For example, if the project is a new chemical plant, projected revenue streams will be based on expected capacity, production levels, sales volume, and so forth.

We then apply to this calculation a *discount rate* based on the firm's cost of capital. The value of that rate is weighted across each source of capital to which the firm has access (typically, debt and equity markets). In this way we weight the cost of capital, which can be calculated as follows:

$$K_{\text{firm}} = (w_d)(k_d)(1 - t) + (w_e)(k_e)$$

The weighted cost of capital is the percentage of capital derived from either debt (w_d) or equity (w_e) multiplied by the percentage costs of debt and equity (k_d and k_e, respectively). (The value t refers to the company's marginal tax rate: Because interest payments are tax deductible, we calculate the cost of debt after taxes.)

There is a standard formula for payback calculations:

$$\text{Payback period} = \text{investment/annual cash savings}$$

The reciprocal of this formula can be used to calculate the average rate of return for the project. However, note that the above formula only works in simple circumstances when cash flows (or annual cash savings) are the same for each year. So, for example, if we invested $150,000 and would receive $30,000 a year in annual savings, the payback period is straightforward:

$$\text{Payback period} = \$150{,}000/\$30{,}000 = 5 \text{ years}$$

On the other hand, when projected cash flows from annual savings are not equal, you must determine at what point the cumulative cash flow becomes positive. Thus:

$$\text{Cumulative cashflow(CF)} = \text{(Initial investment)} + \text{CF(year 1)} + \text{CF(year 2)} + \ldots$$

Once cost of capital has been calculated, we can set up a table projecting costs and revenue streams that are discounted at the calculated rate. The key is to determine how long it will take the firm to reach the breakeven point on a new project. *Breakeven point* represents the amount of time necessary to recover the initial investment of capital in the project. Shorter paybacks are more desirable than longer paybacks, primarily because the farther we have to project payback into the future, the greater the potential for additional risk.

EXAMPLE 12.4 Payback Period

Our company wants to determine which of two project alternatives is the more attractive investment opportunity by using a payback period approach. We have calculated the initial investment cost of the two projects and the expected revenues they should generate for us (see Table 12.10). Which project should we invest in?

SOLUTION

For our example, the payback for the two projects can be calculated as in Table 12.11. These results suggest that Project A is a superior choice over Project B, based on a shorter projected payback period (2.857 years versus 4.028 years) and a higher rate of return (35% versus 24.8%).

TABLE 12.10 Initial Outlay and Projected Revenues for Two Project Options

	Project A		Project B	
	Revenues	Outlays	Revenues	Outlays
Year 0		$500,000		$500,000
Year 1	$ 50,000		$ 75,000	
Year 2	150,000		100,000	
Year 3	350,000		150,000	
Year 4	600,000		150,000	
Year 5	500,000		900,000	

TABLE 12.11 Comparison of Payback for Projects A and B

Project A	Year	Cash Flow	Cum. Cash Flow
	0	($500,000)	($ 500,000)
	1	50,000	(450,000)
	2	150,000	(300,000)
	3	350,000	50,000
	4	600,000	650,000
	5	500,000	1,150,000
Payback = 2.857 years			
Rate of Return = 35%			

Project B	Year	Cash Flow	Cum. Cash Flow
	0	($500,000)	($ 500,000)
	1	75,000	(425,000)
	2	100,000	(325,000)
	3	150,000	(175,000)
	4	150,000	(25,000)
	5	900,000	875,000
Payback = 4.028 years			
Rate of Return = 24.8%			

Net Present Value

The most popular financial decision-making approach in project selection, the **net present value (NPV) method**, projects the change in the firm's value if a project is undertaken. Thus a *positive* NPV indicates that the firm will make money—and its value will rise—as a result of the project. Net present value employs discounted cash flow analysis, discounting future streams of income to estimate the present value of money.

The simplified formula for NPV is as follows:

$$NPV_{(\text{project})} = I_0 + \sum_{n=1}^{t} F_t/(1 + r + p_t)^t$$

where

F_t = net cash flow for period t
r = required rate of return
I = initial cash investment (cash outlay at time 0)
p_t = inflation rate during period

The optimal procedure for developing an NPV calculation consists of several steps, including the construction of a table listing the outflows, inflows, discount rate, and discounted cash flows across the relevant time periods. We construct such a table in Example 12.5 (see Table 12.12).

EXAMPLE 12.5 Net Present Value

Assume that you are considering whether or not to invest in a project that will cost $100,000 in initial investment. Your company requires a rate of return of 10%, and you expect inflation to remain relatively constant at 4%. You anticipate a useful life of four years for the project and have projected future cash flows as follows:

Year 1: $20,000
Year 2: $50,000
Year 3: $50,000
Year 4: $25,000

SOLUTION

We know the formula for determining NPV:

$$NPV = I_0 + \sum_{n=1}^{t} F_t/(1 + r + p)^t$$

We can now construct a simple table to keep a running score on discounted cash flows (both inflows and outflows) to see if the project is worth its initial investment. We already know that we will need the following categories: *Year, Inflows, Outflows,* and *NPV.* We will also need two more categories:

> ***Net flows***: the difference between inflows and outflows
> ***Discount factor***: the reciprocal of the discount rate $(1/(1 + r + p)^t)$

In Table 12.12, if we fill in the *Discount Factor* column assuming that $r = 10\%$ and $p = 4\%$, we can begin work on the *NPV.* Note that *Year 0* means the present time, and *Year 1* the first year of operation.

How did we arrive at the *Discount Factor* for Year 3? Using the formula we set above, we calculated the appropriate data:

$$\textit{Discount factor} = (1/(1 + .10 + .04)^3) = .6749$$

Now we can supply the data for the *Inflows, Outflows,* and *Net Flow* columns.

Finally, we complete the table by multiplying the *Net Flow* amount by the *Discount Factor.* The results give us the data for the *NPV* column of our table. The sum of the discounted cash flows (their net present value) shown in Table 12.13 gives us the *NPV* of the project. The total is a positive number, indicating that the investment is worthwhile and should be pursued.

TABLE 12.12 Running Score on Discounted Cash Flows

Year	Inflows	Outflows	Net Flow	Discount Factor	NPV
0		$100,000	$(100,000)	1.0000	
1	$20,000		20,000	0.8772	
2	50,000		50,000	0.7695	
3	50,000		50,000	0.6749	
4	25,000		25,000	0.5921	

TABLE 12.13 Discounted Cash Flows and NPV (I)

Year	Inflows	Outflows	Net Flow	Discount Factor	NPV
0		$100,000	$(100,000)	1.0000	$(100,000)
1	$20,000		20,000	0.8772	17,544
2	50,000		50,000	0.7695	38,475
3	50,000		50,000	0.6749	33,745
4	25,000		25,000	0.5921	14,803
Total					$ 4,567

Net present value is one of the most common project selection methods in use today. Its principal advantage is that it allows firms to link project alternatives to financial performance, better ensuring that the projects a company chooses to invest its resources in are likely to generate profit. Among its disadvantages is the difficulty in using NPV to make accurate long-term predictions. For example, suppose that we were considering investing in a project with an expectation that it would continue to generate returns during the next 10 years. In choosing whether or not to invest in the project today, we must make some assumptions about future interest rates, inflation, and our **required rate of return (RRR)** for the next 10 years. In uncertain financial or economic times, it can be risky to make long-term investment decisions when discount rates may fluctuate.

Discounted Payback

Now that we have considered the time value of money, as shown in the NPV method, we can apply this logic to the simple payback model to create a screening and selection model with a bit more power. Remember that with NPV we use discounted cash flow as our means to decide whether or not to invest in a project opportunity. Now, let's apply that same principle to the **discounted payback method**. With this method, the time period in which we are interested is the length of time until the sum of the discounted cash flows is equal to the initial investment.

A simple example will illustrate the difference between straight payback and discounted payback methods. Suppose we require a 12.5% return on new investments, and we have a project opportunity that will cost an initial investment of $30,000 with a promised return per year of $10,000. Under the simple payback model, the initial investment should be paid off in only three years. However, as Table 12.14 demonstrates, when we discount our cash flows at 12.5% and start adding them, it actually takes four years to pay back the initial project investment.

The advantage of the discounted payback method is that it allows us to make a more "intelligent" determination of the length of time needed to satisfy the initial project investment. That is, while simple payback is useful for accounting purposes, discounted payback is actually more representative of the financial realities that all organizations must consider when pursuing projects. The effects of inflation and future investment opportunities matter with individual investment decisions; hence, these factors should also matter when evaluating project opportunities.

Internal Rate of Return

Internal rate of return (IRR) is an alternative method for evaluating the expected outlays and income associated with a new project investment opportunity. The IRR method asks the simple question: What rate of return will this project earn? Under this model, the project must meet some required "hurdle" rate applied to all projects under consideration. Without detailing the mathematics of the process, we will say that IRR is the discount rate that equates the present values of a project's revenue and expense streams. If a project has a life of time *t*, the IRR is defined as:

$$IO = \sum_{n=1}^{t} \frac{ACF^t}{(1 + IRR)^t}$$

where

ACF^t = annual after-tax cash flow for time period t
IO = initial cash outlay
n = project's expected life
IRR = project's internal rate of return

TABLE 12.14 Discounted Payback Method

	Project Cash Flow*	
Year	**Discounted**	**Undiscounted**
1	$8,900	$10,000
2	7,900	10,000
3	7,000	10,000
4	6,200	10,000
5	5,500	10,000
Payback Period	4 Years	3 Years

*Cash flows rounded to the nearest $100.

The IRR is found through a straightforward process, although it requires tables representing present value of an annuity in order to determine the project's rate of return. Alternatively, many pocket calculators can determine IRR quickly. Without tables or access to a calculator, it is necessary to employ an iterative process to identify the approximate IRR for the project.

EXAMPLE 12.6 Internal Rate of Return

Let's take a simple example. Suppose that a project required an initial cash investment of $5,000 and was expected to generate inflows of $2,500, $2,000, and $2,000 for the next three years. Further, assume that our company's required rate of return for new projects is 10%. The question is: Is this project worth funding?

SOLUTION

Answering this question requires four steps:

1. Pick an arbitrary discount rate and use it to determine the net present value of the stream of cash inflows.
2. Compare the present value of the inflows with the initial investment; if they are equal, you have found the IRR.
3. If the present value is larger (or less than) than the initial investment, select a higher (or lower) discount rate for the computation.
4. Determine the present value of the inflows and compare it with the initial investment. Continue to repeat steps 2–4 until you have determined the IRR.

Using our example, we know:

Cash investment = $5,000
Year 1 inflow = $2,500
Year 2 inflow = $2,000
Year 3 inflow = $2,000
Required rate of return = 10%

Step One: Try 12%.

Year	Inflows	Discount Factor at 12%	NPV
1	$2,500	.893	$2,233
2	2,000	.797	1,594
3	2,000	.712	1,424
Present value of inflows			5,251
Cash investment			−5,000
Difference			$ 251

Decision: Present value difference at 12% is 250.50, which is too high. Try a higher discount rate.

Step Two: Try 15%.

Year	Inflows	Discount Factor at 15%	NPV
1	$2,500	.870	$2,175
2	2,000	.756	1,512
3	2,000	.658	1,316
Present value of inflows			5,003
Cash investment			5,000
Difference			$ 3

Decision: Present value difference at 15% is $3, which suggests that 15% is a close approximation of the IRR.

If the IRR is greater than or equal to the company's required rate of return, the project is worth funding. In Example 12.6, we found that the IRR is 15% for the project, making it higher than the hurdle rate of 10% and a good candidate for investment. The advantage of using IRR analysis lies in its ability to compare alternative projects from the perspective of expected *return on investment* (ROI). Projects having higher IRR are generally superior to those having lower IRR.

The IRR method, however, does have some disadvantages. First, it is *not* the rate of return for a project. In fact, the IRR equals the project's rate of return only when project-generated cash inflows can be reinvested in new projects at similar rates of return. If the firm can reinvest revenues only on lower-return projects, the "real" return on the project is something less than the calculated IRR. Several other problems with the IRR method make NPV a more robust determinant of project viability:[17]

- IRR and NPV calculations typically agree (that is, make the same investment recommendations) only when projects are independent of each other. If projects are not mutually exclusive, IRR and NPV may rank them differently. The reason is that NPV employs a weighted average cost of capital discount rate that reflects potential reinvestment while IRR does not. Because of this distinction, NPV is generally preferred as a more realistic measure of investment opportunity.
- If cash flows are not normal, IRR may arrive at multiple solutions. For example, if net cash outflows follow a period of net cash inflows, IRR may give conflicting results. If, following the completion of plant construction, it is necessary to invest in land reclamation or other incidental but significant expenses, an IRR calculation may result in multiple return rates, only one of which is correct.

Choosing a Project Selection Approach

What can we conclude from our discussion of project selection methods? First and foremost, we have learned to focus on the *method* that we use in making selection decisions. Have we been consistent and objective in considering our alternatives? The author has worked in a consulting and training capacity with a number of firms that have experienced recurrent problems in their project selections (they kept picking losers). Why? One reason was their failure to even attempt objectivity in their selection methods. Proposed projects, often "sacred cows" or the pet ideas of senior managers, were pushed to the head of the line or, worse, financially "tweaked" until they yielded satisfactory conclusions. Team members knew in advance that such projects would fail because the projects had been massaged to the point at which they seemingly optimized the selection criteria. The key to project selection lies in being objective about the process. If you operate according to the "GIGO" principle—garbage in/garbage out—you'll soon be up to your knees in garbage.

A second conclusion we can draw is that although a wide variety of selection methods exist, certain ones may be more appropriate for specific companies and project circumstances. Some projects require sophisticated financial evidence of their viability. Others may only need to demonstrate no more than an acceptable profile when compared to other options. In other words, any of the previously discussed selection methods may be appropriate under certain situations. Some experts, for example, favor weighted scoring models on the grounds that they offer a more accurate reflection of a firm's strategic goals without sacrificing long-term effectiveness for short-term financial gains.[18] They argue that such important, nonfinancial criteria should not be excluded from the decision-making process. In fact, research suggests that although very popular, financial selection models, when used exclusively, do not yield optimal portfolios.[19] On the other hand, when they are combined with scoring models into a more comprehensive selection procedure, they can be highly effective. It is also critical to match the types of projects we are selecting from to the appropriate screening method. Is it possible to estimate future return on investment? Potential risk? These issues should be carefully thought through when developing a suitable screening model. Perhaps the key lies in choosing a selection algorithm broad enough to encompass both financial and nonfinancial considerations. Regardless of the approach that a company selects, we can be sure of one thing: Making good project choices is a crucial step in ensuring good project management downstream.

PROJECT PROFILE

Project Selection and Screening at GE: The Tollgate Process

General Electric has developed a highly sophisticated approach to project screening and selection that the company calls the Tollgate Process. As you can see from Figure 12.13, Tollgate involves a series of seven formal procedural checkpoints (labeled *100* to *700*) established along the project development time line. Therefore, Tollgate is more than just a project selection methodology; it involves controlling the selection and development of the project as it moves through its life cycle. Each stage in this control process is carefully monitored.

Each of the seven Tollgate stages can be broken down into a so-called *process map* that guides managers and teams in addressing specific necessary elements in the completion of a stage. These elements are the substeps that guide project screening in order to ensure that all projects conform to the same set of internal GE standards.

Figure 12.14 lays out the process flow map that is used to evaluate the progress each project makes at the various stages to final completion. Note that teams must complete all action substeps at each Tollgate stage. Once they have completed a given stage, a cross-functional management review team provides oversight at a review conference. Approval at this stage permits the team to proceed to the next stage. Rejection means that the team must back up and deal with any issues that the review team feels it has not addressed adequately. For example, suppose that the project fails a technical conformance test during field testing at the system verification stage. The technical failure would require the team to cycle back to the appropriate point to analyze the cause for the field test failure and begin remedial steps to correct it. After a project team has received approval from the review team, it needs the approval of senior management before moving on to the next Tollgate stage. Rejection at this point by senior management often effectively kills the project.

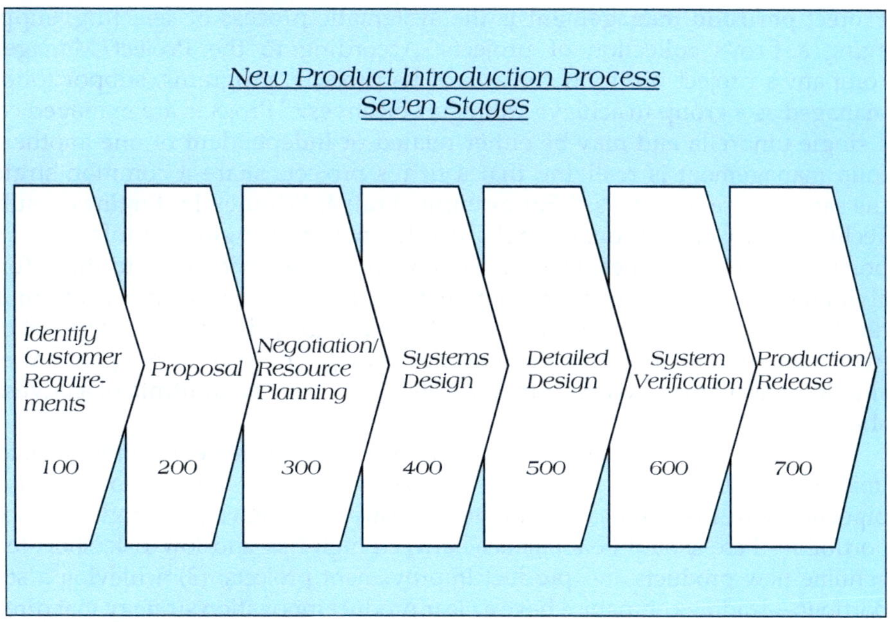

FIGURE 12.13 GE's Tollgate Process

Source: Used with permission of General Electric Company.

(continued)

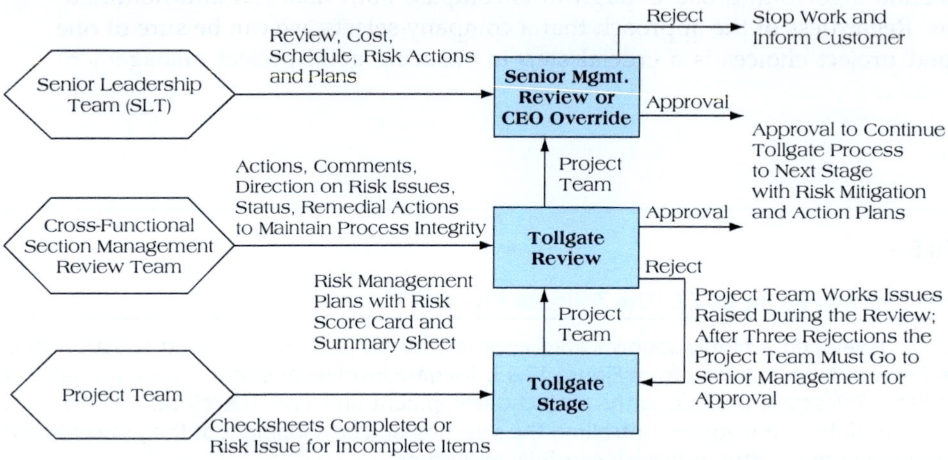

FIGURE 12.14 The GE Tollgate Review Process Flow Map

Source: Used with permission of General Electric Company.

Some critics argue that formalized and sophisticated review processes such as Tollgate add excessive layers of bureaucratic oversight to the project screening process. In fact, the sheer number of actions, steps, checklists, and managerial reviews stipulated by the Tollgate process can add significant delays to projects—a critical concern if a project is needed to address an immediate problem. On the other hand, proponents of such techniques argue that the benefits—standardization across business units, comprehensive step-by-step risk analysis, clear links to top management—more than compensate for potential problems. At GE, the company credits Tollgate with promoting significant improvements in early problem discovery and "real-time" risk management.

12.7 PROJECT PORTFOLIO MANAGEMENT

Project portfolio management is the systematic process of selecting, supporting, and managing a firm's collection of projects. According to the Project Management Institute, a company's project portfolio consists of its projects, programs, subportfolios, and operations managed as a group to achieve strategic objectives.[20] Projects are managed concurrently under a single umbrella and may be either related or independent of one another. The key to portfolio management is realizing that a firm's projects share a common strategic purpose and the same scarce resources.[21] For example, Pratt & Whitney Jet Engines, a subsidiary of United Technologies Corporation, is similar to other major jet engine manufacturers in creating a wide portfolio of engine types, from those developed for helicopters to those for jet aircraft, from civilian use to military consumption. Although the products share common features, the technical challenges ensure that the product line is highly diverse. The concept of project portfolio management holds that firms should not manage projects as independent entities, but rather should regard portfolios as unified assets. There may be multiple objectives, but they are also shared objectives.[22]

Cooper[23] has suggested that project portfolio management should have four goals: (1) maximizing the value of the portfolio—the goal is to ensure that the total worth of projects in the pipeline yields maximum value to the company; (2) achieving the right balance of projects in the portfolio—there should be a balance between high-risk and low-risk, short-term and long-term, genuine new products and product improvement projects; (3) achieving a strategically aligned portfolio—leading companies have a clear product innovation strategy that directs their R&D project investments; and (4) resource balancing—having the right number of projects in the portfolio is critical. Too many firms invest in too many different projects that they cannot simultaneously support. Overextension just drains resources and causes top management to constantly shift their view from new project venture to new project venture, without providing sufficient support for any of them.

Artto[24] notes that in a project-oriented company, project portfolio management poses a constant challenge between balancing long-term strategic goals and short-term needs and constraints. Managers routinely pose such questions as the following:

- What projects should the company fund?
- Does the company have the resources to support them?
- Do these projects reinforce future strategic goals?
- Does this project make good business sense?
- Is this project complementary to other company projects?

Objectives and Initiatives

Each of the questions in the previous list has both short-term and long-term implications, and, taken together, they constitute the basis for both strategic project management and effective risk management. Portfolio management, therefore, entails decision making, prioritization, review, realignment, and reprioritization of a firm's projects. Let's consider each of these tasks in more detail.

DECISION MAKING The decision on whether or not to proceed in specific strategic directions is often influenced by market conditions, capital availability, perceived opportunity, and acceptable risk. A variety of project alternatives may be considered reasonable alternatives during portfolio development.

PRIORITIZATION Because firms have limited resources, they typically cannot fund every project opportunity. Thus they must prioritize. For this task, several criteria may be used:

- ***Cost:*** Projects with lower development costs are more favorable because they come with less upfront risk.
- ***Opportunity:*** The chance for a big payout is a strong inducement for funding.
- ***Top management pressure:*** Political pressure from top management (say, managers with pet projects) can influence decisions.
- ***Risk:*** Project payouts must justify some level of acceptable risk; those that are too risky are scratched.
- ***Strategic "fit":*** If a firm has a policy of pursuing a family of products, all opportunities are evaluated in terms of their *complementarity*—that is, either their strategic fit with existing product lines or their ability to augment the current product family.
- ***Desire for portfolio balance:*** A firm may want to offset risky initiatives by funding other projects. The Boston Consulting Group's product matrix framework, for example, balances company product lines in terms of relative market share and product growth, suggesting that firms can maintain a strategic balance within their portfolios between products with different profiles. A firm might use its profitable but low-growth products to fund investment into projects with high growth prospects. Portfolio balance supports developing a strategy that allows companies the ability to balance or offset risk, explore alternative market opportunities, and fund innovation in other product lines.

REVIEW All project alternatives are evaluated according to the company's prioritization scheme. Projects selected for the firm's portfolio are the ones that, based on those priorities, offer maximum return. For example, at the start of the current economic downturn, DHL Express started evaluating its project portfolio through a new lens. The organization's portfolio review board decided that all ongoing projects had to meet the following criteria: deliver return on investment (ROI) in 2009, be "mission-critical" to running the business, and address government or regulatory issues required to keep the business operational. Following an extensive portfolio review, a number of projects were temporarily discontinued.

REALIGNMENT When portfolios are altered by the addition of new projects, managers must reexamine company priorities. In the wake of new project additions, a number of important questions should be considered. Does the new project conform to strategic goals as characterized by the project portfolio, or does it represent a new strategic direction for the firm? Does a new project significantly alter the firm's strategic goals? Does the portfolio now require additional rebalancing? The decision to change a portfolio by adding new projects restarts the analysis cycle in which we must again reexamine the portfolio for signs of imbalance or updating.

REPRIORITIZATION If strategic realignment means shifting the company's focus (i.e., creating new strategic directions), then managers must also reprioritize corporate goals and objectives. In this sense, then, portfolio management means managing overall company strategy. For example, Bayer Corporation, a global pharmaceutical giant, has found its corporate identity becoming less distinct due to the wide variety of acquisitions and other brands under which it markets its products. The company recently announced its intention to gradually eliminate many of the other brands that it owns under the "Bayer product umbrella" in order to emphasize the Bayer label. They found, after thorough analysis, that supporting a diverse set of brands in the Bayer Group was having the effect of diluting their signature brand. Consumers were confused about what Bayer actually made and that confusion was in danger of altering their perceptions of the quality of Bayer products.

Developing a Proactive Portfolio

Portfolio management, therefore, is an important component in strategic project management. In addition to managing specific projects, organizations plan for profitability, and the road to profitability often runs through the area of strategic project management. One of the most effective methods for aligning profit objectives and strategic plans is the development of a proactive project portfolio, or an integrated family of projects, usually with a common strategic goal. Such a portfolio supports overall strategic integration, rather than an approach that would simply move from project opportunity to opportunity.

A useful model that has been applied to project portfolio management links the two issues of commercial potential and technical feasibility in judging among potential project alternatives to select for a firm's portfolio. This portfolio classifies projects among four distinct types, depending on where they fall in the matrix (see Figure 12.15):[25]

1. *Bread and butter* projects are those with a high probability of technical feasibility and a modest likelihood for commercial profitability. These projects are typically evolutionary improvements to existing product lines or modest extensions to existing technology. A new release of a software product or "new and improved" laundry detergent are examples of bread and butter projects.
2. *Pearls* are projects that offer a strong commercial potential and are technically feasible. These projects can be used to gain strategic advantage in the marketplace. Pearls involve revolutionary commercial applications that have the potential to revolutionize a field while relying on well-known or understood technology. Examples of pearls are projects that involve new applications of existing technology, such as sonar imaging systems to detect deep-water oil reserves.
3. *Oysters* are early-stage projects that have the potential to unleash significant strategic and commercial advantages for the company that can solve the technical challenges. Because oyster projects involve unknown or revolutionary technologies, they are still at the early stages of possible success. If these technical challenges can be overcome, the company stands to make a great deal of money. An example of an oyster project is developing viable fusion power generation or extended life batteries for electric cars.
4. *White elephant* projects are a combination of low technical feasibility coupled with low commercial impact. The question could be asked: Why would a firm select white elephant projects that combine the worst of profitability and technical feasibility? The answer is that they do not deliberately select projects of this sort. Most white elephants start life as bread and butter projects or oysters that never live up to their potential. As a result, although originally undertaken with high hopes, white elephants end up consuming resources and wasting time, but they are often maintained with rationalizations such as, "We've already spent too much on it to just kill it now," or "Influential members of the organization support it."

Project matrixes like the one in Figure 12.15 are a useful means for companies to take a hard look at the current state of their project portfolio. Is there a good balance among project

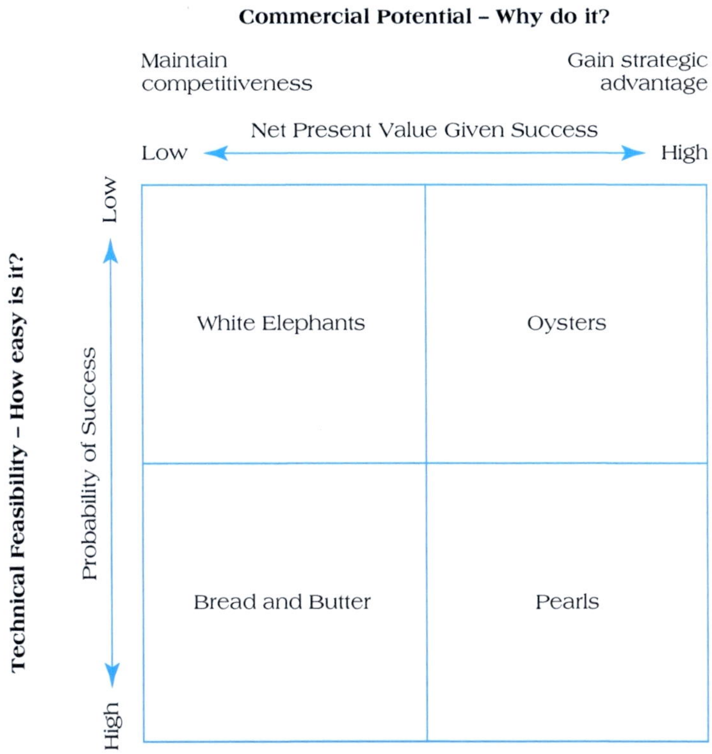

FIGURE 12.15 **Project Portfolio Matrix**

Source: D. Matheson, D. and J. E. Matheson. (1998). *The Smart Organization: Creating Value through Strategic R&D*. Boston, MA: Harvard Business School Press.

types? Are there some obvious white elephants that need to be killed? Should the firm be investing in more (or fewer) strategic projects at the expense of bread and butter projects? Balancing technical risk and potential return are twin goals of the project portfolio matrix and this process should be redone periodically to ensure that the state of the company's portfolio is always updated.

It is also important to avoid making snap judgments or quick opinions of project opportunities in order to classify them on the grid. Classifying your portfolio of projects into a matrix means that a company uses comprehensive and careful methods to identify projects of various types—white elephants, bread and butter, oysters, and pearls. Should we use quantitative scoring or screening models? Financial models? Some combination of several methods? Any of these approaches can be a useful starting point for classifying the current projects in the portfolio and identifying the value of potential new investments.

Consider the example of the large pharmaceutical firm Pfizer.[26] Pfizer and its competitors routinely manage large families of projects in an integrated manner. The overall integration of project management efforts helps the company's managers deal with certain realities of the pharmaceutical industry, such as extremely high development costs and long lead times for new products. In fact, as Table 12.15 shows, the lead time for bringing a new drug to market can easily stretch over 15 years, and the success rate of a drug being commercially developed is estimated to be less than 0.002%.

Therefore, at any particular point in time, Pfizer has numerous projects under research and development, a smaller number of projects entering various stages of clinical trials, and finally, an even smaller line of projects already on the market. Each step in the cycle is fraught with risks and uncertainties. Will a drug work in clinical trials? Will it have minimal negative side effects? Can it be produced in a cost-effective manner? Is it's release time-sensitive (is there, for instance, a limited market opportunity of which to take advantage)? Often the answers to such questions will reduce Pfizer's ongoing portfolio of development projects.

TABLE 12.15 Phases in New Drug Development

Phase	Duration	% of Success	Contents
Discovery	4–7 yrs	1%	Research a selected pool of molecules in computer models and test tubes.
Preclinical research			Test on animals and in test tubes to research the safety, possible indications, toxicology, and metabolism of the molecule.
Phase I	1 yr	70%–75%	Small clinical studies on healthy volunteers to study the safety and ADME characteristics of the molecule.
Phase II	2 yrs	50%	Small studies on patients with the target disease to study the efficacy, dosage, and formulation of the drug.
Phase III	3 yrs	75%–85%	Large clinical studies on patients to confirm the results of phase II. The most expensive phase in the project.
Marketing Application (MA)	1.5–3 yrs	75%–80%	Compile marketing authorization application (MAA) and send to the authorities. After the authorization the drug may be sold and marketed.
Total	12–16 yrs	< 0.002%	

Source: M. Lehtonen (2001). "Resource allocation and project portfolio management in pharmaceutical R&D," in Artto, Martinsuo, and Aalto (Eds.), *Project Portfolio Management: Strategic Management through Projects*, pp. 107–140, figure on page 112. Helsinki, Finland: Project Management Association.

Under the risky circumstances of this industry, in which development time is lengthy, the financial repercussions of failure are huge, and success is never certain, pharmaceutical firms must practice highly sophisticated project portfolio management. Because failure rates are high and washouts constant, the need to take advantage of new product opportunities is critical. Only in this way can the company ensure a steady supply of new products in the pipeline.

The pitfalls and possibilities of the pharmaceuticals development process are illustrated in Figure 12.16. Drug companies compensate for the lengthy lead times necessary to get final

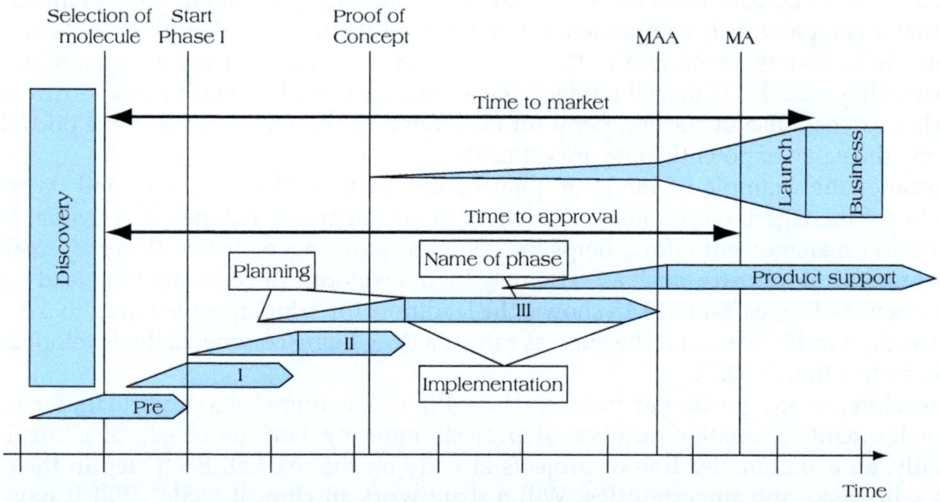

FIGURE 12.16 The Flow of New Drug Development over Time

Source: M. Lehtonen. (2001). "Resource allocation and project portfolio management in pharmaceutical R&D," in Artto, Martinsuo, and Aalto (Eds.), *Project Portfolio Management: Strategic Management through Projects*, pp. 107–140, figure on page 120. Helsinki, Finland: Project Management Association.

approval of new products by simultaneously funding and managing scores of development efforts. Unfortunately, only a small proportion of an R&D portfolio will show sufficient promise to be advanced to the clinical trial stage. Many projects are further weeded out during this phase, with very few projects reaching the stage of commercial rollout.

Pfizer uses portfolio management to manage the flow of new drug development projects, much as Samsung and Erickson use it to keep track of product pipelines that include mobile phones, baseband modems, and firewall systems. Scott Paper manages a large portfolio of products and new project initiatives through the same portfolio management approaches. Project portfolios are necessary because a certain percentage of projects will be canceled prior to full funding, others will be eliminated during development, and still others will fail commercially. This cycle leaves only a few projects to account for a firm's return on all of its investments. In short, any company that puts all its R&D eggs in one project basket runs huge risks if that project fails during development or proves disappointing in the marketplace. As a rule, therefore, companies guarantee themselves fallback options, greater financial stability, and the chance to respond to multiple opportunities by constantly creating and updating portfolios of projects.

Although there are no standard "rules" for the projects a company's portfolio should contain, research into portfolio management across industries has found that for companies in certain industries, there may be general guidelines for the types of projects routinely being developed. For example, in a study of the IT industry, researchers found that the average firm's project portfolio budget consists of 47% spent on infrastructure projects (intended to support essential elements of the organization, its networks, PCs, development tools, training and help desk support, and maintenance). The remaining 53% of the IT portfolio budget is spent on *application projects*, including "frontier" projects to alter the competitive landscape, *enhancement projects* to support better corporate performance, and *utility applications* for improving internal company processes. For the majority of IT firms, nearly 67% of their portfolio budget is spent on infrastructure and utility projects that make no direct business performance improvement but are nevertheless essential for the smooth-running operations of a company.[27] This example demonstrates that it is possible to use research to determine the optimal mix of alternative project types within the portfolios of firms in other industries as a means to guide portfolio-balancing decisions.

Keys to Successful Project Portfolio Management

Although examples of successfully managed portfolios abound, few researchers have investigated the key reasons why some companies are better at it than others. Brown and Eisenhardt[28] studied six firms in the computer industry; all were involved in multiple project development activities. They determined that successfully managed project portfolios usually reflect the following three factors:

FLEXIBLE STRUCTURE AND FREEDOM OF COMMUNICATION Multiple-project environments cannot operate effectively when they are constrained by restrictive layers of bureaucracy, narrow communication channels, and rigid development processes. Successful portfolios emerge from environments that foster flexibility and open communication. When project teams are allowed to improvise and experiment on existing product lines, innovative new product ideas are more likely to emerge.

LOW-COST ENVIRONMENTAL SCANNING Many firms devote a lot of time and money in efforts to hit product "home runs." They put their faith (and financing) in one promising project and aim to take the marketplace by storm, often without sufficiently analyzing alternative opportunities or future commercial trends. As a rule, successful project portfolio strategies call for launching a number of low-cost probes into the future, the idea behind environmental scanning—developing and market-testing a number of experimental product prototypes, sometimes by entering strategic alliances with potential partners. Successful firms do not rely on home runs and narrowly concentrated efforts. They are constantly building and testing new projects prior to full-scale development. Rubbermaid, for example, routinely brings dozens of new product ideas to the market, samples the commercial response, and uses the resulting information to improve potential winners and discard products that don't measure up.

TIME-PACED TRANSITION Successful portfolio management requires a sense of timing, especially as firms make transitions from one product to the next. Successful firms use project portfolio planning routinely to develop long lead times and plan ahead in order to make the smoothest possible transition from one product to another, whether the product lines are diverse or constitute creating a follow-on upgrade. Gillette, for example, has made a lucrative business out of developing and selling new models of shaving razors. Gillette's product life cycle planning is highly sophisticated, allowing it to make accurate predictions of the likely life cycle of current products and the timing necessary for beginning new product development projects to maintain a seamless flow of consumer products.

Problems in Implementing Portfolio Management

What are some of the common problems in creating an effective portfolio management system? Although numerous factors can adversely affect the practice of portfolio management, recent research seems to suggest that the following are among the most typical problem areas.[29]

CONSERVATIVE TECHNICAL COMMUNITIES In many organizations, there is a core of technical professionals—project engineers, research scientists, and other personnel—who develop project prototypes. A common phenomenon is this group's unwillingness, whether out of pride, organizational inertia, or due to arguments supporting pure research, to give up project ideas that are too risky, too costly, or out of sync with strategic goals. Often, when top management tries to trim the portfolio of ongoing projects for strategic reasons, they find engineers and scientists reluctant to accept their reasoning. Data General Corporation, a manufacturer of computers and IT products, found itself increasingly under the dominance of its hardware engineering department, a group intent on pursuing their own new product goals and fostering their own vision for the organization. By the mid-1990s, with one product after another resulting in significant losses, the company could not continue to operate independently and was acquired by EMC Corporation.

OUT-OF-SYNC PROJECTS AND PORTFOLIOS Sometimes after a firm has begun realigning and reprioritizing its strategic outlook, it continues to develop projects or invest in a portfolio that no longer accurately reflects its new strategic focus. Strategy and portfolio management must accurately reflect a similar outlook. When strategy and portfolio management are out of alignment, one or both of two things will probably happen: Either the portfolio will point the firm toward outmoded goals or the firm's strategy will revert to its old objectives.

UNPROMISING PROJECTS The worst-case scenario finds a company pursuing poor-quality or unnecessary projects. Honda, for example, has been pursuing hydrogen fuel technology for over 10 years and is marketing its FCX car in southern California with compressed hydrogen as its fuel source. Unfortunately, while the efficiency of the engine is high, the current difficulties in the technology make the FCX a questionable project choice to continue to support. The tanker trucks that replenish gasoline stations carrying hydrogen refueling pumps can carry about 300 fill-ups. However, hydrogen takes up much more space and requires high-pressure cylinders that weigh 65 times as much as the hydrogen they contain. Therefore, one giant, 13-ton hydrogen delivery truck can carry only about 10 fill-ups! By ignoring this critical flaw in the hydrogen economy idea Honda has a product is grossly inefficient compared to electric cars. Well-to-wheel efficiency analysis of the Honda FCX shows that the Tesla pure electric car is three times more efficient while producing only one-third the CO_2 emissions.[30]

When portfolio management is geared to product lines, managers routinely rebalance the portfolio to ensure that there are a sufficient number of products of differing types to offset those with weaknesses. Revenues from "cash cows," for example, can fund innovative new products. Sometimes critical analysis of a portfolio requires hard decisions, project cancellations, and reallocated resources. But it is precisely this ongoing attention to the portfolio that prevents it from becoming weighted down with unpromising projects.

SCARCE RESOURCES A key resource for all projects is human capital. In fact, personnel costs comprise one of the highest sources of project expense. Additional types of resources include any raw materials, financial resources, or supplies that are critical to successfully completing the project. Before spending large amounts of time creating a project portfolio, organizations thus like to ensure that the required resources will be available when needed. A principal cause of portfolio underperformance is a lack of adequate resources, especially personnel, to support required development.

Portfolio management is the process of bringing an organization's project management practices into line with its overall corporate strategy. By creating complementary projects and creating synergies within its project portfolio, a company can ensure that its project management teams are working together rather than at cross-purposes. Portfolio management is also a visible symbol of the strategic direction and commercial goals of a firm. Taken together, the projects that a firm chooses to promote and develop send a clear signal to the rest of the company about priorities, resource commitment, and future directions. Finally, portfolio management is an alternative method for managing overall project risk by seeking a continuous balance among various families of projects, between risks and return trade-offs, and between efficiently run projects and nonperformers. As more and more organizations rely on project management to achieve these ends, it is likely that more and more firms will take the next logical step: organizing projects by means of portfolio management.

Summary

1. **Explain six criteria for a useful project selection/screening model.** No organization can pursue every opportunity that presents itself. Choices must be made, and to best ensure that they select the most viable projects, firms develop priority systems or guidelines—*selection/screening models* (or a set of models) that will help them make the best choices within the usual constraints of time and money—that is, help them save time and money while maximizing the likelihood of success.

   A number of decision models are available to managers who are responsible for evaluating and selecting potential projects. Six important issues that managers should consider when evaluating screening models are: (1) *Realism:* An effective model must reflect organizational objectives, must be reasonable in light of constraints on resources such as money and personnel, and must take into account both commercial risks and technical risks. (2) *Capability:* A model should be flexible enough to respond to changes in the conditions under which projects are carried out and robust enough to accommodate new criteria and constraints. (3) *Flexibility:* The model should be easily modified if trial applications require changes. (4) *Ease of use:* A model must be simple enough to be used by people in all areas of the organization, and it should be timely in that it generates information rapidly and allows people to assimilate that information without any special training or skills. (5) *Cost:* The cost of gathering, storing, and arranging information in the form of useful reports or proposals should be relatively low in relation to the costs associated with implementing a project (i.e., the cost of the models must be low enough to encourage their use rather than diminish their applicability). (6) *Comparability:* The model must be broad enough that it can be applied to multiple projects and support general comparisons of project alternatives.
2. **Understand how to employ checklists and simple scoring models to select projects.** Checklists require decision makers to develop a list of the criteria that are deemed important when considering project alternatives. For example, a firm may decide that all project alternatives must be acceptable on criteria such as return on investment, safety, cost of development, commercial opportunities, and stakeholder acceptability. Once the list of criteria is created, all project alternatives are evaluated against it and assigned a rating of high, medium, or low depending on how well they satisfy each criterion in the checklist. Projects that rate highest across the relevant criteria are selected. Checklists are useful because they are simple and require the firm to make trade-off decisions among criteria to determine which issues are most important in selecting new projects. Among their disadvantages are the subjective nature of the rating process and the fact that they assume equal weighting for all criteria when some, in fact, may be much more important than others in making the final decision.

   Simple scoring models are similar to checklists except that they employ criterion weights for each of the decision criteria. Hence, all project alternatives are first weighted by the importance score for the criterion, and then final scores are evaluated against one another. The advantage of this method is that it recognizes the fact that decision criteria may be weighted differently, leading to better choices among project alternatives. The disadvantages of the method arise from the difficulty in assigning meaningful values to scoring anchors such as "High = 3, Medium = 2, Low = 1." Thus, there is some uncertainty in the interpretation of the results of simple scoring models using weighted rankings. The usefulness of these models depends on the relevance of the selected criteria and the accuracy of the weight given to them.

3. **Use more sophisticated scoring models, such as the Analytical Hierarchy Process.** The Analytical Hierarchy Process (AHP) is a four-step process that allows decision makers to understand the nature of project alternatives in making selection decisions. Using the AHP, decision makers (a) structure the hierarchy of criteria to be used in the decision process, (b) allocate weights to these criteria, (c) assign numerical values to all evaluation dimensions, and (d) use the scores to evaluate project alternatives. The AHP has been shown to create more accurate decision alternatives and lead to more informed choices, provided the organization's decision makers develop accurate decision criteria and evaluate and weight them honestly.
4. **Learn how to use financial concepts, such as the efficient frontier and risk/return models.** Many projects are selected as a result of their perceived risk/return trade-off potential. That is, all projects entail risk (uncertainty), so project organizations seek to balance higher risk with comparatively higher expectations of return when considering which projects to fund. The efficient frontier concept allows projects to be evaluated against each other by assessing the potential returns for each alternative compared to the risk the firm is expected to undertake in producing the project. The efficient frontier is the set of project portfolio options that offers either a maximum return for every given level of risk or the minimum risk for every level of return.
5. **Employ financial analyses and options analysis to evaluate the potential for new project investments.** Financial analyses using discounted cash flows and internal rates of return allow us to apply the concept of the time value of money to any decision we have to make regarding the attractiveness of various project alternatives. The time value of money suggests that future streams of return from a project investment should at least offset the initial investment in the project plus provide some required rate of return imposed by the company. Options analysis takes this process one step further and considers alternatives in which an investment is either made or foregone, depending upon reasonable alternative investments the company can make in the future. Each of these financial models argues that the principal determinant of an attractive project investment must be the money it promises to return. Clearly, therefore, a reasonably accurate estimate of future streams of revenue is required for financial models to create meaningful results.
6. **Recognize the challenges that arise in maintaining an optimal project portfolio for an organization.** A number of challenges are associated with managing a portfolio of projects, including (a) conservative technical communities that refuse to support new project initiatives, (b) out-of-sync projects and portfolios in which the projects no longer align with overall strategic portfolio plans, (c) unpromising projects that unbalance the portfolio, and (d) scarce resources that make it impossible to support new projects.
7. **Understand the three keys to successful project portfolio management.** There are three keys to success project portfolio management. First, firms need to create or make available a flexible structure and freedom of communication by reducing excessive bureaucracy and administrative oversight so that the portfolio management team maximum has flexibility in seeking out and investing in projects. Second, use of successful portfolio management strategies allows for low-cost environmental scanning, which launches a series of inexpensive "probes" into the future to develop and test-market project alternatives. Finally, successful portfolio management requires a time-paced transition strategy based on a sense of the timing necessary to successfully transition from one product to the next, whether the next product is a direct offshoot of the original or an additional innovative product for the firm's portfolio.

Key Terms

Analytical Hierarchy Process (AHP)
Checklist
Discounted cash flow (DCF) method
Discounted payback method
Efficient frontier
Internal rate of return (IRR)
Lead time
Net present value (NPV) method
Nonnumeric models
Numeric models
Pairwise comparison approach
Payback period
Present value of money
Profile models
Project portfolio
Project portfolio management
Project screening model
Required rate of return (RRR)
Risk/return
Simplified scoring model
Time value of money

Solved Problems

12.1 NET PRESENT VALUE

Your firm is trying to decide whether to invest in a new project opportunity based on the following information. The initial cash outlay will total $250,000 over two years. The firm expects to invest $200,000 immediately and the final $50,000 in one year's time. The company predicts that the project will generate a stream of earnings of $50,000, $100,000, $200,000, and $75,000 per year, respectively, starting in Year 2. The required rate of return is 12%, and the expected rate of inflation over the life of the project is forecast to remain steady at 3%. Should you invest in this project?

SOLUTION

In order to answer this question, we need to organize the following data in the form of a table:

Total outflow = $250,000
Total inflow = $400,000
Required rate of return (r) = 12%
Inflation rate (p) = 3%
Discount factor = $1/(1 + r + p)^t$

The result is shown in Table 12.16. Because the discounted revenue stream is positive ($11,725), the project would be a good investment and should be pursued.

12.2 DISCOUNTED PAYBACK

Your firm has the opportunity to invest $75,000 in a new project opportunity but due to cash flow concerns, your boss wants to know when you can pay back the original investment. Using the discounted payback method, you determine that the project should generate inflows of $30,000, $30,000, $25,000, $20,000, and $20,000 respectively for an expected five years after completion of the project. Your firm's required rate of return is 10%.

SOLUTION

To answer this question, it is helpful to organize the information into a table. Remember that:

Total outflow = $75,000
Required rate of return = 10%
Discount factor = $1/(1 + .10)^t$

Year	Cash Flow	Discount Factor	Net Inflows
0	($75,000)	1.00	($75,000)
1	30,000	.91	27,300
2	30,000	.83	24,900
3	25,000	.75	18,750
4	20,000	.68	13,600
5	20,000	.62	12,400

Payback = 3.3 years

12.3 INTERNAL RATE OF RETURN

Suppose that a project required an initial cash investment of $24,000 and was expected to generate inflows of $10,000, $10,000, and $10,000 for the next three years. Further, assume that our company's required rate of return for new projects is 12%. Is this project worth funding? Would it be a good investment if the company's required rate of return were 15%? Use the following figures to determine the answers to these questions:

Cash investment = $24,000
Year 1 inflow = $10,000
Year 2 inflow = $10,000
Year 3 inflow = $10,000
Required rate of return = 12%

TABLE 12.16 Discounted Cash Flows and NPV (II)

Year	Inflows	Outflows	Net Flow	Discount Factor	NPV
0	$ 0	$200,000	$(200,000)	1.0000	$(200,000)
1	0	50,000	(50,000)	.8696	(43,480)
2	50,000	0	50,000	.7561	37,805
3	100,000	0	100,000	.6575	65,750
4	200,000	0	200,000	.5718	114,360
5	75,000	0	75,000	.4972	37,290
Total					**$ 11,725**

SOLUTION

Step One: Trying 10%.

Year	Inflows	Discount Factor at 10%	NPV
1	$10,000	.909	$ 9,090
2	10,000	.826	8,260
3	10,000	.751	7,510
Present value of inflows			24,860
Cash investment			−24,000
Difference			$ 860

Decision: Present value difference at 10% is $860, which is too high. Try a higher discount rate.

Step Two: Using 12%.

Year	Inflows	Discount Factor at 12%	NPV
1	$10,000	.893	$ 8,930
2	10,000	.797	7,970
3	10,000	.712	7,120
Present value of inflows			24,020
Cash investment			−24,000
Difference			$ 20

Decision: Present value difference at 12% is $20, which suggests that 12% is a close approximation of the IRR. This project would be a good investment at 12%, but it would not be acceptable if the firm's required rate of return were 15%.

Discussion Questions

12.1 Describe the six important issues that managers should consider while evaluating screening models.

12.2 What are the benefits and drawbacks of checklists as a method for screening project alternatives?

12.3 How does use of the Analytical Hierarchy Process (AHP) aid in project selection? In particular, what aspects of the screening process does the AHP seem to address and improve directly?

12.4 What are the benefits and drawbacks of the profile model for project screening? Be specific about the problems that may arise in identifying the efficient frontier.

12.5 How are financial models superior to other screening models? How are they inferior?

12.6 What are the benefits and drawbacks of determining the payback period for a project to assess its viability?

12.7 What advantages do you see in the GE Tollgate screening approach? What disadvantages do you see? How would you alter it?

12.8 How can the project portfolio matrix help an organization to support overall strategic integration?

12.9 What are the keys to successful project portfolio management?

12.10 What are some of the key difficulties in successfully implementing project portfolio management practices?

Problems

12.1 Checklist. Suppose that you work in the pharmaceutical industry and have been asked to undertake a checklist exercise to assess which new drug development project to accept. The organization has decided on the following criteria and you have evaluated them as follows:

Drug A:

Expertise of current research staff	low
Technical facilities	low
Financial return	high
Level of medical innovation	high

Drug B:

Expertise of current research staff	high
Technical facilities	high
Financial return	medium
Level of medical innovation	low

Drug C:

Expertise of current research staff	medium
Technical facilities	low
Financial return	high
Level of medical innovation	low

Construct a table identifying the projects, their evaluative criteria, and ratings. Based on your analysis, which project would you accept? Justify your answer.

12.2 Checklist. Consider the following information in choosing among the four project alternatives below (labeled A, B, C, and D). Each has been assessed according to four criteria:

- Payoff potential
- Lack of risk
- Safety
- Competitive advantage

Project A is rated:

Payoff potential	high	Safety	high
Lack of risk	low	Competitive advantage	medium

Project B is rated:			
Payoff potential	low	Safety	medium
Lack of risk	medium	Competitive advantage	medium
Project C is rated:			
Payoff potential	medium	Safety	low
Lack of risk	medium	Competitive advantage	low
Project D is rated:			
Payoff potential	high	Safety	medium
Lack of risk	high	Competitive advantage	medium

Construct a project checklist model for screening these four alternatives. Based on your model, which project is the best choice for selection? Why? Which is the worst? Why?

12.3 **Scoring Model.** Suppose the information in Problem 2 was supplemented by importance weights for each of the four assessment criteria, where 1 = low importance and 4 = high importance:

Assessment Criteria	Importance Weights
1. Payoff potential	4
2. Lack of risk	3
3. Safety	1
4. Competitive advantage	3

Assume, too, that evaluations of *high* receive a score of 3, *medium* 2, and *low* 1. Recreate your project scoring model and reassess the four project choices (A, B, C, and D). Now which project alternative is the best? Why?

12.4 **Scoring Model.** Now assume that for Problem 3, the importance weights are altered as follows:

Assessment Criteria	Importance Weights
1. Payoff potential	1
2. Lack of risk	1
3. Safety	4
4. Competitive advantage	2

How does this new information alter your decision? Which project now looks most attractive? Why?

12.5 **Screening Model.** Assume that the following criteria relevant to the process of screening various project opportunities are weighted in importance as follows:

Quality (7)
Cost (3)
Speed to market (5)
Visibility (1)
Reliability (7)

Our company has four project alternatives that satisfy these key features as follows:

	Alpha	Beta	Gamma	Delta
Quality	1	3	3	5
Cost	7	7	5	3
Speed	5	5	3	5
Visibility	3	1	5	1
Reliability	5	5	7	7

Construct a project screening matrix to identify among these four projects the most likely candidate to be implemented.

12.6 **Screening Model.** Consider the following weighted criteria that will assess the viability of different charity event project proposals.

Cost (3)
Location (4)
Team expertise (3)
Celebrity endorsement (1)
Likely media coverage (4)
Fundraising potential (5)

Assume that you are required to recommend a charity event to fund. There are three project alternatives that satisfy these key features as follows:

	Music Festival	Fashion Show	Sports Event
Cost	5	4	3
Location	2	1	3
Team expertise	3	1	1
Celebrity endorsement	2	5	3
Likely media coverage	4	5	5
Fundraising potential	5	3	2

Construct a project screening matrix that will assess each event against its weighted criteria and identify among these three projects the most likely candidate to be implemented.

12.7 **Profile Model.** Assume the project profile model shown in Figure 12.17. Define the efficient frontier. The dotted

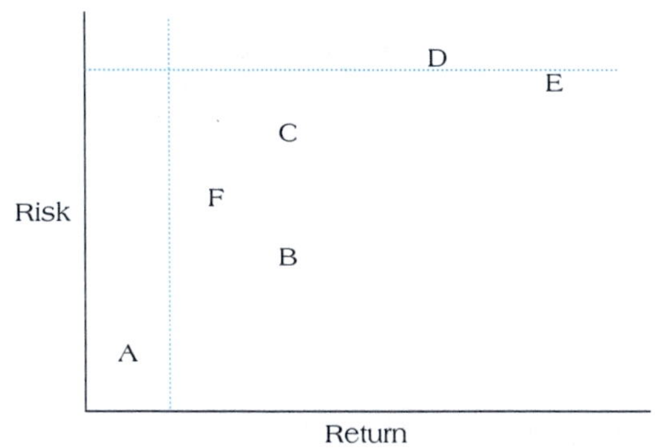

FIGURE 12.17 **Project Profile Model (Problem 7)**

lines represent the minimum return and the maximum risk that the company will accept. Which projects would be suitable for retaining and which should be dropped from the company's portfolio? Why?

12.8 **Profile Model.** Using the information from the profile model in Problem 7, construct an argument as to why project B is preferable to project C.

12.9 **Discounted Payback.** You have been tasked with advising the senior management on whether to invest in a project that will involve the company purchasing a new piece of high-spec software to enable an increased efficiency in supply and demand control. Their main concern is how long it will take for the project to return the initial investment. The software will cost $100,000 and should yield cost savings of $25,000 per year. Calculate the payback period of the investment if the discount rate is 10%.

12.10 **Net Present Value.** Assume that your firm wants to choose between two project options:

- Project A: $500,000 invested today will yield an expected income stream of $150,000 per year for five years, starting in Year 1.
- Project B: an initial investment of $400,000 is expected to produce this revenue stream: Year 1 = 0, Year 2 = $50,000, Year 3 = $200,000, Year 4 = $300,000, and Year 5 = $200,000.

Assume that a required rate of return for your company is 10% and that inflation is expected to remain steady at 3% for the life of the project. Which is the better investment? Why?

12.11 **Net Present Value.** Your organization must decide on whether to accept a project that has been requested by the research and development department. The initial investment is $350,000. You have projected that the cash in-flows from the project will be $65,000 in years 1–3 and $85,000 in year 4–6, with a discount rate of 7%. Should the organization authorize the project to go ahead? Why or why not?

12.12 **Net Present Value.** A company has four project investment alternatives. The required rate of return on projects is 20%, and inflation is projected to remain at 3% into the foreseeable future. The pertinent information about each alternative is listed in the following chart:

Project Carol	Year	Investment	Revenue Streams
	0	$ 500,000	$ 0
	1		50,000
	2		250,000
	3		350,000
Project George	**Year**	**Investment**	**Revenue Streams**
	0	$ 250,000	$ 0
	1		75,000
	2		75,000
	3		75,000
	4		50,000
Project Thomas	**Year**	**Investment**	**Revenue Streams**
	0	$1,000,000	$ 0
	1		200,000
	2		200,000
	3		200,000
	4		200,000
	5		200,000
	6		200,000
Project Anna	**Year**	**Investment**	**Revenue Streams**
	0	$ 75,000	$ 0
	1		15,000
	2		25,000
	3		50,000
	4		50,000
	5		150,000

Which project should be the firm's first priority? Why? If the company could invest in more than one project, indicate the order in which it should prioritize these project alternatives.

12.13 **Portfolio Management.** A large European software training provider has just acquired three smaller IT specialist training companies. The firm has completed an assessment of all current projects for their profitability and alignment with strategic plans using the project portfolio matrix in Figure 12.8. All projects are potential new training programs that are in development. Currently, there are 17 bread and butter, 3 pearls, 24 oysters, and 44 white elephant projects. Based on this model, what recommendations would you make for each category of projects? What other information might you need to help you make a decision? Justify your answer.

12.14 Project Screening. Assume you are the IT manager for a large urban health care system. Lately you have been bombarded with requests for new projects, including system upgrades, support services, automated record keeping, billing, and so forth. With an average of 50 software and hardware support projects going on at any time, you have decided that you must create a system for screening new project requests from the various departments within the health care system. Develop a project selection and screening system similar to GE's Tollgate process. What elements would you include in such a system? How many steps would you recommend? At what points in the process should "gates" be installed? How might a tollgate system for a software development company differ from one used by an architectural firm specializing in the development of commercial office buildings?

CASE STUDY 12.1

Keflavik Paper Company

In recent years, Keflavik Paper Company has been having problems with its project management process. A number of commercial projects, for example, have come in late and well over budget, and product performance has been inconsistent. A comprehensive analysis of the process has traced many of the problems back to faulty project selection methods.

Keflavik is a medium-sized corporation that manufactures a variety of paper products, including specialty papers and the coated papers used in the photography and printing industries. Despite cyclical downturns due to general economic conditions, the firm's annual sales have grown steadily though slowly. About five years ago, Keflavik embarked on a project-based approach to new product opportunities. The goal was to improve profitability and generate additional sales volume by developing new commercial products quickly, with better targeting to specific customer needs. The results so far have not been encouraging. The company's project development record is spotty. Some projects have been delivered on time, but others have been late; budgets have been routinely overrun; and product performance has been inconsistent, with some projects yielding good returns and others losing money.

Top management hired a consultant to analyze the firm's processes and determine the most efficient way to fix its project management procedures. The consultant attributed the main problems not to the project management processes themselves, but to the manner in which projects are added to the company's portfolio. The primary mechanism for new project selection focused almost exclusively on discounted cash flow models, such as net present value analysis. Essentially, if a project promised profitable revenue streams, it was approved by top management.

One result of this practice was the development of a "family" of projects that were often almost completely unrelated. No one, it seems, ever asked whether projects that were added to the portfolio fit with other ongoing projects. Keflavik attempted to expand into coated papers, photographic products, shipping and packaging materials, and other lines that strayed far from the firm's original niche. New projects were rarely measured against the firm's strategic mission, and little effort was made to evaluate them according to its technical resources. Some new projects, for example, failed to fit because they required significant organizational learning and new technical expertise and training (all of which was expensive and time-consuming). The result was a portfolio of diverse, mismatched projects that was difficult to manage.

Further, the diverse nature of the new product line and development processes decreased organizational learning and made it impossible for Keflavik's project managers to move easily from one assignment to the next. The hodgepodge of projects made it difficult for managers to apply lessons learned from one project to the next. Because the skills acquired on one project were largely nontransferable, project teams routinely had to relearn processes whenever they moved to a new project.

The consultant suggested that Keflavik rethink its project selection and screening processes. In order to lend some coherence to its portfolio, the firm needed to include alternative screening mechanisms. All new projects, for instance, had to be evaluated in terms of the company's strategic goals and were required to demonstrate complementarity with its current portfolio. He further recommended that in order to match project managers with the types of projects that the company was increasingly undertaking, it should analyze their current skill sets. Although Keflavik has begun implementing these and other recommendations, progress so

(continued)

far has been slow. In particular, top managers have found it hard to reject opportunities that offer positive cash flow. They have also had to relearn the importance of project prioritization. Nevertheless, a new prioritization scheme is in place, and it seems to be improving both the selection of new project opportunities and the company's ability to manage projects once they are funded.

Questions

1. Keflavik Paper presents a good example of the dangers of excessive reliance on one screening technique (in this case, discounted cash flow). How might excessive or exclusive reliance on other screening methods discussed in this chapter lead to similar problems?
2. Assume that you are responsible for maintaining Keflavik's project portfolio. Name some key criteria that should be used in evaluating all new projects before they are added to the current portfolio.
3. What does this case demonstrate about the effect of poor project screening methods on a firm's ability to manage its projects effectively?

CASE STUDY 12.2

Project Selection at Nova Western, Inc.

Phyllis Henry, vice president of new product development, sat at her desk, trying to make sense of the latest new project proposals she had just received from her staff. Nova Western, Inc., a large developer of business software and application programs, had been experiencing a downturn in operating revenues over the past three quarters. The senior management team was feeling pressure from the board of directors to take steps to correct this downward drift in revenues and profitability. The consensus opinion was that Nova Western needed some new product ideas, and fast.

The report Phyllis was reading contained the results of a project screening conducted by two independent groups within the new product development department. After several weeks of analysis, it appeared that two top contenders had emerged as the optimal new project opportunities. One project, code-named Janus, was championed by the head of software development. The other project idea, Gemini, had the support of the business applications organization. Phyllis's original charge to her staff was to prepare an evaluation of both projects in order to decide which one Nova Western should support. Because of budget restrictions, there was no way that both projects could be funded.

The first evaluation team used a scoring model, based on the key strategic categories at Nova Western, to evaluate the two projects. The categories they employed were: (1) strategic fit, (2) probability of technical success, (3) financial risk, (4) potential profit, and (5) strategic leverage (ability of the project to employ and enhance company resources and technical capabilities). Using these categories, the team evaluated the two projects as shown here. Scores were based on: 1 = low, 2 = medium, and 3 = high.

Project Janus

Category	Importance	Score	Weighted Score
1. Strategic fit	3	2	6
2. Probability of technical success	2	2	4
3. Financial risk	2	1	2
4. Potential profit	3	3	9
5. Strategic leverage	1	1	1
			Score = 22

Project Gemini

Category	Importance	Score	Weighted Score
1. Strategic fit	3	3	9
2. Probability of technical success	2	2	4
3. Financial risk	2	2	4
4. Potential profit	3	3	9
5. Strategic leverage	1	2	2
			Score = 28

The results obtained by this first team suggested that Project Gemini would the best choice for the next new project.

The second team of evaluators presented an NPV analysis of the two projects to Phyllis. In that analysis, the evaluators assumed a required rate of return of 15% and an anticipated inflation rate of 3% over the life of the project. The findings of this team were as follows:

Project Janus

Initial investment = $250,000	
Life of the project = 5 years	
Anticipated stream of future cash flows:	
Year 1	= $ 50,000
Year 2	= 100,000
Year 3	= 100,000
Year 4	= 200,000
Year 5	= 75,000
Calculated NPV = $ 60,995	

Project Gemini

Initial investment = $400,000	
Life of the project = 3 years	
Anticipated stream of future cash flows:	
Year 1	= $ 75,000
Year 2	= 250,000
Year 3	= 300,000
Calculated NPV = $ 25,695	

Thus, according to this analysis, Project Janus would be the project of choice.

The analyses of the two projects by different means yielded different findings. The scoring model indicated that Project Gemini was the best alternative, and the financial screening favored the higher projected NPV of Project Janus. Phyllis, who was due to present her recommendation to the full top management team in the afternoon, was still not sure which project to recommend. The evaluations seemed to present more questions than answers.

Questions

1. Phyllis has called you into her office to help her make sense of the contradictions in the two project evaluations. How would you explain the reasons for the divergence of opinion from one technique to the next? What are the strengths and weaknesses of each screening method?
2. Choose the project that you think, based on the two analyses, Nova Western should select. Defend your choice.
3. What does this case suggest to you about the use of project selection methods in organizations? How would you resolve the contradictions found in this example?

Internet Exercises

12.1 Go to the Web sites for the following organizations:

a. Merck & Company Pharmaceuticals: www.merck.com/about/
b. Boeing Corporation: http://www.boeing.com/boeing/companyoffices/aboutus/index.page
c. Rolls-Royce, Plc.: www.rolls-royce.com
d. ExxonMobil, Inc.: www.exxonmobil.com/Corporate/about.aspx

Based on your review of the companies' posted mission and strategic goals, what types of projects would you expect them to pursue? If you worked for one of these firms and sought to maintain strategic alignment with their project portfolio, what project options would you suggest?

12.2 Access the Web site www-01.ibm.com/software/awd-tools/portfolio/. What is IBM's philosophy regarding project portfolio management as demonstrated by this software product? What do they mean by stating that their goal is to help clients overcome the influence of the loudest voice in the room and use objective information to support decision making?

Notes

1. Texas Department of Transportation (2013). Project Selection Process.
2. Foti, R. (2002). "Priority decisions," *PMNetwork*, 16(4): 24–29; Crawford, J. K. (2001). "Portfolio management: Overview and best practices," in J. Knutson (Ed.), *Project Management for Business Professionals*. New York: Wiley, pp. 33–48; Wheatley, M. (2009). "Making the cut," *PMNetwork*, 23(6): 44–48; Texas Department of Transportation. (2013). *Project Selection Process*, http://ftp.dot.state.tx.us/pub/txdot-info/fin/utp/2013_psp.pdf.
3. Pascale, S., Carland, J. W., and Carland, J. C. (1997). "A comparative analysis of two concept evaluation methods for new product development projects," *Project Management Journal*, 28(4): 47–52; Wheelwright, S. C., and Clark, K. B. (1992, March–April). "Creating project plans to focus product development," *Harvard Business Review*, 70(2): 70–82.
4. Souder, W. E., and Sherman, J. D. (1994). *Managing New Technology Development*. New York: McGraw-Hill; Souder, W. E. (1983). *Project Selection and Economic Appraisal*. New York: Van Nostrand Reinhold.

5. Meredith, J. R., and Mantel, Jr., S. J. (2003). *Project Management,* 5th ed. New York: Wiley.
6. Khorramshahgol, R., Azani, H., and Gousty, Y. (1988). "An integrated approach to project evaluation and selection," *IEEE Transactions on Engineering Management,* EM-35(4): 265–70; Raz, T. (1997). "An iterative screening methodology for selecting project alternatives," *Project Management Journal,* 28(4): 34–39.
7. Cleland, D. I. (1988). "Project stakeholder management," in Cleland, D. I., and King, W. R. (Eds.), *Project Management Handbook,* 2nd ed. New York: Van Nostrand Reinhold, pp. 275–301.
8. Artto, K. A., Martinsuo, M., and Aalto, T. (Eds.) (2001). *Project Portfolio Management: Strategic Management Through Projects.* Helsinki: Project Management Association; Artto, K. A. (2001). "Management of project-oriented organization—Conceptual analysis," in Artto, K. A., Martinsuo, M., and Aalto, T. (Eds.), *Project Portfolio Management: Strategic Management Through Projects.* Helsinki: Project Management Association.
9. Pinto, J. K., and Millet, I. (1999). *Successful Information System Implementation: The Human Side,* 2nd ed. Newtown Square, PA: Project Management Institute.
10. Saaty, T. L. (1996). *The Analytical Hierarchy Process.* Pittsburgh, PA: RWS Publications.
11. Millet, I. (1994, February 15). "Who's on first?" *CIO Magazine,* pp. 24–27.
12. Mian, S. A., and Dai, C. X. (1999). "Decision-making over the project life cycle: An analytical hierarchy approach," *Project Management Journal,* 30(1): 40–52.
13. Foreman, E. H., Saaty, T. L., Selly, M., and Waldron, R. (1996). *Expert Choice.* McLean, VA: Decision Support Software.
14. Millet, I., and Schoner, B. (2005). "Incorporating negative values into the Analytical Hierarchy Process," *Computers and Operations Research,* 12(3): 163–73.
15. Evans, D. A., and Souder, W. E. (1998). "Methods for selecting and evaluating projects," in Pinto, J. K. (Ed.), *The Project Management Institute Project Management Handbook.* San Francisco, CA: Jossey-Bass.
16. Reilly, F. K. (1985). *Investment Analysis and Portfolio Management,* 2nd ed. Chicago, IL: The Dryden Press.
17. Keown, A. J., Scott, Jr., D. F., Martin, J. D., and Petty, J. W. (1996). *Basic Financial Management,* 7th ed. Upper Saddle River, NJ: Prentice Hall; Evans, D. A., and Souder, W. E. (1998). "Methods for selecting and evaluating projects," in Pinto, J. K. (Ed.), *The Project Management Institute Project Management Handbook.* San Francisco, CA: Jossey-Bass.
18. Meredith, J. R., and Mantel, S. J. (2003). *Project Management,* 5th ed. New York: Wiley.
19. Cooper, R. G. (2007). *Doing it Right: Winning with New Products.* Product Development Institute. www.iirusa.com/upload/wysiwyg/2008-M-Div/M2004/White_Papers/Doing-it-right.pdf.
20. Project Management Institute (2013). *A Guide to the Project Management Body of Knowledge,* 5th ed. Newtown Square, PA: PMI.
21. Dye, L. D., and Pennypacker, J. S. (Eds.) (1999). *Project Portfolio Management: Selecting and Prioritizing Projects for Competitive Advantage.* West Chester, PA: Center for Business Practices.
22. Elton, J., and Roe, J. (1998, March–April). "Bringing discipline to project management," *Harvard Business Review,* 76(2): 153–59.
23. Cooper, R. G. (2007), as cited in note 19.
24. Artto, K. A. (2001). "Management of project-oriented organization—Conceptual analysis," in Artto, K. A., Martinsuo, M., and Aalto, T. (Eds.), *Project Portfolio Management: Strategic Management Through Projects.* Helsinki: Project Management Association.
25. Matheson, D., and Matheson, J. E. (1998). *The Smart Organization: Creating Value through Strategic R&D.* Boston, MA: Harvard Business School Press; Cooper, R. G., Edgett, S. J., and Kleinschmidt, E. J. (2001), *Portfolio Management for New Products,* 2nd ed. Cambridge, MA: Perseus Press.
26. Lehtonen, M. (2001). "Resource allocation and project portfolio management in pharmaceutical R&D," in Artto, K. A., Marinsuo, M., and Aalto, T. (Eds.). (2001). *Project Portfolio Management: Strategic Management Through Projects.* Helsinki: Project Management Association, pp. 107–140.
27. Light, M., Rosser, B., and Hayward, S. (2005). *Realizing the Benefits of Project and Portfolio Management.* Stamford, CT: Gartner. www.atlantic-ec.com/edm/edm132/images/gartner_PPM_magic_quadrant_2009.pdf
28. Brown, S. L., and Eisenhardt, K. M. (1997). "The art of continuous change: Linking complexity theory and time-paced evolution in relentlessly shifting organizations," *Administrative Science Quarterly,* 42(1): 1–34.
29. Cooper, R., and Edgett, S. (1997). "Portfolio management in new product development: Less from the leaders I," *Research Technology Management,* 40(5): 16–28; Longman, A., Sandahl, D., and Speir, W. (1999). "Preventing project proliferation," *PMNetwork,* 13(7): 39–41; Dobson, M. (1999). *The Juggler's Guide to Managing Multiple Projects.* Newtown Square, PA: Project Management Institute.
30. Blakeslee, T. R. (2008, September 2). "The elephant under the rug: Denial and failed energy projects," RenewableEnergyWorld.com. www.renewableenergyworld.com/rea/news/article/2008/09/the-elephant-under-the-rug-denial-and-failed-energy-projects-53467; Baime, A. J. (2014, January 14). "Life with a Hydrogen Fuel Cell Honda," *Wall Street Journal.* http://online.wsj.com/news/articles/SB10001424052702304549504579320641877168558

13

Risk Assessment and Management

Chapter Outline

Chapter Objectives

After completing this chapter, you should be able to:

1. Define project risk.
2. Recognize four key stages in project risk management and the steps necessary to manage risk.
3. Understand five primary causes of project risk and four major approaches to risk identification.
4. Recognize four primary risk mitigation strategies.
5. Explain the Project Risk Analysis and Management (PRAM) process.

PROJECT MANAGEMENT BODY OF KNOWLEDGE CORE CONCEPTS COVERED IN THIS CHAPTER

1. Plan Risk Management
2. Identify Risks
3. Perform Qualitative Risk Analysis
4. Perform Quantitative Risk Analysis
5. Plan Risk Responses
6. Control Risks

PROJECT PROFILE

The Building that Melted Cars

Driving a car in London just got a lot more dangerous. A soon-to-be-completed skyscraper in the downtown area is having an impact that no one could have imagined: It is starting fires and melting cars. The building—designed by internationally renowned architect Rafael Viñoly—is a dramatic edifice with curved exterior walls. Built at 20 Fenchurch Street in London's financial center, the 38-story skyscraper is known locally as "the Walkie-Talkie" for its unusual shape.

But that curvilinear shape is exactly what's causing the problem: The south-facing exterior wall is covered in reflective glass, and because it's concave, it focuses the sun's rays onto a small area, not unlike the way a magnifying glass directs sunbeams onto a superhot pinpoint of light.

"Fundamentally it's reflection. If a building creates enough of a curve with a series of flat windows, which act like mirrors, the reflections all converge at one point, focusing and concentrating the light," says Chris Shepherd, from the UK's Institute of Physics. "It's like starting a fire with a parabolic mirror."

The beam caused by the curved skyscraper concentrating the sun's rays was measured at more than 110 degrees Celsius (230 degrees Fahrenheit) in September. So far, the building has been responsible for partially destroying a parked Jaguar XJ luxury car, catching carpets on fire in nearby shops, and shattering slate tiles at local restaurants. This situation is likely to be a recurring problem for any structure built within range of the powerful reflected light coming from the building.

Because the effect is caused by the sun's elevation in the sky at certain times of the day and during a specific time of the year, experts expect the intense light and dangerous heating effect will last about two hours a day over a period of three weeks. To help in the short term, the building's owners have contracted with local authorities to block off a limited number of parking spaces that are right in the reflected beam's path. Longer term solutions are more problematic; the design of the building will not change and of course, the sun's path is not likely to alter in the near future!

This isn't the first time Viñoly's architecture has been the subject of similar controversy: His Vdara Hotel in Las Vegas has been criticized for directing sunbeams onto the swimming pool deck that are hot enough to melt plastic and singe people's hair. The technical term for the phenomenon is a solar convergence, but the hotspot more popularly became known as the "Vdara death ray." The Vdara resolved the "death ray" effect with larger sun umbrellas, but fixing the problem in London might take a lot more work. "There are examples in the past where an architect has had to rebuild the façade," said Philip Oldfield, an expert in tall buildings at the University of Nottingham's Department of Architecture. "If this is serious, then I dread to think how expensive it will be."

Architectural critic Jonathan Glancey says the story is not unprecedented. In 2003, the opening of the Walt Disney Concert Hall in Los Angeles, designed by architect Frank Gehry, had a similar problem. "The building was clad from head to toe, right down to the pavement, in stainless steel panels, and they would send the sun dazzling across the

FIGURE 13.1 **London's Walkie-Talkie Building**

Source: Lionel Derimais/Corbis

sidewalks to hotspots where people were. It was measured up to 60C (140F). Local people living there complained they were having to crank their air conditioning up to maximum to cool things down," he says. Blinding glare also affected drivers passing the building. After computer models and sensor equipment identified the panels causing the problem, they were sanded down to break up the sun's rays.

In the case of the London Walkie-Talkie building, developers could employ a number of possible solutions. "They could coat the windows to reduce reflection—which would be a cheap fix—but the downside of that is it could reduce the light entering the building. Another solution would be for them to misalign the window frames, to slightly alter them by about a millimeter, but that would be very expensive," Chris Shepherd noted.[1]

INTRODUCTION

Projects operate in an environment composed of uncertainty. There is uncertainty regarding project funding, the availability of necessary resources, changing client expectations, potential technical problems—the list is seemingly endless. This uncertainty forms the basis for project risk and the need to engage in risk management. **Risk management**, which recognizes the capacity of any project to run into trouble, is defined as the art and science of identifying, analyzing, and responding to risk factors throughout the life of a project and in the best interests of its objectives. The difference between projects that fail and those that are ultimately successful has nothing to do with the fact that one lacks problems the other has. The key lies in the plans that have been made to deal with problems once they arise. The Project Management Institute defines **project risk** as "an uncertain event or condition that, if it occurs, has a positive or negative effect on one or more project objectives such as scope, schedule, cost, or quality. A risk may have one or more causes and if it occurs, may have one or more impacts." This definition is important because, unlike the past, when project risk was automatically assumed to lead to negative consequences, it is now recognized as the source of either opportunities *or* threats. As a result, whereas in the past leading project management researchers assumed that project risk was "an estimate of the probability of loss from a large population of unwanted circumstances,"[2] risk in the modern sense argues that the uncertainty that exists in any project can result in either positive or negative outcomes. Project managers must acknowledge the possibility that the same risk event may bring several outcomes, of both a positive and detrimental effect on the project. Underlying these definitions is the recognition that many events, both within the organization and outside its control, can affect our best efforts to successfully complete projects.

Risk management consists of anticipating, at the beginning of the project, unexpected situations that may arise that are beyond the project manager's control. These situations have the capacity to severely undermine the success of a project. Broadly speaking, for the manager, the process of risk management includes asking the following questions:

- What is likely to happen (the probability and impact)?
- What can be done to minimize the probability or impact of these events?
- What cues will signal the need for such action (i.e., what clues should I actively look for)?
- What are the likely outcomes of these problems and my anticipated reactions?

This chapter will explore the concept of project risk management in detail. We will address some of the principal sources of uncertainty, and hence risk, in projects. The chapter will also provide information on identifying the key steps to consider in formulating project risk management processes, methods for assessing risk impact, and processes for mitigating negative effects.

Project risk is based on a simple equation:

$$\text{Event Risk} = (\text{Probability of Event})\ (\text{Consequences of Event})$$

In other words, all risks must be evaluated in terms of two distinct elements: the likelihood that the event is going to occur as well as the consequences, or effect, of its occurrence. The risk of a project manager in your company being struck by lightning on the way to work would clearly constitute a high level of consequence to the project, but the probability of such an occurrence is sufficiently low to minimize your need to worry about it. On the other hand, people do change jobs, so an event such as the loss of a key project team member midway through the development phase may have both a potentially serious impact and a high degree of probability in some organizations. Hence, in those project environments, it would be appropriate to develop mitigation strategies to address this risk, given its high likelihood of occurring and the negative consequences it would engender. For example, the project manager could develop a bonus or other incentive program to reward personnel who remain on the project team as a useful response (risk mitigation) for the potential loss of key personnel during the project.

Risk and opportunity are mirror opposites of the same coin—opportunity emerges from favorable project uncertainties and negative consequences from unfavorable events. Figure 13.2 illustrates the dynamics of risk and opportunity over the project life cycle compared to the severity of negative consequences. Early in the life of a project, both risk and opportunity are high. The concept may be thought valuable, and the opportunities are strong, as are the negative risks. This result is due to the basic uncertainty early in a project's life cycle. Until we move forward into the development phases, many unanswered questions remain, adding to overall project uncertainty. On the other hand, the severity of negative consequences (the "amount at stake") is minimal early in the project's life. Few resources have yet been committed to the project, so the company's exposure level is still quite low. As the project progresses and more budget money is committed, the overall potential for negative consequences ramps up dramatically. At the same time, however, risk continues to diminish. The project takes on a more concrete form and many previously unanswered questions ("Will the technology work?" "Is the development time line feasible?") are finding answers. The result is a circumstance in which overall opportunity and risk (defined by their uncertainty) are dropping just as the amount the company has at stake in the project is rising.

The periods of greatest worry shown in Figure 13.2 are the execute and finish stages, at which point uncertainty is still relatively high and the amount at stake is rapidly increasing. The goal of a risk management strategy is to minimize the company's exposure to this unpleasant combination of uncertainty and potential for negative consequences.

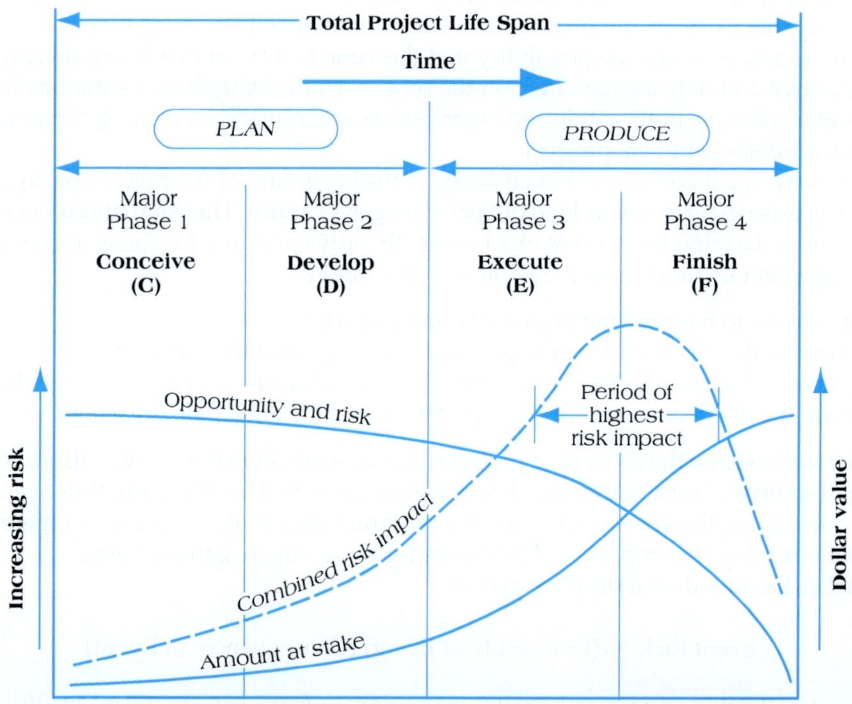

FIGURE 13.2 Risk Versus Amount at Stake: The Challenge in Risk Management

Source: R. Max Wideman. (2004). *A Management Framework for Project, Program and Portfolio Integration.* Victoria, BC, Canada, 2004. Copyright © 2004 by R. Max Wideman, AEW Services Vancouver, BC, Canada: Trafford Publishing. Figure from page 64. Reproduced with permission of R. Max Wideman.

BOX 13.1

Project Managers in Practice

Mathew Paul, General Electric Company

Mathew Paul is the Program Leader for Liquefied Natural Gas (LNG) Locomotives at GE Transportation in Erie, PA. He is currently responsible for leading the introduction of GE's natural gas locomotives for domestic markets from the Engineering function. Mathew completed his Bachelor's in Mechanical Engineering from The University of Kerala, India, in 1998. After a short stint at Cochin Port Trust and Lucent Technologies in India, he decided to pursue his Master's in Mechanical Engineering at The University of Alabama, Tuscaloosa. He also holds a Master's in Business Administration from Fogelman's College of Business at The University of Memphis, Tennessee. He is PMP certified and a Six Sigma Green Belt.

Mathew's career started as an Engineer at Cummins working on new internal combustion engine introduction projects to meet customer requirements and environmental regulations. His specific job was to identify combustion recipes and meet engine performance requirements. However, during the recession of 2008, he was given the responsibility of leading cost reductions as well as identifying profitable projects for the business. Identifying components that either need to be avoided in the engine or redesigned to gain economies of scale was not an easy task due to the wide application and customer base. Project management methodologies had to be implemented to execute the tasks and show the benefits to customers. It was in meeting these challenges that Mathew learned the art of project management and decided to switch careers to project management.

In 2010, Mathew led the introduction of a low-cost Cummins fuel injection system in China for the trucking market to capture market share and reduce dependence on other firms' products. It was the first of its kind for Cummins Fuel Systems and the team quickly realized that a different approach was required to be successful in China. His specific tasks included managing a project comprised of people from both China and the United States in designing, developing, testing, and manufacturing the fuel system. Due to the magnitude of the project, project management methodologies were introduced for the first time at Cummins Fuel Systems. In his words, "The main challenge was to use the data-based approach in communicating with customers, suppliers, and team members as the Chinese culture is mostly customer-centric and saying 'no' was never appreciated. The profit margin per unit was very low and business was based on volume. Maintaining risks—both in quality and cost—was critical for the success of the project."

After the successful implementation of the low-cost fuel system for Cummins, Mathew moved to GE Transportation to introduce PowerHaul™ locomotives in Australia and Korea. Paul recounts, "Even though the product was similar, the challenges were different—while meeting tight schedules was critical for Australia, maintaining customer relations and the highest quality were primary requirements for Korea." Mathew was also tasked to lead GE Transportation's first natural gas locomotive project for domestic markets. Due to the

FIGURE 13.3 An Example of the Next-Generation GE Locomotives that Mathew Paul Supports

Source: Sean Gallup/Getty Images

(continued)

availability of shale gas in the United States, the move to natural gas as the predominant fuel for locomotives seemed a logical next step. However, being a new technology, the safety of personnel and environment was considered as the paramount criteria. "The project was huge as part of my job involved coordinating the work of 250 people from five different countries with an initial investment of over $70 million dollars. We constructed and followed risk analysis and risk mitigation plans that had to be constantly updated—pretty much every day—due to the nature of the project. The project was capital intensive and eagerly awaited by customers, government, and competitors."

Mathew recollects that every project to date had been different and that makes it critical to follow a project management methodology for standard guidelines. He notes that planning is critical for the success of the project and executing the plan is essential; however, the key for any project manager is to have a "sixth" sense about potential risks and be able to respond to it at the earliest. Even with these challenges, the final outcome for any project manager is very fulfilling. "When the first natural gas locomotive was cranked and pulled the load at the desired speed, my eyes watered with joy. I got to experience several firsts in my life. When the first Cummins Tier 3 19L engine was rolled out of their Seymour engine plant, when the first fuel system rolled out of Cummins Wuhan plant, and when the first PowerHaul™ GE engine was unveiled at the customer property in Australia, to cite a few." As Paul has found, that is the moment when years of hard work, volumes of documentation, and hours of meeting converge and only a project manager can envision the final product and strive towards attaining the same on a daily basis.

13.1 RISK MANAGEMENT: A FOUR-STAGE PROCESS

Systematic risk management comprises four distinct steps:

- **Risk identification**—the process of determining the specific risk factors that can reasonably be expected to affect your project.
- **Analysis of probability and consequences**—the potential impact of these risk factors, determined by how likely they are to occur and the effect they would have on the project if they did occur.
- **Risk mitigation strategies**—steps taken to minimize the potential impact of those risk factors deemed sufficiently threatening to the project.
- **Control and documentation**—creating a knowledge base for future projects based on lessons learned.

Risk Identification

A useful method for developing a risk identification strategy begins by creating a classification scheme for likely risks. Remember that risk implies the potential for both positive and negative effects on the project. Risks commonly fall into one or more of the following classification clusters:[3]

- **Financial risk**—Financial risk refers to the financial exposure a firm opens itself to when developing a project. If there is a large up-front capital investment required, as in the case of Boeing or Airbus Industries' development of a new airframe, the company is voluntarily assuming a serious financial risk in the project. Construction companies building structures "on spec" provide another example. Without a contracted buyer prior to the construction, these companies agree to accept significant financial risk in the hopes of selling office space or the building itself after it is completed.
- **Technical risk**—When new projects contain unique technical elements or unproven technology, they are being developed under significant technical risk. Naturally, there are degrees of such risk; in some cases, the technical risk is minimal (modifications to an already-developed product), whereas in other situations the technical risk may be substantial. For example, Goodrich Corporation developed a modification to its electronic hoist system, used for cable hoists in rescue helicopters. Because the company had already developed the technology and was increasing the power of the lift hoist only marginally, the technical risk was considered minimal. On the other hand, the Spanish ship-builder Navantia is currently wrestling with serious performance problems in its newest generation of submarine, the S-80 class, because of the decision to include too many ground-breaking technical upgrades in one ship. The problems with the S-80 are so severe that the submarine itself is considered unsafe and not ready for sea trials (see Case Study 13.2 at the end of the chapter). The greater the level of technical risk, the greater the possibility of project underperformance in meeting specification requirements.

- **Commercial risk**—For projects that have been developed for a definite commercial intent (profitability), a constant unknown is their degree of commercial success once they have been introduced into the marketplace. Commercial risk is an uncertainty that companies may willingly accept, given that it is virtually impossible to accurately predict customer acceptance of a new product or service venture.
- **Execution risk**—What are the specific unknowns related to the execution of the project plan? For example, you may question whether geographical or physical conditions could play a role. For example, developing a power plant on the slopes of Mount Pinatubo (an active volcano) in the Philippines would involve serious execution risks! Likewise, poorly trained or insufficient project team personnel might constrain project execution. Execution risk is a broad category that seeks to assess any *unique* circumstances or uncertainties that could have a negative impact on execution of the plan.
- **Contractual or legal risk**—This form of risk is often consistent with projects in which strict terms and conditions are drawn up in advance. Many forms of contracted terms (e.g., cost-plus terms, fixed cost, liquidated damages) result in a significant degree of project risk. Companies naturally seek to limit their legal exposure through legal protection, but it is sometimes impossible to pass along contractual risk to other parties. For example, most U.S. railroads will not accept penalty clauses for late deliveries of components because they have an almost monopolistic control of the market. Therefore, organizations utilizing rail transportation must accept all delivery risk themselves.

After understanding the broad categories of risk, you want to anticipate some of the more common forms of risk in projects. The following list, though not inclusive, offers a short set of some of the more common types of risk to which most projects may be exposed:

- Absenteeism
- Resignation
- Staff being pulled away by management
- Additional staff/skills not available
- Training not as effective as desired
- Initial specifications poor or incomplete
- Work or change orders multiplying due to various problems
- Enhancements taking longer than expected

Although the broad categories and common types of risk in the preceding lists are both good starting points, you also need to consider common industry-specific risks that run across different types of projects in the specific field in which you are working. A number of methods, both qualitative and quantitative, are available for conducting risk factor identification for industry-specific risks, including:

- *Brainstorming meetings*—Bringing the members of the project team, top management, and even clients together for a brainstorming meeting can generate a good list of potential risk factors. Brainstorming is a qualitative idea-creation technique, not one focused on decision making. In order to be effective, brainstorming meetings must be free of judgments, criticism of others' viewpoints, and pressure to conform. A mini-scenario of risk management is at work. Think about it: Would you be willing to place your most creative ideas on the table in front of 10 other people if you were at risk of being immediately critiqued? Or might you be tempted to hold an idea for later if your boss required that you present it in a fully developed way? In short, the brainstorming environment needs to be made safe for the risk-averse.
- *Expert opinion*—This technique can be used in two alternative ways in assessing project risks. The more quantifiable method, commonly referred to as the Delphi approach, collects and consolidates the judgments of isolated anonymous respondents. For Delphi to be used effectively, some preliminary screening of potential contributors is usually necessary. The collective "wisdom" of the set of experts is then used as the basis for decision making. The simpler, more intuitive method for using expert judgments is based on the principle that "experience counts." You simply identify and consult people within the organization who have had similar experiences in running projects in the past or who have been with the firm long enough to have a clear grasp of the mechanics of project risk analysis. As obvious as this may seem, this opportunity may not be clear to everyone, particularly if management shifts recently have taken place in a firm or if new employees are not aware of the firm's project history.

- ***History***—In many cases the best source of information on future risks is history. Has a firm encountered a consistent pattern of problems while pursuing projects over time? What "storm signals," or events that have preceded past problems, have been detected? Experience can be used to identify not only risk factors but their leading indicators as well. The problem with experience is that it is no guarantee of future events. The issues or conditions that contributed to project risk in the past decade, year, or even month may not be relevant to current market conditions or the state of project work as it is now being conducted. Hence, history can be useful for identifying key project risk factors provided all parties employ a reasonable degree of caution when evaluating current projects through the portal of past events. Rauma Corporation of Finland, for example, developed state-of-the-art logging equipment that worked well in locations with good infrastructure to allow for frequent servicing. When it attempted to use the equipment in remote rain forest regions of Indonesia, however, the company found it had not anticipated the problems involved in routine servicing, including having to fly the machinery hundreds of miles out of the forests to servicing centers. Experience had not prepared the company for new risks.
- ***Multiple (or team-based) assessments***—Using single-case sources to identify project risks is itself a risky proposition because of the potential bias in any one person's viewpoint.[4] It makes sense that no one individual, regardless of her perceived degree of expertise, can possibly discern all sources of threat and project risk. Although an engineer is likely to be more attuned to technical risks, a cost accountant to budgetary risks, and so forth, not even the most seasoned manager with experience in many fields is all-knowing. A team-based approach to risk factor identification encourages identification of a more comprehensive set of potential project risks. At the same time, a collaborative approach can help persuade the half-convinced or uncommitted members of the team to support project goals.[5]

PROJECT PROFILE

Bank of America Completely Misjudges Its Customers

When Bank of America (BofA) decided it would begin to charge customers $5 per month in 2012 just to gain access to their funds via their debit cards, it was unprepared for a response that was far more hostile than it could have imagined. After announcing the new fee in late September 2011, the giant bank anticipated some negative reaction from its customers but thought that after an initial angry response, most would fall in line and grudgingly accept the fee. Perhaps BofA felt secure due to the initial decision by some of its largest competitors, including Wells Fargo, SunTrust, and JPMorgan Chase, to mirror the fees. If BofA thought "might made right," it was in for a giant surprise.

The announcement of a pending new charge just to allow customers to use their debit cards led to massive consumer anger directed at the bank and a pledge that the new fees would not be accepted. These informal protests were galvanized and given a degree of organization by the creation of several viral Internet and Facebook sites to support two major dates in November 2011: "Bank Transfer Day" (November 5) and "Dump your Bank Day" (November 8). Wells Fargo, SunTrust, and JPMorgan Chase banks all dropped their fee-charging plan in the face of these gathering protests, leaving BofA standing alone and continuing to assert its intention of charging the debit card fee. By October 2011, a poll by *TheStreet* showed a whopping 83% of BofA customers said they would indeed take the time out of their busy schedules and dump BofA. Contributing to the poor timing of the BofA announcement was the continuation of the "Occupy Wall Street" protests against financial institutions. Seen in this light, the timing of BofA's decision could not have been worse.

Belatedly realizing its mistake, BofA announced on November 1, 2011, that it was cancelling the $5 debit card fee. Although it is uncertain how many customers BofA lost as a result of this misguided decision, there is no doubt that it sacrificed a huge amount of customer goodwill. In a recession, when Americans were carefully watching their spending, BofA's decisions made no sense. Charging $5 to be allowed to use your own money angered too many and the announcement to drop the charge came too late, causing people to bail on BofA.[6]

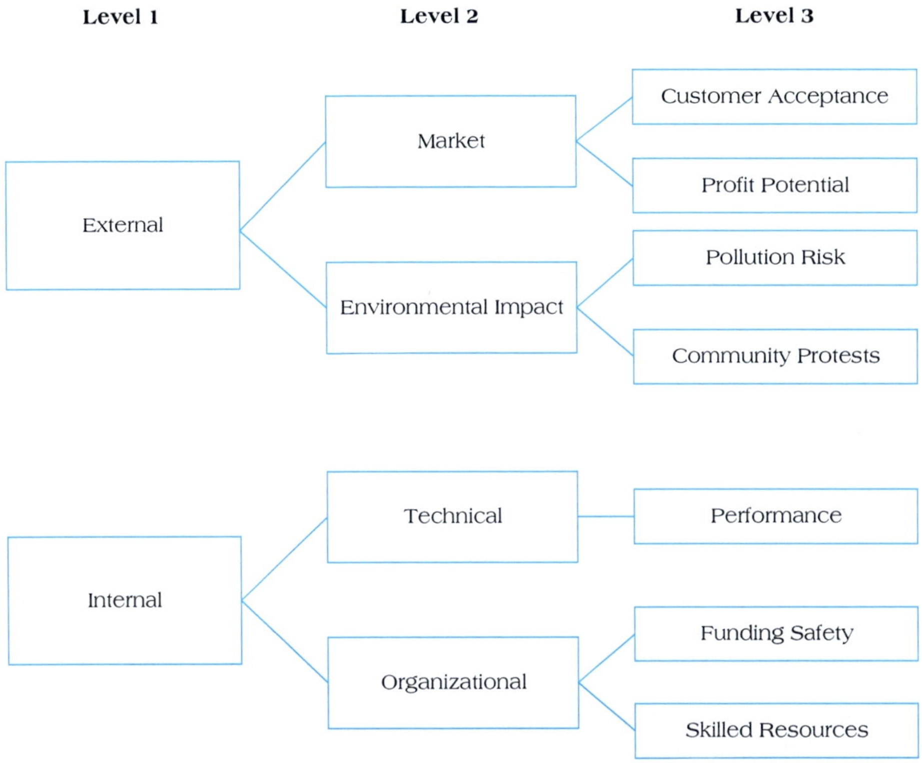

FIGURE 13.4 **Risk Breakdown Structure (RBS)**

Once the process of risk factor analysis is complete and the variety of circumstances or sources of risk have been uncovered, an assessment of potential risk impact can be undertaken.

Risk Breakdown Structures

In identifying and categorizing various project risks, one useful tool is the **Risk Breakdown Structure** (RBS). An RBS is defined as "a source-oriented grouping of project risks that organizes and defines the total risk exposure of the project."[7] We developed the Work Breakdown Structure (WBS) as a means to hierarchically organize and define the various elements of the project scope by breaking up the deliverables into increasingly distinct elements, known as work packages. An RBS employs a similar approach; however, in this case, our goal is to create a hierarchical representation of the project's risks, starting at the higher, general level and breaking the risks down to more specific risks at lower levels. For example, at the highest level, you have both external and internal risks. Specifying more closely, you may identify "Market risks," "Technical risks," "Environmental Impact risks," and "Quality risks" as second level categories. From this first level, your project team breaks out the specific types of risk associated with each of these broader concepts. Figure 13.4 gives an example of an RBS for this hypothetical project. Moving down to more specific risks, we can further classify "Market Risks" as consisting of customer acceptance and profit potential. Likewise, for "Environmental Impact," we have identified two specific risks: pollution risks and community protest potential. A similar de-classification can be conducted across each broader category of project risk. You can see that the advantage of the RBS is that it provides the project team with a visual representation of the critical risks for their project, as well as highlighting the specific components of these risks. This identification method helps with the next step in project risk management: the analysis of probability and consequences associated with each risk.[8]

Analysis of Probability and Consequences

The next step in the process consists of trying to attach a reasonable estimate of the likelihood of each of these risk events occurring. We can construct a risk impact matrix similar to the one shown in Figure 13.5.[9] The matrix reflects all identified project risks, each prioritized according to the probability of its occurrence, along with the potential consequences for the project, the project

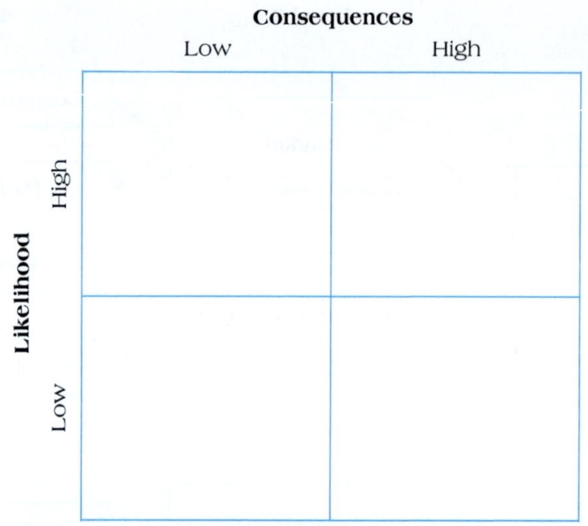

FIGURE 13.5 Risk Impact Matrix

team, or the sponsoring organization should the worst come to pass. Probability combined with consequences provides a sense of overall risk impact. With such a prioritization scheme, the project team is better able to focus their attention where their energy can do the most good.

Figure 13.6 shows a risk impact matrix in use by several *Fortune* 500 companies. Note that instead of a high-low classification, this alternative one features three levels: high, medium, and low. This matrix is further refined by classifying risk impact as either serious, moderate, or minor. The fundamental reason for employing this more complete matrix is to develop a sense of priority in addressing the various risks.

After a project team has worked through and completed a detailed matrix, it is better equipped to recognize the sorts of risks to which the project is subject and the "criticality" of each of those risks in terms of their potential impact on project performance. Clearly, the types of risks that are most relevant to project planning are those that the team classifies as having both high likelihood of occurring (probability) and high potential for harming the project (impact). Risks that fall into this category require detailed contingency planning in order to adequately protect the project's development cycle. Figure 13.6 shows how projects might be classified on the basis of their potential risk impact. The team first identifies the risk factors and then evaluates their impact using the matrix. You can see how the high-low-moderate classification scheme plays out in this example.

It is also useful to revisit our earlier point about the potential opportunities that may emerge from the uncertainty of project risk. That is, when analyzing the probability and consequences of risk events, we should include, as part of our calculation, the ways in which these uncertainties can

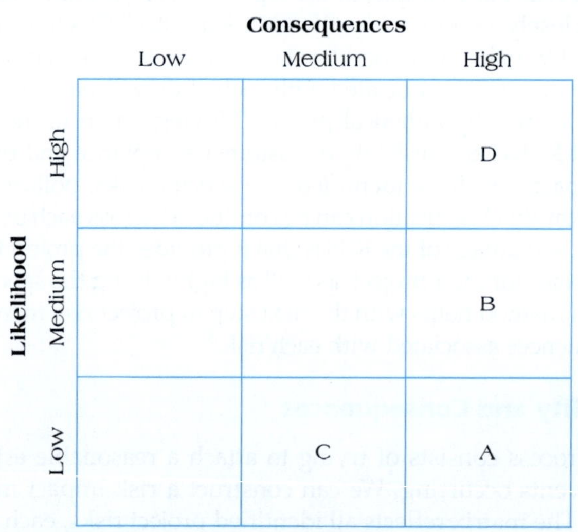

FIGURE 13.6 Classifying Project Risks

open up opportunities for the organization. For example, if our project team identifies several project risks (market, technical, political, etc.), brainstorming sessions can help us determine if these risks are distinctly negative or if they open up the possibility of finding innovative, win-win solutions by transforming them into opportunities. For example, a firm may have concern about the risk from possible governmental regulations regarding reducing greenhouse gases to slow man-made climate change. These concerns can lead a firm to adopt one of two actions: (1) defensive—employing lobbyists to try and derail the legislation to maintain business as usual, or (2) opportunistic—getting out ahead of the regulations by challenging business units to start employing nontraditional, sustainable solutions to technical challenges, leading to new products or processes that they can market to other firms facing similar challenges. As a result, part of our analysis of risk probability consequences should always take into consideration both negative and positive consequences.

Table 13.1 illustrates this quantitative method using the example of a firm developing a new software product for the retail market. The scenario considers both probability of failure and consequences of failure. In *probability of failure,* we are interested in identifying any factors that can significantly affect the probability that the new project can be successfully completed. Think of this category as requiring us to focus on the potential *causes* of failure. For the example in this section, let us assume that the issues identified as potential contributors are (1) maturity of the software design—is it a new product or based on an existing software platform? (2) complexity of the

TABLE 13.1 Determining Likely Risks and Consequences

		Probability of Failure (P_f)	
Score	**Maturity**	**Complexity**	**Dependency**
Low (0.1)	Existing software	Simple design	Not limited to existing system or clients. No external or uncontrollable events are likely to have an impact on the project.
Minor (0.3)	Minor redesign	Minor increase in complexity	Schedule or performance depends on an existing system. Effect on cost or schedule is minor.
Moderate (0.5)	Major change	Moderate increase	Moderate risk to schedule or performance due to dependence on existing system, facility, or processes. Effect on cost is moderate.
Significant (0.7)	Technology is available, but complex design	Significant increase	Schedule or performance depends on new system or process. Significant cost or schedule risk.
Major (0.9)	State of art, some research complete	Extremely complex	Schedule and performance depend on new system and process. Very high cost or schedule risk.

		Consequence of Failure (C_f)		
Score	**Cost**	**Schedule**	**Reliability**	**Performance**
Low (0.1)	Budget estimate not exceeded	Negligible impact on program, no impact on critical path	Minimal or no reliability consequence	Minimal or no performance consequence.
Minor (0.3)	Cost estimate exceeds budget by < 5%	Minor slip in schedule (less than 5%)	Small reduction in reliability	Small reduction in system performance.
Moderate (0.5)	Cost estimate exceeds budget by < 15%	Small slip in schedule starting to impact critical path	Some reduction in reliability	Some reduction in system performance. May require moderate debugging.
Significant (0.7)	Cost estimate exceeds budget by < 30%	Development time slips in excess of 1 month, requires readjustment of critical path	Significant degradation in reliability	Significant degradation in system performance. Guarantees are at risk. Serious debugging required.
Major (0.9)	Cost estimate exceeds budget by > 50%	Large schedule slips ensure the system will miss client time frame	Reliability goals cannot be achieved under current plan	Performance goals cannot be achieved. Results may not be usable.

TABLE 13.2 Calculating a Project Risk Factor

1. Use the project team's consensus to determine the scores for each Probability of Failure category: Maturity (P_m), Complexity (P_c), Dependency (P_d).
2. Calculate P_f by adding the three categories and dividing by 3:

$$P_f = (P_m + P_c + P_d)/3$$

3. Use the project team's consensus to determine the scores for each Consequence of Failure category: Cost (C_c), Schedule (C_s), Reliability (C_r), Performance (C_p).
4. Calculate C_f by adding the four categories and dividing by 4:

$$C_f = (C_c + C_s + C_r + C_p)/4$$

5. Calculate Overall Risk Factor for the project by using the formula:

$$RF = P_f + C_f - (P_f)(C_f)$$

Rule of Thumb:

Low risk	$RF < .30$
Medium risk	$RF = .30$ to $.70$
High risk	$RF > .70$

product—is the design relatively simple or is it highly complex in structure? and (3) dependency—can the product be developed independently of any system currently in place in the company or is it tied to current operating systems or practices? A number of factors can have an impact on the probability of a new project's successful completion. Although our example identifies three (maturity, complexity, and dependency), depending upon the project, a team may identify many unique issues or factors that will increase the probability of failure.

Under the dimension of *consequences of failure,* we are concerned with the issues that will highlight the *effects* of project failure. The consequences of failure require us to critically evaluate the results of a project's success or failure along a number of key dimensions. For this example, the organization has identified four elements that must be considered as critical effects of project failure: (1) cost—budget adherence versus overruns, (2) schedule—on time versus severe delays, (3) reliability—the usefulness and quality of the finished product, and (4) performance—how well the new software performs its designed functions. As with items shown under probability of failure, the set of issues related to the consequences of failure that should be clearly identified will be unique to each project.

Table 13.2 demonstrates the process of creating a project risk score. The scores for each individual dimension of probability and consequence are added and the sum is divided by the number of factors used to assess them. For example, under *probability of failure,* the scores of the three assessed elements (maturity, complexity, and dependency) are totaled to derive an overall score, and that number is divided by 3 to arrive at the probability score. This table shows the overall risk factor formula for the sample project, based on the quantitative assessment. A common rule of thumb assigns any project scoring below .30 as "low risk," projects scoring between .30 and .70 as "medium risk," and projects scoring over .70 as "high risk."

Risk Mitigation Strategies

The next stage in risk management is the development of effective risk mitigation strategies. In a general sense, there are four possible alternatives a project organization can adopt in deciding how to address risks: (1) accept risk, (2) minimize risk, (3) share risk, or (4) transfer risk.

ACCEPT RISK One option that a project team must always consider is whether the risk is sufficiently strong that any action is warranted. Any number of risks of a relatively minor nature may be present in a project as a matter of course. However, because the likelihood of their occurrence is so small or the consequences of their impact are so minor, they may be judged acceptable and ignored. In this case, the decision to "do nothing" is a reasoned calculation, not the result of inattention or incompetence. Likewise, for many types of projects, certain risks are simply part of the equation and must be factored in. For example, it has been estimated that the U.S. recording industry spends millions every year in developing, producing, and promoting new recording artists, knowing full well that of the thousands of albums produced every year, less than 5% are profitable.[10] Likewise, Chapter 12 detailed the extraordinary lengths that pharmaceutical manufacturers must go to and the high percentage of failures they accept in order to get a small percentage of commercially successful drugs to the marketplace. Hence, a high degree of commercial risk is embedded in the systems themselves and must be accepted in order to operate in certain industries.

MINIMIZE RISK Strategies to minimize risk are the next option. Consider the challenges that Boeing Corporation faces in developing new airframes, such as the newly introduced 787 model. Each aircraft contains millions of individual parts, most of which must be acquired from vendors. Further, Boeing has been experimenting with the use of composite materials, instead of aluminum, throughout the airframe. The risks to Boeing in the event of faulty parts leading to a catastrophic failure are huge. For example, several early flights were plagued by meltdowns in the aircraft's lithium ion batteries, manufactured in Japan by GS Yuasa. Consequently, the process of selecting and ensuring quality performance from vendors is a challenge that Boeing takes extremely seriously. One method Boeing employs for minimizing risk in vendor quality is to insist that all significant vendors maintain continuous direct contact with Boeing quality assessment teams. Also, in considering a new potential vendor, Boeing insists upon the right to intervene in the vendor's production process in order to ensure that the resulting quality of all supplier parts meets its exacting standards. Because Boeing cannot produce all the myriad parts needed to fabricate an aircraft, it seeks to minimize the resultant risk by adopting strategies that allow it to directly affect the production processes of its suppliers.

SHARE RISK Risk may be allocated proportionately among multiple members of the project. Two examples of risk sharing include the research and development done through the European Space Agency (ESA) and the Airbus consortium. Due to tremendous barriers to entry, no one country in the European Union has the capital resources and technical skills to undertake the development of the Ariane rocket for satellite delivery or the creation of a new airframe to compete with Boeing in the commercial aircraft industry. ESA and Airbus partners from a number of countries have jointly pooled their resources and, at the same time, agreed to jointly share the risk inherent in these ventures.

In addition to partnerships that pool project risk, ameliorating risk through sharing can be achieved contractually. Many project organizations create relationships with suppliers and customers that include legal requirements for risk to be shared among those involved in the project. Host countries of large industrial construction projects, such as petrochemical or power generation facilities, have begun insisting on contracts that enforce a "Build-Own-Operate-Transfer" provision for all project firms. The lead project organization is expected to build the plant and take initial ownership of it until its operating capacity has been proven and all debugging occurs before finally transferring ownership to the client. In this way, the project firm and the host country agree to jointly accept financial (risk) ownership of the project until such time as the project has been completed and its capabilities proven.

TRANSFER RISK In some circumstances, when it is impossible to change the nature of the risk, either through elimination or minimization, it may be possible to shift the risks bound up in a project to another party. This option, transferring risk to other parties when feasible, acknowledges that even in the cases where a risk cannot be reduced, it may not have to be accepted by the project organization, provided that there is a reasonable means for passing the risk along. Companies use several methods to transfer risks, depending upon their power relative to the client organizations and the types of risks they face. For example, if our goal is to prevent excessive budget overruns, a good method for directly transferring risk lies in developing fixed-price contracts. **Fixed-price contracts** establish a firm, fixed price for the project upfront; should the project's budget begin to slip, the project organization must bear the full cost of these overruns. Alternatively, if our goal is to ensure project functionality (quality and performance), the concept of liquidated damages offers a way to transfer risk through contracts. **Liquidated damages** represent project penalty clauses that kick in at mutually agreed-on points in the project's development and implementation. A project organization installing a new information system in a large utility may, for example, agree to a liquidated damages clause should the system be inoperable after a certain date. Finally, insurance is a common option for some organizations, particularly in the construction industry. Used as a risk mitigation tool, insurance transfers the financial obligation to an insuring agency.

Use of Contingency Reserves

Contingency reserves in several forms, including financial and managerial, are among the most common methods to mitigate project risks. They are defined as the specific provision for unforeseen elements of cost within the defined project scope. Contingency reserves are viewed differently, however, depending upon the type of project undertaken and the organization that initiates it. In construction projects, it is common to set aside anywhere between 10% and 15% of the construction price in a contingency fund. A contract to construct a $5 million building will actually be built to the cost of approximately $4.5 million, with the balance retained for contingency. In other fields, however, project teams are much more reluctant to admit to the up-front need for establishing contingency reserves, fearing that customers or other project stakeholders will view this as a sign of poor planning or inadequate scope definition.

The best way to offset concerns about the use of contingency reserves is to offer documentation of past risk events—unforeseen or uncontrollable circumstances that required the need for such contingency planning. Some of the concerns that might be generated may also be offset if the project team has done its homework and demonstrated in a detailed plan how contingency funds will be released as they are needed. Since the goal of creating contingency funds is to ensure against unforeseen risks, the key to their effective use lies in proactive planning to establish reasonable triggers for their release.[11]

TASK CONTINGENCY Perhaps the most common form of contingency reserve is **task contingency**, which is used to offset budget cutbacks, schedule overruns, or other unforeseen circumstances accruing to individual tasks or project work packages. These budget reserves can be a valuable form of risk management because they provide the project team with a buttress in the face of task completion difficulties. It may be found, for example, that some components or work packages of the project are highly unique or innovative, suggesting that development estimates and their related costs cannot be estimated with anything less than a bound of ±20% or even greater. Hence, task contingency becomes extremely important as a method for offsetting the project team's inability to make an accurate budget estimate.

EXAMPLE 13.1 Calculating Contingency Expected Cost

Suppose a project task is estimated to cost $10,000 to complete, but it is viewed as a high-risk operation. A task contingency multiplier would require our budget to reflect the following:

$$\text{(Task estimated cost)(Task contingency multiplier)} = \text{Expected cost}$$
$$(\$10{,}000)(1.2) = \$12{,}000$$

Naturally, as the project moves forward, it may be possible to reduce budget reserve requirements for task contingency because the project's scope will have been made clearer and its development will have progressed; that is, many of the tasks for which the contingency fund was established will have been completed. As a result, it is quite common for project organizations to assign a budget reserve to a project that is diminished across the project's development cycle.

MANAGERIAL CONTINGENCY While task contingency may involve the risk associated with the development of individual work packages or even tasks, managerial contingency is an additional safety buffer applied at the project level. **Managerial contingency** is budget safety measures that address higher-level risks. For example, suppose a project team has begun development of a new wireless communication device set to operate within guidelines established for technical performance. At some point in the midst of the development process, the primary client requests major scope changes that will dramatically alter the nature of the technology to be employed. Managerial contingency typically is used as a reserve against just such a problem. Another way managerial contingency may be used is to offset potentially disastrous "acts of God," which are natural disasters that, by definition, are unforeseeable and highly disruptive.

One final point about budget reserves at either the task or managerial level: It is extremely important that open channels of communication be maintained between top management and the project manager regarding the availability and use of contingency reserve funds. Project managers must be fully aware of the guidelines for requesting additional funding and how extra project budget is to be disbursed. If either the project manager or top management group uses contingency reserves as a political tool or method for maintaining control, the other party will quickly develop an attitude of gamesmanship toward acquiring those reserves. In this case, the atmosphere and communications between these key stakeholders will become characterized by distrust and secrecy—two factors guaranteed to ensure that a project is likely to fail.

INSURANCE **Insurance** can be a useful means for risk mitigation, particularly in certain types of projects, such as construction. Risks in construction go beyond technical risks or monetary/commercial risks to include health and safety concerns. Not all organizations or countries enforce the same rules regarding occupational health and safety standards. For example, there are countries in the developing world that do not require (or enforce) the use of safety harnesses for workers on skyscrapers, even though a fall would be fatal. Contractors acquire insurance as a means to offset the risks from the project that are often covered under contractual terms. For example, a construction contractor will routinely acquire insurance against loss or theft of building materials, workers' compensation, and professional or general liability. One of the duties of project managers in these settings is to ensure that all certificates of compliance are up to date; that is, all necessary insurance has been acquired and is valid for the life of the project to mitigate against potential risks.

Other Mitigation Strategies

In addition to the set of mitigation strategies already discussed, many organizations adopt practical approaches to minimizing risk through creating systems for effectively training all members of their project teams. One successful method for dealing with project risks involves **mentoring** new project managers and team members. In a mentoring program, junior or inexperienced project personnel are paired with senior managers in order to help them learn best practices. The goal of mentoring is to help ease new project personnel into their duties by giving them a formal contact who can help clarify problems, suggest solutions, and monitor them as they develop project skills. Another method for mitigating risks involves **cross-training** project team personnel so that they are capable of filling in for each other in the case of unforeseen circumstances. Cross-training requires that members of the project team learn not only their own duties but also the roles that other team members are expected to perform. Thus, in the case where a team member may be pulled from the project team for an extended period, other team members can take up the slack, thereby minimizing the time lost to the project's schedule.

Control and Documentation

Once project risk analysis has been completed, it is important to begin developing a reporting and documentation system for cataloging and future reference. Control and documentation methods help managers classify and codify the various risks the firm faces, its responses to these risks, and the outcome of its response strategies. Table 13.3 gives an example of a simplified version of the risk management report form that is used in several organizations. Managers may keep a hard-copy file of all these analyses or convert the analyses to databases for better accessibility.

Having a repository of past risk analysis transactions is invaluable, particularly to novice project managers who may recognize the need to perform risk management duties but are not sure of the best way to do them or where to begin. The U.S. Army, for example, has invested significant budget and time in creating a comprehensive database of project risk factors and their mitigation strategies as part of project management training for their officers. Newly appointed

TABLE 13.3 Sample Risk Management Report Form

Customer: ____________________ Project Name: ____________________

Budget Number: ____________________ Project Team: ____________________

Date of Most Recent Evaluation: ____________________

Risk Description: ____________________

____

____

____

Risk Assessment: ____________________ Risk Factor: ____________________

Discussion: ____________________

____

____

Risk Reduction Plan: ____________________ Owner: ____________________

____

Time Frame to Next Assessment: ____________________

Expected Outcome: ____________________

____

____

officers to Army procurement and project management offices are required to access this information in order to begin establishing preliminary risk management strategies prior to initiating new programs. Figure 13.7 illustrates a contingency document for adjustments to the project plan.

Establishing **change management** as part of risk mitigation strategies also requires a useful documentation system that all partners in the project can access. Any strategy aimed at minimizing

Probable Event	Adjustment to Plans
Absenteeism	
Resignation	
Pull-aways	
Unavailable staff/skills	
Spec change	
Added work	
Need more training	
Vendors late	

FIGURE 13.7 Contingency Document for Adjustments to Project Plan

a project risk factor, along with the member of the project team responsible for any action, must be clearly identified. The sample risk management report form shown in Table 13.3 includes the important elements in such change management. In order to be effective, the report must offer a comprehensive analysis of the problem, the plan for its minimization, a target date, and the expected outcome once the mitigation strategy has been implemented. In short, as a useful control document, a report form has to coherently identify the key information: what, who, when, why, and how.

- *What*—Identify clearly the source of risk that has been uncovered.
- *Who*—Assign a project team member direct responsibility for following this issue and maintaining ownership regarding its resolution.
- *When*—Establish a clear time frame, including milestones if necessary, that will determine when the expected mitigation is to occur. If it is impossible to identify a completion date in advance, then identify reasonable process goals en route to the final risk reduction point.
- *Why*—Pinpoint the most likely reasons for the risk; that is, identify its cause to ensure that efforts toward its minimization will correspond appropriately with the reason the risk emerged.
- *How*—Create a detailed plan for how the risk is to be abated. What steps has the project team member charted as a method for closing this particular project "risk window"? Do they seem reasonable or far-fetched? Too expensive in terms of money or time? The particular strategy for risk abatement should, preferably, be developed as a collaborative effort among team members, including those with technical and administrative expertise to ensure that the steps taken to solve the problem are technically logical and managerially possible.

Documentation of risk analysis such as is shown in Table 13.3 and Figure 13.7 represents a key final component in the overall risk management process.

PROJECT PROFILE

Collapse of Shanghai Apartment Building

The science and engineering principles surrounding the construction of simple apartment blocks are well known and have been practiced for centuries. And yet, even in the most basic of construction projects, events can sometimes transpire to produce shocking results. Just such a story occurred in late June of 2009 in China, when a Shanghai high-rise, 13-story apartment building literally toppled onto its side. The nearly completed structure was part of an 11-building apartment complex in a new development known as "Lotus Riverside." Because the 629-unit apartment building was not yet completed, it was virtually empty. Although one worker was killed in the accident, the tragedy could have been far worse had the building been fully occupied.

FIGURE 13.8 Shanghai Apartment Building Collapse

Source: Imago stock&people/Newscom

(*continued*)

The demand for affordable housing in Chinese cities has never been greater. With the economy humming along and a high demand for workers in economic regions such as Shanghai, there is a critical shortage of available housing. Private and governmental organizations are working to rapidly install new apartment blocks to keep up with this huge demand. Unfortunately, one of the risks with rapid building is the temptation to cut corners or use slipshod methods. When speed is paramount, the obvious concern is whether acceptable standards of building are being maintained.

In the Lotus Riverside building project, unfortunately, the construction firm opted for a procedure that is generally frowned upon (indeed, the method is outlawed in Hong Kong due to its inherent riskiness). Under this system, rather than pour a deep concrete base on which to rest the structure, a series of prestressed, precast concrete pilings were used as a set of anchors to "pin" the building into the ground. Although this system can work effectively with shorter buildings, it has long been considered unsafe for larger, higher structures.

The problem was made critical when the construction crews began digging an underground garage on the south side of the building to a depth of nearly 5 meters. The excavated dirt was piled on the north side of the building to a height of 10 meters. The underground pilings began receiving severe lateral pressure from the excavation, which was further compromised by heavy rainstorms. The storms undermined the apartment building on the south side, causing more soil erosion and putting even greater lateral pressure (estimated at 3,000 tons) on the anchor piling system (see Figure 13.9). Suddenly, the pilings began snapping and the building toppled over on its side. Local officials noted that the only lucky result of the collapse was that the building fell into an empty space. Considering that all the buildings in the complex had been constructed in a similar manner, there was a very real possibility of creating a chain reaction of toppling buildings, much like a set of dominos falling over.

The Chinese government immediately began to aggressively trace the cause of the collapse, questioning the private contractor's use of unskilled workers, questionable construction practices, and overall quality control. China's official news agency, Xinhua, said officials were taking "appropriate control measures" against nine people, including the developer, construction contractor, and supervisor of the project, after it was reported that the company's construction license had expired in 2004. Although it is certain that penalties will be imposed for the building failure, a less certain future awaits the tenants of the other buildings in the complex. After all, what more visible evidence could there be of the unsoundness of the construction in the complex than seeing a "sister building" lying on its side not far from the other structures? Hundreds of prospective tenants have besieged government offices, demanding refunds for apartments in the same complex that they purchased for upward of $60,000 but are now too frightened to live in.

Meanwhile, *China Daily*, the state-run newspaper, published an angry editorial blaming the collapse on the often corrupt relationship between Chinese property developers and local government officials who depend on property taxes and land sales for a significant proportion of their income. The paper raised fears—expressed by some construction industry insiders in China—that many buildings designed to have a 70-year life span "would not stand firm beyond 30 to 40 years" because of corner-cutting during China's rampant construction boom. "It is ironic that such an accident happened in Shanghai—one of the most advanced and international Chinese cities," the paper concluded. "The sheer fact that such a collapse occurred in the country's biggest metropolis should serve as warning to all developers and the authorities to ensure that construction projects do not cut corners and endanger people's lives."[12]

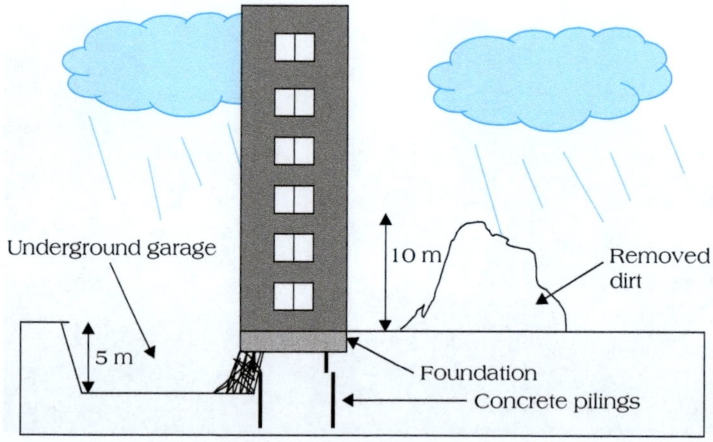

FIGURE 13.9 Schematic of Causes of Collapse

13.2 PROJECT RISK MANAGEMENT: AN INTEGRATED APPROACH

The European Association for Project Management has developed an integrated program of risk management, based on efforts to extend risk management to cover a project's entire life cycle. This program, known as **Project Risk Analysis and Management (PRAM)**, presents a generic methodology that can be applied to multiple project environments and encompasses the key components of project risk management.[13] The ultimate benefit of models such as PRAM is that they present a systematic alternative to ad hoc approaches to risk assessment, and hence can help organizations that may not have a clearly developed, comprehensive process for risk management and are instead locked into one or two aspects (e.g., risk identification or analysis of probability and consequences). The PRAM model offers a step-by-step approach to creating a comprehensive and logically sequenced method for analyzing and addressing project risk.

Among the key features of the PRAM methodology are the following:

- ***The recognition that risk management follows its own life cycle, much as a project follows a life cycle.*** Risk management is integrated throughout the project's entire life cycle.
- ***The application of different risk management strategies at various points in the project life cycle.*** The PRAM approach tailors different strategies for different project life cycle stages.
- ***The integration of multiple approaches to risk management into a coherent, synthesized approach.*** PRAM recommends that all relevant risk management tools be applied as they are needed, rather than in a "pick-and-choose" approach.

Each of the nine phases in the PRAM approach is based on a specific purpose and requires the completion of a comprehensive set of targets (deliverables). Completing PRAM gives the project team a template for getting the most out of risk management and helps them sharpen their efforts in the most productive manner. It also creates a document for merging risk management with overall project planning, linking them in a collaborative sense.

The nine phases of a comprehensive project risk assessment include the following steps:

1. *Define*—Make sure the project is well defined, including all deliverables, statement of work, and project scope.
2. *Focus*—Begin to plan the risk management process as a project in its own right, as well as determining the best methods for addressing project risk, given the unique nature of the project being undertaken.
3. *Identify*—Assess the specific sources of risk at the outset of the project, including the need to fashion appropriate responses. This step requires that we first search for all sources of risk and their responses and then classify these risks in some manner to prioritize or organize them.
4. *Structure*—Review and refine the manner in which we have classified risks for the project, determine if there are commonalities across the various risks we have uncovered (suggesting common causes of the risks that can be addressed at a higher level), and create a prioritization scheme for addressing these risks.
5. *Clarify ownership of risks*—Distinguish between risks that the project organization is willing to handle and those that the clients are expected to accept as well as allocate responsibility for managing risks and responses.
6. *Estimate*—Develop a reasonable estimate of the impacts on the project of both the identified risks and the proposed solutions. What are the likely scenarios and their relative potential costs?
7. *Evaluate*—Critically evaluate the results of the estimate phase to determine the most likely plan for mitigating potential risks. Begin to prioritize risks and the project team's responses.
8. *Plan*—Produce a project risk management plan that proactively offers risk mitigation strategies for the project as needed.
9. *Manage*—Monitor actual progress with the project and associated risk management plans, responding to any variances in these plans, with an eye toward developing these plans for the future.

TABLE 13.4 A Generic Risk Management Process (RMP) Following the PRAM Methodology

Phases	Purposes	Deliverables
Define	Consolidate relevant existing information about the project.	A clear, unambiguous, shared understanding of all key aspects of the project documented, verified, and reported.
Focus	1. Identify scope and provide a strategic plan for the RMP. 2. Plan the RMP at an operational level.	A clear, unambiguous, shared understanding of all relevant key aspects of the RMP, documented, verified, and reported.
Identify	1. Identify where risk might arise. 2. Identify what we might do about this risk in proactive and reactive response terms. 3. Identify what might go wrong with our responses.	All key risks and responses identified; both threats and opportunities classified, characterized, documented, verified, and reported.
Structure	1. Test simplifying assumptions. 2. Provide more complex structure when appropriate.	A clear understanding of the implications of any important simplifying assumptions about relationships among risks, responses, and base plan activities.
Ownership	1. Client contractor allocation of ownership and management of risks and responses. 2. Allocation of client risks to named individuals. 3. Approval of contractor allocations.	Clear ownership and management allocations effectively and efficiently defined, legally enforceable in practice where appropriate.
Estimate	1. Identify areas of clear significant uncertainty. 2. Identify areas of possible significant uncertainty.	1. A basis for understanding which risks and responses are important. 2. Estimates of likelihood and impact on scenario or in numeric terms.
Evaluate	Synthesis and evaluation of the results of the estimate phase.	Diagnosis of all important difficulties and comparative analysis of the implications of responses to these difficulties, with specific deliverables like a prioritized list of risks.
Plan	Project plan ready for implementation and associated risk management plan.	1. Base plans in activity terms at the detailed level of implementation. 2. Risk assessment in terms of threats and opportunities prioritized, assessed in terms of impact. 3. Recommended proactive and reactive contingency plans in activity terms.
Manage	1. Monitoring. 2. Controlling. 3. Developing plans for immediate implementation.	1. Diagnosis of a need to revisit earlier plans and initiation of replanning as appropriate. 2. Exception reporting after significant events and associated replanning.

Table 13.4 shows a generic risk management process following the PRAM methodology. At each of the risk management phases, specific project deliverables can be identified, allowing the project team to create comprehensive project risk management documentation while addressing specific steps along the way. These deliverables are important because they indicate to project managers exactly the types of information they should be collecting at different phases of the project and the materials they should make available to relevant stakeholders.

The PRAM model for risk management is extremely helpful because it offers project managers a systematic process for best employing risk assessment and mitigation strategies. Composed of nine interconnected steps that form a logical sequence, PRAM creates a unifying structure under which effective risk management can be conducted. Because it follows the logic of the project life cycle, PRAM should be conducted not as a "one-shot" activity but as an ongoing, progressive scheme that links project development directly to accurate risk assessment and management.

Finally, in identifying the key deliverables at each step in the process, the PRAM model ensures a similarity of form that allows top management to make reasonable comparisons across all projects in an organization's portfolio.

Project risk management demonstrates the value of proactive planning for projects as a way to anticipate and, hopefully, mitigate serious problems that could adversely affect the project at some point in the future.[14] The value of this troubleshooting process is that it requires us to think critically, to be devil's advocates when examining how we are planning to develop a project. Research and common sense suggest, in the words of the adage, "An ounce of prevention is worth a pound of cure." The more sophisticated and systematic we are about conducting project risk management, the more confident we can be, as the project moves through planning and into its execution phase, that we have done everything possible to prepare the way for project success.

Summary

1. **Define project risk.** Project risk is defined as any possible event that can negatively affect the viability of a project. We frequently use the equation: Risk event = (Probability of event)(Consequences of event). Effective risk management goes a long way toward influencing project development. To be effective, however, project risk management needs to be done early in the project's life. To quote Shakespeare's *Macbeth:* "If it were done, when 'tis done; then 'twere well it were done quickly."[15] As an important element in overall project planning, risk management identifies specific risks that can have a detrimental effect on project performance and quantifies the impact each risk may have. The impact of any one risk factor is defined as the product of the likelihood of the event's occurrence and the adverse consequences that would result. The tremendous number of unknowns in the early phases of a project makes this the time when risk is highest. As the project moves forward, the team continues to address risk with technical, administrative, and budgetary strategies.
2. **Recognize four key stages in project risk management and the steps necessary to manage risk.** There are four distinct phases of project risk management: (1) risk identification, (2) analysis of probability and consequences, (3) risk mitigation strategies, and (4) control and documentation. Risk identification focuses on determining a realistic set of risk factors that a project faces. In analysis of probability and consequences, the project team prioritizes its responses to these various risk factors by assessing the "impact factor" of each one. Impact factors are determined either in a qualitative manner, using a matrix approach and consensus decision making, or in more quantitative ways, in which all relevant probability and consequence parameters are laid out and used to assess overall project risk. The project team begins the process of developing risk mitigation strategies once a clear vision of risk factors is determined. The last step in the risk management process, control and documentation, is based on the knowledge that risk management strategies are most effective when they have been codified and introduced as part of standard operating procedures. The goal is to create systematic and repeatable strategies for project risk management.
3. **Understand five primary causes of project risk and four major approaches to risk identification.** The five primary causes of project risk are (1) financial risk, (2) technical risk, (3) commercial risk, (4) execution risk, and (5) contractual or legal risk. Among the most common methods for risk identification are (1) brainstorming meetings, (2) expert opinion, (3) past history, and (4) multiple or team-based assessments.
4. **Recognize four primary risk mitigation strategies.** Risks can be mitigated through four primary approaches. First, we can simply accept the risk. We may choose to do this in a situation in which we either have no alternative or we consider the risk small enough to be acceptable. Second, we can seek to minimize risk, perhaps through entering partnerships or joint ventures in order to lower our company's exposure to the risk. Third, we can share risk with other organizations or project stakeholders. Finally, when appropriate, we may seek to transfer risk to other project stakeholders.
5. **Explain the Project Risk Analysis and Management (PRAM) process.** PRAM is a generic project risk management approach that offers a model for the life cycle steps a project team might adopt in developing a risk management methodology. Nine distinct steps in the PRAM model present each phase of the process and its associated deliverables.

Key Terms

Analysis of probability and consequences	Control and documentation	Liquidated damages	Risk Breakdown Structure
Change management	Cross-training	Managerial contingency	Risk identification
Commercial risk	Execution risk	Mentoring	Risk management
Contingency reserves	Financial risk	Project risk	Risk mitigation strategies
Contractual or legal risk	Fixed-price contact	Project Risk Analysis and Management (PRAM)	Task contingency
	Insurance		Technical risk

Solved Problem

13.1 QUANTITATIVE RISK ASSESSMENT

Refer to the risk factors shown in Table 13.1. Assume your project team has decided upon the following risk values:

$$P_m = .1 \quad C_c = .7$$
$$P_c = .5 \quad C_s = .5$$
$$P_d = .9 \quad C_r = .3$$
$$C_p = .1$$

You wish to determine the overall project risk using a quantitative method. Following the formulas shown in Table 13.2, we can calculate both the probability of project risk score and the consequences of project risk score, as follows:

$$P_f = (.1 + .5 + .9)/3 = .5$$
$$C_f = (.7 + .5 + .3 + .1)/4 = .4$$
$$RF = .5 + .4 - (.5)(.4) = .70$$

Conclusion: Medium risk to overall project.

Discussion Questions

13.1 Do you agree with the following statement: "With proper planning it is possible to eliminate most/all risks from a project"? Why or why not?

13.2 In evaluating projects across industries, it is sometimes possible to detect patterns in terms of the more common types of risks they routinely face. Consider the development of a new software product and compare it to coordinating an event, such as a school dance. What likely forms of risk would your project team face in either of these circumstances?

13.3 Analyze Figure 13.2 (degree of risk over the project life cycle). What is the practical significance of this model? What implications does it suggest for managing risk?

13.4 What are the benefits and drawbacks of using the various forms of risk identification mentioned in the chapter (e.g., brainstorming meetings, expert opinion, etc.)?

13.5 Discuss the advantages of using the Risk Breakdown Structure (RBS) as a tool to organize risks on a project.

13.6 What are the benefits and drawbacks of using a quantitative risk assessment tool such as the one shown in the chapter?

13.7 Discuss and provide some examples of how a project manager may transfer a risk on a project. Can you identify any limitations with this response?

13.8 Explain the difference between managerial contingency and task contingency.

13.9 Why is it important for the risk management report form to include who should be directly responsible for the risk?

13.10 Consider the following observation: "The problem with risk analysis is that it is possible to imagine virtually anything going wrong on a project. Where do you draw the line? In other words, how far do you take risk analysis before it becomes overkill?" How would you respond?

Problems

13.1 **Risk Identification.** Assume that you are a project manager working for an organization that produces carbonated drinks. It has just decided to break into the confectionary market and you have been assigned a project to develop and launch a new chocolate bar for the company. You are now required to construct a risk breakdown structure, identifying all potential internal and external risks and grouping them into appropriate levels.

13.2 **Qualitative Risk Assessment.** Imagine that you are a member of a project team that has been charged to develop a new product for the residential building industry. Using a qualitative risk analysis matrix, develop a risk assessment for a project based on the following information:

Identified Risk Factors	Likelihood
1. Key team members pulled off project	1. High
2. Chance of economic downturn	2. Low
3. Project funding cut	3. Medium
4. Project scope changes	4. High
5. Poor spec. performance	5. Low

Based on this information, how would you rate the consequences of each of the identified risk factors? Why? Construct the risk matrix and classify each of the risk factors in the matrix.

13.3 Developing Risk Mitigation Strategies. Develop a preliminary risk mitigation strategy for each of the risk factors identified in Problem 2. If you were to prioritize your efforts, which risk factors would you address first? Why?

13.4 Quantitative Risk Assessment. Assume the following information:

Probability of Failure	Consequences of Failure
Maturity = .3	Cost = .1
Complexity = .3	Schedule = .7
Dependency = .5	Performance = .5

Calculate the overall risk factor for this project. Would you assess this level of risk as low, moderate, or high? Why?

13.5 Quantitative Risk Assessment. Assume the following information for an IT project.

Probability of Failure	Consequences of Failure
Maturity = .7	Cost = .9
Complexity = .7	Schedule = .7
Dependency = .5	Performance = .3
Client Concerns = .5	Future Business = .5
Programmer Skill = .3	

Calculate the overall risk factor for this project. Would you assess this level of risk as low, moderate, or high? Why?

13.6 Developing Risk Mitigation Strategies. Assume that you are a project team member for a highly complex project based on a new technology that has never been directly proven in the marketplace. Further, you require the services of a number of subcontractors to complete the design and development of this project. Because you are facing severe penalties in the event the project is late to market, your boss has asked you and your project team to develop risk mitigation strategies to minimize your company's exposure. Discuss the types of risk that you are likely to encounter. How should your company deal with them (accept them, share them, transfer them, or minimize them)? Justify your answers.

13.7 Assessing Risk. You are a project manager that has undertaken a full-risk analysis exercise for designing and installing new customer relationship management software into a medium-sized company, and you are in the process of hiring an IT specialist to create the software. Just before the vacancy is advertised, a senior manager is contemplating outsourcing the whole project to a supplier, but wants your opinion, based on evidence first. Discuss how you would deal with this. What actions would you take to ensure the right decision is made?

CASE STUDY 13.1

Classic Case: de Havilland's Falling Comet

The Development of the Comet

The de Havilland Aircraft Company of Great Britain had long been respected in the aircraft manufacturing industry for its innovative and high-performance designs. Coming off its excellent work during World War II, the company believed that it stood poised on the brink of success in the commercial airframe industry. The de Havilland designers and executives accurately perceived that the next generation of airplane would be jet-powered. Consequently, they decreed that their newest commercial airframe, tentatively called the Comet, would employ jet power and other leading-edge technology.

Jets offered a number of advantages over propeller-driven airplanes, the most obvious of which was speed. Jets could cruise at nearly 450 miles per hour compared with the 300 miles per hour a propeller could generate. For overseas flight, in particular, this advantage was important. It could reduce the length of long flights from a mind-numbing two to three days to mere hours, encouraging more and more businesspeople and tourists to use airplanes as their primary method for travel. Further, jets tended to be quieter than propeller-driven aircraft, giving a more comfortable interior sound level and ride to passengers.

De Havilland engineers sought to create a streamlined airplane that could simultaneously carry up to 50 passengers in comfort, while maintaining aerodynamics and high speed. After working with a number of design alternatives, the Comet began to take shape. Its design was, indeed, distinctive: The four jet engines

(continued)

FIGURE 13.10 The de Havilland Comet

Source: Heanly Mirrorpix/Newscom

were embedded in pairs in the wing roots, at the point where they joined the fuselage. From the front, the aircraft looked as though its wings were literally held in place by the engines. The result of these innovative engineering designs was an aircraft that had remarkable stability in flight, was sleek in appearance, and was very fast.

Another distinctive feature of the aircraft was the pressurized cabin, intended to maintain passenger comfort at cruising altitudes of up to 30,000 feet. In its original testing for safety, de Havilland engineers had pressurized the airframe to more than five times the recommended air density to ensure that there was a clean seal. Consequently, they were confident that the pressurization system would perform well at its lower, standardized settings. Finally, in an effort to add some flair to the design, each window in the passenger cabin was square, rather than the small, round or oval shapes so commonly used.

Knowing that it was facing competition from Boeing Corporation to be first to market with a commercial jet, de Havilland's goal was to introduce its new aircraft as quickly as possible, in order to establish the standard for the commercial airline industry. At first, it appeared the company had succeeded: BOAC (British Overseas Airways Corporation) ordered several Comets, as did Air France and the British military. De Havilland also received some queries from interested American airline companies, notably Pan American Airlines. It looked as though de Havilland's strategy was working; the company was first to market with a radical new design, using a number of state-of-the-art technologies. BOAC's first nine Comet 1 s entered service with the airline on May 2, 1952. The future looked bright.

Troubles

In early May of 1953, a brand new Comet operated by BOAC left Calcutta, India, and flew off into the afternoon sky. Six minutes later and only 22 miles from Calcutta's Dum Dum Airport, the aircraft exploded and plunged to earth, killing all 43 passengers and crew on board. There had been no indication of problems and no warning from the pilots of technical difficulties. Investigators from Great Britain and India tended to believe the crash came about due to pilot error coupled with weather conditions. Evidence from the wreckage, including the tail section, seemed to indicate that the aircraft had been struck by something heavy, but without any additional information forthcoming, both the authorities and de Havilland engineers laid the blame on external causes.

January 10, 1954, was a mild, clear day in Rome as passengers boarded their BOAC aircraft for the final leg of their flight from Singapore to London. When the airplane reached its cruising altitude and speed, it disintegrated over the Mediterranean Sea, near the island of Elba. Most of the airplane was lost at the bottom of the sea, but amid the flotsam 15 bodies of passengers and crew were recovered. A local physician who examined the remains noted: "They showed no look of terror. Death must have come without warning."

As a safety precaution, BOAC instituted a ban on the use of Comets until the airplanes had been thoroughly checked over. Technicians could find nothing wrong with the new aircraft and, following recertification, the airplanes were again brought back into service.

Alas, it was too soon. On April 8, only 16 days after the Comet was reintroduced into service, a third aircraft, operated by South African Airways, departed from Rome's Ciampino airport for Cairo, one of the legs of its regular flight from London to Johannesburg. Under perfect flying weather, the airplane rapidly gained its cruising altitude of 26,000 feet and its airspeed of almost 500 miles an hour. Suddenly, the flight radio went silent and failed to answer repeated calls. A search of the ocean off the island of Stromboli, Italy, turned up an oil slick and some debris. Because of the depth of the water and the time necessary to arrive at the crash site, there was little to be found by search crews. Five bodies were all that were recovered this time, though with an eerie similarity to the victims of the second disaster: Facial expressions showed no fear, as though death had come upon them suddenly.

What Went Wrong?

Investigators swarmed over the recovered wreckage of the aircraft and reexamined the pieces from the first Calcutta accident while also conducting underwater searches at the sight of the second crash near the island of Elba. Guided by underwater cameras, investigators were able to collect sufficient aircraft fragments (in fact, they finally recovered nearly 70% of the airframe) to make some startling discoveries. The foremost finding, from the recovery of the entire, intact tail section, was that the fuselage of the aircraft had exploded. Second, it appeared that engine failure was not the cause of the accidents. Another finding was equally important: The wings and fuselage showed unmistakable signs of metal fatigue, later shown to be the cause of failure in all three aircraft. This point was important because it advanced the theory that the problem was one of structural design rather than simple part failure.

Britain's Civil Aviation Board immediately grounded the entire Comet fleet pending extensive reviews and airworthiness certification. For the next five months, the CAB set out on an extensive series of tests to isolate the exact causes of the mysterious crashes. Before testing was complete, one Comet had been tested literally to destruction, another had its fuel tanks ruptured, more than 70 complete test flights were made in a third, and between 50 and 100 test models were broken up. The results of the extensive tests indicated a number of structural and design flaws.

Although the aircraft's designers were convinced that the structure would remain sound for 10,000 flight hours before requiring major structural overhauling, simulations showed unmistakable signs of metal fatigue after the equivalent of only 3,000 flight hours. Experts argued that even when fatigue levels were revised downward to less than 3,000 hours, Comets would not be safe beyond 1,000 flying hours, a ludicrously low figure in terms of the amount of use a commercial airliner is expected to receive. In addition, testing of the fuselage offered disturbing indications of the cause of failure. Specifically, cracks began developing in the corners of the cabin windows, and these cracks were exacerbated by repeated pressurization and depressurization of the cabin. The investigators noted that this result was most pronounced along the rivet lines near the fuselage windows.

Testing also demonstrated that the wings had a low resistance to fatigue. At a number of stages in the tests, serious cracks appeared, starting at the rivet holes near the wheel wells and finally resulting in rivet heads in the top wing surface actually shearing off. Engineers and investigators were finding incontrovertible evidence in the pieces of recovered wreckage that the cause of the sudden disintegration of the aircraft could only have been due to cabin pressure blowout. Engineers suspected that the critical failure of the aircraft occurred following sudden depressurization, when one or more windows were literally blown out of the aircraft. This led to a sudden "gyroscopic moment" as the aircraft nosed down and began its plunge to earth.

Although at the time no one would admit it, the handwriting was on the wall. After two years, in which Comets carried more than 55,000 passengers over 7 million air miles, the Comet 1 was never to fly again. De Havilland had indeed won the race to be first to market with a commercial jet—a race that it would have been better to have never run at all.[16]

Questions

1. How could risk management have aided in the development of the Comet?
2. Discuss the various types of risk (technical, financial, commercial, etc.) in relation to the Comet. Develop a qualitative risk matrix for these risk factors and assess them in terms of probability and consequences.
3. Given that a modified version of the Comet (the Comet IV) was used until recently by the British government as an antisubmarine warfare aircraft, it is clear that the design flaws could have been corrected given enough time. What, then, do you see as de Havilland's critical error in the development of the Comet?
4. Comment on this statement: "Failure is the price we pay for technological advancement."

CASE STUDY 13.2

The Spanish Navy Pays Nearly $3 Billion for a Submarine That Will Sink Like a Stone

In 2003, shipbuilders at Navantia, Spain's state-owner shipyard, welcomed a contract from their navy to construct four state-of-the-art submarines. The S-80 class was going to be an engineering marvel, filled with the latest and most cutting-edge technology, including a diesel-electric propulsion system that would be 20% lighter than other ships, while delivering 50% more power. As the list of upgrades and new technical gadgetry grew, the delivery date for the Isaac Peral—the lead ship in the S-80 class—continued to ship further behind schedule. Nevertheless, it wasn't the continuous upgrading and addition of new equipment that finally slammed the brakes on the project; it was the startling warning from Navantia's engineers that the Isaac Peral was not seaworthy. The submarine, named in honor of the Spanish man credited by some as the inventor of the underwater vessel, was 75–100 tons overweight, an excess that could make it difficult or impossible for the submarine to surface after submerging. As a result, the Spanish navy was faced with the challenge of fixing a submarine that ran the risk of disaster whenever it decided to submerge!

Navantia admitted the existence of "deviations related to the balance of weight" in the vessel and estimated it would take up to two years more to correct the problem, pushing the new delivery date to late 2018. The firm's engineers are trying to determine their best options at this point. It appears that two choices are most likely: Find a way to trim the design of the overall ship, which would be very difficult at this stage in construction, or lengthen the hull of the already 233-foot submarine to compensate for the extra weight. The problem with this option is that designers have estimated that for every meter the hull is lengthened, it will end up costing nearly 10 million additional euros (about $14 million dollars). Unfortunately for the Spaniards, independent agencies report that they have already sunk the equivalent of $680 million into the Isaac Peral, and a total of $3 billion into the entire quartet of S-80 class submarines.

The buoyancy problem is not the only difficulty facing the program; an analyst said that that submarine's air-independent propulsion (AIP) system reactor is also underperforming. A Strategic Studies Group spokesperson said that the AIP system has been designed to enable the submarine to operate underway for 28 days but is currently able to manage only one week. The Group's memo suggests, "The buoyancy problem alone could cost up to half a billion euros to cover redesign and extra construction, without considering the propulsion problem."

The submarine setback couldn't have come at a worse time for Prime Minister Mariano Rajoy, who was already caught up in a corruption scandal and saw his approval rating hit a record low in 2013. Because of the poor shape of Spain's economy, Rajoy's austerity cuts trimmed the Spanish military budget by 30 percent in 2012, leaving much less room for added ballast. With reports that the S-80 program will be delayed an estimated two years and another general election looming in 2015, Rajoy likely will not see the submarines through to successful launch.

How did such an expensive project get funded at a time when the Spanish military's entire special weapons program received a 98% cut? Sheer pride seems to have been a factor: Spain hoped the S-80 class would be a new homegrown breakthrough achieved without foreign help. Now that Navantia has entered into a $15 million contract with the Electric Boat Division of America's General Dynamics to help with the redesign, that dream seems dead in the water.[17]

Questions

1. Google "Spain's S-80 class submarine" and read some of the articles posted. In your opinion, how does technical risk cause problems with major defense projects?
2. Why do you think it is common for defense contractors to add new features and modifications to current programs? In other words, why do defense agencies contract for one project, only to see it often evolve into something new by the time it is launched?
3. If you were an advisor brought in by the Spanish government, what advice would you offer them in managing their defense projects?

CASE STUDY 13.3

Classic Case: Nicoll Highway Collapse

On April 20, 2004, part of the Nicoll Highway in Singapore collapsed. Six lanes of the highway disappeared into a 100-foot hole when a tunnel being constructed underneath the highway collapsed. Incredibly, no one was driving on the usually congested highway. The tunnel was part of the underground Circle MRT (Mass Rapid Transit) Line, and the supporting structure for the excavation work had failed.

Four workers were killed in the incident and three others were injured. Rescuers hunted in vain for survivors for three days before efforts were called off. By this stage, it was clear that the danger to the rescue teams far outweighed the likelihood of finding any survivors. The other concern was the fact that the ground around the collapse had to be stabilized in order to ensure that no further collapses would occur.[18]

The immediate reason for the collapse was that the retaining wall holding up the evacuation work was insufficient to hold up the tunnel. Two construction cranes had fallen into the hole and there was evidence of twisted steel support beams.

Initial Response

Authorities in Singapore instituted an inquiry into the incident. They also suspended 20 other excavation projects that were ongoing at the time. These were shut down at great expense, and delay as new best-practice codes were put in place. Meanwhile, experts from across the world were brought in to investigate the accident and determine exactly what had happened.

It became clear that a number of factors had contributed to the collapse. Most significant was the fact that geological findings had been misinterpreted. The structure of the tunnel had been under-designed as a direct result of the fact that the engineers had assumed that the soil's shear strength was greater than it actually was. There were also issues with the structural bracing system being used. The collapse had taken place at a point where the bracing was overloaded, and the system lacked the capacity to redistribute the load between the other supports if this part of the bracing failed. The engineers had underestimated the strut loads.

Apportioning Blame

An inquiry committee in May 2005 was told that the disaster was caused by a failure of a connection between horizontal struts and waling beams. The struts and beams supported the diaphragm walls. The general causes of the collapse had already been agreed upon by the Land Transport Authority (LTA) and Nishimatsu-Lum Chang (NLC), who were the main contractors in the joint venture; the NLC lead designer Maunsell Asia; the project engineer Paul Broome; and L&M and Kori (subcontractors).

LTA's View

It had been found that Nishimatsu-Lum Chang (NLC) was negligent, reckless, and dishonest during design and construction, according to the LTA. LTA cited that the design errors had begun with the soil analysis at the earliest stages of the project. According to K. Shanmugam, LTA's counsel: Analysis of the ground conditions had been based on the use of Method A, which looked at the mechanical properties of drained soil.

The soil encountered in the deep excavation was in fact highly plastic marine clay, and NLC should have used data for undrained soils. In using the wrong method, NLC under predicted the forces that would act on the works being carried out. This led to an under-design in the temporary works. As a result of this, the system being installed did not have the capacity required. The incorrect soil analysis also meant that as the excavations got deeper, the errors and potential failures became more acute. The strut connections were under-strength by a factor of two. NLC also substituted C channel shaped steel sections for plate stiffeners in an attempt to strengthen the connections. However, NLC had tried to cut costs by using scrap material to replace the stiffener plates when they had run out of supplies.

LTA went on to claim that NLC had ignored its own risk assessments. Some of the stiffener plates were already buckling, but NLC had hidden this from LTA in order to keep them from insisting on additional works. NLC was already behind schedule in April 2004 and had incurred late penalties of some $25 million. LTA would have undoubtedly ordered NLC to cease work had it known about the problems, and NLC would have had to bear the cost of the extra delays to the work schedule. Similar struts had failed on two other NLC sites, but NLC had insisted that the problem was in hand and pressured the LTA to allow works to continue. It was therefore LTA's contention that NLC had failed to reveal sufficient information for LTA to make an informed judgment.

(*continued*)

NLC's View

NLC was certain that the reason for the collapse was unforeseen downward movement of the diaphragm walls. According to NLC:

- There was a sudden drop in the height of the wall relative to the posts that were supporting the temporary struts.
- This changed the angle at which the struts were connected.
- In turn, this caused the walls to deform and fail.

NLC called this "sway failure," which occurs when violent forces act on the diaphragm walls. The phenomenon had been seen in other parts of the Circle Line, but not at the Nicoll Highway.

NLC maintained that the collapse of the tunnel was not inevitable, but was probably caused because the forced sway mechanism accelerated the failure. NLC admitted that the struts were close to the limit of their performance, but maintained that the loads did not exceed the capacity of the temporary works they had carried out.

Furthermore, NLC expressly countered LTA's suggestion that the soil analysis was the root cause of the disaster, contending:

- It was appropriate to use drained soil data, as it provides a more conservative analysis.
- Although Method A had not been used for deeper excavations in Singapore before, LTA was aware of the method being used and generally agreed with the findings.
- LTA had been specifically briefed about the soil analysis as early as May 2002.
- At that time, LTA's own engineer had stated that other soil analysis types were too conservative.

NLC Admissions

The failure took place at the ninth-level strut connections, which was around 30 meters below the ground and just 3 meters above formation level. As the connections failed, the diaphragm wall deformed. This overloaded the struts which caused them to buckle. In turn, this triggered a gradual and progressive collapse of the tunnel walls. In the event, just one hour elapsed between the failure of the first strut connection and the complete collapse, which triggered devastating damage to the highway.

NLC admitted that there had been a failure in the temporary works. They put this down to under-design and inappropriate detail of the connections. They also admitted that their own engineers had misinterpreted the relevant building code, which had resulted in the use of smaller steels than were actually needed for the struts.

The Greatest Engineering Disaster of the Past Decade?

Although the general causes for the collapse of the highway were agreed upon between all parties in 2005, as of May 2012, just one person had been prosecuted for their part in the disaster. Nonetheless, many lessons had been learned. Work on the MRT has commenced once more, but this time far more heavy-duty temporary works are being demanded. Additional robustness in design is now demanded of contractors.

From the outset, braced excavations were used for transport construction projects in Singapore, and each of the MRT stations were constructed using the "bottom-up" method. This meant excavating and propping up the excavations with steel struts. These were supported at their mid-span by king posts and beams across the face of the diaphragm walls. The struts were placed at 3-meter intervals.

Today, the "top-down" method is preferred. This involves constructing the station with a permanent reinforced concrete roof slab. The slab operates rather like a huge strut, which means that struts are not necessary. At a stroke, the time-consuming installation of struts has been eliminated, and the safety risks are far lower.

Government Response

In the immediate aftermath of the inquiry, the Singapore government accepted the findings in full and was quick to announce a series of new legislation that would improve safety standards in the construction industry. The Joint Review Committee (JRC), made up from various government departments, announced that there would be far stiffer penalties for professionals who had shown dereliction of duty and care. A new licensing scheme was introduced for specialist contractors; additional training and the development of a code of practice for deep excavation work were all part of a raft of new legislation.

The Singapore government was convinced that the failures that led to the collapse of the highway and the deaths had been entirely avoidable and were unacceptable. From this point, all major construction projects would be audited in terms of their safety. The government was determined to point out that small, incremental improvements would not bring about the level of safety that is expected of such projects. As a result, it was necessary for several government departments to prioritize the safety issues and bring in sweeping reforms.

Today, with the reforms in place, the pace of work to extend the MRT system is as rapid as before, but far safer. The Downtown Line is seen as the key to the development of the Marina Bay area. The Bayfront Station will be underneath the leisure and entertainment complex, the Integrated Resort. Here the excavations will be at 24 meters. In order to counter the weak soil, thick diaphragm walls were used and these were stiffened by cross walls and slabs. Even the cut and cover tunnels (just like the one that caused the collapse at Nicholl Highway) have up to seven levels of strutting to support them. Lessons were learned, and legislation has been enacted to back them up.[19]

Questions

1. In what ways were the project's planning and scope management appropriate? When did the planners begin knowingly taking unnecessary risks? Discuss the issue of project constraints and other unique aspects of the tunnel in the risk management process. Were these issues taken into consideration? Why or why not?
2. Conduct either a qualitative or quantitative risk assessment on this project. Identify the risk factors that you consider most important for underground tunnel construction. How would you assess the riskiness of the project? Why?
3. What forms of risk mitigation would you consider appropriate for this project?

Internet Exercises

13.1 Go to www.informationweek.com/whitepaper/Management/ROI-TCO/managing-risk-an-integrated-approac-wp1229549889607?articleID=54000027 and access the article on "Managing Risk: An Integrated Approach." Consider the importance of proactive risk management in light of one of the cases at the end of this chapter. How were these guidelines violated by de Havilland or the Nicoll Highway construction project organization? Support your arguments with information either from the case or from other Web sites.

13.2 FEMA, the Federal Emergency Management Agency, is responsible for mitigating or responding to natural disasters within the United States. Go to www.fema.gov/about/divisions/mitigation.shtm. Look around the site and scroll down to see examples of projects in which the agency is involved. How does FEMA apply the various mitigation strategies (e.g., accept, minimize, share, and transfer) in its approach to risk management?

13.3 Go to www.mindtools.com/pages/article/newTMC_07.htm and read the article on managing risks. What does the article say about creating a systematic methodology for managing project risks? How does this methodology compare with the qualitative risk assessment approach taken in this chapter? How does it diverge from our approach?

13.4 Using the keyword phrase "cases on project risk management," search the Internet to identify and report on a recent example of a project facing significant risks. What steps did the project organization take to first identify and then mitigate the risk factors in this case?

13.5 Go to www.project-management-podcast.com/index.php/podcast-episodes/episode-details/109-episode-063-how-do-risk-attitudes-affect-your-project to access the podcast on risk attitudes on projects. What does the speaker, Cornelius Fichtner, PMP, suggest about the causes of project failures as they relate to issues of risk management?

PMP CERTIFICATION SAMPLE QUESTIONS

1. The project manager has just met with her team to brainstorm some of the problems that could occur on the upcoming project. Today's session was intended to generate possible issues that could arise and get everyone to start thinking in terms of what they should be looking for once the project kicks off. This meeting would be an example of what element in the risk management process?
   a. Risk mitigation
   b. Control and documentation
   c. Risk identification
   d. Analysis of probability and consequences

2. Todd is working on resource scheduling in preparation for the start of a project. There is a potential problem in the works, however, as the new collective bargaining agreement with the company's union has not been concluded. Todd decides to continue working on the resource schedule in anticipation of a satisfactory settlement. Todd's approach would be an example of which method for dealing with risk?
   a. Accept it
   b. Minimize it
   c. Transfer it
   d. Share it

3. A small manufacturer has won a major contract with the U.S. Army to develop a new generation of satellite phone for battlefield applications. Because of the significant technological challenges involved in this project and the company's own size limitations and lack of experience in dealing with the Army on these kinds of contracts, the company has decided to partner with another firm in order to collaborate on developing the technology. This decision would be an example of what kind of response to the risk?
   a. Accept it
   b. Minimize it
   c. Transfer it
   d. Share it

4. All of the following would be considered examples of significant project risks except:
   a. Financial risks
   b. Technical risks
   c. Commercial risks
   d. Legal risks
   e. All are examples of significant potential project risks

5. Suppose your organization used a qualitative risk assessment matrix with three levels each of probability and consequences (high, medium, and low).

In evaluating a project's risks, you determine that commercial risks pose a low probability of occurrence but high consequences. On the other hand, legal risks are evaluated as having a high probability of occurrence and medium consequences. If you are interested in prioritizing your risks, which of these should be considered first?

a. Commercial risk
b. Legal risk
c. Both should be considered equally significant
d. Neither is really much of a threat to this project, so it doesn't matter what order you assign them

Answers: 1. c—Brainstorming meetings are usually created as an effective means to get project team members to begin identifying potential risks; 2. a—Todd is choosing to accept the risk of potential future problems by continuing to work on his resource schedule in anticipation of positive contract talks; 3. d—The firm has decided to share the risk of the new project by partnering with another company; 4. e—All are examples of significant potential project risks; 5. b—Legal risks would be of higher overall significance (high probability, medium consequence) and so should probably be considered first in a prioritization scheme.

INTEGRATED PROJECT

Project Risk Assessment

Conduct a preliminary risk analysis of your project. Use two techniques, one qualitative and one quantitative, in supporting your evaluation of project risk. In order to do this, you will need to:

- Generate a set of likely risk factors.
- Discuss them in terms of probability and consequences.
- Develop preliminary strategies for risk mitigation.

An effective risk analysis will demonstrate clear understanding of relevant project risks, their potential impact (probability and consequences), and preliminary plans for minimizing the negative effects.

SAMPLE RISK ANALYSIS—ABCups, INC.

Among the potential threats or uncertainties contained in this project, the following have been identified:

1. Plant reorganization could take longer than anticipated. Process engineering may be more complicated or unexpected difficulties could arise while the process alterations are underway.
2. A key project team member could be reassigned or no longer able to work on the project. Due to other requirements or top management reshuffling of resources, the project could lose one of its key core team members.
3. The project budget could be cut because of budget cutbacks in other parts of the company. The project budget could be trimmed in the middle of the development cycle.
4. Suppliers might be unable to fulfill contracts. After qualifying vendors and entering into contracts with them, it might be discovered that they cannot fulfill their contractual obligations, requiring the project team and organization to rebid contracts or accept lower-quality supplies.
5. New process designs could be found not to be technically feasible. The process engineers might determine midproject that the project's technical objectives cannot be achieved in the manner planned.
6. New products might not pass QA assessment testing. The project team might discover that the equipment purchased and/or the training that plant personnel received are insufficient to allow for proper quality levels of the output.
7. Vendors could discover our intentions and cut deliveries. Current vendors might determine our intent of eliminating their work and slow down or stop deliveries in anticipation of our company canceling contracts.
8. Marketing might not approve the prototype cups produced. The sales and marketing department might determine that the quality or "presence" of the products we produce are inferior and unlikely to sell in the market.
9. The new factory design might not be approved during government safety inspections. The factory might not meet OSHA requirements.

QUALITATIVE RISK ASSESSMENT

Probability

Consequences	Low	Med	High
High	5		8
Med	3, 9	2	1
Low	4	6, 7	

QUANTITATIVE RISK ASSESSMENT

Probability of Failure

• Maturity	(Moderate)	= .50
• Complexity	(Minor)	= .30
• Dependency	(Moderate)	= .50

Consequences of Failure

• Cost	(Significant)	= .70
• Schedule	(Moderate)	= .50
• Reliability	(Minor)	= .30
• Performance	(Moderate)	= .50

P_m	P_c	P_d		P_f
.50	.30	.50		.43
C_c	C_s	C_r	C_p	C_f
.70	.50	.30	.50	.50
Risk Factor = (.43) + (.50) − (.43)(.50) = .715 (High Risk)				

Risk Mitigation Strategies

High Risk	Mitigation Strategy
1. Plant reorganization takes longer than anticipated.	1. Develop a comprehensive project tracking program to maintain schedule.
2. Marketing does not approve the prototype cups produced.	2. Maintain close ties to sales department—keep them in the loop throughout project development and quality control cycles.
Moderate Risk	
3. New process designs are found to not be technically feasible.	3. Assign sufficient time for quality assessment during prototype stage.
4. A key project team member could be reassigned or no longer able to work on the project.	4. Develop a strategy for cross-training personnel on elements of one another's job or identify suitable replacement resources within the organization.
Low Risk	
5. The project budget could be cut.	5. Maintain close contact with top management regarding project status, including earned value and other control documentation.
6. Factory does not pass OSHA inspections.	6. Schedule preliminary inspection midway through project to defuse any concerns.
7. Suppliers are unable to fulfill contracts.	7. Qualify multiple suppliers at prototyping stage.
8. New products do not pass QA assessment testing.	8. Assign team member to work with QA department on interim inspection schedule.
9. Vendors discover our intentions and cut deliveries.	9. Maintain secrecy surrounding project development!

Notes

1. Lallanilla, M. (2013, September 3). "This London skyscraper can melt cars and set buildings on fire." www.nbcnews.com/science/science-news/london-skyscraper-can-melt-cars-set-buildings-fire-f8C11069092; Smith-Spark, L. (2013, September 3). "Reflected light from London skyscraper melts car," *CNN*. www.cnn.com/2013/09/03/world/europe/uk-london-building-melts-car/; Gower, P. (2014, February 12). "London walkie talkie owners to shield car-melting beam," *Bloomberg*. www.bloomberg.com/news/2014-02-12/london-walkie-talkie-owners-to-shield-tower-s-car-melting-beam.html; BBC News Magazine. (2014, September 3). Chris Shepherd, BBC News Magazine, (2014, Sept. 3). "Who, what, why: How does a skyscraper melt a car?" http://www.bbc.com/news/magazine-23944679. Reprinted by permission from BBC Worldwide Americas Inc.
2. Wideman, M. (1998). "Project risk management," in Pinto, J. K. (Ed.), *The Project Management Institute's Project Management Handbook*. San Francisco, CA: Jossey-Bass, pp. 138–58.
3. Chapman, C. B., and Ward, S. C. (1997). *Project Risk Management: Process, Techniques, and Insights*. Chichester, UK: John Wiley; Kahkonen, K., and Artto, K. A. (1997). *Managing Risks in Projects*. London: E & FN Spon.
4. Chapman, R. J. (1998). "The effectiveness of working group risk identification and assessment techniques," *International Journal of Project Management*, 16(6): 333–44.
5. Martin, P., and Tate, K. (1998). "Team-based risk assessment: Turning naysayers and saboteurs into supporters," *PMNetwork*, 12(2): 35–38.
6. Scheid, J. (2011, December 5). "Risk management meltdowns: A look at some real-world examples." www.brighthubpm.com/risk-management/126793-risk-management-meltdowns-a-look-at-some-real-world-examples/; Bernard, T. (2011, November 1). "In retreat, Bank of America cancels debit card fee," *New York Times*. www.nytimes.com/2011/11/02/business/bank-of-america-drops-plan-for-debit-card-fee.html?_r=0
7. Hillson, D. (2002a, June). "The risk breakdown structure (RBS) as an aid to effective risk management." Proceedings of the 5th European Project Management Conference (PMI Europe 2002), Cannes, France.
8. Viswanathan, B. (2012, June 14). "Understanding the risk breakdown structure (RBS)," *Project Management.com*. http://project-management.com/understanding-the-risk-breakdown-structure-rbs/; Hillson, D. (2002b, October). "Use a risk breakdown structure (RBS) to understand your risks," Proceedings of the 33rd Project Management Institute Annual Seminars & Symposium, San Antonio, TX.
9. Graves, R. (2000). "Qualitative risk assessment," *PMNetwork*, 14(10): 61–66; Pascale, S., Troilo, L., and Lorenz, C. (1998). "Risk analysis: How good are your decisions?" *PMNetwork*, 12(2): 25–28.
10. "MCA spent millions on Carly Hennessy—Haven't heard of her?" (2002, February 26). *Wall Street Journal*, pp. A1, A10.
11. Hamburger, D. H. (1990). "The project manager: Risk taker and contingency planner," *Project Management Journal*, 21(4): 11–16; Levine, H. A. (1995). "Risk management for dummies: Managing schedule, cost and technical risk, and contingency," *PMNetwork*, 9(10): 31–33.
12. http://blogs.wsj.com/chinarealtime/2009/06/29/shanghai-building-collapses-nearly-intact/; http://news.bbc.co.uk/2/hi/8123559.stm; Peter Foster (2009, 29 Jun) Nine held over Shanghai building collapse www.telegraph.co.uk/news/worldnews/asia/china/5685963/Nine-held-over-Shanghai-building-collapse.html.© Telegraph Media Group Limited 2009.
13. Chapman, C. B. (1997). "Project risk analysis and management—The PRAM generic process," *International Journal of Project Management*, 15(5): 273–81; Chapman, C. B., and Ward, S. (2003). *Project Risk Management: Processes, Techniques and Insights*, 2nd ed. Chichester, UK: John Wiley.
14. Artto, K. A. (1997). "Fifteen years of project risk management applications—Where are we going?" in Kahkonen, K., and Artto, K. A. (Eds.), *Managing Risks in Projects*. London: E & FN Spon, pp. 3–14; Williams, T. M. (1995). "A classified bibliography of recent research relating to project risk management," *European Journal of Operations Research*, 85: 18–38.
15. The Tragedy of Macbeth: Act I Scene VII: The same. A room in Macbeth's castle. by William Shakespeare.
16. "Fatigue blamed in Comet crashes." (1954, October 25). *Aviation Week*, 61: 17–18; "Comet verdict upholds RAE findings." (1955, February 21). *Aviation Week*, 62: 16–17; Hull, S. (1954, November 1). "Comet findings may upset design concepts," *Aviation Week*, 61: 16–18; "Fall of a Comet." (1953, May 11). *Newsweek*, 41: 49; "A column of smoke." (1954, January 18). *Time*, 63: 35–36; "Death of the Comet I." (1954, April 19). *Time*, 63: 31–32.
17. Govan, F. (2013, May 22). "£2 billion Spanish navy submarine will sink to bottom of sea," *The Telegraph*, www.telegraph.co.uk/news/worldnews/europe/spain/10073951/2-billion-Spanish-navy-submarine-will-sink-to-bottom-of-sea.html; El Periodico (2013, May 30). "The most modern Spanish submarine sinks for excess weight," www.elperiodico.com/es/noticias/politica/problemas-peso-construccion-submarino-ejercito-espanol-2404561; Davis, C. (2013, May 24). "Spain's S-81 Isaac Peral submarine cost $680 million to build… and can't float," *Huffington Post*. www.huffingtonpost.com/2013/05/24/spain-submarine-s-81-isaac-peral-cant-float_n_3328683.html; "GD to help fix Spanish Navy's overweight issue of S-80 submarine." (2013, June 7). Naval-Technology.com www.naval-technology.com/news/newsgd-to-help-fix-spanish-navy-overweight-issue-s80-submarine
18. "IAP class probes Singapore highway collapse," http://web.mit.edu/newsoffice/2008/collapse-highway-0201.html; "Nicoll highway collapse: Evaluation of geotechnical factors affecting design of excavation support system," http://kb.plaxis.nl/sites/kb.plaxis.nl/files/kb-publications/AJWhittle_RVDavis_2006.pdf; "The Nicollhighway collapse," www.hssmge.gr/HIGHT_The%20Nicoll%20Highway%20Collapse.pdf.
19. "No. 11 Nicoll Highway collapse," http://www.nce.co.uk/features/nce-40-years/no11-nicoll-highway-collapse/8629881.article#.

14 Stakeholder Analysis and Management

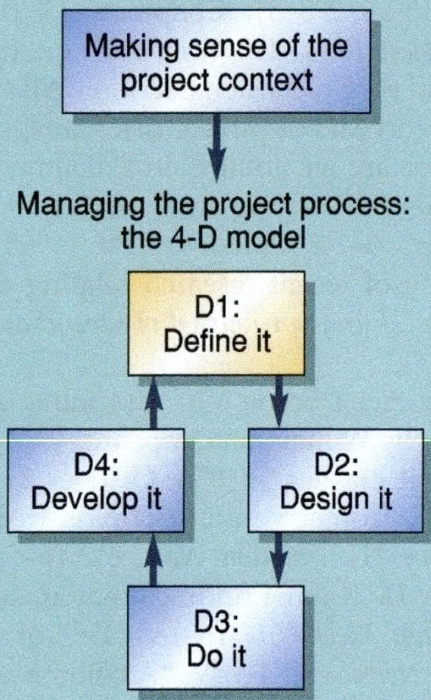

'. . . project managers are the new strategic leaders, who must take on total responsibility for project business results.'[1]

Principles

1. *'Begin with the end in mind.'*[2] Whether a project is a success or failure is rarely universally agreed at the end of a project. However, an agreed statement of what is required provides a good starting point.
2. The perfect result, delivered yesterday and at no cost, is for idealists. The rest of us have to manage the trade-offs between objectives.
3. Projects consume time, energy and resources and in most cases therefore require justification.

Learning objectives

By the time you have completed this chapter, you should be able to:

→ identify appropriate stakeholders and relevant success measures at the outset of a project and recognise their achievement or otherwise at completion

→ demonstrate the need for and the implications of prioritising trade-offs

→ recognise a structured approach to assessing the benefits of and requirements for a project.

Contents

Source: Pierre Mens/Bridgephoto.dk

Source: Sven Rosenhall/Nordic/Getty

The Oresund Link is a 16.4 km road and rail connection between Copenhagen (Denmark) and Malmo (Sweden). This length includes nearly 8 km of bridge, a tunnel and an artificial island. As a project, completing this link is a significant engineering achievement – a combined four-lane road and twin-track rail bridge, with one of the longest cable-stayed main spans in the world. It was opened on time on 1 July 2000, a major management achievement given the scale and complexity of the project. However, the cost of the crossing (c. € 30) has been blamed for the lower than expected traffic figures. This is causing the operators some concern, but politically, the idea of a more integrated region as a result of the bridge appears to be a more important long-term objective than any short-term financial issues.

Introduction

The case of the Oresund Link illustrates an interesting challenge for project managers – how to achieve success in multiple areas. In this case ultimate success would be the achievement of the political, environmental, economic and social objectives, in the short, medium and long term, to the satisfaction of all concerned. Such a requirement represents the ultimate state of perfection for a project. Managing almost any project, not just one as large in scale as the Link, requires project managers to take a pragmatic view as to just how close to this perfection can be achieved.

In this chapter, we will examine how and whether stakeholders can be 'managed' and some approaches that project managers have used to try to do this. Also, while some projects, such as those involved in disaster relief, are 'self-evidently needed', commercial projects in particular are founded upon a good business case. This provides the rationale as to why the project is being carried out and will remain one of the anchors of a project as it moves from conception to execution.

14.1 Stakeholders: success and failure

The challenge to achieving total success comes from the complexity of the objectives and the requirements of many different groups of **stakeholders** for the project, not least because there will be conflicts between the **requirements** of each. We express these requirements as **measures**. Table 14.1 defines and illustrates these.

Measures and requirements are considered together here, as the measures provide an explicit expression of the requirements.

Furthermore, if for instance the initial build-cost of part of the bridge could have been reduced to save money by using inferior materials and make the construction project appear to have performed better, the impact would probably then be seen on the longer-term objectives – when maintenance costs are likely to be higher as a result. There is therefore a **timing** issue here. Three issues will form the basis for the discussion of success and failure here – stakeholders, requirements and measures, and timing.

Starting from a point that a project is unlikely to meet the requirements of all stakeholders all of the time can provide an uninspiring prospect for the project manager. It could be argued that this can be reduced to managing 'how much you are going to fail'. Indeed, the stakeholder management literature appears to have taken this view. Whatever you do, someone somewhere is going to be unhappy. The PM's role is simply to minimise the critical levels of unhappiness.

There is another view. This states that a project is about delivering **value** rather than a *product*. Such an approach considers that the opportunity from a stakeholder analysis is to maximise the overall value of the project. For instance, a project is carried out to change the processes used in a business. During this project, it would be considered that the product (the changed processes) is the main outcome of the process and the project manager should find ways to minimise the level of disruption to members of the organisation. A **value-maximisation** view would take the opportunity to make as many changes as possible in the pursuit of the objective of delivering business benefit from the work being carried out (see section 14.3).

The principle stated at the start of the chapter is from Stephen Covey's *The Seven Habits of Highly Effective People*: begin with the end in mind. In the project environment, mapping the stakeholders and their requirements sets this 'end' and allows focus of the

Table 14.1 Stakeholders, requirements and measures

Item	*Definition*	*Examples*
Stakeholders	Any individual or group with an interest in the project process or outcome	The project customers, the delivery team, the end beneficiaries of the project, anyone affected by the outcome, proponents and opponents of any change
Requirements	What each individual or group wants from the process or outcome	Defined requirements in the form of a specification or contract, implicit requirements (I want this project to be a good place to work), or legal/ethical/moral/commercial/competitive requirements
Measures	The means by which it will be determined during and post project whether those requirements have been met	Level of compliance to specification, customer satisfaction, level of return on investment, staff retention levels

project definition work that follows and the quality management of the project. Such a mapping is worthwhile in most projects. The effort is justifiable as it begins the avoidance of the most often-cited causes of project failure. These include lack of user involvement, lack of top management support, unrealistic user expectations, failing to recognise the real requirements of a key customer group or to gain a shared understanding on the outcomes of the project.[3] The project manager has a major role to play in how stakeholders and this success or otherwise play out in the project.

Stakeholders

A stakeholder, as described in Chapter 7, is any party with an interest in the project process or outcome. Most projects have more than one stakeholder or stakeholder group, presenting the project manager with a major challenge – that of resolving their often divergent and potentially conflicting requirements. Key questions posed here include: Who are the stakeholders? What do they want? What influence is this going to have on the project process or outcome? Mapping these factors does provide a basic means of making sense of project requirements and at least in the first instance having a view on how what will be termed the '**stakeholder landscape**' can be managed.

Who are they?

One aspect of project complexity that was defined in Chapter 7 was that of the role of **external stakeholders**. These are people outside the 'project team' or organisation. Typically, these include the people for whom the project is being provided (a customer group, for instance) or the people paying for the process (termed the 'sponsor'). As will be shown though, this can be an extensive group. **Internal stakeholders** are those associated with the process, typically members of the project team or governance structure.

Who were the stakeholders for the football World Cup in Germany in 2006 (or any other major sporting event for that matter)? A list would include the following:

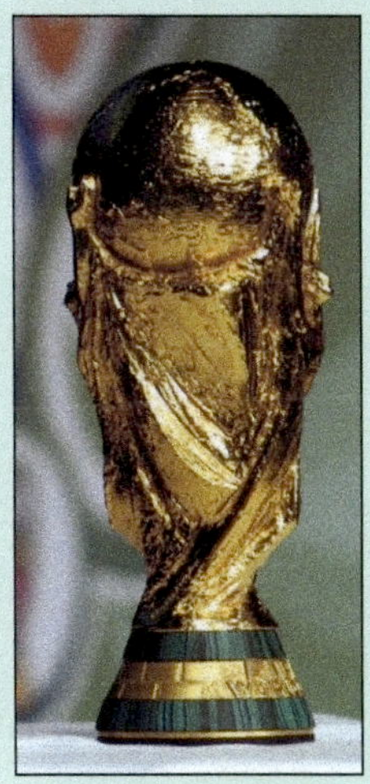

Source: Peter Ending/epa/Corbis

1. The players, referees, coaches, managers, physios and other team support staff.
2. The players' wives and girlfriends, agents, friends and entourage.
3. FIFA – the governing body.
4. The national football associations.
5. Owners of the stadia being used for the event.
6. Fans attending.
7. Police and other law enforcement agencies.
8. Media and press attending (huge numbers).
9. The sponsors.
10. People watching or listening to the games but who did not travel to Germany.
11. People working in the venues.
12. The organising committee.

In the context of development projects, the World Bank (1996) provides the following questions to enable identification:

1. Who might be affected (positively or negatively) by the development concern to be addressed?
2. Who are the 'voiceless' for whom special efforts may have to be made?
3. Who are the representatives of those likely to be affected?

4 Who is responsible for what is intended?
5 Who is likely to mobilise for or against what is intended?
6 Who can make what is intended more effective through their participation or less effective through non-participation or outright opposition?
7 Who can contribute financial and technical resources?
8 Whose behaviour has to change for the effort to succeed?

Source: World Bank, 1996 (http://web.worldbank.org)

The challenge that many project managers face with stakeholder identification is not that of making sure that all relevant groups and individuals are included but deciding where to stop the process. As the questions in the World Bank list show, the 'interest' in the project may be unstated or even unknown, and yet there may be a need to show that these interests have been considered, particularly if an organisation is seeking funding for its work.

Returning to the scenario of a major sporting event, the stakeholders could be viewed as a list that comprises a large percentage of the world's population. For instance, the increase in air travel as a result of the event could be argued to contribute further to climate change, with those being affected in the future being stakeholders. The industries that provide souvenirs of the event but have no direct contractual contact with the organisers are another. The list just goes on. As already noted, the initial challenge for the project manager is the identification of stakeholders. The next step is to make sense of the scale of impact of the stakeholders on the project and the project on the stakeholders. As a first sift on the people whom you have identified, Figure 14.1 gives a basic framework. The internal team are always going to be central to your consideration. The next level out is the core external people – people external to the project but who are crucial for its success – ideally containing a few people or groups. The last layer is '**the rest of the world**' and only requires monitoring to ensure that any new individuals or groups do not unwittingly become core to the project success without appropriate changes being made to the project. For instance, a change of responsibilities between two government departments dramatically changed the nature of the stakeholder environment, with major implications for an IT project being carried out across a number of

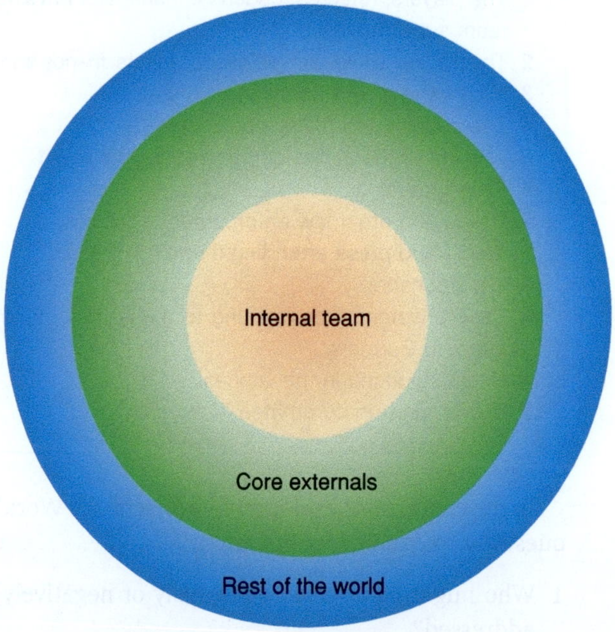

Figure 14.1 Stakeholder groups

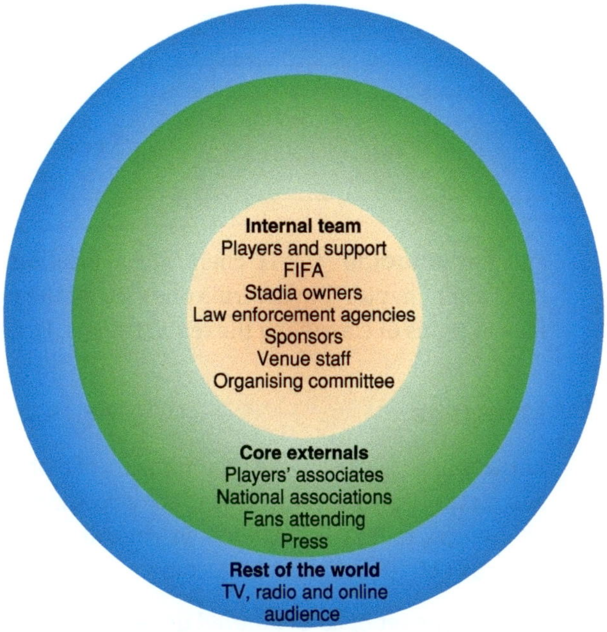

Figure 14.2 Stakeholder grouping for Euro 2006

departments. This resulted in the stakeholders and their requirements and measures changing significantly.

Applying the framework to the Euro 2006 tournament provides the analysis shown in Figure 14.2.

This immediately raises a challenge – whose requirements are paramount? For example, evening games, particularly late evening games, are most popular with the sponsors as the television audiences are likely to be large. However, they are unpopular with the players and even more unpopular with people living around the stadia.

What do they want?

The quotations below illustrate the requirements of different project stakeholder groups.

1 *'This product needs to be developed in the shortest possible time – we need it yesterday.'* (Marketing manager, automotive firm)

2 *'I want a good working solution to the problem, not promises that it will work one day.'* (Main client, IT implementation project)

3 *'I want to work in a stimulating environment with good people and a manager who knows what they want and sticks to it, not changing things all the time.'* (Team member, new product development project)

4 *'We want this project to stay out of the news and out of the public eye until it is finished. The last thing we want here is more bad headlines about this project.'* (Main client, large defence project)

5 *'I want this project to be seen as a success in years to come.'* (Project manager, firm relocation project)

6 *'I am prepared to make a certain level of investment, but when they (the project team) have spent that, there is no more – we will cancel the project.'* (Project sponsor, new business group)

Among these requirements are the ideas that they can be expressed as measures of the **inputs** (the new business sponsor), the **process** (the team member, the defence client)

Table 14.2 Input, process and outcome requirements

	Input	*Process*	*Outcome*
Characteristics	Limit on resources provided (quotes 1, 6)	The environment in which the project is undertaken (quote 3); process resource consumption controlled (quote 4)	Product meets certain requirements (quotes 1, 2, 5)

and the **outcome** (the IT client, the relocation PM). We have used the basic idea of process in Chapter 6 to describe one view of the project environment, and this is a useful idea in terms of classifying the requirements. Examples of these are shown in Table 14.2.

Measures

At the most basic level, the requirements of a project may be stated in terms of time, cost and quality/specification. This triad of requirements is so embedded within the concept of projects that it is included in several well-used definitions. For instance, British Standard 6079[4] defines a project as:

> ***A unique set of co-ordinated activities, with definite starting and finishing points, undertaken by an individual or organisation to meet specific performance objectives within defined schedule, cost and performance parameters.***

At a first level of consideration, time, cost and quality are the most heavily used and do provide the opportunity to consider some requirements. Simply stating the requirements is insufficient from a managerial perspective – these must be prioritised to allow for decisions to be made.

There is, however, a much larger set of measures consistent with the diverse requirements of stakeholders as shown in Table 14.3. Regarding the key concept of project outcome, according to various studies that acknowledged the necessity to measure project success beyond project efficiency (cost, scope and time), project managers were asked to what extent the project achieved its purpose, provided satisfactory benefit to the owner, satisfied the needs of the owner, users and stakeholders, met the pre-stated objectives, was produced to specification, within budget and on time, and satisfied the needs of the project team.

Table 14.3 New product development (NPD) metrics[5]

Type of measure	*Characteristic measured*
Process measures	Product development cost, time and conformance to quality procedures
Short-term outcome measures	Product performance level, desirability to market, flexibility of design to be changed to meet emergent customer needs
Longer-term outcome measures	Payback period, customer satisfaction, percentage of business being generated by the new product, market share, customisability for high-margin markets

Beyond the conventional approach[6]

The following demonstrates the influence of the measures and the involvement of stakeholders in two different approaches to their management. Specifically, the measures set up (described here as 'the end') are then used for monitoring and control as the project

Table 14.4 Conventional versus participatory project monitoring and evaluation

	Conventional M&E	*Participatory M&E*
Who plans and manages the process:	Project managers	Local people, project staff, managers and other stakeholders, often helped by a facilitator
Role of 'primary stakeholders' (the intended beneficiaries):	Provide information only	Design and adapt the methodology, collect and analyse data, share findings and link them to action
How success is measured:	Externally defined, mainly quantitative indicators	Internally defined indicators, including more qualitative judgements
Approach:	Predetermined	Adaptive

progresses. In Table 14.4, the approach of **participatory monitoring and evaluation (PM&E)** is contrasted with the conventional approach.

This example demonstrates a development in the approach to projects more generally. Specifically, the move to 'shared ownership' of the project planning process from one centred on the project manager, from 'telling stakeholders' to 'consulting and adapting according to emergent needs', from success measures (particularly efficiency measures) to a wider range of relevant and often qualitative indicators, and from an approach that suggests that the path of the project can be identified at the outset to one that recognises that the project environment is a dynamic environment.

So not only what do we measure, but how and when do we measure it? There is clearly a range of measures, even within the basic time, cost and quality criteria. Measurement will be discussed further throughout this book, as measurements are vital as the means of checking whether strategy is in fact being implemented.

Timing

It is argued by some that a project manager should not concern themselves with wider issues, that achievement of a limited set of objectives over the project duration alone is sufficient. This may be acceptable in some areas, but we are concerned with project managers having a strategic role as outlined in the previous chapters, and it is consistent with such a strategic role that a wider consideration is appropriate.

So, how do we determine whether a project is a **success**? If we return to the case of the Oresund Link described at the start of the chapter, the timing of the assessment and the perspective of the assessor are critical. Given the wider objectives of the project, this is inevitable. So, what is the role of the project manager in this?

The whole issue of the timings and nature of assessments is crucial to focus the work of the project team. During a project, some notion of 'control' must be imposed on the work. Post completion, there will be reviews and stakeholders will form opinions over time. The challenge for the project manager here is that such a long-term view is not consistent with the nature of project work. Their performance is assessed over a period longer than the project, yet their rewards are usually linked to performance within the project.

One measure at one point in time will not capture the performance of most projects, the managers, project teams or stakeholder views. The challenge then is to put in place an appropriate set of measures, to report performance to date and then to guide in the setting of objectives for the future. Crucial to this is the whole issue of whether perception of success is a good performance measure. Sometimes it just takes longer than has been expected for success to be achieved, as the examples below illustrate.

Sometimes, it just takes longer than expected . . .

There is very little evidence from ancient history that time and budget constraints were set for projects. Instead, emergence of requirements (e.g. evident in the construction of the pyramids) and ongoing provision of resources until the desired outcome was achieved was accepted.

Reviewing major projects in recent history from IK Brunel to the preparations for the 2012 Olympics, there is a consistent theme: *things that change the world usually take longer (and cost more) than we think.*

- **IK Brunel** – most of Brunel's more ambitious schemes ran late and over budget. His tunnel under the Thames and the SS Great Eastern went particularly awry in these terms. However, his legacy has been huge – railways, canals and bridges that are still in use today, delivering benefits decades after the original investments had been repaid.
- **The Apollo missions** – for a series of projects where budget was not a major consideration, the programme was frequently delayed. However, the success was not in terms of conformance to budget, it was in the achievement of the exploration of space.
- **Concorde** – delivered years late and cost over five times the original budget.[7] In service, it was operated commercially for 27 years and transformed the face of global travel. When it was taken out of service, it was doubtful whether supersonic commercial flights would be seen again in this generation.
- **Channel Tunnel** – considered a vital political part of 'the European Project' – delivered over two years late and double its original budget. It was disastrous in project terms, particularly as the over-budget project left a mountain of debt for the operating company (Eurotunnel) such that its shares were virtually worthless for many years. In 2009, the company made its first operating profit and declared its first dividend to shareholders in 23 years. Technically, environmentally and in so many other ways, this was a success.

There are many other examples of course, but these do make the point that on a project management level, all of these are examples of **failure** if we consider them in terms of their out-turn compared with initial predictions. Far more important though is their longer-term impact on their stakeholders.

Managing stakeholders

You can't please all of the people, all of the time . . .

REAL WORLD Jersey Airport

The construction of a new airport terminal building at Jersey Airport started well. The design was approved by all the necessary authorities and contractors were appointed to carry out the work.

The main concern was the deadline for completion – it had to be in the spring, in time for the island's main tourist influx in the summer. This was achieved and everyone was, for a time, very happy with the new facility. That was until a few problems arose.

These all concerned the impact that the new building was having on the operation of the airport. First, the air traffic controllers (ATCs) complained that they were being dazzled by sunlight reflected from the roof of the new terminal building. No problem, said the Chief Executive of the Jersey Airport Authority – well, at least not during the winter.

A further complaint was that the new building affected the accuracy of the airport's wind speed indicator when the wind was in a certain direction. While a new site for the indicator was being sought, the air traffic controllers were having to advise pilots to use their own judgement regarding the wind speed, when it was blowing in a particular direction. Furthermore, the new building obscured the view of parts of the taxiway to the ATCs (they are responsible for aircraft movements on the ground as well as in the air). The solution – install closed-circuit cameras which would relay the obscured area to the control tower.

When questioned about these problems, the Chief Executive reminded his interviewer that safety was still a top priority. In the light of these problems, the *Financial Times* reminded potential visitors to Jersey that 'they can easily go by boat'.[8]

The Real World box shows that the air traffic controllers were clearly a key stakeholder, but their needs were apparently not considered during the design of the new facility. Or if they were, insufficient modelling of the new work environment took place during the design. Also, they would not have been the only stakeholder in this project and clearly there were other requirements that took precedence.

In balancing the precedence given to different stakeholders, many project managers talk about a key aspect of their work in acting as 'mediator' between stakeholders. In Chapter 4, we identified a whole category of managerial complexity devoted to 'stakeholders'. How, then, can we attempt to make some sense of this complexity? One approach is to consider the nature of the **power** or **influence** of a stakeholder on the project and the *interest* or **impact** of the project on that stakeholder.

Power in this context can be in the form of direct authority (e.g. through being the CEO of a company in which a project is carried out), through indirect authority (e.g. a legislative change requiring that a project is carried out) or having an important relationship with the project team (as would be the case of a financial or technical audit function). Interest is the measure of how much that stakeholder knows about the project; impact is how much they will be affected by the process or outcome. Either can be used to produce what is termed a *stakeholder map*.

The stakeholder map provides a rough guide to how to 'manage' particular groups. One commonly used framework is shown in Figure 14.3.

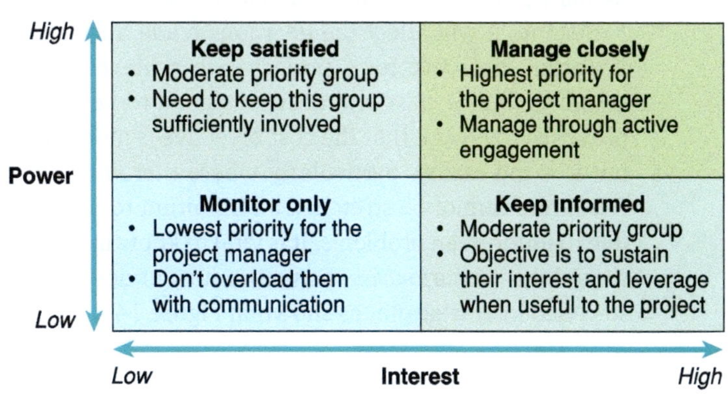

Figure 14.3 Power: interest stakeholder map[9]

An example of the use of such mapping is included in *Project Management in Practice* at the end of this chapter. Another popular means of mapping stakeholders involves the stakeholder potential for cooperation, with the project being plotted against the potential threat of that stakeholder to the project. This is useful where there is likely to be opposition to a project, for instance as is common with organisational change projects.[10]

14.2 Managing strategic choices

In business, there are strategic choices to be made. These choices focus the organisation onto a limited set of objectives, illustrated in Chapter 4 by the cost focus of easyJet. This is stated as, *'We are in business to be the fastest OR the best OR the cheapest.'* The same prioritisation is necessary in projects, as was demonstrated by the strategy framework in Figure 4.1, and is part of the strategy deployment process in organisations.

As described above, the simplest consideration of a project's objectives can be made in terms of time, cost and quality (TCQ). How do we decide which is/are the most important of these three? First, it is necessary to understand the nature of the **trade-offs** that exist in the project.

Consider the following scenario. Your team has been set a task to carry out a piece of market research, for instance. You have a limited time to complete the report on this market for your director. At the outset of the activity, you are able to plan your activities with the objective of delivering the assignment in the time required. The quality of the outcome is dependent on the time that you have – the longer you have, the more research you would be able to do and the more effort you could put into the presentation of the end result. If you have only a very short time, this clearly limits what you can do. You can buy in additional resource, but this costs. This shows clearly the relationship between three elements of project strategy: time, cost and quality. We say that there is a trade-off between these three – that you can have the task completed very quickly, but unless you are prepared to compromise on the quality, you may have to pay more to recruit additional resources to the team.

An example of getting this wrong was the project to build the ship Titanic – it took to sea after its owners had prioritised time over its quality of design. The 'unsinkable' was compromised because emergent issues (ones that could not have been reasonably foreseen or resolved in early design and planning) could not be accommodated in the schedule.[11]

A trade-off is, therefore, the prioritisation of the objectives of a project. It is important at this stage, as there are two major occasions where it will affect the decisions made. The first is during planning. If a customer indicates that a specification for a set of project activities is non-negotiable, the resources of time and cost will need to be manipulated around this central objective. Furthermore, it focuses the project on what is really important, as many projects start with unnecessary assumptions regarding what needs to be achieved.

Second, it will affect the decisions made during execution. For example, if the most important objective for a project is to achieve a particular level of cost performance, where problems exist and decisions need to be made, time and quality could be compromised to ensure that the cost objective is met. This does look like a poor compromise but it is the reality, particularly where there are inherent uncertainties in the project. Resources cannot be stretched ad infinitum to obtain goals that are passing out of sight due to unforeseen problems. It is vital to know in advance what can and cannot be moved should this scenario arise, no matter how undesirable this is in principle. These form the so-called **iron triangle**, as shown in Figure 14.4.

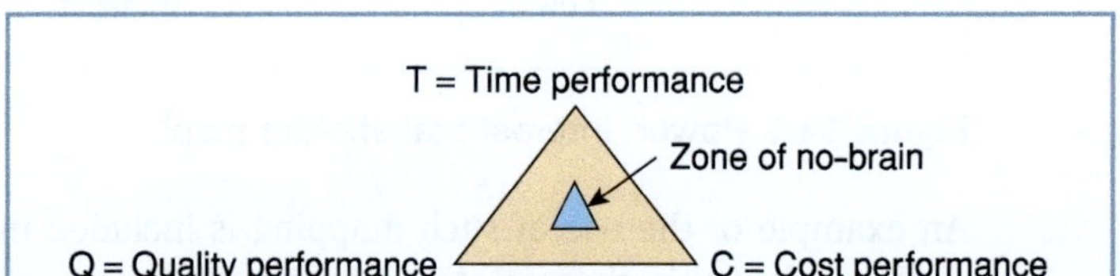

Figure 14.4 Trade-offs in project management

In some cases, it is clear where the position of the project in the iron triangle should lie. For instance, during the second Gulf War, new requirements for the equipment that soldiers were using emerged. These needed to be met with enhanced products in the shortest possible time. The suppliers of that equipment were issued with orders for urgent operational requirements (UOR) by the UK's Ministry of Defence – prioritised work that bypassed much of the normal process associated with product orders, in the interests of getting enhanced equipment into use at the earliest possible time. In such a case, location of the project firmly in the 'time corner' meant that trading off cost and in some instances quality (particularly of process documentation) was necessary (Figure 14.5).

With the Airbus A380, production problems emerged with the wiring systems during 2006. Quite rightly, the delay and additional costs of solving these problems were considered less important than the quality of the completed aircraft. The location of the project in the 'quality' corner was an appropriate response (Figure 14.6).

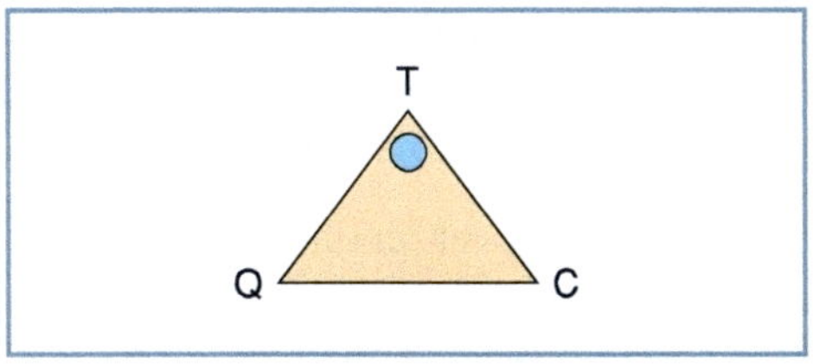

Figure 14.5 Time priority project

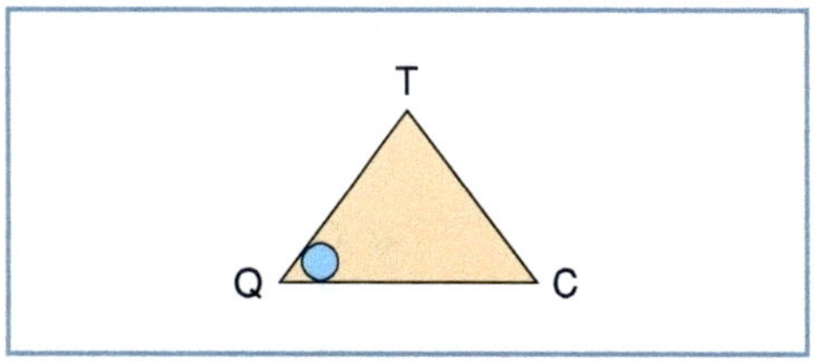

Figure 14.6 Quality priority project

There is a whole category of projects that is cash-limited. For instance, many EU-funded scientific research projects have an absolute maximum funding. Researchers are not allowed to go over that funding limit. Any additional spend has to be funded by their institutions, so there is considerable incentive to stay within allocated budgets resulting in the position shown in Figure 14.7.

Lastly, on the location of the basic priority, many projects have dual requirements. In organising the Sydney Olympics, for instance, the Sydney Olympic Committee (SOC) set out to make it 'the best Games ever'. Given that they could hardly have people turning up at the Games and ask them to 'come back next month, the facilities are not yet finished', the time was immovable. The cost was the only variable and therefore positioned the project somewhere on that side of the triangle. Consistent with this, when the SOC was faced with an advertising revenue shortfall in 1999, it approached the Australian government for further funding. The logic of 'if you want this, it will cost you this' prevailed and an additional A$200 million of funding was approved. Most importantly, the decision was consistent with the strategy and stated objectives of the project as shown by Figure 14.8. The willingness not to cut costs meant the project stayed out of the central region of Figure 14.4, the zone of no-brain.

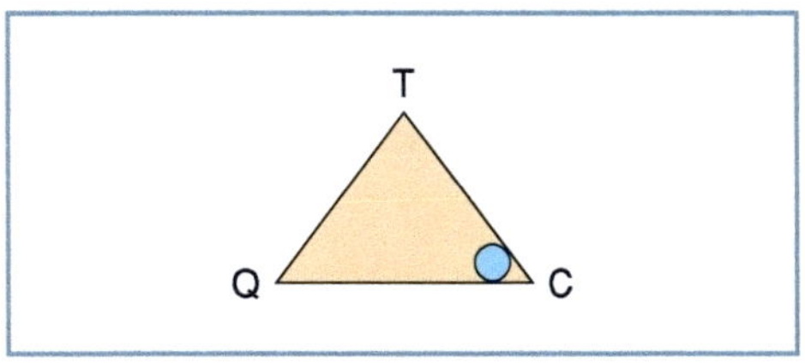

Figure 14.7 Cost priority project

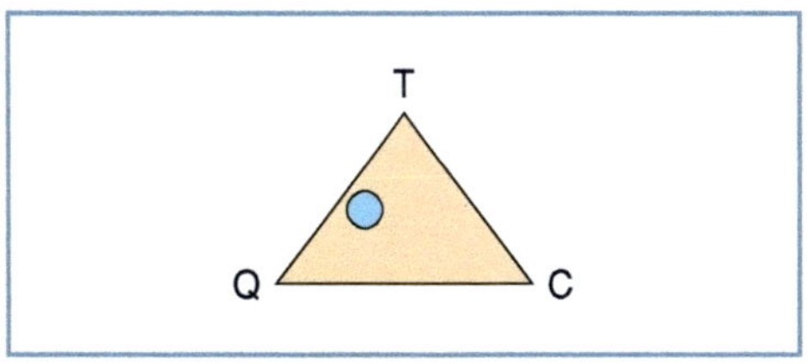

Figure 14.8 Time AND quality priority

Some authors have claimed that the necessity to consider trade-offs has been re-moved by modern management practices.[12] The evidence for this is not as convincing as suggested and the pragmatic project manager is still faced with making these decisions. Before committing to a course of action, the manager should, however, consider the assumptions that underlie each of the criteria. For example, if a project is running up against time constraints, it may be worth considering the sequence of activities to see whether their rearrangement will yield the necessary time savings. This is before any compromise is made on the cost element (reducing time by other means could incur additional costs).

However, such an approach is limited. We will look at whether there is a need to consider the further element of **flexibility** and whether a wider range of measures would, in fact, be beneficial.

The first consideration is to determine the nature of the three key objectives. These have been at the heart of consideration in project management for many years, and while limited on their own, are still the basis for any consideration of project objectives. As a minimum, the project manager must define these and then put in place a project process to ensure that these objectives are met. This approach stresses **conformance** to the stated objectives as being the most important for measuring project success. This is a measure of the *reliability* required of the project system, expressed as:

- Can the project be guaranteed to deliver on time?
- Will the project finish within budget?
- Will the project meet the specified level of quality?

Such reliability measures are a 'good place to start' for many individuals and organisations as they attempt to make sense of a project.

Going beyond this minimalist approach is consistent with the emphasis in many business projects today which has shifted away from just achieving conformance. Still focusing on our three basic criteria of time, cost and quality, excellence is defined in terms of real **performance**, expressed as:

- What is the shortest possible project duration?
- What is the lowest cost?
- What is the highest level of quality that can be achieved?

The mechanisms by which the project manager assures conformance are different from those that ensure performance. For example, by selecting low-cost suppliers, the project manager may attempt to ensure that the project is delivered at minimum cost (performance). Whether it is in fact deliverable is determined by the actions of that manager to secure guarantees that the price (in addition to delivery and quality) will be achieved in practice (conformance). Table 14.5 summarises these characteristics.

Time and cost criteria are relatively straightforward concepts. In practice, determining whether key objectives have been achieved can be a matter of some argument and commercial significance. One of the least understood concepts in projects is *quality*. There are a number of manufacturing and service definitions which we will explore, including the relationship between expectations and perceptions of customers (and other stakeholders) of both the project process and its outcomes.

Table 14.5 Conformance versus performance: attributes of time, cost and quality

	Time	*Cost*	*Quality*
Performance	Shortest possible	Cheapest possible	Highest level
Conformance	As planned	As budgeted	As specified

What lies beyond TCQ?

Looking at the work covered so far, it can be seen that for most projects there are diverse stakeholders with diverse sets of requirements at various stages during and beyond the project lifecycle. Therefore we can say that time, cost and quality are incomplete as a statement of requirements for a project.[13] We cannot assume that such objectives are fixed and known in advance of the project starting and that such diversity of requirements can be reduced to only three measures. In an ideal world (and many project managers' dreams), this would indeed be the case. The process of developing strategy for projects would be easier if customers always knew exactly what they wanted at the outset and were able to communicate this. As will be discussed later, it is the responsibility of the project manager to ensure that customer input is obtained by the project and there are a number of methods available for doing this.

There are, however, many occasions when the requirements of the customer are likely to change as the project progresses. The ability of the project system to address this change is expressed by its flexibility. Such flexibility needs to be accounted for at the outset, as there are penalties in relation to the other objectives – flexibility costs. For example, a firm that makes custom-engineered components is contracted to supply parts to an automotive assembler. It is asked to provide a quotation for new parts, but the specification requires some flexibility, as it will not be determined exactly until the last minute. With this required flexibility, the firm will need to hold back the making up of tooling, requiring this to be made by an express service rather than its normal supplier. This design flexibility therefore has potential cost implications, which, unless built into the estimates, will cause the firm to perform poorly on the cost conformance aspect.

Project performance mapping

Having determined the nature of the trade-offs in the project, the most important ones are determined by our organisational strategy. As stated earlier, this provides the guidance that we compete in a market or market segment by offering projects as the fastest or best or cheapest supplier. If the organisational objective is to be the fastest, then this is a *performance objective*, while the cost and quality criteria are *conformance objectives*. As a minimum, we must hit our conformance objectives. We will focus on improving on our performance objectives. Other objectives can form part of the conformance requirements of the project – not just time, cost and quality. These may be environmental, ethical, legal, health and safety – indeed any of the constraints identified at the start of Chapter 7 can become objectives.

14.3 Benefits analysis, value and justification

In Chapter 4, we explored the idea that it is neither possible nor desirable for an organisation to undertake all of the projects that present themselves. Programme and portfolio management provide the mechanisms by which organisations can reconcile the demands and the capacity to deliver these demands. The objective here is to consider the principles by which projects may be evaluated.

The fundamental idea is that a project should yield value: value to someone at some point in time. Decorating a house may yield value in terms of personal gratification about its improved ambience and may also add financial value, by increasing the price that someone is prepared to pay for it. A social project may not yield any return on the investment, yet may deliver perceived value to those that it tries to help. Business projects will usually have to be justified in hard financial terms, by justifying the timing and **payback** from an investment.

At a high level, the logic behind this is good – payback or **return on investment** should be criteria for determining which projects go into the portfolio of work to be carried out and which should be deferred, amended or rejected. A principle from the previous chapter is that an organisation cannot carry out every project proposed. Determining the kind of benefits that a project can deliver is not always completely straightforward, however. A framework that many organisations use to determine the nature of the return on an investment is the **balanced scorecard.**[14]

The balanced scorecard links four perspectives on business projects. These are:

1 *Shareholders* – what are the intended financial benefits in the short, medium or long term of the project?
2 *Customers and suppliers* – what are the benefits that they will receive from the project, be it direct benefit (reduced costs, for instance) or simply increasing goodwill? Will it enable the organisation to work with a different market of customers or suppliers?
3 *Internally* – how will the project improve our business processes?
4 *Innovation and learning* – how much will we learn from the project?

The last one is particularly interesting and often missed. For instance, the Apollo (and the preceding Mercury) missions were late and budget was 'not a major consideration'. In the development of the Apollo programme, with each successive project in that programme there was considerable learning. There was learning internally for NASA scientists and astronauts. There was learning for the supply chain, both in terms of what worked and what didn't, technically and in process terms.

Overall, these combine to provide a notion of the **value proposition** from a project. Such terminology has become commonplace in the justification of time, energy and resources on business projects. The originators of the balanced scorecard promote a logical cause–effect building of benefits from project work, with the objective to demonstrate how each project will impact organisational strategy. Such construction is consistent with the approach shown in Chapter 4.

Demonstrating such benefits is the purpose of an approach known as **benefits mapping.**[15] Using this, it is possible to work back from the business benefit required, see how this maps to organisational objectives and then determine the changes and supporting actions required to yield those benefits.

One organisation used this approach to demonstrate how an initiative to improve its programme and project management (PPM) capability would benefit the business and produced the map shown in Figure 14.9.

Starting on the right of the figure, the organisational drivers for the change are shown. At the most basic level, improving the organisation's PPM capability is necessary for survival and continued investment in that company and its projects. This drives the benefits requirement – organisational benefits. Externally, it needs to be able to deliver projects in the way planned – its markets and customers are unforgiving when projects are delayed or otherwise compromised. Internally, it wants to demonstrate how improved capability will help the people in the firm who would need to be key participants in any change. It was also noted how it was often forgotten why projects were started – not uncommon in organisations. The next box to the left is the organisational changes that are required – each one can be linked to an element in the organisational benefits box. Similarly, the far left box has elements which are linked to the changes. For instance, before you can have good processes in place (organisational change) it is necessary to define appropriate processes (enabling change).

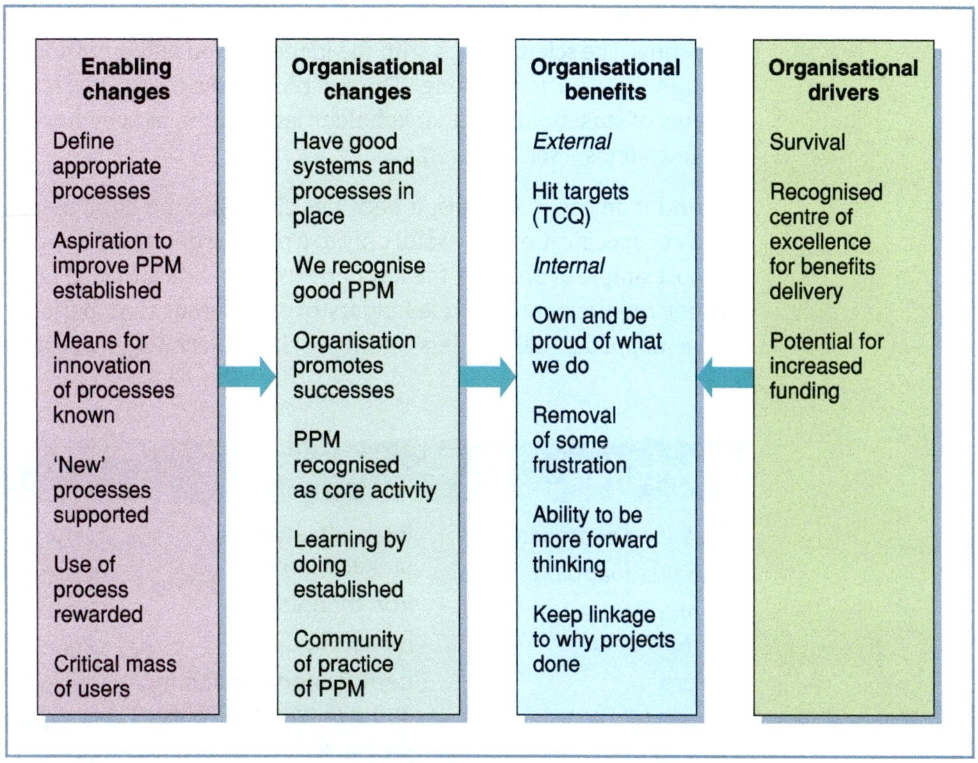

Figure 14.9 Benefits map for PPM capability improvement

From intangible to quantifiable

While there are some benefits that do not require justification (e.g. implement a regulatory change in a bank or be prevented from trading), many project managers struggle with intangible benefits. There are a number of strategies for dealing with this *quantification problem*.[16] These include:

- carrying out a pilot study – determine on a small scale the costs and benefits of the work being proposed before launching into a full-scale project;
- benchmarking and reference sites – other organisations which have carried out similar projects and their costs incurred and benefits gained;
- modelling – build a simulation of the proposed changes – use the data from these to provide evidence of costs and benefits.

Summary

■ Welcome to some of the inherent complexity that goes with running projects. This chapter has sought to show how professional project managers cope with such complexity. The principle of 'beginning with the end in mind' is a good one, and determining this end is a key role for project managers. In doing so, they will need to wrestle with the often indeterminate and conflicting needs of different stakeholder groups. In reality, managing stakeholders can be as much art as science – often referred to in terms of 'herding cats' rather than the traditional view of the process as 'optimising'.

- In projects, the science and art can and should be mutually reinforcing rather than competing. The science helps with the identification and provision of numbers in an effort to help with decision-making. The art recognises that projects and the accompanying 'systems of stakeholders' or stakeholder landscapes, as they have been termed here, are people systems – social systems.

- Working in social systems, it becomes clear that the basic measures of time, cost and quality or specification are useful only to a point in determining project objectives. Beyond the most simple of projects, the key performance indicators (KPIs) used should reflect the broader requirements of stakeholders over different time periods. These requirements can be mapped to help understanding of the project and the requirements.

Key terms

balanced scorecard
benefits mapping
conformance/performance
failure
flexibility
impact
influence
input/process/outcome requirements
internal/external stakeholders
iron triangle
measures
participatory monitoring and evaluation (PM&E)
payback
power
requirements
rest of the world
return on investment
stakeholder landscape
stakeholders
success
timing
trade-offs
value
value-maximisation
value proposition

Relevant areas of the Bodies of Knowledge

Both Bodies of Knowledge are relatively weak on the areas covered in this chapter (Tables 14.6 and 14.7). Part of the reason is due to the definition that they use of project work – that the project doesn't start until such work as is included here has been completed, a business case prepared and the project 'signed off'. The reality for most project managers is that they will and indeed should be involved in the earlier discussions, as described here as phase D1, and not simply pick up the project fully formed in D3.

Table 14.6 Relevant area of the APM Body of Knowledge

Relevant section	*Title*	*Summary*
20	Project success criteria	Defines some of the terms used here, including requirements, critical success factors and key performance indicators.

Table 14.7 Relevant areas of the PMI Body of Knowledge

Relevant section	*Title*	*Summary*
2.2	Project stakeholders	Identifies groups of key stakeholders and their possible relationships with the project.
4.1	Develop project charter	Identifies a process for managing communications within a project.
10.1	Communications planning	States requirements for plan to communicate in an appropriate manner with all necessary stakeholder groups. No tools provided to show how.
10.4	Manage stakeholders	Some good principles for working with stakeholders during (not prior to) a project.

PROJECT MANAGEMENT IN PRACTICE

Managing stakeholders at European transport infrastructure provider

In the development of a strategy for major projects, this organisation spent some time considering how it would work with each of its stakeholder groups. The first stage was to identify these groups. These were:

1. Government – owned the company.
2. Managers – worked in the company.
3. Supervisory board – acted in the role of a regulator of the company's activities.
4. Public authorities – local government organisations.
5. Strategic partners – other transport providers, construction companies.
6. Employees – worked in the company.
7. Suppliers – many organisations, from utility companies to consultants.
8. Press and media – always trying to find a good story.
9. Associations and organisations – groups of interested parties.
10. Local communities – impacted by both the project and the outcomes of the project.
11. Customers – those who actually paid to use the services provided.

Having done this, it then mapped its power and interest, as shown in Figure 14.10. Each stakeholder was represented as an oval on the diagram, with the size of the oval representing the scale of that stakeholder group. 'Government' in these terms is relatively small scale – they were controlled through one single government department that reported directly to a government minister. The press and media were on a larger scale as there were more individual organisations involved: journalists, media companies, etc. The largest group, represented by the largest oval, was the customers.

The company was concerned about the placement of some of its stakeholders as it moved forward. For instance, it appeared that the press and media had more power and influence than one of the most important groups, the customers. As the company developed plans for a major new infrastructure project which would affect all of the groups and particularly customers, it was contemplating whether this arrangement was appropriate.

Points for discussion

1. Outline the role that a government-owned company might take in its management of a major piece of transport infrastructure (could be a road, railway or airport, for instance).
2. Should it be concerned about the placement of customers so low down and in the 'minimal effort' quadrant?
3. Suggest three stakeholders whose positions you would change and outline a strategy for doing so.

→

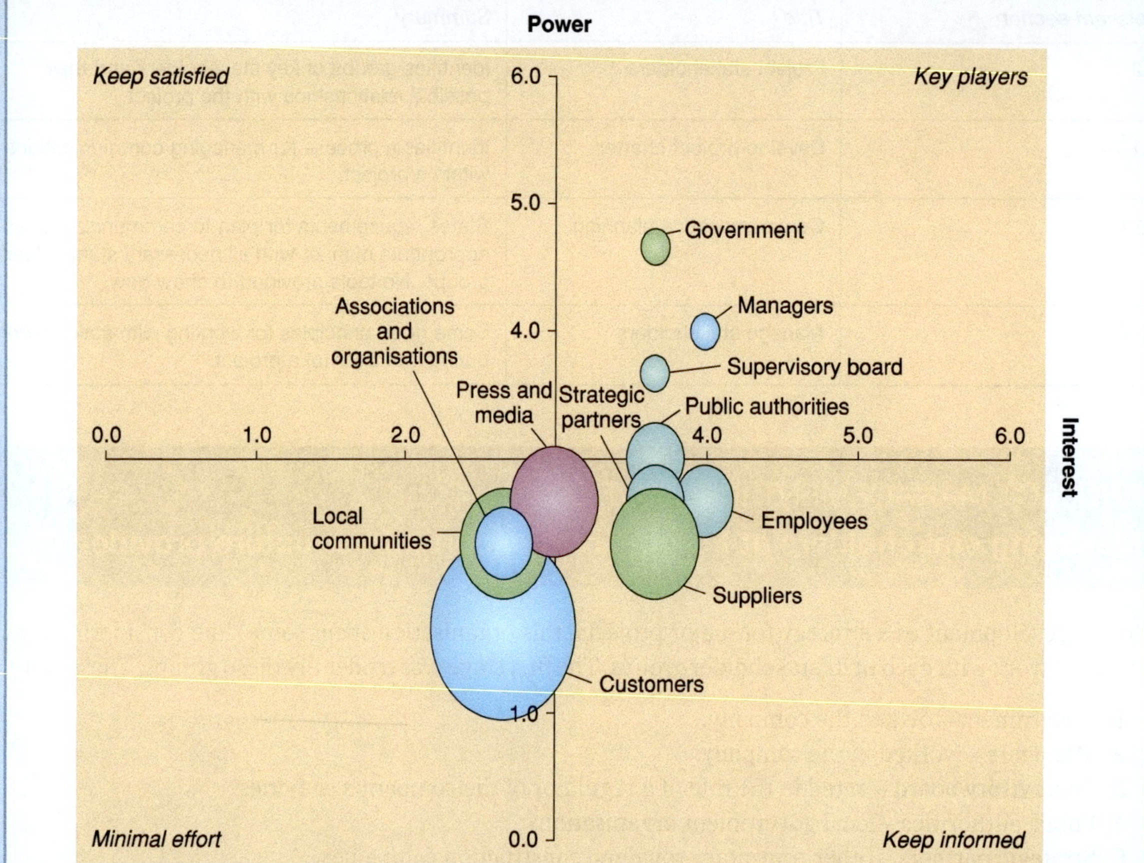

Figure 14.10 Stakeholder map

PROJECT MANAGEMENT IN PRACTICE

A new campus for the University of Rummidge (with apologies to David Lodge[17])

A chance meeting between the leader of the town council of Splot and the Vice-chancellor of the University of Rummidge started a project that would lead to the opening of a new campus in Splot.

This appeared to be an ideal opportunity for both parties – the university was unable to expand further on its existing site, due to local planning restrictions. This was despite having a well-known brand name in the market, particularly for management education. The town was in the process of applying to become a city, a status that would confer additional prestige on the area and almost certain political success for whoever could make it happen. It had been the recipient of around a4 billion of investment in recent years, from leading-edge companies in the automotive and electronics sectors. These new firms were providing a major demand for a wide variety of higher education services that the existing institutions were incapable of providing. Local unemployment was virtually zero and firms were having problems recruiting for all types of work.

A number of opportunities presented themselves to the Splot council. These included setting up their own university, in conjunction with local businesses, and accessing a remote provider through a virtual campus. The first was rejected on the grounds that they did not have the expertise to do this and the second on the basis that despite the low unemployment and prevalence of high-technology industries, the majority of the people of Splot did not have internet access. The availability of school premises in the middle of the town, which could be readily converted into a campus and which were in an area prioritised for redevelopment, sealed the decision. Shutting down the school was a decision eased by the falling numbers of pupils.

For the University of Rummidge, there were likewise other options. Expansion into areas that would relieve the dependence on government funding was always a priority, and operations beyond the physical limitations of the campus were increasingly attractive. Internet-based activities were an option for investment, but there were other initiatives in place to promote these. In addition, forming direct relationships with one or more of the large companies in the area for provision of integrated higher education services was considered. The university's management team favourably viewed the opening of a new campus.

In order to progress the work, a joint venture organisation entitled 'The University of Rummidge in Splot' was established with the brief to 'explore all the various options that will permit the establishment of a permanent and physical presence by the University of Rummidge in Splot'.

Six months later, the joint venture organisation reported, recommending to both the university and the council that the school premises be converted ready for courses to be run the following September. A budget for the conversion of the premises and establishment of the campus (including provision of library and IT facilities) of €15 million was suggested and funding was underwritten by both organisations, subject to grants being approved from central government and sponsorship being obtained from local companies.

The main part of the project is now about to start and the team has 12 months to get the new facility, staffing and all the necessary support services ready. Academic staff at Rummidge are not impressed by this move as much of the negotiation has taken place without their input. Moreover, Splot is around a one-hour drive from Rummidge, traffic permitting. There are also significant reservations about the location of the campus in a relatively run-down district of the town and whether there will be sufficient buy-in from local people to make it worthwhile. In addition, there was debate as to whether courses (both undergraduate and postgraduate) would be run at both sites and whether there would be resources available to assist with the workloads of the departments (both academic and administrative) caused by the new courses. Some of the administrative departments were also unclear as to how the new campus would affect their workloads.

The organisational structures are shown in outline in Figure 14.11.

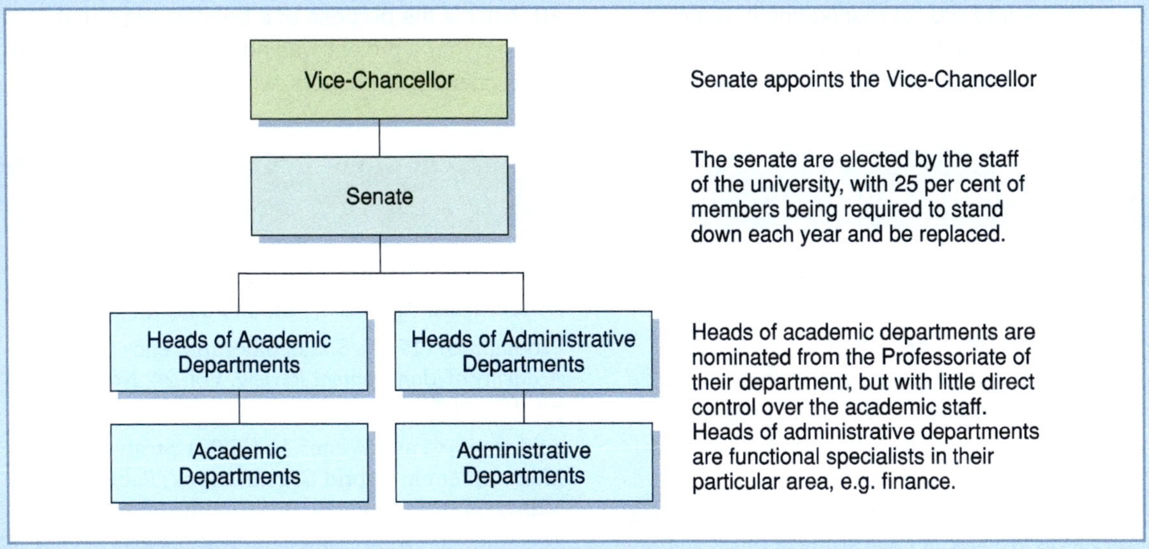

Figure 14.11 Outline structure – University of Rummidge

Points for discussion

1 What are the strategic objectives for each of the organisations involved? Provide a high-level benefits map to structure the objectives and necessary changes.

2 Who are the key stakeholders in such a project? Use one of the maps as in Figure 14.9 to show how each group should be managed.

3 What would appropriate success measures be for the project?

Topics for discussion

1 The Beijing Olympics in 2008 were widely hailed as a great success. Identify the list of majorstakeholders for such an event. Carry out a search of relevant material to determine how the games 'project' performed for each of these stakeholders.

2 What are the implications for a project manager of not having any clear prioritisation of objectives in terms of time, cost and quality?

3 What are the implications for a project manager of being told that the cost of the project was the most important objective for them to achieve?

4 Time, cost and quality measured at project completion have been widely used as performance measures for projects. When might this be useful and how is this a limited approach?

5 How would the use of the balanced scorecard approach to project performance management help a project be 'successful'?

6 Identify the stakeholders for a new masters course in programme and project management. Suggest some key questions that might be asked to make sure that a comprehensive list is achieved.

7 A couple have decided to get married. Being professional project managers, they decide to analyse the stakeholders in the 'wedding project' and to work out any conflicts in advance. List the stakeholders, and provide an interest/influence matrix to determine the strategy for managing the stakeholders in this project.

8 In the launch of a particular product, two key stakeholder groups were identified – the customers and the marketing department of the firm launching the product. As the project manager for this project, identify what the requirements and likely measures are for these two groups and any problems you might face managing these two groups.

9 If a project should be assessed on its long-term performance (beyond the end of the project itself), but project managers have only short-term appointments (usually only up to the end of the project), how should the performance of project managers be measured?

10 What is the purpose of a benefits map? If it showed that a project was not, in fact, contributing to organisational benefits, what would you do?

Further information

Baccarini, D. (1999) 'The Logical Framework Method for Defining Project Success', *Project Management Journal*, Vol. 30, No. 4, pp. 25–32.

Christenson, D. and Walker, D.H.T (2004) 'Understanding the Role of "Vision" in Project Success', *Project Management Journal*, Vol. 35, No. 3, pp. 39–52.

De Lopez, T.T. (2001) 'Stakeholder Management for Conservation Projects: A Case Study of Ream National Park, Cambodia', *Environmental Management*, Vol. 28, No. 1, pp. 47–60.

Freeman, R.E. (1984) *Strategic Management: A Stakeholder Approach*, Pitman Publishing, London.

Frooman, J. (1999) 'Stakeholder Influence Strategies', *Academy of Management Review*, Vol. 24, No. 2, pp. 191–205.

Joldersma, C. and Winter, V. (2002) 'Strategic Management in Hybrid Organisations', *Public Management Review*, Vol. 4, No. 1, pp. 83–99.

McManus, J. (2004) *Managing Stakeholders in Software Development Projects*, Butterworth Heinemann, Basingstoke.

Mitchell, R., Agle, B. and Wood, D. (1997) 'Towards a Theory of Stakeholder Identification and Salience', *Academy of Management Review*, Vol. 22, No. 4, pp. 853–887.

Rasche, A. and Esser, D. (2006) 'From Stakeholder Management to Stakeholder Accountability', *Journal of Business Ethics*, Vol. 65, No. 3, pp. 251–267.

Scott J., Schultz, F.C. and Hekman, D.R. (2006) 'Stakeholder Theory and Managerial Decision-Making: Constraints and Implications of Balancing Stakeholder Interests', *Journal of Business Ethics*, Vol. 64, No. 3, pp. 285–301.

Winstanley, D., Sorabji, D. and Dawson, S. (1995) 'When the Pieces Don't Fit: A Stakeholder Power Matrix to Analyse Public Sector Restructuring', *Public Money & Management*, Vol. 15, No. 2, pp. 19–26.

Wolfe, R.A. and Putler, D.S. (2002) 'How Tight Are the Ties that Bind Stakeholder Groups?', *Organisation Science*, Vol. 13, No. 1, pp. 64–80.

Websites

http://web.worldbank.org – many publications concerning managing stakeholder participation in development projects in particular.

www.dot.ca.gov/hq/projmgmt/documents/pchb/project_communication_handbook_2nd_ed.pdf – excellent project communications handbook.

References

1 Shenhar, A.J., Dvir, D., Levy, O. and Maltz, A. (2001) 'Project Success – A Multidimensional Strategic Concept', *Long Range Planning*, Vol. 34, No. 6, pp. 699–725.

2 Covey, Stephen R. (1990) *The Seven Habits of Highly Effective People*, Free Press, New York.

3 Pinto, J. and Kharbanda, O. (1996) 'How to Fail in Project Management (Without Really Trying)', *Business Horizons*, July–August, pp. 45–53.

4 BS 6079 (2000) *Project Management – Part 1: Guide to Project Management*, British Standards Institute, London.

5 For a fuller list of measures see Griffin, A. and Page, A.L. (1996) 'PDMA Success Measurement Project: Recommended Measures for Product Development Success and Failure', *Journal of Product Innovation Management*, Vol. 13, pp. 478–496.

6 www.ids.ac.uk/ids/bookshop/briefs/Brief12.html.

7 In 1962 the total bill was expected to be between £150 million and £170 million. In December 1974, a written Parliamentary answer disclosed that the cost to Britain and France of developing Concorde up to the point at which it entered service would be £974 million.

8 *Financial Times*, 15 October 1996.

9 There are many variants on this approach and many sources claiming authorship. One easily accessed source is www.mindtools.com/pages/article/newPPM_07.htm.

10 Savage, G.T., Nix, T.W., Whitehead, C.J. and Blair, J.D. (1991) 'Strategies for Assessing and Managing Organizational Stakeholders', *Academy of Management Executive*, Vol. 5, No. 2, pp. 61–75 and more recently, Karlsen, T.J. (2002) 'Project Stakeholder Management', *Engineering Management Journal*, Vol. 14, No. 4, pp. 19–24.

11 For more on this, see Kozak-Holland, M. (2004) *Titanic Lessons for IT Projects*, Multi-media Publications Inc., Chicago; also http://lessons-from-history.com.

12 Notable but not alone in promoting this view was Schonberger, R. (1985) *World Class Manufacturing*, Free Press, New York.

13 See also Atkinson, R. (1999) 'Project Management: Cost, Time and Quality, Two Best Guesses and a Phenomenon, Its [sic] Time to Accept Other Success Criteria', *International Journal of Project Management*, Vol. 17, No. 6, pp. 337–342 and Shenhar et al. 2001 (reference 1).

14 Kaplan, R.S. and Norton, D.P. (2001) *The Strategy Focused Organisation: How Balanced Scorecard Companies Thrive in the New Business Environment*, Harvard Business School Press, Boston.

15 Ward, J., Hemingway, C.J. and Daniel, E.M. (2005) 'A Framework for Addressing the Organisational Issues of Enterprise Systems Implementation', *Journal of Strategic Information Systems*, Vol. 14, No. 2, pp. 97–119.

16 Ward, J. and Daniels, L. (2006) *Benefits Management: Delivering Value from IS and IT Investments*, John Wiley, Chichester.

17 Lodge, D. (2002) *Changing Places*, Penguin, Harlow.

15 Project Management Tools and Techniques

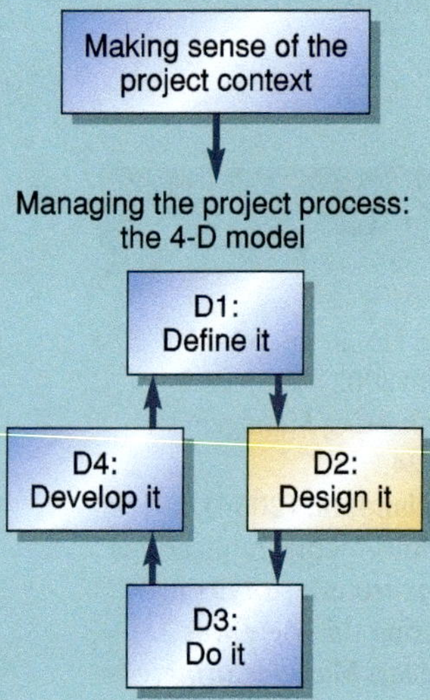

'If you fail to plan, you plan to fail!'
(old adage)

'Planning is an unnatural process. It is much more satisfying to do something and the nicest thing about not planning is that failure comes as a complete surprise rather than being preceded by a long period of worry and depression.'
(Sir John Harvey, c.1800)

Principles

1. The first principle of planning is deconstruction: break the product and the work into tasks.
2. A time plan requires the arrangement of the tasks into a sequence for the purpose of analysis.
3. The most recognised way to communicate a time plan is as a Gantt Chart.

Learning objectives

By the time you have completed this chapter, you should be able to:

- ➔ use the basics of product, task and organisational breakdown and recognise the limitations of these
- ➔ arrange tasks in a simple project into a sequence, and calculate the project duration and critical path
- ➔ display the results of a time plan for communication purposes.

Contents

The Glastonbury Festival has become one of the largest of its kind in Europe. In addition to the performing acts, there is a huge operation to make the festival work, in the management of the media, tickets, security, retail units and general care of the location. Each of these requires a different approach to planning – not just to make sure that all of the acts arrive on a constructed stage at a given time, have all their kit and are able to be heard by the paying guests. In addition to the considerable scale and complexity of the festival, there are always intrinsic uncertainties – will the bands turn up, will the rain turn the place into a mire (2006) or be so hot that people are passing out with heatstroke (2004)? How will the organisers respond in case of a major security alert? All these things are vital considerations for the planners.

Source: Samuel Wordley/Alamy

Introduction

The initial or master plan was constructed and various means provided to communicate and evaluate it. In this chapter, we move into the second major phase of the project process D2: detailed process design. As the opening case demonstrates, this is not a trivial process, as the planner will have to not only deal with the most likely scenarios, but also plan for eventualities – to answer the question 'what happens if . . .?'.

The most basic approach is to deconstruct the project into its constituent products and parts. These then need to be compiled into a time plan and the result of this compilation used to feed into the basic project analysis and communication. This is where one of the most basic tools of the project manager comes into its own – the Gantt Chart.

The opening quotations illustrate a tension between the need to plan a project, and the need to get on with it. The phases of D2 and D3 need to be balanced and on this point there is little to guide the manager as to what constitutes 'sufficient planning'. Determining which items to include in a plan, and how to make them work together, is where the 'art' rather than the 'science' of managing a project is needed.

15.1 Deconstruction of a project

The production of plans is often treated as an end in itself. This misses the point and the value that such an activity can add. Its objectives are twofold. First, it must provide an opportunity for the planner to analyse the project system, to reveal opportunities for improvement and problem prevention, and setting out the basis on which the project will proceed. Second, the benefits of plans are only realised when they are communicated. These two objectives create the rationale for what follows.

Figure 15.1 shows the process that will be used here, and some of the key aspects of planning during this phase.

Having prepared the overview models, it is now the task of the planner to put in place the detail. High-level consideration of the objectives of the various stakeholders and resolution of potential conflicts of the project provide a strong foundation on which to build. This chapter presents the means by which these details can be put in place. Graphical techniques are preferred, as these create the greatest potential for involving others to gain their insight and commitment. However, the objective of such detail must remain at the forefront of the planner's mind. In itself it has little merit. The strength that it offers is in the ability to probe the plans to identify potential improvements to the methods, which may present opportunities for either better performance or risk avoidance.

For the project manager, this is one of the most developed parts of the subject – the methods have been formalised for over 50 years, though in reality have undoubtedly been in use in one form or another since the beginning of civilisation. They must, however, be considered in the light of experience, and this is discussed in the following chapter.

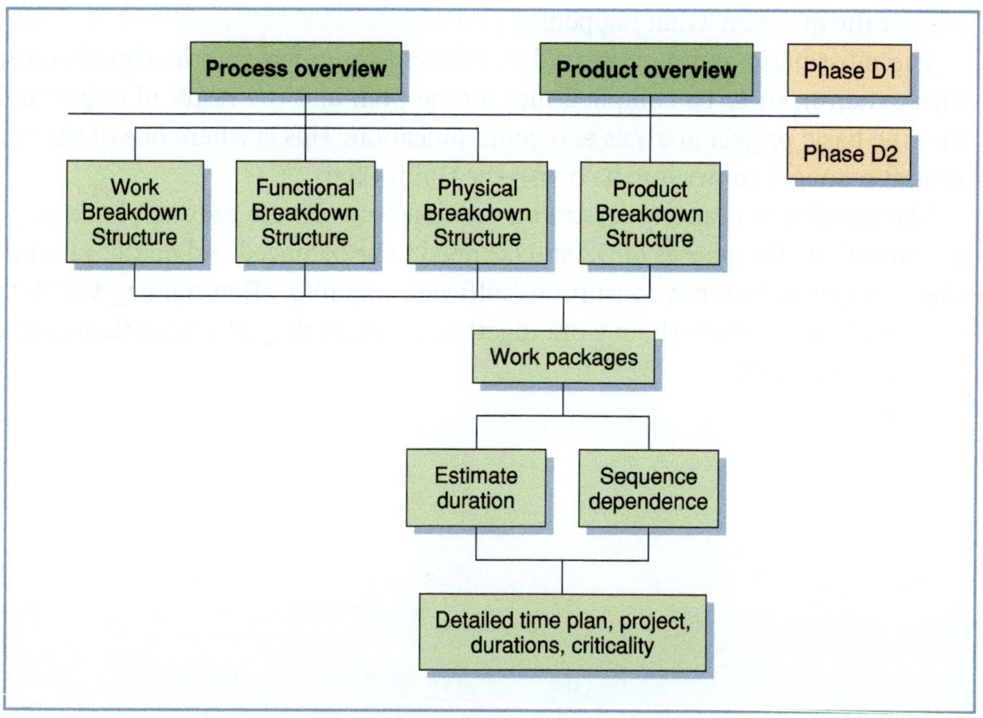

Figure 15.1 Flow of process through this part of the planning

Work breakdown structure

With some small projects, many people are able to break these up into lists of 'things to do' in their heads. This has the advantage of being relatively quick and in many cases works as long as the scale and complexity of the project is relatively limited. The two major downsides of this approach are the vulnerability of the project to that one person, and the inability of this 'plan' to be analysed or communicated. In an attempt to be more systematic about this, the most basic approach for the medium-to-large project is to use a Work Breakdown Structure.

'So how do you eat an elephant (or vegetarian equivalent)?'
'Just one slice at a time.'

The breaking down of large activities (the elephant) into comprehensible or manageable units (the slices) is a fundamental part of project management. Figure 15.2 shows how a systems project – the installation of a new computer system – was broken down into elements that one person or one department could tackle as an activity in its own right at the lowest level in the project. In principle, what could be simpler?! The reality, of course, is never quite so simple.

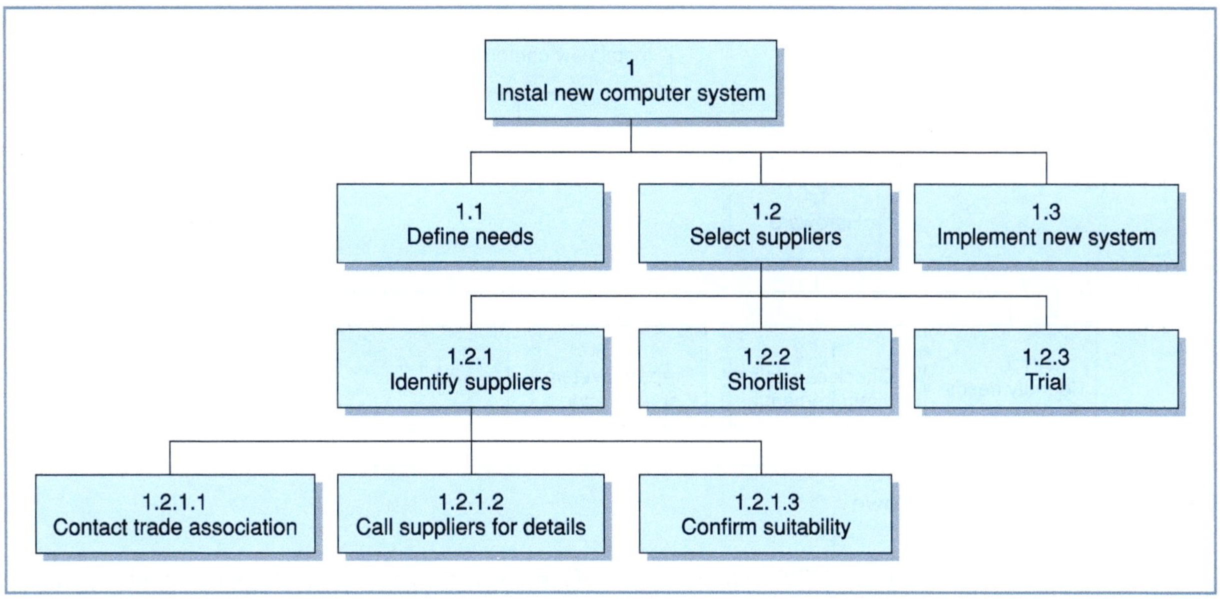

Figure 15.2 Example of a work breakdown structure (WBS)

WBS is also known as 'chunking' or 'unbundling'. This is attractive as it gives people responsibility for a manageable part of the project. WBS also facilitates financial control activities, as individual parts can have their consumption of resources tracked.

Projects can be broken down in a number of ways. The example given above is an activity breakdown – the first level of breakdown is into the major groups of activities that will be undertaken. Other forms of breakdown include a functional breakdown, where the project is divided into its functional areas (in this case IT, finance and operations) and the activities for each area identified. A further type of breakdown is by physical grouping – in this case it could be split up into hardware issues and software issues. These alternatives and the accompanying breakdowns are shown in Figures 15.3 and 15.4.

The role of a WBS is to create a linked, hierarchical series of activities, which are independent units, but at the same time still part of the whole, and here lies the major

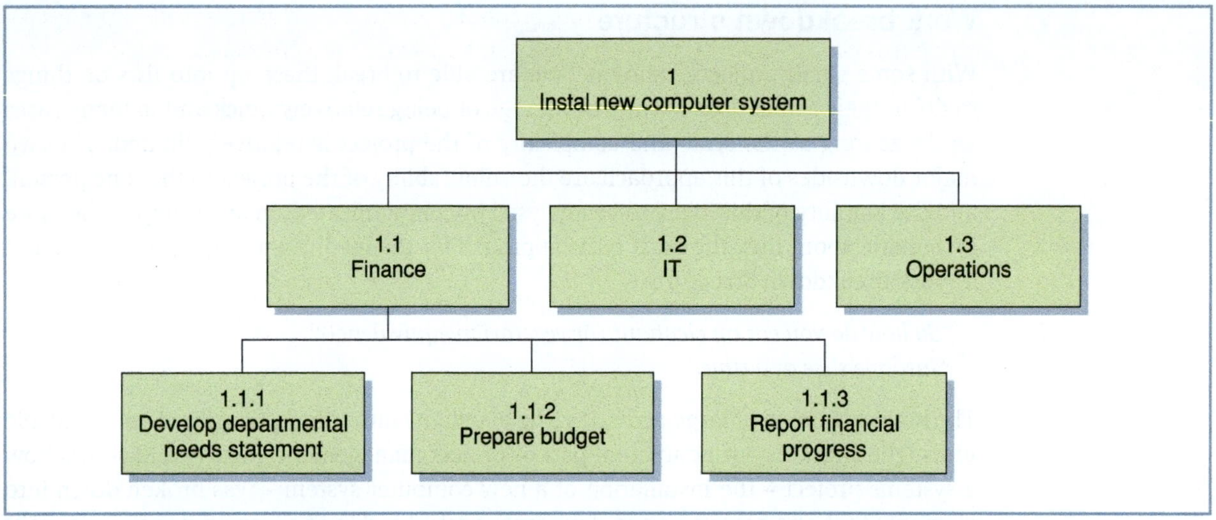

Figure 15.3 Functional breakdown

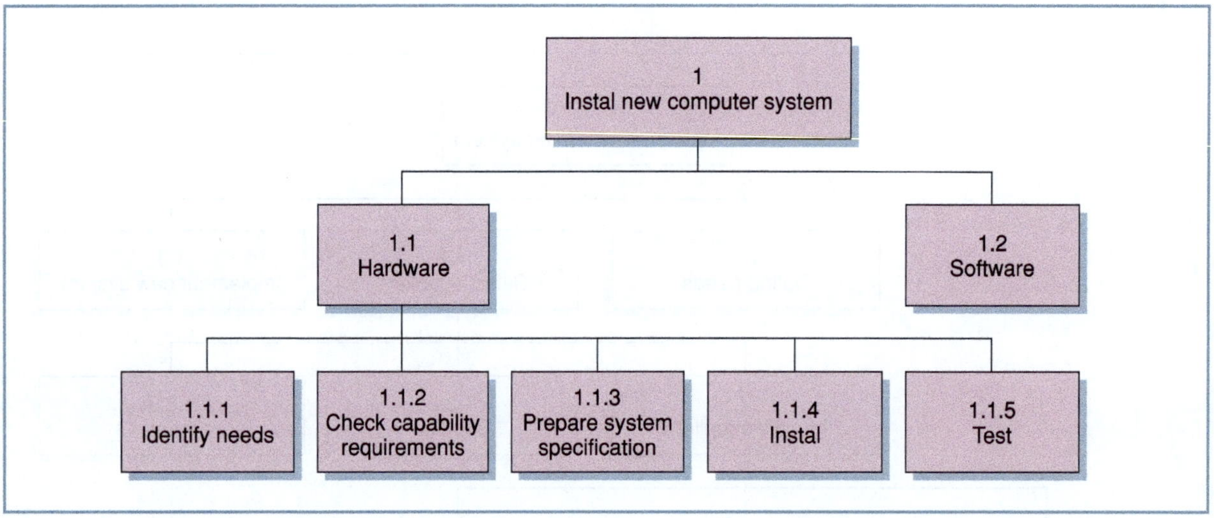

Figure 15.4 Physical breakdown

problem with WBS. Whatever type of structure you choose, there are inevitable conflicts, as demonstrated by the following short case.

Does it matter which type of breakdown you use? Err, yes

During a line refurbishment for London Underground carried out during the 1980s, the project was broken down into track/tunnel units and train/rolling stock units. Communication between the two was problematic, and when the refurbished trains were delivered they did not fit into the refurbished tunnels. Nobody had been assigned to manage the interfaces between the teams during the project, as a result of which everybody relentlessly pursued their own part of the work – regardless of the consequences that it would have elsewhere.

For the project manager, de-constructing a project into constituent elements is not a trivial task. To ensure that the 'product' is delivered requires the production of the product breakdown structure (PBS).

However, a project is not a deconstructionist activity. It is precisely the opposite – it requires construction – building up the project from the sub-projects and activities. Using the metaphor of the elephant, a project is not about slicing it up, but rather about taking the various parts and making them work together. While this is stretching the metaphor, it does illustrate the reality of the challenge for the project manager. They will not only need to manage the delivery of the individual activities or work packages, but also coordinate between the different parts of the breakdown. Practically, this has been achieved through having a liaison person or exchanging staff or through changing the scheduling of activities to run more of them in parallel. This requires much greater interfacing and team-working. Generating the WBS looks like such a simple set of activities, yet the decisions made here are fundamental in achieving success.

The work breakdown structure provides the first attempt at modelling the project process. Whichever type of breakdown is used, at the bottom level will be a list of activities or *work packages* that are passed on to the next stage.

15.2 Constructing a time plan

How long will it take you to complete a major report for your boss, or a 3000-word assignment for a course of study? Many questions then arise, including:

- How precise do you need to be – is a rough/ballpark figure required, or are we using this for detailed planning?
- Do we have any previous experience of doing this? If so, how long did it take last time?
- What are the likely pitfalls that may arise that would cause significant delay?
- What other tasks are going to get in the way of doing this.

Estimating is a key part of project planning, though, as we shall see, it is one that is subject to more games-playing and delusion than almost any other field of human activity. The basics of estimating are discussed here, but it should be remembered that estimates are otherwise called 'guesses'. We should therefore be careful how scientifically we treat the numbers that come from this process, and in particular, not be committed in a hurry to making rough estimates that we later get held to.

The project manager's role in the estimation process will vary from the collection of estimates from other people in the preparation of the proposal to the provision of detailed financial cost–benefit analysis. It is imperative that this function does not operate in a vacuum – that the feedback from previous plans and estimates is used to guide the process. Estimation is an activity which continues during the project life-cycle. As the project nears completion, the manager will have more certainty of the final times, resources and therefore costs. The accuracy of the estimates is therefore going to get better. The types of estimates, their nature, role and accuracies are shown in Table 15.1.

Having the estimates of times and resources required is one part of compiling the plans. In modelling time, these then need to be built into models of the likely project system that will enable key variables such as project duration and then schedules to be established.

Many projects require a planning method, which lends itself to analysis. The most commonly used of these is the '**activity-on-node**' technique. In this, activities from the WBS are represented as tasks on a relatively simple-to-understand diagram, to indicate the way the project is expected to work. The *estimates* have been obtained and a logical analysis of the work packages will usually determine their *sequence*.

Table 15.1 The nature, role and accuracy of estimate types

Name	*Nature*	*Role*	*Accuracy*
Rough/finger-in-the-air/ballpark	Much uncertainty as to what is involved	Early check on feasibility of brief	Very low
As-buts	As was carried out previously, but with the following amendments – some quantitative data exists	With an appropriate contingency factor – can be used for proposals	Moderate
Detailed estimates	Some initial work is carried out to determine what the likely problems are going to be	Proposals	Moderate
. . . to finish	Much of the project is completed and additional funding is needed to complete the tasks	Additional funds request	High

Activity-on-node diagrams and critical path analysis

Using the A-o-N technique, the construction of the project plan combines the work breakdown structure to identify all the constituent activities, the sequence in which they need to be performed, and the estimated duration for each activity.

If the logic of the project can be identified, the project manager can develop a diagram to represent it, allowing better analysis of the activities. Firstly, then, we need to represent the logical sequence in which the activities take place.

Consider a simple example. Figure 15.5 shows two activities, A and B, represented by simple boxes. B cannot start until A has finished and the times for A and B are 6 and 7 days respectively. This logic is known as **dependency**. This dependency means that the total duration of the two tasks is 13 days.

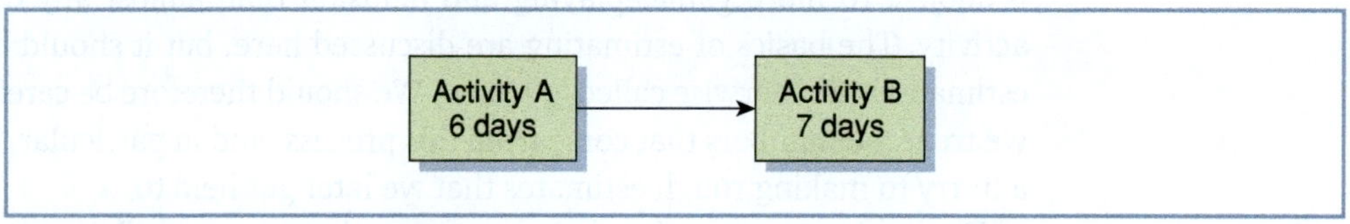

Figure 15.5 Task dependency

The visual clarity of denoting activities as boxes and linking them together is appealing. However, for any two activities, A then B, there are four ways in which they can link (see Figure 15.6). Precedence is indicated by arrows going from:

- the start of an activity (top left-hand or bottom left-hand corner of the box);
- the finish of an activity (middle of right-hand edge of box);

to:

- the start of an activity (middle of left-hand edge of box);
- the finish of an activity (top right-hand or bottom right-hand corner of the box).

The four ways in which activities therefore can link are:

- finish-to-start – the second activity cannot start until the first has finished;
- start-to-start – the second activity cannot start until the first has started;
- finish-to-finish – the second activity cannot finish until the first has finished;
- start-to-finish – the second activity cannot finish until the first has started.

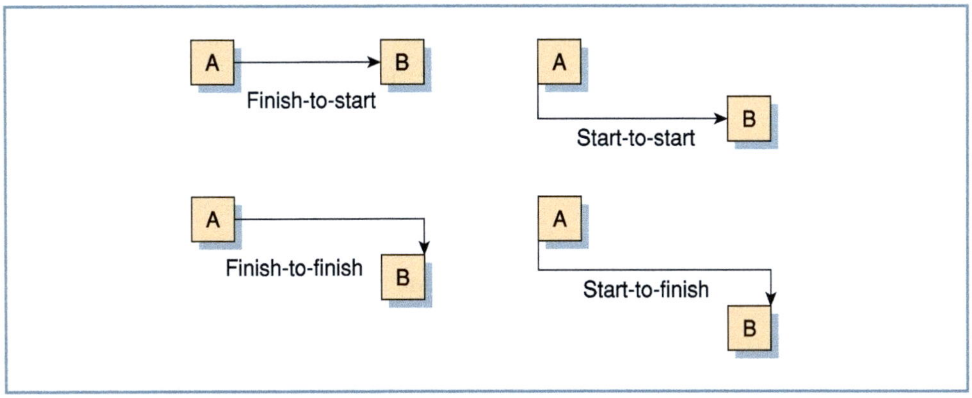

Figure 15.6 Logical activity linkages

The arrows represent a potential time lag in the logic, e.g. if there was a figure, say 2 on the arrow in the start-to-finish case, the second activity could not finish until 2 time units after the first had started.

In the case of the simple activity of washing the car, the statement 'don't drive into the carwash *before* shutting the windows *and* removing the aerial' can be expanded as shown in Figure 15.7. It is represented here as C (drive into the carwash) cannot start until both A (shut windows) and B (remove aerial) are complete. These are finish-to-start activities, and the distinction is important. What could happen if you treated them as the other options in Figure 15.7?

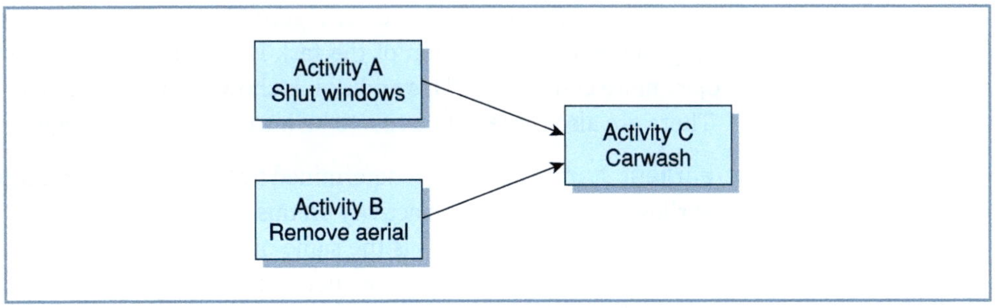

Figure 15.7 Representing multiple dependencies (1)

If the project has multiple activities that need to be completed before another task can start, that can be represented also. Consider the more complicated set of activities in Figure 15.8, which shows that the final activity, H, cannot start until all of E, F and G are finished.

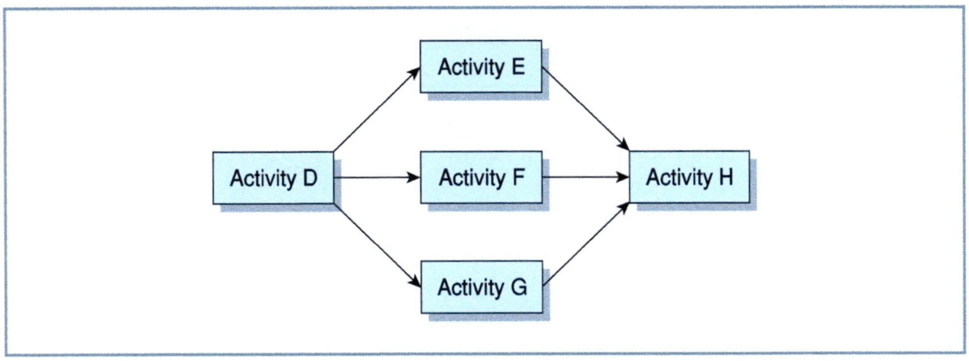

Figure 15.8 Representing multiple dependencies (2)

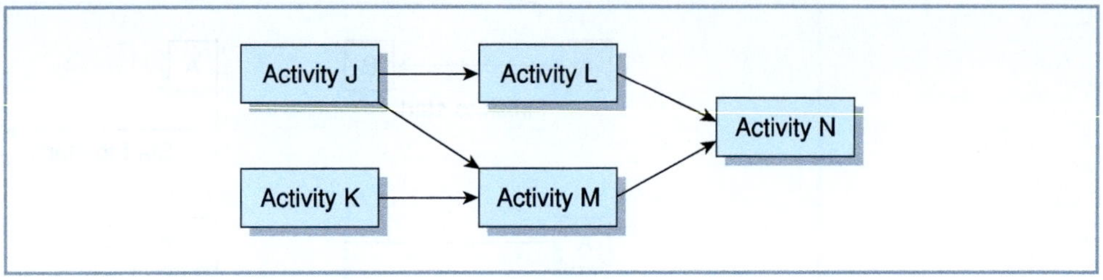

Figure 15.9 Representing multiple dependencies (3)

The plan can be made slightly more complicated. For example, taking the statement that 'activity L is dependent on activity J but activity M is dependent on both activities J and K' would lead to Figure 15.9. In this sequence, L can start once J has finished, but M cannot be started until both J and K are complete.

In order to complete the project with activity N, the project manager needs to schedule the predecessor activities. To understand how best to achieve this, we need more information about the activities within the project. To do this, we add additional information to the activity 'box' and the full detail of the activity-on-node technique becomes apparent. Considering the **network** of Figure 15.9, we already know the activity names (J, K, L, M, N) and we can estimate the time duration that each task will take. Knowing the way the tasks are linked, and the duration of each, we can perform a valuable analysis of the project.

Analysing the network – Critical Path Analysis (CPA)

We can amend the activity boxes of Figure 15.9 to add more information. Specifically, stating the expected duration of the task is the first stage in being able to analyse the project more completely. This addition is shown in Figure 15.10.

There are also three new terms to be introduced to the diagrams:

- **earliest start time** (EST) – determined by the activities preceding the event and is the earliest time at which the activity on this node can start;
- **latest start time** (LST) – is the same or later than the EST and is the latest time at which all the previous activities need to have been completed to prevent the whole project being held up;
- *total* **float** – the difference between the LST and the EST.

How is this used in practice? If we look at the example of Figure 15.11, we see the logic of the activities within this project, and the dependencies between the activities. Bottom-left in each box shows the duration of each activity, and we can use this to determine how long this project is going to take. The path through the activities which takes the longest is known as the '**critical path**' – the longest sequence of dependent activities that need to be completed in order for the project as a whole to finish.

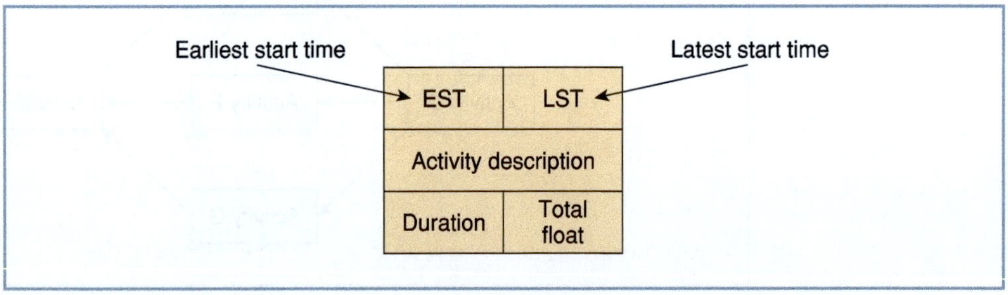

Figure 15.10 Activity notation

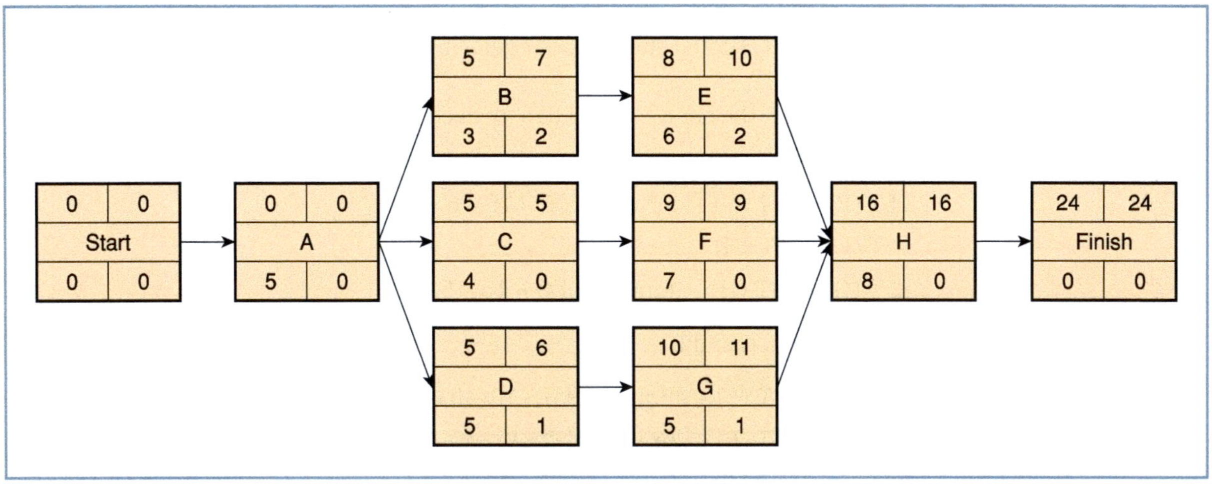

Figure 15.11 Activity network and the critical path

We firstly determine the overall project duration. There are three paths between the start and finish points that need to be examined – A–B–E–H, A–C–F–H and A–D–G–H. This first stage of the analysis is known as the **forward pass**. The subsequent calculation is the **reverse pass** to determine the critical path through the activities.

The forward pass

The forward pass determines the ESTs and starts at the left-hand side of the diagram with the EST for the first activity. This is zero. The next activity, activity A, cannot start until this has finished, and so the EST for A is the EST for the start plus the start duration (0) – zero, as you would expect. Activity A has a duration of 5 days and so the ESTs for B, C and D are all:

$$0 + 5 = 5$$

Continuing with the ESTs, the EST for the E, F and G are as follows:

EST (E) = EST (B) + duration of B = 5 + 3 = 8

EST (F) = EST (C) + duration of C = 5 + 4 = 9

EST (G) = EST (D) + duration of D = 5 + 5 = 10

These are now entered onto the diagram. Activity H presents a small challenge in that there are three possible ESTs. These are:

EST (E) + duration of E = 8 + 6 = 14

EST (F) + duration of F = 9 + 7 = 16

EST (G) + duration of G = 10 + 5 = 15

Activity H cannot start until all three preceding activities have been completed – in this case at time 16 (the *latest* of the ESTs).

Following this through to the end of the network gives the EST (FINISH) as 16 + 8 = 24. This is the project duration.

The reverse pass

The reverse pass starts from the end of the network and assigns the LSTs for each activity. The LST at the finish is assumed to be the same as the LST for that activity – with the meaning that we want the project to be completed as soon as possible. Working backwards, the LST for H is the LST for the finish minus the duration of H. That is, it is the latest time that H could start without delaying the entire project. This is 24 – 8 = 16, the same as the EST.

Continuing with the analysis, the LSTs for each of the activities E, F and G can now be calculated.

LST (E) = LST (H) – duration of E = 16 – 6 = 10

LST (F) = LST (H) – duration of F = 16 – 7 = 9

LST (G) = LST (H) – duration of G = 16 – 5 = 11

and similarly for B, C and D:

LST (B) = LST (E) – duration of B = 10 – 3 = 7

LST (C) = LST (F) – duration of C = 9 – 4 = 5

LST (D) = LST (G) – duration of D = 11 – 5 = 6

The LST for A is another case where there is more than one possibility. The three possible LSTs are:

LST (B) – duration of A = 7 – 5 = 2

LST (C) – duration of A = 5 – 5 = 0

LST (D) – duration of A = 6 – 5 = 1

The choice is the *earliest* of the LSTs – zero. Checking back to the start activity, confirm that this is correct.

The additional task with the Activity-on-Node technique is to calculate the *float* in each activity. This is:

Float = LST – EST

This is then inserted in the bottom right-hand side of the activity box.

Where there is no float, that means that the activity is *critical*, and any delay in this activity will delay the project as a whole. The critical path through the network is therefore:

A – C – F – H

Knowing the critical path has significant implications for project managers. In the example of Figure 15.11, we now know the elements of the project that can tolerate no delay without impacting the end date. This means that the project manager should focus more attention on activities A, C, F and H to ensure they go smoothly. The floats on tasks B, E, D and G mean that they can tolerate a delay of *up to* the float value before they start to impact the critical path.

However, projects rarely run exactly to plan, and if activity C goes better than expected and only takes three days, but task D is delayed by two days, then D's float is lost, and the critical path actually *changes* to A–D–G–H. In this case the overall expected duration increases by one day as well, so it is vital that the project manager does not focus *all* his or her attention on the critical path and lose track of how the other elements are progressing.

The most used package for project planning and the one included with this book, Microsoft Project, uses a slightly different format for its A-o-N diagrams as it takes absolute dates rather than relative times for EST and LST. An example of the format is shown in Figure 15.12.

In Figure 15.12 the activity description is given in the top of the box. The next row down contains the activity number (simply a label) and the activity duration. The bottom row of the box contains the start and the finish times of that activity. In the example, the

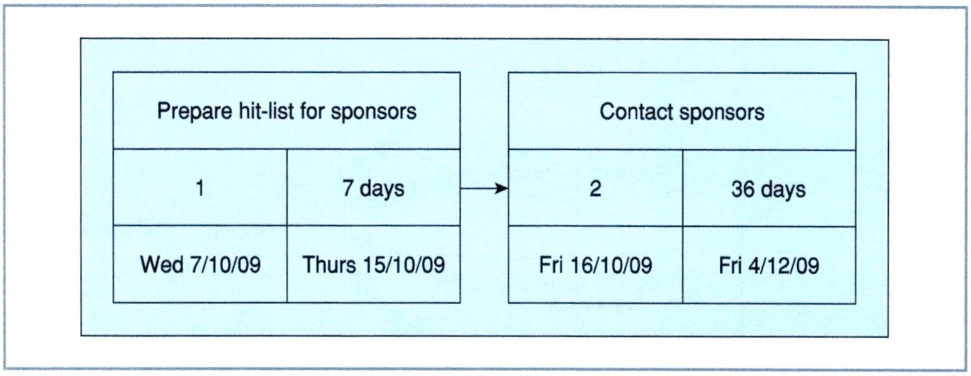

Figure 15.12 Microsoft Project output

duration of 7 days does not include weekend working – hence the start on the Wednesday and not finishing until the Thursday of the following week. The calculation is done for you with this package – hence the apparent lack of detail. This presentation does not allow you to see whether there is any float in the activity, though there are other means of doing this, including showing it in the Gantt Chart for the project, which will be shown in the following section.

One problem with today's project planning software is that sometimes its level of sophistication can add to the confusion of the project team, not reduce it. One multinational company had teams around the world, each working on their section of the WBS in MS Project. All these plans would then be gathered together in the master programme plan in a different package. It all sounds quite sensible, but because the packages recognised different local holidays and individual planners either accounted for or omitted these local factors, milestones always managed to shift by several days. Because of the complexity of the overall plan, many hours would be required to understand where the errors were and correct them to everyone's satisfaction.

If you are involved in working with multinational teams, it is extremely useful to have a wall planner with all the appropriate national holidays clearly highlighted. The more countries involved, the more pens you're likely to need, but at least you can work around the time when other team members are not available. For instance, it is unwise to try to schedule a key Chinese manufacturing activity over their New Year holiday!

Origin of CPA

The 'invention' of the techniques that have been described here as CPA are variously attributed, depending on the particular book you read. The time of first use, 1957/8, is less debated. The first users/developers are credited as being:

- the Catalytic Construction Company for the planning and control of a construction project for DuPont Corporation;
- DuPont Consulting;
- J. Kelly of Remington Rand and M. Walker of DuPont.

Whoever instigated its usage, the applications are now far and wide – it is only a shame that unlike products such as the ring-pull on cans, such methods cannot be patented or the intellectual property otherwise secured. Imagine the impact if they were given just 0.1p every time a company had produced a CPA diagram.

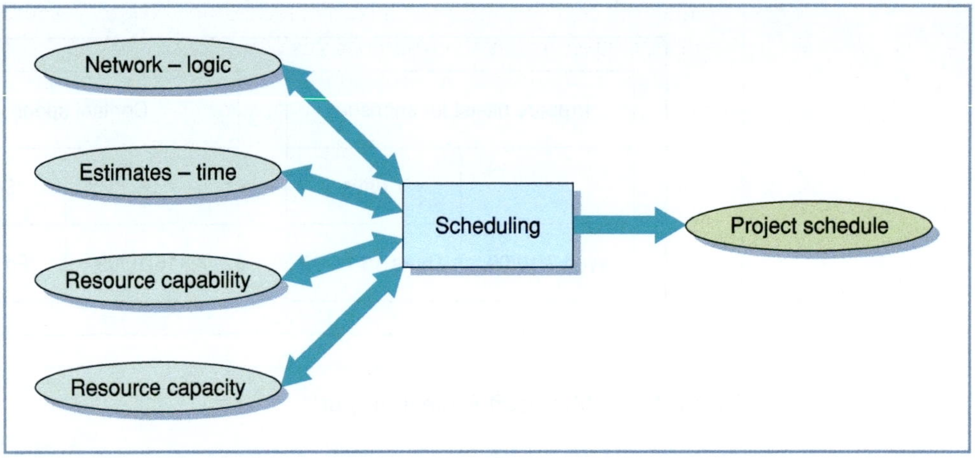

Figure 15.13 Schedule development process

Scheduling

Knowing the sequence and duration of activities is a major step. This does not, however, answer the question of 'When will activities need to be carried out?' The schedule provides this. As already shown by the critical path analysis, critical activities have to take place at a particular time or the entire plan will be disrupted. In order for this to happen, the necessary resources need to be in place in time for the critical activity. In an ideal world, this would allow a very simple schedule to be used for critical activities and everything else arranged around these. The reality is far less appealing – people are not available when you need them, resources have a long lead-time and there are likely to be clashes with other project schedules in a multi-project environment. This provides a constraint on the scheduling process, and as a result of trying this, the activities and sequence will often have to be changed. This is where an additional element of complexity enters and makes a mess of your nice plans!

The process of developing the schedule is shown in Figure 15.13.

The arrows for the inputs to the scheduling process are two-way. The network provides the logic for the order in which activities need to be carried out. Having completed this, the input of the time estimates may show that the time that the project requires for completion is longer than is available. This may necessitate a reconsideration of both the network and the time estimates. As was shown in the previous chapter, planning is inevitably an iterative process.

The **resource capability** is the set of tasks that the resources available to the project manager can reasonably undertake. These resources are often referred to as the **resource pool**. For example, where a project is being undertaken by a particular project team, these are the resource pool. If additional staff can be brought in as needed, they should also be considered as part of that pool. This part of the allocation process requires that the project manager has some knowledge of the capabilities and limitations of the resources concerned.

The **resource capacity** depends on the volume of resources available and issues such as the **resource calendar**. For instance, while a machine may be scheduled for utilisation 24 hours a day, 7 days a week (with time allowed for maintenance), the same cannot be said of humans. The *calendar* is those times that the resource is available, allowing for all the usual times when no work takes place (e.g. weekends, public holidays, personal holidays, sick leave). This does significantly limit when work can be carried out. Again the process of scheduling is iterative, with the schedule being developed, the resource availability checked and subsequently rescheduled. Where resources are over- or under-loaded, corrections may be made at this point.

This iterative process is often supported for medium and large-scale projects by the use of software – allowing rapid calculation of key project times and evaluation of the impact of difference scenarios. The role of such software is discussed in the following section.

15.3 Using Gantt Charts

For some people, the fact that this topic is not covered until over a third of a way through a book on Project Management would be difficult to understand. This is because for many years the Gantt Chart was seen as 'Project Management' by many senior managers. Put simply, if you could construct a Gantt Chart, then you were a project manager by definition. If this is still the case in an environment in which you find yourself, simply take the very excellent tutorial included on the disk with this book and you will be able to generate Gantt Charts in colour in around 20–30 minutes. This will make you an instant expert, people will believe your plans entirely and so it begins . . . Fortunately, in most places there has been considerable development, and this is generally considered to only be a part of the role of a project manager in most organisations today.[1]

The purpose of the Gantt Chart is to illustrate the relationships between the activities and time as in Figure 15.14. This shows activity A represented by the shaded bar starting at time 1 and finishing at time 3. Multiple activities can be built up on the same chart, using the same timescale.

The following example involves a dissertation planning exercise. The student has a number of options as to how to present the information. The supervisor, being a busy person, has asked for the information to be presented in graphical form. The WBS identifies the activities and the time constraints are imposed by the organisation – the start and end dates. The original statement looked as follows:

Activity	*Time*
Project start date	2/5
1 Carry out literature review	2/5–20/6
2 Arrange visits	20/6–4/7
3 Prepare questionnaire	4/7–25/7
4 Review questionnaire	25/7–8/8
5 Deliver questionnaire	8/8–26/9
6 Analyse results	26/9–2/11
7 Write up	2/11–9/12
Hand-in date	9/12

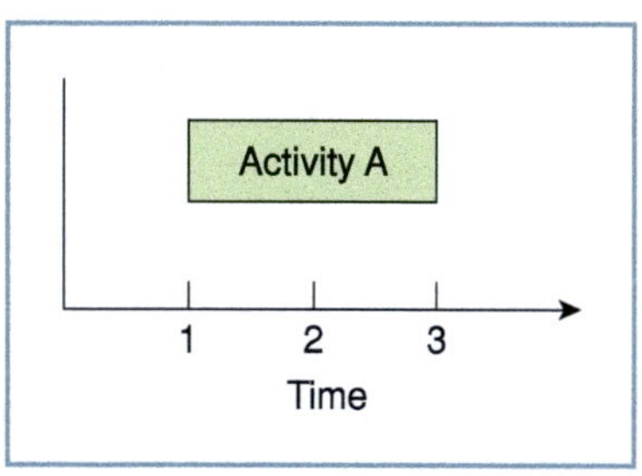

Figure 15.14 Horizontal bar chart: Activity A starts at Time 1 and finishes at Time 3

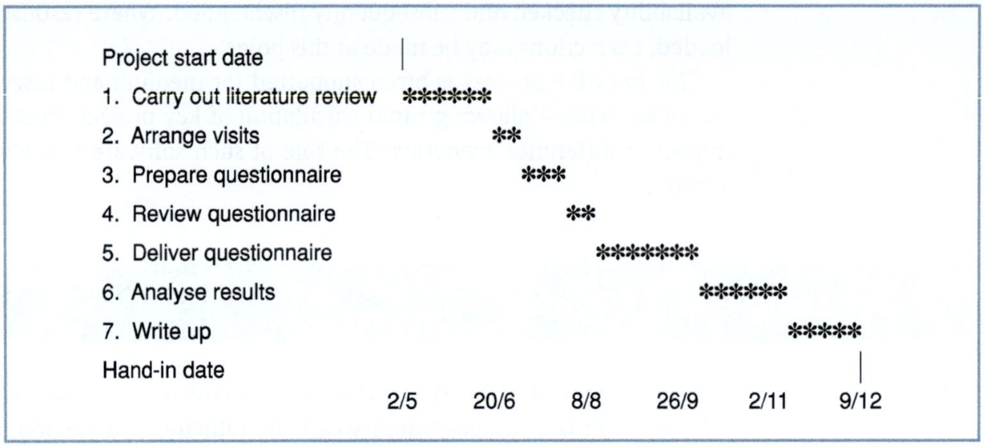

Figure 15.15 Project plan in graphical form

The project is not sufficiently complex to warrant a network, so the next step is to present the plan as a Gantt Chart. In this case, simply showing a week by a star is possible and requires nothing more than pen and paper, a word processor or spreadsheet, as shown in Figure 15.15.

In moving from the WBS to the Gantt Chart, there is:

- a level of logic established; and
- conventions used (time goes from left to right, activities are arranged top to bottom in order of their occurrence).

In addition, the student has had to undertake two critical activities:

- **forward schedule** – started the activities at a given date and followed them forwards in time to determine the end date;
- **backward schedule** – looked at the time by which the project needed to be completed and worked the logic of activities backwards.

The tasks have had rough times allocated to see whether they meet the two constraints of start- and end-times. Where there was insufficient time, activities have been shortened. Any excess time (or slack) is used to lengthen activities.

Figure 15.16 shows an alternative presentation to the above. Logical links are indicated by the use of arrows. The head of the arrow points to an activity that cannot proceed until the activity at the tail of the arrow is completed. The diamond shapes on the chart are used to indicate 'milestones', i.e. important points in the life of the project – in this case the start and the hand-in dates.

Such a chart is often referred to as a **Gantt or linked-bar chart**, as it is part of a family of techniques developed at the turn of the last century by Henry Gantt. They were originally used in industrial planning. Gantt Charts, drawn by hand, are best suited to relatively simple projects, where the number of activities and resources is low, the environment is fairly static and the time periods are relatively long – days and weeks rather than hours.

Their great utility is in their ability to communicate a time plan – they are relatively easy to construct and are readily understood. They do have limitations, however, even when using a computer to generate the charts. Amongst other limitations, the basic charts do not make the link between time and cost and therefore do not provide a method for determining how resources should optimally be allocated, e.g. there are two activities, X and Y, for which the times have been estimated and which use the

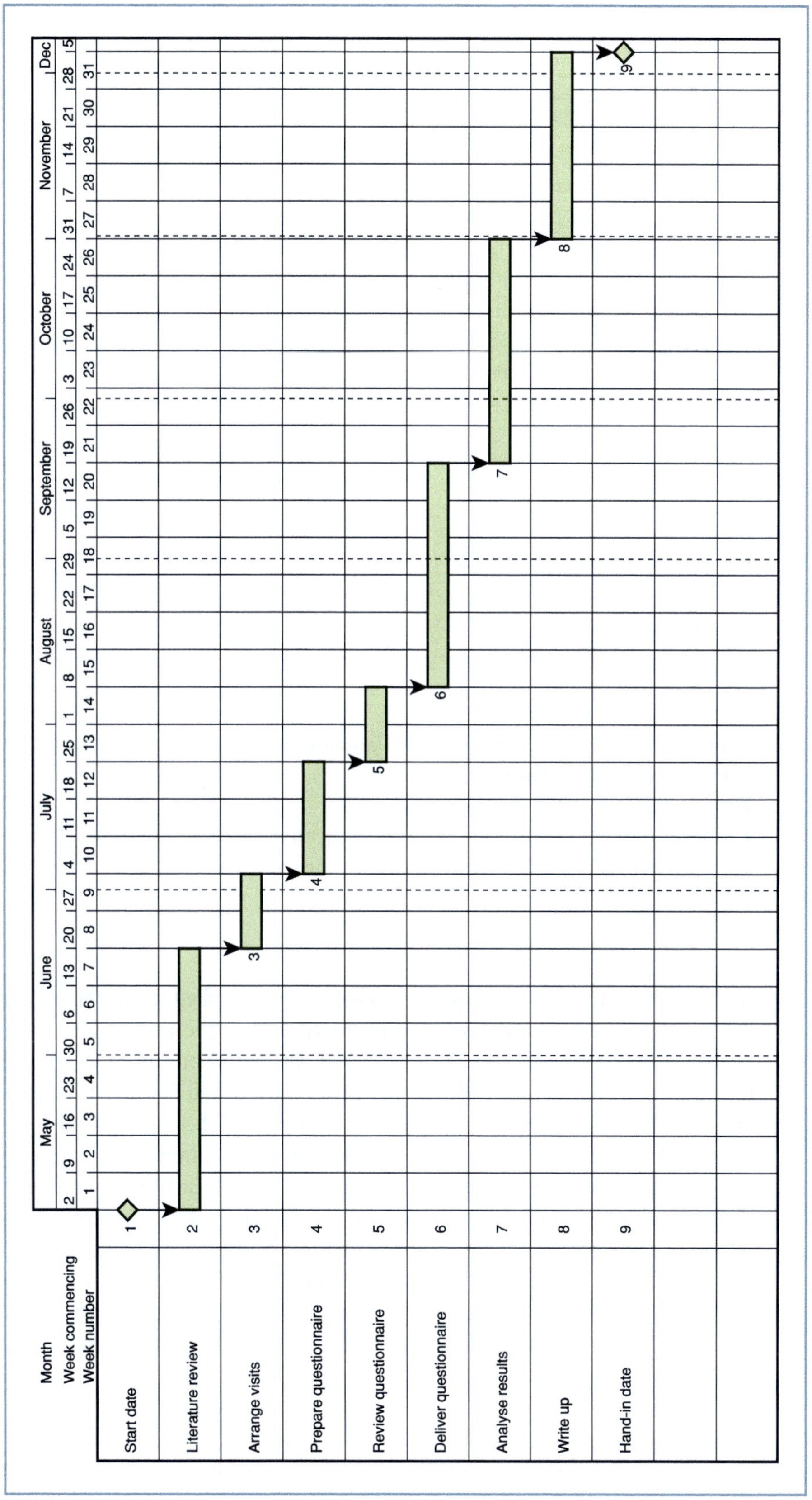

Figure 15.16 Logical links indicated by arrows

same resource. If the resource could be shifted from activity X to activity Y, Y could be completed in a shorter time; X would obviously take longer, but how would this affect the project overall? This kind of analysis is at the root of the other techniques covered earlier in this chapter. The one really great weakness of Gantt Charts is that there is a tendency for the charts to be perceived as a 'statement of reality' (this task will start on this date and finish on that date) rather than a view of 'this is how I would like it to be'. The two are entirely different – one has certainty, the other recognises the fundamental uncertainty that managers in projects have to deal with. In plans prepared using software, the outputs, usually printed in colour, can gain their own legitimacy. Referring back to the start of this chapter, the topic of estimates was discussed. Unless you have substantial data concerning prior projects, these are *guesses*. These provide the inputs to your planning. In IT, the phrase '*Garbage in, Garbage out*' expresses the idea that what you get out is only as good as what you put in. In project planning, there is the danger that we end up with '*Garbage in, Gospel out*', the output being seen in isolation, without concern for the quality of the information that went in to generating it.

Gantt Charts – summary

Good points

- simple to draw and read
- good for static environments
- useful for providing overview of project activities
- very widely used
- the basis of the graphical interface for most project planning software.

Limitations

- difficult to update manually where there are many changes – charts can quickly become obsolete and therefore discredited
- does not equate time with cost
- does not help in optimising resource allocation
- can lead to false sense of certainty about the project.

Computer-assisted project planning

At a recent seminar on organisational change, when asked about the biggest influences on the change process, the speaker responded with 'the people who wrote Microsoft Project'. He continued to justify this statement, based on his experience that the first tool that many organisational change planners reached for in such projects was MS Project. This is an interesting phenomenon in itself – how such tools have influenced organisational practices. The experience, though, is not limited to organisational change. In working with many organisations across all sectors, it was notable in the past that when employees request a training course on 'project management', the organisation offers a course for one of the major software packages. The key ones are listed at the end of this chapter under Further Information, and an example of a medium-scale project (The Balti Experience). More recently, this has been partially replaced by training programmes leading to certification by the professional institutes and PRINCE 2 2009.

There are other issues that occur with using software. With the increasing power and availability of the PC, and increased functionality and interfaceability of the software, there is the tendency for the project manager to become not just 'keeper of the charts' but also computer operator. This will often occur in a vain attempt to keep the computer version of the project plan up to date. Many consider the predominance of planning software not to be as helpful to the profession as the vendors of such systems would have us believe. Indeed, as the projects director of a large construction company recently commented, 'I believe that computer-based project management software has set the subject back 20 years.' This presents an interesting paradox – the capability of the packages has never been greater and yet there is a perception amongst some practitioners and academics that this has not been entirely helpful in improving practices. Given the levels of performance of projects reported in earlier chapters, this is not so hard to understand.

Many truly excellent organisations do not use the critical path analysis (CPA) approach to planning projects. One of Hewlett-Packard's UK plants used whiteboards and Post-it notes for project planning at the top level with individual sub-project managers free to use computerised planning software at the task level. This approach is an adaptation of the principle so well demonstrated by Japanese manufacturers in planning and scheduling – that of ensuring **visibility**. To assist in moving towards more visual methods of planning, there are many tools and techniques available to the project manager. Deployment flow charts described in the previous chapter are just one such example, which allow whole processes to be mapped simply. That said, there is significant power in modern planning packages that can be used to some benefit. They have a vital role, particularly where there are large numbers of tasks. Given the discussion of complexity in Chapter 7, it is however interesting to reflect which aspects of complexity are assisted by these planning tools.

Summary

- The objectives of the planning process are to optimise the project process and to prevent problems in the process. This is achieved through the systematic evaluation of the project's constituent activities, their duration and logical linkage (sequencing). The use of graphical techniques helps in the presentation of the plan and facilitates its review and revision.

- Having identified the activities through the WBS, the next step is arranging them in a logical sequence and then estimating their time requirements. Estimates become more uncertain the further ahead in time the situation is being considered, and range from rough (usually least accurate) to to-finish (usually most accurate).

- The most widely used tools for development of schedules are Gantt Charts and network techniques. A Gantt Chart is a time-scaled graphical planning tool, which gives a static representation of the relationship between activities and their duration. Network techniques provide a graphical means of expressing more complex projects and include activity-on-node (A-o-N) methods of representation of the verbal statement of activities.

- The application of these methods must be in line with the objectives for the process and in themselves they have little merit. The first level of analysis that can be applied to the network diagrams is CPA. This allows determination of the path of activities where, if there is any delay, the whole project will be delayed. The critical path should therefore be the initial focus for management attention – for the purposes of both shortening and control.

- Scheduling is the process that converts the plan into a specific set of dates for individual activities to be started and finished.

Key terms

activity-on-node
critical path
dependency
earliest/latest start times
float
forward/backward schedule
forward/reverse pass
Gantt or linked-bar chart
network
resource capability/ pool/capacity/calendar
visibility

Relevant areas of the Bodies of Knowledge

The Bodies of Knowledge (Tables 15.2 and 15.3) are very different in this respect, with the PMI being relatively comprehensive concerning the nature of the processes involved here and the accompanying tools and techniques. It would be possible in either to lose the reason for carrying out the planning process – to enable optimisation of the project processes and the prevention of problems.

Table 15.2 Relevant areas of the APM Body of Knowledge

Relevant section	*Title*	*Summary*
31	Time scheduling/phasing	This topic is broadly defined and includes activity definition, sequencing, estimating, schedule development and control. The issue of phasing – termed 'the strategic pacing' of the project – is given some prominence and the many techniques including Gantt Charts, A-o-N and CPA are identified.
32	Resource management	It is simply stated that the allocation of resources – be they human, machine or organisational – to a project is a 'fundamental requirement of effective project planning and management'.
42	Estimating	This is identified as an important activity, 'closely related to budgeting and cost management'.

Table 15.3 Relevant areas of the PMI Body of Knowledge

Relevant section	*Title*	*Summary*
6.1	Project time management – activity definition	This process takes in the WBS and all the other project information compiled up to that point. Through consulting with previous similar projects and breaking down the activities further, the outcome is threefold – a list of activities, the information needed to support and define them, and a revised WBS.

Table 15.3 continued

Relevant section	*Title*	*Summary*
6.2	Project time management – activity sequencing	This part of the process considers the activity list, all the constraints on when activities can be carried out, the time requirements for the project. These are used to construct the detailed plans through the *precedence diagramming method* (A-o-N), *arrow diagramming method* (Activity-on-Arrow) or other techniques (see Chapter 12 in this book). As a result of this analysis, the activity lists may have to be updated.
6.3	Project time management – activity duration estimating	It is not clear how this can take place after the sequencing and analysis of 6.2 – these estimates are required to make these decisions. Techniques identified for estimating include *expert judgement*, *analogous estimating* (termed as-buts in this chapter) and *quantitatively based* (termed parametric estimating in Chapter 12).
6.4	Project time management – schedule development	This section presents a wide array of tools and techniques for the development of the network diagrams and activity lists (along with all the associated constraints information) into a schedule for the project.

PROJECT MANAGEMENT IN PRACTICE
The Balti Experience

From critical path time to vaguely realistic schedule in the launch of a new food product

In new product development, time to market can be a key determinant of the success of a product. In the packaged food business, this is especially true, as in excess of 95 per cent of new products last less than 6 months. In this case, the firm concerned were not just launching a new product but a new range of products, to meet Europe's burgeoning appetite for Indian Balti-style ready meals. These were intended as a replacement range for another that had become increasingly difficult to source the materials for, and to meet with environmental requirements of the packaging. Strategically, this was a major change for the company, and required significant investment. The idea had been approved by the board and the firm was now in the phase of detailed planning. The project manager was now tasked by the board with the preparation of plans that would allow them to schedule the launch.

The first step was to prepare a work breakdown structure. The main activities and their sequence were identified, and their durations estimated in weeks. The resulting network is shown in Figure 15.17. The diamonds are included to show the main milestones in the project, i.e. go-ahead and project completion.

The project manager is now ready to present the plan back to the board. She is determined to make a good impression and have answers to their questions.

Points for discussion

1 What is the project duration and what is the critical path?

2 The board were hoping to launch the new range in the next 9 months. From your analysis, could this be achieved?

3 Where would you suggest that gates are put in this process?

→

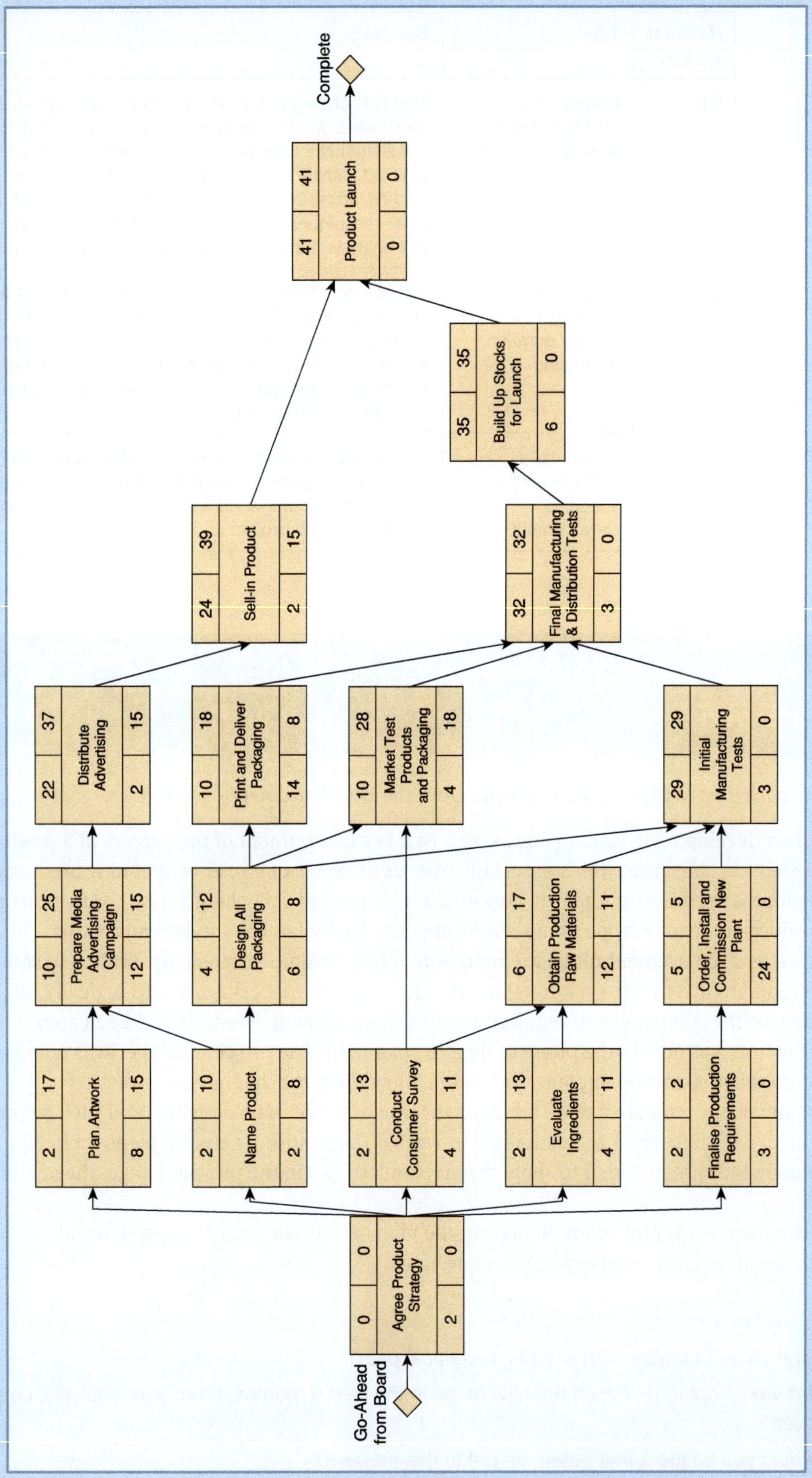

Figure 15.17 Planning the launch of a new food project

PROJECT MANAGEMENT IN PRACTICE
The mobile phone development

The challenge of new product development

A mobile phone company has just promoted a project manager to head up a new product development project.

Developing a mobile phone is a challenging project. Time-to-market is short, the product is technically complicated and there are multiple stakeholders within the phone company. Marketing have strong ideas about new product design, and they have some initial specifications based on their market research. The project is likely to be signed off very shortly, and the finance department are insisting that to be profitable it has to be delivered very quickly, although development funds are tight.

The design team consists of electronics engineers to design the circuitry, software engineers to develop the functionality, interface and features that the customers see and mechanical engineers to create the unit itself. Additionally, manufacturing engineers need to be involved as soon as possible to ensure that the design is going to be suitable for high-volume manufacture.

Suppliers need to be on board quickly so that they can ensure availability of material when volume production starts. Lead times for some parts can be several months, but often there are design changes throughout the project as the detailed design stabilises. You know there will be technical difficulties with the design, and several prototypes need to be planned in so that the phone can be tested during the design phase.

You have been asked to advise and help the new project manager on the best way of planning this project, and what factors he needs to take into consideration.

Points for discussion

1. Use the work covered in Chapter 14 to provide an analysis of the stakeholders and the project strategy.
2. Given your answer to (1), how would this affect the nature of the overview plan that should be presented?
3. What are your recommendations to the project manager to ensure that the project is completed as required?

Topics for discussion

1 You have been put in charge of organising a group trip to visit a company in Japan which has expertise that you and your group are interested in finding out more about. Identify the constituent activities, their sequence and estimate the times that each of the activities will take. Show how you have used forward and backward scheduling to achieve this. Display your plan using a bar chart or similar method.

2 Discuss why graphical techniques for displaying plans are superior to verbal statements.

3 Describe what is meant by 'precedence' and illustrate your answer with an appropriate example.

4 Show the dissertation case example (Figure 15.15) as an activity-on-node diagram.

5 Show the information given in Table 15.4 about a project activity as an activity-on-node diagram.

Table 15.4 Project activities, precedence and duration

Activity	*Description*	*Duration (weeks)*	*Preceding activity*
A	Select software	4	–
B	Select hardware	3	A
C	Install hardware	6	B
D	Install software	2	C
E	Test software	3	D
F	Train staff	5	E
G	System run-up	1	F

(a) From your diagram identify the total project duration.
(b) Show which activities you feel could be run alongside others (in parallel, rather than sequentially). Redraw the network diagram and calculate the new project duration and the critical path.
(c) What further benefits may arise from using parallel activities, rather than sequential?
(d) Assuming that the completion time is critical, identify which activities you would suggest should be the focus for management attention.

6 Table 15.5 considers the development of a short course in project management. From the information, construct the network diagram.

(a) Determine the ESTs, the LSTs, the project duration and the critical path activities.
(b) Show the slack for each activity.
(c) What further factors should be considered in order to give a better view of the realistic timescale for the organisation of the course?

Table 15.5 Project activities, precedence and duration

Activity	*Description*	*Duration (weeks)*	*Preceding activity*
A	Design course overview and publicity	4	–
B	Identify potential staff to teach on course	2	–
C	Construct detailed syllabus	6	–
D	Send out publicity and application forms	10	A
E	Confirm staff availability	2	B
F	Select staff to teach on course	1	C, E
G	Acknowledge student applications	3	D
H	Identify course written material	2	F
J	Preparation of teaching material	20	G, H
K	Prepare room for the course	1	G

7 Why might the critical path change during a project? What happens if it does?

8 What aspects of complexity are assisted by the use of computer-aided project planning and which are not?

9 Using MS Project software, prepare a Gantt chart and critical path network for the example projects in Tables 15.4 and 15.5.

10 What are the benefits and limitations of using software to help with presenting plans?

Further information

Badiru, A.B. (1993) *Quantitative Models for Project Planning, Scheduling and Control*, Quorum, London.

Lock, D. (2000) *Project Management*, 7th edition, Gower, Aldershot, Chapters 7–14.

Lockyer, K. and Gordon, J. (1991) *Critical Path Analysis and Other Project Network Techniques*, 5th edition, Financial Times Pitman Publishing, London.

Randolf, W.A. and Posner, B.Z. (1988) *Effective Planning and Management: Getting the Job Done*, Prentice Hall, Englewood Cliffs, NJ.

Reiss, G. (1992) *Project Management Demystified: Today's Tools and Techniques*, Chapman & Hall, London.

Sapolsky, H.M. (1972) *The Polaris System Development: Bureaucratic and Programmatic Success in Government*, Harvard University Press, Cambridge, MA.

Websites

www.eproject.com – agile PM software site, some interesting articles attached, useful profile of the kind of capability that modern software can offer.

www.extremeplanner.com

www.microsoft.com – for Microsoft Project and enterprise.

www.primavera.com – Primavera is used by many organisations that run large-scale engineering projects.

www.astadev.com/software/powerproject/index.asp – Powerproject.

www.openworkbench.org/ – open source planning and scheduling package.

www.projectinsight.net/ProductInformation/TopTenFeatures.aspx – one of many guides to choosing software.

Reference

1 See Maylor, H. (2001) 'Beyond the Gantt Chart', *European Management Journal*, Vol. 19, No. 1, pp. 92–100.

16

REPORT WRITING

How to select and shape your content appropriately

Writing reports of one kind or another is a part of many degree courses. These often have discipline-specific formats and it is important to follow these and select the correct information to put into the different sub-sections. This chapter considers common formats which may be suitable for the literature survey, the scientific report and the business report.

The purpose of any report is to convey information, usually on a well-defined topic. Conventions have evolved for the structure, style and content of reports in different subjects, and, while the scholarship underlying the report will always be foremost in markers' assessments, presentational aspects are also judged as important, so you should follow the appropriate format very carefully.

?

Why write reports at university?

Report writing is regarded as important because it:

- compels you to complete your work and present it in a neatly organised form for assessment;
- helps you to develop important professional skills;
- provides a record for replication or development of results for future research.

COMMON FEATURES OF REPORT WRITING

Writing a report is often a drawn-out task and may follow a lengthy period of research in the library, on the internet or in the laboratory. However, you should not consider the research and writing phases as separate. Your research must take into account the style and format of the report, while elements of writing up can and should be carried out as you continue to explore your topic.

Keep your focus tight

Students often fall into the trap of being overambitious in their goals. In general, it is better to cover a limited topic well than to write a shallow report covering a wide area.

The following stages are likely to be involved in most exercises culminating in a report:

1 **'Scoping'.** Here, you will be deciding on a topic or a specific aspect of a subject on which to concentrate. Sometimes the topic is decided for you, but in other cases it may emerge as you research. Even in the second situation, having a notional goal when you start is important: this will give you impetus, even though you may change the precise focus later.

2 **Research.** This consists of finding and selecting relevant information. Research may be experimental, as in many science subjects, or it may be desk-based, analysing and evaluating reports, texts and other sources.

3 **Writing.** This involves communicating your work using appropriate language. It's important that your writing provides evidence that you have been thinking at the appropriate level (see tip box below).

4 **Presentation.** You will be expected to present your work to a high professional standard and some marks will normally be awarded for this aspect.

Aspects of report writing

Description: reporting your experiments or summarising facts you have gathered.

Visual summaries: making diagrams, flow charts, graphs or tables to demonstrate your points more clearly.

Analysis: looking at results or facts and possibly working out descriptive or hypothesis-testing statistics.

Discussion: weighing up the pros and cons of a position.

Solution(s): explaining different options to solve an issue or problem being addressed.

Evaluation: deciding what's important and why.

Recommendation: identifying the best solution and giving evidence to support that choice.

Arriving at a conclusion: stating a position on the basis of your research.

REPRESENTATIVE FORMATS FOR REPORTS

Table 16.1 summarises the general components of reports and what they should contain. Reports for different purposes and in different subjects follow different designs and include various components, not always in the same order. Table 16.2 provides some examples, but you should follow closely the guidelines published by your faculty or department.

Table 16.1 Typical components of reports, and notes on the expected content of each part. These are arranged alphabetically and would not appear in this order in any report. For representative examples of report formats, see Table 16.2). *Always adopt the precise format specified in your course handbook.*

Section or part	Expected content
Abbreviations	A list of any abbreviations for technical terms used within the text (for example, 'DNA: deoxyribonucleic acid'). These are also given within the text at the first point of use, for example 'deoxyribonucleic acid (DNA)'.
Abstract	A brief summary of the aims of the experiment or series of observations, the main outcomes (in words) and conclusions. This should allow someone to understand your main findings and what you think they mean. This is normally written last, but is usually positioned at the beginning of the report.
Acknowledgements	A list of people who helped you, sometimes with a brief description of how.
Appendix (pl: appendices)	Includes tabular information, usually, that only an expert would want or need to consult; a section where you can put items such as a questionnaire template, and data or results that would otherwise disrupt the flow of the report or make the results section too lengthy.
Bibliography/references/ literature cited	An alphabetical list of sources cited in the text, following one of the standard referencing styles.
Discussion (or conclusions)	• **Scientific-style reports.** A commentary on the results and an outline of the main conclusions. This could include any or all of the following: – comments on the methods used; – mention of sources of errors; – conclusions from any statistical analysis; – comparison with other findings or the 'ideal' result; – what the result means; – how you might improve the experiment; – how you might implement the findings; – where you would go from here, given more time and resources. Sometimes you might combine the results and discussions sections to allow a narrative to develop – to explain, for example, why one result led to the next experiment or approach. Bear in mind that a large proportion of marks may be given for your original thoughts in this section. • **Non-scientific-style reports.** In this section you might restate the problem or issue to be addressed, outline the key 'solutions' or responses to the problem, and explain the reason for favouring one over another by providing evidence to support that choice. In some, but not all, instances, a set of recommendations might be appropriate and an indication of how they could be implemented.
Executive summary	Takes the place of an abstract in a business report. Gives the key points of the report, usually no more than one A4 page long. It should start with a brief statement of the aims of the report, a summary of the main findings and/or conclusions, perhaps given as bullet points, and a summary of the main conclusions and/or recommendations. You would normally write this part last.
Experimental	A description of apparatus and method, similar to materials and methods.
Glossary	A list of terms that might be unfamiliar to the reader, with definitions.
Introduction	• **Scientific-style reports.** An outline of the background to the experiments, the aims of the experiments and brief discussion of the techniques to be used. Your goal is to orient the reader and explain what you have done and why. • **Non-scientific-style reports.** The context of the study and an outline of the problem or issue to be addressed, in other words, the aim of the report. This may require reference to the literature or other resource material to be used.

continued overleaf

Table 16.1 *(cont'd)*

Section or part	Expected content
Main body of text	Your appraisal of the topic. It should systematically address solutions or issues in response to the report's purpose and provide an analysis of all pertinent matters. It may be subdivided into sections reflecting different aspects. In a scientific literature review, the approach is often to give a chronological account of developments in the field, quoting key authors, their ideas and findings. This section may include tables comparing different approaches or results in different studies. Figures tend to be rare, but may be used to summarise concepts or illustrate key findings.
Materials and methods	A description of what was done. You should provide sufficient detail to allow a competent person to repeat the work.
Results	A description of the experiments carried out and the results obtained, usually presented in either tabular or graphic form (never both for the same data). You should point out meaningful aspects of the data, which need not be presented in the same order in which the work was done.
Table of contents	Effectively an index to allow the reader to find parts in which they are interested. May also include a table of diagrams. More likely to be included in a lengthy report.
Title page	The full names of the author or authors, the module title or code and the date. In a business report this may also include the company logo, client details and classification (for example, 'confidential'). • **Scientific-style reports.** A descriptive title that indicates what was done, indicates any restrictions, and sometimes describes the 'headline' finding. • **Non-scientific-style reports.** A concise but comprehensive title that defines the topic.

Literature surveys

These follow the relatively uncomplicated format shown in Table 16.2(a). Two important formatting aspects to consider are citation of literature references and presenting quotes from your sources.

Scientific reports

Representative formats are shown in Table 16.2(b), (c) and (d). These tend to mirror the format of journal articles in the primary literature for each subject area. Aspects you should bear in mind are that:

- anyone reading your report should be able to assimilate your findings quickly, and should be able to find relevant information in the expected place;
- your text should be objective and balanced, considering all possible interpretations of your results;
- appropriate statistical analysis should be included;
- you should provide enough information to allow another competent scientist to understand and repeat your work.

Reports for non-scientific subjects

Increasingly report writing is becoming a feature in non-scientific subjects. A report-style response could be required for a case study, project or group problem-solving exercise, for

Table 16.2 Designs of different sorts of report. The literature review (a) has a simple structure. The main body is the largest part, and may be subdivided into sections. The general scientific report (b) has a focus on materials and methods, but in some disciplines the components may be presented in a different order, as shown in the model for the report in chemistry (c). An undergraduate lab report (d) will probably be a stripped-down and shorter version of (b). A non-scientific style of report (e) would not focus on materials and methods, but might have a main body of text dealing with the topic being considered. A typical business report (f) includes the conclusions or recommendations as part of the main body and provides an executive summary for quick reading. It often has appendices and a glossary for the non-specialist. See Table 16.1 for details of content for each section.

(a) Literature review	(b) General scientific report	(c) Scientific report in chemistry	(d) Laboratory report in the sciences	(e) Non-scientific report	(f) Typical business report
Title page	Title page	Title page	Title page	Title page	Title page
Abstract	Abstract	Abstract	Introduction	Introduction	Executive summary
Introduction	Abbreviations	Abbreviations	Materials and methods	Main body of text	Acknowledgements
Main body of text	Introduction	Introduction	Results (brief)	Conclusion	Table of contents
Conclusions	Materials and methods	Results	Discussion/conclusions		Main body of text
References or literature cited	Results	Discussion			Recommendations
	Discussion	Materials and methods			Bibliography/references
	Acknowledgements	Acknowledgements			Appendices
	References	References			Glossary

example. Table 16.2(e) shows a representative structure. A good approach for the main body of text in these report-style tasks is to follow the situation–problem–solution–evaluation + (optional) recommendation (SPSER) model. This provides a basic skeleton. You may wish to tailor the headings and sub-headings to fit the context of the topic or problem that you are addressing, but the essence of the SPSER model remains intact 'below the surface' of these headings.

Business-style reports

The main aim of a business report is to provide information that helps decision-making. These reports differ greatly in their style and formality and the chief factor to consider is your audience. Table 16.2(f) illustrates one possible format. Possible variations might include:

- A report aimed solely at a shop-floor manager: relatively short and informal, focusing on production statistics and limitations.
- A business plan aimed at an investor or bank manager: fairly brief, focusing on financial projections given in charts and tables.
- An academic analysis of a business sector: relatively lengthy and formal, quoting many sources and views.

Structurally, a business report is unlike an essay in that you should use headings and sub-headings so that your reader can find relevant information quickly.

PRACTICAL TIPS FOR SELECTING AND SHAPING REPORT CONTENT

Find a model for the layout you need to adopt. This might be given in your course handbook or could be adopted from an example that you feel is well organised. If you are unsure, then you should follow one of the models in Table 16.2.

Be ruthless in rejecting irrelevant information. You must keep your report as short and to the point as you can. Especially if you have spent a long time obtaining information or conducting an analysis, you may be tempted to include it for this reason alone. Don't. Relevance must be your sole criterion.

Consider your writing style. Reports can be dense and difficult to read. Try to keep your sentences relatively simple and your paragraphs short. In reports you can use sub-headings and bullet points to break up the text. All these devices can make the content easier for your reader to assimilate.

Choose appropriate chart types. If you wish to present diagrams and graphs, keep these simple and use the title and legend to explain what you want to show in each case. Use a variety of types of chart if you can.

Think about your likely conclusions from an early stage. This may shape both the research you do and the content. However, make sure you keep an open mind if the evidence points you in another direction.

17

Implementation and Evaluation – People Management

Chapter Outline

Chapter Objectives

After completing this chapter, you should be able to:

1. Understand the steps involved in project team building.
2. Know the characteristics of effective project teams and why teams fail.
3. Know the stages in the development of groups.
4. Describe how to achieve cross-functional cooperation in teams.
5. See the advantages and challenges of virtual project teams.
6. Understand the nature of conflict and evaluate response methods.
7. Understand the importance of negotiation skills in project management.

PROJECT MANAGEMENT BODY OF KNOWLEDGE CORE CONCEPTS COVERED IN THIS CHAPTER

1. Plan Human Resource Management
2. Acquire Project Team
3. Develop Project Team
4. Manage Project Team

PROJECT PROFILE

Engineers Without Borders: Project Teams Impacting Lives

In 2000, Bernard Amadei, a civil engineering professor at the University of Colorado at Boulder, visited San Pablo, Belize, where the sight of little girls hauling water instead of attending school broke his heart. Upon his return to Boulder, he recruited eight civil and environmental engineering students to design and install a clean water system powered by a local waterfall. The total cost, including airfare for him and his students, came to US$14,000.

It was just the beginning for Amadei, who went on to found Engineers Without Borders–USA in 2002. The organization now inspires nearly 14,000 members in over 250 chapters around the country. The more than 350 programs currently underway lean heavily toward civil engineering—a farm irrigation system in Bolivia, a geothermal heating system for a Native American tribe in South Dakota—but some, such as small hydroelectric systems and rooftop solar panel installations, require the skills of electrical engineers. By the latest reckoning, EWB-USA has impacted for the better the lives of over 2.5 million people worldwide.

The U.S. organization follows in the footsteps of a movement that began in France in the 1980s and then spread to Spain, Italy, Canada, and many other countries. The organizations were quite independent, though, sharing only a name and a mission, so in 2004 Amadei created an informal network, EWB-International. Today it has 45 member groups, including ones in Kosovo, Rwanda, and Iran.

"Amadei tapped into a previously unexploited humanitarian passion within the U.S. engineering community," says Peter Coats, a civil engineer and cofounder of EWB-USA's San Francisco chapter, the first to consist of professionals instead of students. That higher purpose is particularly attractive to women, who make up more than 40 percent of student volunteers, twice the proportion of female engineering graduates. "They identify more with people and humanity," says Cathy Leslie, a civil engineer who serves as the executive director of EWB-USA. "Women don't thrive on creating technology for technology's sake."

Communities or local non-government organizations (NGOs) provide EWB-USA with a wish list of needs, and the organization plays matchmaker, helping pair chapters with specific projects. Clean water tops the list—establishing sewage systems, sanitation systems for collecting and disposing of waste, and irrigation canals. Cheap, renewable sources of electricity are also a common need.

These projects can't be built in a day, and like almost all engineering work, they need to be maintained and upgraded, so there is an emphasis on imparting knowledge to local community members and NGOs. For this, project teams include trainers and business folks in addition to engineers. "You establish a sort of trust, which is really powerful," says Eyleen Chou, the president of the University of Wisconsin–Madison's student chapter. "There's no reason why you shouldn't stay 10 years or longer."

Leslie says that successful chapters such as Chou's can build and maintain many projects despite a constant rotation of entering freshmen and departing seniors. They establish training programs and mentorships, devise ways for

(continued)

FIGURE 17.1 EWB Project Team Laying Water Pipes with Local Workers

Source: Dieter Heinemann/Westend61/Corbis

new students to contribute, and find sustainable funding. Chapters are expected to raise the majority of project money themselves, but they work under basic guidelines. At a project's onset, they consult with an EWB-USA technical advisory committee to tweak and finalize plans. Teams must commit five years to a project.

In addition to the student chapters at universities, EWB-USA maintains a number of professional chapters around the country. However, maintaining effective, temporary teams is a challenge; especially for a volunteer organization. Professional chapters have problems of bringing new volunteers up to speed while experienced ones drop out—and their members face the additional challenge of juggling their project work with full-time jobs. For example, the San Francisco chapter's members typically spend at least five hours per week, but this can spike during special events or an actual field visit. Members have on occasion spent over 30 hours a week on EWB activities in addition to working their regular jobs.

In the process of improving others' lives, EWB is also creating a better brand of engineer, says Leslie. "The work we do has educational value for the student," she says, and taking a professional out of the office "makes for a more well-rounded engineer."[1]

INTRODUCTION

The difficulties involved in building and coordinating an effective team can be daunting and highly complex. Becoming technically proficient at scheduling, budgeting, and project evaluation is essential in developing the necessary project management skills; however, it is equally important to develop an appreciation for and willingness to undertake the human challenges of the job. **Team building** and conflict management are two of the most important *people skills* that project managers can cultivate, but they are also two of the most difficult undertakings. We must use our leadership skills to negotiate with department managers for access to skilled personnel for team staffing; we must recognize that no project team comes "fully assembled" and ready to go. Simply grouping a collection of diverse individuals together is not the same thing as building a team.

This chapter offers an overview of some of the key behavioral tasks facing project managers: staffing a project team, building a sense of common purpose and shared commitment, encouraging cross-functional cooperation among team members, and recognizing the causes of and resolving conflicts among all project stakeholders. The bad news is that this is not an easy process; it does not involve formulas or calculations in the same way that task duration estimation does. The "rules" of human behavior often consist of broad generalizations, at best, which should be used only to suggest appropriate managerial actions. The good news is that when carefully evaluated and applied, managing the people side of project management can be just as effective, rewarding, and important for project success as any of the technical duties.

Project staffing, team building, cross-functional cooperation, and conflict management are not supplementary topics in project management; the study of these skills is central to our ability to become proficient in a highly complex and challenging profession. This chapter will not only analyze the team building and conflict processes, but it will also offer some prescriptive advice to readers on how to improve these processes and skills in managing human behavior. One point is clear: If we undertake projects with a project team as our principal resource for getting work done and the project completed, it is vital that we learn everything possible about how to mold people into a high-performing team and how to control the inevitable conflicts that are likely to emerge along the way.

17.1 BUILDING THE PROJECT TEAM

Effective project teams do not happen by accident. A great deal of careful work and preparation goes into the steps necessary to first staff and then develop project team members to the point where they begin to function jointly and the project reaps positive dividends from their collective performance. The best-case scenario for project managers is to take over a project with a unified team composed of individuals who lobbied for and were awarded with membership on the team. Unfortunately, in many organizations, project teams are put together based on other criteria, most notably whoever is available. Regardless of the circumstances, the project manager is faced with the challenge of creating from a set of diverse individuals a high-performing, cohesive project team. The preferred process, however, should be as structured as possible; staffing is ideally aligned with the project manager's judgment of what is best for the project.

Figure 17.2 illustrates how project team personnel may be assigned. Within many organizations, this process emerges as the result of protracted negotiations with functional or departmental supervisors, as we discussed in Chapter 4. The flowchart in Figure 17.2 illustrates several key decision points or critical interfaces in developing a project team.[2]

Identify Necessary Skill Sets

The first stage in project team development is to conduct a realistic assessment of the types of skills the team members will need in order to complement each other and perform their project duties as effectively as possible. For example, in projects with a high technical complexity, it is imperative to ascertain the availability of skilled human resources and their capability of adding value to the project development. No one would seriously embark on a software development project without first ensuring that the technical steps in the project are clearly understood.

Identify People Who Match the Skills

Once a reasonable assessment of the required project skills has been completed, a complementary assessment of the availability of personnel with the requisite skills is necessary. We have two options: (1) hire new personnel for the project (e.g., in many cases, companies will hire contractors on a fixed-term basis for the life of a project), or (2) train current personnel to become proficient in the skills they will need to perform the tasks. The final decision often comes down to a cost/benefit assessment: Who can do the work? Is the cost of hiring or training the person to do the job prohibitively expensive? Once the person has been trained/hired, will these skills be of continuing benefit to the company?

Talk to Potential Team Members and Negotiate with Functional Heads

The third step in the process of building the project team involves opening communication with likely candidates for the team and assessing their level of interest in joining the project. In some cases, personnel have a great deal of authority in assigning their own time to projects. However, in most cases (particularly within functional organizations), all functional specialists are under the authority of departmental heads. Consequently, at some point the project manager must begin

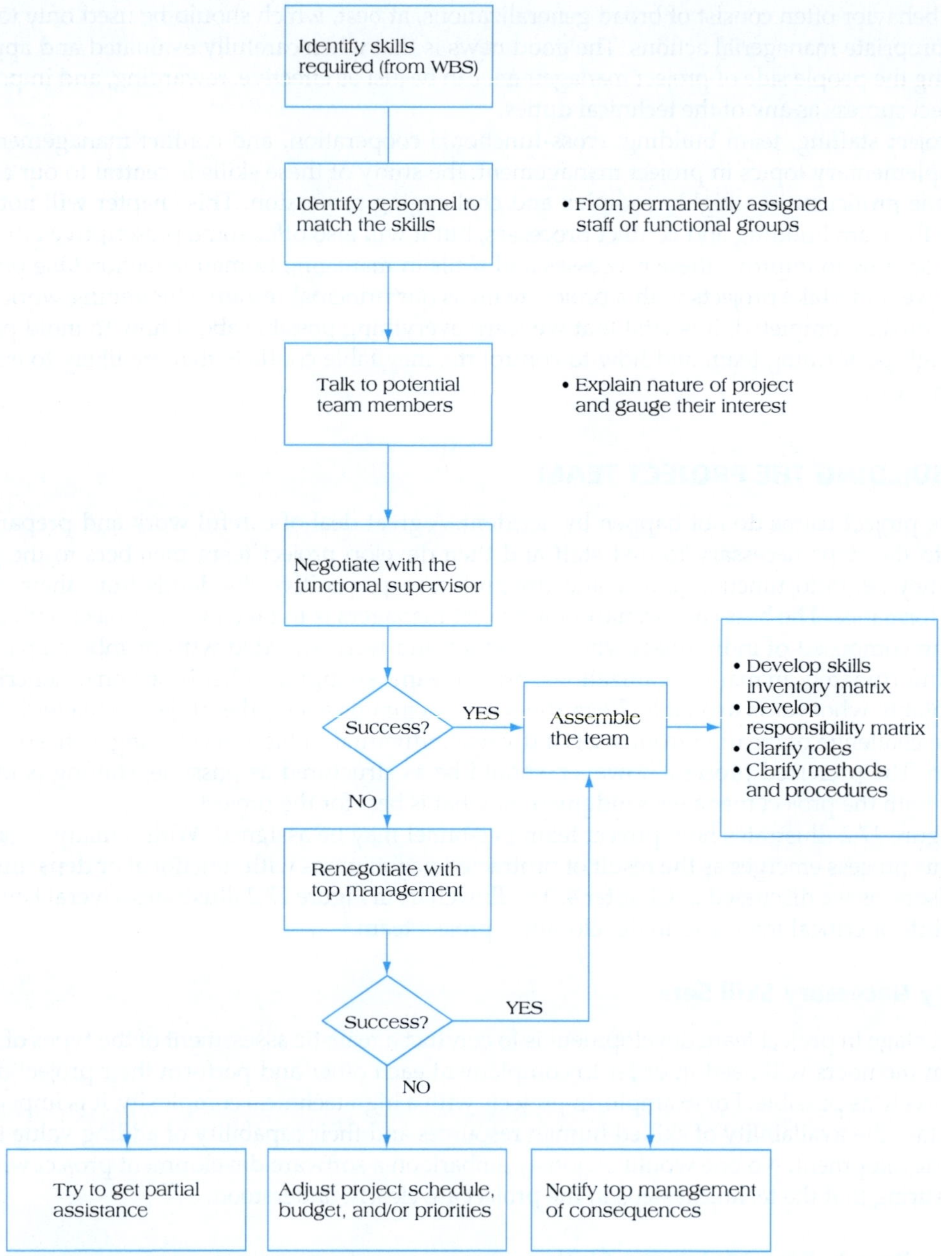

FIGURE 17.2 Basic Steps in Assembling a Project Team

Source: V. K. Verma. (1997). *Managing the Project Team*, p. 127. Upper Darby, PA: Project Management Institute. Copyright and all rights reserved. Material from this publication has been reproduced with the permission of PMI.

to enter into negotiations with these functional heads for the services of prospective project team members. These negotiations can be complex and lengthy.

Departmental managers generally are not opposed to the use of their personnel on projects. They are, however, primarily concerned with the smooth operations of their organizations. Depriving a functional manager of key personnel to serve on a project team can be seen as threatening a smoothly operating department. Hence, negotiations are required. Among the issues to be decided are:

1. ***How long are the team members services required?*** Project team members can be assigned on a full-time basis (40 hours per week) or a part-time basis (less than 40 hours per week). Further, the team member may be assigned for a fixed period (e.g., six months) or for the duration of the project.

2. ***Who should choose the person to be assigned to the project?*** Another point of negotiation is the question of who should select the individual to serve on the project team. The functional manager may have her own ideas as to the best choice, while the project manager may employ different criteria and come up with other possible candidates.
3. ***What happens when special circumstances arise?*** In the event of some emergency or special circumstance, the functional department head may wish to retain control of the team member or have the option of suddenly recalling that individual back to work on departmental activities. How will "emergencies" be defined? If the team member is recalled, how will the department provide a replacement? What is the maximum amount of time a team member can be removed from his project duties? All these questions are important and should be resolved prior to the appointment of project team members.

Most project resources are negotiated with department managers. This point is critical: For the majority of project managers, their outright control over project team members may be limited, particularly early in the process when project team assignments are being made. The best strategy a project manager can engage in at this point is to have thought carefully about the types of expertise and skills that will be required for successful completion of the project and begin bargaining with these clear goals in mind. Treat functional managers as allies, not opponents. The organization supports the project; functional departments will support it as well, but their level of support must be carefully planned in advance.

Build in Fallback Positions

What are your options as the project manager when resources are not available? Suppose, for example, that you need three highly trained design engineers for the project and the head of engineering is unwilling to part with them or negotiate a compromise. As Figure 17.2 demonstrates, in the event that negotiations with functional managers and top managers are not fruitful, the project manager is faced with three basic alternatives.

TRY TO NEGOTIATE FOR PARTIAL ASSISTANCE The best alternative to an outright refusal is to seek some limited assistance. One reason for this approach is that it gets your foot in the door. Once the personnel are assigned to the project, even on limited terms, it forms the basis for your returning to the department head at a later point to ask for them again, while only slowing down the project marginally. This principle argues, in effect, that it is better to have half a loaf than none.

ADJUST PROJECT SCHEDULES AND PRIORITIES ACCORDINGLY When critical resources are not available, the project schedule must be adjusted to reflect this fact. "Resource Management," there is no point in developing a sophisticated project schedule if it is not supported by resources. Or, to put it another way, until we can match people to project tasks, we cannot make progress. With a failure to convince functional managers that their resources are needed to support the project, serious and honest adjustments must be made to all project plans, including scope documents, schedules, risk assessment, and so forth.

NOTIFY TOP MANAGEMENT OF THE CONSEQUENCES Failing to gain necessary resources must be reported to top management, the ultimate sponsors of the project. They may, in the end, become the final arbiters of the resource and staffing question. In the face of persistent resistance from a functional manager, the only recourse may be to present to top management, as candidly as possible, the implications for project success without sufficient support. The final decision then comes down to top management: They will either support the project and require that staffing be completed as requested, suggest a compromise, or support the functional manager. In the first two cases, the project will proceed; in the third, top management is effectively ending the project before it has begun.

Assemble the Team

When the project has been staffed and approved, the final step is assembling the project team. This involves developing a skills inventory matrix that identifies the skills needed for the project against the skills we have acquired and a responsibility matrix using the Responsibility Activity

Matrix (RAM) methodology. Also, all project team roles and responsibilities must be clarified, along with all project team methods, expectations, and standard operating procedures. Where any of these do not exist, it will be necessary to begin establishing them.

17.2 CHARACTERISTICS OF EFFECTIVE PROJECT TEAMS

A great deal of research has investigated the qualities that effective teams possess and how those same qualities are missing from less effective groups. Successful teams share common underlying features, including a clear sense of mission, an understanding of team interdependencies, cohesiveness, a high level of trust, a shared sense of enthusiasm, and a results orientation.

A Clear Sense of Mission

A key determinant of project success is a clear project mission.[3] Further, that sense of mission must be mutually understood and accepted by all team members. Research has demonstrated that a clearly understood project mission is the number one predictor of success as the project is being developed.[4] Two important issues are clear: First, project teams perform well when there is a clear sense of purpose or objectives for their project; and second, the more widely shared and understood those goals, the better the project performance. The alternative is to allow the project manager to function as the hub of a wheel, with each team member as a separate spoke, interacting only through the project manager. This arrangement is not nearly as useful or successful as one in which all project team members understand the overall project objectives and how their performance contributes to achieving those objectives.

A mistake sometimes made by project managers is to segment the team in terms of their duties, giving each member a small, well-specified task but no sense of how that activity contributes to the overall project development effort. This approach is a serious mistake for several important reasons. First, the project team is the manager's best source for troubleshooting problems, both potential and actual. If the team is kept in the dark, members who could potentially help with the smooth development of the project through participating in other aspects of the installation are not able to contribute in helpful ways. Second, team members know and resent it when they are being kept in the dark about various features of the project on which they are working. Consciously or not, when project managers keep their team isolated and involved in fragmented tasks, they are sending out the signal that they either do not trust their team or do not feel that their team has the competence to address issues related to the overall implementation effort. Finally, from a "firefighting" perspective, it simply makes good sense for team leaders to keep their people abreast of the status of the project. The more time spent defining goals and clarifying roles in the initial stages of the team's development, the less time will be needed to resolve problems and adjudicate disputes down the road.

A Productive Interdependency

Interdependency refers to the degree of joint activity among team members that is required in order to complete a project. If, for example, a project could be completed through the work of a small number of people or one department in an organization, the interdependence needed would be considered low. In most situations, however, a project manager must form a team out of members from various functional areas within the organization. For example, an IT project introduction at a large corporation could conceivably require the input or efforts of a team that included members from the Information Systems department, engineering, accounting, marketing, and administration. As the concept of **differentiation** suggests, these individuals each bring to the team their preconceived notions of the roles that they should play, the importance of their various contributions, and other parochial attitudes.

Interdependencies refer to the degree of knowledge that team members have and the importance they attach to the interrelatedness of their efforts. Developing an understanding of mutual interdependencies implies developing a mutual level of appreciation for the strengths and contributions that each team member brings to the table and is a precondition for team success. Team members must become aware not only of their own contributions but also of how their work fits into the overall scheme of the project and, further, of how it relates to the work of team members from other departments.

Cohesiveness

Cohesiveness, at its most basic level, simply refers to the degree of mutual attraction that team members hold for one another and their task. It is the strength of desire all members have to remain a team. It is safe to assume that most members of the project team need a reason or reasons to contribute their skills and time to the successful completion of a project. Although they have been assigned to the project, for many individuals, this project may compete with other duties or responsibilities pulling them in other directions. Project managers work to build a team that is cohesive as a starting point for performing their tasks. Since cohesiveness is predicated on the attraction that the group holds for each individual member, managers need to make use of all resources at their disposal, including reward systems, recognition, performance appraisals, and any other sources of organizational reward, to induce team members to devote time and energy in furthering the team's goals.

Trust

Trust means different things to different people.[5] For a project team, **trust** can best be understood as the team's comfort level with each individual member. Given that comfort level, trust is manifested in the team's ability and willingness to squarely address differences of opinion, values, and attitudes and deal with them accordingly. Trust is the common denominator without which ideas of group cohesion and appreciation become moot. The interesting point about trust is that it can actually encourage disagreement and conflict among team members. When members of a project team have developed a comfort level where they are willing to trust the opinions of others, no matter how much those opinions diverge from their own, it is possible to air opposing views, to discuss issues, and even to argue. Because we trust one another, the disagreements are never treated as personal attacks; we recognize that views different from our own are valuable and can contribute to the project. Of course, before positive results can come from disagreement, we have to develop trust.

There are a number of ways in which project team members begin to trust one another. First, it is important for the project manager to create a "What happens here, stays here" mentality in which team members are not worried that their views will be divulged or confidences betrayed. Trust must first be demonstrated by the professionalism of the project manager and the manner in which she treats all team members. Second, trust develops over time. There is no way to jump-start trust among people. We are tested continuously to ensure that we are trustworthy. Third, trust is an "all-or-nothing" issue. Either we are trustworthy or we are not. There is no such thing as being slightly trustworthy. Finally, trust occurs on several levels:[6] (1) trust as it relates to professional **interaction** and the expectation of another person's competence ("I trust you to be able to accomplish the task"), (2) trust that occurs on an integrity level ("I trust you to honor your commitments"), and (3) trust that exists on an emotional level based on intuition ("It feels right to allow you to make this decision"). Hence, it is important to recognize that trust among team members is complex, takes time to develop, is dependent on past history, and can occur on several levels, each of which is important to developing a high-performing team.

Enthusiasm

Enthusiasm is the key to creating the energy and spirit that drive effective project efforts. One method for generating team enthusiasm is to promote the idea of efficacy, the belief that if we work toward certain goals, they are attainable. Enthusiasm is the catalyst for directing positive, high energy toward the project while committing to its goals. Project managers, therefore, are best able to promote a sense of enthusiasm within the project team when they create an environment that is:

- *Challenging*—Each member of the project perceives his role to offer the opportunity for professional or personal growth, new learning, and the ability to stretch professionally.
- *Supportive*—Project team members gain a sense of team spirit and group identity that creates the feeling of uniqueness with regard to the project. All team members work collaboratively, communicate often, and treat difficulties as opportunities for sharing and joint problem solving.
- *Personally rewarding*—Project team members become more enthusiastic as they perceive personal benefits arising from successful completion of the project. Linking the opportunity for personal advancement to project team performance gives all team members a sense of ownership of the project and a vested interest in its successful completion.

The importance of enthusiasm among project team members is best illustrated by a recently witnessed example. A team leader had been charged with reengineering a manufacturing process at a large production plant in New England. Despite his initial enthusiasm and energy, he was getting increasingly frustrated with his project team, most of them having been assigned to him without any of his input on the assignments. His chief concern became how to deal with the constant litany of "We can't do that here" that he heard every time he offered a suggestion for changing a procedure or trying anything new. One Monday morning, his team members walked into the office to the vision of the words "YES WE CAN!" painted in letters three feet high across one wall of the office. (Over the weekend, the project manager had come in and done a little redecorating.) From that point on, the motto YES WE CAN! became the theme of the team and had a powerful impact on project success.

Results Orientation

Results orientation suggests that each member of the project team is committed to achieving the project's goals. The project manager can influence team performance in many ways, but it is through constantly emphasizing the importance of task performance and project **outcomes** that all team members are united toward the same **orientation**. Some have referred to this phenomenon as the "eyes on the prize" attitude, a commonly held characteristic among successful project teams. The benefit of a results orientation is that it serves to continually rally team members toward the important or significant issues, allowing them to avoid squandering time and resources on problems that may be only peripheral to the major project goals.

17.3 REASONS WHY TEAMS FAIL

Because the challenges involved in creating high-performing project teams are so profound, it is not surprising that project teams fail to perform to their potential in many circumstances. Teams operate at less than optimum performance for a number of reasons, including poorly developed or unclear goals, poorly defined project team roles and interdependencies, lack of project team motivation, poor communication or leadership, turnover among team members, and dysfunctional behavior.[7]

Poorly Developed or Unclear Goals

One of the most common causes of project team failure is the absence of clear and commonly understood project goals. When the project goals are fragmented, constantly changing, or poorly communicated, the result is a high degree of ambiguity. This ambiguity is highly frustrating for project team members for a number of reasons.

UNCLEAR GOALS PERMIT MULTIPLE INTERPRETATIONS The most common problem with poorly developed goals is that they allow each team member to make separate and often differing interpretations of project objectives. As a result, rather than helping the team to focus on the project at hand, these goals actually serve to increase disagreements as each team member interprets the project's goals in different ways.

UNCLEAR GOALS IMPEDE THE WILLINGNESS OF TEAM MEMBERS TO WORK TOGETHER When team members are faced with ambiguous goals, it is common for each person to interpret the goals in the most advantageous way. When goals are used to support individuals rather than team objectives, it often leads to situations in which one person's desire to satisfy the project goals as *he interprets them* actually conflicts with another team member's desire to satisfy her goals.

UNCLEAR GOALS INCREASE CONFLICT Project team conflict is heightened by vague goals that allow for multiple, self-centered interpretations. Rather than working on completing the project, team members expend energy and time in conflict with one another sifting through project objectives.

Poorly Defined Project Team Roles and Interdependencies

Team interdependencies is a state where team members' activities coordinate with and complement other team members' work. To some degree, all team members depend on each other and must work in collaboration in order to accomplish project goals. High-performing teams are well structured in ways that leave little ambiguity about individual roles and responsibilities. When team member assignments or responsibilities are not made clear, it is natural for disagreements to occur or for time to be wasted in clarifying assignments. Another serious problem with poorly defined roles is that it allows for significant time to be lost between project activities. When team members are unaware of their roles and interdependencies in relation to other team members, it is common to lose time on the project through poor transitions, as tasks are completed and successors are expected to begin.

Lack of Project Team Motivation

A common problem with poorly performing project teams is a lack of motivation among team members. Motivation is typically a highly individualistic phenomenon, suggesting that the factors that motivate one member of the project (e.g., technical challenge, opportunities for advancement) may not be motivating for another member. When overall project team motivation is low, however, the project's performance will naturally suffer as team members work at below-optimal performance. Some of the reasons why project team motivation may be low include the following.

THE PROJECT IS PERCEIVED AS UNNECESSARY When projects are viewed by team members as less than critical, their motivation to perform well will naturally be affected. Whether the project team members' perception of a project as "unnecessary" is correct or not, if the organization and the project manager allow this interpretation to become fixed, it is extremely difficult to achieve high motivation from the team. Consequently, project managers need to communicate to the project team, as honestly as possible, the benefits of the project, its goals, and why they are important for the organization.

THE PROJECT MAY HAVE LOW PRIORITY Team members within organizations are often aware of which project initiatives are considered high priority and which are not. Internal company communications, including newsletters, e-mails, and other methods for highlighting activities, clearly identify the projects that top management views as critical. When project team members perceive that they are working on a project of low priority, they adopt a low level of commitment to the project and have low motivation to perform well.

Poor Communication

Poor communication comes about for a variety of reasons. For example, project team members may be uncertain about the structure of the project and the interdependencies among team members so they do not know with whom they are expected to share information. Another reason communication within the project team can break down is that some team members are unwilling to share information, viewing it as a source of power over other members of the team. Communication also may be impeded within the project team due to the different functional or professional orientations of project team members. Technical personnel, such as engineers, are comfortable employing scientific or technical jargon that is hard for nontechnical personnel to understand. Likewise, professionals with financial backgrounds may use business-related terminology that is not clear to technical team members.

The key to resolving many communication problems lies in the project manager's willingness to establish and enforce standards for information sharing among team members, creating an atmosphere within the project team that encourages frank and open exchanges. Other mechanisms for encouraging cross-functional cooperation are examined in greater detail later in this chapter.

Poor Leadership

The importance of the project manager's approach to leadership in great detail. Because this individual is often the linchpin holding the team together, the leadership style chosen by the project manager is a key promoter or inhibitor of project team effectiveness. Project managers who adopt a "one-style-fits-all" approach to leadership fail to recognize that different leadership styles are required in order to get the best performance out of each team member. Further, some project managers adopt a leadership approach that may be completely antithetical to the project team, browbeating, bullying, or threatening team members in the belief that the key to high project team performance is to create an atmosphere of fear and anxiety. Successful project leaders understand that leadership styles depend upon a number of relevant criteria within the project team—including makeup of the team, motivation levels, and experience and skill levels of team members—and modify their leadership style accordingly.

Turnover Among Project Team Members

A common problem in many organizations is that team members are assigned to a project and then unexpectedly pulled off the project for reassignment. The higher the turnover among project team members, the more it disrupts the project manager's ability to create project team cohesion. Further, the act of continually adding to and removing personnel from project teams causes problems with team learning and functioning. Research has found that because of learning curve effects, the act of adding team members to an ongoing project often has the effect of delaying the project. New team members need time to get caught up with the project, they are not clear on structure or team interrelationships, and they do not understand internal team dynamics.

Although the best-case scenario for project managers is to run projects in which team members do not turn over, the practical reality is that we must anticipate the potential for turnover and consider strategies that allow for minimal disruption to the project schedule when turnover does occur. One method of minimizing disruption is for the project manager to require that everyone on the team understands, as clearly as possible, not only her own role but also the roles of other team members to allow the members to support activities that could be delayed due to staff "pullaways." Another option is for the project manager to work closely with functional department heads in order to anticipate the possibility of project team members leaving the team prematurely and to begin prepping possible replacements.

Dysfunctional Behavior

Dysfunctional behavior refers to the disruptive acts of some project team members due to personality issues, hidden agendas, or interpersonal problems. Sometimes the solution simply calls for recognizing which members are engaging in these behaviors and taking steps to correct the problem. Other times, serious cases of dysfunctional behavior may require that a team member be removed from the project team.

17.4 STAGES IN GROUP DEVELOPMENT

The process of group development is a dynamic one.[8] Groups go through several maturation stages that are often readily identifiable, are generally found across a variety of organizations, and involve groups formed for a variety of different purposes. These stages are illustrated in Table 17.1 and Figure 17.3.[9]

TABLE 17.1 Stages of Group Development

Stage	Defining Characteristics
Forming	Members get to know one another and lay the basis for project and team ground rules.
Storming	Conflict begins as team members begin to resist authority and demonstrate hidden agendas and prejudices.
Norming	Members agree on operating procedures and seek to work together, develop closer relationships, and commit to the project development process.
Performing	Group members work together to accomplish their tasks.
Adjourning	Groups may disband either following the completion of the project or through significant reassignment of team personnel.

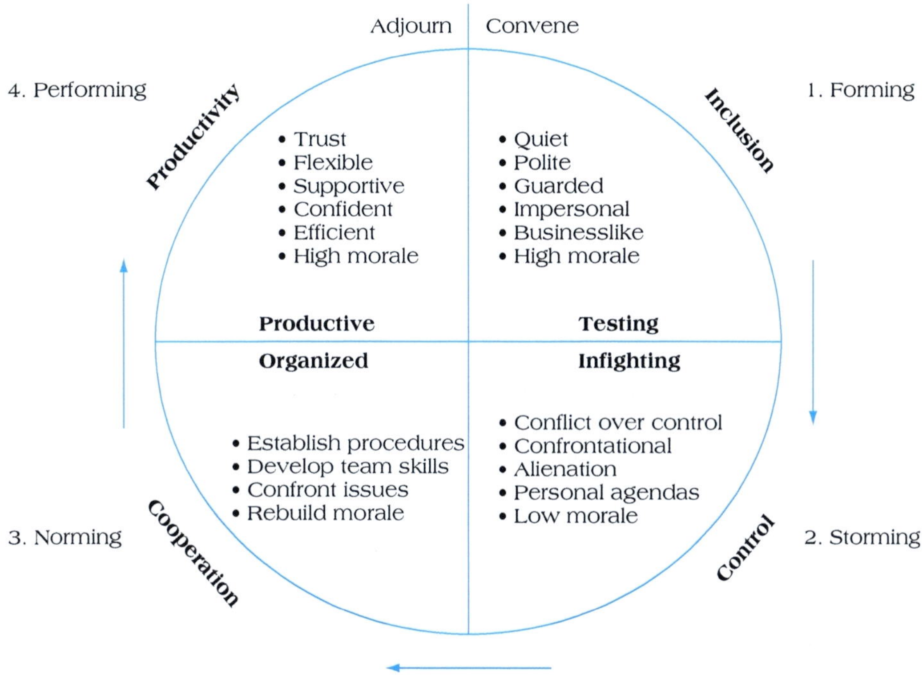

FIGURE 17.3 Stages of Team Development

Source: V. K. Verma. (1997). *Managing the Project Team*, p. 71. Upper Darby, PA: Project Management Institute. Copyright and all rights reserved. Material from this publication has been reproduced with the permission of PMI.

Stage One: Forming

Forming consists of the process or approaches used to mold a collection of individuals into a coherent project team. This stage has sometimes been referred to as the "floundering" stage, because team members are unsure about the project's goals, may not know other team members, and are confused about their own assignments.[10] Team members begin to get acquainted with one another and talk about the purposes of the project, how they perceive their roles, what types of communication patterns will be used, and what will be acceptable behaviors within the group. During the forming stage, some preliminary standards of behavior are established, including rules for interaction (who is really in charge and how members are expected to interact) and activity (how productive members are expected to be). The earlier this stage is completed, the better, so that ambiguities further along are avoided. In these early meetings, the role of the team leader is to create structure and set the tone for future cooperation and positive member attitudes.

Stage Two: Storming

Storming refers to the natural reactions members have to the initial ground rules. Members begin to test the limits and constraints placed on their behavior. Storming is a conflict-laden stage in which the preliminary leadership patterns, reporting relationships, and norms of work and interpersonal behavior are challenged and, perhaps, reestablished. During this stage, it is likely that the team leader will begin to see a number of the group members demonstrating personal agendas, attempting to defy or rewrite team rules, and exhibiting prejudices toward teammates from other functional backgrounds. For example, a team member may unilaterally decide that it is not necessary for her to attend all team meetings, proposing instead to get involved later in the project when she is "really needed." Other behaviors may involve not-so-subtle digs at members from other departments ("Gee, what are you marketing people doing here on a technical project?") or old animosities between individuals that resurface. Storming is a very natural phase through which all groups go. The second half of this chapter addresses ways to handle all types of conflict.

Stage Three: Norming

A *norm* is an unwritten rule of behavior. **Norming** behavior in a group implies that the team members are establishing mutually agreed-upon practices and attitudes. Norms help the team determine how it should make decisions, how often it should meet, what level of openness and trust members will have, and how conflicts will be resolved. Research has shown that it is during the norming stage that the cohesiveness of the group grows to its highest level. Close relationships develop, a sense of mutual concern and appreciation emerges, and feelings of camaraderie and shared responsibility become evident. The norming stage establishes the healthy basis upon which the actual work of the team will commence.

Stage Four: Performing

The actual work of the project team is done during the **performing stage**. It is only when the first three phases have been properly dealt with that the team will have reached the level of maturity and confidence needed to effectively perform their duties. During the performing stage, team relationships are characterized by high levels of trust, a mutual appreciation for one another's performance and contributions, and a willingness to actively seek to collaborate. Morale has continued to improve over the project team's development cycle to this point, at which all team members are working confidently and efficiently. As long as strong task-oriented group norms were established early in the team development and conflict was resolved, the performing stage is one of high morale and strong performance.

Stage Five: Adjourning

Adjourning recognizes the fact that projects and their teams do not last forever. At some point, the project has been completed and the team is disbanded to return to their other functional duties within the organization. In some cases, the group may downsize slowly and deliberately. For example, in the case of developing a systems engineering project, as various components of the system come online, the services of the team's design engineer may no longer be needed and he will be reassigned. In other circumstances, the team will complete its tasks and be disbanded all at once. In either case, it is important to remember that during the final stages of the implementation process, group members are likely to exhibit some concern about their future assignments and/or new duties. Project managers need to be sensitive to the real concerns felt by these team members and, where possible, help smooth the transition from the old team to the new assignments.

Punctuated Equilibrium

In the late 1980s, UCLA researcher Connie Gersick challenged the validity of the standard model of project team development.[11] Through a series of studies, she observed a dramatically different process by which project teams evolve. She referred to her model as *punctuated equilibrium*, based on a similar scientific model proposed by Stephen J. Gould to explain macroevolutionary change in the natural world. **Punctuated equilibrium** proposes that rather than evolution occurring as a steady state of gradual change, real natural change comes about through long periods of stasis, interrupted by some cataclysmic event that propels upward, evolutionary adjustment.

This phenomenon of punctuated equilibrium frequently occurs in the field of group dynamics. Gersick's work suggests that the timing of group process changes is quite consistent across teams and situations. Most teams, she discovered, develop a set of operating norms very quickly, at the time of the first team meeting and on the basis of limited interaction and knowledge of one another or the project mission. These norms, which are often less than optimal, tend to guide group behavior and performance for a substantial period of the project's life. The group will continue to operate as a result of these norms until some trigger event occurs, almost precisely at the halfway point between the initial meeting and the project deadline (see Figure 17.4). The trigger event may be general dissatisfaction with the project's progress to date, a boiling over of interpersonal antagonisms, or some other external force. Nevertheless, once this eruption has occurred, it serves as the motivation to revise group norms, develop better intragroup procedures, and promote better task performance. It is typically during this second phase of the group's life that the majority of effective work gets done and the group begins to function more as a team and less as a collection of individuals.

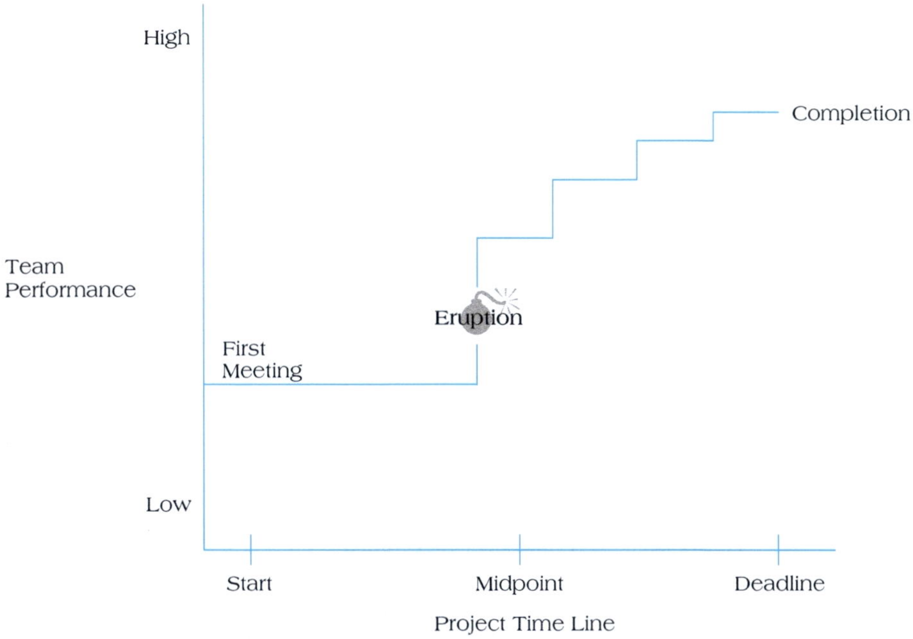

FIGURE 17.4 **Model of Punctuated Equilibrium**

Punctuated equilibrium has some very important implications for project team leaders. First, it suggests that initial impressions are often lasting, as early behaviors and norms quickly solidify and become the controlling force behind the team's behavior. Project team leaders, therefore, need to take a hard look at how they run kickoff meetings and the messages they send (intentional or otherwise) regarding appropriate task and interpersonal behavior. Second, the model suggests that groups collectively experience a form of "midlife crisis" in running their project, because a lack of concrete results, coupled with escalating interpersonal tensions, tends to build to a state of dissatisfaction that finally overflows midway through the development process. Leaders need to plan for these behaviors, recognize the warning signs of their approach, and proactively chart the steps needed for more positive outcomes from the transition. Finally, Gersick's research found that group members tended to feel increased frustration because they lacked a real sense of where the project stood at any point in time. Hence, project managers who wish to avoid the more damaging effects of midlife project transitions need to recognize that the more they plan for interim milestones and other indications of progress, the more they can mitigate the adverse effects of project team blowups.

17.5 ACHIEVING CROSS-FUNCTIONAL COOPERATION

What are some tactics that managers can use for effective team development? One research project on project teams uncovered a set of critical factors that contribute to **cross-functional cooperation**.[12] Figure 17.5 shows a two-stage model: The first set of factors influences cooperation, and the second set influences outcomes. Critical factors that influence cooperation and behavior are superordinate goals, rules and procedures, physical proximity, and accessibility. Through cross-functional cooperation, these influence both high task outcomes (making sure the project is done right) and psychosocial outcomes (the emotional and psychological effects that strong performance will have on the project team).

Superordinate Goals

A **superordinate goal** refers to an overall goal or purpose that is important to all functional groups involved, but whose attainment requires the resources and efforts of more than one group.[13] When Apple developed its iPad tablet, that venture included a number of subprojects, including the creation of a user-friendly operating system, graphical-user interface, a number of unique features and applications for running multiple programs, 4G and wireless capabilities, and so forth.

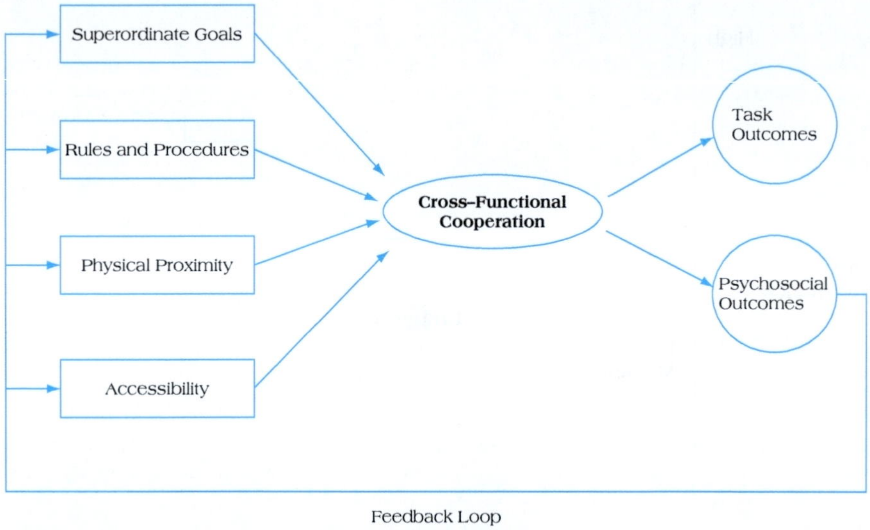

FIGURE 17.5 Project Team Cross-Functional Cooperation

Source: M. B. Pinto, J. K. Pinto, and J. E. Prescott. (1993). "Antecedents and consequences of project team cross-functional cooperation." *Management Science*, 39: 1281–97, p. 1283. Copyright 1993, the Institute for Operations Research and the Management Sciences, 7240 Parkway Drive, Suite 300, Hanover, MD 21076 USA. Reprinted by permission, Project Team Cross-Functional Cooperation.

Each of these subprojects was supported by dozens of electronics engineers, IT professionals, programmers and coding specialists, graphics designers, marketing research personnel, and operations specialists, all working together collaboratively. The iPad could not have been successful if only some of the projects succeeded—they all had to be successful, requiring that their developers maintain strong, collaborative working relationships with one another.

The superordinate goal is an addition to, not a replacement for, other goals the functional groups may have set. The premise is that when project team members from different functional areas share an overall goal or common purpose, they tend to cooperate toward this end. To illustrate, let us consider an example of creating a new software project for the commercial marketplace. A superordinate goal for this project team may be "to develop a high-quality, user-friendly, and generally useful system that will enhance the operations of various departments and functions." This overall goal attempts to enhance or pull together some of the diverse function-specific goals for cost-effectiveness, schedule adherence, quality, and innovation. It provides a central objective or an overriding goal toward which the entire project team can strive.

Rules and Procedures

Rules and procedures are central to any discussion of cross-functional cooperation because they offer a means for coordinating or integrating activities that involve several functional units.[14] Organizational rules and procedures are defined as formalized processes established by the organization that mandate or control the activities of the project team in terms of team membership, task assignment, and performance evaluation. For years, organizations have relied on rules and procedures to link together the activities of organizational members. Rules and procedures have been used to assign duties, evaluate performance, solve conflicts, and so on. Rules and procedures can be used to address formalized rules and procedures established by the organization for the performance of the implementation process, as well as project-specific rules and procedures developed by the project team to facilitate its operations.

The value of rules and procedures suggests that in the absence of cooperation among team members, the company can simply mandate that it occur. In cases where project teams cannot rely on established, organizationwide rules and procedures to assist members with their tasks, they often must create their own rules and procedures to facilitate the progress of the project. For example, one such rule could be that all project team members will make themselves available to one another regarding project business.

Physical Proximity

Physical proximity refers to project team members' perceptions that they are located within physical or spatial distances that make it convenient for them to interact. Individuals are more likely to interact and communicate with others when the physical characteristics of buildings or settings encourage them to do so.[15] For example, the sheer size and spatial layout of a building can affect working relationships. In a small building or when a work group is clustered on the same floor, relationships tend to be more intimate, since people are in close physical proximity to one another. As people spread out along corridors or in different buildings, interactions may become less frequent and/or less spontaneous. In these situations, it is harder for employees to interact with members of either their own department or other departments.

Many companies seriously consider the potential effects of physical proximity on project team cooperation. In fact, some project organizations relocate personnel who are working together on a project to the same office or floor. The term "war room" is sometimes used to illustrate this deliberate regrouping of project team members into a central location. When project team members work near one another, they are more likely to communicate and, ultimately, cooperate.

Accessibility

While physical proximity is important for encouraging cross-functional cooperation, another factor, accessibility, appears to be an equally important predictor of the phenomenon. **Accessibility** is the perception by others that a person is approachable for communicating and interacting with on problems or concerns related to the success of a project. Separate from the issue of physical proximity, accessibility refers to additional factors that can inhibit the amount of interaction that occurs between organizational members (e.g., an individual's schedule, position in an organization, or out-of-office commitments). These factors often affect the accessibility among organizational members. For example, consider a public-sector organization in which a member of the engineering department is physically located near a member of the city census department. Although these individuals are in proximity to each other, they may rarely interact because of different work schedules, varied duties and priorities, and commitment to their own agendas. Such factors often create a perception of inaccessibility among the individuals involved.

Outcomes of Cooperation: Task and Psychosocial Results

As Figure 17.5 suggests, the goal of promoting cross-functional cooperation among members of a project team is not an end unto itself; it reflects a means toward better project team performance and ultimately better project outcomes. Two types of project outcomes are important to consider: task outcomes and psychosocial outcomes. **Task outcomes** refer to the factors involved in the actual implementation of the project (time, schedule, and project functionality). **Psychosocial outcomes**, on the other hand, represent the team member's assessment that the project experience was worthwhile, satisfying, and productive. It is possible, for example, to have a project "succeed" in terms of completing its task outcomes while all team members are so disheartened due to conflict and bad experiences that they have nothing but bad memories of the project. Psychosocial outcomes are important because they represent the attitudes that project team members will carry with them to subsequent projects (as shown in the feedback loop in Figure 17.5). Was the project experience satisfying and rewarding? If so, we are much more likely to start new projects with a positive attitude than in circumstances where we had bad experiences on previous projects. Regardless of how carefully we plan and execute our project team selection and development process, our efforts may take time to bear fruit.

Finally, what are some general conclusions we can draw about methods for building high-performing teams? Based on research, project managers can take three practical steps to set the stage for teamwork to emerge:[16]

1. ***Make the project team as tangible as possible.*** Effective teams routinely develop their own unique identity. Through publicity, promoting interaction, encouraging unique terminology and language, and emphasizing the importance of project outcomes, project managers can create a tangible sense of team identity.

2. ***Reward good behavior.*** There are many nonmonetary methods for rewarding good performance. The keys are (1) flexibility—recognizing that everyone views rewards differently, (2) creativity—providing alternative means to get the message across, and (3) pragmatism—recognizing what can be rewarded and being authentic with the team about how superior performance will be recognized.
3. ***Develop a personal touch.*** Project managers need to build one-on-one relationships with project team members. If they lead by example, provide positive feedback to team members, publicly acknowledge good performance, show interest in the team's work, and are accessible and consistent in applying work rules, project team members will come to value both the manager's efforts and his work on the project.

These suggestions are a good starting point for applying the concept of team building in the difficult setting of project management. Given the temporary nature of projects, the dynamic movement of team members on and off the team, and the fact that in many organizations team members are working on several projects simultaneously, building a cohesive project team that can work in harmony and effectively to achieve project goals is extremely valuable.[17] Using these guidelines for team building should allow project managers to more rapidly achieve a high-performing team.

17.6 VIRTUAL PROJECT TEAMS

The globalization of business has had some important effects on how projects are being run today. Imagine a multimillion-dollar project to design, construct, and install an oil-drilling platform in the North Atlantic. The project calls on the expertise of partner organizations from Russia, Finland, the United States, France, Norway, and Great Britain. Each of the partners must be fully represented on the project team, all decisions should be as consensual as possible, and the project's success will require continuous, ongoing communication between all members of the project team. Does this sound difficult? In fact, such projects are undertaken frequently. Until recently, the biggest challenge was finding a way for managers to meet and stay in close contact. Constant travel was the only option. However, now more organizations are forming virtual project teams.

Virtual teams, sometimes referred to as *geographically dispersed* teams, involve the use of electronic media, including e-mail, the Internet, and teleconferencing, to link together members of a project team that are not collocated to the same physical place. Virtual teams start with the assumption that physical barriers or spatial separation make it impractical for team members to meet in a regular, face-to-face manner. Hence, the virtual team involves establishing alternative communications media that enable all team members to stay in contact, make contributions to the ongoing project, and communicate all necessary project-related information with all other members of the project team. Virtual teams are using technology to solve the thorny problem of productively linking geographically dispersed project partners.

Virtual teams present two main challenges: building trust and establishing the best modes of communication.[18] Trust, as we have discussed, is a key ingredient needed to turn a disparate group of individuals into an integrated project team. Physical separation and disconnection can make trust slower to emerge. Communications media may create formal and impersonal settings, and the level of comfort that permits casual banter takes time to develop. This can slow down the process of creating trust among team members.

What are some suggestions for improving the efficiency and effectiveness of virtual team meetings? Following are some options available to project teams as they set out to use virtual technology.[19]

- ***When possible, find ways to augment virtual communication with face-to-face opportunities.*** Try not to rely exclusively on virtual technology. Even if it occurs only at the beginning of a project and after key milestones, create opportunities to get the team together to exchange information, socialize, and begin developing personal relationships.
- ***Don't let team members disappear.*** One of the problems with virtual teams is that it becomes easy for members to "sign off" for extended periods of time, particularly if regular communication schedules are not established. The best solution to this problem is to ensure that communications include both regular meetings and ad hoc get-togethers, either through videoconferencing or through e-mail and Internet connections.

- ***Establish a code of conduct among team members.*** While it can be relatively easy to get agreement on the types of information that need to be shared among team members, it is equally important to establish rules for when contact should be made and the length of acceptable and unacceptable delays in responding to messages.
- ***Keep all team members in the communication loop.*** Virtual teams require a hyperawareness by the project manager of the need to keep communication channels open. When team members understand how they fit into the big picture, they are more willing to stay in touch.
- ***Create a clear process for addressing conflict, disagreement, and group norms.*** When projects are conducted in a virtual setting, the actual ability of the project manager to gauge team members' reactions and feelings about the project and one another may be minimal. It is helpful to create a set of guidelines for allowing the free expression of misgivings or disagreements among team members. For example, one virtual team composed of members of several large organizations established a Friday-afternoon complaint session, which allowed a two-hour block each week for team members to vent their feelings or disagreements. The only rule of the session was that everything said must remain within the project—no one could carry these messages outside the project team. Within two months of instituting the sessions, project team members felt that the sessions were the most productive part of project communication and looked forward to them more than to formal project meetings.

Beyond the challenges of creating trust and establishing communication methods for dispersed teams, there are other considerations that should be addressed.[20] For example, selecting the appropriate technology tools is an important process. There is no "one best" means for communicating with all team members on all occasions. Communications options include synchronous (occurring in real time) and asynchronous (occurring outside of real time). An example of synchronous communication would be a direct conversation with another party. Asynchronous communication may include e-mail or posting to someone's Facebook wall. The underlying intent behind the communication may be either social or informational. We can use these communication tools to establish relationships with team members in the same way they are useful for passing along important project information.

Other suggestions for effectively using technology to manage a dispersed team include:[21]

- No one technology works for everything; use the technology that fits the task at hand.
- Vary how your team meets; always using teleconferences becomes routine and boring.
- Make sure to intermix meeting types and purposes to keep the team experience fresh. Overemphasizing just one type of meeting (social or informational) can lead to assumptions about the only types of meetings worth having.
- Communication technologies can be combined in various ways; for example, virtual whiteboards work well with videoconferencing.
- Asynchronous technologies tend to become the dominant forms as time-zone differences grow. Find methods for adding a synchronous element whenever possible.
- Training in the proper use of technology is critical to its effectiveness. Whoever facilitates the meetings must be an expert on the technologies employed.

PROJECT PROFILE

Tele-Immersion Technology Eases the Use of Virtual Teams

For many users of videoconferencing technology, the benefits and drawbacks may sometimes seem about equal. Although there is no doubt that teleconferencing puts people into immediate contact with each other from great geographical distances, the current limitations on how far the technology can be applied lead to some important qualifications. As one writer noted:

> I am a frequent but reluctant user of videoconferencing. Human interaction has both verbal and nonverbal elements, and videoconferencing seems precisely configured to confound the nonverbal ones. It is impossible to make eye contact properly, for instance, in today's videoconferencing systems, because the camera and the display screen cannot be in the same spot. This usually leads to a deadened and formal affect in interactions, eye contact being a nearly ubiquitous subconscious method of affirming trust. Furthermore, participants aren't able to establish a sense of position relative to one another and therefore have no clear way to direct attention, approval or disapproval.[22]

(continued)

FIGURE 17.6 Tele-Immersion Technology
HO Marketwire Photos/Newscom

It was to address these problems with teleconferencing that tele-immersion technology was created. Tele-immersion, a new medium for human interaction enabled by digital technologies, creates the illusion that a user is in the same physical space as other people, even though the other participants might in fact be thousands of miles away. It combines the display and interaction techniques of virtual reality with new vision technologies that transcend the traditional limitations of a camera. The result is that all the participants, however distant, can share and explore a life-sized space.

This fascinating new technology, which has emerged very recently, offers the potential to completely change the nature of how virtual project teams communicate with each other. Pioneered by Advanced Network & Services as part of the National Tele-Immersion Initiative (NTII), tele-immersion enables users at geographically distributed sites to collaborate in real time in a shared, simulated environment as if they were in the same physical room. Tele-immersion is the long-distance transmission of life-sized, three-dimensional synthesized scenes, accurately sampled and rendered in real time using advanced computer graphics and vision techniques. The use of this sophisticated representation of three-dimensional modeling has allowed teleconferencing to take on a whole new look; all members of the project literally appear in a real-time, natural setting, almost as if they were sitting across a conference table from one another.

With enhanced bandwidth and the appropriate technology, tele-immersion video conferencing offers an enormous leap forward compared to the current two-dimensional industry standards in use. In its current form, the tele-immersion technology requires the videoconference member to wear polarizing glasses and a silvery head-tracking device that can move around and see a computer-generated 3D stereoscopic image of the other teleconferencers, whereby the visual content of a block of space surrounding each participant's upper body and some adjoining workspace is essentially reproduced with computer graphics. This results in a more fully dimensional and compressible depiction of such real-world environments than is possible with existing video technology. Just how far this technology is likely to go in the years ahead is impossible to predict, but no one is betting against it becoming the basis for an entirely new manner of conducting virtual team meetings.[23]

As Figure 17.6 demonstrates, recent advances in technology have allowed tele-immersion conferencing to sometimes dispense with extra equipment link goggles or tracking devices. The ability to translate and communicate sophisticated images of people, blueprints, or fully rendered three-dimensional models makes this technology unique and highly appealing as an alternative to standard telephone conferencing.

Virtual teams, though not without their limitations and challenges, offer an excellent method for applying the technical advances in the field of telecommunications to the problems encountered with global, dispersed project teams. The key to using them effectively lies in a clear recognition of what virtual technologies can and cannot do. For example, while the Internet can link team members, it cannot convey nonverbals or feelings that team members may have about the project or other members of the project. Likewise, although current videoconferencing allows for real-time, face-to-face interactions, it is not a perfect substitute for genuine "face time" among project team members. Nevertheless, the development of virtual technologies has been a huge benefit for project organizations, coming as it has at the same time that teams have become more global in their makeup and that partnering project organizations are becoming the norm for many project challenges.

17.7 CONFLICT MANAGEMENT

One study has estimated that the average manager spends over 20% of his time dealing with conflict.[24] Because so much of a project manager's time is taken up with active conflict and its residual aftermath, we need to understand this natural process within the project management context. This section of the chapter is intended to more formally explore the process of conflict, examine the nature of conflict for project teams and managers, develop a model of conflict behavior, and foster an understanding of some of the most common methods for de-escalating conflict.

What Is Conflict?

Conflict is a process that begins when you perceive that someone has frustrated or is about to frustrate a major concern of yours.[25] There are two important elements in this definition. First, it suggests that conflict is not a state, but a process. As such, it contains a dynamic aspect that is very important. Conflicts evolve.[26] Further, the one-time causes of a conflict may change over time; that is, the reasons why two individuals or groups developed a conflict initially may no longer have any validity. However, because the conflict process is dynamic and evolving, once a conflict *has* occurred, the reasons behind it may no longer matter. The process of conflict has important ramifications that we will explore in greater detail.

The second important element in the definition is that conflict is perceptual in nature. In other words, it does not ultimately matter whether or not one party has truly wronged another party. The important thing is that one party *perceives* that state or event to have occurred. That perception is enough because for that party, perception of frustration defines reality.

In general, most types of conflict fit within one of three categories,[27] although it is also common for some conflicts to involve aspects of more than one category.

Goal-oriented conflict is associated with disagreements regarding results, project scope outcomes, performance specifications and criteria, and project priorities and objectives. Goal-oriented conflicts often result from multiple perceptions of the project and are fueled by vague or incomplete goals that allow project team members to make their own interpretations.

Administrative conflict arises through management hierarchy, organizational structure, or company philosophy. These conflicts are often centered on disagreements about reporting relationships, who has authority and administrative control for functions, project tasks, and decisions. A good example of administrative conflict arises in matrix organization structures, in which each project team member is responsible to two bosses, the project manager and the functional supervisor. In effect, this structure promotes the continuance of administrative conflict.

Interpersonal conflict occurs with personality differences between project team members and important project stakeholders. Interpersonal conflict sources include different work ethics, behavioral styles, egos, and personalities of project team members.

At least three schools of thought exist about how conflicts should be perceived and addressed. These vary dramatically, depending upon the prevailing view that a person or an organization holds.[28]

The first view of conflict is the *traditional* view, which sees conflict as having a negative effect on organizations. Traditionalists, because they assume that conflict is bad, believe that conflict should be avoided and resolved as quickly and painlessly as possible when it does occur. The emphasis with traditionalists is conflict suppression and elimination.

The second view of conflict is the *behavioral* or contemporary school of thought. Behavioral theorists view conflict as a natural and inevitable part of organizational life. Differentiation across functional departments and different goals, attitudes, and beliefs are natural and permanent states among members of a company, so it is natural that conflict will result. The solution to conflict for behavioral theorists is to manage conflict effectively rather than attempt to eliminate or suppress it.

The third view of conflict, the *interactionist* view, takes behavioral attitudes toward conflict one step further. Where a behavioral view of conflict accepts it when it occurs, interactionists encourage conflict to develop. Conflict, to an interactionist, prevents an organization from becoming too stagnant and apathetic. Conflict actually introduces an element of tension that produces innovation, creativity, and higher productivity. The interactionists do not intend that conflict should continue without some controls, however; they argue that there is an optimal level of conflict that improves the organization. Beyond that point, conflict becomes too intense and severe and begins hurting the company. The trick, to an interactionist, is to find the optimal level of conflict—too little leads to inertia and too much leads to chaos.

Sources of Conflict

Potential sources of conflict in projects are numerous. Some of the most common sources include the competition for scarce resources, violations of group or organizational norms, disagreements over goals or the means to achieve those goals, personal slights and threats to job security, long-held biases and prejudices, and so forth. Many of the sources of conflict arise out of the project management situation itself. That is, the very characteristics of projects that make them unique contribute some important triggers for conflict to erupt among project stakeholders.

ORGANIZATIONAL CAUSES OF CONFLICT Some of the most common causes of organizational conflict are reward systems, scarce resources, uncertainty, and differentiation. *Reward systems* are competitive processes some organizations have set up that pit one group or functional department against another. For example, when functional managers are evaluated on the performance of their subordinates within the department, they are loath to allow their best workers to become involved in project work for any length of time. The organization has unintentionally created a state in which managers perceive that either the project teams *or* the departments will be rewarded for superior performance. In such cases, they will naturally retain their best people for functional duties and offer their less-desirable subordinates for project teamwork. The project managers, on the other hand, will also perceive a competition between their projects and the functional departments and develop a strong sense of animosity toward functional managers whom they perceive, with some justification, are putting their own interests above the organization.

Scarce resources are a natural cause of conflict as individuals and departments compete for the resources they believe are necessary to do their jobs well. Because organizations are characterized by scarce resources sought by many different groups, the struggle to gain these resources is a prime source of organizational conflict. As long as scarce resources are the natural state within organizations, groups will be in conflict as they seek to bargain and negotiate to gain an advantage in their distribution.

Uncertainty over lines of authority essentially asks the tongue-in-cheek question, "Who's in charge around here?" In the project environment, it is easy to see how this problem can be badly exacerbated due to the ambiguity that often exists with regard to formal channels of authority. Project managers and their teams sit "outside" the formal organizational hierarchy in many organizations, particularly in functional structures. As a result, they find themselves in a uniquely fragile position of having a great deal of autonomy but also responsibility to the functional department heads who provide the personnel for the team. For example, when a project team member from R&D is given orders by her functional manager that directly contradict directives from the project manager, she is placed in the dilemma of having to find (if possible) a middle ground between two nominal authority figures. In many cases, project managers do not have the authority to conduct performance evaluations of their team members—that control is kept within the functional department. In such situations, the team member from R&D, facing role conflict brought on by this uncertainty over lines of authority, will most likely do the expedient thing and obey her functional manager because of his "power of the performance appraisal."

Differentiation reflects the fact that different functional departments develop their own mindsets, attitudes, time frames, and value systems, which can conflict with those of other departments. Briefly, differentiation suggests that as individuals join an organization within some functional specialty, they begin to adopt the attitudes and outlook of that functional group. For example, a member of the finance department, when asked her opinion of marketing, might reply, "All they ever do is travel around and spend money. They're a bunch of cowboys who would give away the store if they had to." A marketing member's opinion of finance department personnel might be similarly unflattering: "Finance people are just a group of bean counters who don't understand that the company is only as successful as it can be at selling its products. They're so hung up on their margins that they don't know what goes on in the real world." The interesting point about these views is that, within their narrow frames of reference, they both are essentially correct: Marketing is interested primarily in making sales, and finance is devoted to maintaining high margins. However, these opinions are by no means completely true; they simply reflect the underlying attitudes and prejudices of members of the respective functional departments. The more profound the differentiation within an organization, the greater the likelihood that individuals and groups will divide into "us" versus "them" encampments, which will continue to promote and provoke conflict.

INTERPERSONAL CAUSES OF CONFLICT *Faulty attributions* refer to our misconceptions of the reasons behind another's behavior. When people perceive that their interests have been thwarted by another individual or group, they typically try to determine why the other party has acted as it did. In making attributions about another's actions, we wish to determine if their motives are based on personal malevolence, hidden agendas, and so forth. Often groups and individuals will attribute motives to another's actions that are personally most convenient. For example, when one member of a project team has his wishes frustrated, it is common to perceive the motives behind the other party's actions in terms of the most convenient causes. Rather than acknowledge the fact that reasonable people may differ in their opinions, it may be more convenient for the frustrated person to assume that the other is provoking a conflict for personal reasons: "He just doesn't like me." This attribution is convenient for an obvious and psychologically "safe" reason; if we assume that the other person disagrees with us for valid reasons, it implies a flaw in our position. Many individuals do not have the ego strength to acknowledge and accept objective disagreement, preferring to couch their **frustration** in personal terms.

Faulty communication is a second and very common interpersonal cause of conflict. Faulty communication implies the potential for two mistakes: communicating in ways that are ambiguous and lead to different interpretations, thus causing a resulting conflict, and unintentionally communicating in ways that annoy or anger other parties. Lack of clarity can send out mixed signals: the message the sender intended to communicate and that which was received and interpreted by the receiver. Consequently, the project manager may be surprised and annoyed by the work done by a subordinate who genuinely thought she was adhering to the project manager's desires. Likewise, project managers often engage in criticism in the hopes of correcting and improving project team member performance. Unfortunately, what the project manager may consider to be harmless, constructive criticism may come across as a destructive, unfair critique if the information is not communicated accurately and effectively.

Personal grudges and *prejudices* are another main cause of interpersonal conflict. Each of us brings attitudes into any work situation. These attitudes arise as the result of long-term experiences or lessons taught at some point in the past. Often these attitudes are unconsciously held; we may be unaware that we nurture them and can feel a genuine sense of affront when we are challenged or accused of holding biases. Nevertheless, these grudges or prejudices, whether they are held against another race, sex, or functional department, have a seriously debilitating effect on our ability to work with others in a purposeful team and can ruin any chance at project team cohesion and subsequent project performance.

Table 17.2 illustrates some of the findings from two studies that investigated the major sources of conflict in project teams.[29] Although the studies were conducted more than a decade apart, the findings are remarkably consistent across several dimensions. Conflicts over schedules and project priorities tend to be the most common and intense sources of disagreement. Interestingly, Posner's research found that cost and budget issues played a much larger role in triggering conflict than did the earlier work of Thamhain and Wilemon. The significant changes in the rank ordering of sources of conflict and their intensity may be due to shifts in priorities or practices of project management over time, making issues of cost of greater concern and conflict.[30] Nevertheless, Table 17.2 gives some clear indications about the chief causes of conflict within project teams and the intensity level (1 being the highest and 7 being the lowest) of these conflicts.

TABLE 17.2 Sources of Conflict in Projects and Their Ranking by Intensity Level

	Conflict Intensity Ranking	
Sources of Conflict	**Thamhain & Wilemon**	**Posner**
Conflict over project priorities	2	3
Conflict over administrative procedures	5	7
Conflict over technical opinions and performance trade-offs	4	5
Conflict over human resources	3	4
Conflict over cost and budget	7	2
Conflict over schedules	1	1
Personality conflicts	6	6

Methods for Resolving Conflict

A number of methods for resolving group conflict are at the project manager's disposal. Before making a decision about which approach to follow, the project manager needs to consider several issues.[31] For example, will the project manager's siding with one party to the dispute alienate the other person? Is the conflict professional or personal in nature? Does any sort of intervention have to occur or can team members resolve the issue on their own? Does the project manager have the time and inclination to mediate the dispute? All of these questions play an important role in determining how to approach a conflict situation. Project managers must learn to develop flexibility in dealing with conflict, knowing when to intervene versus when to remain neutral. We can choose to manage conflict in terms of five alternatives.[32]

MEDIATE THE CONFLICT In this approach, the project manager takes a direct interest in the conflict between the parties and seeks to find a solution. The project manager may employ either defusion or confrontation tactics in negotiating a solution. Defusion implies that the project manager is less concerned with the source of the conflict than with a mutually acceptable solution. She may use phrases such as "We are all on the same team here" to demonstrate her desire to defuse the conflict without plumbing its underlying source. Confrontation, which typically involves working with both parties to get at the root causes of the conflict, is more emotional, time-intensive, and, in the short term, may actually exacerbate the conflict as both sides air their differences. In the long run, however, confrontation can be more effective as a mediating mechanism because it seeks to determine underlying causes of the conflict so they can be corrected. Project managers mediate solutions when they are not comfortable imposing a judgment but would rather work with both parties to come to some common agreement.

ARBITRATE THE CONFLICT In choosing to arbitrate a conflict, the project manager must be willing to impose a judgment on the warring parties. After listening to both positions, the project manager renders his decision. Much as a judge would do, it is best to minimize personalities in the decision and focus instead on the judgment itself. For example, saying, "You were wrong here, Phil, and Susan was right," is bound to lead to a negative emotional response from Phil. By imposing an impersonal judgment, however, the project manager can stick with the specifics of the case at hand rather than getting into personalities. "Company policy states that all customers must receive copies of project revision orders within three working days" is an example of an impersonal judgment that does not point the finger of guilt at either party.

CONTROL THE CONFLICT Not all conflicts can be (nor should be) quickly resolved. In some cases, a pragmatic response to a conflict might be to wait a couple of days for the two parties to cool down. This is not a cowardly response; instead it recognizes that project managers must be selective about how they intervene and the optimal manner in which they can intervene. Another way to control conflict is through limiting the interaction between two parties. For example, if it is common knowledge that one member of the project team and the customer have a long history of animosity, good sense dictates that they should not be allowed to communicate directly except under the most controlled of circumstances.

ACCEPT THE CONFLICT Not all conflicts are manageable. Sometimes the personalities of two project team members are simply not compatible. They disliked each other before the project and will continue to dislike each other long after the project has been completed.

ELIMINATE THE CONFLICT We need to critically evaluate the nature and severity of conflicts that occur continually within a project. In some situations, it is necessary, for the good of the project, to transfer a team member or make other changes. If there is a clearly guilty party, a common response is to sanction that person, remove him from the project, or otherwise punish him. If two or more people share a collective guilt for the ongoing conflict, it is often useful to transfer them all—sending a signal that you intend to run the project as impartially as possible.

The important point to bear in mind is that different approaches may be appropriate in different situations. Do not assume that a problem-solving session is always beneficial or warranted, nor is ignoring conflict always "lazy" management. Project managers have to learn to understand their own preferences when it comes to handling conflict. Once we have achieved a greater sense of self-awareness, we will be in a better position first to resolve our own conflicts constructively and then to deal more effectively with subordinate conflicts. The key is flexibility. It is important not to lock into any particular conflict style nor favor one resolution tactic to the exclusion of all others. Each has its strengths and drawbacks and can be an important part of the project manager's tool chest.

Conflict often is evidence of project team progress. As we begin to assemble a group of disparate individuals with various functional backgrounds into a project team, a variety of conflicts are bound to be sparked. Team conflict is natural. Remember, however, that the approaches we choose to employ to deal with conflict say a great deal about us: Are we intolerant, authoritarian, and intransigent, or do we really want to find mutually beneficial solutions? We can send many messages—intentional and unintentional, clear and mixed—to the rest of the project team by the manner in which we approach team building and conflict management.

17.8 NEGOTIATION

One of the central points that this chapter has made is to suggest that much of our future success will rest with our ability to appreciate and manage the variety of "people" issues that are central to life in projects. **Negotiation** is a process that is predicated on a manager's ability to use his influence productively.

Negotiation skills are so important because much of a project manager's life is taken up in bargaining sessions of one type or another. Indeed, stakeholder management can be viewed as the effective and constant mutual negotiation across multiple parties. Project managers negotiate for additional time and money, to prevent excessive interference and specification changes from clients, the loan or assignment to the team of important project team personnel with functional managers, and so forth. Negotiation represents the art of influence taken to its highest level. Because effective negotiation is an imperative for successful project management, it is vital that project managers understand the role negotiation plays in their projects, how to become better negotiators, and some of the important elements in negotiation.

Questions to Ask Prior to the Negotiation

Anyone entering a negotiation needs to consider three questions: How much power do I have? What sort of time pressures are there? Do I trust my opponent?[33]

A realistic self-assessment concerning power and any limiting constraints is absolutely vital prior to sitting down to negotiate. One important reason is that it can show the negotiators where they are strong and, most importantly, what their weaknesses are. A project manager once related this story:

> It was early in June and we were involved in the second week of pretty intense negotiations with a vendor for site considerations before starting a construction project. Unfortunately, the vendor discovered that we do our accounting books on a fiscal basis, ending June 30th, and he figured, correctly, that we were desperate to record the deal prior to the end of the month. He just sat on his hands for the next 10 days. Now it's June 21st and my boss is having a heart attack about locking in the vendor. Finally, we practically crawled back to the table in late June and gave him everything he was asking for in order to record the contract.

This project manager lost out in the power *and* time departments!

How much power do you have going into the negotiation? You are not necessarily looking for a dominant position but a defensive one, that is, one from which the other party cannot dominate you. How much time do you have? The calendar can be difficult to overcome. So, too, can a domineering boss who is constantly telling you to "solve the problem with R&D, marketing, or whomever." Once word gets out that you have a time constraint, just watch your opponent slow down the pace, reasoning correctly that you will have to agree sooner rather than later, and on her terms, not yours.

Is it possible to trust the other party? Will the firm abide by its word, or does it have a reputation for changing agreements after the fact? Is it forthcoming with accurate information? Does it play negotiation hardball? Note that not all of these questions indicate someone who is untrustworthy. Indeed, it is appropriate to play hardball on occasion. On the other hand, the essential question is whether you can sit across a table from your opponent and believe that you both have a professional, vested interest in solving a mutual problem. If the answer is no, it is highly unlikely that you will negotiate with the same degree of enthusiasm or openness toward the other party.

Principled Negotiation

One of the most influential books on negotiation in recent years is *Getting to Yes*, by Roger Fisher and William Ury.[34] They offer excellent advice on **principled negotiation**, the art of getting agreement with the other party while maintaining a principled, win-win attitude. Among the suggestions they offer for developing an effective negotiating strategy are the following.

SEPARATE THE PEOPLE FROM THE PROBLEM One of the most important ideas of negotiation is to remember that negotiators are people first. What this dictum means is that negotiators are no different from anyone else in terms of ego, attitudes, biases, education, experiences, and so forth. We all react negatively to direct attacks, we all become defensive at unwarranted charges and accusations, and we tend to personalize opposing viewpoints, assuming that their objections are aimed at us, rather than at the position we represent. Consequently, in observing the saliency of the notion that negotiators are people first, we must seek ways in which we can keep people (along with their personalities, defensiveness, egos, etc.) out of the problem itself. The more we can focus on the issues that separate us and pay less attention to the people behind the issues, the greater the likelihood of achieving a positive negotiated outcome.

Put yourself in their shoes. An excellent starting point in negotiations is to discuss not only our own position but also our understanding of the other party's position early in the negotiation process. When the other party hears a reasoned discussion of both positions, two important events occur: (1) It establishes a basis of trust because our opponent discovers that we are willing to openly discuss perceptions in the beginning, and (2) it reconstructs the negotiation as a win-win, rather than a winner-take-all, exercise.

Don't deduce their intentions from your fears. A common side effect of almost all negotiations, particularly early in the process, is to construct supporting stereotypes of the other side. For example, in meeting with the accountant to negotiate additional funding for our project, we may adopt a mind-set in which all accountants are penny-pinching bean counters who are only waiting for the opportunity to cancel the project. Notice that even before the negotiation takes place, we have created an image of the accounting department's members and their mind-set based on our own misperception and fears, rather than on any objective reality. When we assume that they will act in certain ways, we subconsciously begin negotiating with them as though money is their sole concern, and before we know it, we have created an opponent based on our worst fears.

Don't blame them for your problems. In negotiations, it is almost always counterproductive to initiate a finger-pointing episode as we seek to attach blame for difficulties our project has encountered. It is far more effective to move beyond the desire to assign blame and search for win-win solutions. For example, suppose that a company has just developed a software program for internal reporting and control that continually crashes in mid-operation. One approach would be for the exasperated accounting manager to call in the head of the software development project and verbally abuse him: "Your program really stinks. Every time you claim to have fixed it, it dumps on us again. If you don't get the bugs out of it within two weeks we're going to go back to the old system and make sure that everyone knows the reason why."

Although it may be satisfying for the accounting manager to react in this manner, it is unlikely to solve the problem, particularly in terms of relations with the software development project team. A far better approach would be less confrontational, seeking to frame the problem as a mutual issue that needs correction. For example, "The reporting program crashed again in midstride. Every time it goes down, my people have to reenter data and use up time that could be spent in other ways. I need your advice on how to fix the problem with the software. Is it just not ready for beta testing, are we using it incorrectly, or what?" Note that in this case, the head of the accounting department is careful not to point fingers. He refrains from taking the easy way out through simply setting blame and demanding correction, and instead treats the problem as a problem that will require cooperation if it is to be resolved.

Recognize and understand emotion: theirs and yours. Although it is often easy to get emotional during the course of a negotiation, the impulse must be resisted as much as possible.[35] It is common in a difficult, protracted negotiation to see emotions begin to come to the surface, often due to anger or frustration with the tactics or attitudes of the other party. Nevertheless, it is usually not a good idea to respond in an emotional way, even when the other party becomes emotional. They may be using emotion as a tactic to get your team to respond in an equally emotional way and allow your heart to begin guiding your head—always a dangerous course. Although emotions are a natural side effect of lengthy negotiations, we need to understand precisely what is making us unhappy, stressed, tense, or angry. Further, are we astute enough to take note of the emotions emanating from our opponent? We need to be aware of what we are doing that is making the other person upset or irritable.

Listen actively. Active listening means our direct involvement in the conversation with our opponent, even when the other party is actually speaking. Most of us know from experience when people are really listening to us and when they are simply going through the motions. In the latter case, our frustration at their seeming indifference to our position can be a tremendous source of negative emotion. For example, suppose a client is negotiating with the project manager for a performance enhancement on a soon-to-be-released piece of manufacturing equipment. The project manager is equally desirous to leave the project alone because any reconfigurations at this time will simply delay the release of the final product and cost a great deal of extra money. Every time the client voices her issues, the project manager speaks up and says, "I hear what you're saying, but...." In this case, the project manager clearly is not hearing a word the client is saying but is simply paying lip service to the client's concerns.

Active listening means working hard to understand not simply the words but the underlying motivations of the other party. One effective technique involves interrupting occasionally to ask a pointed question: "As I understand it, then, you are saying...." Tactics such as this convince your opponent that you are trying to hear what is being said rather than simply adhering to your company's party line no matter what arguments or issues the other side raises. Remember that demonstrating that you clearly understand the other party's position is not the same thing as agreeing with it. There may be many points with which you take issue. Nevertheless, a constructive negotiation can only proceed from the point of complete and objective information, not from preconceived notions or entrenched and intransigent positions.

Build a working relationship. The idea of negotiating as though you are dealing with a party with whom you would like to maintain a long-term relationship is key to effective negotiations. We think of long-term relationships as those with individuals or organizations that we value and, hence, are inclined to work hard to maintain. The stronger the working relationship, the greater the level of trust that is likely to permeate its character.

FOCUS ON INTERESTS, NOT POSITIONS There is an important difference between the positions each party adopts and the interests that underscore and mold those positions. When we refer to "interests," we mean the fundamental motivations that frame each party's positions. As Fisher and Ury note, "Interests define the problem."[36] It is not the positions taken by each party that shape the negotiation nearly as much as it is the interests that are the source of the parties' fears, needs, and desires.

Why look for underlying interests as opposed to simply focusing on the positions that are placed on the table? Certainly, it is far easier to negotiate with another party from the point of our position versus theirs. However, there are some compelling reasons why focusing on interests rather than positions can offer us an important "leg up" in successful negotiations. First, unlike positions, for every interest there are usually several alternatives that can satisfy it. For example, if my major interest is to ensure that my company will be in business over the years to come, I can look for solutions other than simply squeezing every drop of profit from the contractor in this negotiation. For example, I could enter into a long-term relationship with the contractor in which I am willing to forgo some profit on this job while locking the contractor into a sole-source agreement for the next three years. The contractor would then receive the additional profit from the job by paying me less than I desire (my position) while supplying me with long-term work (my interest).

Another reason for focusing on interests argues that negotiating from positions often leads to roadblocks as each party tries to discover their opponent's position while concealing their own. We consume valuable time and resources in making visible our various positions while hiding as long as possible our true intentions. In focusing on interests, on the other hand, we adopt a partnering mentality that acknowledges the legitimacy of both sides' interests and seeks to find solutions that will be mutually satisfying.

Invent Options for Mutual Gain

Managers sometimes put up roadblocks for themselves, making it difficult to consider win-win options when negotiating.

Managers can have premature judgment. We quickly arrive at conclusions about the other side and anything they say usually serves to solidify our impressions. Further, rather than seek to broaden our various options early in the negotiation, we typically go the other direction and put limits on how much we are willing to give up, how far we are willing to go, and so forth. Every premature judgment we make limits our freedom of action and puts us deeper into an adversarial, winners-losers exchange.

Some managers search only for the best answer. A common error made is to assume that buried underneath all the negotiating ploys and positions is one "best" answer that will eventually emerge. In reality, most negotiations, particularly if they are to result in win-win outcomes, require us to broaden our search, not limit and focus it. For example, we may erroneously define the "best" answer to typically mean the best for our side, not the other party. It is important to acknowledge that all problems lend themselves to multiple solutions. Indeed, it is through consideration of those multiple solutions that we are most likely to attain one that is mutually satisfying.

Managers assume that there's only a "fixed pie." Is there really only a fixed set of alternatives available? Maybe not. It is common to lock into a "I win, you lose" scenario that virtually guarantees hardball negotiating with little or no effort made to seek creative solutions that are mutually satisfying.

Thinking that "solving their problem is their problem" is another roadblock. Negotiation breeds egocentrism. The greater our belief that negotiation consists of simply taking care of ourselves, the greater the likelihood that we will be unwilling to engage in any win-win solutions. Our position quickly becomes one of pure self-interest.

If these are some common problems that prevent win-win outcomes, what can be done to improve the negotiation process? There are some important guidelines that we can use to strengthen the relationship between the two parties and improve the likelihood of positive outcomes. Briefly, some options to consider when searching for win-win alternatives include positive and inclusive brainstorming, broadening options, and identification of shared interests.

The use of *positive and inclusive brainstorming* implies that once a negotiation process begins, *during its earliest phase* we seek to include the other party in a problem-solving session to identify alternative outcomes. This approach is a far cry from the typical tactic of huddling to plot negotiation strategies to use against the other team. In involving the other party in a brainstorming session, we seek to convince them that we perceive the problem as a mutually solvable one that requires input and creativity from both parties. Inviting the other party to a brainstorming session of this type has a powerfully disarming effect on their initial defensiveness. It demonstrates that we are interested not in beating the other side, but in solving the problem. Further, it reinforces the earlier point about the necessity of separating the people from the problem. In this way, both parties work in cooperation to find a mutually satisfactory solution that also serves to strengthen their relationship bonds.

The concept of *broadening options* is also a direct offshoot of the notion of brainstorming. Broadening our options requires us to be open to alternative positions and can be a natural result of focusing on interests rather than positions. The more I know about the other party's interests and am willing to dissect my own, the greater the probability that together we can work to create a range of options far broader than those we may initially be tempted to lock ourselves into.

Finally, a third technique for improving chances for win-win outcomes is to *identify shared interests*. A common negotiating approach employed by experienced bargainers is to sometimes table the larger items to a later point in the negotiation, focusing instead on minor or peripheral issues that offer a greater likelihood of reaching agreement. Once the two parties begin to work together to identify their shared interests and gain some confidence from working in a collaborative way, it is possible to reintroduce the larger sticking points. By this time both sides have begun to develop a working rhythm and a level of harmony that makes it easier to look for shared interests within these larger issues.

Insist on Using Objective Criteria

One of the best methods for ensuring that a negotiation proceeds along substantive lines is to frame the discussion around objective criteria.[37] Do not get bogged down in arguing perceptions or subjective evaluations. For example, a project manager recently almost had his new product development (NPD) project canceled because of protracted negotiations with a client over delivering an "acceptable" working prototype. Obviously, the project manager had a far different interpretation of the word *acceptable* than did the client. The project manager assumed that *acceptable* included normal bugs and preliminary technical problems whereas the client had used the word to imply error-free. In their desire to pin the onus of responsibility on the other, neither was willing to back away from her interpretation of the nebulous "acceptable."

Objective data and other measurable criteria often form the best basis for accurate negotiations. When firms or individuals argue costs, prices, work hours, and so on, they are using established standards and concepts that both parties can understand with a minimum of interpretation error. On the other hand, the more vague the terms employed or the more subjective the language, the greater the potential to be arguing at cross-purposes, even if both parties assume that the other is using the same interpretations of these terms.

Develop fair standards and procedures. Whatever standards are used as the basis of the negotiation need to be clearly spelled out and put in terms that are equally meaningful to both parties. This point is particularly relevant in cross-cultural negotiations in that different countries and cultures often attach different meaning to terms or concepts. For example, several American heavy construction firms, including Bechtel Corporation, lodged a protest against a number of Japanese construction firms for their collusion in dividing up biddable contracts (bid rigging) prior to a major airport project in Tokyo Bay. The Japanese companies argued in turn that they were fulfilling the terms of recent free-competition agreements by simply allowing Bechtel to submit a bid. Further, in Japanese society, there is nothing inherently illegal or unethical about engaging in this form of bid rigging. Clearly, both parties had very different interpretations of the idea of fair and clear bidding practices.

Fair standards and procedures require that both parties come together and negotiate from the same basic understanding of the terms and liabilities. In project management, this concept is particularly relevant because construction contracting requires a universally understood set of terms and standards. When the two parties are engaged in negotiating from the point of appropriate standards, it effectively eliminates the source of many potential misunderstandings or misinterpretations.

In visualizing the need to become adept at team building, conflict management, and negotiation, it is important to remember that the greatest challenges project managers typically face in running their projects are the myriad "people" challenges that result from the process of forming a diverse set of project members into a unified and collaborative team, whose goal is to pursue project success. Creating a team and initiating the project development process sows the seeds for a wide variety of conflicts among all project stakeholders. These conflicts are inevitable. They should be treated not as a liability, however, but as an opportunity. Conflict can lead to positive outcomes by solidifying team member commitment and motivation, and generating the energy to complete project activities.

Nevertheless, channeling conflict in appropriate ways requires a sure touch on the part of the project manager. Our ability to sustain influence and use negotiation in skillful ways is a great advantage in ensuring that team development and conflict serve not to derail the project but to renew it. Conflict is inevitable; it is not disastrous. Indeed, the degree to which a conflict disrupts a project's development depends upon the project manager's willingness to learn enough about conflict to deal with it effectively.

Summary

1. **Understand the steps involved in project team building.** The first step in project team building is the selection of personnel to staff the project team. This process can be complicated, particularly due to the high potential for conflict and negotiation with functional managers who may retain effective control over project team members. Following an analysis of skill requirements and staff availability, the team-building process typically involves matching the best people to the identified project tasks, while at the same time understanding the need to make these staffing decisions in collaboration with other top managers or departmental heads.
2. **Know the characteristics of effective project teams and why teams fail.** High-performing teams are typically characterized by (1) a clear sense of mission, (2) an understanding of interdependencies, (3) cohesiveness, (4) trust, (5) enthusiasm, and (6) a results orientation. On the other hand, teams that fail often do so due to poorly developed goals, poorly defined team roles, lack of motivation, poor communication, poor leadership, high project team turnover, and dysfunctional behavior.
3. **Know the stages in the development of groups.** Project teams do not begin their assignments as a unified, cohesive, and motivated body. Rather, their development is a challenge that must be effectively managed if we are to get maximum performance from the team. Teams go through some identifiable stages in their development process, and project managers need to recognize and seek to manage these developmental stages as efficiently as they can. One model of team development posits a five-stage approach—forming, storming, norming, performing, and adjourning—each with its unique challenges and group behaviors. An alternative model that has been validated through research argues that groups adopt a process of "punctuated equilibrium" as they evolve.
4. **Describe how to achieve cross-functional cooperation in teams.** Superordinate goals, rules and procedures, physical proximity, and accessibility are all important factors in motivating people to collaborate. The effects of this cross-functional cooperation are twofold: They can positively impact both project task outcomes and psychosocial project team results. Task outcomes positively affect the project at hand, while psychosocial outcomes mean that team members retain high positive attitudes toward the project experience and will enter new projects with strong motivation to succeed again.
5. **See the advantages and challenges of virtual project teams.** Virtual project teams are defined as the use of electronic media, including e-mail, the Internet, and teleconferencing, to link together members of a geographically dispersed project team, largely because of the globalization of project management. As multinational firms attempt to manage projects from geographically dispersed units, they need sophisticated technical media that support their communications and networking. The sheer physical barriers caused by globalization, coupled with the increase in multiorganizational project teams, have led to the increased use of virtual technologies to link team members. Two of the biggest challenges in effectively creating and managing virtual teams are establishing and reinforcing trust among team members and establishing effective communication patterns.
6. **Understand the nature of conflict and evaluate response methods.** Conflict is an inevitable result when team members with diverse functional backgrounds, personalities, experiences, and attitudes are brought together and expected to work collaboratively. Among the organizational causes of conflict are scarce resources, uncertainty over lines of authority, and differentiation. Interpersonal causes of conflict include faulty attributions, faulty communication, and personal grudges and prejudice. Conflict can be addressed through mediation, arbitration, control, acceptance, or elimination.
7. **Understand the importance of negotiation skills in project management.** Project managers routinely negotiate with a wide variety of organizational stakeholders for resources, contractual considerations, terms and conditions, and so forth. Effective project managers are often those individuals who approach negotiations in a systematic manner, taking the time to carefully analyze the nature of the negotiation, what they hope to achieve, and how much they are willing to offer to achieve their important goal. In principled negotiation, the primary objective is to seek win-win alternatives that allow both parties to negotiate to gain their goals.

Key Terms

Accessibility	Cross-functional cooperation	Goal-oriented conflict	Norming stage
Adjourning	Differentiation	Interaction	Orientation
Administrative conflict	Forming stage	Interdependencies	Outcomes
Cohesiveness	Frustration	Interpersonal conflict	Performing stage
Conflict		Negotiation	Physical proximity

Principled negotiation	Storming stage	Task outcomes	Trust
Psychosocial outcomes	Superordinate goal	Team building	Virtual teams
Punctuated equilibrium			

Discussion Questions

17.1 This chapter discussed the characteristics of high-performing project teams. List the factors that characterize these teams and give examples of each one.

17.2 "Trust can actually encourage disagreement and conflict among team members." Explain why this could be the case.

17.3 Identify the stages of group development. Why is it necessary for project teams to move through these stages in order to be productive?

17.4 Gersick's model of punctuated equilibrium offers an alternative view of group development. Why does she suggest that some defining moment (such as an explosion of emotion) often occurs about midpoint in the project? What does this defining event accomplish for the team?

17.5 Explain the concepts of "task" and "psychosocial" outcomes for a project. Why are psychosocial outcomes so important for project team members?

17.6 What are some of the barriers associated with managing virtual project teams? How could you overcome some of these barriers?

17.7 Imagine you are a project manager and two of your team members are refusing to collaborate on a critical work package. What method of conflict resolution would you use? Why?

17.8 List some examples of why a project manager may need to negotiate on a project.

17.9 Explain the idea that we should "focus on interests, not positions." Can you think of an example in which you successfully negotiated with someone else using this principle?

CASE STUDY 17.1

Columbus Instruments

Problems have been building at Columbus Instruments, Inc. (CIC) (not its real name) for several years now with the new product development process. The last six high-visibility projects were either scrapped outright after excessive cost and schedule overruns or, once released to the marketplace, were commercial disasters. The company estimates that in the past two years, it has squandered more than $15 million on poorly developed or failed projects. Every time a new project venture failed, the company conducted extensive post-project review meetings, documentation analysis, and market research to try to determine the underlying cause. To date, all CIC has been able to determine is that the problems appear to lie with the project management and development process. Something somewhere is going very wrong.

You have been called into the organization as a consultant to try to understand the source of the problems that are leading to widespread demoralization across the firm. After spending hours interviewing the senior project management staff and technical personnel, you are convinced that the problem does not lie with their processes, which are up-to-date and logical. On the other hand, you have some questions about project team productivity. It seems that every project has run late, has been over budget, and has had suboptimal functionality, regardless of the skills of the project manager in charge. This information suggests to you that there may be some problems in how the project teams are operating.

As you analyze CIC's project development process, you note several items of interest. First, the company is organized along strictly functional lines. Projects are staffed from the departments following negotiations between the project manager and the department heads. Second, the culture of CIC seems to place little status or authority on the project managers. As evidence of this fact, you note that they are not even permitted to write a performance evaluation on project team members: That right applies only to the functional department heads. Third, many projects require that team members be assigned to them on an exclusive basis; that is, once personnel have been assigned to a project, they typically remain with the project team on a full-time basis for the term of the project. The average project lasts about 14 months.

One morning, as you are walking the hallways, you notice a project team "war room" set up for the latest new product development initiative within the company. The war room concept requires that project team members be grouped together at a central location, away from their functional departments, for the life of the project. What intrigues you is a hand-lettered sign you see taped to the door of the project

(*continued*)

war room: "Leper Colony." When you ask around about the sign, some members of the firm say with a chuckle, "Oh, we like to play jokes on the folks assigned to new projects."

Further investigation of project team members suggests they are not amused by the sign. One engineer shrugs and says, "That's just their way of making sure we understand what we have been assigned to. Last week they put up another one that said 'Purgatory.'" When you ask the project manager about the signs later in the day, he confirms this story and adds some interesting information: "Around here, we use detached [meaning centralized] project teams. I get no say as to who will be assigned to the project, and lately the functional heads have been using our projects as a dumping ground for their poor performers."

When you question him further, the project manager observes, "Think about it. I have no say in who gets assigned to the team. I can't even fill out a performance review on them. Now, if you were a department head who was trying to offload a troublemaker or someone who was incompetent, what could be better than shipping them off to a project team for a year or so? Of course, you can imagine how they feel when they hear that they have been assigned to one of our project teams. It's as if you just signed their death warrant. Talk about low motivation!"

When you question various department heads about the project manager's assertions, to a person they deny that this is an adopted policy. As the head of finance puts it, "We give the project teams our best available people when they ask." However, they also admit that they have the final say in personnel assignment and project managers cannot appeal their choices for the teams.

After these discussions, you suggest to the CEO that the method of staffing projects may be a reason for the poor performance of CIC's new product development projects. He ponders the implications of how the projects have been staffed in his organization, and then says, "Okay, what do you suggest we do about it?"

Questions

1. What are the implications of CIC's approach to staffing project teams? Is the company using project teams as training grounds for talented fast-trackers or as dumping grounds for poor performers?
2. How would you advise the CEO to correct the problem? Where would you start?
3. Discuss how issues of organizational structure and power played a role in the manner in which project management declined in effectiveness at CIC.

CASE STUDY 17.2

The Bean Counter and the Cowboy

The morning project team meeting promised to be an interesting one. Tensions between the representative from marketing, Susan Scott, and finance, Neil Schein, have been building for several weeks now—in fact, since the project team was formed. As the project manager, you have been aware that Susan and Neil do not see eye to eye, but you figured that over time they would begin to appreciate each other's perspective and start cooperating. So far, unfortunately, that has not happened. In fact, it seems that hardly a day goes by when you do not receive a complaint from one or the other regarding the other team member's behavior, lack of commitment or cooperation, or general shoddy performance.

As the team gathers for the regular project status meeting, you start with an update on the project tasks, any problems the team members are having, and their assessment of the project's performance to date. Before you get too far into the meeting, Susan interrupts, saying, "John, I'm going to be out of town for the next 10 days visiting clients, so I can't make the status meetings either of the next two Fridays."

"That figures," Neil mutters loud enough for all to hear.

Susan whirls around. "I have another job around here, you know, and it involves selling. It may be convenient for you to drop everything and come to these meetings, but some of us have other responsibilities."

Neil shoots back, "That's been your excuse for missing half of the meetings so far. Just out of curiosity," he continues sarcastically, "how many more do you figure on blowing off while hanging out poolside on your little out-of-towners?"

Susan turns bright red. "I don't need to put up with that from you. You bean counters have no clue how this business works or who delivers value. You're so busy analyzing every penny that you have permanent eyestrain!"

"Maybe I could pay attention if I didn't have to constantly stay on the backs of you cowboys in sales," counters Neil. "I swear you would give our products away if it would let you make your quarterly numbers, even if it does drive us into the ground!"

You sit back, amazed, as the argument between Neil and Susan flares into full-scale hostility and threatens to spin out of control. The other team members are looking at you for your response. George, from engineering, has a funny expression on his face, as if to say, "Okay, you got us to this point. Now what are you going to do about it?"

"People," you rap on the table, "that's enough. We are done for today. I want to meet with Susan and Neil in my office in a half hour."

As everyone files out, you lean back in your seat and consider how you are going to handle this problem.

Questions

1. Was the argument today between Neil and Susan the true conflict or a symptom? What evidence do you have to suggest it is merely a symptom of a larger problem?
2. Explain how differentiation plays a large role in the problems that exist between Susan and Neil.
3. Develop a conflict management procedure for your meeting in 30 minutes. Create a simple script to help you anticipate the comments you are likely to hear from both parties.
4. Which conflict resolution style is warranted in this case? Why? How might some of the other resolution approaches be inadequate in this situation?

CASE STUDY 17.3

Johnson & Rogers Software Engineering, Inc.

Kate Thomas, a project manager with Johnson & Rogers Software Engineering, was looking forward to her first project team "meeting." She applied quotes to the term "meeting" because she would not actually be sitting down at a table with any of the other members of the project team. She had been assigned responsibility for a large software development project that would be using team members from both inside and outside the organization, none of whom were currently employed at the same Redlands, California, office where she worked. In fact, as she ticked off the names on the legal pad in front of her, she did not know whether to be impressed or apprehensive with the project she was about to kick off.

Vignish Ramanujam (senior programmer)—New Delhi, India
Anders Blomquist (systems designer)—Uppsala, Sweden
Sally Dowd (systems engineer)—Atlanta, Georgia
Penny Jones (junior programmer)—Bristol, England
Patrick Flynn (junior programmer)—San Antonio, Texas
Erik Westerveldt (subcontractor)—Pretoria, South Africa
Toshiro Akame (customer representative)—Kyoto, Japan

The challenge with this team, Kate quickly realized, was going to involve figuring out how to create an integrated project team with these people, most of whom she had never dealt with before. Although Sally and Patrick worked for Johnson & Rogers at other plant locations, the rest of the "team" were strangers. Erik, from South Africa, was critical for the project because his company had developed some of the specialized processes the project required and was to be treated as an industrial partner. The other members of the team had been assembled either by Erik or through contacts with senior members of her own firm. She did not know, but would soon discover, how they felt about the project and their level of commitment to it.

The first virtual project meeting was scheduled to start promptly at 9 AM Pacific Standard Time. That led to the first problem. As Kate stared at the camera mounted above the video monitor, she kept glancing down at the screen for signs that other members of the team had logged on. Finally, at 9:15, she was joined by Sally, with Toshiro logging in shortly afterward. As they chatted and continued to wait for other members to log on, time continued to pass. When, at 9:30, no one else had signed on, Kate asked the secretary to start making phone calls to verify that other members of the team were trying to access the system. Eventually, by 10:25, the team consisted of five members: Anders, Sally, Penny, Patrick, and Toshiro. It was decided that for the sake of getting something accomplished, those who were logged on would get started.

(continued)

The agenda that Kate had prepared and e-mailed out the day before was produced and the meeting began. Within 10 minutes, the video link to Penny was suddenly lost. The other team members waited for five minutes, shuffling in various states of impatience for Penny to rejoin the meeting. There was still no sign of Vignish or Erik.

The meeting quickly bogged down on technical details as those in attendance realized that several technical issues could not be resolved without input from the missing team members. Though he tried his best to hide it, it became apparent that Toshiro, in particular, was frustrated with the lack of progress in this meeting. Kate suggested that they adjourn until 11, while she made another attempt to contact the missing members, but Toshiro objected, saying, "That is 3 AM in my country. It is now past midnight here. I have been here today for 15 hours and I would like to get home." It was finally agreed to reconvene tomorrow at the same time. Toshiro agreed, but with bad grace: "Can we not find a time that is more accommodating to my schedule?" Kate promised to look into the matter.

The next day's meeting was a mixed success. Although everyone managed to log on to the system within a reasonable period, Penny's connection kept going down, to the exasperation of Vignish, the senior programmer. Although the meeting was conducted with great politeness by all parties, it was equally clear that no one was willing to offer their candid opinions of the project, the goals, and how the team was expected to execute their assignments. After asking members of the team for honest feedback and getting little response, Kate eventually dropped the point. In addition, she had a nagging feeling that there was some unspoken animosity in the manner in which Patrick and Sally interacted with each other.

After some general goal setting and a discussion of team responsibilities, Kate asked if there was a time when they could next meet. In the general silence that followed, Anders spoke up, asking, "Well, how often do you hope to meet like this? To be honest, it is inconvenient for me to attend these sessions regularly, as our telecom equipment is in Stockholm and I have to drive an hour each way."

Toshiro then spoke up as well. "I am sorry to repeat this point," he said, "but these meeting times are extremely inconvenient for me. Could we not find a time that is more generally acceptable?"

Kate replied, "Well, how about 5 PM my time. That's...," Kate paused and quickly consulted her personal planner, "9 in the morning for you."

This suggestion was met by a wave of objections, with the first from Penny who stated, "Uh, Kate, that would be 1 am here in England."

No sooner had she spoken than Anders, Erik, and Vignish chimed in, "Kate, that's 2 AM in Stockholm and Pretoria," and "Kate, are you aware that that is 6 AM here in New Delhi?"

Back and forth the team members argued, trying to find a reasonable time they could all meet. Finally, after going around the group several times to work out a mutually agreeable time for these teleconferences, Erik spoke up: "Maybe we don't all need to meet at the same time, anyway. Kate, why don't you just schedule meetings with each of us as you need to talk?"

Kate objected by saying, "Erik, the whole point of these teleconferences is to get the team together, not to hold one-on-one meetings with each of you."

Erik responded, "Well, all I know is that this is only the first videoconference and already it is becoming a burden."

Penny spoke up, "You're lucky. At least your system works. Mine keeps going up and down at this end."

"Okay, how about just using e-mails?" suggested Erik. "That way it does not matter what the time is at our location."

The other team members agreed that this idea made sense and seemed on the verge of endorsing the use of e-mails for communications. At this point, Kate stepped back into the discussion and stated firmly, "Look, that won't do. We need the opportunity to talk together. E-mails won't do that."

More arguing ensued. Eventually, the team members signed off, agreeing that they needed to "talk further" about these issues. Kate's reaction was one of disappointment and frustration. She sensed reluctance among the other members of the team to talk about these issues and to use the videoconferencing system in the manner she had envisioned. As Kate sat down to lunch that noon, she pondered how she should proceed from here.

Questions

1. How would you advise Kate to proceed? Analyze the conversation she had this morning. What went right? What went wrong?
2. What should Kate's next steps be?
3. How can she use the technology of the Internet and teleconferencing to enhance team development and performance?

Exercise in Negotiation

The following is a negotiation scenario between two firms: SteelFabrik, Inc. (SFI) and Building Contractors of Toledo (BCT). You are asked to take either SFI's or BCT's side of the negotiation. How would you prepare for this negotiation? How would you attempt to create a win-win outcome for both parties?

SteelFabrik's Perspective

You are the project manager for a new steel fabrication plant construction project being built by Building Contractors of Toledo (BCT). Your client is SteelFabrik, Inc. (SFI), a multinational steel products manufacturer. Your timetable calls for completion of the project in 18 months and you have a budget of $6 million. During the last few weeks, it has been increasingly difficult to deal with on-site demands from your client. SFI has insisted on a list of change orders to suit their immediate needs for the plant layout and design. Your counterpart says that because SFI is paying millions for the plant, they are entitled to make appropriate changes to the project for as long as is necessary to "get it right." You are concerned that every day spent in processing change orders adds further delay to your targeted completion date because engineering must approve the changes, design must alter the plans, and fabrication must change the plant's structure.

BCT is already in trouble on this project. In order to win the work, they significantly underbid their local competitors, leaving very little profit margin in the best-case scenario. Unfortunately, now with the list of change requests, both the budget and the schedule are being stretched to the limit. You are under increasing pressure from upper management to complete the job with the expected profit margin. You have $50,000 to work with and still meet your profitability goals. You are personally under pressure within your organization because your track record for the past three years has not been good—several projects that came in over budget and behind schedule have given top management reason to watch your performance on this project very closely. Although no one has said it out loud, you are fully aware that another significant overrun or delay could likely cost you your job with BCT.

Because you view SFI as a potential long-term customer, you are reluctant to simply refuse their demands. You know that a win-win outcome will likely bring future SFI business to your firm and could be the source of a profitable backlog of business for at least the next five years. Your own sales department is aware that this project with SFI could lead to future business and has added to your pressure by constantly stressing the importance of keeping the customer happy. As a result, you have important elements within your own organization, as well as with the customer, all expecting you to successfully complete the project to everyone's satisfaction.

While reading your e-mails over the weekend, you have come upon the latest set of change orders from SFI for adjustments to the plant layout to accommodate enhanced rail traffic into and out of the plant. These changes will require that the current construction work be halted, your own engineers and government regulators meet to discuss these requests, and new assembly and shipping areas be designed. Based on your experience, you estimate that the changes as requested will add $150,000 to the cost of the project and push the completion date back a minimum of six weeks. Worse, as you examine the change requests, you are convinced that these alterations are unnecessarily complicated and add no value to the plant's design. The final line of the e-mail is the most troubling: SFI expects these changes to be made immediately and will not allow any schedule slippage to accommodate them; in fact, they mention that it is imperative that the steel plant become operational on schedule. The only good news is that your sales department has found out that SFI may be willing to spend some additional money for the changes, but they aren't sure how much.

You have just typed out a short note scheduling a meeting for this Wednesday to negotiate an agreement on the requested changes. You are under strong pressure to reach a settlement that preserves BCT's profit margin, but at the same time you must keep SFI happy. As you sit at your home computer this Sunday afternoon, you are already dreading a return to work tomorrow morning. What approach should you take for the upcoming negotiations?

SFI's Perspective

You are a manager with SteelFabrik, Inc. (SFI) and are responsible for overseeing the construction of their fabrication plant in the northwest Ohio region. Recently your management informed you that because of new opportunities, this plant could be extremely valuable to their company, provided the rail spur connecting it with the freight rail system could be modified and upgraded to handle high-volume traffic into and out of the facility. This facility represents a significant investment by your company in the Midwest United States, following several years of contacts with local government officials trying to bring new jobs to the region. As a result, you feel you are entitled to make any necessary adjustments to the project to get the most use out of it. These change requests are, in your opinion, reasonable, necessary, and not prohibitively expensive. However, for the past several weeks, you have been experiencing increasing "push-back" from the BCT project manager to a series of relatively minor change requests. Her approach has been to ridicule the need for the changes, try to use low-cost "quick fixes," or simply talk you out of them. As a result, you are convinced that these latest change requests will also be resisted, and your overall relationship with the BCT project manager has become increasingly strained.

You have casually informed the BCT sales representative that this is the first in what your firm anticipates will be a series of similar plants to be constructed in the Great Lakes region over the next ten years. Although you made no commitments to doing future business with BCT, you have made it clear that successful performance on this project will make them the preferred choice for future work. After all, they understand your needs and have a demonstrated history of project success behind them.

You have been getting pressure from your top management, headquartered in Brussels, to complete the project on time; in fact, finishing on schedule is your greatest concern. SFI has already been bidding construction projects in the Great Lakes region and has several contracts pending, many of substantial size. Further, local politicians are anxious to show the project as an example of a successful public/private partnership and, with local elections coming up, are asking when they can announce its completion. Failure to have the plant ready on time puts you at risk of having to void a series of important construction contracts and slow down hiring, plus it would embarrass you and the region's government. Because the company's construction contract bids are still being reviewed, you are anxious to keep this information confidential to avoid attracting the attention of your competitors.

There is $250,000 in your budget to spend on additional change order costs if necessary, though you are keen to make the best possible impression with your top management by keeping costs as low as possible. You absolutely cannot agree to schedule extensions, however, because of all the pending bids and other pressures to finish the plant on time. Sources in the industry have strongly implied that BCT is in some financial difficulty and needs as much future work as they can get.

Your plant engineers have revised the transportation capacity requirements for the new plant and recommended significant changes to the shipping area to accommodate extra rail traffic. These changes are deemed critical because of the business model projections your firm has developed for getting maximum use and profit from the new fabrication plant. You have sent an e-mail with a detailed set of needed design and construction changes to the BCT project manager late Saturday night and just got back a note requesting a formal meeting on Wednesday morning to discuss these changes and find a way to "resolve our differences." You know that means that she is already trying to decide how to respond to your requests, and you are now planning for the negotiation. As you sit and reflect on the pressures you are feeling from Brussels, you wonder what approach you should use.

Internet Exercises

17.1 Click on the Web page for project teams at www.projectsmart.co.uk/five-steps-to-a-winning-project-team.php. Which of these five steps seem to be easier for a project manager to perform and which seem to be more difficult? Why? How do the ideas in this chapter compare to the advice given in a related link on "five essentials to project team success" at www.projectsmart.co.uk/5-essentials-to-project-team-success.php? What does this suggest about the importance of setting the stage for project success through team development?

17.2 Go to the Web site of a professional sports team and explore the site. What clues do you get regarding the importance of "teams" and "teamwork" from this site? Give two or three specific examples.

17.3 Go to the Web site for a pharmaceutical company. Explore the site, particularly information on new research. What kinds of project teams are used within pharmaceutical companies? Can you identify at least five functional areas within these organizations that should work together in a project team in order to develop a new drug?

17.4 Go to www.ebxml.org/project_teams/project_teams.htm and explore the projects and project teams listed. Notice the size and diversity of some of these project teams. What challenges would you find in attempting to bring these individuals together into a project team? How does the fact that some of the teams are made up of personnel from different organizations affect our best attempts to mold a project team?

17.5 Go to http://tele-immersion.citris-uc.org/ and explore the nature of the project working to develop tele-immersion technology. Connect to the link marked "Projects" and observe the different fields and uses for tele-immersion technology. What are projected advances and uses for this science into the future?

PMP CERTIFICATION SAMPLE QUESTIONS

1. The project manager is experiencing serious, deep-rooted conflict between two key project team members. It is apparent that these differences are based on different interpretations of the project's scope. Which conflict resolution approach would be the most useful for the project manager to employ?
   a. Compromising
   b. Withdrawal
   c. Punishment
   d. Problem solving

2. Which of the following is not an example of a team development strategy?
   a. Creating a WBS for the project
   b. Performance reviews
   c. Project team outing to a sporting event
   d. Team lunches

3. Two programmers are involved in a conflict that is threatening to disrupt the development of the project. The project manager calls the two programmers into her office and

reminds them that they are both "on the same side" in working to develop the software application for the company. Her conflict resolution style would best be seen as:

a. Arbitration
b. Defusion
c. Controlling the conflict
d. Eliminating the conflict

4. Carrie is from the marketing department and she has become increasingly upset with the attitude of the production member of the project team, Andrew. He seems to either ignore her opinions or make disparaging comments every time she speaks, usually referring to marketing in an unpleasant way. Which stage of group development is the project team addressing, as evidenced by the interactions of Carrie and Andrew?
   a. Norming
   b. Performing
   c. Storming
   d. Adjourning

5. Among the useful means to develop a sense of teamwork in personnel from different functional departments are all of the following EXCEPT:
   a. Colocation (physical proximity)
   b. Common goals
   c. Organizational rules governing their interaction
   d. Flexible working hours

Answers: 1. d—Problem solving would be the best alternative when the issues are not so much personal as they are perceptual (based on interpretation of the project's scope). Compromising would be a problem because it could lead to watering down the deliverables; 2. a—The other activities can all result in team development; 3. b—Because the project manager emphasizes commonalties and working together, this would be considered a method of conflict resolution through defusion; 4. c—They are clearly exhibiting behaviors that are associated with storming; 5. d—Flexible working hours have no impact on the willingness of personnel to work cooperatively with members of other departments.

Notes

1. Patel, P. (2009, December 9). "Engineers without borders," *IEEE Spectrum*. http://spectrum.ieee.org/geek-life/profiles/engineers-without-borders
2. Verma, V. K. (1996). *Human Resource Skills for the Project Manager*. Upper Darby, PA: Project Management Institute; Verma, V. K. (1997). *Managing the Project Team*. Newtown Square, PA: Project Management Institute.
3. Hoegl, M., and Parboteeah, K. P. (2003). "Goal setting and team performance in innovative projects: On the moderating role of teamwork quality," *Small Group Research*, 34: 3–19; McComb, S. A., and Green, S. G. (1999). "Project goals, team performance, and shared understanding," *Engineering Management Journal*, 11(3).
4. Pinto, J. K., and Prescott, J. E. (1988). "Variations in critical success factors over the stages in the project life cycle," *Journal of Management*, 14(1): 5–18.
5. Hartman, F. T. (2000). *Don't Park Your Brain Outside: A Practical Guide to Improving Shareholder Value Through SMART Management*. Newtown Square, PA: Project Management Institute; Karlsen, J. T., Grae, K., and Massaoud, M. J. (2008). "The role of trust in project-stakeholder relationships: A study of a construction project," *International Journal of Project Organization and Management*, 1: 105–118; Lander, M. C., Purvis, R. L., McCray, G. E., and Leigh, W. (2004). "Trust-building mechanisms utilized in outsourced IS development projects: A case study," *Information and Management*, 41: 509–28; Kadefors, A. (2004). "Trust in project relationships—inside the black box," *International Journal of Project Management*, 22: 175–82; Smyth, H. J., and Thompson, N. J. (2005). "Managing conditions of trust within a framework of trust," *Journal of Construction Procurement*, 11(1): 4–18.
6. Hartman, F. T. (2002). "Update on trust: A collection of trust-based research findings," in Slevin, D. P., Pinto, J. K., and Cleland, D. I. (Eds.), *Proceedings of the PMI Research Conference 2002*. Newtown Square, PA: Project Management Institute, pp. 247–53.
7. Gido, J., and Clements, J. P. (2003). *Successful Project Management*, 2nd ed. Mason, OH: South-Western.
8. Tuchman, B. W., and Jensen, M. A. (1977). "Stages in small group development revisited." *Group and Organizational Studies*, 2: 419–27.
9. Tuchman, B. W., and Jensen, M. A. (1977), ibid.
10. Verma, V. K. (1997). *Managing the Project Team*, p. 71, as cited in note 2.
11. Gersick, C. (1988). "Time and transition in work teams: Toward a new model of group development." *Academy of Management Journal*, 31: 9–41; Gersick, C. (1989). "Making time predictable transitions in task groups." *Academy of Management Journal*, 32: 274–309.
12. Pinto, M. B. (1988). *Cross-functional cooperation in the implementation of marketing decisions: The effects of superordinate goals, rules and procedures, and physical environment*. Unpublished doctoral dissertation, University of Pittsburgh, PA; Pinto, M. B., Pinto, J. K., and Prescott, J. E. (1993). "Antecedents and consequences of project team cross functional cooperation," *Management Science*, 39: 1281–97.
13. Sherif, M. (1958). "Superordinate goals in the reduction of intergroup conflict," *American Journal of Sociology*, 63(4): 349–56.
14. Galbraith, J. R. (1977). *Organization Design*. Reading, MA: Addison-Wesley.
15. Davis, T. E. (1984). "The influence of the physical environment in offices," *Academy of Management Review*, 9(2): 271–83.
16. Frame, J. D. (2002). *The New Project Management*, 2nd ed. San Francisco, CA: Jossey-Bass.
17. Tjosvold, D. (1993). *Teamwork for Customers: Building Organizations That Take Pride in Serving*. San Francisco, CA: Jossey-Bass; Logue, A. C. (2002). "Building and keeping the dream team," *PMNetwork*, 16(3): 30–36.
18. Adams, J. R., and Adams, L. L. (1997). "The virtual projects: Management of tomorrow's team today," *PMNetwork*, 11(1): 37–41; Kostner, J. (1994). *Knights of the Tele-Round*

Table. New York: Warner Books; Delisle, C. (2001). *Success and communication in virtual project teams*. Unpublished doctoral dissertation. Dept. of Civil Engineering, Project Management Specialization. University of Calgary, Calgary, Alberta; Fagerhaug, T. (2002). "Virtual project organizations—design of and challenges for," in Slevin, D. P., Pinto, J. K., and Cleland, D. I. (Eds.), *Proceedings of PMI Research Conference 2002*. Newtown Square, PA: Project Management Institute, pp. 217–23.

19. Coutu, D. L. (1998). "Organization: Trust in virtual teams," *Harvard Business Review*, 76(3): 20–21.

20. Smith, P. G., and Blank, E. L. (2002). "From experience: Leading dispersed teams," *Journal of Product Innovation Management*, 19: 294–304.

21. Smith, P. G., and Blank, E. L. (2002), ibid.

22. Lanier, J. (2001, April). "Virtually there: Three dimensional tele-immersion may eventually bring the world to your desk," *Scientific American*, 284(4): 66–75.

23. Ditlea, S. (2001, January). "Tele-immersion: Tomorrow's teleconferencing," *Computer Graphics World*, www.cgw.com; (2008). tele-immersion.citris-uc.org/video

24. Posner, B. Z. (1986). "What's all the fighting about? Conflicts in project management," *IEEE Transactions on Engineering Management*, EM-33: 207–11; Thamhain, H. J., and Wilemon, D. L. (1975). "Conflict management in project life cycles," *Sloan Management Review*, 16(3): 31–50; Thamhain, H. J., and Wilemon, D. L. (1977). "Leadership, conflict, and program management effectiveness," *Sloan Management Review*, 19(1): 69–89; Chan, M. (1989). "Intergroup conflict and conflict management in the R&D divisions of four aerospace companies," *IEEE Transactions on Engineering Management*, EM-36: 95–104; Adams, J. R., and Barndt, S. E. (1988). "Behavioral implications of the project life cycle," in Cleland, D. I., and King, W. R. (Eds.), *Project Management Handbook*, 2nd ed. New York: Van Nostrand Reinhold, pp. 206–30.

25. Thomas, K. W., and Schmidt, W. H. (1976). "A survey of managerial interests with respect to conflict," *Academy of Management Journal*, 10: 315–18.

26. Thomas, K. W. (1992). "Conflict and negotiation processes in organizations," in Dunnette, M. D. (Ed.), *Handbook of Industrial and Organizational Psychology*, 2nd ed. Palo Alto, CA: Consulting Psychologists Press, pp. 889–935; Pondy, L. (1968). "Organizational conflict: Concepts and models," *Administrative Science Quarterly*, 12: 296–320.

27. Thamhain, H. J., and Wilemon, D. L. (1975), as cited in note 24.

28. Verma, V. K. (1998). "Conflict management," in Pinto, J. K. (Ed.), *The Project Management Institute's Project Management Handbook*. San Francisco, CA: Jossey-Bass.

29. Verma, V. K. (1996), as cited in note 2; Robbins, S. P. (1974). *Managing Organizational Conflict: A Nontraditional Approach*. Englewood Cliffs, NJ: Prentice-Hall.

30. Thamhain, H. J., and Wilemon, D. L. (1975), as cited in note 24; Posner, B. Z. (1986), as cited in note 24.

31. Verma, V. K. (1998), as cited in note 28.

32. Ware, J. (1983). "Some aspect of problem-solving and conflict resolution in management groups," in Schlesinger, L. A., Eccles, R. G., and Gabarro, J. L. (Eds.), *Managing Behavior in Organization: Text, Cases, Readings*. New York: McGraw-Hill, pp. 101–15.

33. Slevin, D. P. (1989). *The Whole Manager*. New York: AMACOM.

34. Fisher, R., and Ury, W. (1981). *Getting to Yes: Negotiating Agreement Without Giving In*. New York: Houghton Mifflin.

35. Fisher, R., and Ury, W. (1981), ibid.

36. Fisher, R., and Ury, W. (1981), ibid.

37. Fisher, R., and Ury, W. (1981), ibid.

18

Implementation and Evaluation - Cost Management, Evaluation and Impact Analysis

Chapter Outline

Chapter Objectives

After completing this chapter, you should be able to:

1. Understand the various types of common project costs.
2. Recognize the difference between various forms of project costs.
3. Apply common forms of cost estimation for project work, including ballpark estimates and definitive estimates.
4. Understand the advantages of parametric cost estimation and the application of learning curve models in cost estimation.
5. Discern the various reasons why project cost estimation is often done poorly.
6. Apply both top-down and bottom-up budgeting procedures for cost management.
7. Understand the uses of activity-based budgeting and time-phased budgets for cost estimation and control.
8. Recognize the appropriateness of applying contingency funds for cost estimation.

PROJECT MANAGEMENT BODY OF KNOWLEDGE CORE CONCEPTS COVERED IN THIS CHAPTER

1. Plan Cost Management (PMBoK sec. 7.1)
2. Estimate Costs (PMBoK sec. 7.2)
3. Determine Budget (PMBoK sec. 7.3)
4. Control Costs (PMBoK sec. 7.4)

PROJECT PROFILE

Sochi Olympics—What's the Cost of National Prestige?

The Olympics happen every two years and the focus is usually centered mostly on the athletes, but 2012 proved to be different. Instead, topics of overspending, terroristic threats, graft and corruption in high places, and criminal activities took center stage during these winter games. With an initial budget set at $12 billion, the final price tag on the Sochi Olympics is estimated to have surpassed $51 billion, leaving many people scratching their heads. How could the Winter Games become so expensive and where did all the money go?

Previously, the most expensive games were the 2008 Beijing Summer Olympics. However, at an estimated price tag of $40 billion, that total was still far less than the Sochi Olympics. Summer Olympics are also generally more expensive than the Winter Games due to more events being conducted, the need for venue construction, and the higher housing costs for larger teams. When it comes to hosting the Olympics, it seems that preliminary budgets are quickly abandoned, with higher and higher price tags accruing. Countries view hosting the Olympics as an opportunity to showcase their national achievements, so little effort is made to spare expenses. Even by these standards, the Sochi Olympics set a new standard for profligate spending. Historically, the average budget overspending for Olympics between 1960 and 2012 is 179% in real terms and 324% in nominal terms. The final bill for the Sochi games is far worse than these historical averages.

In 2007, when Russia won the bid to host the Winter Olympics against fellow finalists from South Korea and Austria, it promised to spend $12 billion. Although this figure was reasonable (and perhaps even excessive) at the time, it was quickly overtaken by events involved in developing the Sochi site. The key question: How did the original budget of $12 billion become a final price tag of $51 billion? There are several reasons for the escalating cost of the Sochi Games, including:

1. Although host to the Winter Games, Sochi is actually a subtropical climate. Temperatures average 52 degrees in the winter and 75 degrees in the summer. There are even palm trees in this location. So the majority of the skiing events had to be held in the mountains of Krasnaya Polyana, a distance of about 25 miles from Sochi. The cost of constructing the roadway and infrastructure used to transport athletes and spectators back and forth came to a mind-boggling $9.4 billion. At a price of $220 million per kilometer, the roadway was more expensive than the entire budget of the 2010 Vancouver Winter Olympics.
2. Vladimir Putin, President of Russia, had the goal of developing Sochi as a world-class ski resort in an effort to attract winter tourism to the country. As a result, he was a highly visible spectator throughout the project's development, offering suggestions and criticisms of the work being done. Rework on several of the venues and facilities added to the final bill.
3. Fears of terrorism and other disruptions led to an unprecedented level of security around the Sochi site. For example, troops from Russia's Interior Ministry cordoned off the Olympic area to a depth of nearly 20 kilometers to enforce a safe-zone around the Games. The costs of heightened security added significantly to Sochi's costs.
4. Projects needed to be rebuilt several times due to difficulties with terrain or resource management. For example, state planners did not account for streams that ran beneath the location of the venues. This oversight caused an embankment near Olympic Park to collapse repeatedly due to constant flooding, each time having to be rebuilt. Likewise, construction of the ski jump was budgeted for $40 million. However, because of the complex terrain, the placement had to be adjusted many times. It was also alleged that the necessary geological tests were not conducted before construction started. Trees were removed as needed, leaving several structures constructed on fragile soil that was prone to reoccurring landslides, which caused more rebuilding. In the end, the ski jump was completed, but for $265 million, rather than the initial $40 million estimate.
5. Kickbacks and graft were rumored to be rampant during the years of development, with insiders getting "sweetheart" deals from the government, and cronyism running rampant.

How bad was the corruption? As journalist Brett Forrest noted: "The Sochi Internal Affairs department has conducted numerous investigations into Olympstroy [the Russian Olympic organizing commission] and filed criminal complaints, alleging that the Olympic agency and its contractors operated a kickback scheme related to the construction of the Olympic stadium, the main hockey rink, and various other properties. The total in stolen funds, according to prosecutors, approaches $800 million."

(continued)

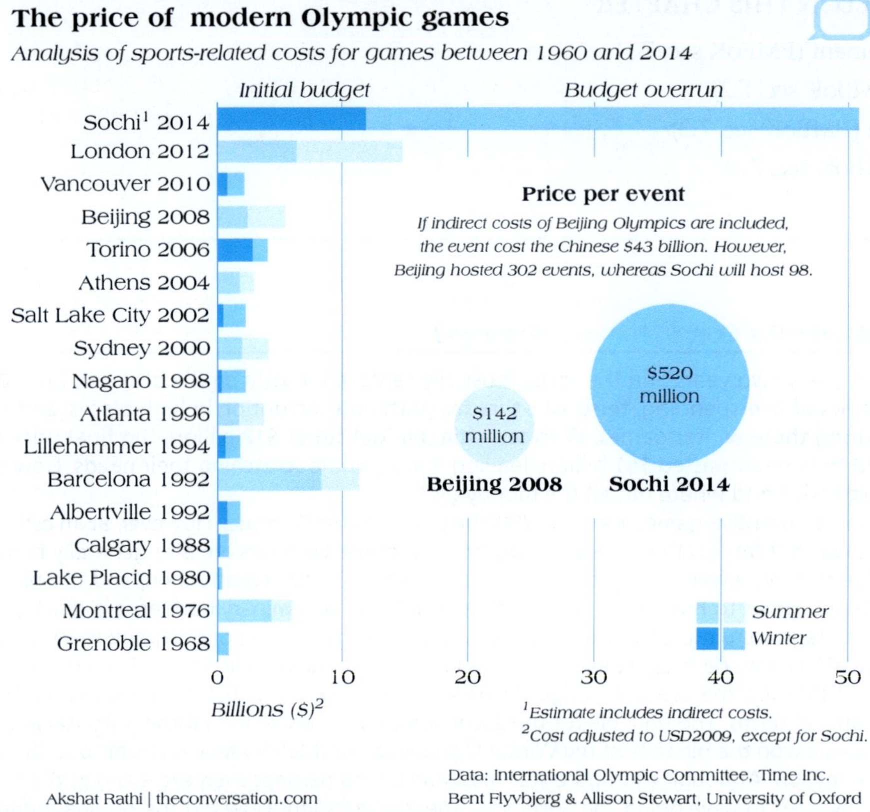

FIGURE 18.1 Sochi Winter Olympics Costs

Source: B. Flyvbjerg and A Stewart. (2012). "Olympic proportions: Cost and cost overrun at the Olympics 1960–2012." Said Business School Working Papers, Oxford: University of Oxford.

This may have been only the tip of the iceberg. Besides the speculated kickbacks, a green light was given to all development schemes around Sochi. Contractors sought to have their projects labeled "Olympic," knowing that way they would receive generous funding, including easements in zoning and building code regulations. There were also widespread allegations of cronyism, as friends and business associates of high-ranking Kremlin officials, including Vladimir Putin, received the choicest contracts. One opposition politician, Boris Nemtsov, criticized the substantial overspending, stating that the total amount embezzled or acquired by Putin's friends was in the range of $25–$30 billion, or more than half of the total budget for the Olympic Games. Construction companies that won contracts would have to inflate their projected costs in order to make the kickback payments to Russian State managers who had originally awarded the contracts. According to Nemtsov, it did not matter if the construction company had sufficient resources and skills for the project. What mattered was the company's willingness to return a percentage to the corrupt officials.

Many issues contribute to the reasons why these Olympics became so expensive. Russia had a concept that was budgeted at $12 billion when it started its preparations. History shows most nations exceed their budgets, though not to the excessive degree experienced by Russia in 2014. Ultimately, though, time is a relentless enemy of Olympic venue preparation; there is no possibility of extensions to the schedule. As a result, with the time moving closer to the opening of the Games, no expense could be (or was) spared in getting Sochi ready. Without question, enormous (and probably unknowable) sums disappeared to corruption and mismanagement. Nevertheless, the Sochi Games came on time and delivered a smoothly running experience to all who participated or came to watch. And yet, at a final price tag of $51 billion, one can still wonder about the costs of maintaining and enhancing national prestige.[1]

18.1 COST MANAGEMENT

Cost management is extremely important for running successful projects. The management of costs, in many ways, reflects the project organization's strategic goals, mission statement, and business plan. *Cost management* has been defined to encompass data collection, cost accounting, and cost control,[2] and it involves taking financial-report information and applying it to projects at finite levels of accountability in order to maintain a clear sense of money management for the project.[3] Cost accounting and cost control serve as the chief mechanisms for identifying and maintaining control over project costs.

Cost estimation is a natural first step in determining whether or not a project is viable; that is, can the project be done profitably? **Cost estimation** processes create a reasonable budget baseline for the project and identify project resources (human and material) as well, creating a time-phased budget for their involvement in the project. In this way, cost estimation and project budgeting are linked hand in hand: The estimates of costs for various components of the project are developed into a comprehensive project budgeting document that allows for ongoing project tracking and cost control.

During the development stage of the proposal, the project contractor begins cost estimation by identifying all possible costs associated with the project and building them into the initial proposal. While a simplified model of cost estimation might only require a bottom-line final figure, most customers will wish to see a higher level of detail in how the project has been priced out, that is, an itemization of all relevant costs. For example, a builder could simply submit to a potential home buyer a price sheet that lists only the total cost of building the house, but it is likely that the buyer will ask for some breakdown of the price to identify what costs will be incurred where. Some of the more common sources of project costs include:

1. ***Labor***—Labor costs are those associated with hiring and paying the various personnel involved in developing the project. These costs can become complex, as a project requires the services of various classifications of workers (skilled, semiskilled, laborers) over time. At a minimum, a project cost estimation must consider the personnel to be employed, salary and hourly rates, and any overhead issues such as pension or health benefits. A preliminary estimate of workers' exposure to the project in terms of hours committed is also needed for a reasonable initial estimate of personnel costs.
2. ***Materials***—Materials costs apply to the specific equipment and supplies the project team will require in order to complete project tasks. For building projects, materials costs are quite large and run the gamut from wood, siding, insulation, and paint to shrubbery and paving. For many other projects, the actual materials costs may be relatively small, for example, the purchase of a software package that allows rapid compiling of computer code. Likewise, many projects in the service industries may involve little or no materials costs whatsoever. Some materials costs can be charged against general company overhead; for example, the use of the firm's mainframe computer may be charged to the project on an "as used" basis.
3. ***Subcontractors***—When subcontractors provide resources (and in the case of consultants, expertise) for the project, their costs must be factored into the preliminary cost estimate for the project and be reflected in its budget. One subcontractor cost, for example, could be a charge to hire a marketing communications professional to design the project's promotional material; another might be costs for an industrial designer to create attractive product packaging.
4. ***Equipment and facilities***—Projects may be developed away from the firm's home office, requiring members of the project team to work "off site." Firms commonly include rental of equipment or office facilities as a charge against the cost of the project. For example, oil companies routinely send four- or five-person site teams to work at the headquarters of major subcontractors for extended periods. The rental of any equipment or facility space becomes a cost against the project.
5. ***Travel***—If necessary, expenses that are related to business travel (car rentals, airfare, hotels, and meals) can be applied to the project as an up-front charge.

Another way to examine project costs is to investigate the nature of the costs themselves. Among the various forms of project costs are those related to type (direct or indirect), frequency of occurrence (recurring or nonrecurring), opportunity to be adjusted (fixed or variable), and schedule (normal or expedited). We will examine each of these types of project costs in turn in this chapter.

Direct Versus Indirect Costs

Direct costs are those clearly assigned to the aspect of the project that generated the cost. Labor and materials may be the best examples. All labor costs associated with the workers who actually build a house are considered direct costs. Some labor costs, however, might not be viewed as direct costs for the project. For example, the costs of support personnel, such as the project's cost accountant or other project management resources, may not be allocated directly, particularly when their duties consist of servicing or overseeing multiple, simultaneous projects. In a nonproject setting such as manufacturing, it is common for workers to be assigned to specific machinery that operates on certain aspects of the fabrication or production process. In this case, labor costs are directly charged against work orders for specific parts or activities.

The formula for determining total direct labor costs for a project is straightforward:

$$\text{Total direct labor costs} = (\text{Direct labor rate})\ (\text{Total labor hours})$$

The direct costs of materials are likewise relatively easy to calculate, as long as there is a clear understanding of what materials are necessary to complete the project. For example, the direct costs of building a bridge or hosting a conference dinner for 300 guests can be estimated with fair accuracy. These costs can be applied directly to the project in a systematic way; for example, all project purchase orders (POs) can be recorded upon receipt of bills of materials or sales and applied to the project as a direct cost.

Indirect costs, on the other hand, generally are linked to two features: overhead, and selling and general administration. Overhead costs are perhaps the most common form of indirect costs and can be one of the more complex forms in estimating. Overhead costs include all sources of indirect materials, utilities, taxes, insurance, property and repairs, depreciation on equipment, and health and retirement benefits for the labor force. Common costs that fall into the selling and general administration category include advertising, shipping, salaries, sales and secretarial support, sales commissions, and similar costs. Tracing and linking these costs to projects is not nearly as straightforward as applying direct costs, and the procedures used vary by organization. Some organizations charge a flat rate for all overhead costs, relative to the direct costs of the project. For example, some universities that conduct research projects for the federal government use a percentage multiplier to add administrative and overhead indirect costs to the proposal. The most common range for such indirect multiplier rates is from 20% to over 50% on top of direct costs. Other firms allocate indirect costs project by project, based on individual analysis. Whichever approach is preferred, it is important to emphasize that all project cost estimates include both direct and indirect cost allocations.

EXAMPLE 18.1 Developing Fully Loaded Labor Costs

Suppose that we are attempting to develop reasonable cost estimation for the use of a senior programmer for a software project. The programmer is paid an annual salary of $75,000, which translates to an hourly rate of approximately $37.50/hour. The programmer's involvement in the new project is expected to be 80 hours over the project's life. Remember, however, that we also need to consider overhead charges. For example, the company pays comprehensive health benefits and retirement, charges the use of plant and equipment against the project, and so forth. In order to cover these indirect costs, the firm uses an overhead multiplier of 65%. Employing an overhead multiplier is sometimes referred to as the *fully loaded* rate for direct labor costs. Thus, the most accurate calculation of the programmer's charge against the project would look like this:

$$\underset{(\$37.50)}{\text{Hourly rate}} \times \underset{(80)}{\text{Hours needed}} \times \underset{(1.65)}{\text{Overhead charge}} = \underset{\$4{,}950}{\text{Fully loaded labor cost}}$$

Some have argued that a more realistic estimate of fully loaded labor costs for each person assigned to the project would reflect the fact that no one truly works a full 8-hour day as part of the job. An allowance for a reasonable degree of personal time during the workday is simply recognition of the need to make personal calls, have coffee breaks, walk the hallways to the restroom, and so forth. Meredith and Mantel (2003) have argued that if such personal time is not included in the original total labor cost estimate, a multiplier of 1.12 should be used to reflect this charge, increasing the fully loaded labor cost of our senior programmer to:[4]

Hourly rate	×	Hours needed	×	Overhead charge	×	Personal Time	=	Fully loaded labor cost
($37.50)		(80)		(1.65)		(1.12)		$5,544

One other point to consider regarding the use of overhead (indirect costs) involves the manner in which overhead may be differentially applied across job categories. In some firms, for example, a distinction is made between salaried and nonsalaried employees. Thus, two or more levels of overhead percentage may be used, depending upon the category of personnel to which they are applied. Suppose that a company applied a lower overhead rate (35%) to hourly workers, reflecting the lesser need for contributions to retirement or health insurance. The calculated fully loaded labor cost for these personnel (even assuming a charge for personal time) would resemble the following:

Hourly rate	×	Hours needed	×	Overhead charge	×	Personal Times	=	Fully loaded labor cost
($12.00)		(80)		(1.35)		(1.12)		$1,451.52

The decision to include personal time requires input from the project's client. Whichever approach is taken, a preliminary total labor cost budget table can be constructed when the process is completed, as shown in Table 18.1. This table assumes a small project with only five project team personnel, whose direct labor costs are to be charged against the project without a personal time charge included.

Recurring Versus Nonrecurring Costs

Costs can also be examined in terms of the frequency with which they occur; they can be recurring or nonrecurring. **Nonrecurring costs** might be those associated with charges applied once at the beginning or end of the project, such as preliminary marketing analysis, personnel training, or outplacement services. **Recurring costs** are those that typically continue to operate over the project's life cycle. Most labor, material, logistics, and sales costs are considered recurring because some budgetary charge is applied against them throughout significant portions of the project development cycle. In budget management and cost estimation, it is necessary to highlight recurring versus nonrecurring charges. As we will see, this becomes particularly important as we begin to develop time-phased budgets—those budgets that apply the project's baseline schedule to projected project expenditures.

Fixed Versus Variable Costs

An alternative designation for applying project costs is to identify fixed and variable costs in the project budget. **Fixed costs**, as their title suggests, do not vary with respect to their usage.[5] For example, when leasing capital equipment or other project hardware, the leasing price is likely not

TABLE 18.1 Preliminary Cost Estimation for Fully Loaded Labor

Personnel	Title	Salary (Hourly)	Hours Needed	Overhead Rate Applied	Fully Loaded Labor Cost
Linda	Lead Architect	$35/hr	250	1.60	$14,000.00
Alex	Drafter—Junior	$20/hr	100	1.60	3,200.00
Jessica	Designer—Intern	$8.50/hr	80	1.30	884.00
Todd	Engineer—Senior	$27.50/hr	160	1.60	7,040.00
Thomas	Foreman	$18.50/hr	150	1.30	3,607.50
Total					$28,731.50

TABLE 18.2 Cost Classifications

	Type		Frequency		Adjustment		Schedule	
Costs	**Direct**	**Indirect**	**Recurring**	**Nonrecurring**	**Fixed**	**Variable**	**Normal**	**Expedited**
Direct Labor	X		X		X		X	
Building Lease		X	X		X		X	
Expediting Costs	X			X		X		X
Material	X		X			X	X	

to go up or down with the amount of usage the equipment receives. Whether a machine is used for 5 hours or 50, the cost of its rental is the same. When entering fixed-rate contracts for equipment, a common decision point for managers is whether the equipment will be used sufficiently to justify its cost. **Variable costs** are those that accelerate or increase through usage; that is, the cost is in direct proportion to the usage level. Suppose, for example, we used an expensive piece of drilling equipment for a mining operation. The equipment degrades significantly as a result of use in a particularly difficult geographical location. In this case, the variable costs of the machinery are in direct proportion to its use. It is common, in many cases, for projects to have a number of costs that are based on fixed rates and others that are variable and subject to significant fluctuations either upward or downward.

Normal Versus Expedited Costs

Normal costs refer to those incurred in the routine process of working to complete the project according to the original, planned schedule agreed to by all project stakeholders at the beginning of the project. Certainly, this planned schedule may be very aggressive, involving extensive overtime charges in order to meet the accelerated schedule; nevertheless, these costs are based on the baseline project plan. **Expedited costs** are unplanned costs incurred when steps are taken to speed up the project's completion. For example, suppose the project has fallen behind schedule and the decision is made to "crash" certain project activities in the hopes of regaining lost time. Among the **crashing** costs could be expanded use of overtime, hiring additional temporary workers, contracting with external resources or organizations for support, and incurring higher costs for transportation or logistics in speeding up materials deliveries.

All of the above methods for classifying costs are linked together in Table 18.2.[6] Across the top rows are the various classification schemes, based on cost type, frequency, adjustment, and schedule. The left-side column indicates some examples of costs incurred in developing a project. Here we see how costs typically relate to multiple classification schemes; for example, direct labor is seen as a direct cost, which is also recurring, fixed, and normal. A building lease, on the other hand, may be classified as an indirect (or overhead) cost, which is recurring, fixed, and normal. In this way, it is possible to apply most project costs to multiple classifications.

18.2 COST ESTIMATION

Estimating project costs is a challenging process that can resemble an art form as much as a science. Two important project principles that can almost be called laws are at work in cost estimation. First, the more clearly you define the project's various costs in the beginning, the less chance there is of making estimating errors. Second, the more accurate your initial cost estimations, the greater the likelihood of preparing a project budget that accurately reflects reality for the project and the greater your chances of completing the project within budget estimates.

One key for developing project cost estimates is to first recognize the need to cost out the project on a disaggregated basis; that is, to break the project down by deliverable and work package as a method for estimating task-level costs. For example, rather than attempt to create a cost estimate for completing a deliverable of four work packages, it is typically more accurate to first identify the costs for completing each work package individually and then create a deliverable cost estimate, as Table 18.3 illustrates.

TABLE 18.3 Disaggregating Project Activities to Create Reasonable Cost Estimates

Project Activities	Estimated Cost
Deliverable 1040—Site Preparation	
Work Package 1041—Surveying	$ 3,000
Work Package 1042—Utility line installation	15,000
Work Package 1043—Site clearing	8,000
Work Package 1044—Debris removal	3,500
Total cost for Deliverable 1040	$29,500

Companies use a number of methods to estimate project costs, ranging from the highly technical and quantitative to the more qualitative approaches. Among the more common cost estimation methods are the following:[7]

1. **Ballpark estimates**—Sometimes referred to as *order of magnitude* estimates, ballpark estimates are typically used when either information or time is scarce. Companies often use them as preliminary estimates for resource requirements or to determine if a competitive bid can be attempted for a project contract. For example, a client may file an RFQ (request for quote) for competitive bids on a project, stating a very short deadline. Managers would have little time to make a completely accurate assessment of the firm's qualifications or requirements, but they could still request ballpark estimates from their personnel to determine if they should even attempt to bid the proposal through a more detailed analysis. The unofficial rule of thumb for ballpark estimates is to aim for an accuracy of ±30%. With such a wide variance plus or minus, it should be clear that ballpark estimates are not intended to substitute for more informed and detailed cost estimation.
2. **Comparative estimates**—Comparative estimates are based on the assumption that historical data can be used as a frame of reference for current estimates on similar projects. For example, Boeing Corporation routinely employs a process known as **parametric estimation**, in which managers develop detailed estimates of current projects by taking older work and inserting a multiplier to account for the impact of inflation, labor and materials increases, and other reasonable direct costs. This parametric estimate, when carefully performed, allows Boeing to create highly accurate estimates when costing out the work and preparing detailed budgets for new aircraft development projects. Even in cases where the technology is new or represents a significant upgrade over old technologies, it is often possible to gain valuable insight into the probable costs of development, based on historical examples.

   Boeing is not the only firm that has successfully employed parametric cost estimation. Figure 18.2 shows a data graph of the parametric estimation relating to development of the Concorde aircraft in the 1960s. The Concorde represented such a unique and innovative airframe design that it was difficult to estimate the amount of design time required to complete the schematics for the airplane. However, using parametric estimation and based on experiences with other recently developed aircraft, a linear relationship was discovered between the number of fully staffed weeks (Concorde referred to this time as "manweeks") needed to design the aircraft and its projected cruising speed. That is, the figure demonstrated a direct relationship between the cruising speed of the aircraft and the amount of design time necessary to complete the schematics. Using these values, it was possible to make a reasonably accurate cost projection of the expected budget for design, demonstrating that in spite of significant changes in airplane design over the past decades, the relationship between cruising speed and design effort had held remarkably steady.

   Effective comparative estimates depend upon some important supplementary sources including a history of similar projects and a detailed archive of project data that includes the technical, budgetary, and other cost information. Adjusting costs to account for inflation simply becomes a necessary step in the process. The key to making comparative estimates meaningful lies in the comparability to previous project work. It makes little sense to compare direct labor costs for two projects when the original was done in a foreign country with different wage rates, overhead requirements, and so forth. Although some argue that comparative cost estimation cannot achieve a degree of accuracy closer

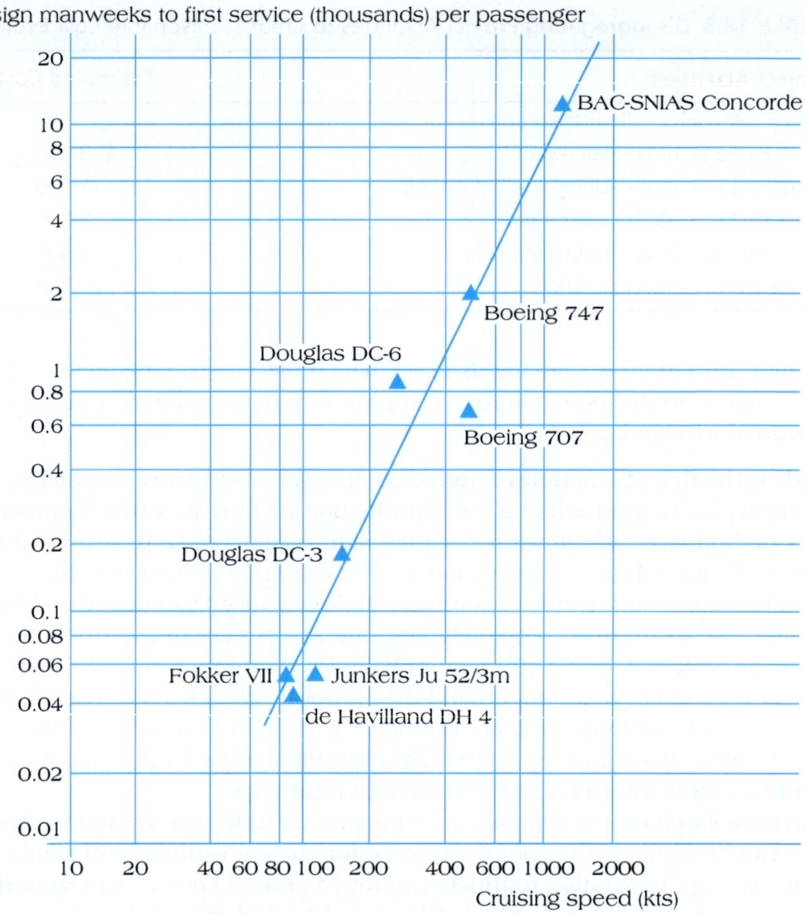

FIGURE 18.2 Parametric Estimate for Design Costs for Concorde

Note: Plot of design effort versus cruising speed for significant commercial aircraft types.

than ±15%, in some circumstances the estimate may be much more accurate and useful than that figure indicates.

3. **Feasibility estimates**—These estimates are based as a guideline on real numbers, or figures derived after the completion of the preliminary project design work. Following initial scope development, it is possible to request quotes from suppliers and other subcontractors with a greater degree of confidence, particularly as it is common to engage in some general scheduling processes to begin to determine the working project baseline. Feasibility estimates are routinely used for construction projects, where there are published materials cost tables that can give reasonably accurate cost estimates for a wide range of project activities based on an estimate of the quantities involved. Because they are developed farther down the life cycle, feasibility estimates are often expressed in terms of a degree of accuracy of ±10%.
4. **Definitive estimates**—These estimates can be given only upon the completion of most design work, at a point when the scope and capabilities of the project are quite well understood. At this point all major purchase orders have been submitted based on known prices and availabilities, there is little or no wiggle room in the project's specifications, and the steps to project completion have been identified and a comprehensive project plan is in place. Because it is understood that cost estimation should naturally improve with time, as more information becomes available and fewer project unknowns remain unresolved, definitive estimates should accurately reflect the expected cost of the project, barring unforeseen circumstances, at completion. Hence, definitive estimates can be expected to have an accuracy of ±5%. We saw in previous chapters that some projects may offer very thin profit margins; for example, in the case of fixed-cost contracts, the project organization assumes almost all risk for completing the project according to originally agreed-on contract terms. As a result, the better the job we do in estimating costs, the more likely we will be to maintain the profit margin contracted.

Which cost estimation approach should a project organization employ? The answer to this question presupposes knowledge of the firm's industry (e.g., software development vs. construction), ability to account for and manage most project cost variables, the firm's history of successful project management, the number of similar projects the firm has completed in the past, the knowledge and resourcefulness of project managers, and the company's budgeting requirements. In some instances (e.g., extremely innovative research and development projects), it may be impossible to create cost estimates with more than a ±20% degree of accuracy. On the other hand, in some projects such as events management (e.g., managing a conference and banquet), it may be reasonable to prepare definitive budgets quite early in the project. For example, while cost estimation can involve significant calculations and some amount of guesswork for certain types of projects, in other cases, project managers and cost estimators are able to calculate project costs with a much greater degree of accuracy. Many construction projects, particularly in standard residential and commercial building, employ estimates based on relatively stable historical data that makes it much easier to determine costs with good accuracy. To illustrate, Internet sites such as RSMeans.com, developed by Reed Construction Data, or CostDataOnLine.com include building cost calculators that are able to predict construction costs (including assumptions about labor rates, cost of living adjustments for location, square footage, type of building) with a reasonable degree of accuracy (see Figure 18.3).

RSMeans QuickCost Estimator

Project Title:	Sample Project
Model:	Apartment, 1-3 Story
Construction:	Face Brick with Concrete Block Back-up/Wood Joists
Location:	VANCOUVER, BC
Stories:	3
Story Height (l.f.):	10
Floor Area (s.f.):	2,500
Data Release:	Year 2012 Quarter 3
Wage Rate:	Union
Basement:	Not included

Costs are derived from a building model with basic components. Scope differences and market conditions can cause costs to vary significantly.

Cost Ranges	Low	Med	High
Total:	$826,650	$918,500	$1,148,125
Contractor's Overhead & Profit:	$206,550	$229,500	$286,875
Architectural Fees:	$82,800	$92,000	$115,000
Total Building Cost:	$1,116,000	$1,240,000	$1,550,000

Do You Need a More Comprehensive Estimate With Current Cost Data and Your Own Detailed Project Specifications?

Access the Custom Cost Estimator, a paid subscription service, to reference a comprehensive library of square foot models updated and localized for the United States to create a customized online estimate specific to your individual project! - All from RSMeans, ***The Industry Source!***

(click here to view a sample report)

Important note: *These costs are not exact and are intended only as a preliminary guide to possible project cost. Actual project cost may vary greatly depending on many factors. RSMeans uses diligence in preparing the information contained here. RSMeans does not make any warranty or guarantee as to the accuracy, correctness, value, sufficiency or completeness of the data or resulting project cost estimates. RSMeans shall have no liability for any loss, expense or damage arising out of or in connection with the information contained herein.*

FIGURE 18.3 Sample Cost Estimator Using RSMeans.com Web Site

Source: Copyright RSMeans 2014- RSMeans Square Foot Models www.rsmeans.com/estimator/qce/qce_result.asp

ESTIMATE AND QUOTATION SHEET				
Project No.	Description:		Type No.	
Work Package No.	Task No.		Estimate No.	
Work Package Description:		Task Description:		
Internal Labor				
Skill	Category	Rate	Hours	Cost
Senior Test Engineer	TE4	18.50	40	$ 740.00
Test Engineer	TE3	14.00	80	1,120.00
Fitter	PF4	13.30	30	399.00
Drafter	DR2	15.00	15	225.00
Drawing Checker	DR3	16.50	3	49.50
Subtotal, Hours and Costs			168	$2,533.50
Labor Contingency (10%)			17	254.00
Total Labor, Hours and Costs			185	$2,787.50
Overhead (80%)				2,230.00
Gross Labor Cost				$5,017.50
Bought-Out Costs				
Materials (Specify): Bolts plus cleating material				$ 20.00
Finished Goods (Specify): N/A				
Services and Facilities: Hire test house; instrumentation plus report				12,300.00
Subcontract Manufacture (Specify): Fixture and bolt modification				250.00
Subtotal				$12,570.00
Contingency (15%)				1,885.50
Total Bought-Out Costs				$14,455.50
Expenses				
Specify: On-site accommodation plus traveling				$ 340.00
Total Bought-Out Costs and Expenses				$14,795.50
Profit %: N/A				
Total Quoted Sum: Gross Labor plus Bought-Out Costs and Expenses				$19,813.00
Compiled by:				
Approved:			Date	

FIGURE 18.4 Sample Project Activity Cost Estimating Sheet

The key to cost estimation lies in a realistic appraisal of the type of project one is undertaking, the speed with which various cost estimates must be created, and the comfort level top management has with cost estimation error. If the information is available, it is reasonable to expect the project team to provide as accurate a cost estimate as possible, as early in the project as possible. Figure 18.4 shows a sample project cost estimation form.

Learning Curves in Cost Estimation

Cost estimation, particularly for labor hours, often takes as its assumption a steady or uniform rate at which work is done. In the case of having to perform multiple activities, the amount of time necessary to complete the first activity is not significantly different from the time necessary to complete the nth activity. For example, in software development, it may be considered standard practice to estimate each activity cost independently of other, related activities with which the programmer is involved. Therefore, in the case of a programmer required to complete four work assignments, each involving similar but different coding activities, many cost estimators will simply apply a direct, multiplicative rule-of-thumb estimate:

Cost of activity	×	Number of times activity is repeated	=	Total cost estimate
($8,000)		(4)		$32,000

When we calculate that each actual coding sequence is likely to take approximately 40 hours of work, we can create the more formal direct cost budget line for this resource. Assuming an overhead rate of .60 and a cost per hour for the programmer's services of $35/hour, we can come up with a direct billing charge of:

$$\frac{\text{Wage}}{(\$35/\text{hr})} \times \frac{\text{Unit}}{(4\text{ iterations})} \times \frac{\text{Overhead Rate}}{(1.60)} \times \frac{\text{Hours/Unit}}{(40\text{ hours})} = \$8{,}960$$

Although this rule of thumb is simple, it may also be simplistic. For example, is it reasonable to suppose that in performing similar activities, the time necessary to do a coding routine the fourth time will take as long as it took to do it the first time? Or is it more reasonable to suppose that the time needed (and hence, cost) of the fourth iteration should be somewhat shorter than the earlier times?

These questions go to the heart of a discussion of how **learning curves** affect project cost estimation.[8] In short, experience and common sense teach us that repetition of activities often leads to reduction in the time necessary to complete the activity over time. Some research, in fact, supports the idea that performance improves by a fixed percentage each time production doubles.[9]

Let us assume, for example, that the time necessary to code a particular software routine is estimated at 20 hours of work for the first iteration. Doing the coding work a second time requires only 15 hours. The difference between the first and second iteration suggests a learning rate of .75 (15/20). We can now apply that figure to estimates of cost for additional coding iterations. When output is doubled from the first two routines to the required four, the time needed to complete the fourth unit is now estimated to take:

$$15 \text{ hrs. } (.75) = 11.25 \text{ hours}$$

These time and cost estimates follow a well-defined formula,[10] which is the time required to produce the steady state unit of output, and is represented as:

$$Y_x = aX^b$$

where

Y_x = the time required for the steady state, x, unit of output
a = the time required for the initial unit of output
X = the number of units to be produced to reach the steady state
b = the slope of the learning curve, represented as: log decimal learning rate/log 2

Assume the need to conduct a project cost estimation in the case of construction, where one resource will be tasked to perform multiple iterations of a similar nature (e.g., fitting, riveting, and squaring). The worker must do a total of 15 of these activities to reach the steady state. Also assume that the time estimated to perform the last iteration (the steady state) is 1 hour, and we know from past experience the learning rate for this highly repetitive activity is .60. In calculating the time necessary to complete the first activity, we would apply these values to the formula to determine the value of a, the time needed to complete the task the first time:

$$\begin{aligned} b &= \log 0.60/\log 2 \\ &= -0.2219/0.31 \\ &= -0.737 \\ 1\text{ hr.} &= a(15)^{-0.737} \\ a &= 7.358\text{ hours} \end{aligned}$$

Note that the difference between the first and fifteenth iteration of this activity represents a change in duration estimation (and therefore, cost) from over 7 hours for the first time the task is performed to 1 hour for the steady state. The difference this learning curve factor makes in project cost estimates can be significant, particularly when a project involves many instances of repetitive work or large "production runs" of similar activities.

EXAMPLE 18.2 Learning Curve Estimates

Let's return to the earlier example where we are trying to determine the true cost for the senior programmer's time. Recall that the first, linear estimate, in which no allowance was made for the learning curve effect, was found to be:

$$(\$35/\text{hr})\ (4\text{ iterations})\ (1.60)\ (40\text{ hours}) = \$8{,}960$$

Now we can apply some additional information to this cost estimate in the form of better knowledge of learning-rate effects. Suppose, for example, that the programmer's learning rate for coding is found to be .90. The steady state time to code the sequence is 40 hours. Our estimate of the time needed for the first coding iteration is:

$$\begin{aligned} b &= \log 0.90/\log 2 \\ &= -0.0458/0.301 \\ &= -0.1521 \end{aligned}$$

$$\begin{aligned} 40\text{ hrs.} &= a(4)^{-0.1521} \\ a &= 49.39\text{ hours} \end{aligned}$$

Thus, the first unit would take 9.39 hours longer than the steady state 40 hours. For this programming example, we can determine the appropriate unit and total time multipliers for the calculated initial unit time by consulting tables of learning curve coefficients (multipliers) derived from the formula with $a = 1$. We can also calculate unit and total time multipliers by identifying the unit time multipliers from 1 to 3 units of production (coding sequences) with a learning rate of .90. We use the units 1 to 3 because we assume that by the fourth iteration, the programmer has reached the steady state time of 40 hours. Based on $a = 1$, the unit time learning curve coefficients are $1^{-0.5121} = 1$, $2^{-0.1521} = 0.90$, and $3^{-0.1521} = .846$, for a total time multiplier of 2.746. Therefore, the time needed to code the first three sequences is:

Total time multiplier		Time required for initial unit		Total time to program first three sequences
(2.746)	×	(49.39)	=	135.62 hours

Because the steady state time of 40 hours occurs for the final coding iteration, total coding time required for all four sequences is given as:

$$135.62 + 40 = 175.62$$

The more accurate direct labor cost for the coding activities is:

$$\begin{array}{c}\text{Wage}\\(\$35/\text{hr})\end{array} \times \begin{array}{c}\text{Overhead Rate}\\(1.60)\end{array} \times \begin{array}{c}\text{Total Hours}\\(175.62\ \text{hours})\end{array} = \$9{,}834.72$$

Compare this figure to the original value of $8,960 we had calculated the first time, which understated the programming cost by $874.72. The second figure, which includes an allowance for learning curve effects, represents a more realistic estimate of the time and cost required for the programmer to complete the project activities.

In some industries it is actually possible to chart the cost of repetitive activities to accurately adjust cost estimation for learning curves. Note the curve relating time (or cost) against activity repetition shown in Figure 18.5.[11] The learning curve effect here shows savings in time as a function of the sheer repetition of activities found in many projects. Some operations management books offer tables that show the total time multiplier, based on the learning rate values multiplied by the number of repetitive iterations of an activity.[12] Using these multipliers, the savings in revising cost estimates downward to account for learning curve effects can be significant. However, there is one important caveat: Learning curve effects may occur differentially across projects; projects with redundant work may allow for the use of learning curve multipliers while other projects with more varied work will not. Likewise, it may be more likely to see learning curve effects apply in greater proportion to projects in some industries (say, for example, construction) than in others (such as research and development). Ultimately, project budgets must be adjusted for activities in which learning curve effects are likely to occur, and these effects must be factored into activity cost estimates.

Increasingly, project contracts are coming to reflect the impact of learning curves for repetitive operations. For example, in the automotive industry, the manufacturer of hydraulic cylinders may be given a contract for the first year to provide cylinders at a price of $24 each. Each year after, the cost of the cylinder sold to the automobile maker is priced at $1 less per year, under the assumption that learning curves will allow the cylinder manufacturer to produce the product at a steadily lower cost. Thus, learning curves are factored into the value of long-term contracts.[13]

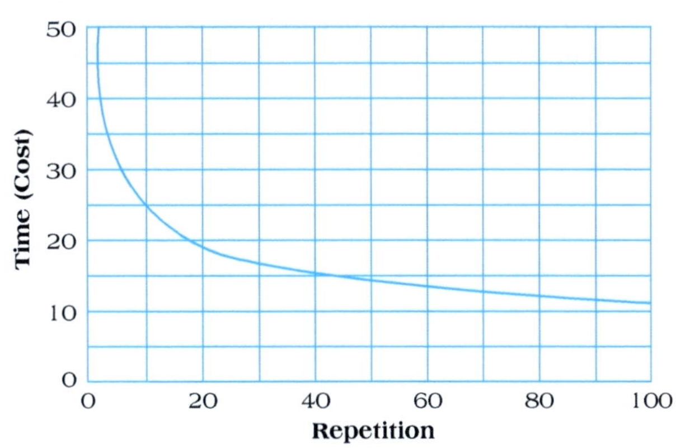

FIGURE 18.5 Unit Learning Curve Log-Linear Model

Source: J. P. Amor and C. J. Teplitz. (1998). "An efficient approximation for project composite learning curves," *Project Management Journal, 29*(3), pp. 28–42, figure on page 36. Copyright © 1998 by Project Management Institute Publications. Copyright and all rights reserved. Material from this publication has been reproduced with the permission of PMI.

Note: Graph on arithmetic coordinates.

Software Project Estimation—Function Points

Evidence from Chapter 6 and Box 18.1 (Software Cost Estimation) highlights the difficulties in developing realistic estimates for large-scale software projects. The track record is not encouraging: More and more software projects are overshooting their schedule and cost estimates, often by significant amounts. One of the reasons is simply due to the nature of uncertainty in these projects. We can make estimates of cost, but without a clear sense of the nature of the software,

BOX 18.1

Project Management Research in Brief

Software Cost Estimation

The software project industry has developed a notorious reputation when it comes to project performance. Past research by the Standish Group[14] found that for large companies, less than 9% of IT projects are completed on schedule and at budget. Over 50% of these projects will cost 189% of their original budget, while the average schedule overrun is 202%. A recent study of 5,400 IT projects conducted by McKinsey and Company and Oxford University found that on average, large IT projects run 45% over budget and 7% over time while delivering 56% less value than predicted. In fact, 17% of IT projects are such a disaster that they can threaten the very existence of the company.[15] Clearly, from both cost and schedule estimation perspectives, the industry is frustrated by unrealistic expectations. In spite of recent improvements in software development cost, schedule, and effort estimation, using Constructive Cost Estimating models (COCOMO II), required by several branches of the federal government when bidding software contracts, our lack of ability to accurately predict software project costs remains a serious concern.[16]

A book by Steven McConnell, president of Construx Software,[17] sheds light on some of the key reasons why software projects suffer from such a poor track record. Among his findings is the common failure to budget adequate time and funding for project activities that are likely to vary dramatically, depending upon the size of the project. He distinguished among six software project activities: (1) architecture, (2) detailed design, (3) coding and debugging, (4) developer testing, (5) integration, and (6) system testing. McConnell determined that for small IT projects of 2,000 lines of code or less, 80% of the project work consisted of just three activities: detailed design, coding and debugging, and unit testing (see Figure 18.6). However, as the complexity of the software projects increased, the proportion of these activities to the overall project cost dropped dramatically. Projects of over 128,000 lines of code required significantly more attention to be paid to the other three activities: architecture, integration, and system testing (about 60% of total effort).

The implications of this research suggest that IT project budgets must consider the size of the project as they calculate the costs of each component (work package). Larger projects resulting in hundreds of thousands of lines of code require that a higher proportion of the budget be allocated to software architecture and testing, relative to the actual cost of construction (design, coding, and unit testing).

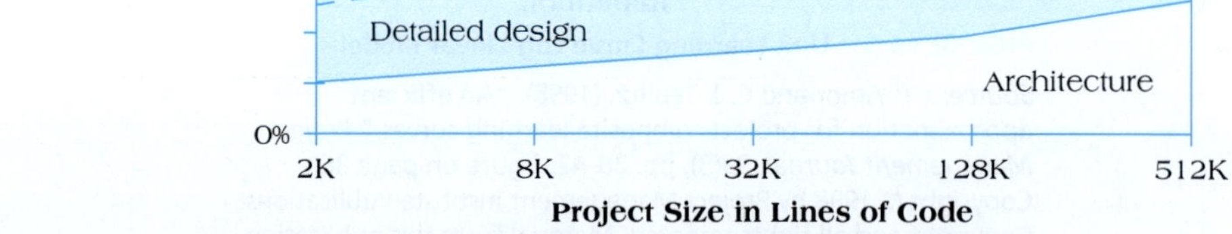

FIGURE 18.6 Software Project Development Activities as a Function of Size

Source: From *Code Complete*, 2d ed. (Microsoft Press, 2004), by Steve McConnell. Used with permission of the author.

the size of the program, and its functionality, these are often just best guesses and are quickly found to be inadequate.

Function point analysis is a system for estimating the size of software projects based on what the software does. To build any system, you need time to create files that hold information and interfaces to other screens (files and interfaces). You also need to create input screens (inputs), enquiry screens (queries), and reports (outputs). If you count all the files, interfaces, inputs, queries, and outputs, you can begin estimating the amount of work to be undertaken. The measure then relates directly to the business requirements that the software is intended to address. It can therefore be readily applied across a wide range of development environments and throughout the life of a development project, from early requirements definition to full operational use.

Simply stated, **function points** are a standard unit of measure that represents the functional size of a software application. In the same way that a house is measured by the square feet it provides, the size of an application can be measured by the number of function points it delivers to the users of the application. As part of that explanation, it is critically important to recognize that the size of the application being measured is based on the *user's view* of the system. It is based on what the user asked for, not what is delivered. Further, it is based on the way the user interacts with the system, including the screens that the user accesses to enter input, and the reports the user receives as output.

We know that it takes different amounts of time to build different functions; for example, it may take twice as long to build an interface table as an input table. Once we have a general sense of the relative times for each of the functions of the system, we have to consider additional factors to weight these estimates. These factor weightings are based on "technical complexity" and "environmental complexity." Technical complexity assesses the sophistication of the application to be built. Are we developing a complex model to determine the multiple paths of geosynchronous orbiting satellites or are we simply creating a database of customer names and addresses? Environmental complexity considers the nature of the setting in which the system is designed to work. Will it support a single user on one PC or a wide-area network? What computer language will the application be written in? A relatively streamlined and commonplace language such as Visual Basic requires less work than a more complex language and, consequently, we would assume that programmers could be more productive (generate more function points). These function points are adjusted for such complexity factors and then summed to determine a reasonable cost estimate for developing the software system.

Let's take a simple example: Suppose a local restaurant commissioned our firm to develop a replenishment and ordering system to ensure that minimum levels of foods and beverages are maintained at all times. The restaurant wants the application to have a reasonable number of input screens, output screens, a small number of query options and interfaces, but large and detailed report generation capabilities. Further, we know from past experience that one programmer working for one month (a "person-month") at our firm can generate an average of 10 function points. Finally, based on our company's past history, we have a set of average system technical and environmental complexity weightings that we can apply across all functions (see Table 18.4). For example, we know that in building an input function for the application, a system with high complexity is approximately three times more complicated (and requires more effort) than one with low complexity.

TABLE 18.4 Complexity Weighting Table for Function Point Analysis

	Complexity Weighting			
Function	**Low**	**Medium**	**High**	**Total**
Number of Inputs	2 × ___ =	4 × ___ =	6 × ___ =	
Number of Outputs	4 × ___ =	6 × ___ =	10 × ___ =	
Number of Interfaces	3 × ___ =	7 × ___ =	12 × ___ =	
Number of Queries	5 × ___ =	10 × ___ =	15 × ___ =	
Number of Files	2 × ___ =	4 × ___ =	8 × ___ =	

TABLE 18.5 Function Point Calculations for Restaurant Reorder System

	Complexity Weighting			
Function	**Low**	**Medium**	**High**	**Total**
Number of Inputs		4 × 15 =		60
Number of Outputs			10 × 20 =	200
Number of Interfaces	3 × 3 =			9
Number of Queries		10 × 6 =		60
Number of Files	2 × 40 =			80
Total				409

With this information, we can apply the specific system requirements from the client to construct a function point estimate for the project. Suppose we determined (from our interviews with the restaurant owners) that the estimate for relative complexity was inputs (medium), outputs (high), interfaces (low), queries (medium), and files (low). Further, we know that the clients require the following number of each function: input screens (15), output screens (20), interfaces (3), queries (6), and report files (40). We can combine this information with our historic weightings for complexity to create Table 18.5.

Table 18.5 shows the results of combining our estimates for complexity of various programming functions with the requirements of the client for system features, including numbers of screens and other elements for each function. The result is our estimate that the project will require approximately 409 function points. We know that our organization estimates that each resource can perform 10 function points each "person-month." Therefore, we calculate the expected number of person-months to complete this job as 409/10 = 40.1. If we assigned only four programmers to this job, it would take approximately 10 months to complete. On the other hand, by assigning our entire staff of 10 programmers, we would expect to complete the job in just over four months. Cost estimation using this information is straightforward: If our average resource cost per programmer is $5,000/month, we multiply this figure by 40.1 to determine that our estimated cost for completing the job is $200,500.

Function point analysis is not an exact science. Complexity determinations are based on historical estimates that can change over time and so must be continuously updated. Further, they may not be comparable across organizations with differing estimation procedures and standards for technical complexity. Nevertheless, function point analysis does give organizations a useful system for developing cost estimates for software projects, a historically difficult class of projects to estimate with any accuracy.[18]

Problems with Cost Estimation

In spite of project management's best efforts, a variety of issues affect the ability to conduct reasonable and accurate project cost estimates. Highly innovative projects can be notoriously difficult to estimate in terms of costs. Surprisingly, however, even projects that are traditionally viewed as highly structured, such as construction projects, can be susceptible to ruinously expensive cost overruns. Among the more common reasons for cost overruns are:[19]

1. ***Low initial estimates***—Caused by misperception of the scope of the project to be undertaken, low initial estimates are a double-edged sword. In proposing the low estimates at the start of a project, management is often setting themselves up to fail to live up to the budget constraints they have imposed. Hence, low estimates, which may be created either willingly (in the belief that top management will not fund a project that is too expensive) or unwillingly (through simple error or neglect), almost always guarantee the result of cost overrun. Part of the reason why initial estimates may be low can be the failure to consider the project in relation to other organizational activities. If we simply cost-out various project activities without considering the other surrounding organizational activities, we can be led to assume the project team member is capable of performing the activity in an unrealistic amount of time.

Low estimates may also be the result of a corporate culture that rewards underestimation. For example, in some organizations, it is widely understood that cost overruns will not derail a project manager's career nearly as quickly as technical flaws. Therefore, it is common for project managers to drastically underestimate project costs in order to get their project funded, continually apply for supplemental funding as the project continues, and eventually turn in a product with huge cost overruns. Political considerations also can cause project teams or top management to view a project through rose-colored glasses, minimizing initial cost estimates, particularly if they run contrary to hoped-for results. The Denver International Airport represents a good example of a community ignoring warning signs of overly optimistic cost estimates in the interest of completing the project. The resulting cost overruns have been enormous.

2. *Unexpected technical difficulties*—A common problem with estimating the costs associated with many project activities is to assume that technical problems will be minimal; that is, the cost estimate is often the case of seeming to suggest that "All other things being equal, this task should cost $*XX*." Of course, all other things are rarely equal. An estimate, in order to be meaningful, must take a hard look at the potential for technical problems, start-up delays, and other technical risks. It is a fact that new technologies, innovative procedures, and engineering advances are routinely accompanied by failures of design, testing, and application. Sometimes the impact of these difficulties is the loss of significant money; other times the losses are more tragic, resulting in the loss of life. The Boeing V-22 Osprey transport aircraft, for example, employs a radical "tilt-rotor" technology that was developed for use by the U.S. Marines and Navy. Prototype testing identified design flaws, contributing to the deaths of test pilots in early models of these aircraft.
3. *Lack of definition*—The result of poor initial scope development is often the creation of projects with poorly defined features, goals, or even purpose. This lack of a clear view of the project can quickly spill over into poorly realized cost estimates and inevitable cost overruns. It is important to recognize that the process of cost estimation and project budgeting must follow a comprehensive scope statement and work breakdown structure. When the first steps are done poorly, they effectively render futile any attempt at reasonable estimation of project costs.
4. *Specification changes*—One of the banes of project management cost estimation and control is the midcourse specifications changes (sometimes referred to as "scope creep") that many projects are so prone to. Information technology projects, for example, are often riddled with requests for additional features, serious modifications, and updated processes—all while the project's activities are still in development. In the face of serious changes to project scope or specification, it is no wonder that many projects routinely overrun their initial cost estimates. In fact, with many firms, initial cost estimates may be essentially meaningless, particularly when the company has a well-earned reputation for making midcourse adjustments to scope.
5. *External factors*—Inflation and other economic impacts can cause a project to overrun its estimates, many times seriously. For example, in the face of a financial crisis or an unexpected worldwide shortage of a raw material, cost estimates that were made without taking such concerns into account are quickly moot. To cite one example, in the early part of this decade, China and India's aggressive modernization and industrialization efforts, coupled with a weak American dollar, had been driving the price of crude oil to near-record highs. Because crude oil is benchmarked against the U.S. dollar, which is currently being kept weak by the Federal Reserve, it was taking more dollars to purchase oil. Further, Chinese and Indian demand for oil had led to higher international prices. A project that requires significant supplies of crude oil would have had to be recalculated upward due to the significant increase in the cost of this critical resource. Other common external effects can occur in the case of political considerations shaping the course that a project is expected to follow. This phenomenon is often found in government projects, particularly military acquisition contracts, which have a history of cost overruns, governmental intervention in the form of oversight committees, multiple constituents, and numerous midcourse change requests.

BOX 18.2

Project Management Research in Brief

"Delusion and Deception" Taking Place in Large Infrastructure Projects

This should be the golden age of infrastructure projects. A recent issue of *The Economist* reported that an estimated $22 trillion is to be invested in these projects over the next 10 years, making spending on infrastructure "the biggest investment boom in history." Because of this long-term commitment to large infrastructure improvements, coupled with the enormous costs of successfully completing these projects, it is critical that the governments and their agents responsible for designing and managing them get things right. In other words, too much is at stake to mismanage these projects.

Unfortunately, as previous examples in this chapter make clear, private organizations as well as the public sector have terrible performance records when it comes to successfully managing and delivering on their large infrastructure cost and performance targets. Examples such as the Sydney Opera House (original projected cost of 7 million Australian dollars; final cost of 102 million), the Eurotunnel (final costs more than double the original projections), and the Boston "Big Dig" (original estimated cost of $2.5 billion; final cost of nearly $15 billion) continue to be the rule rather than the exception when it comes to infrastructure project performance. The long list of incredibly overrun projects begs some simple questions: What is going on here? Why are we routinely so bad at cost estimation? What factors are causing us to continually miss our targets when it comes to estimating project costs?

Professor Bent Flyvbjerg, a project management researcher at Oxford University, and several colleagues have studied the track records of large infrastructure projects over the years and have arrived at some startling conclusions about the causes of their runaway costs: In most cases, the causes come from one of three sources—over-optimism bias, deliberate deception, or simple bad luck.

1. ***Optimism bias***—Flyvbjerg's work showed that executives commonly fall victim to delusions when it comes to projects, something he refers to as the "planning fallacy." Under the planning fallacy, managers routinely minimize problems and make their decisions on the basis of delusional optimism—underestimating costs and obstacles, involuntarily spinning scenarios for success, and assuming best-case options and outcomes. Optimism bias leads project managers and top executives to err on the side of underestimation of costs and time for project activities even in the face of previous evidence or past experiences. In short, we tend to develop overly positive scenarios of schedule and cost for projects and make forecasts that reflect these delusions.
2. ***Deliberate deception***—Large capital investment projects often require complex layers of decision making in order to get them approved. For example, governments have to work with private contractors and other agents who are responsible for making initial cost projections. Flyvbjerg found that some opportunities to inappropriately bias the project (deception) occur when a project's stakeholders all hold different incentives for the project. For example, the construction consortium wants the project, the government wants to provide for taxpayers and voters, bankers want to secure long-term investments, and so on. Under this situation, contractors may feel an incentive to provide estimates that are deliberately undervalued in order to secure the contract. They know that "true" cost estimates could scare off the public partners so they adopt a policy of deliberate deception to first win the contract, knowing that once the government is committed, it is extremely difficult for them to change their minds, even in the face of a series of expanding cost estimates. In short, the goal here is to get the project contracts signed; once the project is "on the books," it tends to stay there.

   Government representatives themselves can play a role in deception when it comes to "greenlighting" expensive projects. They may do this from a variety of motives, including altruism, reasoning that full disclosure of a project's costs will alienate the public, regardless of how much societal good may come from it, or their motives may be more self-serving. For example, the Willy Brandt International Airport in Berlin was scheduled to open in 2010. With a cost that has ballooned to over $7 billion and no fixed opening date in sight, critics have argued that the airport was a politicians' vanity project from the beginning. As one writer noted: "Many politicians want prestigious large-scale projects to be inseparably connected with their names. To get these expensive projects started, they artificially calculate down the real costs to get permission from parliament or other committees in charge."[20]
3. ***Bad luck***—A final reason for escalating project costs is simple bad luck. Bad luck implies that in spite of sound estimates, due diligence from all parties involved in the project, and the best intentions of both the contractors and project clients, there are always going to be cases where circumstances, environmental impacts, and sheer misfortune can conspire to derail a project or severely cripple its delivery. Though there is no doubt that bad luck does sometimes occur, Flyvbjerg warns that it is usually a handy excuse to attribute project problems to "bad luck," when the reality is that overruns and schedule slippage are typically caused by much more foreseeable reasons, as suggested above.

The research on serious project overruns and their causes offers some important insight into reasons why we keep missing our targets for critical projects. It also suggests additional effects that are equally important: Underestimating costs and overestimating benefits from any project leads to two problems. First, we opt to begin many projects that are not (and never were) economically viable. Second, starting these projects means we are effectively ignoring alternatives that actually could have yielded higher returns had we made a better initial analysis. Ultimately, the common complaint about large infrastructure projects ("Over budget, over time, over and over again") is one for which most organizations have no one to blame but themselves.[21]

18.3 CREATING A PROJECT BUDGET

The process of developing a project budget is an interesting mix of estimation, analysis, intuition, and repetitive work. The central goal of a budget is the need to support rather than conflict with the project's and the organization's goals. The **project budget** is a plan that identifies the allocated resources, the project's goals, and the schedule that allows an organization to achieve those goals. Effective budgeting always seeks to integrate corporate-level goals with department-specific objectives; short-term requirements with long-term plans; and broader, strategic missions with concise, needs-based issues. Useful budgets evolve through intensive communication with all concerned parties and are compiled from multiple data sources. Perhaps most importantly, the project budget and project schedule must be created in tandem; the budget effectively determines whether or not project milestones can be achieved.

As one of the cornerstones of project planning, the project budget must be coordinated with project activities defined in the Work Breakdown Structure. As Figure 18.7 suggests, the WBS sets the stage for creating the project schedule; the project budget subsequently assigns the necessary resources to support that schedule.

A number of important issues go into the creation of the project budget, including the process by which the project team and the organization gather data for cost estimates, budget projections, cash flow income and expenses, and expected revenue streams. The methods for data gathering and allocation can vary widely across organizations; some project firms rely on the straight, linear allocation of income and expenses, without allowing for time, while others use more sophisticated systems. The ways in which cost data are collected and interpreted mainly depend upon whether the firm employs a top-down or a bottom-up budgeting procedure. These approaches involve radically different methods for collecting relevant project budget information and can potentially lead to very different results.

Top-Down Budgeting

Top-down budgeting requires the direct input from the organization's top management; in essence, this approach seeks to first ascertain the opinions and experiences of top management regarding estimated project costs. The assumption is that senior management is experienced with past projects and is in a position to provide accurate feedback and estimates of costs for future project ventures. They take the first stab at estimating both the overall costs of a project and its major work packages. These projections are then passed down the hierarchy to the next functional department levels where additional, more specific information is collected. At each step down the hierarchy, the project is broken into more detailed pieces, until project personnel who actually will be performing the work ultimately provide input on specific costs on a task-by-task basis.

This approach can create a certain amount of friction within the organization, both between top and lower levels and also between lower-level managers competing for budget money. When

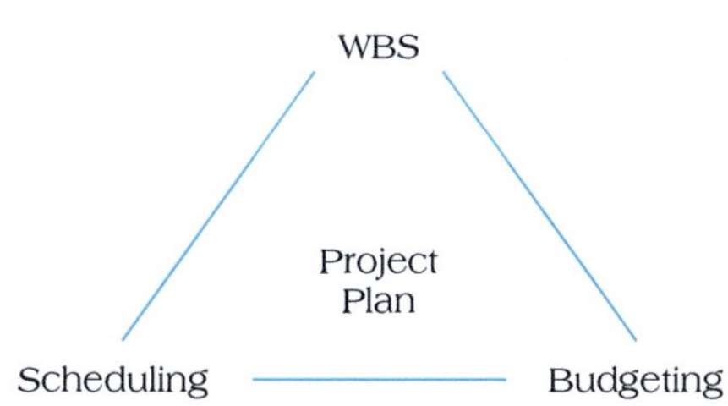

FIGURE 18.7 The Relationship Among WBS, Scheduling, and Budgeting

top management establishes an overall budget at the start, they are, in essence, driving a stake into the ground and saying, "This is all we are willing to spend." As a result, all successive levels of the budgeting process must make their estimates fit within the context of the overall budget that was established at the outset. This process naturally leads to jockeying among different functions as they seek to divide up the budget pie in what has become a zero-sum game—the more budget money engineering receives, the less there is for procurement to use.

On the positive side, research suggests that top management estimates of project costs are often quite accurate, at least in the aggregate.[22] Using this figure as a basis for drilling down to assign costs to work packages and individual tasks brings an important sense of budgetary discipline and cost control. For example, a building contractor about to enter into a contract to develop a convention center is often knowledgeable enough to judge the construction costs with reasonable accuracy, given sufficient information about the building's features, its location, and any known building impediments or worksite constraints. All subcontractors and project team members must then develop their own budgets based on the overall, top-down contract.

Bottom-Up Budgeting

Bottom-up budgeting takes a completely different approach than that pursued by top-down methods. The **bottom-up budgeting** approach begins inductively from the work breakdown structure to apply direct and indirect costs to project activities. The sum of the total costs associated with each activity are then aggregated, first to the work package level, then at the deliverable level, at which point all task budgets are combined, and then higher up the chain where the sum of the work package budgets are aggregated to create the overall project budget.

In this budgeting approach, each project manager is required to prepare a project budget that identifies project activities and specifies funds requested to support these tasks. Using these first-level budget requests, functional managers develop their own carefully documented budgets, taking into consideration both the requirements of the firms' projects and their own departmental needs. This information is finally passed along to top managers, who merge and streamline to eliminate overlap or double counting. They are then responsible for creating the final master budget for the organization.

Bottom-up budgeting emphasizes the need to create detailed project plans, particularly Work Breakdown Structures, as a first step for budget allocations. It also facilitates coordination between the project managers and functional department heads and, because it emphasizes the unique creation of budgets for each project, it allows top managers a clear view for prioritization among projects competing for resources. On the other hand, a disadvantage of bottom-up budgeting is that it reduces top management's control of the budget process to one of oversight, rather than direct initiation, which may lead to significant differences between their strategic concerns and the operational-level activities in the organization. Also, the fine-tuning that often accompanies bottom-up budgeting can be time-consuming as top managers make adjustments and lower-level managers resubmit their numbers until an acceptable budget is achieved.

Activity-Based Costing

Most project budgets use some form of activity-based costing. **Activity-based costing (ABC)** is a budgeting method that assigns costs first to activities and then to the projects based on each project's use of resources. Remember that project activities are any discrete task that the project team undertakes to make or deliver the project. Activity-based costing, therefore, is based on the notion that projects consume activities and activities consume resources.[23]

Activity-based costing consists of four steps:

1. Identify the activities that consume resources and assign costs to them, as is done in a bottom-up budgeting process.
2. Identify the cost drivers associated with the activity. Resources, in the form of project personnel, and materials are key cost drivers.
3. Compute a cost rate per cost driver unit or transaction. Labor, for example, is commonly simply the cost of labor per hour, given as:

$$\text{Cost rate/unit} \longrightarrow \$\text{Cost/hour}$$

TABLE 18.6 Sample Project Budget

Activity	Direct Costs	Budget Overhead	Total Cost
Survey	3,500	500	4,000
Design	7,000	1,000	8,000
Clear Site	3,500	500	4,000
Foundation	6,750	750	7,500
Framing	8,000	2,000	10,000
Plumb and Wire	3,750	1,250	5,000

4. Assign costs to projects by multiplying the cost driver rate times the volume of cost driver units consumed by the project. For example, assume the cost of a senior software programmer is $40/hour and that she is to work on the project for a total of 80 hours. The cost to the project would be:

$$(\$40/\text{hr})(80\,\text{hours}) = \$3{,}200.00$$

As we discussed earlier in this chapter, numerous sources of project costs (cost drivers) apply to both the direct and the indirect costs of a project. Activity-based costing, a technique employed within most project budgets, requires the early identification of these variables in order to create a meaningful control document.

Table 18.6 demonstrates part of a project budget. The purpose of the preliminary budget is to identify the direct costs and those that apply to overhead expenses. It is sometimes necessary to further break down overhead costs to account for separate budget lines. The overhead figure of $500 for *Survey*, for example, may include expenses covering health insurance, retirement contributions, and other forms of overhead, which would be broken out in a more detailed project budget.

Table 18.7 shows a budget in which the total planned expenses given in Table 18.6 are compared against actual accrued project expenses. With periodic updating, this budget can be used for variance reporting to show differences, both positive and negative, between the baseline budget assigned to each activity and the actual cost of completing those tasks. This method offers a central location for the tabulation of all relevant project cost data and allows for the preliminary development of variance reports. On the other hand, this type of budget is a static budget document that does not reflect the project schedule and the fact that activities are phased in following the network's sequencing.

Table 18.8 shows a sample from a time-phased budget, in which the total budget for each project activity is disaggregated across the schedule when its work is planned. The **time-phased budget** allocates costs across both project activities and the anticipated time in which the budget is to be expended. It allows the project team to match its schedule baseline with a budget baseline, identifying milestones for both schedule performance and project expense. As we will see in Chapter 18, the creation of a time-phased budget works in tandem with more sophisticated project control techniques, such as earned value management.

TABLE 18.7 Sample Budget Tracking Planned and Actual Activity Costs

Activity	Planned	Budget Actual	Variance
Survey	4,000	4,250	250
Design	8,000	8,000	- 0 -
Clear Site	4,000	3,500	(500)
Foundation	7,500	8,500	1,000
Framing	10,000	11,250	1,250
Plumb and Wire	5,000	5,150	150
Total	38,500	40,650	2,150

TABLE 18.8 Example of a Time-Phased Budget

	Months					
Activity	**January**	**February**	**March**	**April**	**May**	**Total by Activity**
Survey	4,000					4,000
Design		5,000	3,000			8,000
Clear Site		4,000				4,000
Foundation			7,500			7,500
Framing				8,000	2,000	10,000
Plumb and Wire				1,000	4,000	5,000
Monthly Planned	4,000	9,000	10,500	9,000	6,000	
Cumulative	4,000	13,000	23,500	32,500	38,500	38,500

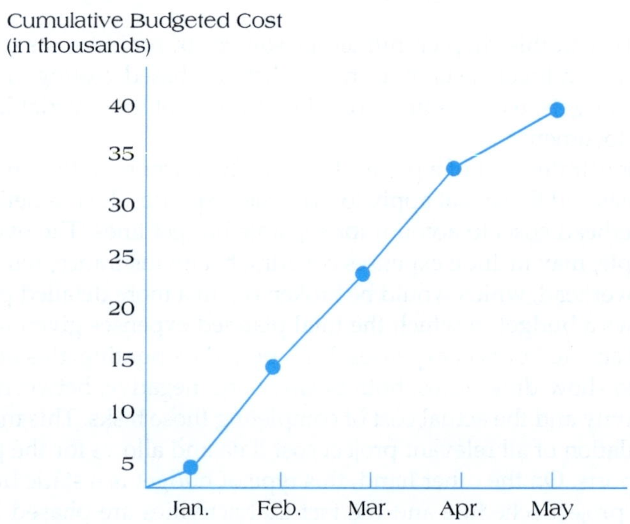

FIGURE 18.8 **Cumulative Budgeted Cost of the Project**

We can produce a tracking chart that illustrates the expected budget expenditures for this project by plotting the cumulative budgeted cost of the project against the baseline schedule. Figure 18.8 is a simple graphic of the plot and is another method for identifying the project baseline for schedule and budget over the anticipated life of the project.

18.4 DEVELOPING BUDGET CONTINGENCIES

Budget contingencies symbolize the recognition that project cost estimates are just that: estimates. Unforeseen events often conspire to render initial project budgets inaccurate, or even useless. (Suppose a construction project that had budgeted a fixed amount for digging a building's foundation accidentally discovered serious subsidence problems or groundwater.) Even in circumstances in which project unknowns are kept to a minimum, there is simply no such thing as a project developed with the luxury of full knowledge of events. A **budget contingency** is the allocation of extra funds to cover these uncertainties and improve the chances that the project can be completed within the time frame originally specified. Contingency money is typically added to the project's budget following the identification of all project costs; that is, the project budget does not include contingency as part of the activity-based costing process. Rather, the contingency is calculated as an extra cushion on top of the calculated cost of the project.

There are several reasons why it may make good sense to include contingency funding in project cost estimates. Many of these reasons point to the underlying uncertainty that accompanies most project cost estimation:[24]

1. ***Project scope is subject to change.*** Many projects aim at moving targets; that is, the project scope may seem well articulated and locked in. However, as the project moves through its development cycle, external events or environmental changes can often force us to modify or upgrade a project's goals. For example, suppose that our organization set out to develop an electronics product for the commercial music market only to discover, halfway through the development, that technological advances had rendered our original product obsolete. One option, other than abandoning the project, might be to engineer a product design upgrade midstream in the project's development. Those scope changes will cause potentially expensive cost readjustments.
2. ***Murphy's Law is always present.*** Murphy's Law suggests that if something can go wrong, it often will. Budget contingency represents one important method for anticipating the likelihood of problems occurring during the project life cycle. Thus, contingency planning just makes prudent sense.
3. ***Cost estimation must anticipate interaction costs.*** It is common to budget project activities as independent operations. Thus, in a product development project, we develop a discrete budget for each work package under product design, engineering, machining, and so forth. However, this approach fails to recognize the often "interactive" nature of these activities. For example, suppose that the engineering phase requires a series of iterative cycles to occur between the designers and the engineers. As a series of designs are created, they are forwarded to the engineering section for proofing and quality assessment. When problems are encountered, they must be shipped back to design to be corrected. Coordinating the several cycles of design and rework as a product moves through these two phases is often not accounted for in a standard project budget. Hence, contingency budgets allow for the likely rework cycles that link project activities interactively.
4. ***Normal conditions are rarely encountered.*** Project cost estimates usually anticipate "normal conditions." However, many projects are conducted under anything but normal working conditions. Some of the ways in which the normal conditions assumption is routinely violated include the availability of resources and the nature of environmental effects. Cost estimators assume that resources required for the project will be available when needed; however, personnel may be missing, raw materials may be of poor quality, promised funding may not materialize, and so forth. When resources are missing or limited, the activities that depend upon their availability are often delayed, leading to extra costs. Likewise, the geography and environmental effects on some projects demonstrate the difficulty in creating a "normal" project situation. For example, a project manager was assigned to develop a power plant in the West Bengal province of India only to discover, upon arrival, that the project was set to begin at the same time that the annual torrential monsoon rains were due to arrive! His first project activity, after reaching the construction site, was to spend three weeks erecting a five-foot retaining wall and coffer dam around the site to ensure it would not flood. Of course, the cost of this necessary construction had not been factored into his initial budget.

While project teams naturally favor contingencies as a buffer for project cost control, their acceptance by project stakeholders, particularly clients, is less assured. Some clients may feel that they are being asked to cover poor budget control on the part of the project firm. Other clients object to what seems an arbitrary process for calculating contingency. For example, it is common in the building industry to apply a contingency rate of 10%–15% to any structure prior to architectural design. As a result, a building budgeted for $10 million would be designed to cost $9 million. The additional million dollars is held in escrow as contingency against unforeseen difficulties during the construction and is not applied to the operating budget. Finally, does the contingency fund apply equally across all project work packages or should it be held in reserve to support critical activities as needed? Where or across what project activities contingency funds should be applied is the final point of contention. Despite these drawbacks, there are several benefits to the use of contingency funding for projects, including:

1. It recognizes that the future contains unknowns, and the problems that do arise are likely to have a direct effect on the project budget. In providing contingency, the project allows for the negative effects of both time and money variance.

2. Provision is made in the company plans for an increase in project cost. Contingency has sometimes been called the first project fire alarm. Allowing contingency funds to be applied to a project is a preliminary step in gaining approval for budget increases, should they become necessary.
3. Application to the contingency fund gives an early warning signal of a potential overdrawn budget. In the event of such signals, the organization's top management needs to take a serious look at the project and the reasons for its budget variance, and begin formulating fallback plans should the contingency prove to be insufficient to cover the project overspend. In large defense-industry contracts, for example, project organizations facing budget overruns often first apply any contingency money they possess to the project before approaching the governmental agency for additional funding. An Army project contract manager will understandably demand full accounting of project expenditures, including contingency funds, before considering additional funding.

Project cost estimation and budgeting are two important components of project control. Because a significant constraint on any project is its budget, the manner in which we estimate project costs and create realistic budgets is critical to effective project planning. Further, the best defense against overrunning our budgets is to prepare project cost estimates as carefully as possible. Although we cannot possibly anticipate every eventuality, the more care that is used in initial estimation, the greater the likelihood that we can create a budget that is a reasonably accurate reflection of the true project cost. Cost estimation challenges us to develop reasonable assumptions and expectations for project costs through clearly articulating the manner in which we arrive at our estimates. Budgeting is the best method for applying project expenditures systematically, with an eye toward keeping project costs in line with initial estimates. Taken together, cost estimation and budgeting require every project manager to become comfortable with not only the technical challenges of the project, but its monetary constraints as well.

Summary

1. **Understand the various types of common project costs.** Project budgeting comprises two distinct elements: cost estimation and the budgeting process itself. Among the well-known expenses in most projects are:
   a. ***Cost of labor***—the charge against the human resources needed to complete the project.
   b. ***Cost of materials***—costs relating to any specific equipment or supplies needed for project development.
   c. ***Subcontractors***—charges against the project budget for the use of consultants or other subcontracted work.
   d. ***Cost of equipment and facilities***—the costs of any plant and equipment, either at the project's location or off-site.
   e. ***Travel***—a sometimes necessary charge for the expense of having project team members in the field or at other sites.
2. **Recognize the difference between various forms of project costs.** The types of costs that a project can incur can be identified in a number of ways. Among the more common types of costs are:
   - ***Direct versus indirect***—Direct costs are those that can be directly assigned to specific project activities performed to create the project. Indirect costs relate to general company overhead expenses or administration. For example, overhead expenses charged to a project may include health benefits or retirement contributions. General administration includes shipping costs, secretarial or computer support, sales commissions, and so on.
   - ***Recurring versus nonrecurring***—Recurring costs are ongoing expenses, such as labor or material costs. They appear across the project's life cycle. Nonrecurring costs are typically one-time expenses related to some special expense or purchase, such as training or purchase of a building.
   - ***Fixed versus variable***—Fixed costs do not vary with respect to their usage. Variable costs generally increase in proportion to the degree they are used.
   - ***Normal versus expedited***—Normal costs are the normally scheduled costs of the project, set in relation to the schedule baseline. Expedited costs are sometimes referred to as "crashing costs" and increase due to the extra resources assigned to speed the completion of a specific project activity.
3. **Apply common forms of cost estimation for project work, including ballpark estimates and definitive estimates.** Cost estimating may follow one of several approaches, usually increasing in accuracy as estimates coincide more closely with the completion of project design work. Preliminary estimates for task completion, sometimes called "ballpark estimates," may be accurate only to ±30%. On the other hand, as the project gets closer to the

completion of the design phase, it is more realistic to expect more accurate, definitive estimates (±5%). One method for cost estimation is through the use of parametric techniques, which compare current project activities to the cost of past, similar activities and then assign a multiplier that considers inflation or other additional cost increases.

4. **Understand the advantages of parametric cost estimation and the application of learning curve models in cost estimation.** Parametric cost estimation allows project managers to develop detailed estimates of current project costs by taking older work and inserting a multiplier to account for the impact of inflation, labor and materials increases, and other reasonable direct costs. Parametric estimation allows project managers to begin formulating cost estimates from a position of past historical record, which can be very helpful in complex projects for which it is difficult to formulate reasonable estimates.

   One element in project cost estimation that cannot be ignored is the effect of learning rates on an individual's ability to perform a project task. Learning curve effects typically are relevant only in cases where a project team member is required to perform multiple iterations of a task. When these situations occur, it is usually easier and faster to complete the *n*th iteration than it was to complete the first, due to the effect of learning on repetitive activities. Using available formulas, we can readjust cost estimates for some project activities to reflect the effect of the learning curve on the cost of an activity.

5. **Discern the various reasons why project cost estimation is often done poorly.** Cost estimation may be poorly done for several reasons, including:
   a. *Low initial estimates*—These are caused by poor knowledge of the project's scope or due to an organizational atmosphere that rewards low initial estimates and does not sanction subsequent cost or schedule overruns.
   b. *Unexpected technical difficulties*—This is a common problem for many projects when technical performance is cutting-edge and unexpected problems emerge.
   c. *Lack of definition*—Poorly specified projects usually lead to poorly budgeted and controlled projects.
   d. *Specification changes*—The continuing distraction of specification change requests can quickly lead to cost overruns.
   e. *External factors*—The uncontrollable effects of inflation or economic or political interference in a project can render initial cost estimates invalid.

6. **Apply both top-down and bottom-up budgeting procedures for cost management.** Project budgeting involves the process of taking the individual activity cost estimates and creating a working document for planned project expenditures. Two approaches to budgeting involve the use of top-down and bottom-up efforts to better identify costs and allocate project budget money. Using activity-based budgeting techniques, project teams typically identify the activities that consume resources and assign costs to them. Second, they determine the cost drivers associated with the activities (usually human resources and materials costs), and third, a cost rate per cost driver is then computed. Activity-based budgeting allows for the creation of project budgets with specific budget lines for each task necessary to complete the project.

7. **Understand the uses of activity-based budgeting and time-phased budgets for cost estimation and control.** Taking activity-based budgeting one step further, we can create time-phased budgets when the specific activity costs are then allocated across the project schedule baseline to reflect the points on the project time line when the budget will be consumed. Using a time-phased budget approach allows the project team to link time and cost into a unified baseline that can be set to serve as the project plan. Project cost control, as the project moves forward, is predicated on creating the time-phased budget.

8. **Recognize the appropriateness of applying contingency funds for cost estimation.** In some projects, it is necessary, for a variety of reasons, to set aside a certain amount of the project budget into an account to handle any uncertainties or unexpected events that could not have been anticipated in the initial cost estimation and budgeting sequence. This account is referred to as a project contingency fund. In many types of projects, particularly construction projects, a contingency fund is a normal part of the project budget. Contingency is not assigned to any specific project activities; rather, it is used as a general project-level emergency fund to handle the costs associated with problems, should any arise.

Key Terms

Activity-based costing (ABC)
Ballpark estimates
Bottom-up budgeting
Budget contingency
Comparative estimates
Cost estimation
Crashing
Definitive estimates
Direct costs
Expedited costs
Feasibility estimates
Fixed costs
Function point analysis
Function points
Indirect costs

Learning curves	Parametric estimation	Recurring costs	Top-down budgeting
Nonrecurring costs	Project budget	Time-phased budget	Variable costs
Normal costs			

Solved Problems

18.1 CALCULATING FULLY LOADED LABOR COSTS

Calculate the fully loaded cost of labor for the project team using the following data. What are the costs for the individual project team members? What is the fully loaded cost of labor?

Name	Hours Needed	Overhead Charge	Personal Time Rate	Hourly Rate	Fully Loaded Labor Cost
John	40	1.80	1.12	$21/hr	
Bill	40	1.80	1.12	$40/hr	
J.P.	60	1.35	1.05	$10/hr	
Sonny	25	1.80	1.12	$32/hr	
	Total Fully Loaded Labor Cost =				

SOLUTION

We use the formula for calculating fully loaded costs, given as:

Hourly rate × Hours needed × Overhead charge × Personal time = Total fully loaded labor cost

Applying each rate given above in turn, we fill in the fully loaded cost table as follows:

Name	Hours Needed	Overhead Charge	Personal Time Rate	Hourly Rate	Fully Loaded Labor Cost
John	40	1.80	1.12	$21/hr	$1,693.44
Bill	40	1.80	1.12	$40/hr	3,225.60
J.P.	60	1.35	1.05	$10/hr	850.50
Sonny	25	1.80	1.12	$32/hr	1,612.80
	Total Fully Loaded Labor Cost =				$7,382.34

18.2 ESTIMATING SOFTWARE COSTS WITH FUNCTION POINTS

Suppose you were required to create a reasonably detailed estimate for developing a new student information and admissions system at a local college. Your firm's programmers average 6 function points on a person-month basis. After speaking with representatives from the college, you know that their request is based on the following screen requirements: inputs (4), outputs (7), interfaces (12), queries (20), and files (16). Further, we have determined that the relative complexity of each of these functions is as follows: inputs (low), outputs (medium), interfaces (high), queries (medium), and files (medium). Using this information and the following table, calculate the number of function points for this project.

	Complexity Weighting			
Function	Low	Medium	High	Total
Number of Inputs	3 × ___ =	6 × ___ =	9 × ___ =	
Number of Outputs	2 × ___ =	6 × ___ =	10 × ___ =	
Number of Interfaces	1 × ___ =	3 × ___ =	5 × ___ =	
Number of Queries	4 × ___ =	8 × ___ =	12 × ___ =	
Number of Files	4 × ___ =	6 × ___ =	8 × ___ =	

SOLUTION

Once we know the number of requirements for each of the five programmer functions and the complexity weighting for the activities, the calculation of total function points requires that we create a table as shown below, in which the relative complexity of the five programming functions is multiplied by the number of screen requirements. The table shows that the total number of function points for this project is 370.

	Complexity Weighting			
Function	**Low**	**Medium**	**High**	**Total**
Number of Inputs	3 × **4** =			**12**
Number of Outputs		6 × **7** =		**42**
Number of Interfaces			5 × **12** =	**60**
Number of Queries		8 × **20** =		**160**
Number of Files		6 × **16** =		**96**

18.3 CALCULATING BUDGET ESTIMATES USING THE LEARNING CURVE

Assume you have a software project that will require the coding services of a senior programmer to complete 14 coding sequences that are relatively similar. We know that the programmer's learning rate is .90 and that the first coding sequence is likely to take her 15 hours to complete. Using the learning curve formula, calculate the steady state time to code these sequences.

SOLUTION

Recall that the learning curve formula for calculating the time required to produce the steady state unit of output is represented as:

$$Y_x = aX^b$$

where

Y_x = the time required for the steady state, x, unit of output

a = the time required for the initial unit of output

X = the number of units to be produced to reach the steady state

b = the slope of the learning curve, represented as: log decimal learning rate/log 2

$$b = \log 0.90/\log 2$$
$$= -0.4576/0.301$$
$$= -0.1521$$
$$Y_x = 15(14)^{-0.1521}$$
$$Y_x = 10.04 \text{ hours}$$

Discussion Questions

18.1 Evaluate the difference between direct and indirect costs when considering your project budget. What other common project costs can you identify?

18.2 How has the global economy affected the importance of cost estimation and cost control for many project organizations?

18.3 Why is cost estimation such an important component of project planning? Discuss how it links together with the Work Breakdown Structure and the project schedule.

18.4 Imagine you are developing a software package for your company's intranet. Give examples of the various types of costs (labor, materials, equipment and facilities, subcontractors, etc.) and how they would apply to your project.

18.5 Give reasons both in favor of and against the use of a personal time charge as a cost estimate for a project activity.

18.6 This chapter suggests that "estimating project costs is a challenging process that can resemble an art form as much as science." Describe the different methods used to estimate costs on a project. How useful are these methods?

18.7 Suppose your organization used function point analysis to estimate costs for software projects. How would the expertise level of a recently hired programmer affect your calculation of their function points on a monthly basis when compared to an older, more experienced programmer?

18.8 Put yourself in the position of a project customer. Would you insist on the cost adjustments associated with learning curve effects or not? Under what circumstances would learning curve costs be appropriately budgeted into a project?

18.9 Consider the common problems with project cost estimation and recall a project with which you have been involved. Which of these common problems did you encounter most often? Why?

18.10 Would you prefer the use of bottom-up or top-down budgeting for project cost control? What are the advantages and disadvantages associated with each approach?

18.11 Explain the concept of activity-based costing (ABC). What steps are involved in this process?

18.12 Describe some of the benefits of developing budget contingencies for projects. Is it advantageous for project managers to apply contingency to every project? Justify your answer.

Problems

18.1 Calculate the fully loaded cost of labor for your project assistant Sally using the following data:

Hourly rate: $25/hr
Hours needed: 260
Overhead rate: 65%

18.2 Suppose that for Problem 1, the overhead rate has changed to 55%. Additionally, you now require Sally's time for 300 hours. Factor in a personal time cost of 12% and recalculate the fully loaded cost of labor for her.

18.3 Calculate the fully loaded cost of labor for the project team using the following data. What are the costs for the individual project team members? What is the fully loaded cost of labor?

Name	Hours Needed	Overhead Charge	Personal Time Rate	Hourly Rate	Fully Loaded Labor Cost
Sandy	60	1.35	1.12	$18/hr	
Chuck	80	1.75	1.12	$31/hr	
Bob	80	1.35	- 0 -	$9/hr	
Penny	40	1.75	1.12	$30/hr	
	Total Fully Loaded Labor Cost =				

18.4 Assume that overhead is charged on a flat-rate basis. Each member of the project is assigned an overhead charge of $150/week. What would the fully loaded cost of labor be for an employee, given that she is assigned to the project for 200 hours at $10.50/hour?

18.5 Assume your senior managers have allocated a labor cost of $30,000 for your project. Using the following data, calculate the fully loaded labor costs for each person. What is the total cost? Can you proceed with the project?

	Hours needed	Overhead charge	Personal Time Rate	Hourly Rate	Fully Loaded Labor Cost
Musa	65	75%	1.12	$12/hr	
Alfie	250	75%	1.12	$25/hr	
Suky	140	50%	1.12	$30.5/hr	
Abigail	100	55%	1.12	$44/hr	
	Total Fully Loaded Labor Cost:				

18.6 Using the following information about work package budgets, complete the overall time-phased budget for your project. (All cost figures are in $000s). Which are the weeks with the greatest budget expense?

Table for Problem 18.6

Task	Budget	Week 1	Week 2	Week 3	Week 4	Week 5	Week 6	Week 7	Week 8
A	5	3	2						
B	8	1	4	3	1				
C	12		2	7	3				
D	7			3	3	1			
E	14				5	5	2	2	
F	6						1	2	3
Plan	52	4	8						
Cumulative		4	12						

18.7 Assume that you are a project manager working on a product launch release. Consider the following information and produce a tracking chart that illustrates the expected budget expenditures against the baseline schedule (all cost figures are in $000s).

Table for Problem 18.7

Work Package Cost per Month

Work package	Budget	April	May	June	July	August
Marketing	35.1	1.5	8	7.6	9	9
Staffing	95.5	15.5	16	16	24	24
Web design	10	10				
Materials	8.5	2.5	5	1		
Prototype	37.5	18	19.5			
Cumulative	186.6	47.5	96	120.6	153.6	186.6

For Problems 8 through 10, refer to the chart of learning curve coefficients (unit and total time multipliers) shown at the bottom of this page.

The simplified formula for calculating learning rate time using the table coefficients is given as:

$$T_N = T_1 C$$

where

T_N = Time needed to produce the nth unit

T_1 = Time needed to produce the first unit

C = Learning curve coefficient

18.8 It took MegaTech, Inc., 100,000 labor-hours to produce the first of several oil-drilling rigs for Antarctic exploration. Your company, Natural Resources, Inc., has agreed to purchase the fifth (steady state) oil-drilling rig from MegaTech's manufacturing yard. Assume that MegaTech experiences a learning rate of 80%. At a labor rate of $35 per hour, what should you, as the purchasing agent, expect to pay for the fifth unit?

18.9 Problem 8 identified how long it should take to complete the fifth oil-drilling platform that Natural Resources plans to purchase. How long should all five oil-drilling rigs take to complete?

18.10 Suppose that you are assigning costs to a major project to be undertaken this year by your firm, DynoSoft Applications. One particular coding process involves many labor-hours, but highly redundant work. You anticipate a total of 200,000 labor-hours to complete the first iteration of the coding and a learning curve rate of 70%. You are attempting to estimate the cost of the twentieth (steady state) iteration of this coding sequence. Based on this information and a $60 per hour labor rate, what would you expect to budget as the cost of the twentieth iteration? The fortieth iteration?

Learning Curve Coefficients (Unit Time and Total Time Multipliers)

	70%		75%		80%		85%	
Steady State Unit	**Unit Time**	**Total Time**	**Unit Time**	**Total Time**	**Unit Time**	**Total Time**	**Unit Time**	**Total Time**
5	.437	3.195	.513	3.459	.596	3.738	.686	4.031
10	.306	4.932	.385	5.589	.477	6.315	.583	7.116
15	.248	6.274	.325	7.319	.418	8.511	.530	9.861
20	.214	7.407	.288	8.828	.381	10.485	.495	12.402
25	.191	8.404	.263	10.191	.355	12.309	.470	14.801
30	.174	9.305	.244	11.446	.335	14.020	.450	17.091
35	.160	10.133	.229	12.618	.318	15.643	.434	19.294
40	.150	10.902	.216	13.723	.305	17.193	.421	21.425

Based on $a = 1$.

18.11 Assume you are a project cost engineer calculating the cost of a repetitive activity for your project. There are a total of 20 iterations of this activity required for the project. The project activity takes 2.5 hours at its steady state rate and the learning rate is 75%. Calculate the initial output time for the first unit produced, using the learning curve formula:

$$Y_x = aX^b$$

where

Y_x = the time required for the steady state, x, unit of output

a = the time required for the initial unit of output

X = the number of units to be produced to reach the steady state

b = the slope of the learning curve, represented as: log decimal learning rate/log 2

18.12 As the manager of the IT group at your insurance firm, you have been asked to develop a cost estimate for upgrades to the computerized accident-reporting and claims adjustment system you have in place. Your system is basic, without many features, but it needs some general modifications, based on complaints from customers and claims adjusters at your firm. You know that your programmer is capable of handling 3 function points in a person-month and your programmer makes $60,000, so her cost is $5,000 per month. The costs for the project are based on the following requirements:

Function	Number of Screens	Complexity
Input	8	Low
Output	3	Low
Interfaces	8	Medium
Queries	6	Medium
Files	10	Low

The complexity weighting for these functions follows a standard formula:

Function	Complexity Weighting			Total
	Low	Medium	High	
Number of Inputs	1 × ___ =	2 × ___ =	3 × ___ =	
Number of Outputs	2 × ___ =	6 × ___ =	10 × ___ =	
Number of Interfaces	10 × ___ =	15 × ___ =	20 × ___ =	
Number of Queries	3 × ___ =	6 × ___ =	9 × ___ =	
Number of Files	1 × ___ =	3 × ___ =	5 × ___ =	

a. Calculate the total estimated number of function points for this project.

b. What is the total expected cost of the project?

18.13 Assume that you are a project manager in a software firm, and you have been asked to calculate the expected cost for a new fast food epos system. Referring to historical information, you know that the developers can handle 8 function points each person-month and that the cost per developer in your company is $5,000 per month. The project whose costs you are estimating is based on the following requirements:

Function	Number of Screens	Complexity
Input	10	Low
Output	4	Low
Interfaces	18	High
Queries	4	High
Files	28	Medium

Additionally, you know that the complexity weighting for these functions follows a standard internal formula, shown as:

a. Calculate the total number of function points for the project.

b. Calculate the total expected cost of the project.

Function	Complexity Weighting			Total
	Low	Medium	High	
Number of Inputs	2 × ___ =	4 × ___ =	6 × ___ =	
Number of Outputs	3 × ___ =	6 × ___ =	12 × ___ =	
Number of Interfaces	5 × ___ =	10 × ___ =	15 × ___ =	
Number of Queries	2 × ___ =	4 × ___ =	6 × ___ =	
Number of Files	2 × ___ =	4 × ___ =	8 × ___ =	

CASE STUDY 18.1

The Hidden Costs of Infrastructure Projects—The Case of Building Dams

In recent years, there has been an upsurge in the development of large dams in both developing and developed countries, including Brazil, Ethiopia, Pakistan, and China. There are a number of reasons for this increased interest in dam building. Demand for electricity is expected to double worldwide between 2010 and 2035. As a result hydroelectric power is seen as a cheap, available option for countries with river systems that allow for dams, particularly as it is a preferred option to dirtier coal-burning plants. Other arguments in favor of building these dams include its use for flood control, crop irrigation, inland transportation, urban water supplies, and as a job creator. These are all powerful and tempting arguments in favor of building large dams; however, there is one important counter-argument to the push toward these hydropower megaprojects. They fail to offer the advantages they are assumed to provide.

There are a number of criticisms of large dam projects. First, megadams take, on average, nearly nine years to complete. As a result, arguments that they will ease the burden of energy demands must be taken on faith; given their long lead times, they certainly are not an option for energy crisis situations. They also assume that all

FIGURE 18.9 Nigeria's Kainji Dam Under Construction

Source: AP Images

current circumstances (energy demand, population growth patterns, water availability, and energy prices) are likely to remain steady, or at least predictable, over the time period in which the dam is developed, which can lead to dangerous assumptions of future benefits. Nigeria's Kainji Dam, for example, has fallen short of generating its expected hydroelectricity levels by as much as 70%. Second, cost and schedule projections to complete these dams are almost always grossly underestimated. In fact, research suggests that cost overruns for large dam projects average 96% higher than estimated costs; that is, actual project costs were nearly double the original estimates. Schedules for these dams averaged overruns of 44%, or 2.3 years. Third, the cost in absolute terms for these large dam projects can nearly bankrupt the countries investing in them. For example, Ethiopia's Grand Ethiopian Renaissance dam on the Nile River was projected to cost $4.8 billion when it was started in 2011. By the time it is completed (projected for 2017), it will end up costing more than $10 billion, or one-quarter of Ethiopia's GDP. Instead of helping the economy and fostering growth, Ethiopia could be facing enormous problems paying off long-term debt from financing the dam. Nor is this a new phenomenon. Brazil's Itaipu Dam was built in the 1970s at a cost of almost $20 billion, or 240% more than projected. Since opening, it has been a drain on the country's finances. Despite producing electricity that is needed to support development in Brazil, it is unlikely that the costs of the Itaipu Dam will ever allow it to break even.

What is the solution? Countries such as Norway, which produces some 99% of its energy from hydropower, have adopted a smaller, more flexible solution to the use of dams. The government encourages the development not of large megadams, but of smaller, more flexible plants designed to produce smaller volumes of electricity but located at more locations within the country. Thus Norway currently supports some 1,000 smaller energy-producing dams that do not disrupt the natural flow of rivers, cause no environmental impact, and produce cleaner energy.

Large megadams of the type that are being developed around the planet are a tempting and expensive pursuit for the majority of countries undertaking them. With poor project development records historically, including huge cost and schedule overruns, these projects are typically undertaken as much for the national prestige they offer. At the same time, countries that have invested precious budget money in creating the dams are frequently disappointed with the results, including underutilization, decades of financial squeeze and debt obligation, and a failure to realize the expected benefits. When it comes to large megadams, the energy they produce is usually neither abundant nor cheap.[25]

Questions

1. Given the history of large cost overruns associated with megadam construction, why do you believe they are so popular, especially in the developing world?
2. Develop an argument in support of megadam construction. Develop an argument against these development projects.

CASE STUDY 18.2

Boston's Central Artery/Tunnel Project

Since the "Big Dig" project was first introduced in the previous edition of this textbook, a number of additional events have occurred that make it important for us to revisit the original story and update the current status of this monumental project. When it was opened in 1959, Boston's Central Artery highway was hailed as a marvel of engineering and forward-thinking urban planning. Designed as an elevated six-lane highway through the middle of the city, the highway was intended to carry a traffic volume of 75,000 vehicles a day. Unfortunately, by the early 1980s, the Central Artery was burdened by a daily volume of more than 200,000 vehicles, a nearly three-fold increase over the anticipated maximum traffic levels. The result was some of the worst urban congestion in the country, with traffic locked bumper to bumper for more than 10 hours each day. At over four times the national average, the accident rate for the Central Artery added to commuters' misery. Clearly, the Central Artery—a crumbling, overused, and increasingly dangerous stretch of highway—had outlived its usefulness.

Michael Dwyer/Alamy

FIGURE 18.10 Boston's Big Dig

The solution to the problem was the advent of the Central Artery/Tunnel (CA/T) project, commonly known to people from the Boston area as the "Big Dig." Under the supervision of the Massachusetts Turnpike Authority and using federal and state funding, the CA/T project comprises two main elements: (1) replacing the aging elevated roadway with an 8- to 10-lane underground expressway directly beneath the existing road, with a 14-lane, two-bridge crossing of the Charles River, and (2) extending Interstate 90 through a tunnel beneath South Boston and the harbor to Logan Airport. Originally conceived and initiated in the early 1980s, the project was a continuous activity (some would say "headache") in the city for more than 20 years.

The technical challenges in the Big Dig were enormous. Employing at its peak about 5,000 workers, the project included the construction of eight miles of highway, 161 lane miles in all, almost half below ground. It required the excavation of 16 million cubic yards of soil, enough to fill the New England Patriots' football stadium 16 times, and used 3.8 million cubic yards of concrete. The second major challenge was to perform these activities without disrupting existing traffic patterns or having a deleterious effect on the current highway system and its traffic flows. Thus, while miles of tunnels were being excavated underneath the old Central Artery, traffic volume could not be slowed on the elevated highway.

The project had been a source of controversy for several years, most notably due to its soaring costs and constantly revised budget. At the time of the project's kickoff in 1983, the original projections for the project's scope assumed a completion date of 1998 and one-time funding from the federal government to cover 60% of the project's original $2.5 billion budget. In fact, the budget and schedule have been revised upward nearly constantly since the project kicked off. Consider the following budget levels:

Year	Budget (in billions)
1983	2.56
1989	4.44
1992	6.44
1996	10.84
2000	14.08
2003	14.63

Final cost projections soared to over $14.5 billion and the project officially wrapped up in late 2004, or seven years late. Cost estimates and subsequent expenditures were so bad that by 2000, a federal audit of the project concluded that the Big Dig was officially bankrupt. One component of the federal audit concluded that a major cause for runaway project costs was due to poor project management oversight. Specifically, it was found that project management routinely failed to hold contractors to their bids or to penalize them for mistakes, resulting in huge cost increases for the Big Dig. Because of the intense public scrutiny and sensitive nature of the project, managers also stopped tracking or publicly acknowledging escalating costs, fearing that the political backlash could cripple the project. In fact, Taxpayers for Common Sense, a nonpartisan watchdog group, charged that the project's economics became so bad that managers delayed budgeting for contracts worth $260 million to a consulting firm because they could not offset such a large cost in the short term. In response to public outcry over the delays and rising costs, the project manager submitted his resignation.

Not surprisingly, the citizens of Boston have viewed the opening of the Big Dig with a genuine sense of ambivalence. Though a technological marvel that will undoubtedly improve the lives of its users, while reducing carbon monoxide emissions and improving the "green" reputation of the city, the project proved to be such a financial morass that public officials quietly canceled a planned celebration of a major section's opening. Finger pointing and a search for the causes of the Big Dig's poor cost estimation and control were vigorous. For its part, the Massachusetts Turnpike Authority planned a $150 million lawsuit against the firms that managed the project, arguing that many of the cost overruns could be attributed to poor project management and oversight.

Increasingly, the question being asked was: Were original cost estimates for the CA/T given in good faith or were they "tuned" to meet political realities? That is, did officials deliberately underestimate true project costs, fearing that the project would not have been approved in the beginning if the public was aware of its likely cost and scope? If so, the result has been to leave a sour taste in the mouths of the taxpaying public, convinced that the CA/T project represents a combination of brilliant technical achievement coupled with poor estimation and lax control. Former Massachusetts House Speaker Thomas Finnerman put the matter directly: "You'd be much, much better off saying upfront, factually, 'Hey, it's going to take umpteen years likely and umpteen billions dollars,' rather than selling it as a kind of smoke and mirrors thing about, 'Oh, it's two billion and a couple of years' work.'"

Aftermath: Reconsidering the Big Dig

Since the completion of the Big Dig, you would expect the commotion to have died down, the complaints to have been resolved, and the people of Boston to have become used to the advantages of this enormous project. Unfortunately, that has not been the case. Since its "completion" in early 2004, bad press, disasters, and accountability continue to dog the Central Tunnel/Artery system.

In 2001, prior to the completion of the project, thousands of leaks began appearing in the ceiling of sections of the tunnel system. The cause? Records suggest that the primary contractor for the concrete pouring, Modern Continental, failed to remove debris prior to pouring concrete, resulting in flaws, cavities, and pockets of weakness in the ceiling and walls of the tunnels. In May 2006, six employees of the main supplier of concrete were arrested for falsifying records.

In fact, 2006 was a very bad year for the Big Dig for a variety of reasons. On July 10, 2006, the bolt and epoxy system holding four sections (12 tons) of concrete ceiling panels failed, causing a section to collapse onto the tunnel roadway and kill a passenger in a car passing beneath the section at the time. That month, a detailed inspection of the ceiling panels throughout the tunnel system identified an additional 242 bolts that were already showing signs of stress! The tunnel system was shut down for the month of August for inspection and repairs. Also in August, the state assumed control of the Central Tunnel/Artery from

(continued)

the Turnpike Authority, citing the TA's poor record of supervision and effective project control.

The tragedy became something close a to farce when the Turnpike Authority and Federal Highway Administration refused to release critical documents to the state, including:

- Deficiency reports flagging initial substandard work
- Construction change orders and contract revisions
- Inspection reports on workmanship and building material quality

Until the court system orders the release of all project documents, we may never know the extent of mismanagement and poor decision making that dogged the development of the CT/A. From a public relations perspective, however, the fighting between state and federal authorities over oversight and control of the troubled project is a continuing black eye for all parties involved.

In early 2008, the contractors for the Big Dig, including primary contractors Bechtel and Parson Brinckerhoff, were ordered to pay $450 million to settle the state's lawsuit over the 2006 tunnel collapse. Though this settlement does not absolve the contractors from future lawsuits, it does settle some of the more egregious failures that occurred while they led the project. Michael Sullivan, the U.S. Attorney who led the lawsuit, noted that the contractors originally made a profit of about $150 million from the Big Dig; however, "They lost money as a result of the failures that occurred under their watch."[26]

Questions

1. Consider the following statement: "Government-funded projects intended to serve as 'prestige projects,' such as the 'Big Dig,' should not be judged on the basis of cost." Do you agree or disagree with this statement? Why?
2. Project success is defined as adherence to budget, schedule, functionality (performance), and client satisfaction. Under these criteria, cite evidence that suggests the "Big Dig" project was a success and/or failure.
3. What are the lessons to be learned from the "Big Dig" project? Was this a failure of project estimation or project control by the contractors and local government?

Internet Exercises

18.1 Go to the Internet and search using the phrase "cost analysis tools." What are some of the links and examples of cost analysis as it applies to projects?

18.2 Go to http://pmworldlibrary.net/ and type "case studies" in the search window. Select a project and report on it from the perspective of its cost estimation, budgeting, and (if applicable) expediting perspectives. Was the project a success or failure? Why?

18.3 Go to www.cityofflint.com/DCED/CDBG2013_14/Budget Detail_sample.pdf and reproduce the summary project budget worksheet. After examining the various elements in the budget, what are the main cost drivers for projects of this sort?

8.4 Go to www.stickyminds.com/articles.asp and click on "Stickyminds.com Original Articles." Search for and click on the article by Karl Wiegers, "Estimation Safety Tips." In the article (found as a pdf link to the site), the author offers tips on making estimates that are accurate and defensible by avoiding common mistakes. Which of these points makes the most sense to you personally? Why does it seem a plausible suggestion?

PMP CERTIFICATION SAMPLE QUESTIONS

1. The project administrator is preparing a preliminary budget for a project and adds in the cost of a new computer for the project team to use. What type of cost would this computer purchase represent?
   a. Variable
   b. Direct
   c. Indirect
   d. Variable direct
2. The project manager for a large project being developed in northern Ontario recognizes that it will be necessary for her to maintain a close presence at the construction site during its development and has negotiated the use of a building for her team near the construction project. The cost of the building must be factored into the project cost and will increase with use; that is, the cost of heating and other utilities is subject to change depending upon weather and team use. What type of cost would this building represent?
   a. Variable direct
   b. Indirect
   c. Nonrecurring
   d. None of the above
3. A project budget identifies $5,000 budgeted for programming costs. The actual amount for programming costs is $5,450. Which of the following statements is correct?
   a. The $450 represents a negative variance to the budget
   b. There is no variance to the budget
   c. The $450 represents a positive variance to the budget
   d. The entire $5,450 represents a positive variance to the budget

4. The project planning phase is moving forward. The project team has solicited the opinions of some senior project managers with experience in similar types of projects to try and develop a cost estimate for the project. This process is an example of:
   a. Activity-based budgeting
   b. Contingency planning
   c. Top-down budgeting
   d. Cost estimation

5. John is putting together his budget for the project and as part of this process, he is actively discussing and soliciting estimates from each member of the project team for the overall budget. He presents his budget to senior management and Susan rejects it, stating, "Team members are always going to pad their estimates. I will give you the figure I want you to shoot for." Susan is employing what method for project cost budgeting?
   a. Bottom-up
   b. Top-down
   c. Parametric
   d. Comparative

Answers: 1. b—A computer purchase would be an example of a direct cost for the project; 2. a—The cost of using a site building varies to the degree it is used and is charged as a direct cost to the project; 3. c—The overrun of $450 would be referred to as a positive variance to the budget; 4. d—The process of asking senior project managers for their best estimates of project costs is part of the cost estimation process; 5. b—Susan is using a top-down method in which she, as the senior manager, is providing the project budget estimate.

INTEGRATED PROJECT

Developing the Cost Estimates and Budget

Develop an in-depth cost estimate to support your initial project proposal narrative and scope statement, including the Work Breakdown Structure. Create a detailed justification of personnel costs, materials costs, overhead, and other forms of costs that are likely to accrue to your project. Be specific, particularly as regards personnel costs and commitment of time. For example, your cost table could look something like the following:

Personnel	Level	Rate	Loaded Rate	Labor-Weeks Needed*	Total Cost
Programmer	Senior	$35	$49/hr	20	$39,200
Sys. Analyst	Junior	$22	$31/hr	10	$12,400

*40-hour work week

Remember that the "loaded rate" assumes that you include the organization's overhead expenses for each employee. A typical multiplier for this figure could run anywhere up to and over 100% of the employee's wage rate. Make sure the course instructor indicates the overhead rate you should apply for your project. So, using the senior programmer example above with a fully loaded rate and assuming an overhead multiplier of 1.40, we get:

$$(\$49)\ (40\ \text{hrs})\ (20\ \text{weeks})\ (1.40) = \$54{,}880$$

Sample Project Plan: ABCups, Inc.

Name	Resource Type	Title	Salary (incl. Benefits) ($)	Hour Rate ($)	Fully Loaded Rate (Overhead = .40)	Time Needed (Hours/ week)	Duration (in weeks)	Total
Carol Johnson	Safety	Safety Engineer	64,600	32.30	45.22	10 hrs/wk	15	$ 6,783
Bob Hoskins	Engineering	Industrial Engineer	35,000	17.50	24.50	20 hrs/wk	35	17,150
Sheila Thomas	Management	Project Manager	55,000	27.50	38.50	40 hrs/wk	50	77,000
Randy Egan	Management	Plant Manager	74,000	37.00	51.80	10 hrs/wk	6	3,108
Stu Hall	Industrial	Maintenance Supervisor	32,000	16.00	22.40	15 hrs/wk	8	2,688
Susan Berg	Accounting	Cost Accountant	45,000	22.50	31.50	10 hrs/wk	12	3,780
Marty Green	Industrial	Shop Supervisor	24,000	12.00	16.80	10 hrs/wk	3	504
John Pittman	Quality	Quality Engineer	33,000	16.50	23.10	20 hrs/wk	25	11,550
Sally Reid	Quality	Jr. Quality Engineer	27,000	13.50	18.90	20 hrs/wk	18	6,804
Lanny Adams	Sales	Marketing Manager	70,000	35.00	49.00	10 hrs/wk	16	7,840
Kristin Abele	Purchasing	Purchasing Agent	47,000	23.50	32.90	15 hrs/wk	20	9,870
							Total	$147,077

Time-Phased Budget for ABCups, Inc. (All values in dollars ($))

Work Packages	June	July	Aug.	Sept.	Oct.	Nov.	Dec.	Jan.	Feb.	Mar.	April	May	Totals
Feasibility	2,500												2,500
Vendor Selection	7,678	3,934	1,960	3,934									17,506
Design			12,563	8,400	5,300								26,263
Engineering					9,992	14,790	15,600						40,382
Prototype Testing						3,250	12,745	7,250					23,245
Sales and Service							1,467	4,467	1,908				7,842
Packaging								2,434	8,101	650			11,185
Assembly									1,676	9,234	890		11,800
Close-out											1,198	5,156	6,354
Monthly Planned	10,178	3,934	14,523	12,334	15,292	18,040	29,812	14,151	11,685	9,884	2,088	5,156	
Monthly Cumulative	10,178	14,112	28,635	40,969	56,261	74,301	104,113	118,264	129,949	139,833	141,921	147,077	147,077

Notes

1. Flyvbjerg, B., and Stewart, A. (2012). "Olympic proportions: Cost and cost overrun at the Olympics 1960–2012. Said Business School Working Papers, Oxford: University of Oxford; Forrest, Brett. (2014, February 23). "Putin's run for gold." *Vanity Fair*. www.vanityfair.com/culture/2014/02/sochi-olympics-russia-corruption; Geere, D. (2014, February 4). "Freezing Sochi: How Russia turned a subtropical beach into a Winter Olympics wonderland." *The Verge*. www.theverge.com/2014/2/4/5377356/sochi-winter-olympics-2014-subtropical-transformation; Rathi, A. (2014, January 30). "The Sochi Olympics are going to be the costliest ever." *Quartz*. http://qz.com/172180/the-sochi-olympics-are-going-to-cost-more-than-the-last-13-olympics-combined/; "Sochi road an engineering marvel." (2014, February 15). *BostonGlobe.com*. | www.bostonglobe.com/sports/2014/02/15/sochi-road-engineering-marvel/dpRwuHty4V35VHR1O5T6SL/story.html; Taylor, A. (2014, January 17). "Why Sochi is by far the most expensive Olympics ever." *Business Insider*. www.businessinsider.com/why-sochi-is-by-far-the-most-expensive-olympics-ever-2014-1; Waldron, T., (2014, February 3). "Sochi Olympics will cost more than every other Winter Olympics combined." *ThinkProgress RSS*. http://thinkprogress.org/sports/2014/02/03/3239131/sochi-olympics-cost-winter-olympics-combined/; Yaffa, J. (2014, January 2). "The waste and corruption of Vladimir Putin's 2014 Winter Olympics." *Bloomberg Business Week*. Bloomberg. www.businessweek.com/articles/2014-01-02/the-2014-winter-olympics-in-sochi-cost-51-billion#p1; Young, J. (2014, February 3). "Money spent on Sochi games raises questions." *VOA*. www.voanews.com/content/money-spent-on-sochi-games-raising-questions/1843380.html.
2. Needy, K. S., and Petri, K. L. (1998). "Keeping the lid on project costs," in Cleland, D. I. (Ed.), *Field Guide to Project Management*. New York: Van Nostrand Reinhold, pp. 106–20.
3. Miller, G. J., and Louk, P. (1988). "Strategic manufacturing cost management," APICS 31st International Conference Proceedings, Falls Church, VA: APICS; Kerzner, H. (1988). "Pricing out the work," in Cleland, D. I., and King, W. R. (Eds.), *Project Management Handbook*, 2nd ed. New York: Van Nostrand Reinhold, pp. 394–410.
4. Meredith, J. R., and Mantel, Jr., S. J. (2003). *Project Management*, 5th ed. New York: Wiley.
5. Needy, K. S., and Petri, K. L. (1998). "Keeping the lid on project costs," in Cleland, D. I. (Ed.), *Field Guide to Project Management*. New York: Van Nostrand Reinhold, pp. 106–20.
6. Source for Table 18.2: Needy, K. S., and Petri, K. L. (1998). "Keeping the lid on project costs," in Cleland, D. I. (Ed.), *Field Guide to Project Management*. New York: Van Nostrand Reinhold, p. 110.
7. Lock, D. (2000). "Managing cost," in Turner, J. R., and Simister, S. J. (Eds.), *Gower Handbook of Project Management*, 3rd ed. Aldershot, UK: Gower, pp. 293–322.
8. Amor, J. P., and Teplitz, C. J. (1998). "An efficient approximation for project composite learning curves," *Project Management Journal*, 29(3): 28–42; Badiru, A. B. (1995). "Incorporating learning curve effects into critical resource diagramming," *Project Management Journal*, 26(2): 38–46; Camm, J. D., Evans, J. R., and Womer, N. K. (1987). "The unit learning curve approximation of total cost," *Computers in Industrial Engineering*, 12: 205–13; Fields, M. A. (1991). "Effect of the learning curve on the capital budgeting process," *Managerial Finance*, 17(2–3): 29–41; Teplitz, C. J., and Amor, J. P. (1993). "Improving CPM's accuracy using learning curves," *Project Management Journal*, 24(4): 15–19.
9. Meredith, J. R., and Mantel, Jr., S. J. (2003). *Project Management*, 5th ed. New York: Wiley.
10. Amor, J. P., and Teplitz, C. J. (1998). "An efficient approximation for project composite learning curves," *Project Management Journal*, 29(3): 28–42.
11. Crawford, J. R. (n.d.), *Learning curve, ship curve, rations, related data*. Burbank, CA: Lockheed Aircraft Corp.
12. Heiser, J., and Render, B. (2001). *Operation Management*, 6th ed. Upper Saddle River, NJ: Prentice Hall.
13. Hackbarth, G. (2005), personal communication.
14. "Extreme chaos." (2001). Standish Group International.
15. Bloch, M., Blumberg, S., and Laartz, J. (2012). "Delivering large-scale IT projects on time, on budget, and on value," *McKinsey Reports*. http://mckinsey.com/MOBT_27_Delivering_large-scale_IT_projects_on_time_budget_and_value%20(1).pdf; Flyvbjerg, B., Budzier, A. (2011). "Why your project may be riskier than you think," *Harvard Business Review*, 89(9): 23–25.
16. For a discussion of COCOMO II standards, see http://csse.usc.edu/csse/research/COCOMOII/cocomo2000.0/CII_modelman2000.0.pdf
17. McConnell, S. (2004). *Code Complete, 2nd ed*. Redmond, WA: Microsoft Press; McConnell, S. (2006). *Software Estimation: Demystifying the Black Art*. Redmond, WA: Microsoft Press.
18. Turbit, N. "Function points overview." www.projectperfect.com.au/downloads/Info/info_fp_overview.pdf; International Functional Points Users Group, www.ifpug.org; Dillibabu, R., and Krishnaiah, K. (2005). "Cost estimation of a software product using COCOMO II.2000 model—a case study," *International Journal of Project Management*, 23(4): 297–307; Jeffery, R., Low, G. C., and Barnes, M. (1993). "A comparison of function point counting techniques," *IEEE Transactions on Software Engineering*, 19(5): 529–32.
19. Hamburger, D. (1986). "Three perceptions of project cost—Cost is more than a four-letter word," *Project Management Journal*, 17(3): 51–58; Sigurdsen, A. (1996). "Principal errors in capital cost estimating work, part 1: Appreciate the relevance of the quantity-dependent estimating norms," *Project Management Journal*, 27(3): 27–34; Toney, F. (2001). "Accounting and financial management: Finding the project's bottom line," in J. Knutson (Ed.), *Project Management for Business Professionals*. New York: John Wiley, pp. 101–27; Shtub, A., Bard, J. F., and Globerson, S. (1994). *Project Management: Engineering, Technology, and Implementation*. Englewood Cliffs, NJ: Prentice-Hall; Smith, N. J. (Ed.). (1995). *Project Cost Estimating*. London: Thomas Telford; Sweeting, J. (1997). *Project Cost Estimating: Principles and Practices*. Rugby, UK: Institution of Chemical Engineers; Goyal, S. K. (1975). "A note of a simple CPM time-cost tradeoff algorithm,"

Management Science, 21(6): 718–22; Venkataraman, R., and Pinto, J. K. (2008). *Cost and Value Management in Projects.* New York: Wiley.

20. Panknin, S., quoted in Grieshaber, K. (2013, April 8). "Berlin's airport delays shame Germans." http://news.yahoo.com/berlins-airport-project-delays-shame-germans-093036692–finance.html
21. Flyvbjerg, B., Garbuio, M., and Lavallo, D. (2009). "Delusion and deception in large infrastructure projects: Two models for explaining and preventing executive disaster," *California Management Review,* 51(2): 170–93; "Building BRICs of growth." (2008, June 7). *The Economist.* www.economist.com/node/11488749; Lovallo, D., and Kahneman, D. (2003). "Delusions of success: How optimism undermines executives' decisions," *Harvard Business Review,* 81(7): 56–63; Flyvbjerg, B., Holm, M. S., and Buhl, S. (2002). "Underestimating costs in public works projects: Error or lie?" *Journal of the American Planning Association,* 68(3): 279–95.
22. Meredith, J. R., and Mantel, Jr., S. J. (2003). *Project Management,* 5th ed. New York: Wiley; see also Christensen, D. S., and Gordon, J. A. (1998). "Does a rubber baseline guarantee cost overruns on defense acquisition contracts?" *Project Management Journal,* 29(3): 43–51.
23. Maher, M. (1997). *Cost Accounting: Creating Value for Management,* 5th ed. Chicago: Irwin.
24. Gray, C. F., and Larson, E. W. (2003). *Project Management,* 2nd ed. Burr Ridge, IL: McGraw-Hill.
25. Flyvbjerg, B., and Ansar, A. (2014, March 19). "Ending the flood of megadams," *Wall Street Journal,* p. A15; Ansar, A., Flyvbjerg, B., Budzier, A., and Lunn, D. (2014). "Should we build more large dams? The actual costs of hydropower megaproject development." *Energy Policy.* http://dx.doi.org/10.1016/j.enpol.2013.10.069
26. "Boston's Big Dig opens to public." (2003, December 20). www.msnbc.com/id/3769829; "Big Dig billions over budget." (2000, April 11). www.taxpayer.net/library/weekly-wastebasket/article/big-dig-billions-over-budget; "Massachusetts to sue Big Dig companies." (2006, November 27). www.msnbc.msn.com/id/15917776; "Big Dig contractors to pay $450 million." (2008, January 23). www.msnbc.msn.com/id/22809747

Project Evaluation and Control

Chapter Outline

Chapter Objectives

After completing this chapter, you should be able to:

1. Understand the nature of the control cycle and four key steps in a general project control model.
2. Recognize the strengths and weaknesses of common project evaluation and control methods.
3. Understand how Earned Value Management can assist project tracking and evaluation.
4. Use Earned Value Management for project portfolio analysis.
5. Understand behavioral concepts and other human issues in evaluation and control.
6. From Appendix 18.1: Understand the advantages of Earned Schedule methods for determining project schedule variance, schedule performance index, and estimates to completion.

PROJECT MANAGEMENT BODY OF KNOWLEDGE CORE CONCEPTS COVERED IN THIS CHAPTER

1. Control Schedule (PMBoK sec. 6.7)
2. Control Costs (PMBoK sec. 7.4)
3. Earned Value System (PMBoK sec. 7.4.2.1)
4. Forecasting (PMBoK sec. 7.4.2.2)
5. Performance Reviews (PMBoK sec. 7.4.2.4)

PROJECT PROFILE

New York City's CityTime Project

"... virtually all of the $600 million that the City paid to SAIC for CityTime was tainted, directly or indirectly, by fraud." In announcing charges filed against several contractors and project overseers for New York City's troubled CityTime automated payroll and time keeping project, Manhattan U.S. Attorney Preet Bharara placed the blame for the massive cost overruns squarely at the feet of corrupt project managers and their shockingly brazen money skimming practices.

In 1998, when former mayor Rudolph Giuliani announced the creation of the CityTime project for New York City's employees, he was seeking to automate an outdated, paper-based time card and payroll system used by some 300,000 city employees. Over the years, this record-keeping system could not keep up with the large employee base, leading to allegations of waste and routinely falsified time sheets, all of which cost the city millions a year. CityTime was supposed to fix this problem by automating and updating the old paper-based methods with the latest electronic, integrated information system. When the city authorized the project, the winning bid was awarded to Science Applications International Corporation (SAIC) for $63 million over a five-year period. SAIC's job as prime contractor was to oversee the development of the new computer-based system and support the migration of all record-keeping and payroll processes to the new system. By the time the dust settled, New York City had spent over $720 million on a system that took 10 years to install. Worse, much of the money appears to have been siphoned off by a string of "consultants" and subcontractors, who all used the project to get rich.

How did things get so bad? Federal prosecutors have said that nearly the entire sum the city spent on the project was stained by an epic fraud that involved hundreds of contractors, systemic overbilling, and an international money-laundering conspiracy.

FIGURE 18.11 New York City
Source: Janniswerner/Fotolia

The project involved numerous stakeholders, all with differing motives and all convinced that others were using the project to push their own agendas. For example, as early as 2003, unions representing city employees were complaining about the new system and the inflated salaries of numerous consultants and officials involved in the project. Still, nothing happened. That was because CityTime had powerful supporters who included the new mayor, Michael Bloomberg; his budget chief Mark Page; and Joel Bondy, the director of the Office of Payroll Administration (OPA). These officials saw the project as a way to control both overtime and pension costs and regarded union complaints as the predictable anger of city employees being stripped of their ability to game the system.

Official oversight for this project rested with a three-person panel including Mark Page, a representative for Comptroller Bill Thompson, and Joel Bondy, who led the Office of Payroll Administration up until he was fired. Despite this oversight, Attorney Baharara says the private contractors and consultants were able to manipulate the terms of their contracts and inflate the costs eleven times the original estimate. Their biggest coup was getting the project terms changed from a fixed-price contract to a fixed-price level of effort contract. This meant that in future, the city would be held responsible for all cost overruns, which quickly became enormous.

Around this time, allegations of fraud and widespread theft were gaining ground. Mark Mazer, for example, was hired in 2004 to streamline and rescue the project, which had been falling behind its original schedule. He is accused of taking more than $25 million in kickbacks in addition to his $4.4 million salary from the CityTime project. His job? Ironically, Mazur was the outside contractor hired by the city to keep a close eye on the other outside contractors who were performing the work; a classic case of the fox being set to guard the chickens! Meanwhile, the prime CityTime contractor, Science Applications International Corp. (SAIC), received more than $600 million from the city. SAIC's project chief, Gerard Denault, is accused of taking $9 million in kickbacks. SAIC's systems engineer, Carl Bell, took more than $5 million and pleaded guilty to doing so.

Much of the bribe money flowed through Technodyne, a subcontractor hired by SAIC and headed by an Indian-American husband and wife team, Reddy and Padma Allen. SAIC paid $450 million to Technodyne, and the Allens responded with a series of illegal cash payments for Denault, Bell, and Mark Mazer, according to the government. In return, investigators say, these individuals worked together to pad the CityTime payroll and prolong the project. The Allens shipped at least $50 million to companies they controlled in India. Part of it was then wired back to the United States to shell companies controlled by Denault and Bell. Mazer was paid off through a larger web of shell companies. Mazer then funneled millions of dollars stolen from the city to bank accounts overseas. Investigators found hundreds of thousands of dollars stashed in safe-deposit boxes around the city that were part of the ill-gotten gains.

Things finally began to unravel in 2010 (over 10 years into the project) when an unhappy CityTime consultant who had been fired went to the city's Department of Investigation and blew the whistle. The Department of Investigation began its own probe and then notified federal authorities who were brought into the case. Federal indictments were returned in 2010 and the cases were finally brought to trial in 2013.

Before he left office, Mayor Michael Bloomberg demanded that SAIC repay the city more than $600 million spent on the scandal-plagued CityTime payroll technology project. In 2012, SAIC came to an agreement with New York City to repay $500 million to avoid federal prosecution. As the U.S. Attorney noted in her indictment, "... the corruption on the CityTime project was epic in duration, magnitude, and scope. As alleged, CityTime served as a vehicle for an unprecedented fraud, which appears to have metastasized over time."

Ironically, a computer system that was developed to make sure that city employees did not cheat on their time card hours resulted in one of the biggest cases of graft, cheating, and outright theft that New York City has ever seen. Project controls and oversight for the project simply did not exist as city officials adopted an attitude that "outside contractors can do it better." If by "doing it better," officials meant "are more capable of theft," then they may have been right. It seems that the echoes of the CityTime scandal are finally starting to fade. Of the 11 people arrested in connection with the fraud and corruption, by 2014, eight had been convicted, the Allens had fled back to India with at least $35 million, and one died prior to the start of his trial. Most recently, a federal judge in Manhattan sentenced three men, including Mark Mazur, to 20 years in prison for their roles in the scandal-ridden project, and he also sharply criticized New York City's contracting procedures for what he called a lack of "adequate and effective oversight."[27]

INTRODUCTION

One of the most significant challenges with running a project has to do with maintaining an accurate monitoring and control system for its implementation. Because projects are often defined by their constraints (i.e., budget and schedule limitations), it is vital that we ensure they are controlled as carefully as possible. Project monitoring and control are the principal mechanisms that allow the project team to stay on top of a project's evolving status as it moves through the various life cycle stages toward completion. Rather than adopting a "no news is good news" approach to monitoring and control of projects, we need to clearly understand the benefits that can be derived from careful and thorough status assessments as the project moves forward.

In order to best ensure that the project's control will be as optimal as possible, we need to focus our attention on two important aspects of the monitoring process. First, we need to identify the appropriate cues that signal project status as well as understand the best times across the project's life cycle to get accurate assessments of its performance. In other words, we need to be fully aware of the *what* and *when* questions: What information concerning the project should be measured, and when are the best times to measure it? Our goal is to have a sense of how to develop systematic project control that is comprehensive, accurate, and timely. Put another way, when we are responsible for a multimillion-dollar investment in our organization, we want to know the status of the project, we want that information as soon as we can get it, and we want it to be as up-to-date as possible.

18.5 CONTROL CYCLES—A GENERAL MODEL

A general model of organizational control includes four components that can operate in a continuous cycle and can be represented as a wheel. These elements are:

1. ***Setting a goal.*** Project goal setting goes beyond overall scope development to include setting the project baseline plan. The project baseline is predicated on an accurate Work Breakdown Structure (WBS) process. Remember that WBS establishes all the deliverables and work packages associated with the project, assigns the personnel responsible for them, and creates a visual chart of the project from the highest level down through the deliverable and task levels. The project baseline is created as each task is laid out on a network diagram and resources and time durations are assigned to it.
2. ***Measuring progress.*** Effective control systems require accurate project measurement mechanisms. Project managers must have a system in place that will allow them to measure the ongoing status of various project activities in real time. We need a measurement system that can provide information as quickly as possible. *What to measure* also needs to be clearly defined. Any number of devices will allow us to measure one aspect of the project or another; however, the larger question is whether or not we are getting the type of information we can really use.
3. ***Comparing actual with planned performance.*** When we have some sense of the original baseline (plan) and a method for accurately measuring progress, the next step is to compare the two pieces of information. A gap analysis can be used as a basis for testing the project's status. *Gap analysis* refers to any measurement process that first determines the goals and then the degree to which the actual performance lives up to those goals. The smaller the gaps between planned and actual performance, the better the outcome. In cases where we see obvious differences between what was planned and what was realized, we have a clear-cut warning signal.
4. ***Taking action.*** Once we detect significant deviations from the project plan, it becomes necessary to engage in some form of corrective action to minimize or remove the deviation. The process of taking corrective action is generally straightforward. Corrective action can either be relatively minor or involve significant remedial steps. At its most extreme, corrective action may even involve scuttling a nonperforming project. After corrective action, the monitoring and control cycle begins again.

As Figure 18.12 demonstrates, the **control cycle** is continuous. As we create a plan, we begin measurement efforts to chart progress and compare stages against the baseline plan. Any indications of significant deviations from the plan should immediately trigger an appropriate response,

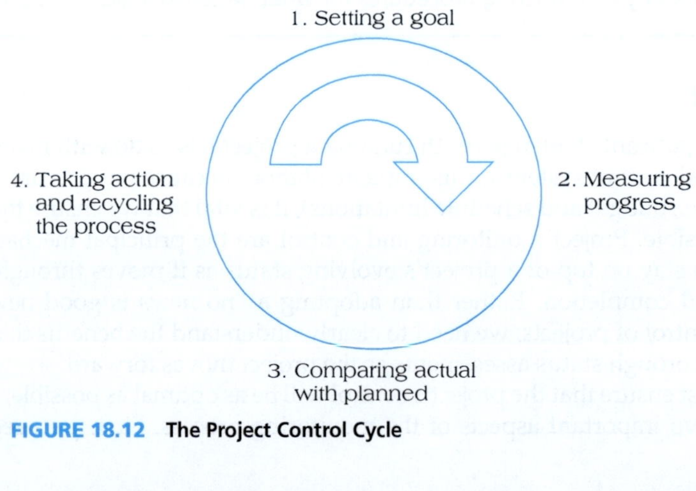

FIGURE 18.12 The Project Control Cycle

leading to a reconfiguration of the plan, reassessment of progress, and so on. Project monitoring is a continuous, full-time cycle of target setting, measuring, correcting, improving, and remeasuring.

18.6 MONITORING PROJECT PERFORMANCE

As we discovered in the chapters on project budgeting and resource management, once we have established a **project baseline** budget, one of the most important methods for indicating the ongoing status of the project is to evaluate it against the original budget projections. For project monitoring and control, both individual task budgets and the cumulative project budget are relevant. The cumulative budget can be broken down by time over the project's projected duration.

The Project S-Curve: A Basic Tool

As a basis for evaluating **project control** techniques, let us consider a simple example. Assume a project (Project Sierra) with four work packages (Design, Engineering, Installation, and Testing), a budget to completion of $80,000, and an anticipated duration of 45 weeks. Table 18.9 gives a breakdown of the project's cumulative budget in terms of both work packages and time. As we discussed in Chapter 18, this type of budget is referred to as a *time-phased* budget.

To determine project performance and status, a straightforward time/cost analysis is often our first choice. Here the project's status is evaluated as a function of the accumulated costs and labor hours or quantities plotted against time for both budgeted and actual amounts. We can see that time (shown on the x, or horizontal, axis) is compared with money expended (shown on the y, or vertical, axis). The classic **project S-curve** represents the typical form of such a relationship. Budget expenditures are initially low and ramp up rapidly during the major project execution stage, before starting to level off again as the project gets nearer to its completion (see Figure 18.13). Cumulative budget projections for Project Sierra shown in Table 18.9 have been plotted against the project's schedule. The S-curve figure represents the project budget baseline against which actual budget expenditures are evaluated.

Monitoring the status of a project using S-curves becomes a simple tracking problem. At the conclusion of each given time period (week, month, or quarter), we simply total the cumulative project budget expenditures to date and compare them with the anticipated spending patterns. Any significant deviations between actual and planned budget spending reveal a potential problem area.

Simplicity is the key benefit of S-curve analysis. Because the projected project baseline is established in advance, the only additional data shown are the actual project budget expenditures. The S-curve also provides real-time tracking information in that budget expenditures can be constantly updated and the new values plotted on the graph. Project information can be visualized immediately and updated continuously, so S-curves offer an easy-to-read evaluation of the project's status in a timely manner. (The information is not necessarily easily interpreted, however, as we shall see later.)

Our Project Sierra example (whose budget is shown in Table 18.9) can also be used to illustrate how S-curve analysis is employed. Suppose that by week 21 in the project, the original budget projected expenditures of $50,000. However, our actual project expenditures totaled only $40,000.

TABLE 18.9 Budgeted Costs for Project Sierra (in thousands $)

	Duration (in weeks)									
	5	**10**	**15**	**20**	**25**	**30**	**35**	**40**	**45**	**Total**
Design	6	2								
Engineer		4	8	8	8					
Install				4	20	6				
Test						2	6	4	2	
Total	6	6	8	12	28	8	6	4	2	
Cumul.	6	12	20	32	60	68	74	78	80	80

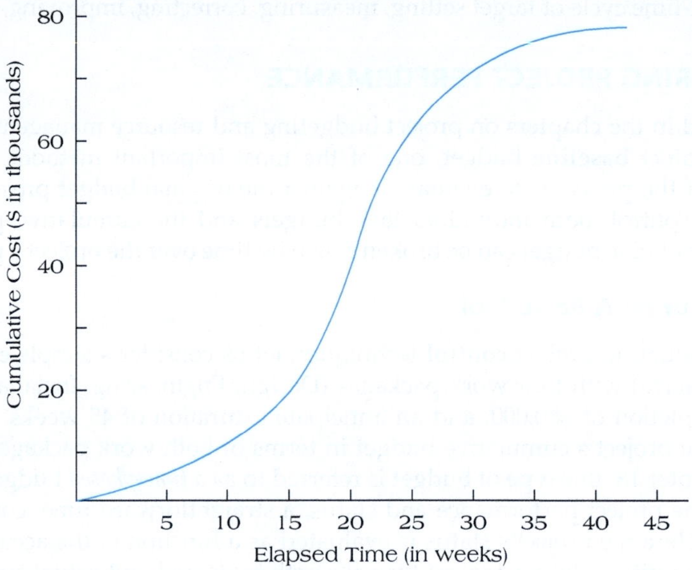

FIGURE 18.13 **Project S-Curves**

In effect, there is a $10,000 budget shortfall, or negative variance between the cumulative budgeted cost of the project and its cumulative actual cost. Figure 18.14 shows the tracking of budgeted expenditures with actual project costs, including identifying the negative variance shown at week 21. In this illustration, we see the value of S-curve analysis as a good visual method for linking project costs (both budgeted and actual) over the project's schedule.

S-Curve Drawbacks

When project teams consider using S-curves, they need to take the curves' significant drawbacks as well as their strengths into consideration. S-curves can identify positive or negative variance (budget expenditures above or below projections), but they do not allow us to make reasonable

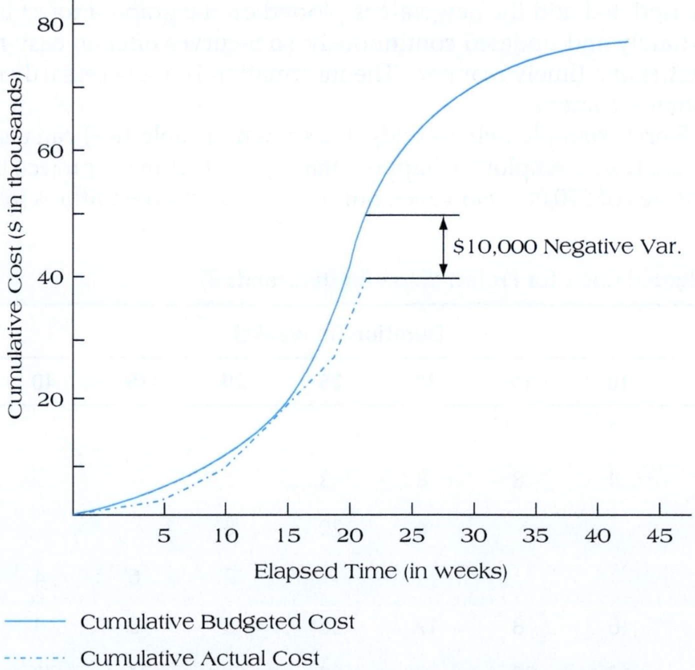

FIGURE 18.14 **Project Sierra's S-Curve Showing Negative Variance**

interpretations as to the cause of variance. Consider the S-curve shown in Figure 18.14. The actual budget expenditures have been plotted to suggest that the project team has not spent the total planned budget money to date (there is negative variance). However, the question is how to interpret this finding. The link between accumulated project costs and time is not always easily resolved. Is the project team behind schedule (given that they have not spent sufficient budget to date) or might there be alternative reasons for the negative variance?

Assume that your organization tracks project costs employing an S-curve approach and uses that information to assess the status of an ongoing project. Also assume that the project is to be completed in 12 months and has a budget of $150,000. At the six-month checkup, you discover that the project S-curve shows significant shortfall; you have spent far less on the project to date than was originally budgeted. Is this good or bad news?

On the surface, we might suppose that this is a sign of poor performance; we are lagging far behind in bringing the project along and the smaller amount we have spent to date is evidence that our project is behind schedule. On the other hand, there are any number of reasons why this circumstance actually might be positive. For example, suppose that in running the project, you found a cost-effective method for doing some component of the work or came across a new technology that significantly cut down on expenses. In that case, the time/cost metric may not only be misused, but might lead to dramatically inaccurate conclusions. Likewise, positive variance is not always a sign of project progress. In fact, a team may have a serious problem with overexpenditures that could be interpreted as strong progress on the project when in reality it signals nothing more than their inefficient use of project capital resources. The bottom line is this: Simply evaluating a project's status according to its performance on time versus budget expenditures may easily lead us into making inaccurate assumptions about project performance.

Another drawback with using S-curves to update a project's progress is that they are providing "reactive" data; that is, we plot the results of expenditures after the money has already been spent. S-curves are a tracking tool that are visually appealing but do not allow the project team to anticipate or take proactive actions because the information only arrives after the fact. Likewise, S-curves do not allow the team to forecast project expenditures or other performance metrics to completion. We know how much we have spent to date, but we only have the initial budget to suggest how much we should have spent and how much we are likely to spend in the future. Once significant variances start appearing in the budget, the question of what our final, likely project costs will be is extremely difficult to determine.

Milestone Analysis

Another method for monitoring project progress is *milestone analysis.* A **milestone** is an event or stage of the project that represents a significant accomplishment on the road to the project's completion. Completion of a deliverable (a combination of multiple project tasks), an important activity on the project's critical path, or even a calendar date can all be milestones. In effect, milestones are road markers that we observe on our travels along the project's life cycle. There are several benefits to using milestones as a form of project control.

1. ***Milestones signal the completion of important project steps.*** A project's milestones are an important indicator of the current status of the project under development. They give the project team a common language to use in discussing the ongoing status of the project.
2. ***Milestones can motivate the project team.*** In large projects lasting several years, motivation can flag as team members begin to have difficulty seeing how the project is proceeding overall, what their specific contribution has been and continues to be, and how much longer the project is likely to take. Focusing attention on milestones helps team members become more aware of the project's successes as well as its status, and they can begin to develop greater task identity regarding their work on the project.
3. ***Milestones offer points at which to reevaluate client needs and any potential change requests.*** A common problem with many types of projects is the nature of repetitive and constant change requests from clients. Using project review milestones as formal "stop points," both the project team and the clients are clear on when they will take midcourse reviews of the project and how change requests will be handled. When clients are aware of these formal project review points, they are better able to present reasonable and well-considered feedback (and specification change requests) to the team.

4. ***Milestones help coordinate schedules with vendors and suppliers.*** Creating delivery dates that do not delay project activities is a common challenge in scheduling delivery of key project components. From a resource perspective, the project team needs to receive supplies before they are needed but not so far in advance that space limitations, holding and inventory costs, and in some cases spoilage are problems. Hence, to balance delays of late shipments against the costs associated with holding early deliveries, a well-considered system of milestones creates a scheduling and coordinating mechanism that identifies the key dates when supplies will be needed.
5. ***Milestones identify key project review gates.*** For many complex projects, a series of mid-term project reviews are mandatory. For example, many projects that are developed for the U.S. government require periodic evaluation as a precondition to the project firm receiving some percentage of the contract award. Milestones allow for appropriate points for these reviews. Sometimes the logic behind when to hold such reviews is based on nothing more than the passage of time ("It is time for the July 1 review"). For other projects, the review gates are determined based on completion of a series of key project steps (such as the evaluation of software results from the beta sites).
6. ***Milestones signal other team members when their participation is expected to begin.*** Many times projects require contributions from personnel who are not part of the project team. For example, a quality assurance individual may be needed to conduct systems tests or quality inspection and evaluations of work done to date. If the quality supervisor does not know when to assign a person to our project, we may find when we reach that milestone that no one is available to help us. Because the quality assurance person is not part of the project team, we need to coordinate her involvement in order to minimize disruption to the project schedule.
7. ***Milestones can delineate the various deliverables developed in the Work Breakdown Structure and thereby enable the project team to develop a better overall view of the project.*** We then are able to refocus efforts and function-specific resources toward the deliverables that show signs of trouble, rather than simply allocating resources in a general manner. For example, indications that the initial project software programming milestone has been missed allow the project manager to specifically request additional programmers downstream, in order to make up time later in the project's development.

Figure 18.15 gives an example of a simple Gantt chart with milestones included. The milestones in this case are simply arbitrary points established on the chart; we could just as easily have placed them after completed work packages or by using some other criteria.

Problems with Milestones

Milestones, in one form or another, are probably the simplest and most widely used of all project control devices. Their benefits lie in their clarity; it is usually easy for all project team members to relate to the idea of milestones as a project performance metric. The problem with them is that, like

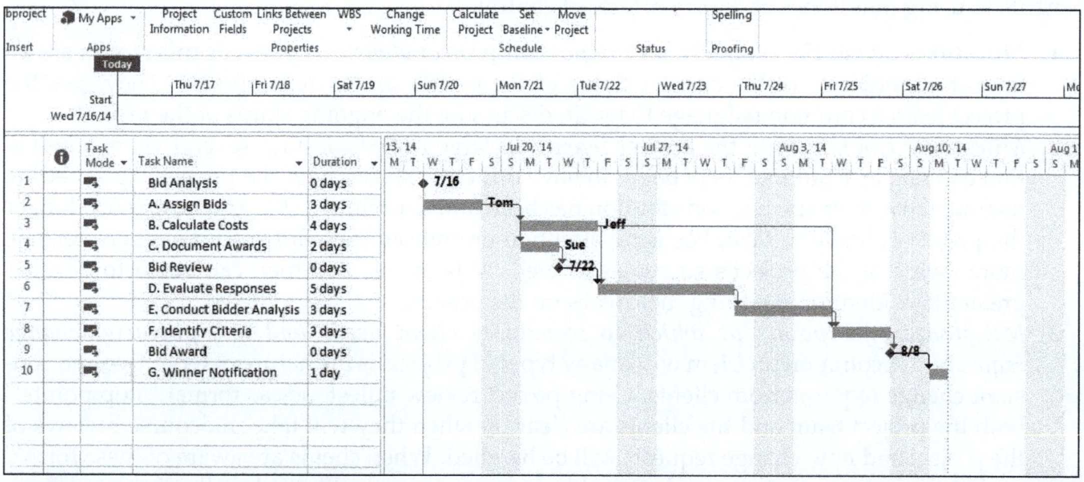

FIGURE 18.15 Gantt Chart with Milestones

Source: MS Project 2013, Microsoft Corporation

S-curves, they are a reactive control system. You must first engage in project activities and then evaluate them relative to your goal. If you significantly underperform your work to that point, you are faced with having to correct what has already transpired. Imagine, for example, that a project team misses a milestone by a large margin. Not having received any progress reports until the point that the bad news becomes public, the project manager is probably not in a position to craft an immediate remedy for the shortfall. At this point, the problems are compounded. Due to the delay in receiving the bad news, remedial steps are themselves delayed, pushing the project even farther behind.

The Tracking Gantt Chart

One form of the Gantt chart, referred to as a *tracking Gantt chart,* is useful for evaluating project performance at specific points in time. The **tracking Gantt chart** allows the project team to constantly update the project's status by linking task completion to the schedule baseline. Rather than monitor costs and budget expenditures, a tracking Gantt chart identifies the stage of completion each task has attained by a specific date within the project. For example, Figure 18.16 represents Project Blue, involving five activities. As the project progresses, its current status is indicated by the vertical status bar shown for Thursday, July 24. To date, activity A (Licensing Agreement) has been 100% completed, while its two subsequent tasks, Specification Design and Site Certification, are shown as having progressed proportionally by the identified tracking date. That is, activity B (Specification Design) is rated as 57% completed, and activity C (Site Certification) as 80% completed. Activities D and E have not yet begun in this example.

It is also possible to measure both positive and negative deviations from the schedule baseline with the tracking Gantt chart. Let us suppose, using our Project Blue example, that activity B remains approximately 57% completed as of the baseline date indicated. On the other hand, activity C has not progressed as rapidly and is only 20% completed as of the July 24 date. The chart can be configured to identify the variations, either positive or negative, in activity completion against the project baseline. These features are demonstrated in Figure 18.17, showing the current date for the project and the delay in progress on activity C.

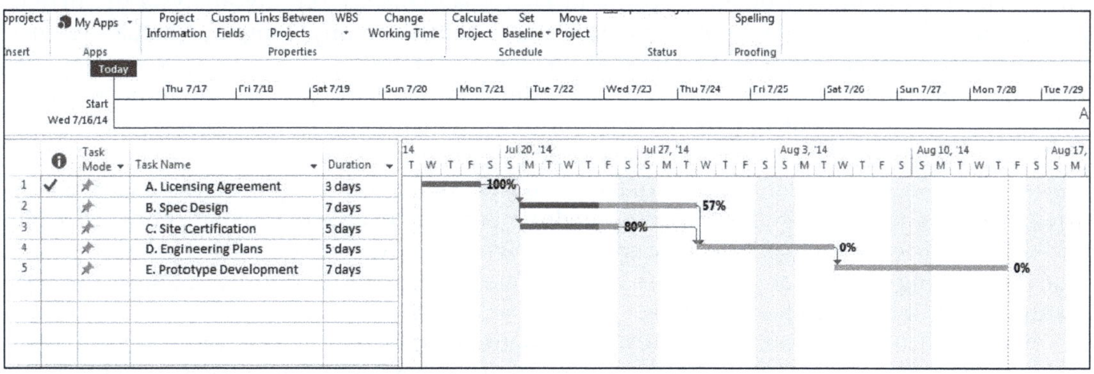

FIGURE 18.16 Assessing Project Blue's Status Using Tracking Gantt Chart

Source: MS Project 2013, Microsoft Corporation

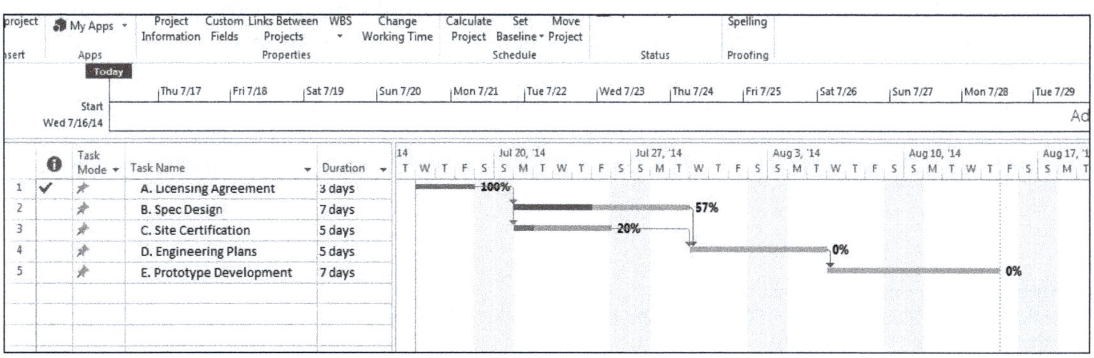

FIGURE 18.17 Tracking Gantt with Project Activity Deviation

Source: MS Project 2013, Microsoft Corporation

Benefits and Drawbacks of Tracking Gantt Charts

A key benefit of tracking Gantt charts is that they are quite easy to understand. The visual nature of the feedback report is easy to assimilate and interpret. This type of control chart can be updated very quickly, providing a sense of real-time project control. On the other hand, tracking Gantt charts have some inherent drawbacks that limit their overall utility. First, although they may show which tasks are ahead of schedule, on schedule, and behind schedule, these charts do not identify the underlying source of problems in the cases of task slippage. Reasons for schedule slippage cannot be inferred from the data presented. Second, tracking control charts do not allow for future projections of the project's status. It is difficult to accurately estimate the time to completion for a project, particularly in the case of significant positive or negative variation from the baseline schedule. Is a series of early finishes for some activities good news? Does that signal that the project is likely to finish earlier than estimated? Because of these drawbacks, tracking charts should be used along with other techniques that offer more prescriptive power.

18.7 EARNED VALUE MANAGEMENT

An increasingly popular method used in project monitoring and control consists of a mechanism that has become known as **Earned Value Management (EVM).*** The origins of EVM date to the 1960s when U.S. government contracting agencies began to question the ability of contractors to accurately track their costs across the life of various projects. As a result, after 1967, the Department of Defense imposed 35 Cost/Schedule Control Systems Criteria that suggested, in effect, that any future projects procured by the U.S. government in which the risk of cost growth was to be retained by the government must satisfy these 35 criteria.[28] In the more than four years since its origin, EVM has been practiced in multiple settings, by agencies from governments as diverse as Australia, Canada, and Sweden, as well as by a host of project-based firms in numerous industries.

Unlike previous project tracking approaches, EVM recognizes that it is necessary to jointly consider the impact of time, cost, and *project performance* on any analysis of current project status. Put another way: Any monitoring system that only compares actual against budgeted cost numbers ignores the fact that the client is spending that money to accomplish something—to create a project. Therefore, EVM reintroduces and stresses the importance of analyzing the time element in project status updates. Time is important because it becomes the basis for determining how much work should be accomplished at certain milestone points. EVM also allows the project team to make future projections of project status based on its current state. At any point in the project's development, we are able to calculate both schedule and budget efficiency factors (the efficiency with which budget is being used relative to the value that is being created) and use those values to make future projections about the estimated cost and schedule to project completion.

We can illustrate the advance in the project control process that Earned Value Management represents by comparing it to the other project tracking mechanisms. If we consider the key metrics of project performance as those success criteria discussed in Chapter 6 (schedule, budget, and performance), most project evaluation approaches tend to isolate some subset of the overall success measure. For example, project S-curve analysis directly links budget expenditures with the project schedule (see Figure 18.18). Again, the obvious disadvantage to this approach is that it ignores the project performance linkage.

Project control charts such as tracking Gantt charts link project performance with schedule but may give budget expenditures short shrift (see Figure 18.19). The essence of a tracking approach to project status is to emphasize project performance over time. Although the

* Note that Earned Value Management (EVM) is used interchangeably with Earned Value Analysis (EVA). EVA is an older term, though still widely in use. EVM has become increasingly common and is used within many project firms.

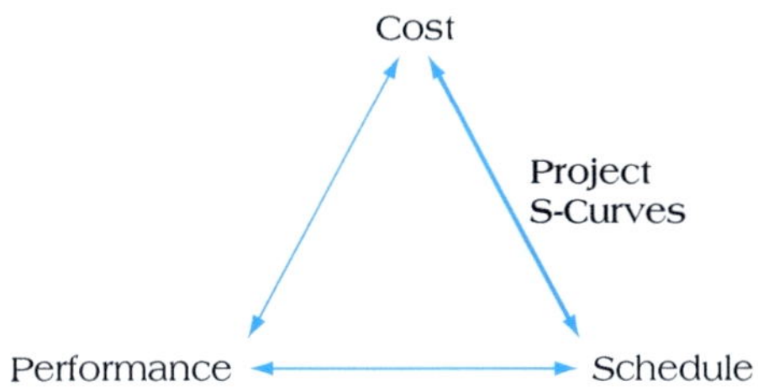

FIGURE 18.18 **Monitoring Project Performance (S-Curve Analysis)**

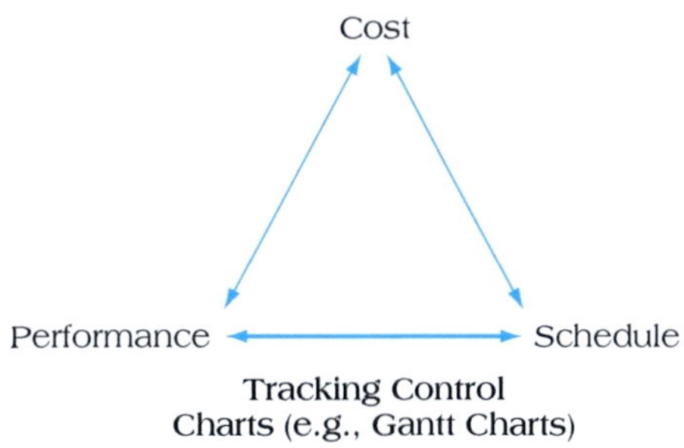

FIGURE 18.19 **Monitoring Project Performance (Control Charting)**

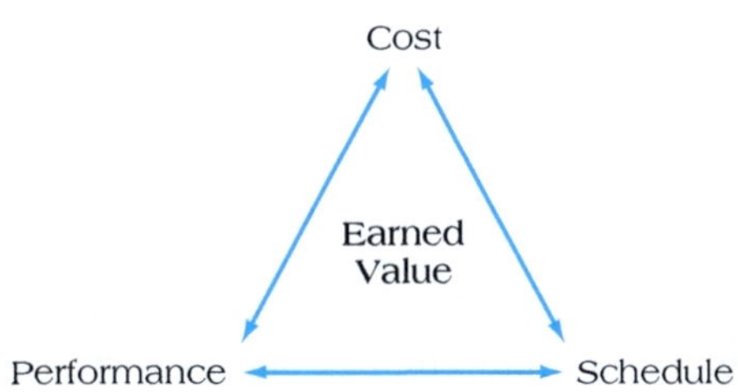

FIGURE 18.20 **Monitoring Project Performance (Earned Value)**

argument could be made that budget is implicitly assumed to be spent in some preconceived fashion, this metric does not directly apply a link between the use of time and performance factors with project cost.

Earned value (EV), on the other hand, directly links all three primary project success metrics (cost, schedule, and performance). This methodology is extremely valuable because it allows for regular updating of a *time-phased* budget to determine schedule and cost variances, as identified by the regular measurement of project performance (see Figure 18.20).

Terminology for Earned Value

Following are some of the key concepts that allow us to calculate earned value and use its figures to make future project performance projections. Many of these definitions are taken from the Project Management Institute's Project Management Body of Knowledge (PMBoK), 5th Edition.

PV **Planned value.** The authorized budget assigned to scheduled work. At any given moment, planned value defines the physical work that should have been accomplished to that point in time. It can also be thought of as a cost estimate of the budgeted resources scheduled across the project's life cycle (cumulative baseline). In older terminology, PV used to be referred to as BCWS (Budgeted Cost of Work Scheduled).

EV **Earned value.** This is a measure of the work performed expressed in terms of the budget authorized for that work. This is the real budgeted cost, or "value," of the work that has actually been performed to date. In older terminology, EV used to be referred to as Budgeted Cost of Work Performed (BCWP).

AC **Actual cost of work performed.** This is the realized cost for the work performed on an activity during a specific time period. It is the cumulative total costs incurred in accomplishing the various project work packages that EV measured. In older terminology, AC used to be referred to as Actual Cost of Work Performed (ACWP).

SV **Schedule variance.** This is a measure of schedule performance expressed as the difference between the earned value and the planned value, or EV – PV. It is the amount by which the project is ahead or behind the delivery date at a given point in time.

CV **Cost variance.** This is a measure of cost performance expressed as the difference between the earned value and the actual cost of work performed, or EV – AC. It is the amount of budget deficit or surplus at a given point in time.

SPI **Schedule Performance Index.** The rate at which project performance is meeting schedule expectations up to a point in time. SPI is expressed as the earned value to date divided by the planned value of work scheduled to be performed (EV/PV). This value allows us to calculate the projected schedule of the project to completion.

CPI **Cost Performance Index.** The rate at which project performance is meeting cost expectations during a given period of time. CPI is expressed as the earned value divided by the actual, cumulative cost of the work performed to date (EV/AC). This value allows us to calculate the projected budget to completion.

BAC **Budgeted cost at completion.** This value represents the total budget for a project.

EAC **Estimate at completion.** The expected total cost of completing all work on the project. This is the projected (forecasted) total cost based on project performance to that point in time. It is represented as the sum of actual costs (AC) plus an estimate to complete all remaining work.

Creating Project Baselines

The first step in developing an accurate control process is to create the project baselines against which progress can be measured. Baseline information is critical regardless of the control process we employ, but baselines are elemental when performing EVM. The first piece of information necessary for performing earned value is the planned value, that is, the project baseline. The PV should comprise all relevant project costs, the most important of which are personnel costs, equipment and materials, and project overhead, sometimes referred to as *level of effort*. Overhead costs (level of effort) can include a variety of fixed costs that must be included in the project budget, including administrative or technical support, computer work, and other staff expertise (such as legal advice or marketing). The actual steps in establishing the project baseline are fairly straightforward and require two pieces of data: the Work Breakdown Structure and a time-phased project budget.

1. The Work Breakdown Structure identified the individual work packages and tasks necessary to accomplish the project. As such, the WBS allowed us to first identify the individual tasks that would need to be performed. It also gave us some understanding of the hierarchy of tasks needed to set up work packages and identify personnel needs (human resources) in order to match the task requirements to the correct individuals capable of performing them.
2. The time-phased budget takes the WBS one step further: It allows us to identify the correct sequencing of tasks, but more importantly, it enables the project team to determine the points in the project when budget money is likely to be spent in pursuit of those tasks. Say, for example, that our project team determines that one project activity, Data Entry, will require a budget of $20,000 to be completed, and further, that the task is estimated to require two months to completion, with the majority of the work being done in the first month. A time-phased budget for this activity might resemble the following:

Activity	Jan	Feb	...	Dec	Total
Data Entry	$14,000	$6,000		-0-	$20,000

Once we have collected the WBS and applied a time-phased budget breakdown, we can create the project baseline. The result is an important component of earned value because it represents the standard against which we are going to compare all project performance, cost, and schedule

TABLE 18.10 Percentage of Tasks Completed for Project Sierra (in thousands $)

	Duration (in weeks)									
	5	10	15	20	25	30	35	40	45	% Comp.
Design	6	2								100
Engineer		4	8	8	8					100
Install				4	20	6				50
Test						2	6	4	2	0
Total	6	6	8	12	28	8	6	4	2	
Cumul.	6	12	20	32	60	68	74	78	80	

data as we attempt to assess the viability of an ongoing project. This baseline, then, represents our best understanding of how the project *should* progress. How the project is actually doing, is another matter.

Why Use Earned Value?

Let us illustrate the relevancy of EVM using our Project Sierra example. Return to the information presented in Table 18.9, as graphically represented on the project S-curve in Figure 18.13. Assume that it is now week 30 of the project and we are attempting to assess the project's status. Also assume that there is no difference between the projected project costs and actual expenditures; that is, the project budget is being spent within the correct time frame. However, upon examination, suppose we were to discover that Installation was only half completed and Project Testing had not yet begun. This example illustrates both a problem with S-curve analysis and the strength of EVM. Project status assessment is relevant only when some measure of performance is considered in addition to budget and elapsed schedule.

Consider the revised data for Project Sierra shown in Table 18.10. Note that as of week 30, work packages related to Design and Engineering have been totally completed, whereas the Installation is only 50% done, and Testing has not yet begun. These percentage values are given based on the project team or key individual's assessment of the current status of work package completion. The question now is: What is the earned value of the project work done to date? As of week 30, what is the status of this project in terms of budget, schedule, *and* performance?

Calculating the earned value for these work packages is a relatively straightforward process. As Table 18.11 shows, we can modify the previous table to focus exclusively on the relevant information for determining earned value as of week 30. The planned budget for each work package is multiplied by the percentage completed in order to determine the earned value to date for the work packages, as well as for the overall project. In this case, the earned value at the 30-week point is $51,000.

Now we can compare the planned budget against the actual earned value using the original project budget baseline, shown in Figure 18.21. This process allows us to assess a more realistic determination of the status of the project when the earned value is plotted against the budget baseline. Compare this figure with the alternative method from Figure 18.14, in which a negative

TABLE 18.11 Calculating Earned Value (in thousands $)

	Planned	% Comp.	Earned Value
Design	8	100	8
Engineer	28	100	28
Install	30	50	15
Test	14	0	0
Cumul. Earned Value			51

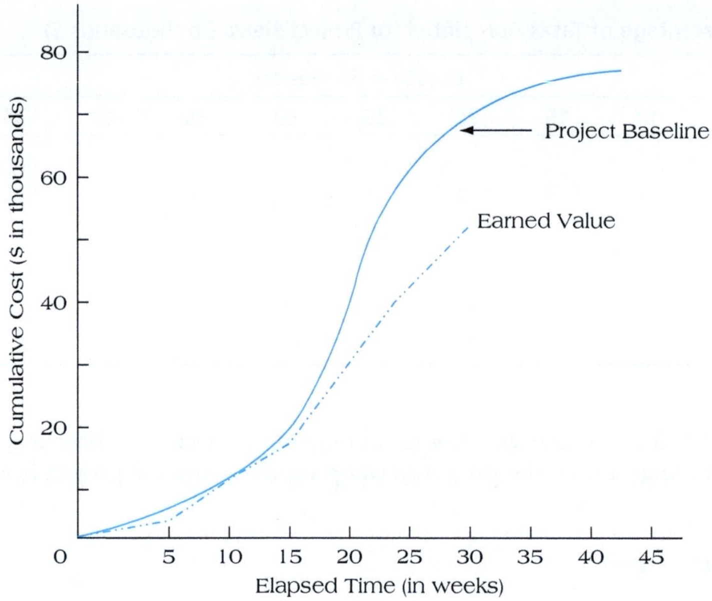

FIGURE 18.21 **Project Baseline, Using Earned Value**

variance is calculated, with no supporting explanation as to the cause or any indication about whether this figure is meaningful or not. Recall that by the end of week 30, our original budget projections suggested that $68,000 should have been spent. Instead, we are projecting a shortfall of $17,000. In other words, we are showing a negative variance not only in terms of money spent on the project, but also in terms of value created (performance) of the project to date. Unlike the standard S-curve evaluation, EVM variance is meaningful because it is based not simply on budget spent, but value earned. A negative variance of $10,000 in budget expenditures may or may not signal cause for concern; however, a $17,000 shortfall in value earned on the project to date represents a variance of serious consequences.

Steps in Earned Value Management

There are five steps in Earned Value Management (EVM):

1. ***Clearly define each activity or task that will be performed on the project, including its resource needs as well as a detailed budget.*** As we demonstrated earlier, the Work Breakdown Structure allows project teams to identify all necessary project tasks. It further allows for each task to be assigned its own project resources, including equipment and materials costs, as well as personnel assignments. Finally, coupled with the task breakdowns and resource assignments, it is possible to create the budget figure or cost estimate for each project task.
2. ***Create the activity and resource usage schedules.*** These will identify the proportion of the total budget allocated to each task across a project calendar. Determine how much of an activity's budget is to be spent each month (or other appropriate time period) across the project's projected development cycle. Coupled with the development of a project budget should be its direct linkage to the project schedule. The determination of how much budget money is to be allocated to project tasks is important. Equally important is the understanding of when the resources are to be employed across the project's development cycle.
3. ***Develop a "time-phased" budget that shows expenditures across the project's life.*** The total (cumulative) amount of the budget becomes the project baseline and is referred to as the **planned value (PV)**. In real terms, PV just means that we can identify the cumulative budget expenditures planned at any stage in the project's life. The PV, as a cumulative value, is derived from adding the planned budget expenditures for each preceding time period.

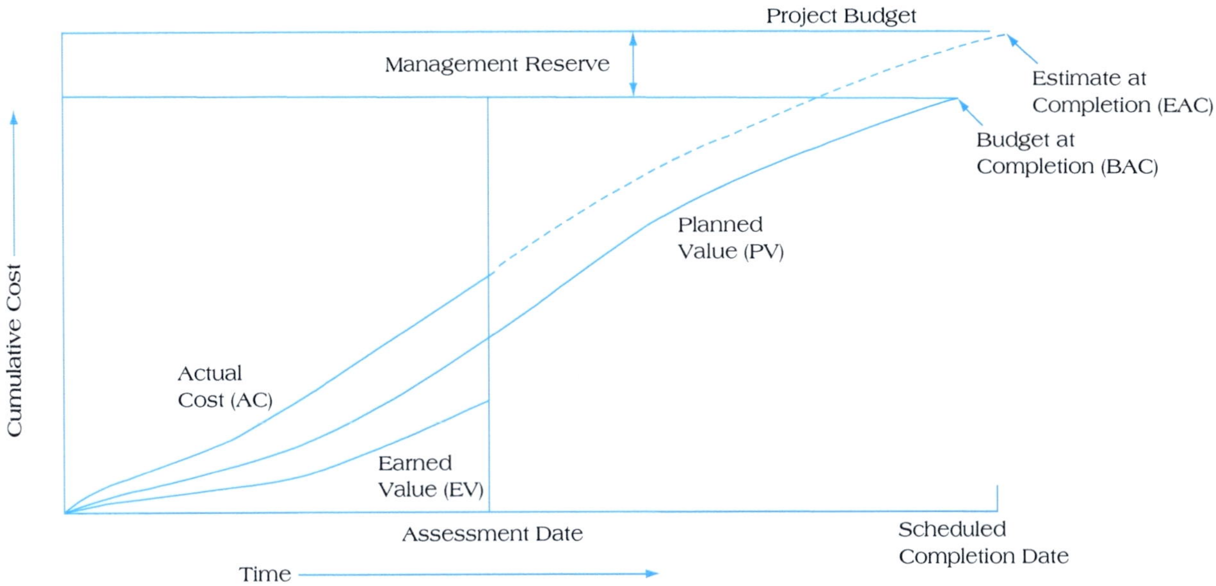

FIGURE 18.22 **Earned Value Milestones**

4. ***Total the actual costs of doing each task to arrive at the actual cost of work performed (AC).*** We can also compute the budgeted values for the tasks on which work is being performed. This is referred to as the earned value (EV) and is the origin of the term for this control process.
5. ***Calculate both a project's budget variance and schedule variance while it is still in process.*** Once we have collected the three key pieces of data (PV, EV, and AC), it is possible to make these calculations. Remember from earlier in the chapter that the **schedule variance** is calculated by the simple equation SV = EV − PV, or the difference between the earned value to date minus the planned value of the work scheduled to be performed to date. The budget, or cost, variance is calculated as CV = EV − AC, or the earned value minus the actual cost of work performed.

A simplified model that fits the principal elements of earned value together (PV, EV, AC, BAC, and EAC) is shown in Figure 18.22. The original baseline data, comprising both schedule and budget for all project tasks, is indicated by the planned value (PV) line and budget at completion (BAC) estimate for the project. Notice that PV follows a standard S-curve outline. Actual costs at the time of this assessment (when the calculations are being made) are shown on the AC line, which has been steadily tracking above the planned value to date. Earned value is illustrated as a line below the PV baseline, suggesting that the project's current earned value is below expectations. The dotted line represents the forecast for project performance to completion (EAC). Note that the line is tracking well above the project's planned value, suggesting that based on current performance, which drives projections to completion, the project is likely to finish over budget and past the scheduled completion date. We will see how these EVM calculations and forecasted projections to completion are actually calculated in the next section.

Assessing a Project's Earned Value

Table 18.12 presents the first components of a calculated earned value analysis on Project Mercury.[29] This project has a planned seven-month duration and a $118,000 budget. The project began in January and we are interested in calculating its earned value as of the end of June. For simplicity's sake, the total work packages for this project are only seven in number. If we know the amount budgeted for each work package and when that work is slated to be done, we can construct a budget table similar to that shown in Table 18.12. Notice that each work package has a fixed budget across a number of time periods (e.g., Staffing is budgeted to cost $15,000 and is to be performed almost equally across the months of January and February, while Blueprinting begins in March, with $4,000 budgeted to be spent, and concludes in April with $6,000).

TABLE 18.12 Earned Value Table (end of June) with $6,000 for Project Mercury (in thousands $)

Activity	Jan	Feb	Mar	Apr	May	June	July	Plan	% Comp.	Value
Staffing	8	7						15	100	15
Blueprinting			4	6				10	80	8
Prototype Development			2	8				10	60	6
Full Design				3	8	10		21	33	7
Construction					2	30		32	25	8
Transfer							10	10	0	0
Punch List						15	5	20	0	0
						$\Sigma =$		118		44
Monthly Plan	8	7	6	17	10	55	15			
Cumulative	8	15	21	38	48	103	118			
Monthly Actual	8	11	8	11	10	30	0			
Cumulative Actual	8	19	27	38	48	78				

If we plot the expenses across each month of the project completed to date (January through June), we find that we can determine the amount budgeted and, through gathering some information from the project team and the accountant, the actual amount spent each month. These sets of figures are added to the bottom four rows of the table. For example, note that by March, we had planned to spend $21,000 in project budget on activities to date. Our actual cumulative costs were $27,000. The obvious question is: Is this good news or bad news? On the surface, we might conclude that it is bad news because we have overspent our budget. However, recall that the chief problem with S-curve methodology is that it only considers actual costs versus planned costs. This simply is not sufficient information for us to make any real determination of the status of the project.

The key pieces of information that allow us to identify earned value are included in the right-hand columns. We are very interested in determining the current status of the project based on the number of tasks completed over the time budgeted to them. Therefore, the last columns show the planned expenditures for each task, the percentage of the tasks completed, and the calculated value. *Value* in this sense is simply the product of the planned expenditures and the percentage of these tasks completed. For example, under the work package Blueprinting, we see that this activity was given a planned budget of $10,000 across two months total. To date, 80% of that activity has been completed, resulting in $8,000 in value. If we total the columns for planned expenditures and actual value (EV), we come up with our project's planned budget ($118,000) and the value realized at the end of June ($44,000).

We now have enough information to make a reasonable determination of the project's status using Earned Value Management. The first number we require is the planned value (PV). This value can be found as the cumulative planned costs at the end of the month of June ($103,000). We also have calculated that the earned value for the project to date (EV) totals $44,000. The schedule variances that are of interest to us are the **Schedule Performance Index (SPI)** and the estimated time to completion. The SPI is determined by dividing the EV by the PV. Table 18.13 shows this calculation ($44,000/103,000 = .43). With the SPI, we can now project the length of time it should take to complete the project. Because the SPI is telling us that we are operating at only 43% efficiency in implementing the project, we take the reciprocal of the SPI multiplied by the original project schedule to determine the projected actual time frame to completion for the project ($1/.43 \times 7 = 16.3$ months). The bad news is: It appears that as of June, we cannot expect to complete this project for an additional 10 months; we are running more than nine months behind schedule.

How about costs? Although we are running more than nine months late, can we make similar projections about the project in terms of how much it is projected to finally cost? The answer, according to EVM, is yes. Just as we can determine schedule variances, we can also compute cost

TABLE 18.13 Schedule Variances for Project Mercury EVM

Schedule Variances	
Planned Value (PV)	103
Earned Value (EV)	44
Schedule Performance Index	EV/PV = 44/103 = .43
Estimated Time to Completion	(1/.43 × 7) = 16.3 months

TABLE 18.14 Cost Variances for Project Mercury EVM

Cost Variances	
Cumulative Actual Cost of Work Performed (AC)	78
Earned Value (EV)	44
Cost Performance Index	EV/AC = 44/78 = .56
Estimated Cumulative Cost to Completion	(1/.56 × $118,000) = $210,714

variances, as long as we have two very important pieces of data—the cumulative actual cost of work **performed (AC)** and the earned value (EV). The earned value figure has already been calculated ($44,000), and now we turn back to Table 18.12 to locate the AC. The cumulative actual cost at the end of June is $78,000. This figure is our AC and is entered into Table 18.14.

As we did in calculating schedule variance, we calculate cost variance by dividing the EV by AC, or $44,000/78,000 = .56. That is the Cost Performance Index (CPI) for this project. Determining the projected cost of the project involves taking the reciprocal of the CPI multiplied by the original project budget ($118,000). The bad news is: Not only is this project well behind schedule, but it also is projected to end up costing more than $210,000, a significant cost overrun.

Finally, we can plot these variance values graphically, showing the difference between EV (earned value) and PV and AC (see Figure 18.23). The intriguing result of this example suggests how misleading simple S-curves can sometimes be. For example, in this case, we have discovered a difference at the end of June of $25,000 between the AC ($78,000) and PV ($103,000). Although the analysis at that point showed that we had underspent our budget slightly, the results were actually more serious when viewed from the perspective of earned value by the end of June ($44,000). In reality, the schedule and cost variances were much more severe due to the lag in earned value on

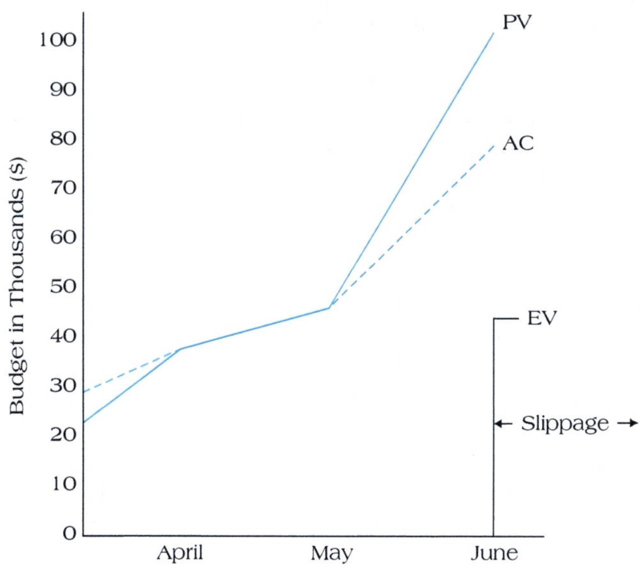

FIGURE 18.23 Earned Value Variances for Project Mercury

TABLE 18.15 Calculating Cumulative CPI for Trend Analysis

	EV	EV^C	AC	AC^C	CPI	CPI^C
July	$27,500	$ 27,500	$20,000	$ 20,000	1.38	1.38
August	$58,000	$ 85,500	$62,000	$ 82,000	0.94	1.04
September	$74,500	$160,000	$69,000	$151,000	1.08	1.06
October	$40,000	$200,000	$35,500	$186,500	1.13	1.07

TABLE 18.16 Calculating Cumulative SPI for Trend Analysis

	EV	EV^C	PV	PV^C	SPI	SPI^C
July	$27,500	$ 27,500	$30,000	$ 30,000	0.92	0.92
August	$58,000	$ 85,500	$60,500	$ 90,500	0.96	0.94
September	$74,500	$160,000	$75,000	$165,500	0.99	0.97
October	$40,000	$200,000	$37,500	$203,000	1.07	0.99

the project, as calculated by the percentage completion of all scheduled tasks. This example clearly shows the advantages of earned value for more accurately determining actual project status as a function of its three component pieces: time, budget, and completion.

Earned value can be employed to measure trends in project performance. Trends are important because we want more than simple, one-time assessments of our project's status; we want to be able to determine whether CPI and SPI are trending up, down, or remaining stationary. So, for example, it is possible to develop cumulative values for CPI and SPI as follows:

$$\text{Cumulative CPI} = \text{Cumulative EV/Cumulative AC, or:}$$
$$CPI^C = EV^C/AC^C$$

$$\text{Likewise, Cumulative SPI} = \text{Cumulative EV/Cumulative PV, or:}$$
$$SPI^C = EV^C/PV^C$$

Let us see how these values can be derived in an actual example. Suppose we collected cost data for our project over four months as shown in Table 18.15.

Our results suggest that after July, CPI dropped significantly for the month of August, before trending upwards in each of the final two months. Further, cumulative CPI (CPI^C) continued to track above the threshold 1.0 level and in recent months has shown a steady positive trend.

Now, using the same data, let's develop the cumulative SPI (SPI^C) table for this example. Suppose that our data is as shown in Table 18.16. We can see from the calculation of SPIC that the project's schedule performance has been steadily improving and by the end of this four-month segment, has improved from 0.92 to nearly 1.0. Cumulative SPI and CPI values are important for updating overall project performance to a master EVM report, rather than relying on a series of discrete "snapshots" of the project at different points in time.

We can also perform Earned Value Management using MS Project 2013. Suppose that we wished to track Project Atlas, shown in Figure 18.24. Notice that as of August 14, the project is beginning to show some signs of delay. By this point, we should have completed four of the six work packages, and yet Testing, for which Stewart is responsible, is only now getting under way. From a monitoring and control perspective, the question we want to answer is: How does EVM indicate the potential delays in our project?

Suppose that, in addition to regularly updating the baseline schedule, we have been tracking the costs associated with each of the work packages and have found, as Figure 18.25 shows, that we have spent all budgeted money allotted to the work packages of Design, Engineering, and

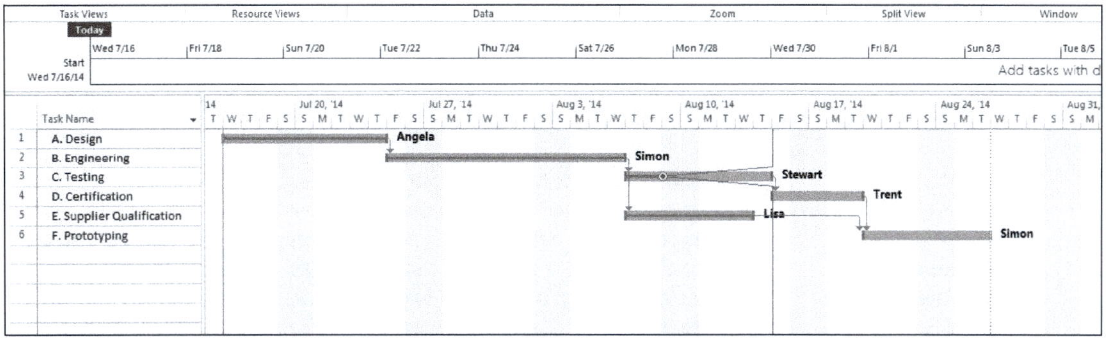

FIGURE 18.24 **Sample Gantt Chart for Project Atlas Showing Status on August 14**

Source: MS Project 2013, Microsoft Corporation

	Task Name	Fixed Cost	Fixed Cost Accrual	Total Cost	Baseline	Variance	Actual	Remaining
1	A. Design	$0.00	Prorated	$1,400.00	$1,400.00	$0.00	$1,400.00	$0.00
2	B. Engineering	$0.00	Prorated	$2,160.00	$2,160.00	$0.00	$2,160.00	$0.00
3	C. Testing	$0.00	Prorated	$864.00	$864.00	$0.00	$288.00	$576.00
4	D. Certification	$0.00	Prorated	$516.00	$516.00	$0.00	$0.00	$516.00
5	E. Supplier Qualificat	$0.00	Prorated	$1,040.00	$1,040.00	$0.00	$1,040.00	$0.00
6	F. Prototyping	$0.00	Prorated	$1,200.00	$1,200.00	$0.00	$0.00	$1,200.00

FIGURE 18.25 **Sample Cost Report for Project Atlas on August 14**

Source: MS Project 2013, Microsoft Corporation

Supplier Qualification. We have only spent $288 of our Testing budget. These are the actual cost values (AC) for these activities. We now have sufficient updated information to determine the earned value for Project Atlas as of August 14.

Figure 18.26 shows an example of an earned value report generated by MS Project 2013 for our Project Atlas.* In addition to providing the key metrics of PV, EV, and AC (see footnote), the report generates both schedule and cost variances. Schedule variance (SV) is simply the difference between earned value and planned value, while cost variance (CV) is the difference between earned value and actual cost. The **Estimate at Completion (EAC)** column shows the expected total cost of the project to completion based on performance across the various tasks up to the status date. Note that for Project Atlas, we are currently projecting schedule and cost variances, suggesting that our project is over budget and behind schedule. In fact, the EAC demonstrates that based on the progress made by August 14, this project is expected to cost $7,180 to completion.

* MS Project 2013 uses the term BCWS (Budgeted Cost of Work Scheduled) for planned value (PV), BCWP (Budgeted Cost of Work Performed) for earned value (EV), and ACWP (Actual Cost of Work Performed) for actual cost (AC). As Figure 18.26 demonstrates, MS Project 2013 employs older terms in conjunction with the newer terminology that has been updated by the Project Management Institute's PMBoK.

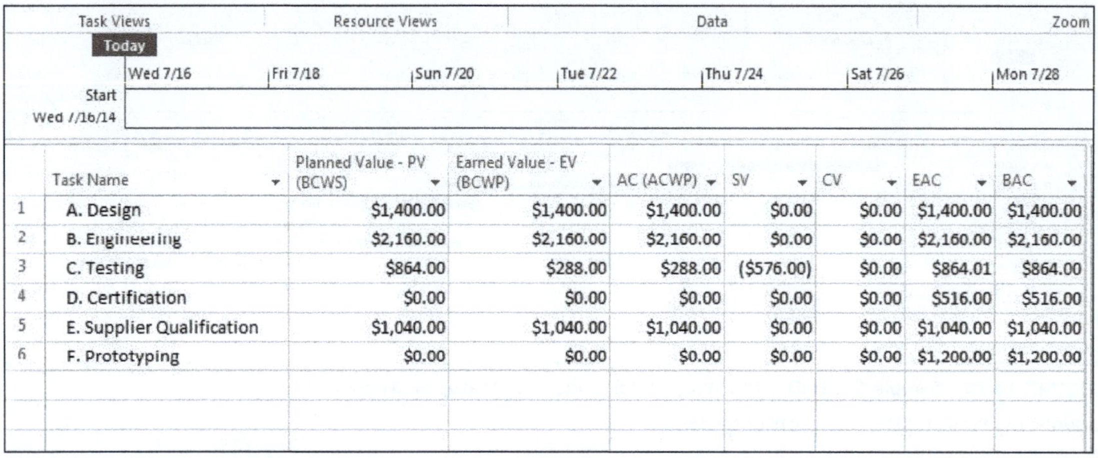

	Task Name	Planned Value - PV (BCWS)	Earned Value - EV (BCWP)	AC (ACWP)	SV	CV	EAC	BAC
1	A. Design	$1,400.00	$1,400.00	$1,400.00	$0.00	$0.00	$1,400.00	$1,400.00
2	B. Engineering	$2,160.00	$2,160.00	$2,160.00	$0.00	$0.00	$2,160.00	$2,160.00
3	C. Testing	$864.00	$288.00	$288.00	($576.00)	$0.00	$864.01	$864.00
4	D. Certification	$0.00	$0.00	$0.00	$0.00	$0.00	$516.00	$516.00
5	E. Supplier Qualification	$1,040.00	$1,040.00	$1,040.00	$0.00	$0.00	$1,040.00	$1,040.00
6	F. Prototyping	$0.00	$0.00	$0.00	$0.00	$0.00	$1,200.00	$1,200.00

FIGURE 18.26 Earned Value Report for Project Atlas on August 14
Source: MS Project 2013, Microsoft Corporation

18.8 USING EARNED VALUE TO MANAGE A PORTFOLIO OF PROJECTS

Earned Value Management can work at the portfolio level as well as with individual projects. The process simply involves the aggregation of all earned value measures across the firm's entire project portfolio in order to give an indication as to the efficiency with which a company is managing its projects. Table 18.17 gives an example of a portfolio-level Earned Value Management control table that identifies both positive and negative cost and schedule variances and, based on these evaluations, projects the cost to completion of each current project.[30]

Other useful information contained in the Portfolio Earned Value Management table includes the total positive variances for both budget and schedule, as well as a determination of the relative schedule and cost variances as a percentage of the total project portfolio. In the example shown in Table 18.15, the company is running average cost and schedule variances on its projects of 7.34% and 6.84%, respectively. The use of Earned Value Management for portfolio tracking and control offers top management an excellent window into the firm's ability to efficiently run projects, allows for comparisons across all projects currently in development, and isolates both the positive and negative variances as they occur. All of this is useful information for top-level management of multiple projects.

TABLE 18.17 Project Portfolio Earned Value (in thousands $)

Project	PV	EV	Time Var ($)	Var	AC	Cost Var ($)	Var +	Plan	Est. at Completion
Alpha	91	73	−18	18	83	−10	10	254	289
Beta	130	135	5	0	125	10	0	302	280
Gamma	65	60	−5	5	75	−15	15	127	159
Delta	25	23	−2	2	27	−4	4	48	56
Epsilon	84	82	−2	2	81	1	0	180	178
	395	373			391				962

Total Schedule Variance 27 | Total Cost Variance 29

Relative Schedule Variance 27/395 = 6.84% | Relative Cost Variance 29/395 = 7.34%

PROJECT PROFILE

Earned Value at Northrop Grumman

"There comes a time to shoot the engineers and get on with production." This statement, commonly voiced in defense industry companies, refers to the engineers' tendency to continually improve but never complete a project. The penchant for continual "tinkering" has enormous implications for companies that live or die by their ability to effectively and efficiently implement their projects. The type of work defense contractors perform further complicates the problem. There is a standing requirement that a company must meet the government's stringent cost and quality control tests as it brings projects through the development cycle. In an effort to regain control of the project development process, defense contractor Northrop Grumman has been committed to the use of Earned Value Management for a number of years.

Northrop Grumman, one of the world's leading defense contractors (see Figure 18.27), has been using Earned Value Management as a key component of its approach to better project tracking and control. Because of the numerous projects the company routinely undertakes, its annual operating budget for projects runs into the billions of dollars. With dozens of projects under way at any time and enormous capital commitments supporting these ventures, it is imperative that the corporation develop and maintain the most sophisticated project control system possible.

Northrop Grumman has selected Earned Value Management as its primary project control device for the following reasons:

1. EVM develops a comprehensive baseline plan for the scope of the program's work over its entire duration.
2. The system incorporates tools to measure work performance and accomplishments based on objective criteria.
3. EVM analyzes and forecasts the impact of significant variances from the plan.
4. It produces managerial decision-making information in ascending levels of management.
5. EVM provides action plans for corrective actions when something digresses from the baseline plan.
6. All parties involved in the plan agree to and document all changes.

The company has developed a four-tier approach for project control using EVM. All projects are classified into one of the following categories, requiring an individualized approach to EVM creation:

Tier One is the most stringent because it requires most of the system's features to be identified. This approach is employed when a contract requires that a large amount of detailed information be produced and reported.

Tier Two is similar to Tier One except that the contract requires close management oversight because the project is risky, and there is a heavier burden to meet profit margin goals.

Tier Three applies to programs of significant size that are mature and running smoothly.

Tier Four applies the benefits of earned value to projects with low administrative costs.

FIGURE 18.27 Northrop Grumman's B-2 Bomber

Source: Mark Meyer/The Life Images Collection/Getty Images

(continued)

Northrop Grumman uses EVM at every stage of a project, from developing the original metrics at the contract proposal stage, to updating them in the form of a full-blown work breakdown structure (WBS) once a project has been won and is under development, to routinely updating the status of project activities on a weekly basis. Over time, the company discovered that monthly reviews were simply too far apart and did not allow for real-time corrective action when it was necessary.

Flow of Earned Value System

Earned value begins early at Northrop Grumman projects. In fact, there is a "flow" to the EVM system, beginning at the proposal stage, moving into a baseline development phase when a contract has been awarded, and then becoming part of a routine maintenance and data generation phase as the project is in development and moving toward successful completion.

Proposal stage. The specifics of the program are determined at this stage. Among the key considerations to be determined is the form of EVM to be applied to the program if the proposal is successful and the contract awarded. Different clients may require different earned value metrics or evaluation windows that have to become part of the proposal.

Contract award. When Northrop Grumman is selected as the successful contractor, all critical elements and requirements of the project are defined, including WBS, scope, delivery schedule, target budgets, as well as an earned value plan that will be used as the basis for status measurement and updates across the project life cycle.

Baseline stage. Once the preliminary scope and deliverables have been agreed to between the contractor and the client, the detailed planning, project schedule, and formal work authorization is developed. The baseline is created now that key work packages and deliverables are identified and budgets are assigned to create a time-phased project budget.

Maintenance phase. Once the project baseline is established and formally signed off by key parties, the project passes to the monitoring and control stage, where the key advantages of EVM are clearly realized. Performance is measured, schedules are updated, and all significant variances are identified and reported. People responsible for the actual performance of the work receive EVM reports at the detailed level and the system is transparent so that government representatives, interested in status updates, can receive real-time data on cost performance (CPI) and schedule performance (SPI) in accordance with contract requirements. Throughout the project life cycle, EVM considerations continue to drive the project forward; shaping the organization of the project, the development of critical planning features, and the manner in which it is controlled.

At Northrop Grumman, EVM is not simply an option, but a corporate mandate. The four-tier approach helps the company tailor the system to each new project in order to apply it correctly for maximum benefit, cost control, and corporate profitability.[31]

18.9 ISSUES IN THE EFFECTIVE USE OF EARNED VALUE MANAGEMENT

As with any other metric that helps us understand the "true" status of an ongoing project, the key to effective use of EVM lies in providing accurate and up-to-date information on the project, particularly in terms of the percentage of work packages completed. Because this information is key to determining the earned value at any point in time, the calculated EV is only as accurate as project team members and managers allow it to be through developing and enforcing an honest reporting system.

In our Project Mercury example shown earlier (Table 18.12), the percentage completion column included values ranging from 100, 80, 60, 33, 25, to zero. In reality, organizations often adopt a simpler decision rule for assigning completion percentages. Among the more common methods for assigning completion values are the following:

1. *0/100 rule*—The simplest and perhaps least effective method requires that a project activity be assigned a value of zero (0) until the point the activity is finished, at which time the value switches to 100%. This rule works best for work packages with very short durations, such as a day or two, but it is not useful for longer work packages because it provides little real-time information on an ongoing basis. It also makes sense for work packages that require vendor deliveries or that depend upon external stakeholders performing required steps. For example, we count a work package as "complete" when the vendor delivers a needed component.
2. *50/50 rule*—Under this decision rule, an activity that has been started automatically receives a valuation of 50% completed. That value remains attached to the work package until the

activity has been completed, at which time it becomes 100% completed. Like the 0/100 rule above, this decision model is used most often for work packages of very short duration.

3. *Percentage complete rule*—Under the percentage complete rule, the project manager and team members mutually agree on a set of completion milestones, whether they are based on quarters (25%, 50%, 75%, 100%), thirds (33%, 67%, 100%), or some other values. Then, on a regular basis, the status of each in-process work package in the project is updated. A new completion value may or may not be assigned to the package, and then the project's EVM is updated based on this new information. As noted earlier, the key to making this process work lies in honest appraisal of the status of ongoing activities, based not on time elapsed or budget spent but on actual percentage of the activity completed.

An important caveat with the percentage complete rule has to do with the controversy surrounding the level of detail to be used in calculating task value. Critics of earned value argue that unless reasonable gradients of completion are acknowledged and used by all parties, there is a high potential to create misleading information through the earned value analysis. For example, one criticism leveled at EVM argues that excessive levels of detail are dangerous and essentially not interpretable. For example, suppose a project uses completion values based on 10% increments (e.g., 10%, 20%, 30%, etc.). As a practical matter, it is fundamentally impossible to successfully delineate between, say, 30% and 40% completion for most project activities; hence, the use of too much detail is more likely to mislead than to clarify the true status of a project.

The chief exception to this difficulty with the project complete rule occurs in projects in which there is a fair degree of prior knowledge of how well delineated the development process is or in situations where it is easier to accurately gauge the amount of work done within any project task. In a simple construction project, for example, where the project steps are well known in advance and rigorously followed, a higher level of detail can be employed. Likewise, in the case of software development where the task consists of writing code, a senior programmer may have an excellent sense of the total number of lines of code needed to complete the task. Therefore, if the total task requires approximately 5,000 lines of code and a programmer completes 500 lines of the program, it would be reasonable to assign a figure of 10% completion of the total task performance requirement.

The importance of establishing a reasonable standard for project performance cannot be overemphasized. In the absence of a clear set of guidelines for identifying cutoff points and the appropriate level of detail, it is possible to derive very different conclusions from the same project information. For example, let us revisit the earlier EVM problem shown in Table 18.12. This time, we will use two decision rules as regards the levels of detail for project activities in calculating value and EV. In the first example, shown in Table 18.18, column 1 gives the original calculations, based on the first set of percentage complete values from Table 18.12. In column 2, I have employed a simple decision rule based on three increments (0, 50%, and 100% complete). Column 3 shows a slightly more precise level of detail, employing levels of 0, 25%, 50%, 75%, and 100% complete. I have rounded the original percentage completion values (shown in column 1) to the closest equivalents in the other two alternatives.

Note what occurs as a result of using alternative levels of detail; rounding the level of completion values to a simplified 0%, 50%, 100% completion scheme results in significantly different results, both for projecting future project schedule and cost deviations. The original schedule overrun that projected a new completion of 16.28 months has been improved to 12.73 months, or a schedule overrun of only 5.73 months. Likewise, the original earned value budget projection for the project ($210,714) has been reduced to $163,889, for a savings of $46,825 due merely to adopting an alternative level of detail for project activity completion. Similarly, using the level of detail with slightly more gradients (0, 25%, 50%, 75%, and 100%), shown in column 3, and rounding the original values to most closely match this alternative, we discover that the future projections for the project, as developed through the SPI and CPI, are more negative than the originals. The new project schedule is forecast to last 17.5 months and the revised project budget has increased to $226,923, or $16,209 more than our first projection. Even more compelling, the absolute difference between the high and low budget projections is more than $63,000, all due to moving from a three-point level of detail (column 2) to one based on five levels of completion (column 3). Is one approach "more correct" than the other? Absent some decision rule or logic for making these determinations, it is virtually impossible to suggest that one level of detail is more representative of the "true" status of project activity completion.

TABLE 18.18 Calculating Project Mercury Earned Value Based on Alternate Levels of Detail (in thousands $)

Activity	Planned Value	Col. 1 (Original) % Comp.	Col. 1 (Original) Value	Col. 2 (0, 50, 100%) % Comp.	Col. 2 (0, 50, 100%) Value	Col. 3 (0, 25, 50, 75, 100%) % Comp.	Col. 3 (0, 25, 50, 75, 100%) Value
Staffing	15	100	15	100	15	100	15
Blueprinting	10	80	8	100	10	75	7.5
Prototype Development	10	60	6	50	5	50	5
Full Design	21	33	7	50	10.5	25	5.25
Construction	32	25	8	50	16	25	8
Transfer	10	0	0	0	0	0	0
Punch List	20	0	0	0	0	0	0
Total EV =			44		56.5		40.75
SPI and Projection to Completion		44/103 = .43		56.5/103 = .55		40.75/103 = .40	
		(1/.43 × 7) = 16.28 mos.		(1/.55 × 7) = 12.73 mos.		(1/.40 × 7) = 17.5 mos.	
CPI and Project to Completion		44/78 = .56		56.5/78 = .72		40.75/78 = .52	
		$210,714		$163,889		$226,923	

As this chapter has noted, earned value management is not a flawless methodology for project tracking and control, particularly as it pertains to the problems in accurately determining the percentage of work packages completed at any time point during the project's development. Nevertheless, EVM does represent a significant step forward in allowing project managers and their teams to gain a better perspective on the "true" nature of a project's status midstream, that is, in the middle of the development and implementation process.[32] This sort of real-time information can be invaluable in helping us gain current information and begin to develop realistic plans for correcting any systematic problems with the development process. The more we learn, and the faster we learn it, of a project's status, the better equipped we will be to take measured and effective steps to get a troubled project back on track.

In recent years, developments in project monitoring and control have led to some modifications and enhancements to the standard EVM processes widely in use. For example, an additional criticism of earned value relates to its use of cost data (budget) to assess not only cost performance but also schedule performance. That is, it has been reasonably argued that earned value does a fine job of monitoring cost performance relative to value earned in a project at any given point in time. We have seen how this information can be used for forecasting project costs at completion. However, there is a philosophical disconnect in the idea of using cost data to measure schedule performance; that is, using this same cost information as a means for forecasting schedule performance has been shown to potentially skewed data, leading to falsely positive or negative status assessments the further into a project we get. One solution recommended is the use of **Earned Schedule (ES)** as a complement to standard EVM analysis.[33] ES is developed in detail in the appendix to this chapter. Another criticism of EVM lies in its potential lack of usefulness for some classes of projects that are more complex or involve uncertain technologies, like R&D or radical new product development projects. For these complex product system (CoPS) projects, authors have suggested that standard metrics of project performance may simply be ineffective and instead, propose a variation of EVM referred to as **Earned Readiness Management (ERM)** that focuses on the maturity of the project and overall system development. Though still in its early stages, ERM shows promise for combining the best features of earned value with a broader perspective needed for these projects.[34]

18.10 HUMAN FACTORS IN PROJECT EVALUATION AND CONTROL

Another recurring problem with establishing accurate or meaningful EVM results has to do with the need to recognize the human factor in all project activity completion projections. That is, there is a strong incentive in most organizations for project team members to continuously report stronger results than may be warranted in the interest of looking good for the boss or sending the right signals about the project's status. Worse, many times implicit or even explicit pressure may come from the project managers themselves, as they find themselves under pressure from top management to show steady results. Hence, the level of detail controversy is not simply one of accurately matching technical performance on the project to the best external indicator or number of gradients. Often it is also a problem rooted in human behavior, suggesting that excessively fine levels of detail not only may be inappropriate for the types of project activities we engage in, but also may be prone to misuse by the project team.

The common feature of control approaches is their reliance on measurable data based on project outcomes; that is, the results of project actions taken in any one time period are collected and reported after the fact. Hence, we determine schedule or cost variance after the information has been collected and reported. Some project management writers, however, have suggested that it is equally essential to maintain a clear understanding of the importance of the management of people in the project implementation process. In other words, the data collected from the various evaluation and control techniques represents important *outcome* measures of the project; however, comprehensive project control also requires that the project organization employ sufficient process evaluations to determine how the development is progressing.

A key component of any process evaluation of project performance must include an assessment of its people, their technical skills, management, teamwork, communication processes, motivation, leadership, and so forth.[35] In short, many evaluation and control techniques (such as EVM) will do an excellent job in answering the "what" questions (What is the status of the project? What is our cost efficiency factor? What tasks are currently running late?), but they do not attempt to answer the "why" questions (Why are activities behind schedule? Why is the project team performing at a suboptimal level?). In an effort to provide answers to the "why" questions, work on the human processes in project management has been initiated and continues to be done.

Past research examining the impact of human factors on project success bears out the importance of considering the wider "management" challenge inherent in managing projects. For example, early work of Baker and colleagues[36] identified a variety of factors that directly predict project success. Included in their list were issues such as:

- Project coordination and relations among stakeholders
- Adequacy of project structure and control
- Project uniqueness, importance, and public exposure
- Success criteria salience and consensus
- Lack of budgetary pressure
- Avoidance of initial overoptimism and conceptual difficulties

Their findings bear out the importance of having a clear knowledge of the managerial challenges involved when implementing projects. These findings have been reinforced by other research that has examined a set of both successful and unsuccessful projects across their life cycle.[37]

The findings of such research are intriguing because of the importance they place on the managerial and human behavioral aspects of project management for project success. As Table 18.19 shows, regardless of whether the project studied was a success or failure, the factors that were of highest importance demonstrate some clear similarities. Issues such as leadership, top management support, team and personal motivation, and client support were consistently linked with project success, suggesting once again that an understanding of the project management *process* is keenly important for determining the likelihood of a project's successful outcome.

One of the key recurring problems, however, with making wider use of nontechnical information as a method for controlling projects and assessing their ongoing status lies in the question of measurement. Although financial and schedule data can be easily acquired and are relatively easy to interpret, measuring human processes such as motivation level, leadership, top management support, and so forth is highly problematic. As a result, even though a number of project management theorists have accepted the argument for inclusion of human process factors in assessing the status of ongoing projects, there has been little agreement as to how best to make such assessments, interpret the results, and use the findings in a prescriptive manner to improve the project processes.

The work of Pinto and Slevin[38] addresses the shortcomings with behavioral assessments of project management processes. They formulated the Project Implementation Profile (PIP), a

TABLE 18.19 Key Success Drivers and Inhibitors

Stage	Successful Projects Factors	Stage	Failed Projects Factors
Formation	Personal ambition	Formation	Unmotivated team
	Top management support		Poor leadership
	Team motivation		Technical limitations
	Clear objectives		Funding problems
	Technological advantage		
Buildup	Team motivation	Buildup	Unmotivated team
	Personal motivation		Conflict in objectives
	Top management support		Leadership problems
	Technical expertise		Poor top management support
			Technical problems
Main Phase	Team motivation	Main Phase	Unmotivated team
	Personal motivation		Poor top management support
	Client support		Deficient procedures
	Top management support		
Closeout	Personal motivation	Closeout	Poor control
	Team motivation		Poor financial support
	Top management support		Unclear objectives
	Financial support		Leadership problems

10-factor instrument that assesses the performance of the project team with respect to 10 critical success factors, that is, those factors they found to be predictive of project success. The advantage of the PIP is that it allows project teams to formally assess their performance on the ongoing project, allowing for midcourse correction and improvement of the management *process* itself. The 10 critical success factors represent an important, supplemental source of information on the project's status. Coupled with other types of evaluation and control information supplied through the tracking of cost and schedule variance against the project baseline, project teams can develop a comprehensive vision of the project's status throughout its development.

Critical Success Factor Definitions

The 10 critical success factors identified by Pinto and Slevin in formulating the Project Implementation Profile (PIP) instrument are (1) project mission, (2) top management support, (3) project plans and schedules, (4) client consultation, (5) personnel, (6) technical tasks, (7) client acceptance, (8) monitoring and feedback, (9) communication, and (10) troubleshooting. Each of these factors is discussed in more detail in the text that follows.

Project mission, the first factor, relates to the underlying purpose for the project. Project success is predicated on the importance of clearly defining objectives as well as ultimate benefits to be derived from the project. Many times, the initial stage of project management consists of a feasibility decision. Are the objectives clear and can they succeed? Project mission refers to a condition in which the objectives of the project are clear and understood, not only by the project team involved, but also by the other departments in the organization. The project manager must be concerned with clarification of objectives as well as achieving broad belief in the congruence of the objectives with overall organizational objectives.

Top management support, the second factor, has long been considered of great importance in distinguishing between ultimate success and failure. Project managers and their teams not only are dependent upon top management for authority, direction, and support, but also are the conduit for implementing top management's plans, or goals, for the organization.[39] Further, if the project is being developed for an internal audience (one within the company), the degree of management support for a project will lead to significant variations in the degree of acceptance or resistance to that project or product. Top management's support of the project may involve aspects such as allocation of sufficient resources (financial, personnel, time, etc.) as well as project management's confidence in support from top management in the event of a crisis.

The third factor, *project plans and schedules,* refers to the importance of developing a detailed plan of the required stages of the implementation process. It is important to remember, however, that the activities associated with project planning and project scheduling are distinct from each other. Planning, which is the first and more general step in developing the project implementation strategy, is composed of scope definition, creation of a Work Breakdown Structure, and resource and activity assignments. Scheduling is the setting of time frames and milestones for each important element in the overall project. The project plans and schedules factor is concerned with the degree to which time schedules, milestones, labor, and equipment requirements are specified. There must be a satisfactory measurement system to judge actual performance against budget allowances and time schedules.

The fourth factor is *client consultation.* The "client" is anyone who ultimately will be using the product of the project, either as a customer outside the company or as a department within the organization. Increasingly, the need for client consultation has been recognized as important in attempting a system implementation; indeed, the degree to which clients are personally involved in the implementation process correlates directly with variations in their support for projects.[40] It is important to identify the clients for the project and accurately determine if their needs are being met.

The fifth factor, *personnel,* includes recruitment, selection, and training of project team members. An important, but often overlooked, aspect of the implementation process concerns the nature of the personnel involved. In many situations, personnel for the project team are chosen with less than full regard for the skills necessary to actively contribute to implementation success. The personnel factor is concerned with developing an implementation team with the ability and commitment to perform their functions.

Technical tasks, the sixth factor, refers to the necessity of having not only the required numbers of personnel for the implementation team but also ensuring that they possess the technical skills and the technology and technical support needed to perform their tasks. It is important that people managing a project understand the technology involved. In addition, adequate technology must exist to support the system. Without the necessary technology and technical skills, projects quickly disintegrate into a series of miscues and technical errors.

The seventh factor, *client acceptance,* refers to the final stage in the project development process, at which time the overall efficacy of the project is to be determined. In addition to client consultation at an earlier stage in the system implementation process, it remains of ultimate importance to determine whether the clients for whom the project has been initiated will accept it. Too often project managers make the mistake of believing that if they handle the other stages of the implementation process well, the client (whether internal or external to the organization) will accept the resulting system. In fact, client acceptance is a stage in the project life cycle process that must be managed like any other.

The eighth factor, *monitoring and feedback,* refers to the project control process by which, at each stage of the project implementation, key personnel receive feedback on how the project is progressing compared to initial projections. Making allowances for adequate monitoring and feedback mechanisms gives the project manager the ability to anticipate problems, to oversee corrective measures, and to ensure that no deficiencies are overlooked. Project managers need to emphasize the importance of constant monitoring and fine-tuning project development; tracking control charts and Earned Value Management are excellent examples of the techniques and types of monitoring and control mechanisms necessary to develop a project.

Communication, the ninth factor, is not only essential within the project team itself, but—as we discussed in regard to stakeholder management—it is also vital between the team and the rest of the organization as well as with clients. Communication refers both to feedback mechanisms and to the necessity of exchanging information with both clients and the rest of the organization concerning the project's capabilities, the goals of the project, changes in policies and procedures, status reports, and so forth. Therefore, channels of communication are extremely important in creating an atmosphere for successful project implementation.

Troubleshooting is the tenth and final factor of the model. Problem areas exist in almost every project development. The measure of a successful project is not the avoidance of problems, but taking the correct steps once problems develop. Regardless of how carefully the implementation effort is initially planned, it is impossible to foresee every trouble area or problem that can possibly arise. As a result, the project manager must include mechanisms in the implementation plan for recognizing problems and for troubleshooting them when they arise. Such mechanisms make it easier not only to react to problems as they arise, but also to foresee and possibly forestall potential problem areas in the implementation process.

Conclusions

This chapter has addressed a variety of approaches to project tracking and control. Although most of the models mentioned have many advantages associated with them, project management professionals should be aware of the concomitant problems and shortcomings with these approaches as well. The key to developing a useful project control process lies in recognizing the strengths and weaknesses of the alternative methods and ultimately developing an approach that best suits the organization, the projects undertaken, and the stakeholders of the project. A project control process should be tailored, to the degree possible, to the specific needs, culture, and uses for which an organization intends it. Thus, under some circumstances, a simplified control system may be sufficient for providing management with the types of information they require. Alternatively, some organizations and/or projects will need to employ highly sophisticated control processes because of either the unique nature of their operating processes or the demands that developing projects place on them (e.g., governmental stipulations and mandates).[41]

The comprehensive and intricate concept of project evaluation and control involves the need to understand alternative evaluation techniques, recognizing their particular usefulness and the types of information they can provide. Ultimately, however, these techniques are merely as good as the project planning process; that is, a good control system cannot make up for inadequate or inaccurate initial plans. Without effective baselines, good project cost estimation and budgeting, and adequate resource commitments, project control simply will not work. However, if the up-front planning has been done effectively, project evaluation and control can work in harmony with the project plans, providing the project team with not only a clear road map to success, but also excellent mileposts along the highway.

Summary

1. **Understand the nature of the control cycle and four key steps in a general project control model.** Accurately evaluating the status of ongoing projects represents a real challenge for project teams and their parent organizations. The process of project control, consisting of a recurring cycle of four steps (setting goals, measuring progress, comparing actual progress with plans, and correcting significant deviations), demonstrates a theoretical framework for understanding the continuous nature of project monitoring and control.
2. **Recognize the strengths and weaknesses of common project evaluation and control methods.** A number of project evaluation and control techniques exist, from the simplistic to the highly sophisticated. The most basic evaluation process, project S-curves, seeks to reconcile the project schedule baseline with planned budget expenditures. The cumulative project budget, resembling the letter *S*, creates a schedule/budget relationship that early project monitoring methods found useful as an indicator of expected progress. Unfortunately, a number of problems with S-curve analysis preclude its use as an accurate evaluation and control technique. Other evaluation methods include milestone analysis and tracking Gantt charts. These approaches link project progress to the schedule baseline, rather than the project budget. As with S-curves, milestones and tracking charts have some advantages, but they all share a common drawback: the inability of these methods to accurately assess the status of ongoing activities, and therefore the "true" status of the project, in a meaningful way. Specifically, because these monitoring and control methods do not link schedule and budget baselines to actual ongoing project performance, they cannot offer a reasonable measure of project status.
3. **Understand how Earned Value Management can assist project tracking and evaluation.** Earned Value Management (EVM) is a powerful tool, developed through a mandate from the federal government, to directly link project progress to schedule and budget baselines. In effect, EVM provides the missing piece of the control puzzle by requiring the reporting of actual project activity status on a real-time basis. Earned Value Management has begun to

diffuse more rapidly within ordinary project-based organizations as they increasingly perceive the advantages of its use.

4. **Use Earned Value Management for project portfolio analysis.** The basic principles that govern the use of earned value on a single project can be applied to a portfolio of projects. Each project is evaluated in terms of the basic efficiency indexes for time and cost, and an overall evaluation can be calculated for a firm's project portfolio. This portfolio model allows us to determine the overall efficiency with which we manage projects, to see which are ahead and which are behind the firm's baseline standards.
5. **Understand behavioral concepts and other human issues in evaluation and control.** A final method for tracking and evaluating the status of ongoing projects lies in the use of alternative control methods, aimed at assessing and managing the "human issues" in project management, rather than focusing exclusively on the technical ones. In other words, EVM and other previously discussed tracking and control mechanisms focus on data-driven measures of performance (budget, schedules, and functionality); but other models that address the managerial and behavioral issues in project management argue that unless we merge these data-driven models with those that assess the project in terms of human interactions (leadership, top management support, communication, and so forth), it is possible to generate a great deal of information on the current status of a project without recognizing the primacy of human behavior in determining the success or failure of project activities. To create a well-rounded sense of the project performance, it is necessary to blend purely data-driven monitoring models with managerial-based approaches.
6. **Understand the advantages of Earned Schedule methods for determining project schedule variance, schedule performance index, and estimates to completion.** The accompanying text should be: Earned schedule represents an alternative method for determining the status of a project's schedule to completion by recognizing that standard Earned Value employs budget data to calculate not only estimates of project cost but also time (schedule). Arguing that "schedule is different," earned schedule identifies the possible schedule estimation errors EVM can be prone to and offers some corrective procedures to adjust these calculations.

Key Terms

Actual cost of work performed (AC)
Budgeted cost at completion (BAC)
Control cycle
Cost Performance Index (CPI)
Earned Readiness Management (ERM)
Earned Schedule (ES)
Earned value (EV)
Earned Value Management (EVM)
Estimate at Completion (EAC)
Milestone
Planned value (PV)
Project baseline
Project control
Project S-curve
Schedule Performance Index (SPI)
Schedule variance
Tracking Gantt chart

Solved Problem

EXAMPLE OF EARNED VALUE

The Project Management Institute, the largest professional organization of project management professionals in the world, has developed a simple example of the logic underlying earned value assessment for a project. It demonstrates, in the following steps, the calculation of the more relevant components of earned value and shows how these steps fit together to contribute an overall understanding of earned value.

Earned value is a management technique that relates resource planning to schedules and to technical cost and schedule requirements. All work is planned, budgeted, and scheduled in time-phased planned value increments constituting a cost and schedule measurement baseline. There are two major objectives of an earned value system: to encourage contractors to use effective internal cost and schedule management control systems, and to permit the customer to be able to rely on timely data produced by those systems for determining product-oriented contract status.

Baseline. The baseline plan in Table 18.20 shows that six work units (A–F) would be completed at a cost of $100 for the period covered by this report.

TABLE 18.20 Baseline Plan Work Units

	A	B	C	D	E	F	Total
Planned value	10	15	10	25	20	20	100

TABLE 18.21 Schedule Variance Work Units

	A	B	C	D	E	F	Total
Planned value	10	15	10	25	20	20	100
Earned value	10	15	10	10	20	—	65
Schedule variance	0	0	0	−15	0	−20	−35, or −35%

TABLE 18.22 Cost Variance Work Units

	A	B	C	D	E	F	Total
Earned value	10	15	10	10	20	—	65
Actual cost	9	22	8	30	22	—	91
Cost variance	1	−7	2	−20	−2	0	−26, or −40%

TABLE 18.23 Spend Comparison Approach Work Units

	A	B	C	D	E	F	Total
Planned spend	10	15	10	25	20	20	100
Actual spend	9	22	8	30	22	—	91
Variance	1	−7	2	−5	−2	20	9, or 9%

Schedule Variance. As work is performed, it is "earned" on the same basis as it was planned, in dollars or other quantifiable units such as labor hours. Planned value compared with earned value measures the dollar volume of work planned versus the equivalent dollar volume of work accomplished. Any difference is called a schedule variance. In contrast to what was planned, Table 18.21 shows that work unit D was not completed and work unit F was never started, or $35 of the planned work was not accomplished. As a result, the schedule variance shows that 35% of the work planned for this period was not done.

Cost Variance. Earned value compared with the actual cost incurred (from contractor accounting systems) for the work performed provides an objective measure of planned and actual cost. Any difference is called a cost variance. A negative variance means more money was spent for the work accomplished than was planned. Table 18.22 shows the calculation of cost variance. The work performed was planned to cost $65 and actually cost $91. The cost variance is 40%.

Spend Comparison. The typical spend comparison approach, whereby contractors report actual expenditures against planned expenditures, is not related to the work that was accomplished. Table 18.23 shows a simple comparison of planned and actual spending, which is unrelated to work performed and therefore not a useful comparison. The fact that the total amount spent was $9 less than planned for this period is not useful without the comparisons with work accomplished.

Use of Earned Value Data. The benefits to project management of the earned value approach come from the disciplined planning conducted and the availability of metrics that show real variances from the plan in order to generate necessary corrective actions.[42]

Discussion Questions

18.13 Why is the generic four-stage control cycle useful for understanding how to monitor and control projects?

18.14 Why was one of the earliest project tracking devices referred to as an S-curve? Do you see value in the desire to link budget and schedule to view project performance?

18.15 What are some of the key drawbacks with S-curve analysis?

18.16 What are the benefits and drawbacks of using tracking Gantt charts as a monitoring tool?

18.17 It has been said that Earned Value Management (EVM) came about because the federal government often used "cost-plus" contractors with project organizations. Cost-plus contracting allows the contractor to recover full project development costs plus accumulated profit from these contracts. Why would requiring contractor firms to employ Earned Value Management help the government hold the line against project cost overruns?

18.18 Identify and describe the five steps that are considered important in implementing EVM into projects successfully.

18.19 Consider the major findings of the research on human factors in project implementation. What common themes seem to emerge from the research on behavioral issues as a critical element in determining project status?

18.20 The 10 critical success factors have been applied in a variety of settings and project types. Consider a project with which you have been involved. Did any of these factors emerge clearly as being the most important for the project's success? Why?

18.21 What are the main issues with being able to use EVM effectively? How can a project manager overcome these issues?

18.22 What do the Schedule Performance Index and the Cost Performance Index demonstrate? How can a project manager use this information to estimate future project performance?

18.23 Consider any project you have been involved in. Which of the control tools described in this chapter would you use? Why?

Problems

18.14 Using the following information, develop a simple S-curve representation of the expected cumulative budget expenditures for this project (figures are in thousands).

	Duration (in days)							
	10	20	30	40	50	60	70	80
Activities	4	8	12	20	10	8	6	2
Cumulative	4	12	24	44	54	62	68	70

18.15 Suppose the expenditure figures in Problem 1 were modified as follows (figures are in thousands).

	Duration (in days)							
	10	20	30	40	50	60	70	80
Activities	4	8	10	14	20	24	28	8
Cumulative	4	12	22	36	56	80	108	116

Draw this S-curve. What does the new S-curve diagram represent? How would you explain the reason for the different, non-S-shape of the curve?

18.16 Assume the following information (figures are in thousands):

Budgeted Costs for Sample Project

	Duration (in weeks)									
	5	10	15	20	25	30	35	40	45	Total
Brief	5	7	1	4						
Release	6	11	6							
Market			12	15	45	9				
Launch					3	9	4	2	1	
Total										
Monthly										
Cumul.										

a. Calculate the monthly budget and monthly cumulative budgets for the project.
b. Draw an S-curve representation of this project.

18.17 Use the following information to construct a tracking Gantt chart using MS Project.

Activities	Duration	Preceding Activities
A	5 days	none
B	4 days	A
C	3 days	A
D	6 days	B, C
E	4 days	B
F	2 days	D, E

Highlight project status on day 14 using the tracking option and assuming that all tasks to date have been completed on time. Print the output file.

18.18 Using the information in Problem 4, highlight the project's status on day 14 but assume that activity D has not yet begun. What would the new tracking Gantt chart show? Print the output file.

18.19 Using the data in the table below, calculate the project schedule variance units:

Schedule Variance Work Units

	A	B	C	D	E	Total
Planned Value (PV)	30	25	10	15	40	120
Earned Value (EV)	25	15	5	15	30	
Schedule Variance (SV)						

18.20 Using the data in the table below, complete the table by calculating the cumulative planned and cumulative actual monthly budgets through the end of June. Complete the earned value column on the right. Assume the project is planned for a 12-month duration and a $250,000 budget.

Activity	Jan	Feb	Mar	Apr	May	Jun	Plan	% Comp.	Value
Staffing	8	7					15	100	___
Blueprinting		4	6				10	100	___
Prototype Development			2	8			10	70	___
Full Design				3	8	10	21	67	___
Construction					2	30	32	25	___
Transfer						10	10	0	___
Monthly Plan	___	___	___	___	___	___	___	___	___
Cumulative	___	___	___	___	___	___	___	___	___
Monthly Actual	10	15	6	14	9	40			
Cumul. Actual	___	___	___	___	___	___	___	___	___

18.21 Using the data from Problem 7, calculate the following values:

Schedule Variances	
Planned Value (PV)	___
Earned Value (EV)	___
Schedule Performance Index	___
Estimated Time to Completion	___
Cost Variances	
Actual Cost of Work Performed (AC)	___
Earned Value (EV)	___
Cost Performance Index	___
Estimated Cost to Completion	___

18.22 Suppose you are working on a project that is estimated to take 5 months to complete and will cost $10,000. Consider the following information, calculating the SPI and estimated time to completion (figures are in thousands). What does this information tell you about the project?

Schedule Variances	
Planned Value of Work Scheduled (PV)	60
Earned Value (EV)	30
Schedule Performance Index	___
Estimated Time to Completion	___

18.23 Suppose, for Problem 9, that your PV was 75 and your EV was 80. Recalculate the SPI and estimated time to completion for the project with this new data.

18.24 You have collected the following data based on three months of your project's performance. Complete the table. Calculate cumulative CPI (CPI^C). How is the project performing after these three months? Is the trend positive or negative?

	EV	EV^C	AC	AC^C	CPI	CPI^C
January	$30,000		$35,000			
February	$95,000		$100,000			
March	$125,500		$138,000			

18.25 You have collected EV, AC, and PV data from your project for a five-month period. Complete the table. Calculate SPI^C and CPI^C. Compare the cost and schedule performance for the project on a month-by-month basis and cumulatively. How would you assess the performance of the project? (All values are in thousands $.)

Table for Problem 18.25

	EV	EV^C	AC	AC^C	PV	PV^C	SPI	SPI^C	CPI	CPI^C
April	8		10		7					
May	17		18		16					
June	25		27		23					
July	15		18		15					
August	7		9		8					

18.26 Consider the following project information. The total budget is $36,000 and it is expected to last 6 months. After four months, you have calculated the following information about the project:

PV = $29,000
EV = $30,500
AC = $28,000

Based on this information, calculate the SPI and CPI. What is the estimated time and cost to completion? What does this information tell you about the project?

18.27 (Optional—Based on Earned Schedule discussion in Appendix 18.1.) Suppose you have a project with a Budget at Completion (BAC) of $250,000 and a projected length of 10 months. After tracking the project for six months, you have collected the information in the table below.

a. Complete the table. How do Earned Value SPI (based on $) and Earned Schedule SPI differ?
b. Calculate the schedule variances for the project for both Earned Value and Earned Schedule. How do the values differ?

	Jan	Feb	Mar	Apr	May	Jun
PV ($)	25,000	40,000	70,000	110,000	150,000	180,000
EV ($)	20,000	32,000	60,000	95,000	123,000	151,000
SV ($)	−5,000					
SPI ($)	0.80					
ES (mo.)	0.80					
SV (t)	−.20					
SPI (t)	0.80					

CASE STUDY 18.3

The IT Department at Kimble College

As part of the effort to upgrade the IT capabilities at Kimble College, the institution initiated a program more than five years ago to dramatically increase the size of the IT department while focusing efforts toward data management and improving administrative functions. As part of the upgrade, Kimble hired a new vice president of information systems, Dan Gray, and gave him wide latitude in identifying problems and initiating projects that would result in improving the IT system campuswide. Dan also was given the final power to determine the development of new projects, which allowed him to field requests from the various college departments, determine which needs were most pressing, and create a portfolio of prioritized projects. Within two years of his arrival at Kimble, Dan was overseeing an IT department of 46 people, divided into four levels: (1) help desk support, (2) junior programmers, (3) senior programmers, and (4) project team leaders. There were only four project team leaders, with the majority of Dan's staff working either at the entry-level help desk or as junior programmers.

In the past three years, the performance of Dan's department has been mixed. Although it has been responsible for taking on a number of new projects, its track record for delivery is shaky; for example, well over half of the new projects have run past their budgets and initial schedules, sometimes by more than 100%. Worse, from the college president's perspective, it does not appear that Dan has a clear sense of the status of the projects in his department. At board meetings, he routinely gives a rosy picture of his performance but seems incapable of answering simple questions about project delivery beyond vague declarations that "things are moving along just fine." In the president's view, Dan's departmental track record is not warranting the additional funding he keeps requesting for new equipment and personnel.

You have been called in, as an independent consultant, to assess the performance of Dan's department and, in particular, the manner in which it runs and monitors the development of its project portfolio. Your initial assessment has confirmed the college president's hunch: The ongoing status of projects in the IT department is not clearly understood. Everyone is working hard, but no one can provide clear answers about how the projects being developed are doing. After asking several project leaders about the status of their projects and repeatedly receiving "Oh, fine" as a response, you realize that they are not being evasive; they simply do not know from day to day how their projects are progressing. When you ask them how they determine project status, the general consensus is that unless the project team leaders hear bad news, they assume everything is going fine. Furthermore, it is clear that even if they wanted to spend more time monitoring their ongoing projects, they are not sure what types of information they should collect to develop better on-time project tracking and control.

(continued)

Questions

1. As a consultant monitoring this problem, what solutions will you propose? To what degree has Dan's management style contributed to the problems?
2. What are some types of project status information you could suggest the project team leaders begin to collect in order to assess the status of their projects?
3. How would you blend "hard data" and "managerial or behavioral" information to create a comprehensive view of the status of ongoing projects in the IT department at Kimble College?

CASE STUDY 18.4

The Superconducting Supercollider

Conceived in the 1980s as a device to accelerate particles in high-energy physics research, the Superconducting Supercollider (SSC) was a political and technical hot potato from the beginning. The technical challenges associated with the SSC were daunting. Its purpose was to smash subatomic particles together at near the speed of light. That would require energy levels of 40 trillion electron volts. Using the physics of quantum mechanics, the goal of the project was to shed light on some of the fundamental questions about the formation of the universe. The SSC was designed to be the largest particle accelerator ever constructed, far bigger than its counterpart at Fermi Laboratory. In order to achieve these energy levels, a set of 10,000 magnets was needed. Each of the magnets, cylindrical in shape (1 foot in diameter and 57 feet long), would need to operate at peak levels if the accelerator were to achieve the necessary energy levels for proton collision. The expected price tag just for the construction of the magnets was estimated at $1.5 billion.

The technical difficulties were only part of the overall scope of the project. Construction of the SSC would be an undertaking of unique proportions. Scientists determined that the accelerator required a racetrack-shaped form, buried underground for easier use. The overall circumference of the planned SSC required 54 miles of tunnel to be bored 165 to 200 feet underground. The initial budget estimate for completing the project was $5 billion, and the estimated schedule would require eight years to finish the construction and technical assemblies.

The SSC's problems began almost immediately after President Reagan's 1988 kickoff of the project. First, the public (including Congress) had little understanding of the purpose of the project. A goal as nebulous as "particle acceleration" for high-energy physics was not one easily embraced by a majority of citizens. The original operating consortium, URA, consisted of 80 public and private American research centers and universities, but it was expected that European and Asian scientists also would wish to conduct experiments with the SSC. Consequently, the U.S. Department of Energy hoped to offset some of the cost through other countries. While initially receptive to the idea of participating in the project, these countries became vague about their levels of contribution and time frame for payment.

Another huge problem was finding a suitable location for the site of the SSC. At its peak, work on the SSC was expected to employ 4,500 workers. Further, once in full-time operation, the SSC would require a permanent staff of 2,500 employees and an annual operating budget of $270 million. Clearly, it was to almost every state's interest to lure the SSC. The result was a political nightmare as the National Research Council appointed a site review committee to evaluate proposals from 43 states. After making their judgments based on a series of performance and capability criteria, the committee narrowed their list to eight states. Finally, in late 1988, the contract for the SSC was awarded to Waxahachie, Texas, on a 16,000-acre tract south of Dallas. While Texas was thrilled with the award, the decision meant ruffled feathers for a number of other states and their disappointed congressional representatives.

The final problem with the SSC almost from the beginning was the mounting federal budget deficit, which caused more and more politicians to question the decision to allocate money at a time when Congress was looking for ways to cut more than $30 billion from the budget. This concern ended up being a long-term problem, as the SSC was allocated only $100 million for 1989, less than one third of its initial $348 million funding request. Budget battles would be a constant refrain throughout the SSC's short life.

Work proceeded slowly on the Waxahachie site throughout the early 1990s. Meanwhile, European financial support for the project was not forthcoming. The various governments privately suspected that the project would never be completed. Their fears were becoming increasingly justified as the cost of the project continued to rise. By 1993, the original $5 billion estimate had ballooned to $11 billion. Meanwhile, less than 20% of the construction had been completed. The process was further slowed when Congress began investigating expenditures and determined that accounting procedures were inadequate. Clearly, control of the project's budget and schedule had become a serious concern.

In a last desperate move to save SSC funding, Energy Secretary Hazel O'Leary fired URA as prime contractor for the construction project. There was talk of replacing URA with a proven contractor—Martin Marietta and Bechtel were the two leading candidates. By then, however, it was a case of too little, too late. Costs continued to climb and work proceeded at such a snail's pace that when the 1994 federal budget was put together, funding for the SSC had been removed entirely. The project was dead. The nonrecoverable costs to the U.S. taxpayer from the aborted project have been estimated at anywhere between $1 billion and $2 billion.

Few questioned the government's capability to construct such a facility. The technology, though leading-edge, had been used previously in other research laboratories. The problem was that the pro- and anti-SSC camps tended to split between proponents of pure research and those who argued (increasingly swaying political support their way) that multibillion-dollar research having no immediate discernible impact on society was a luxury we could not afford, particularly in an era of federal budget cuts and hard choices. The SSC position was further weakened by the activities of the research consortium supervising the project, URA. Its behavior was termed increasingly arrogant by congressional oversight groups that began asking legitimate questions about expenditures and skyrocketing budget requests. In place of evidence of definable progress, the project offered only a sense of out-of-control costs and poor oversight—clearly not the message to send when American taxpayers were questioning their decision to foot a multibillion-dollar bill.[43]

Questions

1. Suppose you were a consultant called into the project by the federal government in 1990, when it still seemed viable. Given the start to the project, what steps would you have taken to reintroduce some positive "spin" on the Superconducting Supercollider?
2. What were the warning signs of impending failure as the project progressed? Could these signs have been recognized so that problems could have been foreseen and addressed or, in your opinion, was the project simply impossible to achieve? Take a position and argue its merits.
3. Search for "superconducting supercollider" on the Internet. How do the majority of stories about the project present it? Given the negative perspective, what are the top three lessons to be learned from this project?

CASE STUDY 18.5

Boeing's 787 Dreamliner: Failure to Launch

It was never supposed to be this difficult. When Boeing announced the development of its newest and most high-tech aircraft, the 787 Dreamliner, it seemed that it had made all the right decisions. By focusing on building a more fuel-efficient aircraft, using lighter composite materials that saved on overall weight and resulted in a 20% lower fuel consumption, outsourcing development work to a global network of suppliers, and pioneering new assembly techniques, it appeared that Boeing had taken a clear-eyed glimpse into the future of commercial air travel and designed the equivalent of a "home run"—a new aircraft that ticked all the boxes.

Airline customers seemed to agree. When Boeing announced the development of the 787 and opened its order book, it quickly became the best-selling aircraft in history, booking 847 advance orders for the airplane. With list prices varying from $161 to $205 million each, depending on the model, the Dreamliner was worth billions in long-term revenue streams for the company. The aircraft was designed for long-range flight and could seat up to 330 passengers. Most industry analysts agreed: With the introduction of the Dreamliner, the future had never seemed brighter for Boeing.

But when the first delivery dates slipped, yet again, into 2012, four years behind schedule, and the company's stock price was battered in the marketplace, Boeing and its industry backers began trying to unravel a maze of technical and supply chain problems that were threatening not just the good name of Boeing, but the viability of the Dreamliner. Derisively nicknamed the "7-L-7" for "late," the project had fallen victim to extensive cost overruns and continuous schedule slippages, and had recently encountered a number of worrisome structural and electrical faults that were alarming airlines awaiting delivery of their aircraft. These events combined to put Boeing squarely on the hot seat, as they sought to find a means to correct these problems and salvage both their reputation and the viability of their high-profile aircraft.

(continued)

FIGURE 18.28 **Boeing's 787 Dreamliner**
Source: Peter Carey/Alamy

The time frame for the development of the Dreamliner offers some important milestones in its path to commercialization, including the following:

- 2003—Boeing officially announced the development of the "7E7," its newest aircraft.
- 2004—First orders were received for 55 of the aircraft from All Nippon Airlines, with a delivery date set for late 2008.
- 2005—The 7E7 was officially renamed the 787 Dreamliner.
- July 2007—The first Dreamliner was unveiled in a rollout ceremony at Boeing's assembly plant in Everett, Washington.
- October 2007—The first six-month delay was announced. The problems identified included supplier delivery delays and problems with the fasteners used to attach composite components of the aircraft together. The program director, Mike Bair, was replaced a week later.
- November 2008—Boeing announced the fifth delay in the schedule, due to continuing coordination problems with global suppliers, repeated failures of fasteners, and the effects of a machinist strike. The first flight was pushed out until the second quarter of 2009.
- June 2009—Boeing announced that the first flight was postponed "due to a need to reinforce an area within the side-of-body section of the aircraft." They further delayed the first test flight until late 2009. At the same time, Boeing wrote off $2.5 billion in costs for the first three 787s built.
- December 7, 2009—First successful test flight of the 787.
- July 2010—Boeing announced that schedule slippages would push first deliveries into 2011. They blamed an engine blowout at a test bed in Rolls-Royce's plant, although Rolls denied that its engines were the cause of schedule delay.
- August 2010—Air India announced a $1 billion compensation claim against Boeing, citing repeated delivery delays for the twenty-seven 787s it had on order.
- November 9, 2010—Fire broke out on Dreamliner #2 on its test flight near Laredo, Texas. The fire was quickly extinguished and the cause was attributed to a fault in the electrical systems. The aircraft were grounded for extensive testing. With that technical mishap, it was feared that the delivery date for the aircraft would be pushed into 2012.
- January 19, 2011—Boeing announced another delay in its 787 delivery schedule. The latest (and seventh official) delay came more than two months after the Dreamliner #2 electrical fire. All Nippon Airways, the jet's first customer, was informed that the earliest it could expect delivery of the first of its 55-airplane order would be the third quarter of 2011, though expectations were high that the airline might not receive any aircraft until early 2012, making final delivery nearly 3½ years late.

There is no question that the Dreamliner is a state-of-the-art aircraft. The 787 is the first commercial aircraft that makes extensive use of composite materials in place of aluminum, both for framing and for the external "skin." In fact, each 787 contains approximately 35 tons of carbon fiber-reinforced plastic. Carbon fiber composites have a higher strength-to-weight ratio than traditional aircraft materials, such as aluminum and steel, and help make the 787 a lighter aircraft. These composites are used on fuselage, wings, tail, doors, and interior sections, and aluminum is used on wing and tail leading edges. The fuselage is assembled in one-piece composite barrel sections instead of the multiple aluminum sheets and some 50,000 fasteners used on existing aircraft. Because of the lighter weight and a new generation of jet engines used to power it, the Dreamliner has a lower cost of operations, which makes it especially appealing to airlines. Additionally, the global supply chain that Boeing established to manufacture components for the aircraft reads like a who's who list of international experts. Firms in Sweden, Japan, South Korea, France, England, Italy, and India all have major contracts with Boeing to supply parts of the aircraft, which are shipped to two assembly plants in the United States (one in Washington and the other planned for South Carolina) for final assembly and testing before being sent to customers. In short, the 787 is an incredibly complicated product, both in terms of its physical makeup and the intricate supply chain that Boeing created to produce it.

So complicated is the 787 program, in fact, that it may be the case that in developing the Dreamliner, Boeing has simply tried to do too much at one time. Critics have argued that creating a new generation aircraft with composite materials while routing an entirely new supply chain, maintaining quality control, and debugging a long list of unexpected problems is simply beyond the capability of any organization, no matter how highly skilled in project management they may be. Suppliers have been struggling to meet Boeing's exacting technical standards, with early test versions of the nose section, for example, failing Boeing's testing and being deemed unacceptable. Boeing has undertaken a huge risk with the Dreamliner. In a bid to hold down costs, the company has engaged in extreme outsourcing, leaving it highly dependent on a far-flung supply chain that includes 43 "top-tier" suppliers on three continents. It is the first time Boeing has ever outsourced the most critical areas of the plane, the wing and the fuselage. About 80% of the Dreamliner is being fabricated by outside suppliers, versus 51% for existing Boeing planes.

Jim McNerney, chief executive of Boeing, has admitted that the 787 development plans, involving significant outsourcing, were "overly ambitious": "While game-changing innovation of this magnitude is never easy, we've seen more of the bleeding edge of innovation than we'd ever care to see again. So we are adjusting our approach for future programs." McNerney continued, "We are disappointed over the schedule changes. Notwithstanding the challenges that we are experiencing in bringing forward this game-changing product, we remain confident in the design of the 787."

Three Years Later—Update on the Status of the Dreamliner

Boeing's 787 officially entered commercial service on September 25, 2011, with Air Nippon of Japan. As of 2014, there were orders placed for 1,031 Dreamliners and a total of 162 had been delivered and were in service worldwide. Since introduction, Dreamliners have logged more than 500,000 hours in the air with 21 carriers. Troubles with reliability continue to dog the Dreamliner, however. Although original concerns about cracks and structural flaws in the composite materials appear to have abated, since its debut in late 2011, the 787 has experienced a series of malfunctions, including a three-month grounding of the global fleet in 2013 after battery meltdowns on two planes. Air India, which hasn't reported an annual profit since 2007, and low-cost airliner Norwegian Air built their growth plans around the composite-material airliner and its promise of more fuel-efficient operation. However, both airlines have reported dissatisfaction with the current state of Dreamliner quality and reliability, throwing their operating strategies into question. Air India, which has ordered 27 of the aircraft, was forced to divert one of its 787s to Kuala Lumpur as recently as February 2014 as a precaution after a software fault on a flight to New Delhi from Melbourne. They recently announced that they would be seeking compensation from Boeing after the carrier found that its Dreamliners are not as fuel efficient as Boeing claimed when selling them. In January 2014, Japan Airlines, one of the biggest operators of the Dreamliner, found a battery cell in an empty jet smoking during preflight maintenance.

Randy Tinseth, Boeing's vice president of marketing, said reliability levels are climbing as the company works closely with airline operations personnel and makes other changes. "All of our customers are seeing improvement in reliability over time," Mr. Tinseth said, but he declined to predict when the 787 would match the 777's track record exceeding 99% reliability.

"We continue on a positive trajectory," he said, "but when we get there, it's difficult to predict."[44]

Questions

1. In evaluating the development of the 787 Dreamliner, what are some of the unique factors in this project that make it so difficult to accurately monitor and control?
2. Comment on the following statement: "In trying to control development of the 787, Boeing should have been monitoring and controlling the performance of its suppliers." Do you agree or disagree that Boeing's project management should have been fully extended to its suppliers? Why?
3. As you read the case, what do you see as the critical issues that appear to be causing the majority of the project delivery and quality problems?

Internet Exercises

18.5 Go to www.brighthubpm.com/monitoring-projects/51982-understanding-the-s-curve-theory-for-project-management-monitoring/ and read the article on the multiple uses of project S-curves. What does the article suggest about the use of different S-curves and analysis methods?

18.6 Go to www.nu-solutions.com/downloads/earned_value_lite.pdf and access the article by Q. W. Fleming and J. M. Koppelman, "Earned Value Lite: Earned Value for the Masses." From your reading, summarize the 10 key steps in EVM and the advantages they argue earned value offers for project control and evaluation.

18.7 Go to www.acq.osd.mil/evm and explore the various links and screens. What does the size and diversity of this site tell you about the acceptance and use of earned value in organizations today?

18.8 Go to www.erpgenie.com/general/project.htm and access the reading on "Six Steps to Successful Sponsorship." Consider the critical success factors it identifies for managing an IT project implementation. How do these factors map onto the 10-factor model of Pinto and Slevin? How do you account for differences?

18.9 Type in the address www.massdot.state.ma.us/highway/TheBigDig.aspx and navigate through the Web site supporting the Boston Tunnel project. Evaluate the performance of this project using the model of 10 critical project success factors discussed in this chapter. How does the project rate, in your opinion? Present specific examples and evidence to support your ratings.

MS Project Exercises

Exercise 18.1

Using the following data, enter the various tasks and create a Gantt chart using MS Project. Assign the individuals responsible for each activity, and once you have completed the network, update it with the percentage complete tool. What does the MS Project output file look like?

Activity	Duration	Predecessors	Resource	% Complete
A. Research product	6	—	Tom Allen	100
B. Interview customers	4	A	Liz Watts	75
C. Design survey	5	A	Rich Watkins	50
D. Collect data	4	B, C	Gary Sims	0

Exercise 18.2

Now, suppose we assign costs to each of the resources in the following amounts:

Resource	Cost
Tom Allen	$50/hour
Liz Watts	$55/hour
Rich Watkins	$18/hour
Gary Sims	$12.50/hour

Create the resource usage statement for the project as of the most recent update. What are project expenses per task to date?

Exercise 18.3

Use MS Project to create a Project Summary Report of the most recent project status.

Exercise 18.4

Using the data shown in the network precedence table below, enter the various tasks in MS Project. Then select a date approximately halfway through the overall project duration, and update all tasks in the network to show current status. You may assume that Activities A through I are now 100% completed. What does the tracking Gantt look like?

Project—Remodeling an Appliance

Activity	Duration	Predecessors
A. Conduct competitive analysis	3	—
B. Review field sales reports	2	—
C. Conduct tech capabilities assessment	5	—
D. Develop focus group data	2	A, B, C
E. Conduct telephone surveys	3	D
F. Identify relevant specification improvements	3	E
G. Interface with marketing staff	1	F
H. Develop engineering specifications	5	G
I. Check and debug designs	4	H
J. Develop testing protocol	3	G
K. Identify critical performance levels	2	J

Project—Remodeling an Appliance (Continued)

Activity	Duration	Predecessors
L. Assess and modify product components	6	I, K
M. Conduct capabilities assessment	12	L
N. Identify selection criteria	3	M
O. Develop RFQ	4	M
P. Develop production master schedule	5	N, O
Q. Liaison with sales staff	1	P
R. Prepare product launch	3	Q

Exercise 18.5

Use the following information to construct a Gantt chart in MS Project. What is the expected duration of the project (critical path)? Assume the project is halfway finished in terms of the schedule (day 16 completed) but activity completion percentages are as shown. Construct a tracking Gantt chart for the project (be sure to show the percentage complete for each activity). What would it look like?

Activity	Duration (in Days)	Predecessors	% Completed (Day 16)
A	6	None	100%
B	2	A	100%
C	4	A	100%
D	7	C	14%
E	10	D	0%
F	6	B, C	33%
G	5	E, F	0%

Exercise 18.6

Using the date for Problem 14, add the resource assignments to each of the activities and input their hourly rates as shown. Construct an earned value chart for the project. Which activities have negative variances? What is the estimate at completion (EAC) for the project? (Hint: Remember to click "Set baseline" prior to creating EVM table. The EVM table is found by clicking on the "View" tab, then "Tables," then "Other Tables".)

Resource Name	Hourly Rate ($)
Josh	12.00
Mary	13.50
Evan	10.00
Adrian	22.00
Susan	18.50
Aaron	17.00
Katie	32.00

PMP CERTIFICATION SAMPLE QUESTIONS

6. Suppose your PV for a project was $100,000 and your EV was $60,000. Your Schedule Performance Index (SPI) for this project would be:
- **a.** 1.52
- **b.** .60
- **c.** You cannot calculate SPI with the information provided
- **d.** 1.66

7. Activity A is worth $500, is complete, and actually cost $500. Activity B is worth $1,000, is 50% complete, and has actually cost $700 so far. Activity C is worth $100, is 75% complete, and has actually cost $90 so far. What is the total earned value for the project?
- **a.** $1,600
- **b.** $1,075
- **c.** $1,290
- **d.** –$1,075

8. Using the information in Question 2, calculate the Cost Performance Index (CPI) for the project.
- **a.** 1.20
- **b.** –1.20
- **c.** 0.83
- **d.** –0.83

9. Which of the following gives the remaining amount to be spent on the project in Questions 2 and 3 based on current spending efficiency?
- **a.** Budget remaining
- **b.** Estimate to complete
- **c.** Cost variance
- **d.** Cost Performance Index (CPI)

10. Activity A is worth $100, is complete, and actually cost $150. Activity B is worth $500, is 75% complete, and has actually cost $400 so far. Activity C is worth $500, is 25% complete, and has actually cost $200 so far. What is the estimated cost to completion for the project?
- **a.** $1,100
- **b.** $750
- **c.** $880
- **d.** $1,375

Answers: **6.** b—SPI is calculated by dividing earned value (EV) by planned value (PV); **7.** b—Earned Value is $1,075 to date; **8.** c—CPI is calculated as earned value (EV) divided by actual cost (AC). In this case, that is $1.075/$1,290, or 0.83; **9.** b—Estimate to complete; **10.** d—Estimate to completion is based on the formula (1/.80) × $1,100, or $1,375.

APPENDIX 18.1

Earned Schedule*

Research and practice using Earned Value Management (EVM) has shown that this method for project tracking and forecasting is reliable and offers the project team an accurate snapshot of both the project's current status and a forecast of its completion conditions. However, in recent years, some critics have noted that EVM also has some important limitations. One of the most important of these limitations is the fact that all project status information is derived in terms of the project's budget, including the project Schedule Performance Index (SPI) and schedule variance. A second concern voiced about EVM is that it becomes less precise (unreliable) the farther a project progresses and that by the latter stages of the project, the information derived from EVM may be either unjustifiably positive or negative. Finally, it has been suggested that EVM becomes an imprecise metric for projects that have already overrun, that is, whose duration has exceeded the original baseline end date. In other words, how do we determine the ongoing status of a project once it is officially "late"?

Let us consider these objections to EVM in turn. First, we know that EVM is derived from the project's budget, not its schedule performance, but intuitively, it makes better sense that a project's schedule performance should be in terms of units of time. For example, remember that Schedule Variance (SV) is calculated by Earned Value (EV) minus Planned Value (PV), and the formula for finding the Schedule Performance Index (SPI) is SPI = EV/PV. Thus, we are assessing the project's schedule performance, not as a function of time, but of money. We can see this graphically by considering Figure 18.29, which shows a generic project EVM measure. The vertical axis of the performance chart is in terms of budget dollars, and the resulting schedule variance is also expressed in terms of the project's budget. The EVM metrics for schedule, then, are Earned Value (EV) and Planned Valued (PV).

The second concern suggests that the closer to completion a project gets, the less precise and useful is the information that EVM provides. The significance of cost-based ratios used with planned duration to predict a project's final duration can be illustrated by a simple example. Assume a project with a budget of $1,000 has completed most of its planned work, with EV = $990, PV = $1,000, BAC = $1,000, and PD (Planned Duration) = 12 weeks. These metrics give an SPI of 0.99, which yields a final duration of 12.12 weeks: Estimate at Completion = $1/.99 \times 12$. We can see from simple inspection that as EV approaches PV, and ultimately BAC, forecasted project duration decreases, because the upper limit for EV is always BAC. Regardless of whether this calculation is performed during week 10 or week 15, the cost-based ratio yields the same results and can show that an

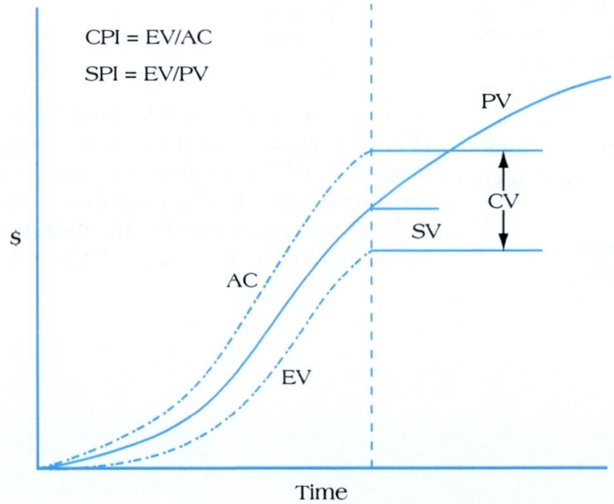

FIGURE 18.29 Earned Value Performance Metrics

Source: Lipke, W. H. (2003, Spring). "Schedule is different," *The Measureable News,* pp. 10–15. Project Management Institute, Schedule is different," The Measureable News " pp. 10–15. Project Management Institute, Inc (2003). Copyright and all rights reserved. Material from this publication has been reproduced with the permission of PMI.

* Portions of this appendix were prepared in collaboration with Bill Mowery, MPM, PMP.

in-progress project has a forecasted completion date in the past. This issue suggests that EVM becomes less precise the closer a project is to its completion. Where early indicators are reasonably accurate, by the final stages of the project's life cycle, the project schedule metric (remember, it is based on monetary units) is likely to show encouraging evidence of completion. However, it is during the final stages of the project that Cost Variance and Schedule Variance data begin to diverge.

Critics of EVM have pointed out this quirk in the system; as a project moves closer to its supposed completion date, its planned value converges on the project's planned cost—that is, PV = BAC (Budgeted at Completion). However, with late projects, the project's planned value has usually already converged on the project's overall budget (i.e., PV = BAC), while EV is still incrementally achieving this value. Once PV = BAC at the project's planned completion date, the project cannot be measured as being "later." In effect, there are measurement errors that do not become apparent until a project is already late.

The solution that researchers have adopted is to introduce the concept of **Earned Schedule (ES)** project management. Earned Schedule recognizes, first, that for accurate forecasts of project schedule, some unit of time must be the metric to consider, rather than EVM's cost-based approach. Earned Schedule uses a relatively simple formulation to achieve its purpose, which is to derive a time-based measurement of schedule performance by comparing a project's EV today (actual time) to a point on the performance measurement baseline (the Planned Value curve) where it should have been earned. The difference in the two times represents a true time-based Schedule Variance, or, in Earned Schedule notation, SV_t. The derivation of Earned Schedule metrics is shown in Figure 18.30. As the figure demonstrates, the Schedule Performance Index for any project can be reconfigured from the original, SPI($) = EV/PV, to the alternative: SPI(t) = ES/AT. In the second equation, the Schedule Performance Index for an Earned Schedule calculation divides the Earned Schedule value by Actual Time. Likewise, in this second configuration, Earned Schedule variance equals Earned Schedule minus Actual Time (ES – AT).

To calculate Earned Schedule, we use the project's current earned value (EV) to identify in which time increment of PV the cost value occurs. The value of ES is then equal to the cumulative time to the beginning of that increment plus some portion of it. For example, suppose we wished, at the end of June, to calculate the ES of a project that began January 1 (see Figure 18.30). We use monthly increments in our calculation; thus, because we are at the end of June, AT = 6. We can see visually that by the end of June, the project's schedule has slipped some degree; in fact, we see that we have completed all of April and some portion of May's work by the end of June. We can use the following formula to determine the project's ES:

$$ES = C + (EV - PV_c)/(PV_{c+1} - PV_c)$$

where C is the number of time increments on the project schedule baseline where EV ≥ PV. In our specific example above, with monthly time increments, the formula becomes:

$$ES = 4 + [EV(\$) - PV(April)]/[PV(May) - PV(April)]$$

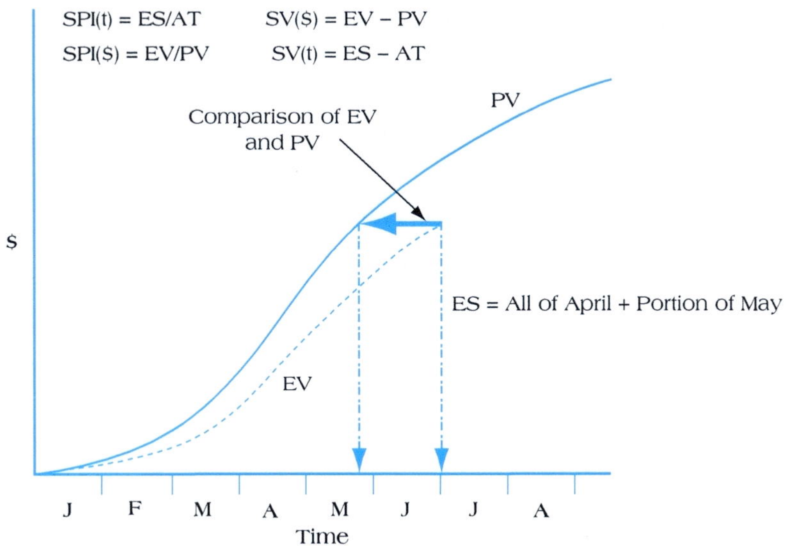

FIGURE 18.30 Earned Schedule Example (end of June)

TABLE 18.24 Earned Schedule Table

	Jan	Feb	Mar	Apr	May	Jun	Jul
PV ($)	105	200	515	845	1,175	1,475	1,805
EV ($)	95	180	470	770	1,065	1,315	
SV ($)	−10	−20	−45	−75	−110	−160	
SPI ($)	0.91	0.90	0.91	0.91	0.90	0.89	
Month Count	1	2	3	4	5	6	7
ES (mo)							
SV (t)							
SPI (t)							

We can see an example of a complete Earned Schedule calculation in the following case. Suppose we have been collecting data on the status of our project for the past six months, using the standard EVM method. Table 18.24 gives this information.

Calculating the ES for January, we have the values:

EV (Jan) = 95

PV (Jan) = 105

We can use this information to calculate ES, SV, and SPI for the project, using the formulas we found previously:

ES = 0 + (95 − 0)/(105 − 0) = 0.90

SV (t) = ES − AT, or 0.90 − 1.0 = −0.10

SPI (t) = ES/C, or 0.90/1 = 0.90

Using this information, let's complete the ES table to the end of June (see Table 18.23). The table now aligns with Figure 18.30.

We can see from the information we have calculated in Table 18.25 coupled with Figure 18.30 that by the end of June, a comparison of the project's PV with actual ES shows a serious slippage. Specifically, by the end of June, we have only completed the project's schedule to approximately halfway through the May period. Furthermore, the schedule variance and SPI values have been worsening over the past four months, suggesting that the slippage is accelerating. This information is not necessarily obvious from the standard earned value table, which uses project budget dollars. Finally, research demonstrates that the SPI based on dollars versus the SPI using time can become very different as the project moves toward completion. Thus, as noted earlier, real data confirm one of the central concerns about EVM, namely, that its estimates for schedule become increasingly imprecise the later into the project we move.

The relative accuracy of Earned Schedule versus EVM can be further illustrated when we use it to anticipate schedule variances and possible project delays. Let's use the following example to compare the results we might find when using EVM versus Earned Schedule. Suppose we have a

TABLE 18.25 Completed Earned Value/Schedule Table

	Jan	Feb	Mar	Apr	May	Jun	Jul
PV ($)	105	200	515	845	1,175	1,475	1,805
EV ($)	95	180	470	770	1,065	1,315	
SV ($)	−10	−20	−45	−75	−110	−160	
SPI ($)	0.91	0.90	0.91	0.91	0.90	0.89	
Month Count	1	2	3	4	5	6	7
ES (mo)	0.90	1.79	2.86	3.77	4.66	5.47	
SV (t)	−0.10	−0.21	−0.14	−0.23	−0.33	−0.53	
SPI (t)	0.90	0.90	0.95	0.94	0.93	0.91	

project planned for 18 months' duration (PD) and a total budget of $231,280 (BAC). At the end of 16 months, $234,080 has been spent (AC) while we only have achieved an EV of $207,470. We first calculate budget performance, or Cost Variance (CV), as CV = EV – AC, or:

$$CV = \$207{,}470 - \$234{,}080, \text{ or } -\$26{,}610$$

Schedule Variance (SV), for our example, also can be calculated based on this information. Recall that SV = EV – PV, or:

$$SV = \$207{,}470 - \$220{,}490, \text{ or } -\$13{,}020$$

The above figures show that the project is over budget and behind schedule, but to what degree over the life of the project? We can also use this information to calculate Schedule Performance Index (SPI) and Cost Performance Index (CPI) for the project. Respectively, these values are found as:

$$CPI = EV/AC, \text{ or } \$207{,}470/\$234{,}080 = .89$$
$$SPI = EV/PC, \text{ or } \$207{,}470/\$220{,}490 = .94$$

We know from earlier in this chapter that the simple interpretation of these values suggests that each dollar spent on the project is only producing 89 cents' worth of work, and each 8-hour day is producing only 7.5 hours of effective work. What would the long-term effects of these values be on the project? One way to determine that is to estimate the final schedule duration, the Estimate at Completion for Time (EAC_t), found through the following formula:

$$EAC_t = \frac{\frac{BAC}{SPI}}{\frac{BAC}{PD}}$$

where

BAC = Budget at Completion ($231,280)
PD = Planned Duration (18 months)
SPI = Schedule Performance Index (0.94)

Solving for EAC_t in our example, we find:

$$\frac{\frac{231{,}280}{0.94}}{\frac{231{,}280}{18}} = 19.15 \text{ months}$$

We can solve a similar equation to find the Estimate at Completion (EAC) for the project's budget. Dividing the BAC of $231,280 by the CPI (0.89) yields an estimated cost at completion for the project of $259,870.

To see how Earned Value and Earned Schedule calculations can lead to important divergence, let's use the same information from the above example, shown in Table 18.26, with ES formulas to determine the project's schedule status when we use *time metrics, not budget data.*

TABLE 18.26 Sample Performance Data (in thousands $)

	Dec	Jan	Feb	Mar
Month	13	14	15	16
Planned Value	184.47	198.72	211.49	220.49
Earned Value	173.51	186.71	198.74	207.47
Cumul. Actual Cost	196.76	211.25	224.80	234.08

Recall that at the end of month 16, we are interested in determining the status of the schedule. Our formula to calculate Earned Schedule (ES) is given as:

$$ES = C + (EV - PV_c)/(PV_{c+1} - PV_c)$$

where

C = the number of time months on the schedule baseline where $EV \geq PV$, or 14 months

$EV = \$207,470$

$PV_{14} = \$198,720$

$PV_{15} = \$211,490$

$ES = 14 + (207,470 - 198,720)/(211,490 - 198,720) = 14.69$ months

Applying our Schedule Variance equation, $SV_t = ES - \text{Actual Time (AT)}$, we find that the project is 1.31 months behind schedule ($SV_t = 16 - 14.69$). We can now apply this information to the Earned Schedule's Schedule Performance Index (SPI_t) formula, given as:

$$SPI_t = ES/AT = 14.69/16 = 0.92$$

Lastly, we can derive our projection for the project's final duration, using the Independent Estimate at Completion for time ($IEAC_t$), and come up with the duration forecast, as shown:

$$IEAC_t = PD/SPI_t$$

where

PD (Planned Duration) = 18 months

$IEAC_t = 18/0.92 = 19.51$ months

Consider the results condensed into Table 18.27. When we compare the variances, performance indexes, and projections to completion for the project using EVM versus Earned Schedule, we can see some important discrepancies. First, note the obvious point that for schedule variance, Earned Schedule provides an actual duration estimate based on time, not dollars. Thus, we can relate to the information more easily. However, it is more intriguing to see the differences when Earned Schedule is applied to the SPI in order to determine the likely overall project duration. In this case, the Earned Schedule value suggests final project duration of 19.51 months, or about half a month later than a similar calculation using EVM.

Earned Schedule is a relatively new concept that has sparked debate within the project management community. To date, most research supporting Earned Schedule has come either from small samples in field tests or through computer models. Nevertheless, the underlying arguments supporting Earned Schedule do bear careful consideration. Research suggests that EVM has a tendency to become unreliable as a project moves to completion, and thus it is important to understand to what degree that is of the ES approach actually improves. Another advantage of Earned Schedule is that the calculations are relatively straightforward and the data can be manipulated from the same information obtained for EVM calculations. Thus, at a minimum, Earned Schedule offers an important "check" to verify the accuracy of EVM for project monitoring, particularly as the project begins to overrun its baseline or move toward completion.[45]

TABLE 18.27 Comparison of EVM and Earned Schedule Metrics for Sample Project

Metric	Earned Value	Earned Schedule
Schedule Variance (SV)	–$13,020	–1.31 months
Schedule Performance Index (SPI)	0.94	0.92
Forecast Duration (IEAC)	19.15 months	19.61 months

Notes

27. Collins, D. (2011, July 5). "CityTime crime is Mayor Bloomberg's shame," *Huffington Post*. www.huffingtonpost.com/daniel-collins/citytime-crime-is-mayor-b_b_890202.html?view=screen; Gross, S. (2011, June 29). "NYC wants $600M from tech giant in scandal," *Huffington Post*. www.huffingtonpost.com/huff-wires/20110629/us-citytime-scandal/; Charette, R. (2011, June 21). "New York City's $720 million CityTime project a vehicle for unprecedented fraud says US prosecutor," *IEEE Spectrum*. http://spectrum.ieee.org/riskfactor/computing/it/new-york-citys-720-million-citytime-project-a-vehicle-for-unprecedented-fraud-says-us-prosecutor; Weiser, B. (2014, April 28). "Three contractors sentenced to 20 years in CityTime corruption case," *New York Times*. www.nytimes.com/2014/04/29/nyregion/three-men-sentenced-to-20-years-in-citytime-scheme.html?_r=0; Hennelly, B. (2011, June 29). CityTime payroll scandal a cautionary tale," *WNYC*. www.wnyc.org/story/143601-citytime-cautionary-tale/ Press Release by United States Attorney, Southern District of New York, "Manhattan U.S. Attorney Announces Charges Against Four New Defendants in an Unprecedented Scheme to Defraud New York City in Connection with CityTime Project," June 20, 2011. Project Management Institute, A Guide to the Project Management Body of Knowledge (PMBOK® Guide)—Fifth Edition. Project Management Institute, Inc (2013). Copyright and all rights reserved. Material from this publication has been reproduced with the permission of PMI
28. Departments of the Air Force, the Army, the Navy, and the Defense Logistics Agency. (1987). *Cost/Schedule Control Systems Criteria: Joint Implementation Guide*. Washington, DC: U.S. Department of Defense; Fleming, Q., and Koppelman, J. (1994). "The essence of evolution of earned value," *Cost Engineering*, 36(11): 21–27; Fleming, Q., and Koppelman, J. (1996). *Earned Value Project Management*. Upper Darby, PA: Project Management Institute; Fleming, Q., and Koppelman, J. (1998, July). "Earned value project management: A powerful tool for software projects," *Crosstalk: The Journal of Defense Software Engineering*, pp. 19–23; Hatfield, M. A. (1996). "The case for earned value," *PMNetwork*, 10(12): 25–27; Robinson, P. B. (1997). "The performance measurement baseline—A statistical view," *Project Management Journal*, 28(2): 47–52; Singletary, N. (1996). "What's the value of earned value?" *PMNetwork*, 10(12): 28–30.
29. Brandon, Jr., D. M. (1998). "Implementing earned value easily and effectively," *Project Management Journal*, 29(2): 11–18.
30. Brandon, Jr., D. M. (1998), ibid.
31. Petro, T., and Milani, K. (2000). "Northrop Grumman's four-tier approach to earning value," *Management Accounting Quarterly*, 1(4): 40–48.
32. Christensen, D. S., McKinney, J., and Antonini, R. (1995). "A review of estimate at completion research," *Journal of Cost Analysis*, pp. 41–62; Christensen, D. S. (1998). "The costs and benefits of the earned valued management process," *Acquisition Review Quarterly*, 5, pp. 373–86; Marshall, R. A., Ruiz, P., and Bredillet, C. N. (2008). "Earned value management insights using inferential statistics," *International Journal of Managing Projects in Business*, 1: 288–94.
33. Lipke, W. J. (2003, Spring). "Schedule is different," *The Measurable News*, pp. 10–15.
34. Magnaye, R. B., Sauser, B. J., and Ramirez-Marquez, J. E. (2010). "Systems development planning using readiness levels in a cost of development minimization model," *Systems Engineering*, 13: 311–323; Magnaye, R., Sauser, B., Patanakul, P., Noqicki, D., and Randall, W. (2014). "Earned readiness management for scheduling, monitoring and evaluating the "Development of complex product systems," *International Journal of Project Management*. http://dx.doi.org/10.1016/j.ijproman.2014.01.009
35. Morris, P. W. G. (1988). "Managing project interfaces—Key points for project success," in Cleland, D. I., and King, W. R. (Eds.), *Project Management Handbook*, 2nd ed. New York: Van Nostrand Reinhold, pp. 16–55.
36. Baker, B. N., Murphy, D. C., and Fisher, D. (1988). "Factors affecting project success," in Cleland, D. I., and King, W. R. (Eds.), *Project Management Handbook*, 2nd ed. New York: Van Nostrand Reinhold, pp. 902–19.
37. Morris, P. W. G. (1988), as cited in note 9.
38. Slevin, D. P., and Pinto, J. K. (1987). "Balancing strategy and tactics in project implementation," *Sloan Management Review*, 29(1): 33–41; Pinto, J. K. (1998). "Critical success factors," in Pinto, J. K. (Ed.), *Project Management Handbook*. San Francisco, CA: Jossey-Bass, pp. 379–95; Slevin, D. P., and Pinto, J. K. (1986). "The project implementation profile: New tool for project managers," *Project Management Journal*, 17(3): 57–70; Belout, A., and Gauvreau, C. (2004). "Factors affecting project success: The impact of human resource management," *International Journal of Project Management*, 22: 1–11; Belout, A. (1998). "Effect of human resource management on project effectiveness and success: Toward a new conceptual framework," *International Journal of Project Management*, 16: 21–26.
39. Beck, D. R. (1983). "Implementing top management plans through project management," in Cleland, D. I., and King, W. R. (Eds.), *Project Management Handbook*. New York: Van Nostrand Reinhold, pp. 166–84.
40. Manley, J. H. (1975). "Implementation attitudes: A model and a measurement methodology," in Schultz, R. L., and Slevin, D. P. (Eds.), *Implementing Operations Research/Management Science*. New York: Elsevier, pp. 183–202.
41. Lock, D. (2000). "Managing cost," in Turner, J. R., and Simister, S. J. (Eds.), *Gower Handbook of Project Management*, 3rd ed. Aldershot, UK: Gower, pp. 293–321.
42. www.acq.osd.mil/pm/evbasics.htm
43. http://psncentral.com/research/SSC.htm; "Superconducting Supercollider project hangs on edge." (1993, September 27). *Boston Globe*, p. 1; "Texas lands the SSC." (1988, November 18). *Science*, 242: 1004; "University consortium faulted for management, accounting." (1993, July 9). *Science*, 261: 157–58.
44. Blass, G. (2008). "Boeing's 787 Dreamliner has a composite problem." www.zimbio.com/Boeing+787+Dreamliner/articles/18/Boeing+787+Dreamliner+composite+problem; Cohan, P. (2010). "Yet another problem for Boeing's 787 Dreamliner." www.dailyfinance.com/story/company-news/yet-another-problem-for-boeings-787-dreamliner/19734254/; Done, K. (2007,

October 10). "Boeing 787 Dreamliner hit by delays," *Financial Times*. www.ft.com/cms/s/0/d42602de-774c-11dc-9de8-0000779fd2ac.html#axzz17R08yXyV; "The 787 encounters turbulence." (2006, June 19). www.businessweek.com/magazine/content/06_25/b3989049.htm; Johnsson, J. (2010, December 4). "787 Dreamliner proving bedeviling for Boeing," *Chicago Tribune*. http://articles.chicagotribune.com/2010-12-04/business/ct-biz-1205-787-delay-20101204_1_dreamliner-teal-group-richard-aboulafia; Lemer, J. (2010, November 12). "Boeing 787 risks further delays," *Financial Times*. www.ft.com/cms/s/0/941df738-ee8a-11df-9db0-00144feab49a.html#axzz17QyTnbm0; Norris, G. (2010, November 15). "787 schedule hinges on fire investigation," *Aviation Week*. www.aviationweek.com/aw/generic/story.jsp?id=news/avd/2010/11/15/09.xml&channel=comm; Norris, G. (2010, November 26). "787 design and software changes follow fire," *Aviation Week*. www.aviationweek.com/aw/generic/story.jsp?id=news/awx/2010/11/24/awx_11_24_2010_p0-272395.xml&channel=comm; Sanders, P., and Cameron, D. (2011, January 19). "Boeing again delays 787 delivery," *Wall Street Journal*, p. B3; Pasztor, A. (2014, July 13). "Boeing Says Dreamliner's Reliability Still Falls Short," *Wall Street Journal*. http://online.wsj.com/articles/boeing-says-reliability-of-787-dreamliner-is-still-falling-short-1405259732; Kotoky, A. (2014, February 11). "Boeing says Air India Unhappy with 787 Dreamliner's Performance," *Bloomberg*. http://www.bloomberg.com/news/2014-02-11/boeing-says-air-india-unhappy-with-787-dreamliner-s-reliability.html "The Courage To Innovate" Wings Club of New York (2010, November). Jim McNerney Chairman, President and Chief Executive Officer, The Boeing Company, Boeing Company, 2010.

45. Lipke, W. H. (2003, Spring). "Schedule is different," *The Measureable News*, pp. 10–15; Lipke, W. H. (2009). *Earned Schedule*. Lulu Publishing; Book, S. A. (2006, Spring). "Earned schedule and its possible unreliability as an indicator," *The Measureable News*, pp. 24–30; Lipke, W. H. (2006, Fall). "Applying earned schedule to critical path analysis and more," *The Measureable News*, pp. 26–30; Book, Stephen A. (2003, Fall). "Issues associated with basing decisions on schedule variance in an earned-value management system," *National Estimator*, Society of Cost Estimating and Analysis, pp. 11–15; www.earnedschedule.com; Vanhoucke, M., and Vandevoorde, S. (2007). "A simulation and evaluation of earned value metrics to forecast the project duration," *Journal of the Operational Research Society*, 58(10): 1361–74.